Environmental Law and Policy:
Nature, Law, and Society

EDITORIAL ADVISORS

Rachel E. Barkow
Segal Family Professor of Regulatory Law and Policy
Faculty Director, Center on the Administration of Criminal Law
New York University School of Law

Erwin Chemerinsky
Dean and Distinguished Professor of Law
Raymond Pryke Professor of First Amendment Law
University of California, Irvine School of Law

Richard A. Epstein
Laurence A. Tisch Professor of Law
New York University School of Law
Peter and Kirsten Bedford Senior Fellow
The Hoover Institution
Senior Lecturer in Law
The University of Chicago

Ronald J. Gilson
Charles J. Meyers Professor of Law and Business
Stanford University
Marc and Eva Stern Professor of Law and Business
Columbia Law School

James E. Krier
Earl Warren DeLano Professor of Law
The University of Michigan Law School

Tracey L. Meares
Walton Hale Hamilton Professor of Law
Director, The Justice Collaboratory
Yale Law School

Richard K. Neumann, Jr.
Professor of Law
Maurice A. Deane School of Law at Hofstra University

Robert H. Sitkoff
John L. Gray Professor of Law
Harvard Law School

David Alan Sklansky
Stanley Morrison Professor of Law
Stanford Law School
Faculty Co-Director
Stanford Criminal Justice Center

ASPEN CASEBOOK SERIES

ENVIRONMENTAL LAW AND POLICY: NATURE, LAW, AND SOCIETY

Fifth Edition

Zygmunt J.B. Plater
Boston College Law School

Robert H. Abrams
Florida A&M University

Robert L. Graham
Jenner & Block, Chicago

Lisa Heinzerling
Georgetown University Law Center

David A. Wirth
Boston College Law School

Noah D. Hall
Wayne State University Law School

Copyright © 2016 Aspen Publishing.

No part of this publication may be reproduced or transmitted in any form or by any means, electronic or mechanical, including photocopy, recording, or utilized by any information storage or retrieval system, without written permission from the publisher. For information about permissions or to request permissions online, visit us at www.AspenPublishing.com.

To contact Customer Service, e-mail customer.service@aspenpublishing.com, call 1-800-950-5259, or mail correspondence to:

> Aspen Publishing
> Attn: Order Department
> PO Box 990
> Frederick, MD 21705

Printed in the United States of America.

3 4 5 6 7 8 9 0

ISBN 978-1-4548-6840-8

Library of Congress Cataloging-in-Publication Data

Names: Plater, Zygmunt J. B., 1943- author. | Abrams, Robert H., 1948- author. | Graham, Robert L. (Lawyer), author. | Heinzerling, Lisa, author. | Wirth, David A., author. | Hall, Noah D., author.
Title: Environmental law and policy : nature, law, and society / Zygmunt J.B. Plater, Boston College Law School; Robert H. Abrams, Florida A&M University; Robert L. Graham, Jenner & Block, Chicago; Lisa Heinzerling, Georgetown University Law Center; David A. Wirth, Boston College Law School; Noah D. Hall, Wayne State University Law School.
Description: Fifth edition. | Frederick, MD: Aspen Publishing, 2016. | Series: Aspen casebook series | Includes bibliographical references and index.
Identifiers: LCCN 2016018945 | ISBN 9781454868408
Subjects: LCSH: Environmental law — United States — Cases. | Environmental policy — United States — Case studies. | Environmental protection — United States — Case studies. | LCGFT: Casebooks.
Classification: LCC KF3775 .E4683 2016 | DDC 344.7304/6 — dc23
LC record available at https://lccn.loc.gov/2016018945

About Aspen Publishing

Aspen Publishing is a leading provider of educational content and digital learning solutions to law schools in the U.S. and around the world. Aspen provides best-in-class solutions for legal education through authoritative textbooks, written by renowned authors, and breakthrough products such as Connected eBooks, Connected Quizzing, and PracticePerfect.

The Aspen Casebook Series (famously known among law faculty and students as the "red and black" casebooks) encompasses hundreds of highly regarded textbooks in more than eighty disciplines, from large enrollment courses, such as Torts and Contracts to emerging electives such as Sustainability and the Law of Policing. Study aids such as the *Examples & Explanations* and the *Emanuel Law Outlines* series, both highly popular collections, help lawstudents master complex subject matter.

Major products, programs, and initiatives include:

- **Connected eBooks** are enhanced digital textbooks and study aids that come with a suite of online content and learning tools designed to maximize student success. Designed in collaboration with hundreds of faculty and students, the Connected eBook is a significant leap forward in the legal education learning tools available to students.

- **Connected Quizzing** is an easy-to-use formative assessment tool that tests law students' understanding and provides timely feedback to improve learning outcomes. Delivered through CasebookConnect.com, the learning platform already used by students to access their Aspen casebooks, Connected Quizzing is simple to implement and integrates seamlessly with law school course curricula.

- **PracticePerfect** is a visually engaging, interactive study aid to explain commonly encountered legal doctrines through easy-to-understand animated videos, illustrative examples, and numerous practice questions. Developed by a team of experts, PracticePerfect is the ideal study companion for today's law students.

- The **Aspen Learning Library** enables law schools to provide their students with access to the most popular study aids on the market across all of their courses. Available through an annual subscription, the online library consists of study aids in e-book, audio, and video formats with full text search, note-taking, and highlighting capabilities.

- Aspen's **Digital Bookshelf** is an institutional-level online education bookshelf, consolidating everything students and professors need to ensure success. This program ensures that every student has access to affordable course materials from day one.

- **Leading Edge** is a community centered on thinking differently about legal education and putting those thoughts into actionable strategies. At the core of the program is the Leading Edge Conference, an annual gathering of legal education thought leaders looking to pool ideas and identify promising directions of exploration.

*To our families and to all
who act to protect this fragile planet.*

There is hardly a political question in the United States which does not sooner or later turn into a judicial one.

— Alexis de Tocqueville, Democracy in America, 1848

All thinking worthy of the name must now be ecological.

— Lewis Mumford, the Pentagon of Power, 1970

Environmentalists are like misers. They are hard to live with, but make great ancestors.

— The India Times

Summary of Contents

Table of Contents	xi
Introduction to the Book	xxv
Acknowledgments	xxxi

Part One — Basic Themes in Environmental Law — 1

Chapter 1	Basic Themes in Environmentalism	3
Chapter 2	Cross-Cutting Themes in Environmental Law	41

Part Two — The Enduring Role of the Common Law in Environmental Protection — 73

Chapter 3	The Common Law in Modern Environmental Law	75
Chapter 4	The Special Challenges of Toxic Tort Litigation	145

Part Three — The Structural Elements of the Regulatory State — 171

Chapter 5	An Overview of Environmental Regulation in the United States	173
Chapter 6	The Administrative Law of Environmental Law & Administrative Agency Process	199
Chapter 7	Sovereignty in the Environmental Law Context	257

Part Four — A Taxonomy of Legal Approaches to Environmental Protection — 311

Chapter 8	Federal Agency Disclosure: NEPA's Stop-and-Think Logic and the Power of Information	313
Chapter 9	Public Planning as a Management Tool: Governmental Oversight of Private & Public Resource Use, and the Challenge of Adaptive Management	343
Chapter 10	Roadblock Statutory Strategies & the Endangered Species Act: Stark Prohibitions and Their Viability	419
Chapter 11	From Harm-Based Standards to Tech-Based Standards: The Clean Air Act	459
Chapter 12	Technology-Based Standard Setting: The Clean Water Act	519
Chapter 13	Using Cost-Benefit Analysis in Agency Rulemaking & Review of Regulations	571
Chapter 14	Market-Enlisting Strategies: Achieving Environmental Protection Through Pollution Trading and Other Economic Incentives	607
Chapter 15	Front-End Strategies: Market Entry Controls, Pollution Prevention, and Toxic Use Reduction	649
Chapter 16	Remedial Liability Regulatory Strategies: CERCLA	687
Chapter 17	Life Cycle Regulatory Strategies: RCRA	755

Part Five	**Overarching Legal Perspectives**	789
Chapter 18	Evolving Patterns of Enforcement and Compliance	791
Chapter 19	Environmental Criminal Law	841
Chapter 20	Public Environmental Rights and Duties: The Public Trust Doctrine	879
Chapter 21	Private Property and Public Rights: Constitutional Limits on Physical and Regulatory Takings	913
Chapter 22	International and Comparative Environmental Law	959

Table of Acronyms, Referents, Pages with Definitions	1017
Table of Cases	1023
Table of Authorities: Books, Articles, Speeches	1039
Table of Authorities: Statutes, Regulations, Constitutions, Treaties	1059
Index	1067

We shall never achieve harmony with land, any more than we shall achieve justice and liberty for [all] people. In these higher aspirations, the important thing is not to achieve, but to strive.

— Aldo Leopold, Sand County Almanac

Table of Contents

Introduction to the Book   xxv
Acknowledgments   xxxi

Part One
Basic Themes in Environmental Law   1

Chapter 1
Basic Themes in Environmentalism   3

A. The Environmental Perspective   3
   1. The Breadth and Scope of Environmentalism   3
   2. The Ecological and Ethical Bases of Environmental Law   7
      a. The Science of Ecology (*MICRO AND MACRO*)   7
            Leopold, A Sand County Almanac   7
            Carson, Silent Spring   8
            Page, A Generic View of Toxic Chemicals & Similar Risks   12
            Sandman, Risk Communication: Facing Public Outrage   15
            Miller, Living in the Environment: Principles,
            Connections & Solutions   17
      b. An Environmental Economics Perspective: *Three Economies*   22
      c. Environmental Ethics   24
            Leopold, A Sand County Almanac   24

B. The Problem of the Commons   28
      Hardin, The Tragedy of the Commons   28

**C. A Salty Paradigm: Road Salt, a Problem That Has Not
Yet Met Its Legal Process**   34
      Wurster, Of Salt . . .   35

Chapter 2
Cross-Cutting Themes in Environmental Law   41

**A. A Milestone Pollution Case in Historical Context:
   Allied Chemical & Its Kepone Pesticide**   41
   1. Allied Chemical's Pesticide Pollution Disaster   42
   2. *Kepone:* A Case Study   42

**B. Beyond *Kepone*: Tracking Several Decades of Environmental
Law Development**   56
   1. The Modern Statutory Array in the Years Since *Kepone*   57

C. Environmental Law Themes & Contexts   64

Part Two
The Enduring Role of the Common Law in Environmental Protection — 73

Chapter 3
The Common Law in Modern Environmental Law — 75

A. Tort Causes of Action in the Environmental Arena — 76
   1. Using Private Law Tort Theories to Remedy Environmental Problems — 76
      a. Trespass — 76
         Borland v. Sanders Lead Co. — 76
      b. Private Nuisance and Negligence — 78
         Roth v. Cabot Oil & Gas Corp. — 79
      c. Strict Liability — 85
         Branch v. Western Petroleum, Inc. — 85
         Mangan v. Landmark 4, LLC — 87
   2. Public Nuisance in Environmental Cases — 89
      a. Conventional Uses of Public Nuisance Addressing Discretely Caused Harms — 89
         New York v. Schenectady Chemical Co. — 90
      b. Non-Conventional Uses of Public Nuisance Addressing Widespread Harm — 94
   3. Defenses Raised in Environmental Tort Cases — 96

B. Causation, and Joint & Several Liability in Conventional Environmental Tort Suits — 100
   1. Causation-in-Fact, Basic Doctrine — 100
   2. Multiple Defendants and the Doctrine of Joint and Several Liability — 101
      Velsicol Chemical Corp. v. Rowe — 101
   3. Proximate Causation — 105
      Pruitt v. Allied Chemical Corp. — 105

C. Remedies in Environmental Litigation — 108
   1. Two Classic Cases Facing Courts with the Difficult Choice of Enjoining a Major Business — 108
      Boomer et al v. Atlantic Cement Co. — 108
      Village of Wilsonville v. SCA Services, Inc. — 117
      Plater, Statutory Violations and Equitable Discretion — 125
   2. Damages — 130
      a. Compensatory Damage Remedies—Past Damages and Permanent Damages — 130
      b. Punitive Damages—Basic Doctrines — 131
         Branch v. Western Petroleum, Inc. — 131
      c. Punitive Damage Awards—Constitutional Due Process and Federal Cause of Action Judicial Limitations — 133
   3. Natural Resources Remedies — 137
   4. Environmental Disasters and Administered Compensation Funds — 142

Chapter 4
The Special Challenges of Toxic Tort Litigation — 145

A. Competing Perceptions? Law & Science — 145

B. Remedies for Victims of Toxic Contamination — 147
    Anderson et al. v. W.R. Grace & Company, Beatrice Foods Company et al. — 149

C. Proof of Complex Causation — 156
    1. Putting Together All of the Facets of Toxic Exposure/Cause-in-Fact — 158
        Donaldson v. Central Illinois Public Service Co. — 158
    2. Plaintiff's Burden of Proof & Proportion of Risk Attributable to Defendant — 166

Part Three
The Structural Elements of the Regulatory State — 171

Chapter 5
An Overview of Environmental Regulation in the United States — 173

A. A Taxonomic Approach to Public Law — The Different Ways That Statutes Work — 175

B. The Advent and Failure of Broad Delegations to Administrative Agencies (Review and Permit Statutes) — 181
    The Utilex Case File — 185
    1. Federalization of the Field and the Blossoming of Regulation — 188
        Elliott, Ackerman & Millian, Toward a Theory of Statutory Evolution: The Federalization of Environmental Law — 188

C. Keeping Score at the Beginning of the Twenty-First Century: Players, Positions, Programs & Policies — 194
    1. Cooperative Federalism — 196
    2. "Command and Control" and "Flexible" Regulatory Strategies — 196

Chapter 6
The Administrative Law of Environmental Law & Administrative Agency Process — 199

A. The Evolution of the Administrative Governing Process — 199

B. Administrative Process and Law in a Nutshell — 201
    1. The Structure of Administrative Agency Power and Process — 202
    2. The *Rybachek* Pollution Case: An Example of Agency Rulemaking, Authorized by Statute, Challenged in Court — 206
        Environmental Protection Agency, Notice of Final Rulemaking — 207
        Rybachek v. U.S. Environmental Protection Agency — 208

3. The *Snail Darter* Case: An Agency Is Brought to Court for Its Own Actions Allegedly Violating Federal Law ... 208
Hiram Hill et al. v. Tennessee Valley Authority ... 208
4. Judges' Handling of Challenges to Federal Agencies ... 209

C. *Overton Park*—A Judicial Review Paradigm ... 212
1. The *Overton Park* Case ... 212
Citizens to Preserve Overton Park, Inc. v. Volpe ... 213

D. Citizen Enforcement in the Courts ... 223
1. The Importance of Citizen Enforcement ... 223
Stewart, The Reformation of American Administrative Law ... 225
2. Standing and the Institutionalization of Citizen Enforcement ... 226
Scenic Hudson Preservation Conference v. Federal Power Commission ... 228
3. Political Resistance to Citizen Enforcement: Removing Courts' Ability to Grant Relief to Citizens ... 240
Department of Interior and Related Agencies Appropriations Act, 1990 ... 240
4. Citizens' Attempts to Expand Agency Procedures ... 242
Vermont Yankee Nuclear Power Corp. v. Natural Resources Defense Council ... 242

E. Statutory Interpretation: How, by Whom?—*Chevron* ... 249
1. Judicial Review of Agency Interpretations of Law ... 249
Chevron U.S.A., Inc. v. Natural Resources Defense Council ... 249

Chapter 7
Sovereignty in the Environmental Law Context ... 257

A. Constitutional Federalism & Environmental Law Controversies in the U.S. ... 257
1. Preemption of State Law ... 260
a. Express Preemption ... 261
b. Conflict & Field Occupancy Preemption ... 264
2. Dormant Commerce Clause Invalidation of State Law ... 268
City of Philadelphia v. New Jersey ... 270
3. Limitations on Federal Power ... 276
4. Concurrent Authority and Cooperative Federalism ... 277

B. Integrating International Agreements into Domestic Law ... 279
1. Shared Natural Resources: Bilateral Treaties ... 280
a. Migratory Birds in North America ... 281
b. The Constitutional Law of Treaty Formation ... 282
Missouri v. Holland ... 283
2. Protecting the Global Commons: Multilateral Treaties & Executive Agreements ... 286
a. Multilateral Treaties to Prevent the Tragedy of the Commons: Saving the Whales ... 287
Whaling in the Antarctic ... 288
b. Executive Agreements: Tensions with Statutory Mandates ... 291
Japan Whaling Association v. American Cetacean Society ... 293
3. International Trade Agreements: The Trade and Environment Problem ... 296

	a. Multilateral Agreements on Trade: The WTO	297
	b. Domestic Implementation of International Trade Agreements: Congressional-Executive Agreements	298
	c. Trade and the Environment: Collision with Domestic Environmental Law?	299
	George E. Warren Corp. v. U.S. E.P.A.	300
	d. The NAFTA Environmental Side Agreement: Citizen Submissions on Enforcement	302
	Final Factual Record for Submission SEM-99-002 (Migratory Birds)	304

Part Four
A Taxonomy of Legal Approaches to Environmental Protection   311

Chapter 8
Federal Agency Disclosure: NEPA's Stop-and-Think Logic and the Power of Information   313

A.	NEPA, the National Environmental Policy Act	314
	Public Law 91-190	315
B.	NEPA in Court: Litigation and Outcomes	320
	1. NEPA Litigation over the Adequacy of an Agency's EIS	320
	Mid-States Coalition for Progress v. Surface Transportation Board	320
	2. NEPA Litigation over an Agency's Decision Not to Prepare an EIS	324
	Center for Biological Diversity v. National Highway Traffic Safety Administration	325
C.	NEPA's State, International, and Transboundary Applications	333
	Hall, Political Externalities, Federalism, and a Proposal for an Interstate Environmental Impact Assessment Policy	333
D.	The Emergency Planning and Community Right-to-Know Act	336

Chapter 9
Public Planning as a Management Tool: Governmental Oversight of Private & Public Resource Use, and the Challenge of Adaptive Management   343

A.	Managing Localized Land Uses	351
	1. Plan-Based Land Use Zoning	351
	2. Critical Areas Designation and Regulation: The CWA §404 Wetlands Example	359
	Bersani v. U.S. Environmental Protection Agency	360
	3. Hazardous Waste Facilities: State and Federal Efforts	365
	a. Hazardous Wastes	365

		b. Nuclear Wastes	369
	4.	"Smart Growth"	370
		Pollard, Smart Growth: The Promise, Politics, and Potential Pitfalls of Emerging Growth Management Strategies	371

B. Planning & Management of Public Lands & Resources — 374
1. Historic Management of Grazing — Managing to Carrying Capacity — 374
2. Managing for "Multiple Use and Sustained Yield" — 377
   Coggins, The Law of Public Rangeland Management IV: FLPMA, PRIA, and the Multiple Use Mandate — 377
3. Public Lands Management Planning in the Supreme Court — 388
   Norton v. Southern Utah Wilderness Alliance et al. — 390

C. Large Scale, Public-Private Resource Management & Broadly Integrated Planning — 396
1. NLUPA: The Fleeting Hope and Promise of a National Land Use Planning Act — 396
2. Intergovernmental Coordination: The CZMA and Its Consistency Requirement — 400
   Ruhl, Biodiversity Conservation & the Ever-Expanding Web of Federal Laws Regulating Nonfederal Lands: Time for Something Completely Different? — 402
3. Federal-State & Public-Private Issues on the Public Lands — 406
   Kleppe v. New Mexico — 407

D. Adaptive Management and Climate Change — 413

Chapter 10
Roadblock Statutory Strategies & the Endangered Species Act: Stark Prohibitions and Their Viability — 419

A. An Introduction to Roadblock Statutes — 419
1. The Delaney Clause — 420
2. Weighing Roadblocks — 420

B. The ESA as a Roadblock Statute — 422
1. The Endangered Species Act — 422
2. A Fish, a Dam, and ESA §7 — 423
   The Snail Darter and the Tellico Dam Case — 423
   Tennessee Valley Authority v. Hiram Hill, et al. — 425
3. ESA §9 and the "No Take" Provision — 432
   Babbitt v. Sweet Home Communities for a Great Oregon — 432

C. "Slippage" and "Roadblock Bypasses" — Subsequent Modifications Temper Stark Standards (and What Conclusions Should Be Drawn from That?) — 436
1. Flexibility Mechanisms in General — 437
2. Flexibility and Slippage in the ESA — 438
   a. The ESA §7 God Committee Amendment — 438

      b. The ESA Prohibitions Get Modified by the ESA §10 "Incidental Take"
         Exemption Amendment   440
      c. A Protective Balance: Avoiding the "Sunk Cost Tactic"   444
      d. "Sunsetting"—The ESA Lives on Borrowed Time   445
   3. The ESA Listing Hurdle and De-Listing   445
   4. Agency Implementation Slippage—Consultation   448
      a. Slippage, Administrative: Flex Mechanisms Added to the ESA   449
      b. The §4(d) Polar Bear Special Rule: ESA Not to Be Used Against
         Global Warming   451
      c. Slippage, Judicial: The Roberts Court Takes Action: *National Association
         of Homebuilders*   453
         *National Association of Home Builders (NAHB) v. Defenders of
         Wildlife, and U.S. E.P.A. Defenders of Wildlife*   453

Chapter 11
From Harm-Based Standards to Tech-Based Standards: The Clean Air Act   459

A. The Clean Air Act: History and Structure   459

B. Harm-Based Ambient Standards Under the CAA   465
   1. What Are the Standards for Setting NAAQS?   468
      Whitman v. American Trucking Associations   470
   2. Transboundary Airflows   477
   3. The Intersection of Agency Action and Environmental Justice   481
      U.S. Environmental Protection Agency, Title VI of the Civil Rights
      Act of 1964: Adversity and Compliance with Environmental
      Health-Based Thresholds   481
   4. Adjusting Requirements for Attainment (PSD) & Nonattainment Areas   486
      Mintz, State and Local Government Environmental Liability   487

C. Technology-Based Standards Under the CAA   489
   1. Technology-Based Standards as a Policy Choice   489
      Michigan v. U.S. Environmental Protection Agency   491
   2. Translating Statutory Obligations into Permits   496
      In re Northern Michigan University Ripley Heating Plant   497

D. Technology-Forcing Under the CAA   507
   1. Reducing Auto Emissions Through CAA Title II   508
      International Harvester v. Ruckelshaus   508

E. Regulation of Greenhouse Gases Under the CAA   512
      Massachusetts v. U.S. Environmental Protection Agency   513

Chapter 12
Technology-Based Standard Setting: The Clean Water Act   519

A. An Overview of the Clean Water Act   519
      U.S. Environmental Protection Agency, National Water Quality
      Inventory: 1994 Report to Congress   521

B.	The Origin and Evolution of TBELs	533
	U.S. Environmental Protection Agency v. California	533
C.	Implementing TBELs Through the NPDES Process	537
	Rybachek v. EPA	537
	Atlantic States Legal Foundation, Inc. v. Eastman Kodak Co.	550
D.	Water Quality-Based Permitting and Management of Nonpoint Source Pollution Under the CWA	555
	Pronsolino v. Nastri	556
E.	A Complex Hypothetical: The Average River	569

Chapter 13
Using Cost-Benefit Analysis in Agency Rulemaking & Review of Regulations — 571

A.	An Overview of Formal Cost-Benefit Analysis	572
	Ackerman & Heinzerling, Pricing the Priceless: Cost-Benefit Analysis of Environmental Protection	572
B.	The Scientific Basis: Risk Assessment	575
C.	Open-Ended Cost-Benefit Balancing: ToSCA	581
	1. ToSCA's Regulatory Design	581
	Toxic Substances Control Act §6	581
	2. Regulation of Asbestos Under a ToSCA Cost-Benefit Analysis	584
	Corrosion Proof Fittings v. U.S. Environmental Protection Agency	584
D.	Formal Cost-Benefit Analysis: SDWA	588
	U.S. Environmental Protection Agency, National Primary Drinking Water Regulations; Arsenic & Clarifications to Compliance & New Source Contaminants Monitoring	589
E.	Cost-Benefit Analysis at the White House	594
F.	Evaluating Cost-Benefit Analysis	596
	1. The Case for Cost-Benefit	596
	American Trucking Associations v. Browner	597
	2. The Case Against Cost-Benefit Analysis	600
	Ackerman & Heinzerling, Pricing the Priceless: Cost-Benefit Analysis of Environmental Protection	600

Chapter 14
Market-Enlisting Strategies: Achieving Environmental Protection Through Pollution Trading and Other Economic Incentives — 607

A.	A Survey of Market Enlistment Devices	607
B.	Domestic Trading Experience in the U.S.	612

Table of Contents

1. Domestic Air Pollution Trading Regimes	612
Ellerman, Joskow & Harrison, Jr., Emissions Trading in the United States: Experience, Lessons and Considerations for Greenhouse Gases	612
2. Flawed Trading Systems and Hot Spots (Adverse Local Effects)	621
Drury, Belliveau, Kuhn, & Bansal, Pollution Trading & Environmental Injustice: Los Angeles' Failed Experiment in Air Quality Policy	622
C. International Trading to Reduce GHG Emissions	**629**
Air Transport Association of America et al. v. Secretary of State for Energy and Climate Change	631
Paris Agreement	633
D. Carbon Taxes	**636**
Naudhaus, The Climate Casino: Risk, Uncertainty, and Economics for a Warming World	638
E. Industry Self-Regulation: The International Organization for Standardization	**643**

Chapter 15
Front-End Strategies: Market Entry Controls, Pollution Prevention, and Toxic Use Reduction — 649

A. Pesticides—FIFRA	**651**
Miller, Federal Regulation of Pesticides	651
Environmental Defense Fund Inc. v. U.S. Environmental Protection Agency	654
B. Toxics—Market Access Regulation: U.S. & Europe, ToSCA & REACH	**663**
1. ToSCA	663
Druley & Ordway, The Toxic Substances Control Act	663
Chemical Manufacturers Association v. U.S. Environmental Protection Agency	665
2. Regulation in the European Union: REACH	679
Fédération des entreprises du commerce et de la distribution (FCD) & Fédération des magasins de bricolage et de l'aménagement de la maison (FMB) v. Ministry of Ecology, Sustainable Development, and Energy	682

Chapter 16
Remedial Liability Regulatory Strategies: CERCLA — 687

A. CERCLA's Liability Rules as Developed Through the Judicial Process of Statutory Interpretation	**690**
1. The Basics of Statutory Remedial Liability for Cleanup of Hazardous Materials	690
Rich, Personal Liability for Hazardous Waste Cleanup: An Examination of CERCLA §107	691
2. Apportionment in CERCLA Actions	696
Burlington Northern and Santa Fe Railway Co. v. United States	697
3. The Government's Relaxed Burden of Proof of Causation in CERCLA Cases	701
United States v. Wade (Wade II)	701
4. The Individual Liability of Managerial Officers	703

    United States v. Northeastern Pharmaceutical & Chemical Co. (NEPACCO)   703
  5. The Classes of Parties Who May Be Held Liable Under CERCLA   711
  6. Corporate Liabilities Under CERCLA   717
   United States v. BestFoods Corp.   717
  7. Private Litigation Under CERCLA §107   724
   United States v. Atlantic Research Corp.   725

B. EPA's CERCLA Administrative Order Process   731

C. Identifying Sites, Funding, and Setting the Standards for Cleanups   735
  Starfield, The 1990 National Contingency Plan—More Detail and More Structure, But Still a Balancing Act   738

D. EPA's Strategy for Cost Recovery and Loss Allocation   745
  O'Neil v. Picillo   747

Chapter 17
Life Cycle Regulatory Strategies: RCRA   755

A. Tracking and Controlling the Lifecycle of Hazardous Waste Materials   756
  1. RCRA's Enactment and Initial Implementation   757
   Florio, Congress as Reluctant Regulator: Hazardous Waste Policy in the 1980s   758
  2. RCRA's Administrative Thicket: Defining Hazardous Wastes   760
  3. Regulating Participants in the Hazardous Waste Life Cycle   764

B. The "Land Ban" and the Use of "Hammers" to Control Agency Action   775
  Hazardous Waste Treatment Council v. U.S. Environmental Protection Agency   776

C. RCRA Citizen Suits to Obtain Cleanup   782
  Meghrig v. KFC Western, Inc.   783

Part Five
Overarching Legal Perspectives   789

Chapter 18
Evolving Patterns of Enforcement and Compliance   791

A. The Continuing Debate over Environmental Enforcement Strategies   791

B. The Governmental Enforcement Process   794
  1. Phases in the Enforcement Process   795
   Mintz, Enforcement at the EPA: High Stakes and Hard Choices   795
  2. The Flow of the Enforcement Process   796
  3. Enforcement Tools   799
  4. Brownfields Federalism and Its Policy of Greater Flexibility and Cooperation   806

Table of Contents

U.S. Environmental Protection Agency, Brownfields Action Agenda	806
Superfund Memorandum of Agreement, Illinois Environmental Protection Agency, U.S. Environmental Protection Agency, Region V	809
5. Administrative Reforms in Environmental Enforcement	812
C. Citizen Enforcement to Complement Governmental Efforts	815
D. Alternative Dispute Resolution Processes	821
1. Why Alternative Dispute Resolution?	821
2. Environmental ADR	823
National Institute for Dispute Resolution, Paths to Justice: Major Public Policy Issues of Dispute Resolution	823
3. Negotiated Rulemaking	825
Susskind & McMahon, The Theory and Practice of Negotiated Rulemaking	825
E. The Impetus to Self-Generated Corporate Compliance	828
1. The Five Primary Triggers for Environmental Compliance	829
a. Permitting and Reporting	829
b. SEC Disclosure Requirements for Public Companies	830
Friedman & Giannotti, Environmental Self-Assessment	830
c. Satisfying Corporate Management Information Needs	831
Frankel, Full Disclosure: Financial Statement Disclosures Under CERCLA	832
d. Borrowing for Ongoing Business Needs	833
e. The Purchase and Sale of a Business or Real Estate	833
2. Due Diligence, Audits, and Other Avenues Toward Voluntary Compliance	836

Chapter 19
Environmental Criminal Law — 841

A. Tactical Rediscovery of Criminal Provisions: The 1899 Refuse Act	843
B. An Increasing Tendency to Prosecute Environmental Crimes	847
People v. Film Recovery Systems, Inc., Metallic Marketing Inc. Charles Kirschbaum, Daniel Rodriguez, Steven O'Neil	847
Ferrey, Hard Time: Criminal Prosecution for Polluters	849
C. Criminal Liability: Problems of Knowledge and Intent	854
United States v. Ahmad	854
United States v. Weitzenhoff	856
D. Problems Raised in Corporate and Executive Prosecutions	864
1. The Fifth Amendment and the Corporation	864
2. Difficulties in Proving Collective Activity Crimes	865
Goldfarb, Kepone: A Case Study	865
3. Executive Liability for Acts or Omissions by Subordinates	870
United States v. Park	870

Chapter 20
Public Environmental Rights and Duties:
The Public Trust Doctrine — 879

A. **Beyond Direct Threats to Human Health & Property: Modern Rediscovery of the Public Trust Doctrine** — 879
    Sax, Defending the Environment: A Strategy for Citizen Action — 883
    Sax, The Public Trust Doctrine in Natural Resource Law: Effective Judicial Intervention — 884
    Marks v. Whitney — 888

B. **Applying the Modern Public Trust Doctrine** — 889
    1. Public Trust Balancing: Diversion — 889
        Paepke v. Building Commission — 889
    2. Public Trust Protections Against Derogation — 892
        National Audubon Society v. Superior Court of Alpine County (The Mono Lake Case) — 892
    3. How Far Does the Public Trust Doctrine Go? — 900
        Defenders of Florissant v. Park Land Development Co. — 900

Chapter 21
Private Property and Public Rights: Constitutional
Limits on Physical and Regulatory Takings — 913

A. **Eminent Domain Condemnations** — 916
    1. The Domain of Deference — 916
    2. Challenging an Eminent Domain Condemnation — 917

B. **Inverse Condemnation: A Constitutional Tort?** — 923
    Thornburg v. Port of Portland — 924

C. **Challenges to Regulations as "Invalid Takings"** — 928
    1. Regulatory Takings — 928
        Pennsylvania Coal Co. v. Mahon — 929
    2. The U.S. Supreme Court's Classic Takings Cases: An Emerging Consensus on Takings Balancing? — 935
        Anthony Palazzolo v. State of Rhode Island — 938
    3. A Takings Role for the Public Trust Doctrine? — 945
    4. Other Property Regulation Issues: Remedies, Exactions & Innocent Landowner Liability — 948
        a. Remedies: If Regulations Are Held to Be Invalid Takings — 948
        b. Amortization, and Offset Alternatives? — 949
        c. Exactions: *Nollan*, *Dolan*, and *Koontz* — 950
        Scro, Navigating the Takings Maze: The Use of Transfers of Development Rights in Defending Regulations Against Takings Challenges — 957

Chapter 22
International and Comparative Environmental Law   959

- A. **Customary International Law**   960
  - *Trail Smelter Arbitration* (*U.S. v. Canada*)   961
- B. **International Conferences & Soft Law**   966
  - Rio Declaration on Environment and Development   968
- C. **Comparative Environmental Law**   972
  - *Mehta v. Union of India*   972
- D. **Multilateral Environmental Agreements & Global Climate Change**   976
  1. Stratospheric Ozone Depletion   977
  2. Global Warming   982
  3. The Global Warming Framework Convention   985
     - United Nations Framework Convention on Climate Change   987
  4. The Kyoto Protocol and the Road to Paris   990
     - Paris Agreement   995
- E. **International Institutions**   999
  1. The World Bank   999
     - Inspection Panel's Report and Findings on the Qinghai Project: Executive Summary   1001
     - World Bank Problem Exercise   1005
  2. The World Trade Organization   1006
     - U.S.— Restrictions on Imports of Tuna   1008
     - Trade & Environment Problem Exercise   1014

Table of Acronyms, Referents, Pages with Definitions   1017
Table of Cases   1023
Table of Authorities: Books, Articles, Speeches   1039
Table of Authorities: Statutes, Regulations, Constitutions, Treaties   1059
Index   1067

Nobody made a greater mistake than he who did nothing because he could only do a little.

— Edmund Burke

Introduction to the Book

We travel together, passengers on a little space ship, dependent on its vulnerable resources of air and soil, all committed for our safety to its security and peace, preserved from annihilation only by the care, the work, and, I will say, the love we bestow on our fragile craft.
—Ambassador Adlai Stevenson, at the United Nations, 1965

"When we try to pick out anything by itself, we find it hitched to everything else in the universe," the wilderness prophet and Sierra Club founder John Muir once said.[1] Indeed, "Everything is connected to everything else" is the First Law of Ecology. That might pose a daunting caution for anyone setting out to learn the art of environmental law, or write a book about it. But there are logical structures and systems within the field that can help us trace a coherent path through the complexity.

Every act of technology or human behavior is likely to have a wide range of interacting effects, direct and indirect, some beneficial, some quite drastic, unpredictable, and long-term or irreversible in their impacts. Environmentalists and their attorneys tend to scrutinize human actions with an eye to accounting the full range of consequences to the public and Nature, not just the upbeat realm of short-term entrepreneurial payoffs. Environmentalism reminds us that everything goes somewhere and remains within the grand system in which we must continue to live, so we need to think broadly and plan thoughtfully for future sustainability.

Environmental law attempts to build foresight into the human decisional system, along with an awareness of costs and values that are typically invisible because, though real, they exist outside the formal market economy. Often environmental law works after the fact, attempting to force accountings for depredations that have already occurred, in hopes of deterring future repetitions. Environmental law has also developed elaborate doctrines attempting to anticipate and prevent environmental disruptions. The goal is to incorporate a process of fair, overall, comprehensive accounting of real societal costs, benefits, and alternatives into major public and private decisionmaking.

Over the past 50 years there has been a dramatic change in the stature of the field. It is no longer dismissable as the fad of a disgruntled minority. It is now the stuff of presidential campaigns and national public opinion poll majorities. There are more environmental lawyers in the U.S. than there are labor lawyers. Given the reality of environmental problems and potentials, the field of environmental protection law will inevitably continue to grow ever more intricate, challenging, and important.

---

1. J. Muir, My First Summer in the Sierra 211 (1911).

The Book's Perspective

This book is designed to track through environmental law according to the structure of the legal process. It uses some of the classic cases and materials of environmental law as its teaching tools, as well as some of the most recent.

There are some necessary admissions—our bias, for example. Every book has its bias, usually unacknowledged. If it isn't already, we wish to make this book's clear. From the start much of environmental protection law has been initiated and shaped by individuals and groups in the active environmental "movement." We believe that in most if not all cases, those who raise environmental protection legal issues are correct in identifying problems that need to be resolved. Most environmental problems arise from a fundamental human tension between short-term marketplace interests and the larger civic-societal public interest. In the dynamic logic that has built the greatest economy the world has ever known, individual human actors behave rationally to maximize their own short-term best interests, without sufficient knowledge, consideration, or accounting of the real natural and societal consequences of their actions. The ecological and civic-societal values affected by such human actions will be most efficiently addressed if they can be brought into the marketplace economy, but the altruism of market players cannot be relied upon to do that. Environmental protection law, in spite of the natural and powerful resistance of market forces, therefore seeks to force facts and public values into the markets of daily life, making human, ecological, and economic systems work successfully and sustainably.

In large part we believe the business marketplace has come to accept and internalize many public environmental values, not just as a result of civic instincts but also because of the credible prospect today of environmental enforcement by agencies and an active citizenry. This book therefore approaches many, though not all, environmental cases from the perspective of those who enforce environmental protection laws—citizens, public interest groups, and agencies. Our approach often is "how can this problem be appropriately managed within the legal system?" presuming in most cases that the targeted problems need to be addressed. Through changing cycles of environmental law—with administrations sometimes more protective, sometimes less—one societal constant is the necessity for nongovernmental citizen environmentalists' continuing oversight and active participation. This book thus makes particular effort to include consideration of the role of citizens, in addition to corporations and governmental officials, in the environmental legal process.

This approach seems realistic and useful as well as defensible. So to get deeper into the swamps of environmental law, in practical terms one must follow the environmental enforcement trail, which often means citizen enforcement actions. Whether readers ultimately view the field from the point of view of plaintiffs or defendants, an understanding of the environmental protection perspective is indispensable to a recognition of what's going on, and how it could be done better.

Structure

The structure of this coursebook should be clear from the table of contents. It surveys environmental law issues throughout the vast range of the U.S. legal process

Introduction to the Book

(with additional consideration of international environmental law principles, which have developed a great deal, often on the U.S. model).

Many books on environmental law have fallen into an organization by physical categories—air, water, toxics, wildlife, energy, land development, groundwater, timber and mining, etc.—not by legal categories. Physical subject categories often produce duplicative and overlapping legal analyses. This book, on the other hand, contains material from many physical subject areas but from the beginning has taken its organization from the elements of the legal system itself, building upon a base of common law and constitutional law, and continuing on to statutory and administrative law. The way the legal system works, not the intricacy of some media-specific physical science area, is our primary concern. The aim is not to teach hyper-technical details of current law, like the specific regulatory parts-per-million hydrocarbon standards for automobile tailpipe emissions, and so on, but to show legal structures and functions. Using this legal process design, the book probes every nook and cranny of the legal system, exploring ways in which environmental attorneys in and out of government must attempt to understand the fascinating complexities of environmental problems in the real world—both human and ecological—using law imaginatively and competently to address them.

Most of the coursebook's explanation and analysis of environmental law is contained within each chapter's introduction, and, more substantially, in the "Commentary & Questions" (we call them "C&Qs") that follow all of the chapters' textual and case excerpts. Although there may be as many as a dozen subtitled entries in a C&Q section, readers should look at all of them in order to get a full sense of the issue being examined in that section, treating the C&Qs as basic explanatory text. (We've also been told that many C&Qs contain very good term paper topics.)

Going Beyond the Book

An environmental law course is broad in scope. The text and commentary in this book often incorporate analysis of source material, cases, and issues extending far beyond the excerpted textual material. In many chapters you will find bulleted notes (•) indicating that extended material on point is available on the coursebook website. The website also has a catalog of links available chapter-by-chapter for further background and analysis of the issues raised in the text. To provide more depth to areas in which they have special research and teaching interests, professors typically add their own further components to this coursebook's materials. Students should also be encouraged to take corollary non-law courses, for example in field biology, toxicology, or environmental policy. Nicholas Ashford & Charles Caldart's ENVIRONMENTAL LAW, POLICY, AND ECONOMICS: RECLAIMING THE ENVIRONMENTAL AGENDA is an excellent field guide in this inquiry, and Glenn Adelson's ENVIRONMENT: AN INTERDISCIPLINARY ANTHOLOGY, presents perspectives from science, literature, and philosophy, economics, law, and politics. To give law students a taste of reality, some classes take on projects or internships with active groups outside academe. Some have carried one chosen problem area through the course of the term or kept track of an ongoing local controversy—a particular toxic disposal case, wildlife or park management issue, or mining, dredging, pipeline, or dam project. Others have assigned short individual research papers, class presentations, field visits, and so on, and each of these has been valuable in providing reinforcing feedback to the analyses and techniques of environmental law set out broadly in the book. Some courses integrate one or more regulatory simulations into the course, giving students an experience of the art and skills of administrative agency regulatory practice, which characterizes so much of modern law. For many this may be the only chance they'll have in law school to pick up this critical administrative process knowledge. Several good sources of hands-on regulatory exercises are available. We have used Anderson & Hirsch's excellent ENVIRONMENTAL LAW PRACTICE: PROBLEMS AND EXERCISES FOR SKILLS DEVELOPMENT to good effect.

Some very fine online services provide information updates on a regular basis. *Greenwire* is an excellent online source of constant updating on important governmental issues, as are the BNA Daily Environmental Report and BNA International Environment Reporter, InsideClimate News, and many more. Industry organizations publish newsletters and are pleased to provide extensive materials in support of their positions. A number of excellent law reviews specialize in environmental law, and Lexis-Nexis, Westlaw, and the Index to Legal Periodicals offer effective access to their contents.

The best environmental law hornbook we know is Professor William Rodgers's HANDBOOK ON ENVIRONMENTAL LAW. Professor Rodgers has also published a very helpful multivolume treatise. Several publishers produce useful annual statutory compilations, and Joseph Sax's DEFENDING THE ENVIRONMENT (1971) continues to be our vivid introduction and guide to the use of law in resolving the pervasive social, economic, and ecological governance problems we call "environmental."

And don't be daunted by the "numbing complexity and detail" of environmental issues and environmental law: Because everything is connected to everything else, if one just picks up a trail and follows it, it will lead to all there is to know.

Note on Editing Conventions Used in This Book

In editing materials for this coursebook we have tried to make the text as smooth as possible to the reader's eye, and to keep the amount of text as short as possible while covering this dauntingly broad and expansive field. This agenda has required quite a bit of editorial surgery on text and excerpted materials.

Within excerpts, many internal citations (especially string citations) are simply excised, with no indication by ellipsis, or are dropped to footnotes. (In some cases in the text itself, when discussing general scientific or other nonlegal data, only limited citations are supplied.) Footnotes in excerpted materials, when they remain, do not have their original numbers unless a footnote holds special importance to subsequent commentators. Judicial opinions are often drastically cut and edited, indicated only by simple ellipsis, and in a few cases portions of text are reordered to make the presentation flow more smoothly. As with most coursebooks, if students wish to delve into a particular case or text, the excerpts here should serve to get the inquiry started, but there's no substitute for going back to the original full text.

Various departures from literary convention and Bluebook style have been incorporated throughout the book to improve scansion (as in eliminating brackets on [i]nitial capitalization changes, or our simplified *above* and *below* references). Case opinion excerpts, however, usually retain the originating court's stylistic idiosyncrasies.

Gender-sensitivity was a virtually unknown editing concept when many classic texts and decisions were written. They and some modern texts as well often address all significant parties as male. In this book the pronouns "he" and "she" when used generically should be understood to refer inclusively to all persons regardless of gender (although in retrospect it seems most polluters still appear here as male).

Help! Acronyms!

Swarms of acronyms have invaded environmental law—EISs, FONSIs, TRIs, NIMBYs, PSD, CERCLA, ToSCA, TMDLs, ad infinitum. To give the student a sobering welcome to the field, and to save trees, we use acronyms throughout the book after their first appearance in these pages. To facilitate the reader's coping with those acronyms, the back reference pages (which contain all reference sections except the Tables of Contents) also include a Glossary of Acronyms & Abbreviations with initial page definitional notations. You may want to tab that page for easy reference.

People Who've Helped Us . . .

This book sometimes seems to have evolved with as much biodiversity of input as any marsh or rainforest. Dozens of people have helped shape and reshape it over the years. For all who know the work of the late Professor Joseph Sax, the mark of his thinking and advice on our efforts will be discernible throughout these pages. This coursebook has always been deeply shaped and guided by his environmental law teachings and vision, and we gratefully acknowledge his impact on our work. In its earliest form the book derives from materials prepared by a committee of law students at the University of Michigan in the early 1970s, including two of the present authors, for a course called Nature, Law, and Society offered to graduate and undergraduate students. In that original group Peter Schroth served not only as a major contributor but also as administrator of the course, a thankless and demanding task. The Nature, Law, and Society project was supported and advised by Joe Sax and Professor William Stapp of the School of Natural Resources. They served graciously and well as mentors and midwives. Prior to its first publication in 1992 with the participation of our marvelous charter member Bill Goldfarb, the book went through repeated reincarnations at a succession of schools at which we taught—the University of Michigan Law School, Boston College Law School, Harvard Law School, Rutgers, the University of Tennessee College of Law, and Wayne State Law School. Before the first edition and since then, we have greatly benefited from suggestions and comments gratefully received from students and colleagues around the country. The book has improved immensely with the addition of Bob Graham, Lisa Heinzerling, and David Wirth, and of Noah Hall, who, we are delighted to say, hereafter will be taking the lead on our book.

Among the many students who contributed to this edition we want to thank especially our Boston College Law School (except as noted) junior colleagues Tyler Archer, Joey Belza, Jacqueline Bertelsen (FAMU College of Law), Wendy Beylik, Yunpeng George Du, Liam Holland, Sonja Marrett, Nelson Nedlin, Michael O'Loughlin, and Graham Welch, and the other members of the Boston College Law School Environmental Law Society who helped compile the Index and tables of cases and authorities under deadline pressures.

The Boston College Law School Library staff too has repeatedly provided indispensable detective work and support, receiving fiendish eleventh-hour requests and calmly coming through for us: Joan Shear, Tuananth Truong, and Kyle Fidalgo.

As for the many authors, photographers, and publishers who graciously granted us permission to reprint portions of their works, a complete listing appears in the Acknowledgments pages, with our gratitude. We also wish to acknowledge the help of Lori Wood and Paul Sobel on this fifth edition, and continuing gratitude for the remarkable group associated with Wolters Kluwer Aspen Publishing who welcomed and coddled the third and fourth editions of the coursebook—especially Carol McGeehan, Melody Davies, and Barbara Roth.

Ultimately, our greatest warm thanks and appreciation must be reserved for our families, who naïvely expressed pleasure when they first heard of this project.

Z.J.B.P.
R.H.A.
R.L.G.
L.H.
D.A.W.
N.D.H.

June 2016

Acknowledgments

Books & Articles

Ackerman, Frank, and Lisa Heinzerling. Pricing the Priceless: Cost-Benefit Analysis of Environmental Protection, 150 University of Pennsylvania Law Review 1553. Copyright © 2002 University of Pennsylvania Law Review. Reprinted by permission.

Carson, Rachel. Silent Spring 54-57, 61. Copyright © 1962 Houghton Mifflin Harcourt. Reprinted by permission.

Coggins, Charles C. The Law of Public Rangeland Management IV: FLPMA, PRIA, and the Multiple Use Mandate, 14 Environmental Law 1. Copyright © 1983 George C. Coggins. Reprinted by permission.

Druley, Ray M., and Girard L. Ordway. The Toxic Substances Control Act, 1-4. Copyright © 1977 BNA/Bloomberg. Reprinted by permission.

Drury, Richard Toshiyuki, Michael E. Belliveau, J. Scott Kuhn, and Shipra Bansal. Pollution Trading and Environmental Injustice: Los Angeles' Failed Experiment in Air Quality Policy, 9 Duke Environmental Law and Policy Forum 231. Copyright © 1999 Duke Environmental Law and Policy Forum. Reprinted by permission.

Ellerman, A. Denny, Richard Schmalensee, Paul L. Joskow, Juan Pablo Montero, Elizabeth M. Bailey. Emissions Trading Under the U.S. Acid Rain Program: Evaluation of Compliance Costs and Allowance Market Performance. Copyright © 1997 Center for Energy and Environmental Policy Research. Reprinted by permission.

Ferrey, Steven. Hard Time Criminal Prosecution for Polluters. Copyright © 1988 The Amicus Journal / Natural Resources Defense Council. Reprinted by permission.

Friedman, Frank, and David Giannotti. Environmental Self Assessment in Law of Environmental Protection, 7-28-7-33. Copyright © 1998 Environmental Law Institute. Reprinted by permission.

Friedman, Thomas. The Inflection Is Near?, The New York Times, March 7, 2009. Copyright © 2009 The New York Times. Reprinted by permission.

Goldfarb, William. Kepone: A Case Study, 8 Environmental Law 645. Copyright © 1978 William Goldfarb. Reprinted by permission.

Goldfarb, William. Changes in the Clean Water Act Since Kepone, 29 University of Richmond Law Review 603. Copyright © 1995 University of Richmond Law Review. Reprinted by permission.

Hall, Noah D. Political Externalities, Federalism, and a Proposal for an Interstate Environmental Impact Assessment Policy, 32 Harvard Environmental Law Review 49, 81-84. Copyright © 2008 Harvard Environmental Law Review. Reprinted by permission.

Hardin, Garrett. The Tragedy of the Commons, 162 Science 1243-48. Copyright © 1968 American Association for the Advancement of Science. Reprinted by permission.

Leopold, Aldo. A Sand County Almanac. Copyright © 1949, 1977 Oxford University Press. Reprinted by permission.

Miller, Marshall. Federal Regulation of Pesticides in Environmental Law Handbook, 14th Edition, 284-30. Copyright © 1997 Government Institutes, Inc. Reprinted by permission.

Mintz, Joel. Enforcement at the EPA, 13-16. Copyright © 1995 University of Texas Press. Reprinted by permission.

Nordhaus, William. The Climate Casino: Risk, Uncertainty, and Economics for a Warming World. Copyright © 2013 Yale University Press. Reprinted by permission.

Sandman, Peter. Risk Communication: Facing Public Outrage, 2 EPA Journal 1-22. Copyright © 1987 United States Environmental Protection Agency. Reprinted by permission.

Sax, Joseph L. Defending the Environment: A Strategy for Citizen Action. Copyright © 1970 The Estate of Joseph L. Sax. Reprinted by permission.

Scro, Jennifer. Navigating the Takings Maze: The Use of Transfers of Development Rights in Defending Regulations Against Takings Challenges, 19 Ocean & Coastal Law Journal 219. Copyright © Jennifer Scro. Reprinted by permission.

Starfield, Lawrence E. The 1990 National Contingency Plan—More Detail and More Structure, But Still a Balancing Act, 20 Environmental Law Reporter 10222. Copyright © 1990 Environmental Law Institute. Reprinted by permission.

Wurster, Charles F. Of Salt . . . and Snow. The New York Times, March 4, 1978. Copyright © 1978 Charles F. Wurster. Reprinted by permission.

Photographs & Illustrations

Average River. Copyright © Philip Scoville. Reprinted by permission.

Bristlecone Pine in the Snake Range of Nevada. G. Thomas / Wikimedia Commons. Used under (CC BY-NC-ND 3.0).

Acknowledgements

Checkerboard and clustered designs in Performance Zoning by Lane Kendig. Copyright © 1980 Planners Press / American Planning Association. Reprinted by permission.

Cuyahoga River Fire, 1952. Copyright © 1952 James Thomas / The Cleveland Press Collection, Michael Schwartz Library, Cleveland State University. Reproduced by permission.

Detroit's Poletown. Copyright © David Turnley / Corbis Historical / Getty Images. Reprinted by permission.

Epcot Spaceship Earth and peppercorn. Copyright © Eric Abrams. Reprinted by permission.

Mono Lake. Copyright © Jim Stroup. Reprinted by permission.

ORV Use in Jawbone Canyon. Copyright © 1989 Howard G. Wilshire. Reprinted by permission.

Scranton, PA coalmine subsidence cave-ins. Copyright © Lackawanna Historical Society. Reprinted by permission.

State Brownfield and Voluntary Cleanup Programs. Copyright © Roy F. Weston, Inc. / Weston Solutions. Reprinted by permission.

Stratospheric chlorine parts per billion. Copyright © University of Wisconsin, Marathon County. Reprinted by permission.

Sustained yield. Copyright © Danielle Sievers. Reprinted by permission.

A Tax in the Gasoline Market. John Welker / Welker's Wikinomics. Used under (CC BY-NC-ND 3.0).

Environmental Law and Policy: Nature, Law, and Society

CLASSIFIEDS. Temperate but endangered planet. Enjoys weather, northern lights, continental drift. Seeks caring relationship with intelligent life form.
F.O.E.

I

BASIC THEMES IN ENVIRONMENTAL LAW

It suddenly struck me that that tiny pea, pretty and blue, was the Earth. I put up my thumb and shut one eye, and my thumb blotted out the planet Earth. I didn't feel like a giant. I felt very, very small.

—Astronaut Neil Armstrong

The first day, we pointed to our countries. Then we were pointing to our continents. By the fifth day we were aware of only one Earth.

—Astronaut Bin Salmon al-Saud, Saudi Arabia

For the first time in my life I saw the horizon as a curved line. It was accentuated by a thin seam of dark blue light—our atmosphere. Obviously this was not the ocean of air I had been told it was so many times in my life. I was terrified by its fragile appearance.

—Ulf Merbold, Federal Republic of Germany

Looking outward to the blackness of space, sprinkled with the glory of a universe of lights, I saw majesty— but no welcome. Below was a welcoming planet. There, contained in the thin, moving, incredibly fragile shell of the biosphere is everything that is dear to you, all the human drama and comedy. That's where life is; that's where all the good stuff is.

—Loren Acton, USA

A Chinese tale tells of some men sent to harm a young girl who, upon seeing her beauty, become her pro-tectors rather than her violators. That's how I felt seeing the Earth for the first time. "I could not help but love and cherish her."

—Taylor Wang, China/USA

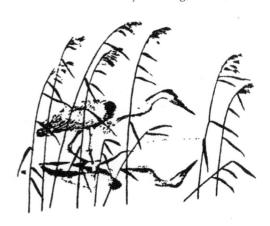

1

Basic Themes in Environmentalism

A. The Environmental Perspective
B. The Problem of the Commons
C. A Salty Paradigm: Road Salt, a Problem That Has Not Yet Met Its Legal Process

A. THE ENVIRONMENTAL PERSPECTIVE

1. The Breadth and Scope of Environmentalism

David Brower, a founding elder of the twentieth-century American environmental movement who had the title role in Encounters with the Archdruid, John McPhee's book about environmentalism in America,[1] was standing on a lakeshore talking to an environmental law class. White-haired and raw-boned with piercing blue eyes, Brower stretched out his arm, with thumb and forefinger held about two inches apart, and said:

> Imagine if our entire planet was reduced to this, the size of an egg.... If Earth was the size of an egg, what do you think, proportionally, all its air, its atmosphere, would be? And what would be the total volume of water, that along with air and sunlight sustains all life on this Earth? ... According to computations I've seen, the sum total of atmosphere swathed around an egg planet Earth would be no more than the volume of a little pea, spread around the globe. And the water? That would be no more than a matchhead, a tiny volume spread thin enough to fill the oceans, rivers and lakes of the world. Our planet is a tremendously vulnerable little system, totally dependent on that fragile tissue of air and water. It's such a thin fabric of life support, and it's all the air and water the Earth will ever have.[2]

But Let's take Brower's metaphor one step further: What would be the proportional relationship between our planet *and the sum total mass of all the humans currently living on Earth*—of Homo sapiens, the unique species that works such drastic impacts upon the earth? Obviously that comparison can't be made in relation to an egg, so let's modify it: What would be the proportional sum total of all of humanity if our planet were the size of

---

1. J. McPhee, Encounters with the Archdruid (1971). David Brower (1912-2000), a seer of environmental activism, founded seven activist citizen organizations. R.I.P.
2. Brower was speaking on a beach on Mission Point Peninsula, Grand Traverse Bay, Michigan, October 1977.

the famous EPCOT Center "Spaceship Earth" globe at Florida's Disney World? One of our faithful research assistants came up with the answer: If Earth were reduced to the size of the EPCOT dome, 165 feet in diameter, then up against it the comparative volume of all human beings on the planet would be roughly the size of a *peppercorn*![3] (See Figure 1-1.) (Note, however, that except in relative mass, humankind is emphatically *not* insignificant and is likely to have dominating effects on that globe for at least a few more centuries.) Earth is indeed one small, limited, totally self-contained entity, a single natural system made up of many interconnected and interdependent systems, containing great richness, diversity, and vulnerability to human actions.

FIGURE 1-1. *Beyond Brower's egg: a juxtaposing thought-experiment: If Earth were reduced to the size of the EPCOT Center globe, the total mass of humanity living on the planet would, proportionally, be the size of a peppercorn. (See footnote 3.) The small human figure at the base of the EPCOT structure, circled, holding out a peppercorn, is one of the founding authors of this coursebook. Photo credit: Eric Abrams.*

3. The average American male's body mass is between .05 and .10 cubic meters (m^3). Based on that, let's assume that the average human's body is at the low end of that spectrum (based on men being bigger than women and Americans being pretty big overall). So let's say the overall average human's body mass is .05 m^3, which is probably pretty generous. Multiply that by the estimated 6.5 billion people currently on planet Earth = 325 million m^3. The mass of Earth is estimated at 1.083 x 10 to the 21st power m^3. Divide the volume of Earth by the volume of its human population and you get 3,332,307,692,307.69. In other words, the ratio of Earth's volume to humans' volume is 3,332,307,692,307.69 m^3 to 1 m^3. "Spaceship Earth," the big EPCOT dome, is 165 feet in diameter. Thus, its volume is 66,603 m^3. Divide 66,603 by 3,332,307,692,307.69 and you get .000000019987 or so. Thus, if Earth was the size of EPCOT's dome, then the volume of all human beings would be 0.000000019987 m^3, or 0.019187 cubic centimeters (cm^3). Something with a volume of 0.019187 cm^3 would have a radius of .166 centimeters (cm), which would be a diameter of around .3333 cm—a peppercorn! Thanks to Tim Landry, Boston College Law, Class of '07, for these calculations.

A. The Environmental Perspective

The ecological future of the planet is constantly being shaped by its geophysical history, of course—by continuing natural forces of sun, rain, wind, water, seismics, vulcanism, the carbon cycle, and the diverse onrolling biological evolution built upon them. But it's also seriously impacted by humans, corporations, and governments. These latter three are very recent arrivals on the global scene as well being relatively trivial in mass. They have proved, however, to have a remarkable capacity for causing planetary effects, for good and ill, and it's upon them that environmental law focuses in doing its work.

Environmental law was born in controversy and has developed in cycles alternating between flourishing growth and retrenchment under bitter counterattack. In the years since the 1960s, it has become a major sector of our legal system and a vivid mirror of the political evolution of our society, operating across a remarkably broad horizon.

What's "environmental"? If you made a mental list of the amazing diversity of situations that are considered "environmental" issues, most of which find their way into the legal system, it could include all of the following and many more. What do they have in common that makes them "environmental"?

- Factories discharging liquid wastes from their drainpipes and smoke from their stacks
- Chemical wastes buried in suburban fields
- Seal puppies clubbed to death on floating ice packs in the Gulf of St. Lawrence
- Uranium fuel rods being shipped thousands of miles to nuclear plants in South Carolina, or India, or North Korea
- A government highway agency cutting a path for an interstate through a park and a low-income neighborhood in Memphis
- A deepwater oil blowout in the Gulf of Mexico hitting ecosystems and economics
- Schools of fish dying in coastal waters from bacterial toxins triggered by waste dumped by upland hog and chicken farmers
- Toxic gases spreading from chemical plants, poisoning surrounding low-income neighborhoods in Italy, India, and Louisiana
- Sprawl development creating towns that resemble parking lots more than communities
- A single-hulled oil tanker more than three football fields long, with an exhausted crew, running at high speed through icebergs in a narrow rocky channel at night
- The imminent extinction of an endangered snapdragon plant in Maine
- Hairdressing salons in Yosemite National Park
- Environmental justice: toxic waste sites and incinerators sited in the midst of low-income minority neighborhoods
- Carcinogenic chemical fire retardants in infant sleepwear
- The cutting of shade trees along rural roads
- Rivers eliminated by federal public works agency dam projects with negative economics
- A centuries-old church bulldozed for a parking lot, and similar historic preservation issues
- Nonreturnable bottles lying along highways and in urban trash
- Disappearing rainforests and desertification in the Third World
- New Jersey's refusal to permit Philadelphia's garbage to be disposed of in New Jersey landfills
- Chlorinated hydrocarbons from consumer products and pesticides disrupting hormones, lowering sperm counts, and harming child development around the world
- Environmental justice: children with rat bites and lead poisoning in urban slums

- Redwood trees turned into tomato stakes and our remnant ancient forests cut for subsidized export
- An internationally known 10 million-year-old paleontological fossil site in Colorado being bulldozed for a resort subdivision
- Asbestos dust in local elementary schools
- Environmental justice: the construction of a new federal prison breaking apart a cohesive low-income neighborhood in New York City
- Chlorofluorocarbons thinning stratospheric ozone, causing increased ultraviolet radiation hazards on Earth
- A primitive tribe in Panama threatened by extension of the Pan-American Highway through its jungle territory
- Space junk in geosynchronous orbit, and possibilities for radioactive and bacterial contamination extending far beyond
- Polar bears stranded by receding sea ice, endangered by changing weather patterns and rising sea levels across the entire planet, caused in substantial part by global warming from human-generated greenhouse gases[4]
- And hundreds more.

In each of these settings noted—especially as we face the unprecedented, existential threats posed by human-caused global climate disruption—environmental law needs to be affirmative as well as critical: How can the human actions that cause these problems be effectively reconfigured to work successfully and sustainably in practical, economic, and ecological terms for future generations?

Is this parade of challenges just *one* field of law? It seems so. All of these widely diverse situations have been called "environmental." For each of them (and hundreds of others), activists identified as "environmentalists" have taken action to improve the situation, often with a modicum of success. Each case involves a highly individualized set of economic and political issues, scientific facts, private or governmental actors, and social and natural consequences. Many of them have no obvious connection with others on the list beyond their environmental label. Because the different areas of environmental law are so voluminously complex, they become compartmentalized and unwieldy. An expert working on water pollution law typically has little time to do anything else. A person studying the science and law of endangered plants may have no special knowledge of any other environmental area and no ties to individuals working on other kinds of environmental cases. Given this diversity, the term *environmental* may seem uselessly broad, describing nothing in particular.

What do these "environmental" examples all have in common? It may be that what makes issues *environmental* is that they all reflect a characteristic battle between two very different ways of looking at the world: Almost every environmental case starts in response to someone's decision to do something: a new product or technology; a construction project; the start, continuation, or cessation of various programs that affect the physical world.[5] A

---

4. This particular environmental challenge is perhaps the most severe and daunting that human society has ever faced. As we will see, however, it will undoubtedly be primarily addressed through some of the already-existing legal approaches studied within this book's "taxonomy" of different legal mechanisms for environmental protection.

5. With regard to some of the largest geophysical issues, of course—such as deforestation or, especially, overpopulation, which produces circumstances where basic natural resources are simply incapable of supporting the geometrically increasing numbers of dependent humans thrust upon them—the operative human decisions are not made consciously, but by tradition, atavistic drives, inertia, and default.

common complaint of environmentalists is that most people who make project proposals do not adequately consider their project's problematic aspects. Resulting decisions thus are often predicated on irrationally and unrealistically narrow grounds, focusing on narrowed advantage to the promoters and unwisely ignoring facts, costs, and impacts on public values that have real importance to the well-being of the community and natural systems.

Environmental analysis in all these cases commonly makes three scrutinizing assessments:

1. What are the true benefits of the proposed project or program?
2. What are its true full costs and consequences?
3. What are the feasible alternatives and their comparative benefits and costs?

One or more of these inquiries typically reveals important questions about the actual public merits of proposals, providing the basis for arguments to improve or halt problematic plans. Unfortunately the environmental perspective often surfaces relatively late in the game, long after the planning stages and well into the implementation stages—that is, at the last minute, when citizens see bulldozers rolling. And environmentalists, because of their instinctive tendency to look for overlooked problems and their often-skeptical view of claimed benefits, often end up sounding chronically negative. It need not be so.

Take the example of the Memphis superhighway studied in the *Overton Park* case.[6] The federal and state highway planners wanted to locate a stretch of Interstate 40 along a route that would minimize the costs of land acquisition and the inconvenience of lawsuits. With that strategy in mind, they planned to run the road straight through an urban park and an older neighborhood. The local citizen environmentalists argued that this official decision took no account of the natural and social values of parkland, especially a park serving low-income communities. If the full costs and values were taken into account, alternative routes existed that were preferable and available. The citizens found a tactical piece of law—an environmental statute limiting highway impacts on parklands—that made their point and won the issue. That citizen-generated legal precedent has subsequently resulted in substantial improvements in the official foresight and advance planning given to major highway projects around the nation.

2. The Ecological and Ethical Bases of Environmental Law

a. The Science of Ecology (*MICRO* and *MACRO*)

Law draws lessons and arguments from ecology and the other flourishing environmental sciences. Modern environmentalists draw particular inspiration and momentum from Rachel Carson and Aldo Leopold, two giants in the field. Here are two brief examples of their work.

Aldo Leopold, A Sand County Almanac
214-220 (1968 ed.)

The image commonly employed in conservation education is "the balance of nature." For reasons too lengthy to detail here, this figure of speech fails to describe accurately what

---

6. *Citizens to Preserve Overton Park v. Volpe*, 401 U.S. 402 (1971) in Chapter 6.

little we know about the land mechanism. A much truer image is the one employed in ecology: the biotic pyramid. . . . Plants absorb energy from the sun. This energy flows through a circuit called the biota, which may be represented by a pyramid consisting of layers. The bottom layer is the soil. A plant layer rests on the soil, an insect layer on the plants, a bird and rodent layer on the insects, and so on up through various animal groups to the apex layer, which consists of the larger carnivores. . . .

In the beginning, the pyramid of life was low and squat; the food chains short and simple. Evolution has added layer after layer, link after link. Man is one of thousands of accretions to the height and complexity of the pyramid. Science has given us many doubts, but it has given us at least one certainty: the trend of evolution is to elaborate and diversify the biota. Land, then, is not merely soil; it is a fountain of energy flowing through soils, plants, and animals. Food chains are the living channels which conduct energy upward; death and decay return to the soil. The circuit is not closed; some energy is dissipated in decay, some is added by absorption from the air, some is stored in soils, peats, and long-lived forests; but it is a sustained circuit, like a slowly augmented revolving fund of life. . . .

The velocity and character of the upward flow of energy depend on the complex structure of the plant and animal community, much as the upward flow of sap in a tree depends on its complex cellular organization. Without this complexity, normal circulation would presumably not occur. Structure means the characteristic numbers, as well as the characteristic kinds and functions, of the component species. This interdependence between the complex structure of the land and its smooth functioning as an energy unit is one of its basic attributes.

When a change occurs in one part of the circuit, many other parts must adjust themselves to it. Change does not necessarily obstruct or divert the flow of energy; evolution is a long series of self-induced changes, the net result of which has been to elaborate the flow mechanism and to lengthen the circuit. Evolutionary changes, however, are usually slow and local. Man's invention of tools has enabled him to make changes of unprecedented violence, rapidity, and scope. . . . The combined evidence of history and ecology seems to support one general deduction: the less violent the man-made changes, the greater the probability of successful readjustment in the pyramid. . . . This deduction runs counter to our current philosophy, which assumes that because a small increase in density enriches human life, that an indefinite increase will enrich it indefinitely. Ecology knows of no density relationship that holds for indefinitely wide limits. All gains from density are subject to a law of diminishing returns.

Rachel Carson, Silent Spring
54-57, 61 (1962)

There are few studies more fascinating, and at the same time more neglected, than those of the teeming populations that exist in the dark realms of the soil. Perhaps the most essential organisms in the soil are the smallest—the invisible hosts of bacteria and threadlike fungi. Statistics of their abundance take us at once into astronomical figures. A teaspoonful of topsoil may contain billions of bacteria. In spite of their minute size, the total weight of this host of bacteria in the top foot of a single acre of fertile soil may be as much as a thousand pounds. Ray fungi, bacteria, [and] small green cells called algae, these make up the microscopic plant life of the soil [and are] the principal agents of decay, reducing plant and animal residues to their component minerals. The vast cyclic movements of chemical

A. The Environmental Perspective

elements such as carbon and nitrogen through soil and air and living tissue could not proceed without these microplants. Without the nitrogen-fixing bacteria, for example, plants would starve for want of nitrogen, though surrounded by a sea of nitrogen-containing air. Other organisms form carbon dioxide, which, as carbonic acid, aids in dissolving rock. Still other soil microbes perform various oxidations and reductions by which minerals such as iron, manganese, and sulfur are transformed and made available to plants.

Also present in prodigious numbers are microscopic mites and primitive wingless insects called springtails. Despite their small size they play an important part in breaking down the residues of plants, aiding in the slow conversion of the litter of the forest floor to soil. The specialization of some of these minute creatures for their task is almost incredible. Several species of mites, for example, can begin life only within the fallen needles of a spruce tree. Sheltered here, they digest out the inner tissues of the needle. When the mites have completed their development only the outer layer of the cells remains. The truly staggering task of dealing with the tremendous amount of plant material in the annual leaf fall belongs to some of the small insects of the soil and the forest floor. They macerate and digest the leaves, and aid in mixing the decomposed matter with surface soil.

Besides all this horde of minute but ceaselessly toiling creatures there are of course many larger forms, for soil life runs the gamut from bacteria to mammals. Some are permanent residents of the dark subsurface layers; some hibernate or spend definite parts of their life cycles in underground chambers; some freely come and go between their burrows and the upper world. In general the effect of all this habitation of the soil is to aerate it and improve both its drainage and the penetration of water throughout the layers of plant growth.

Of all the larger inhabitants of the soil, probably none is more important than the earthworm. Over three-quarters of a century ago, Charles Darwin ... gave the world its first understanding of the fundamental role of earthworms as geologic agents for the transport of soil—a picture of surface rocks being gradually covered by fine soil brought up from below by the worms, in annual amounts running from many tons to the acre in most favorable areas.[7] At the same time, quantities of organic matter contained in leaves and grass (as much as 20 pounds to the square yard in six months) are drawn down into the burrows and incorporated in soil. Darwin's calculations showed that the toil of earthworms might add a layer of soil an inch to inch and a half thick in a ten-year period. And this is by no means all they do: their burrows aerate the soil, keep it well drained, and aid the penetration of plant roots. ... The soil community, then, consists of a web of interwoven lives, each in some way related to the others—the living creatures depending on the soil, but the soil in turn a vital element of the earth only so long as this community within it flourishes.

The problem that concerns us here is one that has received little consideration: What happens to these incredibly numerous and vitally necessary inhabitants of soil when poisonous chemicals are carried down into their world, either introduced directly as soil "sterilants" or borne on the rain that has picked up a lethal contamination as it filters through the leaf canopy of forest and orchard cropland? Is it reasonable to suppose that we can apply a broad-spectrum insecticide to kill the burrowing larval stages of a crop-destroying insect, for example, without also killing the "good" insects whose function may be the essential one of breaking down matter? Or can we use a nonspecific fungicide without also killing

---

7. C. Darwin, The Formation of Vegetable Mould, Through the Action of Worms, with Observations on Their Habits (1897).

the fungi that inhabit the roots of many trees in a beneficial association that aids the tree in extracting nutrients from the soil? . . .

Chemical control of insects seems to have proceeded on the assumption that the soil could and would sustain any amount of . . . poisons without striking back. The very nature of the world of the soil has been largely ignored. . . . A group of specialists who met to discuss the ecology of the soil . . . summed up the hazards of using such potent and little understood tools. . . . "A few false moves on the part of man may result in destruction of soil productivity, and the arthropods may well take over."

COMMENTARY & QUESTIONS

1. Leopold, ecology, and the romantic misnomer of "natural equilibrium." In the years since 1948, when Aldo Leopold first wrote Sand County Almanac, the observations and interconnections he discovered in the Wisconsin countryside helped nurture the new-old science of ecology. The study of organisms as they actually live and interact in living networks over time offers important advantages over the reductionistic study of a creature or a compound or its genetic building blocks isolated on a slide or lab table. The multifactored effects of industrial activities on the people and environments they impact are not realistically predictable through traditional scientific disciplines. For lawyers in the field, a survey course in ecology and environmental science techniques is a good investment of time. The University of Maryland's environmental law program has published a short coursebook on "Environmental Science for Lawyers." Other useful books illustrate the breadth and depth of modern ecological sciences and explain how to ask intelligent questions about them. See, e.g., K.S. Shrader-Frechette & E.D. McCoy, Method in Ecology (1993).

As Leopold noted, the image commonly employed of "the balance of nature" fails to describe accurately what we now know about ecology—that the natural world is composed of dynamic ongoing systems, not of static balances. There is no ideal historical "balance of nature" from which today's environment came and to which natural communities can or should be returned, despite the classical rhetoric of some environmentalists.

> "Equilibrium" was the source of the "balance of nature" premise. . . . It was understood that populations of organisms could swing from low to high in accordance with the seasons and the system's other cycles, but its "equilibrium" levels [supposedly] remained constant over time and the system's pattern did not change. . . . The balance of nature premise has been described as the ecological justification for what was once the dominant principle in environmental law—"let nature be."[8] Equilibrium theory no longer governs ecological thinking. Instead, [it is now understood that] ecosystems . . . do not reach a climax state . . . [but] continue to evolve and change. . . . "Species come and go, climates change, plant and animal communities adapt to altered circumstances, and when examined in fine detail such adaptation and consequent change can be seen to be taking place constantly. The 'balance of nature' is a myth. Our

---

8. 20 Pace Envtl. L. Rev. 675, 687 (2003). See also Botkin, Adjusting Law to Nature's Discordant Harmonies, 7 Duke Envtl. L. & Pol'y F. 25, 26 (1996); and Tarlock, The Nonequilibrium Paradigm in Ecology and the Partial Unraveling of Environmental Law, 27 Loy. L.A. L. Rev. 1121, 1122 (1994). This principle was adopted by legislators, regulators, resource managers, and lawyers, and gradually replaced the progressive conservation movement's ethic of multiple use. Tarlock cites D.L. Feldman, WATER RESOURCES MANAGEMENT: IN SEARCH OF AN ENVIRONMENTAL ETHIC (1991), as providing a good case study of this evolution.

A. The Environmental Perspective

planet is dynamic, and so are the arrangements by which its inhabitants live together."[9] Pardy, Changing Nature: The Myth of the Inevitability of Ecosystem Management.[10]

Environmental law echoes the changing dynamics of human and ecological interconnections.

2. The broad reverberations of Rachel Carson's microcosm. Rachel Carson's perceptive observations revealed a systemic deficiency in the way mid-twentieth-century humans made decisions. Carson changed the way many Americans viewed their world.[11] Reflecting the traditional instinctive perspective of human enterprises, most people plan projects or solve problems using one-shot technology—insulated, narrow, and unidimensional:

"You got bugs? So go get a pesticide." . . .

Zap.

"Now you've got what you wanted. Dead bugs. The End."

But Carson showed us that's not the end of it. There is no such thing as a simple one-shot technology. Everything has continuing long-term consequences. Pesticides don't just disappear after they have killed the target bugs. They linger on and on, blowing in the wind, leaching into groundwater, eliminating the rich, interconnected communities that had naturally evolved in the land to give it its fertility in the first place, moving up through ecological food chains, and diffusing far and wide through the air currents of the hemisphere.[12]

The lessons Carson drew from DDT pesticides are readily applied to many other settings as well—to other kinds of pollution, to resource management issues like timber and grazing, highway and transportation planning, pharmaceuticals and health technology, and by extension to many other areas of national policy like climate change.

Carson showed that the particular results desired from human actions are typically not all that happens. Predictable problems follow when official players, both corporate and governmental, make decisions in traditional terms, seeking short-term benefits with a narrowed, insulated field of vision. Although humans may not take account of the real social and ecological costs of their actions, nature keeps a comprehensive tab, and real consequences follow. Western societies traditionally have tended to view human actors as the central players in the life of the planet, with nature as a subservient and pliant backdrop, but nature is not "outside" our human economy or our jurisprudence.[13] Carson demonstrated

---

9. M. Allaby, BASICS OF ENVIRONMENTAL SCIENCE 154 (1996).

10. 20 Pace Envtl. L. Rev. 675, 687 (2003) (quoting Botkin and Allaby). Prof. Pardy's article explores the policy allegation that, since there is no such thing as natural equilibrium to act as a moral and legal touchstone, human "ecosystem management" activities impacting natural systems do not thereby violate any norm of natural systems, but rather are just one more form of change. But this assertion "is a policy choice masquerading as an inevitability. Neither nonequilibrium nor the absence of pristine systems demands that ecosystems be changed to suit human preferences. . . . Natural is possible. Whether it is preferable is a different debate." Id. at 691.

11. It is remarkable in retrospect how three books written at virtually the same historical moment so powerfully reshaped so much of modern American society's view of life—Jane Jacobs, THE DEATH AND LIFE OF GREAT AMERICAN CITIES (1961); Rachel Carson, SILENT SPRING (1962); Betty Friedan, THE FEMININE MYSTIQUE (1963). What is it they have in common?

12. See T. Colborn, D. Dumanoski & J.P. Myers, OUR STOLEN FUTURE: ARE WE THREATENING OUR FERTILITY, INTELLIGENCE, AND SURVIVAL?—A SCIENTIFIC DETECTIVE STORY (1997).

13. David Westbrook has expressed some frustration at the difficulty of defining a coherent philosophy of environmental jurisprudence. He tried to build a liberal conceptual overview upon the perspectives of individual human rights, collective aggregated rights, and markets but was unable to fit some sectors of environmental law into those realms. Norms protecting endangered species, for instance, seemed to come from an alien, less human-centered domain. See generally Westbrook, Liberal Environmental Jurisprudence, 27 U.C. Davis L. Rev. 619 (1994). As he has commented:

through an ecological lens that the natural backdrop to human activity may be far larger in scale and importance than the human figures pirouetting in the foreground.

Talbot Page, A Generic View of Toxic Chemicals & Similar Risks
7 Ecology Law Quarterly 207 (1978)

... **RELATIVE COSTS: FALSE NEGATIVES AND FALSE POSITIVES.** By definition, the potential costs of environmental risks are great and the benefits are generally modest. Correspondingly, there is asymmetry in the costs of making wrong decisions. For classical pollutants, the asymmetry of potential costs and benefits, and hence the potential costs of wrong decisions, are likely to be less pronounced than for environmental risk problems.

The concept of false negatives and false positives helps to illustrate this distinction. In criminal law, two basic kinds of mistakes can occur: the jury (or judge) can find a guilty man innocent or an innocent man guilty. Testing chemicals for toxicity presents the same problem. Test results may indicate that a toxic chemical is not toxic or that a non-toxic chemical is toxic. The former type of error is called a false negative and the latter a false positive. . . .

[In environmental risk situations,] the cost of a false negative — deciding that the benign hypothesis is true when it is not — is much higher than the cost of a false positive — deciding that the catastrophic hypothesis is true when it is not. . . . Catastrophic results more than offset the modest benefits of erroneously accepting the benign hypothesis. . . .

Acceptable risk . . . Even if the probability of an environmental risk were well defined, our legal, regulatory, and economic institutions must still decide what degree of risk is acceptable. Although there are several approaches for defining acceptable risk, there is little agreement on what is the best approach. This ambiguity presents a major difficulty in managing environmental risk. A few of the approaches are discussed below. . . .

Limiting false positives. The most common approach for risks subject to governmental regulation and court proceedings starts with the assumption that there is no risk and requires that a hazard be proved beyond some standard. Under this approach [of limiting false positives], by definition, if the standard of proof is not met, then the risk is acceptable. The burden of proof is placed on those seeking precautionary action. . . . However, the approach of limiting false positives, although often effective in defining acceptable risk for classical problems, has questionable value for the management of environmental risk. . . .

Most of our law may be (must be) articulable in some liberal language. But the Endangered Species Act cannot be, not really. . . . At some point liberalism's concern for the internal (autonomy, choice), fails to capture environmentalism's sense of the external (ecosystems, nature, etc.). At the end of the day, you cannot explain the outside in terms of the inside. David Westbrook, post on Envprofs listserv, envlawprofs@darkwing.uoregon.edu (Nov. 6, 2001).

Conceptualizing the existence of three interlinked economies, however, explains that environmental jurisprudence operates on the realistic foundation that there *is* no external outside. Environmental law's high purpose and aspiration is to make sense of the First Law of Ecology, that everything is connected to everything else. Environmental law, like all law, ultimately must function in the real world, a world made up of multiple interlocking systems. We humans individually and collectively are indeed significant components of many of these multiple systems. But we are not hermetically separated from the systemic elements and networks that don't operate on our own terms, just as we are not disconnected from the consequences of our own actions.

A. The Environmental Perspective

Limiting false negatives. Limiting false positives is the guiding principle of criminal law. The objective is to limit the chance of a false conviction. The common-sense justification for this objective is that it is better to free a hundred guilty men than to convict one innocent one. . . .

A comparison of criminal law with environmental risk, however, suggests an important difference. The costs of false negatives and false positives are asymmetric for environmental risk as well, but the asymmetry is in reverse order. For environmental risk, the asymmetrically high cost arises from a false negative; in criminal law from a false positive. Similarly, just as a primary good, liberty, is an important concern in criminal law, so another primary good, health, is an important concern in environmental risk management, but again the roles are reversed. Typically, public health is adversely affected under a false negative for environmental risk, while liberty is adversely affected under a false positive for criminal law.

The analogy between criminal law and environmental risk requires that the roles of negatives and positives be reversed. If the emphasis on limiting false positives for criminal law is sensible and based on the asymmetry of costs of wrong decisions and the possible deprivation of a public good, then the implication is that a decision procedure based on limiting false negatives is more appropriate for environmental risk than one based on limiting false positives. . . .

Focusing more attention on the need to limit false negatives brings us back to the importance of modeling the risks and hypotheses, including "credible" worst case modeling. It is clearly infeasible to take precautionary action for each conceivable environmental risk; there would be too many. Requiring some sort of model of the risk provides an entrance barrier against the flood of conceivable risks for which precautionary action should be evaluated. Because of the nature of environmental risk it is senseless to require proof of actual harm; the barrier should be no more than a reasonable basis within the context of the model for believing that there is a risk of harm. The risk itself may be small.

Balancing false positives and false negatives. [Page then recommends a decisionmaking mechanism, which he calls "the expected value approach," that balances the cost of a false negative, weighted by its probability of occurrence, against the cost of a false positive, weighted by its probability of occurrence, and chooses the alternative with the lower weighted cost.[14] Page recognizes the importance and intransigence of "outrage" factors in risk management.]

The hard part is to uncover a social consensus on the appropriate amount of risk aversion and then to build this amount into the institutions which manage environmental risks.

The expected value approach does not require that each environmental risk be regulated, or not regulated, on the sole basis of a detailed and quantified cost-benefit analysis. For example, the internal transfer of benefits tends to be associated with a sharply focused group of proponents of the environmental risk taking, while the external transfer of the potential costs, both spatially and temporally, is associated with a broader but less focused group of opponents.[15] This imbalance in interests, for and against, is likely to lead to an imbalance in decision making, even for an ostensibly neutral cost-benefit analysis, unless the imbalance in interests is recognized and offset by the design of the decision making institutions. Alternatively, in order to come closer to a minimum expected cost of wrong decisions, it is necessary to adjust the rules of the decision process—the standards and

---

14. Once the concepts of "minimizing false negatives" and "minimizing false positives" have been learned, it might be simpler to refer to them as the "proactive" and "reactive" approaches to risk management. [Eds.]

15. This is one of the central tenets of "public choice theory." [Eds.]

burdens of proof, the rules of liability, the incentives for the generation and valuation of information, and so on. For instance, when the potential adverse effects of an environmental risk are many times greater than the potential benefits, a proper standard of proof of danger under the expected cost minimization criterion may be that there is only "at least a reasonable doubt" that the adverse effect will occur, rather than requiring a greater probability, such as "more likely than not," that the effect will occur.

COMMENTARY & QUESTIONS

1. The "Precautionary Principle." The "Precautionary Principle" is an environmental principle reflected in many international and domestic regulatory fields—if a thing is potentially very dangerous and alternatives exist, why wait until all studies are complete before acting to limit exposures? It asserts Page's utilitarian perspective: Unless you collectively are pretty sure that the negative consequences are foreseeable, minor, and mitigatable, and that fundamentally important interconnections will not be disrupted, you'd better be sure that what somebody proposes to do is worth the potential costs. It's generally safer not to take casual risks with the escalating domino consequences that may follow. Moving from a human-centered master-of-nature perspective to the holistic human-species-as-constituent-part-of-nature view is not just an ethical idea—it is fundamentally practical and utilitarian as well, as Rachel Carson argued.

2. "Classical pollution" and "environmental risk." In the same article, Page recommends that the legal system manage risks caused by pollution and resource depletion based on where a particular risk falls on a continuum between what he terms "Classical Pollution" and "Environmental Risk." The former presents the more humdrum problem of dealing with relatively well-understood and innocuous effluent streams and their effects on the environment. The latter is more complex. Page defines environmental risk in terms of nine characteristics: four dealing with the uncertainties surrounding environmental decision-making and five bearing on institutional problems encountered in environmental management. Environmental problems differ as to how intensely they exhibit these characteristics. The first four characteristics of environmental risk are: (1) ignorance of mechanism (i.e., scientific uncertainty as to the generation and transmission of hazards, as well as their environmental impacts), (2) relatively modest benefits, (3) potentially catastrophic costs, and (4) relatively low probability of occurrence of catastrophic outcomes. Hazards manifesting these characteristics often present the "Zero-Infinity Dilemma"—a virtually zero probability of occurrence of a virtually infinite catastrophe.[16]

3. Environmental risk and environmental justice. Since Page wrote this article, environmental justice has emerged as a matter of concern. With that in mind, distributional inequality might qualify as a tenth characteristic of environmental risk. Environmental risks are imposed disproportionately on the least politically powerful members of our society—minorities, the poor, children, and the sick and disabled. The toxic effects of pesticides, for example, are most intensely experienced by farm workers. Most hazardous waste disposal facilities have been located in neighborhoods occupied by disadvantaged groups. Is that form of environmental injustice a form of racism?

---

16. Page's other characteristics are internal benefits, external costs, collective risk, latency (e.g., carcinogenic effects may not manifest themselves until 20 or 30 years after exposure), and irreversibility of effects.

A. The Environmental Perspective

4. Species eradication as a catastrophic ecological cost. The importance of biodiversity, both as a necessity for human survival and as an end in itself, is better understood today than it was even a generation ago. Managing environmental risks entails factoring ecological effects of human behavior into environmental decisionmaking. Extinction is the most profoundly irreversible phenomenon on this planet. How should risks of species extinction be managed? The Endangered Species Act is studied in Chapter 10.

5. External cost transfers and political power. Note how heavily Page, in his definition of environmental risk, relies on the theory of "externalities." Internalization of economic benefits among a focused, knowledgeable, and politically powerful group of producers and consumers leads to concentrated political power that tends to outweigh the weaker political influence exercised by a diffuse, disorganized, unaware, and often politically powerless class of polluted public (which, in theory, includes future generations, which cannot directly participate in the political process). Furthermore, it is difficult to organize members of the general public to oppose the imposition of a collective risk because of the "transaction costs" (e.g., time and money) of participation and the "free rider problem" (i.e., the human tendency to believe that someone else will solve the problem). This political asymmetry is another reason for minimizing false negatives. It also explains the need for politically strong environmental groups to counterbalance the influence of powerful producer and consumer constituencies.

> *Risk* can be defined as a composite measure of (1) the probability that a particular act will cause damage to human health and the environment, and (2) the severity of any damage that may occur. It is a fundamental consideration in many environmental regulatory structures (see Chapter 13). But another human dimension of "risk" involves public perceptions and outrage, as the following article makes clear.

Peter Sandman, Risk Communication: Facing Public Outrage
EPA Journal, Nov. 1987, at 21-22

If you make a list of environmental risks in order of how many people they kill each year, then list them again in order of how alarming they are to the general public, the two lists will be very different. The first list will also be very debatable, of course; we don't really know how many deaths are attributable to, say, geological radon or toxic wastes. But we do know enough to be nearly certain that radon kills more Americans each year than all our Superfund sites combined. Yet . . . millions who choose not to test their homes for radon are deeply worried about toxic wastes. The conclusion is inescapable: the risks that kill you are not necessarily the risks that anger and frighten you. . . .

The core problem is one of definition. To the experts, risk means expected annual mortality. But to the public (and even to the experts when they go home at night), risk means much more than that. Let's redefine terms. Call the death rate (what the experts mean by risk) "hazard." Call all the other factors, collectively, "outrage." Risk, then, is the sum of hazard and outrage. The public pays too little attention to hazard; the experts pay absolutely no attention to outrage. Not surprisingly, they rank risks differently.

Risk perception scholars have identified more than 20 "outrage factors." Here are a few of the main ones:

1. *Voluntariness*: A voluntary risk is much more acceptable to people than a coerced risk, because it generates no outrage. Consider the difference between getting pushed down a mountain on slippery sticks and deciding to go skiing.
2. *Control*: Almost everybody feels safer driving than riding shotgun. When prevention and mitigation are in the individual's hands, the risk (though not the hazard) is much lower than when they are in the hands of a government agency.
3. *Fairness*: People who must endure greater risks than their neighbors, without access to greater benefits, are naturally outraged—especially if the rationale for so burdening them looks more like politics than science. Greater outrage, of course, means greater risk.
4. *Process*: Does the agency come across as trustworthy or dishonest, concerned or arrogant? Does it tell the community what's going on before the real decisions are made? Does it listen and respond to community concerns?
5. *Morality*: American society has decided over the last two decades that pollution isn't just harmful—it's evil. But talking about cost-risk tradeoffs sounds very callous when the risk is morally relevant. Imagine a police chief insisting that an occasional child-molester is an "acceptable risk."
6. *Familiarity*: Exotic, high-tech facilities provoke more outrage than familiar risks (your home, your car, your jar of peanut butter).
7. *Memorability*: A memorable incident—Love Canal, Bhopal, Times Beach—makes the risk easier to imagine, and thus (as we have defined the term) more risky. A potent symbol—the 55-gallon drum—can do the same thing.
8. *Dread*: Some illnesses are more dreaded than others; compare AIDS and cancer with, say, emphysema. The long latency of most cancers and the undetectability of most carcinogens add to the dread.
9. *Diffusion in time and space*: Hazard A kills 50 anonymous people a year across the country. Hazard B has one chance in 10 of wiping out its neighborhood of 5,000 people sometime in the next decade. Risk assessment tells us the two have the same expected annual mortality: 50. "Outrage assessment" tells us A is probably acceptable and B is certainly not.

These "outrage factors" are not distortions in the public's perception of risk. They explain why people worry more about Superfund sites than geological radon, more about industrial emissions of dimethylmeatloaf than aflatoxin peanut butter.

There is a peculiar paradox here. Many risk experts resist the pressure to consider outrage in making risk management decisions; they insist that "the data" alone, not the "irrational" public, should determine policy. But we have two decades of data indicating that voluntariness, control, fairness, and the rest are important components of our society's definition of risk. When a risk manager continues to ignore these factors—and continues to be surprised by the public's response of outrage—it is worth asking whose behavior is irrational.

COMMENTARY & QUESTIONS

1. Reactions to outrage. Commentators who accept the legitimacy of outrage as an element of risk generally recommend two strategies for reconciling the discordances between "expert" and "public" definitions of risk: (1) better "risk communication," the two-way process of information exchange between governmental risk managers and the general public; and (2) involvement of "stakeholders," the parties who are affected by the risk management problem, during all stages of the risk definition and management process. See, e.g., Presidential-Congressional Comm'n on Risk Assessment & Risk Management, Final

A. The Environmental Perspective

Report, vol. 2, chs. 1-3 (1997). Others more skeptical of outrage as a genuine element of risk belittle these approaches. See Cross, The Public Role in Risk Control, 24 Envtl. L. 887, 950 (1994) ("A variety of measures could be taken to facilitate the government's use of scientifically accurate measures of risk rather than mistaken public perceptions. Foremost is the reduction in opportunities for public participation in decisionmaking.").

2. How EPA considers risk in environmental protection. As examined later in several regulatory contexts, risk assessment is a burgeoning field in the realm of environmental regulation. For a summary of the methods of analysis used by EPA in performing risk assessment, see Copeland & Simpson, Considering Risk in Environmental Protection, 8 Cong. Res. Serv. Rev. (No. 10) 7-9 (1987). That article describes the risk quantification procedure the federal government uses to evaluate health risks of hazardous substances. The twofold inquiry first identifies the hazard, usually relying on epidemiologic studies, animal bioassays, short-term bioassays, and chemical structure-activity studies that link the chemical (and its chemically similar cousins) and its properties to diseases in humans and animals. The second prong of the inquiry attempts to look at the exposure side of the problem, considering first the magnitude (frequency and intensity) of the exposure to the substance that will be suffered by the populace, and then trying to assess the likely response of individuals to exposure. This latter effort is fraught with scientific uncertainty, primarily due to: (1) the unknown physical mechanisms at work, and (2) imperfections in the measurement of the exposure. The results of human studies tend to have unusual variability, possibly as a result of the imprecision of measurements of most human exposure data.

3. The law and outrage. Should legal institutions take outrage into account? Is a court better equipped to do so than a politically responsible actor, such as a legislator or an executive branch administrative official? Consider in these coursebook materials whether the legal system ignores, represses, assuages (symbolically or actually) channels into socially productive pathways or is misdirected by public outrage. Keep track of who is making the risk management decisions under review in each situation, government regulators or private project proponents.

A bit more on Ecology as a critical societal understanding: In the excerpt below, a distinguished ecologist reminds his readers of the fundamental practical functionality of ecological principles. Human society is a complex ecosystem surviving within a global network of myriad complex non-human ecosystems, and longterm societal sustainability absolutely requires awareness and maintenance of these interdependent interlocking networks upon which human society depends.

G. Tyler Miller, Living in the Environment: Principles, Connections, & Solutions
105, 247-248 (11th ed. 1999)

None of us live apart from nature. . . . Ecosystems[17] provide us and other species with a number of natural services; ecosystem services, which constitute earth capital, support life

---

17. "An ecosystem is a community of different species interacting with one another and with their nonliving environment of matter and energy. The [expanse] of an ecosystem is somewhat arbitrary; it is defined by the . . . unit of study, . . . small and particular . . . or large and generalized. . . . All of the earth's ecosystems together make up what we call the ecosphere or biosphere. . . ." [citation omitted].

on the earth and are essential to the quality of human life and to the functioning of the world's economies.... Ecosystems...

- Control and moderate climate
- Provide us with and renew air, water, and soil
- Recycle vital nutrients through chemical cycling
- Provide us with renewable and nonrenewable energy sources and nonrenewable minerals
- Furnish us with food, fiber, medicines, timber, and paper
- Pollinate crops and other plant species
- Absorb, dilute, or detoxify many pollutants and toxic chemicals
- Help control populations of pests and disease organisms
- Slow soil erosion and help prevent flooding
- Provide the biodiversity of genes and species needed to adapt to ever-changing environmental conditions through evolution and genetic engineering.

Humans are violating these principles of sustainability.... Biologists have formulated several important principles that can help guide us: Our lives, lifestyles, and economics are totally dependent on the sun and the earth.... The first law of human ecology [is that] everything is connected to everything else: we are all in it together. We are connected to all living organisms through ... our DNA. We are connected to the earth through our interactions with air, water, soil, and other living organisms making up the ever-changing web of life.... The primary goal of ecology is to discover which connections in nature are the strongest, most important, and most vulnerable to disruption.

Earth care is self-care, and we can change our ways. According to environmentalist David Brower, we need to focus on "global CPR ... conservation, preservation, and restoration." This means (1) building societies based on conservation, not waste, (2) preserving what we can't replace, and (3) working with nature to help restore what we have degraded or destroyed.

COMMENTARY & QUESTIONS

1. Living systems, dynamic sustainability, and carrying capacity. The excerpt from Miller's treatise reminds us that no matter how omnipotent some humans and politicians consider themselves, in scientific terms we live in a network of interlocking, interdependent natural systems, and ignore these scientific realities at our peril. All living systems share similar critical features—adaptability, resilience, interdependence, biodiversity, limits, and unpredictability. All living systems are constrained by the carrying capacity of the context in which they exist— Energy is required to sustain life; almost all derive their primary source of energy directly or indirectly from sunlight. If not interrupted, there are natural renewable processes for soil, water, air, plants, and animals. Biodiversity is a fundamental strategy for dynamic ecosystem sustainability; systems need to maintain multiple avenues and strategies to develop, adapt, and survive over time in changing circumstances. Natural systems are limited by the *carrying capacity* of the resource base in which they exist; an ecosystem's population growth or resource overuse that goes beyond carrying capacity triggers draconian limitation, or crashing. Jane Jacobs, the guru of modern planning, made carrying capacity a threshold consideration for rational human development. *See* Witten, Carrying Capacity ... Establishing and Defending Limits to Growth, 28 B.C. Envtl. Aff. L. Rev. 583 (2001).

A. The Environmental Perspective

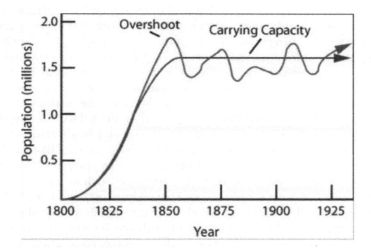

FIGURE 1-2. *Carrying capacity of an ecosystem, in this case human; occasions of consumption overshooting carrying capacity bode ill for an ecosystem's inhabitants. Chart from Samantha Welch, https://www.youtube.com/watch?v=J1Qe5Ad3ap8*

2. "Ecosystem services" and environmental economics. As Miller notes, the richly diverse and dynamic interconnected natural systems that surround us provide extraordinarily valuable and critically important ecosystem services that are largely unrecognized and taken for granted. Robert Costanza and colleagues have analyzed the multi-*trillion* dollar values of "natural capital," the resources and services provided free or far below their true value, without which the marketplace and human life would be impossible. They came up with very impressive "natural capital" numbers:

> We have estimated the current economic value of 17 ecosystem services for 16 biomes, based on published studies and a few original calculations. For the entire biosphere, the value (most of which is outside the market) is estimated to be in the range of US $16-54 trillion per year. . . . Because of the nature of the uncertainties, this must be considered a minimum estimate. Global gross national product total is around $18 trillion per year. Costanza et al., The Value of the World's Ecosystem Services, 387 Nature 253 (1997).[18]

Numbers like these indicate that when we talk about economics we need to include an Economy of Nature, which is more than a charming aesthetic idea and is ignored at our societal peril. See "the three economies" section below.

3. The concept of "ecosystems." You cannot make sense of any piece of nature if you observe it in isolation. Ecology forces us to look beyond just a single bacterium, a cubic centimeter of soil, an earthworm, a tuft of grass, a cow, a wolf, a rancher. An understanding of context, including physical settings and interrelationships with surrounding individuals and communities, is fundamental to understanding reality and the science of ecology. Most ecosystems are complex communities in which all the elements exist and interact in

---

[18]. See also P. Hawken et al., NATURAL CAPITALISM: THE COMING EFFICIENCY REVOLUTION (1998); Costanza & Daly, Natural Capital and Sustainable Development, 6 Conserv. Bio. 37-46 (1992); Hawken, Natural Capitalism, Mother Jones, Mar.-Apr. 1997, at 40. There is a strong body of law review scholarship on ecosystem services. See NATURE'S SERVICES: SOCIETAL DEPENDENCE ON NATURAL ECOSYSTEMS (G.C. Daily ed., 1997); Ruhl & Salzman, The Law and Policy Beginnings of Ecosystem Services, 22 J. Land Use & Envtl. L. 157 (2007); Ruhl, Toward a Common Law of Ecosystem Services, 18 St. Thomas L. Rev. 1 (2005); Salzman, Thompson & Daily, Protecting Ecosystem Services: Science, Economics, and Law, 20 Stan. Envtl. L.J. 309 (2001).

multiple interrelationships characterized overall by extremely high efficiency and relatively high stability so long as fundamental changes do not occur. Disruptions and dislocations cause immediate reverberating effects through the system, leading to adaptive changes and new accommodations, though perhaps with decreased richness in surviving numbers of component species and lowered net productivity. Some elements may be more significant than others. One species may have only a small role in a particular ecosystem, while others may be "indicator species," whose welfare is a barometer for the health of the entire ecosystem, or "keystone species," which if they are removed or altered will force systemic changes throughout the ecosystem. The greater the complexity and biodiversity of the ecosystem, the higher the net primary productivity and adaptive resilience are likely to be.

4. Can the ecosystems metaphor be applied to human systems? The ecosystems metaphor seems applicable to many human social structures such as corporations or political capitals, but it is probably more accurate to say that we humans, whether we like it or not, are part of the ecosystems and biosphere in which we live, uniquely able to observe and manage the way we impact our base and the other systems with which we coexist. To remain ignorant of these systems of ecosystems is likely to be costly and dangerous. Think how staphylococci are increasingly resistant to antibiotics, agricultural soils are losing their fertility and natural regeneration ability, and ocean fish stocks around the world are in precipitous decline.

5. The depressing perspectives of global ecology and the law—and an egregious pun. In the eyes of some observers, these global challenges can be met only through a basic change in attitudes toward use and preservation of natural resources that would dramatically change lifestyles in virtually all parts of the world. What role, if any, would law play in that process? Laws can prohibit directly and indirectly some forms of environmental carnage, as with attempts to protect endangered species. Finding laws that seem capable of effecting larger behavioral changes, such as reducing global emissions of greenhouse gases produced by fossil fuel consumption and deforestation, remains problematic.

Arnold Reitze, in a penetrating article reviewing 20 years of environmental efforts,[19] dourly noted that virtually all global environmental degradation can be traced back to three major human phenomena—population, unwise consumption of resources, and pollution (all three, for example, linked to climate change)—all of which are out of control. Of these, he said, the most devastating is population pressure. Relentless population growth undercuts the hopes of nationbuilders and those who try to apply industrial, social, economic, and legal technology to alleviate the ills of humankind and the planet. Reitze noted that governments find the problems of population and resource consumption so hard to handle that they tend to ignore them and focus instead on pollution,[20] which, though serious, is the least important of the major causes of environmental degradation.

The Pun: It seems to us there's a need to add another one to Reitze's three systemic problems, and not merely for the purpose of making the pun, Four Horsemen of the Eco-palypse.[21] The Fourth Horseman of the Eco-palypse, we would argue, is a critically important procedural/governance problem, particularly within the jurisdiction of the law's art: *It's the gap between what we know and what we do about it.* Despite a truly amazing expansion of ecological knowledge—about pollution, population, resource losses, and the interconnectedness of human and natural systems—and the ability to communicate that knowledge globally at

---

19. Reitze, Environmental Policy—It Is Time for a New Beginning, 14 Colum. J. Envtl. L. 111 (1989).
20. This book to some extent incorporates that mistake. It is far easier to study legal remedies for controlling pollution than for controlling population and resource consumption patterns. This coursebook does look beyond pollution, however, and the legal process approaches examined here can be flexibly extended as far as environmental analysis can go.
21. Plater, Environmental Law as a Mirror of the Future, 23 B.C. Envtl. Aff. L. Rev. 733 (1996).

A. The Environmental Perspective

the speed of light, it's distressing to observe the difference between knowledge and practice. Our capacity to implement what we know about these serious threats consistently falls short, and may even be falling further behind. Looking at the way the realities of climate change science, for instance, have been held at bay, we'd suggest that thoughtful societal responses to what we well know are generally held back by the same powerful market force dynamics that drive human enterprises and cause externalizations in the first place. The same market pressures that make civic regulation necessary assiduously resist it.

In their article Can Selfishness Save the Environment?[22] Bobbi Low and Matt Ridley offer a more optimistic reminder that collective individual self-interests can be mobilized in group mutual support impulses, internalizing the needs of sustainable management, if laws and incentives are crafted to work toward goals of reciprocal advantage.

6. A need for integrated environmental management? Reality exists in the holistic, integrated overview, but knowledge and the capacity to manage discrete problems build from the bottom, from a narrow, incisive, specialized focus. Several strategy reports prepared by the U.S. Environmental Protection Agency[23] argue that EPA should coordinate all protection strategies on the basis of a "systems approach" that views the environment as an integrated whole. The proposal has global implications, which are considered in the last chapter of this book. Perhaps ironically, however, the rest of the EPA report was organized on a medium-by-medium approach — air, water, toxics, noise, land use, and so on. Is it practically inevitable that bureaucrats, legislators, lawyers, litigants, and humans generally will focus on narrow slices of the environmental dilemma? In an increasingly specialized world, how do we keep our eyes open to the whole?

7. Sustainability. Modern environmentalism seeks to implement the concept of "sustainability" — a truly conservative doctrine — as its societal goal.[24] It's a hopeful conceptual approach, holding that thoughtfulness, planning, and luck will enable successive future generations of humankind to sustain and improve our society's collective quality of life in this global setting that supports us. As Professor Dernbach has noted, environmentalism has proactive goals that range far beyond mere defensiveness.

> We often say that the purpose of environmental law is to protect the environment. But it is much more complicated than that. To begin with, environmental law has never been aimed simply at protecting the environment. Environmental law has at least nine major purposes,[25] the most prominent of which is protection of human health. Environmental law also has objectives that are plainly essential to sustainable development, including intergenerational equity and protection of the resource base upon which society rests. Other goals of environmental law include efficiency, national security, preservation for aesthetics or recreation, community stability, biocentrism, and pursuit of scientific knowledge and technology. . . . Sustainable development concepts are embedded in environmental law. Th[ose] nine purposes of environmental law can be organized under the four broad goals of Sustainable Development: Social Well-being, or Equity, . . . Natural Resources Protection, . . . Economic Development, . . . Peace and Security.[26]

---

22. 272 Atl. 76 (Sept. 1993).

23. L. Thomas, Environmental Progress and Challenges: EPA Update (1988).

24. "Sustainability" has become the central principle of the international consensus first enunciated in Our Common Future, the 1987 Report of the World Commission on Environment and Development, echoed since then in the 1992 and 2002 Earth Summits and a succession of international and domestic declarations of policy and law. The concept makes intuitive good sense despite its susceptibility to varying interpretations.

25. C. Campbell-Mohn, OBJECTIVES AND TOOLS OF ENVIRONMENTAL LAW, IN ENVIRONMENTAL LAW: FROM RESOURCES TO RECOVERY §4.1 (C. Campbell-Mohn et al, eds., 1993).

26. Dernbach, Citizen Suits and Sustainability, 10 Widener L. Rev. 503 (2004).

b. An Environmental Economics Perspective: *Three Economies*

A fundamental theme and force in shaping national environmental law, as in most of modern life, is *economics*. That word comes from two Greek words: *oikos*, meaning "household, home, or family place," and *nomos*, meaning "rules." Thus *economics* literally means "the rules governing the human household." Economics could be considered to include the full range of concerns covered by environmental law itself.[27]

Economics usually is given a narrower reach, evoking solely the concerns of the marketplace or the market economy. But consider a useful new analytical perspective: *three* economies. To understand modern societal dynamics, it is helpful to conceptualize three different intersecting economies: (1) the familiar industrial-commercial marketplace economy and all the structures that support it; (2) a separate economy of natural systems; and (3) a human-oriented, civic-societal economy comprised of all the societal values, capital, institutions, and infrastructure not included in the marketplace.[28]

Since the human marketplace economy, broadly defined, generates virtually all environmental problems, environmental law is understood as a comprehensive attempt to control and guide the dynamics of the marketplace economy on behalf of the other two economies. The three-economies construct provides a useful way to talk about an array of long-established concepts of environmental law (and public policy generally), integrating an analysis of societal necessities and ecological realities with the powerful machinery of market dynamics.[29]

Figure 3 offers a schematic view of the three economies. The marketplace economy is the dynamic central core of

FIGURE 1-3.

CENTER SPHERE: *the marketplace economy.*

INTERMEDIARY SPHERE: *the civic-societal economy.*

THE ENCOMPASSING SPHERE: *the economy of nature.*

The rim banding the center sphere represents the governmental role. Relative scale and proportions depend upon observer's perspective.

---

27. On the other hand, the derivation of the word *ecology* connotes a far broader realm—*oikos* again for "home" in the broad figurative sense and *logos*, which means "word" in a sense connoting an all-encompassing sense of thoughtful reckoning narrative, an idea of law and deepened appreciation of reality. As Garrett Hardin wrote, it's ecology that should be the meta-discipline, with economics as just one of its subsidiary parts. "Logically it is obvious that economics is but a small specialty in the much larger science, ecology. Sociologically, it is quite otherwise: the tail wags the dog." G. Hardin, Sweet-Singing Economists, in EXPLORING NEW ETHICS FOR SURVIVAL: THE VOYAGE OF THE SPACESHIP BEAGLE (1972).

28. This idea builds on the work of Joseph L. Sax, who argued that environmental law should recognize an economy of nature as well as the marketplace economy. Sax, Property Rights and the Economy of Nature, 45 Stan. L. Rev. 1433 (1993). See also M. Sagoff, The Economy of the Earth (1988), and the work of a respected consultant on fisheries management policy based in Sequim, Washington, James Lichatowich, "It's the *Economies*, Mr. President," 34 Trout 22 (Summer 1993). Sax uses the phrase "transformative economy" for marketplace economics; Lichatowich uses "industrial economy."

29. For more on the three economies, see Plater, Environmental Law and Three Economies, 23 Harv. Envtl. L. Rev. 359 (1999); Plater, The Three Economies: An Essay in Honor of Professor Sax, 25 Ecology L.Q. 411 (1998).

A. The Environmental Perspective

the three economies' cosmology. It is systematically blind, however, to many important economic elements. For the most part, the marketplace economy deals only with things and services that have a price tag and are bought and sold. It generates waste and externalities as well as profits and products, costs and benefits that are real and need to be included as part of societal economic accounting.

The natural economy is the intricate system of living and geophysical systems that sustains dynamic planetary processes, providing resources and a geophysical base for the human economies. The economy of nature gives and takes, and adjusts as best it can to the marketplace's pollution, resource derogation, and disrupted ecosystem dynamics, while passing the effects of many of these externality impacts onward into the civic economy. The marketplace economy exists *within* the economy of nature, which has hugely significant value to humans even if it is unacknowledged or undervalued by the cash-register economy.[30]

Obvious as this may seem, not everyone sees it. While he was Senior Economist at the World Bank, Herman Daly participated in developing a report on Development and the Environment—

> The chief economist of the World Bank, Lawrence H. Summers [currently financial advisor to President Obama] under whom the report was being written, happened to be on a conference panel at the Smithsonian Institution discussing the book *Beyond the Limits* [Donella H. Meadows, et al.] which Summers considered worthless. In that book there was a diagram showing the relation of the economy to the ecosystem, a diagram exactly like . . . one I had suggested [at the World Bank]. . . . During the question-and-answer time I asked the chief economist if, looking at that diagram, he felt that the question of the size of the economic subsystem relative to the total ecosystem was an important one, and whether he thought economists should be asking the question, "What is the optimal scale of the macro economy relative to the environment?" His reply was immediate and definite: "That's not the right way to look at it."[31]

But beyond linking market economy to the economy of nature we believe that economic analysis, in order to be fully realistic, requires a *third* conceptual economy. The images that launched the environmental law revolution in the 1960s were of pollution directly impacting upon *human* health. The "civic-societal economy"[32] comprises actual social costs, benefits, resources, energy, inputs, outputs, values, qualities, and consequences that are not accounted for in the marketplace but impact human society. Externalized costs exit the marketplace economy, but don't thereby drop into oblivion: By the laws of physics, ecology, and logic, they move through and are internalized into the fabric of one or both of the other economies. Widespread pesticide use, overgrazing, dumping pollutants, chemical exposures that block hormones in our endocrine and reproductive systems, massive layoffs of corporate workers, or a host of other cost externalizations may make powerfully good sense to market players in the narrow market terms of individual gains but be quite irrational in societal economics terms. Healthy societal economic systems are founded upon healthy and sustainable ecological system cycles of soil, water, air, and living communities. When a resource system is derogated or destroyed, some enterprises may prosper greatly, but society is likely to be far less well off. The societal public economy very much needs the market economy, but for the sake of its own short- and long-term interests, society must

---

30. See Costanza and other economic assessments noted above.
31. H. Daly, Beyond Growth: The Economics of Sustainable Development 6 (1997). For a superb quick tour of all the significant economic elements of modern environmental policy, the authors strongly recommend an article by Paul Krugman, Building a Green Economy, N.Y. Times Magazine at page MM34, April 11, 2010, available at http://www.nytimes.com/2010/04/11/magazine/11Economy-t.html.
32. Could someone please come up with a less awkward name for this? We'd be grateful.

somehow contrive to value and incorporate into its governance important elements of civic economic reality that the daily dominant marketplace resists. Toxic spills into watercourses, global warming, lost fisheries, eroded soils, wetlands destruction, pesticide loading, and a multitude of other environmental issues demonstrate important linkages between all three economies.

Where are law and government in the three economies? Many government statutes, agencies, and programs are initiated to protect civic-societal interests. In Figure 2, government is strategically positioned in a schematic circling band at the interface between the civic-societal economy and the marketplace economy. Statutes and regulatory systems are designed to monitor and mediate the dysfunctional impacts of the marketplace economy upon the other two spheres. Public law can lapse and veer, but, like environmental common law, it remains a major element in the interplay of the three economies.

Economic and legal analyses that do not consider civic-societal economics or the impacts of natural economics on society are naïvely or disingenuously narrow, ignoring substantial realities that inevitably are felt by society. The competent practice of both economics and environmental law (not to mention rational democratic governance) implicitly incorporates and requires an understanding of the reality and interdependence of all three economies.

c. Environmental Ethics

Aldo Leopold, A Sand County Almanac

129-130, 203, 224-225 (1968 ed.)

THINKING LIKE A MOUNTAIN . . .
Only the mountain has lived long enough to listen objectively to the howl of a wolf. . . . My own conviction on this score dates from the day I saw a wolf die. We were eating lunch on a high rimrock, at the foot of which a turbulent river elbowed its way. We saw what we thought was a doe fording the torrent, her breast awash in white water. When she climbed the bank toward us and shook out her tail, we realized our error: it was a wolf. A half-dozen others, evidently grown pups, sprang from the willows and all joined in a welcoming mêlée of wagging tails and playful maulings. What was literally a pile of wolves writhed and tumbled in the center of an open flat at the foot of our rimrock.

In those days we had never heard of passing up a chance to kill a wolf. In a second we were pumping lead into the pack, but with more excitement than accuracy. . . . When our rifles were empty, the old wolf was down, and a pup was dragging a leg into impassable slide-rocks. We reached the old wolf in time to watch a fierce green fire dying in her eyes. I realized then, and have known ever since, that there was something new to me in those eyes—something known only to her and to the mountain. I was young then, and full of trigger-itch; I thought that because fewer wolves meant more deer, that no wolves would mean hunters' paradise. But after seeing the green fire die, I sensed that neither the wolf nor the mountain agreed with such a view. . . .

THE LAND ETHIC . . .   There is as yet no ethic dealing with man's relation to land and to the animals and plants which grow upon it. . . . The extension of ethics to this . . . element in human environment is, if I read the evidence correctly, an evolutionary possibility and an ecological necessity. . . . The "key-log" which must be moved to release the evolutionary process for an ethic is simply this: quit thinking about decent land-use as solely an economic problem. Examine each question in terms of what is ethically and esthetically right, as well

A. The Environmental Perspective

as what is economically expedient. A thing is right when it tends to preserve the integrity, stability, and beauty of the biotic community. It is wrong when it tends otherwise.

An Environmental Ethic Beyond Utilitarianism? Leopold's lyrical ecology has inspired generations of environmental scientists and a vigorous ongoing ethical debate. Isn't the environment more than a commodity and medium for human designs? Shouldn't there be a recognized moral and ethical standard extending beyond pure human self-interest, recognizing the normative rights of the planet and of nature itself? It's true, of course, that many environmentalists (like most chapters of this book) do indeed focus on utilitarian arguments for environmental quality: Basic human self-interest, health, and economics should force society not to ignore ecological consequences. Even Leopold himself is ambiguous. He continues the wolf-killing story by showing how wolves are important for controlling populations of deer and other foraging animals that otherwise would strip the forests bare and turn cattle ranges to dustbowls. When he later criticizes current land use policy because "it assumes, falsely, I think, that the economic parts of the biotic clock will function without the uneconomic parts," he is again making a utilitarian argument.

But the fire dying in the she-wolf's eyes, that is something else.

Could it be that humans are not indeed the measure of all things? Are we instead only one part of a larger ecological community, with responsibilities accompanying our undoubted powers and rights? Is there, in other words, a moral-legal basis for environmentalism beyond utilitarianism? This question increasingly reappears in environmental law cases. When a project is stopped because it threatens extinction for some endangered insect or a court considers awards of natural resource damages for ecosystems destroyed by oil spills, the law must reach beyond the normal justifications founded upon net human benefit.

Should we declare that the wolf herself has legal rights, rights that, although not absolute, must nevertheless be substantively weighed in the legal process? Impressive work has been devoted to animal rights and natural rights theories.[33] Nagging problems arise, however, in drawing lines. Is sentiency the litmus? If not, shouldn't plants, rocks, and hills as well be able to claim these rights?[34] Unless the broader view prevails, the ethic ignores the rights of ecosystems. If natural rights can be defined, moreover, who defines them and determines when and how they are to be applied and weighed against human rights and the rights of other entities in the system?

Taking another approach, can it be argued that there is a God who commands ecological sensitivity? Many have criticized the Bible's call for humans to conquer nature:

---

33. See R. Nash, RIGHTS OF NATURE: A HISTORY OF ENVIRONMENTAL ETHICS (1989); H. Rolston, ENVIRONMENTAL ETHICS: DUTIES TO AND VALUES IN THE NATURAL WORLD (1988); R. Nozick, ANARCHY, STATE AND UTOPIA 35-42 (1975); S. Wise, SCIENCE AND THE CASE FOR ANIMAL RIGHTS (2003); and the active literature of environmental ethics including the journal *Environmental Ethics.*

34. See C. Stone, SHOULD TREES HAVE STANDING? (1972). Cf. the view from the self-styled "Wise Use" movement, noted further at the end of the next section: "Environmentalism is the new paganism, trees are worshipped and humans sacrificed at its altar. . . . It is evil . . . and we intend to destroy it." Ron Arnold, chairman of the Center for the Defense of Free Enterprise, Boston Globe, Jan. 13, 1992.

Be the terror and dread of all the wild beasts and all the birds of heaven, of everything that crawls on the ground and all the fish of the sea; they are handed over to you.... Teem over the earth and be lord of it. Genesis 9:1-2, 7.[35]

But other strands in Judeo-Christian theology and other religious cultures cast humans in a less domineering role. Primitive humans were probably animists. The mountains and rivers had spirits, and humans spoke with the trees and animals they were about to kill for their use. In many Eastern and Native American[36] cultures, gods are intimately linked with nature; humans are merely a part of the web, the Tao. Human disruption of nature is deplored as having destroyed "the age of perfect virtue, when men lived in common with birds and beasts, as forming one family."[37] The Dalai Lama, speaking of his Buddhism, said "We have always considered ourselves as part of our environment."[38] The great Jewish philosopher Maimonides dramatically recanted his early Greek-inspired view of human primacy: "It should *not* be believed that all things exist for the sake of the existence of man. On the contrary, all the other beings, too, have been intended for their own sakes and not for the sake of something else."[39]

Christianity, whose God became human, has been more resistant to the diminution of human-centeredness. The Protestant ethic, when it appeared, fit nicely with the Industrial Revolution's conquest of nature. Fundamentalist Christians' resistance to the notion that humans evolved as part of the natural world demonstrates a continuing need to see humans as separate and distinct from nature. But others can now read the Old Testament, particularly the Noah story, as affirming the sanctity and uniqueness of every living species and setting humans the task of preserving the earth's natural heritage. Some Christian scholarship urges an active ethic of human "stewardship" over all Creation.[40] These theological debates between human-centered and more interrelational metaphysics have been paralleled in the dialogues of nonreligious philosophy as well.[41]

Without a clearly divine or natural source of a moral ethic for the environment, the ethic, if it is to exist, must come from humans. Much of any human-based environmental ethic, of

---

35. Calvin and many other Christian theologians have argued that God "created all things for man's sake." Institutes of Religion 182; bk.1, chs. 14, 22 (Battles ed., 1961); see generally J.A. Passmore, MAN'S RESPONSIBILITY FOR NATURE (1974).

36. "Human beings are not superior to the rest of creation. If human beings were to drop out of the cycle of life, the earth would heal itself and go on. But if any of the other elements would drop out—air, water, animal or plant life—human beings and the earth itself would end." Audrey Shenandoan, Onondaga tribe, N.Y. This echoes the "Gaia" hypothesis that the planet Earth itself is a living, self-regulating organism; disruptions will modify the system, and life as we know it may disappear, though the planet will ultimately strike a new balance. J. Lovelock, THE AGES OF GAIA (1988); A. Miller, GAIA CONNECTIONS (1991). In this sense, the planet Earth may not be so "fragile."

37. Chuang Tsu, 4th c. B.C., in Passmore, note 35 above, at 7-8. "When humans interfere with the Tao, the sky becomes filthy, the equilibrium crumbles, creatures become extinct." Lao-tzu, Tao Te Ching (500 B.C.).

38. He continues, "Our scriptures speak of the container and the contained. The world is the container—our house—and we are the contained—the contents of the container.... As a boy studying Buddhism I was taught the importance of a caring attitude toward the environment. Our practice of nonviolence applies not just to human beings but to all sentient beings.... In Buddhist practice we get so used to this idea of nonviolence and the ending of all suffering that we become accustomed to not harming or destroying anything indiscriminately. Although we do not believe that trees or flowers have minds, we treat them also with respect. Thus we share a sense of universal responsibility for both mankind and nature." H.H. the 14th Dalai Lama & G. Rowell, MY TIBET 79-80 (1990).

39. See Passmore, note 35 above, at 12.

40. Fellows of the Calvin Center for Christian Scholarship, EARTHKEEPING: CHRISTIAN STEWARDSHIP OF NATURAL RESOURCES (1980); P. Riesenberg, THE INALIENABILITY OF SOVEREIGNTY IN MEDIEVAL POLITICAL THOUGHT (1956), explores medieval concepts of human (and royal) stewardship.

41. Goethe and Henry More were early outposts in the resistance to the human-centeredness of Bacon, Descartes, and even Kant. See generally Passmore, note 35 above, at 16-23.

A. The Environmental Perspective

course, will continue to be based on utilitarianism—if we want our species' descendants to survive on the planet, we must take the sensitive, cautious long view. But beyond self-interest, further distinctions can extend the ethic. We may indeed currently be the dominant species on Earth, possessing earth-changing knowledge, technology, and physical powers, but along with these powers may come ethical responsibilities. Perhaps these are responsibilities to past generations and to the future, to steward and pass on the extraordinary legacy we have received. A classic legal algorithm holds that for every power there is a countervailing responsibility. The ability to destroy surely does not carry with it the moral right to do so, tempered only by the limitations of self-interest against self-inflicted wounds. That would be too primitive a norm for a species that has been maturing for 2 million years.

From the fact of human intellectual development come other bases for an environmental ethic. On one hand are the arguments that proceed from our superiorities, like the claim for an ecological *noblesse oblige*—because we humans uniquely have been able, in some settings at least, to move beyond the bare demands of food, shelter, and survival to build an abstract culture and to understand the effects of our actions upon the planet, our species has a high calling to protect the less powerful parts of the ecological community in which we live. Aesthetic principles, also a unique human development, likewise argue for an extended stewardship.

On the other hand lie the arguments from humility. The more one knows, the more one realizes one does not know. The greater the expansion of our knowledge and technology, the vaster the realm of the unknown. When we look into the she-wolf's eyes with Leopold, some of what we feel may be anthropomorphic sympathy. But the fire dying there may also spark a recognition that we will never know the world she knows, and that should make us hesitant to make ourselves the measure of it all. Ultimately humans may be impelled to honor an environmental ethic protecting the planet's ecology for the same reason that they are impelled to climb Mt. Everest: because it is there. The very existence—the "is-ness"—of the wolf and her rivers and mountains, separate from humans, makes the ethic fitting and proper for recognition.

When the question arises, as it continually does in legislatures and agencies, courts, and saloons, "Why protect such-and-such particular part of the environment?" environmentalists undoubtedly will continue to argue practically, "Because it may turn out to be important to us or to hurt us if we lose it." But often, when the setting and the light are right, won't many of us also feel a further pull, coming from something more than the stark counsels of daily human utility?

COMMENTARY & QUESTIONS

1. The public trust doctrine. This preceding mix of ethical and practical reasoning is also incorporated within the public trust doctrine. The public trust, studied later in Chapter 20, is a potentially powerful legal doctrine derived from ancient principles that echo environmental law's current mantra of "sustainability." Society must protect certain resources that are owned by humankind through the generations, a legacy received from the past to be stewarded in the present and assured for the future. As Emperor Justinian declared, "By the law of nature, these things are common to humankind: the air, running water, the sea, and . . . the shores of the sea. . . ."[42] Further public trust rights have been

---

42. INSTITUTES OF EMPEROR JUSTINIAN, 2.1.1 (A.D. 529).

acknowledged over the years—in wildlife, in parks, even in fossils and human cultural artifacts. The public trust doctrine includes both the utilitarian perspective that protecting the environment protects human health and welfare, and further resource protections that go beyond strict human utility.

2. Beyond strict utility. The public trust doctrine's direct human utilitarianism is evident when it is applied to protect the quality of drinking water[43] or public access to a river, harbor, or beach. Why is it, however, that environmental law protects groundwater aquifers from pollution *even if they may never be used by anyone* and are not connected to other water bodies? Why do we protect endangered species even when we are virtually certain a particular species will never have any human usefulness? Why do we protect clean environments against minor lowering of air or water quality when some polluting development projects could generate huge economic profits with no danger of reaching the maximum legal levels of harm to health or property?[44] Why do we try to make strip miners in the mountains of Appalachia restore hillsides to pre-mining conditions, when the cost of remediation is ten times the market value of the land per acre before or after the restoration? Protecting a pristine waterfall, an endangered species, a unique prairie, or a wilderness virgin grove of trees in the face of commercial development apparently serves some further societal objectives. How and why does the law assert abstract "legacy" values in addition to utilitarian environmental goals that protect human welfare? The answer in U.S. law, and in emerging international law doctrines such as "intergenerational equity" and the "common heritage of humankind," as we will see, lies in the public trust doctrine.

Environmental law generally has drawn upon standard preexisting legal tools and doctrines to build a body of law incorporating its new perspective, but the public trust doctrine is an exception. It is environmental law's own special ancient and innovative contribution to our legal system.

B. THE PROBLEM OF THE COMMONS

Fortunately or unfortunately, much of the natural world is a commons—air, water, wildlife—which puts it on a collision course with dynamics of human behavior that are based on individually based rational choices.

Garrett Hardin, The Tragedy of the Commons
162 Science 1243, 1243-1248 (1968)

The tragedy of the commons develops this way. Picture a pasture open to all. It is to be expected that each herdsman will try to keep as many cattle as possible on the commons. Such an arrangement may work reasonably satisfactorily for centuries because tribal wars, poaching, and disease keep the numbers of both man and beast well below the carrying capacity of the land. Finally, however, comes the day of reckoning, that is, the day when the

---

43. See Tenn. Code Ann. §§70.324 et seq. (Tennessee Water Pollution Control Act, expressly incorporating the authority of the public trust).

44. PSD rules have been instituted in a number of areas for the "prevention of significant deterioration."

B. The Problem of the Commons

long-desired goal of social stability becomes a reality. At this point, the inherent logic of the commons remorselessly generates tragedy.

As a rational being, each herdsman seeks to maximize his gain. Explicitly or implicitly, more or less consciously, he asks, "What is the utility to me of adding one more animal to my herd?" This utility has one negative and one positive component:

1. The positive component is a function of the increment of one animal. Since the herdsman receives all the proceeds from the sale of the additional animal, the positive utility is nearly +1.
2. The negative component is a function of the additional overgrazing created by one more animal. Since, however, the effects of overgrazing are shared by all the herdsmen, the negative utility for any particular decision-making herdsman is only a fraction of −1.

Adding together the component partial utilities, the rational herdsman concludes that the only sensible course for him to pursue is to add another animal to his herd. And another; and another.... But his is the conclusion reached by each and every rational herdsman sharing a commons. Therein is the tragedy. Each man is locked into a system that compels him to increase his herd without limit—in a world that is limited. Ruin is the destination toward which all men rush, each pursuing his own best interest in a society that believes in the freedom of the commons. Freedom in a commons brings ruin to all.

Some would say that this is a platitude. Would that it were! In a sense, it was learned thousands of years ago, but natural selection favors the forces of psychological denial. The individual benefits as an individual from his ability to deny the truth even though society as a whole, of which he is a part, suffers. Education can counteract the natural tendency to do the wrong thing, but the inexorable succession of generations requires that the basis for this knowledge be constantly refreshed....

In an approximate way, the logic of the commons has been understood for a long time, perhaps since the discovery of agriculture or the invention of private property in real estate. But it is understood mostly only in special cases which are not sufficiently generalized. Even at this late date, cattlemen leasing national land on the western ranges demonstrate no more than an ambivalent understanding, in constantly pressuring federal authorities to increase the head count to the point where overgrazing produces erosion and weed dominance. Likewise, the oceans of the world continue to suffer from the survival of the philosophy of the commons. Maritime nations still respond automatically to the shibboleth of the "freedom of the seas." Professing to believe in the "inexhaustible resources of the oceans," they bring species after species of fish and whales closer to extinction....

POLLUTION ...   In a reverse way, the tragedy of the commons reappears in problems of pollution. Here it is not a question of taking something out of the commons, but of putting something in—sewage, or chemical, radioactive, and heat wastes into water; noxious and dangerous fumes into the air; and distracting and unpleasant advertising signs into the line of sight. The calculations of utility are much the same as before. The rational man finds that his share of the cost of the wastes he discharges into the commons is less than the cost of purifying his wastes before releasing them. Since this is true for everyone, we are locked into a system of "fouling our own nest," so long as we behave only as independent, rational, free-enterprisers.

The tragedy of the commons as a food basket is averted by private property, or something formally like it. But the air and waters surrounding us cannot readily be fenced, and so the tragedy of the commons as a cesspool must be prevented by different means, by coercive laws or taxing devices that make it cheaper for the polluter to treat his pollutants than to discharge them untreated. We have not progressed as far with the solution of this problem as we have with the first. Indeed, our particular concept of private property, which deters us from exhausting the positive resources of the earth, favors pollution. The owner of a factory on the bank of a stream—whose property extends to the middle of the stream—often has difficulty seeing why it is not his natural right to muddy the waters flowing past his door. The law, always behind the times, requires elaborate stitching and fitting to adapt it to this newly perceived aspect of the commons.

The pollution problem is a consequence of population. It did not much matter how a lonely American frontiersman disposed of his waste. "Flowing water purifies itself every 10 miles," my grandfather used to say, and the myth was near enough to the truth when he was a boy, for there were not too many people. But as population became denser, the natural chemical and biological recycling processes became overloaded, calling for a redefinition of property rights.

HOW TO LEGISLATE TEMPERANCE? . . . The laws of our society follow a complex, crowded, changeable world. Our epicyclic solution is to augment statutory law with administrative law. Since it is practically impossible to spell out all the conditions under which it is safe to burn trash in the back yard or to run an automobile without smog-control, by law we delegate the details to [agencies]. The result is administrative law, which is rightly feared for an ancient reason—*Quis custodiet ipsos custodes?*—"Who shall watch the watchers themselves?" . . . Administrators, trying to evaluate the morality of acts in the total system, are singularly liable to corruption, producing a government by men, not laws.

Prohibition is easy to legislate (though not necessarily to enforce); but how do we legislate temperance? Experience indicates that it can be accomplished best through the mediation of administrative law. . . . The great challenge facing us now is to invent the corrective feedbacks that are needed to keep custodians honest. We must find ways to legitimate the needed authority of both the custodians and the corrective feedbacks. . . .

MUTUAL COERCION MUTUALLY AGREED UPON . . . "Responsibility . . . is the product of definite social arrangements." The social arrangements that produce responsibility are arrangements that create coercion, of some sort. Consider bank-robbing. The man who takes money from a bank acts as if the bank were a commons. How do we prevent such action? Certainly not by trying to control his behavior solely by a verbal appeal to his sense of responsibility. Rather than rely on propaganda we . . . insist that a bank is not a commons; we seek the definite social arrangements that will keep it from becoming a commons. That this would infringe on the freedom of would-be robbers we neither deny nor regret. . . .

To say that we mutually agree to coercion is not to say that we are required to enjoy it, or even to pretend we enjoy it. Who enjoys taxes? We all grumble about them. But we accept compulsory taxes because we recognize that voluntary taxes would favor the conscienceless. We institute and (grumblingly) support taxes and other coercive devices to escape the horror of the commons.

An alternative to the commons need not be perfectly just to be preferable. . . . But we can never do nothing. . . . Once we are aware that the status quo is action, we can then compare its discoverable advantages and disadvantages with the predicted advantages and disadvantages of the proposed reform, discounting as best we can for our lack of experience. On the basis of such a comparison, we can make a rational decision which will not involve the unworkable assumption that only perfect systems are tolerable.

B. The Problem of the Commons

RECOGNITION OF NECESSITY . . . Perhaps the simplest summary of this analysis of man's population problems is this: the commons, if justifiable at all, is justifiable only under conditions of low-population density. As the human population has increased, the commons has had to be abandoned in one aspect after another.

First we abandoned the commons in food gathering, enclosing farm land and restricting pastures and hunting and fishing areas. . . . Somewhat later we saw that the commons as a place for waste disposal would also have to be abandoned. Restrictions on the disposal of domestic sewage are widely accepted in the Western world; we are still struggling to close the commons to pollution by automobiles, factories, insecticide sprayers, fertilizing operations, and atomic energy installations. . . .

Every new enclosure of the commons involves the infringement of somebody's personal liberty. Infringements made in the distant past are accepted because no contemporary person complains of a loss. It is the newly proposed infringements that we vigorously oppose; cries of "rights" and "freedom" fill the air. But what does "freedom" mean? When men mutually agreed to pass laws against robbing, mankind became more free, not less so. Individuals locked into the logic of the commons are free only to bring on universal ruin; once they see the necessity of mutual coercion, they become free to pursue other goals. I believe it was Hegel who said, "Freedom is the recognition of necessity."

COMMENTARY & QUESTIONS

1. Common resources, environmental damage, and the "rational maximizer." Looking at the beleaguered cow pasture, Hardin's central metaphor reveals a basic motivation driving each human actor to add to the "tragedy": Operating as self-contained individuals, all human actors instinctively seek to harvest and hold onto the maximum amount of benefits from their actions for themselves and pass as much of the negatives on to others. If environmental social costs can be passed on into the commons where they will not be clearly visible or traceable, the human actors who cause the negative consequences will not be easily called to account for them—thus the entrepreneurial tendency toward "externalization[45] of social costs." What can be done to alter the calculus of those choosing to use the commons? Environmental law's answer has been to seek accounting of those costs back to the people who caused them—"reinternalization" of the costs, or the polluter-pays principle. If the people who are making harmful decisions have to pay for or physically remedy them, the theory goes, over time they will cease their harmful activity or find a more efficient and benign way of doing it.

2. Extrapolating to global scale. Does Hardin's analysis apply beyond the cow pasture to the continental air masses or the oceans? The uses of all these commons are so diverse and diffuse that it is often difficult to demonstrate who is causing what effects. Those individual actions hurting the common resource may be invisible, diffuse, or unaccountable, but cumulatively they can be critical.

Hardin presents two basic scenarios to demonstrate the tendency toward "tragedy." One is pollution of commons, where the private positive benefit is waste disposal and the externalized cost is a cumulative decrease in resource quality. The second paradigm is

---

45. If an individual enterprise absorbs a cost, the cost payment is perceived as "internal" to its business. If it can pass it outside the business where it doesn't have to pay for it, that's "external." The Nobel laureate Ronald Coase relied on the rational actor concept underlying Hardin's tragedy of the commons, that individuals are driven to externalize costs.

overuse via exploitation of the commons: the grass of the cow pasture, fish in the oceans. If users suffer the losses as well as the benefits, their behavioral calculus will be quite different from an open-access commons. Are there ways in which legal rules can be established to force a group of users to act as a single owner would? The law has evolved in this way in several settings, including hydrocarbon development where the owners of land overlying an oil and gas formation are forced to "unitize" the field, extracting oil or gas as if they were a single owner and then sharing the profits of the whole field. This results in greater total production and therefore a greater total benefit to the class of owners than does the wasteful race to capture the resource that occurs in the absence of legally coerced collective action. Some industry advocates have therefore argued that other resources—national forests, fish stocks, minerals on public lands, even national parks—should be "privatized," turned over to single corporate ownership for the sake of efficiency.

Many environmental problems, such as pollution and global warming, are of a scale that refutes privatization.[46] The difficulty of the grand scale lies in discovering the true measure of public costs and what controls may avert the logic of the tragedy, a problem that is nowhere more difficult than in the area Hardin targeted, global population control. Environmental law addresses many different problems of cumulative effects in a wide variety of ways, at different scales. The behavioral logic of the tragedy of the commons, however, permeates virtually all environmental issues.

3. John Locke and a political philosophy of the tragedy of the commons. Under Lockean political theory, if we lived under Eden-like conditions of plenty, there would be no competition for resources, and property law would not be necessary because all desired items would be sufficiently abundant. With increasing populations and limited resources, however, a means for allocating available goods had to be found. To Locke, the institution of exclusive individual property fit nicely with his sense of the order of God's universe and also responded to social needs.[47] Private property induces people to work by granting them ownership of all or some of the fruits of their labors. Nonexclusive rights to property fail to produce work incentives. Like the rational choice theories of modern economics, Locke presumed that human actors generally act in their own rational self-interest. For private property's relationship to a commons, this means that owners will do whatever will maximize their benefits in regard to their own property, and that means passing off the negatives. Externalized costs don't disappear into a vacuum, however, and have serious accumulated public consequences that can end up dwarfing the short-term private logic that spawned them.

4. The pessimism and optimism of the commons. Does Hardin seem too optimistic about the chances for reforming the tragedy of the commons? Some who have considered the matter find Hardin's view—that necessity will induce us to accept protections based on "mutual coercion, mutually agreed upon"—grossly over-optimistic. See W. Ophuls, Ecology and the Politics of Scarcity 145-165 (1977). At the opposite pole are the "cornucopialists." Susan Cox, for example, argues that problems of the commons are not of the magnitude that Hardin fears, and humans will always find new resources and technologies to cope. In her assessment, society has adequately managed such problems throughout the

---

46. It should be noted, however, that the Coase Theorem is based on a sort of privatization proposition: that, for efficiency purposes, plenary rights to pollute could be transferred to polluters, thereafter leaving it up to "consumers" of pollution to try to bargain in the marketplace for the amount of clean air they desired.

47. For a more thorough discussion of John Locke's view of private property, see Sanders, The Lockean Proviso, 10 Harv. J.L. & Pub. Pol'y 401 (1988).

ages, with the major lapses coming only in times of cultural shifts. See Cox, No Tragedy of the Commons, 7 Envtl. Ethics 49 (1985).

5. The commons and positive outcomes. How do you decide which things should be maintained in common ownership rather than being reduced to a form of exclusive private property? As Professor Carol Rose writes:

> The right to exclude others has often been cited as the most important characteristic of private property. This right, it is said, makes private property fruitful by enabling owners to capture the full value of their individual investments, thus encouraging everyone to put time and labor into the development of the resources. Moreover, exclusive control makes it possible for owners to identify other owners, and for all to exchange the fruits of their labors until these things arrive in the hands of those who value them most highly—to the great cumulative advantage of all.[48]

What kinds of things are better suited to public ownership and communal use? Professor Rose cites public libraries and public highways as examples of successful commons. What of lakes and rivers? Forests? Antarctica?

6. Measuring sustainability. Another fundamental problem with the commons is defining the level of sustainability. It isn't easy to define the point where cows exceed the sustainable carrying capacity of the commons. It's far harder to define the acceptable level of imposition on a common resource such as air or water ("assimilative capacity") or an ocean fishery. Is anything less than purity a negative burden on the commons? What constitutes tolerable depreciation, and what constitutes Hardin's downward spiral to disaster? The different approaches to defining and setting appropriate environmental standards are the subject of the chapters in Part IV of this coursebook.

7. Law as mutual coercion. Assuming that much of the commons paradigm is relevant to analyzing environmental policy, note how Hardin sets up a critical role for the law but doesn't specify its operation. If nonmandatory policies or physical privatization are unlikely to work on a pollution commons (are they?), what kinds of legal intervention are likely to be effective and appropriate to avoiding the tragedy of the commons? Criminal sanctions, taxes, individual lawsuits, administrative bureaucracies?

8. The Coase Theorem. One influential argument holds that law's purpose here is to create property rights that are capable of being traded via market exchange. The famous article by Nobel laureate Ronald Coase argues that—assuming the reality of a universal tendency to externalize costs—the same outcomes will be reached through bargaining, starting from a clear legal rule of entitlement, irrespective of which of two different parties holds the legal entitlement. See The Problem of Social Cost, 3 J.L. & Econ. 1 (1960). Coase's demonstration relies on assumptions about equal resources, equal access of all participants to information, and the absence of transaction costs. Is bargaining toward an efficient solution likely to be easy when a large number of parties are joint holders of a legal right, as in the case of a commons used and enjoyed by many? The difficulties of organizing groups of pollution victims to bargain collectively (a form of "transaction costs") poses one problem. Would the bargaining go better if the initial legal right were assigned to the polluter? If that is the case, might some members of the group choose to become "free riders," refusing to participate in the belief that they will be able to reap the shared benefit without active participation? See Farnsworth, Do Parties to Nuisance Cases Bargain After Judgment? A Glimpse Inside the Cathedral, 66 U. Chi. L. Rev. 373 (1999)(an empirical study of 20 "Coasian" lawsuits in which parties to nuisance cases refused to bargain with

---

48. Rose, The Comedy of the Commons, 53 U. Chi. L. Rev. 711, 711-712 (1986).

their adversaries after a legal judgment, as a result of the enmity between the parties and their conviction that legal entitlements were not an appropriate subject of bargaining).

9. The view from "free market" advocates. Juxtaposed against an environmental economics overview is the traditional view of nature as a resource base for dynamic human enterprise. This marketplace logic of industrial and development interests casts resource exploitation and pollution externalities in a far, part of Tea Party history: more upbeat light. Here is part of a manifesto from the self-styled "Wise Use" movement:

> Humans, like all organisms, must use natural resources to survive. This fundamental truth is never addressed by environmentalists. . . . To recognize the legitimacy of the human use of the earth would be to accept the unavoidable environmental damage that is the price of our survival. Once that price is acceptable, the moral framework of environmentalist ideology becomes irrelevant and the issues become technical and economic. . . . The earth and its life are tough and resilient, not fragile and delicate. Environmentalists tend to be catastrophists, believing that any human use of the earth is "damage" and massive human use of the earth is "a catastrophe." An environmentalist motto is "We all live downstream," the viewpoint of helpless or vengeful victims. Wise-Users, on the other hand, tend to be cornucopians. . . . A Wise-Use motto is "We all live upstream," the viewpoint of responsible and concerned individuals. . . .
>
> The only way we humans can learn about our surroundings is through trial and error. . . . Our limitless imaginations can break through natural limits to make earthly goods and carrying capacity virtually infinite. Just as settled agriculture increased goods and carrying capacity vastly beyond hunting and gathering, so our imaginations can find ways to increase total productivity by superseding one level of technology after another. . . . Man's reworking of the earth is revolutionary, problematic and ultimately benevolent. . . . R. Arnold, What Do We Believe?[49]

Where is the commons in this rhetorical context? The marketplace's optimistic focus on the ongoing achievements of human enterprise comes from a totally different way of seeing the world, a perspective from which most environmental regulations based on ecological and civic concepts of the commons appear dismally negativistic, unnecessary, and obstructive. Both perspectives cannot be right.

C. A SALTY PARADIGM: ROAD SALT, A PROBLEM THAT HAS NOT YET MET ITS LEGAL PROCESS

The prosaic environmental controversy that follows has as yet hardly been noticed by the legal system. It nevertheless illustrates a classic environmental law conundrum, with elements that recur throughout the field.[50] Readers in Snow Belt states are living in the midst

---

49. Arnold is a principal spokesman of the "Wise Use" movement and chairman of the Center for the Defense of Free Enterprise, part of the marketplace coalition that attempted to roll back environmental regulation across the board in the 104th Congress. Started in the late 1980s in the West, funded by mining, timber, grazing, and other environment-related industries, Wise Users created coalitions of local and regional groups loudly opposing federal environmental regulation, now often morphed into Tea Party coalitions. "Wise Use" is a slogan hijacked from the conservation creed developed by the eminent conservationist Gifford Pinchot, father of the Forest Service, who used the phrase to emphasize the necessity of tighter sustainability restrictions on resource use.

50. Few environmental issues are as uncomplicated as the salt example—where easily identified externalities and self-interests sustain practices that tend to erode overall societal welfare, with the political context of our governance system making it extremely difficult to change those dysfunctional practices even when the facts are clear. The current opponents of hydrogen-based energy innovations, usually representatives of the traditional coal, oil, and gas industry, echo the salt industry's criticism of innovative de-icing alternatives. Coal, oil, and natural gas

of this exercise. For readers in Sun Belt states, it offers a bemusing and instructive opportunity to observe from a safe distance. The contaminant is highway de-icing salt, which in its own ways can spread almost as widely as harmful chemicals, with some serious human effects including even death.

Charles Wurster, Of Salt . . .
New York Times, March 4, 1978, at A21

The use of salt on roads for snow and ice removal has increased in the years [since the early 1960s]. About nine million tons, more than 10 percent of all salt produced in the world, are applied annually to American highways in snowy states.

The benefits of salt for road de-icing—and its costs—are rarely questioned. A recent report of the EPA, which weighed the costs and benefits of the practice, includes surprises.[51]

The costs of salting begin with $200 million for the salt and its application. Roadside vegetation destroyed by salt, particularly shade trees, was estimated by EPA to add another $150 million. Underground water mains, telephone cables and electric lines are corroded by salt seepage, adding another $10 million in damages. The Consolidated Edison Company, which owns the world's largest underground electrical system, estimated that road salt did $5 million in damages during [a single] winter. . . .

Salt finds its way into drinking-water supplies, especially ground-water aquifers, thereby becoming a health hazard. Recent research implicates salt intake as a causative factor in hypertension, heart disease and other circulatory problems, as well as various liver, kidney and metabolic disorders. It is estimated that at least 20 percent of Americans should restrict salt intake.

Individuals can control the salt that is added to foods, but salt in drinking water is harder to manage. About 27 percent of the drinking water supplies in Massachusetts are contaminated with road salt, and New Hampshire has a state-financed system for replacing contaminated wells. Long Island is especially vulnerable, since its sole drinking water is ground water recharged by precipitation, including highway runoff.

The EPA estimated that 25 percent of the population in the Snow Belt drinks water contaminated with road salt. The cost of providing pure water for these people was put at $150 million, but no objective cost was ascribed to health damage.

Salt damages bridges and other highway structures, best exemplified by the deterioration and collapse of New York City's West Side Highway. Corrosion by salt is believed to have been a major cause of the failure. The EPA estimated the national annual cost of damage to highway structures by salt at $500 million.

But the largest and most obvious cost of road salt is automobile corrosion, estimated by the EPA at $2 billion annually, or an average of about $34 per car per year in the Snow Belt. Heavy salting of highways hastens auto depreciation by about 20 percent. Telephone company vehicles last twice as long in the South as they do in New England.

---

are dominant in the marketplace over environmentally more sustainable renewable energy sources in major part because so many costs are externalized, with both short-term social costs and long-term ecological risks (including global climate change). They also have built up major subsidies that protect the price advantage of traditional energy companies, beginning with tax code provisions that give credits for resource depletion to less direct expenditures for national security policies that appear related to protecting access to sources of supply.

51. EPA Document 600/2-76-105 (May 1976).

Although they are usually assumed without question, the benefits of road salting have proven elusive to substantiate. At temperatures near or slightly below freezing, salt hastens melting and increases traction. But at lower temperatures, salt makes dry snow shiny and more slippery, and causes it to stick on windshields hampering vision. Salt also prolongs street wetness, reducing the friction.

Solid evidence of increased safety is lacking. . . . Salt usually permits faster driving which would benefit emergency vehicles but is a mixed blessing for others. In snow, people tend to drive slowly and have "fender benders," but after salt applications they tend to drive faster and have more serious accidents. The benefits of salt in preventing accidents, if any, are small. Not surprisingly, this conclusion is disputed by the salt industry, which claims great benefits from its use.

An interesting benefit-cost analysis results. Whereas benefits are uncertain but apparently small (except to the salt and automobile industries), costs total nearly $3 billion per year. Only a small amount of the cost is the salt itself, 93 percent consisting of indirect costs, borne especially by owners of motor vehicles.

Road salting should be re-examined. Reduced salting, combined with increased plowing, tire modifications, and driver education in snow driving might yield better results at lower costs.

The EPA report summarized by Dr. Wurster contains many other fascinating details:

- The State of Alaska manages to maintain its highways without any use of road salt.
- The citizens of Michigan, leading the world in auto production, also lead in auto corrosion, losing $198,630,000 each year in salt-caused depreciation, which almost matches the total cost of salt application in the nation.
- Urban shade trees are vulnerable to salt and have substantial monetizable values[52] (a 15" diameter tree was valued at $1767; if a tree starts showing leaf damage from salt, it is beyond saving).
- So much salt has spilled into the Great Lakes that parts of the Lake Michigan depths now have a marine saltwater ecology, including marine fish such as flounder.
- Salt infiltrates through concrete and sets up a powerful pressure reaction with reinforcing steel bars, causing overpass damage and potholes on roadways (as well as pitted sidewalks and crumbling concrete steps when applied by individuals for residential use[53]).
- All things being equal, people favor the "bare pavement" look of salted roads because the visual impression is clearer than that of a scraped and sanded roadway.
- Salt intake is a critical factor in many health afflictions including hypertension, cardiovascular diseases, renal and liver diseases, and metabolic disorders, with likely linkages to increased mortalities, but no studies have focused on the widespread effects of highway salt on drinking water supplies.

---

52. The words *monetized* and *marketized* are used in this text in the informal sense of "having been attributed a market value," not in the technical economics sense of converting to legal obligation.

53. A consumer-protection vignette: Some salt manufacturers, marketing their product for residential de-iceing, label their product as "**Safe for application to concrete and cement!** when used as directed," thereafter stating in the directions' fine print, "In order to avoid harm to concrete and cement, remove slush and moisture associated with this product within 30 minutes of application," a caveat that practically nullifies the premise.

C. A Salty Paradigm: Road Salt, a Problem That Has Not Yet Met Its Legal Process

- The report also notes that highway salt can be harmful to fish and wildlife but doesn't examine these costs.
- The report makes extensive cost comparisons with a "scrape, sand, and selective salting" alternative model. (The net cost of the unlimited salting model was almost twice that of the restricted model.)
- The report doesn't review any of the available salt substitutes for de-icing such as organic CMA (calcium magnesium acetate).

COMMENTARY & QUESTIONS

1. Costs, economic and natural. Environmentalists and resource economists regularly argue that the costs of a targeted proposal are far greater than the limited costs considered by those who make the decision. Here from the EPA report are the (conservative) estimates of some of the total yearly costs of road salting that can be monetarily quantified:[54]

ESTIMATED YEARLY COSTS

Salt Purchase & Application	$200 million
Highway Structures	500 million
Water Supplies	150 million
Vehicles	2,000 million
Utilities	10 million
Vegetation	50 million
TOTAL:	ca. $2.91 billion

This set of costs, of course, is not complete. The EPA report's analysis completely excluded health costs, beyond a factor based on substitute drinking water supplies. Given the severe risks of heart disease posed by salt in water supplies, this would appear to be a strong candidate for heavy cost estimates and application of the "Precautionary Principle." The report also excludes fish and wildlife and other environmental values, and excludes the costs that occur in the production of salt, which typically include local water pollution from mine runoff and leachate.

The point, of course, is that most of these kinds of costs are hidden from direct public view and not chargeable to the persons who decide to impose them. In societal terms the question should be: How many of these costs should rationally be considered as part of the systemic decision to apply or continue applying salt? In operative terms, however, the actual question will be: How many of the salt costs listed above will have to be paid by the road commissions that choose to use salt? If the answer is little or none, then those costs will receive little or no consideration.

2. Is salt an "environmental" problem? Highway salting causes harm to public health, vegetation, fish, and wildlife. But these are the areas least noted in the EPA report. They are indirect and difficult to quantify in money terms. They involve interconnected human and natural effects, are borne in small amounts by a large and dispersed range of recipients,

---

54. All salt figures in the EPA report and the text discussion are given in 1976 dollars: Multiply all numbers by approximately 5.4 to get approximate 2010 dollar figures. Since 1976, no comprehensive report has been issued to update these cumulative national cost estimates.

and the road salting decision that causes them is made on a narrowed basis that doesn't consider them. Doesn't that sound like a typical "environmental" problem?

The nation's road commissions' calculus puts salt on the roads because, for them, it is a completely logical benefit-cost-alternatives decision: They get the *benefits* of bare roads,[55] paying only $200 million a year. But this marketplace decision ignores billions, at least 93% of the true *costs* seen by environmentalists, and ignores some far better *alternatives*.

Salting appears to be a classic example of a human decision thinking in terms of "one-shot" technology. Who wants to bother with thinking about where the salt goes after the zap? Out of sight, out of mind. Environmental science, however, reminds us that everything goes somewhere and has residual consequences. We will live in a natural system with those residuals long after the ice and snow are gone.

3. Benefits. The classic environmental response to a proposal's claimed benefits is to doubt them. The official decisionmakers in the marketplace have decided to go ahead for their own direct market reasons, but is it really necessary that the proposed project or program be done, or done in this particular way? In the case of highway salt, the environmental argument would focus initially on the lack of proof of benefits from the "bare pavement" model. What is the value of a road that appears to be clear, especially if it retains an icy film? What is the value of faster-moving traffic, especially in light of the evidence that accidents on salted road systems are more likely to be fatal than the scrape-and-sand model's "fender-benders"? The environmentalist would acknowledge the benefits of time saved and disruptions avoided by highway salting, but would argue that these benefits should be weighed against foreseeable costs to figure out how best to do the job. In practice, however, the decision is made by highway commissioners whose intuitive judgment is that the "bare-pavement" result of salting is worth more to them than their own yearly $200 million cost of buying and applying salt—and that is the only calculus they consider. In this and other cases where valuation is difficult, moreover, the public tends to leave the calculations to official administrative discretion and the marketplace.

4. Available alternatives: CMA and more. The analysis of a proposal's benefits and costs is meaningless unless it is linked to a comparison of alternatives. Environmentalists can accurately be regarded as narrow-minded negativists if they merely attack proposals without reviewing alternative courses of action. One alternative in every case, of course, is the "no-action" alternative. When developers planned to build a dam that would flood part of the Grand Canyon for power and water supply, environmentalists were able to show that those benefits were not needed at that time and place, in light of the social costs. The better option was to do nothing.

Often the analysis of alternatives turns upon whether the action can better take place with a different design, location, timing, process, and so on. A particular factory might be a better neighbor, for example, if it installed pollution-control mechanisms, used a higher temperature process, or located itself downwind. Beverage bottles would cause less litter and save energy and raw materials if they were returnable. In *Overton Park*, the Memphis highway case in Chapter 6, the citizens argued for location and construction designs that were feasible and prudent alternatives to going through the middle of their park.

In the case of salt, the purpose of the proposed action—removal of snow from the highways so as to allow traffic to move—is clearly necessary. Only the most troglodytic environmentalist would argue that traffic should come to a halt when the snow falls. Rather,

---

55. The highly specific traditional goal definition of highway agencies is to "achieve highway user satisfaction" in terms of "mobility, productivity, and safety," to this end using snow and ice treatments to avoid weather-caused roadway congestion and to "maintain core highway operations priorities."

C. A Salty Paradigm: Road Salt, a Problem That Has Not Yet Met Its Legal Process

the analysis should turn to a comparison of realistic alternatives. Installation of infrared electric melting devices in highway pavements might be effective and avoid all the indirect costs of salting, but the direct costs would be outrageous.

Excellent alternatives to salt exist, however—salt substitutes with the same snow melting characteristics as salt yet lacking its destructive characteristics. CMA (calcium magnesium acetate), invented by Chevron, is a prime example.[56] It can be made from readily available materials including recycled corn wastes or milk whey, it has none of the destructive effects of salt, and in fact it actually rebuilds salt-damaged soils by replacing stripped magnesium and calcium.[57] In 1994 the State of Oregon made a generic switch to using de-icing chemicals including CMA based on an overall analysis of direct and indirect costs, with special consideration of corrosion effects and environmental effects, particularly to the state's protected salmon runs.[58] Even ignoring the public health costs that were not accounted for in the EPA study, it appears reasonable that nonsalt alternatives such as CMA might realize savings of almost $2 billion per year when compared with continued use of salt. This would be true even if the direct costs for de-icing increased fivefold, from $200 million to $1 billion. The actual overall public costs would still drop more than $1.9 billion.

CMA, however, costs the highway officials who budget for roads between $200 and $1000 per ton, as opposed to salt's $20 to $70.[59]" The problem," says Chevron's Dan Walter, "is that the benefit of CMA does not go back to the governmental agency that pays for de-icers, typically state maintenance departments. If a bridge on an interstate highway must be replaced, the federal government will pay 80% of the cost. Therefore the highway department cannot justify paying $600 per ton for CMA."[60] The way the commercial-political marketplace is set up, no one and no forum is in a position to bring the overall public economics to bear upon the operative decisions.

5. Should you believe us on highway salting? Shortly after this highway salting analysis was first published in the coursebook the authors received the following letter from Richard L. Hanneman, president of the Salt Institute lobby, emphasizing a study released in January 1992 concluding that CMA was not—or at least not yet—proved to be a sufficiently economical substitute for highway de-icing to justify a switch away from road salt.[61] Hanneman concluded that—

---

56. Another benign alternative is potassium acetate, which has long been used as a de-icer for airport runways (and is FAA approved for that purpose), and on bridges and other areas especially sensitive to corrosion. Although potassium acetate has the same environmental benefits and risks as CMA, while often being less expensive, CMA has a larger share of the alternative market.

57. See Horner & Brenner, Environmental Evaluation of Calcium Magnesium Acetate for Highway Deicing Applications, 7 Resources, Conserv. & Recyc. 213 (1992).

58. See D. Keep & D. Parker, Tests Clear Snow, Path for Use of Liquid Anti-icing in Northwest, Roads & Bridges (Aug. 1995), reporting significant overall governmental savings (including cleanup costs).

59. In 2002, a survey by one of our research assistants revealed that the majority of road commissions could buy salt for $29.76 per ton. While CMA sold for $200 to $1000 per ton, the similar road treatment, potassium acetate, sold for $330 to $700 per ton.

60. U.S. Water News, Jan. 1990, at 11. If a road commission simply could not find the cash to pay for a 100% switch to CMA, 20 to 60% CMA-to-salt blends are available that buffer much of the salt's negatives but still cost two to three times as much as salt. In 1991, Congress passed the Intermodal Surface Transportation Efficiency Act (ISTEA) providing states with 80% reimbursement for use of CMA on bridges, overpasses, and approaches (because the destruction of these high-value highway features had created public hazards that could not be ignored), but the subsidy has not been uniformly used and is not extendable to highways in general.

61. Transportation Research Board/National Research Council, Highway De-icing: Comparing Salt and Calcium Magnesium Acetate (1991), *available at* onlinepubs.trb.org/onlinepubs/sr/sr235/00i-012.pdf.

There is a strong relationship between the application of de-icing salt and the prevention of about 80 percent of the fatalities and serious injuries that would otherwise occur on untreated highways.... Using highway de-icing salt may prevent huge numbers of tort recoveries, but it still [sic] might be of interest to aspiring attorneys....

Upon examination, the Transportation Research Board report Mr. Hanneman referenced actually concluded that the unaccounted annual externalized costs of salting exceeded $2 billion by an undetermined amount. That report's estimates, moreover, also excluded public costs in human health, particularly problems from salt infiltration into drinking water supplies, and excluded all "environmental damages." Both of these are potentially large in magnitude, but were excluded on grounds of "insufficient information." (As to safety statistics, moreover, it would appear that completely untreated highways are not the appropriate comparison to salted highways.)

6. The political context. Note that, pushed by the road salting industry, it's usually a government agency that makes the salting decision, in virtually the same terms as would a polluting private corporate factory owner.

So assume now that a careful study conclusively proves that the U.S. loses a net $2 billion or more each year, destructively and unnecessarily, because of the use of road salt instead of benign available alternatives. What corrective response can we expect to occur?

Perhaps none. As so often, the important question is *who* if anyone will take up the problem and resolve it? Will the industry itself, and the marketplace economy, take on the problem and solve it? Not likely. Will some government agency do so of its own initiative? Not likely. If not, will activist members of the public do so in the classic process that created environmental law—through media efforts, politics, and creative use of the legal system? Not yet.

Meanwhile, the salt goes on.

* * *

... What if [the economic] crisis ... [is] telling us that the whole growth model we created over the last 50 years is simply unsustainable economically and ecologically, and that ... when we hit the wall [was] when Mother Nature and the market both said: "No more!"? ... "We created a way of raising standards of living that we can't possibly pass on to our children," said Joe Romm, a physicist and climate expert who writes the indispensable blog climateprogress.org. We have been getting rich by depleting all our natural stocks—water, hydrocarbons, forests, rivers, fish and arable land—and not by generating renewable flows.... It has to collapse, unless adults stand up and say, "This is a Ponzi scheme. We have not generated real wealth, and we are destroying a livable climate...." Real wealth is something you can pass on in a way that others can enjoy.... "Just as a few lonely economists warned us we were living beyond our financial means and overdrawing our financial assets, scientists are warning us that we're living beyond our ecological means and overdrawing our natural assets," argues Glenn Prickett, senior vice president at Conservation International. But, he cautioned, as environmentalists have pointed out: "Mother Nature doesn't do bailouts."...

—Thomas Friedman, New York Times, March 7, 2009.

2

Cross-Cutting Themes in Environmental Law

A. A Milestone Pollution Case in Historical Context: Allied Chemical & Its Kepone Pesticide
B. Beyond *Kepone*: Tracking Several Decades of Environmental Law Development
C. Environmental Law Themes & Contexts

A. A Milestone Pollution Case in Historical Context: Allied Chemical & Its Kepone Pesticide

For more than 300 years of our national development, there was little or nothing of environmental law. This is not to say that serious, cumulative environmental problems didn't exist. They did, increasing throughout the pre-environmental law years in number and severity. Today's environmental law came together in a blur of activity during the 1960s and 1970s, spurred by citizen pressures, built on federal legal foundations replacing the states' generally passive stance toward industrial pollution, and growing in depth and breadth in cycles since then.[1]

> In the developmental history of environmental law, many different shifting variables shape the changing profile of public environmental awareness and national law and policy:
>
> - Increasing knowledge of science, of systemic environmental harms, and of the cumulative consequences of cost externalizing behaviors
> - Cyclical shifts in the degree of industry influence on presidential policy, congressional affairs, and state governments
> - Shifts in concepts of the social responsibility and civil obligations of individuals and corporations
> - Shifts in the ability of citizens to sue in court and to intervene in agency proceedings

---

1. (A heavily condensed six-page history of the development of environmental law is posted on the coursebook website in the supplementary materials for this chapter.)

- Accumulation of applicable legal doctrine, starting with basic common law and supplemented over time by public law statutes and regulation
- Oscillations in the relative organizational strength of business lobbies, individual governing figures, and citizen alliances and networks
- Variations in the action levels of different levels of government—federal-state-local
- The degree to which the media actively investigates and covers public interest issues and affects the political process

All of these elements figure into the classic pollution controversy that follows.

1. Allied Chemical's Pesticide Pollution Disaster

The *Kepone* incident in Hopewell, Virginia is a notorious case from the first generation of modern environmental law in the 1970s that set off a media avalanche that galvanized public and regulatory attention and subsequently helped push Congress into making major overhauls of federal environmental statutes. The case illustrates many of the classic determinants of industrial market behavior that made environmental law necessary in the first place. The *Kepone* disaster, however, differs from most major environmental incidents in that very little of the story of what had happened ever appeared in reported court decisions.[2] (Most court cases were settled by the company before they got to a verdict.) The facts presented here were gathered from a wide variety of field and archival sources. As you read the narrative, note the different kinds of serious negative externalities — to occupational health conditions within the factories; to air, water, and environmental quality outside the plants; and to ultimate consumers exposed to pesticides — and consider how the corporate and legal systems should or could have taken account of them.

2. *Kepone*: A Case Study[3]

Hopewell (population approximately 24,000 in the 1970s) is a blue-collar industrial town located on the banks of the James River in southern Virginia. Naming itself "the Chemical

---

2. Within the very limited reported case law on the *Kepone* incident, some details about the case can be gleaned from a Tax Court decision rejecting Allied's attempt to write-off an in-lieu-of-penalties contribution to an environmental trust fund. *Allied-Signal v. Comm'r*, 1992 Tax Ct. Memo LEXIS 204, 241 (T.C. 1992). Personal injury cases such as *Gilbert v. Allied Chem.*, 411 F. Supp. 505 (E.D. Va. 1976, on a collateral motion) never resulted in a reported decision. A federal criminal prosecution resulted in a court-ordered criminal settlement. *U.S. v. Allied Chem.*, 420 F. Supp. 122 (E.D. Va. 1976). A lawsuit filed by fishermen and seafood processors hurt by closure of the James River and Chesapeake Bay has interesting remedy issues (see Chapter 3), but gives little background on the case. *Pruitt v. Allied Chem. Corp.*, 523 F. Supp. 975 (E.D. Va. 1981). An OSHA administrative penalty case focuses primarily on whether Moore and Hundtofte were personally liable for penalties. *Moore, Hundtofte & LSP v. Occupational Safety & Health Comm'n*, 591 F.2d 991 (4th Cir. 1979) (they were held personally liable). A major retrospective symposium on the *Kepone* incident appears in 29 U. Rich. L. Rev. 493 (1995). See Goldfarb, *Kepone*: A Case Study, 8 Envtl. L. 645 (1978), and Goldfarb, Changes in the Clean Water Act Since *Kepone*, 29 U. Rich. L. Rev. 603 (1995); Zim, Allied Chemical's $20-Million Ordeal with Kepone, Fortune, Sept. 11, 1978, at 82; Stone, A Slap on the Wrist for the Kepone Mob, 22 Bus. & Soc'y Rev. 4-11 (1977), reprinted in Corporate Violence 121 (S.L. Hills ed., 1977); Mintz & Klaidman, Creative Settlement or Improper Deal?, Leg. Times, May 11, 1992, at 1; and Facing a Time of Counter-Revolution — The Kepone Incident and a Review of First Principles, 29 U. Rich. L. Rev. 657 (1995).

3. This text is primarily drawn from Goldfarb, *Kepone*: A Case Study, 8 Envtl. L. 645 (1978), and incorporates material from Goldfarb, Changes in the Clean Water Act Since Kepone, 29 U. Rich. L. Rev. 603 (1995).

A. A Milestone Pollution Case in Historical Context

Capital of the South," Hopewell actively recruited large chemical manufacturers to come to the area. Firestone, Hercules, Continental Can, and Allied Chemical (now known as Allied-Signal), with $3 billion in annual sales in the 1970s, located some of their chemical plants there.

Allied Chemical opened its Hopewell plant in 1928, the first industrial plant capable of utilizing atmospheric nitrogen for the production of ammonia and nitrogen fertilizer. Eventually Allied's Hopewell plant became the Hopewell "complex," which in 1975 was Hopewell's largest employer, with 4,000 workers.

The initial batch of 500 pounds of a pesticide named Kepone was produced by Allied in 1949. Two patents for the process were awarded to it in 1952. Kepone is a chlorinated hydrocarbon pesticide, a chemical relative of DDT, Aldrin/Dieldrin, and Mirex (all now banned by the EPA). Kepone is a contact poison, capable of being absorbed through the skin or cuticle; it is lipophilic (fat soluble), but insoluble in water; it is persistent in the environment; and it will bioaccumulate in the fatty tissues of the body. The exact mechanism by which such chlorinated hydrocarbons kill target pests is uncertain. They are nerve poisons, interfering with the transmission of electrical impulses along nerve channels.

Before moving to commercial production, Allied subjected Kepone to toxicity tests necessary in order to obtain registration under the federal pesticide laws for use in the USA.[4] The results of this research revealed Kepone to be highly toxic to all species tested: It caused cancer, liver damage, reproductive system failure, and inhibition of growth and muscular coordination in fish, mammals, and birds. Upon being presented with the test results, Allied voluntarily withdrew its petition to the Food and Drug Administration for the establishment of Kepone residue tolerances for agricultural products, so that the pesticide could only be sold for application outside the USA. Despite the unfavorable toxicity test results, Allied deemed Kepone ready for commercial production for overseas sales, and contracted with the Nease Chemical Company of State College, Pennsylvania to produce it for them.

Allied did not consider Kepone to be a major pesticide. With less than $200,000 in annual sales over a 16-year period, Kepone production never exceeded 0.1% of America's total pesticide production. Kepone was primarily exported to South America to control the Banana Root Borer and to Europe for use against potato beetles. The Kepone sold overseas by Allied from 1958 through 1960 was produced at the Nease plant. Allied entered into a similar production arrangement with Hooker Chemical during the early '60s.

By 1966 even more negative test results had been associated with Kepone, but Allied nevertheless decided to manufacture Kepone on an increased basis in its own Semi-Works facility in Hopewell. In preparation for production, an area supervisor of the Semi-Works developed a production manual containing operating and safety instructions for the production process. The supervisor consulted available toxicity research results, and his recommended precautions reflect the test findings. At Allied, Kepone spills and dust were closely controlled, and workers wore safety glasses, rubber boots and gloves. Allied's Kepone operations were directed by William Moore until 1968, and thereafter by Virgil Hundtofte.

Prior to preparation of the production manual, there had been no recorded case of human exposure of Kepone to the level of acute poisoning. Allied apparently discounted the possibility of such poisoning, regardless of the documented adverse effects of Kepone on animals.

---

4. Registration was required under the precursor statute to the present Federal Insecticide, Fungicide, and Rodenticide Act (FIFRA) (now codified at 7 U.S.C. §§135-136 (1976)). [Eds.]

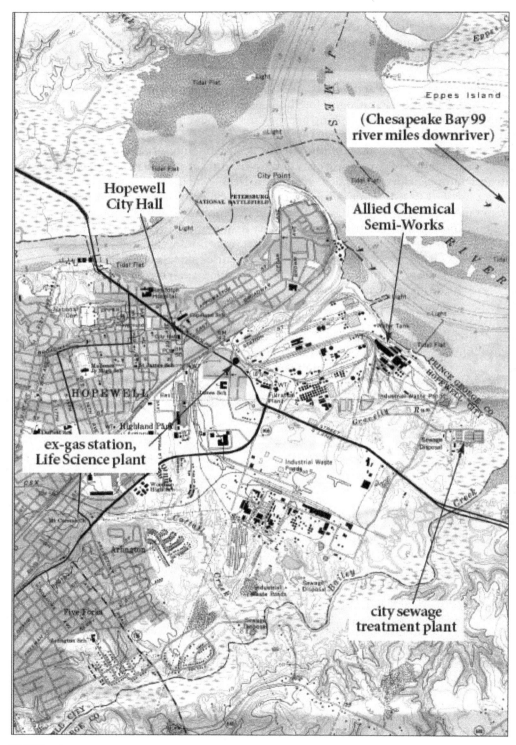

FIGURE 2-1. *Hopewell, Virginia, on the banks of the James River almost 100 river miles from Chesapeake Bay. Adapted from USGS MAP NO. 37077-C3-TF-024 Hopewell Quadrangle.*

A. A Milestone Pollution Case in Historical Context

In 1969, pushed by the first rush of citizen organizations mobilizing for environmental protection, the Federal government resurrected the 1899 Refuse Act requirement that all industries discharging wastes into navigable waters needed to obtain permits from the U.S. Army Corps of Engineers.[5] The Allied complex at Hopewell had three pipes discharging directly into a stream called Gravelly Run, a tributary of the James River. (See Figure 1.) One of these pipes originated at the Semi-Works where Kepone was manufactured. The Refuse Act permit application was discussed by Allied's plant managers and their assistants, who found themselves on the horns of a dilemma. Allied was discharging Kepone process wastes without treatment of any kind, and the installation of pollution control equipment would be quite expensive. Moreover there were plans to build a municipal sewage treatment plant which hopefully would treat the wastes of all industries in Hopewell, but the treatment plant would not be completed before 1975. What should Allied do during the interim period?

Allied decided to list the Semi-Works discharges as "temporary, to be discontinued within two years." The short form Refuse Act application for such "temporary discharges" did not require identification of the substance being dumped. Thus, neither Kepone nor two plastics products (TAIC and THEIC) also manufactured at the Semi-Works were listed by Allied on its Refuse Act application, even though Allied quite clearly did not intend to terminate production at Hopewell and had no plans to treat the wastes until publicly funded treatment would become available five or more years later.

In 1972, the Refuse Act permit program was taken over by EPA, the federal Environmental Protection Agency created in 1970, under the Federal Water Pollution Control Act Amendments of 1972 (FWPCA, soon to be renamed the Clean Water Act). The new permit program was called the National Pollutant Discharge Elimination System (NPDES), and its permits would all be issued in Washington D.C. until such time as EPA certified a state's regulatory program as adequate to exercise the federal law's "cooperative federalism" authority.[6]

In Virginia, the state government did not immediately move to win certification, so in mid-1972 EPA requested data on the nature, volume, and strength of Allied's discharges, and again Allied faced a dilemma about complying. One of Allied's plant managers prepared an option memorandum outlining three strategies which Allied might follow: (1) to do nothing and hope for a lack of enforcement by EPA; (2) to divert the Semi-Works effluent to another outfall pipe for which a permit had been obtained; or (3) to tell EPA about the Kepone discharges and try to strike a deal, making minor improvements to the Semi-Works effluent to "buy time" until completion of the municipal treatment plant. Ultimately Allied chose a fourth option, submitting sketchy data to the federal government, as in 1970, not revealing the composition of the raw Kepone discharges and describing them only as "unmetered, unsampled, temporary outfalls."

In 1973, Allied underwent a corporate reorganization, during which control of the Semi-Works facility was transferred from the Agricultural Division to the Plastics Division. The transfer took place in expectation of the Agriculture Division's impending move to

---

5. The Refuse Act is a subsection of the 1899 Rivers and Harbors Appropriation Act, 30 Stat. §1151 (1899), 33 U.S.C. §407, noted later in this coursebook. In the late 1960s, Representative Henry Reuss of Wisconsin, prodded by early environmental activists, pressured the Corps to interpret industrial pollution as illegal "refuse." For a time thereafter the Refuse Act was the most effective federal water pollution law; it still has enforceable effect in a number of settings. [EDS.]

6. 33 U.S.C. §§1251-1376 (Supp. V 1973); §1342(a)(1) (Supp. V 1975). The federal CWA is studied in Chapter 12. [EDS.]

new facilities in Baton Rouge, Louisiana, an area eagerly competing for chemical plants. Virgil Hundtofte, plant manager of Allied's Agricultural Division at Hopewell, and William Moore, Research Director, made plans to retire from the company rather than relocate. (Hundtofte had been with Allied in Hopewell since 1965, and Moore since 1948.)

One effect of the reorganization was a reorientation of production priorities among the products manufactured at the Semi-Works. Kepone production had decreased steadily, but THEIC plastic, which had been manufactured in small quantities for eighteen years, suddenly found a lucrative market calling for a doubling of production. THEIC and Kepone shared certain production equipment, and with the surge in demand for THEIC a decision was made in 1973 to "toll" Kepone production. Tolling is a common arrangement in the chemical industry whereby another company performs processing work for a fee or "toll" and then returns the final product to the originating company for subsequent sale on the open market. The keynote of a tolling arrangement is that during the processing period legal title to the materials and product remains in the supplier, in this case Allied. (More recently, many U.S. companies have entered into similar tolling agreements with "maquiladora" companies they set up across the border in Mexico to take advantage of looser environmental and labor standards.)

In January 1973, when the decision to toll Kepone was divulged, William Moore saw his opportunity to remain in Virginia and continue in the Kepone manufacturing business. He immediately contacted Hundtofte, who had recently resigned from Allied and gone to work for a fuel oil distributor. Moore and Hundtofte agreed to form a corporation and bid for the Kepone tolling contract. On November 9, 1973, Life Science Products Company (LSP) was incorporated under the laws of the Commonwealth of Virginia. Moore and Hundtofte were the only shareholders, directors, and officers of LSP. Less than a month later, the tolling agreement between Allied and LSP was signed. Allied had solicited bids from Hooker Chemical, Nease Chemical, Velsicol and LSP, but LSP's bid was by far the lowest: 54 cents per pound for 500,000 pounds of Kepone. Nease Chemical (which had manufactured Kepone for Allied from 1958 through 1960) declined to bid, but responded that if it chose to bid on the contract, just disposing of the waste properly would cost Nease 30 cents per pound. Hooker Chemical bid $3.00 per pound.

LSP began producing Kepone for Allied in mid-1973. The details of the tolling agreement are important because the question of Allied's responsibility for LSP's illegal acts affects most subsequent issues of liability. The contract provided that Allied would supply—at its own expense—all of the raw materials for Kepone production, with the title to remain in Allied. Within certain broad limits, Allied would determine the monthly production rate of Kepone, which would be packed in Allied containers and transported in Allied trucks. Allied also agreed to pay LSP's taxes, other than corporate income taxes. LSP was to receive between 32 and 38 cents per pound for 650,000 pounds or more of Kepone. Through a capital surcharge arrangement, Allied was to pay for all of LSP's approved capital expenditures, whether for production or pollution control, except for land and building. If LSP was closed for pollution violations during the first year of the contract, Allied had the option to purchase LSP's assets for $25,000. And if the contract was terminated by either party for any reason, LSP agreed to refrain from producing Kepone for anyone else.

The relationship between Allied and LSP was only partially defined by the tolling agreement. Moore and Hundtofte further promised Allied that they would not dispose of their shares in LSP without Allied's consent. Moreover, Allied assisted LSP in many ways—in obtaining equipment and loans from outside sources (including the mortgage to buy the abandoned gas station in which Kepone would be made), in meeting temporary cash deficits, in augmenting fuel supplies during the oil embargo, and in attaining greater efficiency by the use of Allied facilities. Most importantly, LSP's effluent was sampled and analyzed

A. A Milestone Pollution Case in Historical Context

by Allied personnel after Virginia began to order such testing in October 1974. Before that LSP had "tested" its effluent only by a visual check—if the effluent was cloudy, the presence of suspended Kepone was indicated.

Allied officials regularly toured the LSP plant, and were also informed by mail of the waste disposal problems which LSP faced almost from its inception. Allied had discharged the residues of its Kepone production process directly into Gravelly Run Brook which flows into the James River. LSP at first discharged into a disposal pit on Allied's property, as well as tank-trucking some wastes to the Hopewell landfill. As the possibility increased of inspection by either the state or federal agency, or both, it was decided that LSP would discharge into the Hopewell sewer system, despite the fact that the treatment plant was still unfinished. By this means LSP would avoid having to apply for an NPDES [National Pollution Discharge Elimination System] permit to discharge through a pipe "point source." ("Indirect dischargers" into POTWs—publicly-owned treatment works—are not considered point sources and so don't need a NPDES permit.[7]) Having made the decision to "plug in" to the Hopewell system, LSP contacted C.L. Jones, Director of Hopewell's Department of Public Works, for permission. At the time, Hopewell possessed only a "primary" level waste treatment plant—a series of filters and settling tanks without any biological or chemical treatment other than disinfection and sludge digestion. Such a rudimentary system would not degrade Kepone, but would merely divide Kepone effluent between outfall pipe and sludge. Jones, who had been Plant Manager of Allied's Semi-Works prior to Hundtofte, recommended to Hopewell's City Manager that LSP be permitted to discharge. Permission was granted in November 1973. (LSP was asked by Hopewell to meet a pretreatment standard of three parts per million of Kepone.) Thus, LSP became the only industry in Hopewell allowed to discharge into the municipal sewerage system. Allied Chemical's attorneys participated in these negotiations and agreed to pay for the pollution control equipment that Life Science would require in order to meet the pretreatment standard.

Problems developed as soon as LSP began diverting Kepone wastes into Hopewell's treatment plant. In October 1974, a state inspector discovered that the sludge digester at the plant was inoperative, and his investigation revealed LSP to be the source of contamination. Prior to the plant breakdown, the State was apparently unaware that Kepone was being discharged into the Hopewell system because Hopewell's application for an NPDES permit for its treatment plant (filed a month before plug-in permission was granted to LSP) made no mention of any industrial discharge into the municipal system.[8] LSP's discharges were not halted when the State brought the situation to the attention of LSP and Hopewell officials, even though the pretreatment standard was being violated. Instead, a "study" was commenced to determine a "safe" effluent limit for Kepone.

In September 1974, an LSP employee complained to the Occupational Safety and Health Administration (OSHA) of excessive pesticide fumes and dust in the LSP plant, but based on a phone call to Hundtofte, with no on-site inspection, OSHA found insufficient evidence to support the charge and dismissed it.

In March 1975, the EPA accepted the Commonwealth of Virginia's application for certification to take over by delegation the role of issuing and enforcing NPDES permits governing the discharge of pollutants into navigable waters within the Commonwealth. In June 1975, the state set a pretreatment standard for LSP (.5 parts per billion) that was weaker

---

7. 33 U.S.C. §1317(b) (Supp. V 1975), as amended by CWA of 1977. Pub. L. No. 95-217, 33 U.S.C. §1317(b); 49 F.R. §125.4(a) (1977).

8. The Virginia State Water Control Board was by this time administering the NPDES program pending formal delegation by EPA, under 33 U.S.C. §1342(b). [EDS.]

than EPA wished but stricter than prior standards. EPA, which had been informed of the situation, agreed to this compromise. In order to meet this standard, LSP was supposed to further pretreat its wastes and hold its discharges in "equalization" tanks until such time as discharge would not violate the pretreatment standard (i.e., to even-out the flow). Allied had participated in the negotiations among LSP, Hopewell, Virginia, and EPA, and Allied opted to pay for the necessary pollution control equipment. Allied and LSP then began to discuss the capital costs of expanding Kepone production to 2,500,000 pounds per year in order to meet an increasing demand in the European market. (From the inception of LSP, Allied had constantly requested increased Kepone production.) However, even after the new equipment was installed, the pretreatment standard was violated in 19 out of 21 samplings, though local and state officials appear to have taken no action on the violations.

On July 7, 1975, as LSP was preparing for increased Kepone production, one of its employees visited Dr. Chou, a Hopewell internist, complaining of tremors, weight loss, quickened pulse rate, unusual eye movements, and a tender, enlarged liver. Such symptoms were not unusual among LSP employees, but by now were generally tolerated as a necessary price to be paid for the $5.00 per hour wage they received. Although about twenty physicians had been consulted during the sixteen months of LSP's existence, only Dr. Chou suggested a connection between the ailments and the workplace environment. After questioning his patient and taking a blood sample, Dr. Chou forwarded the sample to the Center for Disease Control in Atlanta, where an analysis for Kepone could be performed. The tests disclosed that the blood sample contained 7.5 parts per million of Kepone, an astounding concentration to be found in human blood. The federal doctors then contacted the Virginia State Epidemiologist, Dr. Robert Jackson, who immediately asked for a meeting with Hundtofte and Moore.[9]

It quickly became clear that Kepone pollution was poisoning workers at the site and contaminating their families with dust brought home in workers' clothing and hair. As a chlorinated hydrocarbon, Kepone can be absorbed through the skin as well as breathed in or swallowed. As it accumulates in the body it generates neurological symptoms, including eye tremors, slurred speech, hand tremors, and serious liver dysfunction, and apparently was the cause of a number of workers' sterility.

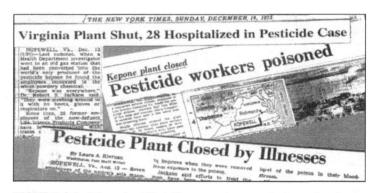

FIGURE 2-2. *When the Allied Kepone story erupted, the national press lavished attention upon the incident and its consequences, fueling popular consciousness of toxic contamination and directly contributing to strengthened federal pollution laws.*

---

9. Meetings had previously been requested by the Virginia State Department of Labor and Industry, but LSP had been successful in postponing them. Only one Federal official, an EPA pesticide inspector, visited LSP before 1973; but he was not authorized to enter the production area. EPA jurisdiction over air and water pollution had been delegated to state officials. At various times representatives of the Virginia Air Pollution Control Board, Water Pollution Control Board, and State Health Department had all visited LSP, but they were not responsible for inspecting LSP's working conditions.

A. A Milestone Pollution Case in Historical Context

When State Epidemiologist Jackson toured the plant he was appalled: Conditions within the LSP workplace were "incredible, . . . might have shocked Charles Dickens," "Kepone dust was everywhere, . . . flying through the air . . . saturating the workers' clothing, getting . . . into sandwiches they munched. . . . "[10] Workers were "virtually swimming in the stuff," were not required to wear protective equipment even when it was available, and no warning signs were posted. Seven out of ten production workers present had "the shakes" so severely that they required immediate hospitalization.[11] One worker, Del White, like many others, now reported that he began to develop tremors within a month of the time he started at LSP. "I thought it was just me, but then I noticed everyone was shaking." He had gone to Moore and Hundtofte and "they assured me that there was nothing in Kepone which could hurt humans. . . . When they told us it wouldn't hurt us, I went back to work." If Kepone had been dangerous, workers reported, they assumed government health officials would require precautions.

On July 25, 1975, LSP voluntarily ended its operations under threat of a closure order by the Virginia Department of Health. In January 1976, the National Cancer Institute released a report implicating Kepone as a possible carcinogen in humans. Investigations revealed seventy-five cases of acute Kepone poisoning among LSP workers and high levels of Kepone in the blood of some of their family members. Some workers showed dramatically lowered sperm counts and low sperm motility.

Outside the plant there was found to be massive contamination of air, soil, and especially water, with the Kepone contamination plume extending 100 miles downstream in the James River. Shellfish and finfish in Chesapeake Bay had dangerous levels of toxic residue. As a result, the State of Virginia closed the James and portions of Chesapeake Bay to fishing. (Parts of the river and Bay remained closed to fishing until 1980.) EPA reported Kepone particulates in the atmosphere as far away as Richmond. Serious levels of Kepone contaminated the Life Science plant, a neighboring building, the soil at the plant site, a section of the Hopewell landfill, and a lagoon adjacent to the Hopewell waste treatment facility. Life Science had declared insolvency as soon as the plant closed, and the officers announced the firm was financially incapable of remedying any consequences of the Kepone contamination.

The *Kepone* case thrust a dramatic new message into the national consciousness. For a dozen years the new environmental movement had been echoing Rachel Carson's warning in Silent Spring that chemicals in the environment threatened the nation's soils and wildlife. Citizen lawsuits had been filed challenging DDT and other chlorinated hydrocarbon pesticides for their effects on populations of birds like eagles and brown pelicans.[12] The chemical industry had mounted a wide-ranging counter-attack, slighting Carson's scientific

---

10. See Harvard Business School, "Allied Chemical Corporation Case" 5 (1979, written by Joseph L. Bodaracco). Interestingly, the HBS case study essentially ignores the role of Allied managers in the *Kepone* affair, treating contamination as the result of isolated renegade acts of the Life Sciences company, which was identified only as a small Allied "supplier," thereby finessing the point that the tolling contract was a carefully considered corporate externalization by Allied itself.

11. In late 1974, the federal Occupational Safety and Health Agency (OSHA) had received a complaint from an LSP worker who claimed to have been fired for refusing to work in the Kepone-laden work setting. OSHA informed the worker that since he was no longer an employee he had no standing to complain under the Act. Miller, Occupational Safety and Health Act, Environmental Law Handbook 517 (17th Ed., 2003). OSHA did send a written inquiry to LSP, but after receiving a mollifying response closed the file without making an on-site inspection.

12. The citizens' pesticide lawsuits, beginning in Long Island, NY, launched the Environmental Defense Fund, a pioneering public interest environmental law organization which now has global activities. See *Yannacone v. Dennison*, 285 N.Y.S.2d 476 (Sup. Ct. 1967) (subsequently settled out of court), *EDF v. Hardin*, 428 F.2d 1093 (D.C. Cir. 1970) (inducing cancellation proceedings), *EDF, Inc. v. Ruckelshaus*, 142 U.S. App. D.C. 74 (1971).

credentials, spreading rumors about her sexual orientation, and characterizing chemical manufacturing as a benign economic enterprise being criticized by an élitist bunch of birdwatcher extremists. But now suddenly the *Kepone* story, coming in a week of summer news-lull, carried the heartbreaking images—of *humans*, ordinary people, suffering neurological shaking and sterility from exposures to chlorinated hydrocarbon pesticide dust—to TV sets across the nation. The story broadened national skepticism about the human consequences of chemical exposures and about the corporate executives who managed the nation's industrial production. In covering the story, the local and national press consistently laid the blame for the *Kepone* incident on Allied. Some news reports and editorials described Life Science as a front for Allied's Kepone manufacture, while others ignored Life Science's role altogether, laying full responsibility directly upon Allied. On December 14, 1975, the CBS program "60 Minutes" aired damaging interviews with Allied officials, tricking them into acknowledging their internal decisions, and sharply criticized the company for creating the *Kepone* incident.

After councilling with industry colleagues about how to address the horrific adverse publicity arising from the *Kepone* incident, Allied planned a major advertising campaign to portray it as a good and concerned corporate citizen. Allied's board of directors took a high level of interest in senior management's responses to the *Kepone* incident and to the negative publicity and litigation that Allied faced. At its February 1976 meeting, the board was informed that Allied's outside auditors had identified the *Kepone* incident as having a potentially significant impact on Allied's financial statements because of the inability to predict what additional costs from pending lawsuits and other liability Allied would incur.

What about law and the legal repercussions of the *Kepone* story? Hundreds of common law personal injury and other damage claims were filed against Allied. Tort claims by Life Science employees, their families, and others aggregated approximately $85 million. Approximately 400 fishermen, alleging that their livelihood was impaired by the closing of the James River and Chesapeake Bay, filed tort claims against Allied aggregating $24 million. In addition, a class action suit was brought against Allied on behalf of some 10,000 fishermen and other members of the Chesapeake Bay-area seafood industry, claiming economic damages of $25 billion.

In terms of public law, OSHA (the Occupational Health & Safety and Health Administration) assessed an administrative fine of $16,500 against LSP for hazards to its workers, which LSP could not pay.[13] As to water pollution, the Virginia Water Control Board brought suit directly against Allied for $3.5 million in civil penalties under the terms of both state and federal statutes. The Commonwealth of Virginia, the City of Hopewell, the EPA, the Army Corps of Engineers, and other governmental agencies involved in the investigation of the *Kepone* incident and its subsequent cleanup also requested reimbursement from Allied for expenses incurred or expected to be incurred in the cleanup. In the aggregate, these cleanup expenses could have exceeded $20 million.

Although the Ford Administration's EPA deferred to the state's civil penalties lawsuit, it decided to file federal criminal charges in the case. In early 1976, the U.S. Attorney for the Northern District of Virginia obtained grand jury criminal indictments against Allied, LSP, Hundtofte, Moore, and the City of Hopewell under the federal water pollution act and the Refuse Act. In the summer of 1976, Judge Robert Mehrige presided over a criminal trial given so much passionate public attention that it had to be moved to West Virginia. [The *Kepone* criminal case is discussed in Chapter 19.]

---

13. It appears that Hundtofte and Moore then were personally assessed the penalties. See *Moore, Hundtofte & LSP v. Occupational Safety & Health Review Comm'n*, 591 F.2d 991 (4th Cir. 1979).

A. A Milestone Pollution Case in Historical Context

Testimony and graphic presentations from the *Kepone* debacle were featured in a series of 1976 congressional hearings leading to passage of two toxics statutes in 1976, RCRA and ToSCA, and the Clean Water Act of 1977 (CWA) establishing the fundamental structure of current federal water pollution law.

Responding to the continuing international sales of stockpiled Kepone and similar hazardous substances, President Jimmy Carter issued an Executive Order prohibiting the overseas export of unregistered chemicals and pharmaceuticals found to be too dangerous to be approved for use in the U.S.[14]

COMMENTARY & QUESTIONS

1. Why did the *Kepone* disaster happen? How did this dramatic widespread poisoning—of workers and their families, neighbors, water, wildlife, air, and soil—come to pass? Was Allied a rogue corporation or just following business norms of the time? The chronology of the *Kepone* story in the years following Allied's 1949 invention of the compound involved dozens of conscious management decisions. Were the corporate leaders ignorant of Kepone's dangers and the hazardous externalities that Allied and Life Science's operations imposed on the workplace, the surrounding environment, and human exposures including consumers overseas? To what extent did their corporate and legal contexts incline them toward ignoring those externalized costs?[15]

Wouldn't the fear of legal liability change corporate executives' calculus? In the *Kepone* era, the prospect of legal accountability was quite unlikely. Who could be expected to keep a close eye on Kepone production? The federal agencies? The local city government? The Commonwealth of Virginia? The working poor of Hopewell? Effective public law requires that appropriate standards, regulatory structures, and enforcement policy are in place and operating. The common law doesn't readily apply before actual injuries occur. In the *Kepone* case, no one acted until a foreign-born outsider doctor blew the whistle. This suggests that then, as now, (1) the practicalities involved in enforcing law, including institutional follow-through, are as vital as the substantive standards on the books; and (2) the realistic prospect of legal accountability is important to the cost-externalizing calculus of business decisionmakers and can vary with political winds.

2. Allied's "tolling" agreement with LSP. Do you see how the tolling agreement for LSP to produce Kepone for Allied produced mutual benefits? As with the *maquiladora* factories along the U.S.-Mexico border, corporations arrange such "independent subcontracting" relationships not only for production cost-cutting but also to limit potential liability for environmental, labor, and other legal consequences.

3. A state-level tendency toward laxity? In *Kepone*, the state's administrative inattention to pollution problems contributed to the scope and severity of contamination. The laxity of Virginia state agencies reflects the interstate competition for industry and jobs that originally prompted Hopewell to advertise itself as "the Chemical Capital of the South." That pressure to compete for jobs undercuts the vigilance of local and state officials. The

---

14. 46 Fed. Reg. 4659 (Jan. 19, 1981). The first Federal Register order published in the name of President Ronald Reagan was a one-sentence Executive Order reversing the Carter ban on export of unregisterable substances. 46 Fed. Reg. 12,943 (Feb. 19, 1981). By 1982, 30% of the nation's chemical pesticide exports were of substances unregisterable in the U.S.

15. See Estes, The Public Cost of Private Corporations, 6 Advances Pub. Int. Acct. 329-351 (1995); and articles prepared by the Program on Corporations, Law & Democracy (POCLAD) as part of the Ending Corporate Dominance Alliance, *available at* www.poclad.org.

race-to-the-bottom continues to be a powerful competitive tendency within the political marketplace at all levels, nibbling away at state regulations as well as the federal laws that attempt to provide a national floor. In most areas of the field, one continues to see arguments of federalism and devolution to the states as a recurring theme of industrial politics.

4. Legal repercussions of the *Kepone* disaster. As noted, one of the major legal consequences of the *Kepone* debacle was congressional action. The legislative debates leading to the 1976 toxics statutes and the 1977 CWA repeatedly invoked the *Kepone* disaster, and four major provisions in the new water act derived from specific reactions against Allied's Hopewell contamination.[16] Regulatory responses were evident too, as federal and state agencies were prompted by the *Kepone* case's notoriety to tighten reporting and enforcement practices against industries around the nation under state and federal pollution laws. In terms of civil litigation, the sum total of Allied's ultimate liability is not known because of confidential sealed settlements. We do know how much the state and local governments collected: $5.25 million to settle all of the claims of the Commonwealth of Virginia and the City of Hopewell for Kepone-related costs that these governmental bodies had incurred, as well as administrative penalties assessed by the Virginia Water Control Board. Embarrassed by the *Kepone* debacle, EPA and the Virginia agency also entered into administrative negotiations with Allied to force the cleanup of contaminated areas. Allied voluntarily decontaminated the Life Science plant site at a cost of close to $1 million. (There were no federal civil recoveries, the federal toxic cleanup statutes not yet existing.)

Allied also sponsored health tests for former Life Science workers and conducted intensive research on methods of retrieving Kepone from the James River and incinerating Kepone residuals. In early 1976, Allied Chemical donated $88,000 to the Medical College of Virginia for monitoring and treating former Life Science employees who had been severely affected by Kepone. (As a result of these studies, the college's medical team perfected a technique for accelerating elimination of Kepone from the human body, thereby speeding the recovery of those persons who had suffered from Kepone poisoning.)

As to civil litigation filed by individual plaintiffs for personal injuries, little was officially reported about the cases or the amounts of damages paid out to private victims of the toxic exposures. After several cases had proceeded through initial stages of tort litigation,[17] in which the most effective cause of action surprisingly turned out to be product liability-based claims for failure to warn (Figure 3, excerpts from plaintiffs' Complaint in Civ. Action 75-0469-R), Allied adopted a policy of settling all suits out of court, each with a strict settlement stipulation that no information ever be provided on the amount of payments.[18] According to one insider, the personal injury settlements totaled about $5 million. The only civil damage action to go to verdict, a suit filed by ten classes of fishermen and other users

---

16. See Goldfarb, Changes in the Clean Water Act Since Kepone, 29 U. Rich. L. Rev. 603, 612-615 (1995), describing Kepone's explicit role in Congress's "mid-course corrections" of water pollution law.

17. A chutzpah common law action filed by LSP's president, William Moore, against Allied alleging "intentional infliction of emotional distress" and "failure to warn" for not telling him of Kepone's dangers unsurprisingly failed. *Moore v. Allied*, 480 F. Supp. 364, 480 F. Supp. 377 (E.D. Va. 1979).

18. In most legal settlement agreements, a standard provision decrees that no details of the settlement are ever to be revealed on pain of forfeiting the cash; some also require plaintiff's attorney to refrain from such representations in the future. The facts of settled cases, however, including investigative research, could be important in warning other injured persons and helping to pursue legal remedies. As a matter of social policy, should such information be open? See Twomey, Breaking the Silence: Examining the Enforceability of Private Settlements Which Conceal Environmental Hazards, 4 New Eng. Envtl. L.F. 109 (1997); Gibeaut, Secret Justice, A.B.A.J., Apr. 1998, at 50 (reporter fined $500,000 for revealing $36 million settlement amount in pollution class action suit against Conoco Inc.).

A. A Milestone Pollution Case in Historical Context

```
                    UNITED STATES DISTRICT COURT
                    EASTERN DISTRICT OF VIRGINIA
                         Richmond Division
DALE F. GILBERT, DELBERT R. WHITE,
EVERETTE L. MESSER, NICKEY F. SHOWN,
JAMES O. ROGERS, JR., JOHN EDWARD COX,
BRUCE W. PRICE, MELVIN L. RUSSELL,            CIV. ACTION NO. CA-75-0469-R
ROBERT W. NEWMAN,                             FILED: Sep 19 1973
FRANK M. ARRIGO
                   Plaintiffs,
             v.
ALLIED CHEMICAL CORPORATION,
a New York corporation,...
                   Defendants
COUNT 1                        COMPLAINT
```

1. Plaintiffs are all citizens of the Commonwealth of Virginia. Defendant, Allied Chemical Corporation, hereinafter referred to as "Allied," is a New York corporation and has its principal place of business in the State of New Jersey;... The matter in controversy..., exclusive of interest and costs, exceeds the sum of Ten Thousand Dollars ($10,000.00).

2. That defendants...beginning in about March, 1974, furnished, sold or supplied certain chemicals to Life Science Products Company of Hopewell, Virginia...which were used by Life Science in the manufacture or production of a chemical substance sold under the Allied trade name of Kepone; that defendants knew or should have known that the said chemicals are imminently and inherently dangerous to life or property, yet defendants negligently supplied said chemicals to Life Science without notice or warning of the defect or danger to the plaintiffs who were users of said chemicals; that defendants failed to exercise a high degree of care and vigilance in dealing with these dangerous chemicals; that it was reasonably foreseeable to the defendants that their failure to warn, explain, instruct and apprise the plaintiffs of the dangers involved would result in serious injuries to them.

3. As a proximate result of the defendants' negligent failure to warn and/or to adequately warn the plaintiffs of the dangers involved, the plaintiffs have suffered severe and permanent injuries to their health, bodies and minds, including, but not limited to, tremors, opisclonus, memory deficits, pleuritic and joint pains, liver damage, cataracts, and injuries to their reproductive systems, and did suffer and will suffer in the future, loses due to being prevented from following their usual course of affairs and the expenditure of large sums of money for medical treatment in an effort to be cured....

...WHEREFOR, plaintiffs demand judgment against Allied...in the sums opposite their respective names, together with costs and interest from date of injury:

Gilbert, Three Million Dollars	$3,000,000.00
White, Three Million Dollars	$3,000,000.00
Messer, Two Million Five Hundred Thousand Dollars	$2,500,000.00
Shown, Three Million Dollars	$3,000,000.00
Rogers, Two Million Five Hundred Thousand Dollars	$2,500,000.00
Cox, Two Million Three Hundred Thousand Dollars	$2,300,000.00
Price, Two Million Three Hundred Thousand Dollars	$2,300,000.00
Russell, Two Million Three Hundred Thousand Dollars	$2,300,000.00
Newman, Two Million Dollars	$2,000,000.00
Arrigo, Two Million Dollars	$2,000,000.00

TRIAL BY JURY IS DEMANDED.   By: _____
                              [Edward W. Taylor, James D. Hundley], Counsel
                              HUNDLEY, TAYLOR & GLASS
                              P.O. Box 518, Richmond, Virginia 23204

FIGURE 2-3. *Excerpts from a personal injury complaint, E.D. Va. Civ. Action 75-0469-R, filed in the aftermath of the* Kepone *incident. Three other counts added to the factual allegations of Count 1 by including claims for negligent supervision of Life Sciences, strict liability personal injury, and strict liability failure to warn. All such private complaints were withdrawn prior to trial on the basis of off-the-record nondisclosure settlements.*

of Chesapeake Bay who suffered economic losses, resulted in damages awarded to two of the plaintiff classes likewise in the neighborhood of $5 million. (*Pruitt v. Allied Chemical,* in Chapter 3.)

In a separate criminal trial before Judge Robert Merhige, Moore and Hundtofte were both convicted of conspiracy to furnish false information to the federal government, conspiracy relating to LSP's discharge of Kepone, and 79 counts under the FWPCA for Kepone discharges into the Hopewell sewer system, for which they were fined $25,000 each. Hopewell was fined $10,000 because, as Judge Merhige stated, "heavy fines would serve no purpose, [taking] money from one pocket of the taxpayer to another." Allied pleaded nolo contendere, was convicted of 940 counts of violating the federal water act, and was fined $13.3 million. (Following up on an indirect suggestion by Judge Merhige, Allied then proposed to set up an $8 million fund for a Virginia Environmental Endowment, a nonprofit corporation that would perform research and implement programs to mitigate the environmental effects of Kepone. As a result, Allied's penalty was reduced to $5 million. Allied's attempt to write off this $8 million as a nonpenal ordinary business expense deduction on its taxes was denied by the Internal Revenue Service.[19]) No one got jail time in the *Kepone* incident.[20] For the *Kepone* event as a whole, Allied's total outlay was reported by a company attorney to have approached $30 million.

To what extent did Allied have to account for the *totality* of the costs its decisions had caused? What about natural resources damages? The judge noted in the *Pruitt* fisheries case that "the costs . . . of Kepone pollution . . . were borne most directly by the *wildlife* of Chesapeake Bay," but no natural resources damages or restoration orders were issued. Are there other legal accountings that could have occurred in this process? The natural resources damages section of Chapter 3 and the public trust materials of Chapter 20 explore those possibilities.

5. Is *Kepone* a tragedy of the commons? To what extent does the *Kepone* story parallel Garrett Hardin's tragedy of the commons in Chapter 1? The waters of the James River and Chesapeake Bay and the air in Hopewell are indeed commons used by all and owned by none, and these commons undoubtedly were polluted by the actions of Allied and Life Science. *Kepone* and other pollution and resource depletion situations do reflect the *behavioral* aspects of Hardin's cow pasture tragedy—the entrepreneurial tendency for each individual actor to pass diffuse harms into the commons to avoid facing their full cost. These cases likewise illustrate the strong practical pressures in the competitive marketplace to continue doing so. But in other ways the Kepone on the banks of the James River is quite different from Hardin's cow pasture. In Hardin's pasture, the degradation of the resource —destruction of the grassland—would ultimately force each of the herdsmen to face the practical consequences of his actions. So far as we know, however, neither Kepone factory ever faced internal production problems from self-polluted air or water supplies, so the "comes-back-around" feature of Hardin's tragedy was missing.[21] Likewise, in many pollution settings, no physical feedback enforces a practical reckoning upon the actors. Unlike overfishing a marine commons, which destroys the industry itself, the physical consequences of chemical pollution do not usually come back through natural physical

---

19. *Allied-Signal v. Comm'r,* 1992 Tax Ct. Memo LEXIS 204, 241 (T.C. 1992).

20. See Chapter 19. Early in the trial, Judge Merhige commented "nobody is going to jail in this case," thereby dampening the prosecutors' attempts to persuade some defendants to turn state's evidence. The criminal case was Crim. Act. No. 76-0129-R, U.S. District Court for the Eastern District of Virginia, Richmond Div. (1977, unreported).

21. Prior to the revelation of Kepone contamination, probably the only self-pollution cost Allied faced was whatever minimal worker health costs it had to absorb through workers' sick pay or company doctors' fees.

A. A Milestone Pollution Case in Historical Context

processes to burden the polluters. Water polluting factories such as Allied are less likely to locate on enclosed lakes where their pollution is drawn back into their own intake pipes than on rivers where their dumped wastes flow away downstream. Given the different positions of parties in relation to the common, and the disparity of power they represent, if there is to be an accounting it probably will have to be imposed by the artifices of law, or the press, or politics.

6. *Kepone* and the role of lawyers. Allied's attorneys worked on the patents, franchise and tolling agreements, withdrawn domestic pesticide application, export permits, occupational health regulations, disposal practices, Refuse Act and NPDES applications, and other critical actions. Could and should they have raised the hazards issues? Environmental cases continually present true moral dilemmas and tough questions of legal ethics. What is the attorney's role and duty upon discovering a significant environmental hazard created by a client that the client refuses to report or correct?

> Despite the threat of harm, the rules of ethics bind you to remain silent if the danger arises from negligence rather than a criminal act.... Which duty should predominate—the duty to maintain the confidences of the client or the duty to avert a danger to the community?... The applicable rule of ethics[22] appears to allow an attorney to remain silent despite significant danger to the public or an individual.... Society has a critical interest in the balance struck between these conflicting duties and in encouraging lawyers to assess environmental dangers rather than blindly adhering to an ethic of silence. Russell, Cries and Whispers: Environmental Hazards, Model Rule 1.6, and the Attorney's Conflicting Duties to Clients and Others, 72 Wash. L. Rev. 409, 411-415 (1997).[23]

For an attorney to raise such sensitive issues is not necessarily conducive to job security, at least not until the risks of huge future liabilities that may follow are acknowledged.

7. *Kepone* and environmental justice. Looking at the map of Hopewell (Figure 1), it perhaps isn't surprising to learn that the residential areas most directly exposed to air and water toxics from the plants that produced Kepone were poor minority neighborhoods. "Poor people and people of color bear the brunt of environmental dangers, from pesticides to air pollution to toxics to occupational hazards. At the same time, poor people and people of color also have the fewest resources to cope with these dangers, legally, medically or politically."[24] The Hopewell neighbors appear to have had only an absorptive role in the story. Issues of environmental justice—the way race, low income, and political disenfranchisement are reflected in environmental impacts—appear in a number of places in this coursebook. It is increasingly clear that many environmental burdens are especially likely to be visited upon communities of color or communities marked by low-level incomes and limited political clout. The burdens range from loss of critical urban amenities and quality of life issues to rat bites and pollution exposure effects. In the years following the *Kepone* case, many people began to see a pattern in the distribution of toxic harms and the characteristics of the people who were most often exposed to them. The correlation was first highlighted in Charles Lee's 1987 study Toxic Wastes and Race in the United States, sponsored by the United Church of Christ Commission for Racial Justice, followed by Dr. Robert Bullard's Dumping in Dixie: Race, Class & Environmental Quality (1990). In these

---

22. ABA Model R. Prof. Conduct 1.6, in its currently diluted form. [Eds.]
23. In her extended analysis of this dilemma, Professor Russell also notes that there is a growing countervailing risk of tort liability to victims for attorneys who fail to warn nonclients of such dangers.
24. Cole, Empowerment as a Key to Environmental Protection: The Need for Environmental Poverty Law, 19 Ecology L.Q. 619 (1992).

and subsequent studies, racial minorities' and low-income groups' risk of exposure to environmental hazards appeared to be both quantitatively and qualitatively greater than that of the general public.

8. A first-generation regulatory setting. The Allied *Kepone* case illustrates a relatively uncomplicated stage in the modern history of environmental regulation. At the time Allied began manufacturing Kepone in Hopewell in 1966, it was regulated only under the common law and the State of Virginia's water pollution statute, which was a permissive 1940s-style law that imposed no significant constraints on industry behavior until it was too late. The federal Refuse Act, a 1890s criminal law that coincidentally fit the needs of environmentalists, rediscovered in the late 1960s, appears to have been the first federal environmental statute to force significant modification in corporate behavior.[25] The Refuse Act provisions were relatively primitive, however, requiring only a simple permit from the U.S. Army Corps of Engineers, and the statutory standards for issuing permits were unclear.

When Congress passed the comprehensively amended FWPCA[26] in 1972, reacting to the interstate race-to-the-bottom, it required each industrial discharge "point source" to obtain a NPDES permit set at levels based on Best Available Technology (BAT) standards. (Under federal water law, because of extensive lobbying from the farm states, "nonpoint sources" such as agricultural runoff and erosion comprise huge volumes of pollution but are not required to have permits, and are thus largely unregulated.) EPA's issuance of point source standards began in 1972 and dragged on for years. Until a state received "cooperative federalism" certification to apply the NPDES program, EPA also had the job of applying its defined pollution standards through federal permits for every point source—every pipe, drain, and drainage channel—in the state. Most states, including Virginia, eventually sought EPA approval to take over implementation of the federal law, often apparently in order to moderate the strictness anticipated under the federal program. Under the provisions of the FWPCA, citizens can bring enforcement actions against violations,[27] but in the *Kepone* case, no citizen actions were filed. In subsequent years, however, citizen enforcement became a major force in shaping and applying pollution standards. Within a few years, in part because of citizen enforcement, the federal water act became an accepted regulatory reality.

The first generation of active federal environmental regulation during the *Kepone* years looked haphazard and unsophisticated. Each regulatory statute begins its life as an unfinished product. Unclear initially how it will work in practice, it evolves over time according to the quality of the enforcement, compliance, political support, and resistance it encounters.

B. BEYOND *KEPONE*: TRACKING SEVERAL DECADES OF ENVIRONMENTAL LAW DEVELOPMENT

The *Kepone* incident captured a moment early in the development of the statutory public law of environmental protection. Although a half-dozen or more significant statutes had

---

25. The strict, simple terms of the Refuse Act's criminal provisions are noted in Chapter 19.
26. 33 U.S.C. §1251ff. The new law set federal minimum standards without which, it is thought, an intense interstate competition for jobs and revenues powerfully induces states to lower their environmental standards. States that enforce environmental protections tend to lose their industries to states that require fewer restrictions. Pollution, moreover, is an interstate problem. More than 20 states receive more than 50% of their water pollution from other states, and an additional 15 states receive between 25-50% from other states.
27. See citizen enforcement of FWPCA and CWA §505, noted further in Chapters 6 and 18.

B. Beyond *Kepone*

been put on the books by 1975, they were then only in their first hesitant stages of implementation. The extent, seriousness, and complexity of statutory systems regulating pollution have grown dramatically in the decades after *Kepone* and Love Canal.

As noted in Chapter 12, the CWA, for example, has continued to expand beyond the 1977 amendments prompted by the *Kepone* scare. Judges now possess stronger criminal sanctions with which to punish knowing violators: "knowing endangerment" that "places another person in imminent danger of death or serious bodily injury" can lead to fines of $250,000 or 15 years imprisonment, doubled for second convictions. 33 U.S.C. §1319.

Kepone also reflected an early period in the development of corporate responses to the new legal restraints on pollution. Allied Chemical's illegal behavior was flagrant, its assimilation of the new legal norms primitive. In some ways, its conduct seems to come from a bygone era. It is important to realize, however, that wrongful corporate conduct of the Allied Chemical variety still occurs. Consider the case of workers in a uranium facility in Paducah, Kentucky, exposed into the 1990s to plutonium, without their knowledge or consent, while the owners of the facility knew of the hazards.[28] Or consider industry decisions to allow widespread asbestos exposure as noted in the next chapter. The examples could be multiplied, and they do not come only from bygone eras. Nevertheless, it is also true that many companies have significantly modified their behavior in response to the modern environmental laws. Yet they have not simply accepted stringent environmental restrictions as a way of life. Rather, their efforts to resist often appear in earlier stages of the legal process, resulting in active lobbying of legislators to reject new (or dilute old) environmental laws, aggressive pressuring of agency regulators to do the same, and sophisticated think-tank and trade association networks aimed, often, at undermining the case for stringent environmental protection of any kind. Many of the proposals for reform introduced later in this chapter grew out of these networks.

1. The Modern Statutory Array in the Years Since *Kepone*

Federal Statutes. One way to track the evolution of environmental statutes is to see how many now apply. Today if Allied Chemical decided to construct a factory to manufacture a twenty-first-century pesticide, for example, it would trigger consideration under virtually all 17 of the federal statutes listed below. Most of these statutes also have a state or local counterpart regulation. Consider this list as a short primer on current statutes, and, scrutinizing the map of Allied's Hopewell location (Figure 1), consider how each might apply to a new Allied Semi-Works. (For a fuller description of these and other significant state and federal environmental statutes and their operation, see the Statutory Capsule Appendix on the coursebook website.)

1. **CWA:** The federal Clean Water Act,[29] administered by EPA. As already seen, CWA is a federal-state partnership where EPA sets permissible levels of discharge for

---

28. In January 2000, Bill Richardson, Secretary of Energy, accepted after decades of denials that thousands of workers at Paducah "had been exposed to radiation and chemicals that produced cancer and early death." Most of the victims displayed symptoms similar to Gulf War veterans, particularly chronic fatigue and joint pain. The workers had been handling uranium contaminated with plutonium and neptunium. Paducah was designed to handle uranium, not plutonium, which is about 100,000 times more radioactive per gram. See Warrick, Study Finds More Hazards at Paducah, Discord Greets Draft Report on Uranium Workers' Radiation Exposure, Wash. Post, Oct. 5, 2000, at A03.
29. 33 U.S.C. §1365 (1972, 1977).

different industrial categories based on the performance of BAT; states with approved laws and programs issue NPDES permits based on the federal standards, backed up by on-site ambient water quality requirements; and state enforcement of permits is backed up by the federal EPA. Criminal prosecutions for violations of the CWA and other laws, lying on pollution reports, as well as "knowing endangerment," can send an executive to jail.[30]

2. **CWA §404:** The federal dredge-and-fill regulation program also falls under CWA, restricting the elimination of wetlands; EPA and the U.S. Army Corps of Engineers also require permits for installing in-stream structures if Allied installs sewerage outfalls.

3. **CAA:** The federal Clean Air Act,[31] administered by EPA. Like the CWA, a federal-state partnership; it has special provisions regulating hazardous air pollutants and holds new air pollution sources to the cleanliness levels of BAT. The basic CAA structure requires enforcement of state implementation plans (SIPs) to prevent ambient levels of pollution from exceeding federal "primary standards" set according to harm-based safety criteria.

4. **FDCA:** The federal Food, Drug, and Cosmetics Act,[32] administered by EPA and the Department of Health and Human Services. This statute provides, among others, protections for food quality by setting permissible tolerances for chemical residues such as pesticides in food products and by monitoring compliance.

5. **EPCRA:** The federal Emergency Planning and Community Right-to-Know Act,[33] passed in 1986 after the Bhopal disaster, administered by EPA. EPCRA requires mandatory public reporting by industry of the nature and characteristics of certain hazardous materials and requires states to establish statewide and local emergency response plans. Hopewell's city government would receive this information, and regular TRIs (toxic release inventory reports) would have to be filed.

6. **RCRA:** The federal Resource Conservation and Recovery Act,[34] a 1976 update of the Solid Waste Disposal Act (SWDA) administered by EPA. RCRA regulates waste disposal in general and certain hazardous wastes (via Subtitle C) in particular, tracking the wastes (not the original chemicals) beginning with their generation and ending with their treatment, storage, or disposal (somewhat imprecisely dubbed "cradle to grave" regulation). RCRA also authorizes EPA to take corrective actions to prevent or remedy contamination; special provisions apply to leaking underground storage tanks and medical wastes.

7. **CERCLA:** The 1980 federal Comprehensive Environmental Response, Compensation, and Liability Act (or "Superfund" Act),[35] administered by EPA. The statute provides for EPA investigations and supervised cleanups of hazardous contaminated sites, paid for by the parties who own or who contaminated the sites, with backup

---

30. It was under these enhanced federal charges that a corporate executive for Smithfield Foods was sentenced on eight counts of destroying records and rendering false information about discharges into the Chesapeake Bay watershed, serving a 30-month prison term starting in January 1997. *U.S. v. Smithfield Foods*, 965 F. Supp. 769, 972 F. Supp. 338 (E.D. Va. 1997).

31. 42 U.S.C. §§7401 et seq. (1970).

32. 21 U.S.C. §§346 et seq. (1954, as amended).

33. 42 U.S.C. §§11001 et seq. (1986).

34. 42 U.S.C. §§6901 et seq. (1976).

35. 42 U.S.C. §§9601 et seq. (1980), as amended by the Superfund Amendments and Reauthorization Act of 1986 (SARA).

B. Beyond *Kepone*

funding from a federal Superfund combining taxes from chemical production, penalties, and taxpayer dollars.

8. **SDWA:** The federal Safe Drinking Water Act,[36] administered by EPA. It sets water quality standards for drinking water suppliers and protection of underground drinking water sources and regulates the deep well injection of wastes, a common industrial practice of pumping chemicals into old wells and drill holes as a method of disposal.

9. **OSHA:** The federal Occupational Safety and Health Act,[37] administered by the Occupational Health and Safety Administration (likewise called OSHA). OSHA addresses safety conditions within industrial workplaces and other work settings. The agency sets general industry standards and monitors and enforces them through agency inspections.

10. **CZMA:** The federal Coastal Zone Management Act,[38] administered by the National Oceanic and Atmospheric Administration (NOAA) in the Department of Commerce. CZMA encourages comprehensive state planning and siting controls in coastal and tidal regions. (A close look at the Hopewell map in Figure 1 reveals that the James River is still "tidal" 100 miles inland.) Federal reinforcement is provided through the requirement that federal actions be "consistent" with state standards.

11. **NEPA:** The National Environmental Policy Act,[39] a generic procedural statute administered by the President's Council on Environmental Quality. NEPA does not stipulate any pollution control measures, nor any direct regulation of any private industry, but levies the significant, litigatable requirement that all federal agencies must prepare an environmental impact statement (EIS) before taking any "major federal action significantly affecting the human environment." Some agency permits, such as permits for Allied's installation of outfall pipes under CWA §404, thus probably would have to go through the EIS process.

12. **PPA:** The 1990 federal Pollution Prevention Act,[40] administered by EPA. This statute is mainly an exhortation to industry to reduce, recycle, or prevent pollution through internal planning, design, and technology adaptations. EPA has the power, however, to impose PPA requirements as permit conditions or as part of violation penalty orders.

13. **ESA:** The federal Endangered Species Act,[41] administered by the U.S. Department of Interior Fish and Wildlife Service (FWS) and NOAA. ESA prohibits harms to endangered and threatened species; if a listed species is present in an ecosystem, pollution discharge permits and construction projects can be forced to go through significant modification procedures or be blocked. Harms caused by private actions are subject to criminal penalties.

14. **ToSCA:** The 1976 federal Toxic Substances Control Act,[42] administered by EPA. This "market access" regulation authorizes the agency to require manufacturers to test chemical substances for hazards to human health and the environment before they are permitted to be manufactured and sold. Failure of EPA to act to restrict use of a

---

36. 15 U.S.C. §§1261 et seq. (1974, as amended).
37. 29 U.SC. §§651 et seq. (1970).
38. 33 U.S.C. §§1251 et seq. (1970).
39. 42 U.S.C. §§4331 et seq. (1970).
40. 42 U.S.C. §§13101 et seq. (1990).
41. 16 U.S.C. §§1531 et seq. (1973, as amended).
42. 15 U.S.C. §§2601 et seq. (1976).

substance acts like a grant of a permit, although with a new pesticide, EPA is unlikely to fail to scrutinize.

15. **FIFRA:** The 1975 Federal Insecticide, Fungicide, and Rodenticide Act,[43] administered by EPA. FIFRA requires persons distributing, selling, offering, or receiving any pesticide to register the poison with EPA after testing for "unreasonable risks to humans and the environment, taking into account the economic, social, and environmental costs and benefits of the pesticide's intended use"; the "market access" registration, once granted with practicable tolerance levels, is akin to a perpetual license to market the product, though registrations can be canceled or suspended.

16. **HMTA:** The 1980 federal Hazardous Materials Transportation Act,[44] administered by the U.S. Department of Transportation. This statute provides for extensive regulation of hazardous substances in transit, with requirements for spill control and prevention, and central reporting in the event of spills of toxic or hazardous substances; it invites concurrent state regulation.

17. **The hazardous materials export controls statute:** One provision of a larger consumer safety statute,[45] this statute requires that a party intending to export a banned hazardous substance notify the Consumer Product Safety Commission at least 30 days prior to exportation. The Commission notifies the government of the country to which the substance is to be exported and informs it of the reasons for which the substance was banned. Regulation, if any, is then solely the responsibility of the receiving country.

At least a dozen additional federal statutes are commonly encountered in environmental practice,[46] including a long list of natural resources management statutes, statutes limiting ocean dumping and export of misbranded products, laws protecting parks and marine sanctuaries, historic preservation regulations, transportation planning requirements, the market disclosure requirements of the SEC and the FTC, significant IRS tax code provisions, and so on.

State and Local Regulatory Systems. To the above federal laws, one must add their state corollaries as well as an array of state laws in areas not covered by federal statutes: land use controls and siting, groundwater protection, recycling and noise regulations, landfill regulations beyond toxics and industrial wastes, toxic product standards, land sale disclosure laws, and more.[47] There is a lot of law here. The following table shows the kind of state and local permits that might be required in setting up a plant like Allied's Semi-Works today.

---

43. 7 U.S.C. §§136 et seq. (1975).
44. 49 U.S.C. §§1801 et seq. (1980).
45. 15 U.S.C. §1273 (1993).
46. For a chronological index of federal statutes in the environmental field promulgated since the late 1800s, see the Chronological Appendix of Statutes on the coursebook website.
47. A number of these state laws are noted in the Statutory Capsule Appendix on the coursebook website, including California's Proposition 65 toxic product labeling law, New Jersey's land transfer disclosure requirements, and waste minimization laws. As for the local level of government, the rapid growth of environmental law in the local realm is chronicled in J. Nolon, New Ground: The Advent of Local Environmental Law (2003).

B. Beyond *Kepone*

AGENCY	REGULATORY REQUIREMENT
State Department of Natural Resources	• Permit for dredging and filling as required on site
	• Permit for construction close to major water body Soil erosion and sedimentation permit
	• Inland streams alteration permit
State Water Resources Commission	• Permit for alteration of channels, floodplains, drains
	• Permit for use of water during plant construction, operation, and sewage treatment (in addition to state water pollution control, or NPDES permit)
State Air Pollution Commission	• Permit for boilers and diesel generators
State Department of Health	• Approval of sanitary sewer system
State Police	• Approval for above-ground storage of flammable liquids
State Department of Aeronautics	• Permit for construction of high smokestacks
State Department of Labor	• Permit for boiler installation
	• Permit for any elevators involved in a plant
State Public Utilities Commission	• Permit for construction of high voltage electric transmission lines
	• Permission for connection to high voltage electric transmission lines
	• Railroad spur construction, alteration, and connection to existing railroad spurs
	• Permits for building grade crossings across railroad tracks
	• Construction permit for operation of electrical substation
State Department of Highways	• Permit for alteration of highway access
County Health Commission	• Permit for alteration of any drains
	• Approval of sewer system
County Road Commission	• Permit for altering or temporary closing of highways for construction
County, and Local Municipality	• Zoning permits
Local Township	• Building, electrical, and plumbing permits
	• Permits for water use and sewerage

COMMENTARY & QUESTIONS

1. The biodiversity of public law, post-*Kepone*. In this parade of regulatory systems, each one has its own story. Some statutes are procedural, some have substantive teeth, some represent a strong initial consensus, some are ragtag pragmatic compromises that pleased no one, some embody a cynical legislative decision to create an empty false impression of action, and so on. Each is typically hatched into law in response to public concern about some perceived threat, then develops over time through a vagarious process of opportunistic administrative and judicial action. The passage of a bill is like the launching of an unguided missile. Only after it has flown for a while, directed this way and that by the forces that continue to act upon it, does it become clearer where it is going and what it may do, with what impact. In virtually all cases, the law's effect depends on agency and judicial interpretation. Most statutes are articulated in greater detail by agency regulations published in the Federal Register or state equivalent (see Chapter 6). Each statute's development is incremental, fractionalized and usually fractious, and idiosyncratically different from others. In Europe, these statutes probably would be collected into one large environmental law "code," a general law drafted by a sober, rational expert law commission, with uniform standard-setting and enforcement procedures, and specialized subparts reserved for the unique features of each area. This is America, however, so our statutes remain a menagerie of different laws reflecting the diversity and happenstance of events that created them and enforced by a variety of agencies in a variety of different ways.

2. Getting a handle on statutes: statutory "taxonomy." Practicing attorneys usually develop extensive checklists of existing statutes and regulations to help them orient their analyses of a major project or program, like the construction of a new chemical factory. In addition, given the different kinds of statute and regulatory systems, in order to develop practical understanding of each relevant statute, it is useful to learn to think about them like biologists, who analyze different species via categories based on their structural elements and essential design. This coursebook is organized according to a variety of discernible statutory taxonomies set out in Chapters 8-20.

3. The standard default regulatory design—the comprehensive "prescriptive-federal-standards" model. Although every statute is different, in the most basic terms, most major modern regulatory systems use a standard conceptual design. As illustrated best by the big federal pollution control statutes and regulations studied in Chapters 11 and 12, the federal government dictates the minimum nationwide standards that must be met, standards are administered through federal permits obtained from federal agencies or delegated state agencies for each regulated source, and enforcement comes from agencies or citizens.

4. Citizen enforcement as part of modern environmental law. In the years after *Kepone* (a case in which, remember, there was no citizen statutory enforcement), the fact of citizen participation in environmental public law has completely permeated the system, both in litigation and in informal and formal participation in agency practice. As noted in Chapters 6 and 18, almost every major federal environmental law since 1970 has included a specific authorization for enforcement by citizens, plus a possibility of reimbursement of enforcement costs. Litigating citizens, acting as "private attorneys general," subsequently have shaped every part of the public law structure. Citizen intervention has been the major element in shifting social governance in environmental law from the old "di-polar" model (where government agencies, on one hand, hold the role and responsibility of counterbalancing the excesses of the marketplace economy on the other) toward a Jeffersonian multicentric pluralism where a diversity of affected interests is able to be actively involved in the legal process, assuring that public and individual values do not get lost in the tangles of the political-economic marketplace.[48] Eliminating citizen enforcement is a main strategy in the "conservative" political resistance to environmental law.

5. Biodiversity of law: the common law's continuing roles. The common law remains a fundamentally important part of modern environmental law. Public law remedies build upon and supplement the common law, but common law stands as the foundational underpinning of the legal system. It is a traditionally open legal forum for affected individuals

---

48. A short overview of the citizen implementation approach to environmental protection law is posted on the coursebook website in materials for this chapter.

and often is more flexible and creative in integrating public civic values into new and significant settings.

6. New expectations, new remedies, new science. Today's pollution statutes are often a strict liability system: Fault need not be proved in order to assess penalties for pollution, and mere recordkeeping violations are subject to serious penalties, including jail. More than two decades after *Kepone* and the first generation of major pollution law enforcement actions, administrative and judicial pollution enforcement cases are far more numerous now than during the 1970s. In *Kepone*, no one went to jail. Today, dozens of individual and corporate defendants have been convicted of criminal offenses for harming the environment. (See Chapter 19.) In the *Kepone* cases, very little scientific data on the off-site poisoning effects of Kepone were ever collected. Nor was a comprehensive quantification made of natural resources damages. No reported *Kepone* case explored the scientific questions that today would be part of the record: How does Kepone enter and affect human metabolisms? How does it react when released into air and water? How does it cumulate in aquatic ecosystems, with what results to fish high on the food chain and humans who eat them? Since the 1970s, environmental sciences and assessment technologies have expanded dramatically. In the twenty-first century, many of the most pressing environmental problems do not even remotely resemble the pollution discharge cases that typified the first generation of environmental law where some definable party chose to dump or spew harmful materials directly into a lake, a river, or the air. The global CO_2 buildup changing Earth's climate or chlorinated hydrocarbons seeping out of consumer products, plastics, and aerosols causing hormone disruption, lowered sperm counts, and other gender and fertility effects are of a different scale entirely.[49]

7. International convergences. Just as problems of environmental pollution and resource depletion spread across international boundaries, so too does environmental law through international conventions and evolving principles of responsibility for sustainability. The pesticide issue reflects this globalization process, with its own dynamics and complexities. Debate at first focused on exports of chemicals and pesticides prohibited for use in the U.S. as in the *Kepone* case, often to countries with little or no regulatory infrastructure that were ill-equipped to police their borders. The "circle of poison" that allowed prohibited pesticides to be exported and then reimported as residues on foods began to attract considerable attention. In the mid-1970s, Congress passed several provisions requiring exporters to notify foreign governments when domestically banned or regulated chemicals and pesticides are being shipped to their ports.

As other countries began to become concerned about the "export of hazard," the locus of policy action shifted to international organizations, including the Organisation for Economic Cooperation and Development (OECD)—a club of 24 industrialized countries—and the United Nations Environment Program (UNEP)—a global organization. At the insistence of industrialized exporting countries, both the OECD and UNEP in the mid-1980s adopted notification requirements similar to the Reagan-weakened U.S. regulations. Developing countries protested, however, leading to the adoption of "prior informed consent" (PIC) as a more rigorous minimum international requirement for toxic pesticides, banned chemicals, and hazardous wastes. Under the PIC scheme, shipments cannot be exported until the government of the importing state consents in writing, a regulatory structure that creates more control for developing countries. Preceded by nonbinding

---

49. See T. Colborn, D. Dumanoski & J.P. Myers, Our Stolen Future: Are We Threatening Our Fertility, Intelligence, and Survival? A Scientific Detective Story (1997).

international "good practice standards," PIC was codified in binding multilateral agreements for hazardous wastes in 1989 (the Basel Convention on the Control of Transboundary Movements of Hazardous Wastes and Their Disposal) and for chemicals and pesticides in 1998 (the Rotterdam Convention on the Prior Informed Consent Procedure for Certain Hazardous Chemicals and Pesticides in International Trade).

More recently, it has become apparent that international trade in chemicals and pesticides is only a piece of the larger international problem. Long-lived chemicals and pesticides — "persistent organic pollutants" (POPs) such as DDT and PCBs, typically containing chlorine as part of their chemical makeup — accumulate in fat, concentrate at higher levels of the food chain, and are often transported literally thousands of miles from the point of their release posing risks of cancer and hormonal disruption. Building on years of work by international nongovernmental organizations (NGOs), the Stockholm Convention on Persistent Organic Pollutants was adopted in 2001, targeting nine chemicals and categories of chemicals for elimination. Although international efforts on chemical pesticides give reason for cautious optimism, there are still significant threats requiring multilateral cooperation.

C. Environmental Law Themes & Contexts

> There is a sprawling array of "cross-cutting themes" in modern environmental law that mark it as a major sector of modern social governance, no longer dismissible as an outlying fad. It's become realistic to think of Environmental Law as a mirror of our society's broadest and deepest contours. Thus, for instance, in every legal opinion, and every legislative or regulatory action, competent legal analysis needs to take informed account of the complex *politics* of the matter; not to do so risks missing important practical realities. It matters what Administration is in office, what political blocks control the legislatures, what lobbies, media, and powerful players are deployed on the issue at hand. The struggles between contending forces — between progressive values of sustainability, quality of life and resource protection on one hand, and the pressures of short-horizon corporate profit maximization, for example, on the other — are daily reflected in the practice of environmental law, and the political tilt is rarely toward society's long-term sustainable needs. Governmental regulation is a natural battleground. Industry groups understandably and powerfully advance their interests; citizen groups launch environmental defenses and counter-initiatives. The result is a never-ending process of back-and-forth political contention. To provide a sense of the many interconnecting threads that weave through and around this field, here **below** in no particular order are a couple of dozen concepts that you will encounter in the world of environmental law.

- **The Polluter-Pays Principle.** As the strict liability character of most of today's pollution legislation shows, a basic premise of most modern regulation here and abroad is that absorbing environmental costs is a responsibility of marketplace industries, not a cost to be absorbed by public subsidies paying for prevention and cleanups, nor by the unpaid subsidy of public toleration of pollution (even if it is more "efficient" to pay industry to end pollution).

C. Environmental Law Themes & Contexts

- **Precaution (a/k/a the Precautionary Principle).** Environmental problems frequently arise at the cutting edge of human knowledge, areas of vigorous scientific inquiry that may be fraught with uncertainty. Environmental risks in such situations, while not precisely known from a scientific point of view, may represent immense potential for harms, like those from global warming of the Earth's climate due to the "greenhouse" effect. Precautionary approaches counsel taking early policy action to avoid uncertain or poorly understood risks, particularly in situations where the consequences may be catastrophic. The concept is frequently espoused in international and domestic law and policy, countered by arguments that disruptive regulations should not be applied to risks until the likelihood of harms and their serious nature have been scientifically established and carefully weighed against the status quo.
- **Administrative Process.** The delegation of pervasive administrative powers to government agencies is a vital part of modern legal process and a part of the perplex of environmental law. Deference to administrative agencies is obviously important in order to allow implementation of public law in a complex world. On the other hand, agencies are vulnerable to the suasions of politics. The skills of managing the administrative process are technically challenging and also raise fundamental questions about democratic governance in modern industrial societies.
- **Sustainable Development and Intergenerational Equity.** Perhaps the phrase that best captures the goal of environmental law and policy is "sustainable development." It was the leitmotif of the Rio Conference on the Environment of 1992, where more than 100 presidents and kings, and hundreds of delegations from around the world, agreed that the momentum and practices of the status quo threaten our common global future and that coherent international planning and action are necessary. "Sustainable development" means many things to different people, but its gravamen seems to be that our societies and legal systems owe it to ourselves and our posterity to live within available resources and not to destroy the environmental birthright of future generations for the needs and profits of today, a theme echoed in the public trust doctrine in Chapter 20 and elsewhere. Development must not be based upon an erosive diminution of global assets, but rather on systems of indefinitely extendable human sustenance and life quality, in balance with the resource capacity of the planet's environments.
- **Uncertainty, Scientific Complexity, and Risk.** These three are endemic problems in environmental policy. Often both the presence and the effects of a harmful human impact are invisible until too late. When chemicals leach through the subsoil killing communities of microscopic soil-building organisms or highway salt poisons the root systems of trees, neither cause nor effect is seen until the soil's productivity crashes or the trees begin to die. When pollution is spread widely through an air or water commons, its concentrations are so diffused that the pollution is not noticed until huge volumes are discharged. When human health begins to show signs of illness and injury from widespread exposures to environmental toxins—sometimes 30 years after the exposure—the individual pathways of contamination and proof of causation are typically so scientifically complicated as to be practically impossible to pin down.

And trying to ascertain and handle "risk," the statistical likelihood of particular perils in particular settings, confronts even greater scientific complexities and subjectivities, as well as psychological and political barriers. Tradeoffs between risks do occur: For example, tradeoffs are made between short-term material welfare and long-term ecological integrity: Some toxic residues can be tolerated in foods in order to have the benefit of crops that are not destroyed by pests; some continuing risks such as global warming are accepted in the short term for the sake of developing economies and consumption desires. Environmentalists, however, continually argue against false tradeoff choices when rational alternatives are available. Is it really true that "You have to choose: either economic progress or environmental quality. You can't have both"? To most modern environmental analysts that universal cliché sounds like the classic false tradeoff. In the long term, both are inseparable; in the short term, they can and, at the very least, must be reconcilable.

Science and law continually work together, but they essentially occupy different worlds. In the complex business of proving "causation," for example—that exposure to chemical X causes malady Y—science requires a certainty level of 95% (a margin of error of no more than 5%), criminal law requires a supermajority ("beyond a reasonable doubt," perhaps somewhat less than 95%), common law requires only 50% plus one ("probable"), and statutory law (which in many cases needs only to be "not arbitrary") can regulate with even less certain proof of causation.[50] This often produces confusion. Navigating these subtle cross-channels of science and law is a continuing challenge.

- **Risk and Cost-Benefit Analyses.** Part of the ongoing debates about enhancing or decreasing environmental protections will continue to be the relativity questions. Given the costs and uncertainties of trying to achieve high degrees of protection, and alternative demands on precious public and private resources of time and money, it is consistently important to gauge the balance of costs, benefits, and alternatives, though the perspectives of the marketplace economy and the civic economy will cast the balance in very different terms.
- **The Many Meanings of Risk.** What is the nature of the risk posed by industrial pollution and toxic chemicals? Can that risk be meaningfully described exclusively by reference to the numerical probability and magnitude of the physical harms these substances produce? Or is it also helpful, for regulatory purposes, to consider as well the qualitative features of the risks posed by them? For decades, Paul Slovic and other cognitive psychologists have studied risk perceptions and their determinants. They have arrived at a fairly compact list of attributes that tend to make a substance or activity seem risky to ordinary citizens. Involuntariness, uncontrollability, unfamiliarity, inequitable distribution, effects on future generations, catastrophic outcomes—these are among the qualities that make particular hazards especially scary. A fierce debate exists as to whether risk regulation should be controlled by reference to quantitative factors alone or should also be informed by the qualitative features of risk.
- **Human Nature and the Externalization of Social Costs.** Hardin's tragedy of the commons and Coase's descriptions of cost externalization illustrate how individual human actors are powerfully motivated to maximize their own gains at the expense of the public and the commons. These drives have produced the biggest marketplace economy the world has known, with all the blessings that follow it, and all the forlorn consequences that arise from not planning for and dealing with the realities of costs that are externalized onto nature and the public.

---

50. Regulatory law often deals with risk situations where government must protect against unproved or unquantified threats, as when it controls releases of genetically altered organisms into the environment. Sometimes these include "zero-infinity" problems, where public law attempts to control the risks of harms that are close to zero in likelihood of happening but that would be catastrophic in scale of harm if they were to occur.

C. Environmental Law Themes & Contexts

- **Environmental Law Attempts to "Internalize" Social Costs.** In effect, Rachel Carson's Silent Spring spread a broad intellectual catch-basket beneath the welfare economists' universe of benefit-maximizing individual actors, so as to collect and take overall account of their jettisoned "externalized" social costs, even if they are indirect and unmarketized. The role of environmental law has been to attempt, through common law, state and federal statutory and regulatory systems, and even constitutional theories, to force externalized environmental and social costs back into the politics and economics of the marketplace.

- **Resistance to Regulation.** Industry-oriented resistance to regulation tends to be a consistent backdrop to the government process. An economic entity naturally tends to resist cost internalization. Multiply this by tens of thousands of economic entities, and one finds a broad concurrent tendency permeating the governance process. Like flowing water, market forces and the behavioral realities that drive them inherently tend to resist any "artificial" barriers that curtail their externalizations of social costs. To place a single sandbag into the current is difficult and not likely to have significant effect. As other sandbags are added with great effort, the inherent pressures of the market economy still pour around them. When finally a working accumulation of sandbags is secured, the waters may turn to a path of less resistance, but they do not stop trying to infiltrate and undercut the obstacles blocking their maximum satisfaction. Across the entire face of the environmental law dike the pressures are felt. Lobbyists, lawyers, media managers, political action committees, and a host of political players apply subtle, comprehensive pressure within all three branches of government. When citizens attempt to get around the phenomenon of agency capture[51] by bringing private enforcement actions in the courts, the forces of the marketplace try to undercut citizen standing and judicial remedies.

- **Biodiversity—of Nature and Law.** From ecological science comes the proposition that natural systems that evolve and maintain a wider diversity of living elements are more likely to be successful in the long run. A rich natural biodiversity means that ecosystems are likely to have more interlocking practical mechanisms and more available adaptive options for coping with ongoing changes.[52] Law too has its biodiversity. A consistent reality in environmental practice is the multiplicity of public law statutes and regulations—not to mention potential common law liabilities—that can come to bear in a particular environmental case. The American legal system has always had as one of its special strengths that it combines statutory, regulatory, constitutional, and common law mechanisms within a single system, and each of these has a rich variety of different approaches and remedies, all employed on occasion by opportunistic environmental law.

- **Laissez-Faire Doesn't Address Long-Term Societal and Environmental Concerns?** There is an instinct in most humans' nature, absent government regulation, to maximize individual profits and avoid thinking of diffused public detriments. If nonstatutory law cannot effectively protect the public interests impacted by the market economy, government regulation of some sort will probably be necessary to bring civic concerns into the daily life of business.

- **Environmental Justice:** As in the *Kepone* case, the ultimate location of many potentially dangerous facilities often turns out to be poorer communities or communities

---

51. On the classic political science phenomenon of "agency capture," see Chapter 6.
52. See discussion of biodiversity in Chapter 10.

of color, the least empowered populations. The reasons include managers' desires to save money and site operations where they will be least likely to face effective environmental opposition; the self-condescension of low-income communities, exhibited in uncritical eagerness to attract jobs at any price; or simple discrimination. Environmental law increasingly has been pressured to take account of environmental justice issues.

- **The Race-to-the-Bottom: State and Federal Jurisdictions.** A basic pressure within environmental law comes from the tendency of states to compete with each other for industrial payrolls by lowering regulatory standards. This race-to-the-bottom is a political kind of tragedy of the commons.[53] Federal statutes have formed the core of environmental law, typically structured to provide federal minimum floors to counter the erosive race-to-the-bottom. Environmental law repeatedly serves as a battleground for economic conflicts in "federalism" debates over the basic allocation of roles between federal and state governments.
- **Common Law and Public Law.** Both common law and statutory public law play a range of potential roles. The structures of the modern administrative state—public law agencies, statutes, and regulations at local, state, and federal levels—are built upon the flexible and evolving foundations of common law. Environmental attorneys often find it necessary to draw upon both systems, sometimes simultaneously.
- **Environmental Statutes Evolve.** Statutes change over time, for better and worse, in the same way as living species evolve, according to the pressures, experience, and changing contexts they encounter.
- **Role of Citizen-Initiated Actions in the Legal System.** Perhaps the core feature in the evolution of U.S. environmental law has been the critical role played by citizens in initiating, shaping, and shepherding the development of environmental protection case law and statutes.[54] Legal standing provisions allowing "private attorneys general" to enforce environmental statutes had an immediate and dramatic effect, and imaginative common law actions built a jurisprudence that became a model for the rest of the world, and citizen litigation continues to be a significant component in 75% of environmental civil cases.
- **Strategic Role of the Media.** A critical part of many or most significant environmental issues, as in the *Kepone* story, is the amount and kind of media coverage they receive. Media climate builds the momentum of citizen organizations, often impels corporate acknowledgment of public concerns, and is particularly helpful in making public law mechanisms responsive. Effective public communication of information plays a significant role in social governance.
- **Systemic Roles of "Outrage."** There is a tension between outrage-driven controversies and cool-headed analysis. Environmentalists often find that they must cast their public arguments in terms of outrage and extremes in order to gain and hold official attention and political credibility. Outrage can skew the subtleties of an issue; it can

---

53. Allied had been persuaded to move some operations to Louisiana, where they became part of a highly polluted industrial area now often known as "Cancer Alley." The concept of race-to-the-bottom is subject to ongoing debate and is explored further in Chapter 5.

54. In many countries, it is up to a government agency to recover such damages for injured citizens. After 2500 people were killed by methyl-isocyanate in Bhopal, India in 1984, it was the government of India that sued Union Carbide, recovering $14,500 per death; after the Seveso dioxin incident in Italy in 1976, the settlement negotiated by the government ended the liability claims. After the *Exxon-Valdez* oil spill disaster in Alaska in 1989, the state government briefly considered recovering on behalf of its injured citizens, but ultimately deferred to normal Anglo-American custom and left private recoveries up to private litigants.

C. Environmental Law Themes & Contexts

also focus necessary attention on issues the public cares about, whereas cool, less passionate discussions may end up missing the public reality.

- **Remedy and Enforcement Choices.** Both private parties and public agencies have a wide choice of potential legal remedies and make their selections based upon the character of acts and actors, the scope of harms, the parties' own agendas, the climate of public reaction, and more. The common law offers a number of forms of damages and creative equitable remedies. Public law provides a further range of civil remedies, plus the possibility of criminal punishments. Administrative options for civil and criminal remedies, or combinations thereof, add a further level of tactical analysis to the complexities of environmental enforcement. See Chapters 18 and 19.
- **Global Interconnections.** Many environmental issues involve international interconnections and repercussions. In some cases, the linkage is through transboundary spillover effects, international standards or obligations tied to legal conventions, or an international reprise of the race-to-the-bottom when U.S. manufacturers threaten to move operations to less-stringent manufacturing locations overseas. In other cases, it is through international business activities, such as Allied's 20 years of Kepone sales to countries that lacked basic safety testing procedures and made no provisions for limiting human exposures. Potential international liability issues arise as environmental law increasingly reflects interconnections transcending national boundaries.
- **Citizen Enforcement, Multicentric Pluralism.** A fundamentally important element of the U.S. legal system, increasingly being adopted abroad, is the legal and practical opportunity for participation in regulation and enforcement by directly affected citizens, a shift from the old di-polar regulatory structure dominated by industry and agencies to a multicentric pluralistic process in which citizen NQOs play a major role.
- **Reaction Against Citizen Pluralism.** Industry-based resistance against citizen involvement in the agency regulatory process, beginning in the Nixon years, is reflected in continuing attempts to create legislative and administrative hurdles against citizen enforcement. In the courts there is a continuing process personified by Justice Scalia (see Chapter 6) to cut back on citizen standing and judicial scrutiny of agency decisionmaking.
- **Resurgence and Ascendancy on the Right.** Environmental law is almost uniformly progressive, a bellwether and target for political storms. The national political landscape in the past half-century has featured the gradual resurgence and ascendancy of a right wing bloc determined to rise from the ashes of the 1964 GOP debacle. Rejecting East Coast Republicanism that had often championed environmental causes, a new coalition of industry, NeoCons, and evangelicals made a pragmatic alliance to mold and mobilize a disgruntled government-distrusting populism to undermine the progressive legacy of the '60s and '70s. The 1972 Powell Memorandum was a guiding action-plan for a movement that ultimately reshaped the GOP, the federal courts, the congressional process, and the media that shapes public opinion,[55] an ascendancy that may have culminated in the intense eight-year reign of the Bush-Cheney Administration. The politics of environmental law continues to be a central element of national political evolution.

---

55. The Powell Memorandum, 1972, a key document in launching the nation's right-wing resurgence, was written by Lewis Powell to guide the U.S. Chamber of Commerce's efforts to oppose "socialistic" anti-market societal tendencies arising in the 1960s. It is available on the coursebook website in the supplementary materials for this chapter. For extensive analyses of challenges to progressive legislation and national policies, see Political Research Associates, Public Eye, http://www.publiceye.org/study_right.html.

- **The Public Trust Doctrine, and Cultural Values Beyond Market Values.** The public trust embodies fundamentally conservative principles. The ultimate measure of a society would seem to be based upon more than just the essential physical needs for survival—to this should be added the full quality of its people's life, and the legacy of ideas, accomplishments, resources, and potentials it seeks to pass on to successor generations. The public trust, whether incorporated in statutes or existing within our nonstatutory jurisprudence, represents and gives legal force to many of the unmarketized present and future social values that often get overlooked in the immediacy of daily life but that are part of the ultimate measure.
- **Stewardship, Intergenerational Equity, and Sustainability.** If a society is to survive and advance over time, like species competing in the Darwinian process of replicating and prolonging their genetic identity over succeeding generations, it must incorporate present realities and the needs of future generations into its present legal norms. Ethical concepts of environmental stewardship described by ecophilosophers evoke concepts of legacy —nations, like most nondysfunctional families, honoring what they have received from the past and trying to pass it on, enhanced, to their posterity. The ancient public trust doctrine thus fits well with modern environmental law's principles and technologies of sustainability.

Climate change adaptation as a special case... Facing the daunting realities of anthropogenic climate change,[56] an article by Prof. J.B. Ruhl reconnoiters the challenges posed by global warming and argues that whatever the prospects may be for *mitigation*—technical approaches for reversing the warming curve—we inevitably will need to pay far more attention to *adaptation*, coping strategies that will be especially demanding of government systems and the legal professionals that run them.[57]

> The path of environmental law has come to a cliff called climate change, and there is no turning around.... In the 1990s... the perceived urgency of attention to mitigation strategies designed to regulate sources of greenhouse gas emissions... snuffed out meaningful progress on the formulation of adaptation strategies designed to respond to the effects of climate change.... Only recently has this "adaptation deficit" become a concern now actively included in climate change policy debate... [owing to] the reality of failed efforts to achieve global mitigation policy.... There is no choice any longer: "mitigation and adaptation are both essential parts of a comprehensive climate change response strategy."[58]

The adaptation component of climate change law has two overarching dynamic goals. First, it is to effectively and equitably manage the harms and benefits of climate change while mitigation policy does its work. Second, it is to put us in a position to resume long term planning for sustainable development when climate change is "over." Adaptation law, in other words, is about building a bridge to get us across the chasm of climate change intact.

In his article Ruhl sets out to describe "how environmental law is likely structurally to be shaped, constrained, and even liberated by the realities and demands of climate change adaptation." He defines a series of predictions on legal trends that will have to be part of society's adaptation strategies. Somewhat simplified, the trends he foresees are these:

---

56. For a remarkable collection of analyses of climate change science, law, economics, and policy, we strongly recommend W. Rodgers, M. Robinson-Dorn, A. Moritz, and J. Barcelos, eds., Climate Change: A Reader (2010).

57. Ruhl, Climate Change Adaptation & the Structural Transformation of Environmental Law, 40 Envtl. L. (2010); Parenteau, Cities on Stilts: The Myth of Large-Scale Climate Adaptation and the Limits of Sustainability, in J. Owley & K. Hirokawa, RETHINKING SUSTAINABILITY TO MEET THE CLIMATE CHANGE CHALLENGE (2015).

58. Quoting U.S. Global Change Research Program, Global Climate Change Impacts in the U.S. 11 (2009), *available at* www.globalchange.gov/impacts.

C. Environmental Law Themes & Contexts

- The top priority = crisis avoidance & development of adaptation response mechanisms
- A shift from preservationism to transitionalism
- An evolution of property rights & liability rules for natural capital adaptation resources
- A blending of water, land use, and general environmental law
- Human rights considerations integrated into climate change adaptation
- A need for constant flexibility: increased variety and flexibility in regulatory mechanisms, frequent reconfiguration of complex linkages and trade-offs, reactive adaptive management when front-end prediction planning comes up short
- Multiscale governance: effort at local, state, regional, national levels, and beyond
- A focus on conciliation mechanisms rather than adversarial postures

And in e-mails with colleagues Ruhl also hypothesized:

- Public health as an overriding factor
- Increased use of structured markets, futility of cost-benefit based regulation
- A resurgence of common law

In implementing these trends toward a future where the cloud of global climate threat can be lifted, Ruhl earnestly hopes we can evolve a system not characterized by polarized tribalisms.[59] "Is it going to be about conflict or conciliation? . . . Climate change adaptation . . . presents an opportunity for environmental law to break free from its culture of litigation and contestation and build back what that culture has eroded most—trust."

And what about "active citizen involvement"? Is there a risk that dynamic adaptive governance models would tend toward unfettered agency discretion, with little or no role for the citizen involvement that has built environmental law and keeps it honest?

Flint, Michigan toxic lead water contamination. Echoing some of the same systemic causes that produced the Allied Chemical Kepone disaster, in the Fall of 2015 a crisis in water supplies in Flint, Michigan hit national news. For 18 months beginning in April 2014, the city had been taking its drinking water from the polluted Flint River, and failing to add required corrosion control treatment. Between 6,000 and 12,000 children in Flint's largely low-income communities of color suffered dangerous and virtually irremediable lead levels in their blood and organs, as well as heavy exposures to coliform bacterial and THMs (trihalomethanes, suspected carcinogens). Lead poisoning is particularly significant for children, where increased lead exposure lowers IQ, increases the risk of ADHD, and has other significant health and behavioral impacts. Negative health outcomes may continue in families long after the initial exposure, and mental diminution is permanent.

Government officials at state and federal levels finally declared a state of emergency in January 2016, alternative water supplies were accessed, and a process of analysis sought to determine who and what had brought this crisis to Flint's citizens. As an expert review panel's report stated:

> The Flint water crisis is a story of government failure, intransigence, unpreparedness, delay, inaction, and environmental injustice. The Michigan Department of Environmental Quality (MDEQ) failed in its fundamental responsibility to effectively enforce drinking water regulations. The Michigan Department of Health and Human Services failed to adequately and promptly act to protect public health. Both . . . stubbornly worked to discredit and dismiss others' attempts to bring the issues of unsafe water, lead contamination, and increased cases of Legionellosis (Legionnaires' disease [that killed 11 people]) to light. . . . EPA delayed

---

59. Kysar and Salzman, Environmental Tribalism, 87 Minn. L. Rev. 1099 (2003); Plater, A Modern Political Tribalism in Natural Resources Management, 11 Pub. Land L. Rev. 1 (1990).

enforcement of the Safe Drinking Water Act (SDWA) and Lead & Copper Rule (LCR), thereby prolonging the calamity. Neither the Governor nor the Governor's office took steps to reverse poor decisions by MDEQ and state-appointed emergency managers until October 2015, in spite of mounting problems and suggestions to do so by senior staff members. Flint Water Advisory Task Force Final Report, http://flintwaterstudy.org/2016/03/flint-water-advisory-task-force-final-report/ (March 2016).

The legal aftermath of the Flint calamity is likely to include many of the legal avenues noted in this chapter—federal and state statutory violations (including criminal as well as civil charges), and significant common law claims filed by impacted citizens and municipal interests. Here are some of the legal considerations:

The Safe Drinking Water Act – The SDWA is the primary law to ensure national public health standards for water supply systems. The act regulates contaminants in public drinking water systems and requires the EPA to set national limits for dangerous contaminants, to be enforced by the state (in Michigan, by MDEQ). Under SDWA, EPA enacted the Lead & Copper Rule (LCR) that protects public health by minimizing those metals in drinking water, primarily by reducing the corrosiveness of water. The LCR requires regular monitoring, reporting, and water treatment.

State and local government failures—Flint was under the control of a state-appointed emergency manager; for reasons unclear he switched its water supply from a Detroit system that draws from Lake Huron, to a local system drawing water from the Flint River, canceling previously-required phosphate-based corrosion controls that could have prevented the crisis.

Federal culpability—State regulators are not the only people at fault. The EPA should have required corrosion control once it learned that the state did not. The federal agency has the power to take regulatory authority away from the state DEQ to protect public health. EPA officials maintain that they did not receive accurate information from state and city officials.

City monitoring failures—Flint was improperly monitoring the water for lead and copper. Independent researchers estimate that there are 15,000 lead service lines supplying drinking water to Flint, but City officials do not know their location. Flint also failed to repeat-test homes that had previously tested high, and improperly instructed residents to flush pipes before taking samples, which would hide high concentrations, and used obfuscative sampling techniques. Federal law requires local water authorities to get state regulators' approval before changing to a water source that could increase the corrosion of lead; this wasn't done.

Legal consequences have come from multiple directions:

1. Class actions and tort suits, coupled with constitutional claims against the government actors (for each of these, see continuing coverage in the blog below);
2. Citizen suits filed by civil rights and environmental groups, focused on enforcement of the Safe Drinking Water Act;
3. Government investigations, both state and federal, that may result in both civil and criminal enforcement actions.

Four state and federal officials had been fired or resigned and three criminal indictments filed as of April 2016.

For continuing information on the resulting legal actions and new developments, see http://www.greatlakeslaw.org/blog/flint-water-crisis/ and the materials on the coursebook website.

This noblest patrimony ever yet inherited by any people must be husbanded and preserved with care in such manner that future generations shall not reproach us for having squandered what was justly theirs.

—The Whig Almanac, 1843

II

THE ENDURING ROLE OF THE COMMON LAW IN ENVIRONMENTAL PROTECTION

If seven maids with seven mops, Swept it for half a year, Do you suppose, the Walrus said, That they could get it clear? I doubt it, said the Carpenter, And shed a bitter tear.

— Lewis Carroll, Through the Looking Glass, 1871

3

The Common Law in Modern Environmental Law

A. Tort Causes of Action in the Environmental Arena
B. Causation and Joint & Several Liability in Conventional Environmental Tort Suits
C. Remedies in Environmental Litigation

The common law provides the foundation and backdrop for many statutes and regulations. Legislatures and agencies rely on the continued existence of common law to fill gaps in public law and to guide courts and agencies in their interpretation of statutes and rules. Each year many environmental cases involving localized pollution are filed under common law theories. By number, these cases constitute the large majority of environmental cases filed. Though localized, the impacts on those affected can be substantial. Common law theories are used to address very high visibility cases as well. When an oil tanker disaster strikes the coastal waters and shores of a state, or when a chemical factory's dump site poisons land and groundwater, the major remedies litigated by injured parties are often likewise based substantially on common law. After the wreck of the *Exxon-Valdez*, for example, the majority of legal claims filed by the State of Alaska and its citizens relied primarily on tort and public trust theories to respond to that catastrophe.[1] The massive 2010 Gulf of Mexico oil spill's legal aftermath followed a bifurcated path that featured a BP-funded multi-billion dollar administrative system that potential tort plaintiffs could elect as an alternative to seeking tort remedies. Even with the administrative system, a considerable amount of tort litigation ensued.[2]

---

1. Public trust law is a non-statutory doctrine so significant in environmental protection theory that it has its own chapter in this book—Chapter 20.

2. The sprawling BP Deepwater litigation—involving thousands of private claims for economic and property damage, and exposure to toxic releases, as well as governmental claims for civil penalties—was consolidated in multi-district litigation. (See *In re: Oil Spill by the Oil Rig "Deepwater Horizon" in the Gulf of Mexico*, on April 20, 2010, MDL No. 2179 E.D. La). The private claims arose under gross negligence and maritime tort doctrines. On September 9, 2014, the court found in favor of the plaintiffs on liability (Phase I Findings of Fact and Conclusions of Law, are available from the court's website at http://www.uscourts.gov/courts/laed/9092014RevisedFindingsofFactandConclusionsofLaw.pdf). The process of quantifying and paying claims is underway and will likely continue for several years. https://www.google.com/search?q=NOAA+BP+photos&biw=1920&bih=955&tbm=isch&tbo=u&source=univ&sa=X&ved=0ahUKEwjvxpzl3-rKAhXHSSYKHUTxCLgQ7AkIMw

The common law raises many fundamental issues of environmental law. The topics are diverse and include questions of proof, uncertainty, balances of risk, fault, liability, foreseeability, standards of care, technological feasibility, causation, long-term residual injuries, remedies, practical deterrence, enforceability, and so on. Despite the existence of innumerable federal and state environmental statutes and reams of administrative regulations, the common law of environmental protections remains vigorous and important.

A. Tort Causes of Action in the Environmental Arena

1. Using Private Law Tort Theories to Remedy Environmental Problems

In a congested society where the actions of one person or corporation, are often likely to affect others, the field of tort law begins from the recognition that in daily life—

> there [will] of necessity be losses or injuries of many kinds sustained as a result of the activities of others. The purpose of the law of torts is to adjust these losses, and to afford compensation for injuries sustained by one person as the result of the conduct of another. Wright, Introduction to the Law of Torts, 8 Cambridge L.J. 238 (1944)[3]

Historically, the common law writ system from which contemporary tort doctrine emerged was highly articulated, where each particular claim of injury was raised by pleading it according to a strict formula associated with a particular kind of writ. That heritage remains. In the environmental field, several distinct causes of action—including trespass, private nuisance, negligence, and strict liability actions—each require a plaintiff to prove certain specific elements to prevail on a claim for that kind of tort. Cases seeking remedies for harmful pollution or exposure to hazardous substances can be based on one or more common law torts.

a. Trespass

Although the nuisance cases pre-date trespass cases in the environmental torts arena, as evidenced in the recounting of precedents in the following case, the trespass cases are an area where some of the most important mid-twentieth century doctrinal growth expanded on cases of a simpler era to fit the modern era.

Borland v. Sanders Lead Co.
369 So. 2d 523 (Ala. Sup. Ct. 1979)

Jones, J. . . . Alabama law clearly provides an appropriate remedy for Plaintiffs who have been directly injured by the deleterious effects of pollutants created by another party's acts. . . . A trespass need not be inflicted directly on another's realty, but may be committed by discharging foreign polluting matter at a point beyond the boundary of such realty. . . .

> In order that there may be a trespass under the rule stated in this Section, it is not necessary that the foreign matter should be thrown directly and immediately upon the other's land. It is

---

3. For a short functional review of tort principles relevant to environmental cases, see the coursebook website for this chapter. See also W.P. Keeton & W.L. Prosser, Prosser and Keeton on Torts §1 (5th ed. 1984).

A. Tort Causes of Action in the Environmental Arena

enough that an act is done with knowledge that it will to a substantial certainty result in entry of foreign matters. Restatement (Second) of Torts, §158

In *Martin v. Reynolds Metals Co.*, 342 P.2d 790 (Ore. 1959), a case remarkably similar to the present case, the Plaintiffs sought recovery . . . for trespass [alleging] that the operation by Defendants of an aluminum reduction plant caused certain fluoride compounds in the form of gases and particulates, invisible to the naked eye, to become airborne and settle on Plaintiffs' property, rendering it unfit for raising livestock. Plaintiffs in the present case allege that the operation of Defendant's lead reduction plant causes an emission of lead particulates, and SO_2, invisible to the naked eye, which emissions have settled on their property, making it unsuitable for raising cattle or growing crops.

The Defendants in *Martin* contended that there had not been a sufficient invasion of Plaintiffs' property to constitute trespass, but, at most, Defendants' acts constituted a nuisance. This would have allowed the Defendants to set up Oregon's two-year statute of limitations applicable to non-possessory injuries to land rather than Oregon's six-year statute for trespass to land. The *Martin* Court pointed out that trespass and nuisance are separate torts for the protection of different interests invaded — trespass protecting the possessor's interest in exclusive possession of property and nuisance protecting the interest in use and enjoyment. The Court noted, and we agree, that the same conduct on the part of defendant may, and often does, result in the actionable invasion of both interests. . . .

The modern action for trespass to land stemmed inexorably from the common law action for trespass which lay when the injury was both direct and substantial. Nuisance, on the other hand, would lie when injuries were indirect and less substantial. . . . If the intruding agent could be seen by the naked eye, the intrusion was considered a trespass. If the agent could not be seen, it was considered indirect and less substantial, hence, a nuisance. . . . The *Martin* Court rejected the dimensional test and substituted in its place a force and energy test, stating:

> The view recognizing a trespassory invasion where there is no "thing" which can be seen with the naked eye undoubtedly runs counter to the definition of trespass expressed in some quarters. It is quite possible that in an earlier day when science had not yet peered into the molecular and atomic world of small particles, the courts could not fit an invasion through unseen physical instrumentalities into the requirement that a trespass can result only from a direct invasion. But in this atomic age even the uneducated know the great and awful force contained in the atom and what it can do to a man's property if it is released. In fact, the now famous equation $E=mc^2$ has taught us that mass and energy are equivalents and that our concept of "things" must be reframed. If these observations on science in relation to the law of trespass should appear theoretical and unreal in the abstract, they become very practical and real to the possessor of land when the unseen force cracks the foundation of his house. The force is just as real if it is chemical in nature. . . . Viewed in this way we may define trespass as an intrusion which invades the possessor's protected interest in exclusive possession, whether that intrusion is by visible or invisible pieces of matter or by energy which can be measured only by the mathematical language of the physicist. We are of the opinion, therefore, that the intrusion of the fluoride particulates in the present case constituted a trespass.

It might appear, at first blush, from our holding today that every property owner in this State would have a cause of action against any neighboring industry which emitted particulate matter into the atmosphere, or even a passing motorist, whose exhaust emissions come to rest upon another's property. But we hasten to point out that there is a point where the entry is so lacking in substance that the law will refuse to recognize it, applying the maxim *de minimis non curat lex* — the law does not concern itself with trifles. In the present case, however, we are not faced with a trifling complaint. The Plaintiffs in this case have suffered, if the evidence is believed, a real and substantial invasion of a protected interest. . . . If the intrusion is direct, then, under our present law, actual damages need not be shown; nominal damages may be awarded and this will support punitive damages. . . .

COMMENTARY & QUESTIONS

1. Access bias when victims consider suing for environmental injuries. There are multiple barriers to bringing a tort claim. Professors James Krier and Clayton Gillette explore that topic more systematically in Risks, Courts, and Agencies, 138 U. Pa. L. Rev. 1027 (1990). Beyond their own personal loss, what are the consequences of having claimants with meritorious cases go without a remedy because the difficulty and expense deter them from seeking it? Do firms that engage in environmentally harmful behavior get off too cheaply? Presumably, if more suits by deserving victims were brought and won, the added internalized cost, if it were great enough, would lead those polluting firms to make greater efforts to prevent the pollution.

2. How far can trespass go? Under *Borland*'s terms, Alabama requires actual and substantial injury for an "indirect" trespass, as in most pollution cases, but most other states do not. If courts apply $E=mc^2$ to determine whether there has been "physical invasion" of plaintiff's property, is there any limit to how far the trespass action might apply? Vibration? Noise? Light photons? Low-frequency electromagnetic radiation from high-voltage transmission facilities? An ugly view? The further down this path a court travels, the more its protection of the right of exclusive possession (trespass) and the right of quiet enjoyment (nuisance) become coextensive.

b. Private Nuisance and Negligence

The best known environmental law nuisance case is *Boomer v. Atlantic Cement Co.*, 257 N.E.2d 870 (N.Y. Ct. App. 1970). *Boomer* appears as a principal case in the remedies section of this chapter. In that case, particulate emissions from a $45 million, newly-constructed cement plant landed on neighbors' farm fields, equipment, and buildings causing significant interference with the neighbors' quiet enjoyment of their property. No health impacts were alleged. The legal issue for which the case is famous relates to remedy—the plaintiffs, consistent with older New York precedents, demanded an injunction that would abate the nuisance. The court's opinion famously declining to issue the injunction appears later in this chapter, in the section on tort remedies in environmental cases. Almost *sub silentio*, the opinion simultaneously "cemented" the important role of nuisance actions in pollution damage cases by raising no question whatsoever regarding the existence of a nuisance by stating simply, "These are actions for injunction and damages by neighboring land owners alleging injury to property from dirt, smoke and vibration emanating from the plant. A nuisance has been found." 257 N.E.2d at 871.

The elements of a prima facie intentional private nuisance case:

To prevail, plaintiffs must prove by a preponderance of the evidence that:

1. plaintiffs suffered substantial unreasonable interference with property use,
2. the interference was caused by defendant's use of its land, and the defendant acted "intentionally."

A. Tort Causes of Action in the Environmental Arena

The elements of a prima facie negligence case:

1. a duty or obligation recognized by the law, requiring the actor to conform to a certain standard of conduct, (usually that which would objectively be required of a reasonable person),
2. a failure to conform to the standard required,
3. a causal connection between the conduct and the resulting injury, and
4. actual loss or damage resulting to the interests of another.

Roth v. Cabot Oil & Gas Corp.

919 F. Supp. 2d 476 (U.S. D. Ct., M.D. Pa. 2013)

JONES, D.J.

Presently pending before the Court is the [Rule 12(b)(6)] Motion to Dismiss filed by Defendants Cabot Oil & Gas Corporation and GasSearch Drilling Corporation. . . .

Plaintiffs Frederick J. and Debra A. Roth are husband and wife and are the owners of property located in Springville, Pennsylvania, where they have resided for more than thirty-five years. Defendant Cabot Oil and Gas Corporation is a Delaware corporation headquartered in Houston, Texas. . . . Defendant GasSearch Drilling Services . . . is a wholly owned subsidiary of Cabot which also engages in the drilling and servicing of oil and gas wells. At all times relevant to this action, Defendants owned and operated several natural gas wells . . . located less than 1,000 feet from the Plaintiffs' Property and residence.

A representative of Cabot visited the Plaintiffs' Property in or about March of 2008 . . . in order to obtain the legal right to drill on or near Plaintiffs' Property and extract natural gas from the Property. Cabot's representative warranted the following to the Plaintiffs in negotiating the lease: that Cabot would test Plaintiffs' pond and water supplies prior to and after commencement of drilling operations to ensure that the water would not be adversely affected; that Cabot would timely and fully disclose the test results to Plaintiffs; that Plaintiffs' persons, property, and land resources would be undisturbed by said operations; that Plaintiffs' quality of life and use and enjoyment of the Property would not be disrupted or adversely affected; that if Cabot's operations do adversely affect the Property, Cabot would immediately disclose that information to Plaintiffs and take, at its sole expense, all steps necessary to return the Property to pre-drilling conditions; and that Cabot would remain at all times in compliance with all state and federal laws and regulations governing safe oil and gas drilling practices.

The Defendants' drilling operations involve a process known as hydraulic fracturing, sometimes referred to as hydro-fracturing or hydro-fracking, which discharge significant volumes of hydraulic fracturing fluids into underground shale formations in order to discharge the gas contained therein. The fracking fluids used by the Defendants in their operations included diesel fuel, lubricating agents, barite, gels, pesticides, and defoaming agents. The Defendants failed to disclose the identity of all chemicals and components used to the Pennsylvania Department of Environmental Protection ("DEP") as required by law. In addition to these hazardous chemicals, other contaminants, such as gas, oil, brine, heavy metals, and radioactive substances naturally present in the shale formations, are dislodged during drilling operations. In order to collect the discharged waste fluids, drilling muds, and other hazardous substances, the Defendants maintain large waste pits at the Wells.

The Defendants began drilling operations at the wells near the Plaintiffs' Property in or about April of 2010. Prior to that time, the Plaintiffs' groundwater supply had always appeared clean, containing no visible gases, malodors, or off-tastes. The Plaintiffs had their groundwater supply tested before the commencement of drilling operations, and those tests revealed that the pre-drilling groundwater supply did not contain detectable levels of methane gas. In August of 2010, the Plaintiffs began to notice that their groundwater supply had diminished in quality, containing excess sedimentation and appearing brown and cloudy. The water supply likewise became malodorous, and in January of 2011, the Plaintiffs began to notice yellow and pink staining in their toilets from the polluted groundwater. These issues continue to date. Because of these issues, the Plaintiffs have ceased drinking from and no longer trust their water supply.

SCHEMATIC RENDERING OF A HYDROFRACKING WELL

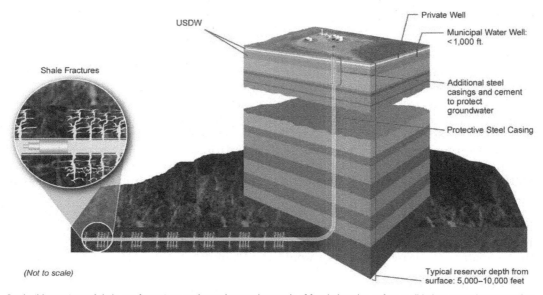

Producible portions of shale gas formations are located many thousands of feet below the surface, well below groundwater aquifers. Modern hydraulic fracturing technology involves sophisticated engineering processes designed to create distinct fracture networks in specific rock strata. Experts continually monitor all aspects of the process, which must comply with local, state and federal laws and regulations.

U.S. Department of Energy from "Shale Gas: Applying Technology to Solve America's Energy Challenges," NETL, 2011.

The DEP has cited the Defendants on several occasions for noncompliance with state law as it governs oil and gas operations. In April of 2010, an inspection of Well #2 revealed that the Well's waste pit liner was riddled with holes and that groundwater was infiltrating the waste pit and permitting hazardous wastewater to enter the soil and contaminate the groundwater. The Defendants were cited for violating Pennsylvania law by failing to dispose of drill fluids in a manner that prevents pollution of the waters of the Commonwealth. At about the same time, DEP representatives also observed negligent cement work and bubbling gas near the surface of Well #2, deficiencies which it required Defendants to remedy. Also in April of 2010, the Defendants caused approximately one-half barrel of waste fluids to be spilled directly on the surface at Well #2. In December of 2010, the Defendants were . . . also cited for failure to report defective casing and cementing within twenty-four hours of discovery. During an investigation in June of 2011, DEP representatives observed that diesel fuel was actively leaking onto a well pad and that a corner of the pad had a breach in

A. Tort Causes of Action in the Environmental Arena

the perimeter berm; the representative also noted that the presence of two other sorbent pads in the area suggested a recent unreported spill. The Defendants were again cited for failure to construct their waste pits and tanks with sufficient capacity to contain pollutants.

The DEP sampled the Plaintiffs' groundwater supply in January of 2011, approximately eight months after the Defendants began their drilling activities. The results of that sampling revealed that levels of dissolved methane in the Plaintiffs' groundwater supply were as high as 15.6 mg/L, rendering the water unsafe and unfit for human consumption. The Plaintiffs believe and aver that the Defendants' noncompliance with the statutory and regulatory frameworks governing oil and gas drilling is responsible for allowing the methane and other harmful contaminants to enter the Plaintiffs' water supply. The Plaintiffs assert that as a result, they have suffered loss of value to their Property, loss of the use and enjoyment of their Property and its land resources, and loss to their quality of life. Plaintiffs also assert that they have suffered damage to appliances which use the contaminated groundwater supply and have had incurred substantial out-of-pocket expenses for water quality monitoring, water sampling, and alternative potable water supplies

NEGLIGENCE

Pennsylvania common law requires a plaintiff to establish the following elements in support of a negligence claim: "(1) a duty or obligation recognized by the law, requiring the actor to conform to a certain standard of conduct; (2) a failure to conform to the standard required; (3) a causal connection between the conduct and the resulting injury; and (4) actual loss or damage resulting to the interests of another."

With respect to the first element, the Plaintiffs assert, and the Defendants apparently do not dispute, that the Defendants are under a legally cognizable duty to conform to certain standards of conduct. The laws and regulations of the Commonwealth of Pennsylvania establish that entities engaging in gas drilling operations must do so in a manner that would not jeopardize the health, safety, and well-being of the citizens of the Commonwealth. . . . The Defendants, as owners and operators of drilling wells, are subject to a certain and articulable standard of conduct, satisfying the first element.

Further, the Plaintiffs satisfy the second element by pleading that the Defendants have used improper drilling techniques and materials and that they have constructed (and failed to remedy) deficient and ineffective well casings and waste disposal pits in violation of this standard of conduct. . . . We thus find that the Defendants have satisfied their pleading burden by establishing that the Defendants breached the applicable standard of conduct.

We turn then to the element of causation. Pennsylvania law presumes that "a well operator is responsible for pollution of a water supply if . . . (i) the water supply is within 1,000 feet of an oil or gas well; and (ii) the pollution occurred within six months after completion of drilling or alteration of the oil or gas well." 58 Pa. Cons. Stat. §3218(c)(1). . . . The temporal and physical proximity of the Defendants' actions to the Plaintiffs' harm, in addition to the lack of contemporaneous and alternative sources of the contamination, permit the reasonable inference that the Defendants were responsible for that harm. . . .

The Plaintiffs' Amended Complaint contains numerous allegations with respect to the harms that they have suffered, including: contaminated groundwater unsafe for human consumption, loss of value to their property, and damage to appliances which utilize the groundwater. Most critically, the Plaintiffs have incurred and will continue to incur substantial costs for water sampling and testing, water quality monitoring, and water treatment systems, in addition to the costs of purchasing alternative water supplies. Thus, the Defendants' contention that the Plaintiffs have failed to plead damages beyond "conclusory allegations" is entirely meritless. For all of these reasons, we will deny the Defendants' Motion to Dismiss the Plaintiffs' negligence claim. . . .

PRIVATE NUISANCE

The Plaintiffs [also] assert a claim for private nuisance, alleging that the Defendants have created and maintained a continuing nuisance in the area of the wells by allowing the wells to exist and operate in a dangerous and hazardous condition and causing the discharge of hazardous chemicals and combustible gases into the Plaintiffs' groundwater supply. The Pennsylvania Supreme Court has adopted Section 822 of the Restatement (Second) of Torts for determining the existence of a private nuisance. This Section provides that:

> One is subject to liability for a private nuisance if, but only if, his conduct is a legal cause of an invasion of another's interest in the private use and enjoyment of land, and the invasion is either (a) intentional and unreasonable, or (b) unintentional and otherwise actionable under the rules controlling liability for negligent or reckless conduct, or for abnormally dangerous conditions or activities.

The Restatement further provides that "There is liability for a nuisance only to those to whom it causes significant harm, of a kind that would be suffered by a normal person in the community or by property in normal condition and used for a normal purpose." Invasions are "significant" if "normal persons living in the community would regard the invasion in question as definitely offensive, seriously annoying or intolerable."

The Defendants again contend . . . that the Plaintiffs have failed to plead an actual and realized injury. . . . We have concluded *supra* that the Amended Complaint contains sufficient facts which, assumed true, establish that the Defendants' negligence in operating their gas wells has caused and continues to cause actual injuries to the Plaintiffs' Property. . . . With respect to whether the alleged invasion is "definitely offensive, seriously annoying or intolerable," the Defendants contend that the Plaintiffs' injuries are speculative and merely "anticipated" as opposed to having been already realized. This contention is belied by the Plaintiffs' allegations that their water supply had already been contaminated as early as August of 2010 and that they have incurred costs for water sampling, water quality monitoring, and purchasing alternative potable water sources for consumption and other residential uses. . . . We conclude that, at this juncture, the Plaintiffs have sufficiently alleged that the Defendants caused a substantial invasion to the Plaintiffs' interest in the private use of their Property causing a "seriously annoying or intolerable" nuisance and satisfying the second prong of the Restatement test. We will thus deny the Defendants' Motion to Dismiss Count IV [private nuisance]. . . .

COMMENTARY AND QUESTIONS

1. **Other claims in the case.** Most of the other claims in the case were either unique to the relationship of the parties (trespass in conjunction with a lease transaction or fraudulent misrepresentation) or unique to the complex of Pennsylvania statutes that were asserted to be applicable to the case. One other more generic tort claim was made for strict liability. That topic is addressed later in this chapter.

2. **Why common law, not statutory regulations?** Hydrofracturing, "fracking," burst onto the fossil fuel scene in the 1990s, often boosted by the misconception that it is more benign and releases less carbon-based greenhouse gases (GHGs) than coal or oil. There are by now more than 1 million fracking wells in the US, often polluting ground and surface water, fouling the air, making neighbors miserable and lucky landowners very wealthy. The states have often been reluctant or unable to apply meaningful supervision or sanctions for the violation of even minimal environmental requirements. What about the federal government? The so-called Halliburton Amendments, inserted by the Bush-Cheney

Administration into the Energy Act of 2005, exempt fracking from a number of federal environmental protection statutes. They forgot, however, to exempt the Clean Air Act, so possibilities still may exist for regulation under CAA §111 if administrations can withstand the ever-present political opposition to fossil fuel regulation. In the meantime, the common law offers opportunities for localized constraints on fracking, and perhaps wider state-based class actions. *A good new book*: J. Dernbach & J. May, Shale Gas & the Future of Energy (2016).

3. Two popular defense tactics at the pleading stage. The attack on the pleading of the claims as insufficient was considered under the comparatively recently announced pleading standards for federal courts established by *Bell Atlantic v. Twombley*, 550 U.S. 544 (2007) and *Iqbal v. Ashcroft*, 556 U.S. 662 (2009). While there is no legal doubt that the classic tort theories of trespass, nuisance, and negligence are properly applied in these cases, this newer federal pleading standard requires a plaintiff to investigate facts sufficiently to be able to allege more than a conclusory, formulaic invocation of the elements of those causes of action. When there is an obvious physical nexus between the defendant's conduct and the plaintiff's claimed injury, the heightened pleading standard can be met. The standard becomes harder to meet in toxic tort cases where the defendant's responsibility for the exposure, and the linkage of exposure to injury are not easily seen or well understood. The *Roth* defendants also sought issuance of a *Lone Pine* order. Seeking those orders also has become a staple in the fracking defendant's playbook. *Lone Pine* orders, when granted, force plaintiffs, at the outset of litigation without aid of discovery, to provide proof specifically linking the defendant's activity to the claimed injury. Requests for *Lone Pine* orders are the subject of increasing scrutiny by courts, particularly in individual or small group suits. See, e.g., *Strudley v. Antero Resources Corp.*, 350 P.3d 874 (Colo. App. 2013). In large mass tort suits, however, where the burden of discovery and mounting a defense is far greater, *Lone Pine* orders can function as a surrogate for dismissals for failure to state a claim in cases presenting plausible claims but that appear to have limited chances of success on the merits. See, e.g., *Acuna v. Brown & Root Inc.*, 200 F.3d 335 (5th Cir. 2000).

4. Negligence, private nuisance, and negligent nuisance—overlaps in the interest protected and distinctions about the role of reasonableness. As the first two elements in the nuisance text box preceding the *Roth* case made clear, that inquiry focuses on the plaintiff landowner's protection against certain classes of invasion—interference with quiet enjoyment that rises above the level of annoyance to a degree that society deems the interference unreasonable. The third element in the text box measures the conduct of the defendant. For an intentional nuisance to be found, the defendant must intend to do the thing that they did (such as drill and engage in hydraulic fracturing) and are thereafter liable for all the natural consequences of the intentional act. It is not necessary that the defendant intend to injure the plaintiff's protected interest. That third element of nuisance also can be satisfied when the defendant's conduct is either reckless or negligent (falls below the standard needed to reasonably protect others against harm) or when the activity in which the defendant is engaging is one that gives rise to strict liability. Thus, in seeking to prove a negligent nuisance, the concept of reasonableness applies twice: once in regard to the extent of the interference with plaintiff's quiet enjoyment, and a second time in setting the standard of care that is claimed to have been breached by the defendant creating the nuisance. Looking at the reported cases over the years, it is a relatively recent development for plaintiffs to allege negligent nuisance rather than intentional nuisance. The simplest explanation for the historic pattern is the comparative ease of proving intent when an industrial facility of the defendant intentionally operates smokestacks or outfalls that add pollutants to the local environment where they are substantially certain to affect neighbors. In more recent cases like *Roth* that also invoke negligent nuisance, the standard of care that is required of defendant has become easier to establish as a result of greater and ever more specific regulatory standards for engaging in the type of conduct involved (in the *Roth* case, hydraulic fracturing and well drilling more generally).

5. Negligence for its own sake. Negligence is seldom the sole theory of recovery in successful environmental cases. Almost all cases involving environmental effects that damage person or property can be brought as intentional or strict liability torts. Since negligence is harder to prove than strict liability or the sort of intentionality required for trespass or nuisance recoveries, plaintiff will join theories of recovery, rather than rely on negligence alone. Of particular interest in the hydrofracking context, in several states, with Oklahoma being the most prominent, wastewater injection wells are causing earthquake activity which is spawning lawsuits. One of the first of these lawsuits relies on allegations that the injections by the energy companies were "negligent, careless, and reckless" in their treatment of the earthquake risks surrounding wastewater injection. See, http://thinkprogress.org/climate/2016/01/12/3738417/oklahoma-earthquake-residents-lawsuit. Plaintiffs also asserted strict liability claims. When plaintiffs include negligence counts, it is usually for one of two reasons — judicial familiarity with negligence and the ability to introduce evidence of defendant's misdeeds. All trial courts have heard many such cases, are well versed in the law of negligence, and even a different type of damage does not make the environmental claim seem unusual. Strategically, negligence shines a spotlight on the defendant's misdeeds, the callousness and disregard for community interests which may influence the attitude the trier of fact. An excellent example of this is the negligence claim in *Hagy v. Allied Chem.*, 265 P.2d 86 (Cal. Ct. App. 1953). In that case, the plaintiffs claimed the defendant-company's failure to warn neighboring citizens of the danger of its operations was negligent when the company was aware of the danger and had its own employees wear protective gear to avoid exposure.

6. Standards of care. The general standard of care in a negligence case is captured in a phrase that often appears in jury instructions — that the defendant must exercise "due care and caution for the safety of plaintiff." That standard is based on an objective (i.e., community standard) view of what is reasonable under the circumstances. Additionally, specific standards of conduct can be imported from regulatory contexts and brought to bear on the defendant's conduct. Most commonly this is done with safety standards that govern aspects of the defendant's operations.

7. Custom, regulatory compliance, and state of the art as satisfaction of the standards of care. Negligence begins with examining defendant's conduct to see if it meets the relevant standard of care. Defendants frequently try to show the exercise of due care by proving that their conduct is what is customary, or that their conduct meets the standard set by a regulation, or that it meets the terms of the permit under which they are operating, or, finally, that they are operating at the "state of the art" level. Essentially, these arguments all seek to rebut plaintiff's assertion that defendant failed to meet the relevant standard of care. Defendants may attempt to label these efforts as affirmative defenses, but that is inaccurate. Proof of custom or regulatory compliance or state of the art operations is simply irrelevant in determining liability in intentional torts or strict liability. In negligence cases, those proofs simply join the issue of whether defendant's conduct is substandard under the circumstances of the particular case.

8. Deterrence, the role of benefit-cost analysis in determining negligence, and cost internalization. Does the threat of negligence verdicts deter would-be polluters? The threat surely deters some negligent conduct by defendants who foresee that reasonably available improvements in their conduct would avoid causing high-cost harms to others who are likely to sue and win. Optimal deterrence, from a total social cost point of view, would result in a level of care that prevents losses to others in excess of the cost of their prevention.[4] Extrapolating from the earlier Commentary and Question about access bias, a rational cost-minimizing polluter, however, would stop well short of that optimal effort to prevent all the injuries that the Learned Hand formula would predict should be avoided. It is a near certainty many of those suffering losses that would be deemed the result of negligence will not sue. A 1991 Rand Corporation study found that only 10% of tort victims actively sought some form of compensation for their losses, and the percentage seeking compensation was highest (only 26% to 31%) in automobile accidents.[5]

c. Strict Liability

RESTATEMENT (SECOND) OF TORTS

CHAPTER 21. ABNORMALLY DANGEROUS ACTIVITIES §519 GENERAL PRINCIPLES

(1) One who carries on an abnormally dangerous activity is subject to liability for harm to the person, land or chattels of another resulting from the activity, although he has exercised the utmost care to prevent such harm.

(2) Such strict liability is limited to the kind of harm, the risk of which makes the activity abnormally dangerous. . . .

§520. Abnormally Dangerous Activities

In determining what constitutes an abnormally dangerous activity, under Restatement §519, the following factors are to be considered:

(a) Whether the activity involves a high degree of risk of some harm to the person, land, or chattels of others;

(b) Whether the gravity of the harm which may result is likely to be great;

(c) Whether the risk cannot be eliminated by the exercise of reasonable care;

(d) Whether the activity is not a matter of common usage;

(e) Whether the activity is inappropriate to the place where it's carried on; and

(f) The value of the activity to the community.

Branch v. Western Petroleum, Inc.

657 P.2d 267 (Utah Sup. Ct. 1982)

STEWART, J. The Branches, the plaintiff property owners, sued for damages for the pollution of their culinary water wells caused by percolation of defendant Western Petroleum's formation waters into the subterranean water system that feeds the wells. . . .

In December 1975, Western purchased forty acres of land in a rural area north of Roosevelt, Utah, which had previously been used as a gravel pit. Western used the property

---

4. This view of due care as aligned with efficiency is derived from the famous passage penned by Learned Hand in *U.S. v. Carroll Towing Co.*, 159 F.2d 169, 173 (2d Cir. 1947), describing a vessel owner's duty to guard against it breaking from its moorings as a function of (1) the probability of the event (P), (2) the gravity of the resulting injury (L, as in loss), and (3) the burden of adequate precautions (B). Liability (negligence) is present when B is less than PL.

5. D.R. Hensler et al., Compensation for Accidental Injuries in the U.S. 116, 121-122 (1991).

solely for the disposal of formation water, a waste water produced by oil wells while drilling for oil. Formation water contains oil, gas and high concentrations of salt and chemicals, making it unfit for culinary or agricultural uses. The formation water was transported by truck from various oil-producing sites and emptied into the disposal pit with the intent that the toxic water would dissipate through evaporation into the air and percolation into the ground. Alternative sites for disposing of the water were available to Western, but at a greater expense.

In 1976, the Branches purchased a parcel of property immediately adjacent to, and at an elevation of approximately 200 to 300 feet lower than Western's property. The twenty-one acre parcel had on it a "diligence" well, which had been in existence since 1929, some outbuildings, and a home. After acquiring the property, the Branches made some $60,000 worth of improvements to the home and premises. Prior owners of the property used the water from the well for a grade A dairy and later a grade B dairy. Both dairy operations required that the water be approved for fitness and purity by appropriate state agencies. The Branches, as had all prior owners since 1929, used water from the diligence well for culinary purposes. The water from the diligence well was described as being sweet to the taste and of a high quality until December of 1976.

Two months after purchasing the property, the Branches noticed that the well water began to take on a peculiar taste and had the distinctive smell of petroleum products. Soap added to the water would no longer form suds. They observed that polluted water from Western's disposal pit was running onto the surface of the Branches' property and, on one occasion, reached their basement, causing damage to food stored there. After testing the diligence well water and finding it unfit for human consumption, and after their rabbits and one hundred chickens had died, apparently from the polluted water, the Branches began trucking water to their property from outside sources. In November, 1977, the Branches dug an additional well south of their home. Water from the new well was tested and found safe for culinary purposes. But after a few months, the new well also ceased producing potable water, and on advice of the State Health Department, the Branches ceased using the new well for culinary purposes and hauled water to their property almost until the time of trial.

The Branches requested Western to cease dumping formation water in the disposal pit, but Western refused unless the Branches would post a bond to cover the costs. . . .

At trial the major issue was whether and how Western's formation waters caused the pollution of the Branches' wells. . . . The Branches' expert, Mr. Montgomery, a state geologist who had spent nine years working for the Utah Division of Water Resources, [said] that the subsurface waters consist of shallow groundwater and a deeper aquifer known as the Duchesne Formation. . . . Water in the disposal pit was percolating into the subsurface waters. . . .

The major substantive dispute is whether the trial court erred in entering judgment against Western on the basis of strict liability for pollution of the Branches' wells. . . .

The landmark case of *Rylands v. Fletcher*, 159 Eng. Rep. 737 (Ex. 1865), aff'd, L.R. 3 H.L. 330 (1868), held that one who uses his land in an unnatural way and thereby creates a dangerous condition or engages in an abnormal activity may be strictly liable for injuries resulting from that condition or activity. Whether a condition or activity is considered abnormal is defined in terms of whether the condition or activity is unduly dangerous or inappropriate to the place where it is maintained. That doctrine was the genesis of §519 of the Restatement of Torts (1939), which, however, limited strict liability to "ultrahazardous activities." . . .

There are two separate, although somewhat related, grounds for holding Western strictly liable for the pollution of the Branches' wells. First, the facts of the case support

A. Tort Causes of Action in the Environmental Arena

application of the rule of strict liability because the ponding of the toxic formation water in an area adjacent to the Branches' wells constituted an abnormally dangerous and inappropriate use of the land in light of its proximity to the Branches' property and was unduly dangerous to the Branches' use of their well water.[6]

[Second], . . . the common law rules of tort liability in pollution cases should be in conformity with the public policy of this state as declared by the Legislature, . . . [and an] industrial polluter can and should assume the costs of pollution as a cost of doing business rather than charge the loss to a wholly innocent party:

> We know of no acceptable rule of jurisprudence which permits those engaged in important and desirable enterprises to injure with impunity those who are engaged in enterprises of lesser economic significance. The costs of injuries resulting from pollution must be internalized by industry as a cost of production and borne by consumers or shareholders, or both, and not by the injured individual. *Atlas Chem. Indus. Inc. v. Anderson*, 514 S.W.2d 309, 316 (Tex. Civ. App. 1974).

We think these reasons adequately support application of the rule of strict liability in this case. In sum, the trial court properly ruled that Western was strictly liable for the damage which it caused the Branches. . . .

Mangan v. Landmark 4, LLC

U.S. District Court for the Northern District of Ohio, 2013 WL 950560

NUGENT, D.J. Plaintiffs allege that beginning in September of 2008, Landmark, an oil and gas well operator, engaged in drilling and hydraulic fracturing activities, . . . near Medina Township, Ohio. The Plaintiffs allege that the . . . wells [are] approximately 2,502 feet from the Plaintiffs' property, home and water supply. Landmark used horizontal drilling and hydraulic fracturing (otherwise known as "fracking"). . . . Plaintiffs claim that [fracking] chemicals were discharged into the ground or into the waters near Plaintiffs' home and water well. . . . Plaintiffs . . . [are] asserting claims of Negligence (Count 1), Strict Liability (Count 2), Private Nuisance/Continuing Trespass (Count 4), Unjust Enrichment (Count 5), Negligence per se (Count 6), Battery (Count 7) and Intentional Fraudulent Concealment (Count 8). . . .

---

6. Even if Western did not know that the formation water would enter the aquifer and cause damage to plaintiffs' wells, it could have determined the likelihood of that consequence. As Professor Davis has stated:

> A polluter should not be absolved from liability just because he may not be able to anticipate the movement of the polluted groundwater he created. . . . Even though precise mapping of groundwater movement in any particular location is still expensive, it is within the reach of any major waste producer which proposes to inject wastes underground. Disposal wells need porous formations for successful waste injection and the appropriate hydrologic tests would insure a successful injection well. . . . If they do not make such tests, they should be charged with the information they would have gained had they made them. Second, it is generally known now that liquids placed on the ground will seep into the soil and may enter the body of groundwater percolating beneath the surface. Persons causing groundwater pollution, in ways other than by deliberate underground disposal, should be charged with such knowledge and should not be insulated from liability for groundwater pollution by claiming that they know nothing more about groundwater movement than was known in 1843 when *Acton v. Blundell* was decided. . . . Davis, Groundwater Pollution: Case Law Theories for Relief, 39 Mo. L. Rev. 117, 145-146 (1974). See also *Wood v. Picillo*, 443 A.2d 1244, 1249 (R.I. 1982).

Landmark now seeks to have the second claim for strict liability dismissed. . . . Landmark argues that Plaintiffs have not alleged facts sufficient to establish that Landmark engaged in "an abnormally dangerous activity" as required for strict liability. In support of this argument, Landmark contends that Plaintiffs failed to address the six factors outlined in Section 520 of the Restatement of Law for determination of what might equate to an abnormally dangerous activity. Further, Landmark argues that Plaintiffs cannot allege a negligence claim for failure to take reasonable precautions, and also maintain a claim for strict liability which exists when there is an inability to eliminate risk of harm by the exercise of reasonable care.

Plaintiffs counter that they have sufficiently pled a claim for strict liability premised on abnormally dangerous activity. . . . A plaintiff is not required to set forth even every element of a claim for negligence or strict liability. The six factors outlined in Section 520 of the Restatement Second of Torts are not elements of a strict liability claim. They are guidelines for the Court to use when determining whether the facts presented . . . establish that the Defendants' activities are abnormally dangerous for purposes of the strict liability laws. . . . Plaintiffs have alleged that Landmark engaged in hydraulic fracturing, using toxic substances, toxic fumes, carcinogens, and otherwise ultra-hazardous materials and injecting those substances below the ground surface under extreme pressure, in the vicinity of private property and public or private water sources during their drilling and production activities. These allegations are sufficient to state a possible claim for strict liability.[7] . . .

The . . . Complaint alleges sufficient facts and information to raise a question as to whether fracking, even in the absence of negligence should be considered an abnormally dangerous activity. . . .

[Eds.—While the case was on remand, the parties settled.]

COMMENTARY & QUESTIONS

1. Why strict liability? Analytically, the *Branch* and *Mangan* cases could have relied on other tort theories (e.g., nuisance, trespass, or negligence) and not invoked strict liability. Look closely at Restatement (Second) of Torts §519. Does this explain the advantages of using strict liability as the basis for the claim?

2. "Abnormally dangerous." What is found in *Branch* to be ultrahazardous or abnormally dangerous under the terms of Restatement §§519-520? Is oil really an abnormally dangerous material? Or is storage of oil-drilling wastewater an abnormally dangerous activity? On the facts of *Branch*, the closest analogy to *Rylands* is disposing of formation waters by placing them in an impoundment near a property line or a recharge area for local wells.

Mangan does not reach a final determination on the issue of abnormally dangerous in relation to hydraulic fracturing due to settlement of the case. When the issue is presented, which way will the courts go? The number of fracking wells in the U.S. has surpassed 1 million.[8] Does that mean the activity has become so common that under Restatement (Second)

---

7. The court distinguished *Hirsch v. CSX*, 656 F.3d 359 (6th Cir. 2011), a case cited by Defendants. In *Hirsch*, the Plaintiffs alleged strict liability for alleged contamination caused when a train derailed and spilled toxic and hazardous chemicals onto the ground. "There is no indication in that case that the transport of the hazardous chemicals was itself alleged to be a strict liability event, or that the chemicals could have caused damage if there had not been a derailment caused by negligence. Further, the transport of hazardous materials by train is an event that is in no way new or uncommon." [Eds.]

8. See, e.g., George E. King, Hydraulic Fracturing 101, http://www.kgs.ku.edu/PRS/Fracturing/Frac_Paper_SPE_152596.pdf.

A. Tort Causes of Action in the Environmental Arena

of Torts §520 factor *d* it is unlikely that fracking will be deemed abnormally dangerous? The cases caution that the §520 factors are to be used as a guide and not all must be met, but once an activity becomes widely practiced and commonplace, isn't that a signal that the dangers are not considered abnormal? The *Hirsch* case mentioned in *Roth*, stands for the proposition that rail transport of toxic materials is not abnormally dangerous even though there is a risk of serious harm when derailments or other accidents occur, as they have in several high visibility train spills over the past several years. Is it the mundane character of the activity—train carriage of materials or fracking—or the gravity of the harm and the difficulty of totally eliminating it with due care (§519 factors *b* and *c*) that should outweigh the other in these cases? Case law seems to indicate that any one factor can outweigh the others. For example, in *Langan v. Valicopters*, 567 P.2d 218 (Wash. 1977), an aerial crop-dusting service had allowed its pesticide sprays to drift onto an organic farm. No crops were killed. Strict liability was applied and the plaintiffs' injury claim, based purely on their crops' loss of "organic" certification caused by the spray, was upheld. See *Koos v. Roth*, 652 P.2d 1255 (Or. 1982) (farmer who employed field burning as an agricultural technique was held strictly liable for damages when the fire destroyed neighbor's property).

3. Defendant's bad attitude in strict liability. The court points out the nonchalance of Western in its attitude toward the Branches' rights and its lack of inquiry into the pollution laws of Utah. Is this relevant in a strict liability case? That evidence is relevant to the Branches' claim for punitive damages, discussed later in this chapter.

4. Defending strict liability by blaming others. As in *Schenectady Chemical*, which follows, at times defendants in strict liability will try to fob off liability onto another party who was engaging in the abnormally dangerous activity. As with other tort theories, the concept of a non-delegable duty applies in the strict liability context as well. See *Loe v. Lenhard*, 362 P.2d 312 (Or. 1961) (liability for extrahazardous activity is non-delegable; farmer and hired crop duster both liable for damage to neighbor's crops).

2. Public Nuisance in Environmental Cases

a. Conventional Uses of Public Nuisance Addressing Discretely Caused Harms

Quite unlike private nuisance, public nuisance is descended from criminal offenses against the public peace. Over time public nuisance became a civil action as well, providing remedies for violations of public rights. Traditionally it has applied to the blocking of public rights-of-way or offenses against public sensitivities and decency, such as boisterous saloons and bawdy houses or, in modern times, pornography shops. Public nuisance also is employed in noxious use cases with public health undercurrents, such as abating the maintenance of slaughterhouses in cities. In typical public nuisance actions, public prosecutors bring lawsuits seeking injunctions against nuisances (often preferring tort law even where statutory remedies are available). Public nuisance is usually litigated as an intentional tort, although in some cases involving the release of toxic contaminants into the environment, it is also litigated on a strict liability theory. Public nuisance actions can be brought by private plaintiffs if they have special injury standing, and often can be filed along with private nuisance claims. Photographs and text on a classic cattle feedlot public nuisance case, *Spur v. Del Webb*, are available on the coursebook website in the supplementary materials for this chapter.

> In the following public nuisance case, the plaintiff is a state agency seeking relief for toxic contamination caused by a poorly sited and operated dumpsite in which defendant chemical company had deposited waste. As you read, consider the tactical advantages the public nuisance tort provides to state officials.

New York v. Schenectady Chemical Co.

459 N.Y.S.2d 971 (N.Y. Sup. Ct., Rensselaer Co. 1983)

HUGHES, J. The court must decide if the State, either by statute or common law, can maintain an action to compel a chemical company to pay the costs of cleaning up a dump site so as to prevent pollution of surface and ground water when the dumping took place between 15 to 30 years ago at a site owned by an independent contractor hired by the chemical company to dispose of the waste material. . . .

The amended complaint contains the following factual assertions. The action is brought by the State in its role as guardian of the environment against Schenectady Chemicals, Inc. with respect to a chemical dump site located on Mead Road, Rensselaer County, New York (the Loeffel site). Since 1906 Schenectady Chemicals has manufactured paints, alkyl phenols, and other chemical products, a byproduct of which is waste, including but not limited to phenol, benzene, toluene, xylene, formaldehyde, vinyl chloride, chlorobenzene, 1,2 dichlorobenzene, 1,4 dichlorobenzene, trichloroethylene, chloroform, ethyl benzene, ethylene chloride, 1,1 dichloroethane, 1,2 dichloroethane, trans-1,2 dichloroethylene, lead, copper, chromium, selenium, and arsenic. These chemical wastes are dangerous to human, animal and plant life, and the defendant was so aware. During the 1950s until the mid-1960s the defendant disposed of its chemical wastes by way of contract with Dewey Loeffel, or one of Mr. Loeffel's corporations. Mr. Loeffel made pick-ups at the defendant's manufacturing plants and disposed of the material by dumping directly into lagoons at the Loeffel site, and in some instances by burying the wastes. It is alleged that with knowledge of the danger of environmental contamination if its wastes were not properly disposed, and knowing of Loeffel's methods, Schenectady Chemicals: (1) hired an incompetent independent contractor to dispose of the wastes; and (2) failed to fully advise Loeffel of the dangerous nature of the waste material and recommend proper disposal methods.

It is alleged that the Loeffel site is approximately 13 acres of low-lying swamp land located in a residential-agricultural area in Rensselaer County with surface soil consisting mainly of gravel and sand. The ground water beneath the site is part of an aquifer which serves as the sole source of water for thousands of area residents and domestic animals. The site drains into two surface streams, one a tributary of the Valatie Kill, and the other a tributary of Nassau Lake. During the period in question approximately 46,300 tons of chemical wastes were deposited at the Loeffel site, of which 17.8 percent, or 8,250 tons, came from defendant. The other material was generated by General Electric Company and Bendix Corporation and has been so inextricably mixed with defendant's as to become indistinguishable. . . .

The complaint alleges that over the years the chemical wastes have migrated into the surrounding air, surface and ground water contaminating at least one area drinking well and so polluting, or threatening to pollute, the area surface and ground water as to constitute an unreasonable threat to the public well-being and a continuing public nuisance. As a result, the Department of Environmental Conservation (DEC) developed a plan to prevent

A. Tort Causes of Action in the Environmental Arena

further migration of chemical wastes from the site, and General Electric and Bendix have agreed to pay 82.2 percent of the costs thereof. Defendant's refusal to pay its portion of the clean-up costs gives rise to this suit. . . .

The fourth through eighth causes of action rely upon a nuisance theory. The "term nuisance, which in itself means no more than harm, injury, inconvenience, or annoyance . . . arises from a series of historical accidents covering the invasion of different kinds of interests and referring to various kinds of conduct on the part of defendants." Nuisances are classified as either private or public. In *Copart Indus. v. Cons. Edison Co.*, the Court of Appeals described a public nuisance as:

> A public, or as sometimes termed a common, nuisance is an offense against the State and is subject to abatement or prosecution on application of the proper governmental agency. It consists of conduct or omissions which offend, interfere with or cause damage to the public in the exercise of rights common to all in a manner such as to offend public morals, interfere with use by the public of a public place or endanger or injure the property, health, safety or comfort of a considerable number of persons. 362 N.E.2d 968, 971 (1977).

While ordinarily nuisance is an action pursued against the owner of land for some wrongful activity conducted thereon, "everyone who creates a nuisance or participates in the creation or maintenance of a nuisance are liable jointly and severally for the wrong and injury done thereby." Even a non-landowner can be liable for taking part in the creation of a nuisance upon the property of another. . . .

The common law is not static. Society has repeatedly been confronted with new inventions and products that, through foreseen and unforeseen events, have imposed dangers upon society (explosives are an example). The courts have reacted by expanding the common law to meet the challenge, in some instances imposing absolute liability upon the party who, either through manufacture or use, has sought to profit from marketing a new invention or product. The modern chemical industry, and the problems engendered through the disposal of its byproducts, is, to a large extent, a creature of the twentieth century. Since the Second World War hundreds of previously unknown chemicals have been created. The wastes produced have been dumped, sometimes openly and sometimes surreptitiously, at thousands of sites across the country. Belatedly it has been discovered that the waste products are polluting the air and water and pose a consequent threat to all life forms. Someone must pay to correct the problem, and the determination of who is essentially a political question to be decided in the legislative arena. As Judge Bergan noted in *Boomer v. Atlantic Cement Co.*, resolution of the issues raised in society's attempt to ameliorate pollution are to a large extent beyond the ken of the judicial branch. Nonetheless, courts must resolve the issues raised by litigants and, in that vein, this court holds that the fourth through seventh causes of action of the amended complaint state viable causes of action sounding in nuisance. . . .

It is argued that the action is untimely. The limitation applicable to a nuisance cause of action is the three-year period provided in N.Y.C.P.L.R. 214. The rule with respect to an ongoing nuisance, as here alleged, is that the action continually accrues anew upon each day of the wrong although the recovery of money damages is limited to the three-year period immediately prior to suit. Defendant's contention that the limitation period should accrue upon the last day of dumping lacks merit since the law has long been settled that, "the right to maintain an action for . . . nuisance continues as long as the nuisance exists. . . ."

The argument that [the governmental plaintiff] lacks standing to maintain the action because the waters are private rather than public cannot withstand scrutiny. The amended complaint alleges that the waste has migrated from the Loeffel site into neighboring surface and ground water, including two streams. By statute, "waters" is defined to include "all other bodies of surface or underground water . . . public or private (except those private waters which do not combine or effect a junction with natural surface or underground waters). . . ."

[As to an attempted constitutional prescriptive rights defense, the New York Court of Appeals has] rejected [the] claim that protecting water from pollution somehow violated a due process property right, stating that the argument was "untenable since such rights do not attach to water itself and in any event are required to yield to public health and public safety. . . ."

As to the request for dismissal for failure to join necessary parties, i.e., other alleged tortfeasors guilty of dumping at the site, the rule is that those contributing to a nuisance are liable jointly and severally and "it is fundamental that a plaintiff . . . is free to choose his defendant." If defendant feels that others may have contributed to plaintiff's damage it should commence the appropriate third-party practice.

The argument that plaintiff has released [co-defendants] General Electric Company and Bendix and thus defendant is released, must fail. First of all the . . . purported releases have not been furnished, lending credence to plaintiff's assertion that they do not yet exist. More importantly, plaintiff has averred that the language of the proposed releases will specifically reserve its rights against defendant; thus, [defendant] will not be discharged.

The defense that the statutory scheme of the Environmental Conservation Law is exclusive and bars common law actions is directly contradicted by §17-1101 of that law. . . .

Likewise, the complaint cannot be dismissed upon defendant's "state of the art" defenses. . . . The fact that a manufacturer may have complied with the latest industry standards is no defense to an action to abate a nuisance since, as stated earlier with respect to public nuisances and inherently dangerous activities, fault is not an issue, the inquiry being limited to whether the condition created, not the conduct creating it, is causing damage to the public.

The final argument for dismissal worthy of discussion is the contention that by hiring a private contractor licensed to dispose of chemical wastes the defendant has met its legal duty and cannot be held liable for the contractor's wrongdoing. . . . Defendant could be found liable for Loeffel's acts if: (1) it was negligent in retaining an incompetent contractor; (2) it failed, with knowledge thereof, to remedy or prevent an unlawful act; (3) the work itself was illegal; (4) the work itself was inherently dangerous; or (5) the work involved the creation of a nuisance. The amended complaint, which must be deemed to be true, makes allegations encompassing all of the above bases of liability. Factual issues requiring a trial are present.

[Eds.—After the defendant's effort to have the case dismissed without trial was denied by the court, the case was settled out of court, with no admission of liability. There was, however, a consent judgment whereby the defendant paid $498,500 in damages. Additionally, the defendant was not excused from paying for future damages if pollution migrated off the site.]

COMMENTARY & QUESTIONS

1. The breadth of public nuisance. Several states have statutes that codify the concept of nuisance. For example, California defines nuisance as: "Anything which is injurious to health, including, but not limited to, . . . [anything that is] indecent or offensive to the senses, or an obstruction to the free use of property, so as to interfere with the comfortable enjoyment of life or property. . . ." Cal. Civ. Code §3479. Section 3480 defines public nuisance by adding, "A public nuisance is one which affects at the same time an entire community or neighborhood, or any considerable number of persons, although the extent of the annoyance or damage inflicted upon individuals may be unequal." Do those statutory provisions enlarge or restrict the common law as it might relate to environmental concerns to any considerable degree? That statute has permitted the novel use of public nuisance to attack gang activities using the obstruction of free use of property provision and language in the statute that includes sale of illegal drugs in the list of proscribed activities.

2. Public nuisance actions for contamination of public drinking water supplies. Is it a public nuisance for a defendant to contaminate a public drinking water supply? There are not many reported cases, but there is no theoretical reason why such cases should not succeed. The damages can be quite substantial, with at least one reported settlement reaching almost $70 million. See *S. Tahoe Pub. Util. Dist. v. Atlantic Richfield Co.*, No. 999128, described at 34 BNA Env't Rep. 817 (Cal. Super. Ct., S.F. Co., Apr. 11, 2003).

3. Using the common law to buttress environmental protection and other public welfare statutes. A distinct modern trend utilizes claims brought by governmental entities sounding in public nuisance as an adjunct to regulatory enforcement. Why? Often the same proof that will constitute a violation of an environmental statute will establish the requisite injury, intent (in the tort sense), and causation for a prima facie case of public nuisance. At that point, the common law remedies that may be available often include relief not available under the statute.

4. Standing to sue in public nuisance. Public nuisance, deriving from criminal law, in the first instance is supposed to be litigated by public prosecutors, but local and state governments often are not enthusiastic about litigating and are sometimes themselves the defendants in public nuisance actions. Private plaintiffs have played a major role in the expansion of public nuisance. Legal standing for private parties, however, traditionally has posed a procedural barrier: In order to sue in public nuisance, private plaintiffs have to show "special injury" different in kind and not just in degree from the public as a whole. This seems a bit paradoxical, since part of the gravamen of public nuisance is precisely the fact that it affects many people in the same way. Recent amendments to the Restatement (Second) of Torts §421c attempt to extend standing in public nuisance, for injunctive relief only, to any person "having standing to sue as a representative of the general public, as a citizen in a citizen suit, or class representative in a class action." Public nuisance actions usually seek equitable relief only; private plaintiffs typically cannot recover public nuisance damages and, unlike the cost sharing sought in *Schenectady Chemical*, public entity plaintiffs normally do not seek damages.

5. Schenectady's liability or vicarious liability? Did Schenectady Chemical create the nuisance in this case or did Loeffel? Here, Loeffel and his various companies were independent contractors, but the court brushes that aside when it quotes the phrase, "everyone who creates a nuisance or participates in the creation or maintenance of a nuisance [is] liable jointly and severally for the wrong and injury done thereby." Even in jurisdictions that do not take so broad a view of responsibility for nuisances, parties may be liable for the acts of their independent contractors in spite of the general rule that one who hires an independent contractor usually will not be vicariously liable for the contractor's acts.[9] Plaintiffs can overcome efforts to hide behind the claim that the wrong was done by an independent con-

---

9. Liability for acts of independent contractors is unlike the more typical vicarious liability of an employer for the acts of an employee, where the acts of the employee are imputed to the employer unless the employee is acting outside the scope of his employment.

tractor by claiming that the party was negligent in hiring that particular contractor. This has the effect of putting the contractor's credentials on trial, which at times can be very harmful to a defendant if the contractor is plainly unqualified to perform the task at hand. A second path around the independent contractor defense arises in relation to the risks surrounding the task being turned over to an independent contractor. When subject matter of the actions of the independent contractor is sufficiently important and risk-laden for the community, the court will term it a non-delegable duty and hold the hiring party vicariously liable for the failings of the independent contractor. A third possibility is that the plaintiff can try to show collusion — that the party who hired the independent contractor was cooperating in the performance of a wrongful act. In the case at hand, do you think Loeffel's creation of a nuisance should be imputed to Schenectady Chemical? Is your answer based on the law of independent contractors or on a sense that the court is not about to let a large chemical concern hide behind a small, probably bankrupt, disposal firm?

b. Non-Conventional Uses of Public Nuisance Addressing Widespread Harm

The common law of public nuisance has a history of adaptation to meet the changed problems of different eras. The antisocial conduct remedied in *Schenactady Chemical* seems like a step along a progression from traditional predecessor cases involving insults to public morality or closing urban slaughterhouses because of their noxious health effects, to protecting the public waters against toxic pollution.

Is public nuisance capable of continued expansion so that it can be used to address broad regional impacts? Starting slightly after the beginning of the twenty-first century, an array of plaintiffs filed cases sounding in public nuisance attacking the conduct of firms that are large greenhouse gas (GHG) emitters. Owing to the interstate and international effects of such pollution, the cases, some brought by governments and some brought by individuals, asserted claims under federal common law as well as state common law. There are pre-Clean Air Act cases that had essentially validated the viability of a federal common law of interstate air pollution nuisance, at least in suits brought by one of the several states against polluters operating in other states. See, e.g., *Georgia v. Tennessee Copper Co.*, 206 U.S. 230, 237 (1907). Based on Supreme Court precedents that arose in regard to interstate federal common law of water pollution nuisance both before and after the passage of the Clean Water Act (see the *Illinois v. Milwaukee cases*[10]), it seemed possible that the Court would hold that federal common law of interstate air pollution would be "displaced" as the federal response to the problem by the Clean Air Act which does to a degree address interstate pollution. What the two *Milwaukee* cases left open was the possibility that state nuisance law would not be preempted, a position that prevailed in *International Paper Co. v. Ouellette*.[11] Eventually one of the state-filed public nuisance cases attacking GHG emissions reached the Supreme Court. In a ruling that is parallel to that in *Ouellette*, the Court held in a GHG public nuisance suit, *American Electric Power Co., Inc. v. Connecticut*, 131 S. Ct. 2527 (2011), that the federal common law had been displaced because the Clean Air Act addressed GHG pollution and that the suits could go forward only under state nuisance law.

Even when allowed to proceed on the basis of state nuisance law, GHG climate suits are highly problematic on their merits and may face challenges based on the redressability

---

10. *Illinois v. Milwaukee*, 406 U.S. 91, 93 (1972) (*Milwaukee I*) and *Milwaukee v. Illinois*, 451 U.S. 304, 316–319 (1981) (*Milwaukee II*).
11. 479 U.S. 481 (1987).

A. Tort Causes of Action in the Environmental Arena

prong of the standing test used in some jurisdictions.[12] A court decision that provided a glimmer of hope that public nuisance suits might be used to attack GHG emissions is *Comer v. Murphy Oil Co.*, 585 F.3d 855 (5th Cir. 2009) vacated, 607 F.3d 1049 (2010).[13] The plaintiffs in *Comer* were residents and owners of lands and property along the Mississippi Gulf coast. They sued numerous defendants whose operation of energy, fossil fuel, and chemical industries in the U.S. caused the emission of GHGs on public and private nuisance theories alleging that:

> defendants intentionally and unreasonably used their property so as to produce massive amounts of GHGs and thereby injure both plaintiffs and the general public by contributing to global warming, which caused the sea level rise and added to the ferocity of Hurricane Katrina, the combined effects of which resulted in the destruction of plaintiffs' private property, as well as their loss of use of certain public property in the vicinity of their dwellings. 585 F.3d at 860-61.

The plaintiffs also raised trespass claims related to the debris that invaded their property due to increased storm surge and negligence claims based on allegations that defendants' actions unreasonably endangered public health and the citizens of Mississippi. The trial court dismissed the action on standing grounds. On appeal from that dismissal, a three-judge panel of the 5th Circuit reversed. In doing so, the opinion rejected both the standing defense and a defense based on non-justiciability. On the standing issue,[14] the three-judge panel found that there was injury in fact suffered by the plaintiffs that was "fairly traceable" to the conduct of the defendants' action and that the injury will likely "be redressed by a favorable decision." The plaintiffs would bear the burden of proof on each of those three aspects of standing, but ruled that the allegations were sufficient to survive a motion to dismiss.

The Circuit opinion also did a careful job of dispatching the non-justiciability/political question defense. The crux of that defense is that the type of problem being presented to the court is one that is not capable of judicial resolution—there being no standards to apply. Viewed slightly differently, the need for a broader more comprehensive solution to the GHG problem meant that the problem was one not capable of solution by the judicial branch and was properly left to the political branches. Essentially the opinion said a nuisance case is just that, and nothing in separation of powers theory limits the authority of courts issuing judgments on legal issues. Since there is no statutory or constitutional assignment of this issue exclusively to the legislature or executive branch, courts retain their

---

12. Standing is covered in greater detail in Chapter 6 and at several other places in this book.

13. The decision to vacate was quite unusual, possibly unique. The appeals court en banc granted a rehearing, 598 F.3d 208 (2010) and thereby vacated the three-judge panel decision that would have allowed the case to go forward. Then, when the en banc hearing was attempted, so many judges disqualified themselves that a quorum was lost. The court of appeals then treated the entire appeal as a nullity and reinstated the previously overturned trial court dismissal.

14. The opinion noted that the Mississippi law of standing differed from that of the federal courts and was easily satisfied:

> The Mississippi Constitution provides that "[a]ll courts shall be open; and every person for an injury done him in his lands, goods, person, or reputation, shall have remedy by due course of law, and right and justice shall be administered without sale, denial, or delay," Miss. Const. art. III §24. Because Mississippi's Constitution does not limit the judicial power to cases or controversies, its courts have been more permissive than federal courts in granting standing to parties. "In Mississippi, parties have standing to sue 'when they assert a colorable interest in the subject matter of the litigation or experience an adverse effect from the conduct of the defendant, or as otherwise provided by law.'" 585 F.3d at 862.

authority to decide cases and controversies within their jurisdiction.[15] It remains important to remember, however, that the three-judge panel *Comer* opinion was vacated without addressing the merits.

COMMENTARY & QUESTIONS

1. Even counting the three-judge panel opinion in *Comer* as correct, will the public nuisance cases be a valuable tool in the legal effort to combat GHG emissions? Not all courts that have considered the matter are persuaded by the *Comer* position on justiciability and political question. That is only a threshold step toward effective relief on the merits. Try to imagine the types of proof and the quantum of proof needed to carry the burden of persuasion on the issues surrounding causation in the case—i.e., persuading the trier of fact (judge or jury) that the defendant's conduct is more likely than not the cause of plaintiffs' injuries. The issues of causation and complex causation are discussed in greater detail later in this chapter and in the next chapter on toxic torts. As a litigation strategy, won't defendants point to all the GHG emissions for which they are not responsible in trying to break down the causal link that plaintiffs must establish?

2. Controlling climate change one public nuisance lawsuit at a time. Does it make any sense to attempt to control GHG emissions in the U.S. through a series of nuisance lawsuits brought by whoever is willing to take the initiative to bring them and can point to some consequential injury they have suffered as a result of climate change? The rolls of potential plaintiffs will be long indeed when some of the consequences of climate change are considered, including all oceanfront owners who lose dryland to a rise in sea level or suffer increased erosion and face increased flooding like the *Comer* plaintiffs. The list also would include farmers in the American West who rely heavily on summer irrigation water that is no longer available to produce their crops. They will say, in accordance with voluminous evidence that is already available, that GHG emissions have resulted in changes in snowpack brought about by warmer winters that deposit more winter precipitation as rainfall, which then runs off and is not "stored" as snowpack, and earlier spring snowmelt that takes additional water downstream before the irrigation season. These lawsuits are not simple, and the stakes for defendants in terms of litigation expense and the possibility of repeated damage awards are potentially debilitating. Does that scenario bear any similarities to the miasma surrounding the judicial determination of the asbestos liability cases? If so, is that a reason to find, as did the lower courts, these cases are not justiciable? Or, instead, should that be a reason prompting Congress or EPA to create a more manageable approach to the problem? After studying the array of regulatory options available to address pollution-caused harms, revisit this question and ask what type of regulation Congress or EPA is likely to enact if cases like these result in repeated imposition of liability and damages on whatever defendants plaintiffs choose to sue.

3. Defenses Raised in Environmental Tort Cases

Recall from the *Schenectady Chemical* case the long list of defenses rejected by the court. They included the failure to state a claim, statute of limitations, lack of standing,

---

15. Not all courts that have considered this issue have ruled in favor of plaintiffs. See *Connecticut v. American Electric Power Co.*, 582 F.3d 309 (2d Cir. 2009), rev'd 131 S. Ct. 2527 (2011).

A. Tort Causes of Action in the Environmental Arena

prescriptive rights, failure to join necessary parties (other tortfeasors who also might be liable for the harm), release of liability, preemption, state of the art, act of an independent third party, and still others that the court did not deem worthy of comment. It's quite an inventory! When defendants uncritically invoke the blunderbuss method of defending a case, few if any of these defenses will merit legitimate attention from the court. Prior to moving on to the consideration of causation and remedies in environmental tort cases, this section will present a thumbnail review of several of the more prominent (and often improperly understood) defenses raised in environmental tort cases.

- **The permit defense.** One common line of attempted defense in environmental cases is the "permit defense." The defendant claims that, because it is operating its facility in compliance with regulatory requirements that have been set out in a permit, it cannot be subjected to tort liability for any resulting pollution. This defense is consistently rejected unless the statute creating the permit system has expressly recognized the defense or the statute is interpreted to have impliedly repealed the availability of common law remedies in the field.[16] Rejecting the permit defense is consistent with the canon of judicial construction to the effect that "statutes in derogation of the common law should be narrowly construed." As discussed in the materials on negligence, courts are willing to take notice of permit compliance into account as evidence tending to show that due care was exercised. Should permit compliance be relevant in the remedial stages? Does permit compliance tend to negate the recklessness or wanton disregard of the safety of others that might lead to punitive damages? Similarly, might permit compliance have some bearing on whether the defendant should be enjoined? Revisit these questions after completing the materials on common law remedies.
- **Primary jurisdiction.** The "primary jurisdiction" defense is less dramatic than the permit defense but equally disliked by environmental plaintiffs. Under this defense, the defendant urges the judge to suspend the common law suit in order to await enforcement by the government agency with jurisdiction over the matter. The argument is not that common law remedies do not coexist with the public law remedy, but rather that courts should defer initially to the expertise, official appropriateness, and uniformity function represented by statutory regulators. The fact that polluters want to be sent to the official agencies gives some indication of which forum is more likely to provide effective remedies against them (as well as giving an ironic twist to familiar corporate arguments denouncing the bureaucratic state). For a careful consideration of the primary jurisdiction doctrine, see Comment, Primary Jurisdiction in Environmental Cases, 48 Ind. L.J. 676 (1973).
- **Statutes of limitation, other time bars, and prescriptive nuisances.** Do statutes of limitations provide a good defense for operators of longstanding nuisances? What if a state has a three-year general torts statute of limitation, and an offending plant commenced operations five years before the suit is brought? Not all state courts have treated the question alike, but the majority position is like *Schenectady Chemical*'s — that if the pollution is a "continuing nuisance," each day is a separate

---

16. For an example of express legislative erection of a permit defense, see Alaska Stat. §09.45.230. Permit defense statutes raise a fascinating question: Can repeal of traditional common law protections of private property create a constitutional breach of rights? See Hasselman, Alaska's Nuisance Statute Revisited: Federal Substantive Due Process Limits to Common Law Abrogation, 24 B.C. Envtl. Aff. L. Rev. 347 (1997). Regarding preemption, see Chapter 7.

injury, so that a lawsuit can recapture all losses within the period of the statute of limitations. When, however, a nuisance is of a "permanent" nature (loosely defined as a nuisance plainly intended from the first to continue to operate for many years in exactly the same way, such as one generated by a major electric generation facility), a few court decisions allow the defendant to use the tort statute of limitations to bar untimely suits. In such cases, the statute begins to run from the time at which the cause of action first accrues to the plaintiff. See *Goldstein v. Potomac Elec. Power Co.*, 404 A.2d 1064 (Md. 1979).

Even where a lawsuit is brought within the statute of limitations, a defendant may claim to have acquired a prescriptive private right to pollute, the prescriptive period usually in the 6- to 20-year range. A few states have "statutes of repose." Those statutes are similar to statutes of limitation but do not honor the discovery rule under which the plaintiff must know of the injury to start the limitation running. Statutes of repose can operate unfairly—their effect can mean that a tort case for injury is time-barred even before victims know their long-latent illness exists.[17]

Other estoppel arguments are also available against injunction suits under the equitable defense of laches. As in *Schenectady Chemical*, however, public rights usually override such private defenses. At least one state, Alabama, has created a degree of statutory protection for prescriptive nuisances by a law that, in effect, gives prescriptive rights to continue operation against intentional nuisance claims if the new operation is not a nuisance within its first year of operation. See Ala. Code §6-5-127(a). Causes of action based on other theories, including trespass and negligence, are not affected. See *Courtaulds Fibers v. Long*, 779 So.2d 198 (Ala. 2000).

- **Coming to the nuisance.** A few states still recognize a special defense (a form of estoppel defense) called "coming to the nuisance." The most prominent modern case utilizing a variant on that doctrine is *Spur Industries v. Del Webb Dev. Co.*, 494 P.2d 700 (Ariz. 1972), in which a developer who located a subdivision well outside of a growing city adjacent to a large animal feedlot was required to pay the cost of relocating the feedlot to a more remote location.[18] The thrust of the "defense" is that the defendant had become established in the area before the plaintiff arrived, so the injury to the plaintiff was, in effect, self-inflicted. As indicated by its lack of widespread recognition, the defense of coming to the nuisance is flawed analytically. Although the defendant may have begun operations that did no palpable harm to neighboring landowners at the time, with the advent of the injury to plaintiff the question is who enjoys the better right —plaintiff to the quiet enjoyment of her land or defendant to continue the operation of its offending activity that casts its wastes and ill effects onto its neighbors' lands? To say, as a defendant does in raising this defense, that plaintiff could have avoided the conflict by settling elsewhere begs the question whether defendant had any legal right to insist that plaintiff do so. In the

---

17. See Ferrer, The Application of Statutes of Repose to Environmentally-Related Injuries, 33 B.C. Envtl. Aff. L. Rev. 345 (2006).
18. The remedy in that case was tailored to the equities between the feedlot owner and the developer. It is not at all certain that the feedlot owner's coming to the nuisance "defense" would have received similar consideration had the lawsuit been brought by an individual homeowner in the development suffering from the odors and flies associated with the feedlot's operation.

A. Tort Causes of Action in the Environmental Arena

last analysis, defendant is seeking to use another's land as its disposal site without ever having purchased that privilege from its neighbor.[19]

- **Releases from liability.** Frequently, as part of a settlement of a dispute, one or both parties will grant releases of liability to the other party in regard to the subject matter of the dispute. Think of a release as the equivalent of a contract between the party giving the release and the party being released. The question that *Schenectady Chemical* raises is whether a release given by the state to General Electric and Bendix in regard to the cleanup also releases Schenectady Chemical. Here the court rejects that defense on a narrow ground—the failure to show that the releases had actually been given. If there is a release that says nothing about Schenectady Chemical, what is the best answer? What rule best encourages settlement? Section 6 of the Uniform Comparative Fault Act states:

    > A release, covenant not to sue, or similar agreement entered into by a claimant and a person liable discharges that person from all liability for contribution, but it does not discharge any other persons liable upon the same claim unless it so provides. However, the claim of the releasing person against other persons is reduced by the amount of the released person's equitable share of the obligation. . . .[20]

    In virtually all jurisdictions, the release also protects the settling tortfeasor against any subsequent suits for contribution, an even more important inducement to settlement.

- **The best defense is a good offense? "SLAPPs."** One interesting environmental defense tactic is the filing of "SLAPPs"—strategic lawsuits against public participation. When public interest citizen activists bring actions to enforce the common law or statutory law against polluters, developers, public utilities, ranchers, or other entrepreneurs using federal lands, a survey covering more than 100 cases taken during the formative years of modern environmental litigation revealed that defendants sued or countersued for damages averaging $7.4 million.[21] Many SLAPP suits sound in tort—defendants claim that the environmental or public interest plaintiffs' allegations amount to libel, slander, defamation, interference with business advantage, and abuse of judicial process.

    On their merits, SLAPPs are overwhelmingly thrown out of court if plaintiffs persevere in resisting them. The fear and burden on volunteer activists of defending against these intimidation suits, however, in practice has resulted in the collapse of many citizen initiatives. Well-heeled defendants can justify spending time and money on SLAPPs as tax-deductible business expenses, knowing that the citizen plaintiffs are likely to be greatly hindered, or halted, in their efforts regardless of

---

19. In contrast to the inherent flaws in the "coming to the nuisance" defense, "right to farm" legislation that has been passed in a majority of states, represents a valid politically enacted judgment defining property rights, determining as a matter of state law that the conflict between farms and encroaching residential development is to be resolved in favor of the farms. See, Terence Centner, Anti-Nuisance Legislation, 30 BNA Envtl. L. Rep. 10253 (2000).

20. Section 4 of the Uniform Contribution Among Tortfeasors Act takes the same position.

21. SLAPPs have also been issued in response to the filing of petitions and testimony by activists in legislative and executive proceedings. See generally Canan & Pring, Studying Strategic Lawsuits Against Public Participation, 22 Law & Soc'y Rev. 385 (1988); Pring, Intimidation Suits Against Citizens: A Risk for Public Policy Advocates, 7 Nat'l L.J. 16 (1985); Comment, Counterclaim and Countersuit Harassment of Private Environmental Plaintiffs, 74 Mich. L. Rev. 106 (1975).

the SLAPP's minimal merits. "SLAPP-back" suits, however, countersuing SLAPPers for damages, do exist.[22]

B. Causation and Joint & Several Liability in Conventional Environmental Tort Suits

Plaintiffs must prove that injuries suffered were *caused* by defendants' tortious conduct. There are two distinct branches of the causation inquiry: cause-in-fact and proximate cause. Sandwiched in between these two discussions here is the issue of joint and several liability, a doctrine that in some cases alters significantly the standard operation of cause-in-fact principles when the actions of more than one tortfeasor combine to cause injury.

1. Causation-in-Fact, Basic Doctrine

The requirement that a defendant's action be the cause-in-fact of the plaintiff's injury is a bedrock requisite of tort law. Remembering that the ultimate goal is to provide remedies for some categories of injuries, the cause-in-fact link is the assurance that the loss is being shifted to an appropriate party, i.e., to one whose act or omission is in some tangible way responsible for the injury, rather than to someone having no part in the chain of events. Except in regard to toxic torts which are considered in the next chapter, cause-in-fact in most tortious injury contexts is a simple concept.

The cause-in-fact inquiry purports to be based solely on facts and deduction, yet a key aspect of the inquiry requires conjecture about what would have happened in the absence of a defendant's action or omission. Indeed, a conclusion that the defendant's act, A, is a cause of plaintiff's loss, B, represents a judgment made by the trier of fact that may be founded alternatively upon experience about the degree of association between A and B, or upon evidence supplied by experts, or even upon mere circumstantial evidence.

In general, the cause-in-fact inquiry seeks to establish a but-for relationship—"but for the defendant's tortious conduct, the plaintiff's injury would not have happened." While helpful, overemphasizing the but-for inquiry at times obscures proper cause-in-fact analysis. A famous example is where a defendant driver drives at grossly excessive speeds, and as a result plaintiff passengers arrive at destination X just in time to have a wall collapse on them, causing injury. Defendant's negligent conduct in driving so recklessly is indeed a but-for cause of the injury, for otherwise plaintiffs would not have been in the location of the collapsing wall at the time of its collapse. Nevertheless, for the purposes of tort law, despite the presence of (1) substandard conduct, (2) but-for causation, and (3) injury to plaintiffs, there should be no recovery against defendant driver because the conduct of the driver did not affect or causally contribute to the events that befell the passengers when they arrived at their destination.

In many environmental torts cases, the cause-in-fact inference is relatively easy to observe and prove. In *Roth*, for example, before the initiation of drilling by Cabot Oil,

---

22. See *Gordon v. Marrone*, 590 N.Y.S.2d 649 (Sup. Ct. 1992) (Nature Conservancy recovers $10,000 for developer's harassing lawsuit challenging its tax exemption). For more on SLAPP-backs, see the California anti-SLAPP statute, 1991 Cal. S.B. 341 §425/66(a) and the article by the father of SLAPP jurisprudence, Professor George "Rock" Pring, in 7 Pace Envtl. L. Rev. 3 (1989), in a symposium on SLAPPs.

B. Causation in Conventional Environmental Lawsurts

the plaintiff's well water had long tested clean and shortly after Cabot's drilling, the water became contaminated with compounds typical of those associated with fracking activities. When more than one cause of pollution is at work, such as the *Velsicol* case that follows, matters become a bit more complicated, but still straightforward in cases where plaintiff can obtain evidence that demonstrates the nature and extent of the link between defendant's emissions or other actions and plaintiff's injuries.[23] Finally, as studied in the next chapter, cause-in-fact can be exceedingly complex in the case of toxic torts where contemporary science cannot definitively link a plaintiff's injury to a particular toxic exposure for which the defendant is responsible.

2. Multiple Defendants and the Doctrine of Joint and Several Liability

When the acts of several parties converge to effect a result that injures plaintiff, tort law must find a way to allocate the loss. Under the classic formulation, the plaintiff has the burden of proof on causation and must show by a preponderance of the evidence, as to each defendant, what damage they have caused. If there were six independent upwind industrial polluters, all using coal for their boiler fuel, a plaintiff would be hard pressed to carry the burden of showing exactly what amount of damage was caused by any one of them. Gradually, the doctrine of joint and several liability developed to allow the plaintiff to obtain full compensation more easily in such circumstances by making the defendants all jointly and severally liable to the plaintiff for the full amount of the injury and, in effect, allowing the plaintiff to select which defendant or defendants to pursue in court and collect the full judgment from any one (or any subset) of the jointly liable defendants. Correspondingly, the law now allows a defendant that has paid more than their equitable share for the plaintiff's injury to bring a claim against the other defendants for contribution. The following case explores the imposition of joint and several liability in a conventional pollution setting.

Velsicol Chemical Corp. v. Rowe
543 S.W.2d 337 (Tenn. 1976)

[The original plaintiffs, residents and homeowners in the Alton Park area of Chattanooga, sued Velsicol Chemical for damages allegedly caused them by pollutants emitted from its chemical manufacturing plant. The complaint alleged that Velsicol's emissions contaminated the air and water, creating a nuisance and a trespass in depositing quantities of chemicals and other pollutants upon plaintiffs' properties. Because plaintiffs alleged that Velsicol had intentionally disregarded past injunctions, they also asked for punitive damages. Velsicol, however, argued that there were five other chemical polluters in the Alton Park area who could have caused or contributed to plaintiffs' injuries. This raised the question, first, whether plaintiffs could choose to proceed only against Velsicol, and second, if they prevailed, whether Velsicol could then sue the other five for contribution in paying damages.]

---

23. When there are two concurrent causes of an injury, each of which is alone sufficient to cause the harm, there is a but-for conundrum: Neither is a but-for cause because as to each one, the injury would have happened even if the tortious act of one of them had not occurred! The law has long solved this problem by holding both such actors to be the cause-in-fact of the loss.

BROCK, J. . . . It has been suggested that joint torts be divided into four basic categories, viz., (1) the actors knowingly join in the performance of the tortious act or acts; (2) the actors fail to perform a common duty owed to the plaintiff; (3) there is a special relationship between the parties (e.g., master and servant or joint entrepreneurs); and (4) although there is no concert of action, nevertheless, the independent acts of several actors concur to produce indivisible harmful consequences. 1 Harper & James, Law of Torts, §10.1. While acknowledging that the last category, which may be termed independent, concurring torts, may not fall within the traditional definition of "joint torts," the authors note an increasing tendency in judicial decisions and among legal commentators to impose joint and several liability for such wrongs and thus to establish such torts as "joint" in their practical or legal effect.

The primary concern in dealing with independent, concurring torts is the proper extent of the liability of such wrongdoers, i.e., when should tortfeasors who do not act in concert, but whose acts combine to produce injury to the plaintiff, be held individually liable for the entire damage? It has been suggested that the proper approach should be to look to the combined effect of the several acts:

> If the acts result in separate and distinct injuries, then each wrongdoer is liable only for the damage caused by his acts. However, if the combined result is a single and indivisible injury, the liability should be entire. Thus the distinction to be made is between injuries which are divisible and those which are indivisible. Jackson, Joint Torts & Several Liability, 17 Tex. L. Rev. 399, 406 (1939).

The requirement of "indivisibility" can mean either that the harm is not even theoretically divisible, as death or total destruction of a building, or that the harm, while theoretically divisible, is single in a practical sense in that the plaintiff is not able to apportion it among the wrongdoers with reasonable certainty, as where a stream is polluted as the result of refuse from several factories.

In *Landers v. East Texas Salt Water Disposal Co.*, 248 S.W.2d 731 (Tex. 1952), the plaintiff sued the defendant salt water disposal company and an oil company jointly and severally for the damage resulting when they independently deposited salt water in his lake. The court, apparently assuming that neither defendant acting alone would have caused the entire damage, extended the liability of such wrongdoers by holding them, in effect, to be jointly and severally liable, with the reservation that any one defendant could reduce his liability by showing the amount of damage caused by his acts only, or the amount that was caused by other defendants. The Texas court said:

> Where the tortious acts of two or more wrongdoers join to produce an indivisible injury, that is, an injury which cannot be apportioned with reasonable certainty to the individual wrongdoers, all of the wrongdoers will be held jointly and severally liable for the entire damages and the injured party may proceed to judgment against any one separately or against all in one suit. 248 S.W.2d at 734.

More recently, in *Michie v. Great Lakes Steel*, 495 F.2d 213 (6th Cir. 1974), residents of LaSalle, Ontario, brought a nuisance action in federal court, claiming that air pollutants from defendants' manufacturing plants across the Detroit River caused diminution of the value of their property, impairment of their health, and interference with the use and enjoyment of their land. Each plaintiff claimed at least $11,000 joint damage against these defendants, charging that the defendants were jointly and severally liable.

Relying upon Michigan automobile cases involving successive collisions, the Court reasoned that in any claim for relief there was a manifest unfairness in "putting on the injured party the impossible burden of proving the specific shares of harm done by each

B. Causation in Conventional Environmental Lawsurts

[defendant]," quoting *Landers*. The Court concluded that the Michigan Supreme Court would extend the principle of the automobile collision cases to the *Michie* facts and held that joint and several liability is applicable in nuisance actions. It is our conclusion that the rule stated and applied in the *Landers* and *Michie* cases is . . . consonant with modern legal thought and pragmatic concepts of justice. . . .

After filing an answer generally denying the plaintiffs' allegations, Velsicol filed a third-party complaint against five third-party defendants, alleging that each of them operated a plant in the Alton Park area, that during the period alleged in the original complaint each of them emitted pollutants of the air and water, and that by reason of these facts the third-party defendants are liable to Velsicol for "whatever amount of recovery is made by said plaintiffs." . . .

The common law rule was that there could be no contribution between those who were regarded as "joint tortfeasors," when one had discharged the claim of the injured plaintiff. . . . Prosser, §50 and n.38. The rule was originally adopted by the English courts in *Merryweather v. Nixan*, 101 Eng. Rep. (K.B. 1799). Apparently, the basis of the rule was the unwillingness of the court to allow anyone to found a cause of action upon his own deliberate wrong, an aspect of the "unclean hands" doctrine. When, in the United States, the codes of civil procedure permitted joinder of defendants who were merely negligent, such defendants came to be called "joint tortfeasors," and the reason for the rule against contribution was lost to sight. The great majority of American jurisdictions applied the rule of no-contribution to all situations, even those in which independent, but concurrent, acts of negligence had contributed to a single resulting injury. A small minority of states—including Tennessee—eventually came to a contrary conclusion, allowing contribution among joint tortfeasors without the aid of legislation. . . .

Any remaining uncertainty regarding the extent of the right of contribution among joint tortfeasors in Tennessee was dispelled by the 1968 enactment of the Tennessee Uniform Contribution Among Tortfeasors Act. TCA §§23-3104, 3105 (1975). Excluding intentional tortfeasors, the Tennessee Uniform Act provides that the right to contribution arises upon the satisfaction of two general conditions. First, there must be "two (2) or more persons . . . jointly or severally liable in tort for the same injury to person or property. . . ." Secondly, one of those jointly or severally liable must have paid more than his pro rata share of the common liability. . . .

COMMENTARY & QUESTIONS

1. Problems of joint liability. In *Velsicol* and in the *Landers* and *Michie* cases it discusses, is it clear that the plaintiffs have suffered a single harm from the air or water pollution? The plaintiffs have suffered a single *type* of harm in each of the three instances, but no single defendant is the cause-in-fact of the entire extent of the harm suffered. What justifies "extending" the liability of each potential defendant to cover the entire loss? Is the extension effectively offset by the availability of an action for contribution? Should the insolvency of one or more jointly and severally liable parties affect the availability of joint and several liability against the others? To answer that question, consider whether it is fairer to make the plaintiff bear the cost of that insolvency or the joint tortfeasors. In a pollution case, as between plaintiff and defendants, who is more likely to have access to proof that might bear on the portion of the harm attributable to each defendant?

2. The "single bullet" problem and proof by statistics. In each of the cases just mentioned, the court presumes that multiple defendants contributed to plaintiffs' injuries. What if it had been a "single bullet" injury, however? The leading case on this subject is *Summers v. Tice*, 199 P.2d 1 (Cal. 1948). In *Summers*, two careless members of a hunting party simultaneously fired shotguns in exactly the same direction. Plaintiff, the third member of the hunting party who at the time was slightly in front of the two other hunters, was hit in the eye by a single pellet. It was impossible to determine which gun had shot that pellet. At a very literal level, this might be a hard case for plaintiff—both defendants are negligent, but only one of them is the cause-in-fact of plaintiff's injury, and plaintiff cannot prove which of the two it was. Moreover, since plaintiff has the burden of proof to show it more likely than not that one defendant or the other was the cause-in-fact, plaintiff cannot meet that burden since it is a 50-50 proposition as to whose pellet struck the plaintiff. Plaintiff won despite this problem, however, because the *Summers* court shifted the burden of proving cause-in-fact from the plaintiff to the defendants, each to attempt to absolve themselves of being the cause-in-fact. If neither defendant could carry that burden, they would be held jointly and severally liable. Isn't the *Summers* result indistinguishable from *Velsicol*? Plaintiff is allowed to finesse the burden of proof on the cause-in-fact issue and the defendants are then left to fight out the issue of apportionment.

Once the plaintiff is able to obtain full compensation, how is the loss allocated among defendants? The action for contribution originated in the equity courts and thus the court is searching for a fair basis on which to apportion the loss. When direct evidence is available to prove which defendant's conduct caused what proportion of plaintiff's injury, that would likely form the basis for an equitable decree. For example, if several upwind polluters have similar coal fired power generating equipment, the amount of coal burned by each during the relevant period, or the number of hours of operation of each, might be used to assign comparative responsibility. In regard to some generic drug reaction cases, courts have looked at defendant's market share in the relevant market when assigning responsibility. See *Sindell v. Abbot Labs.*, 607 P.2d 924 (Cal. 1980). For an assessment of this practice and similar uses of probability in making tort awards, see Nesson, Agent Orange Meets the Blue Bus: Factfinding at the Frontier of Knowledge, 66 B.U. L. Rev. 521 (1986).

3. The power of joint and several liability. What makes the availability of joint and several liability so important to plaintiffs in environmental tort cases? Consider not only the ability to ease plaintiff's burden of proof regarding causation but in choice of litigation strategies as well (e.g., the ability to collect judgments or to coerce defendants to settle or undertake cleanups). The coercive nature of joint and several liability is reprised in the materials of Chapter 16 relating to CERCLA (Superfund) litigation, especially its use by the EPA.

4. Contribution and indemnity. Traditionally, contribution and indemnity, when they were allowed at all, were independent causes of action that became available only after a tortfeasor had paid more than its appropriate share of a judgment to the plaintiff. With the rise of more liberal joinder rules, in particular FRCP 14 impleader and its state court counterparts, defendants who are sued alone may join potential contributors and indemnitors in the original action. This encourages efficiency by joining more of the issues in a single lawsuit, but it does not alter the plaintiff's option to enforce the ensuing judgment in full against a single defendant. When is that option important? Note, however, that defendants may forego that option and later bring an independent action for contribution. By leaving the other tortfeasor(s) out of the case, the defendant may try to take advantage of what is termed "the empty chair defense." Using that defense, the defendant points at the absent tortfeasor as the cause of plaintiff's loss. Usually, if that defendant were joined to the initial lawsuit, the joined defendant would be joining the plaintiff in trying to place blame on the original defendant.

B. Causation in Conventional Environmental Lawsuits

There now are common law and statutory "defaults" that control contribution amounts when sufficient proof of a case-specific basis for apportionment is not available. Under the common law, the Uniform Contribution Among Tortfeasors Act (UCATA), and the Uniform Comparative Fault Act (UCFA), contribution is usually pro rata unless there is some other provable basis on which to apportion the injury. The emergence and growth of comparative negligence in recent years first led to apportionment in accordance with the respective percentages of negligence. In cases founded on nuisance, trespass, and strict liability, comparative fault would seem to be irrelevant, but there, too, courts nevertheless divide responsibility according to the UCFA's comparative fault principles. See, e.g., *Dole v. Dow Chem.*, 282 N.E.2d 288 (N.Y. 1972). See also Phillips, Contribution and Indemnity in Products Liability, 42 Tenn. L. Rev. 85 (1974). What avenues might a polluter in *Velsicol* consider when trying to pay less than a pro rata amount?

3. Proximate Causation

Proximate causation is concerned with the problem of remoteness. At times, but-for causation extends to great distances. The defendant in the next case caused widespread harm to the aquatic resources of the James River and Chesapeake Bay. As the extent of economic harm caused by the defendant ripples out through the web of economic activity surrounding those damaged resources, at some point it may be appropriate to limit the availability of remedies for the far-off consequences of wrongful acts, especially where injuries are purely economic. Where is that line?

The following is excerpted from the only reported civil decision arising from the Kepone disaster.

Pruitt v. Allied Chemical Corp.
523 F. Supp. 975 (U.S. Dist. Ct., E.D. Va. 1981)

MERHIGE, D.J.

Plaintiffs bring the instant action against Allied Chemical Corporation for Allied's alleged pollution of the James River and Chesapeake Bay with the chemical agent commonly known as Kepone....

Plaintiffs allegedly engage in a variety of different businesses and professions related to the harvesting and sale of marine life from the Chesapeake Bay. All claim to have suffered economic harm from defendant's alleged discharges of Kepone into the James River and thence into the Bay. Plaintiffs assert their right to compensation under each of the dozen counts to their complaint [including claims in negligence and strict liability]....

The general rule both in admiralty and at common law has been that a plaintiff cannot recover for indirect economic harm. The logical basis for this rule is obscure. Although Courts have frequently stated that economic losses are "not foreseeable" or "too remote," these explanations alone are rarely apposite. As one well-respected commentator has noted, "the loss to plaintiff in each case . . . would be readily recoverable if the test of duty — or remoteness — usually associated with the law of negligence were applied. . . ."[24]

---

24. James, Limitations of Liability for Economic Loss Caused by Negligence: A Pragmatic Appraisal, 25 Vand. L. Rev. 43 (1972). James has gone on to state that "the prevailing distinction between indirect economic loss and physical damage is probably a crude and unreliable one that may need reexamination if a limitation on liability for pragmatic reasons is to be retained." Id. at 50-51.

The difficulty in the present case is how to measure the cost of Kepone pollution. In the instant action, those costs were borne most directly by the wildlife of the Chesapeake Bay. The fact that no one individual claims property rights to the Bay's wildlife could arguably preclude liability. The Court doubts, however, whether such a result would be just. Nor would a denial of liability serve social utility: many citizens, both directly and indirectly, derive benefit from the Bay and its marine life. Destruction of the Bay's wildlife should not be a costless activity. . . .

Commercial fishermen are entitled to compensation for any loss of profits they may prove to have been caused by defendant's negligence. The entitlement given these fishermen presumably arises from what might be called a constructive property interest in the Bay's harvestable species . . . within a category established in *Union Oil Co. v. Oppen*, 501 F.2d 558 (9th Cir. 1974) (the Santa Barbara oil spill case): they "lawfully and directly make use of a resource of the sea."

The use that marina and charterboat owners make of the water, though hardly less legal, is . . . less direct. . . . Still less direct, but far from nonexistent, is the link between the Bay and the seafood dealers, restaurants, and tackle shops that seek relief (as do the employees of these establishments).

One meaningful distinction to be made among the various categories of plaintiffs here arises from a desire to avoid double-counting in calculating damages. Any seafood harvested by the commercial fishermen here would have been bought and sold several times before finally being purchased for consumption. Considerations both of equity and social utility suggest that just as defendant should not be able to escape liability for destruction of publicly owned marine life entirely, it should not be caused to pay repeatedly for the same damage. The Court notes, however, that allowance for recovery of plaintiffs' lost profits here would not in all cases result in double-counting of damages. Plaintiff . . . seafood wholesalers, retailers, processors, distributors and restaurateurs . . . allegedly lost profits when deprived of supplies of seafood. Those profits represented a return on the investment of each of the plaintiffs in material and labor in their businesses, and thus the independent loss to each would not amount to double-counting. . . . Employees undoubtedly lost wages and faced a less favorable job market than they would have, but for defendant's acts, and they have thus been harmed by defendant. What is more, the number of parties with a potential cause of action against defendant is hardly exhausted in plaintiffs' complaint. In theory, parties who bought and sold to and from the plaintiffs named here also suffered losses in business, as did their employees. In short, the set of potential plaintiffs seems almost infinite.

Perhaps because of the large set of potential plaintiffs, . . . some limitation to liability, even when damages are foreseeable, is advisable. . . . The Court thus finds itself with a perceived need to limit liability, without any articulated reason for excluding any particular set of plaintiffs. Other courts have had to make similar decisions.[25] The Court concludes that [commercial fishermen can recover for their lost profits, but the categories of] plaintiffs who purchased and marketed seafood from commercial fishermen suffered damages that

---

25. See, e.g., Judge Kaufmann's opinion in *Petition of Kinsman Transit Co.*, 388 F.2d 821, 824-825 (2d Cir. 1968), where the court noted that "in the final analysis the circumlocution whether posed in terms of 'foreseeability,' 'duty,' 'proximate cause,' 'remoteness,' etc. seems unavoidable," and then turned to Judge Andrews' well-known statement in *Palsgraf v. Long Island R.R. Co.*, 162 N.E. 99, 104 (N.Y. 1928): "It is all a question of expediency . . . of fair judgment, always keeping in mind the fact that we endeavor to make a rule in each case that will be practical and in keeping with the general understanding of mankind."

B. Causation in Conventional Environmental Lawsuits

are not legally cognizable, because insufficiently direct.... The Court holds that plaintiff ... boat, marina, and tackle and bait shop owners have suffered legally cognizable damages.... Only if some set of surrogate plaintiffs is entitled to press its own claims which flow from the damage to the Bay's sportfishing industry will the proper balance of social forces be preserved.... The Court's conclusion results from consideration of all these factors, and an attempt to tailor justice to the facts of the instant case....

COMMENTARY & QUESTIONS

1. The rationale for barring indirect damages. Is there any compelling reason for the traditional tort law rule that forbade recovery of indirect economic losses in the absence of physical injury? Could the reason be institutional, seeking to limit the number of cases in which courts were called upon to make necessarily speculative determinations about the course of future events? Could the reason instead represent an inductive overgeneralization that in a substantial majority of cases lacking physical damage there is likewise no credible economic damage? The bar against indirect recoveries has been widely applied in maritime tort cases under the rule of *Robins Drydock & Repair Co. v. Flint*, 275 U.S. 303 (1927), and has attracted criticism as a major barrier to oil spill plaintiffs in cases such as the *Exxon-Valdez* spill, although statutory exceptions sometimes apply. See Mulhern, Marine Pollution: A Tort Recovery Standard for Pure Economic Losses, 18 B.C. Envtl. Aff. L. Rev. 85 (1990).

2. Of double-counting and foreseeable losses. What is the double-counting danger that is raised by defendants? The judge is correct in saying that the sum of the lost profits of the several categories of victims, by definition a net figure, is inherently free of double-counting problems. Is it correct to limit the award to "replacement value of a plaintiff's actual investment"? What if a plaintiff bought a going fishing business at an unreasonably low price? Is there any reason to allow defendant to deprive that victim of the anticipated net income the wise investment would have generated?

The judge draws the line at the water's edge. Is that fair to inland plaintiffs who are foreseeable victims of massive contamination of the Bay? How does a recovery by the commercial fishermen in any way redress the interests of the owners and employees of a cannery that can no longer process fish from the Bay? Was the allowance of sport fishery industry recoveries an adequate proxy for natural resource damage? How complete an accounting did Allied Chemical face from private litigation?

3. Proximate cause as loss-shifting policy. Can there be a valid policy reason for not shifting all of the loss caused by a defendant's tortious conduct back to that responsible defendant? Possible policy justifications include large transaction costs that might be incurred in a "full accounting," conservation of authority (i.e., not calling on the cumbersome civil justice system backed by the authority of the state to redress every last little bit of injury), or maintaining "affordable" prices for goods and services by permitting some degree of cost externalization onto victims by denying them compensation for remote injuries. Assume that some or all of these justifications for limiting liability are embodied in the proximate cause inquiry. Does that provide any predictable standard regarding when the limit will be invoked to prevent recovery? Even if the policy-oriented aspect of the proximate cause inquiry seems almost devoid of a standard that can be clearly articulated, could tort law employ some better mechanism than proximate cause when dealing with those policy concerns?

C. REMEDIES IN ENVIRONMENTAL LITIGATION

Many novel issues arise in the context of environmental law remedies. The following sections explore equitable remedies, damages, restoration remedies, and natural resources remedies. Criminal penalties are considered in Chapter 19.

1. Two Classic Cases Facing Courts with the Difficult Choice of Enjoining a Major Business

Boomer et al. v. Atlantic Cement Co.
257 N.E.2d 870 (N.Y. Ct. App. 1970)

BERGAN, J. Defendant operates a large cement plant near Albany. These are actions for injunction and damages by neighboring land owners alleging injury to property from dirt, smoke and vibration emanating from the plant. A nuisance has been found after trial, temporary damages have been allowed; but an injunction has been denied.

The public concern with air pollution arising from many sources in industry and in transportation is currently accorded ever wider recognition accompanied by a growing sense of responsibility in State and Federal Governments to control it. Cement plants are obvious sources of air pollution in the neighborhoods where they operate.

But there is now before the court private litigation in which individual property owners have sought specific relief from a single plant operation. The threshold question raised by the division of view on this appeal is whether the court should resolve the litigation between the parties now before it as equitably as seems possible; or whether, seeking promotion of the general public welfare, it should channel private litigation into broad public objectives.

A court performs its essential function when it decides the rights of parties before it. Its decision of private controversies may sometimes greatly affect public issues. Large questions of law are often resolved by the manner in which private litigation is decided. But this is normally an incident to the court's main function to settle controversy. It is a rare exercise of judicial power to use a decision in private litigation as a purposeful mechanism to achieve direct public objectives greatly beyond the rights and interests before the court. . . .

It seems apparent that the amelioration of air pollution will depend on technical research in great depth; on a carefully balanced consideration of the economic impact of close regulation; and of the actual effect on public health. It is likely to require massive public expenditure and to demand more than any local community can accomplish and to depend on regional and interstate controls. A court should not try to do this on its own as a by-product of private litigation and it seems manifest that the judicial establishment is neither equipped in the limited nature of any judgment it can pronounce nor prepared to lay down and implement an effective policy for the elimination of air pollution. This is an area beyond the circumference of one private lawsuit. It is a direct responsibility for government and should not thus be undertaken as an incident to solving a dispute between property owners and a single cement plant—one of many—in the Hudson River valley.

The cement making operations of defendant have been found by the court of Special Term to have damaged the nearby properties of plaintiffs in these two actions. That court, as it has been noted, accordingly found defendant maintained a nuisance and this has been affirmed at the Appellate Division. The trial judge had made a simple, direct finding that "the discharge of large quantities of dust upon each of the properties and excessive

C. Remedies in Environmental Litigation

vibration from blasting deprived each party of the reasonable use of his property and thereby prevented his enjoyment of life and liberty therein." The judge continued, however: "I have given careful consideration to the plea of plaintiffs that an injunction should issue in this action. Although the Supreme Court has the power to grant and enforce an injunction, equity forbids its employment in this instance. The defendant's immense investment in the Hudson River Valley, its contribution to the Capital District's economy and its immediate help to the education of children in the Town of Coeymans through the payment of substantial sums in school and property taxes leads me to the conclusion that an injunction would produce great public . . . hardship." The total damage to plaintiffs' properties is, however, relatively small in comparison with the value of defendant's operation and with the consequences of the injunction which plaintiffs seek.

The ground for the denial of injunction, notwithstanding the finding both that there is a nuisance and that plaintiffs have been damaged substantially, is the large disparity in economic consequences of the nuisance and of the injunction. This theory cannot, however, be sustained without overruling a doctrine which has been consistently reaffirmed in several leading cases in this court and which has never been disavowed here, namely that where a nuisance has been found and where there has been any substantial damage shown by the party complaining an injunction will be granted.

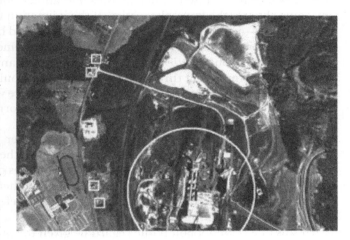

FIGURE 3-1. *Aerial view of Atlantic (now LaFarge) Cement plant (circled) and quarries in Ravena-Coeymans NY. The small squares indicate approximate location of several plaintiffs' homes on Route 9W. Photo: USGS.*

The rule in New York has been that such a nuisance will be enjoined although marked disparity be shown in economic consequence between the effect of the injunction and the effect of the nuisance. The problem of disparity in economic consequence was sharply in focus in Whalen v. Union Bag & Paper Co., 101 N.E. 805. A pulp mill entailing an investment of more than a million dollars polluted a stream in which plaintiff, who owned a farm, was "a lower riparian owner." The economic loss to plaintiff from this pollution was small. This court . . . reinstated the injunction [despite] the argument of the mill owner that in view of "the slight advantage to plaintiff and the great loss that will be inflicted on defendant" an injunction should not be granted. . . . "Although the damage to the plaintiff may be slight as compared with the defendant's expense of abating the condition, that is not a good reason for refusing an injunction." . . . The rule laid down in that case, then, is that whenever the damage resulting from a nuisance is found not "unsubstantial," viz., $100 a year, injunction would follow. . . .

Although the court [at trial in this case] held that an injunction should be denied, it found that plaintiffs had been damaged in various specific amounts up to the time of the trial and damages to the respective plaintiffs were awarded for those amounts. The effect of this was, injunction having been denied, plaintiffs could maintain successive actions at law for damages thereafter as further damage was incurred. The court also found the amount of permanent damage attributable to each plaintiff, for the guidance of the parties in the event both sides stipulated to the payment and acceptance of such permanent damage as a settlement of all the controversies among the parties. The total of permanent damages to all plaintiffs thus found was $185,000. This basis of adjustment has not resulted in any stipulation by the parties.

This [refusal to enjoin] is a departure from a rule that has become settled; but to follow the rule literally in these cases would be to close down the plant at once. This court is fully agreed to avoid that immediately drastic remedy; the difference in view is how best to avoid it.[26]

One alternative is to grant the injunction but postpone its effect to a specified future date to give opportunity for technical advances to permit defendant to eliminate the nuisance; another is to grant the injunction conditioned on the payment of permanent damages to plaintiffs which would compensate them for the total economic loss to their property present and future caused by defendant's operations. For reasons which will be developed the court chooses the latter alternative. If the injunction were to be granted unless within a short period—e.g., 18 months—the nuisance be abated by improved methods, there would be no assurance that any significant technical improvement would occur.

The parties could settle this private litigation at any time if defendant paid enough money and the imminent threat of closing the plant would build up the pressure on defendant. If there were no improved techniques found, there would inevitably be applications to the court at Special Term for extensions of time to perform on showing of good faith efforts to find such techniques.

Moreover, techniques to eliminate dust and other annoying by-products of cement making are unlikely to be developed by any research the defendant can undertake within any short period, but will depend on the total resources of the cement industry nationwide and throughout the world. The problem is universal wherever cement is made. For obvious reasons the rate of the research is beyond control of defendant. If at the end of 18 months the whole industry has not found a technical solution a court would be hard put to close down this one cement plant if due regard be given to equitable principles.

On the other hand, to grant the injunction unless defendant pays plaintiffs such permanent damages as may be fixed by the court seems to do justice between the contending parties. All of the attributions of economic loss to the properties on which plaintiffs' complaints are based will have been redressed.

The nuisance complained of by these plaintiffs may have other public or private consequences, but these particular parties are the only ones who have sought remedies and the judgment proposed will fully redress them. The limitation of relief granted is a limitation only within the four corners of these actions and does not foreclose public health or other public agencies from seeking proper relief in a proper court.

It seems reasonable to think that the risk of being required to pay permanent damages to injured property owners by cement plant owners would itself be a reasonable effective spur to research for improved techniques to minimize nuisance....

The damage base here suggested is consistent with the general rule in those nuisance cases where damages are allowed. "Where a nuisance is of such a permanent and unabatable character that a single recovery can be had, including the whole damage past and future resulting therefrom, there can be but one recovery" (66 C.J.S. Nuisances §140, 947).

---

26. Respondent's investment in the plant is in excess of $45.000,000. There are over 300 people employed there.

C. Remedies in Environmental Litigation

It has been said that permanent damages are allowed where the loss recoverable would obviously be small as compared with the cost of removal of the nuisance (Ky.-Ohio Gas Co. v. Bowling, 95 S.W.2d 1).... Equity will give full relief in one action and prevent a multiplicity of suits....

Thus it seems fair to both sides to grant permanent damages to plaintiffs which will terminate this private litigation. The theory of damage is the "servitude on land" of plaintiffs imposed by defendant's nuisance. (See U.S. v. Causby, 328 U.S. 256, 261, 262, 267, where the term "servitude" addressed to the land was used by Justice Douglas relating to the effect of airplane noise on property near an airport.) The judgment, by allowance of permanent damages imposing a servitude on land, which is the basis of the actions, would preclude future recovery by plaintiffs or their grantees. This should be placed beyond debate by a provision of the judgment that the payment by defendant and the acceptance by plaintiffs of permanent damages found by the court shall be in compensation for a servitude on the land.

Although the Trial Term has found permanent damages as a possible basis of settlement of the litigation, on remission the court should be entirely free to examine this subject. It may again find the permanent damage already found, or make new findings.

The orders should be reversed, without costs, and the cases remitted to Supreme Court, Albany County to grant an injunction which shall be vacated upon payment by defendant of such amounts of permanent damage to the respective plaintiffs as shall for this purpose be determined by the court.

JASEN, J., dissenting.... To now change the rule to permit the cement company to continue polluting the air indefinitely upon the payment of permanent damages is, in my opinion, compounding the magnitude of a very serious problem in our State and Nation today.... The harmful nature and widespread occurrence of air pollution have been extensively documented. Congressional hearings have revealed that air pollution causes substantial property damage, as well as being a contributing factor to a rising incidence of lung cancer, emphysema, bronchitis and asthma.

The specific problem faced here is known as particulate contamination because of the fine dust particles emanating from defendant's cement plant. The particular type of nuisance is not new, having appeared in many cases for at least the past 60 years. (See Hulbert v. Cal. Portland Cement Co., 118 P. 928 (Cal. 1911).) It is interesting to note that cement production has recently been identified as a significant source of particulate contamination in the Hudson Valley. This type of pollution, wherein very small particles escape and stay in the atmosphere, has been denominated as the type of air pollution which produces the greatest hazard to human health. We have thus a nuisance which not only is damaging to the plaintiffs, but also is decidedly harmful to the general public....

The majority is, in effect, licensing a continuing wrong. It is the same as saying to the cement company, you may continue to do harm to your neighbors so long as you pay a fee for it. Furthermore, once such permanent damages are assessed and paid, the incentive to alleviate the wrong would be eliminated, thereby continuing air pollution of an area without abatement.... It is clearly established that the cement company is creating a continuing air pollution nuisance primarily for its own private interest with no public benefit. This kind of inverse condemnation may not be invoked by a private person or corporation for private gain or advantage. Inverse condemnation should only be permitted when the public is primarily served in the taking or impairment of property. The promotion of the interests of the polluting cement company has, in my opinion, no public use or benefit. Nor is it constitutionally permissible to impose a servitude on land, without consent of the owner, by payment of permanent damages where the continuing impairment of the land is for a private use. . . .

I would enjoin the defendant cement company from continuing the discharge of dust particles upon its neighbors' properties unless, within 18 months, the cement company abated this nuisance.[27]

It is not my intention to cause the removal of the cement plant from the Albany area, but to recognize the urgency of the problem stemming from this stationary source of air pollution, and to allow the company a specified period of time to develop a means to alleviate this nuisance.

I am aware that the trial court found that the most modern dust control devices available have been installed in defendant's plant, but, I submit, this does not mean that better and more effective dust control devices could not be developed within the time allowed to abate the pollution. Moreover, I believe it is incumbent upon the defendant to develop such devices, since the cement company, at the time the plant commenced production (1962), was well aware of the plaintiffs' presence in the area, as well as the probable consequences of its contemplated operation. Yet, it still chose to build and operate the plant at this site.

In a day when there is a growing concern for clean air, highly developed industry should not expect acquiescence by the courts, but should, instead, plan its operations to eliminate contamination of our air and damage to its neighbors. Accordingly [I would] grant an injunction to take effect 18 months hence, unless the nuisance is abated by improved techniques prior to said date.

COMMENTARY & QUESTIONS

1. Environmental tort monetary remedies. When plaintiffs successfully establish defendant's liability under an environmental tort cause of action, one remedy is automatic: the award of compensatory damages (if supported by competent proof) for tort injuries suffered. The well-established checklist of compensatory damage categories includes recoveries for health and property damage, lost profits and earnings, pain and suffering, and the like. Environmental cases occasionally add new remedy theories, noted later. The *Boomer* case concerned only property damages but added the relatively novel permanent damage approach to property damages in lieu of an injunction or repetitious periodic suits for damage incurred during succeeding periods of time.

2. A very short explanation of the divide between law and equity. Historically, there was a division in the court system separating courts of equity (where judges sat without a jury and injunctions might be had) and courts of law (where damages were sought and juries could, in most cases, be demanded by the parties). A major tenet of equity jurisprudence is that equitable relief will not be granted if there is an adequate remedy at law. Continuing nuisances offered only a cumbersome remedy in the law courts—sue for damages to the date of judgment and then sue again at a later date for damages incurred since the time of the prior judgment. Many equity courts, including the court in the *Whalen* precedent that plaintiffs tried to use in *Boomer*, found that remedy to be inadequate and would grant the

---

27. The issuance of an injunction to become effective in the future is not an entirely new concept. For instance, in *Schwarzenbach v. Oneonta Light & Power Co.*, 100 N.E. 1134, an injunction against the maintenance of a dam spilling water on plaintiff's property was issued to become effective one year hence.

C. Remedies in Environmental Litigation

injunction against the continuing wrong.[28] After many states and the federal court systems "merged" their law and equity courts, those "merged" courts were empowered to grant all relief to which a party was entitled. Thus, in contemporary merged systems a court in a situation like *Boomer*, once it has found a nuisance, has the full playbook of remedies available.

3. Balancing the equities. Mirroring *Boomer*, the grant of an injunction in virtually all modern courts is never automatic but depends upon a balancing of the equities.[29] Accepting that principle, does an environmental perspective on the *Boomer* case reveal any problems with the court's balance? Should the court consider the cement dust's more general public effects? Would the New York Court of Appeals apply *Boomer* to a public nuisance case? For example, in the Loeffel dumpsite case of *Schenectady Chemical*, the state as plaintiff is clothed with a presumptive authority to speak for the common good. Does that mean that the interests represented by the public official presumptively outweigh the costs to a private nuisance-maker when equities are balanced, or does it merely mean that the public values are allowed onto the scale? In *Boomer*, the majority allowed public interest values onto the defendant's side of the scale but took no account of interests other than those of the named plaintiffs.

4. Deciding to award permanent damages. Traditionally, courts that refused an injunction didn't award permanent damages but instead permitted the plaintiff to return to court periodically over time to prove a new case. What institutional factors relating to the court system workload and judicial competence militate for and against that approach? As a litigant in a case like *Boomer*, how valuable to you is the sense of closure that accompanies the award of permanent damages?

5. What the Boomers eventually won — the judge's initial assessment of permanent damages and the actual outcome. Based on the evidence to the time of trial, the judge, R. W. Herzberg, calculated damages based on lost monthly rental value times the number of months the plant had been in operation. The total for all plaintiffs amounted to $535.00 per month, a cost that Atlantic Cement would gladly pay. In addition, the judge noted that the cement company and the Boomers had stipulated to an award to the Boomers of $14,370 attributable to damage to vehicles stored on their property. That left in dispute the amount to be awarded as permanent damages. The judge, knowing an appeal might be taken, tried to encourage a settlement by calculating a potential award of permanent damages that was founded on Realtor testimony about the change in property values attributable

---

28. Equity courts had another advantage in such cases. Under the "cleanup doctrine," in equity, a court issuing an injunction that would cease the offending behavior also was empowered to award damages for the past effects of the conduct as an incidental part of its full determination of rights.

29. This principle was first famously established in the *Ducktown* cases. See *Madison v. Ducktown Sulphur, Copper & Iron Co.*, 83 S.W. 658 (Tenn. 1904). In that turn-of-the-century case, the court had to deal with an early example of an environmental tradeoff. The smelting industry was getting underway in the foothills of southeastern Tennessee and northern Georgia. It was likely to provide sizable revenues for the entrepreneurs of Atlanta and Chattanooga, jobs for local residents, and copper and other materials for the nation's industrial economy. The copper ore was mined in nearby hills, then smelted in large open-air piles layered with firewood and coal. This firing process, however, produced acidic "sulphuretic" air emissions that eventually turned nearly a hundred square miles of hills into a remarkably stark, denuded desert, its topsoil slowly washing away down sterile, chemical-laden streams. The plaintiffs were farmers whose fields and orchards began to die as the smelting got underway. The Tennessee high court held that the smelting was a continuing private nuisance. But after long and careful deliberation, it allowed the defendant industries to continue operations despite their drastic impact upon the plaintiffs' land and livelihood. The court required only that the mills compensate the plaintiffs for their losses. In common parlance, it awarded legal compensatory damages but denied any injunctive remedy, based on a balancing of equities. The *Ducktown* court certainly balanced the equities.

Plaintiff(s)	Reasonable Market Value		Permanent Damages
	9/1/62	6/1/67	
Oscar H. Boomer and June C. Boomer	$25,000	$12,500	$12,500
Theodore J. Richard and Miriam W. Richard	30,000	12,000	18,000
Avie Kinley, Martha Kinley and Mary Kinley	140,000	70,000	70,000
Kenneth Livengood and Delores Livengood	18,000	7,000	11,000
Floyd W. Millious and Barbara A. Millious	20,000	8,000	12,000
Joseph L. Ventura and Carrie Ventura	25,000	12,500	12,500
James W. McCall	22,000	11,000	11,000
Charles J. Meilak and Angelina Meilak	26,000	12,000	14,000
Total			$185,000

FIGURE 3-2. *Proposed settlement amounts for permanent damages in* Boomer v. Atlantic Cement.

to the presence of the cement plant. The amount proposed to be paid totaled $185,000. See *Boomer v. Atlantic Cement,* 287 N.Y.S.2d 112 (1967).

Over a period of slightly more than two years, all plaintiffs except the Kinleys settled, some of the plaintiffs remaining on their property and granting an easement, and others selling the property outright to Atlantic Cement. The Kinleys eventually won a permanent damage verdict of $125,000 in lost market value plus $50,000 as a fudge adjustment. This was considerably more than the judge had previously proposed. See *Kinley v. Atlantic Cement,* 340 N.Y.S.2d 97, 108 (Sup. Ct. 1972), aff'd, 349 N.Y.S.2d 199 (App. Div. 1973). Bringing the litigation to a close, Atlantic Cement subsequently successfully sued its comprehensive general liability insurer to recoup all of the damages and settlement amounts and its litigation costs in defending the lawsuits. *Atlantic Cement Co. v. Fidelity Cas. Co. of N.Y.,* 459 N.Y.S.2d 425 (App. Div. 1983) (damages "accidentally caused" within meaning of policies' terms despite the fact they were awarded on an intentional tort theory).

6. Possible flaws in the calculation of permanent damages. Is it reasonable to look to property value alone in assessing permanent damages for a continuing nuisance? Judge Herzberg compares the value of the property before construction of the cement plant in 1962 with the present value of the property at the time of trial in 1967 when the property is subject to the nuisance. What if the Boomers' property value—$25,000 before the factory started in 1962—had immediately dropped to $10,000 thereafter, but subsequently climbed back to $25,000 by the time of final judgment in 1967, *only because all property values* in the area had more than doubled by 1967? On the court's reckoning, permanent damages would then cost Atlantic $0! In the *Borland* trespass case, the defendant argued their smelting activities had *increased* the value of plaintiff's land by establishing the area as suitable for industrial use, a use that commanded higher land prices than for the Borlands' use for cattle and farming that had prevailed in the area before the smelter located there. (The argument was rejected there.) Does the Herzberg damage calculation tacitly accept the reasoning rejected in *Borland*? How better should those numbers have been figured?

Do the flaws in the calculation run even deeper? A property's market value is what a willing buyer would pay a *willing* seller for comparable property, based on the testimony of local realtor experts. But the *Boomer* plaintiffs were not willing sellers. If the Boomers

C. Remedies in Environmental Litigation

and the others were willing sellers at the listed prices, they would long ago have accepted a settlement. Can the court assess an extra amount to account for their unwillingness to sell? Must it? See Hiley, Involuntary Sale Damages in Permanent Nuisance Cases: A Bigger Bang from *Boomer*, 14 B.C. Envtl. Aff. L. Rev. 61, 86-91 (1986).

7. Permanent damages as private condemnation or a judge-made right to pollute. The net result of the refusal of an injunction and award of permanent damages is to force the *Boomer* plaintiffs unwillingly to sell to Atlantic Cement Co. an easement to pollute at its court-established market value. Dissenting Judge Jasen in *Boomer* and some commentators therefore have argued that permanent damages are unconstitutional because they amount to private exercise of the condemnation power. Other courts, including the *Borland* court in the continuing trespass context, have summarily noted that private condemnation, "unquestionably, is impermissible." Under the federal Due Process Clause and the constitutions of virtually all states, even a public entity is allowed to use the power of condemnation only in the service of public purposes.

But are permanent damages properly characterized as private condemnation? Cases like *Boomer* are based on common law rather than the police power. Other precedents for forced sales to private parties exist as well—of access easements from landlocked parcels, easements to transport water over neighboring lands in the arid western U.S., or in a far earlier era, easements to build milldams that flooded neighbors' fields—all justified by theories of public necessity. The right to deposit pollution on neighbors, however, is quite a different kind of claimed "necessity."[30] Do permanent damages imply that pollution is acceptable as long as polluters pay, or that economic development trumps the traditional right of a landowner to refuse to sell? Had *Boomer* been decided in the wake of the public uproar over the use of eminent domain to further urban renewal accomplished by private entities, might its result have been different? Cf. *Kelo v. City of New London*, 545 U.S. 469 (2005)(condemnation for privately implemented urban renewal is a public purpose). Perhaps this explains the relatively infrequent use of permanent damages despite much favorable comment in the law and economics literature.

Another argument of polluters seeks to immunize their activities from liability by stressing their utility and importance to the community. Should that argument be accepted as a defense to liability in environmental tort cases? Over the years, several courts have confused the issues of what constitutes a legitimate defense to liability with choice of remedy. Although the *Boomer* court did not fall into this error, other courts have, particularly in nuisance suits where the defense invokes the social utility of defendant's conduct. Those courts mistakenly deny relief altogether on a "balance of utilities," finding defendants' conduct acceptable (not actionable) under the circumstances, as when major industrial facilities have inflicted substantial damage on nearby houses.[31] Even if the characteristics of the emitting facility are not relevant in proving the elements of nuisance, as noted in the trespass materials, the extent of the invasion on quiet enjoyment is relevant, and minor inconvenience is not actionable.

---

30. An argument of "necessity" might follow from the claim that the cement plant was a "state of the art facility" which might be argued to imply that better pollution control was not possible. Certainly Judge Began's opinion suggests as much.

31. In doing so, those courts replicated the oversimplification of an Old English dictum: "Le utilitie del chose excusera le noisomeness del stink," roughly, "The usefulness of the thing will excuse the foulness of the pollution." The legal French appears to be a version of a line from Ranketts case in 1684: "Si home fait Candells deins un vill, per que il caufe un noyfom fent al Inhabitants, uncore ceo neft alcun Nusans, car le needfulnefs de eux difpenfera ove le noifomnefs del fmell." P. 3 Ja. B.R. Rolle's Abridgement, Nusans, 139 (1684). As *Boomer* showed, this may be relevant to the grant or denial of injunctive relief, but it should not affect a finding on the issue of liability.

8. Injunctions as windfalls. Consider the alternative to permanent damages—granting the injunction. Isn't it virtually certain that plaintiffs will use defendant's large sunk capital investment to "extort" a grossly exaggerated price for surrender of their rights to force the plant out of business? How is the court to choose between a forced sale of rights that has all the hallmarks of private condemnation and the immense windfall that is likely to occur if an injunction is issued? Should the cement company have foreseen its peril and purchased a larger parcel or easements from all of its neighbors likely to be affected by its emissions *before* building a $45 million pant?

9. *Boomer* and the cement company's "cost externalization." Besides its interesting holdings on permanent damages and balancing the equities, the *Boomer* case is in many ways a lens for examining polluting behavior and its usual disregard for the environment. For the cement company, doing its own internal benefit-cost analysis, discharging waste dust into the commons costs the least and, therefore, is the most economically rational disposal option. Absent successful legal action, the company would have had to account for almost none of the pollution's cost. Even with the successful action in *Boomer*, only a small part of the total social cost is thrust back on the cement plant. What options are available to change the cement company's behavior, to impose Garrett Hardin's "mutual coercion, mutually agreed upon"? (See Chapter 1.)

One argument favoring the *Boomer* end result can be summed up this way, "Some pollution is necessary to progress, and it has to occur somewhere. The market's accounting dictates that it occur here, in a rural area where only a few relatively low-income people will be affected." Is that a compelling argument? There is no complaint about health effects in *Boomer*, so the effects of cement dust pollution may be relatively slight. The benefits of cement are clearly substantial. Does the rough accounting reached in *Boomer* thus suffice? Does society have the luxury of performing an endless analysis of the benefits and costs of every enterprise like the Atlantic Cement Co., or should such scrutiny be reserved for cases of more dramatic environmental impact? Class actions offer a vehicle for expanded internalization and dramatically increase defendants' incentives to clean up. *Boomer* was not filed as a class action case, although it probably could have been. See Wright, The Cost-Internalization Case for Class Actions, 21 Stan. L. Rev. 383 (1969), on environmental use of class actions.

10. Tactics, politics, and the urge to litigate. If the cement dust pollution was so obvious in this case, why didn't Boomer and his lawyer go straight to the state air pollution agency? Albany, the state capital, was close by, and the official state pollution control agency possessed statutory authority, extensive regulations, public funding appropriated for enforcement, and expertise. What practical advantages in getting relief persuade pollution victims to take on the burdens of litigating in common law courts rather than trusting the official public law system?

Are various public regulatory systems likely to provide people like the Boomers a sympathetic local forum in which to oppose the plant before it is built? The $45 million in local investment weighs heavily on the regulatory balance, just as it did in the court action. Today, communities prostrate themselves in efforts to attract the economic benefits that come with major industrial facilities. There is immense pressure to grant needed permits. As studied later, the state pollution control system addresses pollution control with an emphasis on protecting public health. Those programs seldom provide discrete local remedies for relatively small individual claims.

The *Wilsonville* decision that follows was rendered in a consolidated action of public nuisance cases begun in early 1977 by the village of Wilsonville, the Attorney General of Illinois, and others, seeking injunctive relief. The excerpts include a good deal of description of the testimony of the competing experts in the case. In an effort to limit the length of the excerpt, the editors have changed the order of exposition.

C. Remedies in Environmental Litigation

Village of Wilsonville v. SCA Services, Inc.
426 N.E.2d 824 (Ill. Sup. Ct. 1981)

CLARK, J. . . . The gravamen of the complaints was that the operation of the defendant's chemical-waste-disposal site presents a public nuisance and a hazard to the health of the citizens of the village, the county and the State. . . . The trial court's judgment order concluded that the site constitutes a nuisance and enjoined the defendant from operating its hazardous-chemical waste landfill in Wilsonville. It ordered the defendant to remove all toxic waste buried there, along with all contaminated soil found at the disposal site as a result of the operation of the landfill. Further, the court ordered the defendant to restore and reclaim the site. The defendant appealed. . . .

The defendant initiated the permit process with the Illinois Environmental Protection Agency (IEPA) in 1976 and later that year received development and then operation permits. The defendant's 130-acre chemical waste landfill, roughly 2/3 of which is located within the village limits of Wilsonville, began accepting shipments of waste in November, 1976. Each shipment is the subject of a separate IEPA permit that recites the types of materials to be deposited. By the time of trial in June, 1977, 185 such permits had been granted. The site is bordered on the east, west, and south by farmland and on the north by the village. The site, the village and much of that land is over a coal mine that went out of use in 1954. The coal seam is at a depth of 312 feet. Using the room and panel method, roughly 50% of the coal remains in place as pillars that provide support for the overlying land but do not prevent all subsidence. The defendant contracts with generators of toxic chemical waste to haul the waste away from the generators' locations for disposal at the Wilsonville site, where the wastes are deposited into one of seven trenches. Each [trench] is approximately 15 feet deep, 50 feet wide, and 250 to 350 feet long. Approximately 95 percent of the waste materials were buried in 55-gallon steel drums, and the remainder is contained in double-wall paper bags. After the materials are deposited in the trenches, uncompacted clay is placed between groups of containers and a minimum of one foot of clay is placed between the top drum and the top clay level of the trench. . . .

There are 14 monitoring wells along the perimeter of the site. They are designed to detect liquids which seep through the soil and into the wells. They are not designed to contain liquids, however. In fact, monitoring wells Nos. 5 and 6 are 650 feet apart, which would allow many materials to pass between those two wells and not be discovered. [The wells and other water gathered on the site are sampled quarterly by a private laboratory and test results are submitted to the IEPA.] The surface drainage and the groundwater drainage from the site are to the south, away from the village and toward farmland.

The village does not operate any sewage treatment facilities and buys and pipes in its water from another town. Efforts to pump its water supply from groundwater were abandoned when well drilling efforts failed to produce usable quantities. Nevertheless there are 73 water wells in the village, some of which are used to water gardens or wash cars, and at least one well is used to water pets. One well is used for drinking water and one resident approximately one-half mile away intends to use his well as his water supply when he builds his home. Further south are four more springs used to water livestock.

The materials deposited at the site include polychlorinated biphenyls (PCBs), a neurotoxic, possibly carcinogenic chemical which it has been illegal to produce in this country since 1979. . . . PCBs have been stored at the site in liquid, solid and semi-solid form. . . . Other materials buried at the site in large quantities are solid cyanide, a substance known as C5, 6, paint sludge, asbestos, pesticides, mercury, and arsenic. Considerable evidence was adduced to show that these and other substances deposited at the site are extremely toxic to human beings. Some of the adverse reactions which could result from exposure to these materials are pulmonary diseases, cancer, brain damage, and birth defects.

The general geologic profile of the site shows a surface layer of about 10 feet of loess (wind-blown silt and clay material), under which lies 40 to 65 feet of glacial till. In the till material there is a thin sand layer of a few inches to approximately two feet. Some groundwater has been found in the sand layer. All trenches dug at the site have between 10 to 15 feet of glacial till below them. The glacial till is reported to be very dense and is not very permeable. Thus liquids do not travel through it quickly.

Permeability studies conducted before the site opened by John Mathes, a professional engineer hired by the defendant, indicate permeability results ranging from 7.4×10^{-8} centimeters per second to 1.2×10^{-8} centimeters per second (cm/sec.). (The larger the negative exponent is, the less permeable the soil. E.g., a finding of 10^{-8} cm/sec. indicates that the soil is [ten thousand times] less permeable than would a reading of 10^{-4} cm/sec.) After the site opened, Mathes took permeability samples from or near the bottoms of the trenches that had been dug. His second set of results ranged from 1.4×10^{-7} cm/sec. to $.9 \times 10^{-7}$ cm/sec.

Dr. James Williams, an engineering geologist with the Missouri Geology and Land Survey, also made permeability findings on behalf of the defendant from samples taken from the site after it opened. Dr. Williams' results ranged from 7×10^{-6} cm/sec. to 1×10^{-7} cm/sec. Dr. Williams testified on cross-examination that the general permeability of the site is considered to be greater than 1×10^{-8} cm/sec. and that he would not expect the average permeability of the soil to be as low as that used for samples. In the interim between the opening of the site and the time of trial, the IEPA adopted a suggested permeability standard of 1×10^{-8} cm/sec. for hazardous-waste landfills.

Subsidence of the earth underneath the site is another contention raised by the plaintiffs to support their thesis that the site is unsafe and is therefore an enjoinable nuisance. Dr. Nolan Augenbaugh testified extensively at trial. Dr. Augenbaugh . . . pointed out where subsidence occurred in the pictures he had taken. . . . Dr. Augenbaugh also testified that a subsidence basin lies to the northeast of the disposal site. The pictures also indicate, according to Dr. Augenbaugh, fractures in the ground. One picture depicts a fault, which, Dr. Augenbaugh explained, is a "fracture where there's been differential movement of the two blocks. One block has been moved more than the other block." Sawyer, [a nearby] farmer, told Dr. Augenbaugh the cracks had begun to appear approximately two months before, which would have been spring 1977. Several of these subsidences and fractures are located approximately one-half mile from the western boundary of the lower part of the disposal site. Dr. Augenbaugh testified that, in his opinion, subsidence can and will occur at the disposal site. Further, that ruptures in the earth would occur which, like an open pipe, would act as conduits for artesian water to reach the trenches, thereby contaminating the water.

Dr. Augenbaugh . . . testified that on March 22, 1978, he . . . had a trench dug across the subsidence cracks which he had observed earlier. When the digging was completed, there was a trench 9 feet long and approximately 3 feet wide, with a maximum depth of a little over 8 feet. Photographs were taken and slides prepared of the operation at the site. As the trench was being dug, water began to seep into the trench at a depth of approximately 4 feet. Dr. Augenbaugh testified that the water flowed from subsidence fractures which were below the surface of the ground. Dr. Augenbaugh then poured some green dye into a surface fracture which was located approximately 10 feet away from the trench. The green dye entered the trench through two openings within 25 minutes. [A second expert witness familiar with the region, but who had not visited the area,] offered the opinion that there is a possibility of subsidence wherever coal is mined and underground support is removed.

C. Remedies in Environmental Litigation

Several of the defendant's expert witnesses, James Douglas Andrews, the designer of the site and a consulting engineer for the defendant, John A. Mathes, an engineer, Steven Hunt, a geologist with the Illinois State Geological Survey (ISGS), and Paul B. DuMontelle, an engineering geologist with ISGS and coordinator of environmental geology for the Survey, testified in summary that there would be subsidence at the site, but that it would not be deep, would close in a short time, and could be repaired by means of engineering techniques.

Another of plaintiffs' witnesses, Dr. Arthur Zahalsky, offered the opinion that an "explosive interaction," resulting in chemical explosions, fires, or emissions of poisonous gases, will occur at the site. Dr. Zahalsky is a professor of biochemistry and head of the laboratory of biochemical parasitology at Southern Illinois University at Edwardsville. He testified in essence that if sufficient oxygen could reach the buried chemicals, and he believed it could, then an explosive interaction of unknown date of occurrence, magnitude, and duration is likely. Moreover, Dr. Zahalsky testified that it is unknown what interactions might occur when the waste materials combine after the deterioration of the steel containers and paper bags.

The defendant challenged Dr. Zahalsky's opinion during cross-examination and requested him to diagram the precise chemical formula which would result in an explosive interaction. Dr. Zahalsky testified that a precise formula could not be diagrammed. He stated that the defendant's trench logs indicate that several of the chemical wastes have flash points less than 80 degrees Fahrenheit. Zahalsky reviewed the trench logs and gave examples of chemicals, such as paranitroaniline, which is a strong oxidizing agent and may be explosive, and also paint sludge, which has a flash point of less than 80 degrees Fahrenheit, which could result in a chemical fire. Dr. Zahalsky offered one scenario in which acidic chlorinated degreasers would interact with waste phenolics, releasing the phenolics so that the flash point would be achieved, thereby setting off the paint sludges which, in turn, would set off paint wastes, which would achieve the temperature sufficient for the ignition and combustion of liquid PCBs. All of these materials are deposited together in trench No. 3.

The defendant [to refute the conclusions of Dr. Zahalsky] particularly relies upon the opinion of Dr. Raymond D. Harbison, a professor of pharmacology at Vanderbilt University, a toxicologist and consultant to the U.S. Environmental Protection Agency (USEPA) on toxic-waste handling. Dr. Harbison offered the opinion that the instant site is the most advanced scientific landfill in this country, and that the inventory system and the "absolute confinement" of the materials to the site render the interaction of the chemicals an impossibility. At bottom, Dr. Harbison's opinion is premised upon his belief that the materials at the site will be sufficiently confined so that they will not pose a threat to the health or lives of the residents of the village. Dr. Harbison's opinions were discounted by the trial court, however, due to the substantial evidence which shows that the soil is more permeable than originally thought; that there is migration of water out of the trenches; and that there is subsidence in the area.

Finally, considerable testimony was adduced, much of it conflicting, as to dust, odors, and spills of chemical waste which have occurred in the village. Various residents testified that dust emanating from the site blew toward their houses. Also, odors which caused burning eyes, running noses, headaches, nausea, and shortness of breath were mentioned in testimony. The odors themselves were said to resemble, among other things, fertilizer, insecticide, and burning rubber. There was further testimony that the dust and odors interfered with the witnesses' ability to use their yards for gardening or other recreational uses. The defendant presented witnesses who denied that the disposal site was the source of any odors, and that the odors resulted from the local practices of openly burning refuse and dumping sewage into a nearby creek.

There was testimony that trucks carrying the waste materials to the disposal site via Wilson Avenue, the main street of the village, sometimes spilled toxic liquids onto the street. The evidence is undisputed, both from the defendant's receiving reports and testimony from IEPA inspectors, that many drums arrived on the site leaking waste materials. . . .

The defendant has raised several issues on appeal: (1) whether the finding of the circuit and appellate courts that the waste-disposal site is a prospective nuisance is contrary to the manifest weight of the evidence; (2) whether those courts applied the wrong legal standard in finding that the waste-disposal site constitutes a prospective nuisance; (3) whether the circuit and appellate courts erred in failing to balance the equities, either in finding a prospective nuisance or in fashioning relief; (4) whether the courts erred in failing to defer to, or to otherwise weight, the role of the IEPA, the USEPA, and the ISGS; (5) whether the courts erred in finding that plaintiffs have no adequate remedy at law; (6) whether the courts erred in ordering a mandatory injunction; and, finally, (7) whether the courts' decisions constituted a taking of property without due process of law.

We conclude that the evidence in this case sufficiently establishes by a preponderance of the evidence that the chemical-waste-disposal site is a nuisance both presently and prospectively. . . .

We have reviewed the extensive record compiled in this case. While it is true that the defendant vigorously challenged the evidence concerning an explosive interaction, permeability, and infiltration and migration due to subsidence, the defendant has not overcome the natural and logical conclusions which could be drawn from the evidence. Findings of fact made by the trial court will not be set aside unless they are contrary to the manifest weight of the evidence. . . .

Moreover, the trial court did engage in a balancing process. . . . The Court understands as does counsel that there is a need for disposal of industrial hazardous wastes. However, where disposal of wastes creates a nuisance said disposal site may be closed through legal action. Whether or not a business is useful or necessary or whether or not it contributes to the welfare and/or prosperity of the community are elements to be considered in a serious manner but said elements are not determinative as to whether or not the operation is a nuisance. The importance of an industry to the wealth and prosperity of an area does not as a matter of law give to it rights superior to the primary or natural rights of citizens who live nearby. However, such matters may be considered and have been in this case. . . .

The defendant's next contention is that the courts below were in error when they failed to require a showing of a substantial risk of certain and extreme future harm before enjoining operation of the defendant's site. We deem it necessary to explain that a prospective nuisance is a fit candidate for injunctive relief. Prosser states: "Both public and private nuisances require some substantial interference with the interest involved. Since nuisance is a common subject of equity jurisdiction, the damage against which an injunction is asked is often merely threatened or potential; but even in such cases, there must be at least a threat of a substantial invasion of the plaintiff's interests." (Prosser, Torts §87, at 577 (4th ed. 1971).) The defendant does not dispute this proposition; it does, however, argue that the trial court did not follow the proper standard for determining when a prospective nuisance may be enjoined. The defendant argues that the proper standard to be used is that an injunction is proper only if there is a "dangerous probability" that the threatened or potential injury will occur. (See Restatement 2d of Torts §933(1), at 561, comment b (1979).) The defendant further argues that the appellate court looked only at the potential consequences of not enjoining the operation of the site as a nuisance and not at the likelihood of whether harm would occur. . . .

C. Remedies in Environmental Litigation

In this case there can be no doubt but that it is highly probable that the chemical-waste-disposal site will bring about a substantial injury. Without again reviewing the extensive evidence adduced at trial, we think it is sufficiently clear that it is highly probable that the instant site will constitute a public nuisance if, through either an explosive interaction, migration, subsidence, or the "bathtub effect," the highly toxic chemical wastes deposited at the site escape and contaminate the air, water, or ground around the site. That such an event will occur was positively attested to by several expert witnesses. A court does not have to wait for it to happen before it can enjoin such a result. Additionally, the fact is that the condition of a nuisance is already present at the site due to the location of the site and the manner in which it has been operated. Thus, it is only the damage which is prospective. Under these circumstances, if a court can prevent any damage from occurring, it should do so. . . .

Therefore, we conclude that in fashioning relief in this case the trial court did balance relative hardship to be caused to the plaintiffs and defendant, and did fashion reasonable relief when it ordered the exhumation of all material from the site and the reclamation of the surrounding area. The instant site is akin to Mr. Justice Sutherland's observation that "Nuisance may be merely a right thing in a wrong place — like a pig in the parlor instead of the barnyard." *Village of Euclid v. Ambler Realty Co.*, 272 U.S. 365, 388 (1926).

We are also cognizant of amicus USEPA's suggestion in its brief and affidavits filed with the appellate court which urge that we remand to the circuit court so that alternatives to closure of the site and exhumation of the waste materials may be considered. The USEPA states: "Heavy equipment may damage drums, releasing wastes and possibly causing gaseous emissions, fires, and explosions. Repackaging and transporting damaged drums also risks releasing wastes. Workers performing the exhumation face dangers from contact with or inhalation of wastes; these risks cannot be completely eliminated with protective clothing and breathing apparatus. Nearby residents may also be endangered." It is ironic that the host of horribles mentioned by the USEPA in support of keeping the site open includes some of the same hazards which the plaintiffs have raised as reasons in favor of closing the site. . . .

Accordingly, for all the reasons stated, the judgments of the circuit and appellate courts are affirmed and the cause is remanded to the circuit court to enable it to retain jurisdiction to supervise the enforcement of its order. Affirmed and remanded.

RYAN, J., concurring. While I agree with both the result reached by the majority and the reasoning employed supporting the opinion, I wish to add a brief comment. . . . Any injunction is, by its very nature, the product of a court's balancing of competing interests, with a result equitably obtained. Prosser, in discussing the law of nuisance . . . states: "If the possibility [of harm] is merely uncertain or contingent [the plaintiff] may be left to his remedy after the nuisance has occurred." Prosser, Torts §90, at 603 (4th ed. 1971).

Prosser thus recognizes that there are cases in which the possibility of inflicting harm is slight and where the plaintiff may be left to his remedy at law. However, I believe that there are situations where the harm that is potential is so devastating that equity should afford relief even though the possibility of the harmful result occurring is uncertain or contingent. The Restatement's position applicable to preventative injunctive relief in general is that "the more serious the impending harm, the less justification there is for taking the chances that are involved in pronouncing the harm too remote." Restatement (2d) of Torts §933, at 561, comment b (1979). If the harm that may result is severe, a lesser possibility of it occurring should be required to support injunctive relief. Conversely, if the potential harm is less severe, a greater possibility that it will happen should be required. Also, in the balancing of competing interests, a court may find a situation where the potential harm is such that a plaintiff will be left to his remedy at law if the possibility of it occurring is slight. This balancing test allows the court to consider a wider range of factors and avoids the anomalous result possible under a more restrictive alternative where a person engaged in an ultrahazardous activity with potentially catastrophic results would be allowed to continue until he has driven an entire community to the brink of certain disaster. A court of equity need not wait so long to provide relief.

Although the "dangerous probability" test has certainly been met in this case, I would be willing to enjoin the activity on a showing of probability of occurrence substantially less than that which the facts presented to this court reveal, due to the extremely hazardous nature of the chemicals being dumped and the potentially catastrophic results.

COMMENTARY & QUESTIONS

1. Balancing equities in *Wilsonville* as compared to *Boomer*. Both cases apply the contemporary approach to injunctions in environmental tort cases, balancing the equities. What are the salient factual similarities of the two cases? Both involve siting of a facility in a rural area that has low land values, relatively few close neighbors, and proximity to relevant markets for the product or service that the facility provides. These siting choices are not irrational from the project proponents' point of view, nor are they antisocial from a more general societal point of view. Neither use is appropriate in a congested urban setting, both uses are carried out in furtherance of important functions in modern society. What are their dissimilarities? The *Boomer* plaintiffs are a small group of private individuals. The *Wilsonville* plaintiffs are government entities. Does that explain the difference in relief? Does it seem odd that the *Boomer* court felt itself debarred from considering what might be appropriate regulation of the plant because that is properly a job for expert agencies, and the *Wilsonville* court was quite willing to substitute its assessment of what constitutes the appropriate level of risk from a regulated facility for that of the experts? Looking at the cases as litigated, there is an obvious difference in what evidence was tendered by plaintiffs and credited by the court on the issues that might affect the balance of the equities. In *Boomer*, the risks of continued operation are minimized by the absence of any health effects claimed by the plaintiffs and the refusal of the court to attempt to weigh potentially widespread harms to public health from fine particulate pollution as part of the balance. In *Wilsonville*, if believed, the plaintiffs' experts painted a picture that placed all 600 residents of the village at significant risk of exposure to extremely hazardous wastes and the region's watercourses and aquifers at risk of contamination by those same chemicals. The case involves judicial equitable discretion. Is there only one type of balancing being performed? Consider the defendant's seven allegations of error and see Plater, Statutory Violations and Equitable Discretion, 70 Cal. L. Rev. 524 (1982) (excerpts of which appear later in this chapter, describing three "balances"—threshold assessment of prerequisites for equitable relief, choice among possible course of conduct, and tailoring aspects of remedy).

2. Local politics, community involvement, and environmental risk management. It is easy to understand that siting a hazardous waste disposal facility is going to be unpopular. Many wry acronyms make the point: NIMBY (not in my back yard), LULU (locally unwanted land use), and BANANA (build absolutely nothing anywhere near anyone). SCA Services apparently had gone a step further in angering the local Wilsonville population. At the start, the citizens and officials of Wilsonville claimed they had been told that no hazardous wastes would be disposed of in their village and that the landfill would be made into a park. The citizenry was so outraged by the discovery that wastes were toxic that before the case came to trial armed vigilante groups had blockaded the main streets of the village against waste transport vehicles. The Illinois courts, beginning with the locally elected Circuit Court judge of Macoupin County, assuaged this citizen outrage by ordering the site closed, thoroughly cleaned up (its wastes and contaminated soil to be removed and shipped elsewhere, back to St. Louis as it turned out), and restored.

3. Expert testimony weighed by generalist (non-expert), elected judges. In this litigation seeking equitable relief, the expert testimony of horrific local consequences that might ensue at the SCA disposal site are being evaluated by a non-scientist judge who is answerable in election to the citizens of the rural county that includes Wilsonville. Adding to the pressure on that judge is the presumed credibility and gravitas given to the plaintiffs' case by the presence of the state's Attorney General on the plaintiffs' side. In this era, shortly after the publicity given to hazardous waste debacles like Love Canal, New York and nearby Times Beach, Missouri, would it be a surprise to find that the Attorney General was up for reelection and was campaigning as an environmental champion?

4. There is no "I" in "team," but there is a lot of "junk" in plaintiffs' "science." A careful review offers some reasons to be skeptical of that expert testimony. Dr. Zahalsky's explosive prediction was quite nebulous ("unknown date of occurrence, magnitude, and duration . . . [and resulting from] unknown . . . interactions") and took no account of the clay[32] that was used to seal in wastes after their deposit. Dr. Augenbaugh has frequently been an expert witness. His testimony has been refused in other cases,[33] and his methodology here for proving subsidence and his primitive "bathtub effect" test to demonstrate migration show only that material might move laterally on a fault a short distance. His methodology takes no account of the loess and glacial till that underlie the site that would severely limit migration. His prediction of an "artesian" effect requires groundwater that is under pressure, created by having parts of the same aquifer located at a higher elevation—the regional topography negates that possibility. Even the potentially dangerous fact that the site was more permeable than "advertised" by defendant's original studies as a means of showing a substantial risk of migration of the wastes did not hold up under scrutiny. In the evidence, the most permeable reading was one of several made by Dr. Williams, 7×10^{-6} cm/sec., which calculates out to a rate that allows the waste to travel just over 2 meters per year. Is this site a ticking time bomb or a LULU? Do you expect a generalist judge to be able to know the difference in the face of conflicting expert testimony? If this note was able to raise questions about the plaintiffs' case, was the problem at trial at least in part defendant's poor job of "educating" the judge?

5. The contemporary standards for judicial control over expert testimony. Environmental cases increasingly feature expert testimony. In the *Mangan* case excerpted earlier in this chapter, for example, even in the motion stages there had been several motions by both plaintiffs and defendants seeking to disqualify the other side's experts. Although it has long been a topic of concern, efforts to control the use of questionable expert testimony is now seen as an important judicial function. In the American federal system, the states are not required to follow the lead of the federal courts. In the federal courts, the modern doctrine on the issue was announced in a series of U.S. Supreme Court decisions initiated by *Daubert. v. Merrill Dow Pharm., Inc.*, 509 U.S. 579 (1993) and more fully explicated in later

---

32. The British Geological Survey puts the permeability (also called "hydraulic conductivity") of clay as ranging between 5×10^{-7} meters/day and 1×10^{-3} meters per day. The type of clays best suited for liners, montmonillinite clays, are less permeable still, at 1×10^{-9} meters/day. See http://nora.nerc.ac.uk/7457/1/CR06160N.pdf.

33. See *Berry v. Armstrong Rubber Co.*, 989 F.2d 822 (5th Cir. 1993).

cases.³⁴ Congress, in 2011, wrote the crux of the *Daubert* doctrine directly into the Federal Rules of Evidence. Some states follow *Daubert* or variations on its test and most others use a test that requires the scientific testimony to be "generally accepted" in the relevant scientific community as the standard for admissibility.

**Federal Rules of Evidence:
Rule 702. Testimony By Expert Witnesses**

A witness who is qualified as an expert by knowledge, skill, experience, training, or education may testify in the form of an opinion or otherwise if:
    (a) The expert's scientific, technical, or other specialized knowledge will help the trier of fact to understand the evidence or to determine a fact in issue;
    (b) The testimony is based on sufficient facts or data;
    (c) The testimony is the product of reliable principles and methods; and
    (d) The expert has reliably applied the principles and methods to the facts of the case.

---

6. Judicial injunctions as risk management. By issuing an injunction against a "prospective" nuisance, the court put itself squarely in the position as the ultimate arbiter of the risks involved and the measures to be taken in response. Should the courts have given more credence to U.S. EPA's suggestion that exhumation and removal would pose a greater risk of explosion and escape of the hazardous substances than "containing" the site (e.g., laying a cement cap over the site to prevent further infiltration, building an underground slurry wall around the site with a leachate monitoring system, and installing "pump-and-treat" technology if toxic leaching into the groundwater ever did occur)? Should the courts have considered the comparative economic costs of both alternatives? In fact, it took one year and cost $5 million—in 1981 dollars—to perform the court-ordered remediation. What about the risks of transporting the wastes off-site and depositing them in another landfill that might pose even greater risks than the Wilsonville site due to its proximity to more concentrated populations (that just happen to be in another political jurisdiction)? The Resource Conservation and Recovery Act (RCRA) is the federal law requiring that hazardous waste landfills be upgraded in order to protect the environment. It had been enacted in 1976 but had not yet been fully implemented.³⁵ To what extent are common law courts capable of determining the overall public interest in the context of lawsuits between specific litigants? The Macoupin County Circuit Court and the Illinois Supreme Court in *Wilsonville* did not shy away from the challenge.

7. Private parties as risk promoters and risk managers. The underlying idea and impetus to site the toxic disposal facility in Wilsonville came from SCA Services. In an earlier, less regulation-bound era, SCA's private decision regarding the facility might have been dispositive, in the sense that no governmental pre-approval would have been needed. What factors motivated SCA's decision to select the Wilsonville site as a repository for wastes generated primarily in the nearby St. Louis metropolitan area? Most obvious are economic factors, such as low rural land costs and acceptable transportation costs based on reasonable

---

34. See *General Electric Co. v. Joiner*, 522 U.S. 136 (1997) and *Kumho Tire Co. v. Carmichael*, 526 U.S. 137 (1999).
35. RCRA is studied in greater detail in Chapter 17.

C. Remedies in Environmental Litigation

proximity. Absent tort liability, is there any reason to believe that project proponents will consider the costs they impose on nearby communities?

8. Administrative agencies as risk managers. Are the factors that motivate risk promoters, neighbors of the facility, and courts the same factors that ought to be considered by the IEPA and USEPA in their roles as hazardous waste risk managers? Presumably, expert administrators should be better risk managers than self-interested project proponents, outraged litigants, or inexpert judges and juries. What, then, explains the arguably lackluster performance of the state and federal agencies in the *Wilsonville* case that allowed the facility to be sited with so little leachate monitoring over an abandoned mine shaft? The ongoing comfort level of the expert agencies with the site and its continued operations, seen in the continuing permits, make it incontrovertible that the agencies were aware of the operations at the Wilsonville site and did not believe that they posed undue risk. Did the agencies, perhaps, have a better understanding of the risks of escape than the courts involved?

9. Uncertainty. This is a case of "prospective" nuisance that involves uncertainty about the course of future events. Frequently, environmental cases and risk managers must assess present actions predicated on predictions of future events under conditions of pervasive scientific uncertainty. That uncertainty makes the assessment and management of risk exceptionally difficult. Are there systematic strategies that should be invoked in cases of scientific uncertainty? Is the suggestion of Talbot Page (excerpted in Chapter 1) that advocates avoidance of non-conventional risks really workable? Or should it be read more pragmatically as a call for those risks to be addressed with increased caution?

10. *Wilsonville* as environmental injustice. Apart from the previously identified economic motivation facing SCA Services, are there other factors that might have influenced a decision to site a hazardous waste landfill at this location? Is this a case of environmental injustice? Wilsonville, a poor rural community whose residents included many unemployed ex-miners, had little political leverage compared to that of defendant, its clients (some of whom were highly capitalized hazardous waste generators), and state and federal agencies. Minority status is not an issue in the case. According to the 2000 census, over 98% of Wilsonville's residents are white. Decisions regarding siting are subjected at times to rigorous state hazardous waste disposal facility siting statutes. These are considered in Chapter 9.

The following excerpt delves into the role of equitable discretion and the several balances a court strikes in determining when injunctive relief will issue. It draws on concepts relevant to *Boomer* and *Wilsonville*, and also matters that arose in the famous Snail Darter case that appears in Chapter 10, *TVA v. Hill*, 437 U.S. 153 (1978), in which Professor Plater was counsel to the plaintiff, Hiram Hill.

Plater, Statutory Violations and Equitable Discretion
70 California Law Review 524, 533-544, 545-546 (1982)

The exercise of equitable jurisdiction, particularly the availability of injunctions, has increased over the years. The anachronistic requirement of a property interest in order to invoke equity has been scrapped of necessity, and other impediments have been removed. Despite regular protestations to the contrary, the status of the injunction has become a common, widely used judicial remedy precisely because of its ability to fine-tune the requirements of private conduct in a complex, modern society. Its development parallels the expansion of cases [in environmental law and] in civil rights and other constitutional areas, where damage remedies are insufficient or miss the point. . . .

When equity's application in traditional common law cases is subjected to careful analysis, some basic clarifications emerge. Analytically, it can be argued that the umbrella terms "balancing the equities" and "equitable discretion" obscure what are really three separate areas of balancing, three different functions fulfilled by three different types of equitable relativism. The three areas are:

1. *Threshold balancing*, based in both law and equity, tests whether plaintiffs can maintain their actions. This stage includes questions of laches, clean hands, other estoppels, the lack of an adequate remedy at law, proof of irreparable harm, and similar issues.
2. *Determination of contending conducts* ascertains which conduct will be permitted to continue and which will be subordinated. It often involves the question of abatement, a separate issue from the question of liability for past injuries to protected interests.
3. *Discretion in fashioning remedies* involves a process of tailoring remedies to implement the second stage determination of contending conducts.

Consider, for example, the relatively simple field of private nuisance torts where equity has traditionally played an active role. The classic *Ducktown Sulphur* case demonstrates all three of equity's distinctly different roles. In that turn-of-the-century case, 83 S.W. 658 (Tenn. 1904), the court had to deal with an early example of an environmental tradeoff. The smelting industry was getting underway in the foothills of southeastern Tennessee and northern Georgia. It was likely to provide sizable revenues for the entrepreneurs of Atlanta and Chattanooga, jobs for local residents, and copper and other materials for the nation's industrial economy. The copper ore was mined in nearby hills, then smelted in large open-air piles layered with firewood and coal. This firing process, however, produced acidic "sulphurectic" air emissions that eventually turned nearly a hundred square miles of hills into a remarkably stark, denuded desert, its topsoil slowly washing away down sterile, chemical-laden streams. The plaintiffs were farmers whose fields and orchards began to die as the smelting got underway.

The Tennessee high court held that the smelting was a continuing private nuisance, but after long and careful deliberation allowed the defendant industries to continue operations despite their drastic impact upon the plaintiffs' land and livelihood. The court required only that the mills compensate the plaintiffs for their losses. In common parlance, it awarded legal compensatory damages but denied any injunctive remedy, based on a balancing of equities. The *Ducktown* court certainly balanced the equities. Analytically, however, it did so not once but thrice:

Threshold Balancing. The first type of balancing addresses threshold questions which plaintiffs must survive if a cause of action is to be heard. Some issues appear in the guise of affirmative legal defenses: laches and coming to the nuisance, for example, are legal defenses grounded in principles of equitable estoppel. Other issues—clean hands, additional estoppel principles, proof of irreparable harm, and the inadequacy of legal remedies—are more specifically equitable, brought to bear only where the plaintiff seeks equitable remedies. Each of these threshold issues involves comparisons and balances that are part of the longstanding discretionary processes of equity. The *Ducktown* court made several such determinations, excluding some plaintiffs on laches grounds as to certain defendants, confirming their rights to sue as to others, and noting injuries to land that analytically made equitable remedies potentially available on grounds of irreparability.

C. Remedies in Environmental Litigation

The Determination of Contending Conducts. After plaintiffs survive equity's threshold gauntlet, nonstatutory litigation moves to the application of rules of conduct. The major discretionary function of the equity court at this second stage is the determination of whether the defendant's conduct will be permitted to continue. To reach this abatement determination, however, courts must first consider issues of liability. . . .

The initial question is whether defendants are liable at all, whether their conduct is "illegal" under the common law. . . . Plaintiffs in private nuisance cases and in other common law areas seek equitable remedies — particularly injunctions — as well as damages. In such cases, once tort liability is found, the court turns to the different question of whether defendant's conduct will be abated. . . .

The *Ducktown* abatement question focused on the desirability and consequences of the competing forms of conduct, considering relative hardship between the parties, the balance of comparative social utility between the two competing conducts, and the public interest (which usually amounts to the same thing). The court declared:

> A judgment for damages in this class of cases is a matter of absolute right, where injury is shown. A decree for an injunction is a matter of sound legal discretion, to be granted or withheld as that discretion shall dictate, after a full and careful considerations of every element appertaining to the injury.

Citing a series of equity cases in which the utility of defendant's enterprises weighed against injunctions, the court's "careful consideration" began with a question that virtually answered itself:

> Shall the complainants be granted, by way of damages, the full measure of relief to which their injuries entitle them or shall we go further, and grant their request to blot out two great mining and manufacturing enterprises, destroy half of the taxable values of a county, and drive more than 10,000 people from their homes?

The tort debts owed by one party to the other might be decided by uniformly applicable substantive tort principles, but questions of the life and death of farms and smelting plants — of who must stop and who may go on — were left to the flexible hands and heart of equity. In short, courts have used equity to define and exercise a separate judicial role, grounded upon a rational discretion and working beyond the rigid rules of the law.

Tailoring the Remedies. . . . At this point in a lawsuit, law and equity have determined all the substantive issues, and only the equitable function of implementation remains. If the court had decided in the second stage balance that defendant's conduct may continue, the award of legal damages for past injuries ends the question of remedy. In that situation no equitable remedy is necessary unless required to enforce payment of damages.

When the court determines that defendant's conduct may not continue, on the other hand, a full array of equitable options exists. If defendants agree to abate their activity voluntarily, the court has the option of not issuing any formal equitable remedy at all. This point . . . is taken for granted in the common law setting: an injunction need not issue if the court finds that the abatement decision will be implemented without it, but will usually issue where there is any doubt on the matter. Between these two extremes lies the declaratory judgment, a remedy slightly more formal and more assertive than the no-injunction option but similarly unenforceable through contempt proceedings. Yet in the case of good faith defendants, a declaratory judgment or less may be all that is necessary to implement the court's abatement decision.

The strength and flexibility of injunctions, however, makes them attractive as the remedy of choice in many cases. Equity courts shape injunctions in multifarious forms: injunctions to halt an enterprise completely, to shut down a particular component activity, to scale down overall activity by a certain percentage, to halt a specific offensive effect, to abate after a lapse of a specific term if certain performance standards are not achieved—these are but a few. Injunctions also serve different tactical ends. They can be wielded to drag a rambunctiously recalcitrant defendant into compliance, to tighten the reins on slipshod defendants whose compliance efforts may be sloppy, or merely to add a final reassuring level of certainty to a good faith defendant's compliance. In short, "the plastic remedies of the chancery are molded to the needs of justice."

COMMENTARY & QUESTIONS

1. A range of equitable remedies. When an injunction commands a halt to a polluting activity, it acts like a decisive statutory prohibition. Injunctions decree whatever a court chooses to prescribe, and their prescriptive capabilities are given extra credibility by the criminal contempt-of-court penalties they carry with them. More subtle equitable orders are possible, for example:

- decrees encouraging technological innovation, like Judge Jasen's proposed order in *Boomer*, postponing shutdowns for a set term, to be effective thereafter unless clean technology can be applied;
- decrees ordering, say, a 30% cutback in production until cleaner technology is achieved;
- decrees restricting defendant's activity during times when weather conditions are particularly likely to cause pollution damage;
- decrees requiring ongoing corporate monitoring of offsite pollution;
- decrees requiring that defendants actively clean up their externalized pollution;
- decrees ordering installation of particular specified control technology;
- decrees ordering restitution of profits gained from avoidance of pollution controls;
- decrees requiring periodic reporting to the court;
- decrees ordering "restoration" of trees, soil, personal property, and natural resources;
- appointment of equitable trial masters under Fed. R. Civ. P. 53 for managing complex factual and procedural issues prior to judgment;
- appointment of post-decree monitors to oversee defendant's compliance with court orders, backed by subpoena powers and reporting to the courts;[36]
- environmental receiverships, so that where defendant firms can't or won't comply with environmental requirements, courts will take over and run them through appointed equitable receiverships; and
- other creative applications of this remarkable judicial power.

Courts have not shied away from taking an activist role in crafting remedies. In *Martin v. Reynolds Metals Co.*, 342 P.2d 790 (Ore. 1959), a pre-Clean Air Act aluminum factory trespass case, the court prescribed precisely which pollution control devices defendants had to install and established strict schedules for the defendants to follow. Are courts well-suited to making judgments about the comparative efficacy and appropriateness of a particular pollution control system?

---

36. See Feldman, Post-Decree Judicial Agents in Environmental Litigation, 18 B.C. Envtl. Aff. L. Rev. 809 (1991). The classic *Ducktown* case had a court-appointed monitor remedy to police emissions limits, and the monitor was guaranteed full access to defendant's operations. See *Tennessee Copper*, 237 U.S. at 478, and 240 U.S. 650.

C. Remedies in Environmental Litigation

2. The balance of equities. The *Boomer* case is perhaps most famous for its rejection of the traditional New York common law rule that an injunction would routinely be issued to shut down a continuing nuisance, in favor of the more flexible balancing the equities doctrine. Was the court undercutting environmental protection and sound policy when it reversed the automatic rule? In legal history terms, would you be surprised to find that for 50 years after the tough *Whalen* rule shut down a paper mill, the tendency of trial courts in New York had been to find no nuisance at all, knowing that any finding of nuisance liability would automatically trigger a complete shutdown of industrial operations?

A fundamental canon of equity law is that an equitable decree must do equity. That means it must be sensitive to public as well as private consequences of proposed restrictions. Under the *Ducktown* principle, it was surely fitting and relevant that the *Boomer* court considered public interests weighing in favor of continued plant operation. But which items were allowed into the balance of equities in *Boomer*? Do they appear to include all relevant information for a full-scale balancing? The court weighed items of both public and private concern affirmatively in favor of the defendant, against the proposed injunction. What did it weigh in favor of the injunction for plaintiffs? A more evenhanded approach might have allowed plaintiffs to present evidence of the cement plant's adverse impacts on the community at large. Why does the majority explicitly remove public health issues from its consideration? In light of the public interest element in equitable balancing, which he himself applied in favor of the defendant, doesn't Justice Bergan's refusal to intrude "broad public objectives" into a simple suit between "individual property owners and a single cement plant" ring hollow?

3. Restoration remedies.[37] An innovative prospect for achieving more comprehensive remedies in the environmental protection field is the concept of restoration damages. Historical, ecological, and environmental justice values are often not readily accountable in market terms. Equitable restoration orders tend to rehabilitate natural values that would be excluded from the usual monetary interests balanced in legal actions. Consider the effect of an order requiring Allied to cleanse the polluted sediments of the James River and Chesapeake Bay or Atlantic Cement to reclaim its cement dust. Restoration provides a compelling deterrent in a variety of environmental settings, such as the killing of fish in a river, the wrongful partial demolition of a historic building lacking market value, and so on. In the Colorado *Escamilla* case, a restoration order required a chemical company to remediate contaminated soils and vegetation without regard to the fact that the low-income community's property values did not justify the cost.[38] Restoration cost-based damages are also possible. The Restatement (Second) of Torts §929(1)(a) prescribes, as to measure of damages that for harm to land resulting from a past invasion, "damages include compensation for (a) the difference between the value of the land before the harm and the value after the harm, *or at plaintiff's election in an appropriate case, the cost of restoration that has been or may be reasonably incurred.*" What should be considered in deeming restoration damages "appropriate" in a particular case? For an example where a court refused restoration damages when the values being restored were of minimal value in comparison to the cost, see Ewell v. Petro Processors, 364 So. 2d 604, 608 (La. Ct. App. 1978).

---

37. Further text on restoration damages is available on the coursebook website.
38. See *Escamilla v. Asarco, Inc.*, No. 91 CV 5716 (D.C. Denver, Colo., Apr. 23, 1993); Verdiccio, Environmental Restoration Orders, 12 B.C. Envtl. Aff. L. Rev. 171 (1985); Cox, Reforming the Law Applicable to the Award of Restoration Damages as a Remedy for Environmental Torts, 20 Pace Envtl. L. Rev. 777 (2003) (arguing for broader availability of such awards coupled with application of equitable trust principles that could ensure awards are used for restoration and not mere enrichment of plaintiffs).

4. Restoration and other injunctive relief as legalized extortion. Echoing the judge's suspicions in the *Ewell* case, the potential for extortionate injunctions is a topic increasingly recognized by legal scholars. By asking for restoration injunctions or other remedies that would impose large costs on the defendant, plaintiffs may be seeking to set up an extortionate bargaining position for settlement negotiations. In their article "Threatening Inefficient Performance of Injunctions and Contracts," Ian Ayres and Kristin Madison draw attention to this problem, arguing that it produces inefficiency in the form of negotiation costs, failures to reach a bargain, and inefficient ex ante actions. The article considers legal reforms that could undercut extortionate injunction threats by giving defendants two options: an option to make any injunctive relief inalienable and an option to commit to paying higher damages. See Ayres & Madison, Threatening Inefficient Performance of Injunctions and Contracts, 148 U. Pa. L. Rev. 45 (1999). See also, Cox, Reforming the Law Applicable to the Award of Restoration Damages as a Remedy for Environmental Torts, 20 Pace Envtl. L. Rev. 777 (2003) (arguing for broader availability of such awards coupled with application of equitable trust principles that could ensure awards are used for restoration and not mere enrichment of plaintiffs).

2. Damages

a. Compensatory Damage Remedies—Past Damages and Permanent Damages[39]

The typical tort plaintiff seeks an award of compensatory damages for past injuries, whether or not an injunction is also being sought. Unlike injunctive relief, compensatory damages follow automatically upon a finding of defendant's liability. Compensatory damages can include sums awarded for all forms of property damage, injuries to the plaintiff's health, loss of consortium, and so on.

In *Boomer*, note that the remedy discussion dealt only with the contested permanent damages. The defendant acquiesced to paying all private nuisance damages awarded for past harms not based on decline in market value. Damages included injury to stored automobiles and other personal property, and, as to real property, the "loss of rental value or loss of usable value," averaging $60 per plaintiff per month. The decrease in rental value attempts to gauge the burden imposed by pollution upon the lives of the plaintiffs, assuming that the amount of rent that people would be willing to pay adequately captures the sum total of life-quality values involved.

The elements of damage in the typical personal injury lawsuit are made up of two broad categories: (1) compensation for monetary losses such as lost wages, medical expenses, and automobile repair costs; and (2) compensation for intangibles, especially pain and suffering, but also anxiety and emotional trauma. The *Boomer* damages were limited to the first category. Even though no claim for personal injuries was made, ruling out a typical claim to compensatory damages for pain and suffering accompanying personal injuries, that does not rule out the possibility that the Boomers suffered intangible elements of damage. What if Oscar and June Boomer had long been planning on this farm as their idyllic retreat from the sights and sounds of industrialized America? A number of cases have utilized claims for "hedonic damages" in attempting to seek recoveries for intangible damages associated with loss of enjoyment of various aspects of life, such as a destroyed beautiful view. See Kuiper, The Courts, *Daubert*, and Willingness to Pay: The Doubtful Future of Hedonic

---

39. Permanent damages have already been covered at length in relation to the *Boomer* case.

C. Remedies in Environmental Litigation

Damages Testimony Under the Federal Rules of Evidence, 1996 Ill. L. Rev. 1197, 1204-1206. As the title of that article suggests, the social science methods used in proving hedonic damages are subject to challenge as not being based on a sufficiently grounded scientific methodology.

b. Punitive Damages — Basic Doctrines

Punitive damages are extraordinary in a variety of ways. As seen thus far, before a plaintiff can even recover any damages, the plaintiff must carry the burden of proof on all of the elements of a cause of action. Even when these barriers are scaled, all that is awarded is compensation designed to restore the status quo before the defendants' acts injured the plaintiffs.

Punitive damages are imposed only in cases of egregious conduct by the defendant. When available, they add a new dimension to damage remedies, serving functions quite different from compensation — retributive punishment and enhanced deterrence. In almost all U.S. jurisdictions, punitive damages may exceed the amount of compensatory damages several times over. These awards punish extraordinary disregard for others, even in cases where fault is not an element of the tort. The 40 or so states permitting awards of punitive damages typically prescribe them for cases where the defendant's conduct was found to be "willful," "wanton," "malicious," or "reckless." Because it is the wrongful character of defendant's conduct that is the issue, historically there needed to be no proportionality between the amount of punitive damages and the actual harm inflicted. Modern cases have restricted the size of punitive damage awards on federal constitutional due process grounds.

Punitive damages also may serve other purposes, including camouflaged compensation. To some environmental attorneys, punitive awards are readily justifiable, not only to force defendants to confront the seriousness of environmental concerns, but more practically as a means of capturing and internalizing some of the unrecovered tangible costs, such as ecological injuries to natural resources and property damages to persons downwind for whom injuries were real but insufficient to justify litigation. In the latter cases, punitives are forms of extended compensation for externalities; at other times, punitives can serve as a source from which a plaintiff can recoup litigation costs that are not usually recoverable absent an express statutory authorization. Further, punitive awards serve as a bounty incentive for private citizen enforcement of environmental standards, acknowledging that public officials are often unable (or unwilling) to do so. Injured plaintiffs may also be especially deserving, having suffered disproportionately, but in ways that are not included in the calculation of compensatory damages.

Punitive damages raise serious concerns because of the absence of standards for quantification, the potential for duplication in multiple lawsuits, and the lack of a consistent or direct nexus to the externalities imposed by the defendants.

Branch v. Western Petroleum, Inc.
657 P.2d 267 (Utah 1982)

[After discussing strict liability in the opinion excerpted earlier in this chapter, the court went on to discuss punitive damages for the oil company's failure to protect groundwater.]

Western's final contention on its appeal challenges the award of punitive damages. It argues that punitive damages are appropriate only when willful and malicious conduct is shown and that the court erred in including the phrase "reckless indifference and disregard" in its instruction on punitive damages. However, punitive damages may be awarded when one acts with reckless indifference and disregard of the law and his fellow citizens:

> This presumed malice or malice in law does not consist of personal hate or ill will of one person towards another but rather refers to that state of mind which is reckless of law and of the legal rights of the citizen in a person's conduct toward that citizen. . . . In such cases malice in law will be implied from unjustifiable conduct which causes the injury complained of or from a wrongful act intentionally done without cause or excuse. *Terry v. Zions Coop.*, 605 P.2d 314, 327 (Utah 1979).

The evidence in this case meets that standard. Western discharged the waste water into the disposal pit intending that it seep into and percolate through the soil. Thus, the pollution of the percolating waters was willful and carried out in disregard of the rights of the Branches. Moreover, Western compounded the Branches' problems by its trespass on their land, the spraying of waste water over their land and the failure to comply with state law. In addition, Western continued its dumping activities even after notice of the pollution of the diligence well. The punitive damage award was adequately supported by evidence of reckless indifference toward, and disregard of, the Branches' rights.

Furthermore, there is no merit to Western's contention that the award of punitive damages was excessive and influenced by passion or prejudice rather than reason. The jury was properly instructed that the purpose of exemplary damages is to deter defendant and others from engaging in similar conduct. . . .

COMMENTARY & QUESTIONS

1. Do all intentional torts deserve punitive damages? Could Oscar Boomer have gotten punitive damages against Atlantic Cement? *Boomer* proved that the cement dust pollution was an intentional tort; so wasn't it "willful," justifying punitives? In *McElwain v. Georgia Pacific Corp.*, a pulp mill air pollution case, the court majority allowed punitive damages in a case very much like *Boomer*:

> The intentional disregard of the interest of another is the equivalent of legal malice, and justifies punitive damages for trespass. Where there is proof of an intentional, unjustifiable infliction of harm with deliberate disregard of the social consequences, the question of award of punitive damages is for the jury.
>
> It is abundantly clear from the record that defendant knew when it decided to construct its [paper] mill in Toledo, that there was danger, if not a probability, that the mill would cause damage to adjoining property. . . . The jury could have found that during the period involved in this action the defendant had not done everything reasonably possible to eliminate or minimize the damage to adjoining properties by its mill. 421 P.2d 957, 958 (Or. 1966).

The dissenting justice in *McElwain* strongly disagreed, arguing that actual malice was a necessary and desirable requirement for award of punitive damages.

As another example of the comparatively short step from intentional environmental tort to willful conduct that will support punitive damages, in the *Borland* trespass case that appeared earlier in this chapter the court said, "If the [trespassory] intrusion is direct, then, under our present law, actual damages need not be shown; nominal damages may be awarded and this will support punitive damages." Do *McElwain* and *Borland* really turn those garden-variety intentional torts cases into appropriate cases for punitive damages? What are the dictates of sound remedial policy? In light of those precedents, shouldn't plaintiffs in all environmental intentional tort cases include a count seeking punitive

C. Remedies in Environmental Litigation

damages as, if nothing more, a strong card to be played in settlement negotiations if the punitive damages claim survives the summary judgment stage?

2. Products liability, exposure injuries, and standards for punitive damages. Toxic torts are studied in greater detail in the next chapter, but many cases falling in that general realm include claims for punitive damages for exposure to defendants' products or the environmental contamination they cause. What kind of manufacturer conduct would justify the award of punitive damages? One court, relying on a commentator, stated, "Manufacturer misconduct [justifying punitive damages has been typed] into five categories: (1) fraudulent-type, affirmative conduct designed to mislead the public, (2) knowing violations of safety standards, (3) inadequate testing and quality-control, manufacturing procedures, (4) failure to warn of known dangers, and (5) post-marketing failures to remedy known dangers." *Fischer v. Johns Manville Corp.*, 512 A.2d 466 (N.J. 1968) (citing Owen, Punitive Damages in Products Liability Litigation, 74 Mich. L. Rev. 1257, 1329-1361 (1976)). Analyzing *Branch*, *McElwain*, and factors listed by the *Fischer* court, is the availability of punitive damages restricted to situations where defendants' conduct is extreme and antisocial?

3. Measuring punitives. What is the proper measure of punitive damages? What checks are imposed? In a jury case, the jury instructions explain what constitutes the type of behavior that allows imposing punitive damages and, usually, factors that the jury can take into account in assessing an amount to be awarded. The list of factors varies by jurisdiction, but often includes items such as the reprehensibility of the defendant's conduct and the wealth of the defendant (so that an amount chosen will punish, but not over-punish, the defendant).

Legislated caps on punitives have been increasingly proposed and passed, although at the federal level, Congress has failed to pass several bills containing caps. (See, e.g., 104 H.R. 956, §201(e).) States have been active in the area. See, e.g., Texas S.B. 25 of 1996, capping punitive damages claims at two times economic damages, and also limiting non-economic damages. That legislation further requires a plaintiff to prove fraud or malice by clear and convincing evidence rather than a mere preponderance.

c. Punitive Damage Awards — Constitutional Due Process and Federal Cause of Action Judicial Limitations

The method for calculating punitive damage awards has no obvious benchmark. The twin goals are punishment of socially offensive behavior and deterrence of others from acting with similarly egregious disregard for the safety and welfare of others. Concurrently, the award of punitive damages will help "make plaintiff whole" since in tort cases under the "American Rule" on fees, there is no mechanism that shifts the prevailing plaintiff's attorney's fees to the tortfeasor defendant.

Lacking a benchmark for calculating punitive damages, over time the courts devised narrative standards. Most often, since juries are available and demanded in most tort actions, the case law that summarizes the standard in any given jurisdiction are found either in (1) appellate decisions that rule on the propriety of instructions given to juries or (2) appellate decisions that indicate the standards to be applied when reviewing cases in which punitive damages were awarded in appeals based on claims that the amount was excessive and, adding a federal element, the amount awarded was sufficiently arbitrary that it violated the due process rights of the defendant. Perhaps the leading case arising in that second manner is *Pacific Mutual Life Ins. Co. v. Haslip*, 499 U.S. 1 (1991) in which the U.S. Supreme Court upheld an Alabama punitive damages award against a due process challenge, making note of the clearly articulated basis on which punitive damage awards are reviewed by Alabama's courts. That review expressly relies upon seven criteria:

(1) reasonable relationship between the amount awarded and the harm caused or threatened by defendant's action; (2) reprehensibility, duration, frequency, and consciousness of defendant's conduct; (3) profitability; (4) defendant's financial position; (5) costs of litigation; (6) whether criminal sanctions had been imposed (which mitigate the punitive damage award); and (7) defendant's payment of other civil awards.

The *Haslip* case is also important because even though it upheld the award, in its dicta the Court clearly stated that punitive damages in some cases could violate due process. A crescendo of cases followed,[40] cementing as constitutional not only the use of factors like those in *Haslip*, but also prohibiting a state from imposing "grossly excessive" punishment on tortfeasors. In assessing excessiveness the Court took the step of looking at the ratio of punitive to compensatory damages.[41] Is this apt in environmental cases, where many of the harms cannot be measured by normal compensatory damages? On the ratio issue the Court noted that "[f]ew awards exceeding a single-digit ratio . . . will satisfy due process," and that a ratio of more than 4-to-1 of punitive to compensatory damages may be "close to the line of constitutional impropriety." *State Farm Mut. Auto. Ins. Co. v. Campbell*, 538 U.S. 408, 425 (2003).

The Court has since had the opportunity to consider punitive damages in federal maritime cases, also referred to as admiralty cases. This context is fundamentally different because the Court is not reviewing a state-law based determination against the standards of federal due process, but is instead stating a rule about federal law to be applied by federal courts in cases where punitive damages are awarded. The context was one of the last pieces of the Exxon Valdez oil spill tort litigation in *Exxon Shipping Co. v. Baker*, 554 U.S. 471 (2008).

The Exxon Valdez disaster began on March 24, 1989 when the supertanker *Exxon Valdez* grounded on Bligh Reef off the Alaskan coast, fracturing its hull and spilling millions of gallons of crude oil into Prince William Sound. Exxon settled the claims of the State of Alaska and the U.S. government for environmental damage, with payments totaling less than $1 billion and spent another $2.1 billion in cleanup efforts. Another $300 million was paid in voluntary settlements with some of the region's fishermen, property owners, and other private parties. The unsettled claims went to trial in a consolidated action against Exxon in which the plaintiffs seeking compensatory damages were divided into three classes: commercial fishermen, Native Alaskans, and landowners. Exxon also was able to persuade the court to certify a mandatory class of all plaintiffs seeking punitive damages, a class having more than 32,000 class members. The case was tried in three phases: the first established liability, the second cumulatively awarded slightly more than $500 million dollars to the three categories of plaintiffs, and the third resulted in a $5 billion award of punitive damages.

Appeals followed, and even before reaching the U.S. Supreme Court, the punitive damage award had been cut in half on excessiveness grounds by the Ninth Circuit Court of Appeals. 490 F. 3d 1066 (2007). In the Supreme Court, the award was further reduced by

---

40. These include, *Honda Motors v. Oberg*, 517 U.S. 1219 (1996), *Combustion Eng'g v. Johansen*, 517 U.S. 1217 (1996), *State Farm Mut. Auto. Ins. Co. v. Campbell*, 538 U.S. 408 (2003), and *Phillip Morris USA v. Williams*, 549 U.S. 346 (2007).

41. The Court's logic in this area seems to begin with a phrase penned by Justice Kennedy when he wrote, "It should be presumed a plaintiff has been made whole for his injuries by compensatory damages, so punitive damages should only be awarded if the defendant's culpability, after having paid compensatory damages, is so reprehensible as to warrant the imposition of further sanctions to achieve punishment or deterrence." *State Farm Mut. Auto. Ins. Co. v. Campbell*, 538 U.S. 408, 413 (2003).

C. Remedies in Environmental Litigation

a majority opinion penned by Justice Souter. The key segment of the opinion was devoted to a pseudo-statistical review[42] of the ratio of punitive damages to compensatory damages of prior punitive in prior awards made in judgments of the state and federal courts. Eventually, even though finding almost all states allowed higher maximum ratios and that federal statutory treble damage awards (if one had been applicable) would result in a 2:1 upper bound, the majority adopted a rule applicable in federal maritime cases. The Court stated, "that a 1:1 ratio, which is above the median award [in the studied state and federal cases involving punitive damages], is a fair upper limit in such maritime cases," Using that measure, the Court reduced the punitive damage award by a further 80%.

COMMENTARY & QUESTIONS

1. Punitive damages ratios clash with ecosystem harms. Note how ratio tests like those in *Exxon Mobil* and *State Farm* can have a particularly negative effect in environmental tort cases where defendants may act with egregious disregard for ecological, social, and cultural damage injuries but dollar-value damages measured in terms of cash-register pricing may be quite low. Ecosystem services, for instance, have great economic and ecological values but are not generally subject to any market-pricing compensatory damage awards. A further example: A Michigan defendant intentionally destroyed exotic trees on a neighbor's private arboretum, seeking to pressure the owner to sell the land for development. The defendant demonstrated at trial that the plaintiff's land value had actually been *increased* by

---

42. Exxon mounted an academic attack on punitive damages from the very start. One product of that effort, funded in part by a grant from Exxon, was the work of Harvard Professor W. Kip Viscusi in which he argued that punitive damages should be abolished for corporate risk and environmental cases. Using benefit-cost analysis, Viscusi argued that in these settings punitive damages create more harm than good for society. Viscusi, The Social Costs of Punitive Damages Against Corporations in Environmental and Safety Torts, 87 Geo. L.J. 285 (1998). A powerful critique of the Vicusi assertions was raised by Professor David Luban and others. See Luban, A Flawed Case Against Punitive Damages, 87 Geo. L.J. 359 (1998). Luban concludes that Viscusi ultimately "fails to identify all the potential benefits of punitive damages, fails to establish that punitive damages are ineffective deterrents, and fails to exhibit any significant social harms that punitive damages inflict." Id. at 380. The Court expressly noted its *non*-reliance on Viscusi's Exxon-funded work.

the wrongful tree-clearing. Under the Court's ratios, wouldn't punitive damages be limited to $0?[43]

2. Procedurally, job well done by Exxon. Prior to winning its stunning limitation of punitive damages in admiralty cases, Exxon's success in bundling the matter of punitive damages into a single mandatory (no opt-out) class action was a superb strategy. That maneuver avoided multiple efforts in litigating the issue and forestalled any possibility of having duplicative punishments imposed. Not satisfied with a 90% reduction in the jury's punitive damage award, Exxon kept on the attack, unsuccessfully trying to reduce the amount of interest it was required to pay on the award, saying it had prevailed on the ultimate remedy calculation. *Exxon Valdez v. Exxon Mobil*, 568 F.3d 1077 (9th Cir. 2009).

3. Principled judicial lawmaking vs. arbitrary judicial gut-flopping. Even without reading Justice Souter's majority opinion, can you make a case that the latter characterization better describes Justice Souter's opinion? Here the Court is deciding the issue in advance of congressional legislation, but in the face of 230 years of congressional silence on this particular admiralty issue. Justice Stevens's dissent noted Congress's active hand in admiralty legislation and inferred from it an intent that the check on punitive damages should be the case-by-case due process limitation rather than a judge-made common law rule based on review of academic studies.

4. The magic ascribed to the median award by the majority. What appeared to be the single most important statistical argument to the majority was the median award in the entire universe of punitive damages cases considered by the study being relied upon, which found that the median was 0.62:1. The *median* is the point at which half of the awards have a higher ratio and half have a lower ratio. Are there scenarios that might result in low ratios that have no bearing on what is an appropriate upper bound for the ratio in other cases? Would the punitive damage award, if any was made, be very large in *McElwain* or *Borland*? Is it unfair or inconsistent to punish at a greater ratio when the compensatory damages may understate the value or the nature of the harm done? Why wouldn't the unpredictability problem equally be solved by making the upper bound the *mean* (i.e., the arithmetic average of the total amount awarded as punitives when compared to the total amount awarded as compensatories)? Based on the studies cited that number was 2.90:1, almost five times higher and much closer to the maxima allowed in state courts where the matter had been addressed.

5. These are punitive damages, but they certainly are not going to punish Exxon. In most states, defendant's wealth is relevant in determining the amount of punitive damages to be assessed. Absent that information, the amount awarded might be too small to punish or so severe as to over punish. So, while $507,300,000 would punish most corporations, it represents fewer than 12 hours of then-current Exxon revenue, or roughly one-seventh of one percent of annual revenue. That figure is an even smaller percentage of Exxon's capitalized value. On the plaintiffs' side, more than 20% of the award was consumed by attorneys' fees calculated on a lodestar basis.

6. Creative accounting in damage remedies: ill-gotten gains as an alternative to punitive damages. An intriguing potential for a new theory of damages is disgorgement of benefits. This approach is already a staple in the assessment of regulatory penalties and

---

43. See also Garcia, Remittitur in Environmental Cases, 16 B.C. Envtl. Aff. L. Rev. 119 (1988) (considering the award of punitive damages when no compensatory damages were awarded for natural resource damage).

C. Remedies in Environmental Litigation

setting the amounts of criminal fines. For example, consider 18 U.S.C. §3571, a criminal law enactment:

§3571. Alternative fine based on gain or loss. If any person derives pecuniary gain from the offense, or if the offense results in pecuniary loss to a person other than the defendant, the defendant may be fined not more than the greater of twice the gross gain or twice the gross loss, unless the imposition of a fine under this subsection would unduly complicate or prolong the sentencing process.

If, for example, a factory has avoided a million dollars in waste treatment expenses by violating pollution discharge limits, energetic application of this provision can provide a measure of disgorgement of ill-gotten gains, a dramatically enhanced deterrent to future evasions. Can this same rationale be applied in civil cases under the common law, using, perhaps, a quasi-contract theory of "restitution" of ill-gotten gains or unjust enrichment? So far the courts have not quite bought the theory: *Evans v. Johnstown*, 410 N.Y.S.2d 199 (Sup. Ct., Fulton Co. 1978) (municipal sewage treatment plant), *County Line Inv. Co. v. Tinney*, 933 F.2d 1508 (10th Cir. 1991) (suit against predecessor for landfill remediation by a successor).

In *Combustion Engineering*, a Georgia strip mine acid-drainage case that reached the Supreme Court, the plaintiffs ultimately won $4.35 million in punitives,[44] 100 times the jury's compensatory damages. The disproportionate award was justified in part by the fact that over the span of 11 years of unheeded warnings to correct its waste treatment, defendant had saved a great deal of money by not cleaning up—a savings of $6 million in the last 4 years of operation alone—echoing the *Haslip* test of "profitability of the action." The "ill-gotten gains" recoupment theory of punitive damage awards is likely to find increasingly active use.

3. Natural Resources Remedies

The vast majority of environmental litigation is directed at recouping losses to humans and their property. That tends to obscure ecological reality: Human injuries are not necessarily the major consequences of disruptions of the natural equilibrium. As Judge Mehrige said in *Pruitt*, "Kepone pollution . . . costs were borne most directly by the wildlife of the Chesapeake Bay." 523 F. Supp. at 978. When a wrongdoer destroys or injures natural resources, the law can do an adequate enough job establishing fault or an equivalent basis for liability, but the evaluation of natural resource remedies is more problematic, as demonstrated by the erratic course of restoration efforts after the Exxon Valdez, and ongoing issues after the BP Deepwater Horizon oil platform blowout in the Gulf of Mexico.

There are several solid foundations for awarding natural resources damages (NRDs). The public trust doctrine, explored in Chapter 20, offers a theoretical foundation and justification for equitable restoration remedies and government economic recoveries of NRDs. Public nuisance actions also have supplied authority for NRD remedies, as do a number of state and federal statutes. The CWA, CERCLA, and other federal acts require the federal government to "identify the best available procedures to determine natural resources damages, including both direct and indirect injury, destruction, or loss."[45] Thus, the evolution

---

44. That award was finally upheld after two remittiturs, *Johansen v. Combustion Eng'g*, 170 F.3d 1320 (11th Cir. 1999).

45. CWA, 33 U.S.C. §1321(f)(4)(5); CERCLA, 42 U.S.C. §9651(C)(2). The other federal statutes that authorize NRD are OPA90, 33 U.S.C. §§2701, 2702(b)(2)(A) (1990); Trans-Alaska Pipeline Auth. Act, 43 U.S.C. §1653 (1973, 1988); Deepwater Port Act, 33 U.S.C. §1501 (1974, 1988); Outer Continental Shelf Lands Act Amendments

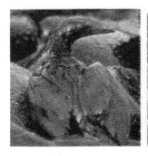

U.S. Seagrant Oiled Wildlife.

of NRD liability theories, evaluation methods, and remedies is occurring concurrently in both common law and public law settings.

The *Exxon-Valdez* oil spill provides a classic example of NRD accounting as well. After the single-hulled supertanker *Exxon-Valdez* sliced into the submerged granite of Bligh Reef in Alaska's Prince William Sound in March 1989, the 11 million gallons of crude oil that spewed from the wreck, pushed by northeasterly winds, spread out over 1000 miles of coastline waters.[46] The ecosystem hit by the *Exxon-Valdez* spill was extraordinarily rich. Affected species included herring, black cod, cutthroat trout, dolly varden, shark, halibut, rock fish, shell fish, fin fish, several species of salmon, sea otters, fur seals, steller's sea lions, harbor porpoises, dall porpoises, killer whales, humpback whales, minke whales, fin whales, blue whales, gray whales, deer, fox, coyotes, black bears, brown bears, bald eagles, several species of gulls, hundreds of thousands of sea birds (such as kittiwakes, puffins, hawks, guillemots, murres, murrelets, loons, grebes, and diving ducks), dungeness crabs, pot shrimp, trawl shrimp—and these were just the upper layers of the ecological pyramid. The waters and wildlife of the Gulf of Alaska were among the most fertile coastal communities on earth, built upon a confluence of ocean currents rich in microorganisms, zooplankton, and phytoplankton.

More than 180 civil suits were filed after the *Exxon-Valdez* spill, almost all by people claiming injury to their economic interests. The State of Alaska's lawsuit included many predictable economic claims—loss of tourism and recreation; reimbursement for out-of-pocket cleanup efforts by towns, Native American tribes, and the State; emotional distress and disruption of citizens' lives; and so on—but the State also asked the trial court to award damages and injunctions that would capture a broader swath of values, based on natural resources losses. As you read Figure 3 containing brief excerpts from the State's 40-page complaint, note the problems faced in defining and separating human and ecological remedies.

---

of 1978, 43 U.S.C. §§1331-1356 (1978, 1988); Marine Protection, Research, and Sanctuaries Act of 1988, 16 U.S.C. §1443 (1988); National Parks Systems Authority Act, 16 U.S.C. §19ii (Supp. V 1993). The doctrines of NRD liability and valuation methods are being actively debated and shaped in judicial review of federal agency NRD regulations.

46. As to fault, the wreck was an accident waiting to happen, attributable to cost-cutting and complacency within the oil industry, abetted by lassitude within the U.S. Coast Guard and state and federal regulatory agencies. See State of Alaska Oil Spill Comm'n, Spill: The Wreck of the *Exxon-Valdez*: Lessons for the Safe Transportation of Oil (1990). Disclosure notice: One of the authors worked for the State of Alaska and for the Oil Spill Commission itself on legal responses to the *Exxon-Valdez* spill.

C. Remedies in Environmental Litigation

IN THE SUPERIOR COURT FOR THE STATE OF ALASKA—THIRD JUDICIAL DISTRICT

THE STATE OF ALASKA, on its own behalf, and as public trustee and as *parens patriae* for the citizens of the State, Plaintiff, vs. EXXON CORPORATION, a New Jersey corporation; EXXON PIPELINE COMPANY, a Delaware corporation; EXXON SHIPPING COMPANY, a Delaware corporation; ALYESKA PIPELINE SERVICE COMPANY, a Delaware corporation; et al. Defendants.	Case No. 3AN8906852CIV

COMPLAINTS FOR COMPENSATORY & PUNITIVE DAMAGES, CIVIL PENALTIES & INJUNCTIVE RELIEF
. . .

20. "Environmental damages" includes, but is not limited to, one or more types of damages to use and enjoyment values derived from State lands, waters, and resources:
(1) Use values, including consumptive and nonconsumptive uses;
(2) Nonuse values, including existence, intrinsic, option, bequest, temporal, and quasi-option values;
(3) Values derived from the existence of management options and the expertise and data to exercise and support same;
(4) Values associated with the necessity or desirability of restoration, replacement, assessment or monitoring;
(5) Other ecosystem existing values. . . .

DAMAGES TO PLAINTIFF

. . . 61. As a result of the oil spill from the EXXON-VALDEZ, over a thousand square miles of State lands, waters, and resources have suffered severe environmental damage. A growing number of coastal and inland sounds and bays, beaches, tidelands, tidal pools, wetlands, estuaries, and other sensitive elements of the ecosystems have been devastated; thousands of mammals, fowl, and fish have been killed or injured; anadromous streams, near shore environments and other fish and wildlife critical habitats have been contaminated; aesthetics and scenic quality have been destroyed or impaired, together with attendant opportunities for recreational experiences; air quality has deteriorated through the escape of evaporating pollutants; commercial fisheries have been sharply curtailed, with adverse biological and economic consequences; the greater ecosystem in the spill area has been deprived of its pristine condition with attendant damage to the condition of, and interrelationship among, living creatures comprising the system; and the management opportunities available through the knowledge and data base generated from prior experience with the ecosystem have been compromised. . . .

RELIEF SOUGHT

WHEREFORE, plaintiff prays that this Court: . . .

Award all compensatory and punitive damages authorized under the common law, including, but not limited to, environmental and economic damages.

Award all compensatory and punitive damages authorized under the general maritime law.

Order that the defendants be permanently enjoined to remove all spilled oil and to restore the surface and subsurface lands, wildlife, waters, fisheries, shellfish and associated marine resources, air and other State lands, waters and resources affected directly or indirectly by the spill;

Order immediate and continuing environmental monitoring and assessment of the conditions of the air, waters and subsurface and surface lands, fisheries, shellfish and the associated marine resources and other natural resources . . . [and]

Award such other and further relief as this Court deems just and proper. . . .

Douglas B. Baily, Attorney General   August 15, 1989

FIGURE 3-3. *Complaint excerpts*, State of Alaska v. Exxon Corp., *Superior Court of Alaska (Aug. 15, 1989).*

COMMENTARY & QUESTIONS

1. NRD precedents from the Alaska oil spill. The *Exxon-Valdez* spill was a milestone event in national environmental policy debates. See J.S. Picou et al., The *Exxon Valdez* Disaster: Readings on a Modern Social Problem (1997). In NRD terms, by 1992, Exxon was told it could stop further cleanup on the beaches of Prince William Sound because it had reached a point of diminishing returns.[47] The state and federal governments negotiated a settlement agreement with Exxon for a $125 million criminal penalty, $12 million of which went to the North American Wetlands Conservation Fund, and civil penalties of $900 million to be paid over ten years into a fund administered by a state-federal Trustee Council.

2. Nonmarketplace human-based remedies. Assuming first that the numerical loss of living resources can be accurately established, natural resources' remedies then go beyond the mere commodity-pricing approach of the marketplace. As the appellate court wrote when Ohio challenged the CWA and Superfund natural resource regulations:

> It is the incompleteness of market processes that give rise to the need for [nonmarket valuation].... While it is not irrational to look to market price as one factor in determining the use value of a resource, it is unreasonable to view market price as the *exclusive* factor, or even the predominant one. From the bald eagle to the blue whale and snail darter, natural resources have values that are not fully captured by the market system.... Option and existence values may represent "passive" use, they nonetheless reflect utility derived by humans from a resource, and thus prima facie ought to be included in a damage assessment.[48]

Note how the court returns to humans. Likewise, although the Alaska complaint begins its narration of damages with environmental losses, even within the definition of "environmental damages" many if not all of the contentions are for *human*-based economic recovery.[49] The term *use value*, for instance, seeks to capture values for things that don't actually trade in the marketplace, but have an attributable market value. *Consumptive value* attributes a value to lost resource uses of sports enthusiasts and tourists who would have taken wildlife in hunting or fishing pursuits. *Nonconsumptive uses* include the ecosystem's value to photographers, birdwatchers, and the like. Some *nonuse values* are based on attributed human value: what it means to people just to know the resource is there, even if they never actively use it; it is *option value* if they may use it. *Bequest value* reflects the resource as a legacy passed by the present generation to its children. *Temporal* and *quasi-option values* assess unknown future values foreclosed. There is a wide range of economic methods for estimating or "shadow pricing" some of these values, including travel cost (the amount that people are willing to spend to travel to such places); hedonic value, using market activity preferences; implied speculative rent values; and contingent valuation methods (CVM) based on public opinion surveys about willingness to pay (as in a hypothetical tax).[50] Fundamentally,

---

47. This assertion is questionable, especially in light of the debate surrounding the continuing effects of the solvents used to produce clean beaches for the visitor's eye and whether the solvents did more harm than good by contaminating the microecology of the beaches far down into the substrates. Oil still remains within the subsurface layers.

48. *Ohio v. U.S. Dep't of Interior*, 880 F.2d 432, 464, petition for reh'g en banc denied, 897 F.2d 1151 (D.C. Cir. 1989) (emphasis in original).

49. Beyond the realm of natural resources, the Alaska complaint also raises environmental questions regarding remedies for the dramatic disruptions to the Alaska Native communities along the coast. The complaint also seeks remedies for noneconomic human losses in psychological stresses suffered by many non–Native Alaskans whose lives were severely impacted by the spill.

50. See Cross, Natural Resource Damage Valuation, 42 Vand. L. Rev. 269 (1989); Cicchetti & Peck, Assessing Natural Resource Damages: The Case Against Contingent Value Survey Methods, 4 Nat. Resources & Env't 6 (Spring 1989).

C. Remedies in Environmental Litigation

each of these approaches creates a hypothetical human market price for resources, an approach that requires the component fish, wildlife, bugs, and microorganisms of an ecosystem be made sufficiently recognizable and attractive to a human audience to deserve monetary recognition.

3. Natural resources' own intrinsic value. None of the preceding remedies pretends to assess the value of the resources in and of themselves. It seems presumptuous, however, to argue that humans are the sole measure of what has been lost in an ecological catastrophe (although only humans, of course, are in a position to raise the intrinsic ethical claims). If courts can look beyond human-based values, as both law and ethics may currently be inviting them to do, serious questions arise. Is it possible to talk intelligently about the lost wildlife's value to itself? First, it's dead; second, it's wildlife, not human. The flora and fauna and their ecosystem leave no probate estates for wrongful death recoveries. Who can sue, for what purpose, and for what measure of relief?

Who can sue? Given our legal system, it would be vastly easier to sue for the loss of resources if they were citizens, or someone owned them. In the absence of either, the State of Alaska can file its claims for remedies based on its *parens patriae* and public trustee roles, and environmentalists can sue as public trust beneficiaries (see Chapter 20), but the nature and extent of standing to recover for intrinsic natural resources losses are not self-evident.

What is the purpose of seeking NRDs? The dead wildlife cannot be brought back to life. In ordinary tort law, the purpose of damages is a delicate mix of restoring plaintiffs to their prior position and taxing wrongdoers for their wrongdoing. "Destruction of the Bay's wildlife should not be a costless activity," said the judge in the *Pruitt* Kepone case in this chapter. To this extent, the punitive damages sought in the Alaska complaint may be an attempt to capture unquantifiable intrinsic losses and deter future wrongful actions. But what is the measure of loss? The wildlife and their ecological pyramid had an "existence value" that is gone. The fact that they used to be there, and no longer are, reflects the disruption of an evolved ecological community that didn't just happen to be there but had adapted and developed over thousands and millions of years. The fundamental problem of damage valuation for the per se loss of wildlife is that the intrinsic worth of natural resources does not conveniently fit the terms of economic accountability.

4. Ecosystem services and natural capital. New conceptualizations of natural resources and their functions have begun a process that is leading toward more comprehensive valuing of natural resources. Building on the concepts presented in Nature's Services: Societal Dependence on Natural Ecosystems (Gretchen Daily ed., 1997), several commentators have worked to develop methods for recognizing and valuing ecosystem services that include such things as air and water purification, soil generation, climate stabilization, photosynthesis, pollination, and waste decomposition. Beyond that scientific and economic effort, those same commentators are urging the legal system to account for those values in appropriate cases, including common law settings and statutes that include provisions for NRDs. See, e.g., J.B. Ruhl, S.E. Kraft & C.L. Lant, The Law and Policy of Ecosystem Services (2007); Salzman, A Field of Green? The Past and Future of Ecosystem Services, 21 J. Land Use & Envtl. L. 133 (2006). See also a 2009 Duke symposium cosponsored by the U.S. Department of Agriculture's Office of Ecosystem Services and Markets.[51] To date no U.S. court cases appear to have relied upon ecosystem services accounting, but the UN Compensation Commission used an ecosystem service-based approach (Habitat Equivalency Analysis) in awarding more than $5 billion to compensate for damage to the

---

51. Duke Envtl. Law & Policy Forum Symposium, Oct. 2009, www.law.duke.edu/webcast.

Kuwait environment from the 1990-1991 Gulf War. See C. Payne, UN Commission Awards Compensation for Environmental and Public Health Damage from 1990-91 Gulf War, ASIL Insights (Aug. 10, 2005), www.asil.org/insights050810.cfm.

In a similar effort to justify a different mode of valuing natural resources, Robert Costanza, among others, has argued for the concept of valuing the services produced by the world's stock of "natural capital." If his premises and figures are correct, a substantial proportion of the world's output of goods and services is not being accounted for by traditional measures. His work found that, for the entire biosphere, the minimum value (most of which is outside the market) is estimated to be in the range of US \$16 to \$54 trillion (10^{12}) per year. As a point of comparison, global gross national product total is around US \$18 trillion per year.[52]

5. Ecological restoration remedies. The shortcomings in human-based valuations, and the perplexities of awarding intrinsic value NRDs, propel the law increasingly toward performance-based relief—restoration or mitigation remedies. Restoration, as an in-kind ecological remedy, represents two different rationales. First, putting things back as they were before defendants' wrongdoing occurred is a satisfying and understandable objective. Second, restoration provides a performance standard as a proxy for the otherwise difficult task of valuing what has been lost. The remedy avoids the vagaries of natural resources valuation by ordering that the wrong be undone. If a piece of forest was wrongfully clearcut, a court can order soil restoration and replanting of mature trees, shrubs, and undergrowth. Natural resources remediation is a way to capture widespread values within judicial relief and raise potent deterrent examples for prospective wrongdoers. Restoration presents serious questions, however, not least the definition of what restoration means and whether it is worth the cost.

6. Mitigation and substituted resources. An early common law suit filed by environmentalists in the Alaska oil spill case, analogizing to CWA provisions, requested the establishment of a fund or foundation for "the acquisition of equivalent [and additional] natural resources" as an alternative remedy where restoration was ecologically or economically infeasible.[53] Is such mitigation-by-acquisition a satisfactory natural resources' remedy? In effect it merely secures (as a park or reserve) existing resources that otherwise might face destruction by economic development. Does it add or replace anything beyond what existed in the aftermath of an ecological catastrophe? Anticipatory mitigation was the approach taken in Alaska's Prince William Sound. The Trustees obligated almost \$500 million of oil spill NRDs to buy up forests surrounding the Sound to prevent the drastic clearcutting that otherwise, laws or no laws, would have choked spawning streams with erosion and debris and altered stream flows and water quality throughout the area.

4. Environmental Disasters and Administered Compensation Funds

The BP Gulf of Mexico Deepwater Horizon oil platform blowout and spill is the most recent and by far the largest attempt to move tort-based environmental disaster claims out of the judicial system into a streamlined administrative tribunal. The basic idea is simple: have the responsible parties create a fund from which claims of persons injured by the environmental damage can be paid with the amounts to be determined through an administrative process rather than a judicial one. In regard to oil spills, prompted by the *Exxon-Valdez*

---

52. Costanza et al., The Value of the World's Ecosystem Services and Natural Capital, Nature, May 15, 1997, at 253. See also Costanza & Daly, Natural Capital and Sustainable Development, 6 Conserv. Bio. 37 (1992); P. Hawken et al., Natural Capitalism: Creating the Next Industrial Revolution (1999).

53. *National Wildlife Fed'n v. Exxon Corp., Alyeska Pipeline Serv. Co.*, 3 AN-89-2533 Civ (Super. Ct. 3d Dist. Alaska 1989).

C. Remedies in Environmental Litigation

experience in which claims were delayed and expensive to pursue, and in which some important types of losses were not covered at all, Congress enacted the Oil Pollution Act of 1990, 33 U.S.C.A. §2701 et seq. (OPA90). Numerous features of the act, including strict liability and recognition of damage claims solely for economic injury (i.e., loss of income claims in the absence of contemporaneous property damage or personal injury claims) ensured the prospect of legal relief for damages to most claimants. Then, to fast track those recoveries so that victims would not be without recompense in the immediate aftermath of the spill while their economic prospects might remain adversely affected by the continuing environmental damage, Congress laid the ground for promptly established polluter-funded and administered claims facilities. The Coast Guard is empowered to designate responsible parties, and within 15 days the responsible parties must then advertise procedures for the victims to submit claims.[54] OPA90 further set rules by which claims are to be addressed, limiting grounds for denial. An important cleavage in the claims process was the division between claims for short-term relief and long-term relief, the idea being to get money in the hands of claimants for short-term losses while leaving the full extent of the claims open for more deliberate handling.

The principal shortcoming of OPA90 as applied to the BP Deepwater Horizon events was that OPA90 had a statutory cap of $75 million placed on the claims facility. On that front, President Obama jawboned BP executives into waiving that cap and instead agreeing to put up to $20 *billion* into the fund. While it may have been the hope of Congress that the OPA90 facility would address all claims (it did allow for governmental claims as well), as indicated by the existence of the federal multidistrict litigation by governments and some private parties, the BP Gulf Coast Claims Facility (GCCF) was not a panacea. Eventually, after disbursing almost $2 billion under the guidance of Kenneth Feinberg (of 9/11-settlement fund renown), the GCCF ceded its role to the Deepwater Horizon Claims Center (DHCC) (see http://www.deepwaterhorizoneconomicsettlement.com/index.php) which is overseen by the multidistrict litigation court. By the end of the summer in 2015, when the deadline for filing claims had run, the GFCC and DHCC had, between them, paid out private claims of $5.6 billion, mostly for economic loss. A total of 368,230 claims had been filed of which 94,600 had been concluded by the payment of recoveries. Comparatively few claims have been denied and the remainder are still pending, although the guidelines for the amount of recoveries are now far clearer.[55] It is perhaps too early to determine whether the GCCF/DHCC process grades out as a success.[56] It has required judicial intervention and supervision that imports some of the same expense and delay that the system is intended to avoid. Offsetting that line of criticism is the fact almost 100,000 claims were fully settled and paid within 5 years putting billions of dollars in the hands of victims and governments to begin the process of rebuilding the regional economy that was so badly disrupted by an environmental disaster. The calamitous impact on the residents of the region and the ecosystem coupled with the difficulty/impossibility of redressing the losses fairly and remediating the environmental harm is a strong argument for increased efforts at prevention. It was said after *Exxon-Valdez* that the disaster was caused by three things: complacency, collusion,

---

54. 33 U.S.C.A. § 2714(b).

55. http://www.nola.com/business/index.ssf/2015/09/bp_oil_spill_claims_56_billion.html.

56. The Department of Justice commissioned an in-depth study of claims handling under the GCCF performed by a major accounting firm. The report identified and corroborated that there were numerous valid concerns of the stakeholders, and an evolutionary process in which the GCCF responded to many of those concerns. The report offers practical guidance should a similar type of facility be established in the future. See http://www.justice.gov/sites/default/files/opa/legacy/2012/06/06/gccf-rpt-find-obs.pdf.

and neglect amongst each of the governmental and corporate actors.[57] After much investigation, it seems apparent that complacency, collusion, and neglect again combined to generate a regional human and ecological disaster in the Gulf. Established safety and operating procedures were ignored, inspections turned a blind eye when they were performed at all, and spill-response preparation was superficial because no one really thought that there was going to be a major problem—until it occurred. For a visual and spatial sense of the magnitude of the BP disaster search: NOAA+BP+photos.

These must be the years when America pays its debts to the past by reclaiming the purity of its air, its water, and our living environment. It is literally now or never.

—Richard Nixon, 1970

*When humans interfere with the Tao,
the sky becomes filthy,
the equilibrium crumbles,
creatures become extinct.*

—Lao-tzu, Tao Te Ching, 500 B.C.E.

---

57. SPILL, a Report of the State of Alaska Oil Spill Commission (1990).

4

The Special Challenges of Toxic Tort Litigation

A. Competing Perceptions? Law & Science
B. Remedies for Victims of Toxic Contamination
C. Proof of Complex Causation

A. COMPETING PERCEPTIONS? LAW & SCIENCE

Science plays a central role in the operation of law, especially in the environmental field. "Conventional" environmental cases like the tort suits in the preceding chapter often touch on subjects grounded in natural and physical science disciplines. Evaluating natural resource damages or other environmental harms demands an understanding of environmental ecology. Proving causation and damage in air pollution nuisance cases like *Borland*, *Boomer*, and *Velsicol* often requires expert scientific witnesses. Environmental law cases involving *toxic chemicals*, however, typically raise scientific issues so much more complex and difficult that they seem qualitatively different, deserving special treatment. Public regulation of hazardous materials is studied in Chapters 15-17.

The "Proof Disparity"

Civil law typically requires that a verdict be based on the conclusion that a fact "is more probable than not"—i.e. that it is 50.01% likely to be true. Scientific conclusions to be considered "significant" usually require a confidence level of 95%.[1] Given that difference in decisional standards, the proof disparity highlights the lack of congruity between the decisional processes in law and science.

---

1. That confidence level is expressed in the form p=.05, which denotes as a statistical matter that there is only a 5% chance that the observed results are a matter of chance rather than (causal) association.

In a very real sense, law and science are contrasting ways of determining truth.

- *Functional Differences.* The major function of the legal system is to resolve disputes efficiently, effectively, and equitably. The major function of science is to make accurate, empirically verifiable predictions about the physical world.
- *Conclusiveness vs. Tentativeness.* Because the primary function of private law (and to a lesser extent public law) is to resolve disputes so that they don't fester and threaten social cohesiveness, the legal system places great value on the finality of decisions. Doctrines of claim and issue preclusion, double jeopardy, statutes of limitations, and a presumption against retroactivity of legislation support the need for finality of legal decisions. Science, seeking to achieve the most accurate predictions possible, can afford to wait. It proceeds by way of tentative (and sometimes conflicting) hypotheses, collecting data through empirical observation and experiments seeking to verify those hypotheses through replicable tests.
- *Moralistic vs. Value-Free Approaches.* Law is unabashedly moralistic. Although law and morality are not always congruent, law is the formalized, enforceable embodiment of public morality. In its heavily prescriptive endeavors, environmental law deals with concepts such as deterrence, compensation, motive, intent, rights, punishment, and environmental justice. Legal decisionmakers seek to implement "average morality" through principles such as the "reasonable person" standard of tort law and institutions such as the jury system. Science, on the other hand, attempts to banish value preferences from application of scientific method because the goal of science is objective prediction of physical phenomena. Science itself—as distinguished from the politics of science or the role of scientists in politics—is descriptive rather than prescriptive.
- *Adversarial vs. Cooperative Mechanisms.* Legal process in general, and private law in particular, often is institutionalized combat. Scientists are profoundly uncomfortable when they appear in the legal arena as expert witnesses or otherwise because they view the pursuit of scientific knowledge as basically a cooperative effort. Acrimonious conflict occurs among scientists, of course, but the ultimate arbiter of scientific disputes is the independent verifiability of empirical experiments reflected in publications read by other scientists. Scientists tend to resolve scientific disputes through cooperation among peer researchers at symposia or in committees of scientific bodies, not in courts or administrative proceedings. The legal system possesses no direct counterpart.
- *Geographic Variability vs. Universality.* Because law is institutionalized morality, and morality is often situational, legal rules frequently differ among jurisdictions. Scientists find it difficult to deal with such variability because good science is universal in the sense that it is nonvaluational, noncontextual, and empirically verifiable within the limits of scientific method.
- *Disparate Rates of Change.* Because law is generated by human beings in order to resolve policy issues perceived to be important to societies, legal rules can change relatively quickly in response to fluctuations in public opinion. The phenomenal growth of environmental law after 1970 is a prime example of how rapidly legal paradigm shifts can occur. Scientists tend to be uncomfortable with the comparative volatility of the legal system, in contrast to the relatively glacial pace of fundamental shifts in scientific theory.
- *Deductive vs. Inductive Approaches.* Deductive and inductive patterns of analysis are important in both law and science. Deduction allows the investigator to compare a new set of facts or circumstances against a known body of laws to arrive at a

conclusion, whereas induction allows investigators to expand the current body of knowledge based on a set of observations. Deduction is on the whole more significant in legal reasoning than induction. Scientific method, in contrast, places heavier emphasis on induction than deduction.
- *Different Conceptions of Causation.* Science accepts statistical evidence (e.g., cigarette smokers contract lung cancer at a rate ten times higher than nonsmokers) as proof of general scientific propositions (e.g., cigarettes cause lung cancer) that facilitate predictability. The common law, with its emphasis on resolving individual disputes in conformity with prevailing social morality, requires particularized proof of causation (e.g., the defendant's cigarettes, in fact, caused plaintiff's cancer).[2] For many years, courts didn't accept statistical epidemiological or toxicological data as evidence of individual causation. Nowadays courts in many jurisdictions accept statistical evidence, but only where plaintiffs also produce individualized evidence of causation (e.g., clinical evidence or negative lifestyle factors). The legal system, in the context of common law tort actions and administrative decisionmaking, thus may refuse to accept generalized conclusions accepted in the scientific community. Conversely, common law courts or administrative agencies, compelled to resolve disputes using the best evidence of probability available, may accept proofs that wouldn't be accepted in the scientific community. As noted in the text box above, scientific method requires that "good science" be validated by a 95% confidence level (or sometimes higher) which is more like the "beyond a reasonable doubt" standard of proof the law requires for criminal convictions, whereas common law courts require only that plaintiff prove probable causation by a preponderance of the evidence. In most settings, administrative law requires only that administrative decisions pass a "fundamental rationality" test (i.e., not "arbitrary and capricious").

B. REMEDIES FOR VICTIMS OF TOXIC CONTAMINATION

Potentially devastating harms to human health are the primary focus of toxic torts. Toxic tort cases arise at varying levels--as localized as a single trough on a farm in which barrels of toxic wastes have been dumped or as ubiquitous as cancer-causing asbestos used for insulation and sound deadening, used in almost all construction for several decades in the twentieth century. Mass tort exposure cases present especially complex legal issues in establishing environmental liability, including challenging issues of civil procedure that will be left to courses on complex litigation, but even smaller scale toxic exposure cases present challenging scientific and litigation issues. In a modern world containing so many voluntary as well as involuntary exposures to so many different kinds of risk, common law toxics cases often face a virtual impossibility in proving that a particular harm was caused by a particular exposure. Proof of causation is difficult not only because of the variety of pathways by which toxics travel and result in human exposure, but also by the latency of the assault between exposure and the onset of illnesses. A chemical may accumulate or lie latent in human bodies over decades before its serious or fatal effects are manifested. The character of toxic threats, however — typically moving unseen and almost undetectably,

---

2. Causation in the legal arena also has a policy element subsumed in the proximate cause inquiry that limits the consequential reach of cause and effect chains.

occurring almost anywhere, and potentially so harmful — creates strong social revulsions toward toxic exposures.

Given the nature of the modern technological marketplace, toxic exposures present a dilemma. Chemicals, including some very powerful compounds, are woven into the fabric of the modern production and consumption economy. The entire population is exposed to a lifelong interacting mélange of at least small amounts of potentially harmful compounds (and some otherwise harmless compounds that become harmful when synergistically combined). Avoiding exposures is impossible. Remedying the horrors of some exposures is impossible. The amounts in damages that could be assessed against the industries that generated toxins over the past 50 years, if ever the "true" causes of all exposure illnesses could be proved, would surely be astronomical.

Some assert that the issue of toxic exposures is a fundamental problem of modern societal governance that should be handled by public law processes, not by common law tort.[3] Until the legislatures discover a scientifically, politically, and constitutionally feasible regime to take over the field, however, people who believe they have been or will be harmed by particular toxic events will continue to plunk down their court filing fees, putting the force of the evolving common law to work on toxic torts. When plaintiffs seek recoveries in toxic tort cases, the nature of the wrongs they have suffered, or the injuries they fear will befall them in the future, give rise to requests for remedies of a somewhat different nature than traditional compensatory damages. In part, the legal system has responded by fashioning appropriate relief, while in the other part fears of runaway liability for speculative injuries have raised special hurdles to recoveries.

Conventional tort cases, such as an auto accident, typically include straightforward damage claims for items of pecuniary loss such as medical expenses, lost wages, property damage to the vehicle and its contents, possibly replacement services while the victim is incapacitated, loss of consortium, and the familiar intangible of conscious pain and suffering. In addition, those same cases at times must address matters requiring valuation of future damage (e.g., lost future earnings, additional medical treatment) and claims for intangible injury linked to emotional distress. Under modern procedure, increased efficiency is obtained by joining all of these damage items into a single recovery that under preclusion rules extinguishes the claims and permits no further litigation. Toxic tort cases for the most part include the same items of damage and are litigated in the exact same manner. Toxic torts cases have a higher incidence and somewhat richer variety of claims for emotional and psychological injuries.

Toxic tort cases, because of the uncertainty of how many of the diseases involved progress from exposure to different stages of impairment and illness, also present matters of future injury that are different from evaluating the future consequences associated with a presently sustained injury. For example, in a conventional automobile crash, a victim suffering facial scars will be allowed to recover for the anticipated cost of later plastic surgery to reduce the visibility of those scars. In toxic torts, by contrast, an exposure may result in a present provable change in the immune system, but the onset of debilitating disease, or the need for treatment if disease later occurs, are not a certainty and the cost of treatment or even an estimate of the conscious pain and suffering is speculative. Also, there is a degree of dread due to that very uncertainty, a psychological injury that is less often present in conventional torts. The materials that follow build on a toxic tort case that grew out of the

---

3. See Huber, Safety and the Second Best: The Hazards of Public Risk Management in the Courts, 85 Colum. L. Rev. 277 (1985).

B. Remedies for Victims of Toxic Contamination

well-known toxic contamination of drinking water wells in Woburn, Massachusetts with known carcinogens that became the subject of a book by Jonathan Harr entitled "A Civil Action" and a movie of the same name starring John Travolta. More extended materials on that case are available on this book's website.

Anderson et al. v. W.R. Grace & Company, Beatrice Foods Company et al.
628 F. Supp. 1219 (U.S. Dist. Ct., D. Mass. 1986)

MEMORANDUM & ORDER ON DEFENDANTS' JOINT MOTION FOR PARTIAL SUMMARY JUDGMENT

SKINNER, D.J. This case arises out of the defendants' alleged contamination of the groundwater in certain areas of Woburn, Massachusetts, with chemicals, including trichloroethylene and tetrachloroethylene. Plaintiffs allege that two of Woburn's water wells, Wells G and H, drew upon the contaminated water until the wells were closed in 1979 and that exposure to this contaminated water caused them to suffer severe injuries.

Of the 33 plaintiffs in this action, five are the administrators of minors who died of leukemia allegedly caused by exposure to the chemicals. They bring suit for wrongful death and conscious pain and suffering. Sixteen of the 28 living plaintiffs are members of the decedents' immediate families. These plaintiffs seek to recover for the emotional distress caused by witnessing the decedents' deaths. Three of the living plaintiffs also contracted leukemia and currently are either in remission or treatment for the disease. The 25 non-leukemic plaintiffs allege that exposure to the contaminated water caused a variety of illnesses and damaged their bodily systems. All of the living plaintiffs seek to recover for their illnesses and other damage, increased risk of developing future illness, and emotional distress. . . . W.R. Grace & Co. and Beatrice Foods Co. (collectively "defendants"), have jointly moved for partial summary judgment on . . . plaintiffs' claims [of emotional distress and risk of future illness]. . . .

Claims for Emotional Distress . . . Defendants move for summary judgment on plaintiffs' claims of emotional distress on the grounds that the non-leukemic plaintiffs' distress was not caused by any physical injury. They also move for summary judgment on the emotional distress claims of plaintiffs who witnessed a family member die of leukemia, arguing that Massachusetts law does not recognize such a claim. . . .

(1) Physical Injury . . . In seeking summary judgment on the non-leukemic plaintiffs' claims for emotional distress, defendants rely on Payton v. Abbott Labs, 437 N.E.2d 171 (Mass. 1982). In Payton, the Supreme Judicial Court answered a certified question as follows:

> In order for . . . plaintiffs to recover for negligently inflicted emotional distress, [they] must allege and prove [they] suffered physical harm as a result of the conduct which caused the emotional distress. We answer, further, that a plaintiff's physical harm must either cause or be caused by the emotional distress alleged, and that the physical harm must be manifested by objective symptomatology and substantiated by expert medical testimony. (437 N.E.2d at 181.)

Defendants attack plaintiffs' claims of emotional distress at three points: they argue that plaintiffs did not suffer physical harm as a result of defendants' allegedly negligent conduct; that, if the plaintiffs did suffer any harm, it was not "manifested by objective symptomatology"; and that any manifest physical harm did not cause the claimed emotional distress. . . .

Each plaintiff states that exposure to contaminants in the water drawn from Wells G and H "affected my body's ability to fight disease, [and] caused harm to my body's organ systems, including my respiratory, immunological, blood, central nervous, gastro-intestinal, urinary-renal systems. . . ." This alleged harm is sufficient to maintain plaintiffs' claims for emotional distress under *Payton*. As used in that opinion, the term "physical harm" denotes "harm to the bodies of the plaintiffs." In requiring physical harm rather than mere "injury" as an element of proof in a claim for emotional distress, the court required that a plaintiff show some actual physical damage as a predicate to suit.

Defendants argue that plaintiffs' alleged harm is "subcellular" and therefore not the type of harm required to support a claim for emotional distress under *Payton*. I disagree. The Supreme Judicial Court requires that plaintiffs' physical harm be "manifested by objective symptomatology and substantiated by expert medical testimony." In setting forth this requirement, the court did not distinguish between gross and subcellular harm. Instead, the court drew a line between harm which can be proven to exist through expert medical testimony based on objective evidence and harm which is merely speculative or based solely on a plaintiff's unsupported assertions. Upon review of the pleadings and the affidavits of plaintiffs' expert, I cannot say as a matter of law that this standard will not be met at trial.

The alleged damages to plaintiffs' bodily systems is manifested by the many ailments which plaintiffs claim to have suffered as a result of exposure to the contaminated water. Dr. Levin apparently will testify to the existence of changes in plaintiffs' bodies caused by exposure to the contaminated water. He will base his testimony on objective evidence of these changes, including the maladies listed. . . . Dr. Levin explicitly states that the changes in plaintiffs' systems have "produced illnesses related to these systems." Although the affidavit does not specifically identify the illnesses suffered by each plaintiff as a result of the changes, nor state that plaintiffs suffered more ailments than the average person would have over the same time span, it is sufficient evidence of harm to support the existence of a factual dispute and bar summary judgment.

Under *Payton*, of course, injury is not sufficient. The harm allegedly caused by defendants' conduct must either have caused or been caused by the emotional distress. . . . However, certain elements of plaintiffs' emotional distress stem from the physical harm to their immune systems allegedly caused by defendants' conduct and [these] are compensable. Plaintiffs have stated that the illnesses contributed to by exposure to the contaminated water have caused them anxiety and pain. The excerpts from plaintiffs' depositions appended to defendants' motion indicate that plaintiffs are also worried over the increased susceptibility to disease which results from the alleged harm to their immune systems and exposure to carcinogens. As these elements of emotional distress arise out of plaintiffs' injuries, plaintiffs may seek to recover for them.

Defendants contend that plaintiffs' physical harm did not "cause" plaintiffs' distress over their increased susceptibility to disease. They argue that the fear arose out of discussions between plaintiffs and their expert witness, Dr. Levin, in which the expert informed plaintiffs of their suppressed immune systems. Assuming, as I must for purposes of the motion, that Dr. Levin is telling the truth, this argument is frivolous.

Plaintiffs can recover "only for that degree of emotional distress which a reasonable person normally would have experienced under [the] circumstances." The Supreme Judicial Court has explicitly stated that the reasonableness of a claim for emotional distress is to be determined by the trier of fact. Accordingly, defendants' motion for summary judgment on the non-leukemic plaintiffs' claims for emotional distress is denied.

(2) Witnessing Death of a Family Member . . . The second issue raised by defendants' motions is whether Massachusetts recognizes a claim for emotional distress for witnessing a

B. Remedies for Victims of Toxic Contamination

family member die of a disease allegedly caused by defendants' conduct. This differs from the question considered in the preceding section because the concern now is whether the plaintiffs can recover for distress caused by witnessing the injuries of others, not by their own condition. The plaintiffs do not claim any physical harm resulted from this emotional distress.

The plaintiffs proceed on alternative theories: (1) that they were in the "zone of danger," Restatement 2d of Torts §313(2), and (2) that they themselves were the victims of an "impact" from the same tortious conduct that caused the death of the children. . . . The Supreme Judicial Court has [held that] damages may be recovered for emotional distress over injury to a child or spouse when the plaintiff suffers contemporaneous physical injury from the same tortious conduct that caused the injury to the close relative. *Cimino v. Milford Keg, Inc.*, 431 N.E.2d 920, 927 (Mass. 1982). . . .

Plaintiffs would be entitled to go forward on the basis of *Cimino*, if it were not for three further prudential limitations on recovery of a bystander for emotional distress resulting from injuries to another. These are the requirements of physical proximity to the accident, temporal proximity to the negligent act, and familial proximity to the victim. The plaintiffs in this case were present during the illness and death of the children, and at least 16 of them . . . are immediate family members of the decedents, but they do not meet the [temporal proximity] test. . . .

For emotional distress to be compensable under Massachusetts law . . . the distress must result from immediate apprehension of the defendant's negligence or its consequences. In each of the cases in which recovery for the emotional distress of a bystander has been allowed, there has been a dramatic traumatic shock causing immediate emotional distress. Such is not the case here. There is no indication in the Massachusetts cases that liability would be extended to a family member's emotional distress which built over time during the prolonged illness of a child.

Imposition of liability in that case, while logically indistinguishable from the trauma situation, would violate the Massachusetts court's demonstrated prudential inclination to keep the scope of liability within manageable bounds. . . .

Claims for Increased Risk of Future Illness . . . Plaintiffs seek to recover damages for the increased risk of serious illness they claim resulted from consumption of and exposure to contaminated water. . . . In Massachusetts,

> . . . a plaintiff is entitled to compensation for all damages that reasonably are to be expected to follow, but not to those that possibly may follow, the injury which he has suffered. He is not restricted to compensation for suffering and expense which by a fair preponderance of the evidence he has proved will inevitably follow. He is entitled to compensation for suffering and expense which by a fair preponderance of the evidence he has satisfied the jury reasonably are to be expected to follow, so far as human knowledge can foretell. *Pullen v. Boston Elevated Ry. Co.*, 94 N.E. 469, 471 (Mass. 1911).

In addition, when there is a "reasonable probability" that future expenses will be required to remedy the consequences of a defendant's negligence, the jury may consider the expense in awarding damages. *Menard v. Collins*, 9 N.E.2d 387 (Mass. 1937). Plaintiffs argue that these cases indicate that Massachusetts accepts the general rule of tort law that "[o]ne injured by the tort of another is entitled to recover damages for all harm, past, present and prospective, legally caused by the tort." Restatement 2d of Torts §910. I agree, subject to two caveats. First, as is indicated by *Pullen* and *Menard*, when an injured person seeks to recover for harms that may result in the future, recovery depends on establishing a "reasonable probability" that the harm will occur. See Restatement 2d of Torts §912.

Second, recovery for future harm in an action assumes that a cause of action for that harm has accrued at the time recovery is sought. See Restatement 2d of Torts §910. . . .

Defendants argue that the cause of action for any future serious illness, including leukemia and other cancers, has not yet accrued because the injury has not yet occurred.[4] This is the rationale of the discovery rule applied to latent disease cases in Massachusetts under which the injury is equated with the manifestation of the disease. The question thus becomes whether, upon the manifestation of one or more diseases, a cause of action accrues for all prospective diseases so that a plaintiff may seek to recover for physically distinct and separate diseases which may develop in the future.

The answer to this question depends on the connection between the illnesses plaintiffs have suffered and fear they will suffer in the future. Unfortunately, the nature of plaintiffs' claim for increased risk of future illness is unclear on two counts. Nothing in the present record indicates the magnitude of the increased risk, or the diseases which plaintiffs may suffer. . . .

A further reason for denying plaintiffs' damages for the increased risk of future harm in this action is the inevitable inequity which would result if recovery were allowed. To award damages based on a mere mathematical probability would significantly undercompensate those who actually develop cancer and would be a windfall to those who do not. In addition, if plaintiffs could show that they were more likely than not to suffer cancer or other future illness, full recovery would be allowed for all plaintiffs, even though only some number more than half would actually develop the illness. In such a case, the defendant would overcompensate the injured class.

Accordingly, action on plaintiffs' claims for the increased risk of serious future illness, including cancer, must be delayed. . . .

COMMENTARY & QUESTIONS

1. Physical harm/emotional distress. What is the relevance of physical harm in a claim for infliction of emotional distress? Is it possible that an individual could be greatly distressed without suffering any injury whatever? The usual rationale for a physical harm requirement is the desire to prevent fictitious claims. The physical harm requirement may be underinclusive in those genuine cases where a victim suffers emotionally without physical damage, and it may be overinclusive in allowing claims of emotional distress by unprincipled plaintiffs who suffer physical harm but no distress at all.

In *Anderson*, satisfaction of the physical harm requirement by subcellular T-cell effects seems to be a needless formality.[5] Are the physical damage requirement and the required causal link between physical injury and emotional distress intended to substitute for a policy debate about whether the defendant's conduct, as a matter of law and policy, should result in liability for this type of injury? Recall that one of the functions of the proximate cause inquiry is to limit the extent of liability that could be imposed using but-for causation carried to extreme lengths. *Pruitt v. Allied Chemical* in Chapter 3, however, shows that proximate cause analyses also may resort to arbitrary rules to guide their application.

---

4. The weight of authority would deny plaintiffs a cause of action solely for increased risk because no "injury" has occurred.

5. The defendants and the court could entertain no real doubt about the plaintiffs' sufferings. The defendants may think that the plaintiffs are suffering needlessly (i.e., that nothing will come of the exposures), but it is hard to believe that they discredit the claims of fear and anxiety.

Even if you are hostile to attempts to limit emotional distress claims for those personally victimized by contamination, is the argument for prudential limitations stronger in the case of those who suffer by witnessing the suffering of others? These claims are no less real to their victims, nor are they any less credible, in the context of watching an immediate family member die an agonizing and unnecessary death, than are first party claims for infliction of emotional distress. Are courts, rather than the legislature, deciding that it is simply too expensive to compensate these noneconomic losses and still maintain affordable prices for goods that produce hazardous materials as by-products of their manufacture?

2. An exposed individual's recovery for fear of cancer.[6] How similar to suffering emotional distress is fear of contracting cancer? Are these two intangibles sufficiently similar to be addressed by the methodology used for emotional distress (i.e., requiring physical harm that is caused or causes the fear of cancer)? Not all courts have required physical harm. See *Sterling v. Velsicol*, 855 F.2d 1188 (6th Cir. 1988). The reluctance of courts to open a floodgate of cases based on fear with no attendant physical injury has led to a high standard in some states, so that the level of distress must be "severe and substantial." *Ironbound Health Rights Advisory Comm'n v. Diamond Shamrock Chem.*, 578 A.2d 1248 (N.J. Super. 1990) (neighbors contaminated by materials from an Agent Orange production facility); see also Gale & Goyer, Recovery for Cancerphobia and Increased Risk of Cancer, 15 Cumb. L. Rev. 734 (1985). Without limiting doctrines, common law liability in fear of cancer cases and other mass tort environmental cases could be extraordinarily extensive. Eminently reasonable, serious fears of chemical contamination can be so widespread that a defendant who pollutes a community might readily face several billion dollars in jury verdicts, which would cause almost any company to fail. For an example of a state that allows recovery of emotional distress compensation caused by exposure alone, but has set an almost insuperable standard based on probability of the injury occurring, see *Potter v. Firestone Tire & Rubber Co.*, 25 Cal. Rptr. 2d 550 (Cal. 1993). When courts raise the threshold barriers to tort recovery in mass toxic tort cases, are they making a social policy judgment that, for reasons of social utility, the damages for nonphysical injuries must remain where they have fallen? Should that decision be reserved to the legislative branch? Is that policy judgment analytically different from the judicial role in enforcing the ordinary private nuisance requirement that the interference with plaintiff's quiet enjoyment be "unreasonable"?

3. Supreme Court allows fear of cancer emotional distress actions under FELA and applies joint and several liability. In *Norfolk & Western Railway v. Ayers*, 538 U.S. 135 (2003), former railroad employees sued the railway under the Federal Employers' Liability Act (FELA), seeking damages for negligent exposure to asbestos that had caused them to contract asbestosis, as well as damages for mental anguish resulting from the fear of developing cancer. The Supreme Court addressed two questions: (1) whether employees can recover damages for asbestosis-related fear of developing cancer, and (2) whether employees may recover their entire damage award from a railroad whose negligence, together with that of others, jointly caused the injury. Relying on common law precedents in this statutory

---

6. Cancerphobia and fear of cancer are not the same thing. *Cancerphobia* is a clinical term used in medicine to describe a phobic reaction or apprehension experienced by its victim stemming from fear of contracting cancer in the future, even in the absence of a specific event that presents an objective danger of contracting cancer. As a medical condition, it requires expert medical testimony to prove its existence, not merely credible lay testimony describing the plaintiff's experience of fear of cancer. See, e.g., Znaniecki, Cancerphobia Damages in Medical Malpractice Claims, 1997 U. Ill. L. Rev. 639, 642. Cancerphobia, as a presently existing and documented medical impairment, is a compensable injury in almost all jurisdictions. Courts, however, frequently use the term *cancerphobia* to describe cases that are merely claims for emotional distress associated with fear of cancer.

FELA case, the Court found that emotional distress precedents consisted of two categories: stand-alone emotional distress claims not provoked by any physical injury[7] and emotional distress claims brought on by a physical injury.[8] The Court noted that recovery is sharply circumscribed in the first category, but more readily permitted in the second category. In determining that *Norfolk & Western* fit into the second category, the Court relied on the Restatement 2d of Torts §456, which states that an actor whose negligence has caused *any* bodily harm to another is also liable for other emotional disturbance resulting from either the bodily harm or the conduct that causes it. The Court accordingly determined that because the asbestosis that the employees had already contracted arose from the same conduct that created their fear of developing cancer, the employees could recover damages for their fear of cancer, provided they could prove that their fear is genuine and serious. The Court also found that, under FELA, an employee who suffers an injury caused in whole or in part by the employer railroad's negligence may recover full damages from the railroad, regardless of whether the injury was also caused in part by the actions of a third party. This finding avoided an apportionment of liability and placed a burden of seeking contribution from other tortfeasors upon the railroad.

As to apportionment versus joint and several liability, the railroad had argued that "the modern trend is to apportion damages between multiple tortfeasors." The Court rejected the attempt:

> Many States retain full joint and several liability, see Restatement 3d of Torts, Apportionment of Liability §17, (1999). Even more retain it in certain circumstances, and most of the recent changes away from the traditional rule have come through legislative enactments rather than judicial development of common-law principles. . . . 538 U.S. at 164-165.

4. Compensation for possible future injury—the discovery rule used in applying statutes of limitation, and the absolutism of statutes of repose. The *Anderson* court addresses these matters in a somewhat rote fashion, relying on allowing present recovery for damages that plaintiff can prove are "reasonably probable," summarily denying the viability of recovery for enhanced risk, and noting that illness that is not reasonably probable will give rise to a new cause of action when and if it occurs. The statute of limitations will not bar such actions due to the operation of the discovery rule that starts the statute running only at the time plaintiff should be aware of the injury and that it is due to defendant's conduct. Preclusion would not apply since a claim for an as-yet-unknown injury would not be ripe at the time of the first litigation. In contrast "statutes of repose" that have been enacted in some states expressly disallow the operation of the discovery rule. See Mass. Gen. Laws ch. 260, §2B (—6 years); 735 Ill. Comp. Stat. 5/13-213(b) (—12 years); Va. Code Ann. §8.01-250 (—5 years).

5. Enhanced risk. Toxic exposure increases the likelihood that a person will suffer serious future illness and earlier death. Can exposed persons sue against identifiable sources of the contamination prior to the onset of disease, not for the disease but for the increased risk of contracting the disease? Such damages could be claimed by a very broad swath of plaintiffs, many of whom in statistical terms surely would never get the illnesses. Treating increased risk as a present injury and allowing that recovery, presumably, would not foreclose future recoveries by those individuals who later actually get sick. Thus, allowing recovery for that genre of pre-illness claims is inherently enigmatic. On one hand, compensation will mulct defendants in damages even in cases where illness never occurs. This results in a

---

7. See *Metro-North Commuter Ry. v. Buckley*, 521 U.S. 424 (1997).
8. See *Consolidated Rail Corp. v. Gottshall*, 512 U.S. 532 (1994).

B. Remedies for Victims of Toxic Contamination

form of systematic overcompensation for a risk that does not mature. On the other hand, to refuse compensation is to ignore the goal of complete compensation because defendant's conduct has made plaintiffs less well off. Consider whether an individual would voluntarily choose to drink contaminated water for several years. See R. Posner, Economic Analysis of Law 149 (6th ed. 2003). Likewise, consider what a prudent insurer of health risks would do if it discovered that an applicant for insurance had suffered a major toxic exposure, as had the plaintiffs in *Anderson*.

6. **Medical monitoring remedies—*Ayers v. Jackson Township*.**[9] Once a novel concept launched in a classic New Jersey toxic contamination case, *Ayers v. Township of Jackson*, 525 A.2d 287 (N.J. 1987), medical surveillance monitoring is becoming a more common response to the problems of long-term toxic torts' latent health effects. Medical monitoring is obviously a prudent, albeit expensive, precaution after a person has suffered a serious toxic exposure. Courts following *Ayers* have held that making defendants pay for monitoring tort victims' health is an appropriate and measured response when it enhances chances that serious illness can be caught and treated at an early stage. This remedy can simultaneously limit the adverse effect of tortious behavior and reduce the feeling of vulnerability and burden felt by wrongfully exposed persons, who otherwise might not be able to provide themselves rigorous medical attention. To obtain medical monitoring, one typical case erected a four-part standard requiring plaintiffs to demonstrate that (1) they were significantly exposed to hazardous materials as a result of the negligence of the defendant; (2) as a proximate result of their exposure, they suffer a significantly increased risk of contracting a serious latent disease; (3) the increased risk makes regular medical monitoring and treatment reasonably necessary; and (4) the monitoring and treatment make early detection and/or prevention of the disease possible. *Paoli R.R. Yard PCB Litig.*, 916 F.2d 829, 852 (3d Cir. 1990). At a practical level, "The indeterminate nature of damage claims in toxic-tort litigation suggests . . . the use of court-supervised funds to pay medical-surveillance claims as they accrue, rather than lump-sum verdicts." *Ayers*, 525 A.2d at 313. See also *Metro-North Commuter R.R. v. Buckley*, 521 U.S. 424 (1997). Would the *Anderson* judge have allowed medical surveillance, although he foreclosed recovery for risk? For a listing of early cases allowing medical monitoring, see Martens & Getto, Medical Monitoring and Class Actions, 17 Nat. Resources & Env't 225, 226 (2003).

7. **Anticipatory fear of toxic facilities, novel toxic tort claims—stigma and the tort of "toxiprox"—and the Sandman analyses.** Owners of land situated in close proximity to hazardous materials sites frequently find that the market values of their land are adversely affected as a result of the nearby presence of the hazardous materials. This is particularly true in the case of sites at which toxic materials have been released into the environment, but it is also true to a lesser extent where a nearby facility is used for the proper treatment or disposal of hazardous materials, or even where the facility is simply one at which hazardous materials are known to be in use. Would-be buyers discount the value of the parcel in consequence of the proximity of the hazardous materials, often without reference to whether those materials pose even a scintilla of risk of harm to the parcel being offered for sale. Compensation increasingly is being sought for losses that are consequent upon toxic proximity alone. Consider the following situations:

- A New Jersey trial court judge certified a class action lawsuit brought by owners of parcels located in close proximity to the infamous Gloucester Environmental

---

9. Further text on the Medical Monitoring remedy is available in this chapter's section of the coursebook website.

Services (GEMS Landfill) hazardous waste site. The principal claim of the suit is that the affected homes are either unsaleable or seriously devalued by their proximity to the contaminated site.[10]
- New York's highest court, in determining how much compensation is due to owners of property condemned for its proximity to high voltage lines, has recognized a compensable interest in favor of property owners who can prove that fear of EMF (electromagnetic field) emissions from high voltage power lines will cause a reduction in the value of their real property, and contemporary cases involving parcel valuation for tax assessment purposes also are beginning to take toxic contamination and its effect on market price into account in valuing the subject parcel.[11]
- New Jersey purchasers of homes in a new development were held to have a cause of action against the builder and brokers who sold them houses without disclosing the proximity to a closed landfill suspected of containing toxic waste.[12]

What is the legal theory supporting recovery in these cases, or are they merely an additional element of damage (similar to fear of cancer claims) being asserted under existing rubrics of negligence, nuisance, and strict liability?

The analyses by Peter Sandman (see Chapter 1) emphasize that thoughtful governance planning and decisionmaking can allay, if not eliminate, the psychological impact on nearby residents and the stigma of the inevitably necessary process of locating of toxic disposal facilities in various locations.

C. Proof of Complex Causation

Often the most difficult initial element in presenting an environmental law analysis to a court or legislature is proving that the actions of particular entities actually caused the harms that have been identified. Human causation of climate change is a prime example. Given the complexity of the science and the political and economic pressures strenuously contesting the general scientific consensus, how can causation be convincingly proved in various legal forums as well as to the public? Similarly, human hormone disruption from chemical exposures in modern life has massive consequences difficult to prove in complex chains of causation, but is critically significant in societal terms.[13] This section focuses

---

10. See *In re GEMS Landfill Super. Ct. Litig.*, No. L-068199-85 (N.J. Super. Ct., Camden County, Feb. 2, 1994), as reported at 8 BNA Toxics L. Rep. 1035-1036 (1994). See also *Exxon Corp. v. Yarema*, 516 A.2d 990 (Md. 1986) (allowing recovery for decreased property value caused by groundwater contamination that did not reach the affected parcel). But see *Adkins v. Thomas Solvent*, 487 N.W.2d 715 (Mich. 1992) (holding that diminished property values caused by negative publicity affecting parcels proximate to, but not themselves subject to, hazardous waste contamination is a loss without legal injury). A California jury awarded $826,500 to a property owner for post-cleanup stigmatization of the property and $400,000 in lost rents. *Bixby Ranch Co. v. Spectrol Elec. Corp.*, No. BC052566 (Cal. Super. Ct., L.A. County, Dec. 13, 1993), as reported at 8 BNA Toxics L. Rep. 955-956 (1994).

11. See *Criscuola v. Power Auth. of N.Y.*, 621 N.E.2d 1195 (N.Y. 1993); *Westling v. County of Mille Lacs*, 512 N.W.2d 863 (Minn. 1994) (assessment included a deduction for the claimed stigma attached to the property because of the pollution).

12. *Strawn v. Incollingo*, No. A-4764-91T3 (N.J. Super. Ct. App. Div., Feb. 22, 1994).

13. See T. Colborn, D. Dumanoski & J. Myers, Our Stolen Future (1996); N. Langston, Toxic Bodies: Hormone Disruptors and the Legacy of DES (2010).

C. Proof of Complex Causation

on proof of causation by specific toxic exposures, but its analysis potentially extends far beyond.

In almost every toxic tort case, proof of causation of harm is a difficult litigation hurdle for plaintiffs. The precise mechanism by which toxic exposure results in disease is not known and is not observable in the same way that a broken bone can be understood and seen to have been caused by an automobile accident. Even where scientific studies are viewed as authoritative because of the large populations studied, and even where previous litigation has been successful in obtaining remedies, proof of causation remains an issue of fact in each case that is likely to be difficult for the plaintiffs. For example, in litigation involving mesothelioma, asbestosis, or other asbestos-related maladies, plaintiffs must still show that their disease was caused by exposure to defendant's asbestos products and not by some other toxic exposure or predisposition to disease.

In *Anderson*, the Woburn toxics case, the obstacle of proving causation was immense. The plaintiffs, unlike in the asbestos and cigarette cases, could not tap into voluminous studies and a rich record of previous plaintiff victories proving that the subject chemicals caused cancer in humans. In the Woburn case the defendants steadfastly denied any such dumping, requiring the plaintiffs to establish that causal link as well. The Woburn victims, like most Americans, were exposed to literally hundreds of possible carcinogens in daily life. A nearby creek that overlay the aquifer from which the well water was drawn itself carried the four toxic chemicals at the heart of the case, though in lesser concentrations than the well water. Leukemia has long been linked to radioactivity exposures, and Woburn had several radium watch-dial factories in the old days. It took serious investigation to exclude the possibility that victims had been exposed to these long-defunct companies' wastes. When plaintiffs filed (eight days before the three-year statute of limitations was set to expire), the best evidence they had was the EPA field memo from the time the wells were closed, saying that from agency groundwater samples, Grace, Beatrice, and Unifirst, the defendants in the case, were PRPs (potentially responsible parties under CERCLA, or Superfund, studied in Chapter 16). The Centers for Disease Control added their statistical conclusion that the leukemias were caused by abnormal exposure, and the Harvard public health students added evidence that some correlation existed between well water and illness, but neither of these data came close to establishing causation by the defendants' chemicals. Even the plaintiffs' tipoff from a Grace employee who lived near the Andersons, revealing the solvent-dumping practices at the Grace plant, did little to tie the defendants specifically to the plaintiffs' illnesses. Based on that summary of the evidence, the case seemed doubtful.

To carry the conventional burden of proof in a toxic tort bodily injury case, the plaintiff eventually must prove, by a preponderance of the evidence ("more likely than not") (1) there is a linkage between exposure to the specific toxic chemicals and the disease that afflicted plaintiffs, (2) that defendant is the source of the exposure, and (3) that the exposure was of a magnitude (concentration) sufficient to be consistent with the plaintiff's injury. None of those three propositions is easily established. The first requires delving deeply into the science of epidemiology, at times seeking to prove linkages of toxins and diseases that are sufficiently rare that they have not previously been studied. The second can be complicated by the fungible nature of toxic products (such as asbestos insulation) or the number of possible sources of the contaminants having similar toxic properties. Plaintiff's case becomes more difficult whenever the defendant is not responsible for all of the relevant exposures. The third requires proof of facts regarding plaintiff's exposure to the toxic substance when, in almost all cases, the plaintiff was unaware that the exposure was occurring and in historic contexts where the extent of the exposure was not being measured.

1. Putting Together All of the Facets of Toxic Exposure/Cause-in-Fact

Donaldson v. Central Illinois Public Service Co.
767 N.E.2d 314 (Ill. Sup. Ct. 2002)

FITZGERALD, J. Plaintiffs are the parents of four children suing, on their own behalf and on behalf of their children, Central Illinois Public Service Company (CIPS), the owner of a former manufactured gas plant in Taylorville, Illinois (Site). The plaintiffs alleged that certain acts or omissions by CIPS and three of its contractors during the cleanup of the Site caused their children to develop neuroblastoma, a rare form of cancer. The litigation spanned six years and included the exchange of hundreds of thousands of documents and more than 250 depositions of numerous witnesses. After a four-month jury trial, at which 77 witnesses testified, a jury returned a $3.2 million verdict for plaintiffs against CIPS. The appellate court affirmed the trial court judgment (730 N.E.2d 68), and we granted CIPS's petition for leave to appeal [and] we now affirm the judgment. . . .

Taylorville, located in Christian County, is a town which recorded 520 live births in 1988. Statistically, a case of neuroblastoma occurs one time every 29 years in a community the size of Taylorville. Between March 1989 and August 1991, during approximately a two–year period, three infants and a teenager in Taylorville were diagnosed with neuroblastoma. Zachary Donaldson was conceived in December 1987 and was born on September 7, 1988. Six months later, in March 1989, Zachary was diagnosed with neuroblastoma. At the time of trial, Zachary was in remission from his illness. Chad Hryhorysak was conceived in April 1989 and was born January 12, 1990. Chad was diagnosed with neuroblastoma six months after his birth, in March 1990. As a result of his illness, Chad is paralyzed from the waist down. Erika May was conceived in February 1989 and was born November 27, 1989. She was diagnosed with neuroblastoma two months later, in January 1990. At the time of trial, she was in remission from her illness. Lastly, Brandon Steele was born on March 17, 1978. On August 9, 1991, at age 13, Brandon was diagnosed with neuroblastoma. Brandon died on January 19, 1993. . . .

Plaintiffs claim that the statistical excess of neuroblastoma cases in Taylorville was caused by their exposure to potent chemical carcinogens released, in part, during the cleanup of the Site. The Donaldsons lived one mile from the Site, the Hryhorysaks lived three miles from the Site, and between 1985 and 1989 the Mays lived in several locations near the Site, the closest one-half mile away and the farthest eight miles away. During his lifetime, Brandon Steele lived two miles from the Site. We now turn to the Site.

[The court reviewed the Site history from 1892, when gas production began. When the plant ceased operations in the 1930s, it was dismantled, but large underground tanks and containers filled with 50,000 gallons of coal tar, a by-product of the coal gasification process, were left in place. In 1961, CIPS sold the Site without disclosing the residual presence of the buried coal tar. Again, in the early 1980s, after federal laws required disclosure of the toxins, CIPS remained silent, despite its knowledge of a warning in the Handbook on Manufactured Gas that some chemicals in coal tar "are among the most powerful carcinogens known to exist."]

Aware of the risk, CIPS, through its environmental affairs department, conducted an independent on-site investigation of its manufactured gas plants and drafted a final report discussing the condition of, and potential risk at, each of its abandoned gas-manufacturing sites, including the Site. CIPS forwarded this report to its insurer and applied for "Gradual Environmental Impairment" insurance to cover "potential claims." CIPS did not report the coal tar sites to any state or federal agency or notify current owners of the potential risk.

C. Proof of Complex Causation

[In 1985, after the then-current owner discovered the contamination and after that owner disturbed the soil, Taylorville authorities recorded complaints about strange odors near the Site and in the adjacent public park. Shortly thereafter, CIPS finally came forward and disclosed the fact of the contamination to the Illinois Environmental Protection Agency (IEPA) and hired contractors to conduct a "Phase I" study of the Site.]

Coal tar may contain up to 10,000 different chemicals; CIPS tested for approximately 190 different compounds. This testing detected the presence of various carcinogenic compounds, including polynuclear organic (aromatic) hydrocarbons (PAHs) and volatile organic compounds (VOCs). . . . Monitoring revealed extremely high concentrations of volatile chemicals on the Site, in the area surrounding the Site, and in the adjacent public park to the east. In some areas, monitoring detected soil contamination at a depth of 95 feet. A Hanson[14] employee recommended "use of the lot south of the building be immediately prohibited." A second contractor, hired by CIPS to detect and minimize emissions, observed that the presence of such high levels of volatile agents, coupled with the Site's close proximity to residents living to the north, required "a strong effort to detect and reduce these emissions." . . . Although contained in initial drafts of the Phase I report, risk assessment and health information was deleted from the final report submitted to the IEPA. [In 1986, IEPA ordered CIPS to commence an "immediate removal action."]

As part of the immediate removal action, CIPS implemented an air-monitoring plan to measure particulate emissions and identify the ambient air quality during the excavation. Emissions particles vary in size, such that matter may be small enough to be easily respirable and undetectable to sensory perception such as smell, taste, or sight. Particles, including coal tar chemicals, may bond to soil particles. Moreover, wind speed and temperature influence emissions. Therefore, CIPS approved the use of stationary equipment placed in trailers to monitor emissions 24 hours a day, while technicians also performed spot testing several times a day with portable hand-held instruments. If the ambient air quality reached certain levels, defined within the remediation plan, workers took safety precautions and the Site was shut down.

CIPS initiated air monitoring, in part, to "minimize liability from 'real' or frivolous lawsuits." Internal documents encouraged "minimal data collection necessary to quantitatively document the principal compounds of concern, thus providing a data base for use in response to potential inquiries or claims from the nearby residents or Manners Park [the public park adjacent to the site] users" because "without (emissions data) they (CIPS) have no data if neighbors claim damages." By the time of discovery [in the lawsuit], the computer data base and original data had disappeared. In its place, CIPS offered a summary of the data, prepared internally, called the Air Monitoring Report, as its "best evidence." The report was offered during trial, and to government agencies during final remediation discussions, as a basis to show that exposure did not occur.

CIPS began the remediation on January 20, 1987. Workers removed building debris, an above-ground gas holder, two underground structures (separators), and 9,000 cubic yards of soil. CIPS required the use of gas masks and protective clothing during removal of the buried structures. Hanson and Parsons, the on-site contractors, recommended relocating residents during removal of the buried structure, but CIPS declined to follow their suggestion. Excavated material and soil were removed from the Site by truck, and soil that was not trucked away at the end of the day was covered with plastic foam.

---

14. Hanson, Parsons, and Haztech are independent contractors hired by CIPS at various stages in the Site investigation and remediation efforts undertaken by CIPS. [EDS.]

Air monitoring detected emissions above the National Air Quality Standards (NAAQS) primary health based standard for particulate emissions on seven days during the first three months of excavation. Additionally, on February 8, 1987, a Site security guard reported that high winds blew dust "all over." Two days later, on February 10, 1987, an air-monitoring station reported a NAAQS exceedance, and a local resident was hospitalized with an intense headache, nausea, blurred vision, and convulsions. She was diagnosed with an acute attack caused by some toxic cause. The Site diary indicates that CIPS was advised of the incident. On February 11, 1987, the Site project manager expressed "great concern" about air emissions at the Site, and "wanted to be on record as pushing for shutdown and resident relocation." During this same time, truck drivers removing the soil and waste complained of nausea. As a result, the drivers were advised to wear respirators once they crossed the railroad tracks near the Site. However, residents living in this same area were not warned or relocated. At trial, CIPS maintained that NAAQS exceedances were the result of other sources, such as truck exhaust and burning leaves, and not the excavated soil.

[Once the excavation and removal of soil was completed in early 1987, activity at the Site halted.] CIPS did not backfill the excavation with soil. CIPS and the IEPA disagreed about the scope of further remediation. . . . During this [two-year] conflict . . . CIPS covered the hole with styrofoam and plywood sheets to reduce dust emissions and volatilization . . . [and] discontinued particulate testing and dismantled the air-monitoring program. . . . Eventually, in April 1989, the IEPA granted CIPS approval to permanently backfill the hole.

The Illinois Department of Public Health (Department) examined the unusually high statistical incidence of neuroblastoma cases in Taylorville. Initially, the Department studied the genetic relatedness between families; scientific testing defeated this theory. In June 1990, the Department prepared a final draft "Preliminary Health Assessment" report for the Site. The report was available to the public for review and made available to CIPS for comment. The report concluded that the Taylorville "population had been exposed to . . . dust entrained contaminants . . . largely as the result of limited remedial action on the part of CIPS." Further, the report stated that the Site "is considered to be of potential public health concern because of the risk to human health caused by the possibility of exposure to hazardous substances. . . . The contaminants are present at the site in large quantities and the presence of significant quantities of contaminated soils represents a source of continuing release to the environment."

CIPS argued to the Department that its report was misleading, stating that more recent CIPS air-monitoring data contradicted the Department's assessment and that the report "should be based on current Site conditions." CIPS maintained that this current data was available in its Air Monitoring Report, the only available source of information regarding ambient air at the Site. Based upon CIPS's Air Monitoring Report, the Department's report was modified to state that "the lack of likely completed exposure pathways makes the CIPS site an unlikely cause of the neuroblastoma excess." The Department's report was finalized as modified despite commentary from the USEPA that because "air emissions occurred during the excavation and likely occurred while the excavation was left open for two years, it appears to be likely that some exposure occurred to residents surrounding the Site."

[Actions were filed in beginning in 1991, containing counts of negligence, nuisance, conspiracy, willful and wanton conduct, spoliation of evidence, conspiracy, and negligent remediation counts. In 1996, after some of the peripheral claims and parties were dismissed or settled, the cases were consolidated in Christian County. Prior to trial] the trial court denied plaintiffs' claims for punitive damages.] At trial, plaintiffs called three experts to connect the neuroblastomas to the toxins at the Site. Plaintiffs called Dr. Shira Kramer, an epidemiologist specializing in childhood cancers; Dr. Harlee Sue Strauss, a toxicologist

C. Proof of Complex Causation

specializing in molecular biology; and Dr. Thomas Winters, a physician specializing in occupational and environmental medicine. CIPS responded with numerous experts and plaintiffs' own treating physicians, all of whom testified that the cause of neuroblastoma is unknown, and that they could not testify within a reasonable degree of medical certainty that exposures from the Site caused the particular neuroblastomas in this case.

At the close of plaintiffs' case, the trial court denied CIPS's motion to strike plaintiffs' expert testimony[15] and its motion for a directed verdict. The jury returned a $3.2 million verdict in favor of plaintiffs against CIPS alone, finding CIPS liable for negligence and public nuisance. The trial court entered judgment on the verdict on March 27, 1998, and CIPS appealed. . . . The appellate court affirmed the judgment. . . . This appeal followed. . . .

CAUSATION. CIPS maintains that plaintiffs failed to satisfy their overall burden to show causation. CIPS points to the record as support, and argues that it shows only a "mere possibility" of causation, rather than that causation is "more probably true than not." According to CIPS, a showing of causation includes both "generic causation"—i.e., coal tar is capable of causing neuroblastoma—and "specific causation"—i.e., exposure to coal tar from the Site did in fact occur and actually caused the neuroblastomas. CIPS also argues that in toxic tort litigation, causation also includes a showing of "exposure," which must be quantified with evidence of the level or dose of exposure. CIPS asserts that a plaintiff may establish this exposure requirement with evidence of biological markers, such as trace fibers or particles found in the body, proximity to the defendant's product, or personal or environmental monitoring.

We disagree with defendant's characterization of Illinois law on causation.[16] First, Illinois law does not define causation in terms of "generic" or "specific" causation. Rather, our case law clearly states that in negligence actions, the plaintiff must present evidence of proximate causation, which includes both "cause in fact" and "legal cause. . . ." A plaintiff may show "cause in fact" under the substantial factor test, showing that the defendant's conduct was a material element and substantial factor in bringing about the alleged injury. . . . "Legal cause" examines the foreseeability of injury—whether the injury is "of a type which a reasonable man would see as a likely result of his conduct." Defendant does not allege that plaintiffs failed to show legal cause.

Turning to "cause in fact," a plaintiff may meet his or her burden of causation with circumstantial evidence—evidence from which a "jury may infer other connected facts which usually and reasonably follow according to . . . common experience." This is to say, Illinois law does not require unequivocal or unqualified evidence of causation. To the contrary, we have held that where "there exists limited medical knowledge of a malady, . . . medical testimony pertaining to causation may not be unqualified and unequivocal."

Additionally, we reject CIPS's assertion that causation includes a showing of exposure, which must be quantified. A plaintiff must establish that he or she came into contact with chemicals produced by the defendant. In this context, however, Illinois law does not require that plaintiffs quantify the level of exposure. CIPS relies upon cases that address exposure to asbestos-containing products in an occupational setting. These cases hold that in order to show causation *in an asbestos case*, a plaintiff must "produce evidence of exposure to

---

15. In a lengthy portion of its opinion, the *Donaldson* court applied the general acceptance test for the admissibility of expert testimony. [EDS.]

16. There are terminological differences between Illinois's causation jurisprudence and the generic tort materials set out in Chapter 3. Substantively, the two are similar. This is typical and underscores the reminder that tort law is state common law and the terminology and substance vary slightly from jurisdiction to jurisdiction. [EDS.]

a specific product on a regular basis over some extended period of time in proximity to where the plaintiff actually worked," commonly called the "frequency, regularity and proximity" test. . . . In this instance, we are not compelled to adopt this rule and depart from traditional concepts of causation. Environmental exposure cases, like the instant case, do not afford litigants the opportunity to specify with such certainty the exact level and dose of exposure. In most instances, the details of exposure, including information of exactly when or where exposure occurred, is not available. . . . Accordingly, we review whether there was evidence from which a jury could conclude that CIPS's conduct was a material element and substantial factor in bringing about the neuroblastomas.

Plaintiffs presented testimony from Dr. Winters, an expert in occupational and environmental medicine. Dr. Winters testified that in the case of environmental exposure, like the instant matter, it is difficult to quantify exposure to individual community members. However, his review of evidence in this case, including the IEPA 4(q) immediate removal action plans, Department reports, USEPA reports, family medical histories and interviews, and Site reports that discussed the level of soil contamination and methods of removal, as well as the open and unmonitored status of the Site for two years, led him to conclude that cumulative exposure occurred here.

Further, plaintiffs presented circumstantial evidence of community exposure. The jury heard evidence regarding the potential of particulate matter to travel undetected for several miles. The jury was advised of Taylorville weather conditions during the period of remediation, including high wind and unseasonably warm weather, which facilitate the travel of air-borne contaminants. Plaintiffs offered evidence that during the period of remediation, on-site workers complained of symptoms consistent with exposure to toxic substances. At that same time, the record shows that a local resident, who lived within several hundred feet of the Site, was hospitalized with dizziness, headaches, vomiting, and seizures, and later diagnosed with exposure to an unknown toxic cause. This individual testified that "everything just reeked from it [coal tar]. It even penetrated into the homes." She later added the Site cast a "heavy mist over the whole area, like a fog" and that workers at the Site dressed in protective gear. [The court recounted next the NAAQS violations and "Draft" state-compiled Health Assessment as further evidence that sustained a finding of exposure.]

Plaintiffs presented testimony from Dr. Kramer, an expert witness who testified regarding causation. [The court recounted Dr. Kramer's extraordinary qualifications as an epidemiologist.] Scientists in this field assume that disease is not distributed randomly in a group of individuals and that identifiable subgroups, including those exposed to certain agents, are at increased risk of contracting particular diseases. Dr. Kramer explained that epidemiology concerns whether a particular agent is capable of causing a disease or injury. Further, she testified that an epidemiologist may conduct one of many studies to determine whether an agent is related to the risk of disease or adverse health effects. As she explained, study design varies depending upon the circumstances, including resource limitations, time constraints, or the subject of the study. Both parties agree that under the current scientific literature, several epidemiologic criteria are used to judge the relation between an agent and the risk of disease, including the temporal relationship between the disease and the exposure; the statistical strength of association; the dose-response relationship; the replication of findings; the biologic plausibility; alternative causes; cessation of exposure; the association of exposure with a single disease; and consistency with other knowledge. According to Dr. Kramer, however, scientific literature also explains that the science of epidemiology does not demand satisfaction of each criteria, rather on occasion some may be irrelevant or impossible to determine.

Dr. Kramer testified that the carcinogens contained in coal tar and coal tar related carcinogens from the Site were the most likely cause of the plaintiffs' neuroblastomas. She later

C. Proof of Complex Causation

quantified this as a "greater than 50 percent probability." Dr. Kramer admitted that no scientific consensus exists to support the theory that coal tar causes neuroblastoma. However, in great detail she outlined the methodology used to generate her conclusion, including her own published studies on neuroblastoma, scientific literature on risk factors for nervous system cancers, animal studies regarding nervous system cancer, studies regarding the risks of expectant mothers and infants, and her Taylorville case-specific study that was based upon family history questionnaires and Illinois Cancer Registry data. Her research ruled out random variability as the cause for the sudden increase of Taylorville neuroblastoma cases.

Dr. Kramer discussed the temporal relationship between the release of ambient air emissions from the Site and the onset of neuroblastoma. However, Dr. Kramer did not rely solely on an abstract temporal connection. Dr. Kramer also examined the increased incidence of neuroblastoma through standard scientific calculation, and calculated the probability that the onset of neuroblastoma was due to random chance; she concluded that the possibility of chance was one in 10,000. Further, Dr. Kramer discussed that coal tar is a multipotential carcinogen that can cause cancer at multiple sites in the body. Dr. Kramer addressed alternative sources, and determined that although alternative sources are potential causes of neuroblastoma, only the Site was a common risk factor among all plaintiffs. Consistent with the science of epidemiology, Dr. Kramer performed a cancer incidence rate analysis to measure the rate of development of neuroblastoma and adult cancers in Taylorville. The incidence rate examines whether the sudden or dramatic increase in cases is more likely due to chance. In order to complete this study, Dr. Kramer studied the incidence of neuroblastoma in four different comparison groups during the period 1986 through 1991, including: the National Cancer Institute Surveillance Epidemiology and End Results Program Rates (SEER, a national cancer registry), the State of Illinois, demographically similar zip codes without manufactured gas plant sites, and demographically similar zip codes with manufactured gas sites. At the conclusion of her study, Dr. Kramer testified that there was a one in 10,000 probability that chance caused the neuroblastomas in this case. Further, Dr. Kramer discussed fetal nervous system cancers and the increased sensitivity of expectant mothers and young children to carcinogens. Based upon medical research animal studies, she testified that the fetal nervous system is 50 times more sensitive to carcinogens. Dr. Kramer also testified that there is no safe level of exposure to known sensitive populations, and argued that this was a "known scientific fact" cited in the literature.

Plaintiffs also presented Dr. Strauss, a molecular biologist and toxicologist.... Her field of study, toxicology, examines the adverse effects of chemicals on living organisms, and is otherwise called the "science of poisons." Dr. Strauss explained that toxicological studies, by themselves, rarely offer direct evidence that a disease in any one individual was caused by a chemical exposure. However, toxicology can rule out other risk factors known to cause a disease and provide scientific information regarding the increased risk of contracting a disease at any given dose.

Dr. Strauss testified that coal tar and its general chemical constituents were the cause of plaintiffs' neuroblastomas. Dr. Strauss based her conclusions upon animal studies and medical research in the area of nervous system tumors, soil samples from the Site, health and safety diaries from the Site, and air-monitoring logs from the Site. Additionally, Dr. Strauss discussed the volatile potential of coal tar compounds, using studies that discussed manufactured gas plant sites with similar site histories and VOC contamination profiles. From this data, she compiled the potential toxicity of the Site and the cancer potency of the coal tar. Further, Dr. Strauss discussed the complex chemical compounds contained in coal tar, and the "synergistic" effect that occurs when these compounds interact to form more potent compounds. She stated that these same compounds are multipotential, affecting several organ sites, and transplacental, meaning that the carcinogen may pass from the placenta to a developing fetus.

This case presents the classic "battle of the experts" frequently seen in toxic tort litigation. Plaintiffs' experts testified that the Site was a substantial factor in bringing about plaintiffs' neuroblastomas, while defendants' experts testified that medical science does not associate coal tar with neuroblastoma. When viewing this evidence in the light most favorable to the plaintiffs, we do not find that the evidence so overwhelmingly favors CIPS that no contrary verdict based on that evidence could ever stand.[17] Clearly, there was sufficient evidence from which a jury could conclude that CIPS's conduct was a material element and substantial factor in bringing about the alleged injury.

DUTY. CIPS next claims that plaintiffs failed to satisfy [their] burden to show CIPS violated any duty. CIPS does not deny the existence of a duty; it argues that the evidence was insufficient to establish that it breached its duty. We find sufficient evidence of a breach.

In their complaint, plaintiffs alleged a breach of duty beginning in 1939 and ending in 1989. Jury instructions incorporated specific acts and omissions alleged in plaintiffs' complaint: (1) the abandonment of coal tar in the underground tanks in 1938; (2) failure to monitor the Site before contaminants migrated off-site and were discovered by local authorities; (3) failure to warn local authorities or residents after CIPS discovered contamination in 1985; (4) failure to control airborne pathways before beginning its immediate removal action in 1987; (5) increasing volatile air and dust emissions during the immediate removal action in 1987; (6) failure to control the volatile air and dust emissions after the immediate removal action between 1987 and 1989; (7) failure to warn residents of any risk to human health resulting from exposure to the Site while it remained open between 1987 and 1989; and (8) failure to provide reliable air monitoring of emissions while the Site remained open between 1987 and 1989. [The court with little discussion found sufficient evidence that a jury could find that CIPS had breached its duty.]

PUBLIC NUISANCE. Last, CIPS claims that plaintiffs' nuisance claims were defective. . . . At the time plaintiffs filed their complaint, plaintiffs had a common law right to claim damages for public nuisance. At common law, a public nuisance included:

> an unreasonable interference with a right common to the general public. Earlier cases recognized that the public had a right to clean, unpolluted air and that any deprivation of that right was actionable as a private injury and indictable as a public wrong. However, the notion of pure air has come to mean clean air consistent with the character of the locality and the attending circumstances. Whether smoke, odors, dust or gaseous fumes constitute a nuisance depends on the peculiar facts presented by each case. *City of Chicago v. Commonwealth Edison*, 321 N.E.2d 412 (1974). . . .

We find, therefore, that plaintiffs' nuisance claim was proper.

The second issue presented for our review is whether IEPA direction and supervision bar nuisance liability. CIPS maintains that the extension of nuisance liability in this context will damage State interests by discouraging the private sector from cooperating with the

---

17. The latter half of this sentence describes the usual standard appropriate when an appellate court is asked to rule that the trial court erred in failing to grant either a directed verdict or a judgment notwithstanding the verdict. The first half of the sentence is usually associated with the posture to be taken by a trial court (i.e., viewed in the light most favorable to the nonmoving party) in considering materials offered in support and opposition to a motion for summary judgment. [EDS.]

IEPA. At the heart of CIPS's albeit brief argument is the contention that it is "unfair" to reward cooperation with exposure to liability. CIPS warns that if this court permits liability here, it will slow down or reduce future clean-up efforts.

First, we reject CIPS's argument based upon the language of the Illinois Environmental Protection Act §45(a), [which] states that "no existing civil or criminal remedy for any wrongful action shall be excluded or impaired by this Act." . . . We are, however, compelled to respond further. CIPS was not held liable for the mere release of toxins into the ambient air during remediation. In an industrial society, odors, film, dust, and smoke may exist. This logic is equally true in the case of an environmental remediation. In this instance, however, plaintiffs allege a substantial injury different from the general public, and claim that this injury is not based solely on ordinary clean-up efforts, but rather negligent remedial conduct. We need only look to plaintiffs' allegations: CIPS is liable for the "release of 'coal tar' into the soil, groundwater and air *in violation of the IEPA*; contamination of public water supplies *in violation of the IEPA*; release of airborne carcinogens, clastogens, and mutagens from the Site before its 'Immediate Removal Action'; release of airborne carcinogens, clastogens, and mutagens from the Site during its 'Immediate Removal Action'; release of airborne carcinogens, clastogens, and mutagens after its 'Immediate Removal Action'; maintaining an open pit resulting in erosion of soil and collection of surface water which allowed the further release of volatile air and fugitive dust emissions for two years after its 'Immediate Removal Action.'" (Emphasis added by the court.) We do not find that liability in this case will frustrate future remedial efforts or deter cooperation. To the contrary, it may encourage cooperation with government agencies, and heighten care and concern for public safety during remedial actions. As a final matter, we reject CIPS's argument that it should not be liable because the release of emissions was solely the result of IEPA oversight. The record demonstrates otherwise. . . . Affirmed.

[Concurrence of McMorrow, J., omitted.]

COMMENTARY & QUESTIONS

1. Plaintiff's theories and the relevance of defendant's efforts at concealment. CIPS's behavior demonstrates a consistent pattern of attempting to conceal information about the contamination from the authorities and the public. Why is this concealment relevant? Which legal issues does CIPS's concealment affect? The court relies on the concealment to find a breach of duty, but it also is relevant to plaintiffs' claims for punitive damages. Based on the precedents set out in the previous chapter, was the dismissal without trial of the punitive damage claim correct? The court also references the concealment evidence in relation to the nuisance claim and plainly finds a *negligently* created public nuisance. But could the court have sustained a nuisance finding based on *intentionality* alone? Recall that the legal rubric for intentionality — that CIPS intended the natural consequences of its acts — is quite straightforward. However, the somewhat harder question is just what should be included among the "natural consequences." If CIPS's only act had been leaving the coal tar in the ground decades ago, the issue might be a difficult one for plaintiffs. As the events played out, however, the carcinogenicity and amount of coal tar, coupled with the necessity of disturbing the soil to remediate the site, make potential exposures resulting from volatilization and particulate pollution a natural consequence of intended actions. Care in performing the remedial activity, therefore, is not relevant to an intentional tort theory. Likewise, even carrying out a cleanup according to IEPA requirements that might be evidence of due care in a negligence claim is plainly not relevant if the plaintiffs' claims sound in intentional nuisance or strict liability.

2. Linking exposure to disease and reaching novel conclusions. In *Donaldson*, what is the most convincing evidence and testimony linking coal tar exposure to neuroblastomas? Could the jury have found for plaintiffs without the testimony of the epidemiologist? Although it is not yet a universal position, many courts are requiring that plaintiffs be able to produce epidemiological testimony to avoid summary judgment on the issue of causation. The exception to that rule would be cases in which there is direct proof, such as the "fibers or residual traces" that CIPS argued were missing in this case. An example of an older case that does not require epidemiological testimony is *Chevron Chem. Co. v. Ferebee*, 736 F.2d 1529 (D.C. Cir. 1984).

3. Litigation involving rare cancers and litigation involving more common cancers. In light of the importance of epidemiological evidence to proving linkage of exposure and disease, which cases are likely to be easier to litigate, cases involving relatively rare cancers, such as *Donaldson*, or cases involving more prevalent and therefore more frequently studied cancers? One variable that affects the answer is resources. If the plaintiff is able to obtain painstaking case-specific research and testimony relating to a rare cancer, such as that done by Dr. Kramer in *Donaldson*, the rarity of the cancer may become a plus. There is likely to be no other research that addresses the subject, thereby reducing the grounds for debating the conclusion of linkage and causation offered by plaintiff's expert. Lacking the resources, however, plaintiff either will have to forgo epidemiological testimony, which could easily result in losing the case on summary judgment, or rely on testimony that collects and opines on the instant case by relying on studies that are not quite on-point. This latter technique is referred to by the experts and the court in *Donaldson* as *extrapolation* and is considered by the court to be a generally accepted methodology where more direct data are not available. Even more confounding for the victim of a rare cancer, could a plaintiff win a case like *Donaldson* if there is only one victim in the locality of the exposure? In such a case, the statistical possibility that the cancer can be explained as a random event is 100%. With more common cancers, there are likely to be more studies. As already noted, the studies may appear equivocal if they do not all reach similar results. If some studies support the plaintiff, that is sufficient to avoid summary judgment, but may not suffice if the great weight of the studies favors defendant.

2. Plaintiff's Burden of Proof & Proportion of Risk Attributable to Defendant[18]

Epidemiology studies the relationship between a disease and a factor suspected of causing the disease, using statistical methods to determine the likelihood of causation.[19] Epidemiology is a study of groups, not individual victims of disease, and for that reason its conclusions are expressed in terms of degrees of statistical association between the presence of the risk factor (i.e., exposure to the harmful agent) and the incidence of disease. These are studies of correlation, not proofs of what the *Donaldson* defendants and laypeople might label *specific causation*. While statistical correlations do not *prove* causation, at times the epidemiological evidence can strongly, even compellingly, support an inference of causation.

---

18. The textual material here borrows heavily from the court's opinion in *Landrigan v. Celotex Corp.*, 605 A.2d 1079 (N.J. 1992). That case features a careful exposition of these concepts in the context of linking a death from colon cancer to asbestos exposure.

19. See Black & Lilienfeld, Epidemiologic Proof in Toxic Tort Litigation, 52 Fordham L. Rev. 732, 750 (1984).

C. Proof of Complex Causation

The factors that control the power of the inference of causation are (1) the strength of the statistical association and (2) the consistency of the association with other knowledge. The court in *Landrigan v. Celotex Corp.*, 605 A.2d 1079 (N.J. 1992), quoted a leading text on the subject as follows:

> In general, the stronger the association, the more likely it represents a cause-and-effect relationship. Weak associations often turn out to be spurious and explainable by some known, or as yet unknown, confounding variable. . . . Strength of an association is usually measured by the relative risk or the ratio of the disease rate in those with the factor to the rate in those without. The relative risk of lung cancer in cigarette smokers as compared to nonsmokers is on the order of 10:1, whereas the relative risk of pancreatic cancer is about 2:1. The difference suggests that cigarette smoking is more likely to be a causal factor for lung cancer than for pancreatic cancer.
>
> If the association makes sense in terms of known biological mechanisms or other epidemiologic knowledge, it becomes more plausible as a cause-and-effect relationship. Part of the attractiveness of the hypothesis that a high-saturated fat, high-cholesterol diet predisposes to atherosclerosis is the fact that a biologic mechanism can be invoked. Such a diet increases blood lipids, which may in turn be deposited in arterial walls. A correlation between the number of telephone poles in a country and its coronary heart disease mortality rate lacks plausibility as a cause-and-effect relationship partly because it is difficult to imagine a biologic mechanism whereby telephone poles result in atherosclerosis.[20]

In addition to *relative risk*, epidemiological studies can be used to describe *attributable risk*. As the term suggests, *attributable risk* refers to the proportion of the disease that is statistically attributable to the risk factor. Relative risk (RR) and attributable risk (AR) are, in a sense, reciprocal measures. When the relative risk is 2.0 (sometimes expressed as 2:1), the attributable risk is 50% (sometimes expressed as .5). What this relative risk of 2.0 or 2:1 means in popular parlance is that a person with that risk factor is twice as likely as someone without the factor to have the correlated harm occur. The precise equation that relates the two values is RR-1/RR=AR. When relative risk is 10:1, as it is for the association of smoking cigarettes and lung cancer, the attributable risk is .9 or 90%. Be sure to remember in using these concepts that they are merely statistical averages based on studies of whole populations. Attributable risk calculated by that formula, for example, does not take into account the degree of exposure of any particular member of the exposed class; it is an aggregate, or average, indicator. For a good introductory discussion to the forms of epidemiological data and their use in toxic tort litigation, see Dintzer & Mosher, Epidemiological Evidence in Toxic Tort Cases, 17 Nat. Resources & Env't 222 (2003).

COMMENTARY & QUESTIONS

1. Legal causation and epidemiological statistical proof: comparing apples and pears. What makes a relative risk value of 2.0 appear to be particularly important in the legal arena? A relative risk value in excess of 2.0 makes it appear more likely than not that the risk factor is the operative cause of the injury. This linguistic formulation tracks the standard that the plaintiff must meet to carry the burden of proof on the issue of causation-in-fact. That is, the plaintiff has the burden of persuading the trier of fact that defendant's action is more likely than not the cause of plaintiff's injury. Using the term *attributable risk*

---

20. Gary D. Friedman, Primer of Epidemiology 1, 183-84 (3d ed. 1987).

makes this linguistically even clearer; when the risk attributable to defendant is more than half (>50%) of the total risk, it is easy to conclude that the defendant's act is more likely than not the cause of the plaintiff's injury.

Two very different lines of inquiry undercut reliance on a relative risk of 2.0 or below carrying so great a significance. First, as should be very clear, individual factors relating to the plaintiff, such as exposure to the defendant's toxic substance, other exposures or risk factors (or their absence), are all variables that affect the probative value of the epidemiological evidence. In *Donaldson*, for example, plaintiffs were able to provide very compelling proof on a range of key issues. These included proof about exposure both in terms of proximity to the site in time and space based on location and weather conditions; effective testimony explaining exposure pathways and heightened neuro-susceptibility of young persons including the transplacental exposure in utero of the three children who suffered. It also was helpful to the strength of the case that the four plaintiffs were not related and therefore did not share a familial genetic predisposition to neuroblastomas (i.e., negating a risk factor for which defendant is not responsible). Finally, because the victims were children, plaintiffs could more easily minimize other exposures and risk factors.

Second, conceptually, most courts, as did the *Donaldson* court, now treat causation in toxic tort cases in much the same way that they treat joint causation of a single injury in conventional tort cases, and for many of the same reasons relating to the nature of proof that a plaintiff reasonably can be expected to be able to provide. As the *Donaldson* court said:

> Environmental exposure cases, like the instant case, do not afford litigants the opportunity to specify with such certainty the exact level and dose of exposure. In most instances, the details of exposure, including information of exactly when or where exposure occurred, is not available. . . . Accordingly, we review whether there was evidence from which a jury could conclude that CIPS's conduct was a material element and substantial factor in bringing about the neuroblastomas. 767 N.E.2d at 332.

In *Allen v. U.S.*, 588 F. Supp. 247 (D. Utah 1984), rev'd on other grounds, 816 F.2d 1417 (10th Cir. 1987), the court was faced with horrifying facts but little available proof of the extent of individual exposures. Unannounced and unadmitted atmospheric testing of atomic weapons had resulted in mass exposure of the general public to radioactive fallout released by the test. The government's lack of warning and haphazard monitoring of fallout levels made it impossible for citizens to avoid the exposure and, likewise, impossible for them to reliably prove their level of exposure. (The government's feckless efforts had not recorded reliable measures.) Still, based on the epidemiological studies, the relative risk levels (a term not used in the *Allen* litigation) were far lower than 2.0. Although its precise ruling is elusive and not easy to summarize, the court allowed the plaintiffs to shift the burden of proof on the cause-in-fact issue (which the *Allen* court refers to as the factual connection issue) to the defendant by proving that the defendant's conduct was a substantial risk-increasing factor. Once plaintiff makes that showing, the defendant is to come forward with evidence that tries to weaken the factual connection between its acts and the plaintiff's injuries. In the end, no fixed rule is announced: "Whether any of these factual connections will lead to liability is, as Professor Thode reminds us, 'an issue involving *the scope of the legal system's protection afforded to plaintiff* and not an issue of factual causation.' Thode, Tort Analysis: Duty-Risk v. Proximate Cause and the Rational Allocation of Functions Between Judge and Jury, 1977 Utah L. Rev. 1, 6." (Emphasis by the court.) In short, the key issue becomes one of policy regarding the extent of protection offered by the legal system, the very essence of the proximate cause inquiry.

2. Legal causation and statistical significance: comparing apples and pear melba. When the term *significant* appears in legal discourse, it usually has its lay meanings that

C. Proof of Complex Causation

speak to the importance of a factor or that contrast the central with the peripheral. In relation to scientific studies that find a correlation significant (as between an exposure and the subsequent onset of disease), the word *significant* is a term of art that describes the reliability of the linkage. To be more precise, the significance of a correlation is the likelihood that the data observed are not the product of mere random chance. In a case of radiation exposure, the judge in the *Allen* case explained statistical significance this way:

> Where there is an increase of observed cases of a particular cancer or leukemia over the number statistically "expected" to normally appear, the question arises whether it may be rationally inferred that the increase is causally connected to specific human activity. The scientific papers and reports will often speak of whether a deviation from the expected numbers of cases is "statistically significant," supporting a hypothesis of causation, or whether the perceived increase is attributable to random variation in the studied population, i.e., to chance. The mathematical tests of significance commonly used in research tend to be stringent; for an increase to be considered "statistically significant," the probability that it can be attributed to random chance usually must be five percent or less ($p=.05$). In other words, if the level of significance chosen by the researcher is $p=.05$, then an observed correlation is "significant" if there is 1 chance in 20—or less—that the increase resulted from chance. In scientific practice, levels of significance of .01 or .001 are used providing an even more stringent test of a chosen hypothetical relationship. *Allen v. U.S.*, 588 F. Supp. 247, 416 (D. Utah 1984).

Accordingly, from the legal viewpoint, a causal hypothesis that narrowly fails to satisfy a .05 level of statistical significance is not insignificant. For instance, data for which there is only a 1 in 19 chance of its being random fails a .05 significance test but nevertheless evidences a relationship for which "the probability is 94.73 percent or 18 chances out of 19 that the observed relationship is not a random event . . . [and] the certainty that the observed increase is related to its hypothetical cause rather than mere chance is still far more likely than not." Id. What does all this mean for the trial of toxic tort cases? Even causal hypotheses that are not statistically significant at traditional p-values used in scientific research may be significant and highly probative proof that helps establish causation-in-fact.

3. The pitfalls of probabilistic proof. A hot debate in the legal literature surrounds the advisability of allowing proof of probabilities to establish causation-in-fact. There are numerous good articles on this subject, two of the classics being Tribe, Trial by Mathematics: Precision and Ritual in the Legal Process, 84 Harv. L. Rev. 1329 (1971), and Nesson, Agent Orange Meets the Blue Bus: Factfinding at the Frontier of Knowledge, 66 B.U. L. Rev. 521 (1986).

Consider the following hypotheticals:[21] Following exposure to defendant's toxic waste that leached into an aquifer, the cancer rate in a community rises from 10 per year to 19 per year (hypo 1) or 21 per year (hypo 2), *and* all other possible causes have been ruled out by undisputed expert testimony. If probability is translated uncritically into plaintiffs' failure or success in carrying the burden of proof on the cause-in-fact issue, then in hypo 1 defendant goes free of liability to any of the 19 victims, and in hypo 2 defendant must compensate all 21 victims. Is such a result absurd? Do the hypotheticals make it clear why *Landrigan* and other cases are chary of making a relative risk of 2.0 a litmus for recovery? Should plaintiffs be relieved of their usual burden of proof because of these proof problems? In *Allen* the court fashioned a more lenient standard that adapted the "substantial factor" doctrine developed in the joint and several liability context to allow for proof of cause-in-fact in toxic exposure cases.

---

21. The hypotheticals are adapted from Delgado, Beyond *Sindell*, 70 Cal. L. Rev. 881, 885 (1982).

III

THE STRUCTURAL ELEMENTS OF THE REGULATORY STATE

Regulations, the wisdom, necessity, and validity of which, as applied to existing conditions, are...apparent,... probably would have been rejected as arbitrary and oppressive...a century ago or even a half century ago.... While the meaning of the constitutional guaranties never varies, the scope of their application must expand or contract to meet the new and different conditions which are constantly coming within the field of their operation. In a changing world it is impossible that it should be otherwise.

— Sutherland, J., in *Euclid v. Ambler*, 272 U.S. 386, 387 (1926)

The U.S. Chamber of Commerce is the nation's biggest lobby, spending an average of $400,000 a day in a single legislative session.

— Center for Responsive Politics

5

An Overview of Environmental Regulation in the United States

A. A Taxonomic Approach to Public Law—
   the Different Ways Statutes Work
B. The Advent and Failure of Broad Delegations to Administrative
   Agencies (Review and Permit Statutes)
C. Keeping Score at the Beginning of the Twenty-first Century:
   Players, Positions, Programs & Policies

The most dynamic source of environmental protection law today is "public law"—legal structures and mechanisms built upon statutes and administrative regulations at federal, state, and local levels, and occasionally at the global level as well—rather than the common law. *Boomer* and the TCE groundwater contamination in the Woburn, Massachusetts area demonstrate that tort law alone does not fully address the problems of modern environmental protection. That requires public law, standing alone or reinforcing and expanding upon the common law of environmental protection.

The previous chapters demonstrate that common law environmental litigation will surely continue to play an important role in providing remedies for injuries that are broadly considered to be environmental. The scope of harms associated with toxic contamination and global climate change make it obvious, however, that common law can't be relied upon to serve as society's primary environmental law strategy. Common law in most cases operates retrospectively. The range of common law remedies is inadequate to the demands of public necessities. Common law rules vary among jurisdictions and are administered by generalist judges and court administrative personnel who lack the specialized knowledge and the continuity necessary for implementation of environmental protection systems. The burden of proof in common law cases, moreover, requires plaintiffs to prove specific causation by a preponderance of the evidence in almost all instances, a constraint that makes broad responsive or proactive precautionary policies infeasible. Finally, common law systems lack the territorial reach broad enough to cope with environmental problems that increasingly are transnational, regional, and even global in scope.

"Public law" contrasts with both "private law" and "common law." Environmental public law is built from hundreds of legislative enabling statutes delegating authority to administrative agencies to promulgate and enforce regulations, and to perform quasi-judicial adjudicatory functions with regard to permitting and enforcement. That pattern of legislatively delegating power to government agencies to implement statutes is the paradigmatic model of almost all regulation, including environmental regulation, although the U.S. has also pioneered the concept of active citizen enforcement of public law.

Environmental regulation is centuries old. London had smoke-control ordinances in the 1600s. But environmental regulation was neither varied nor sophisticated until the final third of the twentieth century. Since 1970, environmental regulation has broadened its reach in terms of subjects addressed and has developed a rich amalgam of types of regulatory approaches—a "taxonomy" surveyed by this coursebook. The standard modern mode of U.S. pollution control regulation has been a Washington-dominated "cooperative federalism" in a "command-and-control" regulatory format. Despite constant efforts to delegitimize this approach, it appears to have achieved notable successes in some areas, with the public benefits of the Clean Air Act (CAA) being the most studied and perhaps easiest to assess in economic terms. A study required by its 1990 amendments stated as follows:

> The direct benefits [in excess of costs] of the Clean Air Act from 1970 to 1990 include reduced incidence of a number of adverse human health effects, improvements in visibility, and avoided damage to agricultural crops. Based on the assumptions employed, the estimated economic value of these benefits ranges from $5.6 to $49.4 trillion, in 1990 dollars, with a mean, or central tendency estimate, of $22.2 trillion. These estimates do not include a number of other potentially important benefits which could not be readily quantified, such as ecosystem changes and air toxics-related human health effects. The estimates are based on the assumption that correlations between increased air pollution exposures and adverse health outcomes found by epidemiological studies indicate causal relationships between the pollutant exposures and the adverse health effects.[1]

The litany of improvements in environmental outcomes produced by regulation is extensive. Besides significant air and water quality improvements, fewer hazardous substances are discharged into the environment, and hazardous residuals that are still discharged must be treated to high levels of quality and publicly reported. Accidental spills and releases of hazardous materials must be reported and immediately contained and cleaned up. Most abandoned hazardous waste disposal sites have already been, or are in the process of being, remediated. Federal activities that might have significant environmental impacts must be documented and publicly disclosed and their alternatives analyzed. Pesticides must be registered and their uses justified. Endangered species, federal public lands, and critical areas such as wetlands and marine sanctuaries have received some legal protection. And several international environmental threats have been addressed. The U.S. environmental regulatory model was so successful that most modern democracies have established similar regulatory systems, often more protective than their U.S. model.

Despite these manifest achievements, subsequent chapters illustrate the reality that great room for improvement remains. Aspects of U.S. environmental regulatory law are inadequate, ineffectual, suboptimal, merely symbolically reassuring, and even counterproductive. The effectiveness of federal resource management programs, for example, is compromised by statutory loopholes, political pressures on the agencies that administer the law, insufficient governmental resources, and systematic nonenforcement. (See Chapter 9.) The federal Clean Water Act (CWA) cannot presently be used to address the major remaining sources of water pollution—nonpoint sources—because most of these dischargers are exempt from the Act's provisions. Major environmental threats, including sprawl and

---

1. Quoted from the EPA study, *available at* www.epa.gov/air/sect812/copy.html.

widespread chemical disruption of human hormonal conditions, remain virtually unregulated by federal environmental law. Effective regulation of GHG emissions is still in the process of taking form. Although its necessity has gained substantial acceptance, political resistance will continue to be fierce.

In short, although the U.S. (and, to some extent, the world community) has made substantial progress in recognizing and controlling environmental pollution and natural resource depletion, there is still a long way to go. The fight against environmental degradation appears to be ever-changing and perpetual.

A. A Taxonomic Approach to Public Law— The Different Ways Statutes Work

A wide array of public law regulatory approaches is used to address environmental problems. An effort to isolate the key elements of various regulatory approaches has been the organizing force for this casebook in all of its editions. Taking a taxonomic approach to the techniques has important benefits, not the least of which is the emphasis on how the statute is constructed instead of a focus on the often intricate linguistic way in which complex environmental statutes are written by Congress, administered by the agencies, and interpreted by courts. This approach also stresses the potential transferability of the techniques for application to additional settings, an important point in facing the future. Complex statutes that address a variety of problems, such as the CAA, frequently embody a combination of these regulatory techniques, using one or more to address facets of the larger problem. Environmental law is a dynamic field in which regulatory initiatives do not remain fixed. By conceptualizing the contemporary regulatory system as a taxonomy of techniques, the evolving regulatory future will, in the main, be understandable as an adaptation and recombination of the techniques that are already in use with the possible addition of a small number of regulatory innovations that have yet to be tried.

In the environmental area, virtually every regulatory effort has two somewhat distinct elements: a regulatory technique and a procedure for implementation. As used in this book, those techniques are the items in the taxonomic list, the various strategies that are used to address environmental problems. To given an example, harm-based ambient standards are a regulatory technique. This taxonomic device operates by:

1. correlating concentrations of pollutants in the receiving body with undesirable human health and environmental effects (the most obvious receiving bodies for this type of regulation are air and water);
2. selecting a target level, an ambient quality standard, for concentrations that the regulator deems safe (i.e., a level at which the harms are reduced to an acceptable level of harm or risk); and
3. prescribing the amount of pollution that individual polluters whose pollution affects the receiving body may emit or discharge in such a way that if each polluter complies, the ambient standard will be attained.

Since this regulatory technique prescribes limits for individual polluters and needs compliance with those limits to be successful, there also needs to be a procedure for implementation. In this case, the implementing procedure can most easily be a permit to emit or discharge only a certain amount of pollutants. Moreover, to make compliance likely, there have to be penalties for unpermitted pollution.[2] Distinct regulatory techniques may share highly similar implementing procedures.

The distinction between the taxonomic regulatory technique and the implementing procedure is self-evident in most cases. The two principal exceptions arise in regard to some of the many statutes that incorporate permits and to some of the statutes that impose outright bans on activities. This book classifies permit systems as a separate type of taxonomic technique when the legislation creating the permit system does not provide sufficient guidance regarding how the content of any particular permit is going to be ascertained. In essence, in those systems the actions taken by the administrative agency in the permit process itself creates the regulatory standard that is being imposed and the permit is not being used to implement a standard that was derived employing another technique. A statute of this type is featured later in this chapter. In the case of outright bans, under almost all permit statutes, failure to have a permit is intended to proscribe the activity, just like a ban would. Nevertheless, for some statutes, such as the Endangered Species Act (ESA), the interdiction of otherwise lawful activity lies at the heart of the regulatory technique and is intended as a "roadblock," not a mere implementing process.

The listing that follows includes the major regulatory techniques studied in this book in roughly the order in which they appear. The list is not encyclopedic; there are other approaches that could be appropriately included. Also, it is important to keep in mind that a single statute can, and most of the major environmental statutes in the U.S. do, combine techniques in addressing the problems they seek to solve.

Review and Permit (Chapter 5, Part B). The essential features of this technique are identification of an environmental problem area by the legislature, a very broad statement of public policy in that regard, and the delegation to an agency of authority to make case-by-case determinations in regard to environmentally degrading behavior with the power to permit, condition, or deny the proposed action. The agency "reviews" the data in relation to the activity and its environmental effects, the possibility of controls, etc., and issues its decision in the form of a "permit" (that may contain conditions limiting harmful environmental effects) or a denial of a permit.

Disclosure (Chapter 8). This technique was pioneered by the National Environmental Policy Act (NEPA). In that form, it applied to all of the agencies of the federal government and required that they prepare and disclose a full inventory of the environmental impacts of a proposed action as part of the planning process and that their study also consider alternatives to the proposed action and their environmental impacts. Disclosure laws take other forms as well, such as the TRIs of the Emergency Planning and Community Right-to-Know Act (EPCRA), which requires firms to list the substances that they have on hand and those that are released into the environment. Disclosure increases the level of environmental knowledge about a proposal, raises visibility of actions, and brings considerable public and political pressure to bear on what might otherwise be underinformed or insular decisions.

---

2. In thinking about the procedure for implementation, the FRCPs offer a useful analogy. In litigation, no matter what the cause of action, the defendant must receive a summons, a part of which coercively threatens entry of a default judgment and its subsequent enforcement if the defendant fails to respond. Permits, and the penalties for not having a permit or violating a permit, create a similar form of coercion that must underlie a regulatory program. In contrast to implementation, the means by which the permit terms are determined is often one of the key differentiators among regulatory techniques.

Planning Statutes (Chapter 9). Planning is not itself a taxonomic device, but within the array of planning statutes, several types of regulatory techniques can be identified. *Land use regulation* is among the most traditional environmental regulatory devices. With a heritage of seeking to preserve and enhance amenity values (and reduce the likelihood of nuisances), zoning regulations become an environmental technique when zones are drawn with reference to a particular environmental or health and safety issue, such as flood plains. Within zones, activities allowed under the zone regulation may proceed, others are barred. It is a short step from zoning to *critical areas management* regulation. Like zoning, certain areas have a regulatory plan attached to them, but the lines are drawn with explicit reference to a particular environmental problem, such as the loss of wetlands. *Facility siting laws* are another planning tool, usually addressing the common problem of finding a suitable spot for facilities that are necessary for society but are locally unwanted and pose environmental risks. These siting laws contain safety requirements that try to limit environmental risks and to create community-acceptance mechanisms that assign the affected communities a relevant participatory role in the siting to improve their degree of acceptance of the outcome of the process. *Resource management statutes* are also a major planning area. The national government owns vast tracts of land, particularly in the West, and how it manages the resources on those lands has a profound environmental effect. Over the years, a number of management techniques have been tried; the three canvassed here are *dominant use, multiple use,* and *managing to master plan.* Finally Chapter 9 takes up the very difficult problem of coordinating activities that are regulated by multiple authorities. Featured in that context is the Coastal Zone Management Act (CZMA), a *consistency statute.* Consistency laws coordinate activities by requiring that actions permitted under one regulatory regime also be consistent with the requirements of another. Consistency is also involved with managing to a master plan, though in that context it might be considered an implementation device.

Roadblock Statutes (Chapter 10). The dominant element of roadblock statutes is that the legislative branch has put down a fixed line, a flat prohibition on environmentally damaging behavior. Such an unyielding approach is reserved for problems of particular gravity, such as the irreversibility of species eradication that is prohibited by the ESA. Under that law, pursuant to a complex process, a federal agency generates a list of endangered and threatened species. Then, under §7 of the Act, federal agencies are required to utilize their authorities (construction, permitting, etc.) to avoid jeopardy to the listed species. If they cannot eliminate the risk of harm to the listed species, the agency cannot proceed. That is the roadblock. Similarly, under §9 of the Act, all persons are prohibited from "taking" listed species, even when it is done indirectly by altering habitat in a way that adversely affects the species' breeding, feeding, and sheltering. That, too, is a roadblock. The starkness of the result in these cases creates pressure for workarounds that allow the desired activity to proceed without sacrificing the imperative of species protection. Under the ESA, the workaround adjustment processes have in general been quite successful.

Harm-Based Ambient Standards (Chapters 11 and 12). As described in the introduction to this section, harm-based approaches begin with the goal of preventing some identified harm based on levels of exposure to conventional or toxic agents that are present in the environment generally.[3] A concentration is set for the allowable limit of the pollutant

---

3. The term *ambient* refers to the general receiving medium. At times, smaller areas might be allowed to have harmfully high concentrations of a pollutant, such as "mixing zones" under the CWA.

in the receiving body, which is the key regulatory standard in this type of technique. From there, the regulatory program accounts for the contributing sources of the pollution and regulates those sources in a way that ensures the total loadings result in ambient quality at least as good as that required by the standard, which should avoid unacceptable levels of harm.[4] Both the CAA and the CWA employ harm-based ambient standards as a prominent feature of their regulatory regimes. This technique implicitly allows pollution up to the regulatory limit and, standing alone, the harm-based ambient standards approach does not require efforts to reduce pollution beyond that point, even when additional pollution reductions are technologically and economically feasible. These statutes are almost always implemented through permits issued to the regulated facilities.

Technology-Based Standards (Chapters 11 and 12). Technology-based standards set performance levels for pollution control based on available technologies. The ambient quality result thus becomes a function of the number of facilities in a locale and the characteristics of the receiving body. There is no guarantee of any certain level of risk prevention, nor is there any consideration given to the possibility that the receiving body might be able to "assimilate" additional pollution without adverse consequences. The goal in these statutes is usually the minimization of pollution, so the standards are usually set with reference to the "best" technology for controlling the particular category of polluting facility. The standards are measured as levels of performance achieved by those technologies and do not require the use of any specific way of achieving that level of performance, leaving room for innovation and cost savings if more efficient ways to meet the standard are available. These statutes are almost always implemented through permits issued to the regulated facilities.

Technology-Forcing (Chapter 11). This technique is used when the legislature desires to achieve a pollution reduction result that cannot be met by any existing in-use technology. The two most notable instances of technology-forcing in the United States were in regard to vehicle tailpipe emissions and the elimination of the use of certain types of chlorofluorocarbons (CFCs). The legislature picks a time in which it thinks a new, more effective pollution control technology or environmental protection system can be brought on-line, and mandates a performance standard based on the new technology that will be able to be achieved by that future date. Those subject to the technology-forcing regulation are threatened with being put out of business if they do not develop a means by which to comply. Technology-forcing is a little bit like a game of "chicken" that the legislature is playing with the regulated industry. Since shutting down a major industry is not a politically realistic legislative choice, there is a considerable risk to employing the technique and actually following through if the needed innovation has not been achieved in the time allowed. Both the legislature and the regulated community understand that, so usually technology-forcing is employed when there is strong evidence that the needed technology can be implemented by the appointed time and the industry, for whatever reason, has delayed or opposed its commercial utilization. The most recent use of technology-forcing, setting of aggressive gas mileage standards, follows this pattern. Even without innovation,

---

4. There is similarity in these first steps, i.e., having an environmental goal and an upper limit on emissions or discharges that will attain that goal, between the harm-based ambient standards and the cap-and-trade market enlistment technique. In cap-and-trade, one of the key regulatory decisions is to select an allowable amount of emissions or discharges from the entities being regulated under the program. The means of obtaining the desired result is radically different. Also, in some cap-and-trade settings, the initial cap is chosen by rollback (e.g., 50% reduction from the baseline of current emissions) or some other method that is not extensively correlated with harm that is occurring at particular ambient levels of pollution.

the auto manufacturers can comply with the standards by marketing a different mix of vehicles, but the new standard also provides a powerful incentive to spur vastly improved GHG-reducing vehicle technologies that would allow the continued production of more profitable larger and more powerful and luxurious vehicles that, to date, have had generally poor fuel efficiencies.

Cost-Benefit Analysis (Chapter 13). Most commonly, cost-benefit analysis is a tool used for setting policy, wherein the decisionmaker wants to be assured that a particular course of action will provide benefits in excess of its costs. If the project or proposal under review can't pass that simple test, it seems that society is better off not to go forward with a losing proposition. Historically, cost-benefit analysis was used as a regulatory tool to rein in pork-barrel construction spending by federal agencies, such as the Army Corps of Engineers and the Bureau of Reclamation. It was not particularly successful because of the manipulation of the numbers those agencies practiced to justify questionable projects. In contemporary times, the technique has been applied to government regulation under the same premise: Regulatory efforts ought to create net benefits in excess of costs imposed. Whether that technique is well suited to environmental regulation is an important policy question taken up in the chapter. There are two important environmental laws that require cost-benefit analysis as part of their bureaucratic execution. The Office of Information and Regulatory Affairs, housed in the executive branch's Office of Management and Budget, has often been active in using cost-benefit analysis to prevent regulation proposed by many agencies (especially EPA) from going into effect.

Market-Enlisting Regulatory Strategies (Chapter 14). The goal of the regulations studied in the book is to alter behavior that adversely affects the environment. Most of the techniques mentioned thus far rely on what is often pejoratively labeled "command-and-control" techniques. Although that description overstates the degree of specificity with which parties are regulated, market-enlisting techniques try to influence polluter behavior by aligning the marketplace economic incentives with the behaviors that will result in the desired environmental outcome. There are several of these techniques. The two simplest to understand are *subsidies* and *pollution taxes*. If the environmental goal is clean up the countryside by getting old discarded vehicles picked up and hauled to the scrap yard, offering a bounty for scrapped cars will increase the rate at which those cars are found and taken to scrap yards. Pollution taxes also rely on easily understandable principles of cost avoidance. If a firm faces a $100/ton pollution tax for emitting carbon dioxide to the atmosphere, if there is a pollution reducing option that decreases emissions at a cost of less than $100 per ton, the tax creates an incentive to reduce emissions. Pollution taxes are really quite common (e.g., disposal fees reduce the volume of trash or hazardous waste sent to landfills or disposal facilities, and also promote recycling).

Another market-enlistment technique is *emissions trading*. The idea here is a bit like harm-based ambient standards:

1. set an upper limit on the amount of pollution that the regulated entities can emit;
2. issue tradable allowances that represent that amount of pollution;
3. require all of the regulated entities to have an allowance to cover each unit of pollution it emits; and
4. establish penalties for having insufficient allowances to cover the pollution that are greater than the cost of compliance with the requirement.

At the beginning of the program, the total emissions exceed the number of allowances. After a short phase-in period, however, the simple behavioral choices will result in the following actions: High-cost pollution avoiders will buy allowances and not substantially reduce their pollution. Low-cost pollution avoiders will decrease their pollution by large amounts and avoid needing many allowances, and, if they have extra allowances after reducing their emissions, they will sell the extras to the high-cost pollution avoiders. The beauty of this result is that the emissions are reduced and the amount of money spent on the reductions is less, because the low-cost avoiders were the ones making the reductions. As the chapter shows, the means of implementing an effective trading system are considerably more complex than those basic steps.

Hazardous Substance Regulation to Protect Land and Groundwater from Pollution (Chapters 16 and 17). Many of the taxonomic regulatory techniques for dealing with pollution that are described above are used primarily, although not exclusively, in relation to air and water. Congress has enacted two major statutes, and one or two lesser ones, that seek to prevent the contamination of soil and groundwater by hazardous substances.[5] The Resource Conservation Recovery Act (RCRA) applies what this book calls a *life cycle* technique to the generation, transport, and disposal of hazardous wastes. The idea is fairly simple, if all of the hazardous waste is always accounted for and in the custody of someone who has the facilities to keep it contained, it will not be out loose in the environment contaminating soil and groundwater. In fact, RCRA accomplishes that feat by combining an amalgamation of several taxonomic types, some already listed, some not. It has very extensive *technology-based* requirements applicable to treatment, storage, and disposal facilities (TSDFs), and it has *market-enlisting* waste reduction aspects because the cost of disposal at a licensed TSDF is so high that waste reduction is a less expensive alternative for many generators. A key part of this system is a *tracking* or *manifest system*, which makes generators responsible for seeing that their waste arrives at the TSDF. RCRA relies heavily on a *roadblock provision*, the so-called land ban to force EPA and the regulated community to take action to implement the statute's provisions without interminable objection and litigation. Action-forcing legislative provisions (like the land ban that works by threatening dire consequences) are sometimes referred to as hammer clauses.

CERCLA (aka Superfund) is the leading U.S. embodiment of the *polluter pay principle*, which might more taxonomically be labeled *cost internalization* or *cleanup liability*. Conceptually, Superfund is in a complementary relationship to RCRA: RCRA is the prevention law; CERCLA is the cure for past improper disposal.[6] CERCLA's most prominent provision frequently imposes joint and several liability for cleanup costs on all those whose actions played a role in the release of a hazardous substance into the environment. CERCLA, too, has several parts, including a *revolving fund* to pay initially for cleanups that are orchestrated under an elaborate set of substantive and procedural *planning* standards that reside in the National Contingency Plan, which has community involvement aspects similar to those present in some siting statutes. Under CERCLA, EPA is granted an *extraordinary administrative order power* backed by *treble damage awards* as an inducement to cooperation, and more.

---

5. See, e.g., the Pollution Prevention Act of 1990, 42 U.S.C. §§13101 et seq. This statute declares a national policy of waste prevention and lists a hierarchy of strategies by which that goal can be accomplished. It is a hortatory call for action.

6. RCRA has its own cleanup provisions that apply to TSFDs.

B. The Advent and Failure of Broad Delegations to Administrative Agencies

COMMENTARY & QUESTIONS

Studying the regulatory techniques. This long list of taxonomic techniques used in environmental regulation is a testament to the richness and complexity of the field. What lies ahead in this book are examples of these techniques applied in one or more ways to address environmental problems. In studying those regulatory programs, try to discern what makes a technique effective or ineffective. Is its effectiveness limited in its application, or is it transferrable? When techniques are ineffective or imperfectly applied, look for ways to correct the problems or consider what other contexts might allow a technique to be better used. The environmental future will demand such adaptive thinking.

B. THE ADVENT AND FAILURE OF BROAD DELEGATIONS TO ADMINISTRATIVE AGENCIES (REVIEW AND PERMIT STATUTES)

Public law has a long history, but its principal growth and development in the environmental field begins in the last half of the twentieth century. Slightly less than a century before that, American environmental law had a somewhat limited beginning as public health-based local smoke control ordinances in cities. While those ordinances might have had some effect as Professor Laitos pointed out:

> Although the ordinance typically declared that the emission of thick, dense smoke was a public nuisance, no public official was empowered either to locate or abate these nuisances. . . . Unfortunately, whatever advantage there was in having dense smoke recognized as a nuisance per se was outweighed by the fact that such a narrowly focused prohibition ignored the more harmful invisible pollutants present in the smoke. J. Laitos, Legal Institutions & Pollution: Some Intersections Between Law & History, 15 Natural Resources Journal 423 (1975).

Whatever the benefit of those localized ordinances, their coverage and enforcement was woefully incomplete in the face of what had by 1950 become widespread incidence of health and environmental impairment due to pollution. A more comprehensive response was needed. Initially, that response began at the state level, and eventually moved to the national level.

As a function of institutional capacity, the initial legislated response took largely predictable channels Under U.S. democratic and constitutional arrangements, the legislature is the primary law making institution and holds the power to establish environmental regulations. Institutionally, of course, due to lack of bandwidth alone, the legislature lacks the capacity to implement and operate any meaningful regulatory program. To solve that problem, the legislature empowers administrative agencies (as their agents) to take on those tasks.

While the use of agencies is necessary at the operational and implementation level, the relationship between the legislature and the agencies in determining the substantive content of the regulatory program varies. As studied in the administrative law materials, the legislature, under constitutional commands forbidding the unlawful delegation of their authority to others, cannot simply identify an area for regulation, create an agency, give it carte blanche, and walk away. The legislature must, at a minimum, provide guidance regarding the regulatory policy and manner in which it is to be pursued. When public environmental law enactments were in their infancy, however, the legislature was hard pressed to offer sufficient guidance.

Consider, as an example, water pollution regulation in Michigan, which adopted a state program. Two aspects of the statute are what make it typical of its generation of environmental regulation—the generality of the policy guidance and the choice of "review and permit" as the regulatory methodology. A third aspect of the statute, its lack of effectiveness, is also typical of its sister statutes of that era. As the primary forum shifted from the municipal level to the state level, state pollution control statutes such as the Michigan Water Resources Commission Act (WRCA), as it stood from 1929 to the early 1970s,[7] became prevalent. Derived from an older public health statute, the Michigan statute established a seven-member, part-time Water Resources Commission (WRC),[8] "to prohibit the pollution of any waters of the state."

> **Michigan Water Resources Commission Act of 1929**
>
> The commission shall protect and conserve the water resources of the state and shall have control of the pollution of surface or underground waters of the state and the Great Lakes which are or may be affected by waste disposal. . . . The commission shall enforce this act and shall promulgate rules as considered necessary to carry out its duties under this act.

To go along with its broad mandate, the WRC was given investigatory power and the power to bring actions at law and in equity. The legislation in general terms prohibited discharges that harmed public health or destroyed fish life in the water, and granted the WRC the power to regulate discharges into the state's waters by setting and enforcing pollution standards, in terms common to other review-and-permit programs:

> The commission shall establish such pollution standards for lakes, rivers, streams and other waters of the state in relation to the public use to which they are or may be put, as it shall deem necessary. . . . It shall have the authority to make rules and orders [i.e., permits] restricting the polluting content of any waste material or polluting substance discharged or sought to be discharged into any lake, river, stream or other waters of the state. It shall have the authority to take all appropriate steps to prevent any pollution which is deemed by the commission to be unreasonable and against public interest in view of the existing conditions in any lake, river, stream or other waters of the state.

With the broad authority to implement a review-and-permit process thus set, the statute also addressed some of the more critical details. Since the first enactment of the statutory plan, the WRC had enjoyed the power to make orders (permits) that would limit discharges. What might be called the "burden of initiation" of action under the WRC Act became explicit. As to existing facilities, the WRC had the burden of initiating standard-setting and

---

7. The Water Resources Commission Act, Pub. Act 245 of 1929. The statute has since been repealed by P.A. 1994, No. 451, §90101, Eff. March 30, 1995. While in effect it was codified at Mich. Comp. Laws. Ann. §323.1 et seq. Subsequent citations to the old act and its repealers are omitted. The control over water pollution was transferred to the Michigan Department of Natural Resources and updated to satisfy the rigorous requirements for state laws imposed by the federal CWA. See Act 293 of 1972 Mich. Pub. Acts.

8. The composition of the Commission, as spelled out in the legislation, comprised the directors of the state departments of natural resources, public health, highways, and agriculture; and three citizens of the state to be appointed by the governor, by and with the advice and consent of the state senate: one from groups representative of industrial management; one from groups representative of municipalities; and one citizen from a group "representative of conservation associations or interests."

B. The Advent and Failure of Broad Delegations to Administrative Agencies

permitting procedures. If it did not make standards and apply them to specific polluters, there was no need for the polluters to seek WRC approval of their practices. As to new or increased discharges only, a mandatory review and permit process was added that required an application "setting forth the nature of the enterprise or development contemplated, the amount of water required to be used, its source, the proposed point of discharge of said wastes into the waters of the state, the estimated amount so to be discharged, and a fair statement setting forth the expected bacterial, physical, chemical and other known characteristics of said wastes." Upon receipt of an application, the WRC had 60 days in which to deny or issue an order [permit] that could contain conditions "necessary to guard adequately against such unlawful uses of the public waters."

The vague generality of these standards poses two different obstacles to preventing pollution. The first obstacle is interpretive—to the extent that the standards are vague (e.g., "injurious to public health or to the conducting of any industrial enterprise"), the WRC had to come up with more precise enforceable definitions. Recalling that the WRC was not a politically powerful agency—and by its very composition was somewhat sympathetic to industrial and commercial interests—suggests that it would tend not to interpret those terms stringently. Only the clearest cases of injury would be defined by the WRC as violating the threshold of harm that triggered its regulatory powers.

The second obstacle lay in the steps required in going from a case of probable unlawful discharge (i.e., a finding that the application, if granted without conditions, would result in an unlawful discharge) to the regulatory application of adequate permit conditions to prevent the proscribed harm from occurring. The WRC, for political reasons already described, was hesitant to deny permit applications outright. In general, the WRC could be expected to insert permit conditions that would allow the discharger to go forward with the overall project but that would also require that the effluent be treated in some manner before discharge. Here the WRC's lack of staff and technical expertise was a major barrier to effective operation.[9] Industrial permit applicants generally possess engineering expertise and use it well in negotiating permit conditions. The WRC, and most similar agencies or commissions, were, in the period under discussion, simply overmatched in that process.[10]

COMMENTARY & QUESTIONS

1. Identifying the Michigan WRC Act as a review-and-permit statute—procedural methodology. Under the WRC Act, the Commission issued "orders" that are functionally identical to what in most contemporary statutes are termed "permits." By whichever name, those Commission actions amounted to administrative agency adjudications—applying a regulatory standard to the conduct of a regulated party. The "review" amounts to the agency action of looking at some relevant body of case-specific information as part of the adjudicatory process. The usual review-and-permit statute begins with a permit application

---

9. Recall that the Commission was not a line agency, but was instead a group of commissioners whose staff had to be cobbled together from any available capacity in the state agencies whose heads served on the Commission. In Michigan, that staff was drawn primarily from the Department of Natural Resources, which at that period in its history was a land and game management agency, not a pollution control agency.

10. Despite the many shortcomings of the Michigan WRCA, it was in some ways a remarkably enlightened piece of legislation. One noteworthy feature is that it applied to both groundwater and surface water. Few pollution control laws, either past or present (and most notably the CWA), address groundwater contamination. Second, the law applies to water quantity concerns pertaining to the environmental effects of diminished stream flows. This, too, was extraordinary.

of some sort. Typically, the procedure places the burden on the regulated party to use that application to build the record for review from which the agency will be able to determine whether the proposed activity of the applicant is consistent with the legal standards the agency is in place to enforce. As described previously in the administrative law materials, most contemporary review-and-permit statutes on all levels (federal, state and local) require at least a minimal degree of public notice of the application, and interested citizens who manage to learn of the application usually have an opportunity to participate via written or oral comment, submission of materials, and, in some limited instances, formal intervention in the proceedings. As a sign of its times, the Michigan WRC Act did not require notice or opportunities for public participation. The "permit" part of the process refers to the agency action, usually in the form of some certification evidencing agency permission to proceed, a conditional grant, or a denial.

2. Standards of decision in review-and-permit statutes. The review-and-permit methodology operates independently of the content of the standard that serves as the basis for review. The standard can be as broad as "in the public interest" or "injurious to public health or to the conducting of any industrial enterprise," or as specific as "will not result in a concentration exceeding X parts per billion of Y pollutant in any receiving water body measured Z meters from the outfall pipe." The review-and-permit implementation mechanism is so generic it is used in many settings besides environmental regulation.

3. Negative permit decisions. Permit systems all share a common element, a requirement that the regulated activity cannot proceed without obtaining a permit. To make the holding of a permit a true necessity, there must be a credible threat of a penalty substantial enough to deter noncompliance, which may also take the form of an injunction ordering cessation of the offending activity.[11]

4. Are review-and-permit statutes their own taxonomic type, or does the way in which standards are set differentiate one taxonomic type that uses the review-and-permit technique of regulation from another? The answer that this book gives is both, but with the emphasis on the latter. Most environmental regulatory approaches utilize permits or their equivalents as an implementing device. How the standards are set, by whom and why that particular standard is appropriate in the particular environmental context is a significant differentiator among regulatory approaches. Much of the chapter organization of this book tracks these differences in statutory approaches. At the same time, review-and-permit statutes with very broadly stated standards are a stand-alone category in their own right. In that type of regulatory program the content of the regulation resembles an administratively created common law, summing up the actions taken by the agency that amounts to the environmental law of the area. The eventual regulatory results are largely unchecked by the legislature that erected the vague standard in the first place. The results are also largely unchecked by the courts that review agency actions deferentially and that are hesitant to invalidate the broad delegation of power to the agency because the nature of many environmental subject matters makes it difficult for the legislature to have the expertise needed to wisely erect a more tightly controlled policy.

Now viewing the Michigan WRCA as an early prototype of a broad standard review-and-permit statute, it is time to consider its effectiveness and the potential for improved statutes like it to be used successfully in other environmental contexts.

---

11. This aspect of all permit statutes, the blocking of the activity in the absence of a permit, is a rudimentary "roadblock" device that is needed for effective enforcement. Looking ahead to Chapter 10, "roadblock statutes" are treated as a separate taxonomic category.

B. The Advent and Failure of Broad Delegations to Administrative Agencies

The Utilex Case File

As part of a project undertaken by the University of Michigan Environmental Law Society in the early 1970s, law students examined a typical case file on one particular WRC permit issued to the Utilex Company of Fowlerville, Michigan, a small electroplating plant. The following chronology of file entries reveals a typical story of how state agencies enforced state pollution laws before the federal pollution statutes became law.

MICHIGAN DEPARTMENT OF NATURAL RESOURCES ENFORCEMENT FILE #MI 0003727: UTILEX-HOOVER BALL BEARING
[A descriptive digest of file entries:]

- December, 1952: The Utilex Company, in connection with new plating operations, requests a "new use" permit to allow dumping of cyanide, copper, zinc, nickel and other matter into the adjoining Looking Glass River.
- January, 1953: WRC makes order granting permit, attaching [weak] standards for water quality.
- July, 1953: Staff field report: effluent violates permit standards.
- September, 1953: Staff field report: effluent violates permit standards.
- September, 1954: Staff field report: effluent violates permit standards.
- March, 1955: Staff field report: effluent violates permit standards. Staff writes letter to company suggesting new control equipment.
- March, 1956: Staff field report: effluent violates permit standards.
- November, 1956: Staff field report: effluent violates permit standards.
- June, 1957: Violation noted for nickel only.
- June, 1959: Staff field report: effluent violates permit standards in all categories.
- January, 1960: Staff field report: effluent violates permit standards in all categories.
- October, 1960: Staff field report: effluent violates permit standards in all categories.
- May, 1961: Staff field report: effluent violates permit standards in all categories. Biological test shows long-term toxic effect; fifteen river miles required for recovery of water quality in river.
- June, 1963: Staff field report: effluent violates permit standards.
- September, 1963: Staff field report: effluent violates permit standards.
- January, 1964: Biological test shows no sign of life to three and one-half miles downstream; near-lethal cyanide levels.
- October, 1964: WRC writes company that controls would be "most desirable."
- November, 1965: Staff field report: concentrations exceeding standards 9.3 miles downstream.
- September, 1966: Citizen complaints [others have apparently been received, but are not copied in file] lead to staff field report: effluent violates permit standards.
- November, 1966: University biological test shows complete eradication of life to 4.7 miles downstream.
- March, 1968: Staff field report: excess effluents in all categories.
- May, 1968: In response to public environmental concern, WRC asks company for stipulation of new standards; company accepts, "prefers to have voluntary stipulation"; no mention of previous violations of permit.
- December, 1968: Excess effluents; company submits plans for control equipment to meet new standards by April, 1969.

- July, 1969: Company fails to install equipment by promised date due to "changed engineering plans." WRC sets new due date: April, 1970.
- February, 1970: Staff field report: effluent violates both old and new standards.
- April, 1970: Staff field report: effluent violates both old and new standards; no equipment installed by due date.
- June, 1970: Company requests postponement of due date; WRC notes the company "is moving expeditiously."
- September, 1970: Equipment installed.
- October, 1970: Staff field report: excess heavy metals in violation of 1953 standards.
- December, 1970: Staff field report: effluent violates permit standards.
- Spring, 1971: Environmental Law Society has been investigating WRC files; at next meeting WRC passes resolution limiting citizen access to its files.
- March, 1972: Staff field report: effluents exceed standards up to two miles downstream. Company writes letter explaining difficulty of cleaning up. Effluents do not meet 1953 permit standards.
- [October 1972]: [Congress passes CWA, requiring states in the National Pollution Discharge Elimination System (NPDES) program to upgrade their state pollution regulatory systems.]
- February 28, 1974: NPDES discharge permit issued; includes stricter standards.
- August 9, 1974: NPDES discharge permit issued on 02/28/74 found to be in error.
- January 8, 1976: Monitoring requirements are revised. Verification that cadmium was no longer present in detectable quantities; cadmium monitoring requirement could be deleted.
- January 20, 1977: New NPDES permit is issued to Utilex on nickel and chromium discharges.
- January 28, 1977: Utilex receives an "I" rating for inadequate permit compliance; effluent violates NPDES permit.
- February 7, 1977: A waste water treatment construction project is begun at Utilex.
- June 22, 1977: A sulfuric acid spill occurs at Utilex.
- June 30, 1977: Revised draft permit for Utilex. Standards of original NPDES permit based on Michigan Waste Criteria were more stringent than EPA guidelines. WRC agrees to loosen standards.
- July 11, 1977: Completion of waste water treatment system at Utilex.
- July 13, 1977: A letter from Utilex explaining corrective actions taken in response to the acid spill of 06/22/77. Utilex installed a lining for a retaining wall and replaced storage tanks.
- July 29, 1977: Completion of water waste treatment project is confirmed.
- September 13, 1977: Field waste water survey done; shows violations of NPDES permit.
- October 4, 1977: Notice of non-compliance and Order to Comply sent to Utilex. Utilex found to have exceeded both its chromium and oil & grease maximums during July. Letter of explanation requested.
- October 12, 1977: Utilex writes that the parameters set forth by the permit have been attained.
- November 8, 1977: Utilex exceeds permit limits on pH acidity, zinc, and copper.
- November 9, 1977: Utilex writes that DNR [Department of Natural Resources] limits for chrome, acid, and nickel had been exceeded due to a crack in a pipe sustained during demolition and replacement of roof.

B. The Advent and Failure of Broad Delegations to Administrative Agencies

- December 6, 1977: Letter from Water Quality Division stating that waste water survey of 09/13/77 indicated that limits on NPDES permit had been exceeded. A letter of explanation is requested.
- December 22, 1977: Notice of non-compliance with permit issued on 01/20/77. Chromium and nickel levels exceeded limits during the period from 10/14 to 10/25/77.
- 1978: Utilex closes, still in violation of standards.

COMMENTARY & QUESTIONS

1. The administrative explanation. When asked about the Utilex file in 1972, the WRC Executive Director complained that he "didn't have sufficient manpower and budget to enforce the law" and that his agency also lacked sufficient legal authority. By 1972, the WRC was administering thousands of permits with a mere handful of staff (but note that staffing was adequate to do almost 20 years of violation reports). The claim of insufficient legal authority seems to be contradicted by the broad grant of enforcement authority set forth in the WRCA noted above. The WRC, however, had no legal counsel on its own staff, and its only method of seeking enforcement was to refer cases to the offices of the Attorney General or local county prosecutors for action. Perhaps ironically, a number of cases like *Utilex* were not referred for prosecution because the WRC staff held the erroneous belief that legally, in order to mount a prosecution, they had to be able to prove fish kills, and, as one field inspector said in the 1970s, "all of the fish were poisoned out of there in the 1950s."

And politics is surely part of the explanation. One staffer told the researchers that "every time it looked as if maybe our boss was going to let us crack down on Utilex, it seems like the entire male population of Fowlerville—almost all of them worked at Utilex—would come up to our office here in Lansing to talk with the Executive Director about how much they needed that plant. And they'd be accompanied by their state Senator, who made it clear that tightening our enforcement against Utilex would trigger some payback at appropriations time."

2. The post-1929 mandatory permit system. Why did the legislature decide to require a mandatory new and enlarged source permit system when it did? One explanation was that the cumulative effects of pollution on aquatic ecosystems by then were becoming a visible concern, as was the economic impact of deteriorating water quality on all forms of water use. The statute was expanded to protect a wider range of environmental harms and also to prohibit any water use "which is injurious to the public health or to the conducting of any industrial enterprise or other lawful occupation." Why was this permit process imposed only on new and increased sources? Plainly, this was not a trivial loophole, given that by that time existing pollution already was severe enough to be causing readily identifiable undesirable effects. It seems irrational to exclude all existing sources from the permit system; some countervailing political force probably explains that compromise. Many regulatory programs grandfather existing uses, presumably because of their political power. Thus, waiting to regulate until the environmental destruction is substantial enough to spur political action may be more symbolic than effective if there is not sufficient political will to include all sources, old and new.

3. Improving the system—standard-setting. The WRC case study drawn from the Utilex file is a paradigm of why enforcement of pollution control laws was problematic during the pre-1970 years of traditional broad standard review-and-permit statutes. A number of changes in the regulatory approach had to be made if pollution control was to improve significantly, for example, by moving toward more definite standards. What is likely to be different when standards are more definite?

4. Improving the system—changing the dipolar paradigm. This traditional review-and-permit process is strictly "dipolar"—a dialogue between the regulated corporation and the administrative agency alone. Where was the public? The only gesture to other constituencies was in the representative composition of the WRC itself, which might include a sportsman or garden club representative along with industrial appointees. How could the regulatory process be changed to incorporate a broader "multi-polar" conception of the public interest? Almost universally, administrative law improvements have injected opportunities for broader participation into review-and-permit procedures. What is needed to make those opportunities meaningful?

5. Improving the system—intra-agency changes. The agencies that administered the midcentury permit systems were the forerunners of modern environmental protection agencies, and they pioneered changes in the bureaucratic landscape. In the case of Michigan and the WRC, the agency added in-house technical expertise. The WRC staff originally was drawn from the DNR, which historically was concerned with fish and game management, not pollution control. Over time, DNR and similar agencies throughout the nation added staff with environmental and pollution control expertise. These agencies, by introducing a new technocratic class into the regulatory process, heralded a new era in which regulatory agencies possess their own environmental and technical expertise. The commission composition and the Act's cumbersome procedures, however, hampered effective regulation.

1. Federalization of the Field and the Blossoming of Regulation

Donald Elliott, Bruce Ackerman & John Millian, Toward a Theory of Statutory Evolution: The Federalization of Environmental Law

1 JOURNAL OF LAW, ECONOMICS & ORGANIZATION 313 (1985)

... An extraordinary outburst of lawmaking related to pollution and the environment occurred at the national level during the 1960s and 1970s as a dozen major federal pollution control statutes were enacted. This network of national statutes—together with a much larger body of implementing regulations—now constitutes one of the most pervasive systems of national regulation known to American law. Today every discharge into the land, water, or air—from the smallest smokestack to the largest landfill for the disposal of toxic chemicals—requires direct or indirect permission from the national government....

What accounts for this "dramatic plunge forward"? After decades of incrementalism and accommodation, why did Congress suddenly enact a series of relatively extreme federal environmental statutes in the early 1970s?...

It is a non sequitur to assert—as lawyers frequently do—that Congress passes statutes "because" policy problems exist. The existence of a real or perceived policy problem may be a necessary condition for the passage of a statute, but the existence of a problem alone does not a statute make; additional conditions must be satisfied, which explains why Congress passes statutes addressed to certain problems while other equally pressing problems go unaddressed. Conversely, when the Clean Air Act was passed [in 1970], at least some air pollution problems were getting better as a result of the gradual substitution of oil for coal during the 1960s....

The first significant statutes regulating air pollution, the Motor Vehicle Pollution Control Act of 1965 and the Air Quality Act of 1967, were not passed because of the political power of environmentalists at the national level but because two well-organized industrial groups, the automobile industry and the soft coal industry, were threatened with a state of affairs even worse from their perspective than federal air pollution regulation—namely, inconsistent and progressively more stringent environmental laws at the state and local level. As a consequence of the structure of our federal lawmaking system, environmentalists were able to organize industry to do their bidding for them. Thus, the first federal legislation regulating air pollution was passed not because environmentalists solved their organizational problems on the national level but because environmentalists exploited the organizational difficulties of their industrial adversaries at the state and local level.

The auto industry and the soft coal industry undoubtedly would have preferred no government regulation of air pollution rather than federal legislation. When faced with the threat of inconsistent and increasingly rigorous state laws, however, they [used] their superior organizational capacities in Washington to preempt or control the environmentalists' legislative victories at the state level. . . .

COMMENTARY & QUESTIONS

1. The auto companies might have gotten more stringent regulation than they had anticipated. Under the Clean Air Act of 1970 Congress required auto manufacturers to reduce some auto tailpipe emissions by 90% within 5 years. In addition, their factories became subject to a complex system where plant emissions were reduced under plans designed to achieve ambient air quality protective of public health. See Chapter 11.

2. The eruption of environmentalism. During the late 1960s and early 1970s, a volcanic outburst of public sentiment against environmental degradation and in favor of strong, national environmental laws swept traditional, well-entrenched political interests away on its molten flow. Three formerly separate but powerful subsets of interest groups—the resource conservationists, the aristocratic wilderness preservationists, and public health protection groups—joined forces with newly minted Rachel Carson populists to capture the attention of the media and general public as "the environmental movement." This eruption of public opinion was generated by (1) blatant and well-publicized environmental abuses such as Allied's Kepone discharges in Hopewell, Virginia; construction of homes and schools on an abandoned and leaking hazardous waste disposal site in New York's Love Canal neighborhood; water pollution so extreme that Ohio's Cuyahoga River caught fire twice near Cleveland; the fouling of 30 miles of California beaches by a massive oil spill from a blown offshore oil well off Santa Barbara; and air pollution-caused "killer fogs" in London, England and Donora, Pennsylvania, that killed and injured hundreds of people; (2) the emergence of a credible and persuasive environmentalist literature—notably Carson's 1962 book SILENT SPRING—that identified environmental stressors and recommended reasonable solutions; and (3) an already angry and mistrustful public that was antagonized by the U.S government's involvement in the unpopular war in Vietnam. The U.S. political system tends to accommodate such torrents of public opinion, and great progress followed.

3. The federalization of environmental law. A role for the federal government began to take shape in the 1960s as the midcentury primacy of state governments—operating 50+ independent review-and-permit systems (as in the *Utilex* case study)—increasingly revealed its shortcomings. Some of the shortcomings were technical, posed by the geographic scope and complexity of pollution. Awareness and public arousal regarding environmental quality in this era was focused initially on dramatic events, such as fish kills near a factory's outfall, or fumes and smoke invading a neighborhood, or raw sewage polluting beaches, and so on. Broader public health issues began to surface indicating that pollution not only appeared in isolated hot spots but also affected large areas of the U.S. Data from many cities began to show increased incidence of respiratory disease linked to increased air pollution. Fish populations were in decline almost everywhere.

No single city or state was in a position to collect or process the overall data, which could best be done and funded on a national level. In the aftermath of World War II, the national government had taken its first tentative steps in the field. In 1948, Congress had enacted the Federal Water Pollution Control Act,[12] establishing funding for basic water pollution control research and funding some cleanup programs.[13] On the air side, the same evolution was occurring. In 1955, the federal Department of Health, Education, and Welfare (HEW) was assigned a major research role into the effects of air pollution.[14] Federal studies of automobile pollution began a few years later,[15] and in the 1963 version of the CAA,[16] HEW was directed to publish advisory national air quality criteria. These "criteria" documents, based on epidemiological and other research that correlated levels of air quality with public health effects, later became the federal ambient air quality standards.[17] In 1956, the states successfully lobbied the federal government for larger subsidies for sewage treatment, singled out for federal funding because of the interstate flow of many rivers. Federal expertise and funding were clearly necessary, but a need for federal regulation was also becoming obvious.

State-by-state control of pollution did not address the increasingly serious problem of cross-border spillover effects.[18] Downwind and downstream states had no power, other than persuasion and invocation of the doctrine of comity (voluntary respect by one state for the interests of a sister state) by which to protect themselves from transboundary pollution. The upwind and upstream states had little incentive to use scarce political capital to regulate their near-border polluters whose waste streams would have little or no effect on the state's own citizens. These scenarios also supported a more extensive federal role in environmental regulation.

4. The race of laxity as a justification for federal regulation. By the late 1960s, it was also becoming apparent that many states could not or would not regulate pollution adequately for political reasons. Some of the inadequacies of state programs could be attributed to the generic difficulty of pushing marketplace economic powers toward respecting public needs for environmental quality. In the minds of many, however, the low levels of many state-mandated pollution controls had an even more sinister aspect that argued for federal minimum standards—the "race of laxity," also called the "race-to-the-bottom" or "the Mississippi Syndrome," after the industrial recruitment strategy of the poorest state in the nation.

---

12. Act of June 30, 1948, ch. 758, 62 Stat. 1155 (1948).

13. FWPCA's one foray into providing substantive remedies was to establish a convoluted, and ultimately unsuccessful, public nuisance cause of action that could be enforced only by federal officials in cases of proven interstate water pollution.

14. Act of July 14, 1955, ch. 360, 69 Stat. 322 (1955).

15. Act of June 8, 1960, Pub. L. No. 86-493, 74 Stat. 162 (1960).

16. Clean Air Act of 1963, Pub. L. No. 88-206, 77 Stat. 392 (1963).

17. The role of HEW was expanded to include the delineation of air quality control regions in the Air Quality Act of 1967, §108, 81 Stat. 490-497. The statute also upgraded the criteria documents from being merely "advisory" to a status as air quality standards. Three years later, in 1970, these standards became the federal government's nationwide mandatory minimum standards.

18. Interstate pollution is still a substantial problem, even after the federalization of environmental law.

B. The Advent and Failure of Broad Delegations to Administrative Agencies

The race of laxity was perceived as a state-by-state lowering of standards in order to attract new industry. To be sure, environmental laws were but one of several components of state efforts to woo industry, along with hospitable tax rates, labor costs, corporate laws, and so on. Nevertheless, a failure to join in the race of laxity in environmental regulation posed a major threat of lost economic prosperity to those states enforcing more burdensome environmental regulations than those enacted by their sister states.[19]

By the beginning of the 1970s, the conviction that states were being pressured into keeping down their environmental control standards by an invidious race of laxity competition for marketplace economics prompted Congress to initiate a dramatic federal takeover of the job of setting nationwide minimum standards.

Relatively little direct evidence supports the race of laxity's existence.[20] Whether an intentional race of laxity occurred during the midcentury period is largely beside the point. Standards did vary, and state officials thought and reacted with the presumption that their compatriots in other states were using lowered environmental standards as a lure. Sophisticated firms considering major plant investment surely considered costs of environmental compliance in their decisional process. Most important, however, members of Congress from the populous and industrialized states, states having the greatest concentrations of existing factories and the attendant pollution, worried about interstate competition over pollution. For instance, in debates over the CAA of 1970, which imposed national standards, Representative Vanik of Ohio declared:

> To date, the States have been left to establish their own air quality standards. In all too many areas, there has been delay and foot dragging—and ridiculously low standards set to accommodate local industries and interests. The establishment of national standards will ensure action throughout the Nation on a rapid basis. . . . National standards of pollution control would prevent another State from attracting any industries because of a greater pollution tolerance. Such competition is unfair and against the public interest. 116 Cong. Rec. 19,218 (91st Cong., 1st Sess., June 10, 1970).

By virtue of their voting strength in Congress, the senators and representatives from populous, industrialized states who perceived the race of laxity as a threat could enact laws of nationwide scope that limited the race.[21] These new nationally oriented federal laws having very detailed methods for standard-setting marked the end of the midcentury review-and-permit era.

---

19. As noted previously, state regulation of automobile emissions generated fears on the part of the automakers of a race of stringency. Voting for ever tighter control offered legislators in states not having significant auto production facilities a politically popular vote for improved public health and a cleaner environment with no perceptible in-state consequences.

20. A governmental report provided evidence demonstrating a continuing race of laxity despite current federal floors designed to prevent it. See USGAO, Differences Among the States in Issuing Permits Limiting the Discharge of Pollutants 9 (1996), and Professor Engel's study discussed below. Anecdotal evidence is abundantly available. In 1965, for example, Governor Ross Barnett of Mississippi gave a speech at Princeton University (attended by one of this book's authors) in which he lauded the state's lax environmental laws, low tax rates, and weak labor protections to a group of students whom he believed might become future corporate decisionmakers making plant siting decisions.

21. As will be seen in the more detailed studies of the laws enacted, some regulatory elements plainly addressed race of laxity issues, such as uniform national performance standards that applied to new facilities wherever built. Other regulatory approaches, such as those focusing on the overall quality of the air or water, may disadvantage areas where there is already concentrated pollution. Again, given the voting power in Congress of the more industrialized and congested areas of the nation, the degree of disadvantage in environmental regulatory programs was not large.

5. Federal law, the race of laxity, and modern devolutionism. Fear of a race of laxity among the states motivated Congress to give the federal government a dominant role in environmental regulation, rather than confining it to research, funding, and policing interstate pollution externalizations. During the 1990s a revisionist academic and political debate arose over the question of whether such a race ever existed or, beyond that, whether it leads to negative results. The leading revisionist voice belongs to Professor Richard Revesz:

> Contrary to prevailing assumption, competition among the states for industry should not be expected to lead to a race that decreases social welfare; indeed, as in other areas, such competition can be expected to produce an efficient allocation of industrial activity among the states. It shows, moreover, that federal regulation aimed at dealing with the asserted race to the bottom, far from correcting evils of interstate competition, is likely to produce results that are undesirable. Rehabilitating Interstate Competition: Rethinking the "Race-to-the-Bottom" Rationale for Federal Environmental Regulation, 67 N.Y.U. L. Rev. 1210, 1211-1212 (1992).

The argument is important for contemporary environmental policymaking. If one agrees with the Revesz analysis,[22] the modern federal role in environmental regulation should be scaled back and returned to the states, changing much of what will be studied in this book (and in all other current environmental law texts) about environmental standard-setting and policymaking, shifting it into 50 different systems. Many regulated industries, which often have disproportionate power in their home communities, employ Revesz' theoretical inquiry to legitimize their calls for "devolution." They argue that the federal government should restore greater state regulatory autonomy in the environmental arena.[23]

6. Responding to Revesz' theory with both theory and empiricism. An extensive reply and counterargument to Revesz and others questioning the race-to-the-bottom is made in Engel, State Environmental Standard-Setting: Is There a "Race" and Is It "to the Bottom?" 48 Hastings L.J. 271 (1997).[24] Professor Engel's article challenges Revesz' revisionist theory. She suggests that there are already well-established theoretical economic models that do predict a race-to-the-bottom. Her principal criticism of Revesz' theory attacks its reliance on the strong neoclassical economic assumptions of purely competitive behavior. Engel instead argues for the use of game theory in explaining states' strategic behaviors:

> The argument that interstate competition leads to a race-to-the-bottom and the revisionists' argument that it does not are both based on long-standing theoretical traditions. A principal argument for the existence of a race-to-the-bottom is based upon game theory, of which the classic Prisoner's Dilemma model is a simple but frequently cited example. According to this

---

22. Professor Revesz cautioned in his article that his claims against the race of laxity were predicated on models of behavior and that "modeling, by necessity, involves making strong sets of assumptions." 67 N.Y.U. L. Rev. at 1211-1212, 1244. This limitation has been ignored by devolution proponents who cite the Revesz article as if it provided conclusive evidence of the nonexistence of a race-to-the-bottom.

23. For example, in the failed attempt to promote and obtain passage of H.R. 961 in the 104th Congress (a bill popularly referred to as the Dirty Water Act), the two groups that drafted and pushed the bill through the House—"Project Relief" and the "Alliance for Reasonable Regulation"—designed the bill to undercut pollution controls primarily by shifting ultimate standard-setting and enforcement to the states. The corporations making up these groups include more than 500 of the nation's largest dischargers of water pollutants.

24. Revesz' article has gathered a number of critics in addition to Professor Engel. See, e.g., Esty, Revitalizing Environmental Federalism, 95 Mich. L. Rev. 570 (1996); Sarnoff, The Continuing Imperative (But Only from a National Perspective) for Environmental Protection, 7 Duke Envtl. L. & Pol'y F. 225 (1997); Swire, The Race of Laxity and the Race to Undesirability: Explaining Failures in Competition Among Jurisdictions in Environmental Law, 14 Yale J. on Reg. 67 (1996). See Revesz in reply, The Race-to-the-Bottom and Federal Environmental Regulation: A Response to Critics, 82 Minn. L. Rev. 535 (1997). The devolution debate is a continuing feature of environmental policy analysis.

B. The Advent and Failure of Broad Delegations to Administrative Agencies

model, competition among a small number of players makes each player worse off than if he or she had not been a player in a game. . . . Game theory was invented fifty years ago to address shortcomings in traditional neoclassical economics, which could not handle situations in which market participants interacted strategically. Thus, the revisionists' return to the neoclassical economic framework to understand interstate competition, a problem many theorists were already solving through the application of game theory, is, historically speaking, a conceptual step backward. 48 Hastings L.J. at 298-298.

Professor Engel did an empirical survey analysis of state officials and corporate executives. She found very few corporate executives who would say that environmental laxity was a major inducement to their location decisions, but she also found that many state officials acted under the assumption that the comparative stringency of state environmental laws did influence corporate location decisions. As a result, "a substantial minority of officials influential in the state standard-setting process concede that their state has relaxed its standards and permit procedures in order to attract or retain industrial firms." 48 Hastings L.J. at 351-352.

7. Inverting the race of laxity. Recalling the fear of the auto industry in the mid-1960s, is it possible that states could or would invert the race of laxity into a race for enhanced environmental quality generally, a race-to-the-top?[25] For that to happen, states raising their environmental standards would have to provide some offsetting benefits to firms that would more than outweigh the increased cost of doing business there. Is the value of a cleaner, healthier environment a sufficient lure? To some executive decisionmakers, who themselves would be living in the preferred setting, higher environmental standards might be a plus, and perhaps those same benefits would be useful in personnel recruitment. A more likely path by which states can raise environmental standards is market power, such as that enjoyed by California and described in the Elliott et al. excerpts above. California's economy is so large that if it were an independent nation, its economy would be among the ten largest in the world. Most large firms doing business in the U.S. will act in ways that accommodate California if the alternative is to limit their access to California's market. In the environmental field, that market power has occasionally allowed California to invert the race of laxity to suit its will. For example, California developed its own higher-than-national standards for automobile emissions and had both the market power to force the automakers to manufacture to California standards and the political power to keep Congress from preempting those standards in the CAA. Even more of an inversion of the race of laxity has occurred in the wake of California's Proposition 65, which requires disclosure of use of hazardous chemicals. Many producers serving the California market have chosen to adapt their products to meet California's most-stringent-in-the-nation regulations and have made the decision to market the identical products nationwide. The economic logic is built upon economies of scale in having to manufacture and distribute a unitary line of products, rather than separate (but similar) products designed to meet both higher and lower regulatory standards. There are not many states with market power like California's, so for other states to act in that manner would probably require joint action of several states. Due to the Compact Clause of Article I, §10, of the U.S. Constitution, states cannot formally join forces in regulatory matters absent congressional approval. States can independently adopt parallel or identical regulatory regimes, but obtaining that much voluntary cooperation among several states and maintaining it over time makes the likelihood of it happening very remote.

---

25. Elsewhere in the excerpted article, Elliott and his coauthors call for just this path of statutory growth in which loosely organized coalitions of environmental activists concentrate on passing state legislation that threatens industries with inconsistent state pollution control standards, to the point where industry itself lobbies for preemptive federal legislation.

C. Keeping Score at the Beginning of the Twenty-First Century: Players, Positions, Programs & Policies

Just as the evolution of federal environmental regulatory law follows several general political patterns, the major political actors in these environmental regulatory issues are predictable, although their political positions on particular environmental issues may not be formulaic.

EPA is the major pollution regulatory institution in the U.S. It was formed in 1970 by a Reorganization Plan (a type of executive order) that centralized the pollution control functions that had previously resided in several federal agencies (e.g., prior to 1970, air and water pollution control were under the jurisdiction of separate federal agencies). EPA is an agency that is headquartered in Washington, D.C. with ten regional offices dispersed throughout the U.S. EPA is headed by an Administrator, who is located in the main office in Washington, D.C. Each regional office is run by a Regional Administrator. The relationships among the EPA regions and the main EPA office, and among the regions themselves, are complex. For example, political administrations differ with regard to allocations of administrative authority between central EPA and the regions. As to the regions themselves, some are traditionally more enthusiastic regarding pollution control than are others. Some of the environmental regulatory functions performed by EPA are (1) promulgating pollution control regulations; (2) providing technical assistance and program funding to state pollution control agencies; and (3) issuing permits and performing monitoring (both ambient quality and compliance monitoring), surveillance, and administrative enforcement activities, where states do not.

EPA also possesses some regulatory authority on the "conservation" (as distinguished from pollution control) side of environmental law (e.g., EPA's authority to protect wetlands and marine sanctuaries), but other federal agencies bear the major responsibility for conservation regulation at the federal level. For example, the U.S. Fish and Wildlife Service and the National Marine Fisheries Service, in the U.S. Department of the Interior (DoI), administer the federal ESA; the Bureau of Land Management, also located in DoI, administers federal grazing laws; and the Forest Service, located in the U.S. Department of Agriculture, administers the National Forest Management Act (NFMA). The most significant environmental statutes and the federal agencies that hold primary responsibility for implementing them are listed in Figure 1.

Each state has established its own set of pollution control and conservation regulatory agencies. In some states, these functions are included in a single agency, but in others they are separated into two or more agencies. The constitutional power relationships between federal and state environmental regulatory agencies are governed by the federalism concepts of Chapter 7, but as described below, the provisions of several major federal environmental protection statutes institutionalize a degree of "devolution" of regulatory power to states.

Local environmental protection agencies, at the county and municipal levels of government, perform many environmental regulatory functions relating to local activities, such as land use permitting and monitoring of on-site septic systems. Having been created by state law, county and municipal governments possess only those regulatory powers that have been delegated to them by state legislative enactments.

At all levels of government, legislative committees with authority to review environmental bills, and the legislators who sponsor or oppose those bills and chair or sit on those committees, are important actors in the environmental political process.

On the nongovernmental side of environmental politics, the major actors at the federal level are the national environmental groups, industry, and organized labor. National

C. Keeping Score at the Beginning of the Twenty-First Century

FEDERAL STATUTE	ADMINISTERING AGENCY	FEDERAL STATUTE	ADMINISTERING AGENCY
GENERAL		**WILDLIFE & WILDERNESS**	
NEPA	CEQ	ESA	DoI-FWS; DoC-NOAA, NMFS
EPCRA	EPA	MMPA	DoC-NOAA; DoI-FWS
PPA	EPA	MBTA	DoI-FWS
OSHA	DoL	NMRAA	DoI-FWS
Consumer Prod. Safety Act	CPSC	FWCA	DoI-FWS
National Historic Preservation Act	DoI-NPS	Wilderness Act of 1964	DoI; USDA-USFS
AIR		WSRA	DoI-NPS, BLM, FWS; USDA-USFS
CAA	EPA	**PUBLIC LANDS**	
WATER		FLPMA	DoI-BLM
CWA	EPA; DoD-Army COE	NFMA	USDA-USFS
SDWA	EPA	**MINING**	
MPRSA	EPA; DoC-NOAA	SMCRA	doi-OSM
CZMA	DoC-NOAA, OOCRM	Mining and Minerals Policy Act	DoI
CBRA	DoI-FWS	Mining Act of 1872	DoI-BLM
OPA	EPA; DoD/DHS-U.S. Coast Guard; DoC-NOAA	Mineral Leasing Act of 1920	DoI-BLM
Refuse Act	DoD-U.S. Army COE	Federal Cola Leasing Amendments of 1975	DoI-BLM
Watershed Act	USDA; DoI	**FARM BILLS**	
HAZARDOUS MATERIALS & HAZARDOUS WASTE		Conservation Reserve Program	USDA
RCRA	EPA	Wetlands Reserves	USDA
CERCLA	EPA	**ENERGY**	
ToSCA	EPA	NWPA	DoE
HMTA	DOT	AEA	DoE-NRC
Pesticides:		PURPA	DoE-FERC
FIFRA	EPA	**TRANSPORTATION**	
FDCA	HHS-FDA	ISTEA	DoT
FQPA	EPA	§4(f) the Parklands Act	Dot-FHWA

FIGURE 5-1. *Some major federal environmental statutes and the agencies that have major responsibility for them.*

environmental groups differ with regard to (1) preferred strategies (e.g., legislative lobbying, electoral politics, media utilization, litigation, cooperative problem solving with industry, intervention in administrative proceedings, land purchases and leases, political demonstrations); (2) priority issues (e.g., pollution, protection of public lands, protection of fish and wildlife, international issues); and (3) political stridency and willingness to enter into coalitions with other environmental groups and compromise with industry. Industry is also not monolithic in terms of its behavior on environmental regulatory issues. For example, manufacturing industries, which are designated as regulated point sources under the CWA, are sometimes in political conflict with large agricultural operations, which are unregulated nonpoint sources of water pollution, over who should bear the costs of the enhanced water pollution controls that are required by the CWA. Organized labor sometimes sides with industry on environmental regulatory issues, especially where jobs might be threatened by proposed environmental regulation. At other times, unions oppose industry on issues such as workplace health and safety or environmental justice for workers who live in neighborhoods close to existing or proposed industrial facilities.

1. Cooperative Federalism

Cooperative federalism, or the "federal-state partnership," is the legal and institutional model that underlies most environmental regulatory statutes in the U.S.[26] Cooperative federalism entails nationwide environmental planning, research and demonstration, and standard-setting at the federal level, with subsequent delegation (also "devolution") of legal authority ("primacy") to consenting states to perform localized environmental planning and research, set more stringent standards, administer environmental permit systems, and carry out first-line monitoring, surveillance and enforcement activities within their boundaries. Cooperative federalism includes the concept of "federal floor" standards, whereby a state can set stricter, but not less strict, environmental protection standards than the federally designated "floor" standards. A federal agency will delegate primacy to a state that makes a satisfactory showing that it possesses the necessary legal authority, financial resources, and political will to effectively and efficiently administer a particular regulatory program. Approximately 75% to 80% of the pollution control permits authorized by federal law are actually issued by state agencies. After delegation has taken place, the lead federal agency remains in an oversight capacity—providing program grant funding and technical assistance to state agencies, supervising state performance, and intervening with regard to permitting, monitoring and surveillance, and enforcement, only where the state program is shown to be inadequate in general or in a particular instance. Where a state does not consent to accept programmatic primacy, the lead federal agency directly administers permitting, monitoring and surveillance, and enforcement in that state.

In most instances, cooperative federalism operates smoothly to allocate the elements of the elaborate system of pollution control regulatory activities among the levels of government that are capable of performing them most efficiently, effectively, and equitably.[27]

2. "Command and Control" and "Flexible" Regulatory Strategies

Since the mid-1970s, U.S. industry has faced an intensive coordinated system of federal pollution regulation. Prescriptive federal standards applied comprehensively, source by source, became the nation's standard regulatory approach. The mandatory compliance aspect of the program earned it the descriptor "command," and the demanding performance standards, somewhat unfairly and pejoratively, earned the program the descriptor "control." In fact, performance standards do not specify a particular method of control.[28] Performance standards, instead, require a level of performance in reducing emissions; the choice of means resides with the regulated party.

---

26. Cooperative federalism relationships, and their variations, are described more fully in Chapter 7.

27. Two case studies available on the coursebook website, one relating to state foot-dragging in fully regulating concentrated animal feeding operations (CAFOs) and one involving the regulation of a steel mill, illustrate some of the problems of cooperative federalism.

28. Standards that prescribe a specific method of operation are termed *specification standards*. They are relatively uncommon in the major federal environmental laws. Their most prominent use is in RCRA's regulation of the design of hazardous waste landfills.

C. Keeping Score at the Beginning of the Twenty-First Century

"Command and control" has become a catch phrase in a larger ideological debate about how environmental regulation ought to operate. Demanding equivalent levels of pollution control of all polluters is argued by some to be inefficient, leading to unnecessary costs in achieving the desired degree of emission reduction. The debate on that point is legion and has been joined by several leading environmental law scholars.

COMMENTARY & QUESTIONS

1. **The Command and Control Debate.** Two very well-known law review articles framed the debate over the wisdom of the federal pollution control approach. On the one side were Professors Bruce Ackerman and Richard Stewart, and their article Reforming Environmental Law, 37 Stan. L. Rev. 1333 (1985). Taking the other side was Professor Howard Latin in his article, Ideal versus Real Regulatory Efficiency: Implementation of Uniform Standards and "Fine-Tuning" Regulatory Reforms, 37 Stan. L. Rev. 1267 (1985). As the latter title implies, Ackerman and Stewart had argued that the generally inflexible uniform national standards of the major federal legislation were inefficient and far too costly when more fine-grained standards would accomplish at least as much at a far lower total cost. Latin argued that the fine-tuning ideal was, in effect, at best a theoretical advantage and overlooked the real-world advantages of uniform standards:

> There are numerous advantages of uniform standards in comparison with more particularized and flexible regulatory strategies. These advantages include decreased information collection and evaluation costs, greater consistency and predictability of results, greater accessibility of decisions to public scrutiny and participation, increased likelihood that regulations will withstand judicial review, reduced opportunities for manipulative behavior by agencies in response to political or bureaucratic pressures, reduced opportunities for obstructive behavior by regulated parties, and decreased likelihood of social dislocation and "forum shopping" resulting from competitive disadvantages between geographical regions or between firms in regulated industries. . . . Well-intentioned scholars often recommend "fine-tuning" because they focus on ideal efficiency, while [antiregulatory activists] may advocate "fine-tuning" precisely because they believe it will seldom work in practice and would therefore accomplish sub rosa deregulation. 37 Stan. L. Rev. at 1273.

2. **Making room for industrial innovation and lower cost solutions.** One focus of Ackerman and Stewart is on decisionmakers; they want to remove bureaucrats from technological decisionmaking and place that in the hands of the regulated firms under incentives that can spur innovation.[29] Drawing upon the book Clean Coal, Dirty Air (1981), Congress passed a major experiment in the 1990 CAA Amendments setting up a power plant sulfur oxides trading system. The CAA's Title IV allows utilities to innovate and trade surplus clean air credits around the country, so that each can adjust the amount of cleanup it wants to pay for, and efficiencies will be rewarded with profit-generating tradable credits. This and other market-enlisting mechanisms studied in Chapter 14, such as netting and banking of pollution credits, have now become part of the air pollution regulatory structure.

---

29. The jury is out on whether non-command-and-control programs have produced the predicted levels of innovation. See, e.g., Driesen, Is Emissions Trading an Economic Incentive Program? Replacing the Command and Control/Economic Incentive Dichotomy, 55 Wash. & Lee L. Rev. 289 (1998); Driesen, Does Emissions Trading Encourage Innovation? 33 Envtl. L. Rep. 10094 (2003); Steinzor, Toward Better Bubbles and Future Lives: A Progressive Response to the Conservative Agenda for Reforming Environmental Law, 32 Envtl. L. Rep. 11421 (2002).

After completing the chapters exploring both command and control and other regulatory methods, reconsider the strength of the claims that less command and control results in greater innovation.

3. Standards: one-size-fits-all or adjusted case-by-case?[30] How should environmental standards be set in each case? What is lost if account is made for localized differences, special circumstances, and differential calculations of costs, benefits, and risk? Not requiring the employment of available pollution reduction methodologies in reliance on receiving body characteristics means that opportunities are lost for the receiving media to be even cleaner than is true under case-by-case approaches. The one-size-fits-all has a distributional consequence by leveling the playing field across the nation in regard to the stringency of regulation, which already has been shown to be important at the political level. Most tellingly, the command-and-control system undoubtedly has produced measurable and significant improvements in the quality of air, water, and control of toxic contamination.

4. Beware the ghost of *Utilex*. The *Utilex* case study presented earlier in this chapter illustrated an ineffective midcentury review-and-permit system that was handicapped by ambiguous standards, unenergetic dipolar negotiations between the state agency and the industry, and selective nonenforcement. Does a move toward case-by-case regulation recreate a dynamic in which the regulatory agency without a fixed regulatory standard will be overmatched in the negotiation process by the regulated entity? Even under command and control, the lessons of *Utilex* bear remembering. See Steinzor, EPA and Its Sisters at 30: Devolution, Revolution, or Reform? 31 Envtl. L. Rep. 11086 (2001). Professor Steinzor's case study of the pollution control at a Bethlehem Steel plant finds immense regulatory slippage despite the command-and-control federalization of environmental law.

Unfortunately, our affluent society has also been an effluent society.

—Hubert H. Humphrey, Gannon College, 11 October 1966

I was always taught as I was growing up that democracy is not something you believe in, not something you hang your hat on. Democracy is something you do.

—Abbie Hoffman, closing argument to jury in *Commonwealth v. Hoffman, et al.*, Amherst, Mass 1988

Why all this talk about efficiency? The last thing the "Founding Fathers" were after was efficiency. They were after freedom. And they understood that freedom implied a certain tolerance for messy conflict.

—John Culver, quoted in N.Y. Times Mag., 12 March '89, at 101

The simple plan: That they should take, who have the power, and they should keep, who can.

—*Meeker v. City of East Orange*, 74A. 379, 385 (N.J. 1909)

---

30. Although all three are termed command and control regulation by their critics, there are distinctive differences in cost and implementation consequences of (1) a harm-based nationwide ambient standard that must be achieved by having the states issue permits that will result in its attainment, (2) requiring results that achieve a certain level of effluent reduction in a waste stream, and (3) telling firms exactly what pollution control equipment they must select. These differences are explored in Chapters 11 and 12.

6

The Administrative Law of Environmental Law & Administrative Agency Process

A. The Evolution of the Administrative Governing Process
B. Administrative Process and Law in a Nutshell
C. *Overton Park*—A Judicial Review Paradigm
D. Citizen Enforcement in the Courts
E. Statutory Interpretation: How, by Whom?—*Chevron*

A. THE EVOLUTION OF THE ADMINISTRATIVE GOVERNING PROCESS

The history of the administrative process in the U.S. divides analytically into at least six different stages.[1] Environmental protection administrative law was mostly nonexistent until the fifth stage.

1st • The Passive Era The first stage would begin at the birth of the republic, or earlier, before the Revolution, when the private marketplace economy, it can be argued, was in fact the predominant "government" of the U.S. Many historians assert the Revolution was more an economic than a political phenomenon: The colonies and their economies matured "like ripe fruit," and dropped away from Great Britain when the colonies became self-sufficient market entities. In terms of domestic governance, the colonial structures and then the state, federal, and local governments initially merely attended to minor governmental chores. Government's major early role was to facilitate the private marketplace. Government agencies built roads, canals, and a postal system, and provided a defense of borders and international trade.

2d • 1880+ The second stage, the advent of regulatory agencies, can be traced to the 1880s, when federal and state governments reacted to the perceived excesses of the Industrial Revolution's unregulated marketplace, including child labor, railroad gouging of farmers and shippers, and the like. Society discovered that there was a civic realm beyond the structures of the marketplace economy. Regulatory agencies were invented to correct

---

1. This historical analysis builds upon ideas in Stewart, The Reformation of American Administrative Law, 88 Harv. L. Rev. 1669 (1975).

"market failures" by imposing a dipolar theory of social governance: The marketplace on one hand would supply economic strength, and government on the other would protect citizens and society from the excesses of the marketplace in specific regulated areas. Reaction against governmental regulation, coming from the marketplace's major players, was immediate and passionate in the 1890s (and continues in much the same rhetorical terms today). From the beginning, however, private regulated interests in the marketplace did not merely oppose governmental regulatory agencies: They also moved to co-opt them.[2] In this era, government involvement in the economy remained the exception, not the rule. As Calvin Coolidge is supposed to have said in 1925, "The business of government is business."

3d • 1930+ The third stage, in the 1930s, marked a shift from regulatory agencies as mere occasional correctives, to the theory that agencies can be given a primary directive role in the economy, at least during national traumas such as the Great Depression and the Second World War. The New Deal produced a host of agencies that were managers as well as regulators. It was at this point that "the administrative state" became a tangible entity. The powers of government reached into areas never before regulated. (This is not to say that the process was systematically rational or even that government became the dominant factor in U.S. society. The relatively unfettered private economy remained the preeminent force in the daily life of the nation.)

4th • 1946+ In 1946, a reaction against regulatory agency high-handedness resulted in the passage of the federal Administrative Procedures Act (APA),[3] copied in many states. There had always been a reaction against governmental interference with the marketplace because so much human energy and passion is invested in private property and income-generating activities, and government tends to get in the way. The APA's clear and dominating purpose was to prevent the exercise of agency peremptory power through required procedures and judicial control of the agency process. Nevertheless the U.S., faced with postwar complexities of life as a great power, melting pot, social experiment, and economic dynamo, continued to develop its administrative substructure at every level of government. By 1968 the federal agencies comprised more than 130 agencies and 2 million civil servants.

5th • 1960s+ The next phase in the evolution of administrative law is quite closely linked to the growth of environmentalism: It was a 1960s shift from the dipolar model—regulatory agency versus regulated industry—to a far more realistic pluralistic, multicentric model. Citizen outsiders began to use the legal tools created by industry for challenging government agency powers, but deployed them against defendants who now were often agencies and industries working together (the "Establishment" that was targeted by 1960s activists). Beginning in 1966, the federal courts in particular began to be much more open to citizens—to environmentalists, consumers, civil rights activists, and so on—and the administrative process, responding to the courts, began to follow suit. From

---

2. As the Attorney General of the U.S. wrote to the president of a railroad in 1892 in response to the latter's plea for abolition of the "socialistic" Interstate Commerce Commission (ICC): "The Commission . . . is or can be made of great use to the railroads. It satisfies the popular clamor for government supervision of railroads, at the same time that the supervision is almost entirely nominal. Further, the older such a commission gets to be, the more inclined it would be found to take the business and railroad view of things. It thus becomes a sort of barrier between the railroad corporations and the people, and a sort of protection against hasty and crude legislation hostile to railroad interests. . . . The part of wisdom is not to destroy the Commission, but to utilize it." Letter from Attorney General Richard Olney to Charles Perkins, in Jaffe, The Effective Limits of the Administrative Process, 67 Harv. L. Rev. 1105, 1009 (1954).

3. 5 U.S.C. §§501 et seq. (1946).

that pluralistic opening-up of the administrative law system came many of the significant social changes of the second half of the twentieth century.

6th • 1976+ The year 1976, however, provided early steps in an initiative of retrenchment against pluralistic democratic involvement in the administrative process. The *Vermont Yankee* case later in this chapter lent early support to this trend. The Supreme Court has since moved in a variety of ways to limit opportunities for citizens to involve themselves in judicial challenges when agency actions are overly linked to regulated interests,[44] reflecting themes echoed in subsequent right-wing campaigns for deregulation.

These stages in the evolution of administrative law overlap one another, so that in modern society one can still simultaneously see a tendency to turn to governmental agencies to handle newly identified societal problems, a reaction against governmental agencies, a pluralistic tendency toward a continuing democratization of the administrative process, and counter-tendencies attempting to limit outsider citizen participation.

This quick excursion through history gives a sense of how environmental law, which has consistently been shaped by private citizens' activist efforts, reflects major cross-currents in the development of U.S. government. The administrative state, built upon a foundation of common law, forces environmentalists to deal with all the varied advantages and disadvantages of the government process.

Because environmentalism has been so ready to rock the boat—persistently trying to force an evasive status quo to confront a broad range of important concerns in the civic-societal economy, about pollution, chemical exposures, and dwindling resources—environmental law has tended to be on the cutting edge of a wide range of fields, including equity, tort, civil procedure, and others already encountered. Administrative law is a prime example on this list. A modern administrative law course could be taught using environmental cases exclusively.

This chapter does not purport to be a course in administrative law. It is a glimpse at the field, meant to inform subsequent consideration of various environmental regulatory programs in later chapters.

B. ADMINISTRATIVE PROCESS AND LAW IN A NUTSHELL

Practical questions of administrative law boil down to three broad areas of inquiry that analyze the following:

1. The process by which government agencies (at all levels—local, state, federal, and perhaps even international) receive the powers that they apply in their various regulatory settings—this is the *delegation* issue.
2. The methods by which they exercise their powers in particular cases. The three primary modes of agency action that impact upon third parties outside government are *monitoring* (including inspections and data collection), *adjudication* (which includes

---

4. See Scalia, The Doctrine of Standing as an Essential Element of the Separation of Powers, 17 Suffolk U. L. Rev. 881, 897 (1983) (arguing that citizen standing should be restricted, in order to prevent enforcement of "lots of [ill-advised] once-heralded programs [that] ought to get lost or misdirected in [the] vast hallways [of bureaucracy].").

the vast majority of agency decisionmaking), and *rulemaking*; all three can be undertaken in *formal trial-type* or *informal* procedures.
3. How such agency exercises of power can be mobilized, demobilized, directed, overturned, or circumvented (by the process of applying pressures within the legislative and executive branches of government, before or after decisions are made, as well as by judicial review litigation second-guessing particular agency decisions).

1. The Structure of Administrative Agency Power and Process

The Source of Power: Delegation. Agencies are just that: agents. Their only reason for existence, since they are not provided for in the federal Constitution or most state constitutions, is that the constitutionally-created branches of government had too much detailed work to do than they could conveniently do themselves. The constitutionally-created branches accordingly delegated some of their powers to standing agents in order to spread the workload and drudgery of performing investigations, day-to-day oversight, and the hands-on administrative tasks of running a society.

This reality reflects the utilitarian assumption, common to all modern nations, that government has to take an active part in running a modern society. The market and various social relationships are incapable of managing the required scope and complexity. Without the external imposition of governmental powers into the market system, some important needs and values would not be adequately addressed. Without government, there would not be adequate machinery for defending our borders against enemies and building roads and schools for all. Without government, factories might well still be using the labor of children (which in market terms made compelling good sense) and disposing of pollution by dumping it willy-nilly.

Most government programs, therefore, originate in recognition of market failure—where the marketplace and processes of social accommodation failed to do a job that a politically significant number of people think need doing. But virtually all such tasks turn out to be too much for the constitutionally established officials (a couple thousand or so legislators and judges in the federal government, and a handful of executives) to handle. So they create agents. (And then, of course, more can be done, so then even more new tasks can be undertaken by government, so then more agents have to be created, and so on. But then, that's another issue.)

Agencies can be created by each branch of government, acting alone. Courts can set up "special masters" to handle administrative tasks; legislatures can set up their own budget-analysis and investigatory offices, such as the Congressional Budget Office (CBO), the Government Accountability Office (GAO), and the Office of Technology Assessment (OTA); chief executives can set up councils of economic advisors, security advisors, budget advisors, and environmental advisors. But in the vast majority of cases where an agency is set up to manage affairs that directly affect people outside of government, including most agencies affecting the environment, the agency is created by an act of the legislature signed into law by the chief executive; it will be placed more or less into the bailiwick of the executive branch.

A basic question: Were the powers an agency seeks to exercise in a particular case validly delegated to the agency? The powers and duties of most agencies must be set out and guided by the statutes that create them (their respective "organic acts"). Agencies hold only subsidiary powers; they can make only subsidiary rules. Their actions must be authorized by and conform to the requirements of the statutes (and, beyond the statutes, of course, to the Constitution).

Delegation has often provided fertile ground for attacks on agency actions, especially at the state level, and especially rulemaking. Judges who dislike an agency action may turn to the "non-delegation doctrine" to void it: "Did the statute give the agency the particular power it is attempting to exercise? Do the legislature and the chief executive have the right to delegate a particular role or power to an agent? Is the legislature's delegating language too broad or vague to give adequate definition of the powers for guidance of the agency and reviewing courts?" In some cases, delegations to agencies have been voided under the separation of powers theory: The statute has impermissibly delegated legislative or judicial power to an agent that is a non-legislature and non-court. In some cases, agency actions have been struck down under the ultra vires ("beyond the powers") principle: The delegating statute did not grant a power specifically enough or extend it broadly enough to cover the particular kind of thing that the agency is attempting to do.

In the vast majority of federal cases, however, the non-delegation doctrine now is only a minor background constraint on agency action. After a number of attempts to use non-delegation to strike down environmental regulations for lack of a sufficiently clear delegated definition of "safety," even Justice Rehnquist rejected the non-delegation argument in the 2001 *American Trucking* decision, thereby substantially reducing its utility as a weapon against agencies.[5]

The Exercise of Agency Powers. An administrative agency is an ongoing, functioning organism. As such, it exercises a variety of powers, both internally, within the agency, and externally, impacting upon people outside the agency. The external powers include the power to investigate, require submission of information, etc., and these can be important. Day in and day out, however, the primary exercises of an agency's external powers occur in two ways—rulemaking (the issuance of regulations[6]), and adjudication (the process of making operative agency decisions by applying legal standards set out in statutes or regulations to the facts of particular cases). Most agencies are delegated the power to act in both ways, often according to their own choice of how best to proceed.

The life of the administrative state can be tracked through millions of reams of official paper each year. RCRA, which is 96 pages long, for instance, has been arduously articulated through more than 150 pages of regulations. Each rulemaking reflects hundreds of hours of agency process and disputation. Administrative "adjudications"—which includes the process of applying statutes and rules to tens of thousands of cases each year—multiply the scope geometrically. And a large number of these agency processes are controversial, which makes their details important to lawyers. The Administrative Procedure Act (APA) is the blueprint of modern federal administrative law, used almost universally as a model by the states as well. It sets out many (although not all) of the basic definitions and prescriptions for how an agency is to run itself—how to promulgate rules, how to give notice to the public, how hearings examiners (administrative law judges) are to proceed, and so on. APA Chapter 7 prescribes the basis for judicial review of challenged agency actions.[7] The federal courts in the D.C. Circuit handle a large majority of all litigation involving federal agencies.

---

5. See *Indus. Union Dep't, AFL-CIO v. Am. Petroleum Inst.*, 448 U.S. 607 (1980) (the *Benzene* case, Rehnquist, J., concurring opinion); *Am. Textile Mfg. Inst. v. Donovan*, 452 U.S. 490 (1981) (the *Cotton Dust* case, Rehnquist dissent). What would happen if courts held legislatures to a strict rule that the terms of all statutes must be "as precise as feasible"? In *American Trucking* (examined in depth in Chapter 11), however, the Court, including Justices Rehnquist and Scalia, emphatically overrode the circuit court's attempt to void a major EPA pollution standard with that restrictive delegation logic. *Whitman v. Am. Trucking Assocs.*, 531 U.S. 457 (2001).

6. Rules and regulations: What is the difference between a rule and a regulation? Nothing.

7. 5 U.S.C. §§701-706.

Both rulemaking and agency adjudication can be accomplished "formally," that is, they can be done with full trial-type process—discovery, motions, production of evidence, cross-examination, stenographic record, and a decisionmaker bound to decide in a reasoned judgment only on the basis of the record produced. Both can also be undertaken "informally" through less than formal procedures and without full trial-type process. They also can be "hybrid," part trial-type process and part informal procedure. Hybrid procedures are not prescribed in the APA; they are applied when required by some other particular statute, by the voluntary decision of the agency itself, or, in some cases, by court order.

The following sections of the APA set out partial prescriptions for how these functions will be exercised (state codes have similar provisions):

	RULE MAKING	*ADJUDICATION*
Informal	§553, notice-and-comment, or less	(no prescribed process)
(hybrid, in-between)	§553, plus selected parts of §556-557	(no prescribed process)
Formal	§553, plus full §§556-557 trial-type procedures, "TTP"	§554, plus full §§556-557 trial-type procedures, "TTP"

APA §553 says that informal rulemaking, when it affects parties outside government, at a minimum must provide for public notice and opportunity to comment prior to publication of a rule in the Federal Register.[8] Sections 556 and 557 are the add-ons for formal trial-type process—discovery, cross-examination, a reasoned decision on the full record, and so on—that can be added on to either adjudication or rulemaking. Section 554 is the prescription for formal adjudication, which always triggers the formal trial-type processes of §§556-557. There is no required process for informal adjudications, however even though these are certainly the vast majority of agency actions. Where an agency, for example, says "Yes, you may build a house there," or "No, you may not drain a swamp," or "Yes, you may treat pollution abatement as a tax-deductible business expense," or "No, you may not file a late application"—all these are typically informal adjudications, applying law to facts without trial-type procedures.

Battles are often fought between agencies and regulated parties, or intervening parties, about which kind of procedure the agency should follow, since often there is no express statutory requirement that an agency act through formal or informal rulemaking or adjudication. Sometimes parties want rulemaking rather than adjudication (because then an agency directive can be prospective only). More often parties try to get more formalized trial-type procedures, regardless of whether the agency is proceeding in rulemaking or adjudication. (Attorneys apparently consider that, at least in most cases, the more procedure they get, the better the ultimate deal they'll get for their clients.)

---

8. Rulemaking typically moves through a series of public notice stages before a regulation becomes law. After having been developed within a labyrinth of internal agency procedures, a draft rule is finally published in the Federal Register in an NPR (Notice of Proposed Rulemaking) with an explanation of what formal or informal procedures will be applied. At minimum, the public has the opportunity to send in comments by mail. After at least 30 days, the agency can process the comments received and publish an NFR (Notice of Final Rulemaking) in the Federal Register, along with its summarized reactions to public comments received. Every year or so, regulations are codified into the Code of Federal Regulations (CFR) (a woefully poorly organized compilation; thankfully, regulations can now be searched through Westlaw and Lexis, and Federal Register notices through HeinOnline).

B. Administrative Process and Law in a Nutshell

The arguments for more procedure usually come down to one of a couple constitutional issues. Procedural due process is the prime argument, though it is not easy to force an agency to give procedure it doesn't want to give.[9] The other constitutional argument is grounded upon the basic judicial review jurisdiction of Article III of the U.S. Constitution: It is reflected in holdings that a court should require more procedure in a given case for the sake of the integrity of its own judicial review role, in order to produce a sufficient body of data (on a formal or informal agency record) to permit it to make an adequately incisive, though deferential, review of the agency action.

Contending Forces—Five Blocs. As noted throughout this coursebook, to understand the realities of modern environmental law's policy and practice, one must take note of the various political players that shape the outcomes of particular issues in the governance process. In operative terms, on any given issue there are typically four significant blocs likely to be actively involved and playing significant roles in the determination of administrative outcomes—*industrial-commercial interests* acting individually or through their various organizations, the *administrative agency* or agencies, the *activist citizen associations*, the *legislature* and the *legislators*, and the *courts*, which often have the final say. (To these could be added the media, although these purport to play less directive roles in the process.) In every administrative law case, diagramming out these blocs of players and their potential positions and tactical agendas, whether obvious or latent, is a sage practical reconnaissance process that usually makes attorneys much more effective.

Pressuring Agencies. There are very few significant legal or economic issues that do not turn in substantial part upon the decisions of governmental agencies—local, state, or federal. Since agencies wield such broad-ranging powers in modern society, pressuring them in one direction or another has become a fundamental task of hundreds of thousands of attorneys and other citizens, most concerned with particular private and corporate interests but a significant number serving avowed public interests. Pressure can be applied before or after a particular agency decision in a variety of forums. Agencies respond to lobbying, to the media, to internal or external politicking, and of course to the legislature that created them and annually can cut them down through the budget process, oversight hearings, and amendments to agencies' statutory authority.

Regulatory Agency Action—Rulemaking. In the regulatory setting, the first stage of official agency action often is the issuance of a regulation detailing permissible behaviors under a statute—for instance, setting out the maximum allowable discharge of particular pollutants. Some statutes are enforceable without further elaboration of details, but most aren't, and even in such cases adjectival rules are usually issued, procedural and substantive. Notices of Proposed Rulemaking are published in the Federal Register, followed by a time for at least written public comment, then a Notice of Final Rulemaking accompanied by written agency responses to comments received, with the rule later codified in the Code of Federal Regulations (CFR).[10] But what initiates this rulemaking? In some cases, the base

---

9. The basic three-point balancing argument comes from *Mathews v. Eldridge*, 424 U.S. 319 (1976)—a court reviewing how much procedure an agency must constitutionally give a claimant should weigh (1) the hardship to the claimant in not receiving additional process, (2) the hardship to the government in having to provide additional process, and (3) the risk of error in not having particular additional procedures apply. The last of these is the key argument.

10. Learning to move through the forest of regulatory materials is a complicated but necessary part of being an effective attorney. An excellent guidebook to this process is J. Anderson & D. Hirsch, Environmental Law Practice

statute mandates rulemaking within certain deadlines, but more often the agency has to be prompted to start the rulemaking. Sometimes the initiation comes from within the agency leadership or staff, sometimes from industries and other lobbies that will be benefited by a rule if it is drafted in their favor. Sometimes agency rulemaking is forced by citizens under APA §553(e), as in Chapter 11's *NRDC v. Train*, in which EPA was court-ordered to commence rulemaking and ultimately issue air pollution standards for lead.[11]

Regulations occupy a median position between statutes and mere agency guidelines. In the hierarchy of laws, the *U.S. Constitution* comes first, then *statutes*, then *regulations* that are issued by agencies as adjectival to statutes and that cannot contradict or exceed the terms of the statute.

At a level below regulations are *guidelines* (or, more commonly, *guidance* in current EPA rubric). Guidance documents are issued to set out agency definitions and procedures that affect parties outside the agency, but they are deemed not to be binding. They are generally followed by the agency, however, and have been occasionally forced into §553 rulemaking by judges who believe they are de facto regulations.[12]

Regulatory Agency Action — "Adjudication." The concept of administrative adjudication does not necessarily involve anything resembling a court's procedure. Since it covers any occasion upon which agency staffers apply a morsel of their operative law — from statutes, regulations, agency practices, common sense — to a set of facts presented to them, it can be very informal indeed.

Enforcement of environmental statutes, usually under the terms of regulations issued under the statutes, is initiated by agency staffers in a variety of formal or informal internal administrative procedures or directly in judicial proceedings. If agencies fail to enforce legal standards against violators, citizens can initiate enforcement themselves, for practical reasons, almost always in court. (See congressional grants of standing for citizen enforcement later in this chapter.)

2. The *Rybachek* Pollution Case: An Example of Agency Rulemaking, Authorized by Statute, Challenged in Court

The Statute The Clean Water Act (1972), codified at 33 U.S.C. §1251ff:

§301(a).[13] Illegality of pollutant discharges except in compliance with law.

Except as in compliance with [sections of] this title, the discharge of any pollutant by any person shall be unlawful. 33 U.S.C. §1311(a). . . .

(2d ed. 2003), especially pages 6-52, which carry you through an administrative definition problem and provide a primer on using online databases for researching administrative materials.

11. *NRDC v. Train*, 545 F.2d 320 (D.C. Cir. 1976). Under APA §553(e), any person has a right to petition an agency for promulgation of a rule, and, especially if the petition actually proposes a title and draft language, this can be tactically very useful. If the agency declines, its basis for declining to move forward with the rule can then be challenged in court under APA §§555(e) and 706. See *Baur v. Veneman*, 352 F.3d 625 (2d Cir. 2003) (plaintiff who filed §553(e) petition seeking USDA rule banning processing of sick "downed" cows into consumer food products is entitled to judicial review of agency's refusal to do so).

12. See *Gen. Elec. Co. v. EPA*, 290 F.3d 377, 379 (D.C. Cir. 2002) ("On its face the Guidance Document imposes binding obligations upon applicants to submit applications that conform to the Document and upon the Agency not to question an applicant's use of the 4.0 (mg/kg/day) −1 total toxicity factor. This is sufficient to render it a legislative rule [i.e. requiring notice-and-comment rulemaking if it is to be valid].").

13. The short section number reflects the section numbering of the original bill as passed, typically used as a familiar nickname by those who regularly work with the section.

B. Administrative Process and Law in a Nutshell

§304(b). **Effluent limitation guidelines.** ... The [EPA] Administrator shall, after consultation with appropriate Federal and State agencies and other interested persons, publish ... regulations providing guidelines for [water pollutant] effluent limitations. ... Such regulations shall— (1)(A) identify ... the degree of effluent reduction attainable through the application of the best practicable control technology currently available.[14] ... 33 U.S.C. §1314(b).

EPA Issues a Regulation: After months of study on November 20, 1985, EPA issued an NPR (a Notice of Proposed Rulemaking) (50 Fed. Reg. 47982) proposing a pollution effluent standard for placer mining under the statutory authority of §304, thus beginning a "notice-and-comment" rulemaking procedure.[15] As often happens, the agency was avalanched with comments, mostly industry objections to the proposed rule's putative harshness. After 32 months processing comments on the NPR (a longer delay than usual for most rules), EPA issued a 3-page rule that, after 23 pages summarizing comments received and EPA responses, set out final official water pollution limitations for placer mining, including the following subsection provision on "settleable solids."

Environmental Protection Agency, Notice of Final Rulemaking

53 Federal Register 18764 (May 24, 1988) [subsequently codified into 40 C.F.R. §440]

ORE MINING AND DRESSING; POINT SOURCE CATEGORY; EFFLUENT LIMITATIONS GUIDELINES, PRETREATMENT STANDARDS, AND NEW SOURCE PERFORMANCE STANDARDS. ...

§440.143. Effluent limitations representing the degree of effluent reduction attainable by the application of the best available technology economically achievable (BAT). ...

Any existing point source subject to this subpart must achieve the following effluent limitations. ...

(b) The volume of process wastewater which may be discharged from a dredge plant site shall not exceed: ... *Settleable solids*: 0.2 ml/liter. ...

The Regulated Industry Challenges the Regulation: When regulated industries deem an agency rule too restrictive, or citizen environmentalists deem it too lenient, one side or the other (sometimes both) are likely to challenge it in court. (Many formal or informal agency "adjudicatory" decisions[16] are challenged too, usually by regulated parties.) In the following court case (discussed further in Chapter 12), the Alaska placer mining industry

---

14. Under this and other subsections of CWA §304 the Administrator was directed to set a variety of effluent limitations (permit standards) for various water pollutants from various sources, many of them "technology-based" as in §304b)(1)(A), e.g., certain toxic pollutants "shall require application of the *best available technology economically achievable* for such category or class. ..." §301(2)(A)(i). See Chapter 12.

15. This was "informal" rulemaking under APA§553, i.e., only written proceedings; no open or formalized hearing was held. A placer mine is a mining operation located in the middle of a river or stream thought to contain gold particles and nuggets. Like a giant variation on a prospector's gold pan, placer mining equipment shovels up benthic gravels from the river, mixes in a flocculant chemical to clump up gold particles (nineteenth-century gold panners used mercury), sluices the mix around to allow the gold clumps to settle out, then usually dumps the residue back into the watercourse.

16. Familiar suits against agency adjudication decisions include challenges leveled against permits with tough standards, decisions that a particular corporate action must stop, etc.

filed a court challenge against the placer mining Settleable Solids Rule just noted above, and the case went for direct review[17] to the Ninth Circuit.

Rybachek v. U.S. Environmental Protection Agency
904 F.2d 1276 (U.S. Ct. App., 9th Cir. 1990)

O'SCANNLAIN, J. The Alaska Miners Association and Stanley and Rosalie Rybachek timely petitioned this court for review of the EPA's regulations . . . promulgating final effluent-limitation . . . standards. . . . [As to settleable solids,] the EPA determined that the settleable solids level achievable with settling ponds was 0.2 ml/l. The Rybacheks assert that the EPA has inadequate support for this determination and was required to set instead a higher level. . . . Between 1983 and 1986, the EPA took 73 samples of full-scale settling ponds at 39 different gold placer mines; 50 of these samples indicated levels of settleable solids at or below 0.2 ml/l after treatment. . . . Ponds not achieving this level had discernible design or operating deficiencies. . . . Because . . . the proper factors were considered, and because . . . the EPA's determination of the 0.2 ml/l level [and each of the rule's other challenged effluent limitations] is supportable by the record, we uphold the EPA's determination. . . .

3. The *Snail Darter* Case: An Agency Is Brought to Court for Its Own Actions Allegedly Violating Federal Law

Agencies are taken to court in two very different settings—cases in which a court, at the request of a challenger, is *reviewing an agency regulatory action,* as in the *Rybachek* challenge in the preceding paragraphs, and cases in which the agency is sued *as itself a defendant* (i.e., not a "reviewee") *because of its own allegedly illegal programmatic actions,* as in the following case. Compare the settings of the following judicial challenge—similar to literally thousands of U.S. cases since 1970 in which citizen plaintiffs have enforced federal environmental laws against both private and public violators—where the agency wins again. The case ultimately came to the Supreme Court, however, in a decision noted in Chapter 10.

The Statute The Endangered Species Act §7, codified at 16 UCS §1536:

> §1536 . . . All . . . federal agencies shall . . . ensure that actions authorized, funded, or carried out by such agencies do not jeopardize the continued existence of . . . endangered species . . . or result in the destruction or modification of habitat of such species. . . .

The agency is sued by citizens for its actions alleged to violate the statute.

Hiram Hill et al. v. Tennessee Valley Authority
419 F. Supp. 753, 755-758, 763-764 (U.S. Dist. Ct., E.D. Tenn. 1976)

TAYLOR, J. Plaintiffs, the Association of Southeastern Biologists, the Audubon Council of Tennessee, Hiram Hill, Zygmunt Plater and Donald Cohen seek to enjoin the completion of the Tellico Dam and consequent impoundment of the Little Tennessee River. Plaintiffs

---

17. By statute, judicial reviews of some regulations go directly to a Circuit Court of Appeal rather than initial review in a federal trial court.

B. Administrative Process and Law in a Nutshell

allege that defendant TVA, a wholly-owned corporation of the United States, is acting in violation of §7 of the Endangered Species Act of 1973 by bulldozing and clear-cutting trees and foliage along the banks of the Little Tennessee River and by proceeding with plans to impound the river, [thereby jeopardizing] a small, tannish-colored fish which is commonly known as the *snail darter*.... [The fish was] placed on the [Department of Interior's] endangered species list November 10, 1975 on the ground that there was a present or threatened destruction of the snail darter or its habitat....

We conclude that it is highly probable that closure of the Tellico Dam and the consequent impoundment of the river behind it will jeopardize the continued existence of the snail darter.... We conclude ... that the preponderance of the evidence demonstrates that closure of the Tellico Dam ... will result in the adverse modification, if not complete destruction, of the snail darter's critical habitat....

We conclude that TVA has not acted arbitrarily, capriciously or otherwise not in accordance with the law in continuing further implementation of the Tellico Project. It has acted within the scope of authority given it by Congress and ... has consulted with other agencies about the problem....

It is ordered that the plaintiffs' request for a permanent injunction in this action be, and hereby is, denied ... [and] that the action be, and hereby is, dismissed on the merits....

4. Judges' Handling of Challenges to Federal Agencies

In *Rybachek*, the first preceding example of an agency being challenged in court, the agency defendant's regulatory action clearly is being subjected to judicial *review*, and in the second, the *Snail Darter* case, the agency is itself straightforwardly the *statutory defendant*. As noted below, the distinction often can and should make a difference in the posture of the case and the amount of deference the court pays to the agency.

Judicial review of agencies' formal or informal adjudications and rulemaking is the most visible and commonly encountered constraint on agency freedom of action. A disgruntled person in most cases can request judicial review of a particular agency action, as in *Rybachek*, and judicial review can operate to cramp an agency's style even if ultimate reversal of the agency decision is not usually likely.

> **Deference:** When agency actions undergo judicial review, the degree to which federal judges will scrutinize — or alternatively defer — to the agencies can tend to become quite outcome-determinative. Debate over the appropriate degree of a court's deference or scrutiny occur in several different arenas: agencies' determinations of the facts in a case, agencies' legal interpretations of the relevant statutes, and agencies' interpretations of their own regulations. There is no one standard in any of these arenas, and not a little judicial political strategizing.

Judicial review of federal agency action operates under Chapter 7 of the APA, 5 U.S.C. §701ff. The challenging party must show standing and reviewability under §702, and fulfill a few other judge-made threshold requirements (ripeness for review, exhaustion of agency remedies, etc.).

Standard of Review. Section 706 then sets out a catalogue of different inquiries courts are directed to make: the "arbitrary, capricious, or abuse of discretion" test (for informal rulemaking or adjudication), the requirement of "substantial evidence" supporting the decision (in the case of most formal proceedings), and an array of other possible tests.[18]

Most substantive challenges of agency decisions are reviews that use the "arbitrary & capricious" standard of review or the "substantial evidence" standard, reviewing the rather subjective question of whether the agency's decision was reasonable in the circumstances. In some environmental cases, to be sure, challenges to agency action come down to straightforward application and interpretation of statutes: Did the agency violate a provision of some particular law? In far more cases, however, the question is not so easy, instead turning on the assertion that the agency has exercised bad judgment. Courts understandably do not usually like to second-guess agencies, instead preferring to defer to agency discretion and expertise. But their Article III judicial mandate requires them to examine cases validly presented to them.

Degrees of Deference. Issues constantly arise about what "standard of review" should be applied. In challenges to agency findings of fact, the judicial scrutiny can range from the rather minimal "arbitrary" test all the way to judicial takeover of the question (trial de novo). A little-remarked threshold question, noted above, is "What is the agency's role that brought it to court?" Analytically there is a distinction between whether the agency's action is merely being *reviewed* or whether the agency is itself being sued as a direct defendant. As self-taught "citizen attorney general" Richard "Max" Strahan once said:

> Hey, why is the judge deferring to the Coast Guard's judgment about how to run their boats in the whales' critical habitat? We're not talking here about the agency as a regulator. We're talking about the agency as a *perpetrator!* They're violating a federal statute themselves by killing whales! Shouldn't that make a difference?[19]

---

18. §706 . . . To the extent necessary to decision and when presented, the reviewing court shall decide all relevant questions of law, interpret constitutional and statutory provisions, and determine the meaning or applicability of the terms of an agency action. The reviewing court shall—

    (1) compel agency action unlawfully withheld or unreasonably delayed; and
    (2) hold unlawful and set aside agency action, findings, and conclusions found to be—
        (A) arbitrary, capricious, an abuse of discretion, or otherwise not in accordance with law;
        (B) contrary to constitutional right, power, privilege, or immunity;
        (C) in excess of statutory jurisdiction, authority, or limitations, or short of statutory right;
        (D) without observance of procedure required by law;
        (E) unsupported by substantial evidence in a case subject to sections 556 and 557 of this title or otherwise reviewed on the record of an agency hearing provided by statute; or
        (F) unwarranted by the facts to the extent that the facts are subject to trial de novo by the reviewing court.

In making the foregoing determinations, the court shall review the whole record or those parts of it cited by a party, and due account shall be taken of the rule of prejudicial error.

19. The distinction was echoed in the 2009 *Otero Mesa* case:

> In challenging that proceeding, the plaintiffs did not contend that BLM [as a *regulator*] wrongfully adjudicated their rights, but rather that its policymaking process [in issuing oil and gas leases] was contrary to law and injured their interests. For that reason, BLM appeared in the district court as *a traditional adversarial party, defending its own actions* against challenges by the State and NMWA [plaintiffs], *rather than defending a ruling made by the Agency in a controversy between parties appearing before it.*" Richardson et al. v. BLM, 565 F.3d 683, 698 (10th Cir. 2009) (emphasis added).

Nonlawyer "Max, the Prince of Whales" Strahan has spent more than two decades as an intelligent, persistent, annoying, endangered species activist litigating cases (usually pro se, by leave of court) that have gone as far as the Supreme Court. See *Strahan v. Linnon*, 966 F. Supp. 111 (D. Mass. 1997); *Strahan v. Linnon*, 1998 U.S. App. LEXIS 16314 (1st Cir. 1998); *Strahan v. Coxe*, 939 F. Supp. 963 (D. Mass. 1996), mostly aff'd in *Strahan v. Coxe*, 127 F.3d 155

B. Administrative Process and Law in a Nutshell

Strangely there is little academic or judicial recognition that the two different settings deserve different postures of deference. When an agency is being sued for its allegedly illegal physical or programmatic actions rather than reviewed for its regulatory decisions, the posture of the case would seem to indicate less judicial deference to the agency. In *Overton Park*, which follows, the Supreme Court seems to regard the agency as a project construction agency rather than a regulator, and shows little deference. It is difficult, however, to find courts expressly discussing this sliding-scale deference issue. Whether the agency is acting as regulator being reviewed or as an alleged perpetrator, court challenges often confront issues about the scope of agency "discretion." Discretion and deference are often paired in administrative law, but they are different concepts, not always exactly congruent.

Most court cases against agencies, however, whether rightly or wrongly, are referred to in terms of judicial "review." In all cases a major question is how deeply will the court pry into the particulars of an agency decision, especially when it realizes that the closer it looks, the more it is second-guessing and taking over the agency's decisional process? In all but de novo cases, the question usually comes down to the same judicial determination: "Could a reasonable agency official have reached this decision on this record of facts?" The practical difference between various standards of judicial review comes down to differences in degrees and moods of deference to agencies in each case, reflecting different sensitivities to separation of powers issues. In the minuet of contending powers, moreover, courts can use the choice of different standards of review—"arbitrary" for loose review, "substantial evidence" for tougher—to effectuate a result that they personally prefer. Politics and ideology in this way can insinuate themselves into courtroom challenges of agency actions.

The same sort of scale applies in challenges to agencies' interpretations of law, although a bit less predictably. Judges often don't seem quite so inclined to defer to agencies' decisions about law (the agencies' interpretation of what a statute or regulation requires) as they do to agencies' decisions about questions of fact. See *Chevron* and *Mead* below.

Scope of Review. Issues also arise on "scope of review": How broadly will the court look in scrutinizing the agency action? How much data and "record" will it require? Will it allow new evidence to be introduced in court proceedings that was not brought before the agency? Normally the scope of judicial review is limited to the record of whatever was compiled and presented in the challenged agency proceedings. In some cases, a court may say that its necessary scope of review requires more evidence to be prepared and presented.

Remedies. Finally there are questions of remedies. If an enforcement action reaches a successful end in an agency or a court, what remedy should be issued? penalties, fees, criminal penalties,[20] injunctive orders? If judicial review of an agency action finds it to be faulty, what sanction should the reviewing court apply against the agency? injunction,

---

(1st Cir. 1997), cert. denied sub nom. *Coates v. Strahan*, 525 U.S. 978 (1998). See also Strahan, A New Paradigm for Conservation of Great Whales, 36 B.C. Envtl. Aff. L. Rev. 431 (2009). A longtime graduate student in physics, he is the transient public citizen agitator who filed the petition with the FWS that forced the listing of the northern spotted owl as an endangered species; he has obtained injunctions against practices threatening northern right whales and other endangered whales, and inspired the fictional character portrayed by Joe Pesci in the movie *With Honors*. See Allen, Devil Doing Angels' Work? Irascible Environmentalist Winning Battles in His War to Save the Right Whale, Boston Globe, Jan. 13, 1997, at C1.

20. One of the authors once briefly researched the possibility of convicting an agency head on a statutory felony charge. Some of the legal reasons, beyond politics, why such attempts are quixotic are set out in Smith, Shields for the King's Men: Official Immunity and Other Obstacles to Effective Prosecution of Federal Officials for Environmental Crimes, 16 Colum. J. Envtl. L. 1 (1991).

declaratory judgment, remand to the agency, or something else? Environmental administrative cases have sometimes fashioned quite creative remedy packages.

Summary. As this quick excursion should make clear, administrative law and administrative process make up a separate legal ecosystem that is intricately intertwined with hundreds of important environmental and jurisprudential issues, and differs in many regards from the standard litigation model that dominates the law school curriculum.

Whatever substantive area of practice a case arises in, it should by now be evident that a familiarity with underlying administrative law principles is a basic requirement of legal literacy. In no area is this truer than in environmental law.

C. *Overton Park*—A Judicial Review Paradigm

Administrative agencies are intimately woven into the power fabric of the nation, and accordingly are linked to most of the environmental issues discovered and decried over the past few decades by environmentalists. Within themselves, agencies mirror many of the forces, procedures, and vested interests that cause environmental problems. It therefore comes as no surprise that environmentalists often find themselves launching challenges against agency actions at all three levels of government—federal, state, and local. Because of their political context, citizen interventions often get short shrift in agency processes,[21] so citizen activists end up taking agencies to court.

In administrative law litigation environmental plaintiffs are usually not asking the court to take over the matter and make the "right" decision itself. Rather, when a court is asked to look at an agency decision in most cases it is only applying judicial *review*, and that limitation has consequences. Judicial review of agency actions differs from review of decisions made by lower court judges or juries. An agency is a creature of a different branch of government, so more deference is required. Too much deference, however, would mean that courts abdicate their judicial role. So the critical question of administrative law is how, and how much, the court will scrutinize what an official agency has done.

Plaintiffs challenging administrative action in court, at least if it's a judicial *review* process, must first successfully pass a series of threshold obstacles—standing, reviewability, ripeness, exhaustion, and others. The reviewing court then turns to scrutiny of the procedural and substantive merits of the government actions being challenged.

1. The *Overton Park* Case

In the following case, note the plaintiffs' array of arguments—that they did not receive adequate procedures, that the agency decision was substantively wrong, and that the Court should extend the most probing, least deferential, level of scrutiny to the agency's fact-finding and decisions of law. They lost on all these battle points but won their road war.

---

21. In a fairly typical Michigan case, for instance, the citizens were rebuffed by the environmental protection agency, which deemed itself the rightful public representative in deciding that a forest reserve should be drilled for oil, and so they had to face the agency and the oil company standing together when they took the case to court, ultimately blocking the drilling. *W. Mich. Envtl. Action Council v. NRC* (*Pigeon River* case), 275 N.W.2d 538 (Mich. 1979).

C. *Overton Park*—A Judicial Review Paradigm

Citizens to Preserve Overton Park, Inc. v. Volpe
401 U.S. 402 (1971)

[The "Parklands Act," §4(f) of the Department of Transportation Act of 1966 and §138 of the Federal Aid to Highways Act of 1968,[22] provide as follows:

> §4(f) . . . It is hereby declared to be the national policy that special effort should be made to preserve the natural beauty of the countryside and public park and recreation lands, wildlife and waterfowl refuges, and historic sites. The Secretary of Transportation . . . shall not approve any program or project which requires the use of any publicly owned land from a public park, recreation area, or wildlife and waterfowl refuge of national, State, or local significance as determined by the Federal, State, or local officials having jurisdiction thereof, or any land from an historic site of national, State, or local significance . . . unless (1) there is no feasible and prudent alternative to the use of such land, and (2) such program includes all possible planning to minimize harm to such park, recreational area, wildlife and waterfowl refuge, or historic site resulting from such use.]

MARSHALL, J. The growing public concern about the quality of our natural environment has prompted Congress in recent years to enact legislation designed to curb the accelerating destruction of our county's natural beauty. We are concerned in this case with §4(f) of the Department of Transportation Act of 1966, as amended. . . .

Petitioners, private citizens as well as local and national conservation organizations, contend that the Secretary has violated these statutes by authorizing the expenditure of federal funds for the construction of a six-lane interstate highway through a public park in Memphis, Tennessee. . . .

Overton Park is a 342-acre city park located near the center of Memphis. The park contains a zoo, a nine-hole municipal golf course, an outdoor theater, nature trails, a bridle path, an art academy, picnic areas, and 170 acres of forest. The proposed highway, which is to be a six-lane high-speed expressway, will sever the zoo from the rest of the park. Although the roadway will be depressed below ground level except where it crosses a small creek, 26 acres of the park will be destroyed. The highway is to be a segment of Interstate Highway I-40, part of the National System of Interstate and Defense Highways. I-40 will provide Memphis with a major east-west expressway which will allow easier access to downtown Memphis from the residential areas on the eastern edge of the city.

Although the route through the park was approved by the Bureau of Public Roads in 1956 and by the Federal Highways Administration [FHWA] in 1966, the enactment of §4(f) of the Department of Transportation Act [in 1966] prevented distribution of federal funds for the section of the highway designated to go through Overton Park until the Secretary of Transportation determined whether the requirements of §4(f) had been met. Federal funding for the rest of the project was, however, available, and the state acquired a right-of-way on both sides of the park. In April 1968, the Secretary announced that he concurred in the judgment of local officials that I-40 should be built through the park. And in September 1969 the State acquired the right-of-way inside Overton Park from the city. Final approval for the project—the route as well as the design—was not announced until November 1969, after Congress had reiterated in §138 of the Federal-Aid Highway Act that highway construction through public parks was to be restricted. Neither announcement approving the route and design of I-40 was accompanied by a statement of the Secretary's

---

22. 49 U.S.C. §1653(f) and 23 U.S.C. §138. The two sections embody exactly the same language.

factual findings. He did not indicate why he believed there were no feasible and prudent alternative routes or why design changes could not be made to reduce the harm to the park.

Petitioners contend that the Secretary's action is invalid without such formal findings and that the Secretary did not make an independent determination but merely relied on the judgment of the Memphis City Council. They also contend that it would be "feasible and prudent" to route I-40 around Overton Park either to the north or to the south. And they argue that if these alternative routes are not "feasible and prudent," the present plan does not include "all possible" methods for reducing harm to the park. Petitioners claim that I-40 could be built under the park by using either of two possible tunneling methods,[23] and they claim that, at a minimum, by using advanced drainage techniques the expressway could be depressed below ground level along the entire route through the park including the section that crosses the small creek.

Respondent [FHWA argues] that it was unnecessary for the Secretary to make formal findings, and that he did, in fact, exercise his own independent judgment which was supported by the facts. In the District Court, respondents introduced affidavits, prepared specifically for this litigation, which indicated that the Secretary had made the decision and that the decision was supportable. . . .

We agree that formal findings were not required. But we do not believe that in this case judicial review based solely on litigation affidavits was adequate.

A threshold question—whether petitioners are entitled to any judicial review—is easily answered. Section 701 of the APA provides that the action of "each authority of the Government of the United States," which includes the Department of Transportation, is subject to judicial review except where there is a statutory prohibition on review or where "agency action is committed to agency discretion by law." In this case, there is no indication that Congress sought to prohibit judicial review and there is most certainly no "showing of 'clear and convincing evidence' of a . . . legislative intent" to restrict access to judicial review. *Abbott Labs. v. Gardner,* 387 U.S. 136, 141 (1967).

Similarly, the Secretary's decision here does not fall within the exception for action "committed to agency discretion." This is a very narrow exception. The legislative history of the APA indicates that it is applicable in those rare instances where "statutes are drawn in such broad terms that in a given case there is no law to apply." S. Rep. No. 752, 79th Cong., 1st Sess., 26 (1945).

Section 4(f) of the Department of Transportation Act and §138 of the Federal-Aid Highway Act are clear and specific directives. Both provide that the Secretary "shall not approve any program or project" that requires the use of any public parkland "unless (1) there is no feasible and prudent alternative to the use of such land, and (2) such program includes all possible planning to minimize harm to such park. . . ." This language is a plain and explicit bar to the use of federal funds for construction of highways through parks—only the most unusual situations are exempted.

Despite the clarity of the statutory language, respondents argue that the Secretary has wide discretion. They recognize that the requirement that there be no "feasible" alternative route admits of little administrative discretion. For this exemption to apply the Secretary must find that as a matter of sound engineering it would not be feasible to build the highway along any other route. Respondents argue, however, that the requirement that there be

---

23. Petitioners argue that either a bored tunnel or a cut-and-cover tunnel, which is a fully depressed route covered after construction, could be built. Respondents contend that the construction of a tunnel by either method would greatly increase the cost of the project, would create safety hazards, and, because of increase in air pollution, would not reduce harm to the park.

C. *Overton Park*—A Judicial Review Paradigm

no other "prudent" route requires the Secretary to engage in a wide-ranging balancing of competing interests. They contend that the Secretary should weigh the detriment resulting from the destruction of parkland against the cost of other routes, safety considerations, and other factors, and determine on the basis of the importance that he attaches to these other factors whether, on balance, alternative feasible routes would be "prudent."

But no such wide-ranging endeavor was intended. It is obvious that in most cases considerations of cost, directness of route, and community disruption will indicate that parkland should be used for highway construction whenever possible. Although it may be necessary to transfer funds from one jurisdiction to another, there will always be a smaller outlay required from the public purse when parkland is used since the public already owns the land and there will be no need to pay for right-of-way. And since people do not live or work in parks, if a highway is built on parkland no one will have to leave his home or give up his business. Such factors are common to substantially all highway construction. Thus, if Congress intended these factors to be on an equal footing with preservation of parkland there would have been no need for the statutes.

Congress clearly did not intend that cost and disruption of the community were to be ignored by the Secretary. But the very existence of the statute indicates that protection of parkland was to be given paramount importance. The few green havens that are public parks were not to be lost unless there were truly unusual factors present in a particular case or the cost or community disruption resulting from alternative routes reached extraordinary magnitudes. If the statutes are to have any meaning, the Secretary cannot approve the destruction of parkland unless he finds that alternative routes present unique problems.

Plainly, there is "law to apply" and thus the exemption for action "committed to agency discretion" is inapplicable. But the existence of judicial review is only the start: the standard for review must also be determined. For that we must look to §706, which provides that a "reviewing court shall . . . hold unlawful and set aside agency action, findings, and conclusions found" not to meet six separate standards. In all cases agency action must be set aside if the action was "arbitrary, capricious, an abuse of discretion, or otherwise not in accordance with law," or if the action failed to meet statutory, procedural, or constitutional requirements. In certain narrow, specifically limited situations, the agency action is to be set aside if the action was not supported by "substantial evidence." And in other equally narrow circumstances the reviewing court is to engage in a de novo review of the action and set it aside if it was "unwarranted by the facts."

Petitioners argue that the Secretary's approval of the construction of I-40 through Overton Park is subject to one or the other of these later two standards of limited applicability. . . . Neither of these standards is, however, applicable.

Review under the substantial-evidence test is authorized only when the agency action is . . . based on a [trial-type] hearing. See 5 U.S.C. §§556, 557. . . . The only hearing that is required by either the APA or the statutes regulating the distribution of federal funds for highway construction is a public hearing conducted by local officials for the purpose of informing the community about the proposed project and eliciting community views on the design and route. 23 U.S.C. §128. The hearing is nonadjudicatory, quasi-legislative in nature. It is not designed to produce a record that is to be the basis of agency action—the basic requirement for substantial-evidence review.

Petitioners' alternative argument also fails. De novo review of whether the Secretary's decision was "unwarranted by the facts" is authorized by §706(2)(F) in only two circumstances. First, such de novo review is authorized when the action is adjudicatory in nature and the agency factfinding procedures are inadequate. And there may be independent judicial factfinding when issues that were not before the agency are raised in a proceeding to enforce nonadjudicatory agency action. Neither situation exists here.

Even though there is no de novo review in this case and the Secretary's approval of the route of I-40 does not ultimately have to meet the substantial-evidence test, the generally applicable standards of §706 require the reviewing court to engage in a substantial inquiry. Certainly, the Secretary's decision is entitled to a presumption of regularity. But that presumption is not to shield his action from a thorough, probing, in-depth review.

The court is first required to decide whether the Secretary acted within the scope of his authority. This determination naturally begins with a delineation of the scope of the Secretary's authority and discretion. As has been shown, Congress has specified only a small range of choices that the Secretary can make. Also involved in this initial inquiry is a determination of whether on the facts the Secretary's decision can reasonably be said to be within that range. The reviewing court . . . must be able to find that the Secretary could have reasonably believed that in this case there are no feasible alternatives or that alternatives . . . involve unique problems.

Scrutiny of the facts does not end, however, with the determination that the Secretary has acted within the scope of his statutory authority. Section 706(2)(A) requires a finding that the actual choice made was not "arbitrary, capricious, an abuse of discretion, or otherwise not in accordance with law." To make this finding the court must consider whether the decision was based on a consideration of the relevant factors and whether there has been a clear error of judgment. Although this inquiry into the facts is to be searching and careful, the ultimate standard of review is a narrow one. The court is not empowered to substitute its judgment for that of the agency.

The final inquiry is whether the Secretary's action followed the necessary procedural requirements. Here the only procedural error alleged is the failure of the Secretary to make formal findings and state his reason for allowing the highway to be built through the park.

Undoubtedly, review of the Secretary's action is hampered by his failure to make such findings, but the absence of formal findings does not necessarily require that the case be remanded to the Secretary. Neither the Department of Transportation Act nor the Federal-Aid Highway Act requires such formal findings. Moreover, the APA requirements that there be formal findings in certain rulemaking and adjudicatory proceedings do not apply to the Secretary's action here. See 5 U.S.C. §§553(a)(2), 554(a). Although formal findings may be required in some cases in the absence of statutory directives . . . , those situations are rare. . . .

Petitioners contend that although there may not be a statutory requirement that the Secretary make formal findings, . . . Department of Transportation regulations require them. This argument is based on DOT Order 5610.1, which requires the Secretary to make formal findings when he approves the use of parkland for highway construction but which was issued after the route for I-40 was approved. Petitioners argue that even though the order was not intended to have retrospective effect the order represents the law at the time of this Court's decision and under *Thorpe v. Housing Auth.*, 393 U.S. 268, 281-282 (1969), should be applied to this case. . . . The general rule [when government rules change in favor of private individuals] is "that an appellate court must apply the law in effect at the time it renders its decision." 393 U.S. at 281. While we do not question that DOT Order 5610.1 constitutes the law in effect at the time of our decision, we do not believe that *Thorpe* compels us to remand for the Secretary to make formal findings. Here, unlike the situation in *Thorpe*, there has been a change in circumstances—additional right-of-way has been cleared and the 26-acre right-of-way inside Overton Park has been purchased by the State. Moreover, there is an administrative record that allows the full, prompt review of the Secretary's action . . . without additional delay which would result from having a remand to the Secretary.

C. *Overton Park*—A Judicial Review Paradigm

That administrative record is not, however, before us. The lower courts based their review on litigation affidavits that were presented. These affidavits were merely "post hoc" rationalizations, which have traditionally been found to be an inadequate basis for review. *Burlington Truck Lines v. U.S.*, 371 U.S. 156, 168-169 (1962). And they clearly do not constitute the "whole record" compiled by the agency, the basis for review required by APA §706.

Thus it is necessary to remand this case to the District Court for plenary review of the Secretary's decision. That review is to be based on the full administrative record that was before the Secretary at the time he made his decision. But since the bare record may not disclose the factors that were considered or the Secretary's construction of the evidence it may be necessary for the District Court to require some explanation in order to determine if the Secretary acted within the scope of his authority and if the Secretary's action was justifiable under the applicable standard.

The court may require the administrative officials who participated in the decision to give testimony explaining their action. Of course, such inquiry into the mental processes of administrative decision-makers is usually to be avoided. *U.S. v. Morgan*, 313 U.S. 409, 422 (1941). And where there are administrative findings that were made at the same time as the decision, as was the case in *Morgan*, there must be a strong showing of bad faith or improper behavior before such inquiry may be made. But here there are no such formal findings and it may be that the only way there can be effective judicial review is by examining the decision-makers themselves.

The District Court is not, however, required to make such an inquiry. It may be that the Secretary can prepare formal findings including the information required by DOT Order 5610.1 that will provide an adequate explanation for his action. Such an explanation will, to some extent, be a "post hoc rationalization" and thus must be viewed critically. If the District Court decides that additional explanation is necessary, that court should consider which method will prove the most expeditious so that full review may be had as soon as possible. Reversed and remanded.

BLACK, J., joined by **BRENNAN, J.**, concurring separately. . . . I agree with the Court that the judgment of the Court of Appeals is wrong and that its action should be reversed. I do not agree that the whole matter should be remanded to the District Court. I think the case should be sent back to the Secretary of Transportation. It is apparent from the Court's opinion today that the Secretary of Transportation completely failed to comply with the duty imposed upon him by Congress. . . . That congressional command should not be taken lightly by the Secretary or by this Court. It represents a solemn determination of the highest law-making body of this Nation that the beauty and health-giving facilities of our parks are not to be taken away for public roads without hearings, factfindings, and policy determinations under the supervision of a Cabinet officer—the Secretary of Transportation. . . . I regret that I am compelled to conclude for myself that, except for some too-late formulations, apparently coming from the Solicitor General's office, this record contains not one word to indicate that the Secretary raised even a finger to comply with the command of Congress. It is our duty, I believe, to remand this whole matter back to the Secretary of Transportation, . . . whose duty has not yet been performed.

DOUGLAS, J., took no part in the consideration or decision of this case.

COMMENTARY & QUESTIONS

1. Administrative realities: The "sunk cost" strategy. What was really going on here? In planning the east-west route of I-40, the federal, state, and local agencies specifically wanted the highway to come straight through Memphis through the park. Why? Civic leaders and agency officials who promote such highways traditionally assume that putting an interstate through the middle of a metropolis will relieve traffic jams and bring added prosperity.[24] In perverse economic motivation, moreover, parklands have affirmatively attracted highways, transmission lines, and similar public facilities because the governmental promoters consider them free. Further, while 90% of federal interstate highways costs are paid by Washington from tax revenues and the federal Highway Trust Fund, states are allowed to count the value of provided land toward their required 10% contribution. This makes parklands even more seductive. If Tennessee contributes 26 acres of cost-less parkland to the highway project, it gets to value that parkland as if it were a cash contribution of its fair market value—the value of 26 acres of downtown urban land. For this reason, parks tended to attract their own destruction, and it is for precisely that reason that environmentalists had found it so necessary to fight to put §4(f) into the highway legislation.[25]

FIGURE 6-1. *Memphis, Tennessee, 2010, showing Overton Park and original I-40 road construction built right to the eastern edge of the park; to the west, at left, the I-40 bridge across the Mississippi River built directly on the park route alignment; and the present I-240 that detours around the park. USGS photo annotation by Taylor Black, BCLS '12.*

So what's the "sunk cost" strategy? The governmental agencies in this case knew that local citizens, who were urging alternative routes north or south of Overton Park, would try to bring a §4(f) lawsuit to protect the park. The authorities proceeded to condemn and bulldoze homes in the planned corridor, building the highway right-of-way right up to the eastern boundary of the park. They also built a multimillion dollar I-40 bridge across the Mississippi River on the planned highway alignment though the Park. (See Figure 1.) None of that work violated express words of the statute. It was only then that they officially turned to the Secretary to ask approval for the park route, saying that now it was the only feasible and prudent alternative remaining.[26]

---

24. The experience of many cities, however, has been that new highway routes are rapidly congested by traffic newly generated by their existence and travelers lured away from mass transit, and arteries into the hearts of cities often serve to sever or empty the center city of a stable mixed residential and economic basis by accelerating commuting and a shift to the suburbs.

25. Thus the official argument in *Overton Park* for overriding §4(f), based on "prudent" limiting of acquisition costs, replayed the problem that required §4(f) in the first place.

26. Does it seem likely that the *Overton Park* plaintiffs could have succeeded in getting an injunction against the earlier highway activities—against the condemnation of land and highway construction up to the edge of the

C. *Overton Park*—A Judicial Review Paradigm

The sunk cost strategy is frequently encountered in environmental controversies, as corporate or agency project promoters quite naturally try to get as much momentum and construction as possible irreversibly underway before citizen opposition can get organized to raise questions about a project or program's legality, expecting that any court balancing on remedies will tilt in favor of the fait accompli.

2. Threshold administrative law issues in citizen suits. Before plaintiffs can get to the merits of challenges to agency decisions, they must pass a number of threshold tests.

(a) *Justiciability/Reviewability*. When challenged by citizen suits, agency attorneys often (as in the *Overton Park* case) initially argue that their challenged agency decisions are unreviewable or "unjusticiable" because they contain discretionary elements. The courts, however, have demonstrated extreme hesitation in finding nonreviewability. In *Abbott Laboratories* the Court held: "The enactment of the Administrative Procedures Act . . . embodies the basic presumption of judicial review to one 'suffering legal wrong because of agency action. . . .' The Act's 'generous review provision' must be given a 'hospitable' interpretation. . . . Only upon a showing of 'clear and convincing evidence' of a contrary legislative intent should the courts restrict access to judicial review." *Abbott Labs. v. Gardner*, 387 U.S. 136, 141 (1967). Sovereign immunity barriers to reviewability of federal agency actions were specifically removed in 1976 by amendments to APA §702. Since APA §706 specifically authorizes the court to "hold unlawful and set aside action . . . found to be . . . an abuse of discretion," discretionary acts are clearly not unreviewable.

(b) *Standing*. In *Overton Park*, as in many environmental cases, there is no problem with standing. Some or all of the Tennessee plaintiffs would be directly affected by the consequences of the agency decision. It has long been established that plaintiffs' "injury in fact" necessitated by Article III's case-or-controversy requirement does not have to be economic or legal but can extend to recreational, aesthetic, and other injuries.[27] Although courts may deny standing when particular persons are not injured, or are injured only to the same extent as millions of other citizens, the Supreme Court has occasionally allowed fairly broad standing to sue, in part to allow troublesome environmental questions to be debated.[28]

(c) *Exhaustion of remedies and ripeness*. In *Overton Park*, the legal issues were clearly ready for review when plaintiffs went to court. In some environmental cases it's argued that citizens should exhaust internal remedies within the agency before going to court; in other cases, the argument is that an agency decision, though it has been made, is not yet "ripe" for judicial review because it has not actually been applied or is not yet completely final. These arguments generally have not been successful defenses against environmental litigation. Courts often seem to reflect the legal system's interest in resolving important legal questions at an efficient early stage, before major investments and commitments of resources are wasted. But not always.[29]

A composite of these threshold hurdles was used in the Supreme Court's rejection of a citizen suit trying to force the federal Bureau of Land Management (BLM) to prevent

---

park—as a violation of §4(f)? Probably not. The defense would have been that the issue was not yet "ripe" (see below), the law was not yet violated. A NEPA suit might offer better prospects in such cases (see Chapter 8).

27. *Sierra Club v. Morton*, 405 U.S. 727, 734 (1972).

28. See, e.g., *Duke Power v. Carolina Envtl. Study Group*, 438 U.S. 59 (1978); *U.S. v. SCRAP*, 412 U.S. 669 (1973).

29. As in the *Overton Park* history, where citizens were unable to bring the on-rolling imminent violation of the statute into court prior to the final moment the money was released for the final thrust into the park because no final agency decision on point was ripe for court action until that last sunk cost moment. Could a judge in the *Overton Park* circumstances have acknowledged the factual realities and considered the case for an injunction as soon as the corridor construction began?

destructive ORV (off-road vehicle) use in protected wilderness candidate areas. *Norton v. Southern Utah Wilderness Alliance (SUWA)*, 542 U.S. 55 (2004). Though the Wilderness Act required BLM to prevent "impairment" of the wilderness areas, and BLM's official plan required the agency to monitor use and protect the areas against destructive ORV intrusions, BLM did nothing to control ORV use. Justice Scalia held, however, that the statutory requirements and the plans were too general to create any mandatory duties, and thus if no actions were mandatory the agency's failure was not reviewable under the APA, nor was there any particular action ripe for review. APA §706(1) "empowers a court only to compel an agency to perform a ministerial or non-discretionary act," and the Court said there was none such act. (See *SUWA* in Chapter 9.)

3. The administrative law of *Overton Park*: tactics and standard of review. *Overton Park* is a classic administrative law case with many interesting details. Note how easily the Court in *Overton Park* accepts the plaintiffs' threshold showings allowing them to get into court. As to procedure, however, the plaintiffs did not succeed in their request for formal findings, nor did they get hearings before the Secretary. Both of these procedures obviously would have been helpful in sharpening their case against the highway through the park and obtaining closer judicial review of the subsequent decision. (The Supreme Court opinion, like many lawyers, seems to consider that all agency "adjudications" are formal adjudications, when in fact informal adjudications constitute the vast majority of government agency decisions.)

As to the substantive standard of review to be applied to the agency's factual decision, the plaintiffs didn't get de novo review,[30] the toughest standard, nor even the substantial evidence test. They got only review under the arbitrary and capricious test, and they never got a judicial ruling that the Secretary had indeed been arbitrary and capricious in approving the parkland route.

So why didn't the Department of Transportation (DOT) win? While the Court says that "the ultimate standard of review is a narrow one," thus adopting a continued deference to the agency's expertise on fact-finding, it nevertheless recognizes that judges examining an agency's actions under the Constitution's Article III judicial power need to see enough facts to "be able to find that the Secretary could reasonably have believed that in this case there are no feasible alternatives." The Court orders a *plenary* review on remand to build such a record. The *Overton Park* plaintiffs thus were able to bootstrap an injunction against the highway based on the thinness of the agency record for Article III review purposes.

If environmental lawyers can convince reviewing judges that the factual evidence considered by an agency would not be enough to allow the judges themselves to make intelligent decisions on critical points, then judges are likely to send the case back to the agency even if they are not ready to declare that the agency decision was indeed arbitrary. This invites environmental attorneys to search out points of decision that do not appear to be adequately supported by the agency's formal or informal record, and to leverage these strategic quibbles about thin areas in the record into persuasive arguments for remand. In the tactics of lawyering, a remand on technical points is not as good as a substantive victory, but is far from a hollow victory. The challengers are perceived to have beaten the agency in court, an accomplishment in itself. Additionally, challengers now get another bite at the

---

30. No one is very sure when it is that the de novo standard applies under the terms of the APA, and Justice Marshall's oft-quoted explanation isn't very helpful. If triggered it can mean either *review de novo*, where the court re-decides the matter based upon the agency's record, or *trial de novo* where the court itself calls witnesses, etc., and builds its own judicial record for decision.

C. *Overton Park*—A Judicial Review Paradigm

bureaucratic apple, presenting an opportunity for bringing political and public opinion pressures to bear.

4. Interpreting statutory language: who does it, and how to have applied an incorrect interpretation of the statutory words "feasible and prudent." Are you satisfied with the Court's interpretation of the statutory term "feasible and prudent alternative"? Shouldn't judges defer to an expert agency in its interpretation of law to the same extent they do on fact-finding? In part, it may be that judges consider themselves the experts in interpretation of law, and if a statute's meaning seems obvious to the judges, that's the interpretation the court will require. The "plain meaning" rule is an old maxim of statutory interpretation founded upon the assumption that in some cases the words of a statute are unambiguously clear and hence must be effectuated, whatever their results, because each word of a statute (as opposed to common law terms) is binding law. Ambiguity, however, is the norm. See *Chevron*, Part E below. Could it also be, as Justice Black implies, that courts will defer less to those agencies that demonstrate institutional resistance to statutory requirements?

5. "Arbitrary and capricious"? Like many courts that decide to overturn a particular agency decision, the *Overton Park* Court did not want to declare the Secretary's decision arbitrary and capricious, and so it remanded the case for development of a better record supporting the decision. Could it have found the decision "arbitrary"? The answer depends on what the term "arbitrary" means. The courts have applied the term to a confusingly wide range of substantive and procedural holdings.[31] Applied as a test of the substantive merits of a decision, it is best defined in terms of rationality: "Does the agency decision have rational support on the record reviewed by the court?" or "could a rational official have reached that decision on this record?"[32]

Even limited to application as a test of substantive rationality, analytically the arbitrary and capricious test can be applied in at least five different settings:

1. where the agency has no legal standard to apply to the evidence, or uses an incorrect standard;
2. where the agency may have had enough evidence back home in its files to support a decision, but just didn't show it to the court;
3. where the agency did not have enough evidence to support its decision;
4. where the agency had enough evidence to support its decision rationally, if it were accurate, but plaintiffs prove that the evidence is wrong;
5. where the agency failed to consider the "relevant factors" set by the statute, or based its decision on irrelevant factors.

In *Motor Vehicles Mfrs. Ass'n v. State Farm Mut. Life Ins. Co.*, 463 U.S. 29 (1983), the Supreme Court dramatically declared a DOT reversal of a prior administration's seat belt and air bag rule to be arbitrary and capricious because the agency hadn't considered, and failed to present to the Court, evidence supporting the need for a new rule. This would seem to fit the (2) or (3) definitions of arbitrary. Which would have applied to *Overton Park*? The Court

---

31. See Plater & Norine, Through the Looking Glass of Eminent Domain: Exploring the "Arbitrary and Capricious" Test and Substantive Rationality Review of Governmental Decisions, 16 B.C. Envtl. Aff. L. Rev. 661, 712-722 (1989).

32. Thus, viewed conceptually, the arbitrary and capricious test and the stricter-sounding "substantial evidence" test come down to the same thing; the latter may just require a greater quantum of evidence to prove the point. Id. at 716-718.

could probably have used one or more of the first three of these tests. In other cases, after examining the record basis of agency decisions, plaintiffs can sometimes prove the fourth.[33]

Challenging agency actions under the arbitrary and capricious test, however, is no easy task because judges consider it such a deferential standard of review. In practical terms, in most cases, when a court begins reviewing an agency action under the arbitrary and capricious test, that means that the agency decision is shortly going to be upheld. Even if their case convinces the court, attorneys can reasonably expect that the agency, instead of being declared arbitrary, will receive the kind of face-saving remand that defendants got in *Overton Park* (although that proved to be enough for plaintiffs).

When plaintiffs are alleging that an agency is itself "a perpetrator" violating a statute, shouldn't APA §706's "arbitrary and capricious" standard be replaced by the "not in accordance with law" standard? How can a judge, as in the *Snail Darter* trial court opinion, hold an agency action found to be in violation of law *not* to be arbitrary? Should a court defer to an agency and decline to "substitute its judgment" when it believes that an agency is violating federal law?

6. "Feasible and prudent" as a public trust standard. The "feasible and prudent" standard captures well the idea of a strong presumption in favor of protection, to be factored into decisions about how parkland public trust resources should be developed. By extension it can be read into the public trust generally. But what does it mean? Does it mean that questions of cost are not to be considered at all? Presumably there is always an alternative, if cost is no object. But "prudent" implies some attention to money factors.[34] If money is to be considered, how is it to be weighed against intangible natural values? Money tends to be an all-or-nothing factor. If you consider cost, going through parks will virtually always be the preferable option, and a test that incorporates the prudence of cost saving negates the protective purpose and effect. The Court suggests that only an "extraordinary magnitude" of expense would justify going through the park. What would that mean? Is part of the balance of feasible and prudent the question whether the project should be built at all? Might a decision *not* to build an interstate highway through Memphis be a feasible and prudent alternative?

7. The subsequent history of *Overton Park*. After the Supreme Court's ruling, the case bounced around in the lower courts for a few more years. Finally, after new hearings and an EIS, Secretary Volpe announced in January 1973 that he could not find that there was no feasible and prudent alternative to going through the park. The Tennessee DOT thereupon challenged his decision, demanding that he specify what the feasible and prudent alternative was, but the Sixth Circuit upheld the Secretary's ruling as it stood and the Supreme Court denied certiorari.[35] Congress has not disturbed the judicial results, so I-40 will never be built through Overton Park. Today, as shown in Figure 1, the original interstate highway corridor comes to an ignominious, disruptive halt at the edge of the park. A loop bypass to the north now carries I-40's thru traffic.

8. Tradeoffs. Memphis had already purchased 160 acres of private land in the northern part of the city to be made into parks to replace the 26 acres of Overton Park used for the highway, and indicated that it probably would acquire still more. Doesn't this mean there

---

33. See *Motor Vehicle Mfrs. Ass'n of U.S. v. EPA*, 768 F.2d 385 (D.C. Cir. 1985) (by granting a methanol use permit based on a failed test, and tests of three dissimilar gas additives, EPA acted arbitrarily).

34. Note that the standard is *feasible* as well as prudent; agencies thus would want to argue that this includes economic feasibility, in order to expand their range of discretion.

35. *Citizens to Preserve Overton Park v. Brinegar*, 494 F.2d 1212 (6th Cir. 1974), cert. denied, *Citizens to Preserve Overton Park v. Smith*, 421 U.S. 991 (1975).

would have been a lot more parkland with the highway project through the park than without it? Was that relevant to the Secretary's decision?

D. CITIZEN ENFORCEMENT IN THE COURTS

1. The Importance of Citizen Enforcement

Woven through much of this book are examples of the central role of active citizen efforts (often resisted at each step by public and private entities) in creating and shaping environmental law, whether through common law strategies or public law pressuring.

In the *Overton Park* setting, who would have enforced the federal statute if a bunch of low-income citizens had not rallied to carry the case up through the federal courts? The FHWA? The Governor of Tennessee? The Congress that had passed the Parklands Act? No.[36] Within the administrative processes that constitute the bulk of positive law in the administrative state, citizen efforts have been critically important.

Environmentalists operate within the administrative process in two basic ways: (1) by "intervention," formal or informal, in ongoing agency procedures; and (2) by bringing agency actions to court for judicial scrutiny. Once a state or federal wetlands act, for instance, is passed on the strength of citizen lobbying, it can be neutered, or strengthened, depending on the regulations and administrative implementation given to it by the administering agency. Agency officials hear persistently and powerfully from regulated vested interests. Within the day-to-day administrative process, agencies now sometimes also hear a great deal from concerned citizen activists. If rigorous, enforceable wetlands regulations are produced, it is altogether likely that citizen expertise and political pressure helped produce them. If environmental groups think agency regulations subvert the legislative mandate, they can sue, seeking to hold the agency to the original terms of the statute.

The federal air and water acts studied in Chapters 11 and 12, for example, were initially created through extraordinary citizen pressures on Congress, supported by a few notable congressional leaders. The strength and breadth of the statutes' subsequent antipollution regulatory programs, moreover, were fundamentally shaped and driven by citizen groups, through extensive interventions and litigation.[37]

Knowing the Players. To understand any administrative process litigation, one has to figure out the respective roles and status of the various competing participants.

---

36. The point is that enforcement of public law provisions by the official organs of government is often highly unlikely. Perhaps the Sierra Club, NRDC, or another national group could have picked up the immense burdens of litigating the case (and in fact national environmental groups did help in the later stages of the litigation), but these organizations' capabilities are severely limited. They litigate only a fraction of the deserving cases referred to them each year. That means that most cases deserving judicial attention either never get launched or founder along the way.

37. For instance, in the early stages of the CAA, the federal EPA decided, over environmental protests, to write rules allowing polluting industry to comply with the CAA by moving to clean air states like Wyoming and Idaho that had pristine air quality, thereby spreading pollution around but not abating it. It was only because of citizen litigation and negotiation that a nationwide "nondeterioration" policy was established. *Sierra Club v. Ruckleshaus*, 344 F. Supp. 253 (D.D.C.), aff'd, 412 U.S. 541 (1973). (Note in this controversy the interstate replay of a scene from the tragedy of the commons.)

The plaintiffs in the *Overton Park* case were exceptional in that they were a small group of disgruntled neighbors who were able to hold the case together all the way to the U.S. Supreme Court. Far more typical are national environmental citizen organizations designed for sophisticated advocacy in courts, agencies, and the legislature.

Faced with resistance from industry lobbyists and hesitancy on the part of federal regulators, a "shadow government" has sprung up, including notably the Natural Resources Defense Council, EarthLaw, Environmental Defense, the National Wildlife Federation, National Audubon Society, Friends of the Earth, and EarthJustice[38] — national public interest law groups that commit themselves to monitor, negotiate, litigate, and lobby for rigorous, enforceable regulatory programs. Beginning in 1970, a few young law graduates, many from Yale, laid the foundations for such groups, attempting to hold federal government agencies to the terms of the environmental statutes so painfully won in the halls of Congress. The groups evolved to enroll thousands of subscribing members, with legal staffs and budgets of sufficient depth and strength to allow them to play an oversight role in many important administrative programs. The critical role these organizations have played in the securing of environmental protection in the U.S. is impressive, and their example is now being followed around the world, as the international environmental law movement begins to develop 20 years behind the U.S. lead.

As to defendants, note how in many of these environmental cases there is no clear distinction between the regulatory agency entrusted with the environmental protection mandate and the industry and regulated interests that it is assigned to supervise. In the atomic energy field, for instance, the alignment of the Atomic Energy Commission (AEC) with the nuclear industry was so incestuous that Congress ultimately split the agency into two parts, the promotional Energy Research and Development Agency (ERDA), and the protective Nuclear Regulatory Commission (NRC). The environmental community does not necessarily believe that such organizational splits end the affinity of regulator and regulatee.

Of the Iron Triangle, the Pork Barrel, and the Establishment. The *Overton Park* case reminds environmental observers that environmental quality initiatives, even when they are backed by statutory provisions, run into the opposition of vested interests, public as well as private. Some environmentalists call it the "pork barrel," others the "iron triangle" — in either case referring to the interlocking structure and political process linking private construction and industrial interests, government agencies that service the industry, and congressional delegations that want to attract particular public expenditures into their backyards. The momentum of that combination makes the pork barrel one of the most consistently powerful and resistant forces of environmental alteration. Environmentalists are often underfinanced, politically powerless neighborhood agitators who come along late in the game seeking to stop the momentum of the good ol' boys establishment steamroller.

By successfully, against the odds, putting the Parklands Act onto the federal books, environmentalists did not automatically succeed in enlisting the federal government on the side of parkland preservation. Quite the contrary; federal program agencies often adopt a recalcitrant posture toward statutes that limit their standard operating procedures. Agencies that measure their success in terms of accomplishing their mission in pouring concrete and building road mileage understandably treat conservation legislation as a technicality, an annoyance, and often as a frustrating and contradictory obstacle that must be overridden in order to do their jobs.

---

38. This list covers most of the most frequent broad-spectrum environmental litigation groups. Many other groups, including groups focused on just one area of the law, are significant players as well.

D. Citizen Enforcement in the Courts

The "Capture" Phenomenon. Environmentalists repeatedly identify the problem of governmental agencies' "capture" by market forces as a disturbing backdrop to many administrative process cases. A regulatory agency created in the fervor of a popular movement to regulate some designated problem may begin its life energetically pursuing the overall public interest, but over time its initiative gradually may be eroded into narrower views, intimately linked with the industry and problems it was intended to solve.

Richard Stewart, The Reformation of American Administrative Law
88 Harvard Law Review 1669, 1684-1687 (1975)

Critics have repeatedly asserted . . . that in carrying out broad legislative directives, agencies unduly favor organized interests, especially the interests of regulated or client business firms and other organized groups at the expense of diffuse, comparatively unorganized interests such as consumers, environmentalists, and the poor. In the midst of a "growing sense of disillusion with the role which regulatory agencies play," many legislators, judges, and legal and economic commentators have accepted the thesis of persistent bias in agency policies. At its crudest, this thesis is based on the "capture" scenario, in which administrations are systematically controlled, sometimes corruptly, by the business firms within their orbit of responsibility, whether regulatory or promotional. But there are more subtle explanations of industry orientation, which include the following:

First—The division of responsibility between the regulated firms, which retain primary control over their own affairs, and the administrator, whose power is essentially negative and who is dependent on industry cooperation in order to achieve his objectives, places the administrator in an inherently weak position. The administrator will, nonetheless, be held responsible if the industry suffers serious economic dislocation. For both of these reasons, he may pursue conservative policies.

Second—The regulatory bureaucracy becomes "regulation minded." It seeks to elaborate and perfect the controls it exercises over the regulated industry. The effect of this tendency, particularly in a regime of limited entry, is to eliminate actual and potential competition and buttress the position of the established firms.

Third—The resources—in terms of money, personnel, and political influence—of the regulatory agency are limited in comparison to those of regulated firms. . . . Hence, the agency must compromise with the regulated industry if it is to accomplish anything of significance.

Fourth—Limited agency resources imply that agencies must depend on outside sources of information, policy development, and political support. This outside input comes primarily from organized interests, such as regulated firms, that have a substantial stake in the substance of agency policy and the resources to provide such input. By contrast, the personal stake in agency policy of an individual member of an unorganized interest, such as a consumer, is normally too small to justify such representation. . . . As a somewhat disillusioned James Landis wrote in 1960, the result is industry dominance in representation, which has a "daily machine-gun like impact on both [an] agency and its staff" that tends to create an industry bias in the agency's outlook.

These various theses of systematic bias in agency policy are not universally valid. Political pressures and judicial controls may force continuing agency adherence to policies demonstrably inimical to the interests of the regulated industry. . . . Moreover, the fact that agency policies may tend to favor regulated interests does not in itself demonstrate that such policies are unfair or unjustified, since protection of regulated interests may be implicit in the regulatory scheme established by Congress. Nonetheless, the critique of agency discretion as unduly favorable to organized interests—particularly regulated or client firms—has sufficient power and verisimilitude to have achieved widespread contemporary acceptance.

COMMENTARY & QUESTIONS

The context of citizen environmental enforcement. The context in which environmental law developed, as noted in Chapter 2, was a shift away from the old dipolar regime in which government agencies were presumed to be the preclusive primary defenders of the public interest. Starting in the 1960s, it became clear that agencies could not exclusively be relied upon to fulfill that role. When the Woodstock Generation accused agencies of being part of the industrial economy's "Establishment,"[39] were they just being paranoid? Agencies in a dipolar system often have tended to resist citizens' calls for rigorous enforcement of laws against the excesses of the marketplace. The history of environmental law can be traced in the oscillating willingness of agencies to enforce statutory standards, as in the 1970s, or to defer to industry, as in the Bush II Administration's environmental policies. Since the beginning of the environmental era, the agencies' various stances have been played out against a backdrop of citizen initiatives pushing agencies to enforce statutes stringently or taking over the enforcement role themselves.

2. Standing and the Institutionalization of Citizen Enforcement

Standing, one of the threshold constitutional and statutory tests citizens have to meet in order to obtain judicial scrutiny of agency actions, is ultimately a judicial doctrine. It is courts that determine when citizens can claim standing and when they cannot, even under statutory grants of standing. The plaintiffs' premise in environmental standing cases often is that the government agency is not eager to enforce the law, or itself has violated the law, and so there will be no enforcement unless the courts support the citizens' standing to sue. The practical motivation of anti-standing advocates seems to reflect precisely the same premise as its intended result.

Standing principles can be broadened to permit litigation on issues for which judges want to have dispositive determinations, and conversely can be narrowed to nip off challenges that courts would rather not have to decide. The law of standing in recent years has often been made through environmental cases. In all standing cases, plaintiffs' standing to sue will be tested under:

- Article III's requirement that federal courts can only hear cases where there is a case or controversy (usually a basic a claim of injury, but also whatever other elements the Court holds to be constitutionally required); plus

---

39. The "Establishment" rubric appears to have been coined by Henry Fairlie, writing in *The Spectator* in the 1950s:

> By "the Establishment" I do not mean only the centres of official power—though they are certainly part of it—but rather the whole matrix of official and social relations within which power is exercised. The exercise of power . . . cannot be understood unless it is recognised that it is exercised socially.

Fairlie, The Establishment at Work, Spectator, Sept. 23, 1955. The label soon was picked up to describe official players being opposed by citizen civil rights activists, and subsequently by environmental activists.

D. Citizen Enforcement in the Courts

- "prudential limitations" based on judicial discretion, invented by the Supreme Court to restrict standing, not applicable if a statute overrides them (prudential principles include "no standing to enforce rights of third parties," a requirement of "imminent" injury, and so on, but new ones continue to be added, and the Court since 1980 has converted some, like "redressability," to "constitutional" Article III status so that statutory grants of standing cannot override them); and either
- statutory requirements for judicial review in the specific statute being applied, like "aggrieved" under §313(b) of the Federal Power Act in *Scenic Hudson* below (typically no more than the Article III requirements) or special citizen-enforcement authorizations for "any person" who files a 60-day notice (included in many environmental statutes as noted below, they are far more liberal than the Article III "injury" requirement and override prudential limitations); or
- the general statutory requirements for standing under definitions of APA §702's "person adversely affected or aggrieved... within the meaning of a relevant statute" (much the same as Article III but subject to prudential principles).

The law of standing for citizens, in courts and agencies, lies at the heart of the evolution of environmental law and is often the target for latter-day marketplace reactions against environmental protections. The condensed chronology of standing cases that follows reflects the changing context of the field.

The *Storm King* Case. The first major milestone for environmental citizens' participation in administrative law and process—involving citizen enforcement of federal statutes, and citizen standing in agency proceedings as well as in subsequent judicial review of agency decisions—occurred in the mid-1960s in the shadow of Storm King Mountain on the shores of New York's Hudson River.[40] Consolidated Edison (Con Ed) and the Federal Power Commission (FPC) had been planning Con Ed's construction of a "pumped storage" hydroelectric project cutting a crater reservoir out of the top of Storm King Mountain so that water could be pumped up in hours of slack electricity use, to be released through generator turbines (as "peaking power") when energy needs were greatest. Disturbed by the prospect, a group of local citizens formed the Scenic Hudson Preservation Conference and began to question the utility company and the agency about the project's negative effects—loss of a beautiful mountain, scour, sedimentation, and other impacts on fish and the river when huge volumes of water were sucked up and down through turbines. Neither Con Ed nor the federal agency wanted the citizens to participate in the various permit procedures required to license the Storm King project. The agency would not allow citizens to put several studies on the project's negative consequences into the agency record. When the Storm King license was granted, the citizens went to court. In a remarkable Second Circuit opinion, Judge Hays had to weigh the project's troubling facts against the agency's demand for deference. As a threshold matter, he first had to consider the agency's argument that citizens had no right to judicial review because they were not aggrieved parties under the relevant statutory requirements for judicial review or under Article III's case or controversy clause. Judge Hays wrote an innovative decision for the court:

---

40. A detailed chronicle of the Storm King legal saga is available at the Marist Environmental History Project: http://library.marist.edu/archives/mehp/scenicdecision.htmlhttp://library.marist.edu/archives/mehp/scenicdecision.html.

Scenic Hudson Preservation Conference v. Federal Power Commission
354 F.2d 608 (U.S. Ct. App., 2d Cir. 1965), cert. denied, 384 U.S. 941 (U.S. Sup. Ct. 1966)

HAYS, J. . . . The Storm King project is to be located in an area of unique beauty and major historical significance. The highlands and gorge of the Hudson offer one of the finest pieces of river scenery in the world. . . . Respondents argue that "petitioners do not have standing to obtain review" because they make no claim of any personal economic injury resulting from the Commission's action. . . ." [only aesthetic injuries, and thus are not "aggrieved" within the meaning of administrative law standing requirements.] The Commission takes a narrow view of the meaning of "aggrieved party." . . . Scenic Hudson has some seventeen miles of trailways in the area of Storm King Mountain. Portions of these trails would be inundated by the construction of the project's reservoir. . . . The "case or controversy" requirement of Article III §2 of the Constitution does not require that an "aggrieved" or "adversely effected" party have a personal economic interest. . . . In order to insure that the FPC will adequately protect the public interest in the aesthetic, conservational, and recreational aspects of power development, those who by their activities and conduct have exhibited a special interest in such areas must be held to be included in the class of "aggrieved" parties. . . . We see no justification for the Commission's fear that our determination will encourage "literally thousands" to intervene and seek review in future proceedings. . . . Our experience with public actions confirms the view that the expense and vexation of legal proceedings [are] not lightly undertaken. . . .

A party acting as a "private attorney-general" can raise issues that are not personal to it. . . . Especially in a case of this type, where public interest and concern is so great, the Commission refusal to receive the [citizens' power study] testimony, as well as proffered information on fish protection devices and underground transmission facilities, exhibits a disregard of the statute and of judicial mandates instructing the Commission to probe all feasible alternatives. . . .

In this case as in many others the Commission has claimed to be the representative of the public interest. This role does not permit it to act as an umpire blandly calling balls and strikes for adversary groups appearing before it; the right of the public must receive active and affirmative protection at the hands of the Commission.

[Reasoning that without citizen participation and agency follow-up on the citizens' substantiated concerns the agency decision was not rationally supported on the record, the court set aside the license and remanded the project to the district court and the Commission, where it died.[41]]

Mineral King **(1972).** The first major Supreme Court case encouraging citizen participation through expanded judicial standing was *Sierra Club v. Morton*, 405 U.S. 727 (1972) (basing the standing question only on the Article III and APA "aggrieved" standard, with no mention of prudential limitations). The Walt Disney Corporation sought to develop ski runs, lodges, and a winter resort on national forest public lands at Mineral King Mountain in the California Sierras. The environmental plaintiffs, trying to enforce federal conservation statutes, asked to be heard based only on their general interest in environmental

---

41. A number of books and law review articles have commented on *Scenic Hudson*. See, e.g., A. Talbot, Power Along the Hudson: The *Storm King* Case & the Birth of Environmentalism (1972). The full case deserves reading by anyone interested in the history of environmental law. For a scathing criticism of the case in terms of its putative antidemocratic elitism, see Tucker, Environmentalism and the Leisure Class, 255 Harpers 49-56, 73-80 (Dec. 1977).

D. Citizen Enforcement in the Courts

protection, with no claim of individual injury.[42] They argued that a real case or controversy clearly existed between the parties; they would clearly commit substantial effort to litigating the issues fully. Previously the Supreme Court had extended standing only to persons who had a clearly defined economic injury or a "legal interest" specifically protected by statute or constitution. Justice Stewart wrote for the Court:

> The complaint alleged that the development "would destroy or otherwise adversely affect the scenery, natural and historic objects and wildlife of the park and would impair the enjoyment of the park for future generations." We do not question that this type of harm may amount to an "injury in fact" sufficient to lay the basis for standing. . . . The trend of cases arising under the APA and other statutes authorizing judicial review of federal agency action has been toward recognizing that injuries other than economic harm are sufficient to bring a person within the meaning of the statutory language, and toward discarding the notion that an injury that is widely shared is ipso facto not an injury sufficient to provide the basis for judicial review. . . . The interest alleged to have been injured "may reflect aesthetic, conservational, and recreational, as well as economic values. . . ." Aesthetic and environmental well-being, like economic well-being, are important ingredients of the quality of life in our society, and the fact that particular environmental interests are shared by the many rather than the few does not make them less deserving of legal protection through the judicial process. *Mineral King*, 405 U.S. at 734, 738.[43]

The *Mineral King* Court, however, declined to adopt the broadest definition of private attorneys general set out in *Scenic Hudson*, instead requiring the Sierra Club to allege member injuries from the proposed government action, which it quickly did on remand.[44] Proof of a specific harm, however small, was confirmed as the simplistic test of standing. Note how the *Mineral King* Court nevertheless greatly broadened the constitutionally cognizable injuries that could be the basis of citizen lawsuits. Citizens no longer needed to show an economic injury or violation of a constitutional right.

SCRAP (1973). Several years later, a group of law students in Washington, D.C., decided to challenge ICC rate-making decisions that discouraged use of recycled materials by assigning lower transport tariffs to raw materials. *U.S. v. Students Challenging Regulatory Agency Procedures (SCRAP)*, 412 U.S. 669 (1973). The Court, in another Stewart opinion, found that SCRAP had alleged sufficient individual harm to get standing:

> Standing is not to be denied simply because many people suffer the same injury. . . . To deny standing to persons who are in fact injured simply because many others are also injured would mean that the most injurious and widespread Government actions could be questioned by nobody. We cannot accept that conclusion.

---

42. There have been numerous attempts to extend standing to nonliving things. Could the plaintiffs have filed the lawsuit in the name of the mountain itself? In a ringing dissent in *Mineral King*, Justice Douglas urged the adoption of Professor Chris Stone's argument that standing should be granted to organizations that speak knowingly and will commit resources in defense of inanimate trees, mountains, or wildlife. C. Stone, Should Trees Have Standing? (1974). Why might the Sierra Club have wanted to have the mountain itself as the plaintiff? To some extent, such attempts may reflect a philosophical stance, an attempt to focus attention on the real long-term issues. In part, such a claim might reflect the fact that members do not always live or hike in areas where citizen enforcement efforts are necessary, as in Arctic tundra threatened by oil drilling or in outer space where some energy planners suggest dumping radioactive wastes.

43. Citing dicta in *Ass'n of Data Processing Servs. v. Camp*, 397 U.S. 150, 154 (1970). The Court did not buy Professor Stone's argument that "trees should have standing," see 45 S. Cal. L. Rev. 450 (1972).

44. On remand, the Club readily supplied available evidence of direct use of the mountain by its members and got standing. Were the original pleadings badly designed or a grab for the brass ring?

But the injury alleged here is [not] direct and perceptible. . . . Here, the court was asked to follow a far more attenuated line of causation to the eventual injury of which the appellees complained—a general rate increase would allegedly cause increased use of nonrecyclable commodities as compared to recyclable goods, thus resulting in the need to use more natural resources to produce such goods, . . . resulting in more refuse that might be discarded [along hiking trails used by the students] in national parks in the Washington area. . . .

Of course, pleadings must be something more than an ingenious academic exercise in the conceivable. A plaintiff must allege that he has been or will in fact be perceptibly harmed by the challenged agency action, not that he can imagine circumstances in which he could be affected by the agency's action. And it is equally clear that the allegations must be true and capable of proof at trial. . . . If proved, [however, plaintiffs' allegations] would place them squarely among those persons injured in fact by the Commission's action. *SCRAP*, 412 U.S. at 687-690. [Standing was granted!]

Understandably, *SCRAP* was viewed as an expansion of citizens' rights to sue against governmental abuses. Potential harms to plaintiffs had to be alleged, but the linkage of such harms to challenged agency actions could be quite indirect. Plaintiffs didn't have to prove that they were "within the zone of interests" of a relevant statute,[45] nor did plaintiffs have to show a likelihood that the court's orders would "redress" the harms. Citizens could go to court to enforce statutes and the public values they embodied, even where official enforcement agencies had been rendered quiescent by the politics of the marketplace. Citizen standing, and the pluralistic democracy it represented, provided a powerful mechanism for protecting civic and environmental interests, counteracting the marketplace's neutralizing pressures upon regulatory programs. In the absence of citizen action, many government agencies could not or would not do a sufficient job of enforcing federal law.

Congressional Grants of Standing for Citizen Enforcement. Though not involved in *Mineral King* or *SCRAP*, more than a dozen environmental statutes passed since the early 1970s specifically authorized citizen standing.[46] Building on the example of Martin Luther

---

45. The "zone of interests" test is drawn from words in APA §702, not from Article III constitutional grounds, and initially was liberally interpreted:

The [APA] should be construed "not grudgingly but as serving a broad remedial purpose." . . . The "zone of interest" formula [originally mentioned in *Data Processing*, 397 U.S. 153 (1970)] has not proved self-explanatory, but significant guidance can be drawn from that opinion. First, the Court interpreted the phrase "a relevant statute" in §702 quite broadly (indeed even using a different statute from the one sued under). . . . Second, the Court approved the "trend . . . toward [the] enlargement of the class of people who may protest administrative action." . . . The test is not meant to be especially demanding; in particular there need be no indication of congressional purpose to benefit the would-be plaintiff. *Clarke v. Securities Indus. Ass'n*, 479 U.S. 388, 395-400 (1987).

46. See Toxic Substances Control Act §§19(d), 20(c)(2), 15 U.S.C. §§2618(d), 2619; Endangered Species Act of 1973 §11(g)(4), 16 U.S.C. §1540(g)(4); Surface Mining Control and Reclamation Act of 1977, 30 U.S.C. §1270(d); Deep Seabed Hard Mineral Resources Act §117(c), 30 U.S.C. §1427(c); Clean Water Act (Federal Water Pollution Control Act Amendments of 1972 §505), 33 U.S.C. §1365(d); Marine Protection, Research, and Sanctuaries Act, 33 U.S.C. §1415(g)(4); Deepwater Port Act of 1974, 33 U.S.C. §1515(d); Safe Drinking Water Act §1449(d), 42 U.S.C. §300j-8(d); Noise Control Act of 1972 §12(d), 42 U.S.C. §4911(d); Energy Sources Development Act, 42 U.S.C. §5851(e)(2); Energy Policy and Conservation Act, 42 U.S.C. §6305(d); Solid Waste Disposal Act, 42 U.S.C. §6972(e); Clean Air Act §304, 42 U.S.C. §§7604, 7607(f); Powerplant and Industrial Fuel Act, 42 U.S.C. §8435(d); Ocean Thermal Energy Conservation Act, 42 U.S.C. §9124(d); Outer Continental Shelf Lands Act, 43 U.S.C. §1349(a)(5). The Marine Mammal Protection Act, however, lacks such a provision.

Significantly, most of these grants of enforcement standing also provide for certain litigation fee awards if appropriate, e.g. "The court, in issuing any final order in any suit brought pursuant to [this Act] may award costs of

D. Citizen Enforcement in the Courts

King, Jr.'s use of citizen enforcement provisions under nineteenth-century civil rights laws, these laws authorized citizen enforcement so citizens could take on the task of enforcing federal statutes when official agencies failed to do so. Here's a fairly typical statutory provision from the federal water pollution statute:

> **§505(a)** ... Any citizen may commence a civil action on his own behalf—(A) ... (1) against any person (including (i) the United States, and (ii) any other government instrumentality or agency ...) who is alleged to be in violation of (A) an effluent standard or limitation under this chapter or (B) an order issued by the Administrator or State with respect to such a standard or limitation, or (2) against the Administrator where there is alleged a failure of the Administrator to perform any act or duty under this chapter which is not discretionary with the Administrator....
>
> **§505(b)** No action may be commenced—(1) ... (A) prior to sixty days after the plaintiff has given notice of the alleged violation (i) to the Administrator, (ii) to the State in which the alleged violation occurs, and (iii) to any alleged violator of the standard, limitation, or order,[47] or (B) if the Administrator or State has commenced and is diligently prosecuting a civil or criminal action in a court of the United States or a State to require compliance with the standard, limitation, or order, but in any such action in a court of the United States any citizen may intervene as a matter of right.... CWA, 33 U.S.C. §1365 (1972).

Federal courts have been quite attentive to these citizen suit provisions, generally acknowledging the strength of the congressional intent to encourage citizen enforcement as a parallel national strategy for achieving implementation of federal regulatory programs.[48] Starting in the late 1970s, however, Supreme Court decisions inclined toward rolling back citizen enforcement, retreating to the narrowed industry-agency terms of traditional administrative process.[49]

Retrenchment in the Scalia Court. In the years immediately following *SCRAP*, standing doctrine initially shifted toward *SCRAP*'s accommodating terms, and then with Republican appointees the Court began a steady retrenchment against citizen enforcement.[50] Almost as

---

litigation (including reasonable attorney and expert witness fees) to any party, whenever the court determines such award is appropriate." ESA §11(g), 42 U.S.C. §1540(g)(4).

47. The 60-day waiting period does not apply in cases of toxic and pretreatment standards or national performance standards. Environmentalists have argued that waivers to the 60-day waiting period should also be granted or liberalized in other settings where the public interest and congressional policy require it. Irvin, When Survival Is at Stake: A Proposal for Expanding the Emergency Exception to the Sixty-Day Notice Requirement of the Endangered Species Act's Citizen Suit Provision, 14 Harv. Envtl. L. Rev. 343 (1990) (the article presents interesting examples of the necessity for citizen enforcement where industry and government remain passive).

48. "[Where the] only public entities that might have brought suit ... [are] named as defendants ... and vigorously [oppose] plaintiffs, ... only private citizens can be expected to guard the guardians." *La Raza Unida v. Volpe*, 57 F.R.D. 94, 101 (N.D. Cal. 1972). The nation's "regrettably slow progress in controlling air pollution is blamed on [both] the scarcity of skilled personnel available to enforce control measures and on a lack of aggressiveness by EPA's predecessor agency.... The public suit seems particularly instrumental in the statutory scheme [in cases forcing agency compliance], for only the public—certainly not the polluter—has the incentive to complain if the EPA falls short...." *NRDC v. EPA*, 484 F.2d 1331 (1st Cir. 1973).

49. *Hallstrom v. Tillamook County*, 493 U.S. 20 (1989); *Gwaltney of Smithfield v. Chesapeake Bay Found.*, 484 U.S. 49. (1987). *Gwaltney*'s holding—that citizen suits can be filed only where an ongoing violation continues when the lawsuit is filed, but not for past violations—was specifically overridden by Congress as to the CAA. The 1990 CAA Amendments provided for citizen lawsuits upon evidence that past violations have been repeated. Pub. L. No. 101-549, §707(g) (amending §304(a) of the CAA, 42 U.S.C. §7410).

50. Sometimes generous standing rulings, as in *Duke Power v. Carolina Envtl. Study Group*, 438 U.S. 59 (1978), have reflected the Supreme Court's apparent desire to hear an environmental argument in order to quash it, to remove uncertainty from the marketplace. Id. at 78.

soon as he was put on the Court, the late Justice Antonin Scalia began to play a dominant role in restricting citizen standing. In a 1983 law review article, Scalia sharply criticized citizen enforcement of environmental protection laws. Reacting to the language of Judge J. Skelly Wright in the classic *Calvert Cliffs* decision (which declared that the goal of citizen suits was to assure that important congressional intentions to reduce pollution not be "*lost or misdirected in the vast hallways of the federal bureaucracy*"), Justice Scalia asked:

> Does what I have said mean that . . . "important legislative purposes, heralded in the halls of Congress, [can be] lost or misdirected in the vast hallways of the federal bureaucracy?" Of course it does—and a good thing, too. . . . Lots of once-heralded programs ought to get lost or misdirected, in vast hallways or elsewhere. . . . Scalia, The Doctrine of Standing as an Essential Element of the Separation of Powers, 17 Suffolk U. L. Rev. 881, 897 (1983).

With Justice Scalia's vote and pen, new majority opinions followed several strategies—applying broadened prudential limitations where Congress has not granted specific standing rights,[51] requiring that plaintiffs be within "the zone of interests" that the statute was intended to protect,[52] holding statutory grants of citizen standing to their narrowest terms,[53] and adding more restrictive principles as constitutional requirements so as to override statutory grants and tighten standing generally.[54]

***Gwaltney of Smithfield* (1987).** In *Gwaltney of Smithfield v. Chesapeake Bay Found.*, 484 U.S. 49 (1987), the Court narrowed citizen enforcement standing by strict construction of the statutory grant. In a case where a defendant swine-processing plant had been violating water pollution standards for years but had stopped its discharges shortly after the environmental plaintiffs filed their 60-day notice letter, the Court said the statutory text required an ongoing violation or proof of future likelihood of violations for citizens to have standing. CWA §505(a), noted above, grants standing to "any citizen . . . against any person . . . who is alleged to *be in violation* of . . . an effluent standard or limitation" (emphasis added). This interpretation cast a shadow over citizen suits by raising the possibility that groups taking on the extensive efforts of preparing an enforcement action might find themselves non-suited, with no prospect of regaining expert witness and attorneys' fees, by defendants who move into compliance at the last moment under threat of the citizen suit.

***Lujan I* (1990).** In *Lujan I* (*Lujan v. National Wildlife Fed'n*, 497 U.S. 871 (1990)) (a case where there was no statutory grant of citizen standing), the Court used constitutional arguments on standing to require environmentalists challenging agency actions to allege highly particularized injuries, and made suits against alleged programmatic violations extremely difficult. The Reagan Administration had proposed to open western public lands to grazing, timber, and mining operations. Justice Scalia dismissed the case:

---

51. For example, the proposition that plaintiffs cannot claim injury from harm to third parties was launched in *Warth v. Seldin*, 422 U.S. 490 (1975).
52. See *Air Courier Conference v. Am. Postal Workers Union*, 498 U.S. 517 (1991) (Rehnquist, J., denying standing).
53. See *Gwaltney*, 484 U.S. 49, 52 (1987), and *The Steel Co. v. Citizens for a Better Env't*, 523 U.S. 83 (1998).
54. "The constitutional component of standing doctrine incorporates concepts concededly not susceptible of precise definition. The injury alleged must be, for example, 'distinct and palpable,' and not 'abstract' or 'conjectural' or 'hypothetical.' The injury must be 'fairly' traceable to the challenged action, and relief from the injury ['redressability'] must be 'likely' to follow from a favorable decision." *Allen v. Wright*, 468 U.S. 737 (1984). *SCRAP*, in other words, is history. By calling these tests constitutional rather than prudential, the Court can use them to limit congressional standing grants.

D. Citizen Enforcement in the Courts

> To support the [plaintiffs' standing] the Court of Appeals pointed to the affidavits of two of respondent's members . . . which claimed use of land "in the vicinity" of the land covered by two of the listed actions. . . . There is no showing that [their] recreational use and enjoyment extends to the particular 4500 acres covered by the decision to terminate classification. . . . Respondent alleges that violation of the law is rampant within this program—failure to revise land use plans in proper fashion, failure to submit certain recommendations to Congress, failure to consider multiple use, inordinate focus upon mineral exploitation, failure to provide adequate environmental impact statements. Perhaps so. But respondent cannot seek wholesale improvement of this program by court decree. . . . The flaws in the entire "program"—consisting principally of the many individual actions referenced in the complaint, and presumably actions yet to be taken as well—cannot be laid before the courts for wholesale correction under the APA, simply because one of them that is ripe for review adversely affects one of respondent's members. . . . Respondent must seek such programmatic improvements from the BLM or Congress. *Lujan I*, 497 U.S. 880-894 (1990).

***Lujan II* (1992).** In *Lujan II* (*Lujan v. Defenders of Wildlife*, 504 U.S. 555 (1992)), Justice Scalia extended his stringent theories of Article III standing even to cases where Congress had specifically authorized citizen standing. Environmentalists were trying to apply the protections of the federal ESA to overseas projects of U.S. agencies that ignored ecological issues and endanger species. The Act's §7 forbids agencies to jeopardize species or destroy their habitat (see Chapter 10) and requires formal consultations when there is a risk. ESA §11 authorizes "any person" to enforce the Act in court. In 1986, the Reagan Administration had issued a regulation relieving federal agencies from any duty to comply with ESA §7(a)(2) when participating in projects in other countries.

> The Court of Appeals focused on the affidavits of two Defenders' members. . . . Ms. Skilbred averred that she traveled to Sri Lanka in 1981 and "observed th[e] habitat" of "endangered species such as the Asian elephant and the leopard" at what is now the site of the Mahaweli Project funded by the Agency for International Development (AID) [which] "will seriously reduce endangered, threatened, and endemic species habitat including areas that I visited" . . . but confessed that she had no current plans . . . to go back to Sri Lanka. . . . "There is a civil war going on right now." . . . These affidavits . . . contain no facts . . . showing how damage to the species will produce [the] "imminent" injury to Ms. Skilbred . . . that our cases require.
>
> Besides failing to show injury, respondents failed to demonstrate redressability. . . .[55] Since the agencies funding the projects were not parties to the case, the District Court could accord relief only against the Secretary: He could be ordered to revise his regulation to require consultation for foreign projects. But this would not remedy respondents' alleged injury unless the funding agencies were bound by the Secretary's regulation, which is very much an open question. . . .
>
> The Court of Appeals found that respondents had standing for an additional reason: because they had suffered a "procedural injury." The so-called "citizen-suit" provision of the ESA provides, in pertinent part, that "any person may commence a civil suit . . . to enjoin any person, including . . . any . . . governmental instrumentality or agency . . . who is alleged to be in violation." . . . This is not a case where plaintiffs are seeking to enforce a procedural requirement the disregard of which could impair a separate concrete interest of theirs. . . . Nor . . . is it the unusual case in which Congress has created a concrete private interest in the outcome of a suit against a private party for the government's benefit, by providing a cash bounty for the victorious plaintiff. Rather, the court held that the injury-in-fact requirement had been satisfied

---

55. This paragraph is from segment IIIB of the opinion, which drew only four votes: Scalia, Rehnquist, White, and Thomas. The redressability concept had been launched in *Simon v. Eastern Ky. Welfare Rights Org.*, 426 U.S. 26, 38, 41 (1976). [EDS.]

by congressional conferral upon all persons of an abstract, self-contained, noninstrumental "right" to have the Executive observe the procedures required by law. We reject this view. . . . Vindicating the public interest (including the public interest in government observance of the Constitution and laws) is the function of Congress and the Chief Executive. . . . To permit Congress to convert the undifferentiated public interest in executive officers' compliance with the law into an "individual right" vindicable in the courts is to permit Congress to transfer from the President to the courts the Chief Executive's most important constitutional duty, to "take Care that the Laws be faithfully executed." *Lujan II,* 504 U.S. at 568-578.

The *Lujan II* decision was strongly criticized for undercutting the Court's previous acceptance of congressional definitions of generalized injury as a base of citizen standing.[56] Justice Blackmun, joined by Justice O'Connor, dissented, saying "I cannot join the Court on what amounts to a slash-and-burn expedition through the law of environmental standing." In subsequent years, however, Justice Scalia was not uniformly restrictive of citizen standing. When two cattle ranchers sought to challenge the Department of Interior's enforcement of the ESA on the Klamath River, the Court, in an opinion by Justice Scalia, gave the ranchers standing. *Bennett v. Spear,* 520 U.S. 154 (1997).

***The Steel Company* (1998).** Standing was again further restricted when citizens sued in a case involving a factory that had long failed to file information required by EPCRA on its use of toxics, but then filed the reports under threat of the citizens' notice of intent to sue. Do citizens suffer a sufficient specific and concrete Article III injury from a polluter's monitoring and reporting violations? In *The Steel Co. v. Citizens for a Better Env't,* 523 U.S. 83 (1998), the Court decided that the citizens' injury, if it existed, had already been redressed by the late-filed reports and so would not be further redressed by a court order, so standing was barred. To environmentalist plaintiffs, the *Steel Company* decision, like *Gwaltney,* undercut an important purpose of each citizen enforcement case—to provide a deterrent example of effective citizen prosecution to other violators.

***Laidlaw* (2000).** To the pleasant surprise of many environmentalists who had glumly watched a succession of constrictive standing decisions, in 2000 citizen standing received a strong affirmation from the Court, over Justices Scalia and Thomas's fervent dissent. In *Friends of the Earth v. Laidlaw Envtl. Servs.,* 528 U.S. 167 (2000), the majority opinion applied a broader, commonsense definition of Article III injury and scrutinized the political realities of a state agency's collusion with an industrial defendant, in order to allow citizen prosecution to go forward. A South Carolina hazardous waste incinerating plant had repeated violated its CWA permit by dumping excess toxic wastes including mercury into the Tyger River on 489 occasions over an eight-year span. The corporation argued that plaintiffs' enforcement action should be dismissed on four standing grounds (each echoed in Justice Scalia's dissent):

1. There had been no proof of substantial ecological harms from the dumping, so if the environment wasn't injured there was no Article III injury.
2. Since there was no demonstrated health or environmental harm, plaintiffs had no personal cognizable injury.
3. Because the company had quickly reached a small settlement with the state agency as soon as the citizens filed their 60-day notice letter, the citizen suit was foreclosed

---

56. Sunstein, What's Standing After *Lujan?,* 91 Mich. L. Rev. 163 (1992); Nichol, Justice Scalia, Standing, and Public Law Litigation, 42 Duke L.J. 1141 (1993); Pierce, *Lujan v. Defenders,* 42 Duke L.J. 1170 (1993).

D. Citizen Enforcement in the Courts

under CWA §505(b), above, which bars suits where the agency "has commenced and is diligently prosecuting a civil or criminal action."
4. Since the plant's operations had subsequently shut down and plaintiffs were not seeking injunctive relief, the plaintiffs' request that the company pay penalties to EPA would do nothing to redress their claimed harms.

Any one of these arguments could previously have been expected to doom the citizens' suit. Remarkably, however, a strong body of scholarship had begun to emerge scrutinizing the line of constrictive standing decisions and clarifying basic principles underlying Article III. Influential studies of standing jurisprudence raised serious questions about whether increased restrictions on standing were the result of evolving doctrinal interpretation or organic agenda-driven decisionmaking.[57] To many scholars, standing decisions were an embarrassing departure from neutral principles for defining what constituted an Article III case or controversy, seeming to turn more upon which team was at bat than upon principle. As Professors Davis and Pierce asked:

> Why does the Court sometimes use a . . . test that is impossible to meet? What distinguishes these cases from the many cases in which the Court uses a logical and pragmatic test for determining [standing]? . . . The Court uses standing . . . to preclude federal courts from intervening in disputes [that the majority] considers inappropriate for federal judicial intervention. K. C. Davis & R. Pierce, ADMINISTRATIVE LAW TREATISE §16.5, at 38-39 (1994).[58]

In *Laidlaw*, writing for a new Court majority in an opinion that reads like a primer on citizen standing, Justice Ginsburg rejected all four arguments, in each case directly refuting the assertions being made in dissent by Justice Scalia:

1. The relevant showing for purposes of Article III standing is not injury to the environment but *injury to the plaintiff*. . . .
2. The affidavits and testimony presented by FOE in this case assert that Laidlaw's discharges . . . directly affected those affiants' recreational, aesthetic, and economic interests. . . . Kenneth Lee Curtis averred . . . that he lived a half-mile from Laidlaw's facility; that he occasionally drove over the North Tyger River, and that it looked and smelled polluted; and that he would like to fish, camp, swim, and picnic in and near the river. . . .
3. [As to the claim that the state's settlement barred the citizens' suit:] Plaintiff-petitioners [FOE] . . . sent a letter to Laidlaw notifying the company of their intention to file a citizen suit against it under §505(a) of the Act after the expiration of the requisite 60-day notice period. . . . Laidlaw's lawyer then contacted DHEC [the state enforcement agency] to ask whether DHEC would consider filing a lawsuit against Laidlaw . . . to bar FOE's proposed citizen suit through [§505](b)(1)(B) [diligent

---

57. Is the Scalian line of restrictive holdings "conservative"? Note that they insulate big government agencies from judicial review. The insulation admittedly is not against marketplace players but against citizens, without whom there is no practical likelihood that collusive agency-industry violations—like the exploitation of western lands in *Mineral King* and *Lujan I*, or destructive public works projects in *Scenic Hudson*, *Lujan II*, and many other cases—would ever be held accountable for ongoing violations of law.

58. See Echeverria & Zeidler, Barely Standing: The Erosion of Citizen "Standing" to Sue and Enforce Environmental Law, Geo. Envtl. L. & Pol'y Inst. (1999), *available at* http://www.law.georgetown.edu/gelpi/research_archive/standing/BarelyStanding.pdf; Buzbee, Expanding the Zone, Tilting the Field: Zone of Interests and Article III Standing Analysis After *Bennett v. Spear*, 49 Admin. L. Rev. 764 (1997); Carlson, Standing for the Environment, 45 UCLA L. Rev. 932 (1998); Coplan, Refracting the Spectrum of Clean Water Act Standing in Light of *Lujan v. Defenders of Wildlife*, 22 Colum. J. Envtl. L. 170 (1997).

prosecution]. DHEC agreed to file a lawsuit against Laidlaw; the company's lawyer then drafted the complaint for DHEC and paid the filing fee. On June 9, 1992, the last day before FOE's 60-day notice period expired, DHEC and Laidlaw reached a settlement requiring Laidlaw to pay $100,000 in civil penalties and to make "every effort" to comply with its permit obligations.... In imposing the civil penalty of $100,000 against Laidlaw, DHEC failed to recover, or even to calculate, the economic benefit that Laidlaw received by not complying with its permit.... Laidlaw had gained a total economic benefit of $1,092,581 as a result of its extended period of noncompliance with the mercury discharge limit in its permit.... After [the state settlement], but before the district court rendered judgment, Laidlaw violated the mercury discharge limitation in its permit 13 times [more, and] committed 13 monitoring and 10 reporting violations.... The district court held that DHEC's action against Laidlaw ["entered into with unusual haste, without giving the Plaintiffs the opportunity to intervene"] had not been "diligently prosecuted"; consequently, the court [properly] allowed FOE's citizen suit to proceed....

4. [And as to mootness and a lack of redressability for the plaintiffs, because the plant had closed and payment of penalties would be to the government, not to plaintiffs:] Penalties in Clean Water Act cases ... also deter future violations.... To the extent that civil penalties encourage defendants to discontinue current violations and deter them from committing future ones, they afford redress to citizen plaintiffs who are injured or threatened with injury as a consequence of ongoing unlawful conduct.

Winter and Summers (2008, 2009). Justice Scalia's unhappiness with *Laidlaw's* grant of citizens' standing to enforce federal laws against ongoing violations was somewhat allayed by two later cases. In *Winter v. Natural Resources Defense Council*, 555 U.S. 7 (2008), environmentalists sought to apply Marine Mammal Act protections against Navy sonar practice using extremely loud, explosive underwater noise bursts where studies conducted around the world showed the piercing underwater sounds cause whales to flee in panic or fatally dive too deeply and post-sonar necropsies showed signs of internal bleeding in the whales' ears. The Ninth Circuit granted standing based on the "possibility" of serious damage to an unknown number of whales. The Roberts' majority opinion held that was too lenient a standard: plaintiffs had to show that irreparable injury was "likely" in the absence of an injunction. In *Summers v. Earth Island Institute*, 555 U.S. 488 (2009), where environmentalists sought to levy a general challenge against a Forest Service policy that would exempt major forest-cutting operations from APA notice-and-comment procedures. Justice Scalia wrote a 5-4 decision holding that the "deprivation of a procedural right without some concrete interest that is affected by the deprivation ... is insufficient to create Article III standing."

In subsequent years, the Court has been inconsistent. In *Monsanto v. Geertson Seed Farms*, 130 S. Ct. 2743 (2010), the Court allowed standing for farmers who, fearing that they would have to test their crops annually to avoid exposure to genetically-modified seed strains, opposed federal deregulation of genetically-modified seeds. The Court said this was a "significant risk" that was a sufficiently "concrete interest." But in a 2013 non-environmental case, *Clapper v. Amnesty Int'l*, 133 S. Ct. 1138, the Court refused standing to journalists who argued that federal electronic surveillance of their overseas communications would chill their relationships with international sources and clients. The *Clapper* Court said that standing required proof that possible future injuries asserted by plaintiffs were "*certainly impending.*" Perhaps it's relevant to remember that in a classic standing case, the Court observed that "generalizations about standing to sue are largely worthless as such." *Association of Data*

D. Citizen Enforcement in the Courts

Processing, 397 U.S. 150, 151 (1970). The standard for standing in many cases appears to be merely a reflection of a particular majority's political stance on the matter at hand.

COMMENTARY & QUESTIONS

1. ***Laidlaw* survives as a basis for citizen standing.** Has the standing inquiry post-*Laidlaw* now turned to a realistic basis for assessing whether there is a genuine noncollusive legal case or controversy that will be competently presented for the Court to decide, which after all is what Article III seeks? The *Laidlaw,* Court did not back away from the simplistic traditional focus on the need to prove some injury, reaffirmed in *Winters,* nor from the *Lujan II* requirement that it must be a present specific discrete harm or risk of harm to the plaintiff, not just a "likely, possibly in the future" harm, as noted in *Summers.* But the *Laidlaw* Court gave significant weight to the plaintiffs' claims that they would use and enjoy the river "but for," and seemed to be impressed that some of the plaintiffs had done so before the pollution. The "I-might-go-back-someday-to-see-the-endangered-animals" of *Lujan II* is probably still too remote a claim of harm, as the Scalia majority held in *Summers.* (Note that *Laidlaw* is a citizen enforcement suit, not a citizen suit seeking judicial *review* of agency action, but for standing purposes this does not seem to make any difference.)

2. **How much harm must a plaintiff now show? Would a trivial $5 bounty do it?** The *Laidlaw* majority accepted the sufficiency of standing allegations when plaintiffs said they would like to use a specifically affected resource located close to where they lived. But the definition of sufficient Article III standing interest or injury is nebulous in part because it looks only to the existence of a linkage between the plaintiff and the thing, not gauging the weightiness of the interest. Not that adding such a subjective relative balancing test would be a good idea.

But the current state of the law allows the constitutional threshold to be determined by trivialities. According to the Scalia opinion in *Lujan II,* constitutional standing would exist "[where] Congress has created a concrete private interest in the outcome of a suit[59] . . . by providing a cash bounty for the victorious plaintiff." So if Congress authorized payment of a $5 reward for successful law enforcement, even Justice Scalia would apparently have allow standing — which makes the injury-based standing test seem rather superficial, disingenuous, and beside the point.

If a small money bounty would be sufficient to give a citizen Article III standing in *Lujan* terms, then why not likewise the authorizations for prevailing parties to collect attorneys' fees and expert witness fees? Those provisions already exist in almost every major environmental statute's grant of citizen enforcement standing as noted above for CWA §505. Especially where plaintiffs are public interest attorney groups, the prospect of recovering tens of thousand dollars for their labors enforcing the law would seem to be a tangible enough interest to assure a solid controversy.

How do government agencies satisfy Justice Scalia's specific interest or injury standard? We all assume that when Congress passes a statute and gives an independent federal agency the authority to prosecute it, the agency has Article III standing — for example, the CPSC is given authority to prosecute antitrust violations and is assumed to have standing to do

---

59. The quote says "a suit against a private party," but it is difficult to see any Article III difference between suits against private defendants and public defendants.

so. Why? What is the CPSC's constitutional injury or interest[60] if it is not the enforcement standing created by Congress' delegation of authority-to-sue to the agency? If Congress can delegate statutory enforcement authority to the CPSC, then why can't it also delegate that authority to private organizations similarly dedicated to enforcing public law? (There is no administrative law bar against delegation to private parties.) Could Justice Scalia have been wrong in asserting that a congressionally created procedural interest is not sufficient for standing, especially if he admits that a paltry bounty would support standing? Professor Sunstein has called into question the focus on "injury" as the necessary and sufficient threshold test for standing. "At least in general," Sunstein's article advises, "standing depends on whether any source of law has created a cause of action." If Congress can create new causes of action, it would seem that it generally could also create standing for their enforcement as it chooses and deny standing when it likes. Sunstein, What's Standing after *Lujan?*—Of Citizen Suits, "Injuries," and Article III, 91 Mich. L. Rev. 163 (1992).

3. Redressability. The concept of redressability—asking whether the harms claimed by plaintiffs as a basis for standing are likely to be resolved by a judicial remedy—was previously considered a court-made "prudential principle" subject to being overridden by congressional mandates expanding standing. In *Lujan II,* Justice Scalia had clearly converted redressability into an Article III requirement that must be met even if a statute purports to grant standing without it. In *Lujan II* the defendants were federal agencies. Is it unlikely that agencies would honor the court's rulings? Is redressability an invitation to political science predictions? After *Laidlaw*, it appears that the Court has at least liberalized the concept of redressability.

4. Standing and the "diligent prosecution" jurisdictional defense? Note how on the facts of *Laidlaw* the Court mocked the "diligently prosecuting" defense. *Laidlaw* illustrates the judiciary's ability to look critically at the quality of state enforcement of environmental laws and distain state enforcement if it is weak. Considering Laidlaw's transparently disingenuous use of alleged state agency "enforcement" as a shield, what conclusions do you draw about the importance of citizen suits in undercutting the race-to-the-bottom?

5. Ripeness, exhaustion, financing, and other barriers to citizen enforcement. The extended analysis of standing issues here should not obscure the fact that virtually every tactical issue in administrative law plays a frequent role in environmental litigation. "Ripeness" is a prime example—the question whether the agency has made a sufficiently final decision to be reviewed. See *Ohio Forestry v. Sierra Club*, 523 U.S. 726 (1998) (agency planning would not be ripe for review on whether it conformed with NFMA planning requirements until the plan actually authorized particular trees to be cut). "Exhaustion of remedies" is another, asking whether citizens should seek all appropriate remedies in an agency before trying to pull the issues into court.[61] As to the tactics of financing litigation, when citizens embark as "private attorneys general" attempting to enforce existing law in agencies and courts, they often face substantial administrative and financial burdens, against opponents who are either public officials or well-financed corporate entities writing off expenses against revenues. Expert witnesses and attorneys cost money. For plaintiff groups like the citizens in *Overton Park*, this often means having to raise funds through bake sales, raffles, logo tee-shirt sales, or passing the hat. Statutory enforcement raises many practical and logistical issues for citizens. Paying the costs of litigation is one major concern, only partially offset by the possibility of recovery of attorney and expert witness fees.

---

60. The CPSC is an independent agency and thus could not say it has constitutional standing as an executive subordinate of the President who holds the Article II duty to "see that the laws are faithfully executed."

61. See *EDF v. Hardin*, 428 F.2d 1093 (D.C. Cir. 1970), where both issues arose in an environmental group's attempt to get an agency to curtail DDT as a pesticide.

D. Citizen Enforcement in the Courts

6. Ripeness: pre-enforcement review implications for stalling EPA protective actions—the *Sackett* case. The EPA often has issued on-site "compliance orders" against companies it determined had violated environmental statutes, orders that would lead to subsequent formal enforcement actions. The opportunity to challenge the EPA's determinations by judicial review was delayed on ripeness grounds until after the "final decision" in the EPA's formal enforcement processes confirmed the violation. If judicial review upheld the agency's finding, penalties were assessed from the day of the original compliance order. Companies hit by compliance orders complained that the orders were "final" enough to be ripe for judicial review as soon as they were issued, because otherwise they'd have to gamble against additional penalties that would accrue in the interim before formal enforcement.

Under the current test of ripeness, two conditions must be satisfied for agency action to be "final." First, the action must mark the consummation of the agency's decision-making process. Second, the action must be one by which rights or obligations have been determined, or from which legal consequences will flow. *Bennett v. Spear*, 520 U.S. 154, 177-178 (1997).

The Supreme Court's unanimous decision in *Sackett v. EPA*, 132 S. Ct. 1567 (2012) held that an EPA compliance order under the CWA was subject to pre-enforcement judicial review under the APA, enhancing regulated parties' future pre-enforcement challenges against EPA compliance orders generally.

Project proponents, like the foreign-owned Pebble Partnership gold mine project in the Alaskan wilderness, continue to mount judicial challenges to the EPA's pre-enforcement decisions based in part on *Sackett*, seeking to delay or deflect regulation and avoid compliance costs as early in the regulatory process as possible. Pebble tried to get judicial review of the EPA's initial administrative steps that would set high regulatory standards for the waters potentially impacted by the mine.[62] From an environmental protection perspective, successful *Sackett* claims in cases like *Pebble Partnership* would create extended delays of environmental enforcement, undermining administrative efficiency and effectiveness. Since *Sackett*, the lower courts have decided both for and against pre-enforcement judicial review of agency decisions, depending on circumstances; the Ninth Circuit denied the Pebble's *Sackett* claim. In late 2015, the Supreme Court granted certiorari in *U.S. Army Corps of Engineers v. Hawkes Co.*, 782 F.3d 994, reversing 963 F. Supp. 2d 868 (which had decided that a Corps determination that the property-owner's land was a jurisdictional wetland under the CWA was not enough of a "final agency action" to support judicial review prior to any regulatory action.

7. Is citizen standing a mistake?—Where's prosecutorial discretion? One of the most ancient elements of governmental power is the grace to *withhold* punishment. Prosecutorial discretion allows appropriate governmental officials to decide where best the society's enforcement efforts should be focused, and what violations should be overlooked for reasons of policy or of fairness (echoing Aristotle's *aequitas*—asserting that to provide for the occasions when laws apply harshly or unwisely there must be an avenue for selective absolution). The Court in *Heckler v. Chaney*[63] confirmed that federal agencies enjoy a fundamental power of prosecutorial discretion. What happens to that discretion if

---

62. *Pebble Limited P'ship v. EPA*, No. 14-35845, 2015 WL 3407186, at *2 (9th Cir. May 28, 2015). See Craig Johnston, *Sackett*: The Road Forward, 42 Envtl. L. 993, 1005 (Fall 2012). For more on Pebbele Mine, see http://www.savebristolbay.org/about-the-bay/about-pebble-mine.

63. 470 U.S. 821 (1985). The facts of the case are bemusing. FDA rules prohibit use of pharmaceuticals unless they have been tested for pain and "safety" for a particular use. Drugs used to euthanize animals have to be so certified. In *Heckler*, death row inmates sought to apply the rules to bar the use of drugs used for human lethal

citizens using statutory standing grants can decide to enforce environmental statutes and regulations against violators? Some violations undoubtedly do not deserve active prosecution. Some environmentalists—we'll name no names—can clearly be loose cannons, undermining the credibility of environmental positions in national policy debates. Literal enforcement of every provision on the statute books is pretty clearly not a good idea. On the other hand, a significant lesson of the twentieth century was that agencies cannot be relied upon to be driven by the public interest in the face of the focused suasions and resistance of the marketplace. How to winnow the wheat from the chaff? The cost of litigating is an unreliable filter to screen out improvident litigation, but why is the Court's rather haphazard harm-based standing criterion any more rational? This argues for the proposition that organized citizen efforts must continue to be a significant part of a modern industrial democracy—and legal standing in court probably is citizens' single most significant institutional instrumentality for guaranteeing their public interest commitments an active role in governance.

3. Political Resistance to Citizen Enforcement: Removing Courts' Ability to Grant Relief to Citizens

Department of Interior and Related Agencies Appropriations Act, 1990
Public Law Number 101-121 (1989)

> §318(g) . . . No restraining order or preliminary injunction shall be issued by any court of the United States with respect to any decision to prepare, advertise, offer, award, or operate . . . timber sales in fiscal year 1990 from the thirteen national forests in Oregon and Washington and Bureau of Land Management lands in Western Oregon known to contain northern spotted owls. The provisions of 5 U.S.C. §705 [authorizing courts to stay agency actions] shall not apply to any challenge to such a timber sale. Provided, that the courts shall have authority to [issue permanent injunctions for timber sales found to be] arbitrary, capricious, or otherwise not in accordance with law. . . .

[Other provisions of this appropriations rider required the agencies to sell off increased annual quotas of timber, insulated from judicial review Forest Service and BLM decisions shown to be based on outdated information, and made quasi-judicial findings to reverse two injunctions against timber cutting.[64] In recent years, similar riders have surfaced fairly regularly.]

---

injections, which had not been so tested and certified. The Court said the Secretary of Health and Human Services could exercise prosecutorial discretion whether to apply the law.

64. See §§314, 318(b)(6), 103 Stat. at 743, 747. In practice, these timber sales typically auction off the public forests at below-cost subsidized prices. Section 318's quasi-judicial findings were held unconstitutional on separation of powers grounds, *Seattle Audubon v. Robertson*, 914 F.2d 1311 (9th Cir. 1990), rev'd, 503 U.S. 429 (1992).

Section 318 is a "rider" because it was tacked onto the on-rolling spending bill. In fact, attaching substantive law provisions onto appropriations bills violates House Rule 23 and Senate Rule 16, but through parliamentary maneuvers the rules were not applied.

Timber lobbyists rather cynically tacked similar riders onto the Oklahoma bombing and Hurricane Katrina disaster relief bills. See *Or. Nat'l Resources Council v. Jack Ward Thomas*, 92 F.3d 792 (9th Cir. 1996); *Northwest Forest Resource Council*, 82 F.3d 825 (9th Cir. 1996).

D. Citizen Enforcement in the Courts

COMMENTARY & QUESTIONS

1. The spotted owl appropriations rider. What's going on here with §318g? The provision was inserted into a DoI appropriations bill in reaction to environmentalists' successes in protecting the northern spotted owl under a variety of environmental statutes (see Chapter 10). Environmentalists had repeatedly been able to demonstrate that the endangered owl was threatened by illegal clearcutting operations in various old-growth national forests in the Pacific Northwest. The appropriations rider was intended to end the citizens' disruption of ongoing practices.

What is the theory of such riders? They are the legislative parallel to judicial attempts to restrict citizen enforcement standing so that business can go on as usual. They do not repeal or amend laws that stand in the way of promoters' enterprises. (Repeals or amendments are straightforward legislative alternatives available to Congress, but they can be difficult to pass.) Instead riders such as §318 merely remove the citizens' ability to get preliminary injunctions (and limit permanent injunctions to extraordinary cases where citizens are able to prove on the restricted merits that agency action was arbitrary, capricious, etc.).[65]

The rider's apparent assumption is that—absent citizen enforcement—neither the private industry logging the lands nor the two federal agencies supervising the logging will need to comply with federal laws. In order to nullify the laws, one doesn't have to repeal them (there weren't enough votes to do that), but only needs to eliminate the citizen enforcers.

2. Can Congress foreclose judicial review? Beyond the question of legislating on appropriations bills, is there any constitutional limit to the ability of special interest riders to foreclose judicial review of targeted agency practices? A broad-ranging review of provisions overriding judicial review ended its constitutional and statutory analysis with the plaint that "it is crucial that courts apply a heightened standard of review in examining measures that limit judicial review.... Judicial review is fundamental to the 'very essence of liberty' [citing *Marbury v. Madison*, 5 U.S. 137, 163 (1803)]. The Supreme Court has held that any 'statutory preclusion of judicial review must be demonstrated clearly and convincingly.'"[66] If Congress doesn't change the law, but removes judicial jurisdiction to consider violations in whole or in part, does that violate the Article III judicial power and the separation of powers doctrine? Absent a clear constitutional barrier to such legislative shortcuts, special interest attempts to foreclose citizen enforcement will continue.

---

65. In the timing of such citizen efforts, practically speaking, preliminary injunctions are the entire battle. If preliminary relief staying the agency action is not ordered, the forest is stripped bare before plaintiffs can get to trial on the permanent injunctions. Such appropriations riders are effective federal law for only one fiscal year, although when lobbyists successfully add them to an appropriations bill for one year, they tend to reappear thereafter.

After 458 law professors from 61 schools in 41 states and the District of Columbia sent a letter to leaders of the House and Senate protesting §318 as a "dangerous precedent" for undermining protective federal laws, however, §318 was not re-promulgated for the following fiscal year. The fight was successfully led by Senators Baucus and Chaffee, who not coincidentally were the ranking members of the standing committees bypassed by the appropriations stratagem and by the Sierra Club.

66. Sher & Hunting, Eroding the Landscape, Eroding the Laws: Congressional Exemptions from Judicial Review of Environmental Laws, 15 Harv. Envtl. L. Rev. 435, 481 (1991) (citing *NLRB v. United Food & Comm'l Wkrs. Union*, 484 U.S. 112, 131 (1987)).

4. Citizens' Attempts to Expand Agency Procedures

> History has shown the indispensable role of citizens in assuring the implementation of federal environmental statutes. As in the standing cases, regulated entities and their like-minded judicial brethren assiduously try to constrict citizen participation. In *Overton Park*, the citizen plaintiffs were ultimately unsuccessful in persuading the courts to grant extended procedural opportunities to challenge the highway project within the agency or to require formal findings, but were able to leverage the Court's own need for a sufficient record to apply Article III judicial review to the agency decision. In subsequent years, many federal courts, led by the D.C. Circuit, began to expand the procedures owed to citizen challengers—sometimes on claims of individual due process, especially in matters of "Great Public Import." The following case involved both a citizen attempt to increase the administrative procedures on a matter of great public import, and a claim that the record was insufficient for adequate review by the courts. Note the tone of the Supreme Court opinion, the political alignments among the various parties, and how the citizen environmentalists focused their arguments on procedural claims as much as, or more than, attacking the substantive agency decision.

Vermont Yankee Nuclear Power Corp. v. Natural Resources Defense Council
435 U.S. 519 (U.S. Sup. Ct. 1978)

REHNQUIST, J. In 1946, Congress enacted the Administrative Procedure Act, which as we have noted elsewhere was not only "a new, basic and comprehensive regulation of procedures in many agencies," *Wong Yang Sung v. McGrath*, 339 U.S. 33 (1950), but was also a legislative enactment which settled "long-continued and hard-fought contentions, and enacts a formula upon which opposing social and political forces have come to rest." . . . Interpreting [§4 of the Act, now codified as §553] in *U.S. v. Allegheny-Ludlum Steel Corp.*, 406 U.S. 742 (1972), and *U.S. v. Fla. E. Coast Ry. Co.*, 410 U.S. 224 (1973), we held that generally speaking this section of the Act established the maximum procedural requirements which Congress was willing to have the courts impose upon agencies in conducting rulemaking procedures. Agencies are free to grant additional procedural rights in the exercise of their discretion, but reviewing courts are generally not free to impose them if the agencies have not chosen to grant them. This is not to say necessarily that there are no circumstances which would ever justify a court in overturning agency action because of a failure to employ procedures beyond those required by the statute. But such circumstances, if they exist, are extremely rare. . . .

In December 1967, after the mandatory adjudicatory hearing and necessary review, the Commission granted petitioner Vermont Yankee a permit to build a nuclear power plant in Vernon, Vt. Thereafter, Vermont Yankee applied for an operating license. Respondent Natural Resources Defense Council (NRDC) objected to the granting of a license, however, and therefore a hearing on the application commenced on August 10, 1971. Excluded from consideration at the hearings, over NRDC's objection, was the issue of the environmental effects of operations to reprocess fuel or dispose of wastes resulting from the reprocessing operations. This ruling was affirmed by the Appeal Board in June 1972.

D. Citizen Enforcement in the Courts

In November 1972, however, the Commission, making specific reference to the Appeal Board's decision with respect to the Vermont Yankee License, instituted rulemaking proceedings "that would specifically deal with the question of consideration of environmental effects associated with the uranium fuel cycle in the individual cost-benefit analyses for light water cooled nuclear power reactors" [i.e., the rule would stipulate a waste storage evaluation factor that thereafter could be incorporated into formal plant licensing proceedings without re-opening the whole messy question in each licensing]. The notice of proposed rulemaking offered two alternatives, both predicated on a report prepared by the commission's staff entitled Environmental Survey of the Nuclear Fuel Cycle. The first would have required no quantitative evaluation of the environmental hazards of fuel reprocessing or disposal because the Environmental Survey had found them to be slight. The second would have specified numerical values for the environmental impact of this part of the fuel cycle, which values would then be incorporated into a table, along with the other relevant factors, to determine the overall cost-benefit balance for each operating license.

Much of the controversy in this case revolves around the procedures used in the rulemaking hearing which commenced in February 1973. . . . All participants would be given a reasonable opportunity to present their position and could be represented by counsel if they so desired. Written and, time permitting, oral statements would be received and incorporated into the record. . . . More than 40 individuals and organizations representing a wide variety of interests submitted written comments. . . . The major substantive issue was the [rulemaking choice between the two hazard evaluation options in] the Environmental Survey.

In April 1974, the Commission issued a rule which adopted the second of the two proposed alternatives. . . . The Commission also approved the procedures used at the hearing, and indicated that the record, including the Environmental Survey, provided an "adequate data base for the regulation adopted." . . . Respondents appealed from both the Commission's adoption of the rule and its decision to grant Vermont Yankee's license to the Court of Appeals for the District of Columbia Circuit.

The court . . . examined the rulemaking proceedings and, despite the fact that it appeared that the agency employed all the procedures required by 5 U.S.C. §553 and more, the court determined the proceedings to be inadequate and overturned the rule [and the operating license]. . . .

The Court of Appeals struck down the rule because of the perceived inadequacies of the procedures employed in the rulemaking proceedings. The court first determined the intervenors' primary argument to be "that the decision to preclude 'discovery or cross-examination' denied them a meaningful opportunity to participate in the proceedings as guaranteed by due process." The court then went on to frame the issue for decision thus: "Thus, we are called upon to decide whether the procedures provided by the agency were sufficient to ventilate the issues." The court conceded that absent extraordinary circumstances it is improper for a reviewing court to prescribe the procedural format an agency must follow, but it likewise clearly thought it entirely appropriate to "scrutinize the record as a whole to insure that genuine opportunities to participate in a meaningful way were provided. . . ." The court also refrained from actually ordering the agency to follow any specific procedures, but there is little doubt in our minds that the . . . court's decision is that the procedures afforded during the hearings were inadequate. This conclusion is particularly buttressed by the fact that after the court examined the record, particularly the testimony of Dr. Pittman, and declared it insufficient, the court proceeded to discuss at some length the necessity for further procedural devices. . . .

This much is absolutely clear: Absent constitutional constraints or extremely compelling circumstances the "administrative agencies 'should be free to fashion their own rules of procedure and to pursue methods of inquiry capable of permitting them to discharge their multitudinous duties.'" *FCC v. Schreiber*, 381 U.S. 279, 290 (1965)....

Respondent NRDC argues that [§553] of the Administrative Procedure Act merely establishes lower procedural bounds and that a court may routinely require more than the minimum when an agency's proposed rule addresses complex or technical factual issues or "Issues of Great Public Import."...

Our decisions reject this view.... We also think the legislative history... does not bear out its contention, ... [leaving] little doubt that Congress intended that the discretion of the agencies and not that of the courts be exercised in determining when extra procedural devices should be employed. . . . [The circuit court's] Monday morning quarterbacking not only encourages but almost compels the agency to conduct all rulemaking proceedings with the full panoply of procedural devices normally associated only with adjudicatory hearings....

The court below uncritically assumed that additional procedures will automatically result in a more adequate record because it will give interested parties more of an opportunity to participate and contribute to the proceedings. . . . Nothing in the APA, . . . the circumstances of this case, the nature of the issues being considered, past agency practice, or the statutory mandate under which the Commission operates, permitted the court to review and overturn the rulemaking proceeding on the basis of the procedural devices employed (or not employed) by the Commission so long as the Commission employed at least the statutory minima, a matter about which there is no doubt in this case.

There remains, of course, the question of whether the challenged rule finds sufficient justification [on the record of] the administrative proceedings that it should be upheld by the reviewing court. Judge Tamm, concurring in the result reached by the majority of the Court of Appeals, thought that it did not. There are also intimations in the majority opinion which suggest that the judges who joined it likewise may have thought the administrative proceedings an insufficient basis upon which to predicate the rule in question. We accordingly remand so that the Court of Appeals may review the rule as the Administrative Procedure Act provides.... The court should . . . not stray beyond the judicial province to explore the procedural format or to impose upon the agency its own notion of which procedures are "best" or most likely to further some vague, undefined public good....

[The Court of Appeals' procedural requirements] border on the Kafkaesque. Nuclear energy may some day be a cheap, safe source of power or it may not. But Congress has made a choice to at least try nuclear energy, establishing a reasonable review process in which courts are to play only a limited role. . . . Time may prove wrong the decision to develop nuclear energy, but it is Congress or the States within their appropriate agencies which must eventually make that judgment. Reversed and remanded.

[On February 24, 2010, the Vermont legislature voted to terminate the Vermont Yankee Nuclear Plant's state operating permit when it expires in 2011, based upon problems with its "reliability and economics" (i.e., not "safety" since state regulation of "safety" is preempted by the Atomic Energy Act).]

COMMENTARY & QUESTIONS

1. Tactics: in procedural terms, what was the NRC attempting to do in *Vermont Yankee*? By shifting the safety and radiation waste disposal questions into an informal rulemaking proceeding, thereafter to be published as a regulation that could be simply incorporated by reference, the agency would avoid having to face citizen organizations' questioning and

D. Citizen Enforcement in the Courts

cross-examination on the waste issue in future formal adjudications when utilities sought operating licenses. If the nuclear waste disposal question remained part of each licensing case, it would be subject there to trial type procedures: full notice, full discovery, full cross-examination, full right to present contrary evidence. In this particular rulemaking proceeding, the agency did in fact allow some hybrid procedures, more than mere notice-and-comment rulemaking, but it prohibited discovery and much cross-examination. Would those really have made much difference to the agency's ultimate decision? After the *Vermont Yankee* decision, can agencies push environmental intervenors back into the closet, or do the continuing requirements of a record for judicial review keep the intervenors as active players?

2. What was the holding of *Vermont Yankee*? *Vermont Yankee* is a ringing denunciation of the Court of Appeal's requirement for added agency procedures to benefit citizen environmental intervenors. Justice Rehnquist held that the APA's procedural minimum requirements for agencies were now also the maximum procedures that courts could require. (Ironically, in doing so he cited cases such as *Wong Yang Sung* in which the Court had actually granted extended procedures far beyond statutory requirements in order to protect individuals against agency excesses.) What narrow exceptions to the new rule against court-expanded procedures would the Rehnquist opinion allow? He notes several situations in which courts may force agencies to grant more process.[67] But note the penultimate paragraph in the *Vermont Yankee* excerpt. The entire rulemaking was sent back for further review on the adequacy of the factual record: whether the NRC had shown enough facts so that a court could determine that reasonable NRC officials could or could not have decided as they did. This is a second kind of procedural argument—that for the courts' own sake, rather than for citizens, agencies must produce a sufficient formal or informal review record to permit judges to apply whatever standard of substantive review applies to the decision. The needs of Article III judicial review thus can still become the tail that wags the dog (as in *Overton Park*).

3. The substantive question on the *Vermont Yankee* record. The factual issue that triggered the *Vermont Yankee* remand appears to have been the shakiness of the report by Dr. Pittman, which was the basis of the NRC decision. Dr. Pittman had devoted most of his report to proposed federal repositories for above-ground waste storage, and less than two pages to the problem of geologic waste disposal. The NRC subsequently abandoned above-ground storage and turned to geologic disposal solutions (although these have also been almost impossible to site). The further problem was that the Pittman report, upon which the NRC rule was based, had been produced with little time or research. Might cross-examination, if it had been available, have usefully revealed the thinness of this particular piece of evidence?

4. *Vermont Yankee*, remand and back. What ultimately happened with the nuclear waste rule? The NRC prepared a revised rule with further documentation and research, reasserting its determination of an extremely low risk factor, based on an assumption that nuclear wastes would never be released into the environment. When the case returned to the Court it upheld this optimistic determination against skeptical citizen challenge:

> The zero-release assumption—a policy judgment concerning one line in a conservative Table designed for the limited purpose of individual licensing decisions—is within the bounds of reasoned decisionmaking. It is not our task to determine what decision we, as Commissioners,

---

67. Since the APA provides no standards for less-than-formal *adjudications*, courts are not limited by the *Vermont Yankee* rationale in their ability to require that various procedures be added to agencies' informal adjudications.

would have reached. Our only task is to determine whether the Commission has considered the relevant factors and articulated a rational connection between the facts found and the choice made. Under this standard, we think the Commission's zero-release assumption, within the context of Table S-3 as a whole, was not arbitrary and capricious. *Baltimore Gas & Elec. v. NRDC*, 462 U.S. 87 (1983).

5. The "hard look" doctrine. Prior to *Vermont Yankee*, and subsequent to the decision as well, federal courts have enunciated what is called the "hard look" doctrine: When Congress has set a statutory standard for agencies to apply, courts must see enough evidence on the record to be satisfied that the agency itself took a "hard look" at all relevant facts and the statutory standards that applied to them. The "hard look" determination is obviously subjective. Does *Vermont Yankee* do anything to dampen the courts' scrutiny of an agency's hard look?

6. Rulemaking/adjudication: tactical considerations. Other settings illustrate other tactical uses of the rulemaking/adjudication distinction. In some cases, unlike the NRC in *Vermont Yankee*, an agency will seek to proceed by adjudication, rather than by rulemaking, because subsequent courts do not hold agencies to the terms of their adjudicative precedents as strictly as they do to published rules. Conversely, regulated parties sometimes want to have rulemaking on a matter because, unlike adjudication, rulemaking is prospective and cannot penalize past activities. Regulated parties, on the other hand, sometimes prefer adjudication because of the protective trial-type procedures that normally accompany agency adjudicative processes.

The distinctions between rulemaking and adjudication, and their tactical consequences, emphasize that administrative law is surprisingly young and evolving. Interesting administrative law issues arise in many areas of environmental law and will be repeatedly encountered in later chapters.[68]

7. Citizens intervening in agency proceedings. In *Vermont Yankee*, the citizen group understandably wanted to participate in the heart of the agency process. Section 6 of the APA, 5 U.S.C. §555(b), provides that "so far as the orderly conduct of the public business permits, an interested person may appear before an agency or its responsible employees for the presentation, adjustment, or determination, request, or controversy in [any] proceeding." Section 555(b), however, is little known and little used, at least in non-formal, non-trial-type proceedings. What does the "orderly conduct of public business" limitation mean, and who is legally an "interested" party? *Scenic Hudson* presumed the validity of citizen participation in FPC proceedings.[69] Intervention is a vital part of citizen involvement in the administrative process, allowing a pluralist debate to begin early in the process rather than later in retrospective judicial review. The future development of APA §555(b) will reflect the evolution of intervention in informal as well as formal proceedings. Environmentalists' motions to intervene in ongoing agency proceedings are reinforced by the fact that subsequent reviewing courts might say that a record made without active participation is not

---

68. Chapter 10, for instance, considers whether, when citizen environmentalists have proved a statutory violation, courts may permit violations to continue, based on traditional common law balancing of the equities (i.e., which party's interests and which policy considerations are more important). The Supreme Court, with one dissent, has said that judges can override legislation they consider to be outweighed by other judicial considerations.

69. As a noted administrative law practitioner observed, "today, at least in my experience, intervention is seldom denied.... In light of the role that the courts have carved out for intervenors, and the risks inherent in denying interested citizens the right to be heard, intervention has assumed the proportions of a right, even where the applicable statute or rules are phrased permissively." Butzel, Intervention and Class Actions Before the Agencies and the Courts, 25 Admin. L. Rev. 135, 136 (1973).

D. Citizen Enforcement in the Courts

sufficiently comprehensive and does not cover certain critical features sufficiently to support the agency action in judicial review. A citizen's right to intervene in an agency, under APA §555(b) or otherwise, is arguably broader than standing for judicial review because administrative agency process is not constitutionally limited by Article III's "case or controversy" requirement.

8. The role of an agency when citizens intervene. Note that in the *Scenic Hudson* standing case excerpted in the previous section, the court criticized the agency for treating citizen intervention not as a helpful contribution, but as a resented disruption; the commission had stepped back and acted like "an umpire blandly calling balls and strikes" between the industry and the small ad hoc group of citizen intervenors. Responding to the same problem, Judge Burger roundly criticized the agency proceedings on remand from a prior order of his:

> [The agency] seems to have regarded [the citizen intervenors] as "plaintiffs," and the licensee as "defendant," with burdens of proof allocated accordingly.... We did not intend that intervenors representing a public interest be treated as interlopers. Rather... a "public intervenor" is..., in this context, more nearly like a complaining witness who presents evidence to police or a prosecutor whose duty it is to conduct an affirmative and objective investigation.... In our view the entire hearing was permeated by... the pervasive impatience—if not hostility—of the examiner... which made fair and impartial consideration impossible.... The public intervenors, who were performing a public service under a mandate of this court, were entitled to a more hospitable reception in the performance of that function. As we view the record the examiner tended to impede the exploration of the very issues which we would reasonably expect the Commission itself would have initiated; an ally was regarded as an opponent.... The administrative conduct reflected in this record is beyond repair. [The agency decision was revoked and the case remanded to the agency. *Office of Communication of United Church of Christ v. FCC*, 425 F.2d 543, 546-550 (D.C. Cir. 1969).]

9. Citizens' access to information: FOIA. Information is power, or, at least, it is clear that without basic specific information, interested parties and intervenors will not be effective. In 1966, Congress dramatically reversed the prior widespread agency presumption that government information should be withheld unless there was specific legal authority for its release. The Freedom of Information Act (FOIA), 5 U.S.C. §552, provides that:

> Each agency upon any request for records which . . . reasonably describes such records and [follows certain simple procedures] shall make the records promptly available to any person. 5 U.S.C. §552(a)(3).

FOIA restricts withholding to nine fairly narrow exceptions. 5 U.S.C. §552(b)(1)-(9). Environmentalists have often found FOIA critically helpful in obtaining agency information through formal requests or, perhaps even more usefully, in prompting informal release of information. Federal courts have applied the Act with stringency in a number of environmental cases,[70] although the development of the Act's disclosure mandate, and its provisions

---

70. See *Soucie v. David*, 448 F.2d 1067 (D.C. Cir. 1971) (negative reports on the predicted effects of a supersonic transport plane must be released); cf. *Nat'l Parks & Conservation Ass'n v. Morton*, 498 F.2d 765 (D.C. Cir. 1974) (financial data from national park concessionaires need not be released).

for waiving data retrieval fees for requests "primarily benefiting the public interest,"[71] are still evolving, often facing marked official resistance.[72]

10. Official public participation policies. In December 2009, the Obama Administration issued its "Open Government Directive." EPA's Public Involvement Policy had initially been initiated by the Clinton Administration. Before leaving the Bush II Administration EPA Administrator Christine Todd Whitman attempted to implement the Policy, but it slipped into low priority. The new policy applies to all EPA environmental programs and seeks to provide guidance to EPA staff on effective ways to involve the public in EPA's regulatory and program implementation decisions. It is available at www.epa.gov/publicinvolvement.

11. "Internalizing costs" through public law? In approaching pollution and other environmental harms caused by private individuals and industries, environmental law often follows the strategy of cost internalization, attempting to force private decisionmakers to account for environmental costs in their economic market behavior. Is there an equivalent accounting strategy in the public law setting, where decisionmakers are not involved in a market enterprise? In *Vermont Yankee*, the environmentalists' ultimate aim was to make the agency take full account of the daunting and potentially overwhelming costs and risks of nuclear waste storage.

To an extent, government decisionmakers often seem to share the functional frame of reference of private corporate entrepreneurs. To the minds of promoters, whether private or public, accounting for negative external consequences is dysfunctional, hence to be avoided, because it gets in the way of the enterprise's mission. Development agencies funded by taxpayer dollars, however, may tend to be institutionally less sensitive to cost accounting.

How are agency officials practically induced to consider consequential public costs in their internal calculus? One approach is political. The currency of the bureaucratic marketplace is politics—who has power, who has momentum, who is under fire. Agencies can foresee that if they attract severe media criticism, or legislative committee oversight hearings, or negative reactions from an executive office, they will feel the heat, and so they act accordingly. Another internalizing approach is personal accountability, a rarity in government except at the highest levels. FOIA's §552(a) provides:

> Whenever the court orders the production of any agency records improperly withheld from the complainant . . . and . . . issues a written finding that the circumstances surrounding the withholding raise questions whether agency personnel acted arbitrarily . . . with respect to the withholding, the Special Counsel [of the Civil Service merit system review process] shall promptly initiate a proceeding to determine whether disciplinary action is warranted. . . . 5 U.S.C. §552(a)(4)(F).

Such personal sanctions catch and hold bureaucratic attention, but are infrequent. Ultimately it is legal constraints likely to be enforced against agencies, in many cases only by citizen efforts, that constitute the backbone of administrative accountability.

---

71. 5 U.S.C. §552(a)(4)(A). The Act's serious intent to compel an open governmental process is underscored by its provisions for advancing FOIA cases to the top of federal court dockets, 5 U.S.C. §552(a)(4)(D); award of attorneys' fees against the agencies, 5 U.S.C. §552(a)(4)(E); and personal accountability as in the next text note.

72. Official reluctance to make proceedings open and disclose document on request long predates the Department of Homeland Security and the Patriot Act, but recent years have seen renewed barriers. See Echeverria & Kaplan, Poisonous Procedural "Reform": In Defense of Environmental Right to Know, 12 Kan. J.L. & Pub. Pol'y 579 (2002-2003).

E. STATUTORY INTERPRETATION: HOW, BY WHOM? — CHEVRON

1. Judicial Review of Agency Interpretations of Law

Chevron U.S.A., Inc. v. Natural Resources Defense Council
467 U.S. 837 (U.S. Sup. Ct. 1984)

[Section 111 of the CAA,[73] requires that tougher permit standards, based on BAT (see Chapter 11), must be applied to any "new source" of pollution in areas that violate existing air quality standards. A "source" was defined in the statute as "any building, structure, facility, or installation which emits or may emit any air pollutant." In 1980, the latter statutory phrase had been interpreted by EPA to mean that every new subunit or smokestack of a factory was a source that had to meet those higher standards. In 1981, however, the Reagan Administration changed the definition by a rulemaking applying a regulatory "bubble"[74] concept: The new regulation defined the statutory term "source" to mean "all of the pollutant-emitting activities which belong to the same industrial grouping, are located on one or more contiguous or adjacent properties, and are under the control of the same person or persons." The result was that EPA could now view an entire industrial site as a single source. If a company offset new emissions within a plant by closing old dirtier units, there would be no net increase of pollutants coming from within the bubble, so new construction did not count as a new source and did not have to meet the tougher standards. The NRDC sued.]

STEVENS, J. The question presented by this case is whether EPA's decision to allow states to treat all of the pollution-emitting devices within the same industrial grouping as though they were encased within a single "bubble" is based on a reasonable construction of the statutory term "stationary source."

When a court reviews an agency's construction of the statute which it administers, it is confronted with two questions.

First, always, is the question whether Congress has directly spoken to the precise question at issue. If the intent of Congress is clear, that is the end of the matter; for the court, as well as the agency, must give effect to the unambiguously expressed intent of Congress.[75]

If, however, the court determines Congress has not directly addressed the precise question at issue, the court does not simply impose its own construction on the statute, as would be necessary in the absence of an administrative interpretation. Rather, if the statute is silent or ambiguous with respect to this specific issue, the question for the court is whether the agency's answer is based on a permissible construction of the statute.[76] "The power of

---

73. 42 U.S.C. §7411, as amended in 1977 and 1990.

74. See Chapter 11.

75. The judiciary is the final authority on issues of statutory construction and must recheck administrative constructions which are contrary to clear congressional intent. If a court, employing traditional tools of statutory construction, ascertains that Congress had an intention on the precise question at issue, that intention is the law and must be given effect [as a matter of the judges' own statutory interpretation]. [This is footnote 9 in the original opinion.]

76. The Court need not conclude that the agency construction was the only one it permissibly could have adopted to uphold the construction, or even the reading the court would have reached if the question had initially arisen in a judicial proceeding.

an administrative agency to administer a congressionally created . . . program necessarily requires the formulation of policy in the making of rules to fill any gap left, implicitly or explicitly, by Congress."

The principle of deference to administrative interpretations has been consistently followed by this Court whenever decision as to the meaning or reach of the statute has involved reconciling conflicting policies, and a full understanding of the force of the statutory policy on the given situation has depended upon more than ordinary knowledge respecting the matters subjected to agency regulations. *Hearst*, 322 U.S. 111 (1944). . . . "If this choice represents accommodation of conflicting policies that were committed to the agency's care by the statute, we should not disturb it unless it appears from the statute or its legislative history that the accommodation is not one that Congress would have sanctioned. . . ." *U.S. v. Shimer*, 367 U.S. 374, 382 (1961).

Our review of the EPA's varying interpretations of the word "source"—both before and after the 1977 amendments—convinces us that the agency primarily responsible for administering this important legislation has consistently interpreted it flexibly—not in a sterile textual vacuum, but in the context of implementing policy decisions in a technical and complex arena. . . . When a challenge to an agency construction of a statutory provision, fairly conceptualized, really centers on the wisdom of the agency's policy, rather than whether it is a reasonable choice within a gap left open by Congress, the challenge must fail. In such a case, federal judges—who have no constituency—have the duty to respect legitimate policy choices made by those who do. Responsibilities for assessing the wisdom of such policy choices and resolving the struggle between competing views of the public interests are not judicial ones: "Our Constitution vests such responsibilities in the political branches." *TVA v. Hill*, 437 U.S. 153, 195 (1978). Reversed.

COMMENTARY & QUESTIONS

1. The strategics of definitions. Note how critical differences can often turn on agency interpretations of key statutory terms: "source" in *Chevron*, "feasible and prudent" in *Overton Park*, "aggrieved" in *Scenic Hudson*, "point source" in the CWA, and so on. In one famous example, EPA concurrently improved the average gas mileage of the Chrysler Corporation's "passenger vehicle" and "light truck" fleets by redefining minivans as the latter, not the former, thereby shifting them from embarrassment in one category to enhancement of another. Independent judicial scrutiny of these interpretations obviously could make significant differences for good and ill.

In *Chevron* the interpretation of the term "source" as incorporating air pollution "bubbles" had immediate and far-reaching effects on U.S. industry and air quality. The agency had strong arguments in favor of the bubble interpretation. Do you see how a bubble might result in cleaner air, despite allowing lower standards? If an industry considering upgrading its physical facilities knows it will be held to the highest standards, might it decide not to add new plant modifications at all? The question in every case is whether the agency's interpretation is to be second-guessed by the courts or be deferred to.

> The complexities of judicial deference to agency interpretations of statutes and regulations take on particular subtleties when you consider that interpretations made in one administration may be quite unappealing to a subsequent, politically-opposite administration, yet courts presumptively treat agency interpretations as objective and

E. Statutory Interpretation: How, by Whom? — Chevron

> consistent over time. Changes in agency interpretations usually must be justified with new facts or changes in context. *State Farm Mutual*.[77]

2. Judicial deference to agency interpretations of law, in *Chevron*. Does *Chevron* set out a principle of general deference to agency interpretations of statutes, or just for agency gap-filling? The Court holds that the agency can so interpret the term "source," "making . . . rules to fill any gap left, implicitly or explicitly, by Congress," because EPA is following Congress's overall statutory mandate to clean up the air and there is no evidence of any congressional intention on the particular question of bubbling. The *Chevron* rule has spread far beyond gap-filling, however, and is often thought to be a general deference rule.

The standard analysis drawn from *Chevron* has two steps, with a great deal of room for fudging in each:

- Step One: Given the statutory language, is the intent of Congress (in the eyes of the reviewing court) clear? If so, the court will itself declare that interpretation, whether the agency agrees or not.
- Step Two: If the court decides the meaning is not clear, then the court must review the agency's interpretation deferentially, upholding it if the court thinks the agency's answer is based on "a permissible construction of the statute."

In Step One, great flexibility lies in the judicial determination whether Congress has "directly spoken" to the "precise question at issue" or "unambiguously expressed" its intent. There is even more flexibility in what courts will look at in deciding whether the congressional intent is clear or ambiguous: Will a court look only at the specific words of the challenged statutory provision standing alone, or also at other relevant language in the statute, or at the provision in the full context of the statute, or at the legislative history of the provision in Congress, or at congressional policy on point, or is it open to all the other contextual analysis tools used in statutory interpretation? If courts close their eyes to anything but the specific words, they are in an irrational vacuum, but if they open their eyes to all that is relevant to determining intent, deference is minimal.

In Step Two, the question whether the agency's answer is based on "a permissible construction of the statute," likewise incorporates highly subjective weighing. Courts tend to go through all the traditional elements anyway, replicating a full judicial interpretation process, in order to see if the agency's interpretation is "permissible."[78] Judges tend to believe that courts are always competent to interpret statutes. Deference is decided case by case by

---

77. *Motor Vehicles Manufacturers Ass'n v. State Farm Mut. Ins. Co*, 463 U.S. 29 (1983) (nullifying the Reagan Administration's reversal of the Carter Administration's decision that auto safety as defined in the NHSTSA statute required seat belts).

78. That in fact was what was done in the leading administrative law case declaring deference to agency interpretations of statutes, *Hearst v. NLRB*, 322 U.S. 111 (1944). In *Holly Farms v. NLRB*, 517 U.S. 392 (1996), the Court said, "Administrators and reviewing courts must take care to assure that exemptions . . . are not so expansively interpreted as to deny protection . . . the Act was designed to reach." Note that this implies that if the agency *broadened* the exemptions, courts could appropriately, on a *policy* analysis, defer much less to the agency interpretations. The Court also said, "courts . . . must respect the judgment of the agency empowered to apply the law to varying fact patterns, even if the issue 'with nearly equal reason [might] be resolved one way rather than another.'" The word "even" missed the point. Can courts *decline* to defer when the interpretations are *not* "nearly equal"? In this labor case, at least, Justices Rehnquist, Scalia, O'Connor, and Thomas declared in dissent that "the deference owed to an expert tribunal cannot be allowed to slip into a judicial inertia. . . ."

the deferrers themselves. And what of the widely varying relationships between particular agencies and particular statutes? In his post-*Chevron* analysis, Professor Colin Diver noted that still "the decision to grant deference depends on various attributes of the agency's legal authority and functions, and of the administrative interpretation at issue."[79] Should courts defer to interpretations of the FWHA, as in *Overton Park*, where the §4(f) parkland environmental protection provision was an unwelcome burr under the agency's bureaucratic saddle, to the same degree as they defer to EPA on toxicity definitions? Even after *Chevron*, would it be a permissible argument against judicial deference to an agency interpretation watering down a statutory provision, to show that the same agency, disliking that particular provision's strictness, had given extensive testimony against its passage in the first place?

3. Post-*Chevron* judicial review of agency interpretations of law, and the *Mead* addendum. The *Chevron* first step is the most common point at which courts themselves take over the question, holding that a statute's meaning is sufficiently clear that the court can determine it correctly on its own. Since *Chevron*, the Supreme Court has repeatedly demonstrated that it will dictate its own interpretation of statutory meaning, not deferring to agencies' interpretations, if it believes that standard norms of statutory construction, as interpreted by the Court, would lead to a different answer. See *INS v. Cardoza-Fonseca*, 480 U.S. 421 (1987). The line between deference and judicial takeover of the fundamental decision can thus get quite hazy.

Deference to agencies' legal interpretations is most likely where a legislative scheme seems highly technical, with a wide range of details delegated to the agency's special expertise. *Chevron*, with its intricate air pollution technicalities, was a particularly apt subject for deference to the agency on legal as well as factual matters. The less daunting the legal provisions faced by the courts, the less likely they are to be deferential on questions of law. Within judicial chambers, the tendency is to apply the familiar judicial methods to reach an interpretation, then to consider whether the agency's interpretation agrees with the judge's view of the term's meaning, plain or fancy.[80]

The *Chevron* deference formulation nevertheless continues to be one of the most-cited holdings in modern administrative law generally, not just in the environmental field. State and federal courts use it continually as a general touchstone for deferring to agency determinations (including some judges not deeply familiar with administrative law who apply it to agency decisions of fact as well as of law).

U.S. v. Mead Corp., 533 U.S. 218 (2001), has somewhat affected the *Chevron* field. In *Mead*, a nonenvironmental case that nonetheless has importance for its potential shift in the administrative law of judicial review, the Court declined to apply *Chevron* deference in a case involving a customs classification ruling. The Court's decision to reject the *Chevron* standard turned primarily on the premise that Congress had not intended the administrative classifications to have the legal force of regulations. Deference will be greatest, using *Chevron*, where Congress has expressed an intent to delegate broad authority to the agency to carry out the goals of the enabling legislation or when strong evidence suggests such an implicit congressional delegation. Yet, even when the *Chevron* standard is inapplicable, the Court will consider the "degree of the agency's care, its consistency [in *Mead* the agency had changed its position], formality, and relative expertness, and . . . the persuasiveness of the agency's position." 533 U.S. at 228. This seems to reopen the door to extended

---

79. Diver, Statutory Interpretation in the Administrative State, 133 U. Pa. L. Rev. 549, 562 (1985).
80. Id.

E. Statutory Interpretation: How, by Whom?—Chevron

arguments over whether agency determinations of law in a particular case should receive great, medium, or light deference in future judicial reviews.

4. The "plain meaning" finesse. It is interesting to see how courts since *Chevron* can avoid deferring to agency interpretations of law when they disagree with them. One of the approaches is the "plain meaning" theory—that if the legal meaning of a term is clear to a court on the face of a statute or regulation, then the court will apply that interpretation regardless of the expert agency's differing opinion.[81] In *Hercules v. EPA*, 938 F.2d 276, 280, 281 (D.C. Cir. 1991), the court said it would only weigh the words of the contested clause, but nevertheless proceeded to review legislative history, contextual analysis, policy analysis of congressional intent in the Act, the statute's broad remedial purposes, the limited agency burdens that would be imposed by the notice requirement, and the legislative purpose of dealing fairly with subsequent purchasers. This typical exercise in statutory interpretation in *Hercules* demonstrates how ready courts are to embark on the familiar task of interpreting legal language, going far beyond plain meaning.

5. Deference to agencies' interpretations of their own regulations? *Chevron* was the Court's quite successful attempt to set out a conceptual matrix for determining when courts would intrude upon agencies' interpretations of statutes. *Auer* deference on agency interpretations *of their own regulations* followed up on *Chevron's* formula on deference to agency interpretations of *statutes*. Under *Auer*,[82] an agency's interpretation of its own regulation becomes of controlling weight unless it is plainly erroneous or plainly inconsistent with the regulation. This deference has been long considered equivalent to *Chevron* deference, helping to insulate agency action from legal challenges and a powerful tool for agencies in the enforcement context.[83] In *Decker v. Northwest Envtl. Defense Ctr.*, 133 S. Ct. 632 (2013), Justice Scalia, after years of applying *Auer* deference, denounced it in his dissent—because per *Marbury v. Madison* the purpose of interpretation is to "say what the law is," the province of the judiciary. Chief Justice Roberts (joined by Justice Alito) filed a separate concurrence suggesting that *Auer* deference should be re-visited. (This apparent invitation to challenge *Auer* may have been politically motivated by their concerns about actions of the Obama administrative state.)

6. Differential deference? How much deference for guidance documents? To improve its internal efficiency, speed up regulatory management adjustments, and free up its regulatory hands, EPA often avoids official §553 rulemaking and sets out informal standards via guidance documents.[84] In 2004, the Court had to determine the relative authority of interpretations of the CAA made by a state agency and EPA. In *Alaska Dep't of Envtl. Conservation (ADEC) v. EPA*, 540 U.S. 461 (2004), the state agency had interpreted an air pollution requirement for BACT (Best Available Control Technology) more leniently than EPA. EPA relied on a prior guidance to show its continuing right to intervene to assure that state interpretations are "based on a reasoned analysis." With its strong states-rights advocates, would the Court extend deference to the federal agency's interpretation if EPA was overriding a state agency? Writing for the majority, over a dissent by Justices Rehnquist, Scalia, and Thomas, Justice Ginsburg said:

---

81. See Murphy, Old Maxims Never Die: The Plain Meaning Rule and Statutory Interpretation in Modern Federal Courts, 75 Colum. L. Rev. 1299 (1975).

82. *Auer v. Robbins*, 519 U.S. 452 (1997).

83. Ben Snowden, Has *Auer*'s Hour Arrived?, Nat. Resources & Env't, Spring 2014, at 31.

84. Sometimes courts reject EPA's use of guidance on the theory that they have too much practical binding effect and therefore require §553 rulemaking, the holding in *General Elec. Co. v. EPA*, 290 F.3d 377, 379 (D.C. Cir. 2002), footnoted earlier in note 12.

We "normally accord particular deference to an agency interpretation of 'long-standing' duration," recognizing that "well-reasoned views" of an expert administrator rest on "a body of experience and informed judgment to which courts and litigants may properly resort for guidance" [quoting *Skidmore v. Swift & Co.*, 323 U.S. 134, 139-140 (1944)]. We have previously accorded dispositive effect to EPA's interpretation of an ambiguous CAA provision. See *Chevron* and *Union Electric*. The Agency's interpretation in this case, presented in internal guidance memoranda, however, does not qualify for the dispositive force described in *Chevron*. "Interpretations such as those in . . . policy statements, agency manuals, and enforcement guidelines, all of which lack the force of law—do not warrant *Chevron*-style deference"; accord, *U.S. v. Mead Corp.* Cogent "administrative interpretations . . . not [the] products of formal rulemaking . . . nevertheless warrant respect." We accord EPA's reading of the relevant statutory provisions . . . that measure of respect. 540 U.S. at 487-488.

Analyzing the basis of the EPA guidance and the statutory scheme, the Court majority accepted the position of the EPA guidance and approved the override of the state standard. What remains unclear in such cases is how and how much deference is given to the guidance, since the Court's decision may well have been largely based on its own interpretation of the statutory language and context.

7. Organic decisionmaking? The *Chevron* tests can operate to insulate government agencies' interpretations of key statutory provisions from judicial scrutiny. If judges incline toward overriding an agency interpretation, on the other hand, under *Chevron* they can find a "plain meaning" for the statutory term that differs from the agency's, and override. The process of finding that "plain meaning," moreover, apparently does not have to take place on the face of the text but can be based on the full range of judicial statutory interpretation techniques.

Flexibility exists, moreover, beyond the terms of *Chevron* analysis. If a court dislikes an agency position on an ambiguous term but cannot say that an agency's interpretation is not a "permissible" reading of the statute, the court can utilize the old "delegation doctrine" restriction on agency actions. See Justice Rehnquist's arguments in the OSHA benzene and cotton dust cases, attempting to reject OSHA's definition of "unsafe" environmental exposures on delegation grounds—that Congress had not given the agency sufficient details on how to regulate—in effect rejecting the agency's gap-filling function.[85]

8. When statutes appear to conflict. When statutes appear to conflict, courts can apply a variety of interpretive canons to resolve the matter—including interpreting both to coexist, applying whichever statute is more recent, applying whichever statute is more specific, applying whichever statutory mandate appears most substantive or important, adopting agency interpretations that address the question, etc. These choices leave judges a lot of leeway to vote for outcomes they personally prefer. In *National Association of Home Builders v. Defenders of Wildlife*, 551 U.S. 644 (2007), noted in Chapter 10, Justice Alito used a self-serving agency regulation and a theory favoring earlier statutes over later statutes in order to undercut protections of endangered species set out in prior Court opinions.

9. Administrative law as a game of craps? As this chapter's descriptive and analytical materials reflect, administrative law principles provide judges with a wide range of opportunities to fudge decisions toward outcomes they prefer. A court's rulings on judicial review issues are often discretionary and usually outcome-determinative—particularly as to the

---

85. *Indus. Union Dept., AFL-CIO v. Am. Petroleum Inst.*, 448 U.S. 607 (1980) (Rehnquist, J., concurring opinion); *Am. Textile Mfg. Inst. v. Donovan*, 452 U.S. 490 (1981) (Rehnquist, dissent) (both opinions arguing that the agency had too much leeway filling gaps in the regulatory definition). For delegation arguments from the opposite pole, see Schoenbrod, The Delegation Doctrine: Could the Court Give It Substance?, 83 Mich. L. Rev. 1223 (1985).

E. Statutory Interpretation: How, by Whom? — Chevron

validity and definition of delegation, standing, exhaustion, ripeness, standard of review, scope of review, procedural quibbles, and tailoring of remedies. Is this an indictment of the field, or a realistic assessment that reinforces the desirability of understanding the complex elements of each issue and scoping out the political and programmatic contexts in which these cases arise? Administrative law demands both technical acuity and consciousness of political context, and the issues it deals with go deep. In the environmental administrative law area, as in environmental law generally, scratch away at almost any case and you soon find yourself contemplating fundamental issues of democratic governance.

7

Sovereignty in the Environmental Law Context

A. Constitutional Federalism & Environmental Law Controversies in the U.S.
B. Integrating International Agreements into Domestic Law

Just as environmental issues cross state and national boundaries, environmental law crosses those same borders. Accordingly, in an age of heightened globalization and knowledge of the transboundary nature of many environmental concerns, understanding inter-sovereign legal relationships is a critical component of environmental law. Within the U.S., environmental authority and responsibility is distributed among domestic sovereigns, primarily the federal government and the states, and to a far lesser extent, tribes and a broad array of local and special governmental units. Concurrently, international agreements contribute to the resolution of environmental problems. This chapter starts with the more familiar doctrines delineating the roles of the states and the federal government in environmental matters within the U.S. and then canvases the key ways in which international elements are grafted onto that system of power relationships.

A. CONSTITUTIONAL FEDERALISM & ENVIRONMENTAL LAW CONTROVERSIES IN THE U.S.

The doctrines and case law of U.S. constitutional federalism emanate from the inter-sovereign power relations described in the U.S. Constitution. Constitutional decisions that define contemporary federalism norms originally were crafted to resolve disputes involving subjects as remote and diverse as Revolutionary War debts,[1] nineteenth-century steamboat

---

[1] Raising questions of federal judicial power to issue judgments against states and ushering in the Eleventh Amendment. See *Chisholm v. Georgia*, 2 Dall. 419 (1973). The jurisprudence in this area is unusually arcane.

monopolies,[2] Depression-era price stabilization,[3] and mid-twentieth-century immigration issues.[4] In more recent history, many of the same doctrines have attracted attention in the environmental law context and led to decisions that delineate limits on the regulatory powers of both the state and national governments. The resulting power relationships have great practical importance for the modern environmental lawyer. A perhaps surprising aspect of these doctrines is that a great deal of authority is concurrent, allowing both state and federal regulation of the environment to coexist. Over time, a pattern of exclusive and shared authority has evolved. Exactly how inter-sovereign relations are worked out by the state and federal actors is in many eras a response to the temper of their times. The Supreme Court, the ultimate arbiter of these inter-sovereign relations, has also moved through periods where its majority has held different views on the proper constitutional division of authority between the state and the national governments.

Through much of the nation's history, environmental quality was the province of the states, acting through their police power authority over health, safety, and general welfare. In the latter third of the twentieth century, the initiative switched to the federal government, which, in a 15-year period starting around 1970, passed an array of environmental laws that remain the most far-reaching of any nation in the world. Even so, most recently the initiative seems to have shifted back to the states, several of which have been far more aggressive than the federal government, particularly in the Bush II era, in addressing global warming, environmental quality, and hazardous substance regulation.

At the most fundamental level, in a constitutional democracy, as a matter of elementary political theory, whatever is enshrined in the Constitution takes precedence over "mere" legislation or other efforts to alter constitutionally established norms. In the U.S., the judiciary is the branch of government that serves as the guardian of constitutional norms. Exercising judicial review, the courts will invalidate laws and regulations that are inconsistent with constitutional requirements. Judicial review relies heavily on discerning the intent of the Framers when the Court interprets and applies constitutional doctrine to specific cases.

In regard to federal-state relations, the intent of the Framers is well understood at a general level. The Framers were keenly aware of the potential for conflict between the central government and the states and of the potential jealousies of overlapping sovereignty. The Constitution itself established a division of authority that has remained largely intact for two centuries, altered only by a few duly ratified amendments. The core concept is that the federal government is not given general powers, but only specific enumerated powers. If this principle was not made sufficiently clear by a carefully drawn list of powers granted to the central government, the Tenth Amendment, ratified almost as the ink was drying on the original document, stated:

> The powers not delegated to the United States by the Constitution, nor prohibited by it to the States, are reserved to the States respectively, or to the people.

On a structural level, this arrangement reflected the political reality. At the time they formed the nation to secure their independence from England, the states were a group of

---

2. Raising questions of state regulation that burdens interstate commerce and giving rise to what is now termed "dormant Commerce Clause" jurisprudence. See *Gibbons v. Ogden*, 22 U.S. (9 Wheat.) 1 (1824).

3. Raising questions of the scope of the commerce power and the limits imposed by the Tenth Amendment. See *Wickard v. Filburn* 317 U.S. 111 (1942).

4. Raising questions of federal preemption of state regulatory authority under the Supremacy Clause. See *Hines v. Davidowitz*, 312 U.S. 52 (1941).

A. Constitutional Federalism in the U.S.

independent sovereigns. They therefore wanted to continue their sovereignty to the fullest extent, with only a limited cession of power to the newly created national entity. Thus, the states retained the general, all-purpose police power to regulate for health, safety, and welfare within their respective borders. Environmental regulation, which grew out of public health concerns, was and is well within the ambit of the states' police power. Similarly, the state police power was the font of common law, the source of many remedies for environmental harms.

At the same time as reserving a great deal of power in the states, the Constitution granted considerable power to the federal government. To avoid a narrow view of the enumerated powers from being an impediment that hamstrung the newly formed entity, the Framers included the Necessary and Proper Clause, supplementing the enumerated powers with such lesser powers as are needed to effectuate the specifically granted ones. Even more significant to federal-state relations is the Supremacy Clause:

> This Constitution, and the Laws of the United States which shall be made in Pursuance thereof; and all Treaties made, or which shall be made, under the authority of the United States, shall be the supreme Law of the Land; and the Judges in every State shall be bound thereby, any Thing in the Constitution or Laws of any State to the Contrary notwithstanding.[5]

The supremacy of federal law against a background of reserved state police power to regulate health and welfare creates potential tension between the national government and the states in regard to environmental regulation. Assume, as is now authoritatively established, most environmental regulation fits within the federal government's interstate and international commerce power.[6] From this alone, because of the Supremacy Clause, Congress is empowered to enact environmental regulation that takes precedence over state regulation of the same conduct.

The potentially antagonistic concepts of federal and state supremacy can be, and often are, reconciled by creating a presumption in favor of concurrent federal and state regulation.[7] The presumption of concurrency means, most simply, that state regulation is permitted in the presence of federal regulation in the same sphere, absent additional indications that the federal government intends to employ its supremacy to block concurrent state activity.[8] This presumption does not do violence to the constitutional division of power. In the environmental field, which lies near the heart of the traditional state police power, it would be odd if some regulatory action by the federal government completely displaced state authority. The Court has created a presumption of concurrency, one that the federal government can overcome.

Over time, two lines of cases have emerged that delineate the extent to which federal laws and regulation displace state authority because of federal supremacy. The more general line of cases addresses the subject in terms of "federal preemption." The narrower line

---

5. U.S. Const. art. VI, cl. 2.
6. See, e.g., *Hodel v. Va. Surface Mining & Reclamation Ass'n*, 452 U.S. 264 (1981) (intrastate federal regulation of strip mining activities).
7. The Tenth Amendment has erected a limit on some federal regulatory mechanisms that address environmental problems by requiring states to act in a federally specified manner. See *N.Y. v. U.S.*, 505 U.S. 144 (1992) (invalidating a provision of the federal Low Level Radioactive Waste Policy Act Amendments of 1985 that required the states to take title to wastes if no statutorily permitted disposal alternative was achieved).
8. The one generic setting in which additional factors need not be present in finding a denial to the states of concurrent regulatory power is in the judge-made "dormant Commerce Clause" doctrine. For environmental law, the dormant Commerce Clause doctrine affects natural resources and the movement of solid waste.

of cases applies to state efforts that directly affect the interstate movement of goods and services and is described as involving the "dormant Commerce Clause."

As a doctrinal matter affecting environmental law, there is more to federalism than just preemption and dormant Commerce Clause cases. There are two more pieces to the "power puzzle": (1) defining what falls within the enumerated powers of the U.S. (and what is beyond those powers) and (2) mapping out the very complex issue of state sovereign immunity in cases that are litigated in federal courts. The scope of federal power to regulate the environment is considered in other chapters, which allow its study in specific regulatory contexts. State immunity is left for courses devoted to the federal courts and jurisdiction.[9]

1. Preemption of State Law

Establishing concurrent regulation as the norm does not negate the power of supremacy. If Congress expressly states that there shall be only federal law on an environmental topic, state laws to the contrary are preempted. Congressional action of this type, called *express preemption*, is not used often in the environmental field, but one prominent example is the Atomic Energy Act of 1954 (AEA).

Express preemption is not the only way in which the effect of the Supremacy Clause can lead to the invalidation of state environmental regulation. The U.S. Supreme Court, in a case involving pesticide regulation, summarized the general framework of preemption analysis as follows:

> Under the Supremacy Clause, . . . state laws that "interfere with, or are contrary to the laws of Congress, made in pursuance of the constitution" are invalid. *Gibbons v. Ogden*, 9 Wheat. 1, 211 (1824, Marshall, C.J.). The ways in which federal law may preempt state law are well established and in the first instance turn on congressional intent. Congress' intent to supplant state authority in a particular field may be express in the terms of the statute. Absent explicit preemptive language, Congress' intent to supersede state law in a given area may nonetheless be implicit if a scheme of federal regulation is "so pervasive as to make reasonable the inference that Congress left no room for the States to supplement it," if "the Act of Congress . . . touch[es] a field in which the federal interest is so dominant that the federal system will be assumed to preclude enforcement of state laws on the same subject," or if the goals "sought to be obtained" and the "obligations imposed" reveal a purpose to preclude state authority. *Rice v. Santa Fe Elevator Corp.*, 331 U.S. 218, 230 (1947). See *Pac. Gas & Elec. v. Cal. Energy Res. Conservation & Dev. Comm'n*, 461 U.S. 190, 203-204 (1983). When considering preemption, "we start with the assumption that the historic police powers of the States were not to be superseded by the Federal Act unless that was the clear and manifest purpose of Congress." *Rice*, 331 U.S. at 230.[10]

Three categories of federal preemption of state laws:

(1) express preemption,
(2) field occupancy (implied preemption), and
(3) conflict preemption.

Even when Congress has not chosen to occupy a particular field, preemption may occur to the extent that state and federal law actually conflict. Such a conflict arises when "compliance with both federal and state regulations is a physical impossibility"[11] or when a state law "stands as an obstacle to the accomplishment and execution of the full purposes and

---

9. For an environmental case presenting an Eleventh Amendment issue, see *Pa. v. Union Gas*, 491 U.S. 1 (1989).
10. *Wis. Pub. Intervenor v. Mortier*, 501 U.S. 597, 605 (1991).
11. *Fla. Lime & Avocado Growers v. Paul*, 373 U.S. 132, 142-143 (1963).

A. Constitutional Federalism in the U.S.

objectives of Congress."[12] Beyond preemption lies potential federal override under the "Dormant Commerce Clause," noted below.

a. Express Preemption

In principle, the most straightforward case for preemption is one in which Congress explicitly provides that state regulation is superseded by federal law. Even here, however, ambiguities arise. Congress seldom speaks with perfect clarity, and often it seeks to displace some, but not all, state regulation in a particular area. Add to this the Court's oft-stated (but not always applied) presumption against preemption, and cases can become very complicated indeed.

Regulation of radiological safety in the nuclear power industry is a prototypical example of express federal preemption of state regulation of an environmental hazard. Without a division of power between the federal government and the states, the industry likely would not exist. Nuclear generation is a risk-laden enterprise demanding extensive safety regulation. Moreover, if a major accident happens, the astronomical tort liability would bankrupt virtually any private entity. It is also an industry that faces immense costs of facility construction, and operation, which act as further barriers to entry for commercial nuclear power generators. To encourage commercial nuclear generation in the face of those risks and barriers to entry, and to limit the possibility of varying state regulations and tort liability, the federal government in the 1950s created a federalized legal environment. Congress granted the Atomic Energy Commission (now bifurcated with the regulatory control being vested in the Nuclear Regulatory Commission) exclusive authority to regulate radiological hazards. In that way, firms entering the field had a single, uniform, national standard to meet rather than 50 different state regulations that responded to local concerns such as in-state coal producers or strong antinuclear lobbies. Based on numerous indications of Congress's intent to put the federal agency in exclusive charge of the radiological hazards of nuclear power, the statute was held to preempt state regulation.[13] Congress explicitly limited the scope of preemption: 42 U.S.C. §2021(k) provides that "nothing in this section shall be construed to affect the authority of any State or local agency to regulate activities for purposes other than protection against radiation hazards." In addition to ensuring uniform radiological regulation, in 1957, in the Price-Anderson Act,[14] Congress used its affirmative authority to limit the total liability for a nuclear accident to $560 million. If safety breaches at nuclear facilities that the states are forbidden to regulate result in damage, state common law remedies, including the availability of punitive damages, are still permitted.[15]

Look again at the disclaimer language of §2021(k). Try to build a catalog of regulations that the states remain free to impose. Zoning and rate regulation come immediately to mind. In *Pac. Gas & Elec. v. Cal. Energy Res. Conservation & Dev. Comm'n*, 461 U.S. 190 (1983), a California law blocked licensure of a power plant on purportedly economic grounds, finding that the proposed facility might prove uneconomic because of the unknown cost of permanent fuel rod waste disposal. The law did not permit licensure until a special state commission made a finding that adequate means were available for the permanent storage and disposal of nuclear waste, a topic that the state admitted it could not regulate directly. In response to a preemption challenge, the Court accepted the state's characterization of

---

12. *Hines v. Davidowitz*, 312 U.S. 52 (1941).
13. See, e.g., *N. States Power Co. v. Minn.*, 447 F.2d 1143 (8th Cir. 1971), aff'd, 405 U.S. 1035 (1972).
14. Pub. L. No. 85-256, 71 Stat. 576 (1957).
15. *Silkwood v. Kerr-McGee Co.*, 464 U.S. 238 (1984).

its law as motivated by economic concerns, an area in which the AEA had preserved state authority. Some passages in *Pacific Gas & Electric* gave the impression that if a state regulation were inspired by a purpose different from allegedly preemptive federal regulation, the state regulation would stand. Subsequent cases, however, have made clear that so broad a reading of *Pacific Gas & Electric* is incorrect. In *English v. Gen. Elec. Co.*, 496 U.S. 72, 84 (1990), the Court explained: "Even as the [*Pacific Gas & Electric*] Court suggested that part of the pre-empted field is defined by reference to the purpose of the state law in question, it made clear that another part of the field is defined by the state law's actual effect on nuclear safety."

COMMENTARY & QUESTIONS

1. Do the express preemption cases achieve results consistent with the Constitution? That question is rather easily answered in the affirmative. The Constitution demands that when Congress uses an enumerated power to preempt, the Supremacy Clause, and hence the preemption, must be honored. The cases all apply that principle, but the cases also present issues of divining just how much preemption Congress intended. Does the Tenth Amendment suggest that it is always appropriate in assessing preemptive intent to take a narrow view that preserves the maximum amount of state autonomy, or is the *English* Court correct when it insists the actual effects on the federal program count, too? What if a state, by a public initiative, passed a "no nukes" law? Does that law regulate radiological safety? What if the same law is passed by the legislature and the legislative history reveals that the animating reason for the statute is to eliminate nuclear risks from the state?

2. Another environmental context in which the state's purpose is relevant. *Huron Portland Cement Co. v. Detroit*, 362 U.S. 440 (1960), remains a key precedent in environmental preemption litigation.[16] That case upheld a local Detroit smoke abatement ordinance that was applied to ships that docked at Detroit. The cement company owned and operated ships whose boilers had to remain fired while in port in order to operate the deck equipment for loading and unloading. The particular boilers in question had operational characteristics that caused them to violate Detroit's Smoke Abatement Code. Those same boilers were regulated for safety by federal law; they were inspected by the Coast Guard and found to meet all applicable federal requirements. The Court stated that the relevant federal legislation

> make[s] clear that inspection of boilers and related equipment is for the purpose of seeing to it that the equipment "may be safely employed in the service proposed." . . . By contrast, the sole aim of the Detroit ordinance is the elimination of air pollution to protect the health and enhance the cleanliness of the local community. 362 U.S. at 445.

In *Huron Portland Cement*, it was conceded that the boilers could not easily be retrofitted to meet the Detroit standards and might have to be replaced. Thus the "different purposes" test, as it might be called, does not sit easily alongside the line of cases studied in the next subsection, which invalidate state regulations because of the difficulty or impossibility of complying with both federal and state rules.

---

16. Excerpted text from the *Huron Portland* decision is posted on the coursebook website for this chapter.

A. Constitutional Federalism in the U.S.

3. Federal nonpreemption of tort remedies. In *Silkwood v. Kerr-McGee*, 464 U.S. 238 (1984), sizable awards of state common law damages, both compensatory and punitive, were awarded to a worker who had been exposed to radioactive materials in a regulated processing facility. The awards were upheld against a claim of federal preemption of nuclear safety issues. In *English v. General Electric Co.*, the Court revisited the subject of preemption of tort remedies in another case involving a nuclear materials processor as defendant. In that case, the plaintiff reported workplace safety violations and eventually was fired. She sought a statutory remedy under a federal whistleblower's provision but was denied relief on procedural grounds. She subsequently filed a state common law tort suit for intentional infliction of emotional distress and was met with the claim of federal preemption. A unanimous Supreme Court rejected the preemption argument:

> Although the decision in *Silkwood* was based in substantial part on legislative history suggesting that Congress did not intend to include in the preempted field state tort remedies for radiation-based injuries, we think it would be odd, if not irrational, to conclude that Congress intended to include tort actions stemming from retaliation against whistleblowers in the preempted field but intended not to include tort actions stemming from radiation damage suffered as a result of actual safety violations. 496 U.S. at 85.

The Court also rejected the narrower argument that the enactment of a federal whistleblower remedy precluded the availability of additional state law-based remedies that served a similar purpose.

4. Do savings clauses save anything anymore? The savings clause, a tool extensively used by the federal environmental statutes, ostensibly preserves the ability of states to adopt requirements different from—and typically more stringent than—those imposed by the federal program. They attempt to prevent, in other words, the preemption of state requirements by the federal program. Recently, however, the Supreme Court has found some savings clauses inadequate to the task.

In a unanimous decision in *U.S. v. Locke*, 529 U.S. 89 (2000), the Court held that federal law preempted Washington State's regulations covering oil tankers in state waters, enacted in the oily wake of the *Exxon-Valdez*. Washington had earlier adopted similar rules, but the Supreme Court held them preempted by the Ports and Waterways Safety Act of 1972 (PWSA), 86 Stat. 424, in *Ray v. Atlantic Richfield Co.*, 435 U.S. 151 (1978).

Title I of the Oil Pollution Act of 1990 (OPA), 33 U.S.C. §2701, includes several savings clauses that appear to grant states leeway to adopt more stringent standards than those prescribed by OPA. Washington contended that these clauses had altered the preemptive effect given the PWSA in *Ray*. The Court read the clauses narrowly and found that *Ray's* holding was unaffected by OPA. It found that their placement in a title captioned "Oil Pollution Liability and Compensation" indicated that they were not intended to cover tanker regulation as a whole, but rather were limited to preserving state rules relevant to the subject matter of Title I: "The evident purpose of the savings clauses is to preserve state laws which, rather than imposing substantive regulation of a vessel's primary conduct, establish liability rules and financial requirements relating to oil spills." *Locke*, 529 U.S. at 105. The Court also found the clauses too weak to defeat a long history of comprehensive federal regulation in the field:

> We think it quite unlikely that Congress would use a means so indirect as the savings clauses in Title I of OPA to upset the settled division of authority by allowing states to impose additional unique substantive regulation on the at-sea conduct of vessels. We decline to give broad effect to saving clauses where doing so would upset the careful regulatory scheme established by federal law. Id. at 106.

The logic of *Locke* has found its way into the interpretation of savings clauses that guarantee the continued availability of tort remedies.[17] Savings clauses of that sort are common in environmental statutes and guarantee that those harmed by pollution and other environmental insults may avail themselves of any available state common law remedies.[18] This sort of clause goes toward preventing pollution hot spots by allowing affected parties to bring tort suits to respond to the distributional elements of pollution that may go unconsidered in programs predicated on ensuring environmental quality at regional, state, and national levels.

5. Other environmental preemptions—automobiles and more. Preemption issues have a relatively recent and voluminous history in regard to automobiles. (Air pollution from motor vehicles is addressed in Chapter 11.) It is fairly plain why preemption issues arise in that context. Manufacturers would lose economies of scale if the products they mass-produced for a national market had to meet unique requirements imposed by each state. (This potential consequences of fragmented state-specific regulation was a motivating factor for the automobile industry's support of the Clean Air Act (albeit support for an act with less rigorous requirements for them).) Viewed from a defendant's point of view, preemption is a way to use federal law to trump state or local regulations (or state law to trump local regulations).

Defendants, with varying success, have brought preemption cases to prevent local town governments from passing ordinances requiring stricter standards of herbicide and pesticide applicators,[19] to prevent states from banning potentially harmful fuel additives,[20] and to prevent states from passing hazardous materials cleanup laws.[21]

b. Conflict & Field Occupancy Preemption

Conflict preemption is straightforward—if a state law or regulation conflicts with a validly promulgated federal law or regulation, the state effort is preempted. Cases where it is difficult or impossible to comply with both regulatory commands are easy cases for invalidation of the state enactment. Determining when different or additional state requirements pose a conflict, rather than complementary concurrent regulation, can be difficult, and the methodology used in deciding those cases tends to resemble that of the field occupancy cases. What a court is trying to determine is whether the state enactment hinders or is antagonistic to the federal action that has the force of supremacy behind it.

A fertile ground for field occupancy preemption cases grows out of the late nineteenth-century federal mining acts and the creation of the National Forest system on the federal public lands. It was an era in which Congress established numerous federal resource management programs designed to promote a variety of declared national interests. When states try to regulate the environmental impacts of federal programs and their licensees, thorny preemption issues arise.

---

17. See *Geier v. Am. Honda Motor Co.*, 529 U.S. 861 (2000) (tort remedy would conflict with federal transportation safety regulatory program).

18. See, e.g., 33 U.S.C. §1365(e) (CWA); 42 U.S.C. §7604(e) (CAA).

19. See, e.g., *Wis. Pub. Intervenor v. Mortier*, 501 U.S. 597 (1991).

20. See, e.g., *Oxygenated Fuels Ass'n v. Davis*, 331 F.3d 665 (9th Cir. 2003) (upholding California's ban on fuel additive MTBE against preemption challenge based on CAA).

21. See, e.g., *Boyes v. Shell Oil Prods. Co.*, 199 F.3d 1260 (5th Cir. 2000) (preempting Florida statute prohibiting individual's suit for remediation of property contaminated with petroleum from nearby service stations); *CSX Transp. v. Pub. Util. Comm'n of Ohio*, 901 F.2d 497 (6th Cir. 1990) (preempting most of the state hazardous material transport law).

A. Constitutional Federalism in the U.S.

Generically, these cases most often raise claims that the state law interferes with the accomplishment of federal objectives. In broad terms, the argument goes like this: The federal agency, by licensing the private activity as part of its resource management program, has affirmatively authorized the activity; state laws that bar or burden the activity therefore conflict with federal law. The counterargument rests on the view that federal licenses or permits are not intended to divest states of their traditional police power authority, including environmental quality regulation.

Many of these cases are complicated by the fact that many federal licensing programs include their own environmental standards and reviews. If a federal agency imposes environmentally protective conditions on its licensees, the preemption argument against additional state environmental regulation is strengthened. At that point, the additional state environmental review may be redundant and, more tellingly, inconsistent with federal determination of the proper balance between environmental quality and other national programmatic objectives. In this situation, concurrent state regulation arguably constitutes an interference with the federal program.

In a leading case on this subject, *California v. Federal Energy Regulatory Comm'n (FERC)*, 495 U.S. 490 (1990), a proposed hydroelectric facility on a tributary of the American River in California (Rock Creek) threatened to reduce stream flows in a way that would adversely affect fisheries. FERC, as part of its licensing process and pursuant to congressional directives,[22] reviewed information on these issues and granted the applicant a license that prescribed specified minimum stream flows. FERC's minimum flow standard allowed stream flows to decline to less than a third of the state's proposed minimum requirements. The Supreme Court held that FERC's standards governed. The Court applied and thereby reaffirmed the arguments of *First Iowa Hydro-Elec. Coop. v. FPC*, 328 U.S. 152 (1946), interpreting §27 of the Federal Power Act, which specifically disclaims any congressional aim to "affect[] or intend[] to affect or in any way to interfere with the laws of the respective States relating to the control, appropriation, use, or distribution of water used in irrigation or for municipal or other uses, or any vested right acquired therein." Faced with the seemingly clear intent of Congress to preserve state water regulatory powers, the *First Iowa* decision had narrowed the clause's meaning, holding that its preservation of state jurisdiction is "confined to rights of the same nature as those relating to the use of water in irrigation or for municipal purposes." 328 U.S. at 175-176. With this case as its guide, the Supreme Court held in *California v. FERC* that California could not impose its own more environmentally protective stream flow requirements.[23]

California Coastal Comm'n v. Granite Rock Co., 480 U.S. 572 (1987), presented a similarly subtle preemption problem that resulted in a decision allowing concurrent state regulation. Granite Rock had obtained a permit from the U.S. Forest Service to mine for pharmaceutical grade white limestone in a portion of the Los Padres National Forest near Big Sur

---

22. The Electric Consumers Protection Act of 1986, Pub. L. No. 99-495, codified as part of the Federal Power Act at 16 U.S.C. §§797(e) and 808(a), requires FERC to consider fish and wildlife effects in making its licensure determinations, although in practice the statutory standards are neither substantively nor procedurally rigorous.

23. In *Nugget Hydroelec. Co. v. SWRCB*, Civs-90-0203 EJG/EM (E.D. Cal. July 9, 1991), the preemptive effect of *California v. FERC (Rock Creek)* was extended to divest the California State Water Resource Control Board (SWRCB) of the authority to require the FERC licensee to submit information to the state on issues other than the availability of water. The SWRCB had required Nugget to provide more thorough analyses of the in-stream impacts of its project than those provided to FERC, at which point Nugget withdrew its application for a SWRCB permit and went to federal court seeking a preemption-based order to save it from having to "jump through a never-ending series of hoops [that] relate to matters already reviewed by FERC," adding that "the delay and cost impose a tremendous hardship on plaintiff [Nugget]." The court preempted the SWRCB efforts.

(California). Due to the land's proximity to the Pacific coast, the area was also within the jurisdiction of the California Coastal Commission (CCC), a state agency having extensive land use planning and environmental protection powers. Despite the existence of the federal permit, CCC directed Granite Rock to apply to it for an additional permit, a request that was met with a lawsuit claiming that the CCC's authority had been preempted.

The Supreme Court rejected Granite Rock's argument that the state process was preempted by federal law and required Granite Rock to submit to the state permit proceeding. One key to the ruling lay in the language of the Forest Service regulations, several of which called for federal licensees to comply with applicable state environmental quality standards; one regulation specifically mentioned state permits' usefulness for proving such compliance with state regulations. See 36 C.F.R. §§228.5(b), 228.8(a)–(c), (h).

The licensee's second major contention was that the CCC's actions were a thinly veiled effort to reverse the Forest Service's choices under its land use planning mandate, contained in the NFMA, 16 U.S.C. §§1600-1614. Granite Rock claimed that CCC was trying to prohibit mining in an area that the Forest Service had determined was appropriate for mining. The majority found this challenge speculative; CCC had not acted to impose any conditions or requirements on Granite Rock prior to the filing of the lawsuit.

Justice O'Connor's majority opinion also drew a rather fine semantic distinction between land use planning and environmental protection:

> The [CCC] alleges that it will use its permit requirement to impose reasonable environmental regulation. . . . Federal land use statutes and regulations, while arguably expressing an intent to preempt state land use planning, distinguish environmental regulation from land use planning. 480 U.S. at 593.

COMMENTARY & QUESTIONS

1. The case for finding preemption in *Granite Rock*. *Granite Rock* presents a strong case for displacement of state authority. The parallel state authority that is to be exercised affects lands in federal ownership that are part of the National Forest system and that are being managed under an articulated "multiple use" mandate that establishes federal policies regarding the administration of National Forest tracts. See Chapter 9. To whatever extent the CCC might thwart a federally approved project, there is both an arguable intrusion upon federal government planning and de facto imposition of state land use controls on federal land. These points motivated a dissent by Justice Powell (joined by Justice Stevens) and a dissent by Justice Scalia (joined by Justice White). Even so, a majority of the Court was willing to support concurrent regulatory control as long as there was no concrete conflict of regulations. What can the CCC now impose by way of conditions that would not be in conflict with the Forest Service plan? Would erosion and dust emission control requirements that forced Granite Rock to keep excavated materials covered during mining operations, or a strict post-mining reclamation requirement, be allowed? Does it matter how much compliance with such requirements would cost? What if, for example, the increased cost made the proposed mining project more expensive than other feasible alternative sites?

2. Local expertise and pluralism. What makes concurrent levels of regulatory authority attractive? Concurrency almost surely is less efficient, adding costs for dual filings, studies, and processing and constantly posing opportunities for delay and possibly harassment by project opponents. Does concurrency sustain the traditional view of the states as primary regulators of environmental matters? In an era of massive federal statutory intervention in

A. Constitutional Federalism in the U.S.

the environmental field, it sometimes seems hard to resist the conclusion that Congress and the federal bureaucratic army have become the primary regulatory system. Is local expertise at issue here? Is there any indication that the CCC is better apprised of the environmental consequences of the proposed action than the federal District Ranger? A different justification for concurrency lies in the desire to respect the sovereignty of the states. Making concurrency the norm arguably does not undercut federal authority; it simply places the burden on the federal government to announce its intentions to exercise unilateral control. It may be that the environmental perspective is benefited by concurrency. The theory is that two forums are better than one. The public environmental perspective may receive a more hospitable reception in one place rather than the other, and a potentially destructive project must survive the rigors of both tests.

3. State regulation of the federal public lands. As a historical matter in the public lands area, it is only recently that the Property Clause of the U.S. Constitution has been recognized as supporting active federal management authority over federal lands. Nineteenth-century cases frequently regarded that clause merely as an authority to own on the same basis as any other landholder, i.e., subject to state regulation. For an excellent discussion of this topic and many others relating to the federal public lands, see Cowart & Fairfax, Public Lands Federalism: Judicial Theory and Administrative Reality, 15 Ecology L.Q. 375, 439-476 (1988).

4. Is preemption analysis better applied on a local (site-by-site) or a national (programmatic) level? Consider the following criticism of the *Granite Rock* approach:

> The Court focused on the preemptive effect of the governing federal statutes and nationwide regulations. Some vehicle was needed, it rightly assumed, to avoid giving the states a veto over federal land uses. But the Court could better have addressed the issue by instead considering the preemption of state law at the lowest level—the preemption that occurs when a federal agency at the local level lawfully acts in a way that causes conflict with a state or local law. So long as federal action preempts at that level, preemption at a higher level is unneeded and, in this setting at least, undesirable. From an institutional perspective, preemption at the lowest level can best foster cooperative land planning on the scene. For a variety of reasons, preemption should occur only when a federal agency concludes, in a site-specific determination made in the course of statutory land-planning processes, that a particular federal use should override contrary state and local rules. Freyfogle, *Granite Rock*: Institutional Competence and the State Role in Federal Land Planning, 59 U. Colo. L. Rev. 475, 477 (1988).

What could be the "variety of reasons" for site-by-site preemption to which Professor Freyfogle refers? Would such an approach better respect state sovereignty? Would his approach lead to regulatory uncertainty, thereby increasing costs?

5. Concurrent regulatory programs—vessel regulation as an example. Federal authority over interstate and international commerce and admiralty has generated numerous federal regulatory programs that address vessels, their design, and their operation. At the same time, vessels call at ports throughout the nation, each of which has many local interests that are affected by those vessel operations, which gives rise to state and local regulatory efforts. Sometimes the regulatory impulse is environmental and not merely economic. Oil spill prevention through tanker design regulation is one example, and invasive species prevention through ballast water regulation is another. Arguably, benefits flow from uniformity and the consistency provided by unitary regulation. This is certainly the view of the regulated community, which goes a step further and argues that even in the absence of express preemption, federal regulations in this area ought to enjoy a presumption favoring preemption. The case law is somewhat mixed. As to ship design, where it could be difficult to follow the guidelines of many regulatory masters, the Supreme Court has found conflict preemption of supertanker design.[24] In *U.S. v. Locke*, 529 U.S. 89 (2000), involving the federal PWSA, the Court edged a bit further toward blanket preemption. It noted that there is no presumption of concurrency of state and federal regulation in the maritime arena, but that is not quite the same thing as erecting a presumption in favor of preemption. That last point was important in a decision upholding Michigan state regulation of ballast water to prevent the introduction of invasive species against a preemption claim founded on federal statutes and Coast Guard regulations addressing that same subject.[25] In *American Trucking Assoc. v. City of Los Angeles*, 133 S. Ct. 2096 (2013), the Court struck down as preempted by the Federal Aviation Administration Authorization Act (FAAAA) two city-imposed requirements regulating placards on trucks and off-street parking of trucks serving the city-owned and-operated Port of Los Angeles. This part of the decision was largely unsurprising in light of the statutory language. 49 U.S.C.A. §14501(c)(1) preempts a state "law, regulation, or other provision having the force and effect of law related to a price, route, or service of any motor carrier . . . with respect to the transportation of property." The parties agreed that provision would be preemptive if the manner in which the city imposed its regulation, which was as part of a contract allowing truckers to serve the port, had "the force and effect of law." Justice Kagan writing for the Court had no difficulty finding those provisions did indeed have the force of law because they could be enforced by criminal penalties.

6. State regulation of federal facilities. To what extent can states and local governments apply their environmental regulations to federal facilities in their territories? The question has recurred over the years, as military posts allow toxins to leach into groundwater, federal hospitals violate air pollution standards, federal authorities authorize the construction of mammoth power transmission towers or radio transmission towers in historic zones, and so on. The simplest answer seems to be that the federal action trumps state and local regulations unless the basic federal statute accepts state jurisdiction, or unless the federal government has voluntarily agreed to accommodate state and local restraints.

7. Preemption of local municipal laws. The preemption arguments between federal and state governments often are echoed in cases where local municipal ordinances are challenged as being in violation of state law, even in the face of so-called "Home Rule" provisions that operate in a manner roughly analogous to savings clauses. The case law tends to track the same analysis as federal-state preemption arguments.

2. Dormant Commerce Clause Invalidation of State Law

Preemption cases begin with an affirmative act by Congress or the Executive. Before the states—the traditional full-purpose sovereigns in the U.S. system—can be displaced through preemption, the federal government must use its enumerated powers. That is, the mere fact that the Constitution permits federal action does not alone prevent state action. There is one major exception to this precept as it applies to the interstate commerce power, and it is an exception that has frequent application in the environmental and natural resources area.

One of the important goals of the Constitution was to permit the development of a national economy. A common practice in the late eighteenth century (and thereafter) was for nations to erect a variety of barriers to trade with other nations, be it in the form of

---

24. See *Ray v. Atl. Richfield Co.*, 435 U.S. 151 (1978).
25. See *Fednav, Ltd. v. Chester*, 547 F.3d 607 (6th Cir. 2008). (The *Fednav* case is available in an edited version on the coursebook website as a recent example of a carefully structured conflict and field occupancy preemption case. *Fednav* also addresses the operation of a savings clause in light of the approach taken in *Locke*.

A. Constitutional Federalism in the U.S.

tariffs, prohibitions on the movement of goods of certain types, pilotage requirements, or other like devices. The states, in the pre-constitutional period and to the present, similarly have engaged in trade-restrictive efforts, usually with the aim of protecting local industries from outside competition by laying tariffs, by requiring outside entities to make use of local goods and services, or by ensuring that certain natural resources or other natural advantages remained at home. Even without the passage of federal legislation in furtherance of the interstate and international commerce power, state and local efforts at economic protectionism work at cross purposes to a constitutionally established national policy.

Recognizing that state and local laws burdening interstate commerce are contrary to constitutional policy is one step toward allowing courts to declare such laws unconstitutional. The second step, which is sometimes stated explicitly in judicial opinions, is more pragmatic. Congress cannot be expected to be aware of all such burdensome state and local laws, far less analyze them all and pass judicious legislation permitting some state and local laws to operate and preempting others. Since Congress lacks the time and resources to effectuate the national interest in this vital constitutional sphere, the courts, at the behest of persons adversely affected by the parochial state and local laws, take on the job. The area gets its name because the Commerce Clause, even in its "dormant" state (i.e., without legislation or executive action to effectuate the Commerce Clause) controls cases presented to the courts, which can strike down protectionist state and local laws.

In the courts, the clause has been anything but dormant. State laws that explicitly distinguish between domestic commodities and consumers and out-of-state commodities and consumers are almost invariably struck down. State laws that are facially evenhanded but that burden interstate commerce are subject to a somewhat more complicated test. The state or local law must have a proper public purpose, not an improper one (e.g., like favoring local businesses); its design must be reasonably related to achieving that purpose; and the burden on interstate commerce must not be "excessive" when balanced against the public interests being protected.[26]

The dormant commerce clause has been used to challenge a wide range of state environmental policies, in two general categories:

(1) restrictions on pollution sources and other environmental harms entering the state, from automobiles and toxic consumer products to trash and invasive species; and
(2) restrictions on natural resources and other environmental goods leaving the state, from water and hunted game to renewable energy and technology.

Natural resource cases have been a staple of dormant Commerce Clause jurisprudence for at least a century, beginning with a famous opinion by Justice Oliver Wendell Holmes (since overruled) that allowed Connecticut to restrict the export of wild fowl captured by hunters.[27] The formal doctrine in this area is now fairly well settled and permits states very little latitude in attempting to block the interstate movement of goods and services. That,

---

26. This series of inquiries is similar to those undertaken in determining when a regulatory taking has occurred. See Chapter 21.
27. See *Geer v. Conn.*, 161 U.S. 519 (1896), overruled in *Hughes v. Okla.*, 441 U.S. 322 (1979).

however, has not kept the states from trying, especially in regard to the movement of solid and hazardous waste.

City of Philadelphia v. New Jersey
437 U.S. 617 (U.S. Sup. Ct. 1978)

STEWART, J. A New Jersey law prohibits the importation of most "solid or liquid waste which originated or was collected outside the territorial limits of the State. . . ." In this case we are required to decide whether this statutory prohibition violates the Commerce Clause of the United States Constitution.

The statutory provision in question is Chapter 363 of 1973 N.J. Laws, which took effect in early 1974. In pertinent part it provides:

> No person shall bring into this State any solid or liquid waste which originated or was collected outside the territorial limits of the State, except garbage to be fed to swine in the State of New Jersey, until the commissioner [of the State Department of Environmental Protection] shall determine that such action can be permitted without endangering the public health, safety and welfare and has promulgated regulations permitting and regulating the treatment and disposal of such waste in this State. N.J. Stat. Ann. §13:1I–10.

As authorized by Ch. 363, the Commissioner promulgated regulations permitting four categories of waste to enter the State. Apart from these narrow exceptions, however, New Jersey closed its borders to all waste from other States.

Immediately affected by these developments were the operators of private landfills in New Jersey, and several cities in other States that had agreements with these operators for waste disposal. . . .

Although the Constitution gives Congress the power to regulate commerce among the States, many subjects of potential federal regulation under that power inevitably escape congressional attention "because of their local character and their number and diversity." *S.C. State Highway Dept. v. Barnwell Bros.*, 303 U.S. 177, 185. In the absence of federal legislation, these subjects are open to control by the States so long as they act within the restraints imposed by the Commerce Clause itself. The bounds of these restraints appear nowhere in the words of the Commerce Clause, but have emerged gradually in the decisions of this Court giving effect to its basic purpose. That broad purpose was well expressed by Mr. Justice Jackson in his opinion for the Court in *H.P. Hood & Sons, Inc. v. Du Mond*, 336 U.S. 525, 537-538:

> This principle that our economic unit is the Nation, which alone has the gamut of powers necessary to control of the economy, including the vital power of erecting customs barriers against foreign competition, has as its corollary that the states are not separable economic units. As the Court said in *Baldwin v. Seelig*, 294 U.S. 511, 527, "What is ultimate is the principle that one state in its dealings with another may not place itself in a position of economic isolation."

The opinions of the Court through the years have reflected an alertness to the evils of "economic isolation" and protectionism, while at the same time recognizing that incidental burdens on interstate commerce may be unavoidable when a State legislates to safeguard the health and safety of its people. Thus, where simple economic protectionism is effected by state legislation, a virtually per se rule of invalidity has been erected. The clearest example of such legislation is a law that overtly blocks the flow of interstate commerce at a State's borders. But where other legislative objectives are credibly advanced and there is no patent discrimination against interstate trade, the Court has adopted a much more flexible

A. Constitutional Federalism in the U.S.

approach, the general contours of which were outlined in *Pike v. Bruce Church, Inc.*, 397 U.S. 137, 142:

> Where the statute regulates evenhandedly to effectuate a legitimate local public interest, and its effects on interstate commerce are only incidental, it will be upheld unless the burden imposed on such commerce is clearly excessive in relation to the putative local benefits. . . . If a legitimate local purpose is found, then the question becomes one of degree. And the extent of the burden that will be tolerated will of course depend on the nature of the local interest involved, and on whether it could be promoted as well with a lesser impact on interstate activities. . . .

The crucial inquiry, therefore, must be directed to determining whether Ch. 363 is basically a protectionist measure, or whether it can fairly be viewed as a law directed to legitimate local concerns, with effects upon interstate commerce that are only incidental.

The purpose of Ch. 363 is set out in the statute itself as follows:

> The Legislature finds and determines that . . . the volume of solid and liquid waste continues to rapidly increase, that the treatment and disposal of these wastes continues to pose an even greater threat to the quality of the environment of New Jersey, that the available and appropriate land fill sites within the State are being diminished, that the environment continues to be threatened by the treatment and disposal of waste which originated or was collected outside the State, and that the public health, safety and welfare require that the treatment and disposal within this State of all wastes generated outside of the State be prohibited.

The New Jersey Supreme Court accepted this statement of the state legislature's purpose. The state court additionally found that New Jersey's existing landfill sites will be exhausted within a few years; that to go on using these sites or to develop new ones will take a heavy environmental toll, both from pollution and from loss of scarce open lands; that new techniques to divert waste from landfills to other methods of disposal and resource recovery processes are under development, but that these changes will require time; and finally, that "the extension of the lifespan of existing landfills, resulting from the exclusion of out-of-state waste, may be of crucial importance in preventing further virgin wetlands or other undeveloped lands from being devoted to landfill purposes." Based on these findings, the court concluded that Ch. 363 was designed to protect, not the State's economy, but its environment, and that its substantial benefits outweigh its "slight" burden on interstate commerce.

The appellants strenuously contend that Ch. 363, "while outwardly cloaked 'in the currently fashionable garb of environmental protection,' . . . is actually no more than a legislative effort to suppress competition and stabilize the cost of solid waste disposal for New Jersey residents. . . ." The appellees, on the other hand, deny that Ch. 363 was motivated by financial concerns or economic protectionism. . . .

This dispute about ultimate legislative purpose need not be resolved, because its resolution would not be relevant to the constitutional issue to be decided in this case. Contrary to the evident assumption of the state court and the parties, the evil of protectionism can reside in legislative means as well as legislative ends. Thus, it does not matter whether the ultimate aim of Ch. 363 is to reduce the waste disposal costs of New Jersey residents or to save remaining open lands from pollution, for we assume New Jersey has every right to protect its residents' pocketbooks as well as their environment. And it may be assumed as well that New Jersey may pursue those ends by slowing the flow of all waste into the State's remaining landfills, even though interstate commerce may incidentally be affected. But whatever New Jersey's ultimate purpose, it may not be accomplished by discriminating against articles of commerce coming from outside the State unless there is some reason, apart from their origin, to treat them differently. Both on its face and in its plain effect, Ch. 363 violates this principle of nondiscrimination.

The Court has consistently found parochial legislation of this kind to be constitutionally invalid, whether the ultimate aim of the legislation was to assure a steady supply of milk by erecting barriers to allegedly ruinous outside competition, or to create jobs by keeping industry within the State, or to preserve the State's financial resources from depletion by fencing out indigent immigrants. In each of these cases, a presumably legitimate goal was sought to be achieved by the illegitimate means of isolating the State from the national economy.

Also relevant here are the Court's decisions holding that a State may not accord its own inhabitants a preferred right of access over consumers in other States to natural resources located within its borders. These cases stand for the basic principle that a "State is without power to prevent privately owned articles of trade from being shipped and sold in interstate commerce on the ground that they are required to satisfy local demands or because they are needed by the people of the State." *Foster-Fountain Packing Co. v. Haydel*, 278 U.S. 1, 10.

The New Jersey law at issue in this case falls squarely within the area that the Commerce Clause puts off limits to state regulation. On its face, it imposes on out-of-state commercial interests the full burden of conserving the State's remaining landfill space. It is true that in our previous cases the scarce natural resource was itself the article of commerce, whereas here the scarce resource and the article of commerce are distinct. But that difference is without consequence. In both instances, the State has overtly moved to slow or freeze the flow of commerce for protectionist reasons. It does not matter that the State has shut the article of commerce inside the State in one case and outside the State in the other. What is crucial is the attempt by one State to isolate itself from a problem common to many by erecting a barrier against the movement of interstate trade. . . .

Today, cities in Pennsylvania and New York find it expedient or necessary to send their waste into New Jersey for disposal, and New Jersey claims the right to close its borders to such traffic. Tomorrow, cities in New Jersey may find it expedient or necessary to send their waste into Pennsylvania or New York for disposal, and those States might then claim the right to close their borders. The Commerce Clause will protect New Jersey in the future, just as it protects her neighbors now, from efforts by one State to isolate itself in the stream of interstate commerce from a problem shared by all.

REHNQUIST, J., dissenting. . . . The Court recognizes that States can prohibit the importation of items "'which, on account of their existing condition, would bring in and spread disease, pestilence, and death, such as rags or other substances infected with the germs of yellow fever or the virus of small-pox, or cattle or meat or other provisions that are diseased or decayed, or *otherwise, from their condition and quality, unfit for human use or consumption.*'" *Bowman v. Chicago & Northwestern R. Co.*, 125 U.S. 465, 489 (1888). As the Court points out, such "quarantine laws have not been considered forbidden protectionist measures, *even though they were directed against out-of-state commerce.*" (Emphasis added.)

In my opinion, these cases are dispositive of the present one. Under them, New Jersey may require germ-infected rags or diseased meat to be disposed of as best as possible within the State, but at the same time prohibit the *importation* of such items for disposal at the facilities that are set up within New Jersey for disposal of such material generated *within* the State. The physical fact of life that New Jersey must somehow dispose of its own noxious items does not mean that it must serve as a depository for those of every other State. Similarly, New Jersey should be free under our past precedents to prohibit the importation of solid waste because of the health and safety problems that such waste poses to its citizens.

A. Constitutional Federalism in the U.S.

The fact that New Jersey continues to, and indeed must continue to, dispose of its own solid waste does not mean that New Jersey may not prohibit the importation of even more solid waste into the State. I simply see no way to distinguish solid waste, on the record of this case, from germ-infected rags, diseased meat, and other noxious items. . . .

COMMENTARY & QUESTIONS

1. States try other tacks. Recognizing that simple bans on out-of-state waste were legally doomed, state and local governments became more inventive. One common method was to charge out-of-state operators higher prices for waste disposal than in-state operators. States claimed the differential was justified to offset the costs imposed by the waste, i.e., the potential environmental harms and cost of remediation if the disposal site experienced future problems. Put differently, the higher fees attempted to internalize on out-of-state contributors of waste the costs of long-term waste management that were otherwise likely to be borne by the receiving state and its citizens. In *Chemical Waste Mgmt. v. Hunt*, 504 U.S. 334 (1992), and again in *Oregon Waste Sys. v. Oregon Dep't of Envtl. Quality*, 511 U.S. 93 (1994), differential tipping fees were held unconstitutional. In both instances, the Court treated the regulations as "discriminatory" and therefore prohibited under Philadelphia's virtual per se rule of invalidity. Undeterred, states attempted to erect other barriers to the entry of out-of-state wastes. Michigan, for example, erected a comprehensive statewide waste management system that gave local officials an optional veto power over nonlocal wastes. This was invalidated by the Supreme Court in *Fort Gratiot Sanitary Landfill v. Michigan Dep't of Natural Res.*, 504 U.S. 353 (1992). The Supreme Court quoted *Philadelphia* in stating that, "the evil of protection can reside in the legislative means as well as the legislative ends." 504 U.S. at 360.

2. Criticism of the nondiscrimination principle. Few judges or legal scholars have questioned the Supreme Court's nondiscrimination principle, requiring the almost automatic invalidation of state or local laws that facially discriminate against out-of-state commodities. Here is one dissenting view:

> The nondiscrimination principle serves none of the objectives commonly cited in favor of it—neither economic efficiency, representation reinforcement, nor national unity. . . . Where, as here, the dominant justification for invalidating state and local legislation is that this practice serves important purposes, purposelessness alone would warrant reconsideration of the Court's doctrine. Nonetheless, the nondiscrimination principle is imperiled not only by what it does not achieve, but by what it does: a mandated preference for markets over regulation, where "regulation" is identified by an interference with the market as shaped by common-law entitlements. Thus the nondiscrimination principle is not an unassuming rule designed to rein in outlaw state and local governments, but a *Lochner*-style incursion on their legislative autonomy.
>
> The cases applying the nondiscrimination principle to invalidate the political judgments of state and local governments are not the only examples of the current Court's usurpation of the legislative function. Some have also seen a repetition of *Lochner*'s mistakes in the Court's recent decisions on takings, standing, and the scope of Congressional power under the Commerce Clause. With *Lochner* everywhere, it is perhaps not surprising that it should appear even in such a seemingly mundane and uncontroversial setting as the Court's review of laws that discriminate against interstate commerce. What is more surprising is that its presence there has gone largely unremarked. Heinzerling, The Commercial Constitution, 1995 Sup. Ct. Rev. 217, 275-276.

You may recall from your constitutional law course that in *Lochner*, the Supreme Court invalidated a New York law that set maximum hours for certain workers, concluding that the law conflicted with the right to freedom of contract. The Court has since repudiated the reasoning in *Lochner*, and the decision has become a pariah, symbolizing the worst kind of judicial interference with legislative prerogative.

3. Presumptions of invalidity and congressional authorization of discrimination. An interesting way to characterize the contrast between preemption and dormant Commerce Clause cases is to say that the presumption of concurrency is reversed. In preemption cases, the presumption, applied in most cases, is that the state law is to coexist with the federal interest; in dormant Commerce Clause cases, the presumption is that the state law is to be invalidated if it has an overt, adverse effect on the national interest. In the former case, courts defer to state efforts if there is any basis on which to avoid preemption, and Congress has to step in to alter that outcome if it wishes to do so. In dormant Commerce Clause cases, courts do not defer to state efforts if they discriminate against interstate commerce, and Congress has to step in to alter that outcome if it wishes to do so. Congress occasionally does act to authorize state laws that otherwise would violate the dormant Commerce Clause. The power to do so is inherent in Congress's plenary control over interstate commerce. The authorization claim is occasionally made in environmental dormant Commerce Clause cases but usually fails. See, e.g., *South-Central Timber Dev. Co. v. Wunnicke*, 467 U.S. 82 (1984) (rejecting claim that ban on export of raw timber was authorized by Congress).

4. Evenhanded legislation and legislative purpose. Regulation that is not deemed facially discriminatory against interstate commerce is subjected to the test set forth in the quotation from *Pike v. Bruce Church* that appeared in the Philadelphia case. The purpose of the legislation must be legitimate (in furtherance of local public interest), the burden on interstate commerce must be only "incidental," and the local benefits must outweigh the burdens on commerce. Courts also will inquire whether there is an available alternative that is less burdensome on commerce.

5. The dormant Commerce Clause's balance of burdens. As just noted, even when a state passes the first part of the *Pike* test, the burden on interstate commerce must be weighed against local benefits in a fairly complex calculus that seeks to account for the importance of the local benefit and the extent of the burden on interstate commerce. In *Minnesota v. Clover Leaf Creamery Co.*, 449 U.S. 456 (1981), an attack on state legislation contended that it was prompted by mixed environmental and protectionist motives. The Minnesota statute restricting plastic milk containers arguably favored pulpwood manufacturers (a major Minnesota industry) and disfavored plastics manufacturers (a non-Minnesota industry). The Court found that the statute was not discriminatory and proceeded to measure the burdens on interstate commerce under the *Pike* test, eventually concluding that "even granting that the out-of-state plastics industry is burdened . . . we find that this burden is not 'clearly excessive' in light of the substantial state interest in promoting conservation of energy and other natural resources and easing solid waste disposal problems. . . ." Id. at 473.

6. "A barrier is a barrier is a barrier," or is it sometimes a quarantine? Does it make any difference for dormant Commerce Clause purposes whether *Philadelphia* is an import ban (blocking the import of waste) or an export ban (blocking the export of landfill space)? The simple answer would seem to be no. State efforts to exclude undesirable items and to hoard valuable ones equally interfere with treating the nation as "one economic unit." Even so, the Court in *Philadelphia* was careful to distinguish the situation there from what it viewed as valid state quarantine laws. The Court found the two situations different because quarantine laws "did not discriminate against interstate commerce as such, but simply prevented traffic in noxious articles, whatever their origin." 437 U.S. at 629. The states have not experienced success in limiting waste movement on quarantine theories. In *C&A Carbone*

A. Constitutional Federalism in the U.S.

v. Town of Clarkstown, 511 U.S. 383, 389 (1994), the Supreme Court showed how little it thought of the quarantine theory as applied to solid waste:

> The town says that its ordinance reaches only waste within its jurisdiction and is in practical effect a quarantine: It prevents garbage from entering the stream of interstate commerce until it is made safe. This reasoning is premised, however, on an outdated and mistaken concept of what constitutes interstate commerce.

Carbone, which involved a privately owned waste transfer facility to which all locally generated wastes were required to flow held that "a so-called flow control ordinance, which require[d] all solid waste to be processed at a designated transfer station before leaving the municipality," discriminated against interstate commerce and was invalid under the Commerce Clause because it "depriv[ed] competitors, including out-of-state firms, of access to a local market." 511 U.S. at 386. More recently, on facts that are highly similar to those of *Carbone* but involving a publicly owned transfer facility rather than a privately owned facility, Justice Roberts, writing for a six-member majority, upheld a flow control ordinance that required all locally generated trash to be processed at the local facility. Justice Alito, joined by Justices Stevens and Kennedy, dissented, questioning the importance of that distinction. See *United Haulers Ass'n v. Oneida-Herkimer Solid Waste Mgmt. Auth.*, 550 U.S. 330 (2007).

In regard to quarantines in environmental cases, the Court has upheld only one environmental embargo based on a quarantine theory. *Maine v. Taylor*, 477 U.S. 131 (1986), was exceptional when it was decided and remains so today. The Court upheld a naked import ban on out-of-state seined baitfish, based on very favorable fact-finding that will be difficult to replicate in other cases. The trial court found, and the Supreme Court accepted the finding, that the import ban was necessary to prevent introduction of nonnative parasites into the Maine ecosystem.

7. Insisting on cleaner, leaner garbage. Do *Pike v. Bruce Church* and *Maine v. Taylor* open the door a crack to state laws that have the effect of discriminating against out-of-state interests? Can these "exceptions" to the pattern of invalidation of commerce-restricting state laws be adapted to aid the states in their efforts to enforce differential tipping fees or otherwise disfavor out-of-state waste? There is, of course, very little that distinguishes an in-state pile of garbage from an out-of-state pile of garbage unless something has been done to the in-state garbage that makes it either safer or more economical to manage. Suppose a state, by statute, requires predisposal treatment of waste as a precondition to disposal or as a basis for obtaining a lower tipping fee. Pretreatment could include mandatory recycling (to reduce volume) or segregation of waste streams to eliminate the presence of small-volume hazardous materials such as household batteries and noncommercial volumes of paints and solvents. Are such laws evenhanded? Do they remain evenhanded if the state also makes pretreatment mandatory within its borders? *National Solid Waste Mgmt. Ass'n v. Meyer*, 63 F.3d 652 (7th Cir. 1995), squarely considered a provision requiring mandatory recycling as a precondition to Wisconsin's disposal of solid waste; the court invalidated the provision on a variety of grounds. The key flaw, in the court's view, inhered in the fact that if any waste in an out-of-state community was Wisconsin-bound, all of the waste in that community had to be pretreated to satisfy the Wisconsin law. That amounted to impermissible extraterritorial regulation. The court found the law discriminatory against out-of-state waste haulers "simply because [their waste] comes from a community whose ways are not Wisconsin's ways." 63 F.3d at 662. Finally, even under a nondiscriminatory *Pike* analysis, the court found that Wisconsin had available to it less burdensome alternatives, such as having nonrecycled out-of-state wastes subject to disposal after first being taken to a recycling facility.

8. The "market participant" exception. In a resource hoarding case, *Reeves Inc. v. Stake*, 447 U.S. 429 (1980), the Supreme Court held that a state-owned and -operated cement factory could discriminate in favor of in-state customers during a time of regional cement shortages. What about a state being a market participant is different from a state regulating that same market? Cost is one obvious factor: The state may decide to "spend" its money by providing subsidized cement to its citizens. Nothing in the dormant Commerce Clause bars a state from spending money it collects for the benefit of its citizens, even if that "spending" takes the form of subsidizing their waste disposal activities. In *Swin Res. Sys. v. Lycoming County, Pa.*, 883 F.2d 245 (3d Cir. 1989), cert. denied, 493 U.S. 1077 (1990), a 2-1 majority applied the *Reeves* precedent to the local preference of a county-operated landfill.

3. Limitations on Federal Power

In the same way that the Constitution prescribes enforceable limitations on state authority, it also imposes limits on federal authority. The limitations arise in two quite different ways. The first involve arguments that the federal action is not supported by the enumerated power on which it is claimed to rest. In the environmental field, and in several others, the power that most often forms the basis for federal action is the commerce power. In this book, that subject is viewed primarily in materials in Chapter 12 regarding the jurisdictional reach of the CWA's wetlands program. Second, the Constitution, in the Tenth and Eleventh Amendments, includes language preserving state authority and limiting of federal authority. On relatively rare occasions, the Court has applied those provisions to limit the federal power in the environmental area. The Tenth Amendment is discussed briefly below and is more fully considered in materials appearing on the book's website. The Eleventh Amendment, which imposes a complex and arcane limitation on federal judicial power to grant monetary relief against state governments, is largely peripheral to the study of environmental law.

The Tenth Amendment, in relevant part, declares that "powers not delegated to the United States by the Constitution, nor prohibited by it to the States, are reserved to the States respectively, or to the people." There has long been debate as to whether the Tenth Amendment alters, in any way, the power relation between the states and the federal government established by the grants of power to the federal government, the Necessary and Proper Clause, and Supremacy Clause. The claim made for giving the Tenth Amendment some bite in the matter of federal-state relations is that somehow the amendment erects an area of state sovereignty, immune from federal encroachment.

The conventional wisdom and the vast majority of cases reject that claim. The rejection is captured in a phrase, often repeated in cases raising the issue: "[The Tenth Amendment] states but a truism that all is retained [by the states or the people] which has not been surrendered [to the federal government]."*U.S. v. Darby*, 312 U.S. 100, 124 (1941). The "truism" confirms federal supremacy (within the sphere of the federal government's enumerated powers) and the abdication of a reciprocal degree of state sovereignty on nationhood, but notes the fact that the remainder of state sovereignty was unaffected.

Nevertheless, the idea of state sovereignty is an important one in the federal system. There has been one environmental case in which the Supreme Court has been willing to restrict the federal government's encroachment on the states, even when the federal government is pursuing national objectives that are within its sphere of constitutional competence. In *N.Y. v. U.S.*, 505 U.S. 144 (1992), a federal statute required states that did not conform with a federal program for the disposal of low-level radioactive wastes to "take title" to any such wastes in their state, which would have obligated the affected states to find a

A. Constitutional Federalism in the U.S.

legal method for disposing of the wastes. That, in turn, would probably have resulted in the states overcoming the NIMBY phenomenon, which had prevented the creation of sufficient capacity for the safe disposal of that type of waste. The Court's majority found that requiring specific conduct by state officials was not permissible under the Tenth Amendment.

Much more typically, federal environmental mandates that impact the states and their regulatory programs are upheld. A leading example of this is *Hodel v. Va. Surface Mining & Reclamation Ass'n*, 452 U.S. 264, 288 (1981). In *Hodel*, the Court upheld the Surface Mining Control and Reclamation Act of 1977 against a Tenth Amendment challenge. In that case the federal statute set standards that the states must follow, but the federal law did not "commandeer"[28] the states into regulating mining. The Court found that "the States are not compelled to enforce the steep-slope standards, to expend any state funds, or to participate in the federal regulatory program in any manner whatsoever. If a State does not wish to submit a proposed permanent program that complies with the Act and implementing regulations, the full regulatory burden will be borne by the Federal Government."

4. Concurrent Authority and Cooperative Federalism

The preceding sections have focused primarily on ways in which inter-sovereign conflicts or questions of sovereign authority in environmental disputes are resolved pursuant to the division of authority established by the U.S. Constitution. That focus tends to obscure the far larger category of modern regulatory cases where, by design, the federal government and the states regulate environmental matters concurrently, often harmoniously sharing regulatory authority.

Since at least the 1970s, concurrency of state and federal authority is the norm in environmental matters. The state police power and its role in protecting public health, safety, and welfare, areas that encompass environmental matters, is as old as the nation itself. As the preemption materials indicate, that state power is very seldom displaced entirely by federal action. Similarly, the common law, a staple of state authority, is almost never displaced by environmental statutes, whether enacted by the federal government or by the states themselves.

As described in Chapter 5, the form and degree of federal involvement in environmental matters changed radically around 1970. Until then, most federal environmental programs were intended to support state and local regulation by providing funds for such things as sewage treatment facilities and by undertaking critical but costly scientific research that was best done on a national scale. That role changed in response to public pressure for federal action when citizens became aware of the declining quality of their state-regulated environments.

---

28. The Court has employed the martial metaphor in this area. In a dissent in a public utility regulation case where the federal law favored co-generation and imposed terms that would constrict state activity, Justice O'Connor stated:

> I agree with the Court that the Commerce Clause supported Congress' enactment of the Public Utility Regulatory Policies Act of 1978 (PURPA). I disagree, however, with much of the Court's Tenth Amendment analysis. Titles I and III of PURPA conscript state utility commissions into the national bureaucratic army. This result is contrary to the principles of *National League of Cities v. Usery*, 426 U.S. 833 (1976), antithetical to the values of federalism, and inconsistent with our constitutional history. *FERC v. Miss.*, 456 U.S. 742, 775 (1982).

National League of Cities, a Tenth Amendment case, was overruled by *Garcia v. San Antonio Metro. Transit Auth.*, 469 U.S. 528 (1985), but the issue of the outer limit of federal power remains contested.

The federal government's power to regulate environment and public health was well-established by the 1970s. In responding to the public outcry for more effective environmental regulation, however, Congress remained acutely aware of traditional state prerogatives in the field, and also knew that implementing such a vast regulatory effort needed more personnel and local expertise than the federal government could bring to bear. The resulting programs embraced shared state and federal responsibility, in a combination that is usually referred to as "cooperative federalism."[29] In the major pollution control laws covering the three principal media—air (CAA), water (CWA), and land (RCRA)—the form of cooperative federalism employed follows a similar pattern.

Under these and some other environmental laws, the federal government sets standards for environmental and public health protection, establishes the form that the regulatory systems will have, and pushes states to take primacy in implementing their programs. States are offered the incentive of monetary grants (which have shrunk over the years); if these fail to sufficiently motivate, the federal government pressures states into taking primacy by threatening to operate the regulatory programs itself, thus affecting the states' industries and constituents and creating a very bitter pill for states to swallow. Once primacy is granted to the states, the federal government, usually through EPA, oversees state decisions to ensure that the state is implementing and enforcing the federal standards. Those statutes also expressly authorize the states to use state law to erect environmental protections that are even more stringent than those required by the federal program. The federal government also serves in an arbitral role when state actions under these environmental laws have extraterritorial impacts that may adversely affect sister states.

COMMENTARY & QUESTIONS

1. The federal hammer in "state primacy" cooperative federalism. The threat of a federal takeover may induce the states to accept primacy, but the real force behind these statutes is the Supremacy Clause. That overriding authority allows the federal government to set uniform national standards, limit the race of laxity, and overcome the political imbalance between locally important firms and industries and state regulators that doomed many state pollution control efforts before the federal statutes came into force.

2. Cooperative federalism is not always comfortable or universally effective. There are numerous possible points of friction in the dominant type of environmental cooperative federalism. Initially, the states may believe the federal standards are not appropriate to

---

29. The imprecision of that term has grown considerably. For example, Hope Babcock identifies three distinct varieties of cooperative federalism:

> The first is the "dual regulation" or "state primacy" model, under which states are administratively delegated regulatory primacy to enforce federal laws through existing state laws and institutions. The second is the "collaborative management" or "consensus-based" model, under which a joint federal, multi-state institution is created for the sole purpose of developing consensus derived plans that will be used by the various jurisdictions to manage federal designated natural resources. The final model is the "layered federalism" or "consistency" model, under which individual states develop and administer natural resource management plans with which proposed federal activities must be consistent.

Babcock, Dual Regulation, Collaborative Management, or Layered Federalism: Can Cooperative Federalism Models from Other Laws Save Our Public Lands?, 14 Hastings W.-Nw. J. Envtl. L. & Pol'y 449, 461 (2008). The version of cooperative federalism most prevalent in environmental regulation is the "dual regulation or "state primacy" form.

their situation. More pointedly, the federal oversight and potential rejection of state actions where states have taken primacy is an obvious bone of contention. See, e.g., *Alaska Dep't of Envtl. Conservation v. EPA*, 540 U.S. 461 (2004) (EPA rejection of a state PSD permit based on rejection of state's selection of a particular technology as BACT for that installation). States can, and frequently do, evade the federal commands by underenforcement, inaction, and other forms of passive resistance. EPA lacks sufficient resources to actively superintend its myriad responsibilities and must rely heavily of the states' good faith efforts to comply with the federal program. Enforcement issues and remedies for underenforcement and nonenforcement are considered in Chapter 18.

B. INTEGRATING INTERNATIONAL AGREEMENTS INTO DOMESTIC LAW

> The United States is primarily a dualist system, in which the international and domestic legal orders do not intersect except through the operation of some mechanism linking the two. Binding international agreements, whose parties are states, operate as the legal equivalent of a contract or compact in the international legal order, making law for the states that are parties to them. Treaties have binding effect on the domestic level as well, typically with the legal force of a statute.

As anyone who has skimmed a newspaper, surfed the Internet, or turned on the television in the last decade and a half knows, we are living in a world that is rapidly globalizing. Greater interconnectedness in a worldwide marketplace benefits businesses and consumers by increasing access to goods. But it also contributes to a wider spread of environmentally harmful "bads," including invasive species, pollution from the transportation of products over great distances, unwitting importation of contaminated food, and the migration of industry to jurisdictions with less stringent environmental policies.

Realizing the benefits of international economic activity requires coordinated action among the countries of the planet. But unlike our domestic system, on the international level there is no multilateral legislature with the power to make rules, no global police power to enforce rules that do exist, and no court with comprehensive jurisdiction to compel performance by individuals or private entities. The international legal and political system consequently presents unusual challenges to crafting and implementing environmental law and policy.

These impediments nonetheless must be addressed, not ignored. There is now a critical need for international cooperation to combat the increasingly lengthy list of environmental hazards that threaten the future of the planet, including:

- global warming from the greenhouse effect, which threatens the habitability of the planet over the remainder of this century;
- depletion of the stratospheric ozone layer, which protects life on Earth from harmful levels of ultraviolet radiation;
- wholesale conversion of productive land in developing countries to desert;
- global dispersion of pollutants that threaten human health and reproduction;
- acid rain, which endangers lakes and forests in North America, Europe, and other continents;
- and many more, some likely yet to be discovered.

Environmental problems like these, truly global in scope, demand a global response. No single country can prevent catastrophe by itself. Nor are individual countries likely to find it in their national self-interest to act alone unless they are confident that others will act in accordance with a coordinated plan. These global hazards cry out for legal structures and institutions that respond effectively to the next generation of environmental challenges threatening us in the new century.

Although environmental awareness is relatively new to international politics, there has long been interaction and cooperation among the nations of the world. Since the mid-seventeenth century, international law—very different from domestic or national law—has evolved to govern and mold these relationships. The principal actors in this system are typically referred to in international jurisprudence as "states"—not the constituent states of the U.S., but sovereign nations or countries. Coequal sovereign states are both the primary and the highest legal authority in the international legal order, with no international legislature or court of general jurisdiction superior to that of the state. A legal structure in which independent states not only make the law, but also interpret and apply it to themselves and each other, requires legal approaches different from those found in most municipal legal systems.

We now live in a legal world in which international norms play an increasing role, not just in the rarefied realm of international relations, but increasingly in domestic law and litigation as well. The call to "think globally, but act locally" presents a challenge for environmental lawyers, who must develop a toolbox for transferring global expectations into domestic law and vice versa. International and domestic law can influence each other in complex ways, often reinforcing each other but sometimes conflicting. A U.S. environmental lawyer therefore needs to be familiar not only with the operation of statutes and regulations adopted by domestic legislatures and agencies, but also with international agreements that the U.S. concludes with other states.

This section analyzes how the U.S. legal system applies international agreements on the environment by addressing several issues of pressing current importance—safeguards for migratory birds, international cooperation to save whales, and conflicts with trade agreements. As part of that analysis, we canvass a variety of legal instruments until recently rarely thought to concern domestic lawyers—bilateral and multilateral treaties, executive agreements, and congressional-executive agreements. These issues are as broad as the planet, and the policy tools for tackling them are gateways to international legal concepts of increasing sophistication and burgeoning importance to environmental law in the twenty-first century.

1. Shared Natural Resources: Bilateral Treaties

An international agreement is nothing more than a contractual deal between sovereign states. Like most contracting parties, states expect to be better off as a result of the deal, even when reaching agreement has required them to compromise on goals based on their self-interest alone. Political scientists often speak of international treaties as designed to overcome "collective action problems" in which states that are unlikely to take action by themselves are willing to do so in collaboration with others. In the environmental field, for example, arguments are often made against costly unilateral action to control pollution on the theory that competitive disadvantages will result. If, by contrast, two states, all the countries in a region, or the entire international community make pollution control investments on the same schedule, then competitive distortions are reduced or eliminated.

By negotiating an international agreement, states can establish rules governing each other's behavior, much as parties to a private contract can memorialize the terms of a deal in writing. Also in much the same manner as a contract, the rules contained in an

B. International Agreements in Domestic Law

agreement between states are legally binding on the states that are party to it and enforceable under international law.[30] To carry the private contract analogy even further, one often speaks of a treaty as establishing a flow of rights and obligations. Important differences, of course, exist between private contracts and international agreements. For example, there is no court of general jurisdiction in the international legal system, which means that in the event of a dispute or breach, no neutral third-party tribunal automatically has the authority to adjudicate the controversy. In many important respects, however, principles of contract law carry over in a form that readily applies to treaties.

a. Migratory Birds in North America

Natural resources that span the borders between states, including migratory animals and lakes and rivers that straddle or cross an international border, have long been appreciated as ready candidates for international environmental cooperation. Natural watersheds and patterns of air flow occupy ecological zones that do not necessarily correspond to the arbitrary political boundaries drawn by human hands and may require coordinated action by more than one state for their protection. One state's lackadaisical policies with respect to a shared natural resource can adversely affect or even destroy the benefits provided by the resource to the other, whether economic, ecological, or aesthetic.

The U.S. has made treaties to protect one kind of shared resource, migratory birds, with a variety of countries, including Mexico (1936), Japan (1972), and Russia (1976). All these pacts are modeled on a 1916 convention (a somewhat lofty term for *treaty*) on migratory birds with Canada, on whose behalf the agreement was concluded by Great Britain. Consistent with standard international practice, the text of the Convention for the Protection of Migratory Birds was agreed upon between the U.S. representative, Robert Lansing, Secretary of State of the U.S., and the British negotiator, Cecil Spring Rice, the British Ambassador to the U.S., in Washington on August 16, 1916. The two men certified the terms and authenticity of the text they had settled upon by signing it, very much as they might a private contract.

An editorial from the *New York Times* of September 2, 1916, praises the agreement as "the first of its kind ever negotiated by the United States. . . . This shows commendable progress in a movement that is distinctly for the benefit of the American people." The piece is surprisingly contemporary in identifying the need for the agreement and its approach to addressing the problems of migratory birds:

> The chief purpose of . . . the treaty . . . is to save from extinction the migratory game birds, whose number has been reduced by more than one-half in the last forty years, and to protect those birds which help the farmer by eating the insects that prey upon his crops. . . . It has been estimated by the Department of Agriculture that the American farmer's annual loss which is due to insects exceeds $800,000,000. Protection is given by the law and the treaty to the insectivorous birds whose presence in the fields tends to prevent a part of this loss. They aid the farmer, and thus are friends of the consumer. . . .

Notwithstanding the Convention, the fate of migratory birds continues to be a serious environmental concern. According to the Defenders of Wildlife, nearly 80% of the 313 species considered "at risk" in Canada either migrate or range across the U.S.-Canada border.

---

30. While international agreements are a principal source of international law, particularly from the point of view of its domestic relevance, international law operates in a number of other settings as well, as discussed in Chapter 22.

The content of the 1916 migratory bird treaty with Canada is remarkably modern in tone. The introductory preamble voices concern for "species . . . of great value as a source of food or in destroying insects which are injurious to forests and forage plants . . . [and] agricultural crops . . . but nevertheless are in danger of extermination through lack of adequate protection during the nesting season or while on their way to and from their breeding grounds." The agreement establishes certain dates for closed seasons on migratory birds, prohibits the taking of nests or eggs of migratory birds, prohibits hunting insect-eating birds, and allows the two governments to issue special permits authorizing the killing of migratory birds that have been determined to be harmful to agriculture.

From the point of view of domestic law, however, the agreement has substantial gaps. Hunters and poachers were expected to inflict most of the harm to migratory birds. The agreement does not spell out the form of domestic implementation, which could differ substantially in the U.S. and Canada; nor does it deal with domestic matters that are neither part of the international agreement nor of any concern to the other treaty partner.

As is common in such situations, the U.S. Congress in 1918 adopted the Migratory Bird Treaty Act (MBTA), 16 U.S.C. §§703-711, as "implementing legislation" to give domestic life to the convention with Canada. The MBTA defines the offenses of taking, killing, and possessing migratory birds. The Act makes violation of the statute a federal crime and in certain cases a felony. Traps and other equipment may be confiscated by the Department of the Interior, whose agents are given the authority to make warrantless arrests to prevent a violation in progress. As domestic legislation, the MBTA is among the more powerful tools available for the protection of wildlife in the U.S.

b. The Constitutional Law of Treaty Formation

As a matter of domestic U.S. law, only the President, as head of the executive branch, has the authority to negotiate international agreements. In practice, this means that negotiations are conducted on behalf of the U.S. by the Department of State—the Cabinet department that represents U.S. interests abroad and serves as a conduit for communications from foreign governments—together with other executive branch agencies that may have an interest in the subject matter. Article II, §2, of the Constitution confirms that the President "shall have Power . . . to make Treaties. . . ." That same section also limits the President's power, specifying that treaties must be adopted "by and with the Advice and Consent of the Senate . . . provided two thirds of the Senators present concur. . . ."

The Framers purposely divided treaty power between the President and the Senate, in part because the treaty-making process reverses the usual roles for the President and the Congress. Instead of Congress's adopting legislation subject to the President's approval, as for a statute, the President as treaty negotiator holds the pen as the drafter of new law. The President—or, in practice, executive branch agencies as represented by the State Department—negotiates the treaty for the U.S. and then presents it as a concluded agreement to the Senate for its subsequent advice and consent prior to ratification. The President may then ratify the agreement, perfecting the obligations in it.[31] At this point,

---

31. The President, and only the President, may ratify a treaty on behalf of the U.S. Even though frequently encountered, the statement that "the Senate ratifies treaties" is consequently incorrect. Occasionally, the Senate gives its advice and consent, but the President nonetheless withholds ratification. The Basel Convention on the Control of Transboundary Movements of Hazardous Wastes and Their Disposal is one such example in which the Executive refrained from ratifying due to the lack of implementing legislation and active opposition from industry.

B. International Agreements in Domestic Law

and only at this point, does the treaty become binding as a matter of both international and domestic law.

From the point of view of the effective and efficient conduct of foreign relations, it is sensible to give an authoritative President the capacity to deal confidently and free of domestic discord to foreign powers, some of which may be hostile. The Framers had also experienced the unsatisfactory precedent of the Articles of Confederation, under which Congress had done a poor job of handling foreign relations. If, however, a treaty could take effect without Congress's participation, the President, in effect, could make domestic law through his power to negotiate treaties with no checks and balances. The Framers consequently specified that treaties would take effect for the U.S. only after the subsequent confirmation or "ratification" of their terms. The requirement for a supermajority of two-thirds in the Senate in theory assures that the President strikes deals that are responsive to the interests of the states and the public. The process of ratification based on domestic legal processes was also well understood in international practice at the time, so the Constitution meshes smoothly with international law as well.

Consistent with the U.S. Constitution, Article IX of the migratory bird treaty with Canada states that the signatures on the text are provisional only, subject to subsequent ratification. The Senate gave its advice and consent to ratification by a two-thirds vote on August 29, 1916, and the President ratified the agreement on September 1. Great Britain ratified the Convention for Canada on October 20, and the parties exchanged instruments of ratification (documents perfecting the obligations in the agreement) on December 7. As specified in the agreement, the contractual rights and obligations of the two treaty partners became effective— "entered into force"— as of that date.

Any treaty, including an environmental pact, has domestic legal effect similar to a federal statute. An international agreement fully ratified by the federal government is both binding under international law and, like federal legislation, operates as "the supreme Law of the Land" through the Supremacy Clause of the Constitution. The "federalization" of policy on migratory birds, however, ran counter to U.S. tradition, in which the regulation of hunting has been generally thought to be a matter of state and local concern. The legal effect of the migratory bird convention with Canada was challenged in the following famous case, arguably the most important Supreme Court decision on the domestic legal effect not just of environmental agreements, but of treaties on any subject matter. (You might at this point also note the map of intercontinental bird migration routes, Figure 1 which appears later in this Chapter.)

Missouri v. Holland

252 U.S. 416 (U.S. Sup. Ct. 1920)

HOLMES, J., delivered the opinion of the Court. This is a bill in equity brought by the State of Missouri to prevent a game warden of the United States [Holland] from attempting to enforce the Migratory Bird Treaty Act of July 3, 1918, 40 Stat. 755, and the regulations made by the Secretary of Agriculture in pursuance of the same. The ground of the bill is that the statute is an unconstitutional interference with the rights reserved to the States by the Tenth Amendment, and that the acts of the defendant done and threatened under that authority invade the sovereign right of the State and contravene its will manifested in statutes. . . . A motion to dismiss was sustained by the District Court on the ground that the Act of Congress is constitutional. . . . The State appeals.

On December 8, 1916, a treaty between the United States and Great Britain was proclaimed by the President. It recited that many species of birds in their annual migrations traversed many parts of the United States and of Canada, that they were of great value as a source of food and in destroying insects injurious to vegetation, but were in danger of extermination through lack of adequate protection. It therefore provided for specified closed seasons and protection in other forms, and agreed that the two powers would take or propose to their lawmaking bodies the necessary measures for carrying the treaty out. 39 Stat. 1702. The above mentioned act of July 3, 1918, [intended] to give effect to the convention, prohibited the killing, capturing or selling any of the migratory birds included in the terms of the treaty except as permitted by regulations compatible with those terms, to be made by the Secretary of Agriculture. Regulations were proclaimed on July 31, and October 25, 1918. It is unnecessary to go into any details, because, as we have said, the question raised is the general one whether the treaty and statute are void as an interference with the rights reserved to the States.

To answer this question it is not enough to refer to the Tenth Amendment, reserving the powers not delegated to the United States, because by Article 2, §2, the power to make treaties is delegated expressly, and by Article 6 treaties made under the authority of the United States, along with the Constitution and laws of the United States made in pursuance thereof, are declared the supreme law of the land. If the treaty is valid there can be no dispute about the validity of the statute under Article 1, §8, as a necessary and proper means to execute the powers of the Government. The language of the Constitution as to the supremacy of treaties being general, the question before us is narrowed to an inquiry into the ground upon which the present supposed exception is placed.

It is said that a treaty cannot be valid if it infringes the Constitution, that there are limits, therefore, to the treaty-making power, and that one such limit is that what an act of Congress could not do unaided, in derogation of the powers reserved to the States, a treaty cannot do. An earlier act of Congress that attempted by itself and not in pursuance of a treaty to regulate the killing of migratory birds within the States had been held bad in the District Court. *U.S. v. Shauver*, 214 Fed. 154. *U.S. v. McCullagh*, 221 Fed. 288. Those decisions were supported by arguments that migratory birds were owned by the States in their sovereign capacity for the benefit of their people, and that under cases like *Geer v. Connecticut*, 161 U.S. 519, this control was one that Congress had no power to displace. The same argument is supposed to apply now with equal force.

Whether the two cases cited were decided rightly or not they cannot be accepted as a test of the treaty power. Acts of Congress are the supreme law of the land only when made in pursuance of the Constitution, while treaties are declared to be so when made under the authority of the United States. It is open to question whether the authority of the United States means more than the formal acts prescribed to make the convention. We do not mean to imply that there are no qualifications to the treaty-making power; but they must be ascertained in a different way. It is obvious that there may be matters of the sharpest exigency for the national well being that an act of Congress could not deal with but that a treaty followed by such an act could, and it is not lightly to be assumed that, in matters requiring national action, "a power which must belong to and somewhere reside in every civilized government" is not to be found. . . . When we are dealing with words that also are a constituent act, like the Constitution of the United States, we must realize that they have called into life a being the development of which could not have been foreseen completely by the most gifted of its begetters. It was enough for them to realize or to hope that they had created an organism; it has taken a century and has cost their successors much sweat and blood to prove that they created a nation. The case before us must be considered in the light of our whole experience and not merely in that of what was said a hundred years ago. The treaty in question does not contravene any prohibitory words to be found in the Constitution. The only question is whether it is forbidden by some invisible radiation from the general terms of the Tenth Amendment. We must consider what this country has become in deciding what that amendment has reserved. . . .

Here a national interest of very nearly the first magnitude is involved. It can be protected only by national action in concert with that of another power. The subject matter is only transitorily within the State and has no permanent habitat therein. But for the treaty and the statute there soon might be no birds for any powers to deal with. We see nothing in the Constitution that compels the Government to sit by while a food supply is cut off and the protectors of our forests and our crops are destroyed. It is not sufficient to rely upon the States. The reliance is vain, and were it otherwise, the question is whether the United States is forbidden to act. We are of opinion that the treaty and statute must be upheld.

COMMENTARY & QUESTIONS

1. Migratory birds and states' rights. *Missouri v. Holland* continues to be controversial because of its strong suggestion that the federal government can supersede state prerogatives through the treaty power when an identical statute would unconstitutionally exceed Congress's power to preempt state law through legislation. In other words, *Missouri v. Holland* means that the President, with a two-thirds vote of the Senate, can cut a deal with a foreign government that represents an unconstitutional intrusion on the reserved powers of the states if attempted by legislation enacted by Congress. If so, the case raises the possibility that the President need merely find a willing foreign power as a pretext for disrupting domestic principles of federalism. The magnitude of the controversy is a little difficult for us in the modern era to appreciate, since nowadays the MBTA likely would be widely regarded as a valid exercise of congressional authority under the Commerce Clause. Recent Commerce Clause cases including *Lopez v. U.S.*, however, in which the Supreme Court has curtailed Congress's constitutional authority to supersede state law, might indicate a greater federal need for the doctrine of *Missouri v. Holland* in the future.

2. Avoiding a "flap" with Canada: Are wild geese a matter of national security? If both treaties and domestic statutes must operate within constitutional limits, what justification is there for distinguishing between the reach of these two forms of lawmaking? What other, perhaps somewhat more compelling, situations might Justice Holmes have in mind when he states, "here a national interest of very nearly the first magnitude is involved"? Are wild geese really that important? Suppose the case had come out the other way—that is, holding that the federal government did *not* have the power to enter into the Convention with Canada. What adverse consequences might there be for national security? What unusual difficulties might courts encounter in reviewing the treaty to determine whether it exceeds constitutional limits? Who should decide this question, and what standards should courts apply in addressing it? Are the benefits to national security from Justice Holmes's position worth the potential interference with the domestic legal order of the 50 states?

Under the doctrine of the "supremacy of international law," even if the Supreme Court were to hold that the Convention with Canada exceeded the treaty power under the Constitution, that agreement would still remain in force as a matter of international law. How does this doctrine affect the outcomes available to Justice Holmes? What unpleasant political and legal consequences could you imagine if the Court were to hold for the State of Missouri and conclude that the agreement exceeded constitutional limits? How would you expect Canada to react? If you are the President, what does that scenario imply to you in terms of practical, real-world dealings with Canada and other foreign powers?

3. The long-range impact of migratory birds. In the early 1950s, Senator Bricker of Ohio proposed a constitutional amendment to overrule the preemptive effect of *Missouri v. Holland* on state law. A floor vote in the Senate in February 1954 on a version of the Bricker Amendment was 60 to 31 in favor of the amendment, one vote shy of the two-thirds requirement in Article V of the Constitution. Although the Bricker Amendment was never adopted, the federal government has tended to avoid preempting state law through treaties as a policy matter where possible. Is the doctrine of *Missouri v. Holland* environment-friendly or hostile to goals of environmental protection? As a Senator opposed to the Bricker Amendment, how would you argue that the Bricker Amendment is either unnecessary or a bad idea?

2: Protecting the Global Commons: Multilateral Treaties & Executive Agreements

Why do we think of shared natural resources such as boundary waters or migratory species, as well as shared "bads" in the form of pollution, as international issues? The physical entity concerned—water, an animal, or a pollutant—is either localized on the boundary between countries or moves across that boundary. While a bilateral or regional approach is helpful in dealing with many problems that are geographically localized, environmental threats to areas beyond national jurisdiction, such as the high seas, or those that are truly global in nature present additional challenges.

International law has addressed marine resources from the beginning. Every international lawyer knows the name of Grotius, often described as the "father of international law," who vigorously advocated freedom of the seas.[32] Inherent in the notion of the high seas is the existence of an area beyond the national jurisdiction of any state, the first global commons. Difficulties in managing the resources of the high seas stem not only from the law but also from the physical reality that many marine resources require common management schemes for effective conservation. The alternative all too often is rapacious overexploitation. As Garrett Hardin wrote, "the oceans of the world continue to suffer from the survival of the philosophy of the commons. Maritime nations still respond automatically to the shibboleth of the 'freedom of the seas.' Professing to believe in the 'inexhaustible resources of the oceans,' they bring species after species of fish and whales closer to extinction."[33]

The international law of the sea, framed in terms of rights and obligations of states, poorly reflects the need for collective action to conserve marine biological resources. States nevertheless have evolved a number of mechanisms to overcome collective action problems of the sort described by Hardin, principal among them the multilateral treaty. Unlike the U.S.-Canada migratory bird treaty, multilateral agreements may have numerous parties. In addressing global commons issues, typically every state on the planet is eligible to become party, in which case the agreement is said to be "universal." In principle, a multilateral treaty consists of a huge number of bilateral relationships among the various parties, with a flow of rights and obligations among them. In practice, however, multilateral agreements

---

32. See generally H. Grotius, The Freedom of the Seas (*Mare Liberum*) (J. Brown Scott ed. & R. van Deman Margoffin trans., 1916) (1633).
33. Hardin, The Tragedy of the Commons, 162 Science 1243, 1245 (1968).

B. International Agreements in Domestic Law

tend to have much more of a legislative character, establishing norms of expected behavior for the parties that agreed to be bound by them.

Despite their undoubted utility, multilateral treaties present their own impediments to efficacious management of shared or common resources. Multilateral treaties are similar to the bilateral U.S.-Canada migratory bird treaty in terms of formalities such as signature and ratification. Most multilateral agreements have formal procedures for signature of the text as a preliminary indication of an intent to be bound, followed by subsequent ratification that perfects the obligations for a particular party. But treaty negotiations with a large number of participants risk delay or collapse. Treaties by definition apply only to those states that indicate their affirmative intent to be bound by those obligations, a system that often rewards free riders, holdouts, scofflaws, and laggards. In contrast to lawmaking techniques in many municipal legal systems, the texts of multilateral treaties are ordinarily adopted by consensus, meaning unanimity. Even after acquiescing in the agreement's adoption, any state may decline to be bound by most multilateral agreements merely by withholding approval in a subsequent domestic ratification process. International treaty-making characterized by these multiple junctures at which the consent of states is necessary can produce disappointingly diluted, "least common denominator" obligations determined by the more reluctant, rather than the more ambitious, participants.

Entry into force for a multilateral treaty tends to be somewhat more complex than in a bilateral situation. Consistent with a contractual theory of treaties, a treaty must have a minimum of two parties. While Zen Buddhism might entertain the possibility of the sound of one hand clapping, under international law there is no such thing as a treaty with only one party. Many multilateral treaties establish a higher threshold, usually phrased as a number of ratifications that serve as a "trigger" or condition precedent for entry into force. While not a legal necessity, the policy motivation for relatively rigorous numerical conditions for entry into force is often strong. States entering into potentially costly obligations may well be prepared to accept those constraints only if potential treaty partners do the same, particularly when the potential for competitive disadvantage is strong. On the other hand, raising the bar for entry into force may increase the time lag until the required critical mass of ratifications is obtained, an effect sometimes known as the "slowest boat" phenomenon.

a. Multilateral Treaties to Prevent the Tragedy of the Commons: Saving the Whales

Preservation of whales is a classic tragedy of the commons. It is probably in the best interests of all to prevent the extinction of whales, but because every market participant can make short-term profit by ignoring long-term resource destruction, and none trusts the others to forebear, the resource is exploited in a downward spiral. In the case of many endangered species, moreover, the rarer the remaining individuals, the higher the unit price that is likely to be offered for them, which only accelerates the extinction.

The International Convention for the Regulation of Whaling, originally crafted as a vehicle for divvying up the global pie in whales as a resource, over time has metamorphosed into the principal international instrument for protecting these unique creatures. The Convention was adopted on December 2, 1946, in Washington. The Senate subsequently gave its advice and consent to ratification on July 2, 1947. The U.S. was consequently one of the initial parties to the Convention when it entered into force on November 10, 1948. The Convention created a subsidiary body, the International Whaling Commission (IWC). The IWC has the power to set limits on the harvesting of various whale species. In 1982, the Commission established a zero quota for commercial whaling, effectively prohibiting it altogether.

The following case in the International Court of Justice concerns an interpretation of Article VIII, paragraph 1, an exception to the zero commercial whaling quota which allows a state party to the Convention to "grant to any of its nationals a special permit authorizing that national to kill, take, and treat whales for purposes of scientific research . . ." This exception for "scientific" whaling has been controversial, as a potential vehicle for allowing what is effectively a resumption of some commercial whaling under the guise of scientific research. The case, initiated by Australia with New Zealand intervening, challenges the second phase of Japan's program, known as "JARPA II," to allow lethal "sampling" of fin, humpback, and minke whales in the Southern Ocean Sanctuary,

Whaling in the Antarctic

Australia v. Japan, New Zealand intervening
2014 I.C.J. 148

127. [T]he Court . . . finds that the JARPA II activities involving the lethal sampling of whales can broadly be characterized as "scientific research." There is no need therefore, in the context of this case, to examine generally the concept of "scientific research". Accordingly, the Court's examination of the evidence with respect to JARPA II will focus on whether the killing, taking and treating of whales in pursuance of JARPA II is *for purposes of* scientific research and thus may be authorized by special permits granted under Article VIII, paragraph 1, of the Convention. To this end and in light of the applicable standard of review . . . , the Court will examine whether the design and implementation of JARPA II are reasonable in relation to achieving the programme's stated research objectives. . . .

144. The Court concludes that the papers to which Japan directed it reveal little analysis of the feasibility of using non-lethal methods to achieve the JARPA II research objectives. Nor do they point to consideration of the possibility of making more extensive use of non-lethal methods in order to reduce or eliminate the need for lethal sampling, either when JARPA II was proposed or in subsequent years. Given the expanded use of lethal methods in JARPA II, as compared to JARPA, this is difficult to reconcile with Japan's obligation to give due regard to IWC resolutions and Guidelines and its statement that JARPA II uses lethal methods only to the extent necessary to meet its scientific objectives. In addition, the 2007 paper to which Japan refers the Court suggests a preference for lethal sampling because it provides a source of funding to offset the cost of the research. . . .

156. These weaknesses in Japan's explanation for the decision to proceed with the JARPA II sample sizes prior to the final review of JARPA lend support to the view that those sample sizes and the launch date for JARPA II were not driven by strictly scientific considerations. These weaknesses also give weight to the contrary theory advanced by Australia —that Japan's priority was to maintain whaling operations without any pause, just as it had done previously by commencing JARPA in the first year after the commercial whaling moratorium had come into effect for it.

157. [T]he Court turns next to the evidence regarding the way that Japan determined the specific target sample sizes for each of the three species in JARPA II. . . .

172. In considering these contentions by the Parties, the Court reiterates that it does not seek here to pass judgment on the scientific merit of the JARPA II objectives and that the activities of JARPA II can broadly be characterized as "scientific research." . . . With regard to the setting of sample sizes, the Court is also not in a position to conclude whether a particular value for a given variable (e.g., the research period or rate of change to detect) has scientific advantages over another. Rather, the Court seeks here only to evaluate whether

the evidence supports a conclusion that the sample sizes are reasonable in relation to achieving JARPA II's stated objectives. . . .

181. The Court finds that the JARPA II Research Plan overall provides only limited information regarding the basis for the decisions used to calculate the fin and humpback whale sample size. These sample sizes were set using a 12-year period, despite the fact that a shorter six-year period is used to set the minke whale sample size and that JARPA II is to be reviewed after each six-year research phase. Based on Japan's own calculations, the sample sizes for fin and humpback whales are too small to produce statistically useful results. These shortcomings . . . , in addition to the problem specific to the decision to take fin whales . . . , are important to the Court's assessment of whether the overall design of JARPA II is reasonable in relation to the programme's objectives, because Japan connects the minke whale sample size . . . to the ecosystem research and multi-species competition objectives that, in turn, are premised on the lethal sampling of fin and humpback whales. . . .

198. Taken together, the evidence relating to the minke whale sample size, like the evidence for the fin and humpback whale sample sizes, provides scant analysis and justification for the underlying decisions that generate the overall sample size. For the Court, this raises further concerns about whether the design of JARPA II is reasonable in relation to achieving its stated objectives. These concerns must also be considered in light of the implementation of JARPA II, which the Court turns to in the next section. . . .

212. Japan's continued reliance on the first two JARPA II objectives to justify the target sample sizes, despite the discrepancy between the actual take and those targets, coupled with its statement that JARPA II can obtain meaningful scientific results based on the far more limited actual take, cast further doubt on the characterization of JARPA II as a programme for purposes of scientific research. This evidence suggests that the target sample sizes are larger than are reasonable in relation to achieving JARPA II's stated objectives. The fact that the actual take of fin and humpback whales is largely, if not entirely, a function of political and logistical considerations, further weakens the purported relationship between JARPA II's research objectives and the specific sample size targets for each species —in particular, the decision to engage in the lethal sampling of minke whales on a relatively large scale. . . .

219. The Court notes that the Research Plan uses a six-year period to obtain statistically useful information for minke whales and a 12-year period for the other two species, and that it can be expected that the main scientific output of JARPA II would follow these periods. . . . Japan points to only two peer-reviewed papers that have resulted from JARPA II to date. These papers do not relate to the JARPA II objectives and rely on data collected from respectively seven and two minke whales caught during the JARPA II feasibility study. While Japan also refers to three presentations made at scientific symposia and to eight papers it has submitted to the Scientific Committee, six of the latter are JARPA II cruise reports, one of the two remaining papers is an evaluation of the JARPA II feasibility study and the other relates to the programme's non-lethal photo identification of blue whales. In light of the fact that JARPA II has been going on since 2005 and has involved the killing of about 3,600 minke whales, the scientific output to date appears limited.

222. The Court notes that . . . some further evidence of co-operation between JARPA II and other domestic and international research institutions could have been expected in light of the programme's focus on the Antarctic ecosystem and environmental changes in the region.

223. In light of the standard of review set forth above . . . , and having considered the evidence with regard to the design and implementation of JARPA II and the arguments of the Parties, it is now for the Court to conclude whether the killing, taking and treating of whales under the special permits granted in connection with JARPA II is "for purposes of scientific research" under Article VIII of the Convention.

224. The Court finds that the use of lethal sampling per se is not unreasonable in relation to the research objectives of JARPA II. However, as compared to JARPA, the scale of lethal sampling in JARPA II is far more extensive with regard to Antarctic minke whales, and the programme includes the lethal sampling of two additional whale species. Japan states that this expansion is required by the new research objectives of JARPA II, in particular, the objectives relating to ecosystem research and the construction of a model of multi-species competition. In the view of the Court, however, the target sample sizes in JARPA II are not reasonable in relation to achieving the programme's objectives. . . .

227. Taken as a whole, the Court considers that JARPA II involves activities that can broadly be characterized as scientific research . . . , but that the evidence does not establish that the programme's design and implementation are reasonable in relation to achieving its stated objectives. The Court concludes that the special permits granted by Japan for the killing, taking and treating of whales in connection with JARPA II are not "for purposes of scientific research" pursuant to Article VIII, paragraph 1, of the Convention. . . .

247. For these reasons,

THE COURT, . . .

By twelve votes to four,

Finds that the special permits granted by Japan in connection with JARPA II do not fall within the provisions of Article VIII, paragraph 1, of the International Convention for the Regulation of Whaling; [and] . . .

By twelve votes to four,

Decides that Japan shall revoke any extant authorization, permit or licence granted in relation to JARPA II, and refrain from granting any further permits in pursuance of that programme.

COMMENTARY & QUESTIONS

1. Judicial review of questions of science in international tribunals. The International Court of Justice (ICJ) in the *Antarctic Whaling* case was charged with direct review of determinations of a sovereign state, Japan, on questions of policy-relevant science. This is reminiscent of the analogous question in the domestic federal law of judicial review that is considered in Chapter 6. Unlike federal courts in the United States, the ICJ has no Administrative Procedure Act or analogous jurisprudence on which to rely in crafting an appropriate standard of review. How does the Court address this issue? What questions does it ask, and what does it refrain from asking? Why? The ICJ does not ordinarily hear testimonial evidence, but instead has to rely on the "facts"—including scientific evidence—presented to it by the parties to the dispute. For the reliance on scientific information in this case, see, e.g., Guillame Gros, The ICJ's Handling of Science in the Whaling in the Antarctic Case: A Whale of a Case? 6 J. Int'l Dispute Settlement 578 (2015). The ICJ shares this dilemma with many other international organizations, including in particular WTO dispute settlement panels and its Appellate Body. More on this topic is available in Chapter 22.

2. Any effect from the ICJ's ruling? One knowledgeable commentator has suggested that "the ICJ ruling represents little more than a temporary setback for Japan . . . Japan's whaling will continue much as before." Clapham, Japan's Whaling Following the International Court of Justice Ruling: Brave New World—Or Business as Usual?, 51 Marine Pol'y 238 (2015). How can that be consistent with the ICJ's opinion? At first blush, the opinion and the Court's findings and decisions read like a prohibition on continued whaling. As Legal Adviser to the Japanese foreign minister, can you suggest an alternative reading of the opinion, and an interpretation that might allow Japan legally to resume scientific whaling?

3. Long-term impacts of the *Japan Whaling* case. The ICJ, the "World Court," is more correctly understood as an arbitral body—that is, it exercises jurisdiction over "contentious" cases such as this one only with the consent of the parties to the dispute. This case was initiated by Japan under the so-called "compulsory" jurisdiction of the International Court, according to which any state may make a declaration accepting the court's jurisdiction broadly and prospectively, without necessarily taking into account the nature of the particular dispute. Apparently in response to the Court's judgment in the Antarctic Whaling case, Japan in October 2015 amended its declaration to exclude "any dispute arising out of, concerning, or relating to research on, or conservation, management or exploitation of, living resources of the sea." The United States and France withdrew their consent to the Court's "compulsory" jurisdiction over high-profile disputes over Nicaragua and nuclear testing in the South Pacific, respectively. What does this mean for the future of international arbitration? Should international tribunals avoid controversial judgments in difficult cases in the interest of maintaining their longer-term institutional integrity?

b. Executive Agreements: Tensions with Statutory Mandates

> Article II §2 of the Constitution requires the advice and consent of the Senate, by a two-thirds majority, to the President's ratification of concluded international agreements. But upwards of 90% of the internationally binding agreements concluded by the United States are done without Senate or any other Congressional participation as "executive agreements." An executive agreement requires legal authority in the form of: (1) congressional legislation; (2) an Article II, §2 treaty; or (3) the President's own constitutional powers.

Like the process of drafting multilateral treaties, most international institutions, whose members are states as represented by their governments, operate by consensus, which in practice means unanimity. This is a practical principle of international relations not required by international law, whose purpose is to encourage a high degree of buy-in by states, which are sovereign authorities subject to no higher legal order. One consequence of the "rule" of consensus is that any one state with sufficient motivation or enough political clout can block or impede the entire process. The Whaling Convention is one of the few international instruments that incorporate non-consensus processes, specifically in the adoption of the IWC's all-important catch limitations or quotas. After a specified "opt-out" period, those actions then become binding on all states that have not objected to them.

As a result of concern for enforcement of the IWC's quotas, the United States enacted domestic legislation to buttress the Whaling Convention and to enhance the international momentum for compliance. The Pelly and Packwood Amendments, federal statutory requirements, reinforce the Whaling Convention on the domestic level by requiring the Secretary of Commerce to monitor the whaling activities of foreign nationals and to investigate potential violations of the Whaling Convention. Upon completion of this investigation, the Secretary must promptly decide whether to certify conduct by foreign nationals that "diminishes the effectiveness" of the Whaling Convention. After certification by the Secretary, the Packwood Amendment directs the Secretary of State to reduce the offending nation's fishing allocation within the U.S. fishery conservation zone by at least 50%. This unilateral strategy relies on a more vigorous domestic statutory framework that emphasizes negative disincentives or punishments for violations of IWC quotas, even if the offending state has opted out of them.

In 1981, the IWC established a zero quota for harvests of sperm whales. During the next year, the Commission ordered a five-year moratorium on commercial whaling to begin in the 1985-1986 season and to continue until 1990. Japan "opted out" of the moratorium by filing timely objections that effectively relieved it, as an international legal matter, from compliance with the sperm whale quotas for 1982 through 1984. Nonetheless, the potential sanction under the Pelly and Packwood Amendments by the U.S. threatened Japanese whaling for the 1984-1985 season. In response to this situation, the executive branch concluded an executive agreement with Japan, which entered into force without Senate advice and consent, in which that country agreed to abide by the spirit but not the letter of multilaterally agreed whaling quotas, implementing the international prohibitions on a more protracted schedule than contemplated by the IWC. Japan agreed to catch no more than 400 sperm whales in each of the 1984 and 1985 seasons and to stop commercial whaling by 1988, three years after the date specified by the IWC. The U.S. in return promised that it would not impose its domestic statutory sanctions so long as Japan was adhering to the executive agreement, regardless of Japan's violation of the IWC quotas. Several environmental organizations brought suit to compel the Secretary of Commerce to certify Japan.

The crucial point in this scenario is that the agreement with Japan was concluded with no express congressional participation and, in particular, without Senate advice and consent by a two-thirds majority. Not every international agreement concluded by the U.S. receives Senate advice and consent under Article II, §2, of the Constitution. Notwithstanding the constitutional requirement for Senate advice and consent to ratification, fewer than 10% of international agreements are ever submitted to the Senate.[34] These instruments, done unilaterally by the executive branch, are known as "executive agreements." Although the text of the Constitution makes no reference to such a possibility, the practice of concluding some international agreements without Senate approval has been accepted since soon after the adoption of the Constitution.

International law makes no distinction among domestic processes for implementation of international compacts, all of which are binding and enforceable under international law. Foreign relations lawyers for this reason generally prefer the term *international agreements* when referring to all agreements governed by international law, reserving the term *treaty* to describe the subset that are submitted to the Senate. The term *executive agreement* has purely domestic significance and does not affect the instrument's status in international law.

Circumventing Senate advice and consent and eliminating the possibility for delay or rejection might have substantial appeal from a political point of view. An environmentally conscious President, having negotiated an international agreement, would see his policies implemented immediately, arguably to the benefit of the environment. For example, the U.S. failed to become a party to the Kyoto Protocol on global warming (discussed in Chapters 14 and 22), negotiated and signed by the Clinton Administration, for lack of Senate advice and consent. The UN Convention on Biological Diversity, adopted in 1992 and signed by the Clinton Administration in 1993, has languished in the Senate ever since.

---

34. From 1939 through 2013, the United States concluded about 17,300 executive agreements, by contrast with approximately 1100 treaties in the constitutional sense. Michael John Garcia, Cong. Research Serv., International Law and Agreements: The Effect Upon U.S. Law 5 (2014). *See also* Wirth, "The International and Domestic Law of Climate Change: A Binding International Agreement Without the Senate or Congress?" 39 Harv. Envtl L. Rev. 515 (2015).

B. International Agreements in Domestic Law

Despite their expediency, executive agreements—which on the domestic level are similar to executive orders issued by the President without congressional approval—can raise substantial legal questions. The Constitution directs the President to "take Care that the Laws be faithfully *executed*," while reserving "all legislative powers" to the Congress. Starting from the proposition that every action of the President must be supported by some domestic legal authority, the black letter rule is that executive agreements must find legal support in: (1) statutes enacted by Congress; (2) an Article II, §2, treaty, which has the same force as a statute thanks to Senate advice and consent; or (3) the President's own constitutional powers. See Restatement of the Foreign Relations Law of the U.S. §303 (1987). In environmental matters typically governed by detailed statutory schemes, the first of these options is the most likely.

The test for choosing the form of an international agreement—known as the choice of instrument problem—is whether there is legal authority for the agreement absent Senate advice and consent to ratification. While legal considerations play a role in this decision, political factors also come into play. Congress does not always explicitly authorize the Executive to enter into international agreements. The executive branch also enters into some executive agreements that rely on existing statutory authority but are neither expressly authorized by statute nor approved by the Congress after the fact. In situations like the executive agreement with Japan on whaling, the authority to enter into the agreement with a foreign power is implied and the obligations in any resulting agreement may not exceed the statutory boundaries. As a structural matter, the President is in the driver's seat, controlling the decision whether to submit an agreement to the Senate and consequently the form of the agreement.

The dispute that arose over the agreement with Japan on whales is a volatile mix of an Article II treaty, an executive agreement, and a domestic statute, each expressing differing and sometimes competing policies for protecting endangered whales. As you read the opinion, think about how the executive agreement's relationship to the statute would be described (a) by the plaintiffs, an organization dedicated to preserving whales; and (b) by the executive branch, the defendant in the case.

Japan Whaling Association v. American Cetacean Society
478 U.S. 221 (U.S. Sup. Ct. 1986)

WHITE, J. The issue before us is whether, in the circumstances of these cases, either the Pelly or Packwood Amendment required the Secretary to certify Japan for refusing to abide by the IWC whaling quotas. We have concluded that certification was not necessary and hence reject the Court of Appeals' holding and respondents' submission that certification is mandatory whenever a country exceeds its allowable take under the ICRW Schedule.

Under the Packwood Amendment, certification is neither permitted nor required until the Secretary makes a determination that nationals of a foreign country "are conducting fishing operations or engaging in trade or taking which diminishes the effectiveness" of the ICRW. It is clear that the Secretary must promptly make the certification decision, but the statute does not define the words "diminish the effectiveness of" or specify the factors that the Secretary should consider in making the decision entrusted to him alone. Specifically, it does not state that certification must be forthcoming whenever a country does not abide by IWC Schedules, and the Secretary did not understand or interpret the language of the Amendment to require him to do so. Had Congress intended otherwise, it would have been a simple matter to say that the Secretary must certify deliberate taking of whales in excess of IWC limits. . . .

The Secretary, of course, may not act contrary to the will of Congress when exercised within the bounds of the Constitution. If Congress has directly spoken to the precise issue in question, if the intent of Congress is clear, that is the end of the matter. *Chevron U.S.A. Inc. v. Natural Res. Defense Council, Inc.*, 467 U.S. 837, 843 (1984). But as the courts below and respondents concede, the statutory language itself contains no direction to the Secretary automatically and regardless of the circumstances to certify a nation that fails to conform to the IWC whaling Schedule. The language of the Pelly and Packwood Amendments might reasonably be construed in this manner, but the Secretary's construction that there are circumstances in which certification may be withheld, despite departures from the Schedules and without violating his duty, is also a reasonable construction of the language used in both Amendments. We do not understand the Secretary to be urging that he has carte blanche discretion to ignore and do nothing about whaling in excess of IWC Schedules. He does not argue, for example, that he could refuse to certify for any reason not connected with the aims and conservation goals of the Convention, or refuse to certify deliberate flouting of schedules by members who have failed to object to a particular schedule. But insofar as the plain language of the Amendments is concerned, the Secretary is not forbidden to refuse to certify for the reasons given in these cases. Furthermore, if a statute is silent or ambiguous with respect to the question at issue, our long-standing practice is to defer to the "executive department's construction of a statutory scheme it is entrusted to administer," *Chevron*, unless the legislative history of the enactment shows with sufficient clarity that the agency construction is contrary to the will of Congress.

Contrary to the Court of Appeals' and respondents' views, we find nothing in the legislative history of either Amendment that addresses the nature of the Secretary's duty and requires him to certify every departure from the IWC's scheduled limits on whaling. . . . The discussion on the floor of the House by Congressman Pelly and other supporters of the Amendment . . . demonstrates that Congress' primary concern in enacting the Pelly Amendment was to stave off the possible extermination of both the Atlantic salmon as well as the extinction of other heavily fished species, such as whales, regulated by international fishery conservation programs. 117 Cong. Rec. 34752-34754 (1971) (remarks of Reps. Pelly, Wylie, Clausen, and Hogan). The comments of Senator Stevens, acting Chairman of the reporting Senate Committee and the only speaker on the bill during the Senate debate, were to the same effect. See id., at 47054 (if countries continue indiscriminately to fish on the high seas, salmon may become extinct). Testimony given during congressional hearings on the Pelly Amendment also supports the conclusion that Congress had no intention to require the Secretary to certify every departure from the limits set by an international conservation program. . . .

Enactment of the Packwood Amendment did not negate the Secretary's view that he is not required to certify every failure to abide by IWC's whaling limits. There were hearings on the proposal but no Committee Reports. It was enacted as a floor amendment. It is clear enough, however, that it was designed to remove executive discretion in imposing sanctions once certification had been made—as Senator Packwood put it, "to put real economic teeth into our whale conservation efforts," by requiring the Secretary of State to impose severe economic sanctions until the transgression is rectified. 125 Cong. Rec. 21742 (1979). But Congress specifically retained the identical certification standard of the Pelly Amendment, which requires a determination by the Secretary that the whaling operations at issue diminish the effectiveness of the ICRW. 16 U.S.C. §1821(e)(2)(A)(i). See 125 Cong. Rec. 21743 (1979) (remarks of Sen. Magnuson); id., at 22083 (remarks of Rep. Breaux);

B. International Agreements in Domestic Law

id., at 22084 (remarks of Rep. Oberstar). We find no specific indication in this history that henceforth the certification standard would require the Secretary to certify each and every departure from IWC's whaling Schedules. . . .

We conclude that the Secretary's construction of the statutes neither contradicted the language of either Amendment, nor frustrated congressional intent. See *Chevron*, 467 U.S., at 842-843. In enacting these Amendments, Congress' primary goal was to protect and conserve whales and other endangered species. The Secretary furthered this objective by entering into the agreement with Japan, calling for that nation's acceptance of the worldwide moratorium on commercial whaling and the withdrawal of its objection to the IWC zero sperm whale quota, in exchange for a transition period of limited additional whaling. Given the lack of any express direction to the Secretary that he must certify a nation whose whale harvest exceeds an IWC quota, the Secretary reasonably could conclude, as he has, that, "a cessation of all Japanese commercial whaling activities would contribute more to the effectiveness of the IWC and its conservation program than any other single development."

We conclude, therefore, that the Secretary's decision to secure the certainty of Japan's future compliance with the IWC's program through the 1984 executive agreement, rather than rely on the possibility that certification and imposition of economic sanctions would produce the same or better result, is a reasonable construction of the Pelly and Packwood Amendments. Congress granted the Secretary the authority to determine whether a foreign nation's whaling in excess of quotas diminishes the effectiveness of the IWC, and we find no reason to impose a mandatory obligation upon the Secretary to certify that every quota violation necessarily fails that standard. Accordingly, the judgment of the Court of Appeals is reversed.

MARSHALL, J., with whom **BRENNAN, BLACKMUN,** and **REHNQUIST, JJ.**, join, dissenting. . . . I would affirm the judgment below on the ground that the Secretary has exceeded his authority by using his power of certification, not as a means for identifying serious whaling violations, but as a means for evading the constraints of the Packwood Amendment. Even focusing, as the Court does, upon the distinct question whether the statute prevents the Secretary from determining that the effectiveness of a conservation program is not diminished by a substantial transgression of whaling quotas, I find the Court's conclusion utterly unsupported. I am troubled that this Court is empowering an officer of the executive branch, sworn to uphold and defend the laws of the U.S., to ignore Congress' pointed response to a question long pondered: "whether Leviathan can long endure so wide a chase, and so remorseless a havoc; whether he must not at last be exterminated from the waters, and the last whale, like the last man, smoke his last pipe, and then himself evaporate in the final puff." H. Melville, Moby Dick 436 (Signet ed. 1961).

COMMENTARY & QUESTIONS

1. Unilateral action versus multilateralism. The Pelly and Packwood Amendments are examples of unilateral domestic law measures taken to reinforce and fill gaps in the multilateral Whaling Convention. In response to failures of political will and structural barriers to the effective preservation of common resources like whales, environmental groups have advocated unilateral self-help to create incentives for more effective international cooperation. These unilateral measures generally identify a juncture at which governmental action by one state leverages performance by another. One sometimes hears the criticism that these unilateral measures are "inconsistent with multilateralism"—in other words, that a state like the U.S. should seek action from international bodies like the IWC and refrain from resorting to the international version of vigilantism. Are the Pelly and Packwood Amendments just an example of the U.S. throwing its weight around under a cloak of global altruism? Under what circumstances might such unilateral actions be appropriate? Necessary? Inappropriate? Remember that Japan had no international legal obligation to refrain from taking whales.

2. Executive branch scare tactics. Because international law makes no distinction between a treaty in the constitutional sense and an executive agreement like the one challenged in this case, the agreement with Japan would remain binding as an international legal matter regardless of the outcome—an unusual twist on the frequent perception that international instruments have less legal force than domestic statutes. In a case like *Japan Whaling* challenging the legality of an executive agreement, the executive branch—the defendant in the case—will often expressly or impliedly raise the specter of judicial disruption of foreign affairs. If the conservation organization plaintiff were to win, the U.S. would still be obliged to refrain from sanctioning Japan, while at the same time the Executive would be subject to a judicial order directing it to impose sanctions. Arguments about the lack of judicial competence in foreign affairs and the constitutional separation of powers in which the President is the sole voice of the nation in foreign relations are often tossed in for good measure. Based on the extraordinarily low number of cases in which courts have held executive agreements to lack domestic legal authority, these arguments are quite a powerful weapon in discouraging judicial intervention. At the same time, recall that the President makes the choice of form as between a treaty and an executive agreement, and judicial deference to that choice undoubtedly invites executive abuse. If the President had chosen to submit the bilateral agreement with Japan to the Senate for its advice and consent, there would have been no dispute because the Senate's action would have provided the necessary legal authority. On behalf of the plaintiff conservation organization, how would you respond to the government's argument? Why do you think the deal with Japan was concluded as an executive agreement and not a treaty in the constitutional sense? Suppose the Court had held for the conservation organization and declined to give legal effect to the agreement with Japan. What response would you expect from the Japanese government?

3. Lessons for Congress. As a member of Congress, would you view the result in *Japan Whaling*, in which the Court seemed to interpret the statutory mandates in light of unilateral executive branch action, as constructive engagement with the needs of Japan, or as a disingenuous sell-out of environmental values? The texts of the Pelly and Packwood Amendments specifically tie those enactments to the multilateral Whaling Convention, suggesting that Congress not only meant what it said but also clearly said what it meant. If you were a member of Congress, or advising one, how would you frame amendments to Pelly and Packwood that would prevent the problem encountered in *Japan Whaling* from arising in the future? What actions short of adoption of new legislation could Congress take to alter the outcome? In actuality, only Senator Packwood of the 535 members of Congress took the trouble to object to the bilateral agreement.

3. International Trade Agreements: The Trade and Environment Problem

As long ago as the early nineteenth century, the British economist David Ricardo, reacting to the prevalent mercantilist and colonialist views of the time, hypothesized that countries that reciprocally open their borders to foreign trade will inevitably be better off than countries that impede or prohibit trade. Ricardo observed that free trade in goods (not to be confused with trading of emissions allowances discussed in Chapter 14)

B. International Agreements in Domestic Law

encourages specialization and global economic efficiency, both of which benefit the public. The Ricardo theory of comparative advantage is alive and well today in modern trade agreements, including the General Agreement on Tariffs and Trade (GATT),[35] the agreement creating the World Trade Organization (WTO),[36] the North American Free Trade Agreement (NAFTA),[37] and the recently-concluded Trans-Pacific Partnership (TPP).[38]

a. Multilateral Agreements on Trade: The WTO

The obligations in international trade agreements—including the GATT, WTO agreements, and NAFTA—are basically ones of nondiscrimination and are expressed legally in three principal ways. The first of the basic obligations or "disciplines" found in international trade agreements is the requirement for most favored nation (MFN) treatment. For countries that have MFN status with the U.S., the U.S. has promised to not treat those countries' goods differently from the goods of other MFN nations. So, if the U.S. is carrying on trade relations with the fictional countries of Fredonia and Ruritania, and both have MFN status, the U.S. is obliged to treat Ruritania no less well than it treats Fredonia, and vice versa. The second principal discipline—the national treatment obligation—requires treatment of imported products no less well than similar, domestically manufactured products. If the U.S. imports widgets from Fredonia, it must treat the imported Fredonian widgets no less well than it treats the domestically manufactured widgets.

The national treatment requirement, taken together with the MFN obligation, results in a kind of Equal Protection Clause for goods in international trade. A third discipline, the prohibition on quantitative restrictions, can be thought of as a corollary to the national treatment obligation. If a country does not have restrictions on the quantity of a certain product that can be produced domestically, it cannot place numerical limits on imported versions of that product. Collectively, these three nondiscrimination obligations operate something like the dormant Commerce Clause under the U.S. Constitution, which restricts the capacity of a state to regulate in ways that interfere with interstate trade within the U.S.

International trade agreements in legal form are similar to multilateral environmental agreements, but the dynamics of the negotiating process are quite different. Assume both Ruritania and Fredonia have trade barriers of whatever kind—tariffs, embargoes, regulations—that impede the free movement of goods between the two countries. Neither of them acting on its own is likely to lower those trade barriers, a classic collective action problem. Ricardo teaches that if Ruritania and Fredonia collaborate by promising to reduce their trade barriers reciprocally, those states and the public in both countries will all be better off. Each side agrees to reduce its trade barriers in return for a promise from the other side to lower its obstacles to trade. Large multilateral trade agreements, including the WTO suite of agreements, are somewhat more complicated, but in principle have a similar structure.

The obligations in these reciprocal trade agreements are significant for a state's economic well-being. If Ruritania agrees to lower its trade barriers in return for similar promises from Fredonia, Fredonia has a legitimate expectation that Ruritania will perform on those obligations. The possibility that Ruritania might not perform raises the need to craft

---

35. General Agreement on Tariffs and Trade, Oct. 30, 1947, 61 Stat. (5), (6), T.I.A.S. No. 1700, 55 U.N.T.S. 194, 4 General Agreement on Tariffs and Trade, Basic Instruments and Selected Documents (1969).
36. Agreement Establishing the World Trade Organization, Apr. 15, 1994, 33 I.L.M. 1144.
37. North American Free Trade Agreement, Dec. 8, 11, 14 & 17, 1992, U.S.-Can.-Mex., 32 I.L.M. 296, 612.
38. For details on this agreement, see https://ustr.gov/trade-agreements/free-trade-agreements/trans-pacific-partnership/tpp-full-text.

effective means for settling disputes in some binding third party process like a court proceeding. In response to this concern, the GATT eventually created a dispute settlement mechanism in which complaints can be forwarded to a panel of three experts, typically trade specialists, for a hearing. One of the principal innovations in the WTO in 1995 was to strengthen dispute settlement procedures by creating a standing Appellate Body, consisting of seven members.

b. Domestic Implementation of International Trade Agreements: Congressional-Executive Agreements

From a constitutional perspective, even the phrase *international trade agreement* presents something of a conundrum. The Constitution divides authority over international trade between Congress and the President. Under Article I, §8, of the Constitution, Congress has the exclusive power to regulate international trade (e.g., by prohibiting importation, placing fees (tariffs) on foreign goods, or allowing importation only under certain circumstances). But without the power to negotiate with other states to overcome the collective action problems that characterize international trade, Congress is poorly positioned to engage in international bargains. Article II, §2, of the Constitution gives the President the exclusive authority to conduct foreign relations and to make treaties, but the President does not have the unilateral power to legislate. So, in the usual case, the President negotiates an international agreement and then presents it to the Senate for its advice and consent to ratification by a two-thirds majority as specified in the Constitution.

From the point of view of international trade policy, there are significant problems with this approach. First, the Senate can use the ratification process to alter the terms of the agreement. Since most trade agreements reduce or eliminate protectionist trade barriers such as tariffs and subsidies, it is well nigh inevitable that some provisions will negatively affect industries or other constituencies that benefit from these trade barriers; these pejoratively dubbed *protectionists* are likely to object to their removal. The result is a high probability that a trade agreement may be subject to significant revision in the Senate. A second criticism of the Article II, §2, treaty approach is that it leaves out the House of Representatives, which ordinarily would have a say in legislation affecting trade.

To remedy these difficulties, the Executive and legislative branches have crafted an innovation called a *congressional-executive agreement*, which is the form in which trade agreements have been adopted since 1974. Congress, exercising its Article I, §8, powers, authorizes the President, by prior statute, to negotiate an international trade agreement on general terms, provided that the agreement not enter into force until Congress adopts subsequent implementing legislation. The President carries out the negotiations, brings home an agreement, and then presents the agreement to Congress, along with implementing legislation that is typically drafted by the executive branch.

The principal innovation in this scheme is the last step, in which implementing legislation is adopted on the fast track (now known as *trade promotion authority*), which allows for no amendments and only limited public participation. Although most constitutional scholars believe that congressional-executive agreements are fully the equivalent of treaties that have gone through the Senate advice-and-consent process, the agreements in fact provide Congress with a much smaller role. Under fast-track procedures, Congress has only one very unattractive remedy if it does not like an agreement—disapprove it altogether. Congress has essentially forgone the normal domestic statutory processes, thereby

B. International Agreements in Domestic Law

substantially increasing the executive's role in the lawmaking function with respect to international trade.[39]

c. Trade and the Environment: Collision with Domestic Environmental Law?

What does all this mean for the environment? International obligations on trade are almost exclusively "negative" in the sense that they place constraints on governmental action. Trade agreements encourage liberalized or free trade through obligations that limit governmental intrusion into what otherwise would be a free market. From an environmental point of view, this phenomenon is the equivalent of deregulation—in the sense of reducing the level of governmental intrusion in the market—and trade agreements by virtue of their negative obligations are inherently deregulatory. This deregulatory momentum largely explains the phenomenon of globalization, at least as it has been defined for the past decade or so: getting governments out of the business of impeding private interactions and transactions, thereby facilitating their global reach.

Environmental protection anticipates affirmative governmental interventions in the marketplace to offset market failures. That in a nutshell is the clash between the two approaches: one operates to disable governmental action; the other depends on invigorating government. Obligations in trade agreements *proscribe* certain governmental behavior that impedes trade, while environmental statutes *prescribe* other governmental actions to protect public health and ecosystems. International environmental agreements operate in a similar way. For example, the Montreal Protocol on Substances that Deplete the Ozone Layer requires ratifying states to intervene in their domestic jurisdictions to accomplish certain concrete results in the form of prohibitions on private actions. Trade agreements therefore generally create no affirmative rulemaking authority. Unlike international trade agreements, in domestic legal systems such as that created by the U.S. Constitution, there is normally some affirmative governmental regulatory authority to offset the externalities created by market liberalization.

One regulation challenged in this way was a rule, promulgated in 1994 by EPA under the CAA, dealing with "reformulated" gasoline. The regulations specify the composition of reformulated gasoline and require reductions in the emissions of certain pollutants. For gasoline to qualify as reformulated, it must be compared to a baseline unreformulated state. In its rule, EPA specified that domestic refiners could choose from a variety of baselines. Because there were fewer data about foreign refiners, making enforcement much more difficult, EPA did not give foreign refiners a choice but instead assigned them a baseline. The Venezuelan national oil company, Petróleos de Venezuela (PDVSA), protested that the EPA rule discriminated against imported gasoline in violation of the U.S.' WTO obligations. As a matter of trade law, this was a relatively easy case of facial discrimination for the newly created Appellate Body of the WTO in its very first case.[40]

The real issue, however, was what happened after the WTO dispute settlement panel report on the rule came out. As a matter of domestic U.S. law, dispute settlement panel reports have no domestic legal effect. To be implemented domestically, the WTO Appellate Body's report had to go back to EPA for remedial action. The agency subsequently started

---

39. In a case seeking compliance with the National Environmental Policy Act for the negotiation of NAFTA, the D.C. Circuit held that the judicial branch has no role in reviewing the fast-track trade agreement process. *Pub. Citizen v. Office of the U.S. Trade Rep.*, 5 F.3d 549 (D.C. Cir. 1993), cert. denied, 510 U.S. 104 (1994). So, in addition to Congress's reduced role, the courts essentially are cut out of the process, further enhancing the presidential prerogative.

40. U.S.—Standards for Reformulated and Conventional Gasoline, 35 I.L.M. 603 (1996).

a new rulemaking process by publishing a notice of proposed rulemaking, soliciting comments, and the like. At the same time that the rulemaking was going on, another part of the executive branch, the U.S. Trade Representative, was reassuring Venezuela that the new regulation would comply with the WTO report. This tended to attenuate, if not entirely undermine, the rights of public participation that we are accustomed to in the ordinary administrative process and that have given domestic environmental law such vigor. Later, the amended rule, promulgated in 1997, was challenged by a coalition of domestic refiners and environmental organizations in the following case.

George E. Warren Corp. v. U.S. E.P. A.
159 F.3d 616 (U.S. Ct. App., D.C. Cir. 1998)

GINSBURG, J. The petitioners argue the rule is beyond the EPA's statutory authority because (1) allowing foreign refiners the option to petition the EPA for an individual baseline may result in a degradation of air quality; [and] (2) in promulgating the rule the EPA considered factors other than air quality, namely (a) the WTO's decision that the 1994 rule was inconsistent with the GATT, and (b) the likely effect of regulation upon the price and supply of gasoline in the U.S. market. . . .

Because the EPA is charged with administering the Clean Air Act, we evaluate a challenge to its statutory authority under the familiar two-step analysis of *Chevron*. Under *Chevron* step one the court asks "whether Congress has directly spoken to the precise question at issue"; if so, then we "must give effect to the unambiguously expressed intent of Congress." If the Congress has not addressed the issue, however, then under *Chevron* step two we will defer to the agency's interpretation if it is reasonable in light of the structure and purpose of the statute.

We review a challenge to the agency's actions as arbitrary and capricious under the same standards that we apply when reviewing a rule pursuant to the Administrative Procedure Act. As we have pointed out before, this inquiry may overlap with our analysis under step two of *Chevron*, see *Republican Nat'l Comm. v. FEC*, 76 F.3d 400, 407 (1996); so it does to some extent in this case.

The petitioners base all their challenges to the EPA's statutory authority upon the premise that any rule that does not guarantee the maintenance or improvement of air quality violates the anti-dumping provision of 42 U.S.C. §7545(k)(8). For this they rely upon our remark in *American Petroleum Inst. (API) v. EPA*, 52 F.3d 1113, 1119 (1995), that the "sole purpose of the [reformulated gasoline] program is to reduce air pollution." In doing so, however, the petitioners misjudge the applicability of that precedent.

The overall goal of the reformulated gasoline program is, of course, to improve air quality by reducing air pollution; the means chosen to achieve that end are, first, requiring that only reformulated gasoline be sold in nonattainment areas, and second, prohibiting the transfer of pollutants in the refining process from reformulated to conventional gasoline. . . . In sum, although the general purpose of the antidumping provision is to maintain average emissions per gallon from conventional gasoline at no more than 1990 levels, the specific approach adopted by the Congress makes full achievement of that goal less than certain. This result apparently reflects a legislative compromise between two potentially conflicting goals—avoiding degradation of air quality and not disrupting the market for conventional gasoline. . . .

Again proceeding from the mistaken premise that the maintenance or improvement of air quality is the sole focus of the anti-dumping provision, the petitioners argue that the EPA may not consider factors other than air quality in promulgating rules under §7545(k)(8). Thus do they challenge the EPA's consideration both of the WTO's decision interpreting the GATT and of the comments of the Department of Energy concerning the economic effects of the alternatives before the agency.... The EPA responds that nothing in the statute precludes consideration of such factors, and that its approach is congruent with that employed by the Congress when it enacted the anti-dumping provision.

The petitioners do not direct our attention to anything in the text or structure of the statute to indicate that the Congress intended to preclude the EPA from considering the effects a proposed rule might have upon the price and supply of gasoline and the treaty obligations of the United States. Under step two of *Chevron*, therefore, we must defer to the agency's construction if it is reasonable....

Under step two of *Chevron*, we think the agency's interpretation is permissible. Section 7545(k)(8) specifically allows foreign refiners that produced dirtier than average gasoline in 1990 to continue importing gasoline of that quality, presumably in order to prevent the disruption that might ensue were those refiners forced to choose between producing cleaner gasoline than they did in 1990 or quitting the U.S. market. The agency, following the lead of the Congress, similarly sought to prevent its rule from disrupting the market.

In the particular circumstances of this case our usual reluctance to infer from congressional silence an intention to preclude the agency from considering factors other than those listed in a statute is bolstered by the decision of the WTO lurking in the background. "Since the days of Chief Justice Marshall, the Supreme Court has consistently held that congressional statutes must be construed wherever possible in a manner that will not require the United States 'to violate the law of nations.'" *S. African Airways v. Dole*, 817 F.2d 119, 125 (D.C. Cir. 1987) (quoting *The Schooner Charming Betsy*, 6 U.S. (2 Cranch.) 64 (1804)); see also *Vimar Seguros y Reaseguros, S.A. v. M/V Sky Reefer*, 515 U.S. 528, 539 (1995) ("If the U.S. is to be able to gain the benefits of international accords and have a role as a trusted partner in multilateral endeavors, its courts should be most cautious before interpreting its domestic legislation in such manner as to violate international agreements").

In sum, we conclude the EPA's consideration of factors other than air quality is not precluded by anything in §7545(k)(8); in this case, moreover, that consideration appears to be congruent with both the congressional purpose not to disrupt the market for imported gasoline and the Supreme Court's instruction to avoid an interpretation that would put a law of the U.S. into conflict with a treaty obligation of the U.S. For these reasons we deem the EPA's interpretation of the anti-dumping provision a reasonable one; pursuant to *Chevron* step two, therefore, we must uphold it.

COMMENTARY & QUESTIONS

1. Judicial review in a foreign policy setting. As implicitly recognized by the *Warren* court, adverse reports of WTO dispute settlement panels and its Appellate Body have no domestic legal effect and therefore cannot affect the statutory mandate in the CAA. To that extent, this case has a similar posture to *Japan Whaling*. Nonetheless, the D.C. Circuit seemed to give that report considerable weight. Exactly what was the legal significance of the report, and how did it play a role in the decision from an analytical point of view? Is the D.C. Circuit's approach a good or bad thing from a principled point of view? Is it likely to foster or hinder efforts to protect the environment? What, if anything, does this case add to your understanding of the *Chevron* rule? Was this an appropriate case for application of the *Chevron* approach?

2. The WTO and the rule of law. Although it did not expressly say so, the D.C. Circuit seems to have relied on a general inclination of the courts to defer to the executive in matters of foreign relations. One of the motivations behind the creation of the WTO was to shift toward a more rule-based system than in the old GATT, with the creation of the Appellate Body a principal component of that agenda. While removal of the governmental action—the "measure" in the parlance of trade agreements—is the preferred remedy, there is disagreement even among eminent trade scholars as to whether there is a legal obligation to do so. WTO panels have the power to award compensation to the prevailing party, suggesting that WTO member states may instead choose to maintain the measure and to pay compensation instead. What arguments would you make to the D.C. Circuit on behalf of your clients, U.S. environmental groups and domestic petroleum refiners, in support of the proposition that the court should give effect to the domestic statutory mandate notwithstanding the foreign policy consequences?

3. Trade-based measures to protect the environment. Environmental measures that employ trade sanctions have been a particular focus of concern under the WTO regime. These include unilateral measures such as the Pelly Amendment, as well as multilateral ones. Do you see why these might be considered to violate the basic GATT/WTO disciplines—MFN, national treatment, and the prohibition on quantitative restrictions? To deal with such situations, the GATT contains exceptions in Article XX, an "escape clause" that in effect authorize states to maintain measures even if they violate the trade disciplines. Two paragraphs of Article XX are of particular relevance to environmental measures:

> Subject to the requirement that such measures are not applied in a manner which would constitute a means of arbitrary or unjustifiable discrimination between countries where the same conditions prevail, or a disguised restriction on international trade, nothing in this Agreement shall be construed to prevent the adoption or enforcement by any contracting party of measures: . . .
> (b) necessary to protect human, animal or plant life or health; [or] . . .
> (g) relating to the conservation of exhaustible natural resources if such measures are made effective in conjunction with restrictions on domestic production or consumption.

Can you argue on behalf of an environmental group that trade restrictions adopted under the Pelly Amendment meet this test? How would you formulate an argument on behalf of a government challenging U.S. restrictions under Pelly? Can you make similar arguments for the trade restrictions in the Montreal Protocol, which provide trade advantages to states party to the Protocol and discriminate against nonparties? Based on the text of Article XX, can you make an argument that multilateral measures such as those in the Protocol ought to be more likely to meet the test for application of the exceptions than unilateral measures, including sanctions under the Pelly Amendment?

d. The NAFTA Environmental Side Agreement: Citizen Submissions on Enforcement

Public debate over NAFTA was fierce. From the environmental side, concerns arose over the vulnerability of environmental regulations like that on reformulated gasoline, the potential for a race-to-the-bottom as environmental regulations are relaxed, the lack of institutional capability on environmental matters, and the possibility that even multilateral environmental agreements such as the Montreal Protocol might face trade-based challenges. From the trade point of view, there were symmetrical worries over the abuse of environmental measures for protectionist purposes, the deployment of unilateral trade-based actions

B. International Agreements in Domestic Law

including the Pelly Amendment to address international environmental challenges, and the consideration of trade measures in multilateral instruments or by multilateral bodies dealing with environmental hazards. The implication of much of the public policy discussion was that there was a zero-sum set of tradeoffs between the two.

Upon assuming office as President, Clinton declined to renegotiate the NAFTA text—crafted by the earlier George H.W. Bush Administration—instead advocating the adoption of new "side agreements" on environment and labor. According to President Clinton, the principal environmental concern was not a divergence in national standards among the three NAFTA countries and a potential race-to-the-bottom. According to the three governments negotiating the Side Agreement, the more pressing need was to provide effective enforcement mechanisms for fully implementing existing national laws. The resulting North American Agreement on Environmental Cooperation (NAAEC, the "Side Agreement")[41] did not alter, amend, or clarify the NAFTA text.

Instead, the NAAEC establishes a trilateral Commission for Environmental Cooperation (CEC) headed by a council consisting of the environment ministers of the three NAFTA states, which in the case of the U.S. is the Administrator of EPA. The CEC is serviced by a professional secretariat in Montreal and advised by a committee of Canadian, Mexican, and U.S. nationals appointed in their personal capacities.

The Side Agreement assigned the CEC Secretariat the responsibility to receive and process citizen submissions alleging that one of the NAFTA parties has failed effectively to enforce its domestic law, as specified in Articles 14 and 15 of the agreement. The CEC citizen submission process is a major innovation in public international law, which ordinarily is confined to articulating a flow of rights and obligations among states and acknowledges no role for individuals, environmental organizations, and corporations that are not "subjects" of international law.

The NAFTA Article 14/15 process begins when a nongovernmental organization or individual lodges a submission with the CEC Secretariat alleging that one of the three NAFTA governments "is failing to effectively enforce its environmental law." The Secretariat first conducts an initial consideration of the admissibility of the submission, determines whether the submission warrants developing a factual record, and transmits its recommendation to the CEC Council. The Council, by two-thirds vote, then instructs the Secretariat whether to prepare a factual record. After the Secretariat prepares a factual record the Council, by two-thirds vote, decides whether to make the factual record public.

At the time of the negotiations on the Side Agreement, the emphasis on enforcement and implementation was primarily directed at Mexico. In the years since, however, several high-profile cases have involved Canada, including one alleging that the government of Canada had failed to ensure the protection of fish and fish habitat in British Columbia's rivers from environmental damage caused by hydroelectric dams. The first submission against the U.S. was filed in 1999. Bringing the subject matter of this section full circle, that submission alleges that the U.S. government is failing to effectively enforce §703 of the MBTA, which prohibits the killing of migratory birds without a permit.

---

41. Sept. 8-14, 1993, U.S.-Can.-Mex., 32 I.L.M. 1482 (1993). The NAAEC was not authorized by the fast-track legislation that preceded negotiation of NAFTA, leading some to question the legal authority for the Side Agreement's inclusion in the NAFTA package submitted to Congress.

Final Factual Record for Submission SEM-99-002 (Migratory Birds) (2003)

www.cec.org/files/pdf/sem/MigratoryBirds-FFR_EN.pdf

The first case involved the destruction of a great blue heron rookery near Arcata, California, in April 1996. The logging took place under the direction of the owner of the land containing the rookery and it destroyed at least five great blue heron nests, at least some of which contained eggs, plus at least one fledgling great blue heron. A registered professional forester [named Scott Feller] prepared a Notice of Conversion Exemption Timber Operations on the basis that the timber harvest involved less than three acres, but the Notice was not approved by the California Department of Forestry and Fire Protection (CDF) prior to the logging, as required by California law. Consistent with state law, the Notice required that no sites of rare, threatened or endangered plants or animals or species of special concern, such as great blue herons, be disturbed, threatened or damaged during the logging.

After neighbors contacted state wildlife enforcement authorities, the CDF and the [California Department of Fish and Game (CDFG)] launched an investigation on 10 April 1996. These neighbors later sent the [federal Fish and Wildlife Service (FWS), an agency of the Department of the Interior] a letter, dated 16 April 1996, regarding the rookery destruction. The FWS did not participate in the investigation, but the CDFG investigating officer was a deputized US deputy game warden with authority to investigate both state and federal violations of law, including violations of MBTA §703. After the landowner pleaded no contest to six misdemeanor violations of state law, the district attorney recommended the maximum sentence of six months in jail and a $2,700 fine. The county probation office recommended that the landowner be ordered to pay $310,000 in restitution as well. On 9 December 1998, the landowner was sentenced to 120 days in county jail, a fine of $540 and three years' probation, with no order of restitution. . . .

The FWS first became aware of the destruction of the great blue heron rookery upon receipt of the 16 April 1996 letter from the landowners' neighbors. The FWS had no MBTA permitting program that applied to the logging activity that took place, and had no ongoing program for inspecting or monitoring logging operations to determine compliance with the MBTA. . . .

In the view of the FWS, once the state's prosecution of the landowner was completed, it was inappropriate for the FWS to seek federal prosecution under the U.S. Department of Justice's "Petite Policy." The Petite Policy establishes guidelines for deciding whether to bring a federal prosecution based on conduct involved in a prior state or federal proceeding. The Petite Policy provides an explanation for why the U.S. believes federal enforcement would have been inappropriate. The U.S. informed the Secretariat that the Petite Policy was applicable to the landowner, who was convicted and sentenced in a state proceeding. By contrast, it is not clear that the Petite Policy was applicable in connection with the registered professional forester, as to whom the state dismissed criminal charges and sought administrative sanctions.

Under the Petite Policy, for federal prosecution to have proceeded following completion of the state's action against the landowner, the federal government would have had to determine that the case involved a substantial federal interest, that the state prosecution left that interest demonstrably unvindicated, that the landowner's conduct constituted a federal offense, and that he could be convicted on admissible evidence. In addition, the Assistant Attorney General for Environment and Natural Resources, U.S. Department of Justice, would have had to approve a federal prosecution. Last, federal prosecutors would still retain discretion not to pursue the case.

B. International Agreements in Domestic Law

In regard to whether the case involved a substantial federal interest, one might consider the FWS's conclusion that the case was a high priority for investigation because it involved a wild population of a species protected under the MBTA. One might also consider the view of FWS officials that great blue herons are likely to be given special consideration in regard to enforcement of the MBTA because they are colonial nesters.

Regarding whether the state prosecution left the federal interest in protecting migratory birds demonstrably unvindicated, one might consider the district attorney's opinion that the maximum punishment available under state law is insufficient given the nature of the crime in assessing whether additional federal penalties could or should have been sought under the MBTA. Although significant penalties were imposed in MBTA cases that the U.S. describes as similar, it is not clear that significant additional punishment could have been obtained against the landowner with an MBTA prosecution. The U.S. and the CDF believe that the state enforcement action adequately addressed the landowner's conduct.

As to the likelihood of success, the evidence that led to the landowner's conviction under state charges might have supported a federal MBTA prosecution as well. The United States asserts that the case would have been a high priority for investigation and that logging that kills birds will be prosecuted in appropriate circumstances when a violation of the MBTA can be proven. However, a federal MBTA prosecution might have raised significant legal issues. As far as the United States is aware, a prosecution against the landowner would have been the first MBTA §703 prosecution ever sought in connection with a logging operation since the MBTA was enacted in 1918. One possible outcome would be a broad ruling that the MBTA does not apply to any unintentional, yet direct takes, contrary to the United States' successful prosecutions, none involving logging, of unintentional takes resulting from otherwise lawful activities. Such an outcome would be a significant setback to the FWS's overall program for enforcing the MBTA. The law in the United States on the applicability of the MBTA to unintentional takings, as opposed to intentional takings resulting from activities such as hunting, is conflicting and unsettled, at least in the context of timber harvesting. . . .

The cases interpreting §703 of the MBTA have unanimously rejected the proposition that habitat modification or loss alone is sufficient to amount to a violation of the taking prohibition. The cases are split, however, on the question of whether §703 of the MBTA prohibits unintentional as well as intentional takes, at least in the context of logging. . . .

A central assertion in submission SEM-99-002 is that it is the unofficial policy and practice of the U.S. government not to enforce §703 of the MBTA in connection with logging operations. The Submitters rely chiefly on responses to Freedom of Information Act (FOIA) requests indicating that the U.S. has never sought a prosecution under MBTA in connection with a logging operation, and on an unsigned, unofficial memorandum from the Chief of the FWS that states:

> The [FWS] has had a longstanding, unwritten policy relative to the MBTA that no enforcement or investigative action should be taken in incidents involving logging operations that result in the taking of non-endangered, non-threatened migratory birds and/or their nests. . . . The Service will continue to enforce the MBTA in accordance with this longstanding policy.

The U.S. informed the Secretariat that to the best of its knowledge, the U.S. has never sought to prosecute under the MBTA an incident involving a logging operation. The U.S. confirms that in response to FOIA requests, it found no record of any such prosecutions. Representatives of the U.S. also informed the Secretariat that, to the best of their knowledge, federal prosecutions of either of the two cases referenced in Council Resolution 01-10 would have been the first ever prosecution of the MBTA in connection with a logging operation. The U.S. asserts that the absence to date of any federal prosecutions of the MBTA in connection with logging operations reflects an exercise of prosecutorial discretion and allocation of resources to higher enforcement priorities. . . .

On one hand, the U.S. asserts that logging that kills birds will be prosecuted in appropriate circumstances when a violation of the MBTA can be proven. The U.S. informed the Secretariat that "appropriate circumstances" are more likely in cases involving the taking of colonial nesters such as great blue herons, or destruction of their nests or eggs. As noted above, the evidence might have supported a successful federal MBTA prosecution against Wallace [the landowner] as well, putting aside the legal issues that might have been raised. Therefore, the Wallace case might have provided an opportunity to set a precedent in regard to enforcement of the MBTA in connection with logging operations. The district attorney's conclusion that the state's case against Feller lacked sufficient evidence linking Feller with the taking of birds might be taken into account in considering the likelihood of a successful MBTA case against Feller.

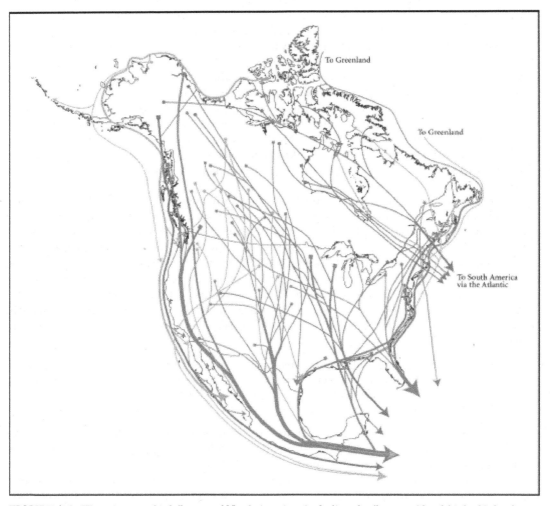

FIGURE 7-1. *The migratory bird flyways of North America, including the flyways of land birds, birds of prey, waterfowl, seabirds, shorebirds, and wading birds. Source: North American Commission for Environmental Cooperation, State of the Environment Report (2002).*

B. International Agreements in Domestic Law

Evidentiary considerations aside, a federal MBTA action against Wallace would have been, as far as the U.S. is aware, the first case ever brought under the MBTA in connection with a logging operation. As noted above, the U.S. explains that the lack to date of any MBTA prosecutions in connection to logging operations is the result of enforcement discretion. . . . These examples are consistent with the federal government's record to date of never having enforced the MBTA in regard to logging operations. . . .

COMMENTARY & QUESTIONS

1. **"Factual records" on "failures to enforce"—law, fact, or paper tigers?** As the NAAEC blue heron file excerpt indicates, NAFTA's Side Agreement provides, as a remedy, the production of a "factual record" in response to allegations that one of the three government parties to the agreement "is failing to effectively enforce its environmental law." The blue heron factual record demonstrates the tension inherent in this formulation. The Secretariat collects "facts" concerning effective enforcement but is constrained from reaching a conclusion by reference to the legal test of "failing effectively to enforce." The Secretariat phrases its findings by preceding them with the apparently tepid observation "one might. . . ." The last section of the migratory birds factual record is not entitled "Conclusion," but merely "Closing Note." Is this likely an oversight on the part of the drafters of the NAAEC? In the U.S., an allegation of failure to enforce the law is very difficult to prove in a suit for judicial review of administrative action. Although regulatory norms governing the behavior of private parties established by administrative agencies such as the FWS can be attacked, the government's exercise of its enforcement discretion is largely shielded from review. As demonstrated by the MBTA factual record, the Article 14/15 process, by contrast, anticipates at least modest inquiries into this sensitive area in which the CEC Secretariat evaluates the effectiveness of enforcement efforts and reflects on their likely outcome. Does the NAAEC Article 14/15 process provide an effective vehicle for closing this gap in domestic law? Does the MBTA factual record succeed in convincing you one way or the other as to the effectiveness of U.S. enforcement despite the fact that it does not come to a formal conclusion on this point?

2. **Assuring the effectiveness of the NAAEC.** The independence of the professional Secretariat, which in principle reports to the trilateral Commission and not to individual governments, and the three governments' attempts to constrain or micromanage the process of preparing a factual record, has been an ongoing theme in the implementation of the citizen submission process. The process is particularly susceptible to political manipulation at the interim step at which the three governments decide whether to authorize the Secretariat to move to the next phase, the preparation of a factual record. In the MBTA case, the U.S. refused to authorize a wide-ranging inquiry into its alleged failure to enforce the statute, instead confining the Secretariat to examining only those specific instances that had been identified in the submission. Can you explain why the process might have been drafted to put representatives of the three NAFTA parties in this crucial gatekeeping role? As an advocate representing a citizen submitter in the Article 14/15 process, what actions would you take to improve the likelihood that the three ministers comprising the CEC Council would authorize the Secretariat to prepare a factual record?

3. **Safe harbors for delinquent governments.** The NAAEC provides a number of jurisdictional exceptions for:

- "any statute or regulation . . . directly related to worker safety or health" (Article 45(2)(a)(iii)); and
- domestic measures "the primary purpose of which is managing the commercial harvest or exploitation . . . of natural resources" (Article 45(2)(b)).

There are other defenses, invoked by the U.S. in the MBTA case, available to governments that justify nonenforcement in a situation that:

- "reflects a reasonable exercise of . . . discretion in respect of investigatory, prosecutorial, regulatory or compliance matters" (Article 45(1)(a)); or
- "results from bona fide decisions to allocate resources to enforcement in respect of environmental matters determined to have higher priorities" (Article 45(1)(b)).

Governments may rely on these criteria as a basis for explaining their own decisions to vote against the preparation of a factual record. Assuming a factual record is prepared, the Secretariat then applies these defenses related to the exercise of enforcement discretion and allocation of enforcement resources. One might think that these defenses would justify almost any action and that the Article 14/15 process would consequently be a "nothing-burger." The information related to those justifications, however, is almost exclusively in the hands of governments, which may then find themselves in something of a Catch-22: either provide sensitive enforcement information to the Secretariat for its evaluation as to whether the governmental decisions were "reasonable" and "bona fide," or withhold it and forgo the defense. If you were representing a government alleged to be failing to effectively enforce its domestic environmental law in a situation like the MBTA case, how would you structure your client's case in light of these considerations? What constraints would you expect to encounter, both from the text of the NAAEC and from the broader institutional and political setting? As a representative of one of the organizations that sponsored the submission, how could you put these insights to use in structuring your case?

4. What's it good for anyway? A factual record in an Article 14/15 case has no domestic legal force. Under what circumstances might this channel serve as a useful advocacy tool? Is there anything going on here beyond the "mobilization of shame"? If you were representing one of the organizations that sponsored the submission in the MBTA case, how, and in what institutional settings, could you use the Secretariat's factual record in your efforts as a policy advocate on behalf of the environment?

5. Do NAAEC factual records return home to roost as supplements to domestic law? As noted in Chapter 6, obtaining judicial review of executive branch enforcement is not always easy. Against this backdrop, an Article 14/15 factual record dealing with the U.S. serves the very useful purpose of providing an external, independent evaluation of agencies' enforcement of environmental laws that can rarely, if ever, be obtained under domestic law. A CEC factual record could be interpreted as filling a gap in our national legal system by providing an international remedy where the domestic counterpart is inadequate or lacking—a well-accepted approach supported by the U.S. in such areas as human rights. Although the agreement is silent as to subsequent follow-up, viewed in this light the NAAEC would complement domestic environmental statutes in a meaningful way by providing a standard against which environmental groups, Congress, and the public can measure executive branch performance on environmental enforcement.

This issue came to a head in September 2003 when the CEC Working Group on Environmental Enforcement and Compliance Cooperation was preparing a strategic plan to shape its future efforts. One of this coursebook's authors, a member of a federal advisory committee overseeing the work of the CEC, suggested in a formal comment that the

B. International Agreements in Domestic Law

Working Group should itself keep track of and publicize the subsequent implementation of factual records by the NAFTA countries. The Working Group declined to do so on the theory that appropriate follow-up for factual records was up to national governments and not the multilateral CEC. The U.S. Justice Department stated that it intended to follow up on factual records with relevant agencies, but only "informally" and with no explanation to the public. Since then, only one other citizen submission against the U.S. has proceeded to a full factual record. Does this mean that the whole CEC Article 14/15 process is a waste of time?

IV

A TAXONOMY OF LEGAL APPROACHES TO ENVIRONMENTAL PROTECTION

—*"taxonomy"—systematics; the orderly scientific classification of plants and animals according to their physical structure and presumed relationships. (see above, pages 187-192.)*

I know of no safe repository of the ultimate powers of the society but the people themselves; and if we think them not enlightened enough to exercise their discretion; the remedy is not to take it from them, but to inform their discretion.

— Thos. Jefferson to William Charles Jarvis, 28 September 1820

For a successful technology, reality must take precedence over public relations, for nature cannot be fooled.

— Richard Feynman

8

Federal Agency Disclosure: NEPA's Stop-and-Think Logic and The Power of Information

A. NEPA, the National Environmental Policy Act
B. NEPA in Court: Litigation and Outcomes
C. NEPA's State, International, and Transboundary Applications
D. The Emergency Planning and Community Right-to-Know Act

This chapter focuses on the broadest, most widely applicable, and best-known statutory model of an environmental disclosure statute—the National Environmental Policy Act (NEPA). NEPA is intended to force federal agencies to stop and think before making decisions and taking actions that harm the environment. NEPA enforces that objective with environmental impact statement (EIS) information-disclosure procedures enforced by citizen litigation.

NEPA is by no means the only environmental statute to have an information disclosure element, although it is more central in NEPA than in many others. Much of environmental law is concerned with obtaining information, organizing it, and directing it to where it can do the most legal and political good. "Information is power" in environmental policymaking because if the media and the public have critical information about a government decision, the public inclinations toward environmental protection may produce a corrective decision in court or in the political arena. Getting strategic information into open public debate is often more than half the battle, especially where the availability of direct citizen enforcement mechanisms can make information regarding environmental threats actionable by members of the public, without the intervention of governmental agencies.

Thus information-disclosure components can be found in many environmental statutes. The biological assessment mechanism of §7 of the Endangered Species Act (ESA) pressures federal wildlife agencies to examine and publish the factual biological vulnerabilities of endangered species populations, forcing many potential conflicts into the open that otherwise would be lost in bureaucratic bogs. Pollution statutes often are linked to public information, requiring submission of data to governmental agencies with a strong presumption in favor of public availability.[1] Product-regulation and market-access statutes typically require the intensive development and production of information regarding product safety as a core regulatory element. Market-enlisting statutes can succeed or fail depending on the availability of good data on the physical conditions to be addressed as well as the economic and financial impacts of taxes and incentives. Effective enforcement and informal dispute resolution demand reliable data of all varieties. And international law often operates far more by information generation and production than by mandate.

A. NEPA, THE NATIONAL ENVIRONMENTAL POLICY ACT

NEPA[2] is a statute that provokes a wide diversity of reactions. To some it is a paper tiger, of awesome but toothless aspect. To others, it is a ringing statutory declaration of environmental protection and rational human governance that sets a precedent of international significance. To some it is an unproductive attempt to intrude on productive public-private enterprises. To others, it is a legislative accident (whether fortunate or unfortunate) that was created and continues to evolve by happenstance. As usual, there is probably some truth in all of these perspectives. Ultimately, NEPA's successes may be impossible to measure, in part because its effectiveness includes the anonymous thousands of destructive federal projects that are withdrawn, or never proposed in the first place, in anticipation of NEPA scrutiny.

In taxonomic form, NEPA provides a distinct new model of statutory environmental management. NEPA is a broad stop-and-think, disclose-to-the-public administrative law. It is general in its statutory commands, establishing a general and simple set of directives that apply across the board to all federal agencies. Its operative terms require agencies to contemplate the context and consequences of their actions before acting, in effect mandating a particularized process of program planning, intended to begin early in the genesis of agency decisions.

Public disclosure is NEPA's complementary mandate: Agencies must produce a publicly reviewable physical document reflecting the required internal project analysis. Preparation of this document is supposed to ensure that the agency has given "good faith consideration" to the environmental consequences of its proposed action and its reasonable alternatives, but in practice, this assumption is frequently false. The rationality of this requirement—requiring documented formal consideration of negatives and alternatives as well as benefits before acting—may be obvious now, but NEPA was its pioneer. Its logic has subsequently been adopted in many international and domestic systems. The potent bureaucratic forces that NEPA attempts to control, however, have kept up a running resistance to its statutory mandates, with some successes over the years.

NEPA at its best becomes a component of the administrative process, shaping the environmentally related content of the administrative decision-making record on proposals for major federal actions that might produce significant environmental consequences. As discussed in Part B, when a federal agency fails to comply with NEPA, courts can invalidate the agency's decision as arbitrary and capricious because the agency has not adequately explained the environmental implications of its decision-making process.

---

1. See, e.g., CWA §308(a), 33 U.S.C. §1318(a)-(b).
2. 42 U.S.C. §§4321 et seq., Pub. L. No. 91-190 (1970).

A. NEPA, the National Environmental Policy Act

Here is the text of NEPA as it was signed into law by President Richard Nixon on January 1, 1970 (it was passed by Congress in 1969). Note how it was written to fulfill the bold promise of its title, to establish a new environmental policy embracing environmental values for the nation. Also note the few actionable provisions that allow citizens to enforce this policy on the federal government.

Public Law 91-190 (1970)

AN ACT: To establish a national policy for the environment, to provide for the establishment of a Council on Environmental Quality, and for other purposes. Be it enacted by the Senate and House of Representatives of the United States of America in Congress assembled, that this Act may be cited as the "National Environmental Policy Act of 1969."

TITLE I. DECLARATION OF NATIONAL ENVIRONMENTAL POLICY.

Sec. 101 (a) The Congress, recognizing the profound impact of man's activity on the interrelations of all components of the natural environment, particularly the profound influences of population growth, high-density urbanization, industrial expansion, resource exploitation, and new and expanding technological advances and recognizing further the critical importance of restoring and maintaining environmental quality to the overall welfare and development of man, declares that it is the continuing policy of the Federal Government, in cooperation with State and local governments, and other concerned public and private organizations, to use all practicable means and measures, including financial and technological assistance, in a manner calculated to foster and promote the general welfare, to create and maintain conditions under which man and nature can exist in productive harmony, and fulfill the social, economic, and other requirements of present and future generations of Americans.

(b) In order to carry out the policy set forth in this Act, it is the continuing responsibility of the Federal Government to use all practicable means, consistent with other essential considerations of national policy, to improve and coordinate Federal plans, functions, programs, and resources to the end that the Nation may — (1) fulfill the responsibilities of each generation as trustee of the environment for succeeding generations; (2) assure for all Americans safe, healthful, productive, and esthetically and culturally pleasing surroundings; (3) attain the widest range of beneficial uses of the environment without degradation, risk to health or safety, or other undesirable and unintended consequences; (4) preserve important historic, cultural, and natural aspects of our national heritage, and maintain, wherever possible, an environment which supports diversity and variety of individual choice; (5) achieve a balance between population and resource use which will permit high standards of living and a wide sharing of life's amenities; and (6) enhance the quality of renewable resources and approach the maximum attainable recycling of depletable resources.

(c) The Congress recognizes that each person should enjoy a healthful environment and that each person has a responsibility to contribute to the preservation and enhancement of the environment.

Sec. 102. The Congress authorizes and directs that, to the fullest extent possible:

(1) The policies, regulations, and public laws of the United States shall be interpreted and administered in accordance with the policies set forth in this Act, and

(2) all agencies of the Federal Government shall —

(A) utilize a systematic, interdisciplinary approach which will insure the integrated use of the natural and social sciences and the environmental design arts in planning and in decisionmaking which may have an impact on man's environment;

(B) identify and develop methods and procedures, in consultation with the Council on Environmental Quality established by title II of this Act, which will insure that presently unquantified environmental amenities and values may be given appropriate consideration in decisionmaking along with economic and technical considerations;

(C) include in every recommendation or report on proposals for legislation and other major Federal actions significantly affecting the quality of the human environment, a detailed statement by the responsible official on — (i) the environmental impact of the proposed action, (ii) any adverse environmental effects which cannot be avoided should the proposal be implemented, (iii) alternatives to the proposed action, (iv) the relationship between local short-term uses of man's environment and the maintenance and enhancement of long-term productivity, and (v) any irreversible and irretrievable commitments of resources which would be involved in the proposed action should it be implemented. Prior to making any detailed statement, the responsible Federal official shall consult with and obtain the comments of any Federal agency which has jurisdiction by law or special expertise with respect to any environmental impact involved. Copies of such statement and the comments and views of the appropriate Federal, State, and local agencies, which are authorized to develop and enforce environmental standards shall be made available to the President, the Council on Environmental Quality and to the public as provided by section 552 of Title 5, United States Code, and shall accompany the proposal through the existing agency review processes;

NEPA §102(2)(C) — the statute's key procedural provision: Requires federal agencies to prepare an Environmental Impact Statement (EIS) for all proposed major federal actions significantly affecting the quality of the environment.

(D) study, develop, and describe appropriate alternatives to recommended courses of action in any proposal which involves unresolved conflicts concerning alternative uses of available resources;

(E) recognize the worldwide and long-range character of environmental problems and, where consistent with the foreign policy of the United States, lend appropriate support to initiatives, resolutions, and programs designed to maximize international cooperation in anticipating and preventing a decline in the quality of mankind's world environment;

(F) make available to States, counties, municipalities, institutions, and individuals, advice and information useful in restoring, maintaining, and enhancing the quality of the environment;

(G) initiate and utilize ecological information in the planning and development of resource oriented projects; and

(H) assist the Council on Environmental Quality established by title II of this Act.

Sec. 103. All agencies of the Federal Government shall review their present statutory authority, administrative regulations, and current policies and procedures for the purpose of determining whether there are any deficiencies or inconsistencies therein which prohibit full compliance with the purposes and provisions of this Act. . . .

Sec. 104. Nothing in Section 102 or 103 shall in any way affect the specific statutory obligations of any Federal agency (1) to comply with criteria or standards of environmental quality, (2) to coordinate or consult with any other Federal or State agency, or (3) to act, or refrain from acting contingent upon the recommendations or certification of any other Federal or State agency.

A. NEPA, the National Environmental Policy Act

Sec. 105. The policies and goals set forth in this Act are supplementary to those set forth in existing authorizations of Federal agencies.

[Title II establishes the President's Council on Environmental Quality (CEQ), which gathers information and conducts studies on environmental trends and conditions, reviews federal government programs in light of NEPA's substantive goals, and recommends national policies for environmental improvement. The CEQ issues regulations for coordinating federal agency compliance with NEPA.[3]]

COMMENTARY & QUESTIONS

1. NEPA as paper tiger. Note that NEPA, as finally passed, contains a great deal of aspirational policy language and precious little that is mandatory. There are declarations of policy and commitments to processes of scientific rationality, especially in §101, and in most of §102. Does all this amount to anything? Is there anything in §101 that has any legal effect? Professor Oliver Houck concludes that §101 is not lawmaking in the ordinary sense: "Motivational as [the NEPA policies] may be, they lack the precision that would allow someone in our system, ultimately a reviewing court, to say, 'this is over the line.'"[4]

There is, of course, the small matter of §102(2)(C) — NEPA's "procedural" subsection. Note that even that subsection is filled with vague verbiage; the instrumental words are limited to a couple of dozen out of two hundred. If you parse it carefully, however, §102(2)(C) levies a sole, narrow, statutory requirement: An EIS shall be prepared for all major federal actions significantly affecting the quality of the human environment. That deceptively simple requirement has produced virtually all NEPA case law. However, even this enforceable EIS requirement is merely procedural and does not purport to dictate substantive results. NEPA thus provides a right to have information considered, but not to have particular decisions made. A central question for examining NEPA is whether this procedural information requirement produces better substantive decisions. As Professor Joe Sax wrote about NEPA, "I think the emphasis on the redemptive quality of procedural reform is about nine parts myth and one part coconut oil...."[5]

2. Interpreting NEPA as non-substantive. Although some early lower court decisions included language suggesting that federal agencies bore some responsibility to take the environmental information revealed by an EIS into account in making the substantive decision on a proposed project, in *Strycker's Bay Neighborhood Council v. Karlen*, 444 U.S. 223 (1980), the Supreme Court put that possibility to rest. In that case, the EIS for a low-income housing unit found serious environmental consequences (including social and economic ghettoization) would result from a proposed site in Manhattan. (Courts have consistently held that the urban environment is within the purview of NEPA.) The EIS also showed alternative sites available, that did not have such adverse environmental effects, but those alternatives would have required a two-year delay to shift the project. The agency chose to build as planned. The Second Circuit said that in light of NEPA's policy, the two-year time factor could not be treated as "an overriding factor"; "environmental factors . . . should be

---

3. Exec. Order No. 11514 (1970), as amended by Exec. Order No. 11991 (1977); 40 C.F.R. §§1500-1508. These regulations are the most complete guide to the interpretation of NEPA; when an important NEPA court decision is handed down, it is customarily codified here.

4. Houck, Is That All? A Review of the National Environmental Policy Act, An Agenda for the Future, By Lynton Keith Caldwell, 11 DUKE ENVTL. L. & POL'Y F. 173, 180-181 (2000).

5. Sax, The (Unhappy) Truth About NEPA, 26 OKLA. L. REV. 239 (1973).

given determinable [sic] weight." *Karlen v. Harris*, 590 F.2d 39, 44 (1978). The Supreme Court in a per curiam decision reversed, saying "once an agency has made a decision subject to NEPA's procedural requirements, the only role for a court is to insure that the agency has *considered* the environmental consequences."

3. NEPA as accidental legislation. The politics underlying NEPA's legislative history began with a late-1960s groundswell of popular attention to problems of environmental quality. Facing upcoming elections, Congress and President Nixon hastened to adjust to the issue. "The 1970s must be the years that America pays its debts to the past by reclaiming the purity of its air, its water, and our living environment. It is literally now or never," said Nixon. A number of legislative details, however, reveal the moderate intent of the President and Congress. As the various draft bills that became NEPA moved through the legislature in 1969 (as S. 1075 and H.R. 12549, 91st Cong., 1st Sess.), they initially were quite innocuous. Section 101 read then much as it does now; §102 merely called for governmental funding for environmental studies. Where teeth seemed to exist, they were pulled. Section 101(c) originally read: "The Congress recognizes that each person has a fundamental and inalienable *right* to a healthful environment . . . ," language that was weakened in the final legislation.

On April 16, 1969, however, in one of a seemingly endless series of small committee hearings, Professor Lynton Caldwell, a political scientist from Indiana University, mentioned in testimony before Senator Jackson's Interior Committee that he "would urge that in the shaping of such policy it have an action-forcing, operational aspect. . . ." Chairman Jackson, to the surprise of his staff, picked up on this: "I agree with you that realistically what is needed in restructuring the governmental side of this problem is to legislatively create those situations that will bring about an action-forcing procedure that departments must comply with. Otherwise these lofty declarations are nothing more than that. . . . I am wondering if I may broaden the policy provision in the bill so as to lay down a general requirement that would be applicable to all agencies?"[6] Based on this brief interchange, Caldwell sat down with several staffers and drafted the text of the present §102.

The underlying mood of Congress continued to be felt, however. Jackson accepted an amendment inserting the phrase "to the fullest extent possible" into §102, a phrase apparently intended to modify the otherwise strict command of its first sentence. In §102(2)(C), Jackson's language originally read that there had to be an environmental "finding" by the responsible official, a term that was amended to read "statement," apparently to avoid the implication that an agency "finding" may require findings of fact that would be judicially reviewable.[7] Imagine the shock of Richard Nixon and many members of Congress when, early in 1970, they discovered that these apparently innocuous words of §102 could be the basis of very real lawsuits. Section 102, like a snake in the grass, contained the hidden but potent EIS requirement. Since then there have been thousands of NEPA lawsuits, affecting federal projects and programs running into billions of dollars. Why didn't Congress recognize this potential? If Congress didn't recognize NEPA's potential, can courts nevertheless enforce the statute to give it precisely the judicial effect that Congress had tried to eliminate? In the years immediately following NEPA's passage, almost 200 bills were introduced

---

6. National Environmental Policy Act, 1969: Hearings on S. 1075, S. 233, and S. 1752 before the Senate Committee on Interior and Insular Affairs, 91st Cong., 1st Sess. 116–117 (1969) (statement of Lynton Caldwell, Professor of Government, University of Indiana).

7. For a complete history of NEPA's legislative genesis, see R.N.L. Andrews, Environmental Policy and Administrative Change (1976).

A. NEPA, the National Environmental Policy Act

to weaken or repeal it. None passed. This indicates that, once passed, a "motherhood" statute is no less sacred for having been unintended.

4. NEPA's de facto statutory strategy. Despite NEPA's legislative history, one can still analyze the provisions that emerged from Congress as embodying a novel de facto statutory strategy. First, whatever NEPA requires is government-wide, not a series of directives specifically tailored to particular governmental agencies. Similarly, NEPA is not focused on or limited to specific types of pollution or environmental harms, allowing it to be used as new environmental issues arise. Second, NEPA asserts a strong general declaration of policy that might be made relevant to a wide range of substantive interpretations and applications of various statutes, although this has not noticeably been the case. Third, the EIS procedure requires an internal process of overview accounting, specifying a detailed analysis of agency proposals. It pins down this required process with the EIS, a specific work product that provides tangible, reviewable evidence of the agency's compliance. The notion, moreover, that the EIS will accompany proposals through the decisional process may impose a practical timing requirement bringing environmental impact accounting into the earlier project stages. A hoped for benefit of that timing feature is that the agency's own self awareness of the environmental impacts will occur at an early stage in the process, where it is easier to modify or even abandon the project before the agency becomes "invested" in pursuing the project, or pursuing it in a particular manner. There is anecdotal evidence that this happens, but no systematically collected empirical evidence.

Also note that there is no enforcement mechanism in NEPA itself. Congress presumed that NEPA would be actively enforced by the President, acting through the Office of Management and Budget (OMB) and the Council of Environmental Quality (CEQ). In reality, as the following cases demonstrate, enforcement came through citizen litigation under the Administrative Procedure Act (APA). Nevertheless, the statutory framework can be viewed as incorporating a coherent and quite novel regulatory logic. Through its provisions, even low-visibility agency decisions that might significantly impact the environment would have to be "ventilated" within and outside the agency, and made accessible in published form to the President, Congress, other relevant federal agencies, and the public for their review and response.

5. The political science of NEPA. Note that the only enforceable section of NEPA targeted its requirements on federal agencies, not the industrial polluters who previously had been the primary focus of public attention. Federal agencies, however, happen to be intimately involved with a host of major production and development activities across the face of the economy and the territory of the United States. Federal agencies are involved in the logging of national forests, in water resources, minerals and mining, the construction of highways and airports, urban redevelopment, and the oil industry and offshore oil development. The wisdom of targeting federal agencies grew after NEPA was enacted, when the federal environmental laws of the 1970s gave rise to hundreds of federal rulemakings and thousands of federal permit decisions, all potentially subject to NEPA and environmental review.

6. The role of citizens. The history of each statute is unique. NEPA was written in broad terms, achieved support, and passed through Congress as a product of its unique times. It is impossible to overestimate the importance of public opinion in pushing NEPA into law. NEPA would never have moved beyond its first drafts without the environmental fervor of hundreds of thousands of citizens in the late 1960s. Even more than most statutes, however, NEPA was only an incipient force when it was signed in January 1970. Its growth and development once again depended upon citizens' efforts, this time in the courts. Turning to NEPA in the courts, it is important to remember a basic irony: When the terms of a statute require interpretation, courts put their primary reliance upon the intention of the legislature, but in the case of NEPA there really *wasn't* any discernible intent beyond a vague articulation of environmental goals accompanied by an incompletely defined mandatory process lacking an explicit enforcement mechanism. Thus NEPA jurisprudence is primarily judge-made, decisional law (referred to as the "common law of NEPA"), as refined and codified by the CEQ in its regulations.

7. NEPA's establishment of the Council on Environmental Quality. NEPA created the Council on Environmental Quality, an executive branch agency that oversees NEPA and promulgates rules for its implementation. While founding such an agency was of great political moment in 1970, the CEQ's regulations addressing agency compliance with NEPA have a considerable influence on the statute's performance because the regulations are used by courts when they review the actions of agencies that are subject to NEPA. Those regulations are codified at 40 C.F.R., Parts 1500-1517. Other federal agencies may also promulgate NEPA regulations, consistent with CEQ policy.

B. NEPA IN COURT: LITIGATION AND OUTCOMES

Whenever a new statute is enacted, an elaborate series of further questions must be answered. Has it created a new cause of action? If so, who can file lawsuits? Against what defendants? What is the statute of limitations? What actions can be attacked? What are potential defendants required to do under the Act? What do plaintiffs have to show in their complaint and at trial? What defenses are available? What remedies are provided for, and what outcomes can be sought? The evolving answers to these questions create a common law of the statute. Depending upon how they are answered in court, a statute can flourish or wither on the vine. NEPA litigation, from the beginning, has focused upon the one clear requirement of the Act – a proposal for a major federal action significantly affecting the human environment must be accompanied by an EIS. This requirement is triggered when an agency decides to undertake a physical action (such as building a highway) and when an agency decides to make a regulatory decision (promulgating a rule or issuing a permit).

There are two primary issues that give rise to NEPA litigation. First, when an agency does prepare an EIS, litigants may challenge the adequacy of the agency's EIS if the EIS fails to disclose sufficient information about the environmental impacts of the agency's decision. Second, it is possible an agency may decide that its action will not significantly impact the environment, and thus it will not have to prepare an EIS. These two scenarios are analyzed separately in the following two sections of the chapter.

1. NEPA Litigation over the Adequacy of an Agency's EIS

Mid-States Coalition for Progress v. Surface Transportation Board
345 F.3d 520 (8th Cir. 2003)

ARNOLD, J. Petitioners challenge the decision of the Surface Transportation Board issued January 30, 2002, giving final approval to the Dakota, Minnesota & Eastern Railroad Corporation's (DM&E) proposal to construct approximately 280 miles of new rail line to

B. NEPA in Court: Litigation and Outcomes

reach the coal mines of Wyoming's Powder River Basin (PRB) and to upgrade nearly 600 miles of existing rail line in Minnesota and South Dakota. They maintain that in giving its approval the Board violated . . . the National Environmental Policy Act (NEPA) (42 U.S.C. §§4321-4347). . . . The Board has exclusive licensing authority for the construction and operation of rail lines. . . .

In this case, the Board made an initial determination that DM&E's proposal was merited . . . because it would offer a shorter and less expensive method by which to transport coal from the PRB mines to power plants. . . . [T]he Board instructed its Section of Environmental Analysis (SEA) to examine the potential environmental effects resulting from the construction and continuing operation of the proposed project. SEA, in coordination with five cooperating federal agencies, then produced a nearly 5,000-page draft environmental impact statement (DEIS) examining the effects both of constructing the rail line extension to the PRB mines and rehabilitating DM&E's existing lines in Minnesota and South Dakota to accommodate the coal traffic anticipated as a result of the project. SEA initially allowed 90 days for public review of and comment on the DEIS, but later extended this period by 60 days to ensure that the large number of persons and entities who wished to comment had ample opportunity to do so. The environmental review culminated with the issuance of a final environmental impact statement (FEIS), which contained further analysis in response to the comments received on the DEIS. The FEIS also made recommendations to the Board regarding environmentally preferable routing alternatives and mitigation measures. In all, the environmental review process took nearly four years and generated roughly 8,600 public comments.

The NEPA mandates that a federal agency "take a 'hard look' at the environmental consequences" of a major federal action before taking that action. To comport with this standard, an agency must prepare a "detailed statement" (generally, an EIS), 42 U.S.C. §4332(2)(C), "from which a court can determine whether the agency has made a good faith effort to consider the values NEPA seeks to protect." In reviewing the agency's decision, we are not free to substitute our judgment for that of the agency. Our role in the NEPA process "is simply to ensure that the agency has adequately considered and disclosed the environmental impact of its actions and that its decision is not arbitrary or capricious."

The Sierra Club [which challenged the STB's decision along with Mid-States Coalition for Progress] argues that SEA wholly failed to consider the effects on air quality that an increase in the supply of low-sulfur coal to power plants would produce. Comments submitted to SEA explain that the projected availability of 100 million tons of low-sulfur coal per year at reduced rates will increase the consumption of low-sulfur coal vis-à-vis other fuels (for instance, natural gas). While it is unlikely that this increase in coal consumption would affect total emissions of sulfur dioxide (which are capped nationally at maximum levels by the Clean Air Act Amendments of 1990), the Sierra Club argues that it would significantly increase the emissions of other noxious air pollutants such as nitrous oxide, carbon dioxide, particulates, and mercury, none of which is currently capped as sulfur dioxide is.

Before this court, the Board admits that because of the need to comply with the restrictions in the Clean Air Act Amendments on sulfur dioxide emissions, many utilities will likely shift to the low-sulfur variety of coal that the proposed project would make available. It argues, however, that this shift will occur regardless of whether DM&E's new line is constructed, since the proposed project will simply provide a shorter and straighter route for low-sulfur coal to be transported to plants already served by other railroad carriers. But the proposition that the demand for coal will be unaffected by an increase in availability and a decrease in price, which is the stated goal of the project, is illogical at best. The increased availability of inexpensive coal will at the very least make coal a more attractive option to future entrants into the utilities market when compared with other potential fuel sources, such as nuclear power, solar power, or natural gas. Even if this project will not affect the short-term demand for coal, which is possible since most existing utilities are single-source dependent, it will most assuredly affect the nation's long-term demand for coal as the comments to the DEIS explained. Tellingly, DM&E does not adopt the Board's argument that the proposed project will leave demand for coal unaffected: Instead, it adopts the more plausible position that SEA was not required to address the effects of increased coal generation because these effects are too speculative.

NEPA requires that federal agencies consider "any adverse environmental effects" of their "major . . . actions," 42 U.S.C. §4332(C), and the CEQ regulations, which are binding on the agencies, explain that "effects" include both "direct effects" and "indirect effects," 40 C.F.R. §1508.8. Indirect effects are defined as those that "are caused by the action and are later in time or farther removed in distance, but are still reasonably foreseeable." "Indirect effects may include . . . effects on air and water and other natural systems, including ecosystems." The above language leaves little doubt that the type of effect at issue here, degradation in air quality, is indeed something that must be addressed in an EIS if it is "reasonably foreseeable." As in other legal contexts, an environmental effect is "reasonably foreseeable" if it is "sufficiently likely to occur that a person of ordinary prudence would take it into account in reaching a decision."

DM&E argues in its brief that "if the increased availability of coal will 'drive' the construction of additional power plants . . . the [Board] would need to know where those plants will be built, and how much coal these new unnamed power plants would use. Because DM&E has yet to finalize coal-hauling contracts with any utilities, the answers to these questions are pure speculation—hardly the reasonably foreseeable significant impacts that must be analyzed under NEPA." Even if this statement is accurate (the Sierra Club has asserted that it is not), it shows only that the *extent* of the effect is speculative. The *nature* of the effect, however, is far from speculative. As discussed above, it is reasonably foreseeable—indeed, it is almost certainly true—that the proposed project will increase the long-term demand for coal and any adverse effects that result from burning coal.

Contrary to DM&E's assertion, when the *nature* of the effect is reasonably foreseeable but its *extent* is not, we think that the agency may not simply ignore the effect. The CEQ has devised a specific procedure for "evaluating reasonably foreseeable significant adverse effects on the human environment" when "there is incomplete or unavailable information." 40 C.F.R. §1502.22. First, "the agency shall always make clear that such information is lacking." Then, "[i]f the information relevant to reasonably foreseeable significant adverse impacts cannot be obtained because the overall costs of obtaining it are exorbitant or the means to obtain it are not known," the agency must include in the environmental impact statement:

> (1) A statement that such information is incomplete or unavailable; (2) a statement of the relevance of the incomplete or unavailable information to evaluating reasonably foreseeable significant adverse impacts on the human environment; (3) a summary of existing credible scientific evidence which is relevant to evaluating the reasonably foreseeable significant adverse impacts on the human environment, and (4) the agency's evaluation of such impacts based upon theoretical approaches or research methods generally accepted in the scientific community.

We find it significant that when the Board was defining the contours of the EIS, it stated that SEA would "[e]valuate the potential air quality impacts associated with the increased availability and utilization of Powder River Basin Coal." Yet, the DEIS failed to deliver on this promise. Interested parties then submitted comments on the DEIS explaining, for the reasons that we have summarized, why this issue should be addressed in the FEIS. These

B. NEPA in Court: Litigation and Outcomes

parties even identified computer models that are widely used in the electric power industry to simulate the dispatch of generating resources to meet customer loads over a particular study period. According to the commenting parties, these programs could be used to forecast the effects of this project on the consumption of coal. These efforts did not convince SEA, which asserted that "[b]ecause the 1990 Clean Air Act Amendments mandate reductions in pollutant emissions . . . an assumption of SEA's analysis was that emissions will definitely fall to the mandated level, producing whatever effect the emissions will have on global warming." SEA's "assumption" may be true for those pollutants that the amendments have capped (including, as we have said, sulfur dioxide) but it tells the decision-maker nothing about how this project will affect pollutants not subject to the statutory cap. For the most part, SEA has completely ignored the effects of increased coal consumption, and it has made no attempt to fulfill the requirements laid out in the CEQ regulations.

The Board has stated that this project "is the largest and most challenging rail construction proposal ever to come before [us]," and that the total cost of the project is estimated to be $1.4 billion, not counting the cost of environmental mitigation. We believe that it would be irresponsible for the Board to approve a project of this scope without first examining the effects that may occur as a result of the reasonably foreseeable increase in coal consumption.

[The court remanded the matter to the Surface Transportation Board to correct the deficiencies in the EIS.]

COMMENTARY AND QUESTIONS

1. NEPA in the context of substantive regulation. In the *Mid-States Coalition* case, the sufficiency of the Surface Transportation Board (STB) EIS was assessed in the context of existing law. That context included the 1990 amendments to the Clean Air Act, which cap total sulfur dioxide emissions from most major sources (including the existing and future power plants likely to be served by the new rail lines) and allow trading to allocate emission reduction credits such as those that might be earned by switching to low sulfur coal. In that context, should STB be allowed to claim that reductions attributable to the switch to low sulfur coal are an environmental benefit of the project? As plaintiffs argued and the court recognized, the salient environmental effect of coal switching would be the likely increase in other pollutants associated with coal burning that are not necessarily capped or prevented by existing law. The omission of analysis of those effects was a major failing of the EIS. More generally, to what extent are an agency's EIS obligations limited by the existence of other regulatory laws addressing a potential environmental impact of a proposed action? Failing to mention such impacts, even if they are within the regulatory limits set by the other law seems to violate the full disclosure policy of NEPA. Must the EIS address the possibility that the other law may not be fully enforced, or obeyed, or is that inquiry too speculative?

2. NEPA as an alternative to substantive regulation and as a "small handle" on other environmental problems. The Sierra Club and other plaintiffs in the *Mid-States Coalition* case are primarily concerned with emissions of greenhouse gases (especially carbon dioxide) and mercury, neither of which was adequately regulated under the CAA at the time of the litigation. Should it matter for purposes of NEPA whether the environmental impacts are regulated (or unregulated) under another federal statute?

Because of its universal application to the federal government, NEPA frequently comes into play in cases that have very little federal involvement. For example, assume that a major western water transfer between private parties intends to make use of a canal that traverses federal land, and therefore requires a permit from a federal agency, such as the Bureau of Land Management. Assuming that the canal itself has no significant environmental impacts, should an EIS be required that addresses the impacts of the water transfer. This is sometimes referred to as using NEPA as a "small handle" to get environmental review of a project that is otherwise not subject to such a review. As an ethical matter is using NEPA as a small handle to obstruct a project that is otherwise legally unassailable an appropriate tactic?

3. Timing and scope. The railroad company, DM&E, argues that the environmental impacts of burning coal in power plants should be studied plant-by-plant, once the locations and technologies of those plants are certain. More specific information could lead to a more informed environmental decision, so why require an EIS at this early stage? Does a deferred plant-by-plant assessment tend to minimize the impacts of the project that should be assessed in the aggregate at the programmatic level? The CEQ regulations do not expressly require agencies to prepare programmatic impact statements, but they do describe a process called "tiering" that contemplates preparation of one broad EIS and a "subsequent statement or environmental assessment [to] summarize the issues discussed in the broader statement and incorporate discussions from the broader statement by reference and . . . concentrate on the issues specific to the subsequent action." 40 C.F.R. §1502.20. See also 40 C.F.R. §1508.28.

4. NEPA results, or lack therof. NEPA is a procedural statute, and the court's ruling does not prevent the railroad project from being built. It simply requires the STB to consider the environmental impacts of greenhouse gas and mercury emissions. The STB subsequently prepared a supplemental EIS in 2005 that was ultimately upheld. See *Mayo Found. v. Surface Transp. Bd.*, 472 F.3d 545 (8th Cir. 2006). Perhaps that result was foreseeable in light of *Stryker's Bay* and similar precedents. If NEPA does not prevent an agency from choosing an environmentally destructive alternative, what's the point of the litigation? In some cases preparing a more complete environmental accounting has influenced the agency to mitigate impacts or alter the project. An EIS that reveals embarrassingly bad environmental impacts can galvanize public opinion against the project or, in rare cases, affect congressional willingness to fund the agency project or proposal. However, it is worth noting that the DM&E project was eventually scrapped in late 2009, with the company citing the combination of environmental concerns and economic factors to explain its decision.

2. *NEPA Litigation over an Agency's Decision Not to Prepare an EIS*

> The NEPA process:
>
> The federal agency proposing a major federal action typically begins with an EA, which is less detailed and involved than a full EIS.
> The EA results in either a finding of no significant impact (FONSI), which ends the process and can trigger litigation, as seen in the *Center for Biological Diversity v. NHTSA* case below, or a decision to prepare an EIS.
>
> While the decision to prepare an EIS is not subject to judicial review, the adequacy of the EIS is commonly challenged in court, as seen in the *Mid-States Coalition* case above.

The threshold decision of an agency—whether to prepare an EIS—involves an interpretive application of key terms in §102(2)(C), deciding what is a "major federal action significantly affecting the quality of the human environment." In the early years of NEPA, the courts, on a somewhat ad hoc basis, grappled with that issue as citizen groups and other

B. NEPA in Court: Litigation and Outcomes

parties sued federal agencies that had not compiled EISs in relation to agency actions. The CEQ regulations have since provided a procedural framework and guidance—agencies perform a less comprehensive review of environmental effects called an Environmental Assessment (EA). See 40 C.F.R. §§1501.4 & 1508.9. Based on the EA, the agency thereafter makes a formal determination to prepare an EIS or, if none is to be prepared, files a finding of no significant impact (FONSI). See 40 C.F.R. §1508.13. The next case arises from a challenge to a FONSI.

Center for Biological Diversity v. National Highway Traffic Safety Administration

538 F.3d 1172 (9th Cir. 2008)

FLETCHER, J. Eleven states, the District of Columbia, the City of New York, and . . . public interest organizations [Center for Biological Diversity, Sierra Club, Public Citizen, Environmental Defense, and Natural Resources Defense Council] petition for review of a rule issued by the National Highway Traffic Safety Administration (NHTSA) entitled "Average Fuel Economy Standards for Light Trucks, Model Years 2008-2011." Pursuant to the Energy Policy and Conservation Act of 1975 (EPCA), the Final Rule sets corporate average fuel economy (CAFE) standards for light trucks, defined by NHTSA to include many Sport Utility Vehicles (SUVs), minivans, and pickup trucks, for Model Years (MYs) 2008-2011. . . . Petitioners challenge the Final Rule under the EPCA and the National Environmental Policy Act of 1969 (NEPA). [The petitioners substantively challenged the rule by alleging that it was contrary to EPCA because the agency's cost-benefit analysis did not set the CAFE standard at the "maximum feasible" level. They also alleged NHTSA failed to consider—among other things—the benefits of reduced energy consumption and excluded certain vehicles from regulation. The court first held the rule arbitrary, capricious, and contrary to EPCA, then addressed the NEPA claims.]

Petitioners argue that NHTSA's Environmental Assessment is inadequate under NEPA because it fails to take a "hard look" at the greenhouse gas implications of its rulemaking and fails to analyze a reasonable range of alternatives or examine the rule's cumulative impact. Petitioners also argue that NEPA requires NHTSA to prepare an Environmental Impact Statement. . . . [We] hold that the Environmental Assessment was inadequate and that Petitioners have raised a substantial question as to whether the Final Rule may have a significant impact on the environment. Therefore, we remand to NHTSA . . . to prepare either a revised Environmental Assessment or an Environmental Impact Statement.

FACTUAL AND PROCEDURAL BACKGROUND

CAFE Regulation Under the Energy Policy and Conservation Act

In the aftermath of the energy crisis created by the 1973 Mideast oil embargo, Congress enacted the Energy Policy and Conservation Act of 1975. Congress observed that "[t]he fundamental reality is that this nation has entered a new era in which energy resources previously abundant, will remain in short supply, retarding our economic growth and necessitating an alteration in our life's habits and expectations." The goals of the EPCA are to "decrease dependence on foreign imports, enhance national security, achieve the efficient utilization of scarce resources, and guarantee the availability of domestic energy supplies at prices consumers can afford." These goals are more pressing today than they were thirty years ago: since 1975, American consumption of oil has risen from 16.3 million barrels per day to over 20 million barrels per day, and the percentage of U.S. oil that is imported has risen from 35.8 to 56 percent.

In furtherance of the goal of energy conservation, Title V of the EPCA establishes automobile fuel economy standards. [A corporate] "average fuel economy standard" (often referred to as a CAFE standard) is "a performance standard specifying a minimum level of average fuel economy applicable to a manufacturer in a model year." Only "automobiles" are subject to fuel economy regulation, and passenger automobiles must meet a statutory standard of 27.5 mpg, whereas non-passenger automobiles must meet standards set by the Secretary of Transportation . . . at "the maximum feasible average fuel economy level that the Secretary decides the manufacturers can achieve in that model year." . . .

In response to a request from Congress, the National Academy of Sciences (NAS) published in 2002 a report entitled "Effectiveness and Impact of Corporate Average Fuel Economy (CAFE) Standards." The NAS committee made several findings and recommendations. It found that from 1970 to 1982, CAFE standards helped contribute to a 50 percent increase in fuel economy for new light trucks. In the subsequent decades, however, light trucks became more popular since domestic manufacturers faced less competition in the light truck category and could generate greater profits. The "less stringent CAFE standards for trucks . . . provide[d] incentives for manufacturers to invest in minivans and SUVs and to promote them to consumers in place of large cars and station wagons." When the CAFE regulations were originally promulgated in the 1970s, "light truck sales accounted for about 20 percent of the new vehicle market," but now they account for about half. This shift has had a "pronounced" effect on overall fuel economy. As the market share of light trucks has increased, the overall average fuel economy of the new light duty vehicle fleet (light trucks and passenger automobiles) has declined "from a peak of 25.9 MPG in 1987 to 24.0 MPG in 2000." Vehicle miles traveled (VMT) by light trucks has also been growing more rapidly than passenger automobile travel.

The . . . committee found that the CAFE program has increased fuel economy, but that certain aspects of the program "have not functioned as intended," including "[t]he distinction between a car for personal use and a truck for work use/cargo transport," which "has been stretched well beyond the original purpose." The committee also found that technologies exist to "significantly reduce fuel consumption," for cars and light trucks and that raising CAFE standards would reduce fuel consumption. Significantly, the committee found that of the many reasons for improving fuel economy, "[t]he most important . . . is concern about the accumulation in the atmosphere of so-called greenhouse gases, principally carbon dioxide. Continued increases in carbon dioxide emissions are likely to further global warming." In addition, the committee found "externalities of about $0.30/gal of gasoline associated with the combined impacts of fuel consumption on greenhouse gas emissions and on world oil market conditions" that "are not necessarily taken into account when consumers purchase new vehicles."

National Environmental Policy Act

NEPA requires a federal agency "to the fullest extent possible," to prepare "a detailed statement on . . . the environmental impact" of "major Federal actions significantly affecting the quality of the human environment." 42 U.S.C. §4332(2)(C)(i). The purpose of NEPA is twofold: "ensure[ ] that the agency . . . will have available, and will carefully consider, detailed information concerning significant environmental impacts[, and] guarantee [ ] that the relevant information will be made available to the larger [public] audience." "NEPA expresses a Congressional determination that procrastination on environmental concerns is no longer acceptable." NEPA "is our basic national charter for protection of the environment."

B. NEPA in Court: Litigation and Outcomes

If there is a substantial question whether an action "may have a significant effect" on the environment, then the agency must prepare an Environmental Impact Statement (EIS). An EIS should contain a discussion of significant environmental impacts and alternatives to the proposed action. As a preliminary step, an agency may prepare an Environmental Assessment (EA) in order to determine whether a proposed action may "significantly affect[ ]" the environment and thereby trigger the requirement to prepare an EIS. An EA is "a concise public document" that "[b]riefly provide[s] sufficient evidence and analysis for determining whether to prepare an environmental impact statement or a finding of no significant impact [FONSI]." 40 C.F.R. §1509(a)(1) (2007). An EA "[s]hall include brief discussions of the need for the proposal, of alternatives as required by sec. 102(2)(E), of the environmental impacts of the proposed action and alternatives, and a listing of agencies and persons consulted." Id. §1509(b).

Whether an action may "significantly affect" the environment requires consideration of "context" and "intensity." Id. §1508.27. "Context . . . delimits the scope of the agency's action, including the interests affected." *Nat'l Parks & Conservation Ass'n v. Babbitt*, 241 F.3d 722, 731 (9th Cir. 2001). Intensity refers to the "severity of impact," which includes both beneficial and adverse impacts, "[t]he degree to which the proposed action affects public health or safety," "[t]he degree to which the effects on the quality of the human environment are likely to be highly controversial," "[t]he degree to which the possible effects on the human environment are highly uncertain or involve unique or unknown risks," and "[w]hether the action is related to other actions with individually insignificant but cumulatively significant impacts." 40 C.F.R. §1508.27(b)(2), (4), (5), (7).

NHTSA's Proposed Rulemaking and Draft Environmental Assessment

In August, 2005, NHTSA issued proposed CAFE standards for light trucks MYs 2008-2011 of 22.5 mpg for MY 2008, 23.1 mpg for MY 2009, and 23.5 mpg for MY 2010. . . . NHTSA [also] issued a Draft Environmental Assessment. . . . The Draft EA analyzed three alternatives to the proposed rule[, including an alternative that] would extend the MY 2007 standard of 22.2 mpg through MY 2011 [essentially a no action alternative].

The Draft EA noted that "CO_2 . . . has started to be viewed as an issue of concern for its global climate change potential." With regard to biological resources, the Draft EA stated, "emissions of criteria pollutants and greenhouse gases could result in ozone layer depletion and promote climate change that could affect species and ecosystem." . . . The Draft EA concluded that the proposed standards would "result in reduced emissions of CO_2, the predominant greenhouse gas emitted by motor vehicles," "reductions in contamination of water resources," and "minor reductions in impacts to biological resources." In addition, "the cumulative effects estimated to result from both the 2005-2007 and 2008-2011 light truck rulemakings over the lifetimes of the vehicles they would affect are projected to be very small."

NHTSA received over 45,000 comments on the NPRM [notice of proposed rulemaking] and Draft EA from states, consumer and environmental organizations, automobile manufacturers and associations, members of Congress, and private individuals. . . . The states and environmental and consumer organizations generally argued that . . . NHTSA's draft EA is inadequate and fails to consider the proposed rule's impact on climate change.

Commenters also submitted to NHTSA numerous scientific reports and studies regarding the relationship between climate change and greenhouse gas emissions and the expected impacts on the environment. Emissions from light trucks make up about eight percent of annual U.S. greenhouse gas emissions. The transportation sectors account for about 31 percent of human-generated CO_2 emissions in the U.S. economy. "Overall, U.S.

light-duty vehicles [passenger cars and light trucks] produce about 5 percent of the entire world's greenhouse gases. . . . Since the United States produces about 25 percent of the world's greenhouse gases, fuel economy improvements could have a significant impact on the rate of CO_2 accumulation in the atmosphere." [NAS Report, supra, at 14, 20]. [The court further described evidence in the record linking GHG emissions to major adverse environmental consequences, and including reference to studies that indicate the range of scenarios may be non-linear, i.e., that there may be "mechanisms that push global warning past a dangerous threshold (the 'tipping point')."]

[The Final Rule issued on April 6, 2006, set CAFE standards for light trucks at 22.5 mpg for MY 2008, 23.1 mpg for MY 2009, and 23.5 mpg for MY 2010. For MY 2011, the CAFE standards would vary according to a vehicle's size.]

STANDARD OF REVIEW

The Administrative Procedure Act (APA), 5 U.S.C. §§701-706, provides that agency action must be set aside by the reviewing court if it is "arbitrary, capricious, an abuse of discretion, or otherwise not in accordance with law." . . .

NHTSA's compliance with NEPA is reviewed under an arbitrary and capricious standard pursuant to the APA. With respect to NEPA documents, the agency must take a "hard look" at the impacts of its action by providing "a reasonably thorough discussion of the significant aspects of the probable environmental consequences." We must determine whether the EA "foster[s] both informed decision-making and informed public participation."

DISCUSSION
[Section A discussed EPCA issues and the Final Rule.]

National Environmental Policy Act

The EPCA does not limit NHTSA's NEPA obligations

. . . NHTSA argues both that it has broad discretion to balance the [EPCA] factors in setting fuel economy standards and that the EPCA constrains it from considering more stringent alternatives in the EA. NHTSA can't have it both ways. Its hands are not tied, as demonstrated by its discretionary, substantive decisions to, among other things, value the benefit of carbon emissions reduction at zero. . . . NHTSA clearly has statutory authority to impose or enforce fuel economy standards, and it could have, in exercising its discretion, set higher standards if an EIS contained evidence that so warranted. Although NEPA does not demand substantive environmental outcomes, NHTSA possesses the power to act on whatever information might be contained in an EIS. This court has recognized that "NEPA's legislative history reflects Congress's concern that agencies might attempt to avoid any compliance with NEPA by narrowly construing other statutory directives to create a conflict with NEPA. Section 102(2) of NEPA therefore requires government agencies to comply "to the fullest extent possible."

Moreover, the CAFE standard will affect the level of the nation's greenhouse gas emissions and impact global warming. NHTSA does not dispute that light trucks account for a significant percentage of the U.S. transportation sector, that the U.S. transportation sector accounts for about six percent of the world's greenhouse gases, and that "fuel economy improvements could have a significant impact on the rate of CO_2 accumulation in the atmosphere," which would affect climate change.

In sum, the EPCA does not limit NHTSA's duty under NEPA to assess the environmental impacts, including the impact on climate change, of its rule. EPCA's goal of energy conservation and NEPA's goals of "help[ing] public officials make decisions that are based on

B. NEPA in Court: Litigation and Outcomes

understanding of environmental consequences, and take actions that protect, restore, and enhance the environment," and "insur[ing] that environmental information is available to public officials and citizens before decisions are made and before actions are taken," are complementary. NEPA prohibits uninformed agency action. "The procedures included in §102 of NEPA are not ends in themselves. They are intended to be 'action forcing.' The unequivocal intent of NEPA is to require agencies to consider and give effect to the environmental goals set forth in the Act, not just to file detailed impact studies which will fill governmental archives."

Sufficiency of the Environmental Assessment

We examine the EA with two purposes in mind: to determine whether it has adequately considered and elaborated the possible consequences of the proposed agency action when concluding that it will have no significant impact on the environment, and whether its determination that no EIS is required is a reasonable conclusion.

Even though an EA need not "conform to all the requirements of an EIS," it must be "sufficient to establish the reasonableness of th[e] decision" not to prepare an EIS. An EA "[s]hall include brief discussions of the need for the proposal . . . [and] the environmental impacts of the proposed action and alternatives." 40 C.F.R. §1508.9(b) An EA "must in some circumstances include an analysis of the cumulative impacts of a project. . . . An EA may be deficient if it fails to include a cumulative impact analysis. . . ."

A. Cumulative Impacts of Greenhouse Gas Emissions on Climate Change and the Environment

A cumulative impact is defined as "the impact on the environment which results from the incremental impact of the action when added to other past, present, and reasonably foreseeable future actions regardless of what agency . . . or person undertakes such other actions. Cumulative impacts can result from individually minor but collectively significant actions taking place over a period of time." . . . We conclude that the EA's cumulative impacts analysis is inadequate. While the EA quantifies the expected amount of CO_2 emitted from light trucks MYs 2005-2011, it does not evaluate the "incremental impact" that these emissions will have on climate change or on the environment more generally in light of other past, present, and reasonably foreseeable actions such as other light truck and passenger automobile CAFE standards. The EA does not discuss the *actual* environmental effects resulting from those emissions or place those emissions in context of other CAFE rulemakings.

NHTSA does not dispute that the CAFE standard will have an effect on global warming due to an increase in greenhouse gas emissions. The new rule will not actually result in a decrease in carbon emissions, but potentially only a decrease in the rate of growth of carbon emissions. NHTSA concedes that "the new CAFE standards will not entirely offset the projected effect of increases in the number of light trucks." However, NHTSA contends that Congress is "the cause of that shortfall," not the agency, since it "is Congress's decision in EPCA to require that CAFE standards be technologically feasible and economically practicable." NHTSA concludes from this that it has no obligation to assess the cumulative impact of its rule on climate change.

This argument is without merit for the reasons already discussed. NHTSA has the power to change the CAFE standards based on information contained in an EIS. We agree with Petitioners that "[b]y allowing particular fuel economy levels, which NHTSA argues translate directly into particular tailpipe emissions, NHTSA's regulations are the proximate cause of those emissions just as EPA Clean Air Act rules permitting particular smokestack emissions are the proximate cause of those air pollutants and are unquestionably subject to NEPA's cumulative impacts requirements." Thus, the fact that "climate change is largely a global phenomenon that includes actions that are outside of [the agency's] control . . . does not release the agency from the duty of assessing the effects of *its* actions on global warming within the context of other actions that also affect global warming." The cumulative impacts regulation specifically provides that the agency must assess the "impact of the action when added to other past, present, and reasonably foreseeable future actions *regardless of what agency (Federal or non-Federal) or person undertakes such other actions.*"

The impact of greenhouse gas emissions on climate change is precisely the kind of cumulative impacts analysis that NEPA requires agencies to conduct. Any given rule setting a CAFE standard might have an "individually minor" effect on the environment, but these rules are "collectively significant actions taking place over a period of time." Thus, NHTSA must provide the necessary contextual information about the cumulative and incremental environmental impacts of the Final Rule in light of other CAFE rulemakings and other past, present, and reasonably foreseeable future actions, regardless of what agency or person undertakes such other actions.

Reasonable Alternatives

NHTSA must "[r]igorously explore and objectively evaluate all reasonable alternatives." The alternatives section is the "heart" of an EIS. Although "an agency's obligation to consider alternatives under an EA is a lesser one than under an EIS, NEPA requires that alternatives . . . be given full and meaningful consideration," whether the agency prepares an EA or an EIS. The agency must "provide sufficient evidence and analysis for determining whether to prepare an environmental impact statement or a finding of no significant impact." 40 C.F.R. §1508.9.

In the EA, NHTSA considered a very narrow range of alternatives. All the alternatives evaluated were derived from NHTSA's cost-benefit analysis. [The EA contained five alternatives using different combinations of MY standards and weight-based fuel economy targets. The court found the alternatives were not significantly different from the Final Rule.]

NHTSA acknowledged that "the range of impacts from the considered alternatives is very narrow and minimal." However, the agency justified its choice of range and refusal to consider other alternatives on the ground that "standards more stringent than those represented by the alternatives would not satisfy the statutory requirement to establish standards . . . that are both technologically feasible and economically practicable. . . . NEPA's requirements must be applied in light of the constraints placed on the agency by EPCA." Once again, NHTSA falls back on its contention that it had no discretion to consider setting higher CAFE standards. As before, we conclude that this argument is flawed.

NHTSA also erroneously contends that Petitioners have not identified any specific alternative the agency should have considered. [The court found petitioners had submitted material identifying reasonable alternatives.]

NHTSA must Prepare either a Revised Environmental Assessment or, as necessary, an Environmental Impact Statement

An agency must prepare an EIS "if substantial questions are raised as to whether a project . . . *may* cause significant degradation of some human environmental factor." Petitioners "need not show that significant effects *will in fact occur*," but only that there are "substantial questions whether a project may have a significant effect." "If an agency decides not to prepare an EIS, it must supply a 'convincing statement of reasons' to explain why a project's impacts are insignificant. 'The statement of reasons is crucial to determining whether the agency took a "hard look" at the potential environmental impact of a project.'" NHTSA's EA is markedly deficient in its attempt to justify the refusal to prepare a complete EIS.

[NHTSA argued that its proposed rule would result in only a slight decrease in CO_2 emissions from light duty trucks, and therefore the rule did not have a significant environmental impact. The court again rejected that argument as not accounting for the context, i.e., whether the failure to adopt a more stringent set of CAFE standards might avoid having cumulative emissions exceeding the environmental tipping point, a difference that would be highly significant.]

Petitioners have raised a "substantial question" as to whether the CAFE standards for light trucks MYs 2008-2011 "*may* cause significant degradation of some human environmental factor," particularly in light of the compelling scientific evidence concerning "positive feedback mechanisms [i.e., crossing the tipping point]" in the atmosphere. . . . [The court's list of petitioners' evidence in support of that possibility is omitted.]

Finally, Petitioners have satisfied several of the "intensity" factors listed in 40 C.F.R. §1508.27(b) for determining "significant effect." For example, the Final Rule clearly may have an "individually insignificant but cumulatively significant" impact with respect to global warming. Evidence that Petitioners submitted in the record also shows that global warming will have an effect on public health and safety. Petitioners do not claim (nor do they have to show) that NHTSA's Final Rule would be the *sole* cause of global warming, and that is NHTSA's only response on this point.

Petitioners have also satisfied the "controversy" factor. NHTSA received over 45,000 individual submissions on its proposal. . . .

Nowhere does the EA provide a "statement of reasons" for a finding of no significant impact, much less a "convincing statement of reasons." For example, the EA discusses the amount of CO_2 emissions expected from the Rule, but does not discuss the potential impact of such emissions on climate change. . . .

Nor is there any analysis or statement of reasons in the section of the EA that discusses environmental impacts. The EA states that reduction in fuel production and consumption would reduce "contamination of water resources," acid rain, risk of oil spills and contamination, and "lead to minor reductions in impacts to biological resources . . . includ[ing] habitat encroachment and destruction, air and water pollution, greenhouse gases, and oil contamination from petroleum refining and distribution."

NHTSA's EA "shunted aside [significant questions] with merely conclusory statements," failed to "directly address[ ]" "substantial questions," and most importantly, "provide[d] no foundation" for the important inference NHTSA draws between a decrease in the rate of carbon emissions growth and its finding of no significant impact. NHTSA makes "vague and conclusory statements" unaccompanied by "supporting data," and the EA "do[es] not constitute a 'hard look' at the environmental consequences of the action as required by NEPA." Thus, the FONSI is arbitrary and capricious. . . .

Finally, we must decide the appropriate remedy given NHTSA's inadequate EA. We have previously recognized that preparation of an EIS is not mandated in all cases simply because an agency has prepared a deficient EA or otherwise failed to comply with NEPA. If, for example, an EA is so procedurally flawed that we cannot determine whether the proposed rule or project may have a significant effect, the court should remand for the preparation of a new EA. If an agency completely fails to prepare an EA before deciding that a proposed project or rule will have no significant environmental impact, remand for preparation of an EA is likewise the proper remedy. And where an agency determines that consideration of certain factors are legally irrelevant to the agency's action, rendering it impossible for the reviewing court to determine the accuracy of the FONSI, we also remand for preparation of an EA on a complete record.

By contrast, if the court determines that the agency's proffered reasons for its FONSI are arbitrary and capricious and the evidence in a complete administrative record demonstrates that the project or regulation may have a significant impact, then it is appropriate to remand with instructions to prepare an EIS.

[The court opted to remand to the NHTSA to determine for itself whether to improve the EA or jump right to the EIS. An important consideration was the passage, in the interim, of the Energy Independence and Security Act of 2007, 49 U.S.C. §32902(b)(2)(A), which requires NHTSA to increase fuel economy standards for passenger and non-passenger automobiles to reach a combined average of at least 35 mpg by model year 2020. Since NHTSA had already begun an EIS for its CAFE rulemaking under that law, the court felt NHTSA was in a position to rectify the deficiencies of the current EA based on materials developed for that effort, or might use those same materials as part of an EIS related to the rulemaking reviewed in this case.]

COMMENTARY & QUESTIONS

1. NEPA and rulemaking. NEPA predated almost every major federal environmental statute, including EPCA, and has become a key aspect of federal rulemaking pursuant to environmental statutes. In *Center for Biological Diversity v. NHTSA*, the petitioners successfully challenged the rule itself as inconsistent with the governing statute, and the agency's environmental review pursuant to NEPA. In other cases, interest groups opposed to a new federal rule may have more success challenging the agency's environmental review of the rule's impact, rather than the rule itself. This pattern is also seen in litigation challenging an agency's permitting decision. However, NEPA's environmental review requirements also apply to non-regulatory agency actions, such as the decision to build or fund a new highway. In these circumstances, NEPA litigation may be the only option to challenge the agency in court.

2. Environmental assessments versus environmental impact statements. Early in NEPA's history, EAs were simple and short evaluations to determine whether there was the potential for an environmental impact warranting a more comprehensive EIS. Over time, EAs have become lengthy documents to justify the agency's FONSI. Does this trend further NEPA's goals or undermine them? Does it matter if the agency's and public's discussion of a project's environmental impact occurs through an EA or an EIS?

3. After the NHTSA litigation, what purpose would an EIS serve? The point of an EIS is to force the agency to make itself aware of the environmental consequences of its decisions and to educate the public and interest groups. But to prevail in a NEPA challenge against an agency, litigants in this case seemingly needed to have persuasive evidence of the significant environmental impacts of the agency's decision—precisely the type of information that an EIS is supposed to provide. The petitioners offered many hundreds of pages of documentation regarding the environmental impact of the proposed CAFE standards and climate change. If the petitioners had to demonstrate the environmental impacts of the agency's decision to prevail in a case requiring the agency to disclose the environmental impacts of its decision, what benefit will be obtained by making the agency prepare an EIS that catalogs environmental impacts? Can an EIS showing environmental harms galvanize political opposition to a project? Can delay eventually change the environmental outcome? For private projects requiring a governmental permit, funding sources for a project can dry up in the face of delays. At the governmental level, a change in administrations, from Clinton to Bush II, and then from Bush II to Obama, changes that also altered some environmental attitudes in the agencies, has affected many regulatory positions.

4. New executive action on CAFE standards. As if to confirm the court's belief that the agency itself might eventually take a different approach to CAFE standards, President Obama's administration ultimately raised CAFE standards to 54.5 mpg for model year 2025, reducing the carbon intensity of vehicles by 40% from 2012 to 2025.

5. Law students making environmental law. In addition to the states and public interest organizations that are named parties in the case, the litigation is notable for the key role that students played. The Stanford Law School Environmental Law Clinic, directed by Professor Deborah Sivas, performed work on the NEPA issues for the public interest groups in the lawsuit. The Stanford clinic, like many other environmental law clinics in the country, allows law students in their second and third years to engage in practical legal work in the environmental law field. This work will vary depending on the needs of the clinic and the experience of the students participating, but will generally include researching substantive areas of the law, drafting pleadings, motions, and Freedom of Information Act requests, and otherwise preparing a case that will eventually be litigated on behalf of a public interest group or the clinic itself. These clinics provide students with invaluable "real world" experience and show the critical roles students often can and do play in shaping the developing field of environmental law. As noted elsewhere in this book, NEPA is not the only environmental law area in which law students and clinics have played key roles.

C. NEPA's State, International, and Transboundary Applications

Noah D. Hall, Political Externalities, Federalism, and a Proposal for an Interstate Environmental Impact Assessment Policy

32 Harvard Environmental L. Rev. 49, 81-84 (2008)

NEPA has already served as a model for advancing the general concept of environmental impact assessment under state law.... Thirty-two states have some form of an environmental impact assessment policy modeled after NEPA. Not only do these state laws provide for environmental impact assessment of state projects and permit decisions, but many of these NEPA-inspired state laws offer improvements over the original federal act.[8]

> NEPA as model for environmental impact assessment at home and abroad:
>
> Over 30 states have an environmental impact assessment law, some of which apply to local governments.
>
> Over 100 nations have an environmental impact assessment law, some of which include substantive requirements and protections.
>
> Transboundary environmental impact assessment has been widely adopted in international law as a way of preventing disputes and harms.

---

8. For a listing of the state environmental impact assessment laws, *see* Daniel R. Mandelker, NEPA LAW & LITIGATION §12.02[1] (2d ed. 1992).

Two key differences between some of the state laws and NEPA are worth noting. . . . First, while NEPA is purely procedural and does not require a specific outcome based on the EIS, a few states have established substantive requirements in their environmental impact assessment laws that require mitigation of environmental impacts.[9] . . . Second, in addition to covering state projects and decisions, some of the state laws also apply to local governments.[10] This is particularly important in addressing interstate environmental harms from sprawl, since most land use decisions are made by local governments. . . .

The concept of environmental impact assessment first provided by NEPA has not only spread to state law, but also to other countries. Since NEPA was enacted in the United States, over one hundred countries have established some form of domestic environmental impact assessment laws. The widespread adoption of domestic environmental impact assessment law has facilitated growth of the concept of transboundary environmental impact assessment under international law. . . . International transboundary environmental impact assessment is a logically required first step to prevent international transboundary pollution, since addressing a harm requires knowing something about it. The importance of transboundary environmental impact assessment under international law is evident in the United Nations Conference on Environment and Development Rio Declaration of 1992: "States shall provide prior and timely notification and relevant information to potentially affected States on activities that may have a significant adverse transboundary environmental effect and shall consult with those States at an early stage and in good faith."

Despite the widespread adoption of domestic environmental impact assessment laws and the Rio Declaration supporting the principle of transboundary environmental impact assessment, there is still no global treaty on transboundary environmental impact assessment. There are however several regional models worth noting. [One example is the] Convention on Environmental Impact in a Transboundary Context, known as the Espoo Convention [signed by the United States, Canada, and European countries] in 1991. It requires parties to perform an environmental impact assessment for any activity that is likely to cause a significant transboundary environmental impact. The Espoo Convention also provides a significant role for public participation. . . .

In the transboundary context, where externalities are all but inevitable, public access to environmental information may be one useful mechanism to force States to take into account the views of all those who are impacted by actions taken within their borders, whether the affected persons are voting citizens or residents of other States. Information can help affected populations shine light on governmental decisions and rally political support in favor of their interests, even when the political entities making the decisions are not directly accountable to them.

Information and public participation could similarly be used to directly address the underlying political externality causes of interstate environmental harms. In some respects, interstate environmental impact assessment is more promising than the international proposals, as the systems of law and principles of non-discrimination are more firmly established

---

9. The states that have a substantive requirement to reduce or mitigate negative environmental impacts identified in the environmental impact assessment are California, New York, Minnesota, Massachusetts, and the District of Columbia. *See* Cal. Pub. Res. Code §21,002.1(b); N.Y. Envtl. Conserv. Law §8-0109(1); Minn. Stat. §116D.04(6); Mass. Gen. Laws ch. 30, §61; and D.C. Code Ann. §6-981.

10. The states that subject local governments to environmental impacts assessment requirements are California, New York, Minnesota, Massachusetts, and the state of Washington. *See* Cal. Pub. Res. Code, §§21,003(a), 21,063, 21,151; N.Y. Envtl. Conserv. Law, §8-0105; Minn. Stat., §116D.04(1)(a); Mass. Gen. Laws ch. 30, §62; Wash. Admin. Code, §43.21C.020.

C. NEPA's State, International, and Transboundary Applications

among the American states than among the many nations of the world. Further, as even this brief review of environmental impact assessment law makes clear, there is a tremendous legal tradition for use of information and public process to minimize environmental impacts. The concept of environmental impact assessment, first established in the United States, spread relatively quickly to over a hundred other legal systems. This facilitated the use of transboundary environmental impact assessment as a way to address the challenge of transboundary environmental harms under international law. Now the domestic legal system should "rediscover" the concept and apply it to the century-old problem of interstate environmental harms in the United States.

COMMENTARY AND QUESTIONS

1. Imitation is flattery, but is it deserved? Given that NEPA is one of the most imitated environmental laws in the world, it's worth asking if NEPA itself deserves such flattery. Why have states and other countries been so enthused with environmental review as a legal response to environmental problems? Is NEPA's primary weakness, that it only requires information disclosure and not a different substantive outcome, also its primary selling point for other countries?

2. Making NEPA better—improving on the original. One benefit of the widespread adoption of NEPA-like statutes by states and other countries is that improvements are often made on the original. Professor Bradley Karkkainen has surveyed the state and foreign laws and offers several recommendations for a "smarter" NEPA: "require monitoring, ongoing policy and project reassessment, [and] adaptive mitigation." He argues that NEPA is based on a "1960s-style faith in comprehensive bureaucratic rationality." This "naive faith in the predictive capacities of rational bureaucrats" should be modernized with "'post project assessment,' that is, ongoing monitoring, reevaluation, or project adjustments or adaptations in response to new information or changing conditions."

3. Getting it wrong the first time; making it better later. Decades of experience with environmental review has shown that pre-project assessments, the central feature of NEPA and most other environmental impact assessments, are often wrong. According to one recent study of EISs performed pursuant to NEPA, most environmental impact predictions failed to accurately forecast the direction and the magnitude of the actual harm.[11] This is not a criticism of predictive environmental impact assessments, but a recognition of their limitations. Predictions are simply that, and environmental decisions should be based on both predictions of anticipated impacts and information learned after the initial decision has been made.

This leads to two of Professor Karkkainen's specific recommendations. First, post-decision monitoring is necessary to determine the actual environmental consequences of the project or decision. Second, using the information learned through post-decision monitoring, the agency should use adaptive management to avoid unpredicted harms. While this may seem to create an additional burden, it could actually make the initial environmental assessment cheaper and easier, since less up-front certainty and conservatism in predictions would be needed. These concepts have been used in the Canadian Environmental Assessment Act and the California Environmental Quality Act, two prominent examples of NEPA's progeny. The adaptive management concept also complements the role of agency planning, discussed in the following chapter.

---

11. Paul J. Culhane et al., Forecasts and Environmental Decisionmaking: The Content and Predictive Accuracy of Environmental Impact Statements, at 111-112 (1987).

D. THE EMERGENCY PLANNING AND COMMUNITY RIGHT-TO-KNOW ACT

The Emergency Planning and Community Right-to-Know Act (EPCRA)[12] was enacted in 1986 in response to media coverage of a tragic series of toxic chemical releases, especially the methyl isocyanate release in Bhopal, India that killed 2000 people. Section 313 of the Act establishes the Toxic Release Inventory (TRI). TRI requires certain facilities that "manufacture . . . , process . . . , or otherwise use" listed toxic chemicals in amounts above designated thresholds, and that employ ten or more full-time workers, to file annual reports with EPA. EPCRA §§313(a)(1)(A), 313(b)(2). TRI reports detail the use and release of nearly 650 listed toxic chemicals above yearly threshold amounts.[13] A facility submits its TRI information for persistent, bioaccumulative, and toxic (PBT) chemicals[14] on a so-called Form R, which must include the following information:

> (i) Whether the toxic chemical at the facility is manufactured, processed, or otherwise used, and the general category or categories of use of the chemical. (ii) An estimate of the maximum amounts (in ranges) of the toxic chemical present at the facility at any time during the preceding calendar year. (iii) For each waste stream, the waste treatment or disposal methods employed, and an estimate of the treatment efficiency typically achieved by such methods for that waste stream. (iv) The annual quantity of the toxic chemical entering each environmental medium. EPCRA §313(g).

Facilities must also report offsite transfers of TRI chemicals (e.g., to sewage treatment plants or hazardous waste facilities), as well as source reduction, recycling, and waste minimization efforts. (For non-PBT chemicals, facilities may use a shorter form, Form A, only if the "annual reporting amount" of the chemical is 500 pounds or less, and the chemical was manufactured, processed or otherwise used in an amount not exceeding 1 million pounds during the reporting year.) More than 21,000 U.S. corporate facilities submit TRI reports to the EPA annually. EPA's TRI report compilation is made available to the general public through published reports and an online database system (TRI Explorer) available via the Internet.[15] Published TRI information is organized by total releases and transfers, chronological trends, geographic distributions, and industry-by-industry comparisons. While there has historically been a two-year lag between submissions of the forms and EPA's published TRI reports, this trend appears to be disappearing. The 2008 TRI National Analysis was the first to be published in the same calendar year as when EPA received the data.

---

12. 42 U.S.C. §§11001-11050 (1986).

13. See generally EPA's 2008 TRI National Analysis webpage at http://www.epa.gov/TRI/tridata/tri08/national_analysis/index.htm.

14. PBTs include dioxins, mercury and lead. The vast majority of PBTs released or disposed of are lead and lead compounds.

15. EPA's comprehensive TRI database is available at http://www.epa.gov/triexplorer. In addition, Environmental Defense (ED) has installed an online database, called the "Scorecard," that links chemical release and toxicology data with maps locating facilities that use certain chemicals. A user need only enter a zip code in order to see a map highlighting local sources of pollution. More than 400 public databases are linked to create this database. The Scorecard is now owned and operated by Green Media Toolshed and is available at http://www.scorecard.org.

D. The Emergency Planning and Community Right-to-Know Act

> Community right-to-know laws may improve corporate environmental performance by:
>
> - Forcing companies to audit their processes and emissions systematically, thus revealing opportunities to prevent pollution and probably save money by doing so;
> - Providing local citizens and municipalities with important information about potential hazards and contingency planning;
> - Providing information to that increasing segment of the American public that practices green consumerism, giving a company that achieves pollution prevention a competitive public relations advantage; and
> - Informing corporate shareholders, who can use their votes to stimulate corporate environmental performance to achieve positive gains and avoid potential negative costs and liabilities.

In addition to the community right-to-know functions listed above, Congress explicitly intended EPCRA to make citizens aware of health and safety risks in their communities in order to facilitate emergency planning and notification procedures to cope with potential chemical releases. Consequently, local police and fire departments, public health officials, and citizen participants, organized into local emergency planning committees, are significant users of TRI material. Local citizen groups also use TRI data to establish cooperative relationships with local industries so as to promote pollution prevention, obtain limited community surveillance and inspection of facilities, and improve community warning systems.

> How can citizens use the information from right-to-know laws?
>
> - to lobby legislatures and agencies for stricter pollution control requirements;
> - to supervise compliance with emissions permits and bring citizen suits where violations are occurring; and
> - to perform environmental justice analyses to determine whether members of racial, ethnic, or economic minority groups are being disproportionately exposed to toxic chemicals.

COMMENTARY AND QUESTIONS

1. TRI data in detail. The latest TRI data showed that almost 21,700 U.S. facilities reported the disposal or release of 3.9 billion pounds of TRI chemicals in 2008. The majority of these chemicals were disposed of on-site, either through air emissions or land disposal. Nearly 22.6 billion pounds of production-related waste were managed by facilities in 2008 and the majority of these wastes were recycled on-site. The largest disposal of chemicals came from the metal mining industry and electric utilities.[16]

---

16. See U.S. EPA Toxics Release Inventory Reporting Year 2008 National Analysis Summary of Key Findings (2009), available at http://www.epa.gov/TRI/tridata/tri08/national_analysis/pdr/TRI_key_findings_2008.pdf.

2. Evaluating EPCRA. EPCRA, according to many observers, has been remarkably successful in reducing emissions of toxic chemicals without resort to full-fledged command-and-control regulatory systems. Reported toxic chemical disposal or other releases have decreased by 65% since 1988. While some of this decrease has been caused by more accurate reporting and stringent regulation, there is broad agreement among industry and environmentalists that most of the reduction is due to EPCRA and other disclosure laws. According to the U.S. General Accounting Office (GAO), the public availability of TRI data, which assures that year-to-year changes in a firm's environmental performance are transparent, is a key factor in stimulating firms to use pollution prevention and improve community and public relations. GAO, EPA Should Strengthen Its Efforts to Measure and Encourage Pollution Prevention (01-283) (2001).

On the negative side, EPCRA, like NEPA, is plagued by the major flaw in all mandatory disclosure strategies: The entities that are required to disclose the data have an inherent incentive either not to disclose or to disclose inaccurate or misleading information. Violations of TRI reporting obligations are allegedly widespread. Enforcement of TRI reporting requirements is difficult because agencies and citizen groups seldom know enough about facility operations to form a basis for asserting with confidence that mandated disclosures are missing or incomplete. Limitations on citizen suits, such as the need to allege "continuing violations," have hampered citizen efforts to enforce EPCRA. In *Steel Co. v. Citizens for a Better Environment*, 523 U.S. 83 (1998), plaintiffs alleged that defendant had violated EPCRA by failing to file chemical reports for past years. By the time the complaint was filed, however, defendant had brought its filings up to date. The Supreme Court held that none of the requested relief would remedy plaintiffs' alleged injury. The Court suggested that plaintiffs must allege continuing violations of EPCRA reporting requirements in order to bring citizen suits.

EPCRA also has its weaknesses and critics. As one commentator has summarized:

> [EPCRA] does not and cannot achieve its ostensible goal of accurately informing the public about toxic releases. It omits many environmentally significant chemicals and focuses on [large] sources that account for a small fraction of releases. It largely fails to note distinctions between more and less risky pollutants and modes of release. Finally, EPA has administered TRI in isolation, without coordination with other programs that might correct its defects. As a result, TRI fails to portray accurately the extent and the possible impacts of the chemical releases it purports to cover or to provide a basis for comparing those impacts with other uncovered risks.[17]

3. Should "materials accounting" data be reported? On October 1, 1996, EPA issued an Advance Notice of Proposed Rulemaking (ANPR) announcing its intention to expand the TRI requirements to include "materials accounting" data. 61 Fed. Reg. 51,322. Materials accounting would involve a complete thorough analysis of toxic chemicals, identifying the amounts of TRI chemicals (1) coming into the facility; (2) being transformed into products and wastes; and (3) leaving the facility as products, releases, and offsite transfers. New Jersey and Massachusetts require materials accounting data under their state community right-to-know statutes.[18]

Is disclosure of materials accounting data necessary to identify opportunities for pollution prevention and protect against nondisclosure and inaccurate disclosure? Or is it

---

17. Pedersen, Regulation and Information Disclosure: Parallel Universes and Beyond, 25 Harv. Envtl. L. Rev. 151, 152 (2001).
18. N.J. Stat. Ann. §§34:5A-1 to 34:5A-31; Mass. Gen. Laws Ann. ch. 211 §§1-23.

a superfluous, inappropriate intrusion on a facility's confidential business information? Some observers argue that "the collection of [materials accounting] data is an unjustified, fundamental change in the TRI program that is not in harmony with the intent or purpose of EPCRA."[19] EPA received over 40,000 responses to its ANPR, and the materials accounting issue has not, to say the least, been resolved quickly. EPA has still not taken further action with regards to the proposed rule.

4. TRI and performance benchmarking. TRI marks a watershed, pioneering the use of performance monitoring and benchmarking as regulatory tools. By creating an objective performance metric, TRI compels firms to self-monitor even as it enables them to benchmark performance among operating units and against their competitors. For an article exploring the strengths and limitations of this innovative approach, and its implications for future environmental regulation, see Karkkainen, Information as Environmental Regulation: TRI and Performance Benchmarking, Precursor to a New Paradigm?, 89 Geo. L.J. 257 (2001).

5. Information disclosure in other contexts: coal ash sites. In December 2008, a massive spill of coal ash spread across 300 acres, damaging or destroying 40 homes, as the result of the structural failure of a containment pond at a TVA power plant in Kingston, Tennessee. Coal ash is a residue of coal burning, in slurry form, containing a variety of toxics, including arsenic, lead, and mercury. There are nearly 600 coal ash sites spread throughout 35 states and spills have occurred at 34 of these sites in the past decade. Sparked by the Tennessee disaster and public outcry, in 2009 EPA released the locations of "high hazard potential" coal ash sites. "High hazard potential" means that if the containment structure is compromised, there is a high risk of resulting loss of human life. Currently, the EPA has listed 49 sites on an online inventory.[20] The locations of the sites had previously been kept secret by the federal government, and many public interest groups are demanding that the EPA begin to regulate storage and disposal of coal ash. The agency has indicated that it is considering proposing new regulations.

6. International right-to-know. Right-to-know transparency principles are reflected internationally in a number of settings. The North American Commission for Environmental Cooperation established by the environmental side agreement to NAFTA has been working on the issue of pollutant release and transfer registers, of which the U.S. TRI is one example. The U.S. and Canada have already "harmonized" their programs, making them compatible with each other. Mexico, however, has lagged behind. Unlike the U.S. and Canadian efforts, Mexico's requirements are voluntary rather than mandatory, apply only to facilities regulated by the federal government and not the states, do not guarantee public access, and require reporting in terms of production figures instead of environmental discharges. One of the issues during the NAFTA negotiations was the potential for a "race to the bottom" in a situation such as this, in which those countries with higher standards make them compatible with those of others by relaxing their domestic requirements.

To protect against this dynamic, the Commission's governing treaty specifies that "each Party shall ensure that its laws and regulations provide for high levels of environmental protection and shall strive to continue to improve those laws and regulations." While that is perhaps a useful sentiment, what problems might you expect to encounter in implementing it in practice? For example, how would the governments of Canada and the U.S. encourage

---

19. Clay, The EPA's Proposed Phase-III Expansion of the Toxic Release Inventory (TRI) Reporting Requirements, 15 Pace Envtl. L. Rev. 293, at 297.

20. See U.S. EPA Fact Sheet: Coal Combustion Residues (CCR) — Surface Impoundments with High Hazard Potential Ratings, available at http://www.epa.gov/epawaste/nonhaz/industrial/special/fossil/ccrs-fs/index.htm.

Mexico to "harmonize up?" What does harmonizing up mean in any event? How does one compare regulations in situations in which the metrics are incommensurable? For instance, Mexico might well argue that reporting production of hazardous chemicals as opposed to discharges is in fact a more meaningful measure, on the theory that measurement of discharges is subject to error or misrepresentation.

European countries have also been active in fostering international information disclosure. The Arhaus Convention, which entered into force in 2001, creates rights to information on the part of the public and obligations for public authorities regarding access to this information. The U.S. is not a party to the Convention. A meeting of the parties held in Kiev, Ukraine in 2003 adopted a Protocol on Pollutant Release and Transfer Registers (PRTRs)—a subsidiary instrument to the Aarhus Convention—setting out international obligations corresponding to the TRI approach in the U.S., involving the collection and dissemination of toxic emissions released into the environment. The Protocol is the first legally binding international instrument on PRTRs. According to article 1, the agreement's objective is "to enhance public access to information through the establishment of coherent, nationwide pollutant release and transfer registers (PRTRs)." While the Protocol is a significant achievement, the U.S. is not a party, and the instrument still lacks the requisite ratifications to enter into force.

7. Information disclosure and national security. One of the potential drawbacks of a disclosure strategy is that it arguably might disclose too much.[21] Under CAA §112(r), 42 U.S.C. §7412(r), more than 65,000 companies were required to submit accident prevention and response plans ("risk management plans"), including "worst-case accident scenarios," to EPA by mid-1999. EPA announced, however, that this data would not be placed on the Internet because of the possibility that terrorists might use the information to plan attacks on vulnerable sites. The data will, however, be made available to local emergency response officials and also to members of the public through FOIA requests. On August 5, 1999, President Clinton signed S. 880, which for one year suspended FOIA disclosures of information on off-site consequences associated with risk management plans required under CAA §112(r). Certain public officials continue to have access to this information.

After the 9/11/2001 attacks, the government removed previously available information regarding toxics from the Internet, and some of these documents are still unavailable. Some have argued, on the other hand, that the possibility of terrorist attacks on chemical plants should strengthen our resolve to gather information about chemical releases and to reduce use of toxic chemicals. A study by the Surgeon General of the Army conducted shortly after 9/11/2001 found that as many as 2.4 million people could be killed or injured in a terrorist attack on a chemical plant in a densely populated area in the United States.[22]

In response to these concerns, Congress authorized the Department of Homeland Security to issue Chemical Facility Anti-Terrorism Standards (CFATS) in 2007. The standards require chemical facility owners to perform a preliminary screening to help the Department determine the level of risk posed by individual facilities. Depending on the level of risk, the Department may require a facility to identify vulnerabilities and create a site security plan. CFATS also provide that the Department will audit and inspect facilities to assess risk and police compliance. In November, 2009, the House passed the Chemical

---

21. On striking the balance between information disclosure and national security, see Katherine Chekouras, *Balancing National Security with a Community's Right to Know: Maintaining Public Access to Environmental Information Through EPCRA's Non-Preemption Clause*, 34 B.C. Envtl. Aff. L. Rev. 107 (2007).

22. See Pianin, *Study Assesses Risk of Attack on Chemical Plant*, Wash. Post, Mar. 12, 2002, at A8.

D. The Emergency Planning and Community Right-to-Know Act

and Water Security Act, H.R. 2868, to revise the legislative requirements and extend CFATS authorization. The bill now moves to the Senate Committee on Homeland Security and Governmental Affairs for approval.

8. TRI data and environmental justice. In addition to providing the public with a wide range of information on toxic chemicals, EPCRA has implications for the disproportionate effects of these chemicals on certain segments of the population. A study published in the American Journal of Public Health[23] compared survey data on race, income, gender, and other demographic factors with the location of chemical facilities listed in the TRI. The authors then used statistical analysis to draw associations between the demographic factors and residences within one mile of the TRI facilities. The results showed that African Americans were significantly more likely than White Americans to live within a mile of a facility. For example, in the Midwest, 58% of African American respondents lived within a mile of a facility, compared to 35% of White respondents. Similar disparities were found in the Southern and Western regions of the country. Socioeconomic disparities between the races only gave a partial explanation for the results, suggesting that racial factors, such as housing segregation and racially motivated facility siting, are at work. What are your thoughts on the results of the study? Is proximity to a facility a good predictor of exposure to toxic chemicals?

---

23. The study was conducted by the University of Michigan Survey Research Center. The full article is available at http://www.greatlakeslaw.org/files/mohai-ej-article.pdf.

9

Public Planning as a Management Tool

GOVERNMENTAL OVERSIGHT OF PRIVATE & PUBLIC RESOURCE USE, AND THE CHALLENGE OF ADAPTIVE MANAGEMENT

A. Managing Localized Land Uses
B. Planning & Management of Public Lands & Resources
C. Large Scale, Public-Private Resource Management & Broadly Integrated Planning
D. Adaptive Management and Climate Change

Planning—the creation, implementation, and ongoing use of plans to guide human actions—is a fundamentally rational and useful practice for both private and public actors, amply deserving attention in a taxonomic analysis of environmental protection law. Planning, of course, is only as good as the data, process, and standards applied in creating and implementing the plan, whether it addresses private, corporate, or governmental activities and resources. This chapter's goal, then, is an examination of how legally enforceable planning may best be designed for optimal civic outcomes.

Environmental management planning by government agencies, especially when it deals with resources 100% owned by the public, should be a straightforward and effective means to achieve rational environmental protections and sustainable development. It isn't.

Our national culture applauds sound planning of private enterprises and individuals—good business plans, life plans, career plans, retirement plans—yet often seems suspicious about any directive governmental planning that impacts upon private actors. When that happens, opponents often castigate government planning as a "socialistic" design suspiciously like modern European social systems, a harbinger of totalitarian Soviet-style five-year plans. Government planning for the objective management of *publicly* owned resources arouses equally powerful resentments, largely coming from the private corporate interests that tend to dominate and profit from the use of particular public resources—timberlands, rangeland, minerals, water.[1] Antipathy to government planning is strong even when government owns the resources in question and is under an obligation to manage them as steward and trustee for the people.

In a complex world, however, effective, enforceable, objective planning is quite clearly a necessity. *Laissez-faire* policies determined by individual decisions of thousands of private market actors aren't sufficient to handle the interconnected physical and economic realities that challenge societies today. Land use decisions impact flood and hurricane disasters, energy and transportation policy impact climate change, growth and economic development patterns impact water supplies and national quality of life. These and myriad other linked critical concerns affirm a need for effective planning-based coordination of activities, rather than a regime of narrowly focused atomistic individually profit-driven decisions.

All governmental programs, of course, to some extent involve planning. This chapter addresses governmental management programs in which "a plan" of some sort is a major, prescriptive, enforceable feature of agency action. Some of these planning structures work, some don't. This chapter addresses different planning structures as part of the taxonomy of regulatory approaches, and explores how planning systems are designed and why they succeed or fail in particular settings.

Land use and natural resources management processes in the U.S. provide a limited number of significant examples of the history, strengths, and weaknesses of governmental planning. Here are some notable examples of American environmental planning:

> 1914*ff*: nationwide campaign to encourage local governments to plan and control land use development patterns — notably by county and municipal zoning, which remains the nation's most widespread public planning mechanism
>
> 1916-18 & 1940-45: intensive governmental wartime planning; aside from securing war materiel, no meaningful environmental/land use/natural resource planning
>
> 1956: the Interstate Highway System; began as a national plan seeking to "connect the U.S.A." and eventually became the single most prominent federal determinant of land use patterns in the nation's history
>
> 1970: the CWA's §208[2] Water Quality Management Planning program, focused on wastewater; federal government encourages states to plan with regional and local units to build and maintain sewerage facilities and monitor impacted waters; the program has had a tangible effect on development patterns[3]
>
> 1970: NLUPA, the National Land Use Planning Act, a fascinating congressional proposal that never became law but possessed an intriguing potential to foresee and avoid the dysfunctions of sprawl that plagues so many greater metropolitan regions
>
> 1974: CZMA,[4] providing federal support and backup for state plans for the coastal zone
>
> 1976: FLPMA ("flip-ma"),[5] some planning for federal lands

---

1. A thoughtful exploration of many of the issues presented in this chapter is Owen, Probabilities, Planning Failures, and Environmental Law, 84 Tulane L. Rev. 265 (2009). For a sense of regulated industries' powerful reaction against civic planning for public resources, note some of the history of the "Wise Use" movement. Plater, Environmental Law as a Mirror of the Future: Civic Values Confronting Market Force Dynamics in a Time of Counter-Revolution, 23 B.C. Envtl. Aff. L. Rev 733, 772-777 & n. 143 (1996).

2. 33 U.S.C. §1251.

3. The planning required by the CWA is large-scale and relatively open-ended in the management mandates it dictates. Other statutes require "plans" but, many, like the CAA's SIPs, are largely adjectival, brokering pollution allocations within a strictly delimited set of objective statutory criteria.

4. Coastal Zone Management Act, 16 U.S.C. §§1451 et seq.

5. Federal Land Policy and Management Act of 1976, 43 U.S.C. §§1701 et seq.

- 1976: NFMA ("nifma"),[6] under which the U.S. Forest Service (USFS) must prepare Land and Resource Management Plans (LRMPs)
- 1977: the Carter Administration National Energy Planning initiative, which came to naught
- 1986: EPCRA[7] (see Chapter 8), includes toxics emergency planning
- 1990: OPA-90's National Contingency Plan for oil pollution — shown to be faulty, 2010
- 1991: ISTEA ("ice-tea"),[8] includes limited transportation planning
- 2003: the Cheney-Bush National Energy Policy (primarily deregulatory *laissez-faire*, planning for energy subsidies)
- 2009: UN Copenhagen Conference on Climate Change, the summit-level endeavor to reach agreement on a global plan for reduction of atmospheric carbon concentrations; only vague goals emerge, and the U.S., like most nations, works on an ambiguous and politically tenuous domestic plan
- 2015: the Obama Administration's Clean Power Plan, and the USA's major contribution to the COP-21 Paris accord — as a plan, the Clean Power Plan has aspirational timelines and textual policy standards, pivots away from natural gas fracking and nuclear energy toward sustainables such as solar and wind, but is launched in a context of immediate massive political resistance and cannot purport to bind future administrations; the COP-21 consensus accord contains timelines with aspirational targets but no legally binding standards; it includes an interesting program of five-year adaptive climate effort reviews (see the last unit on this chapter on adaptive management) — an international experiment that will be closely and hopefully watched.

It's astonishing to note in this selection of major wide-scale U.S. environmental planning endeavors that there haven't actually been very many over the nation's 200-plus years, and that at least half of them have failed in whole or part. As the 2010 Gulf oil episode showed — 20 years after the Exxon Valdez spill prompted Congress to require planning, in the OPA-90 statute — a process of corporate and regulatory agency entropy and resistance tends to erode legal planning requirements.

The erratic record of public planning reflects the underlying reality that public planning programs tend to be powerfully impacted by the nongovernmental economic and institutional establishments they attempt to regulate. Public planning efforts are designed to achieve broad civic, communal goals, while the processes they attempt to regulate often are driven by powerful narrower interests. Public attempts to coordinate and guide economic and institutional behavior toward optimally rational public outcomes therefore often are buffeted by internal and external political pressures. Public planning tends to be shaped from the start by political context. Stringent provisions tend to be resisted and eroded over time. Enforcement can be extremely problematic. Our current form of "democracy" gives such extraordinary power to large economic interests, and has made Congress such a polarized obstruction to progressive policies, that achieving effective apolitical planning in broad areas of societal concern is extremely difficult.

Long-term societal sustainability, however, will require effective mechanisms of public planning, weighing societal necessities, refining alternatives, developing and implementing rationalized decisional matrices for meeting societal needs over long periods of time.

National energy planning. Where contrary industrial pressures are substantial, the most common experience of large-scale public planning in the U.S. has been a political process of avoidance and erosion. A prime example of important and necessary planning

---

6. National Forest Management Planning Act, 16 U.S.C. §§1601 et seq.
7. Emergency Planning & Community Right to Know Act, 42 U.S.C. §§11001 et seq.
8. Intermodal Surface Transportation Efficiency Act, 23 U.S.C. §§101 et seq.

attempts faltering under political pressures is the failure to implement any sort of national U.S. energy plan.

Today, in the second decade of the twenty-first century, it is undeniable that serious national energy planning is a societal necessity. The history of energy planning in the U.S., however, is a troubling example of public policy foot-dragging and regressive politics—

- Initially, as in most areas of human enterprise, the process of "planning" for energy supply and consumption was an uncoordinated default system resulting from the unregulated actions of market-driven industries. In the mid-twentieth century, spurred by war, government hydropower projects were the rare and limited example of public energy planning. By the 1960s, the fossil fuel and nuclear industries had successfully built a structure of production and supply, government subsidies, and tax advantages that produced healthy profits while keeping the cost of energy for consumers relatively low. Until the Arab oil embargo of 1973 and the worldwide "oil shock" it created, the word *energy*[9] was not even generally recognized as a major policy concept or public concern.
- Faced with the oil embargo, developed nations suddenly discovered their prodigal dependence and serious vulnerability regarding energy supply. President Nixon created an Energy Advisory Council composed of six energy researchers and ten representatives of industry. The Council recommended deregulation of energy industries with continuation of subsidies to increase domestic fossil energy supplies.
- The Ford Administration followed Nixon's policy of decreasing the taxation and regulation of energy industries, and signed the Energy Policy and Conservation Act of 1975 (P.L. 94-163) that increased fossil fuel subsidies but also authorized a variety of potential conservation measures.
- In 1977, with consumption continually straining supply despite rising energy costs, the Carter Administration created a Cabinet-level Department of Energy and promised to establish a National Energy Plan within 90 days, along with an Energy Mobilization Board. Instead of a Board and a Plan, however, Carter eventually settled for an announced National Energy Policy emphasizing conservation efforts. He promulgated significant energy-efficiency (CAFE, corporate average fuel economy) standards for automobiles and consumer appliances, and pushed major research and development subsidies for energy-efficiency technologies and alternative energy sources. These initiatives were enthusiastically replicated by nations in the European Community.
- The Reagan Administration rescinded the Carter conservation policies, substantially loosening CAFE standards and other energy regulations, cutting back R&D for alternative energy and conservation, and asserting a strong military presence in the Middle East (referred to as "strong reserves, strong forces"). Natural gas was substantially deregulated.
- The Bush I Administration passed the Energy Policy Act of 1992, adding new incentives for domestic oil production, increased subsidies for nuclear power, deregulated electric utilities, and increased federal support for alternative energy R&D. Still no National Energy Plan.
- The Clinton Administration attempted to reimpose heightened CAFE standards, fund increased R&D for renewable energy, prevent fossil fuel development in the Alaska National Wildlife Reserve, and limit CO_2 emissions to 1990 levels (signing

---

9. Like the word *environment*, which was practically unknown as a referent for *nature* until well into the 1960s.

the 1997 Kyoto Protocol). Most of these initiatives were blocked by energy lobbyists in the congressional process. Still no National Energy Plan.
- The Bush II Administration announced its National Energy Plan in 2001, the "Reliable, Affordable, and Environmentally Sound Energy Plan for America's Future," drafted by a task force assembled by Vice President Cheney. Less a plan than a generalized policy statement, it encouraged domestic gas, oil, nuclear, and "clean coal" development, and loosened environmental regulations to accelerate new energy production, opened new lands for drilling, increased tax breaks for energy industries, and expanded western gas, oil, and coal leasing on wilderness-quality lands. Many of its provisions were passed into law in the 2005 Energy Policy Act.
- The Obama Administration asserted its intention to address the critical need for a National Energy Plan and created a new White House position for a Coordinator of Energy & Climate Policy. With stimulus funds it accelerated support for alternative energy source R&D and modernization of the national electricity grid, promising to double renewable energy production, improve energy efficiency and conservation programs, raise CAFE standards, and create a national cap-and-trade system to control GHG emissions. Faced with economic straits and intractable obstruction from energy-backed opposition in the Senate, however, the Administration's efforts to advance international energy agreements and achieve an operable national energy plan proved wistful. And the BP Deepwater Blowout appears not to have catalyzed better planning.

In the rest of the world, in modern industrial democracies as well as in more autocratic regimes, governmental planning mechanisms tend to be far more widespread and determinative than in the U.S. in the energy field and beyond. In the European Union and Anglo-inspired legal systems like Canada and Australia, national and provincial environmental planning tends to be closely integrated with regulatory systems that implement the plans' provisions on public and private development projects.[10] China, though still deeply mired in the coal-dominated energy technology of past centuries, began an accelerating program of alternative energy research, development, and investment in 1998 that has brought it to a leadership position significantly ahead of the U.S.[11]

The lobbying logjams and obstructions of objective planning in the U.S. energy field caused Thomas Friedman, a triple Pulitzer Prize–winning journalist to dream, half seriously, "if only we could be China for a day (but not for two)!" China's dictatorial government has been able to coordinate and launch a modern energy-efficiency campaign that is making China, despite its current massive dependence on coal, a pioneering global leader in sustainable long-term green energy technology. Not the U.S.—

> Rather than having a national energy strategy we have instead what the energy expert Gal Luft called "the sum of all lobbies." Whichever lobby generates the most campaign cash wins. To put it another way, "We have energy *politics*, not energy *policy*." . . . It means that the politics of the issues (that is, who will benefit specifically) drive the policy priorities (what is really best for the country as a whole), not the other way around. It is very difficult to produce a coherent and viable long-term strategy in such an environment. . . . What you have instead is a lot of blather

---

10. The British Town & Country Planning Act of 1948 was a dramatic imposition of governmental planning on nationwide development patterns. The German one-stop Bergamt permitting process created a multilevel forum for development planning. See Plater, Coal Law from the Old World, 9 Land Use & Env't L. Rev. (1978). In the European Union, substantial support for intra-Union planning is based in the Directive on Strategic Environmental Assessment, coupled with the EU "Infrastructure for Spatial Information in Europe" and GMES (Global Monitoring for Environment and Security) programs.

11. See Osnos, "Green Giant," New Yorker, Dec. 21-28, 2009, at 54-65.

about "clean" coal and a lot of money pouring into corn ethanol programs, out of all proportion to what makes national sense. T. Friedman, China for a Day, in Hot, Flat, and Crowded: Why We Need a Green Revolution—and How It Can Renew America 437 (2008).

On the other hand, a number of energy planning efforts outside the federal government have been remarkably effective. Almost half the states have passed energy facility siting statutes, and these programs, notably those in California, Oregon, and Massachusetts,[12] have demonstrated how the process of building an infrastructure of large energy units can integrate extensive public standards of economic accounting, science, coordination, and safety—with meaningful public participation—into business decisions involving hundreds of millions of dollars.

Water quality planning. There are also affirmative examples on a national scale of effective major planning initiatives overcoming the clash of interests and jurisdictions, producing significant beneficial operating results. Good exemplars are the CWA's §208 planning mandate and the Safe Drinking Water Amendments of 1986. In CWA §208 Congress authorized comprehensive watershed planning to address problems with point and nonpoint source pollution controls.[13] Section 208 requires states to designate the boundaries of each area "which as a result of urban industrial concentrations or other factors has substantial water quality control problems" and to designate representative governmental and nongovernmental agencies "capable of developing effective areawide waste treatment management plans for such area." 33 U.S.C. §1288(a)(1)-(2) (1995).

> §208 contains unique authority to control water pollution from point sources (e.g., factory or pipe discharge) . . . and from nonpoint sources (e.g., mining or agricultural runoff). Its implementation features [don't limit] State efforts to stationary sources of pollution. The Section is intended to coordinate and integrate other planning, construction, and discharge permit provisions of the Act. Section 208 charts a course not only for the cleaning up of polluted waters but also for the prevention of future pollution by identifying problem sources, regulating construction of certain industrial facilities, and developing processes to control runoff sources of pollution." *NRDC v. Costle*, 564 F.2d 573, 577 (D.C. Cir. 1977).

There are no stipulated penalties if a state fails to conform to §208 planning requirements, but the Act nevertheless has encouraged a great deal of coordinated state and regional land use planning.

The Safe Drinking Water Act (SDWA) requires states to develop "source water protection" programs to ensure that the land areas providing recharge to drinking water supplies (both ground and surface waters) are protected against inappropriate land uses within delineated "wellhead protection areas" and surface watersheds. As land uses are rarely regulated comprehensively at the state level, states have imposed "source water protection" planning requirements on their respective municipalities, which, in turn, have adopted plans and regulations consistent with those plans to protect drinking water resources. Safe Drinking Water Act Amendments of 1986, 42 U.S.C. §300f (1994).

Initially the SDWA required states to adopt comprehensive planning programs focused on protecting public water supply "wellheads" to avoid groundwater contamination. This

---

12. See Cal. Pub. Res. Code §§25213ff (a complex but "one-stop" permitting process); Or. Rev. Stat. §§469.300ff; Mass. Gen. Laws chap. 164, §69S; and regulations issued thereunder.

13. The 1987 amendments to §319 of the CWA further required states to adopt plans to reduce nonpoint source pollution, including the adoption of what has become commonly referred to as "best management practices" (BMPs) for agricultural activities and residential, commercial, and industrial developments—noted further in Chapter 11.

developed into a highly successful planning effort, the Source Water Protection Program, extending planning to the protection of entire watersheds, including both surface and groundwaters. SDWA §1453(2)(A). The Source Water Protection Program sets forth a highly logical planning approach to natural resource protection by requiring states and their respective local governments to (1) delineate the watersheds that provide recharge to specific water bodies, (2) identify all sources of contamination, (3) analyze the relative susceptibility of the water resource to contamination (e.g. through an analysis of underlying geology and distance to/from known contamination sources), and (4) adopt management solutions to protect the water resource (e.g., adoption of land plans and regulatory and nonregulatory planning techniques).[14]

The combined effect of §208 and SDWA planning mandates has been to provide one of the few effective large-scale guidance structures for development patterns in the U.S., with tangible effects on private as well as public development planning.[15] Why have these planning efforts been successful when so many others have not? It may have something to do with the fact that it's hard for anyone to oppose clean drinking water and wastewater treatment, and there are few politically powerful economic interests positioned to resist such planning.

The successes of planning under CWA §208 and the SDWA, however, have not been fully replicated in the CWA's regulations based on planning for "carrying capacity," in part perhaps because those rules assign stringent numerical standards to state waterways, potentially imposing direct impacts on an array of corporate polluters. CWA §303(d) requires states to establish "waste load allocations" for point and nonpoint sources for particular waterbodies, defining the "total maximum daily load" (TMDL) of pollutants for each waterbody. State and local governments are required to adopt land use plans and regulations designed to ensure that the carrying capacity of the water resource is not exceeded. As noted in Chapter 11, however, states and courts have been hesitant to require active enforcement of TMDL plans.

Reduced to its bare bones, governmental planning ideally duplicates the elements of private planning, with the difference that it is externally enforced. Seven essential elements can be discerned in sequence or in blended form in virtually all "rational planning" systems—

1. Defining the terrain and the goals: what is the focal problem and scope of concern, and what are the goals and objectives the planning effort is supposed to address?
2. Data collection: statistical data, maps, charts, relevant expert research, historical data, solicitation and collection of relevant input from private and public sources, new and ongoing research, policy literature and debates, polls of public attitudes, etc.
3. Formulation of potential alternative approaches to optimal achievement of the goals, with consideration of different arrays of actions, technologies, timing, locations,

---

14. See Am. Planning Ass'n, A Guide to Wellhead Protection, PAS Rep. 457/458 (1995), and Am. Water Works Ass'n, Source Water Protection: Effective Tools and Techniques You Can Use (1999).

15. Our colleague Prof. Jon Witten, a trained planner as well as law professor to whom we are indebted for advice on this section, argues that regulation of the water resource is one of the strongest existing legal leverages on land development patterns. See Witten, Carrying Capacity and the Comprehensive Plan: Establishing and Defending Limits to Growth, 28 B.C. Envtl. Aff. L. Rev. 4 (2001).

management structures and approaches, etc. (Public participation from this point on is appropriate, useful, and necessary for a variety of reasons.)

4. Evaluating and winnowing options, choosing the planning design; "satisficing" — weighing the available alternative hypotheses, and choosing and defining an optimal pattern or path for management of the subject given the data, the objectives, the political and institutional constraints, and context.
5. Developing principles, enforceable standards, and procedures to be applied: articulating the selected applicable regulatory and management standards, patterns, paths, timelines, and the management regime.
6. Putting it all into a coherent plan: consolidating the operative principles, standards, and procedures into a structured mechanism to guide future action, defining actions permitted or required, actions forbidden, procedural sequences mandated, benchmark standards, etc.
7. Implementation, application, monitoring, responsive enforcement, ongoing adaptation: applying the plan to the targeted range of actions as mandatory guidance (or not); protocols for collecting and processing continuing feedback on how the implementation and application of the plan are working in practice, including information on successful achievements, violations, failures, new conditions, etc., with responsive reactions to incoming monitoring information; in enforcement terms, violations must be addressed and remedies implemented; feedback loops include responsive amendments of original plan terms to adapt to new information and improve the continuing process.

Further significant organic questions include— *Who?* What entity at what level, with what grant of authority, will develop and implement the planning?— *What?* What power mechanism and remedies will be authorized to implement the planning system? and— *When?* Is the planning system to be relatively static, laying out and enforcing a determined pattern or path at the outset, with few ongoing changes, or is it designed to be a dynamic, constantly evolving management process?

Each of these bland-sounding elements can trigger a welter of controversial questions and debates. This chapter samples a wide variety of past environmental planning efforts, some successful, most less so, and also addresses the very modern challenge presented by highly fluid and unpredictable conditions, noting the adaptive management approach (also known as ARM, adaptive resource management).

Analyzing successes and failures can improve future planning efforts to manage environmental problems. This chapter considers governmental planning systems that attempt to regulate both public and private interests—

- Regulation of private land use—government planning directly targeting and shaping private actions, primarily focusing on local regulation of private land use around the nation.
- Public natural resource management—officially developed plans for government agencies managing the use and exploitation of natural resources, principally on the federal public lands.
- Regulation of mixed public-private interactions—planning designed to control mixed public and private resources and the initiatives, using examples from energy planning, the CZMA, the CWA §404, and ill-starred NLUPA.
- Adaptive management—in the context of a world with highly fluid and unpredictably changing and interacting conditions, planning cannot be static but must anticipate and respond to evolving circumstances. Adaptive management theories present

challenges to the technology of planning but to ideals of democratic governance as well.

In all these planning settings it becomes obvious, for public resources as well as private, that it is almost always the private market players whose actions and reactions impact planning efforts and subsequent legal controversies most strongly. Understanding the planning design and implementation process at different levels of government, and the problematic political contexts in which these legal initiatives play out, will inevitably be essential to environmental law as it develops, as it must, thoughtful, proactive, dynamic planning regimes to cope with the stringent challenges of the twenty-first century.

A. MANAGING LOCALIZED LAND USES

In day-to-day practice, the overwhelming majority of land use planning and management occurs in the form of local county and municipal government regulation. Although local land use law is quite variable from jurisdiction to jurisdiction, there are two ubiquitous tools, zoning and subdivision regulation, both of which provide positive and negative lessons. Almost invariably, local planning systems are heavily impacted by those they regulate. The most directly affected well-organized constituency tends to be land development interests whose political influence is often dominant and quick to launch legal attacks on restrictive regulations, including constitutional claims that legal controls violate Due Process and Takings Clauses under the Fifth and Fourteenth Amendments.[16] (See Chapter 21.)

The role of local governments in localized land regulation in zoning and subdivision regulation has received dramatic supplementation by federal regulation coming from an unexpected quarter, §404 of the CWA, and by the aftershocks of publicized toxic contaminations that have led to state siting interventions, noted later in this section.

1. Plan-Based Land Use Zoning

Most zoning is locally based, reflecting original policy decisions embodied in the Standard State Zoning Enabling Act (SSZEA),[17] a 1922 federally suggested model act adopted by virtually all states, delegating the zoning power down to local government units. To guide local zoning, the federal government promoted the Standard City Planning Enabling Act (SCPEA),[18] whereby states authorized local units to set up planning commissions alongside zoning boards to adopt official comprehensive plans.

The most common form of zone ordinance is the Euclidean model, named for the Supreme Court case that established zoning's general validity, *Village of Euclid v. Ambler Realty Co.*, 272 U.S. 365 (1926). Euclidean zoning is based upon (1) a comprehensive plan analyzing existing land uses and specifying community development directions; (2) a (separate) zone ordinance creating a catalog of zone district categories, defining the range of

---

16. Cynthia Barrett, though focused on Florida water resources in her book Mirage (2007), eloquently catalogs land developers' effective and comprehensive resistance to regulations in every era of that state's history.

17. SSZEA, drafted as a national model for state implementation by the U.S. Department of Commerce in 1922. P.E. Salkin, Authority to Enact Land Use Regulations: Delegation of Power; The Enabling Acts, 1 Am. Law of Zoning §2:11 (5th ed. 2009).

18. Drafted by the U.S. Dept. of Commerce in 1928.

permitted uses, densities, and structural characteristics in each category; (3) an official zone map, incorporated as part of the ordinance, mapping out the districts on the ground; and, finally, (4) a zone enforcement agency to interpret and apply the zone requirements throughout the community, reviewing and determining enforcement issues, special exceptions, and variances as required. (See Figure 1.)

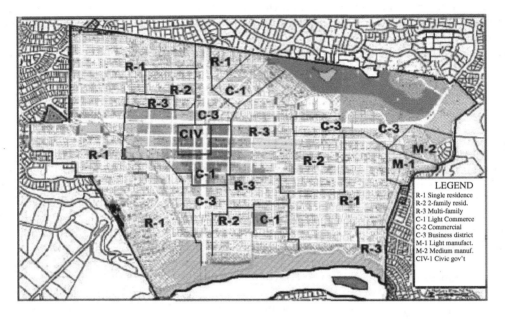

FIGURE 9-1. *A standard municipal Euclidean zone arrangement in a California city with an area of two square miles. See analysis in Commentary & Questions that follow.*

This form of planning places zone designations on every square inch of the jurisdiction, specifying in advance which uses will automatically be allowed without permits, which added uses will be allowed by special-exception permit, and which uses are prohibited.

Some flexibility is built in through ordinance provisions that allow defined "special exceptions" if specified procedures are followed and by hardship "variances" to prevent unconstitutionally excessive "regulatory takings;" the local government can also legislatively amend the map or the ordinance, though the changes must accord with the official plan.[19] Zoning's broad area designations reflect a theory that if like activities are grouped with one another, and unlike activities prohibited, there will be fewer cases in which incompatible land uses are located conflictingly close to one another. Traditional zones prescribe minimum lot sizes, height limits, and required side setbacks as well as use restrictions for residential zone districts.

Zoning directly affects private property decisions, which explains why from its inception it has stirred up a hornet's nest of opposition. Nevertheless, the land use problems of American communities were seen as sufficiently serious that, of all major American cities, only Houston has refused to employ zoning, paying a price in chaotic land-development patterns.

---

19. Illegal "spot zoning" occurs if a change is not in conformity with the plan. Several states, however, unfortunately either don't require a plan or do not require consistency with the plan. See Witten & Curtin, Windfalls, Wipeouts, Givings, and Takings in Dramatic Redevelopment Projects: Bargaining for Better Zoning on Density, Views, and Public Access, 32 B.C. Envtl. Aff. L. Rev. 325, 328-345 (2005).

A. Managing Localized Land Uses

Zoning both explicitly and implicitly incorporates some environmental values. This simple form of use segregation tends to reduce the likelihood of nuisances and negative externalities attributable to proximity of incompatible activities. Not only does it prevent most residential development immediately adjacent to industrial areas, if a zone planning agency knows which way the political and meteorological winds are blowing, it will not locate residential areas downwind from its industrial zone districts. "Densities" (concentrations of permitted structures) designated for various districts can have direct consequences for local quality of life. In many cases, however, "Home Rule" laws induce each community to perceive itself as a separate little city-state, incorporating prime residential areas, industrial zones to capture tax base, no waste disposal sites, and no coordination on a county or regional basis to determine how and where larger settlement and economic development patterns should be located.

Over the years, a variety of other more overtly environmental regulations have emerged as overlays to basic zoning ordinances, capitalizing upon zoning's established political and legal acceptability. When some communities want to protect wetlands or flood plains, for sake of convenience they add the new regulations as overlay districts upon their zone maps. (See Figure 2.) Land in any location that is within a historic district overlay, for instance, must comply with the overlay regulation as well as the underlying zone requirements. Some communities add "open space" overlays or "green belt" requirements to the basic zone ordinance and map, or erosion and sedimentation restrictions using setbacks and other requirements to protect water quality of adjacent waterbodies, historic preservation controls, and similar modern environmental resource protections. As local zoning increasingly reflects the growing sophistication of the land use planning and landscape architecture specialties, more and more environmentally oriented elements are likely to be incorporated in the planning and implementation of local zone ordinances.

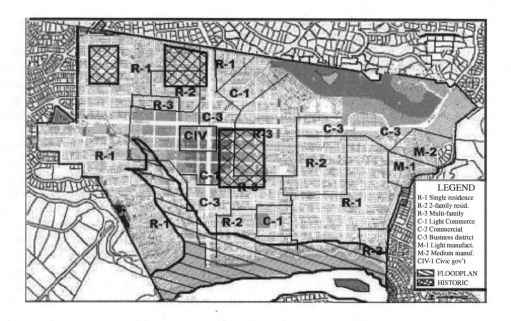

FIGURE 9-2. *"Overlay" regulatory designations for flood plain and historic area land use limitations are superimposed upon the base zone map.*

COMMENTARY & QUESTIONS

1. Plan-based zoning: advantages as a taxonomic device. The design of zoning regulation—starting with a plan, an implementing ordinance, and an official map stipulating different uses for different areas—provides a practical way to translate civic policy decisions into practice on the ground. The technology of plan-based zoning is relatively straightforward and simple, and it produces tangible effects in controlling land use decisions.

Process: The official plan is typically developed by land planning professionals in an open process with public input, and the zone ordinance with map are adopted in open city legislative procedures. The process typically follows an intensive inventory of the community's physical and social context, and incorporates community objectives.

Clarity: Looking at Figure 1, note how the city plan's provisions enforced by the zoning are clearly presented on the zone map, avoiding confusion. Because automatically permitted uses are set out in each of the zone ordinance's districts, potential buyers, developers, and municipal enforcement officials can easily see what can be done with each parcel of land without a zone permit or by special permit. They can then adapt their development planning in advance to comply with zone requirements.

Enforceability: Relatively straightforward. Most structures and uses won't need a permit. Most violations are easy to spot, and citizen complaints act as a built-in enforcement mechanism.

Some flexibility: All plans need to incorporate a potential for flexibility to meet changing needs and conditions. In Euclidean zoning, in addition to takings hardship variances and legislative amendments of plans and zone ordinances, the special-exception permit process sets out requirements and a range of permitted flexibility, and provides for public input.

Because of these advantages, local zoning has ultimately been adopted in the vast majority of U.S. communities

2. Plan-based zoning: shortcomings. Plan-based zoning incorporates potential disadvantages that may provide lessons for other planning-based regulatory schemes.

Scale limitations: Again looking at Figure 1, note that the local zone covers only the two square miles of the subject community. The surrounding areas are apparently densely populated, but belong to other local government jurisdictions. Each zoned community tends to plan and zone itself as a self-contained independent kingdom, taking little or no account of the regulations and needs of neighboring communities. (Note the location of the manufacturing zones; it's quite likely that prevailing winds blow left to right.)

To counter the dysfunctions of fractionalized plans and zones, a number of initiatives have been tried. State governments have tried to raise the profile of state planning agencies, or have tried to establish regional planning structures or metropolitan regional processes (some involving more than one state), to integrate planning for large areas, especially urban areas containing many dozens of separate government units. Rational analysis indicates that some issues need to be dealt with at higher levels of planning than others. (See "The 'Subsidiarity' Principle," below.) Some issues like affordable housing have prompted state courts to require local governments to incorporate statewide considerations into local planning and zoning, following the innovative lead of the New Jersey Supreme Court in *Township of Mount Laurel v. NAACP*, 67 N.J. 151 (1975). But although many issues presented by local zoning have statewide and even nationwide significance, land use controls have nevertheless remained overwhelmingly local, and the federal government does virtually no national land use planning.

Static planning, needs for flexibility: A common problem of planning, and zoning in particular, is that plans do not adequately foresee changing needs and circumstances. Evolving

A. Managing Localized Land Uses

transportation issues or economic activity often require amended provisions not provided for in original planning, zone districts, and defined special-exception provisions. Non-Euclidean zoning has been one answer: to add new highly flexible multiple-use districts to the ordinances, by which developers can apply for special master permits to be applied in special amendments to the zone map. Typically these "PUDs" (planned unit developments), "floating zones," or "contract zonings" require new planning analysis and extensive negotiation with planners, local officials, and the public. When well-coordinated with planning processes, such non-Euclidean devices can provide useful examples of "adaptive management" (see Section D below).

Politics—pressure from the regulated industry: Regulatory provisions that limit market forces (virtually all, since most regulations are designed to correct market failures) inevitably attract strong political impacts from regulated interests. Planning thus is rarely dominated only by planning "science"—the application of objective criteria to objective factual conditions—but rather typically includes ample consideration of what is politically possible.

Regulated market interests—typically, in the case of zoning, real estate developers—exert great focused pressures upon administrators and agencies set up to design and implement planned regulatory regimes.

Subsequent modifications in plan-based zoning are thus often products of ad hoc pressures rather than comprehensive analysis. Zoning "variances," for example—supposedly extraordinary devices instituted to relieve unconstitutional burden effects on particular private properties—often become politically pressured trump cards that summarily override restrictions. Issued by administrative staff rather than elected or judicial bodies, and tinged by the uncertainties of what is or isn't an invalid regulatory taking (see Chapter 21), variances often derive from focused political threats or are followed by rumors of under-the-table financial inducements. Locally legislated zone amendments often are accused as unjustified "spot zoning," bypassing official plans under pressure from individual entrepreneurs.

Stultifying uniformity: Plan-based zoning as it developed in mid-twentieth-century America has often been criticized as an unrealistic broad-brush simplification of human communities. Miles of white-bread, cookie-cutter housing developments—each lot with unusable zoning-decreed front yards and side yards, and the same single-family demographic—have created sprawlingly consumptive and inefficient land uses (based on the premise of automobile transportation and cheap gas prices), and a de facto social segregation often based upon income and other like-with-like regulatory parameters.

Reacting to such perceptions of traditional zoning, a number of innovative planning concepts have been taking hold—"New Urbanism" theories of mixed demographics and mixed uses,[20] human-scaled development, "smart growth," and others. Many current planning concepts derive from urban planning ideas reflecting the perceptions of the late Jane Jacobs, who observed how community life and economics flourished in helter-skelter neighborhoods like her Greenwich Village in New York City[21] with a heady mixture of people and enterprises evolved in a natural human process over the years. Planning is necessary to screen out dysfunctional initiatives and excesses beyond an area's "carrying capacity," while encouraging efficiencies and benefits of clustered uses and mixed populations.

3. Subdivision regulations. Subdivision of land and the ensuing construction of residential housing constitute a major industry in the U.S. A variety of environmental problems,

---

20. For an introduction to New Urbanism, see A. Duany, E. Plater-Zyberk, et al., Suburban Nation: The Rise of Sprawl and the Decline of the American Dream (2000).
21. See J. Jacobs, The Death and Life of Great American Cities (1961).

some severe, commonly ensue when subdividers take large parcels of land (often farms or ranches purchased in large blocks) and divide them up legally into many small lots (often a quarter-acre or less) to be resold as many separate commodity units. Developers' practices are a basic cause of widespread sprawl. Seeking out large, cheap parcels of land to develop, they tend to "leap-frog" their developments out and away from existing cities and towns, wastefully eliminating farmland and open space, dysfunctionally creating far-flung needs for utilities and new transportation facilities, and diluting opportunities for planned growth and community coherence. Developers frequently lack design sophistication, ignoring topography and natural processes like flooding. These developments usually impose costs on the larger community because the developers, in most instances, are not legally responsible for providing basic services. Other externalized costs of this type of development can arise from site disruptions that cause erosion and septic overflows that degrade lakes and rivers.

Regulation of the market-driven subdivision process is a major land use tool that, given the political will to implement it, is often more nuanced and useful than zoning. Subdivision regulations incorporate generic planning requirements rather than comprehensively mapped planning processes.

Subdivision regulations use the developer's private act of recording a master deed with its multi-lot plot-plan chart ("plat") in the local registry of deeds as the regulatory fulcrum. Before these private law subdivision documents can be recorded and lots sold, a subdivision regulation ordinance mandates that they must meet a variety of specified legal requirements — sewerage, utilities, road criteria, etc. The ordinance's requirements are often applied in the form of required certificates issued by departments of the local government that must be annexed and noted on the master plat itself. Many subdivision requirements are environmental in nature. Beyond the basics, some more sophisticated subdivision regulations anticipate the potential cost externalizations developers might otherwise impose and require erosion and sedimentation controls, dedication of park land and other "exactions" offsetting burdens placed on the community, certified landscape architects' plans with analyses of groundwater flows and slope configurations, and the like.[22] Having a subdivision law in places achieves regulatory economies of scale for the community, as the planning law attaches a range of significant requirements to all subdivisions in a jurisdiction.

Subdivision regulations can also require that developers put enforceable restrictive covenants and other private law devices on the master deed, such as requirements for open space protection, density controls, and other use restrictions which can be made specifically enforceable both by other lot owners and by the local government as a third party beneficiary. Subdivision regulations often are more acceptable to the developer than other forms of land use regulation because they can result in higher-value properties.

4. Land planning innovations. Beyond non-Euclidean concepts, smart growth, and New Urbanism as noted above, there are a host of new planning techniques and innovations, including transportation-based planning, water-resource-based planning, and multilayered electronic geographic information systems (GIS) that permit coordinated consideration of statistical and photographic data superimposed on graphic maps.

---

22. Design standards can encourage site plans that "cluster" residential structures to preserve the maximum amount of amenities and useful space for the inhabitants of the subdivision, rather than cutting up the parcel into the allowable number of standardized front, back, and side lots covering the site like a checkerboard.

A. Managing Localized Land Uses

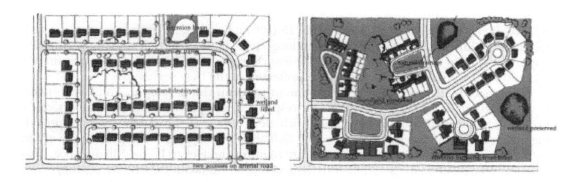

FIGURE 9-3. *Same parcel of land, two development alternatives: traditional checkerboard or clustered design. Reprinted with permission from Lane Kendig et al., Performance Zoning (1980).*

One technique developed over past decades is the planning concept of "cluster development" by which particular parcels of land (and potentially larger territories up to the level of regional development) can apply more dynamic and efficient designs by defining constituent parcels in smaller terms, with alignments adjusted to terrain or transportation designs, and imaginative use of opened-up spaces. As shown in Figure 3, compared to a standard subdivision design covering maximal area with diminished utility, the clustered "performance" design retains natural features, more amenities, less roadway, the same or greater population, and higher unit prices. Applying the same principles across broader geographical areas can promote effective anti-sprawl smart growth development patterns.

5. TDRs—mixing zoning with economic incentives to accomplish land use steering. A number of local governments have set up creative systems of transferable development rights (TDRs), to give developers and the public a measure of design flexibility. Similar to tradeable pollution credits studied in Chapter 14, TDRs represent unused development density at one site that can be transferred and sold to other sites that wish to build beyond standard regulatory limits.

> TDR programs aim to direct development away from environmentally sensitive land to land more suitable for development by creating a market for development rights. Logistically, TDR programs achieve this result by quantifying the development potential of sensitive properties ("sending sites"), and providing that this development potential may be sold to landowners to increase building density in areas suitable for development ("receiving sites"). *Good v. U.S.*, 39 Fed. Cl. 81, 107 (1997).

New York City has a complex system of TDRs, featured in the *Penn Central* case, 438 U.S. 104 (1978) (see Chapter 21), where the Supreme Court held that the value of TDRs is relevantly weighed in regulatory takings challenges. The theory was charted out in Professor John Costonis's Development Rights Transfers: An Exploratory Essay, 83 Yale L.J. 75 (1973). For an environmental TDR primer, see McEleney, Using Transferable Development Rights to Preserve Vanishing Landscapes and Landmarks, 1995 Ill. B.J. 634.

A particularly interesting environmental application of TDRs has been implemented in the Lake Tahoe Basin. The Tahoe Regional Planning Agency, created through a bi-state compact between Nevada and California, seeks to prevent overdevelopment of the watershed in order to reduce erosion and sewage discharges into the lake. Under the terms of its integrated Basin management plan, designed to protect the lake's remarkably pure waters, owners of restricted parcels may sell TDRs within the Basin, even across the state line. See Fink, Structuring a Program for the Lake Tahoe Basin, 18 Ecology L.Q. 485 (1991); *Suitum v. Tahoe Regional Planning Agency*, 520 U.S. 725 (1997); Lazarus, Litigating *Suitum* . . . , 12 J. Land Use & Envtl. L. 179 (1995). One challenge is to assure a sufficient array of transfer-importing sites to maintain a market, while assuring that the TDR transfers serve and not undermine the public values sought to be protected in the base regulation.

6. Impact fees: internalizing development costs on the developer. Similar to subdivision exactions noted below, impact fees respond to the problem that developers often locate high-density developments without sufficient regard to the public's costs of providing utilities and amenities. Impact fees are calculated by analyzing the imposed costs of the use being initiated. The governmental entity requires the fees to be paid in advance, providing funds to defray costs of added parks and recreation facilities, schools, drainage and sewer construction, roads and other transportation infrastructure, groundwater recharge facilities, and an infinitely expandable range of other imposed costs.[23] In planning terms, what is the precise role of impact fees? In economic terms, what role do impact fees play? Do they force the project proponent to internalize costs, or are they instead merely a form of governmental extortion? Like other land use devices currently applied at the local level, impact fees can mobilize the expertise and defensive instincts of local communities. They hold larger intercommunity and regional potential as well.

7. The "Subsidiarity" Principle, local zoning, and the NLUPA bill. In terms of levels of government, the local focus of zoning reflects a taxonomic concept called the "Subsidiarity Principle," which can be seen in many environmental settings including land use, federal pollution statutes' cooperative federalism, and international environmental control.

The Subsidiarity Principle holds that for reasons of information knowledge and democratic governance, decisions should be determined at the *lowest level* of decisionmaking at which they can most rationally be made. In extreme form it supports the argument that it's the *individual* who is best situated to make land use decisions, but in many settings it is rationally obvious that certain decisions have to be made at various higher levels, up to the federal government level (and beyond).

The federal government generally stays far away from regulating land use, which traditionally is viewed as being under the state police power, not granted to the federal government under the Constitution. State governments also typically avoid direct land use regulation, with a few exceptions leaving it up to the lowest levels of government.[24] Efforts to set up regional land use controls have largely failed, due to the balkanized nature of intergovernmental relations and the traditional norms of local government home rule. Zoning usefully reflects local knowledge of the community and landscape in which it applies. It can often serve as a useful vehicle for carrying modern environmental ideas into practical land development practice. But zoning's area-wide designation of uses and its local focus cause serious dysfunctions as well. Fracturing national land use controls into tens of thousands of small, uncoordinated jurisdictions invites skews and gaps. The trend of the future is likely to be elevation of planning horizons to the state level, as in the NLUPA initiative noted later in this chapter.[25]

---

23. See Blasser & Kentopp, Impact Fees: The Second Generation, 38 J. Urb. & Contemp. L. 55 (1990).

24. Hawaii and Maine have state-based land use regulatory systems that, at least in theory, cover the entire state.

25. See Section C(1), below.

A. Managing Localized Land Uses

2. Critical Areas Designation and Regulation: The CWA §404 Wetlands Example

Critical areas designation and regulation is, in many cases, a more overtly resource-oriented application of zoning principles.[26] The element that makes the area "critical" has an environmental or resource foundation. That resource aspect defines the area governed by the regulatory program, and the management goal for the resource is effectuated by regulations designed to obtain that desired result. To give a very simple example, critical groundwater management areas are now fairly commonplace, where too much pumping has either caused unsustainable overdraft (withdrawals in excess of recharge) or threatens the aquifer with saline intrusion. The area covered would be lands overlying the aquifer, and the regulations put in place (well spacing, pumping limits, etc.) control allowable pumping in order to protect the resource from injurious overuse.

In terms of planning, critical area regulation applies criteria opportunistically. When an area is designated and defined as critical, an array of previously established standards and procedures come into play.

Wetlands regulations have long been the best-known example of critical area management. The most prominent reasons for this are their ubiquitous presence in virtually every part of the nation. Wetlands are a central part of the ecological web, providing extraordinary "eco-system services" worth billions of dollars annually—retarding floods, providing spawning and living habitat to commercial and noncommercial wildlife, filtering toxins, supplying and storing water, etc. The magnitude of wetlands loss in this country is staggering. Since its founding the nation has lost more than half of the 221 million acres of wetlands that existed in the contiguous 48 states to development. For a time the loss continued at a rate between one-half and one-quarter million acres per year, though in recent years the estimated loss is down to about 100,000 acres per year.[27]

The major modern wetlands regulatory program is §404 of the CWA.[28] In an unusual power allocation, §404 is primarily administered by the U.S. Army Corps of Engineers, not EPA, as a result of the Corps' historic authority over dredge and fill activities in the nation's "navigable waters." Despite that historic linkage to navigable waters, in the spirit of the CWA, EPA regulations define *wetlands* as—

> those areas that are inundated or saturated by surface or ground water at a frequency and duration sufficient to support, and that under normal circumstances do support, a prevalence of vegetation typically adapted for life in saturated soil conditions. 40 C.F.R. §230(t).

A wetland thus is an area, including an area constructed by human beings, that exhibits some combination of hydric soils, wetland vegetation, and wetland hydrology. This leaves a great deal of vagueness in the regulatory definition, and the precise identification of individual wetlands depends on interpretive manuals and on-the-ground judgment by Corps and EPA officials.

The disjunction between the functional definition of wetlands and the commerce power "navigable waters" predicate for federal regulation of land use activity on nonfederal lands has prompted numerous challenges to the reach of §404. These challenges have produced several Supreme Court opinions on the scope of the federal authority, the most

---

26. Flood plain zoning, for example, can be seen as either zoning or critical areas management.
27. See U.S. EPA, Wetlands, Status and Trends, www.epa.gov/OWOW/wetlands/vital/status.html. See also U.S. GAO, Wetlands Protection: The Scope of the §404 Program Remains Uncertain (1993).
28. 33 U.S.C. §1344.

prominent in recent years being *Solid Waste Agency of N. Cook County (SWANNC) v. U.S. Army Corps of Eng'rs* 531 U.S. 159 (2001), and *Rapanos v. U.S.*, 547 U.S. 715 (2006). This aspect of §404 is covered in greater depth in Chapter 12.

The current goal of §404 implementation has been summed up in the phrase "no net loss," a policy that is meant to be implemented by a mitigation program that matches permits to destroy wetlands with requirements to replace them with artificial wetlands or enforceable protection from development of existing high-quality wetlands. Both prongs of the program are problematic. Artificial wetlands seldom provide equivalent ecological benefits, even when ratios of trade are greater than 1:1, and preserving already extant wetlands does not avoid net loss.

The following short excerpt shows the CWA §404 program in controversial action.

Bersani v. U.S. Environmental Protection Agency

850 F.2d 36 (2d Cir. 1988), cert. denied, 489 U.S. 1089 (1989)

TIMBERS, J. [Pyramid, a shopping center developer, sought a permit to fill more than 60% of a 49.6 acre parcel located in Sweeden's Swamp, "a high quality red maple swamp" located along I-95 in Attleboro, Massachusetts, a parcel that clearly fell within the jurisdictional definition of navigable waters of the U.S. Acting under the CWA, EPA vetoed the approval by the Corps of a permit to build the mall because EPA found that an alternative site had been available to Pyramid at the time it entered the market to search for a site for the mall, although the available site became unavailable during the course of the regulatory process.]

One of the sections of the CWA relevant to the instant case is §301(a), which prohibits the discharge of any pollutant, including dredge or fill materials, into the nation's navigable waters, except in compliance with the Act's provisions, including §404. . . . Section 404 of the Act, focusing on dredge or fill materials, provides that the U.S. Army and EPA will share responsibility for implementation of its provisions. . . .

As with virtually all critical areas regulatory programs, applicants seeking permit approval to build a development in the regulated area must submit site plans, various traffic, economic, and environmental analyses, and propose mitigation measures as necessary. Section 404(a) authorizes the Secretary of the Army, acting through the Corps, to issue permits for the discharge of dredged or fill materials at particular sites. Section 404(b) provides that, subject to §404(c), the Corps must base its decisions regarding permits on guidelines (the "§404(b)(1) guidelines") developed by EPA in conjunction with the Secretary of the Army.

The §404(b)(1) guidelines, published at 40 C.F.R. §230 (1987), are regulations containing the requirements for issuing a permit for discharge of dredged or fill materials. 40 C.F.R. §230.10(a) covers "non-water dependent activities" (i.e., activities that could be performed on non-wetland sites such as building a mall) and provides essentially that the Corps must determine whether an alternative site is available that would cause less harm to the wetlands. Specifically, it provides that "no discharge of dredged or fill material shall be permitted if there is a practicable alternative" to the proposal that would have a "less adverse impact" on the "aquatic ecosystem." It also provides that a practicable alternative may include "an area not presently owned by the applicant which could reasonably be obtained, utilized, expanded, or managed in order to fulfill the basic purpose of the proposed activity." It further provides that "unless clearly demonstrated otherwise," practicable alternatives are (1) "presumed to be available," and (2) "presumed to have less impact on

A. Managing Localized Land Uses

the aquatic ecosystem." Thus, an applicant such as Pyramid must rebut both of these presumptions in order to obtain a permit. Sections 230.10(c) and (d) require that the Corps not permit any discharge that would contribute to significant degradation of the nation's wetlands and that any adverse impacts must be mitigated through practicable measures.

In addition to following the §404(b)(1) guidelines, the Corps may conduct a "public interest review." 33 C.F.R. §320.4 (1987). This public interest review is not mandatory under §404, unlike consideration of the §404(b) guidelines. In a public interest review, the Corps decision must reflect the "national concern" for protection and use of resources but must also consider the "needs and welfare of the people."

Under §404 of the Act, EPA has veto power over any decision of the Corps to issue a permit. It is this provision that is at the heart of the instant case. Specifically, §404(c) provides that the Administrator of EPA may prohibit the specification of a disposal site "whenever he determines, after notice and opportunity for public hearings, that the discharge of materials into such area will have an unacceptable adverse effect" on, among other things, wildlife. An "unacceptable adverse effect" is defined in 40 C.F.R. §231.2(e) as an effect that is likely to result in, among other things, "significant loss of or damage to . . . wildlife habitat. . . ." The burden of proving that the discharge will have an "unacceptable adverse effect" is on EPA.

In short, both EPA and the Corps are responsible for administering the program for granting permits for discharges of pollutants into wetlands under §404. The Corps has the authority to issue permits following the §404(b)(1) guidelines developed by it and EPA; EPA has the authority under §404(c) to veto any permit granted by the Corps. The Corps processes about 11,000 permit applications each year. EPA has vetoed five decisions by the Corps to grant permits. . . .

On appeal, the thrust of Pyramid's argument is a challenge to what it calls EPA's "market entry" theory, i.e. the interpretation by EPA of the relevant regulation, which led EPA to consider the availability of alternative sites at the time Pyramid entered the market for a site, instead of at the time it applied for a permit. . . .

We hold (1) that the market entry theory is consistent with both the regulatory language and past practice; (2) that EPA's interpretation, while not necessarily entitled to deference [because the other federal agency administering §404, the Corps, disagreed with EPA's interpretation], is reasonable; and (3) that EPA's application of the regulation is supported by the administrative record. . . . [A highly fact-specific recitation of why the appeals court majority found that this case fit within the EPA regulation is omitted. The dissent argued that the decision on practicable alternatives should be made at the time of agency decision.]

COMMENTARY & QUESTIONS

1. Timing theories in *Bersani*. Should the "practicable alternative" test be applied at the time of "market entry," permit application, or "time of decision"? There are several problems with the "time of decision" test (advocated in a dissent). First is the question of which of many decision points is applicable? In this case, is it the Massachusetts Department of Environmental Quality Engineering's original rejection, its subsequent approval, the Corps' original rejection, its subsequent approval, the EPA decision, or the decisions of the two state courts or two federal courts that considered this matter on judicial review? Second, since the "time of decision" comes rather late in the process, it is doubtful that a developer would take a substantial financial risk in the face of possible permit denial based on distant events that it can neither control nor predict. Third, the developer will have invested so much in project preparation by the time of decision that agencies will be reluctant to deny it a permit based on the availability of a site that has only recently come on the market. But if, as a general matter, the "time of decision" test is problematic, does that mean that the "time of entry" test is necessarily the proper one to apply in all cases? The real issue here is whether the developer, in good faith, considered non-wetland sites. Would it perhaps be better not to adopt a formal timing rule but to encourage the agencies to determine the matter of good faith consideration of alternatives on a case-by-case basis?

2. The "practicable alternative" test. Is the §404 "practicable alternative" test a good one? The dissent pointed out that the practicable alternatives test has nothing to do with the desirability of building in a wetland. Developers, unfortunately, are drawn to wetlands because they are conveniently located, available, and relatively cheap. Professor Oliver Houck demonstrates how an applicant can manipulate the "practicable alternative" test by defining a project so narrowly that only the proposed site will accommodate it.[29] What if Pyramid had proposed a "unique shopping experience in a magnificent aquatic setting"? Since 1989, the Corps has somewhat modified its previous position of deferring to the applicant's statement of purpose and need. Professor Houck considers the *Bersani* decision "the most tough-minded [judicial] interpretation of alternatives analysis under §404":

> To the *Bersani* court, then, an alternative to a large commercial development was feasible although it was neither the developer's choice nor the developer's most profitable option; the availability of this alternative would be measured at the time the developer's own, internal choice is being made; and offers of mitigation would not finesse this alternatives analysis but, rather, would follow it to offset losses that could not otherwise be avoided. . . . The *Bersani* dissent, however, found this result more than remarkable. In its view, the majority mistook §404's "basic purpose," which is not to provide an incentive for developers to avoid choosing wetlands but, rather, to provide a balancing analysis between the "biological integrity" of a wetland area and "commerce and other economic advantages." Alternatives are but a "factor" in this determination. This relatively free-wheeling balancing approach is, of course, reminiscent of the Corps public interest review regulations and has found a secure home in a second line of cases interpreting the alternatives requirement of §404.[30] 60 U. Colo. L. Rev. at 806-807.

Professor Houck concludes that, because the "practicable alternative" test is fatally flawed, §404 should be amended to "make the water dependency test dispositive. . . . Unless this type of activity needs to be located in waters of the United States, it will not be." Id. at 830.

3. An uncomfortable partnership. Despite the rarity of EPA vetoes, the sharing of §404 implementation responsibility between the Corps and EPA has been cumbersome and contentious, and the effectiveness of §404 has suffered as a result. The Corps is responsible for permit issuance and initial enforcement, while EPA is authorized to (1) develop the environmental guidelines used to evaluate permit applications, (2) veto proposed permits with unacceptable environmental impacts, (3) oversee state assumption of the §404 program, (4) interpret statutory exemptions, (5) determine the jurisdictional reach of the program, (6) set aside areas where no disposal of fill will be permitted, and (7) enforce in cases where

---

29. Houck, Hard Choices: The Analysis of Alternatives Under §404 of the Clean Water Act and Similar Environmental Laws, 60 U. Colo. L. Rev. 773, 788-789, 832-836 (1989).

30. See *La. Wildlife Fed'n v. York*, 761 F.2d 1044 (5th Cir. 1985), and *Fund for Animals v. Army Dep't*, 85 F.3d 535, 543 (11th Cir. 1996) (". . . the Corps' . . . practicable alternatives analysis is not subject to numerical precision, but instead requires a balancing of the applicant's needs and environmental concerns").

A. Managing Localized Land Uses 363

the Corps has not adequately done so. As a construction-oriented agency, the Corps historically has not been a zealous defender of wetlands:

> The Corps receives about 15,000 individual permit applications annually [and] issues approximately 10,000 individual permits (67%). The Corps denies approximately 500 individual permit applications, or about 3% of the applications it receives. The remaining 30%, about 4,500 applications, are either withdrawn or qualify for letters of permission or general permits. In addition, the Corps authorizes about 40,000 activities under regional or nationwide general permits each year. U.S. GAO, Wetlands Protection: The Scope of the §404 Program Remains Uncertain 12 (1993).

The GAO also found that Corps enforcement of §404 has been sporadic. EPA, on the other hand, does not possess the resources to adequately supervise the Corps' performance. As of 2008, EPA had used its §404(c) veto power only 12 times since 1972! Only two states, Michigan and New Jersey, have received delegation from EPA to administer the §404 program.[31]

4. Using §404 as an end run around the pollution control requirements of the CWA. In *Coeur Alaska, Inc. v. S.E. Alaska Conservation Council*, 129 S. Ct. 2458 (2009), a Supreme Court majority held that discharging massive quantities of mine slurry containing arsenic and heavy metals into an artificial lake was the deposit of "fill" (because it would eventually raise the bottom of the lake by 50 feet), subject only to a simple §404 permit, not a permit for the discharge of "pollutants" into the waters of the U.S. as required by §402 of the CWA. See Chapter 12.

5. Mitigation of environmental damage. Mitigation of wetlands loss is a highly controversial device:

> In the context of existing wetland regulation, mitigation generally refers to avoidance, minimization, and compensation. These steps are frequently applied in a sequential manner. First, a party seeking a permit for a project that affects wetlands must demonstrate that the least environmentally damaging alternative will be used. Second, the permit applicant must develop a plan to minimize the environmental harm from any unavoidable impacts. Finally, the applicant must compensate for or offset any harm done to wetland functions and values which is not avoided or minimized. The applicant satisfies the compensation requirement by enhancing, restoring, creating, or preserving other wetlands that may be located on or off the project site. [There is a] preference for on-site mitigation and for in-kind [restoring the type of wetland function that a development project affects] mitigation, [as well as a preference for] restoration and enhancement, rather than creation or preservation. . . . Mitigation banking involves mitigating for wetland impacts before an activity causes environmental harm. Mitigation banking occurs when one restores, enhances, creates, or preserves wetlands, thereby generating mitigation credits. A regulatory agency determines the amount and value of the mitigation credits which the credit generator may use to offset the adverse wetland impacts of its own development projects, [or] in a more complex scenario, . . . a private entity generates credits, which a third party purchases to meet its own unrelated mitigation requirements. Gardner, Banking on Entrepreneurs: Wetlands, Mitigation Banking, and Takings, 81 Iowa L. Rev. 531, 531-537 (1996).

---

31. In an omitted portion of the *Bersani* opinion, the court refers to an additional state wetland regulation program operated by Massachusetts. For an analysis of existing delegation programs under §404, see Houck & Rolland, Federalism in Wetlands Regulation: A Consideration of Delegation of Clean Water Act Section 404 and Related Programs to the States, 54 Md. L. Rev. 1242 (1995). The authors argue that if delegation "is done carefully and with the proper mix of federal inducements and safeguards, it could succeed." Id. at 1314.

According to Professor Gardner, "The failure of compensatory mitigation is wetland regulation's dirty little secret." Id. at 540. Parties agreeing to perform mitigation often lack the technical or economic resources to fulfill their obligations. Noncompliance is common and enforcement is sporadic. Moreover, scientific uncertainties regarding wetlands ecology militate against the success of mitigation through creation or preservation. Environmentalists also complain that mitigation sends the wrong message to the American public and glosses over the need for humility and restraint with the natural world. Two federal agency reports cast doubt upon the effectiveness of mitigation efforts under §404 and suggest means of improving this process, including better data collection and enforcement. National Research Council, Compensating for Wetland Losses Under the Clean Water Act (2001), and U.S. GAO, Wetlands Protection Assessments Needed to Determine Effectiveness of In-Lieu Fee Mitigation, USGAO-01-325 (2001). A New Jersey study concludes that only 78% of the freshwater wetland acreage lost to development at 75 New Jersey sites studied has been replaced with newly constructed wetlands, despite a requirement of New Jersey law that degraded or destroyed wetlands be replaced at a 2:1 ratio.[32]

6. Evaluation of §404 as an example of site-by-site permitting. Section 404 undoubtedly has been successful in preserving some wetlands from development, but the site-by-site approach, as illustrated by §404, nevertheless has significant disadvantages as a critical area protection mechanism. To reiterate a point made above, §404 applies only to the deposit of dredged or fill material in wetlands; it does not apply to all wetland development activities. See, e.g., *Save Our Community v. EPA*, 971 F.2d 1155 (5th Cir. 1992), where a permit was not required for draining a wetland.[33] Neither does §404 apply to activities on neighboring non-wetland areas that lead to impairment of wetlands functions. Second, §404 administration is replete with statutory exemptions (e.g., for many agricultural activities) and general permits (both nationwide and regional) that limit the scope of the program. See 40 C.F.R. §323.3 (Activities Not Requiring Permits), and 33 C.F.R. §330 (Corps of Engineers Nationwide Permit Program Regulations). Of the approximately 50,000 projects that are currently covered by §404 permits, roughly 35,000 are operating under either nationwide or regional permits, which entail a minimum of paperwork and are desultorily enforced. Nationwide permits involving discharge of dredged or fill material into headwaters wetlands (including Corps determinations allowing "mountaintop removal" in strip mining areas[34]) and construction of single-family homes in wetlands have been especially controversial. Third, cumulative impacts of past, proposed, and potential projects are also systematically neglected in the §404 permitting process. The U.S. GAO Report cited above commented, "case files we reviewed indicated that Corps districts generally considered the impacts of projects on a case-by-case basis, and that cumulative impacts were sporadically addressed...." This is plainly a matter of Corps choice, for *Buttrey v. U.S.*, 690 F.2d 1170 (5th Cir. 1982), indicates that the Corps is authorized to, and sometimes does, consider cumulative impacts in making §404 permitting decisions. Thorough critical area protection can be assured only through a preventive land use planning and management program

---

32. N.J. Dep't of Envtl. Protection, Creating Indicators of Wetland Status (Quantity and Quality): Freshwater Wetland Mitigation in New Jersey (2002).

33. The use of mechanized earth-moving equipment to conduct land clearing, drainage, ditching, channelization, in-stream mining, or other development activities in wetlands (at least in "adjacent wetlands") is covered by §404, unless only "incidental fallback" results. But wetlands drainage without utilizing heavy equipment (e.g., through hydraulic conveyance devices such as pipes, hoses, or tile drains) is not subject to §404 permitting.

34. By defining the process of strip mining by which mountains are scalped and the soil and rocks overlying coal dumped into adjoining valleys as "fill," the Corps was able to avoid federal regulation of the resulting severe pollution of mountain streams. See Mitchell, When Mountains Move, Nat'l Geo., Mar. 2006.

administered by an institution that possesses jurisdiction over an area that includes the entire resource to be protected. In the wetlands context, one commentator has suggested that EPA could achieve biodiversity protection through the §404 process by "exercis[ing] its *advance* veto authority, which can be used to protect relatively intact ecosystems in advance of a 404 permit application." Fischman, Biological Diversity and Environmental Protection: Authorities to Reduce Risk, 22 Envtl. L. 435, 496 (1992). Whether EPA will have the political leverage to exercise this authority is another matter entirely.

7. Wild and Scenic Rivers as another instance of critical areas management. The federal Wild and Scenic Rivers Act of 1968 (WSRA), 16 U.S.C. §§1271 et seq., has been somewhat effective in protecting certain values on segments of designated rivers on federal lands. The scope of the WSRA is limited to designated "Wild," "Scenic," and "Recreational" Rivers, with their "immediate environments," defined as narrow corridors extending approximately one-quarter mile from the ordinary high-water mark on both sides of the rivers. Once a river is admitted to the system, certain tangible protections follow. Most important, a "roadblock" (see Chapter 10) is placed in the way not only of Federal Energy Regulatory Commission licensing of any dam "on or directly affecting" a designated river, but also in the way of any other federal agency that proposes to assist—by loan, license, permit, or otherwise—"in the construction of any water resources project that would have a direct and adverse effect on the values for which such river was established...." 16 U.S.C. §1278. Rivers that flow through federal land receive special protection under the WSRA. Federal agencies that manage lands "which include, border upon, or are adjacent to" any designated river—including lands outside the management corridor—"shall take such action respecting management policies, regulations, contracts, [and] plans, affecting such lands . . . as may be necessary to protect such rivers. . . ." 16 U.S.C. §1283. The statute has done little, however, to protect rivers and riverine ecosystems from incompatible private development. See generally Raffensperger & Tarlock, The Wild and Scenic Rivers Act at 25: The Need for a New Focus, 4 Rivers 81 (1993). Even within the narrow management corridor the WSRA provides no federal regulatory authority over private lands along the designated rivers. In addition, federal land acquisition power within the corridors is sharply limited. Similarly, wider watershed impacts of development on private lands outside the management corridors, such as polluted runoff caused by residential development or agricultural operations, are beyond the WSRA's scope.

8. Taking stock of critical areas management. The examples of critical area management do not lend a great deal of confidence in that mechanism as an effective regulatory technique. Is the problem endemic to the technique, or is it merely a function of the particular examples, such as the politically unpopular shared feature of federal regulation of nonfederal lands? In theory, there is no reason that adequate political and regulatory will cannot enact and implement strong protection of critical areas. In practice, however, that will, even if present for a period of time, is hard to maintain against the inexorable focused pressure of those who benefit tangibly and directly from eroding the protections. As Joe Sax wrote in his important book, Defending the Environment: A Strategy for Citizen Action 51 (1970), "As the man said, 'Money can always wait.'"

3. Hazardous Waste Facilities: State and Federal Efforts

a. Hazardous Wastes

Siting facilities for disposal of solid waste, hazardous waste, and nuclear waste has become extraordinarily difficult because of the way that LULUs (Locally Undesirable

Land Uses) trigger the NIMBY (Not In My Back Yard) syndrome local reaction.[35] Waste management tragedies such as Love Canal, New York and Times Beach, Missouri—along with the close participation of state and federal government officials in the siting and permitting of some of these misplaced and mismanaged facilities[36]—have created a mood of deep public skepticism about whether waste can be safely disposed of, and cynicism about whether state or federal governments are sufficiently competent and objective to protect the health and safety of host communities. In addition, local residents harbor reasonable fears that a waste disposal facility will create few jobs, produce little additional tax revenue, overburden local services (e.g., fire, police) and infrastructure (e.g., roads, sewerage facilities), and negatively affect property values. Proposals to site a waste disposal facility are almost certain to be met by a combination of local zoning prohibitions, political opposition, media denunciation, lawsuits, and civil disobedience. Quite often, resistance to siting has been successful, but the battle goes on because any disposal site that manages to achieve a RCRA federal toxics disposal license possesses a cash cow, a license to make huge profits.[37] Only highly capitalized firms need apply, however, because they are the only ones that can meet RCRA's financial responsibility requirements.[38] RCRA's regulation also imposes safety requirements that take the form of site design and location criteria that must be met, further escalating the cost of facility siting and construction.

Beginning around 1990, a small number of states enacted hazardous waste disposal facility siting statutes. The purpose of these laws was fairly straightforward—make it possible to safely site facilities in a manner that was perceived as reasoned and equitable. The statutes varied considerably and employed a creative mix of incentives and palliatives attempting to assuage community fears, raise community confidence, and provide community incentives as a means of getting communities to accept facilities. The statutes also included technical review that addressed safety concerns.[39] Despite their many statutory features, several of which are described below, none of the state siting laws that were enacted have ever succeeded in siting a facility. Virtually all new facilities built since 1990 have been built in states that do not have a siting law.

The four state hazardous waste facility siting statutes described here stand out as contrasting types. Minnesota's law gives the community—broadly defined as the county —control over final siting decisions. Minn. Stat. §115A.191. New Jersey has what might be called a "top-down" approach, in which the state Hazardous Waste Facility Siting Commission has the power to obtain a site by eminent domain and override local zoning where necessary to site a facility. N.J. Stat. Ann. §§13.1E-52 & 59. In Wisconsin, the developer chooses the site and, with a complicated exception for ordinances enacted more than 15 months prior to the developer's choice, a negotiation of terms ensues under the threat of binding, "winner

---

35. Some other common acronyms inspired by LULU and NIMBY are OOMBY (Out Of My Back Yard), NIFYE (Not In My Front Yard Either), NIMTOO (Not In My Term Of Office), NOPE (Not On Planet Earth), and BANANA (Build Absolutely Nothing Anywhere Near Anyone).

36. The public reaction in Chapter 3's Wilsonville case, brought on by the dishonest and bungling way in which the facility was permitted, makes it a classic example of the incendiary nature of siting such facilities, even if the site was not as poor a choice as the court's opinion made it out to be.

37. See Chapter 17. It is no surprise that Tony Soprano found wealth in illegal waste disposal.

38. That aspect of RCRA was intended to ensure that operators of facilities had the wherewithal to engage in cleanup and response efforts if needed. Also, having deep pocket target defendants as facility operators who have a major investment and capital at risk avoids the risks posed by impecunious dumpsite operators. Recall in this regard Dewey Loeffel's inability to pay even a small share of the cleanup costs at his site in the *Schenectady Chemical* case in Chapter 3.

39. RCRA's Subtitle C standards are not preemptive of state regulation in this area.

take all" arbitration. Wis. Stat. §289.01. In Massachusetts, the state has taken the dominant role by preempting local ability to use ordinances, permit requirements, or other forms of land use laws to block siting of a facility. Mass. Gen. Laws 21D §3-15. Operationally, the state Hazardous Waste Facility Siting Council reviews applications ("Notices of Intent") by developers after which the Council may issue a finding that the proposal is "feasible and deserving" in terms of the developer's financial capability and past management practices, technical feasibility of the proposal, need for the facility, and compliance with state and federal laws. After that, the community, aided by state technical assistance grants, is required to negotiate with the developer and the state. The state is a party to the negotiations because the outcome may include state incentives to a host community. If the negotiations result in impasse, an arbitrator prepares a draft settlement for public comment. The final settlement is submitted to the Council and is subject to judicial review.

COMMENTARY & QUESTIONS

1. Incentives to communities. What sorts of incentives might be sufficient to negate concerns about safety or about the adverse economic impact of having such a facility? In New Jersey, for example, the host community is entitled to at least 5% of the gross receipts of any facility constructed within its boundaries in order to mitigate the effects of the facility. In Minnesota a county that accepts a facility receives $150,000 a year for two years.

2. Overcoming "outrage" factors and building community confidence. Waste management companies have grown far more sophisticated in "risk communication" and have tried to explain how their facilities will operate and the ways in which the redundant control systems will prevent releases of the hazardous wastes into the environment. The statutes offer small amounts of money to the potential host communities to be used for the community to hire experts to advise them about the technical issues affecting safety. If the amounts were more realistic, would the presence of community-hired experts lead to greater willingness to accept the facility?

3. Negotiations—between whom, over what, and with what pressure to succeed? Each of the four statutes mentioned include some form of negotiations with the site developer. It is plausible that in a rational world a representative of the concerned community (whether a community-appointed representative or one selected by the statute) and the site developer could negotiate and agree on changes in the proposal that make it more agreeable to the host community without making the project infeasible or otherwise unattractive for the developer. Changes that benefit both parties, should they exist, should emerge from negotiation. Beyond that, most parties can be expected to negotiate with reference to what will happen if no further progress is made. The statutes make varied choices. For example, in Wisconsin, the community and developer that cannot agree are sent to binding arbitration in which the arbitrator selects the position of one side or the other. In Massachusetts, impasse in three-way negotiations involving the host community, the site developer, and the state results in arbitration in which the arbitrator decides what is appropriate subject to judicial review (Massachusetts). What variables are most likely to affect the usefulness of the negotiation process?[40]

---

40. See, e.g., Wheeler, Negotiating NIMBYs: Learning from the Failure of the Massachusetts Siting Law, 11 Yale J. Reg. 241, 244 (1994).

4. **Explaining the track record of siting statutes.** In spite of these sophisticated statutes, no major hazardous waste disposal facility has been sited, using their procedures, in any of these four states or in any of the other approximately eight states that have enacted similar hazardous waste facility siting statutes.[41] One major reason for the virtual nonuse of these siting statutes was the decline in demand for hazardous waste disposal brought about by federal environmental statutes—most notably RCRA. RCRA, enacted in 1976 and made far more effective by amendments passed in 1984, set very high technical standards for hazardous waste disposal facilities. Those regulations effectively raised the barriers to entry in the waste disposal field and very significantly increased the cost of disposal, which decreased waste generation, an effect that was reinforced by offshore migration of manufacturing facilities. EPCRA's effect is harder to ascertain, but its Toxics Release Inventory (TRI) program raised the level of visibility of the use and presence of hazardous materials at plants throughout the nation. By 2000, hazardous waste releases (including transfers to offsite hazardous waste treatment, storage, and disposal facilities) had declined over 75%. (EPA, TRI, 2003.)

5. **Choosing the site and the attraction of low-income communities.** Should a developer be permitted to choose a site, or should the state or the locality screen and propose sites? Hazardous waste disposal facilities have been disproportionately sited in low-income and minority communities. See Cole, Empowerment as the Key to Environmental Protection: The Need for Environmental Poverty Law, 19 Ecology L.Q. 619, 622 (1992). Is it equitable or acceptable for a developer to select a disadvantaged community that is poorly organized and desperate for development? Is it necessarily inequitable to locate LULUs in disadvantaged communities, or is the problem one of unequal access to information and political power that could be remedied by the grants to the proposed host community to study the matter for itself? Will a state be more likely than a developer to pick a site in a wealthy, politically well-connected community? If communities volunteer, which ones will do so?

6. **Environmental Justice siting debates.** From the beginning, siting of facilities that process, store, or release toxic materials has provided the most dramatic focus for the Environmental Justice movement, which criticizes the disproportionate cumulative impacts suffered by low-income communities and communities of color. Charles Lee's Toxic Wastes and Race in the United States (1987), written for the United Church of Christ Commission for Racial Justice, and Dr. Robert Bullard's Dumping in Dixie: Race, Class & Environmental Quality (1990), presented data showing that risk of exposure to toxic waste hazards appeared to be both quantitatively and qualitatively greater for communities of color and low income than for the general public, a conclusion backed by much subsequent research. Some scholars, however, have criticized the studies' accuracy and argue that even if LULUs disproportionately affect minorities, that is not necessarily the result of racism, and even if perfectly neutral objective procedures result in locating a site in a higher-income area, market forces will devolve the surrounding area to lower-income within a short number of years.[42]

Litigation intended to prove discrimination on the basis of race and poverty in toxics facilities siting decisions has generally been unsuccessful. Courts (unlike EPA, which has

---

41. For the first two examples of "successful" siting in the immediate wake of the passage of the several state laws mentioned above, see *Polumbo v. Waste Techs.*, 989 F.2d 156 (4th Cir. 1993), and *Coalition for Health Concern v. LWD, Inc.*, 60 F.3d 1188 (6th Cir. 1995) (hazardous waste incinerator sitings in Ohio and Kentucky upheld over public opposition).

42. See Prof. Vicki Been's milestone article, Locally Undesirable Land Uses in Minority Neighborhoods: Disproportionate Siting or Market Dynamics? 103 Yale L.J. 1383 (1994).

A. Managing Localized Land Uses

issued "discriminatory effect" regulations under Title VI of the 1964 Civil Rights Act[43]) generally require a showing of "discriminatory *intent*," which is most difficult to prove.[44] Is it racism for corporate managers to seek out (1) the most inexpensive land and (2) areas where they will face the least effective political opposition and the most desperate welcome for jobs and economic activity? The correlation of toxics facilities sitings with race and low income thus may well derive from cold marketplace logic rather than discriminatory bias.[45] Because of judicial discouragement of environmental injustice lawsuits without showings of discriminatory intent, it is likely that future environmental justice disputes in the toxics facilities siting context will be resolved within federal, state, and local administrative siting and permitting processes.

b. Nuclear Wastes

Disposal of high-level nuclear wastes, primarily produced by commercial nuclear power plants and government defense-related activities, presents an especially complex and contentious siting dilemma. Currently 70,000 metric tons of nuclear waste is being stored in large water-filled pools at 80 power plants in 35 states, with an increase to 153,000 metric tons expected by 2055, raising potential pollution and security threats. Despite the enactment of a federal siting statute, the Nuclear Waste Policy Act (NWPA), 42 U.S.C. §§10101 et seq., there is currently no ultimate disposal facility for high-level nuclear wastes generated by nuclear power plants.[46] The Waste Isolation Pilot Plant (WIPP), located in southeastern New Mexico, has begun accepting transuranic waste produced by defense-related activities. As plans for siting temporary and permanent high-level nuclear waste disposal facilities in the Southwest have become bogged down by NIMBY-type, as well as national environmental group, opposition, the Mescalero Apache Tribe of New Mexico and the Goshute Tribe of Central Utah have proposed the construction of interim hazardous waste storage facilities on their lands.[47]

In 2002, Congress designated Nevada's Yucca Mountain as the repository for 70,000 metric tons of nuclear waste, but due to state lawsuits and political opposition that facility

---

43. Title VI of the 1964 federal Civil Rights Act, 42 U.S.C. §2000d, reads:

No person in the United States shall, on the ground of race, color, or national origin, be excluded from participation in, be denied the benefits of, or be subjected to discrimination under any program or activity receiving Federal financial assistance.

Title VI was long thought not to offer serious remedies for the kinds of problems involved in environmental justice. Since 1993, however, the EPA's Office of Civil Rights has reversed that position and opened investigatory files on more than a dozen major cases alleging violations of Title VI; and EPA regulations, 40 C.F.R. §7.35, and the Browner Guidance have strengthened internal consideration of environmental justice issues.

44. See, e.g., *Alexander v. Sandoval*, 532 U.S. 275 (2001), and *South Camden Citizens in Action v. Shinn*, 274 F.3d 771 (3d Cir.), cert. denied, 536 U.S. 939 (2002) (the Civil Rights Act of 1964 does not create a private right of action for judicial enforcement without a showing of discriminatory intent). For the difficulty of proving discriminatory intent, see *Arlington Heights v. Metro. Hous. Dev. Corp.*, 429 U.S. 252, 265 (1977).

45. For an example of the apparent lack of political power of low-income minority communities being a clear factor in a siting decision, see Cole, Civil Rights, Environmental Justice and the EPA: The Brief History of Administrative Complaints Under Title VI of the Civil Rights Act of 1964, 9 J. Envtl. L. & Litig. 309, 382-383 (1994) (Flint Incinerator's approval by the same state board that denied a permit in a nonminority area on lesser objections).

46. See *Indiana-Michigan Power Co. v. DOE*, 88 F.3d 1272 (D.C. Cir. 1996) (Dept. of Energy was told to provide for disposal of high-level nuclear waste by Jan. 31, 1998; it didn't happen).

47. See Leonard, Sovereignty, Self-Determination, and Environmental Justice in the Mescalero Apache's Decision to Store Nuclear Waste, 24 B.C. Envtl. Aff. L. Rev. 651 (1997).

did not become operational in 2010 as targeted.[48] If ever opened, at its authorized volume, it will be insufficient to hold present stored waste totals, not to mention future waste.

The Yucca Mountain issue almost inevitably renews the debate over the desirability of nuclear-fueled electric power plants, which have been anathema since the 1980s. Nuclear plants are preferable to fossil-fueled counterparts because nuclear power generation does not produce greenhouse gases or other air pollutants, conventional (SO_x or NO_x), or hazardous (e.g., mercury). Nuclear power advocates also argue that contemporary nuclear plants are considerably safer and less expensive than their predecessors. Nevertheless, "anti-nuke" critics respond that extraction, processing, transportation, fission, and waste disposal stages of uranium-derived nuclear power present insurmountable pollution and national security problems, as well as issues of siting.

The facilities siting outlook is no brighter with regard to disposal of low-level radioactive wastes produced by, for example, hospitals and research laboratories. Under the Low-Level Radioactive Waste Policy Act, 42 U.S.C. §§2021(b) et seq., states are required to dispose of their own commercially generated waste, either individually or in interstate compacts. Since the statute was enacted in 1980, ten regional low-level nuclear waste compacts, covering 41 states, have been approved by Congress, but no new disposal facilities have been constructed under any of these compacts.[49] As a "hammer clause" that was intended to force the states to take swift action, the original legislation included a "take title" requirement. That provision involuntarily transferred ownership of low level hazardous waste to the state in which it was generated if that waste was not disposed of according to statutory standards. That provision was invalidated by the Supreme Court on Tenth Amendment grounds in *N.Y. v. U.S.*, 505 U.S. 144 (1992) (see Chapter 7).

4. "Smart Growth"

The best developers have visions that extend beyond the single site or project to what makes a better neighborhood, a better community, and a better quality of life.

—National Governors' Association, 2000

Especially with rising prices of gas at the pump, there is growing public recognition that urban sprawl development—the post–World War II American ideal—can severely undermine a society's overall quality of life and a sustainable environmental and economic future. The "Smart Growth" Movement is one expression of public frustration with urban sprawl development. In the following excerpt, the author describes the basic tenets of "Smart Growth" and assays the potential of "Smart Growth" to change U.S. patterns of land development and use.[50]

---

48. In 2004, the U.S. Court of Appeals for the District of Columbia held that EPA violated the Energy Policy Act by choosing only a 10,000-year compliance period for its radiation-exposure standards, which did not comply with the recommendations of the National Academy of Sciences. *Nuclear Energy Institute, Inc. v. EPA*, 373 F.3d 1251 (D.C. Cir. 2004). In 2009, the Obama Administration put an end to the 22-year debate about the Yucca Mountain facility by cutting the project's funding and declaring that Yucca Mountain was no longer viewed as an option for storing reactor waste. On January 29, 2010, U.S. Secretary Steven Chu announced the formation of a Blue Ribbon Commission on America's Nuclear Future to provide recommendations for developing a safe, long-term solution to manage nuclear waste.

49. See U.S. GAO, Radioactive Waste: Status of Commercial Low-Level Facilities (1995); McGinnis, Collective Bads: The Case of Low-Level Radioactive Waste Compacts, 34 Nat. Res. J. 563 (1994).

50. For perspectives on Smart Growth that are generally more affirmative than Pollard's, see http://smartgrowth.org/about/default.asp.

Oliver A. Pollard III, Smart Growth: The Promise, Politics, and Potential Pitfalls of Emerging Growth Management Strategies

19 Virginia Environmental Law Journal 247 (2000)

... Although growth can bring jobs, wealth, tax revenues, and amenities, more people are recognizing the link between accelerating suburban sprawl and pervasive problems such as traffic congestion, overcrowded schools, deteriorating neighborhoods, air and water pollution, higher taxes, and communities that are being transformed by changing development and population patterns, regardless of whether they are declining or struggling to keep pace with growth....

Current land use and transportation policies have become a major issue of environmental concern as evidence of the heavy toll sprawling development patterns take on the environment continues to mount. Virtually every environmental problem—from air and water pollution to the destruction of wetlands and wildlife habitat, from global climate change to overflowing landfills—has been linked to the land consumption and pollution that result from current land use and transportation patterns....

A more nuanced view of economic development is emerging. Citizens and politicians increasingly recognize that they face choices about the pace, scale, and location of development they wish to permit and attract. There is also greater recognition that development decisions are not merely the result of the free market, but are influenced by a broad range of federal, state, and local policies. Further, in a more mobile, information-based economy, it is increasingly evident that the quality of life in an area can have a significant impact on its ability to attract and retain businesses. These changing views of development have sparked efforts throughout the country to capture the benefits of economic growth while minimizing the costs.... Many of these strategies are being lumped together under the label "smart growth."...

The goals of smart growth [are] to balance economic development and limit sprawl by channeling growth to areas that have already been developed; to revitalize and prevent the decline of existing urban and suburban areas; to promote more compact urban form; to protect open space, farmland, forests, and environmentally sensitive areas from suburban encroachment; to reduce the public cost of providing infrastructure and services to new development by making more efficient use of existing resources; to protect the natural environment; and to provide affordable housing....

In contrast [to state growth management acts], smart growth approaches, at least at this point in the evolution of the concept, do not place as much emphasis on regulation to shape long-term growth patterns. Land use controls, such as zoning codes, and environmental regulations remain important, but smart growth typically seeks to supplement these provisions using incentives rather than additional regulation. The model state smart growth statute is Maryland's Priority Funding Areas Act [Md. Ann. Code State Fin. & Procurement Act §5-7B-(1-10)], part of a broader "Smart Growth and Neighborhood Conservation" initiative. This statute does not identify specific measures local governments must adopt. Instead, it targets the flow of state funds for "growth related" projects (such as highways and water and sewer lines) to existing communities and to additional areas where growth is planned as long as these additional areas meet minimum state criteria for average residential density and for provision of public water and sewer. Development is not prohibited outside the designated growth areas, but by limiting state financial assistance outside of these areas, the statute creates a strong incentive for localities to guide growth to existing communities. The premise is that guiding growth to areas with existing infrastructure is more efficient than incurring the expense of building new infrastructure to serve development in outlying areas. In addition, encouraging the revitalization of existing communities both strengthens these communities and reduces pressure on undeveloped areas by providing attractive, alternative places to live and work.

In general, the smart growth approach tends to be less proscriptive and less regulatory-intensive than previous growth management efforts. It tends to discourage, rather than to forbid, undesired development. . . .

A second, related distinction between smart growth and more traditional growth management approaches is that smart growth focuses more on the role federal, state, and local government policies and practices play in influencing land use development patterns.

Although the causes of scattered development patterns are numerous and complex, a cornerstone of the smart growth approach is the recognition that public investments (such as funding for highways and water and sewer lines), regulatory policies (such as zoning and street design requirements), and tax policies (such as estate taxes and the tax treatment of easements) strongly influence the pace, scale, and location of development. . . .

Subsidies distort market and individual behavior. There are a host of federal, state, and local public subsidies that arguably have fueled sprawling development for decades, including transportation funding policies that emphasize highway construction; public funding for water and sewer extensions that open new land in outlying areas to development; cash payments and tax breaks to lure new businesses to outlying areas; mortgage policies that subsidize and favor single-family suburban homes; tax deductions for mortgage interest and property taxes; and school construction spending that favors building new schools in new suburban areas over expanding and renovating existing structures. . . .

The smart growth approach seeks to limit or eliminate subsidies that fuel development in outlying areas and undermine existing cities, towns, and suburbs, and to use government expenditures and tax policy to promote more sensible growth patterns in two ways: First, development is guided toward existing communities, encouraging more concentrated, pedestrian- or transit-friendly development within these communities. Measures that promote this objective include providing incentives for infill development, historic preservation, and the development of abandoned industrial sites or "brownfields";[51] directing government funds for roads, water, sewer, and other infrastructure to existing communities; and allocating a higher percentage of transportation funding to transit, bicycling, and pedestrian projects. . . .

Second, smart growth investments seek to preserve open space, farmland, and environmental areas through tools such as the purchase of property or development rights, or by providing tax incentives for private donations of agricultural or conservation easements. . . .

POLITICAL AND POLICY OBSTACLES TO SMARTER GROWTH. Despite the popular support smart growth has enjoyed, it will be difficult to make the fundamental changes in deeply entrenched land use and transportation policies, processes, perceptions, and agencies that are necessary to achieve more sensible growth. The inertia of fifty years of land use and transportation policies that have favored scattered development will not be easy to overcome; bureaucracies are resistant to change, and powerful corporate and other financial interests have an enormous stake in continuing current policies and practices.

Efforts to shift decades of transportation policies emphasizing road building offer an instructive example. Congress made fundamental changes to federal transportation law

---

51. See Chapter 16. [EDS.]

A. Managing Localized Land Uses

when it adopted the landmark Intermodal Surface Transportation Efficiency Act, 23 U.S.C. §§134 et seq. (ISTEA, commonly pronounced "Ice-Tea").[52] Among other things, ISTEA placed greater emphasis on maintaining the existing transportation system, allowing states to spend a larger share of the federal funds they receive on a broader range of transportation options (such as mass transit), increased local authority over transportation decisions, and dedicated transportation funds to air quality improvements in areas that do not meet the requirements of the Clean Air Act. . . . Yet the practical impact of ISTEA has been limited: although some states broadened the focus of their transportation programs as envisioned . . . , most have continued to focus on building and expanding roads as the response to their transportation problems and have limited the local role in transportation decisionmaking. . . .

Another factor that may limit the prospects for success of smart growth measures is that growth problems rarely respect political boundaries. Scattered development patterns, as well as the traffic congestion, environmental degradation, fiscal stresses, and other problems that accompany them, tend to be regional in nature, extending beyond the boundaries of any one locality. Consequently, many growth problems are best addressed through regional solutions that federal, state and local smart growth measures may not provide. Although there is evidence of increasing cooperation among localities as they realize that sprawl problems cross political boundaries, localities are often unwilling to cooperate with one another, jealously guarding their autonomy.

COMMENTARY & QUESTIONS

1. Smart growth and the takings issue. Which aspects of smart growth might raise constitutional takings questions? (See Chapter 21.) Would your property be "taken" if a change in a local zoning ordinance abolishes "single-use" zoning in your neighborhood, significantly reducing your property's value? Is smart growth élitist?

2. Are we ready for smart growth? Identify the economic and political constituencies for current sprawl growth patterns. Is this an invincible political coalition? What economic mechanisms might encourage these interests to support smart growth? For example, might transferable development rights for development in smart growth areas be distributed to real estate companies that have purchased farmland and are holding it for development? How might municipalities be encouraged to relinquish their devotion to "Home Rule" and participate in regional growth management strategies? Could new revenue-sharing strategies be devised that would discourage the race-to-the-bottom that often accompanies the "rateables game"? Smart growth could be expensive. For example, government must either purchase open space outright or purchase or lease development rights from landowners. How will these expenditures be funded? Open space taxes? If so, who should be required to pay them? In the long run, will smart growth only reinforce our current glorification of unsustainable and inequitable concepts of economic growth? Or should "growth" be redefined in order to include quality of life concerns, including environmental protection?

---

52. See also the discussion of ISTEA below in the Commentary & Questions following Professor Ruhl's article. [EDS.]

B. Planning & Management of Public Lands & Resources

As noted earlier, one might expect that planning and management of resources completely owned by the public would be straightforward and effective, most likely to achieve objective rational policies of sustainability and environmental protections. But that's not the case. Public resources—national forests and rangelands, minerals on public lands, parks, public monuments, beds and banks of navigable waterbodies, the waters themselves,[53] fish and wildlife, and much more—represent a huge fraction of the nation's wealth. Fully one-third of the nation is owned outright by the federal government.[54] West of the Mississippi, it's one-half. Theoretically, land is owned by the federal government in trust for all members of the society, as a public legacy from the past, presumptively to be passed on in some form to future generations. Virtually all public resources, however, have developed strong corporate interest blocks based on specialized private exploitation of the resource. For historical and political reasons these industries typically obtain public resources for free, or at costs far below their actual market value. Attempts to impose long-term sustainability standards (instead of short-term private profit decisionmaking) face extraordinarily powerful resistance from well-established "iron triangles"—industry lobbying, accommodating agencies, and industry-aligned blocs of legislators.[55]

To avoid the tragedy of the commons in public resource exploitation in the U.S.,[56] a variety of governmental initiatives have attempted to impose resource management controls, in Hardin's terms—"mutual coercion, mutually agreed upon."[57] Federal resource management statutes delegate responsibility to the federal agencies through enabling or organic legislation, to regulate resource use consistent with legislative goals and requirements. In many cases the statutory standards are very broad, resulting in case-by-case management determinations buffeted by market force pressures without significant guidance from an objective plan.

1. Historic Management of Grazing—Managing to Carrying Capacity

Raising cattle is a storied activity in the western United States. Vast, sparsely populated public lands could support a substantial number of cattle, grazing season after season without the need for artificial feeding methods. As larger and larger numbers of privately owned cattle were added to public lands, however, public rangelands were soon overgrazed with ruinous consequences for ranchers, inadequate food for their cattle, and destruction of the rangeland base, a classic tragedy of the commons problem. Denuded areas that did not

---

53. Most states are the owners of the waters themselves and water rights created under state law are usufructuary (rights of use) only. See, e.g., J. Sax, B. Thompson, J. Leshy & R. Abrams, Legal Control of Water Resources 365 (4th ed. 2004).

54. Like most environmental casebooks, we focus on the federal government, but invite analogies to state, local, and international and comparative resource regulation.

55. See discussion of "iron triangles" in Chapter 6.

56. Internationally, most industrial democracies are far more militant in stewarding their public natural resources than the U.S., in part because they lack the history of wide open spaces. Between nations, where binding legislation is absent, negotiations sometimes lead to international agreements that place restrictions on consenting nations regarding the management of transboundary public resources, such as migratory birds.

57. See Garrett Hardin's Tragedy of the Commons in Chapter 1. For a review of contemporary social science research on the commons tragedy and a discussion of possible nonregulatory strategies for addressing the inherent psychological, sociological, and economic obstacles to commons management, see Thompson, Tragically Difficult: The Obstacles to Governing the Commons, 30 Ecology L.Q. 241 (2000).

B. Planning & Management of Public Lands & Resources

re-vegetate produced dustbowl conditions and erosion of what little soil there was. Many such rangelands are among the 170 million acres of arid or semiarid federal land in the 11 western states under the control of the federal Bureau of Land Management (BLM), a lesser known agency housed in the Department of Interior. Overgrazing made regulatory attempts unavoidable, first in the Taylor Grazing Act of 1934[58] and later in FLPMA.[59] The two statutes took different regulatory tacks in addressing overgrazing and the environmental problems it causes.

Until 1934, the federal government maintained a *laissez-faire* attitude toward public lands, perpetuating an unregulated commons that deteriorated into a severely overgrazed range. A combination of drought and the New Deal prompted reevaluation of federal range policy, resulting in the Taylor Grazing Act of 1934. Congress had two avowed purposes in enacting the Taylor Act: to end overgrazing and to stabilize the livestock industry. Federal policies that appeared laudable in theory were inconsistent in practice.

The Taylor Act did stabilize the livestock industry but did little to alleviate range deterioration. It had three main components: (1) it authorized the Secretary of the Interior to withdraw unappropriated public lands from homesteading and organize them into grazing districts; (2) it gave preference in obtaining and renewing grazing permits to adjacent landowners; and (3) it established district advisory boards, composed mainly of ranchers, that had to be consulted before management decisions were made. The Act resulted in agency "capture." Large-operation ranchers dominated the agency through advisory boards and lobbying power in Washington, gaining for themselves excessive grazing allotments at fees far below market value:

> The first round of grazing permit decisions set a pattern for the next four decades. Adjacent ranchers first received temporary one-year permits. Later hearings to determine carrying capacity for purposes of permit adjustments were conducted by the ranchers through the advisory boards. Ten-year permits—the maximum allowed by statute—soon became the norm.
>
> By early 1936, board representatives and the Grazing Division (which had already issued thousands of permits) worked out rules for preference and fees.... The Division set grazing fees at five cents per month for cows and one cent for sheep. The permits were theoretically limited to "carrying capacity." That term, however, turned out to have a different meaning in practice than in science because capacity was determined (primarily by the stockmen) within the first year or two of Taylor Act administration without benefit of survey or biological opinion. In most districts permits had been issued for many more livestock than the range could properly support. When later scientific information, however inadequate, indicated the need for downward revision, ranchers often effectively opposed cuts.[60]

Instead of affording security to the livestock industry in exchange for responsible grazing practices on public lands, the Taylor Act provided further subsidies to ranchers—primary access to the public lands, preferential permits, federal funds for "range improvements" (fencing, re-vegetation, etc.), and low grazing fees—to continue their traditional overuse of the federal range resource.

The BLM, created in 1946 by the merger of the federal Grazing Division and the General Land Office (an agency with strong disposal inclinations), did little to limit the exploitation dynamic. A 1970 report of the Public Land Law Review Commission revealed the terribly deteriorated condition of a substantial amount of BLM lands, implicitly criticizing BLM as

---

58. 43 U.S.C. §§315 et seq.
59. 43 U.S.C. §§1701 et seq.
60. Coggins & Lindeberg-Johnson, The Law of Public Rangeland Management II: The Commons and the Taylor Act, 13 Envtl. L. 1, 58-59 (1982) (hereafter cited as Coggins II).

a servant of grazing interests (and of the mining and timber industries), and recommending that grazing allotments be required to be consistent with the productivity of the land.[61] There was little change in BLM range policies until 1974, however, when a NEPA lawsuit, *NRDC v. Morton*, 388 F. Supp. 829 (D.D.C. 1974), transformed the theory of federal range management. BLM had prepared a programmatic environmental impact statement on its grazing program after the enactment of NEPA in 1970. The NRDC alleged the programmatic EIS was inadequate because it did not address the physical impacts of grazing in its various grazing districts. The federal district court ordered BLM to prepare EISs for each district. Compelled to study rangeland conditions openly and "go public" with its findings, BLM "had no choice but to reduce allotments down to carrying capacity."[62] *NRDC v. Morton* also alerted Congress to the deplorable condition of BLM lands and the failure of the Taylor Act, leading directly to 1976 passage of FLPMA.

COMMENTARY & QUESTIONS

1. Is carrying capacity a flawed planning standard? The abstract idea of managing a resource "to carrying capacity" is a sound one, designed to provide sustainability over time, but its success or failure depends on implementation. That begins with setting the upper bound limit at a level that is at or below the actual carrying capacity, which requires good data and scientific understanding of the resource and the stressors—plainly wanting or ignored under the Taylor Grazing Act process.

2. Allocating beneficial uses. The second element in a "carrying capacity" form of management is a method for allocating beneficial uses within the carrying capacity. Future chapters will also explore statutory techniques for allocating who uses a public resource up to a defined maximum level, particularly the CAA's "state implementation plan" process for regulating stationary source emissions, and cap-and-trade systems. In regard to grazing, what factors would be relevant if the agency itself were to assign the grazing rights to interested parties? Particularly in the original historical context, where all previous users were trespassers whose actions resulted in pillaging the public domain, it seems a little odd to reward past use (although analogous rewards for past polluting behavior has not prevented similar allocation in the CAA cap-and-trade program). Does the difficulty of defining and applying factors for allocation suggest an auction might be best? List the pros and cons for an auction as the initial allocation of grazing rights under a cap-and-trade system.

3. Permits for a limited term. What management benefits result from putting limited terms on grazing permits, whether one year or a few years at a time? At a very fundamental level, if permits are not term-limited, the overall result is not too greatly different from an outright alienation of the public resource to private use, raising serious public trust issues. (Note, however, the further logic that users who don't own the land, or have only short-term permissions, may be even more likely to drive the resource into desolation.) When permits expire, the management of the resource reverts to the exclusive control of the agency. Even if a holder is favored for renewal by the rules of the program, the agency can refuse renewal if the permit holder has not followed resource protection terms in the permit, and should be free to reduce or eliminate permit allowances based on the condition of the resource.

---

61. Public Land Law Review Commission, One-Third of the Nation's Land 106-108 (1970).
62. Coggins, Evans, & Lindeberg-Johnson, The Law of Public Rangeland Management I: The Extent and Distribution of Federal Power, 12 Envtl. L. 536, 555 (1982) (hereafter cited as Coggins I).

4. Is resource management agency capture inevitable? Even though BLM manages 170 million acres of land, decisions on individual permits devolved to the local level so local conditions could be taken into account. At that level, considering the dynamics of the process, who, if anyone, is likely to argue against grazing extra cattle?

2. Managing for "Multiple Use and Sustained Yield"

Formal statutory planning processes increasingly are central features of public resources management on the federal lands under a variety of statutes. In 1976, FLPMA[63] attempted for the first time to impose meaningful planning and controls on public land management, and under NFMA,[64] the USFS and BLM must prepare LRMPs[65] for all lands they manage. Both FLPMA and NFMA require formal, public-participation land use planning, and resulting plans are supposed to be legally binding, with agencies' on-the-ground management consistent with adopted plans.

George Coggins, The Law of Public Rangeland Management IV: FLPMA, PRIA, and the Multiple Use Mandate

14 Environmental Law 1, 5-6 (1983)

FLPMA does not repeal the major Taylor Act provisions. Instead, the 1976 Act superimposes a new management system, with more diverse goals and emphases. FLPMA requires the multiple use-sustained yield that the BLM has long claimed to practice. The 1976 Act mandates intensive planning; of equal importance, specific management decisions made after the land use plans are completed must accord with the plans. The Act also protects grazing permittees to a limited extent. On the whole, however, FLPMA represents a condemnation of past stewardship and requires that the BLM utilize a broader approach to public rangeland management....

FLPMA resolves two fundamental issues: Congress decided to retain the public lands in public ownership and to manage the lands in ways that avoid the "unnecessary or undue degradation" so common in the past.

The framework of FLPMA apparently originated in the 1970 report of the Public Land Law Review Commission (PLLRC). Senator Henry Jackson later claimed that FLPMA embodies the enactment of over 100 PLLRC recommendations into law. In the area of range management, however, the dissimilarities between the report and the final legislation are at least as prominent. The PLLRC recommended that Congress authorize the sale to permittees of lands chiefly valuable for grazing, give ranchers greater security of tenure while requiring them to pay higher fees to use the retained lands, and make livestock grazing the "dominant use of retained lands where appropriate." FLMPA secures

---

63. 43 U.S.C. §§1701 et seq.

64. Pub. L. No. 94-588, now codified as parts of 36 U.S.C. §§1600 et seq. NFMA planning will be primarily discussed in this section because it has evolved much further than FLPMA planning by the BLM.

65. The LRMP defines the "management direction" for the forest. It constitutes a program for all natural resource management activities and establishes management requirements to be employed in implementing the plan. It identifies the resource management practices, the projected levels of production of goods and services, and the location where various types of resource management may occur. Implementation of the LRMP is achieved through individual site-specific projects and all projects must be consistent with the LRMP. 16 U.S.C. §1604, 36 C.F.R. §219.

permittee tenure in some ways and holds down grazing fee increases, but Congress rejected the generous PLLRC attitude toward ranchers in those other respects. FLMPA adopts the PLLRC recommendations that sought consistency between grazing and land "productivity," that put "priority on the rehabilitation of deteriorated rangeland where possible," that required more administrative flexibility, and that paid more attention to public values, including wildlife. Congress arguably stopped short of adopting the PLLRC recommendation to exclude livestock from "frail lands" and did not make the permittee responsible for the frail condition of the land. . . .

Section 1701(a) of FLPMA declares thirteen sweeping policies. Although it contains some apparent inconsistencies, the section is Congress' most thorough and unambiguous statement of public land policy. The statement is qualified by the proviso in §1701(b) that FLPMA policies are not "effective" until specifically enacted in the Act itself or elsewhere. The courts faced with questions involving §1701(a), however, have uniformly assumed that the policies are binding and effective in the absence of contrary provisions. Whatever their precise legal status, the congressional policies ought to serve as fundamental range management guidelines.

Congress first stated that the public lands will remain in federal ownership unless planning determines that the "national interest" requires disposal of "a particular parcel." . . . The second policy is that "the national interest will be best realized if the public lands and their resources are periodically and systematically inventoried and their present and future use is projected through a land use planning process coordinated with other Federal and State planning efforts." . . . [Policies Three to Six involve reviews of existing federal land classifications, restraints on executive withdrawals, encouragement of public participation in BLM decision-making, and judicial review of public land adjudications.]

The seventh congressional statement should be, but has not yet become, the touchstone of public rangeland management. Congress declared that "goals and objectives be established by law as guidelines for public land use planning, and that management be on the basis of multiple use and sustained yield unless otherwise specified by law." Congress specifically enacted these general requirements, but the BLM has neither understood nor carried out these commands.

The eighth statement of policy is a radical departure from all prior rangeland management understanding. Congress required that:

> the public lands be managed in a manner that will protect the quality of scientific, scenic, historical, ecological, environmental, air and atmospheric, water resource, and archeological values; that, where appropriate, will preserve and protect certain public lands in their natural condition; that will provide food and habitat for fish and wildlife and domestic animals; and that will provide for outdoor recreation and human occupancy and use.

Whether or to what extent Congress specifically enacted this goal is unclear. Some sections of FLPMA and other statutes support an argument that this policy binds public land managers, but all the statutory provisions are qualified in some way.

In its ninth policy, Congress sought "fair market value" for public land uses and resources "unless otherwise provided by statute." This policy is definitely not law; not only are grazing fees set at a fraction of market value, but the United States probably does not receive full value for any of the nation's resources. . . . Congress's tenth policy statement calls for uniform procedures for disposal, exchange, or acquisition of public lands. This policy was enacted in other FLPMA sections. . . . The eleventh policy seeks rapid protection of "areas of critical environmental concern"; the statute provides that protection.

B. Planning & Management of Public Lands & Resources

The twelfth congressional policy balances or counteracts the eighth by emphasizing use instead of preservation. Congress required that "the public lands be managed in a manner which recognizes the Nation's need for domestic sources of minerals, food, timber, and fiber from the public lands." . . . The thirteenth and final policy calls for equitable reimbursement to states for the local tax burden caused by federal immunity from taxation. This policy was enacted in the Payment in Lieu of Taxes Act of 1976. . . .

For the first time, the BLM is forced by law to develop land use plans in fairly precise ways and, after the plans are promulgated, to act in accordance with the guidelines established in the plans. Section 1711 commands a detailed inventory of all public land resources, and §1712 requires preparation of land use plans for all public land areas. . . . Section 1732(a) negates any implication that the plans are to be just public relations makework by making the plans binding on all subsequent multiple use decisions. . . .

FLPMA emphatically rejects the grazing-as-dominant-use tradition in public rangeland management in favor of multiple use-sustained yield principles. . . . In theory, the standard requires the agency to give all listed resources roughly equal consideration and weight in all decisionmaking. Multiple use-sustained yield is basically a utilitarian principle requiring high-level annual production of all resources in combination.[66] Congress defined both multiple use and sustained yield in sweeping terms. Apparently, however, the legislature never debated precisely how those management concepts were to be applied. Congress assumed instead that the standard was a significant, environmentally-oriented advance over existing authorities. Contrary to the opinions of several commentators, and to BLM predilections, multiple use and sustained yield are more than idle slogans allowing the agency to do as it professionally pleases. If courts begin reviewing multiple use decisions with any depth or insight, the standard as applied through planning processes will reverse the course of public rangeland management. . . .

Before investigating the limitations on management discretion inherent in the multiple use standard, the uses or resources themselves should be defined. In the Multiple Use-Sustained Yield Act (MUSY, 1960),[67] the "renewable surface resources" include only "outdoor recreation, range, timber, watershed, and wildlife and fish purposes." In 1976, Congress broadened the list of uses to "renewable and nonrenewable resources including, but not limited to, recreation, range, timber, minerals, watershed, wildlife and fish, and natural scenic, scientific, and historical values." . . .

Most of the listed resources are "renewable," meaning that they regenerate in some biological or climatological fashion. Although minerals are now included in the list, both hardrock mining and mineral leasing remain primarily governed by other statutes that have given mineral exploitation legal or de facto priority over other uses. Water itself, the key resource, was omitted,[68] probably because water allocation was seen as a state function. Wilderness, or "preservation," is not specifically listed, but is supplied in §1782. . . .

The key to multiple use-sustained yield management as a land management system is in the statutory definition of the two phrases. FLPMA borrows heavily from the MUSY Act:

---

66. Multiple use-sustained yield standards do not necessarily apply to each management unit where multiple use would be inconsistent with the nature of the resource base. In such cases, multiple use-sustained yield must be maintained on the level of some larger, more inclusive planning unit. [EDS.]

67. The Multiple-Use, Sustained Yield Act of 1960, 16 U.S.C. §§528 et seq., along with other statutes, governs the activities of the USFS. [EDS.]

68. Watershed protection, in multiple use legislation, means preservation of the soil and vegetation conditions necessary to provide adequate supplies of clean water. [EDS.]

43 U.S.C. §1702 . . . (c) the term "multiple use" means the management of the public lands and their various resource values so that they are utilized in the combination that will best meet the present and future needs of the American people; making the most judicious use of the land for some or all of these resources or related services over areas large enough to provide sufficient latitude for periodic adjustments in use to conform to changing needs and conditions; the use of some land for less than all of the resources; a combination of balanced and diverse resource uses that takes into account the long-term needs of future generations for renewable and nonrenewable resources, . . . and harmonious and coordinated management of the various resources without permanent impairment of the productivity of the land and the quality of the environment with consideration being given to the relative values of the resources and not necessarily to the combination of uses that will give the greatest economic return or the greatest unit output. . . .

(h) The term "sustained yield" means the achievement and maintenance in perpetuity of a high-level annual or regular periodic output of the various renewable resources of the public lands consistent with multiple use.

The main differences between the 1960 and 1976 definitions, apart from the inclusion of additional resources and values in 1976, are the congressional emphasis on intergenerational equity, the clear directive to achieve long-term conservation, and the requirement of environmental nonimpairment. . . .

[After discussing numerous discretionary aspects of these statutory definitions, Professor Coggins comments on what he considers to be their enforceable aspects: (1) avoiding impairment of productivity of land and the quality of the environment; and (2) managing for sustained yield.] . . . This [nonimpairment] standard is fairly precise, and it ought to be enforceable. In a sense, the limitation is a restatement of the watershed value because rangeland productivity requires both water to grow grass and grass to keep the soil in place. "Productivity" is the capacity of the land to support flora and fauna and to furnish "the various renewable resources" in the future. The two key elements in production are soil and water. Therefore, soil and water quality and quantity should be the central focus of public rangeland management attention, but that has not been the case so far.

If the manager were to allow a practice, such as prolonged overgrazing, that causes permanent reductions in future grass production, the nonimpairment limitation would make that action illegal as well as arbitrary. Moreover, when enjoyment of a listed use depends on a rare or unique attribute of an area, the manager must safeguard (or preserve) that attribute to ensure nonimpairment. For example, if a particular vista is especially attractive for hikers or tourists (the "outdoor recreation" resource), actions that seriously and permanently interfere with those scenic qualities arguably violate the nonimpairment standard. . . . The nonimpairment standard is clear, mandatory and nondiscretionary. . . .

The most significant management limitation in FLPMA is the definition of "sustained yield" in §1702(h). The phrase means *perpetual, high level* annual resource outputs of *all* renewable resources. Sustained yield is a separate, binding standard that makes continuing resource productivity the highest management criterion. The plain meaning of sustained yield . . . is that administrators may not sacrifice the future output of any renewable resource in present resource allocations. The "permanent" impairment provision qualifies the sustained yield limitation by ensuring that only serious, longlasting damage is prohibited. . . . In other words, the agency must plan to accommodate recreation, timber, watershed, wildlife, and natural values, as well as grazing, at high levels in perpetuity, and then act according to that plan. . . .

The search for compatible use combinations at optimum production levels will encounter more conflict than harmony. The main point of multiple use decisionmaking is conflict resolution, with all of the political problems that phrase implies. The manager must try to accommodate all resource uses to the extent possible, giving priority to none — at least on the broad scale — and consideration to all. Sustained yield in compatible combinations does resolve conflicts by theoretically forbidding the optimization of one resource at the expense of others. Such optimization of one resource could leave multiple use decisions vulnerable to attack on sustained yield grounds....

Multiple use-sustained yield management was meant to be more than a "succotash syndrome." Inherent in the concept are detailed and comprehensive commands to force thinking before acting and to mold individual actions into a long-range scheme for the public benefit. FLPMA does not allow the manager to do whatever appears politic or expedient at the time....

COMMENTARY & QUESTIONS

1. Public land management philosophies. "Multiple use-sustained yield" is the management philosophy mandated for all BLM lands, and national forests managed by the USFS. Its major rival is "dominant use," a standard recommended by the Public Land Law Review Commission for BLM lands but disavowed by Congress in FLPMA. In a dominant use management system, a primary use is selected for a portion of the public lands; after that, only those secondary uses that are compatible with the dominant use will be allowed there. Where grazing or mining are set as dominant uses, environmental values would be broadly precluded. By nature of that kind of planning, however, presumably only smaller delimited areas would be designated as available for exploitation, rather than all agency-managed lands. In a continuation of BLM's historic capture by the grazing industry and its supporters, Congress's multiple use directive has been superseded in practice by a de facto unlimited dominant use system favoring grazing. What are the major advantages and disadvantages of multiple use-sustained yield versus dominant use as public land management philosophies?

2. Multiple use-sustained yield reconsidered. Despite his earlier enthusiasm for the concept, Professor Coggins has given up on multiple use-sustained yield:

> [Multiple use-sustained yield] is a product of history: it is the latter-day offshoot of Gifford Pinchot's utilitarian maxim, the most benefits for the most people in the long run. Still, however, nobody knows what multiple use really means.... To the resource exploitation industries, multiple use means full speed ahead on the development of all surface and subsurface resources. To the managers on the ground, it means that they are free to decide every question according to their expert judgment without legal standards or judicial review. Neither ever mention sustained yield, except in the context of timber. This commentator once argued that multiple use laws actually meant something — not much, but something — but no court or agency has ever taken that argument seriously. Fortunately (from this perspective), multiple use as an operational standard is already dying a slow death, even without statutory repeal or revision.... Multiple use is obsolete.[69]

---

69. Coggins, Commentary: Overcoming the Unfortunate Legacies of Western Public Land Law, 29 Land & Water L. Rev. 381, 389 (1994).

Professor Michael Blumm concurs that multiple use-sustained yield has failed. In his view, it has resulted, under heavy industry pressure, in the federal agency's "allocation of dominant uses to fulfill [a] preexisting commitment to sustained commodity production."[70]

Other commentators declare the demise of multiple use from entirely different causes:

> The traditional commodity uses identified with Western folklore—timber, grazing, and mining operations—play a relatively less important role in the modern economy of the West than in past times. For instance . . . livestock grazing in the West is down from 17 million head in 1934 to 2 million today. . . . The decrease in commodity use parallels an emerging fact about public lands—they are chiefly valuable for non-consumptive uses. Outdoor recreation is a $350 billion industry (in terms of gross national product), with approximately $140 billion attributable to public lands. Consequently, there is a growing demand for public lands from recreational users, and a corresponding commitment towards environmental preservation. . . . The looming conflict in public land use will be between two former allies—recreation and preservation interests. Such a conflict is particularly likely to arise between low-impact, human-powered recreational users (preservationists) and high-impact, motorized recreational users (recreationists).[71]

An unusually forthright judge in a national forest case made the political problem explicit:

> One example of bias is particularly illustrative. The Forest Service argues that its [clearcutting] plan is based on evidence that timbering will provide new opportunities for recreation that will, in turn, preserve and enhance the diversity of plant and animal communities in the Wayne [Ohio] National Forest. . . . Timbering simply does not promote the kind of recreational activities that are in demand in the Wayne; in fact, recreation like fishing and hiking is harmed by clearcutting. . . . [But] it is not surprising that the Forest Service came to this conclusion. . . . Rather than being a neutral process which determines how the national forests can best meet the needs of the American people, forest planning, as practiced by the Forest Service, is a political process replete with opportunities for the intrusion of bias and abuse.[72]

3. Privatize public resources so private enterprises can manage them more profitably? A colleague who studies natural resource management from a generally market-oriented perspective has argued forcefully that industry political pressures may be too great for agencies to resist, so perhaps the wiser policy may be to turn the resources over to industry to manage for most efficient economic return. "The fact that economically powerful industries have had a major influence on the allocation of public lands resources only underscores the influence of money in our political system. The problem . . . is political. . . . So long as the federal government . . . is the owner and manager of lands and resources, politics will govern." Prof. Huffman asks, "Where does the foregoing perspective lead me . . . ?" and decides that in many instances "some form of private ownership will be better." Huffman, Public Lands: The Case for Privatization, 6.2 NRLI News 10 (1995). See also Huffman, The Inevitability of Private Rights in Public Lands, 65 U. Colo. L. Rev. 241, 245 (1994).

4. Dominant use management on public lands: mining, logging, wilderness. National Wildlife Refuges are managed by the FWS of the Department of the Interior, primarily

---

70. Blumm, Public Choice Theory and the Public Lands: Why "Multiple Use" Failed, 18 Harv. Envtl. L. Rev. 405, 426 (1994).

71. Laitos & Carr, Transformation on Public Lands, 26 Ecology L.Q. 140, 144-146 (1999) (see following section on ORVs).

72. *Sierra Club v. Thomas*, 105 F.3d 248 (6th Cir. 1997), rev'd for lack of ripeness, 523 U.S. 726 (1998).

for the benefit of fish and wildlife conservation. A refuge manager may "permit the use of any area within the System for any purpose, including but not limited to hunting, fishing, public recreation and accommodations, and access whenever he determines that such uses are compatible with the major purposes for which such areas were established."[73] Is hunting appropriate in a wildlife refuge? What about off-road vehicle (ORV) or motorboat use? Would dominant use justify opening a wildlife refuge for oil recovery operations that impinge on only a small part of the surface area, but drain a pool of oil that underlies the entire refuge?[74] What about agriculture? (Forty percent of the Tule Lake and Klamath Lake Wildlife Refuges have been turned over to agriculture, eliminating wetlands, withdrawing large amounts of water for irrigation, and feeding a virulent campaign against downstream water flows for endangered fish populations.[75])

Perhaps the best-known dominant use statute is the Wilderness Act of 1964, 16 U.S.C. §§1131 et seq. Under the express terms of this statute, all commercial logging and permanent roads and most structures and installations, temporary roads, commercial enterprises, and motorized equipment and forms of transportation are prohibited, but the following secondary uses are explicitly permitted: mining claims; mineral leases, and grazing permits obtained before January 1, 1964; water resources projects approved by the President; commercial services provided by guides, packers, and river runners; and hunting and fishing. Are these secondary uses compatible with a wilderness area, which is defined by the Act as "an area where the earth and its community of life are untrammeled by man, where man is himself a visitor who does not remain," 16 U.S.C. §1131(c)?

Hard-rock mining on public lands represents an extreme form of dominant use. It is still substantially governed by the General Mining Law of 1872, which declares all unreserved public lands open to mineral exploration and extraction.[76] Under this statute, a prospector locating minimum amounts of valuable minerals on public lands can stake a mining claim, exclude other prospectors and interfering recreationists from it, build a house on the property, and use whatever timber exists there for mining purposes. After several years of negligible work, and payment of a modest fee, the locator can be granted a federal patent that will entitle her to outright ownership of the former mining claim. Once a claim has been patented, the owner can do whatever she wants with the property, including using it or selling it for nonmining purposes. At no time is a locator-patentee required to make rental or royalty payments to the U.S. Environmental abuses on mining claims and patented lands have been frequent and serious, sometimes resulting in abandoned mines that pose threats to local water supplies.[77]

---

73. National Wildlife Refuge Administration Act, 16 U.S.C. §668dd(d)(1). This Act was amended by Pub. L. No. 105-57 (1997), which strengthened the conservation mandate of the FWS in National Wildlife Refuges.

74. See Michigan's Pigeon River case, *W. Mich. Envtl. Action Counsel v. Natural Res. Comm'n*, 275 N.W.2d 538 (Mich. 1979).

75. See Oregon Wild, Commercial Agriculture on Klamath Refuges: Background on the Klamath's Leaseland Agriculture Program—Impacts of Leaseland Agriculture on Klamath Basin National Wildlife Refuges, http://oregonwild.org/waters/klamath/refuges.

76. 30 U.S.C. §§22 et seq. In the Mineral Leasing Act of 1920, 30 U.S.C. §§181 et seq., Congress removed fuel minerals from the ambit of the General Mining Law and established a leasing system, based on competitive bidding, including provisions that authorize the BLM (which also oversees mineral leases on federal lands) to insert environmentally protective provisions in mineral leases.

77. For a portrait and analysis of the General Mining Law in operation, see C. Wilkinson, Crossing the Next Meridian ch. 2 (1992).

Although logging in National Forests is ostensibly regulated by the multiple use-sustained yield standard of the NFMA, many would argue that, like the BLM lands, the National Forests have been managed according to a de facto dominant use for timber production.[78]

Water is the key to other land uses in the arid West, but water allocation is not listed as one of FLPMA's multiple uses because water diversion on federal land has traditionally been governed by state law. West of the Mississippi River, almost all state water allocation laws are based on the "prior appropriation" principle ("first in time is first in right"). Until comparatively recently, environmental protection has been difficult to achieve under western state water allocation systems.[79]

5. Unenforceable policies and mixed mandates. FLPMA, like almost every other federal and state statute, has a section entitled "Declaration of Policy." Section 102(b) states that "the policies of this Act shall become effective only as specific statutory authority for their implementation is enacted by this Act or by subsequent legislation. . . ." As the above excerpt points out, some of FLPMA's policies have been enacted, some have been conditionally enacted, some have not been enacted, and some—e.g., the "fair market value" policy—are being ignored by the BLM. Moreover, FLPMA §102 contains policies encouraging both preservation and consumption. What are the functions of legislative policy statements such as these? Are they intended to mislead an unwary public? Are they media "sound bites"? Do they serve to mollify interest groups that have not received all they wanted? Or are they statements of long-term goals that may or may not now be practicable? In fact, all of these concerns, among others, motivate draftspersons when drafting statutory declarations of policy. Consequently, in reading statutes, one must be sensitive to the difference between hortatory, emotive, and political statements, on the one hand, and enforceable commands on the other.

6. The public trust and the public lands. Does the public trust doctrine (see Chapter 20) impose obligations on federal land managers supplementary to those found in their management statutes? Compare *Sierra Club v. Dep't of the Interior*, 376 F. Supp. 90 (N.D. Cal. 1974), and *Sierra Club v. Dep't of the Interior*, 398 F. Supp. 284 (N.D. Cal. 1975) (the public trust doctrine applies to the activities of the National Park Service with regard to the management of Redwood National Park), with *Sierra Club v. Block*, 622 F. Supp. 842 (D. Colo. 1985), vacated on other grounds *sub nom. Sierra Club v. Yeutter*, 911 F.2d 1405 (10th Cir. 1990) (where Congress has set out statutory duties, they comprise all the responsibilities of a federal land management agency). The public trust doctrine has been applied, however, to a state allocation of water rights that detrimentally affected federal public lands. (See the *Mono Lake* decision in Chapter 20.)

As a remarkable feature of federal public trust powers in public lands management, note the President's inherent stewardship power to withdraw lands into reserves. Teddy Roosevelt withdrew almost 130 million acres from the public domain between 1901-1908 to set up wildlife, forest, and oil reserves, a power validated in *U.S. v. Midwest Oil Co.*, 236 U.S. 459 (1915). The Executive apparently has affirmative power to declare such protections unless limited by congressional action (a political process that confronted the Clinton Administration's unilateral extension of rangeland protections).

7. "Cooperative management" and the BLM. In the Public Rangelands Improvement Act of 1978, 32 U.S.C. §§1901 et seq., Congress found that "vast segments" of the public lands were in "unsatisfactory condition" because they were "producing less than their

---

78. Wilkinson, id., ch. 4; S. Yaffee, The Wisdom of the Spotted Owl (1994).
79. See generally J. Sax, R. Abrams & B. Thompson, Legal Control of Water Resources ch. 3 (2d ed. 1991).

potential" for the multiple uses detailed in FLPMA. The congressional prescription was improved management by the BLM, including discontinuance of grazing on stressed lands and "explor[ation of] innovative grazing management policies and systems which might provide incentives to improve range conditions." Relying on this language, BLM established a Cooperative Management Agreement (CMA) program authorizing BLM to enter into special permit arrangements with selected ranchers who had demonstrated "exemplary rangeland management practices." The purpose of the CMA program was to allow these exemplary ranchers to "manage livestock on the allotment as they determine appropriate" for ten-year periods. "Exemplary practices" were not defined in the regulation, nor were the agreements required to contain performance standards or any other limiting terms or conditions. If a permittee did not comply with the nebulous goals of the program, BLM's only remedy was to deny renewal of the agreement after its ten-year term had elapsed. In *NRDC v. Hodel*, 618 F. Supp. 848, 868 (E.D. Cal. 1985), the court, finding that "the CMA program is *not* an experiment, but is a permanent system of permit issuance aimed at a group of favored permittees," struck down the CMA regulations as inconsistent with BLM's statutory obligation to "prescribe the manner in and the extent to which livestock practices will be conducted on public lands."

8. Grazing fees and other public land use subsidies. All attempts to raise the grazing fee to a figure approaching market value (the current federal grazing fee is less than $2 per cow, per month, in contrast with current forage market rates of over $10 per cow, per month) have been unsuccessful. Other subsidies for resource use on public lands include below-cost timber sales from the National Forests, federal payments to timber companies for logging road construction when they buy timber in the national forests,[80] extraction of hard-rock minerals from the public lands without paying royalties to the federal government, below-cost sales of water from federally constructed dams, cost-free water diversions from federal lands, free access to ORVs, and below-cost fees for public access to National Parks.[81] Are there good reasons for subsidizing resource use on public lands? Should the USFS sell timber below cost as benign support for the economies of timber-dependent communities?[82] Should fees for National Park access be kept low in order to attract low- and middle-income visitors? Should grazing fees remain low in order to preserve the economic viability of the small rancher?[83]

9. The planning "shell game." Professor Robert Feller, a keen observer of BLM grazing management practices, noted that—

> concerned citizens and environmental organizations who urge BLM and the Forest Service to assess the appropriateness of grazing on particular parcels of public lands find themselves engaged in a bureaucratic shell game in which the agencies avoid the issue by sliding it back

---

80. In February 1998, the Clinton Administration imposed a moratorium on logging road construction in most national forests, even if timber companies are willing to build the roads without federal subsidies. The Bush II Administration suspended this moratorium and in May 2009 the Obama Administration reinstated the moratorium on roughly 50 million acres of forest.

81. See generally Wilkinson, Crossing the Next Meridian (1992), for a discussion of subsidies for ranchers, miners, and water users.

82. See the discussion in Anderson, Below-Cost Timber Sales & Community Economic Subsidies: A Conflict of Values, 5 Md. J. Contemp. Legal Issues 129 (1995).

83. Only 12% of grazing permit holders are listed by the Interior Department as small operators. Ten percent of permit holders—including the Metropolitan Life Insurance Company (800,000 acres), the Mormon Church, a Japanese conglomerate, the Nature Conservancy, and some of the wealthiest families in the nation—control about half of all public grazing land. Egan, Wingtip "Cowboys" in Last Stand to Hold On to Low Grazing Fees, N.Y. Times, Oct. 29, 1993, at 27.

and forth between their land use planning processes and their decision making processes for individual grazing allotments. When citizens request that a land use plan include a review of the appropriateness of grazing on particular sites or allotments within a planning area, they are typically informed that the land use planning process is not designed to address such site-specific issues, and that they should raise the issue when allotment management plans (AMPs) are developed for the allotments in question. However, when the issue is raised during the development of an AMP or the issuance of a permit for an allotment, the agency responds that it is a land use planning issue that should have been raised during the development of the applicable land use plan. In fact, the issue is never addressed, and grazing continues without ever being seriously questioned. Feller, 'Til the Cows Come Home: The Fatal Flaw in the Clinton Administration's Public Lands Grazing Policy, 25 Envtl. L. 703, 748 (1995).

10. The more things change . . . The BLM continues to defy the dictates of federal law in its regulation of cattle grazing on federal lands in the West. In *Idaho Watersheds Project v. Hahn*, 307 F.3d 815 (9th Cir. 2002), several environmental groups sued the BLM for, among other things, violating NEPA in the issuance of grazing permits to ranchers grazing cattle on federal lands in the Owyhee Resource Area in southwestern Idaho. The district court held that the BLM had violated NEPA and granted a permanent injunction imposing interim environmental protection conditions (e.g., protection of riparian vegetation) on grazing and imposing a timetable for the BLM to issue new permits in compliance with NEPA. The Ninth Circuit Court of Appeals, in affirming the district court's judgment, extolled the Owyhee Area as "over one million acres of ruggedly beautiful landscape . . . [including] spectacular and wild canyonlands." In addition, the area "provides habitat for bighorn sheep, elk, mule deer, antelope, peregrine falcon, redband trout, sage grouse, and hundreds of other species. Startling in its ecological diversity, from arid sagebrush desert to lush juniper woodlands, the Owyhee shelters the world's largest population of nesting raptors and a variety of rare and endangered species." Cattle ranching has been a traditional land use in the Owyhee Area: "Ranching families are an important part of the local community with many family members participating actively in civic life as local elected officials, volunteer firefighters, and school board members. Well over four hundred people currently depend on cattle grazing in the Owyhee for their livelihood." 307 F.3d at 821.

But BLM has managed the Owyhee Area as if cattle grazing were the dominant use of this region:

> Water is life, and the health of the Owyhee depends on the health of its streams. Unfortunately, cattle overgrazing now threatens the life of the Owyhee. . . . In 1981, the BLM identified livestock overgrazing as a significant problem in the Owyhee and concluded that approximately ninety percent of the Owyhee rangeland was in poor or fair ecological condition. In 1981, the BLM also found over one hundred and forty miles of streams to be in poor condition, due in large part to overgrazing. In 1996, the BLM again examined the health of the streams in the Owyhee and found that ninety-one percent of the stream miles inventoried were in unsatisfactory condition. Despite the BLM's own findings, the BLM failed to address destruction of riparian habitat caused by cattle overgrazing in the fifteen years between 1981 and 1996 and the condition of stream banks in the Owyhee continued to deteriorate during this period. . . . In 1997 . . . the BLM issued sixty-eight grazing permits covering about one million acres. The BLM sought to comply with NEPA by filling out pre-printed one page forms for each permit, and stating on the form that the permit complied with the then 16-year-old EIS that had been adopted in 1981. Grazing on the allotments covered by these permits continued uninterrupted and continues today. 307 F.3d at 822.

11. The holy grail of maximum sustained yield. Obscured behind the political compromises and slippage in resource planning is the goal and concept of maximum sustained

B. Planning & Management of Public Lands & Resources

yield, MSY (a standard not at all like MUSY). Wherever reproducing natural resources are involved, MSY, as the term implies, represents the highest harvestable benefit for human society that can be expected to be maintained continuingly year after year.
In Figure , at what approximate level would you estimate that MSY would be found?

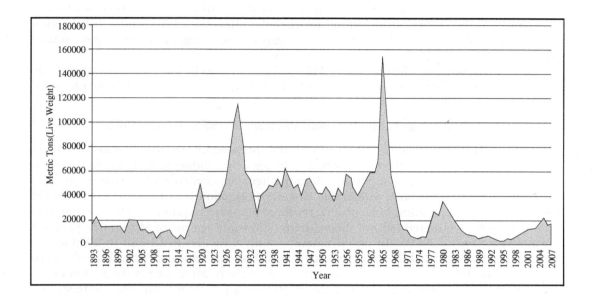

FIGURE 9-4. *Chart showing annual tonnage of groundfish (haddock) harvested from the Gulf of Maine & Georges Bank of New England since 1893. Overfishing in the 1920s made the population drop, but it recovered when the relatively small American fishing fleet backed off for a few years, turning to other available prime species. Thereafter, 24 years of a relatively stable harvest of roughly 45,000 to 50,000 tons annually ended in a dramatic spike driven by a competitive rush brought on by entry and predation by foreign fishing boats and factory ships. The resulting drastic crash was temporarily reversed by a statutory limitation on foreign fleets in the 1970s, but subsequent major expansion in the U.S. fleet in the late 1970s made the resource crash again. Limited mid-1990s restrictions on "TAC," total allowable catch, allowed the population to recover somewhat by 2009, although political pressures for continued harvesting and against stricter limits have not allowed the resource to return to its former annual levels. The annual catch is currently roughly 15,000 tons a year, roughly 30,000 tons a year less than it could be if it were politically possible to apply a five-year total moratorium to allow the resource to recover fully to MSY.*[84] *Chart compiled and created by Danielle Sievers, BCLS '11.*

Looking at Figure 4, the dysfunctionality of political pressures blocking scientific management becomes obvious. The successful pressuring of resource agencies by fishermen and industry lobbyists perpetrates chronically excessive fishing quotas that prevent recoverable stocks from recovering up to their maximum sustainable level. That is shortsighted. If objective science were the basis of regulation, a lifecycle moratorium of five to ten years could triple or quadruple the total harvest in terms of societal protein and money

---

84. Data in this section from E. Dorsey, A Brief History of the New England Fisheries Crisis(1998); NOAA, A Brief History of the Groundfishing Industry of New England (2004), www.nefsc.noaa.gov/history/stories/groundfish/grndfsh2.html; and NOAA, Fishwatch (2009), www.nmfs.noaa.gov/fishwatch/species/haddock.htm; and see Plater, Facing a Time of Counter-Revolution—The Kepone Incident and a Review of First Principles, 29 U. Rich. L. Rev. 657, 674-678 (1995).

for fishermen. In a classic replay of Hardin's Tragedy of the Commons, however, the present players in the industry all feel competitively locked into a downward spiral. "I feel like the last buffalo hunter," one fisherman said sadly.[85] But how does one say to small-boat fishermen "Stop for five years to allow the fish stocks to treble!" when they know that a moratorium for long-term sustainability would mean they'll go bankrupt in the very short term, unable to pay mortgages and buy food for their families, forced to give up fishing altogether. Does this present a conundrum that suggests, for a time, a policy of government payments to fishermen not to fish?

In general, however, the concept of MSY will continue to be a powerfully rational policy goal that can serve as an objective scientific beacon for resource management planners.

3. Public Lands Management Planning in the Supreme Court

FLPMA and NFMA require the USFS and BLM to prepare LRMPs for all lands they manage. Plan preparation is taken very seriously by agencies, industry, and citizens—and is often the subject of sharp contention—because agency permissions for exploitative uses of public lands are extremely vulnerable to citizen litigation if not authorized in a valid LRMP. Because preparation of an official resource plan also requires an EIS, environmental plaintiffs have targeted most of their dozens of lawsuits against BLM resource plans on alleged violations of NEPA. In one dramatic example, the Tenth Circuit in 2009 struck down the supplemental EIS for a plan opening 518 square miles of New Mexico's Otero Mesa Management Area to oil and gas drilling. The Otero Mesa area is the nation's largest remaining Chihuahuan Desert grassland, providing habitat for numerous rare species and overlying a major groundwater aquifer. BLM had issued an initially limited plan with an EIS, then adopted a plan amendment greatly expanding the size and locations of drilling lease areas without covering the changes in an SEIS, saying that environmental effects would be the same. The appeals court said that given the impacts of the expansion, the NEPA statement "need[ed] to analyze the specific land use plan that the BLM eventually selected," blocked the plan, and halted the oil and gas leasing. See *Richardson et al. v. BLM*, 565 F.3d 683 (10th Cir. 2009).

Once a plan is deemed valid, to what extent does an agency have to follow it? That is the issue raised by a recent Supreme Court decision on the use of ORVs on wilderness study areas managed under a BLM plan.

The same kinds of internal institutional and external industry pressures on agency resource management evident in the oil and gas, grazing, mining, and timberlands settings likewise occur with regard to ORVs. Along with water-borne thrill craft jet skis and snowmobiles, two-, three-, and four-wheeled motorized all-terrain vehicles have become a major commercial recreation industry, beloved by millions and often supporting local tourist economies. Unfortunately, part of the thrill of these machines is the joy of racing through undisturbed natural settings, and the machines' fleeting passage can leave scars and consequences that seriously disrupt the natural environment, sometimes for decades to come.

> Off-road vehicles have damaged every kind of ecosystem found in the United States.... In some cases the wounds will heal naturally; in others they will not, at least for millennia.... The ready availability of federal land has profoundly shaped the ORV phenomenon.... ORVs eat land. It is because ORVs attack the relatively thin layer of disintegrated rock and organic material to which all earthly life clings —soil— that they can have such a devastating effect on natural

---

85. Declining Fisheries, (NPR broadcast, Weekend Edition, Dec. 3, 1994) (quoting Ed Miller of Montauk, NY).

resources.... A major difficulty with ORVs... is that the terrain which truly challenges the capability of these machines, and which is therefore most attractive to many ORV operators, is exactly that which is most highly sensitive to erosional degradation.... ORVs damage vegetation [and] disrupt animal life.... ORV and snowmobile use of the land conflicts with other human uses of the land, [and] the conflicts engendered by these machines can be quite bitter.... The most serious conflicts arise between ORV operators and nonmotorized picnickers or campers, hikers, backpackers, sightseers, and so on —or between ORVers and persons using the land for educational purposes—students, teachers, researchers.... David Sheridan, Off-Road Vehicles on Public Lands 7-12 (1979).

FIGURE 9-5. *ORV use on public lands. This ridge in California's Jawbone Canyon has been stripped of vegetation by heavy ORV recreational use. The plume of dust marks the uphill run of an all-terrain motorcycle. In the desert, even in cases of low-volume ORV use, noise levels can be deafening, and the tire track ruts made by just one machine in one 15-minute run through the fragile ecology of the desert floor may remain visible from the air for more than 50 years. ©1989 Howard Wilshire.*

In addition to the Plans required by FLPMA and NFMA, the Wilderness Act of 1964[86] required federal agencies to review all roadless federal lands for candidacy for wilderness designation[87] (ultimately identifying nearly 80 million acres as prime wilderness or WSAs, "wilderness study areas"). Many of these areas were highly attractive to ORV users, and the agencies were hesitant to exclude them. The agencies were required by law, however, to protect the identified areas' wilderness characteristics against "impairment" pending congressional votes on whether or not to formally proclaim them wilderness areas.

These legally mandated plans were thought to be legally binding, with agencies' actions required to be consistent with the plans.[88] The question was whether the plans would be enforced. As so often

---

86. 16 U.S.C. §§1131 et seq.
87. The RARE process (Roadless Area Review and Evaluation, RARE I, RARE II, etc.).
88. The LRMP defines the "management direction" for the forest. It constitutes a program for all natural resource management activities and establishes management requirements to be employed in implementing the plan. It identifies the resource management practices, the projected levels of production of goods and services, and the location where various types of resource management may occur. Implementation of the LRMP is achieved through individual site-specific projects and all projects must be consistent with the LRMP. 16 U.S.C. §1604, 36 C.F.R. §219.

where the government does not police its own agencies, the issue comes down to whether citizen enforcement will be possible.

In the following case BLM's Plan had stated that BLM *"will conduct use supervision and monitoring"* of ORV use in several WSAs in Utah, but BLM had not done so, tolerating extensive and expanding ORVs access within the wilderness study areas.

Norton v. Southern Utah Wilderness Alliance et al.

542 U.S. 55 (2004)

Scalia, J. In this case we must decide whether the authority of a federal court under the Administrative Procedure Act to "compel agency action unlawfully withheld or unreasonably delayed," 5 U.S.C. §706 (1), extends to the review of the U.S. Bureau of Land Management's stewardship of public lands under certain statutory provisions and its own planning documents. . . .

FLPMA establishes a dual regime of inventory and planning. Sections 1711 and 1712, respectively, provide for a comprehensive, ongoing inventory of federal lands, and for a land use planning process. . . . Congress made the judgment that some lands should be set aside as wilderness at the expense of commercial and recreational uses. . . . The Wilderness Act of 1964 provides that designated wilderness areas, subject to certain exceptions, "shall [have] no commercial enterprise and no permanent road," no motorized vehicles, and no manmade structures. . . . The Secretary of Interior has identified so-called "wilderness study areas" (WSAs), roadless lands of 5,000 acres or more that possess "wilderness characteristics," as determined in the Secretary's land inventory [to be] subjected to further examination and public comment in order to evaluate their suitability for designation as wilderness. In 1991, out of 3.3 million acres in Utah that had been identified for study, 2 million were recommended as suitable for wilderness designation. This recommendation was forwarded to Congress, which has not yet acted upon it. Until Congress acts one way or the other, FLPMA provides that "the Secretary shall continue to manage such lands . . . in a manner so as not to impair the suitability of such areas for preservation as wilderness." 43 U.S.C. §1782(c). This nonimpairment mandate applies to all WSAs. . . .

Aside from identification of WSAs, the main tool that the BLM employs to balance wilderness protection against other uses is a land use plan—what the BLM regulations call a "resource management plan." Land use plans, adopted after notice and comment, are "designed to guide and control future management actions." 43 U.S.C. §1712. Generally, a land use plan describes, for a particular area, allowable uses, goals for future condition of the land, and specific next steps. Under FLPMA, "the Secretary shall manage the public lands under principles of multiple use and sustained yield, in accordance with the land use plans . . . when they are available." 43 U.S.C. §1732(a). . . .

In 1999, respondents Southern Utah Wilderness Alliance and other organizations (collectively SUWA) . . . sought declaratory and injunctive relief for BLM's failure to act to protect public lands in Utah from damage caused by ORV use. SUWA made three claims that are relevant here: (1) that BLM had violated its nonimpairment obligation by allowing degradation in certain WSAs; (2) that BLM had failed to implement provisions in its land use plans relating to ORV use; and (3) that BLM had failed to take a "hard look" at whether, pursuant to [NEPA], it should undertake supplemental environmental analyses for areas in which ORV use had increased. SUWA contended that it could sue to remedy these three failures to act pursuant to the APA's provision of a cause of action "to compel agency action unlawfully withheld or unreasonably delayed."

B. Planning & Management of Public Lands & Resources

[After extensive analysis of the APA, the Scalia opinion concluded that] a claim under APA §706(1) can proceed only where a plaintiff asserts that an agency failed to take a discrete agency action that it is required to take. . . .

With these principles in mind, we turn to SUWA's first claim, that by permitting ORV use in certain WSAs, BLM violated its mandate to "continue to manage [WSAs] . . . in a manner so as not to impair the suitability of such areas for preservation as wilderness." . . . [The nonimpairment provision] is mandatory as to the object to be achieved, but it leaves BLM a great deal of discretion in deciding how to achieve it. It assuredly does not mandate, with the clarity necessary to support judicial action under §706(1), the total exclusion of ORV use. SUWA argues that [FLPMA] does contain a categorical imperative, namely the command to comply with the nonimpairment mandate. It contends that a federal court could simply enter a general order compelling compliance with that mandate, without suggesting any particular manner of compliance. . . . [But] general deficiencies in compliance . . . lack the specificity requisite for agency action.

The principal purpose of the APA limitations we have discussed . . . is to protect agencies from undue judicial interference with their lawful discretion, and to avoid judicial entanglement in abstract policy disagreements which courts lack both expertise and information to resolve. If courts were empowered to enter general orders compelling compliance with broad statutory mandates, they would necessarily be empowered, as well, to determine whether compliance was achieved—which would mean that it would ultimately become the task of the supervising court, rather than the agency, to work out compliance with the broad statutory mandate, injecting the judge into day-to-day agency management. To take just a few examples from federal resource management, a plaintiff might allege that the Secretary had failed to "manage wild free-roaming horses and burros in a manner that is designed to achieve and maintain a thriving natural ecological balance." . . . The prospect of pervasive oversight by federal courts over the manner and pace of agency compliance with such congressional directives is not contemplated by the APA.

SUWA's second claim is that BLM failed to comply with certain provisions in its land use plans, thus contravening the requirement that "[the] Secretary shall manage the public lands . . . *in accordance with the land use plans* . . . when they are available." . . .

The statutory directive that BLM manage "in accordance with" land use plans and the regulatory requirement that authorizations and actions "conform to" those plans, prevent BLM from taking actions inconsistent with the provisions of a land use plan. Unless and until the plan is amended, such actions can be set aside as contrary to law. The claim presently under discussion, however, would have us go further and conclude that a statement in a plan that BLM "will" take this, that, or the other action, is a binding commitment that can be compelled under §706(1). In our view it is not—at least absent binding commitment in the terms of the plan.

FLPMA describes land use plans as tools by which "present and future use is projected." The implementing regulations make clear that land use plans are a preliminary step in the overall process of managing public lands—"designed to guide and control future management actions and the development of subsequent, more detailed and limited scope plans for resources and uses." 43 C.F.R. §1601.0-2 (2003). The statute and regulations confirm that a land use plan is not ordinarily the medium for affirmative decisions that implement the agency's "project[ions]." Title 43 U.S.C. §1712(e) provides that "the Secretary may issue management decisions to implement land use plans"—the decisions, that is, are distinct from the plan itself. Picking up the same theme, the regulation defining a land use plan declares that a plan "is not a final implementation decision on actions which require further specific plans, process steps, or decisions. . . ." 43 C.F.R. §1601.0-5(k) (2003). . . .

The San Rafael plan provides an apt illustration of the immense scope of projected activity that a land use plan can embrace. Over 100 pages in length, it presents a comprehensive management framework for 1.5 million acres of BLM-administered land. Twenty categories of resource management are separately discussed, including mineral extraction, wilderness protection, livestock grazing, preservation of cultural resources, and recreation. The plan lays out an ambitious agenda for the preparation of additional, more detailed plans and specific next steps for implementation. Its introduction notes that "an [ORV] implementation plan is scheduled to be prepared within 1 year following approval of the [plan]." Similarly "scheduled for preparation" are activity plans for certain environmentally sensitive areas, "along with allotment management plans, habitat management plans, a fire management plan, recreation management plans . . . , cultural resource management plans, [etc.]. The projected schedule set forth in the plan shows "anticipated implementation" of some future plans within one year, others within three years, and still others, such as certain recreation and cultural resource management plans, at a pace of "one study per fiscal year."

Quite unlike a specific statutory command requiring an agency to promulgate regulations by a certain date, a land use plan is generally a statement of priorities; it guides and constrains actions, but does not (at least in the usual case) prescribe them. . . .

Of course, an action called for in a plan may be compelled when the plan merely reiterates duties the agency is already obligated to perform, or perhaps when language in the plan itself creates a commitment binding on the agency. But allowing general enforcement of plan terms would lead to pervasive interference with BLM's own ordering of priorities. . . . Its predictable consequence would be much vaguer plans from BLM in the future—making coordination with other agencies more difficult, and depriving the public of important information concerning the agency's long-range intentions.

We therefore hold that the [plan's] statements to the effect that BLM will conduct "use supervision and monitoring" in designated areas—like other "will do" projections of agency action set forth in land use plans—are not a legally binding commitment enforceable under §706(1). [The Court's decision also dismissed plaintiffs' NEPA claim. Surprisingly, apparently due to the APA issue, the decision was unanimous![89]]

COMMENTARY & QUESTIONS

1. What remains of FLPMA's planning "consistency clause" (the requirement that public lands shall be managed in accordance with completed land use plans)? The Court states that allowing a court to order general compliance with plan terms would result in the preparation of vague plans. But won't the *SUWA* Court's decision lead to the same result, treating plans as vague "goals" rather than operational guidance? Preparing valid land use plans that pass NEPA muster will still be necessary because proposed intensive uses will have to be authorized in the plans. In terms of plan safeguards,

---

89. The Supreme Court's *SUWA* decision has attracted strong academic criticism. See Blumm & Bosse, *Norton v. SUWA and the Unraveling of Federal Public Land Planning*, 18 Duke Envtl. L. & Pol'y F. 105 (2007-2008); Keiter, Breaking Faith with Nature: The Bush Administration and Public Land Policy, 27 J. Land Res. & Envtl. L. 195 (2007); Sakashita, . . . A Failure to Protect Wilderness in Redrock Country, 32 Ecology L.Q. 391 (2005); Konrad, The Shrinking Scope of Judicial Review in *Norton v. Southern Utah Wilderness Alliance*, 77 U. Colo. L. Rev. 515 (2006); Kappler, Off-Roading Without a Map: The Supreme Court Drives over NEPA in *Southern Utah Wilderness Alliance*, 24 Ga. St. U. L. Rev. 533 (2007-2008).

however, will they be merely precatory documents with only symbolic meaning? Or is there some point in the development of plans and sub-plans where agency declarations become legally binding commitments? If so, what is that line of demarcation, if not at the "will-do" stage?

2. Is nonimpairment really mandated? After *SUWA*, what remains of the so-called "nonimpairment mandate" regarding management of WSAs? Do you agree that federal courts cannot legally issue general compliance orders, even where the defendant agency's departure from plan requirements clearly leads to destruction of the area's wilderness character, thus violating the statutory nonimpairment mandate? Would it avoid undue judicial interference with agency discretion if a court allowed a reasonable time to remedy the impairment and then evaluated whether the responsive agency action had been arbitrary and capricious?

3. Dilemmas underlying public resource management. This chapter does not provide clear answers to the generic questions it raises: Are public resources to be a continuing legacy, or will interested constituencies continue to be able to convert those national resources to benefit their short-term profit-maximization interests? Are the resources to be assigned to single or multiple uses, to be used for local or nationwide benefit? What mechanism should be used, if any, to harmonize competing interests? Statutes such as the Wilderness Act and FLPMA attempt to establish long-term basic principles to guide resource management, which inevitably collide with the pressures of economic interests that focus, as we all do, on the short-term specific.

It doesn't make much difference to the mayor of a small Northwest logging town whether the surrounding mountains are public or private; the old-growth forests that remain there are a source for perhaps just a half dozen more years of economic life for the community on the only terms that are available—clearcutting according to prevailing corporate practice. For as long as these last forests are allowed to be cut, by just so long will local citizens be able to pay their mortgages and taxes and avoid having to go on welfare or move away. The practices of the timber industry, and its failures to implement successful long-term renewable, sustainable timber supply, are matters beyond the control of the community.

What is lost when an ancient forest is gone, beyond a localized depreciation of natural environment? Are there public losses other than those that occur in terms of recreation, tourism, water quality, etc.? What exactly is the value of the oldest living tree on Earth? Such questions become even more abstract when it isn't a tree or the last carrier pigeon, but thousands of acres comprising the last 5% of our original natural forest—or when human actions do not destroy the resource but change its context. Joe Sax once was startled as he climbed up a tortuous ridge in Tennessee to look out over a sprawling, forested, mountain-girded gulf in the Great Smokies National Park, to see a white high-rise Sheraton hotel thrusting up in the middle distance of the Park, built on an inholding. See also J. Sax, Mountains Without Handrails: Reflections on the National Parks (1980); Sax, Helpless Giants: The National Parks and the Regulation of Private Lands, 75 Mich. L. Rev. 239 (1976). What kind of experiential or aesthetic issues did this commercial intrusion raise? What is a "wilderness experience"?

Or, for another situation raising a composite of these issues, consider the reintroduction of wolves, grizzlies, and other endangered predator species to areas from which they had previously been exterminated. Montana, Wyoming, Minnesota, and other northern tier states have seen a number of attempts to restore large predators on public lands, especially national parks. For ranchers grazing cattle on nearby public and private rangelands, these ecological experiments represent the height of public policy folly.[90] Killing bears, mountain lions, and wolves seems to be an atavistic human instinct, coupled with a farmer's vivid sense of emotional and economic injury upon finding a calf slaughtered in an early morning meadow. Doesn't a policy to bring back the predators seem irrational? To shoot the animal that killed your calf, however, runs the risk of fine and imprisonment.

At the very least we owe future generations an attempt to clarify what our national public resources policies are.

4. Future resource planning needs to incorporate rational triage? Rational resource triage is possible. The field of water law provides examples in recognition of the fact that we can no longer tolerate chaotic, fractionalized approaches to critical societal resources. Rivers and subsurface aquifers run dry while subsidized water supplies allow farmers to maintain rice paddies in deserts. The most imperative water needs of the nation and competing uses can be prioritized in hierarchical order.[91] (1) The first-order use would be to ensure population security—water that people need to live and support themselves economically[92] in concentrated areas.[93] (2) The second-order use, ecological security: the collapse of ecosystems from dewatering or water resources mismanagement carries devastating and often irreversible costs, whether the example is the Owens Valley in California, the devastation of the Everglades that now threatens the ability of Florida to meet its freshwater needs for population security, the loss of species, or saline intrusion into coastal aquifers.[94] (3) The third-order use, energy security: Water resources are intimately linked to energy production, a nexus that is increasing as the nation attempts to combat its dependence on insecure foreign sources of oil and reduce its production of greenhouse gasses.[95] (4) The fourth-order use, food security: roughly 85% of the water consumed in the United States is for irrigated agriculture,[96] but this is a very low-value use of water.[97] Food is perhaps the most essential item to survival, but the U.S. has a land and climate base that permits it to shift food production away from water-stressed regions to humid regions where dry land farming is feasible or to well-watered locales where minimal irrigation can greatly increase crop yields.

---

90. Keiter & Holscher, Wolf Recovery Under the Endangered Species Act: A Study in Contemporary Federalism, 11 Pub. Land L. Rev. 19 (1990).

91. For a more complete exposition of this approach, see Abrams & Hall, Framing Water Policy in a Carbon Affected and Carbon Constrained Environment, 50 Nat. Res. L.J. (2010).

92. The idea of population support includes water for household use and industrial and commercial use that provides economic sustenance for the people living there. It does not include water for excessive residential or recreational irrigation, and, of course, the amounts can be minimized by sound conservation measures.

93. In the U.S., most dispersed populations rely on tiny amounts of self-supplied groundwater withdrawals and, if groundwater were not available, there would not be serious social dislocations if those areas did not support people.

94. A more comprehensive catalog of the values of ecosystems is found in an extensive literature surrounding ecosystem services and natural capital. See, e.g., J.B. Ruhl, S.E. Kraft & C.L. Lant, The Law and Policy of Ecosystem Services (2007); Costanza et al., The Value of the World's Ecosystem Services and Natural Capital, 387 Nature 253 (1997). Two courts have dealt with the value of ecosystem services. See *Palazzolo v. State*, 2005 WL 1645974 (R.I. 2005) (the state trial court on remand from the Supreme Court), and *Avenal v. State*, 886 So. 2d 1085 (La. 2004), noted in Ruhl, The "Background Principles" of Natural Capital and Ecosystem Services, 22 J. Land Use & Envtl. L. 525, 540-547 (2007).

95. This linkage of water and energy security is explored at length in Abrams and Hall, supra note 91.

96. See W.B. Solley et al., Estimated Use of Water in the United States, 1995 U.S. Geological Survey Circular 1200, at 19 fig. 7 (USGS 1998), available at http://water.usgs.gov/watuse/pdf1995/html. The 1995 data is offered since that is the last of the five-year USGS water use estimates that compiled figures for both withdrawal and consumption of water. More recent reports include only withdrawals.

97. See, e.g., R.A. Young, Determining the Economic Value of Water: Concepts and Methods (2005).

B. Planning & Management of Public Lands & Resources

Other water uses like navigation and recreation are important, but not on the same plane as these four "securities." Recreation and navigation uses, moreover, will often be supported by the presence of water protected in the use hierarchy as part of ensuring ecological security. The resource management goal ought to be to provide secure supplies of water to meet the four needs in hierarchical priority.[98] The essence of planned resource management is to ensure that most important uses are satisfied first on a predictable basis upon which resource users can rely and make their own planning decisions.

5. More on ORV policy. As noted, ORVs create policy and planning conflicts difficult to compromise. There is a real thrill in being able to propel oneself with great speed through otherwise impassable natural settings in deep snow, open water, and rugged terrain. The technology to do so has created a new, expansive form of outdoor recreation, and substantial manufacturing and commercial activity with a powerfully focused political lobby. The recreational and preservationist interests negatively impacted by ORVs, however, tend to be quieter, more contemplative, and more diffuse. One kid on an ORV can spoil the enjoyment of a hundred or more passive recreationists using the same resource. When the uses conflict, technology usually wins, the passive recreationists tending to look elsewhere to find quieter undisturbed places of natural quality.

Compromise is difficult. Time rationing — limiting the hours or days per week ORVs can operate in an area — is difficult to enforce and does little to prevent physical degradation of the resource. For many ORVers, area restrictions — designating and controlling limited trails or water zones for ORV and thrill craft use — apparently contradict the joys of individual transport through nature, taming the illusion of mastery of the wild and encouraging "outlaw" operation that technology so easily permits in legally unpermitted areas.

The Clinton Administration's National Park Service (NPS), after almost a hundred hearings with several thousand witnesses (most supporting closure), banned snowmobile use from nearly 30 national parks, recreation areas, and monuments where snowmobiles had previously been permitted. The ORV industry counterattacked, and in 2002 the Bush II Administration nullified major provisions of the rule. Legal challenges continue.[99]

The NPS and the USFS have also issued limited bans on personal watercraft (jet skis, jet boats) in 21 National Recreation Areas. See *Hells Canyon Alliance v. USFS*, 227 F.3d 1170 (9th Cir. 2000)(USFS did not act arbitrarily and capriciously in approving a jet boat ban for three days every other week on the Snake River in Hells Canyon National Recreation Area; this ban survived counterattack).

FLPMA gave ORVs cursory and ambiguous attention. FLPMA §601 established a "multiple use" planning process for designated areas "to conserve these resources for future generations, and to provide present and future use and enjoyment, particularly outdoor recreation uses, *including the use, where appropriate, of off-road recreational vehicles.*" President Carter issued an executive order[100] ordering federal agency reviews to designate lands on which ORVs should be *permitted*, with management plans, and to immediately ban ORV use where it would "cause or is causing considerable adverse effects." BLM immediately

---

98. When the mechanisms used to deliver water to those preferred uses includes dam and reservoir operations, flood control enters the management calculus and often competes with hierarchical uses for storage capacity. For example, population security might call for keeping reservoirs as full as possible as a hedge against summer drought. Fears that a spring may prove unusually wet and flood prone may require spilling water from those reservoirs to ensure there is space to capture potential flood water.

99. See *Fund for Animals et al. v. Norton*, Civ. No. 02-2367EGS (D.D.C., Dec. 16, 2003).

100. Exec. Order No. 11989 (1977); see generally Bleich, Chrome on the Range: Off-Road Vehicles on Public Lands, 15 Ecology L.Q. 159, 166-167 (1988).

backtracked, interpreting the order as applying only to "fragile areas which are actually threatened with serious damage," shifting the presumption so that the designation process would identify lands on which ORV use would be *prohibited*, and stressing voluntary action on the part of ORV users. As in the *SUWA* case, citizen attempts to force an agency to enforce restrictions where ongoing damage was proved have not generally been successful. See *Sierra Club v. Clark*, 756 F.2d 686 (9th Cir. 1985) (court defers to agency's decision to tolerate sacrifice area in Dove Springs Canyon).

C. Large Scale, Public-Private Resource Management & Broadly Integrated Planning

Here we consider planning efforts that try to deal with the reality of overlapping planning and regulatory efforts, seeking to manage them for the achievement of larger goals, and avoiding conflicts of crossed purposes.

1. NLUPA: The Fleeting Hope and Promise of a National Land Use Planning Act

After successfully steering NEPA into law in 1969, Senator Henry "Scoop" Jackson of Washington, beginning the following year, introduced a series of bills to create a National Land Use Policy Act (NLUPA)[101] as a complement to NEPA. Senator Jackson had become one of the nation's most holistic legislative thinkers about environmental protection, and also hoped to run for president.

Unlike NEPA, the proposed NLUPA gave the major role to *states* and their land use planning.[102] By pushing state governments to undertake rational statewide planning and mandating national and local coordination with state plans, Jackson believed the nation could vastly improve its land use decisionmaking in an area plagued then and now by the chaos, overlaps, and inconsistencies of uncoordinated local government planning.[103]

The first element of Jackson's approach was to encourage the creation of statewide comprehensive plans and state-level coordination of land use programs, through a federal grant-in-aid program allocating $100 million annually for eight years among states that made a bona fide effort to implement comprehensive planning. All states that accepted federal planning money for state and local planning efforts were encouraged to create comprehensive state plans, establish programs for coordinating local land use planning

---

101. S. 3354, 91st Cong., 2d Sess. (1970), available in S. Rep. No. 91-1435, Calendar No. 1446, Dec. 14, 1970. Versions of the bill were submitted in subsequent congressional sessions, and in 1973 passed in the Senate, 64 to 21, but not the House, as S. 268, 93d Cong., 1st Sess., the "Land Use Policy and Planning Assistance Act of 1973." See also Daly, A Glimpse of the Past—A Vision for the Future: Senator Henry M. Jackson and National Land-Use Legislation. 28 Urb. Law. 1, 9, 26 (1996).

102. This section draws upon an unpublished Boston College Law School research paper by David Kirchblum, BCLS '09, "NLUPA: Senator Henry Jackson's Ill-Fated National Land Use Planning Act, and Its Continuing Echoes in the Coastal Zone Management Act" 5-7 (2009). The NLUPA bill was first brought to the authors' attention in 2007 by a research paper written by Marika M.B. Plater, Bard College '08.

103. See Daly, Glimpse of the Past, supra note 101, at 18; see also Nolon, Fusing Economic and Environmental Policy: The Need for Framework Laws in the United States and Argentina, 13 Pace Envtl. L. Rev. 685, 719 (1995).

C. Large Scale, Public-Private Resource Management

and regulation, and submit their state plans to a Department of Interior Land & Water Resources Council for review, suggestions, and approval.

To prepare state plans funded by NLUPA, states would inevitably have undertaken fundamental planning activities that previously were often scanted, ineffective, and eclipsed by the dominant land use role of the local governments. To create approved plans states would do substantive statewide inventories of their land and natural resources. They would collect data on transportation corridors, energy transmission and supply, location and availability of health facilities, population trends, development trends and effects, and more. NLUPA included further requirements to "identify large scale and regional benefit developments, to inventory and designate areas of critical environmental concern and those impacted by key facilities, to coordinate programs and services of state and local agencies affecting land use, and hold public hearings on the planning process." Implicitly but inevitably the consequence of such a statewide inventory process would be to develop statewide policies for present and future development. As to the role of local governments, state planning programs funded by NLUPA would have to include unprecedented provisions for reviewing and coordinating local government units' land use planning, requiring local plans to be in conformity with surrounding local jurisdictions and state policy goals. The NLUPA process would fundamentally increase the role of state planning, ending the fractionalized land use consequence of land use decisionmaking by hundreds and even thousands of separate, uncoordinated, hermetically insulated local units.

The second strategic element in Jackson's NLUPA bill came from its §307.[104] Whereas NEPA gained its functional impact from its (initially low-profiled) §102 EIS requirement pressuring federal agencies, the NLUPA bill's significant kick came from a state-federal leverage contained in §307. Once approved, state plans would take on a potentially very powerful political role. Consider the practical and political impact of NLUPA's kicker as it appeared in the 1970 version of the NLUPA bill:

§307(a). **Coordination of Federal Programs.** All Federal agencies conducting or supporting activities involving land use in an area subject to an approved statewide land use plan *shall operate in accordance with the plan....*[105]

(b) State and local governments submitting applications for Federal assistance for activities having significant land use implications in an area subject to an approved statewide land use plan shall indicate the views of the State land use planning agency as to the consistency of such activities with the plan. *Federal agencies shall not approve proposed projects that are inconsistent with the [state] plan.*

(c) All Federal agencies responsible for administering grant, loan, or guarantee programs for activities that have a tendency to influence patterns of land use and development, including but not limited to home mortgage and interest subsidy programs and water and sewer facility construction programs, *shall take cognizance of approved statewide land use plans....* [Emphases added.]

---

104. As numbered in the December 1970 version of S. 3354.

105. This was not an absolute: "The Council may approve a federally conducted or supported project, a portion or portions of which may be inconsistent with the plan, if it finds that (1) the project is essential to the national interest and (2) there is no reasonable and prudent alternative which would not be inconsistent with an approved statewide land use plan.... The President may approve projects inconsistent with a statewide land use plan only when overriding considerations of national policy require such approval." §307(a).

COMMENTARY & QUESTIONS

1. NLUPA's taxonomic design: plans and consistency requirements. What would NLUPA §307 change? States previously had the ability to prepare statewide plans, and still would. Local governments previously had the power to make binding local plans, and still would. NLUPA's federal money grants certainly had the power to encourage increased planning activity, but aren't the bill's potential political effects far more significant? Note the strategic shift in the role of state governments: If local governments' planning now would have to be consistent with statewide planning, which level of government will be dominant, and what will happen to the previous model of uncoordinated local planning for development, infrastructure, and provision of civic services? Further, note that the consistency requirements applied to federal actors as well as local. What strategic shift in credibility and authority would NLUPA §307 bestow upon states vis-à-vis both their local governments and the federal government? NEPA had shown how pervasively federal agency actions are involved in the daily context of life in the U.S. If states via their officially adopted plans exercised a dominant voice and presumptive veto over federal agency projects and programs, a broad increase in state-level power would be inevitable. (Does §307 really give state plans that dominance? What legal meaning(s) do you find in the phrases "in accordance with ...," "[not] inconsistent with ...," and "shall take cognizance of ..."?) The consistency device is considered further in the next section, using today's CZMA as its prime functioning example.

2. NLUPA and federalism. Land use planning generally operates under state authority and isn't plainly included in any of the express grants of authority to the national government. Nevertheless, the overall environmental welfare of the nation, coordination of resources management, and preventing incompatible uses from spilling over state lines are plainly topics that impact interstate and international commerce. Why does the federal NLUPA, unlike NEPA, target the state level? The federal power to tax and spend for the general welfare supports NLUPA's design of "paying" the states to participate in the overall planning system. Would the federal aid suggested be enough to defray the state's out-of-pocket costs of participating and creating statewide plans, and the political cost of requiring state land use plans to pass minimum federal standards? Is there any reason to think that the states would ever voluntarily agree to participate in a system that imposes even the limited federal oversight of whether the state has properly implemented NLUPA? Contemplate how a version of NLUPA could be made politically acceptable in the current political context.

Even though other nations and even groups of nations practice planning at the national level,[106] the American psyche and federal structure appear to be aligned against it. Feasible forms of national planning may in the future grow out of environmental or other defined problems which, unlike land use, are publicly perceived as significant national threats. Climate change and its potential effects in rising sea levels, energy insecurity, transportation gridlock, and such are more likely to galvanize political will to pass federal regulation that, to be effective, reaches down and requires coordination of decisions historically made at the local level, such as transportation planning, growth management, energy generation choices, and so on.

3. NLUPA: why did it fall into a black hole? In the early 1970s the U.S. looked as if it was shifting into a progressive profile. NEPA and the parade of major environmental

---

106. See generally Nolon, Comparative Land Use Law: Patterns of Sustainability, 37 Urb. Law. 807 (2005).

C. Large Scale, Public-Private Resource Management

statutes passed rapidly through Congress and were signed into law by none other than Richard Nixon. President Nixon actually urged Congress to pass NLUPA in his 1973 State of the Union Address.[107] Soon after that Address, however, industrial and business lobbyists realized the sweeping limiting effect NLUPA might have upon their relatively unrestricted ability to determine land use decisions, and persuaded him to turn against the bill. In a pivotal meeting Nixon told his Cabinet that it was time to "get off the environment kick,"[108] and the federal government backed off its leading role in this area of environmental protection and many others.

4. Where would we be today if NLUPA had passed? Would the state-level process of basic inventorying, planning, and coordinating land use decisions have changed the way

FIGURE 9-6. *Nighttime North America from space, 2009. Note the coastline effect, and the East-West distinction. Might this image have looked different if NLUPA-prompted coordination in the early 1970s had increased public transportation infrastructure and de-emphasized the primacy of gasoline-fueled automobiles for individual transport? Photo: NASA.*

---

107. "Our greatest need is for comprehensive new legislation to stimulate State land use controls. We especially need a National Land Use Policy Act authorizing Federal assistance to encourage the States, in cooperation with local governments, to protect lands of critical environmental concern and to regulate the siting of key facilities such as airports, highways and major private developments. Appropriate Federal funds should be withheld from States that fail to act." Richard M. Nixon, State of the Union Message to the Congress on Natural Resources & Environment, Feb. 15, 1973, available at www.presidency.ucsb.edu/ws/index.php?pid=4102&st=union&st1=state.

108. J.B. Flippen, The Nixon Administration, Politics, and the Environment 316-317 (Ph.D. diss., U. Md., 1994), cited in R.J. Lazarus, The Making of Environmental Law 9 (2004).

A key document believed to have influenced Nixon was a memorandum prepared by Lewis Powell for the U.S. Chamber of Commerce. The Powell Memorandum urged the business community to take back the media and the universities from their "socialistic" attitudes, through right-wing think tanks, PR, and other campaigns that became core features of the post-1980 right-wing resurgence. (See the 1972 "Powell Memorandum" on the coursebook website.)

the U.S. now looks from outer space at night? Might our society have avoided the sprawl, leapfrogging development, poorly located availabilities of civic services, and other major dysfunctions arising from the unthought-out land development patterns, many fueled by nevermore low gasoline prices, that pose major national challenges today?

2. Intergovernmental Coordination: The CZMA and Its Consistency Requirement

The CZMA[109] does not authorize federal land use controls, but it is explicitly land use legislation. It is fundamentally a planning statute remarkably like the failed NLUPA model of 1970. The CZMA authorizes federal matching grants for the purpose of assisting coastal states in the development of management programs for the land and water resources of their coastal zones, and requires the "consistency" of federal agency actions in states to conform to officially adopted state plans.

The CZMA explicitly attempts to coordinate local, state, and federal actions affecting the environmentally sensitive coastal zone. The land area it covers extends inland from the shorelines "to the extent necessary to control shorelands, the uses of which have a direct and significant impact on the coastal waters, and to control those geographical areas which are likely to be affected by or vulnerable to sea level rise" thus extending inland as far as tidal effects are felt. (Note that in the map for the Allied Chemical case materials (see Chapter 2, Figure 2-1), the tidal effects extended 100 miles inland along the James River.) The CZMA applies to states and territorial possessions with saltwater coasts and the Great Lakes states. It encourages states to draw up plans for the protection and development of the coastal zone by offering grants and other support for state planning efforts,[110] and by requiring federal agency actions affecting the coastal zone to be "consistent" with state plans approved by the Secretary of Commerce.[111]

> Each federal agency activity within or outside the coastal zone that affects any land or water use or natural resource of the coastal zone shall be carried out in a manner which is consistent to the maximum extent practicable with the enforceable policies of approved state management programs.[112]

The "consistency" requirement has become the main driver of implementation of the CZMA.[113] The states, however, do not get the benefit of CZMA consistency requirements without taking on burdens within their own sphere of influence. Local planning and regulations, not just the actions of federal agencies, must be consistent with the state plan, and the plans' binding elements must be embodied in "enforceable policies," not merely hortatory guidelines.[114] Moreover, Congress, as part of the price states must pay to enjoy the

---

109. Pub. L. No. 89-454, Title III, §301, codified at 16 U.S.C. §§1451-1456 (2004). This law has been amended several times, most recently by the Coastal Zone Protection Act of 1996, Pub. L. No. 108-415.

110. See, e.g., 16 U.S.C. §1455(a) (matching grants for program administration). There also are numerous year-to-year appropriations for study and research and other financial incentives for which participating states are eligible.

111. The Commerce Department is the home agency for NOAA, the National Oceanic and Atmospheric Administration.

112. 16 U.S.C. §1456(c)(1)(A).

113. See Cheston, Comment, An Overview and Analysis of the Consistency Requirement under the CZMA, 10 U. Balt. J. Envtl. L. 135, 136 (2003).

114. See 16 U.S.C. §1455(d)(1) (local participation in planning); 16 U.S.C. §1455(d)(3) (plan must control state and local activities). States have been held to have violated their own Coastal Zone Management Plans, see

C. Large Scale, Public-Private Resource Management

benefits of the CZMA and its consistency provision, has used the CZMA to prompt states to take regulatory actions that Congress does not require under other statutes. For example, Congress conditioned continued federal approval of state plans on state implementation of coastal nonpoint source water pollution plans.[115] CZMA's power incentives have worked. More than 30 states and territories have implemented CZMA plans.[116]

Washington gets a quid pro quo for "surrender" of its supremacy clause-backed powers in favor of state plan consistency. The nation benefits from soundly planned utilization of coastal resources that the federal government cannot easily regulate under its powers over admiralty, navigation, and commerce.[117] Moreover, the national government is far from abdicating its control and authority to ensure its interests are fully protected. Consider all of the "checks and balances" the federal government has over state CZMA powers:

- State plans must obtain federal approval pursuant to standards promulgated by the lead federal agency, the Department of Commerce.
- Federal funding can be suspended if a coastal state fails to adhere to its management program.
- The state plans cannot single out federal activities for differential and less favorable treatment, and state and local activities must also be consistent with the state plan.[118]
- The states cannot claim inconsistency of a federal action without a supportable basis.[119]
- When a dispute regarding consistency does arise there are two options:
    The federal agency and the state may opt for mediation by the Secretary of Commerce;[120] or the disputants may opt for immediate judicial review,[121] in which case courts are divided over who bears the burden of proof on the consistency/inconsistency issue.[122]
- In the wake of administrative or judicial review that upholds an inconsistency finding, the President has a power of exemption for federal actions that are "in the paramount interest of the United States."[123]
- Finally, Congress, can always repeal the law or, more narrowly, override a particular inconsistency determination by legislative exemption.

The CZMA consistency provision, although it has its detractors,[124] "works" without too much friction or federal frustration. The President has never had to use the exemption

---

Cook Inlet Keeper v. Alaska, 46 P.3d 957 (Alaska 2002).

115. Section 6217 of the Coastal Zone Act Reauthorization Amendments of 1990, codified at 16 U.S.C. §1455b.
116. Patricia E. Salkin, 1 Am. Law of Zoning §3.3 (5th ed., database update of May 2009).
117. The scope of those powers when they affect local land uses is frequently challenged. See, e.g., *Solid Waste Agency of N. Cook County v. U.S. Army Corps of Eng'rs,* 531 U.S. 159 (2001).
118. See 15 C.F.R. §930.6(a).
119. See Duff, The Coastal Zone Management Act: Reverse Pre-emption or Contractual Federalism?, 6 Ocean & Coastal L.J. 109, 113 (2001) ("the state must do more than merely object; it must articulate some rational basis for doing so . . .").
120. 16 U.S.C. §1456(h).
121. 15 C.F.R. §930.116.
122. Compare *La. v. Lujan,* 777 F. Supp. 486, 488-489 (E.D. La. 1991) (burden on state), with *Conservation Law Found. v. Watt,* 716 F.2d 946 (1st Cir. 1983) (burden on federal agency); see also LaLonde, Note, Allocating the Burden of Proof to Effectuate the Preservation and Federalism Goals of the Coastal Zone Management Act, 92 Mich. L. Rev. 438 (1993) (arguing that burden should be on the federal agency objecting to an inconsistency finding by the state).
123. 16 U.S.C. §1456(c)(1)(B).
124. See Kuhse, The Federal Consistency Requirement of the Coastal Zone Management Act of 1972: It's Time to Repeal This Fundamentally Flawed Legislation, 6 Ocean & Coastal L.J. 77 (2001); Gibbons, Too Much of

power, and the Secretary, in mediation cases, has used the veto power on only limited occasions, not so many as to undercut the credibility of state plans.[125] Congress has regularly reauthorized the act, and even strengthened it when a Supreme Court decision[126] restricted the right of a state to consider *indirect* effects of federal activities in inconsistency determinations.[127]

In the following excerpt, Professor J. B. Ruhl summarizes the CZMA and argues that it is an example, under a "Three-Cs" analysis, of a "Cooperation" strategy, preferable to both the "Coercion" approach (e.g., §404 of the CWA seen earlier in this chapter and the ESA noted in Chapter 10), and the "Coordination" model (e.g., under NEPA). As viewed through this book's "taxonomic" classification, the CZMA's key regulatory technique is the consistency provision and its operation.

J. B. Ruhl, Biodiversity Conservation and the Ever-Expanding Web of Federal Laws Regulating Nonfederal Lands: Time for Something Completely Different?
66 University of Colorado Law Review 555, 616-623 (1995)

The CZMA was enacted in 1972 to promote the "national interest in the effective management, beneficial use, protection, and development of the coastal zone." Ecological protection was paramount among the concerns Congress expressed as reason for addressing the "increasing and competing demands upon the lands and waters of our coastal zone." . . . Congress stated as its principal goal for the CZMA "to preserve, protect, develop, and where possible, to restore or enhance, the resources of the Nation's coastal zone for this and succeeding generations."

The approach Congress took in the CZMA, however, is decidedly different from the regulatory structures of the Endangered Species Act and §404 of the Clean Water Act. Congress was convinced that "the key to more effective protection and use of the land and water resources of the coastal zone is to encourage the states to exercise their full authority over the lands and waters in the coastal zone." The CZMA does this by establishing a method by which the states, in cooperation with federal and local governments, can establish "unified policies, criteria, standards, methods, and processes for dealing with land and water use decisions of more than local significance." . . .

Sections 305 and 306 of the CZMA provide federal grants to . . . coastal states for developing and implementing their coastal management plans ("CMPs"). A CMP must be consistent with guidelines established by the Secretary of Commerce, which must require "identification of the means by which the State proposes to exert control over the land uses and water uses" and the "priorities of uses in particular areas." A state's CMP development must be conducted "with the opportunity of full participation by relevant [governmental agencies and private persons]" and must provide "an effective mechanism for continuing consultation and coordination" between those entities. The CMP must define permissible land and water uses in the coastal zone and identify in that regard "areas of particular

---

a Good Thing? Federal Supremacy & Devolution of Regulatory Power: The Case of the Coastal Zone Management Act, 48 Naval L. Rev. 84 (2001).
125. See Duff, supra note 119, at 115 n. 25 (listing 8 vetoes).
126. *Secretary of Interior v. Cal.*, 464 U.S. 312 (1984).
127. See Cheston, supra note 113, at 139-140, and sources cited there.

concern." The CMP also must demonstrate that land and water uses can be controlled and coordinated through either state establishment of standards for local implementation, direct state regulation, state review of all state, local, and private development proposals for consistency with the CMP, or a combination of those three general approaches.

The Secretary's CZMA regulations, promulgated through NOAA, elaborate on each of those key statutory elements for CMP development and approval. Significantly, NOAA's rules for special management areas address in detail the "areas of particular concern" feature of the CMP. NOAA's rules recognize that a state's set of controls for the coastal zone may vary throughout the zone in intensity, scope, and detail. NOAA requires that "where these policies are limited and non-specific, greater emphasis should be placed on areas of particular concern [in the CMP] to assure effective management and an adequate degree of program specificity." . . .

Once a state's CMP is in place, the CZMA requires that all actions carried out by federal agencies directly, or by nonfederal entities requiring some form of federal approval or funding, be concurred with by the state or its designated agency as consistent with the CMP. Significantly, the consistency review requirement applies not only to activities physically located within the CMP boundary, but also to activities outside the boundary which may affect the coastal zone. NOAA's regulations implement a detailed consistency review procedure. . . .

The chief advantage the CZMA presents for promoting biodiversity protection is its flexibility, which operates on many levels. The CZMA allows a state flexibility to adopt the management approach . . . most consistent with that state's general style of land use regulation and management. . . .

The CZMA also exhibits flexibility in terms of geographic emphasis and intensity of the regulatory program. The program for areas of particular concern allows states to focus regulatory efforts on specified areas in need of close attention, such as those needing intense biodiversity protection. The CZMA also inherently recognizes that land and water uses will occur in the coastal zone and must be accommodated. Hence, rather than requiring a uniform level of regulation throughout the coastal zone ecosystem, the CZMA recognizes that some areas will require more development than others and some will require a greater degree of protection than others. Also, the CZMA recognizes that activities outside the coastal zone boundary may affect coastal resources and thus need to be addressed. . . .

The CZMA's flexibility, however, also imposes burdens in terms of developing and implementing the CMP according to the loosely-stated federal guidelines. The danger exists that goals such as biodiversity protection will become diffusely enforced and thus ineffective as management tools. In that sense, then, if the detailed consistency review procedures are not closely followed, the CZMA could prove ineffective for biodiversity protection in the coastal zone. . . .

The Cooperation model offers some measure of balance between Coercion and Coordination model statutes, holding traits of each. The essence of the Cooperation model is the expression of strong federal goals and policies in the context of a flexible partnership between federal, state, and local interests in seeing to it that the federal policies are implemented in the form of substantive legal requirements. Cooperation model statutes often hold out some form of regulatory carrot or stick, or blend of both, as an incentive for the partners to act together within the framework of the federal goals and policies, but substantive review criteria and outcomes generally are not prescribed. Rather, it is left to the cooperative process to formulate a regulatory response directed at the particular state or local planning area.

The Cooperation model statutes thus are expensive to operate. They involve substantial transaction costs and time as the cooperating partners forge consensus over the final substantive shape of the regulatory policy. But the final result offers promise of achieving the substantive outcome with greater impact than the Coordination model offers, and with greater consensus than the Coercion model offers. . . .

COMMENTARY & QUESTIONS

1. Comparing the CZMA, where the states and territories have opted in, to the never-enacted NLUPA. In its 2006 annual report on the CZMA, NOAA reported that 34 coastal states (including the Great Lakes state) and territories have approved coastal management programs. NLUPA, in contrast, lost its political support before enactment, and, as contemplated, offered inadequate incentives for state participation. What explains that contrast? The two statutes share important similarities as to goals and overall design. Both seek to encourage broad state-level land use and/or resource planning. Both leave the content of those state plans largely in the hands of the state. Finally, and somewhat misleadingly, both effectuate the plans that are generated by requiring consistency of activities with the state plan. Both the CZMA and NLUPA require consistency to conform federal activities and the activities of federal licensees to the dictates of the state plan. This element is critical in terms of state buy-in because this type of required consistency enlarges state power at the expense of the federal government, which cedes some, but not all, of its power to act independently of the state plan.[128]

2. The operation of other federal laws and the federal "veto." The CZMA expressly preserves the force of other federal laws, including interstate and international agreements. See 16 U.S.C. §1456(e). So, for example, even if a state plan would allow for the siting of an oil terminal in the coastal zone, and the state had issued all necessary permits, the CAA requirements for controlling air emissions would still remain in full force. Similarly, a state could not use its CZMA plan and authorities to undercut the protections of the ESA, nor could it exempt a project requiring a federal license from compliance with the NEPA.

The other facet of the CZMA that maintains a supervening level of federal authority is a provision, 16 U.S.C. §1456, that provides authority for a federally authorized activity to go forward even if it is found inconsistent with a state CZMA plan. The standard to be met appears high. One such exemption can be had "if the President determines that the activity is in the paramount interest of the United States." Id. §1456(c)(1)(B). Under §1456(c)(3)(A), the CZMA provides that the Secretary of Commerce must override a state's objection to a proposed project that requires a federal license or permit if the project is "consistent with the objectives of the CZMA . . . or necessary in the interest of national security." The implementing regulation, 15 C.F.R. §930.121, makes the exemption power appear to be fairly broad, it can be issued if—

> . . . a Federal license or permit activity . . . which, although inconsistent with a State's management program, is found by the Secretary to be permissible because it satisfies the following four requirements.
>
> (a) The activity furthers one or more of the competing national objectives or purposes contained in section 302 or 303 of the [the broad congressional findings and policies sections of the CZMA],

---

128. Recall from the materials presented in Chapter 7 that the federal government's programmatic interests can form a basis for conflict preemption of state law.

C. Large Scale, Public-Private Resource Management

(b) When performed separately or when its cumulative effects are considered, it will not cause adverse effects on natural resources of the coastal zone substantial enough to outweigh its contribution to the national interest,

(c) The activity will not violate any requirements of the Clean Air Act, as amended, or the Federal Water Pollution Control Act, as amended, and

(d) There is no reasonable alternative available (e.g., location, design, etc.) which would permit the activity to be conducted in a manner consistent with the management program.

Despite the breadth of the regulation, there are only a small number of reported cases, and some of those are ones in which the Secretary is sued for refusing to override the state finding of inconsistency. See, e.g., *Millennium Pipeline Co. v. Gutierrez*, 424 F. Supp. 2d 168 (D.D.C. 2006) (upholding Secretary's refusal to invoke the override).

3. Leveraging the CZMA to serve additional state interests. Since consistency review applies to activities outside the coastal zone boundary that affect the coastal zone, states can and sometimes do object to activities that are being pursued in other nearby states. Since state plans can and do vary, it is possible that the state where an activity is taking place might find an activity consistent while a sister state objected that the activity was inconsistent with its CMP. As a federalism matter, the extraterritorial reach of the objecting state would have the force of federal law and the Supremacy Clause behind it. North Carolina made just such an attempt by denying CZMA consistency certification to a Federal Energy Regulatory Commission action that confirmed its licensee's grant of a right of way for a pipeline that would carry 60 million gallons per day of drinking water from the Roanoke River to the city of Virginia Beach, Virginia. The diversion was to be made from Lake Gaston, which is located in Virginia upstream of the point at which the river flows into North Carolina and at a considerable distance from the river's estuary. In that case, the Secretary overrode North Carolina's effort to block the project on CZMA grounds, and that veto was upheld. See *N.C. v. Brown*, 42 Env't Rep. Cas. 1254, 1995 WL 852123 (D.D.C. 1995).

4. Mixed mandates and diffuse expectations. Professor Ruhl suggests that the CZMA can serve as a model for protecting biodiversity, a broad, hard to define environmental objective by having states identify and nominate biological resource zones (BRZs) "corresponding to local and regional ecosystems requiring the greatest levels of protection because they are unique, sensitive, or threatened." The state could then enforce consistency with its plan from local units of government and, with a CZMA-like federal enactment, it could control many activities of federal lands that are inconsistent with the state's plan. Is it possible to see that path as a way around the long-entrenched pattern of environmentally destructive uses of federal public lands?

5. Has the CZMA worked? An ambivalent assessment. "As a vehicle for promoting state and local land use planning along coastal America, the CZMA has largely succeeded."

> As for the tough, nasty business of land use regulation, there is evidence that difficult decisions are being made and, at times, against economic and development interests. Spurred forward by CZMA grants of money and authority, some states have passed highly-controversial set-back ordinances, made generous provisions for public access to coastal resources, and banned certain development altogether. On the other hand, states have been almost equally free to look the other way. Houck & Rolland, Federalism in Wetlands Regulation: A Consideration of Delegation of Clean Water Act Section 404 and Related Programs to the States, 54 Md. L. Rev. 1242, 1297, 1297-1298 (1995).

Nevertheless, this statute has been unsuccessful in curbing what Professor Houck calls "America's Mad Dash to the Sea."[129] According to Professor Houck, "we are expecting state regulation, under the [CZMA], to overcome formidable economic and political pressures without the safeguard of a clear, national mandate."

6. ISTEA, subsidies, and consistency applied to transportation planning. America's dependence on the automobile, facilitated by massive governmental investments in roads (3 million miles) and interstate highways (45,000 miles), has fostered urban sprawl development, which, in addition to the impacts outlined above, has also led to a lack of affordable housing and the decline of central cities and their systems of mass transit. In 1991, Congress tentatively responded to this phenomenon by enacting ISTEA, 23 U.S.C. §§134 et seq.

Perhaps the most important aspect of ISTEA was its funding flexibility.[130] Whereas federal transportation funding traditionally had been restricted to highway projects, ISTEA made over half of its $155 billion authorization available for any surface transport mode, including construction and maintenance of intracity mass transit systems, bikeways, and pedestrian systems. Second, ISTEA invigorated regional transportation planning by requiring states to develop statewide Transportation Improvement Programs (TIPs) that must be consistent with transportation plans formulated by metropolitan planning organizations (MPOs), with participation by all affected stakeholders. The purpose of this planning process was to promote the development of intermodal transportation systems that "will efficiently maximize mobility of people and goods within and through urbanized areas and minimize transportation-related fuel consumption and air pollution." Planners were required to consider the "overall social, economic, energy, and environmental effects of transportation decisions." Third, TIPs had to be consistent with State Implementation Plans (SIPs) under the CAA (Chapter 11) in order for transportation projects included in TIPs to be eligible for federal funding. The CAA itself bars federal licenses or permits for activities that are inconsistent with SIPs.[131]

ISTEA was reauthorized by the Transportation Equity Act of the 21st Century (TEA-21), Pub. L. No. 105-178 (1998). In addition to retaining the anti-sprawl elements of ISTEA, TEA-21 authorized funding for mitigation of water pollution from road construction or maintenance, restoration of wetlands and other environmental resources impacted by transportation projects, integration of transportation and community planning, and research on the relationship between highway density and ecosystem health. Environmentalists are concerned, however, that a provision of TEA-21 requiring federal agencies to streamline environmental reviews of transportation projects will weaken existing federal agency responsibilities under NEPA (Chapter 8) and other statutes.

3. Federal-State & Public-Private Issues on the Public Lands

The following Supreme Court decision is the classic case in a century of vitriolic litigation regarding federal versus state power and public versus private rights on the public lands, and reflects a chapter in the antifederal "Sagebrush Rebellion." As you read the opinion, consider which legal questions have been definitively settled and which are still open.

---

129. Amicus J., Summer 1988, at 21-36.

130. The following summary of ISTEA is, in part, based on Pelham, Innovative Growth Control Measures: The Potential Impacts of Recent Federal Legislation and the *Lucas* Decision, 25 Urb. Law. 881 (1993).

131. 45 U.S.C. §7506(c).

C. Large Scale, Public-Private Resource Management

Kleppe v. New Mexico
426 U.S. 529 (U.S. Sup. Ct. 1976)

MARSHALL, J. At issue in this case is whether Congress exceeded its powers under the Constitution in enacting the Wild Free-Roaming Horses and Burros Act, 16 U.S.C. §§1331-1340, . . . in 1971 to protect "all unbranded and unclaimed horses and burros on public lands in the United States" from "capture, branding, harassment, or death." The Act provides that all such horses and burros on the public lands . . . are committed to the jurisdiction of the respective Secretaries, who are "directed to protect and manage [the animals] as components of the public lands . . . in a manner that is designed to achieve and maintain a thriving natural ecological balance on the public lands." If protected horses or burros "stray from public lands onto privately owned land, the owners of such land may inform the nearest Federal marshal or agency of the Secretary, who shall arrange to have the animals removed. . . ."

On February 1, 1974, a New Mexico rancher, Kelley Stephenson, was informed by BLM that several unbranded burros had been seen near Taylor Well, where Stephenson watered his cattle. Taylor Well is on federal property, and Stephenson had access to it and some 8,000 surrounding acres only through a grazing permit. . . . After BLM made it clear to Stephenson that it would not remove the burros and after he personally inspected the Taylor Well area, Stephenson complained to the [New Mexico] Livestock Board that the burros were interfering with his livestock operation by molesting his cattle and eating their feed. Thereupon the Board rounded up and removed 19 unbranded and unclaimed burros pursuant to the New Mexico Estray Law. Each burro was seized on the public lands of the United States. . . . On February 18, 1974, the livestock Board, pursuant to its usual practice, sold the burros at public auction. After the sale, BLM asserted jurisdiction under the Act and demanded that the Board recover the animals and return them to the public lands.

On March 4, 1974, appellees [New Mexico public officials] filed a complaint . . . seeking a declaratory judgment that the [Act] is unconstitutional and an injunction against its enforcement. . . . [The District Court held the Act unconstitutional and granted the injunction; the Supreme Court reversed.]

The Property Clause of the Constitution provides that "Congress shall have Power to dispose of and make all needful Rules and Regulations respecting the Territory or other Property belonging to the United States." In passing the Wild Free-Roaming Horses and Burros Act, Congress deemed the regulated animals "an integral part of the natural system of the public lands" of the United States, and found that their management was necessary "for the achievement of an ecological balance on the public lands." According to Congress, these animals, if preserved in their native habitats, "contribute to the diversity of life forms within the Nation and enrich the lives of the American people." Indeed, Congress concluded, the wild free-roaming horses and burros "are living symbols of the historic and pioneer spirit of the West." Despite their importance, the Senate Committee found that—

> [these animals] have been cruelly captured and slain and their carcasses used in the production of pet food and fertilizer. They have been used for target practice and harassed for "sport" and profit. In spite of public outrage, this bloody traffic continues unabated, and it is the firm belief of the committee that this senseless slaughter must be brought to an end.

For these reasons, Congress determined to preserve and protect the wild free-roaming horses and burros on the public lands of the United States. The question under the Property Clause is whether this determination can be sustained as a "needful" regulation "respecting" the public lands. In answering this question, we must remain mindful that, while courts must eventually pass upon them, determinations under the Property Clause are entrusted primarily to the judgment of Congress.

Appellees argue that the Act cannot be supported by the Property Clause. They contend that the Clause grants Congress essentially two kinds of power: (1) the power to dispose of and make incidental rules regarding the use of federal property; and (2) the power to protect federal property. According to appellees, the first power is not broad enough to support legislation protecting wild animals that live on federal property; and the second power is not implicated since the Act is designed to protect the animals, which are not themselves federal property, and not the public lands. As an initial matter, it is far from clear that the Act was not passed in part to protect the public lands of the United States[132] or that Congress cannot assert a property interest in the regulated horses and burros superior to that of the State.[133] But we need not consider whether the Act can be upheld on either of these grounds, for we reject appellees' narrow reading of the Property Clause. . . .

In brief . . . appellees have presented no support for their position that the [Property] Clause grants Congress only the power to dispose of, to make incidental rules regarding the use of, and to protect federal property. This failure is hardly surprising, for the Clause, in broad terms, gives Congress the power to determine what are "needful" rules "respecting" the public lands. And while the furthest reaches of the power granted by the Property Clause have not yet been definitively resolved, we have repeatedly observed that "the power over the public land thus entrusted to Congress is without limitations." *U.S. v. San Francisco*, 310 U.S. 16, 29 (1940).

The decided cases have supported this expansive reading. It is the Property Clause, for instance, that provides the basis for governing the territories of the United States. And even over public land within the States, "the general government doubtless has a power over its own property analogous to the police power of the several states, and the extent to which it may go in the exercise of such power is measured by the exigencies of the particular case." *Camfield v. U.S.*, 167 U.S. 518, 525 (1897). We have noted, for example, that the Property Clause gives Congress the power over the public lands "to control their occupancy and use, to protect them from trespass and injury, and to prescribe the conditions upon which others may obtain rights in them. . . ." *Utah Power & Light Co. v. U.S.*, 243 U.S. 389, 405 (1917). . . . In short, Congress exercises the powers both of a proprietor and of a legislature over the public domain. Although the Property Clause does not authorize "an exercise of a general control over public policy in a State," it does permit "an exercise of the complete power which Congress has over particular public property entrusted to it." *U.S. v. San Francisco*, 310 U.S., at 30. In our view, the "complete power" that Congress has over public lands necessarily includes the power to protect the wildlife living there.

Appellees argue that if we approve the Wild Free-Roaming Horses and Burros Act as a valid exercise of Congress' power under the Property Clause, then we have sanctioned an impermissible intrusion on the sovereignty, legislative authority and police power of the State and have wrongfully infringed upon the State's traditional trustee powers over wild animals. The argument appears to be that Congress could obtain exclusive legislative jurisdiction over the public lands in the State only by state consent, and that in the absence of such consent Congress lacks the power to act contrary to state law. This argument is without merit. . . .

---

132. Congress expressly ordered that the animals were to be managed and protected in order to "achieve and maintain a thriving natural ecological balance on the public lands." [This is footnote 7 in the original.]

133. The Secretary makes no claim here, however, that the United States owns the wild free roaming horses and burros found on public land. [This is footnote 8 in the original.]

C. Large Scale, Public-Private Resource Management

While Congress can acquire exclusive or partial jurisdiction over lands within a State by the State's consent or cession [under the so-called Enclave Clause of the Constitution, Article I §8, cl. 17], the presence or absence of such jurisdiction has nothing to do with Congress' powers under the Property Clause. Absent consent or cession a State undoubtedly retains jurisdiction over federal lands within its territory, but Congress equally surely retains the power to enact legislation respecting those lands pursuant to the Property Clause. And when Congress so acts, the federal legislation necessarily overrides conflicting state laws under the Supremacy Clause. As we said in *Camfield v. U.S.*, 167 U.S., at 526, in response to a somewhat different claim, "A different rule would place the public domain of the United States completely at the mercy of state legislation." . . .

Appellees' fear that the Secretary's position is that "the Property Clause totally exempts federal lands within state borders from state legislative powers, state police powers, and all rights and powers of local sovereignty and jurisdiction of the states," is totally unfounded. The Federal Government does not assert exclusive jurisdiction over the public lands in New Mexico, and the State is free to enforce its criminal and civil laws on those lands. But where those state laws conflict with the Wild Free-Roaming Horses and Burros Act, or with other legislation passed pursuant to the Property Clause, the law is clear: the State laws must recede. . . .

Appellees are concerned that the Act's extension of protection to wild free-roaming horses and burros that stray from public land onto private land will be read to provide federal jurisdiction over every wild horse or burro that at any time sets foot upon federal land. While it is clear that regulations under the Property Clause may have some effect on private lands not otherwise under federal control, *Camfield v. U.S.*, 167 U.S. 518 (1897), we do not think it appropriate in this declaratory judgment proceeding to determine the extent, if any, to which the Property Clause empowers Congress to protect animals on private lands or the extent to which such regulation is attempted by the Act. . . .

COMMENTARY & QUESTIONS

1. The statutory policy. The Wild Free-Roaming Horses and Burros Act is a statute that causes mixed feelings amongst both ranchers and environmentalists. On one hand these animals, brought from Europe by Spanish and English pioneers, are living symbols of the historic or mythical frontier West and creatures that deserve humane treatment. On the other, they have multiplied so successfully in some niches of their transplanted habitat that they destroy the forage and threaten the survival of native species in the western ecosystem, such as antelope and black-footed ferrets, as well as private livestock.

A vivid, highly focused citizens' campaign—using video footage of dog food suppliers stampeding and butchering terrified wild horses—pushed the statute through Congress, and as law it must be enforced by federal land managers. But the statute does not acknowledge the policy contradictions it presents, with endangered species laws for instance. Some environmentalists have suggested the compromise of inserting IUDs in wild horses and burros (as birth control-laced pigeon food has been advocated in somewhat analogous urban settings), but the issues are likely not to be so easily resolved.

2. Public land and private land. Consider a situation where a herd of free-roaming horses and burros strays from public land onto adjacent private land, and the rancher informs the BLM, which fails to remove the animals. The Act specifies that the Secretary "shall arrange to have the animals removed," but it contains no time limitation for BLM action. If the animals injure the private range, can the rancher sue the federal government in inverse condemnation? In *Mountain States Legal Found. v. Hodel*, 799 F.2d 1423 (10th Cir. 1986), cert. denied, 480 U.S. 951 (1987), the court rejected a takings claim by a grazing association in a similar situation on the grounds that: (1) wild horses are wild animals, not instrumentalities of the federal government; (2) "of the courts that have considered whether damage to private property by protected wildlife constitutes a 'taking,' a clear majority have held that it does not and that the government does not owe compensation"; and (3) the plaintiffs had not shown a deprivation of substantially all economically viable uses of their lands. See also *Christy v. Hodel*, 857 F.2d 1324 (9th Cir. 1988), cert. denied, 490 U.S. 1114 (1989) (the ESA's protection of grizzly bears did not effect a taking of sheep owner's property where a grizzly bear killed domestic sheep). Federal courts have consistently held that a grazing permit is not a vested property right but merely a revocable privilege, and thus cancellation or substantial modification of a grazing permit cannot constitute a taking of property without just compensation. See, e.g., *Fed. Lands Legal Consortium v. Agriculture Dep't*, 195 F.3d 1190 (10th Cir. 1999).

3. Helpless giants? Does the Property Clause give the federal government the authority to regulate activities on state, local, or private lands within ("inholdings") or outside federal landholdings when those activities are interfering with the uses of the federal lands? For example, assume that the FWS seeks an injunction that forbids a promoter from holding rock concerts just outside a National Wildlife Refuge, or that the NPS wants to prevent the construction of a hideously ugly commercial structure adjacent to and painfully visible from a national battlefield.[134]

Camfield v. U.S., 167 U.S. 518 (1897), cited frequently in *Kleppe*, would appear to authorize the federal government to protect its property against external threats. In *Camfield*, an owner of alternate, odd-numbered sections (purchased from a railroad) effectively gained exclusive use of 10,000 acres of federal land by carefully building a zigzag fence on the outer boundary of the checkerboard parcels containing both federal and his private lands (see Figure 7). The Supreme Court, declaring that the federal government has the constitutional power under the Property Clause to protect its land against nuisances, held that the fence violated a federal statute prohibiting enclosures of public lands. The Tenth Circuit Court of Appeals has since ruled that it is a violation of the Unlawful Enclosures Act to construct a *Camfield*-type fence that effectively excludes pronghorn antelope from their critical winter range on federal land. *U.S. v. Lawrence*, 848 F.2d 1502 (10th Cir. 1988), cert. denied, 488 U.S. 980 (1989). Since *Camfield*, federal circuit courts of appeals have consistently upheld federal regulation of external threats. See *Stupak-Thrall v. U.S.*, 70 F.3d 881 (6th Cir. 1995), and cases cited. The federal land management agencies, however, have been unenthusiastic about exercising these powers. See Sax, Helpless Giants: The National Parks and the Regulation of Private Lands, 75 Mich. L. Rev. 239 (1976). If the federal government has the legal power to regulate external activities, how far does the power extend? Can the NPS promulgate a regulation requiring a large agricultural operation, 50 miles upriver of a national park, to cease discharging nutrients because these pollutants are causing the river in the park to become eutrophic (prematurely aged)?

---

134. The latter reference is to a tall neon-emblazoned sightseeing tower that loomed over the national cemetery and battlefield park at Gettysburg, which ultimately was purchased and razed by the federal government. See *Commonwealth of Pennsylvania v. National Gettysburg Tower, Inc.*, 311 A.2d 588 (Pa. 1973). (Further text on the *Gettysburg Tower* case is available on the coursebook website in materials for Chapter 20.)

C. Large Scale, Public-Private Resource Management

4. Access problems. On checkerboard land grants, can private owners of alternate, odd-numbered sections deny access to recreationists traveling on a BLM-constructed road through sections 14, 22, and 16 (see Figure 9-7) in order to reach a federal reservoir, even though the public road touches their sections 15, 21, and 23 only at the corners? In *Leo Sheep Co. v. U.S.*, 440 U.S. 668 (1979), the Supreme Court rejected express or implied easements across private lands, thus requiring the BLM to purchase or condemn road easements. Justice Rehnquist, writing for the majority, distinguished *Camfield* in unconvincing fashion. Isn't the Leo Sheep Company really enclosing public lands? In a condemnation proceeding, would the fair market value of Leo Sheep's land include its proximity to the water supply and recreation provided by the federally funded reservoir?[135]

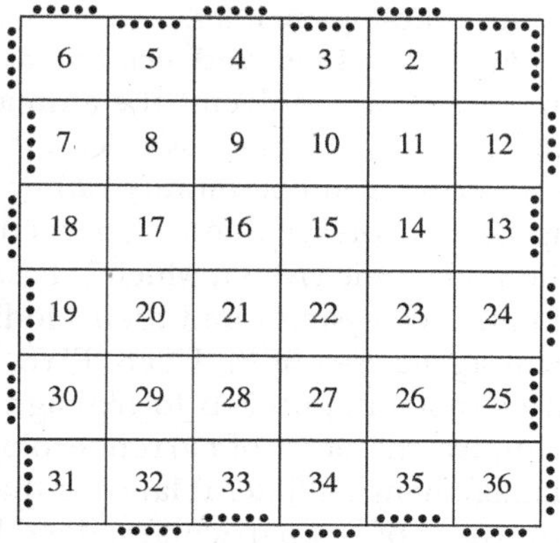

FIGURE 9-7. *From Camfield v. U.S., 167 U.S. 518 (1897)—illustrating the checkerboard federal/private land ownership pattern, and the strategic fence placement employed by Camfield, shown by the dotted lines, always putting the actual fence on his own private property, to double his amount of fenced grazing land to 20,000 acres. The publicly owned parcels are even-numbered; Camfield's private parcels are odd-numbered.*

5. The "Sagebrush Rebellion" and the "Wise Use" movement. Problems caused by interspersed federal and private lands, exacerbated by FLPMA's declaration that the federal lands will generally remain in federal ownership and be managed for multiple use and sustained yield, generated a reaction known as the "Sagebrush Rebellion," one manifestation of which consisted of a number of western states contesting the constitutionality of federal ownership of the public lands. In 1978, the State of Nevada sued the federal government, claiming that federal land ownership was a violation of both Nevada's Tenth Amendment rights and its right to be admitted on an "equal footing" with the original 13 states, in which there is comparatively little federal land. While that case was pending, the Nevada legislature enacted a statute claiming title to most of the federal lands (excepting wildlife refuges and Native American reservations) in the state. The federal district court dismissed Nevada's claim on the merits, *Nevada State Bd. of Agric. v. U.S.*, 512 F. Supp. 166 (D. Nev. 1981), aff'd for lack of justiciability, 699 F.2d 486 (9th Cir. 1983). *Nye County*, Nevada's attempt to assert county ownership of federal lands, met the same fate. *U.S. v. Nye County, Nev.*, 920 F. Supp. 1108 (D. Nev. 1996). The Ninth Circuit Court of Appeals has reaffirmed federal ownership of federal public lands. *U.S. v. Gardner*, 107 F.3d 1314 (9th Cir. 1996) (involving a defense to an enforcement action for unauthorized grazing on public lands). The so-called Wise Use movement, the loosely organized but high profile anti-environmental and anti-regulatory coalition of mostly western populist groups, funded by industry, continued to pursue the Sagebrush Rebellion agenda of "Local Sovereignty," along with a focus on private property rights, through the media, the political process, and the courts. Although the phrases *Sagebrush Rebellion* and *Wise Use movement* are no longer used, the Bush II Administration proved far more responsive than

---

135. For a case holding against the landowner on far more favorable facts, see *Branch v. Oconto County*, 109 N.W.2d 105 (Wis. 1961).

previous administrations to the demands of the extractive and libertarian interests that espouse these principles.

6. Public land and ecosystem management. The Wild Free-Roaming Horses and Burros Act, which deems the animals to be "an integral part of the natural system of the public lands," is Congress's clearest acceptance to date of Aldo Leopold's concept of land as an ecological community rather than a commodity. Increasingly, Americans are looking beyond preservation of particular species or resources (e.g., endangered species or wild and scenic rivers), which is based on a variety of "zoo" mentality, toward preservation of entire ecosystems and their biodiversity.[136] All four of the federal public land management agencies—BLM, USFS, FWS, and NPS—have announced that they will implement an ecosystem approach to managing their lands and natural resources. Apart from the primitive character of current ecological data, the most obvious impediment to ecosystem management on federal lands is that ecosystems transcend jurisdictional boundaries, not only those of any particular federal land management agency, but also those of the federal government itself:

> While ecosystem management will require unparalleled coordination among federal agencies, disparate missions and planning requirements set forth in federal land management statutes and regulations hamper such efforts. And although ecosystem management will require collaboration and consensus-building among federal and nonfederal parties within most ecosystems, incentives, authorities, interests and limitations embedded in the larger national land and natural resource use framework—many beyond the ability of the federal land management agencies individually or collectively to control and affect—constrain these parties' efforts to work together effectively. U.S. GAO, Ecosystem Management: Additional Actions Needed to Adequately Test a Promising Approach 5 (1994).

Is ecosystem management consistent with a multiple use-sustained yield statutory mandate? What about a dominant use directive?

7. Can states regulate resource extraction and wildlife management on federal lands? In *California Coastal Comm'n v. Granite Rock Co.*, 480 U.S. 572 (1987), the Supreme Court drew a distinction between land use planning and environmental regulation, holding that the NFMA preempts state land use planning in National Forests, but not state environmental regulation.[137] Is there a discernible difference between land use planning and environmental regulation in the context of public lands management?

Except in federal enclaves, such as National Parks, states typically regulate hunting and fishing on federal lands unless the federal government has declared otherwise, as in the Wild Free-Roaming Horses and Burros Act. In a *Kleppe*-like standoff between federal and state wildlife officials, the State of Wyoming challenged the FWS's refusal to permit state officials to vaccinate elk on the National Elk Refuge against brucellosis, a serious disease that threatens not only free-ranging elk but also domestic cattle on neighboring ranches. The Tenth Circuit Court of Appeals held that: (1) the Tenth Amendment to the U.S. Constitution does not reserve to the states the absolute right to manage wildlife on federal lands, and (2) the National Wildlife System Improvement Act of 1997 permits federal land management officials to preempt state wildlife management activities in wildlife refuges. *Wyoming v. U.S.*, 279 F.3d 1214 (10th Cir. 2002).

---

136. For a critique of the resource-by-resource preservation approach, in the context of the ESA, and an examination of the potential legal means of protecting biodiversity, see Doremus, Patching the Ark: Improving Legal Protection of Biological Diversity, 18 Ecology L.Q. 265 (1991).

137. See the discussion of *Granite Rock* in Chapter 6.

D. Adaptive Management and Climate Change

Here's a recent twist on environmental planning theory: Most planning systems presume a relatively stable factual context, permitting the creation of relatively stable plans to reach stable goals, with merely a need for minor tweaking adjustments as the program rolls along. The problem is that today in many areas of environmental planning unpredictably dramatic changing circumstances and uncertainty mean that relatively static plans can quickly become anachronistic. Surging energy prices, updated knowledge like discoveries of unanticipated toxicities, and a host of other shifts in fundamental conditions can make carefully constructed traditional plans suddenly obsolescent. And climate change in particular presents a gigantic adaptive challenge.

Adaptive management theory (also known as ARM, adaptive resource management) is an attempt to cope with contextual volatility.

Take, for instance, the example of planning for protection of endangered species or ecosystems: In recent years we not only have discovered significant unforeseen interactions — the arrival of exotic species invading native ecosystems, the effects of previously unsuspected chemical residues on species genetics, etc. — but global climate change as well, making dramatic, rapid, and probably irreversible tectonic shifts in ambient habitat conditions.

Globally, due to global warming, species in the northern hemisphere are moving northward at the rate of roughly 4 to 10 miles a decade — or, in the presence of mountains, sectors of species ratchet roughly 100 feet upward to higher elevations each decade, where some will become stranded on the heights and eventually disappear. For every increase of 1.8° Fahrenheit in average seasonal temperatures, vegetation belts shift roughly 60 to 100 miles northward, or 550 to 600 feet higher. The result is not just physical migration of plant and animal species. Reproduction patterns change as well. Some animal species hatch and bear young an average of five days sooner than they did several decades ago, and trees and other plants are blooming earlier.[138] Invasive newcomer species previously excluded by habitat conditions can now enter and disrupt prior ecosystem diversity. When species and the food they rely on mature at different rates, the result is disruption of lifecycle interactions, migration behaviors, and established ecological patterns.

The traditional approach to species protection under the ESA typically analyzes species' current location — and particularly their "type habitat," the basic paradigmatic place and condition in which they are located — and also considers prior lost habitat. (Future habitat is normally considered merely in terms of recovery into prior lost habitat.) Official recovery plans are drafted and implemented, and official regulatory requirements are locked in by ESA §10 permits, on this relatively static planning basis. (See Chapter 10.)

But what happens when many of the basic ecological premises become invalid, when changed conditions no longer fit the presumed fundamental habitat profiles?

Adaptive management provides a matrix for continually updating critical scientific information and for dynamically flexible planning. The underlying premise is that upon acquiring new substantive information, planners can incorporate that knowledge into a continually evolving interacting approach to natural resources management planning. Adaptive management thus seeks to reduce uncertainty over time by monitoring ecosystems,

---

138. For more on ecological consequences of climate change, see Thorson, On Thin Ice: The Failure of the United States and the World Heritage Committee to Take Climate Change Mitigation Pursuant to the World Heritage Convention Seriously, 38 Envtl. L. 139 (2008).

testing assumptions, and continually adjusting plans to best integrate newly acquired information into evolving management actions over time. In the endangered species setting this may mean that species recovery plans must be proactive in surveying necessary migrations into new habitat and new management elements. Fixed agreements between agencies and private property interests may become obsolete or require updating, where often contracted responsibilities have been permanently defined as fixed and unalterable.

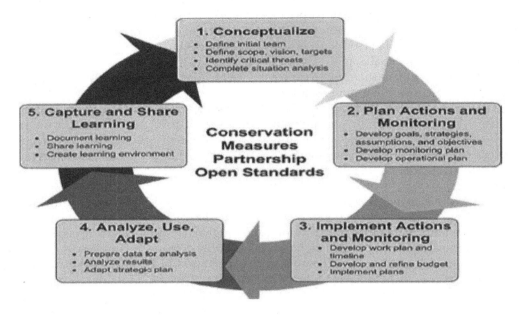

FIGURE 9-8. *CMP Adaptive Management Process, Conservation Measures Partnership, www.conservationmeasures.org. Used by permission.*

Agencies adopting adaptive management systems commit themselves to updating and amending management plans according to evolving scientific knowledge. The Department of Interior and the USFS have developed complex institutional procedures to integrate adaptive management practices into their programs.[139]

In 2004, after creating a model Analysis and Adaptive Management Program, the Conservation Measures Partnership (CMP) developed a common set of standards and guidelines for applying adaptive management to conservation projects and programs. These Open Standards for the Practice of Conservation[140] have received a positive reception from a large number of resource management agencies in the U.S. and abroad.

How does adaptive management work? Adaptive management is best conceived as cyclical. The process begins when the relevant agency identifies and assesses an ecosystem or natural resource problem. From that evaluation, the agency produces and implements a management plan to address that particular issue. The course of action called for in the plan is continually monitored, evaluated, and adjusted as new information becomes available. The cycle then renews again, as the government reassesses the issue and tests the plan's assumptions in light of what has been uncovered along the way. In its conceptual

---

139. See U.S. Dep't of Interior Adaptive Management Tech Guide, www.doi.gov/initiatives/Adaptive-Management/TechGuide.pdf; USFS Adaptive Management Services Unit, www.fs.fed.us/adaptivemanagement.

140. Available at http://conservationmeasures.org/CMP/Site_Docs/CMP_Open_Standards_Version_2.0.pdf.

D. Adaptive Management and Climate Change

theory facing rapid changes and uncertainty, ARM often reflects what is referred to as "Bayesian logic," a modern approach to a theoretical process conceived in the eighteenth century for updating statistical analyses in light of new scientific data and prior statistical patterns.[141] (Bayesian logic, for example, is likely to play a key role in global climate change analysis over coming decades.)

Given the increasing complexity of knowledge about ecological and environmental sciences, it makes fundamental common sense that modern resource management planning programs over time will inevitably need to incorporate the dynamic updating procedures of adaptive management.

COMMENTARY & QUESTIONS

1. Will agencies plan objectively under ARM systems? ARM systems make perfect rational sense: Science is given the dominant role for addressing and achieving civic goals. The history of resource management planning, however, constantly reflects the dominating role of industry-driven politics over science. Will the logic of rational necessity change the political context? Given the Supreme Court's *SUWA* decision, isn't it likely that continually evolving, mutable ARM plans would be deemed even less mandatory than traditional resource plans when political pressures tug the other way?

2. Democracy: What's the role of citizens in adaptive management? Note that it's agencies that do adaptive management. An unspoken premise of ARM programs appears to be that government agencies will scrupulously implement the entire process, seeking and updating relevant information, applying objective standards to the data and principles of the program, and implementing all required protective procedures on the ground, free of agency turf wars and opposition from resource industry lobbies and private property interests. Is this believable? In prior decades active citizen enforcement has been the indispensably necessary catalyst and backstop for all environmental protection efforts in the U.S., often opposed by "iron triangle" alliances of industry, agencies, and politicians.

In a series of useful articles, Professor Alejandro Camacho addresses the unfortunate realities. The experience in programs such as the ESA's Habitat Conservation Program "is that there is a distinct lack of adaptive pressure toward direct achievement of regulatory goals. Existing studies reveal—and recent Inspector General investigations corroborate —that the most acute evolutionary [internal agency] pressures . . . have been political rather than biological factors, a phenomenon echoed in other regulatory programs.[142]

Camacho argues forcefully that, especially because citizen enforcement is more difficult, the ARM process must by regulation be rigorously transparent, and further that a role for public interest citizens must be intensively integrated into ARM procedures throughout the dynamic evolving planning and implementation process.

That is a consummation devoutly to be desired. A basic lesson drawn from the experience of most planning initiatives to date is that objective science-based planning is critically important for sustainability in many critical societal areas. Such objective planning

---

141. In 1742, the Reverend Thomas Bayes, an enigmatic figure in the history of mathematics, was elected a Fellow of the Royal Society of London, which published his essential work in 1764, three years after he died. For a detailed introduction to the resurrected Bayes Theorem, see Eliezer S. Yudkowsky, An Intuitive Explanation of Bayesian Reasoning (2003); see also http://yudkowsky.net/rational/bayes.

142. Alejandro Camacho, Can Regulation Evolve? Lessons from a Study in Maladaptive Management, 55 UCLA L. Rev. 293, 344 (2007).

regimes, however, may be difficult to maintain in modern democratic governance as we know it.[143]

3. Oil: contingency plans, adaptive management, and RCAC citizen councils. A number of systemic reforms will surely follow in the wake of the Gulf of Mexico BP Deepwater Blowout spill, and oil disaster contingency plans will be one of the targets. As in the *Exxon Valdez* case, the official contingency planning for Gulf of Mexico oil discharges was found to be sadly ill-prepared and ineffective, based on overly-optimistic premises, vague empirical information, false assurances, and little or no operational preparedness. In the future, contingency plans are likely to be held to far more stringent standards. They will also necessarily be designed as adaptive management plans, rather than static plans. The complexity and change encountered with weather, currents, differential technology requirements, and the different character and intensity of discharges mean that a contingency plan must continually be modified to cope with changing conditions. The federal and state incident command centers will have the decisive role in this process.

To mitigate the problem noted in the preceding Comment, the agency role may well be complemented by the interesting innovation of RCACs — regional citizens advisory councils. These watchdog councils were proposed and adopted in OPA-90, the Oil Pollution Act of 1990, 33 U.S.C. §2732(d). Councils are comprised of representatives of local coastal communities, fishermen, local businesses, and other interests that will suffer the harms of systemic breakdowns that produce and fail to contain oil spills and blowouts, and have the power to investigate and publicize strategic information within corporate and agency operations.

As institutional entities outside the "di-polar" system of industry and regulatory agency management, these citizens councils operate as a strategic third party participant, countering the di-polar tendency toward "complacency, collusion, and neglect" described by the Exxon Valdez Oil Spill Commission back in 1990,[144] and ensuring that adaptive management does not bypass active public involvement.

In the lobbying that accompanied the passage of OPA-90 after the Exxon Valdez calamity, these innovative citizen councils were restricted to Alaska waters. There they have served an extremely useful function in helping to prevent discharges, and to ensure preparedness for response efforts if and when spills occur. Amongst the aftermath repercussions of the BP Deepwater Blowout spill, the RCAC innovation (imported from Alaska) fits well into the planning designs for updates to OPA-90, and beyond.

4. The huge adaptation challenges posed by global climate disruption. It is not now, if it ever was, possible to return the earth's atmosphere to a level of carbon content that would start to reverse climate disruption effects within anyone's lifetime. Mitigation efforts must continue, but in the meantime the need for adaptive strategies is avoided by only the most benighted thinkers.

Sea level rise is only one of the unavoidable climate-driven realities as the world's perched glaciers melt. It's a big one, but there are other big ones. Ocean acidification is changing the global ecology of the seas, killing coral protective barrier reefs, affecting millions of tons of fish and other biomass, and lessening the seas' carbon sink functionality. Wild dislocations of the jet stream make weather trends and events less predictable and

---

143. For an affirmative projection of how adaptive management could improve BLM's management of oil and gas extraction in the West, focusing on Wyoming's Powder River Basin, see Benson, Adaptive Management Approaches by Resource Management Agencies in the U.S., 29 J. Energy & Nat. Res. 87 (2010).

144. See State of Alaska Oil Spill Commission, SPILL: The Wreck of the Exxon Valdez — Implications for Safe Transportation of Oil (1990), available at http://www.arlis.org/docs/vol1/B/33339870.pdf.

D. Adaptive Management and Climate Change

massively more disruptive. Climate zones of animal and plant ecosystems, and farms, shift inexorably toward the poles, disrupting ecological contexts that evolved over tens of thousands of years in mere decades.

Sea level rise probably has attracted most attention, in part because of the vividness of world-wide mapping that demonstrates the physically accurate effect of different sea level elevations.[145] To stay in place, much of Bangladesh, New Orleans, Shanghai, and a thousand other intensely developed human locations would have to be floodproofed to an unimaginably demanding level. Floodproofing big cities is a slogan rather than a feasible initiative for sprawling metropolitan areas near coasts. See Parenteau, Cities on Stilts: The Myth of Large-Scale Climate Adaptation and the Limits of Sustainability, in J. Owley & K. Hirokawa, RETHINKING SUSTAINABILITY TO MEET THE CLIMATE CHANGE CHALLENGE (2015). (Even the Dutch, with centuries of experience and a relatively tiny geographic area to protect, may not be able to withstand a possible five-meter rise in sea levels.) With entire Pacific island states being inundated to the point of being uninhabitable, the world community will have to figure how and where nation state transplantations can occur, or face disastrous ad hoc flotillas of environmental refugees.

The Paris COP-21 accord offers a vast global climate plan (explored in detail in Chapter 22). It includes an innovative adaptive management program. In order to address the goal of holding global average temperatures short of a 2° Celsius increase over pre-industrial global temperatures, the nation states each agreed to a control program establishing "nationally determined contributions" to carbon control (NDCs) — which they will report to a central secretariat. But these programs are not to be static. They will each be revised upward every five years, guided by a process for monitoring progress, reported with enhanced transparency so that actual efforts and results are assessable and continual meaningful adaptive development is maintained. As Prof. John Dernbach wrote —

> These processes may be understood in terms of "reflexive" law and governance. Reflexive approaches . . . improve the capacity of governmental institutions . . . to learn about themselves and their actions [and] stimulate them to use this information to make appropriate changes. They create spurs to action. In the context of the Paris Agreement, reflexive governance seems intended to perform at least four key tasks. First, it should encourage or prod governments to be more ambitious over time, without being prescriptive about what they should do. . . . Second, it will provide information to governments and others about what other governments are actually doing, as well information about the effectiveness and impacts of particular laws and policies. This information can then be used to modify those laws and policies. Third, because this information will be public, it means that governments are more likely to honestly and openly share what they are doing, and be responsive to the views of nongovernmental organizations and businesses as well as the public in general. Finally, there are few areas in law and policy in which the playing field is changing faster than in climate change. . . . These and other processes in the Paris Agreement are more likely to survive, accommodate, and address this shifting landscape in the years ahead.[146]

Adaptive management — which is sometimes treated rather dismissively as a wistful academic seminar theory — is about to get a tryout on the world's largest stage, the planet itself.

---

145. See, for instance, the Climate Central interactive mapping that upon request reveals the degree of flooding of coastal and inland sites anywhere on the planet at http://sealevel.climatecentral.org.
146. http://johndernbach.com/2015/12/470/ Dec. 13, 2015.

The best developers have visions that extend beyond the single site or project to what makes a better neighborhood, a better community, and a better quality of life.

National Governors' Association, 2000

Environmentalists should make good urbanists, since they understand systems, diversity, connectivity and interdependence.

— Caryl Terrell

There are two types of environmentalists: those who understand that the city is part of the environment and those who do not.

— Paul Soglin, Mayor of Madison, Wisconsin

The compact neighborhood is the true architecture of nature. . . . The loss of a forest or a farm is justified only if it is replaced by a village. A subdivision and a shopping center is not an even trade.

— Andres Duany

We don't want to be a regulatory agency. We want to be a development agency on our national lands.

— Secretary of Interior Manuel Lujan, speaking to coal executives, N.Y. Times, 29 Nov. 1992 at 30.

Animals are not brethren, they are not underlings. They are other nations caught with ourselves in the net of life and time.

— Henry Beston

Humans think they are smarter than dolphins because we build cars and buildings, and start wars, etc., and all that dolphins do is swim in the water, eat fish, and play around. Dolphins believe that they are smarter for exactly the same reasons.

—Douglas Adams, THE HITCH-HIKER'S GUIDE TO THE GALAXY

10

Roadblock Statutory Strategies & the Endangered Species Act

STARK PROHIBITIONS AND THEIR VIABILITY

A. An Introduction to Roadblock Statutes
B. The ESA as a Roadblock Statute
C. "Slippage" and "Roadblock Bypasses"—Subsequent Modifications Temper Stark Standards (and What Conclusions Should Be Drawn from That?)

A. AN INTRODUCTION TO ROADBLOCK STATUTES

"Roadblock" laws—statutory provisions that in stark, direct, easily litigatable flat-out terms declare "*Thou Shalt Not* . . . "—have been a continuing part of the statutory history of environmental law from its beginning in the 1960s. Although sometimes created by accident, they often play a critically important role. There are times when a problem is so complex, so incapable of careful measurement and fine tuning, or so politically difficult to shift away from the old status quo that a stark flat prohibition provision may be necessary to achieve effective environmental protection.

The federal Endangered Species Act (ESA),[15] is the prime example used in this chapter, where threatened animals and plants can present the roadblock question. (A number of other roadblock statutes exist in the environmental realm—the 1899 Rivers and Harbors Act, which makes it a crime to dump any refuse into the nation's waters without a permit; the Wilderness Act of 1964, which prohibits virtually all development and motorized uses in declared wildernesses; and the Delaney Clause of the Federal Food, Drug, and Cosmetic Act (FDCA), which banned any food additive that has caused cancer in test animals.) Other statutes can contain prohibitions that permit very limited exceptions (such as *Overton Park*'s Department of Transportation Act §4(f) provision in Chapter 6, the CAA's Title II prohibition of auto emissions beyond 10% of 1970 levels, in Chapter 11, and more).

---

1. 16 U.S.C. §§1531 et seq. (1973, as amended).

1. The Delaney Clause

Take the example of the Delaney Clause: Despite some scientists' skepticism about the usefulness of high-dosage animal tests, the terms of the clause (passed in 1958 at the urging of Representative James Delaney who made the provision a personal crusade) declared that—

> No [food] additive shall be deemed to be safe if it is found . . . to induce cancer in man or animal. . . . 21 U.S.C. §348(c)(3) (1958), FDCA §409.

In the years after its passage, the Delaney Clause forced the nation's food industry to be far more conscious of potential carcinogenicity, but in some cases the zero-risk ban was clearly too strict. Some cancer-linked additives posed extremely trivial risks of actual harm, arising only in the case of huge overdoses, and were far less dangerous than the toxic but noncarcinogenic additives being used as substitutes. The FDA quietly allowed the use of some additives that posed cancer risks of less than one-in-a-million. When the NRDC blocked the FDA's informal flexibility with an injunction enforcing the statute's absolute ban,[2] Congress and President Clinton decided to overturn the Delaney Clause roadblock, substituting a statutory standard providing that—

> as used in this section, the term "safe" . . . means that the Administrator has determined that there is a *reasonable certainty* that no harm will result from aggregate exposure to the pesticide chemical. . . . 21 U.S.C. §346a(b)(2)(A)(ii), Food Quality Protection Act of 1996 (FQPA) (emphasis added).

The subsequent effect of the FQPA amendment is subject to debate. Some argue that public health and safety are now undercut by the loosened constraints on the agency; others argue that overall it improves them.[3] Either way, note the strategic shifts that have occurred: The amendment shifts from a clear absolute standard to a subjective balancing—from an objective test litigatable by citizens to a discretionary agency determination of "reasonable" that courts will review deferentially, and from a pluralistic setting where the roadblock norm is enforceable by a wide variety of interested parties, back to a "dipolar" setting where in practical effect the regulatory outcome is primarily determined between industry and the Administrator, whoever that may be.

2. Weighing Roadblocks

Statutory histories like that of the Delaney Clause open up a range of questions:

- In its strict roadblock form, to what extent does the standard achieve the desired environmental or public health protection? If it is effective, why? Does it overprotect? If so, by how much, and at what relative systemic costs?
- If the roadblock gets amended, is it because the original environmental or public health goal has been found in whole or part to have been wrong-headed from the start? If not, is the new moderated statutory standard as effective as the old in achieving the public's environmental and public health interests? For instance, is it still readily enforceable by citizen plaintiffs if the designated agencies refuse to do it? The familiar phenomenon of "regulatory slippage," where strict statutory

---

2. *Les v. Reilly*, 968 F.2d 985 (9th Cir. 1992) (EPA had no discretion to permit the use of such food additives).

3. The negative argument is that in actual administrative practice the FQPA's word *reasonable* spreads over to modify the *no harm* phrase as well. The positive argument is that the agency now can allow minimalist carcinogens that are far less risky than the alternatives.

A. An Introduction to Roadblock Statutes

commands are modified over time, can sometimes be a constructive process of progressive adaptation, and sometimes an erosive, backsliding abandonment of public interest goals.
- And there are questions of timing and politics: For legal standards to be effective over spans of years requires an accumulation of political momentum, experience, credibility, acceptance, and support as well as workable technical terminology and enforcement mechanisms. If the roadblock survives over time, how does it do so? What political support has it collected to sustain it? If the roadblock has been moderated by amendments, could the public's environmental and public health interests have been just as well served if it had been legislated this way in the first place? Or was it necessary first to "establish a beachhead," consolidating the standard's political strength as a crude blunt roadblock in order to implant its mandate forcibly into the established political and industrial legal order?
- If the roadblock is amended, is the new format more or less open to public participation and public confidence?

Roadblock statutes may offer a good answer to many environmental problems, but they also raise this chain of important questions.

Are roadblock laws a good idea? They demonstrate the virtues of crude strength as well as some serious potential vices. On occasion they certainly have been effective, as in the §4(f) protection of parklands and the stark 90% rollback in auto emissions. For the same reason, however, they may be especially subject to the problems of the unguided missile: The tradeoff for decisive effectiveness is the risk that they may hit too hard, in not exactly the right place, or with disruptive or disproportionate consequences that weren't predicted. Roadblocks typically arouse immediate backlashes labeling them too extreme and inflexible, sometimes with good reason. Should environmental statutes be drafted from the very beginning to be less stark and draconian, "eco-pragmatically" seeking "the reasonable middle"?[4] Rather than enforcing crude, stringent prohibitions, should we build eco-pragmatic regulatory programs around standards that incorporate careful balances between ecology and industrial economics? That way, won't these laws have greater "social sustainability," avoiding destructive backlashes? The sharpness of a law's terms, however, can make a large difference in whether it will be implemented. If it does not have a continuing political force supporting it, often its major chance for effective implementation will be citizen lawsuits, and that often requires terms that are clear and simple.

Statutes evolve. Over time, many strict roadblocks have been softened by mellowing amendments, with varying results depending on your point of view. Sometimes this "slippage"[5] or "fine-tuning" modification process consolidates or improves the law's effectiveness, sometimes it reduces it, and sometimes it guts it. The trick in designing statutes is to determine when and how strict environmental protection standards should initially be imposed, and how they should be maintained thereafter over time.

---

4. Professor Dan Farber prompted the question with Ecopragmatism (1999), which stimulated Prof. J.B. Ruhl's Working Both (Positivist) Ends Toward a New (Pragmatist) Middle in Environmental Law, 68 Geo. Wash. L. Rev. 522 (2000); Ruhl, A Manifesto for the Radical Middle, 38 Idaho L. Rev. 385 (2002); and others. For a critical appraisal, see Heinzerling, Pragmatists and Environmentalists, 113 Harv. L. Rev. 1421 (2000).

5. See Farber, Taking Slippage Seriously: Noncompliance and Creative Compliance in Environmental Law, 23 Harv. Envtl. L. Rev. 297 (1999).

B. The ESA as a Roadblock Statute

1. The Endangered Species Act

> The militant environmentalist movement in America today is a new homosocialism, communism. What these people are is against private property rights. They are trying to attack capitalism and corporate America. . . . And they're trying to say that we must preserve . . . virgin trees because the spotted owl and the rat kangaroo and whatever live in them, and it's the only place they can live, the snail darter and whatever it is.
>
> — Rush Limbaugh, *The Rush Limbaugh Show*, Dec. 7, 1993

The Endangered Species Act of 1973 was a revolutionary legal document. It was the first major piece of legislation in any legal system that sought to put teeth into the protection of endangered species domestically and internationally. The ESA has been a model for subsequent wildlife conservation efforts throughout the world.

The critical initial step in the ESA process is the listing of a species as "endangered" or "threatened" on the federal Endangered Species List, via ESA §4. The Act provides three basic regulatory approaches:

1. A commercial ban limiting the importation and domestic sale of endangered species and their parts.[6]
2. A provision forbidding federal agencies from harming endangered or threatened species—ESA §7, the original roadblock hidden within the ESA's text.
3. A provision forbidding the killing or "taking" of endangered species—ESA §9, which also creates a major roadblock.

As to the first, market pressures encourage the destruction of many endangered species by raising the exploitation value of each remaining animal as a species approaches extinction. To the extent that the ESA ban on commercial trade in endangered species reduces the market, it lessens the pressure on species that provide the market with fur coats, exotic pets, and other market luxuries.

Section 7 of the 1973 ESA contained a hidden roadblock, a direct congressional prohibition against federal agency projects and programs that harm endangered species. The resemblance between ESA §7 and NEPA §102 is remarkable. Both provisions target federal agency actions. Both contained hidden teeth that subsequently emerged to the surprise of most members of Congress who had voted for them. NEPA requires only procedural compliance. The roadblock terms of ESA §7, however, are substantive, precise, and mandatory, and the Act specifically authorizes enforcement by citizens acting as private attorneys general.

ESA §9 looks like a straightforward prohibition against "taking" any endangered species, a prohibition that attaches heavy criminal sanctions to the act of killing or capturing endangered animals. But the interpretive rule issued by the Department of Interior's Fish and Wildlife Service (FWS) defines habitat modification or degradation as a "harm" that can constitute an illegal "take."[7] (This makes ecological sense. Habitat alteration is the number one cause of extinction of species on the face of the earth, a far more important threat than hunting and killing.) As a result of the broad agency definition of *harm* under

---

6. This ban on the importation or sale of endangered species is a straightforward domestic law implementation of CITES, the Convention on International Trade in Endangered Species, probably the most effective international environmental treaty ever.

7. 50 C.F.R. §17.3.

B. The ESA as a Roadblock Statute

ESA §9, however, the ESA has become a potentially wide-ranging roadblock against private as well as public development, arousing a firestorm of political opposition.

As we'll see later in this chapter, faced with a perceived need for flexibility, Congress ultimately passed amendments somewhat loosening the ESA's roadblocks—notably the God Committee procedures for §7 in 1978, and a §10 incidental take permit process to bypass §9 in 1982.

2. A Fish, a Dam, and ESA §7

> The ESA's roadblocks first reached the U.S. Supreme Court in a classic confrontation between a small, endangered fish and the Tennessee Valley Authority's Tellico Dam.

The strict roadblock in the terms of ESA §7 as it was originally written in 1973 lay camouflaged. When parsed carefully, however, its words absolutely prohibited certain harmful federal agency actions. As you read through the original text of §7 (while noting the clunky prose style that made it unlikely that many members of Congress realized what they were approving), take a pencil and underline the series of words below that, pulled together by environmental litigators, created a substantive mandate and at least two separate causes of action for citizen lawsuits:

> **§7. Interagency Cooperation.** The [Interior] Secretary shall review other programs administered by him and utilize such programs in furtherance of the purposes of this chapter. All other Federal agencies shall, in consultation with and with the assistance of the Secretary, utilize their authorities in furtherance of the purposes of this chapter by carrying out programs for the conservation of endangered species and threatened species listed pursuant to section 1533 of this title and by taking such action necessary to ensure that actions authorized, funded, or carried out by such agencies do not jeopardize the continued existence of such endangered species or threatened species or result in the destruction or modification of habitat of such species which is determined by the Secretary, after consultation as appropriate with the affected States, to be critical. 16 U.S.C. §1536 (1973).

THE SNAIL DARTER AND THE TELLICO DAM CASE

The Supreme Court's dramatic first encounter with ESA §7 arose from a typical environmental controversy between a citizens' group—including farmers, sportsmen, archaeologists, and Cherokee Indians—rallying behind an endangered fish to oppose the Tennessee Valley Authority's Tellico Project.[8] TVA, a federal multipurpose agency, had designed the land development project to support its final dam.

A member of the perch family, the snail darter is a small, brownish fish, rarely more than two-and-a-half inches at maturity, with highly specific habitat requirements —shallow, clean, cool, and rapid-flowing big river habitat with rocky substrates containing tiny snails and caddis larvae as food sources. As so often happens, the snail darter was endangered because of habitat alteration. At one time it had lived throughout the Tennessee river system between the Appalachians and the Mississippi. Little by little its populations were extirpated

---

8. *Disclosure Notice.* As the length and tone of this section probably reveal, one of the authors was both attorney and a party plaintiff in the snail darter case, beginning in 1974 and continuing up through the Supreme Court and three rounds of congressional review. See Z. Plater, THE SNAIL DARTER AND THE DAM (2013), the saga of the small endangered fish's travels through the corridors of American power. For images and more on the case, see goo.gle/ecQ158, and associated website materials.

by damming. By 1973, TVA and the Army Corps had built 68 dams, turning 2500 linear river miles in that relatively flat, gently rolling region into serpentine impoundments. This left the 33 un-dammed miles of the Little Tennessee River as the darter's last significant habitat.

The river valley was likewise extraordinary in human terms — rolling meadows with more than 300 family farms on 38,000 acres of some of the richest soils left in the region, unique archaeological and historical features, and great potential for recreation and tourist development at the edge of the Great Smoky Mountains National Park.

TVA's final dam project arose in a classic public works context often called the "pork barrel." Since the marginal final dam couldn't be cost-justified for normal dam purposes like power, water supply, or flood control (because it was small and surrounded by other dams), the agency promoted the project on a novel economic theory.[9] Most of the valley lands were condemned from the farmers at low prices, for resale to corporate developers of Timberlake, a hypothesized model industrial city to be funded by federal taxpayers and built by the Boeing Corporation at some point in the future. (See map and description of land condemnation in Chapter 21.) The reservoir plan claimed speculative profits from development of the condemned lands, along with recreation gains, as its two major "benefit" justifications.

The project calculations were economically unsupportable,[10] and Boeing soon bowed out. With continuing appropriations from Congress's appropriations committees, however, TVA pressed on. The farmers, fishermen, and environmentalists advanced the usual critical environmental analysis — that the project's claimed benefits were greatly exaggerated and unrealistic, the project's economic costs were severely underestimated and took no notice of social and ecological costs, and far better alternatives existed that maximized public and natural values. The citizens tried to demonstrate the project's economic dysfunctionality in congressional testimony, in media outreach, and in court through condemnation defenses and a NEPA lawsuit, all without success.[11]

Then one afternoon, wading at a wide shoal in the river with a snorkel and facemask, ichthyology professor David Etnier discovered the snail darter. Hiram Hill, a law student, heard about it from Etnier's grad students and wrote an environmental term paper arguing that Tellico Dam violated ESA §7. The term paper quickly turned into a federal court lawsuit filed by Hill and his professor on behalf of the darter and the river valley's defenders. TVA responded with accelerated construction and bulldozing in the valley, trying to moot the case with a strategy of sunk costs.

As reported in the resulting cascade of stories in the press, the case was consistently portrayed as a simple caricature: the snail darter, a two-inch minnow, discovered at the last possible moment and misused by extremist environmentalists, halting completion of a massive valuable $150 million hydroelectric dam project. This caricature stuck to the case throughout the following years, affecting the final outcome, but on the factual record every element of that story was wrong.[12] The trial court judge concluded that the dam was likely to eliminate the fish and

---

9. All such projects must claim a positive economic benefit-cost ratio, earning at least $1.01 for every $1.00 of federal money spent, estimated over a span of up to 100 years with limited attributed interest figured in. This requirement, intended to control "logrolling" by congressional public works politics, prompts highly imaginative agency calculations that typically expand claimed benefits and trivialize costs. See F. Powledge, Water: The Nature, Uses, and Future of Our Most Precious and Abused Resource 291-302 (1982).

10. See the economic verdict of the God Committee later in this chapter.

11. A citizen lawsuit halted the project for 16 months by forcing TVA to do an EIS. *EDF v. TVA*, 339 F. Supp. 806 (E.D. Tenn.), aff'd, 468 F.2d 1164 (6th Cir. 1972); *EDF v. TVA*, 371 F. Supp. 1004 (E.D. Tenn. 1973), aff'd, 492 F.2d 466 (6th Cir. 1974).

12. In actual fact, the darter was a perch, closer to three inches long, discovered when only 20% of project costs had been incurred. The core citizen opponents were farmers and sportsmen as well as environmentalists. And

B. The ESA as a Roadblock Statute

its habitat but declined to issue an injunction against the reservoir project. The Sixth Circuit Court of Appeals, however, enjoined the dam,[13] and the case went to the Supreme Court.

Tennessee Valley Authority v. Hiram Hill, et al.
437 U.S. 153 (U.S. Sup. Ct. 1978)

BURGER, C.J. We begin with the premise that operation of the Tellico Dam will either eradicate the known population of snail darters or destroy their critical habitat. Petitioner does not now seriously dispute this fact.

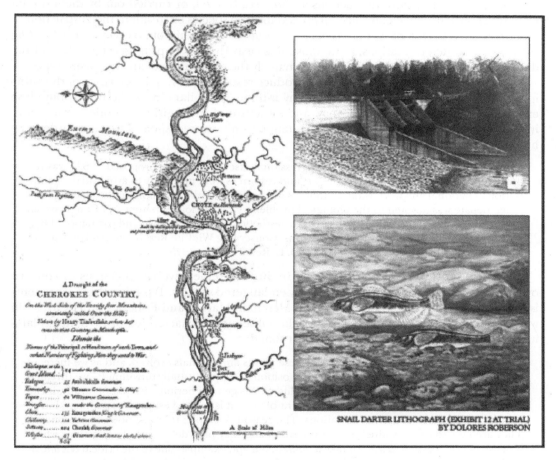

FIGURE 10-1. *The Little Tennessee River Valley, the dam, and the snail darter. The river and valley were sacred to the Cherokee, whose towns and sanctuaries appear on the 1762 colonial map. Prior to the* Tellico *case, TVA had dammed all of the river through and beyond the Enemy (Smoky) Mountains, and below this area all the way to the Mississippi.*

---

the dam was small, ca. $5 million in concrete and steel out of a total budget of ca. $150 million, most of which was being spent for land, roads, and bridges. The project was built for possible real estate development and recreation, not hydroelectric generation—and was expected to destroy prime farmlands and a beautiful river as well as the darter's prime habitat. The existence of the darter as a basis for stopping the dam, the citizens argued, was like a canary in a coal mine. Its precarious survival in the Little Tennessee River, after elimination under 68 dams elsewhere, made the fish species a sensitive barometer of a wide range of threatened public values in the river valley.

13. *Hill v. TVA*, 549 F.2d 1064 (6th Cir. 1977), rev'g 419 F. Supp. 753 (E.D. Tenn. 1976).

Starting from the above premise, two questions are presented: (a) would TVA be in violation of the Act if it completed and operated the Tellico Dam as planned? (b) if TVA's actions would offend the Act, is an injunction the appropriate remedy for the violation? For the reasons stated hereinafter, we hold that both questions must be answered in the affirmative.

It may seem curious to some that the survival of a relatively small number of three-inch fish among all the countless millions of species extant would require the permanent halting of a virtually completed dam for which Congress has expended more than $100 million. . . .

One would be hard pressed to find a statutory provision whose terms were any plainer than those in §7 of the Endangered Species Act. Its very words affirmatively command all federal agencies "to insure that actions authorized, funded, or carried out by them do not jeopardize the continued existence" of an endangered species or "result in the destruction or modification of habitat of such species. . . ." This language admits of no exception. Accepting the Secretary's determinations, as we must, it is clear that TVA's proposed operation of the dam will have precisely the opposite effect, namely the eradication of an endangered species.

Concededly, this view of the Act will produce results requiring the sacrifice of the anticipated benefits of the project and of many millions of dollars in public funds, but close examination of the language, history, and structure of the legislation under review here indicates beyond doubt that Congress intended endangered species to be afforded the highest of priorities.

> The dominant theme pervading all Congressional discussion of the proposed [ESA] was the overriding need to devote whatever effort and resources were necessary to avoid further diminution of national and worldwide wildlife resources. Much of the testimony at the hearings and much debate was devoted to the biological problem of extinction. Senators and Congressmen uniformly deplored the irreplaceable loss to aesthetics, science, ecology, and the national heritage should more species disappear. Coggins, Conserving Wildlife Resources: An Overview of the Endangered Species Act of 1973, 51 N.D. L. Rev. 315, 321 (1975).

The legislative proceedings in 1973 are, in fact, replete with expressions of concern over the risk that might lie in the loss of any endangered species. Typifying these sentiments is the Report of the House Committee on Merchant Marine and Fisheries on HR 37, a bill which contained the essential features of the subsequently enacted Act of 1973; in explaining the need for the legislation, the Report stated:

> As we homogenize the habitats in which these plants and animals evolved, and as we increase the pressure for products that they are in a position to supply (usually unwillingly) we threaten their and our own genetic heritage. The value of this genetic heritage is, quite literally, incalculable. From the most narrow possible point of view, it is in the best interests of mankind to minimize the losses of genetic variations. The reason is simple: they are potential resources. They are keys to puzzles which we cannot solve, and may provide answers to questions which we have not yet learned to ask. To take a homely, but apt, example: one of the critical chemicals in the regulation of ovulations in humans was found in a common plant. Once discovered, and analyzed, humans could duplicate it synthetically, but had it never existed — or had it been driven out of existence before we knew its potentialities — we would never have tried to analyze it in the first place. Who knows, or can say, what potential cures for cancer or other scourges, present or future, may lie locked up in the structures of plants which may yet be undiscovered, much less analyzed? . . . Sheer self-interest impels us to be cautious. The institutionalization of that caution lies at the heart of HR 37. . . . H.R. Rep. No. 93-412.

Congress was concerned about the unknown uses that endangered species might have and about the unforeseeable place such creatures may have in the chain of life on this planet. In shaping legislation to deal with the problem thus presented, Congress started from the finding that "the two major causes of extinction are hunting, and destruction

B. The ESA as a Roadblock Statute

of natural habitat." Sen. Rep. No. 93-307, p. 2 (1973). Of these twin threats, Congress was informed that the greatest was destruction of natural habitats.

It is not for us to speculate, much less act, on whether Congress would have altered its stance had the specific events of this case been anticipated. In any event, we discern no hint in the deliberations of Congress relating to the 1973 Act that would compel a different result than we reach here.

One might dispute the applicability of these examples to the Tellico Dam by saying that in this case the burden on the public through the loss of millions of unrecoverable dollars would greatly outweigh the loss of the snail darter. But neither the Endangered Species Act nor Article III of the Constitution provides federal courts with authority to make such fine utilitarian calculations. On the contrary, the plain language of the Act, buttressed by its legislative history, shows clearly that Congress viewed the value of endangered species as "incalculable." Quite obviously, it would be difficult for a court to balance the loss of a sum certain—even $100 million—against a congressionally declared "incalculable" value, even assuming we had the power to engage in such a weighing process, which we emphatically do not.

Having determined that there is an irreconcilable conflict between operation of the Tellico Dam and the explicit provisions of §7 of the Endangered Species Act, we must now consider what remedy, if any, is appropriate. It is correct, of course, that a federal judge sitting as a chancellor is not mechanically obligated to grant an injunction for every violation of law. [But] once Congress, exercising its delegated powers, has decided the order of priorities in a given area, it is for the Executive to administer the laws and for the courts to enforce them when enforcement is sought.

Here we are urged [in Justices Rehnquist and Powell's dissents] to view the Endangered Species Act "reasonably," and hence shape a remedy "that accords with some modicum of common sense and the public weal." But is that our function? We have no expert knowledge on the subject of endangered species, much less do we have a mandate from the people to strike a balance of equities on the side of the Tellico Dam. Congress has spoken in the plainest of words, making it abundantly clear that the balance has been struck in favor of affording endangered species the highest of priorities, hereby adopting a policy which it described as "institutionalized caution."

Our individual appraisal of the wisdom or unwisdom of a particular course consciously selected by the Congress is to be put aside in the process of interpreting a statute. Once the meaning of an enactment is discerned and its constitutionality determined, the judicial process comes to an end. We do not sit as a committee of review, nor are we vested with the power of veto. The lines ascribed to Sir Thomas More by Robert Bolt are not without relevance here:

> The law, Roper, the law. I know what's legal, not what's right. And I'll stick to what's legal. . . . I'm not God. The currents and eddies of right and wrong, which you find such plain-sailing, I can't navigate. I'm no voyager. But in the thickets of the law, oh there I'm a forester. . . . What would you do? Cut a great road through the law to get after the Devil? . . . And when the last law was down, and the Devil turned round on you, where would you hide, Roper, the laws all being flat? . . . This country's planted thick with laws from coast to coast—Man's laws, not God's—and if you cut them down . . . d'you really think you could stand upright in the winds that would blow then? Yes, I'd give the Devil benefit of law, for my own safety's sake. R. Bolt, A Man for All Seasons, Act I, 147 (Heinemann ed. 1967).

We agree with the Court of Appeals that in our constitutional system the commitment to the separation of powers is too fundamental for us to pre-empt congressional action by judicially decreeing what accords with "common sense and the public weal." Our Constitution vests such responsibilities in the political branches. Affirmed.

POWELL, BLACKMUN, and **REHNQUIST, JJ.**, dissent.

COMMENTARY & QUESTIONS

1. Is this an "environmental" opinion? Much of the snail darter majority opinion looks at the ESA to determine, via statutory construction, only the bald questions of whether it applied to the dam and whether a court had to obey the statute. The Court does not provide the citizens with a forum to review the factual merits of the dam and its alternatives, just a roadblock. Justice Burger does echo congressional declarations of the high purposes of endangered species preservation and "institutionalized caution," a critical environmental principle, but when he announced the decision in court he invited Congress to repeal protection for the fish. And the media coverage of the Supreme Court decision predictably chorused a "little fish bites dam" theme, casting the case and plaintiffs in damaging terms of extreme environmentalism. On balance, did the snail darter litigation aid the cause of conservation or undercut it?

2. Rationales for endangered species protection. Why might a nation consider it sufficiently important to pass a statute with such patent and latent strengths in an abstract area of natural science? The question is made all the more pointed by the fact that protection of endangered species inevitably causes a head-on confrontation with marketplace politics.

It is easiest to say that the ESA of 1973 was passed to satisfy a vague popular clamor, beginning in the 1960s, to conserve natural resources. Endangered species had the good fortune to be represented by such mediagenic figures as the bald eagle, polar bear, whale, and whooping crane, all of which were sentimentally appealing, fairly remote from market considerations affecting most people, and dramatic or beautiful. Further, there were international conventions ratified by the U.S. that in broad, hortatory terms expressed an international intention to conserve such species and all endangered and threatened wildlife. Part of the impetus came from the well-organized nationally based conservation groups that have long made the U.S. a leader in international conservation.

But political pressure and aesthetics alone do not represent a sufficient explanation for why the ESA of 1973 became domestic law. The argument for protection of endangered species represented not only protection of the aesthetic beauties of certain species, but also ecological and philosophical principles asserting the value of the survival of the widest possible number of species, some of them quite homely, in the context of the continuing loss each year of hundreds of species worldwide. In utilitarian terms, preserving endangered species can be directly or indirectly important for the continued survival of human beings. An endangered species may possess chemical or medical properties that will never be discovered if the creatures are rendered extinct. We preserve species because of lessons they may teach us in the future; at some point, "they may reveal a cure for cancer." Another argument is that the more diversity that exists in the natural world, the more adaptable that world is to continuing stresses. This argument reflects a fundamental law of ecology that the more diverse a gene pool or ecosystem, the greater the natural bank of adaptive diversity on which society can draw.

Unfortunately, as repeatedly demonstrated in subsequent hearings on the Act, it is very difficult to show the utility of many species, especially species previously unknown that happen to confront a specific expensive development project. Therefore, beyond the strict utility argument, endangered species protection often draws on a variety of quasi-religious principles emphasizing the sanctity of life. This latter philosophical principle was

B. The ESA as a Roadblock Statute

the most difficult to articulate amidst congressional hearings or agency proceedings, but it reflects an important thread running through the endangered species cases—humans are stewards of their natural environment and ultimately are only constituent members of the community of life of the globe. The ESA, which made no distinction between species that have a commercial value or direct human utility and those that do not, affirmed a variety of abstract interests in protecting species because they were endangered. The statute gave legal value to an abstraction. The survival of species, insofar as possible, was declared a valid and important national goal, backed up with §7's teeth.

The roadblock terms of §7 forced the abstract value of species protection into the heart of the political calculus in a way that traditional review-and-permit regulatory approaches were unlikely to do (in the same way that the parkland protection policy litigated in *Overton Park* needed the absolutism of FDCA §4(f) to be taken seriously).

Are the ESA's rationales dwarfed by the current reality of global climate change? If it were possible to show that over the next century as many as half of all endangered species were likely to be rendered extinct by global warming, a condition that appears to be human-augmented but quite impervious to legal liability, would the ESA become an obsolete footnote or continue to be a practicable tool, a worthwhile declaration of principle, and a utilitarian "canary in a coal mine"?

3. "Canaries in a coal mine": the practical utility of endangered species. Whatever the moral and philosophical arguments for species protection, it is clear that the everyday logic of the political process responds far more readily to practical economic self-interest than to abstract principle; endangered species are generally considered to reflect the latter more than the former. During the snail darter-Tellico Dam oral argument,[14] Justice Powell skeptically inquired:

> Apart from biological interest, which I do not challenge, what purpose is served, if any, by those little darters? Are they used for food? . . . Are they suitable for bait?[15]

Many advocates defending strong endangered species protections therefore try to stress human utilitarian reasons for doing so. In the spotted owl debates, environmentalists emphasize the useful function played by the owl in maintaining the ecological and water-cycle balance in Pacific Northwest forests.[16] They tell how the Pacific yew tree (*Taxis brevifolia*), a slow-growing, endangered plant living under the ancient forest canopy, is the only known source of taxol, a promising new drug for treating ovarian and breast cancer. Protection of endangered species' habitat protects the critical sources of useful medicines and other products, some of which will remain unknown until future scientists find them, if the trees survive. But most endangered species will not cure cancer, so utilitarian arguments must range further. The environmentalists answered Justice Powell's question with a utilitarian argument:

> This species turns out to be a highly sensitive indicator of precisely the qualities of the habitat that citizens were fighting about in this case for years before the snail darter was known to exist.[17]

This is the now-familiar "canary in a coal mine" argument. Like the canaries carried down into the mines (the birds were sensitive to odorless methane coal gas, so when they

---

14. Transcript of Oral Argument, Apr. 18, 1976, at 43-44.
15. Id.
16. D. Kelly & G. Braasch, Secrets of the Old Growth Forest 32 (1988). The owl's droppings spread critically important water-storing fungus spores to root systems throughout its habitat.
17. Transcript of Oral Argument, Apr. 18, 1976, at 43-44.

began to asphyxiate it was time for miners to flee), endangered species can be vivid living indicators of important human concerns. Endangered birdlife and frogs revealed the danger of DDT and other pesticides to humans. The snail darter, like most endangered species, thus acts as a sensitive physical and legal barometer of endangered human habitat values as well as of the ecological qualities in its habitat niche.[18]

4. Roadblocks' superior citizen litigatability. The roadblock character of ESA §7 was important because a looser standard would have been much tougher for citizens to enforce. What exactly was the legal cause of action in *TVA v. Hill*? Did TVA violate §7's requirements (a) that agencies "shall [carry] out programs for the conservation of endangered species," (b) that agency actions "shall not jeopardize the continued existence of endangered species," and (c) that agency actions "shall not . . . result in the destruction or modification of [critical] habitat"? The initial "conservation" count (a) is rather vague and open-ended and hasn't been used much by citizen litigants.[19] The latter two provisions are both roadblocks, however, and are the basis of most ESA litigation. As in *TVA v. Hill*, they often arise concurrently. Thinking like a litigator, which of the two is analytically easier to prove?

What if the operative verb in §7 had been written *may* instead of *shall*? What if the 1973 ESA had retained the phrase from the 1966 ESA, "insofar as practicable and consistent with the [agency's] purposes"? Would endangered species protection under either of these phrases ever reach the Supreme Court? Would agencies and industry today be taking endangered species protection seriously?

5. Denouement for the snail darter: the little fish gets the third degree, wins, and loses. As noted later in this chapter, the snail darter's roadblock effect, widely ridiculed by Washington lobbyists and the media, led to the creation of the so-called God Committee — an unprecedented Cabinet-level economic review exemption process that could create bypasses to the roadblock. After four months of intensive fact-finding into the snail darter–*Tellico Dam* case (the plaintiffs' first chance to argue their full case before a legal forum charged with making a comprehensive judgment on the project's real merits), the God Committee unanimously denied an exemption for the snail darter on explicitly economic grounds.[20] As Charles Schultze, then-Chairman of the Council of Economic Advisors and a member of the Committee said:

> Here is a project that is *95 percent complete*, and if one takes just the cost of finishing it against the [total project] benefits, and does it properly, it still doesn't pay, . . . which says something about the original design! [*Laughter.*]

---

18. See The Embattled Social Utilities of the Endangered Species Act—A Noah Presumption, and a Caution Against Putting Gas Masks on the Canaries in the Coal Mine, 27 Envtl. L. 845 (1997).

19. Do agencies have affirmative conservation duties under this clause, which now is generally known as ESA §7(a)? In *Carson-Truckee Water Conservancy Dist. v. Clark*, 741 F.2d 257 (9th Cir. 1984), the court held that the Department of Interior was required not only to protect existing habitats and endangered species but also to "use programs administered by [the Department] to further the conservation purposes of [the ESA]." The Department must "conserve threatened and endangered species to the extent that they are no longer threatened" and "halt *and reverse* the trend toward species extinction, whatever the cost." 741 F.2d at 262 (the emphasis is the court's). See also *Palila v. Hawaii Dep't of Land & Natural Res.*, 852 F.2d 1106 (9th Cir. 1988). But finding case settings where this vague provision will be enforced is difficult.

20. Decision of Endangered Species Committee, Jan. 23, 1979 (in archives of the Secretary of Interior, sitting as Chair, and with the coursebook authors) (remarkably, this transcript is unreported).

B. The ESA as a Roadblock Statute

Committee Chairman Secretary of Interior Cecil Andrus added:

> I hate to see the snail darter get the credit for stopping a project that was so ill-conceived and uneconomic in the first place.

Is it possible to believe that citizens, so lacking in funding, political power, and media clout, could have achieved this national-level review of the true merits of a powerful agency's pork-barrel project without a stark clear litigatable statutory roadblock provision to enforce? The possibility lay open for an innovative redevelopment of the valley and its river resource—prime agricultural lands and the valley's historic, touristic, and recreational assets

It was not to be. On June 18, 1979, in 42 seconds in a nearly empty House chamber, the House appropriations committee slipped a rider onto an ongoing bill explicitly overriding the Supreme Court decision and all other federal or state protective laws as they applied to the Tellico Project and ordering the reservoir's immediate completion. President Jimmy Carter threatened to veto the bill, but signed it on September 25, 1979, with an abject telephone call thereafter apologizing to the plaintiffs.

Of the last major natural population—25,000 darters that had lived in the Little Tennessee prior to dam construction—none survived. Small relict populations were discovered in several sites downstream, and two substantial transplanted populations are being sustained on life support (oxygen bubbling equipment is needed in low-water summer months), and on that basis, the Department of Interior downlisted the darter to threatened status. (The condemned valley lands produced no model industrial city. Today, its primary economic activity is the development of upper-income retirement communities with a country club and golf courses, and an industrial park located as proposed in the citizens' river-based alternative.[21])

6. The precedential results of *TVA v. Hill*'s enforcement of the §7 roadblock. Due in no small measure to its notoriety in the dam-blocking case, ESA §7 became a significant regulatory program in the years immediately following the snail darter decision, with substantial increases in annual FWS budget allocations and a new degree of (sometimes grudging) respect for its regulatory potency from agency bureaucrats and industrial lobbyists. Scientific surveys for endangered species impacts became an accepted part of agency project planning and permit application processes. In many cases courts have strictly interpreted the ESA to the detriment of powerful market forces. Oil well leases have been delayed, a major East Coast refinery was scuttled in part because of endangered species problems, western water reclamation allocations have been changed to favor species protection over industrial and municipal use, and the courts have enforced the Act without reference to the "significance" of the species concerned. How strong would the courts have been in these cases had not the Supreme Court held such a strong line in a highly publicized case poising an "insignificant" species against a purported multimillion dollar project? The snail darter precedent seems to have secured a basic protection for endangered species likely to be with us for a long time, and the roadblock provisions of ESA §7 deserve credit.

The process of "slippage" in environmental statutory protection, however, is a familiar part of the history of progressive regulations, as noted in Section C, below.

---

21. TVA strove to sell the condemned lands for development, but without much success. The first development proposal after two years of stagnation was to create a regional toxic waste facility on the valley lands; the citizens quashed it. Subsequently, TVA transferred a substantial portion of the valley, on a subsidized basis, to a second-home vacation housing developer. The industrial park (smaller than the industrial park included as part of the citizens' non-dam alternative plan) has attracted a number of businesses.

7. A tactical footnote on ESA legislative history. Would it change your view of ESA §7 if you were told that it had been consciously drafted by a legislative aide and several ardent wildlife advocates in a form that would avoid its being recognized as a substantive roadblock statute? If §7, which has become one of the landmark environmental protections in federal law, would never have been passed without a virtually impenetrable verbal camouflage, what does that say about Congress and the legislative process? What does it say about the ethics of the provision's drafters, who successfully slipped it into federal law? Is it a satisfactory excuse that the opponents of environmental protection regularly slip exceptions and destructive undercutting amendments into ongoing legislation? The tactical questions that arise when environmentalists actively participate in the legislative process continually force thoughtful people to reconsider their philosophy of government, views of public interest advocacy, and ethics. And the text at the beginning of this chapter virtually admits that the plaintiffs used the snail darter as a convenient "handle" to raise public issues about farmland, historic values, river recreation, and economics. As Justice Burger said during the oral argument, "the snail darter was discovered, and became a handy handle [for dam opponents] to hold onto. . . . I'm sure that they just don't want this project!" Was this litigation a misuse of the law, one that moreover selfishly risked the destruction of the ESA itself?

3. ESA §9 and the "No Take" Provision

> The ESA contains another major roadblock provision, ESA §9, potentially even more politically explosive because it can impact human activity on private land as well as federal agencies. Once the Supreme Court upheld §7 in *TVA v. Hill*, the political players worried about the leveraging effect of endangered species upon development and resource exploitation activities sought to limit the looming threat of ESA §9, as in the following case where the Northern Spotted Owl[22] and Red Cockaded Woodpecker could bring scrutiny to the operations of timber, oil and gas, mining, big agriculture, and many other major enterprises.

Babbitt v. Sweet Home Communities for a Great Oregon
515 U.S. 687 (U.S. Sup. Ct. 1995)

STEVENS, J. The Endangered Species Act of 1973 contains a variety of protections designed to save from extinction species that the Secretary of the Interior designates as endangered or threatened. . . . Section 9(a)(1) of the Endangered Species Act provides the following protection for endangered species:

> With respect to any endangered species of fish or wildlife listed pursuant to §1533 of this title it is unlawful for any person subject to the jurisdiction of the United States to . . . (B) take any such species within the United States or the territorial sea of the United States. 16 U.S.C. §1538(a)(1).

Section 3(19) of the Act, 16 U.S.C. §1532(19), defines the statutory term "take":

> The term "take" means to harass, harm, pursue, hunt, shoot, wound, kill, trap, capture, or collect, or to attempt to engage in any such conduct.

---

22. Some material on the spotted owl is posted on the coursebook's website.

B. The ESA as a Roadblock Statute

The Act does not further define the terms it uses to define "take." The Interior Department regulations that implement the statute, however, 50 C.F.R. §17.3, define the statutory term "harm":

> "Harm" in the definition of "take" in the Act means an act which actually kills or injures wildlife. Such act may include significant habitat modification or degradation where it actually kills or injures wildlife by significantly impairing essential behavioral patterns, including breeding, feeding, or sheltering. . . .

Respondents in this action are small landowners, logging companies, and families dependent on the forest products industries in the Pacific Northwest and in the Southeast, and organizations that represent their interests. They brought this declaratory judgment action against petitioners . . . to challenge the statutory validity of the Secretary's regulation defining "harm," particularly the inclusion of habitat modification and degradation in the definition. . . . Their complaint alleged that application of the "harm" regulation to the red-cockaded woodpecker, an endangered species, and the northern spotted owl, a threatened species, had injured them economically. . . .

We assume respondents have no desire to harm either the red-cockaded woodpecker or the spotted owl; they merely wish to continue logging activities that would be entirely proper if not prohibited by the ESA. On the other hand, we must assume arguendo that those activities will have the effect, even though unintended, of detrimentally changing the natural habitat of both listed species and that, as a consequence, members of those species will be killed or injured. Under respondents' view of the law, the Secretary's only means of forestalling that grave result—even when the actor knows it is certain to occur—is to use his §5 authority to purchase the lands on which the survival of the species depends. . . .

The text of the Act provides three reasons for concluding that the Secretary's interpretation is reasonable. . . . The dictionary definition of the verb form of "harm" is "to cause hurt or damage; to injure." In the context of the ESA, that definition naturally encompasses habitat modification that results in actual injury or death to members of an endangered or threatened species. . . . The dictionary definition does not include the word "directly" or suggest in any way that only direct or willful action that leads to injury constitutes "harm." . . .

Second, the broad purpose of the ESA supports the Secretary's decision to extend protection against activities that cause the precise harms Congress enacted the statute to avoid. In *TVA v. Hill*, 437 U.S. 153 (1978), we described the Act as "the most comprehensive legislation for the preservation of endangered species ever enacted by any nation," . . . among its central purposes is "to provide a means whereby the ecosystems upon which endangered species and threatened species depend may be conserved." "The plain intent of Congress in enacting this statute," we recognized, "was to halt and reverse the trend toward species extinction, whatever the cost. This is reflected not only in the stated policies of the Act, but in literally every section of the statute." Although the §9 "take" prohibition was not at issue in *Hill*, we took note of that prohibition, placing particular emphasis on the Secretary's inclusion of habitat modification in his definition of "harm." . . . Respondents . . . ask us to invalidate the Secretary's understanding of "harm" in every circumstance, even when an actor knows that an activity, such as draining a pond, would actually result in the extinction of a listed species by destroying its habitat. . . .

Third, the fact that Congress in 1982 authorized the Secretary to issue permits for takings that §9(a)(1)(B) would otherwise prohibit, "if such taking is incidental to, and not the purpose of, the carrying out of an otherwise lawful activity," 16 U.S.C. §1539(a)(1)(B), strongly suggests that Congress understood §9(a)(1)(B) to prohibit indirect as well as deliberate takings. . . . Several of the words that accompany "harm" in the §3 definition of "take," especially "harass," "pursue," "wound," and "kill," refer to actions or effects that do not require direct applications of force. . . . The statutory context of "harm" suggests that Congress meant that term to serve a particular function in the ESA, consistent with but distinct from the functions of the other verbs used to define "take." . . . The House Report underscored the breadth of the "take" definition by noting that it included "harassment, whether intentional or not. . . ." When Congress has entrusted the Secretary with broad discretion, we are especially reluctant to substitute our views of wise policy for his. See *Chevron*. . . . Based on the text, structure, and legislative history of the ESA, . . . the Secretary reasonably construed the intent of Congress when he defined "harm" to include "significant habitat modification or degradation that actually kills or injures wildlife." . . . Reversed.

    O'CONNOR, J., concurring. . . . The challenged regulation is limited to significant habitat modification that causes actual, as opposed to hypothetical or speculative, death or injury to identifiable protected animals. . . . I do not find it as easy as Justice Scalia does to dismiss the notion that significant impairment of breeding injures living creatures. To raze the last remaining ground on which the piping plover currently breeds, thereby making it impossible for any piping plovers to reproduce, would obviously injure the population (causing the species' extinction in a generation). But by completely preventing breeding, it would also injure the individual living bird, in the same way that sterilizing the creature injures the individual living bird. To "injure" is, among other things, "to impair." . . . To make it impossible for an animal to reproduce is to impair its most essential physical functions and to render that animal, and its genetic material, biologically obsolete. This, in my view, is actual injury. . . .

    SCALIA, J., joined by REHNQUIST, C.J., and THOMAS, J., dissenting. I think it unmistakably clear that the legislation at issue here (1) forbade the hunting and killing of endangered animals, and (2) provided federal lands and federal funds for the acquisition of private lands, to preserve the habitat of endangered animals. . . . To "take," when applied to wild animals, means to reduce those animals, by killing or capturing, to human control . . . , a class of acts (not omissions) done directly and intentionally (not indirectly and by accident) to particular animals (not populations of animals). . . . "Harm" is merely one of 10 prohibitory words . . . and the other 9 fit the ordinary meaning of "take" perfectly. To "harass, pursue, hunt, shoot, wound, kill, trap, capture, or collect" are all affirmative acts . . . which are directed immediately and intentionally against a particular animal. . . .

    The regulation . . . produces a result that no legislature could reasonably be thought to have intended: A large number of routine private activities—farming, for example, ranching, road building, construction and logging—are subjected to strict-liability penalties when they fortuitously injure protected wildlife, no matter how remote the chain of causation. . . . [Justice Scalia, who (justifiably) is often skeptical about excessive reliance upon legislative history, then dismisses the majority's use of congressional committee reports that suggested "take" should be defined in "the broadest possible manner," as an "empty flourish."] Habitat modification can constitute a "taking," but only if it results in the killing or harming of individual animals, and only if that consequence is the direct result of the modification. This means that the destruction of privately owned habitat that is essential, not for the feeding or nesting, but for the breeding, of butterflies, would not violate the Act, since it would not harm or kill any living butterfly. . . . I respectfully dissent.

B. The ESA as a Roadblock Statute

COMMENTARY & QUESTIONS

1. Is the "take" prohibition a statutory roadblock or a reg-created roadblock? Note that in ESA §9, the roadblock was not created by the statute alone. It required agency elaboration of the meaning of the word *harm*, reinforced by *Chevron* deference. The potential consequences of the *Sweet Home* decision are dramatic. Land development, which traditionally has been one of the most unregulated, politically charged economic ventures, can now come under federal government scrutiny forcing intense review of the particular facts of a development site and plan, subject to heavy civil and criminal penalties. The definition of *harm* is subjective and potentially extremely broad ranging, and property that is determined important to endangered species may in effect be frozen. Is the roadblock primarily attributable to the statute or to the regulatory interpretation? Is this case a seminar on statutory interpretation or an administrative law exercise deciding whether to defer to an agency's interpretive regulation?

Sweet Home reflects one pitched battle in the ongoing war between western "Wise Use" local sovereigntyists, resource exploitation corporations, and private property rights activists, on the one hand, and the federal government, environmental preservationists, and others who think that endangered species law may provide the only effective forum for obtaining overall public accounting of challenged activities, on the other. The defenders won this round, but as Justice O'Connor noted, "Congress may, of course, see fit to revisit this issue. And nothing the Court says today prevents the agency itself from narrowing the scope of its regulation at a later date." 515 U.S. at 714.

2. Statutory interpretation games. The question is about the meaning of one of ten words—the meaning of *harm* in the statutory definition of *take*, as to "harass, harm, pursue, hunt, shoot, wound, kill, trap, capture, or collect." Is this another example of legislative legerdemain—*harm*, an environmentally protective phrase, being slipped into a statute by indirection, in this case on the Senate floor after *habitat destruction* had been stricken from the bill in committee? Or is it fairly within the central mandate of the Act? And what of conflicting canons of interpretation? *Noscitur a sociis*, "a word gathers meaning from the words around it," is a canon that the majority used to establish an interpretive context. *Sweet Home*'s dissenting narrow interpretationists had in mind the stricter *ejusdem generis*—"a word should be defined like the others in the same series, without independent meaning." Given the way lawyers in legislatures write statutes, which canonic interpretation should govern?

3. Administrative law: *Chevron* creates a roadblock. The *Sweet Home* majority and dissenting opinions treat the *Chevron* precedent differently. The majority said that "our conclusions that Congress did not unambiguously manifest its intent to adopt respondents' view, and that the Secretary's interpretation is reasonable, suffice to decide this case. *Chevron*. The latitude the ESA gives the Secretary in enforcing the statute, together with the degree of regulatory expertise necessary to its enforcement, establishes that we owe some degree of deference to the Secretary's reasonable interpretation," citing Breyer, Judicial Review of Questions of Law and Policy, 38 Admin. L. Rev. 363, 373 (1986). In dissent, Justice Scalia, a consistent supporter of broad *Chevron* deference to agencies, argued that here the Secretary's decision need not be deferred to because "the regulation . . . dispense[s] with a [necessary] proximate-cause requirement. . . . This Court . . . may not uphold a regulation by adding to it even the most reasonable of elements it does not contain." 515 U.S. at 733. Justice Scalia implied that he could ignore *Chevron* deference because he would find either that the agency interpretation was unreasonable or that it violated an express congressional mandate. For the majority, however, the agency's interpretation, backed with *Chevron* deference, created a strong statutory roadblock.

4. "Critical habitat" as another tooth in the ESA's bite. Looking back at the text of ESA §7 as it was in 1973 (all the elements of which remain in the current statute, but with much added—the section has grown from just 128 words to more than 4,400 words), note that there are two prohibitions, not just one. The familiar one is: Thou shalt not "jeopardize the continued existence" of an endangered or threatened species. But there's a second: Thou shalt not act in a manner that "result[s] in the destruction or modification of habitat of such species . . . determined critical." Which of the two is easier to prove in a contested case? And what exactly does it mean? At base, it requires consultation when an agency action may threaten to create habitat impacts. But to many ESA opponents it has been characterized as a potential federal lock-up against development in vast swathes of the nation, and over the years, the politics of critical habitat have been rocky, as noted below.

5. Protecting ecosystems instead of just individual species? If we want to preserve biodiversity, why don't we simply set aside bioreserves instead of indirectly attempting to preserve ecosystems through protection of individual endangered species? Much scholarly comment has been directed to the preferability of protecting entire ecosystems. The ESA, perhaps mistakenly, wasn't primarily targeted to preserve ecosystem habitats. Are we being fair, not only to ourselves but also to the spotted owls and snail darters of the world, when we use indicator species as legal "handles" to preserve critical ecosystems? Or does our political system, which functions to muddle through and "satisfice" conflicting demands, militate against attacking the habitat issue directly? If it is difficult to define and prohibit hazards to individual species, how much more difficult would it be to base protections on ecosystems? Is the species-oriented ESA only a stopgap measure while we build a political constituency for broader ecosystem and bioreserve protections?

C. "Slippage" and "Roadblock Bypasses"—Subsequent Modifications Temper Stark Standards (and What Conclusions Should Be Drawn from That?)

> As with many progressive statutes passed in a moment of focused popular political awareness, roadblock statutes like the Delaney Clause and the ESA almost immediately are faced with long-running campaigns of organized resistance within the daily political life of the capital, powerfully mounted by the parties and institutions that the statutes seek to constrain. On the other hand, the terms of laws passed in moments of passion and haste may turn out to be problematic or unworkable as drafted. No law remains static in a changing, politically-pressured world, and like other statutes the ESA continues evolving.[23] After some general notes on flexibility, this section uses some of the ESA's pressured evolutions as a case study in "slippage"[24] for good and ill.

---

23. For an intensive history of the process see D. Goble, J. Scott, and F. Davis, THE ENDANGERED SPECIES ACT AT THIRTY. Vols. 1 and 2 (2005).

24. See Farber, Taking Slippage Seriously: Noncompliance and Creative Compliance in Environmental Law, 23 Harv. Envtl. L. Rev. 297 (1999).

C. "Slippage" and "Roadblock Bypasses"

1. Flexibility Mechanisms in General

The realities of politics and the legal process have produced a variety of explicit and implicit flexibility mechanisms that can loosen strict roadblocks. Each mechanism presents the drawbacks and potential advantages of deviations from a clear rule.

Balancing accommodations can be made in the following ways, among others:

- Private ordering: When private parties—prompted by idealism, business judgment, public or media pressure, or apprehension about the costs of contesting a civic standard—decide to accept it, they are often able to construct practical and beneficial accommodations to eliminate the conflict.
- Agency conflict-resolving procedures: Interior, for example, has successfully resolved hundreds of potential endangered species conflicts through formal or informal ESA §7 interagency "consultation" processes,[25][28] pushing project agencies to alter harmful elements of their plans to adjust to the needs of species protection; there have been hundreds of similar negotiations with private parties under §9.
- Administrative interpretations of legal terms or facts: Agencies can, in practice, make or break a statute in the vast number of decisions that are made in the daily process of implementation—including how they define the terms of a statute or regulation, such as *harm* in *Sweet Home*, or by findings of fact that acknowledge, or evade, critical elements of the statutory mandate. The degree of transparency of the internal agency process can make a great difference in outcomes.
- Judicial interpretations of legal terms or facts: As with agency decisions, the role of courts in enforcement actions and judicial review can vary the strictness given to a roadblock. In the snail darter case, Justices Rehnquist and Powell were clearly ready to take on the legislative balancing act themselves. Court grants or denials of standing, reviewability, deference, narrow scope of review, and equitable relief can operate sub rosa to strengthen or weaken roadblocks.
- "Slippage" in administrative process, negative or positive, where agencies allow departures from the strict terms of statutes: In many cases, the logistics and politics of particular cases are such that administrative accommodations are made for a variety of reasons, salutary or corrosive, and neither official nor citizen strict-enforcement action occurs. In these settings, the practical state of the roadblock law is mutated by default.
- Legislative amendments that incorporate more or less rigorous balancing mechanisms: As noted below, the ESA offers prime examples, in the 1978 §7 God Committee exemption amendments and in the 1982 "incidental take" amendments to §9. Private property interests further pushed campaigns at the end of the 1990s to expand the incidental take exemptions to incorporate substantial "habitat conservation plan" bargaining into ESA enforcement, allowing moderate harms to endangered species. If balancing is consigned to agency discretion, the species protection process is likely to be narrowed, if not undercut.
- Legislative amendments that eliminate the roadblock provision: Faced with roadblocks, affected interests often seek to repeal the obstruction. Thus numerous environmental provisions that block industry practices, including wetlands and endangered species protections, are regularly targeted for repeal. Marketplace

---

25. There is always the possibility, of course, that the agency is diluting the law's standards in order to avoid controversy.

lobbying in the legislatures and agency rulemaking likewise try to rescind the procedures that implement a roadblock (as in Chapter 6's §318, selectively eliminating citizen enforcement of the ESA and forestry laws) or to override laws as applied to particular cases (as in the appropriations rider ultimately repealing the ESA insofar as it prevented TVA from building the Tellico Dam).

In each and every case, of course, the nature of the balance can vary widely, and opportunities for fudging in each direction are constantly presented. For this reason, no flexibility mechanism can be meaningfully evaluated without realistic consideration of its political context.

2. Flexibility and Slippage in the ESA

ESA §§7 and 9, as originally passed and as upheld by the Supreme Court in *TVA v. Hill* and *Sweet Home*, both embodied stark statutory roadblock prohibitions. This set up a classic dilemma of democratic process. Often in the history of important civic statutory innovations, after passage they face erosion bit by bit over the years by continued resistance from regulated interests. In addition to the ESA, NEPA and FOIA are examples of broad-coverage statutory restrictions of agency behavior that have experienced nibbling diminutions of their terms and enforceability under pressure from agency-industry blocs. The statutes' original protective terms encounter erosive efforts acting within the administrative process, congressional politics, and in the federal courts. As noted at the start of this chapter, any stark rule is likely to be a blunt instrument that falls short of perfect rationality, yet without the strength of such a strict clear rule the pressures of marketplace politics can often neutralize the nonmarket-based civic values that the law seeks to protect. The trick is to know when and how, if at all, a strict statutory standard should be altered.

Industry lobbyists have often used the snail darter case and the §9 cases leading to *Sweet Home* as "extreme examples" supporting a need for amending the ESA. Several legislative and administrative modifications of the ESA roadblocks have occurred, including §7 and §9 flexibility mechanisms noted in the following pages. A question in the ESA context, as in any roadblock setting, is whether and to what extent loosening provisions are necessary and appropriate.

a. The ESA §7 God Committee Amendment

As noted, after the Supreme Court's decision in *TVA v. Hill,* in response to a lobbying furor against "extremist" endangered species protections for the snail darter and its kind, Congress added a major exemption procedure to ESA §7,[26] creating a Cabinet-level review board comprised of the Administrators of EPA and NOAA, the Chair of the Council of Economic Advisors, a state representative, and the Secretaries of Army, Agriculture, Transportation, and Interior (sitting and judging the case themselves with no proxies). The Committee soon was dubbed the God Committee (and sometimes even more irreverently, the God Squad) because of its authority to permit extinction of a species if an agency satisfactorily proved a stringent set of criteria.

16 U.S.C. §1536(h) . . . The Committee shall grant an exemption . . . if, by a vote of not less than five of its [seven] members voting in person—

---

26. See 16 U.S.C. §1536 (e)-(o).

C. "Slippage" and "Roadblock Bypasses"

> (A) it determines on the record [after a full review of the data] that—
>   (i) there are no reasonable and prudent alternatives to the agency action;
>   (ii) the benefits of such action clearly outweigh the benefits of alternative courses of action consistent with conserving the species or its critical habitat, and such action is in the public interest;
>   (iii) the action is of regional or national significance; and
> (B) it establishes . . . : reasonable mitigation and enhancement measures, including, but not limited to, live propagation, transplantation, and habitat acquisition and improvement. . . .

The amendment stipulated that the snail darter – *Tellico* Dam case would be the subject of the God Committee's first meeting.[27]

COMMENTARY & QUESTIONS

1. The God Committee §7 amendment: tough tests or a sellout? The drafters' inclusion of two tests seriously examining and weighing alternatives (§A(i) and (ii) above)[28] forces the God Committee process to go into the heart of these project-species conflicts. As in NEPA cases, it is clear that one of the alternatives that must be considered is "no action." Thus the §7 God Committee's endangered species protections provide a forum to explore objective questions about whether a project or program substantively makes common sense, questions that often cannot be meaningfully raised anywhere else in the political or judicial system. Is this exemption process a regressive slippage, or a reasonable consolidation of the ESA's mission? In a rational world no rule can realistically be absolute. The standards are stringent, and could such a protective procedure have been legislated at the start absent the original roadblock?

2. The God Committee after the snail darter: the spotted owl. For more than a dozen years after the God Committee's rigorous review and unanimous decision in the snail darter case, no federal projects sought God Committee exemptions. In 1992 in the Northern spotted owl cases, however, facing inevitable §7 injunction actions, the Bush I Administration's Interior Secretary Manuel Lujan decided to seek a Committee exemption for the spotted owl. In a proceeding featuring accusations of improper pressure, God Committee members granted ESA exemptions for 13 timber-cutting contracts. In a citizen challenge of the decision, *Portland Audubon Soc'y v. Endangered Species Comm.*, 984 F.2d 1534, 1538 (9th Cir. 1993), the court noted the environmentalists' contention "that improper ex parte contacts between the White House and members of the Committee tainted the decision-making process. . . . According to two anonymous administration sources, at least three Committee members had been 'summoned' to the White House and pressured to vote for the exemption . . . [which] may have changed the vote of at least one Committee member." But because the timber sales were also blocked by NEPA and NFMA injunctions, the court did not issue a final ruling on the validity of the God Committee overrides. Subsequently President Clinton negotiated a Northwest Forests Initiative settling the litigation. See U.S. Forest Service & Bureau of Land Mgmt., Record of Decision for Amendments to Forest

---

27. The first convocation of the Committee was also directed to review Prof. Parenteau's injunction against the Greyrocks Dam that threatened the whooping crane.

28. Coincidentally, the Senate staffer who produced the first draft of the God Committee amendment with its requirements for scrutinizing project alternatives, like Hank Hill (the lead plaintiff), had studied environmental law with an early version of this coursebook in a University of Michigan natural resources course that emphasized the *Overton Park* balance.

Service and Bureau of Land Management Planning Documents Within the Range of the Northern Spotted Owl (1994).

In practice, the God Committee's exemption process is perceived as so rigorous and embarrassing that agencies will only rarely even consider undertaking the difficulties of obtaining one. In 2003, when protection for the Rio Grande silvery minnow threatened established water rights, the opponents obtained an appropriations bill rider exemption rather than face the scrutiny and extended procedures of God Committee review.[29] If the God Committee is a bypass to §7's roadblock, it is a tortuous one that does not easily circumvent the obstacle of §7. The net result seems to be a pragmatic compromise that leaves the U.S. with a potent legal provision protecting endangered species against harm caused by any federal agency actions.

b. The ESA Prohibitions Get Modified by the ESA §10 "Incidental Take" Exemption Amendment

The spotted owl, like the snail darter, aroused strong industry protests about the ESA's alleged irrational extremism. The spotted owl cases, as the later *Sweet Home* case showed, raised issues under the ESA §9 "take" prohibition as well as under ESA §7. In 1982, Congress was induced to pass further exemption balance mechanisms to shield certain private property owners from the §9 roadblock. The 1982 amendments created a new §10:[30]

> **16 U.S.C. §1539(a)(1). Permits [Incidental Take Permits (ITPs)].** The Secretary may permit, under such terms and conditions as he shall prescribe—
> ... (B) any taking otherwise prohibited by §9 if such taking is incidental to, and not the purpose of, the carrying out of an otherwise lawful activity.
> (2)(A) No permit may be issued by the Secretary authorizing any taking referred to in paragraph (1)(B) unless the applicant therefore submits to the Secretary a conservation plan [EDS.—universally referred to as an "HCP," a habitat conservation plan] that specifies—
> (i) the impact which will likely result from such taking;
> (ii) what steps the applicant will take to minimize and mitigate such impacts, and the funding that will be available to implement such steps;
> (iii) what alternative actions to such taking the applicant considered and the reasons why such alternatives are not being utilized; and
> (iv) such other measures that the Secretary may require as being necessary or appropriate for purposes of the plan.
> (B) If the Secretary finds, after opportunity for public comment, with respect to a permit application and the related conservation plan that—
> (i) the taking will be incidental;
> (ii) the applicant will, to the maximum extent practicable, minimize and mitigate the impacts of such taking;
> (iii) the applicant will ensure that adequate funding for the plan will be provided;
> (iv) the taking will not appreciably reduce the likelihood of the survival and recovery of the species in the wild; and

---

29. See *Rio Grande Silvery Minnow v. Keys*, 333 F.3d 1109 (10th Cir. 2003), vacated as moot, 2004 U.S. App. LEXIS 56 (10th Cir. 2004); Energy and Water Development Appropriations Act of 2004, Pub. L. No 108-137 §208(a), 117 Stat. 1827 (2003). The latter rider immunized only one federal water supply project from the trial court's intensive analysis and injunction, but the residuum was rendered moot by the end of drought conditions, governmental water use adjustments, and the injunction's own limited duration.

30. Pub. L. No. 95-632 (1982). The amendments also created a simpler incidental take exemption process for federal agencies, who can apply for and receive an immunity "incidental take statement" without binding promises or a conservation plan. 16 U.S.C. §1536(b)(4)(B) & (C).

C. "Slippage" and "Roadblock Bypasses"

> (v) the measures, if any, required under subparagraph (A)(iv) will be met; and he has received such other assurances as he may require that the plan will be implemented, the Secretary shall issue the permit. The permit shall contain such terms and conditions as the Secretary deems necessary or appropriate. . . .

This incidental take exemption provision theoretically allows the Secretary to modify unnecessary burdens placed on property owners by §9, but it also reflects many of the potential risks that lie in retrenchments from roadblocks.

Was this flexibility amendment a good idea? Note the elements that may be quite permissive: Almost any harm to species from habitat destruction will be "incidental" since virtually no market projects set out purposefully to harm species. The requirement that harms to species must be minimized "to the maximum extent practicable" could be a major loophole, interpreted to allow the developer's own practicalities to dominate the balance. The element requiring that "the taking . . . not appreciably reduce the likelihood of survival and recovery" retreats from the statutory goal of improving the chances for recovery, and "not appreciably" is an indeterminate measure. Ultimately the rationality of the balance struck under §10 depends completely on the Secretary. If he or she wishes to hold applicants to high standards for HCPs and strict terms for extensive mitigations, and is stringent in setting "such other measures that the Secretary may require as being necessary and appropriate," then the balance may be sufficiently protective of species. If a Secretary doesn't like the Act, however, he or she in practice can use the permissive terms to eviscerate §9. The Secretary's decisions, moreover, are effectively immune from citizen suits, so the amendment rolls the law back to the old dipolar system where the public interest depends totally on bureaucratic enforcement.[31]

For a decade after the incidental take amendments to the §9 roadblock, surprisingly few permits were granted—less than 20 from 1982 to 1994—but beginning in 1993 the Clinton administration dramatically accelerated the volume of §10 HCP exemptions, with more than 500 approved by 2002 with 200 pending. Most of the early HCPs covered areas of less than 1000 acres. In applications after 1996, 25 exceeded 10,000 acres in size, 25 exceeded 100,000 acres, and 18 exceeded 500,000 acres. The volume and character of permits mean that it is extremely difficult to gauge how the balancing process works in practice.[32] Some HCPs and §10 permits appear to be biologically sophisticated and carefully

---

31. The elements of the exemption are determined by relatively unreviewable agency discretion, HCPs are designed to exclude citizen enforceability (the FWS itself expressly proposes that the public not be granted the status of third party beneficiaries (see HCP Handbook App. 9 Template Agreement §14.8.)), and the most citizens can do is try to prove that particular exemption shortcomings "jeopardize the existence" of endangered species, a tough burden. The legal opponents are likewise tough: The property owners who take advantage of §10 are unlikely to be the little guys who can least bear the burdens of ESA restrictions and whose limited property holdings have limited impacts. It takes a lot of time, money, biologists, and lawyers to negotiate a §10 exemption, and those who do so will fight to defend their permits.

32. See Hood, Frayed Safety Nets: Conservation Planning Under the ESA (1998), Symposium, 27 Envtl. L. 755-877 (1997). A number of studies have concluded that because of political pressures and other constraints, the federal agencies with jurisdiction over endangered species — Interior's FWS and Commerce's NOAA— are underprotecting species in their recovery planning under the ESA. Tear et al., Status and Prospects for Success of the Endangered Species Act: A Look at Recovery Plans, Sci., Nov. 1993, at 976.

balanced to protect the species while accommodating human uses.[33] Others appear to be hapless political capitulations.[34]

> A group of scientists funded by the National Science Foundation released the results of the first comprehensive study of HCPs.... Among the more disturbing findings of the study are these: over three-quarters of the plans lacked such basic information as the population size of species and whether it was growing or shrinking; a third of the plans did not know the life spans of the species at issue; over half did not have adequate monitoring, without which, of course, there is no way to tell whether the measures are working or not; of the 44 plans studied in depth, many prescribed mitigation measures that would do more harm than good. Parenteau, Vermont Law School, Letter to New England Senators, Mar. 3, 1998.

In the subsequent 15 years, the quality of official HCPs did not appreciably improve. Nevertheless, a number of committed environmental leaders have urged further regulatory changes to the ESA. Some wish to strengthen protections by encouraging multispecies and ecosystem-wide protections rather than species-by-species regulation.[35] Ecosystem and biodiversity concepts[36] are far more realistic measures of natural habitat qualities than are single-species indicators, but their subtleties make them less feasible as legal concepts. Other environmentalists, traumatized by the close call the ESA barely survived in the 104th Congress and noting that Interior is barely enforcing the politically explosive take prohibitions, urge further preemptive modification of the strictness of §9. "Eco-pragmatism" is not only a recognition that climatic change will require some inevitable trade-off sacrifices, but also that practical politics will render some compromises in what is protected and how. Given the dramatic goals of the ESA and the widespread human-based character of species endangerment, it is inevitable that major political conflicts arise in ESA enforcement. It is probably equally inevitable that some agency officials will avoid strong enforcement of their statutory mandate in order to avoid exacerbating the political context. Is this a problem or a solution?

COMMENTARY & QUESTIONS

1. The §10 incidental take statutory standards. Where are the legal teeth in the §10 amendment? Note how its legal elements effectively move away from citizen enforceability in courts to a reliance on the energy and judgment of the Secretary of Interior. A tough

---

33. The authors have been impressed, for instance, by the Atlantic Coast Piping Plover HCP and Massachusetts's three-year experimental permit allowing restricted dune buggy use of the plover's beach habitat.

34. HCPs and permits allowing large timber companies to cut down nest trees of red-cockaded woodpeckers after waiting 60 days for them to find alternative homes seem to verge on the cynical.

35. The ecosystem approach makes sense: "By overemphasizing the role of single chemicals, and single media in pollution policy, and of single species in land management policy, we underestimate the interactive effects of chemicals, the cross-media effects of emissions, and the interdependence of habitats." Chertow & Esty, Environmental Policy: The Next Generation, Issues in Sci. & Tech., Fall 1997, at 74. Ecosystem proposals, however, run the practical risk of magnifying what already are very difficult scientific requirements for proposing and defending species protections.

36. *Biodiversity* as a regulatory concept can be difficult to define. It means something more than merely having larger numbers of species: If a road is cut through a wilderness rainforest or tundra, it *increases* the net number of species but extirpates unique native indicator species. Conservation biologists prefer a concept of *native biodiversity* or *continuum biodiversity* to capture the goal of diverse natural communities evolving as much as possible without anthropogenic disturbances, but the regulatory complexities that would be required have militated five initiatives in that direction. See D. Perlman & G. Adelson, Biodiversity: Exploring Values & Priorities in Conservation (1997).

C. "Slippage" and "Roadblock Bypasses"

conservation-minded Secretary could hold the incidental take permit process to a very rigorous standard, but an antiregulationist, business-minded Secretary could apply the terms extremely permissively. In either case, note how subjective the decision is likely to be, and given judicial deference to agency discretion and expertise, not easily reversible in court. One scholar of agency decisionmaking and the §10 habitat conservation plan program has concluded that "the experience of the HCP program is that there is a lack of will and incentives for the Services and permittees to engage in earnest contingency planning or adaptive management," and the limitation of citizen participation indicates that statutory standards are unlikely to be met. Camacho, Can Regulation Evolve? Lessons from a Study in Maladaptive Management, 55 UCLA L. Rev. 293, 344 (2007).

2. Klamath Basin suckerfish and the expedited federal agency incidental take bypass. Under the terms of the ESA's incidental take permit amendment, the standard for federal agency exemptions is easier than for private parties. For federal agencies, all that is required to permit takes that hurt members of the species is a biological opinion letter ("incidental take statement") from the Secretary asserting that the action would not jeopardize the species' existence, thus overriding the agency's obligations under both §7 and §9.[37] This process was used in the rancorous Klamath Basin case. In July 2001, a district judge ordered a halt to federal irrigation water withdrawals because low water conditions caused by several years of drought and increasing small farm withdrawals from the Klamath River severely threatened three endangered species. (In the outcry that followed, which of the three affected species—the bald eagle, the coho salmon, or the Klamath suckerfish—inevitably received the vast majority of press and talk-radio mention?) The Bush II Administration quickly issued an incidental take statement permitting irrigation water withdrawals, killing 33,000 salmon and uncounted other fish. In 2009, a negotiation between many but not all stakeholders, produced a Klamath Basin Restoration Agreement that may allocate water sufficiently to protect the river, and remove four dams by 2020, *if* $40 million in annual federal funding is consistently provided.

3. The "critical habitat" roadblock gets bypassed. Destruction and modification of habitat are the most significant causes of species extinction. Remember that the ESA §7 roadblock provisions forbid not only federal actions that "jeopardize" species existence but also the "destruction or modification of [critical] habitat." The Department of Interior began listing geographic areas in which existing endangered species lived and some further areas into which species populations could re-expand in order to achieve "recovery."

Critical habitat, the second §7 roadblock, however, has been far more of a political football than the "jeopardy" provision. As Professor Parenteau has noted:

> Critical habitat designation has always been controversial. State and local governments may see it as an unwelcome federal intrusion into local land use matters. Private landowners see it as diminishing the value and development potential of their property. Wary of this political mine field, the wildlife agencies have found lots of reasons not to designate critical habitat—not possible, not prudent, not now.[38] Consequently, despite the statutory command that "the Secretary shall designate critical habitat," and shall do so "concurrently" with the listing, only one-fifth

---

37. ESA §7(b)(4) implicitly authorizes federal agency "incidental takes" based on consultation and a biological opinion letter.

38. The 1978 ESA amendments required that critical habitat always be officially listed at the same time as a species is listed, unless the Secretary finds that the geographic area is "not determinable" or listing is "not prudent" or will produce more costs than benefits. ESA §4(b). The amendment was offered by Senator Garn, a staunch foe of the Act, perhaps in the hope that the political and scientific difficulties of listing critical habitat would serve to constrain the listing of species as well. [EDS.]

of listed species have had critical habitat declared. As with listing decisions, citizens can and do use the ESA's citizen suit provision to challenge the agencies' failure to designate critical habitat. On the other side of the coin, opponents of critical habitat designations have had some success arguing that such designations [require] preparation of an environmental impact statement. Parenteau, Rearranging the Deck Chairs: Endangered Species Act Reforms in an Era of Mass Extinction, 22 Wm. & Mary Envtl. L. & Pol'y Rev. 227, 262-263 (1998).

The potential force of the critical habitat roadblock thus gets bypassed by administrative nonlisting and underenforcement. Critical habitat protection particularly serves the ESA purpose of promoting species recovery, not simply bare survival, in viable sustainable populations. In 1999, however, Secretary Bruce Babbitt's Department of Interior signaled its desire to get out of the habitat-listing business by suggesting that the jeopardy test was all that was necessary:

> We have long believed that, in most circumstances, the designation of "official" critical habitat is ... duplicative, ... of little additional value for most listed species, yet it consumes large amounts of conservation resources.... For almost all species, the adverse modification and jeopardy standards are the same, resulting in critical habitat being an expensive regulatory process that duplicates the protection already provided by the jeopardy standard. 64 Fed. Reg. 31871-74 (June 14, 1999).

Subsequent courts have held, however, that it is improper to conflate and collapse the two protections into one.[39] Yet the politics of critical habitat continue.

c. A Protective Balance: Avoiding the "Sunk Cost Tactic"

Mechanisms for statutory balancing like the God Committee can easily become politicized tactical battlegrounds. One congressional response to this problem was a later ESA §7(d) amendment. In a host of major cases such as the *TVA v. Hill* battles over the Little Tennessee River and Chapter 6's *Overton Park* case, project promoters try to accelerate construction in the face of potential legal constraints, pouring so much concrete or cutting so many trees before a citizen group can finally get to a court hearing that the proponents can then argue that the balance now tips decisively in their favor, or that statutory compliance has regrettably become irrational or moot. ESA §7(d) was added to prevent just such disingenuity:

> **16 U.S.C. §1536(d).** After initiation of consultation ... the Federal agency and the permit or license applicant shall not make any irreversible or irretrievable commitment of resources with respect to ... agency action which has the effect of foreclosing the formulation or implementation of any reasonable or prudent alternative measures....

This provision is intended to undercut the sunk-cost strategy that can foreclose the God Committee balancing process. It is not well understood, however. See Kopf, Steamrolling §7(d) of the ESA: How Sunk Costs Undermine Environmental Regulations, 23 B.C. Envtl. Aff. L. Rev. 393 (1996); Houck, The "Institutionalization of Caution" under §7 of the Endangered Species Act: What Do You Do When You Don't Know?, 12 Envtl. L. Rep. 15001 (1982); and cf. *Bays' Legal Fund v. Browner*, 828 F. Supp. 102 (D. Mass. 1993) (court ignores ongoing construction despite §7(d), saying $4 billion sewage system could be abandoned later if species threat makes it advisable to do so).

---

39. See *NRDC v. U.S. Dep't of the Interior*, 113 F.3d 1121 (9th Cir. 1997); *Sierra Club v. FWS*, 245 F.3d 434 (5th Cir. 2001); *Gifford Pinchot Task Force v. U.S. Fish & Wildlife Serv.*, 378 F.3d 1059 (9th Cir. 2004).

C. "Slippage" and "Roadblock Bypasses"

d. "Sunsetting"—The ESA Lives on Borrowed Time

Many public interest statutes on the verge of passage are saddled by their opponents with last-minute "sunset" provisions, typically terminating the law after a given amount of time unless Congress can be persuaded to reauthorize it. (This is how the assault weapon ban was removed from federal law by the NRA's successful effort to block reauthorization.) The 1973 ESA was passed with a sunset provision of five years, which virtually guarantees its awkward status as a political football. The ESA has not been reauthorized since 1982, but survives on yearly "continuing resolution" funding bills. The ESA, despite broad public support, appears to be much more congressionally embattled than other federal environmental statutes. With only occasional exceptions, the political marketplace has generally come to accept the validity and permanence of pollution and toxics statutes. But the ESA is still regularly subjected to plenary denunciations on the floor of Congress, faces serious nonreauthorization initiatives, was hit by a sweeping one-year listing moratorium, and has faced hundreds of restrictive amendments. Between 2011 and 2015, "there have been at least 164 legislative attacks on endangered species, for an average of 33 per year,"[40] most sponsored by the timber, oil and gas, and big agriculture industries. In the 15 years prior there were fewer than 5 per year.

Why is it that the ESA suffers from this particular precariousness? Pollution and toxics statutes have come to be accepted by agencies and industry, primarily because their direct human utility is intrinsically obvious to public opinion. The societal rationale for endangered species conservation, on the other hand, is generally characterized in terms of philosophy, emotions, and aesthetics—often regarded as heartfelt but not so substantially significant when weighed against the "practical" world of production, payrolls, and profits.

The ESA would clearly gain political strength if it were publicly recognized to fulfill significant utilitarian functions as well. Utility arguments can be made far beyond the physical or medicinal use of individual species.[41] The predominant cause of endangerment is not hunting or trapping or market harvesting. It is the alteration and destruction of habitat. Because of this, endangered species often play a role serving human utility by identifying problems and triggering protections for habitat areas and conditions that hold threatened human values as well.

The "canary in the coal mine" indicator role is not necessarily the primary or an omnipresent function of the ESA, but it deserves recognition as a tangible and systemically important function lying within the logic of endangered species protection generally, one that is at least potentially relevant in every case. The ESA's provisions are likely to wax or wane in its current political gauntlets depending on how the various utilities of species protection are publicly perceived.

3. The ESA Listing Hurdle and De-Listing

The key to the ESA is the §4 listing process. If a species is not on the official federal Endangered Species List, none of the Act's protections will apply. The Secretary of

---

40. See J. Pang and N. Greenwald, THE POLITICS OF EXTINCTION (July 2015).
41. "Traditionally, endangered species protection is not viewed as pollution control. It is, however, in a larger sense exactly that. Endangered species are useful, though incomplete, indicators of the health stems and of the earth we share. While the best indicators may often be mollusks, plants and lower life forms, the decline of the bald eagle from the effects of chlorinated hydrocarbons is a good indication of the impact of those chemicals on human life. As water quality becomes inadequate to protect the delta smelt, it will also become inadequate for human uses." Houck, Why Do We Protect Endangered Species, and What Does That Say About Whether Restrictions on Private Property to Protect Them Constitute "Takings"?, 80 Iowa L. Rev. 297, 327-328 (1995).

Interior, the federal official overseeing the ESA (acting on the expertise of Interior's FWS and NOAA's National Marine Fisheries Service), plays a strategic decisional role in creating roadblocks—or not—each time a species is considered for official ESA listing. ESA §4 says:

> The Secretary shall . . . determine whether any species is an endangered species or a threatened species because of any of the following factors:
> (A) the present or threatened destruction, modification, or curtailment of its habitat or range;
> (B) overutilization for commercial, recreational, scientific, or educational purposes;
> (C) disease or predation;
> (D) the inadequacy of existing regulatory mechanisms; or
> (E) other natural or manmade factors affecting its continued existence. [and] shall, concurrently . . . designate [critical] habitat. . . . ESA §4(a)(1, 3), 16 U.S.C. §1533(a)(1), (3).

And from the Definitions section:

> "Endangered species" means any species which is in danger of extinction throughout all or a significant portion of its range. . . . 16 U.S.C. §1532(6).[42]

The statute says "shall," but are the definition and criteria objectively clear? What degree of endangerment of extinction crosses the line to require listings? The regulations, 50 C.F.R. §17.1ff, add some specificity to the statutory definitions but still leave room for agency discretion. Coupled with the large numbers of species potentially deserving listing (tens of thousands according to some scientists) and the political storms that listings can provoke, any flexibility in the decision to list or not inevitably becomes contentious. In numerous lawsuits, the gatekeeping listing process has been challenged from both directions. Are Pacific Northwest salmon species endangered if the wild natives are dying out and the bulk of a run is dependent on continual hatchery stocking?[43] Is the Northern spotted owl really a separate population and truly declining? What about Western gray wolves which were listed, then de-listed, and their non-re-listing reflects subtleties of biology in a mixed political context?[44] The emerging doctrine is that science, not politics, should dominate the listing process, but practicalities and pressures will continue to focus on the threshold §4 decision.

> Almost since the passage of the ESA in 1973 . . . there has been a backlog of species needing protection but not receiving it, in many cases for decades. This problem became particularly acute during the Bush II Administration. In total, the administration only protected 62 species over the entire 8 years, despite a list of over 250 candidate species, of which many had been waiting for protection for 20 or more years. . . . At least 42 species have gone extinct waiting for protection.[45]

---

42. "Species" includes "any subspecies of fish or wildlife or plants, and any *distinct population segment* (DPS) of any species of vertebrate fish or wildlife which interbreeds when mature." §1532(16) (emphasis added). In 1991, NMFS issued a Policy Statement defining a DPS as an "evolutionarily significant unit" (ESU) "of the biological species." 56 Fed. Reg. 58612, 58618 (Nov. 20, 1991). "'Threatened species' means any species which is likely to become an endangered species within the foreseeable future throughout all or a significant portion of its range." §1532(20). "'Critical habitat' . . . means the specific areas within the geographical area occupied by the species . . . essential to the conservation of the species and . . . [specially designated] areas outside the geographical area occupied. . . ." §1532(5).

43. See *Alsea Valley Alliance v. Lautenbacher*, No. 06-6093-HO (D. Or. 2007) (salmon listing), www.earthjustice.org/library/legal_docs/salmon-ruling-81407.pdf; *Ctr. for Biological Diversity v. Norton*, No. 05 CV 1988 BEN (S.D. Cal. 2005) (dune scarab beetle); *Ctr. for Biological Diversity v. FWS*, No. CV 03-1110 JDB (D.D.C. 2004) (arctic grayling).

44. See 74 Fed. Reg. 15123 (Apr. 2, 2009) for a fascinating exploration of the puzzle.

45. Noah Greenwald, Center for Biological Diversity, message to authors, 27 Dec. 2015.

C. "Slippage" and "Roadblock Bypasses"

In 2011, a coalition of environmental groups led by the Center for Biological Diversity and WildEarth Guardians in a multi-species, multi-district litigation[46] forced the Department of Interior to negotiate a national settlement agreeing that the agency would make decisions on 757 species that had been languishing in the FWS bureaucracy. Many of the species in the files had been scientifically determined to deserve listing, but the agency had classified them as "warranted-but-precluded" under a statutory amendment authorizing delay in listing due to restricted agency resources, so long as the agency acted as expeditiously as possible,"[47] and the groups had prevailed in prior actions determining that the agency was not moving expeditiously.[48] As of the beginning of 2016, the agency had made decisions on close to 700 of the 757 species, issuing positive decisions for roughly 88% of these species.

But some FWS decisions on long-lingering species files raise a sensitive question: Can the FWS rely upon promises in unenforceable voluntary agreements to decide that a species does not require protective listing?

Among other recent examples[49] is the case of the greater sage grouse. For many years the grouse had been fully scientifically determined to deserve listing on the factual record. It was spread over 11 states, with virtually all its populations stressed by roads, oil and gas operations, and wind turbines so that its numbers had declined from millions to low thousands. The pressure from the oil and gas and agriculture industries in particular induced the Obama Administration's Department of Interior to find that "listing the greater sage-grouse is not warranted at this time" based on a multi-state voluntary agreement.[50] Fish and Wildlife Service, the agency that made the grouse decision, presented it as ecologically preferable because its effects would not only protect the grouse but also "more than 350 other species that share the landscape. And preserving such habitats means that important natural processes continue, like pollination and the storage in vegetation of carbon dioxide from the atmosphere." The video release declared the decision a substantial victory for the environment; it did not note that the government plan depended on the potential vagaries of voluntary enforcement by 11 Western states.[51]

The *de-listing* of species is likewise a substantial ESA issue. The gray wolf is a focal example: In 2009, FWS published separate rules removing protections in the northern Rockies and western Great Lakes, allowing wolf-hunting to move forward in both regions where political opposition to wolves was intense. The agency used the terms of "distinct population segments" (DPSs) — originally intended to extend protections to specific areas where a species was endangered while not endangered in other areas; bald eagles, for instance, exist in abundant, stable, sustainable populations in Alaska — to justify lifting protections from gray wolves in those areas on the theory that those populations were sustainable. Initially, the de-listings were overruled by court action, but quite unprecedentedly in April 2011 Congress attached a rider to a budget bill that stripped ESA protections from wolves in Montana, Idaho, eastern Washington and Oregon, and part of northern Utah, removing

---

46. Misc. Action No. 10-377 (EGS), MDL Docket No. 2165 (D. D.C. Sept. 9, 2011). See Jesup, Endless War or End This War? The History of Deadline Litigation Under Section 4 of the Endangered Species Act and The Multi-District Litigation Settlements, 14 Vt. J. Envtl Law 327 (2013).

47. ESA 16 U.S.C. §§1533(b)(3)(B)(iii)(I).

48. *Biodiversity Conservation Alliance et al. vs. Kempthorne*, Civ No. 1:04-CV-02026 (GK) (D. D.C. 2006).

49. See, e.g., Defenders of Wildlife White Paper, The Dunes Sagebrush Lizard: The Cautionary Tale of a Candidate Species Denied (2013).

50. 80 FR 59857, October 2, 2015. See the voluntary plan, issued May 28, 2015: Department of Interior, Fact Sheet: BLM, USFS Greater Sage-Grouse Conservation Effort.

51. Dept. of Interior video announcement, Sept. 22, 2015, by Secretary of Interior Sally Jewell, available at https://www.youtube.com/watch?v=OHUsVfmyXhg.

listing for those areas without supporting scientific evidence. In 2013, moreover, the Obama Administration issued a proposal to remove ESA protections from gray wolves across all the lower 48 states (except for the Southwest's Mexican gray wolf). In 2014, however, federal court rulings restored federal protections to wolves in Wyoming and the western Great Lakes states, in effect stalling federal plans to remove gray wolf protections across the lower 48 states except where the congressional rider had de-listed them.

4. Agency Implementation Slippage — Consultation

The ESA §7 roadblock provision in its original form contained a bare requirement for endangered species "consultation" between the Department of Interior and other agencies. When it became clear that §7 was strictly enforceable, the consultation process evolved quickly in agency practice to mediate conflicting interests. The formal consultation process has been elaborated and regularized by amendments and regulations. 16 U.S.C. §1536(b)(3) (1978); 50 C.F.R. pt. 402. If agencies, field staff, or concerned citizens believe that a possible species problem exists, they request the Department of Interior to do a Biological Assessment (BA) to ascertain if it is so. If the BA finds a threat to an endangered species, the project agency requests formal consultation, which triggers a strict time schedule. FWS undertakes active consultation and must issue a Biological Opinion ("BiOp," or "Jeopardy Opinion"), analyzing the conflict and suggesting alternatives, if necessary, within 90 days. In the aftermath of *TVA v. Hill*, compliance with these procedures became far more consistent. When a BiOp Jeopardy Opinion is issued indicating a threat to a species' continued existence, agencies tend to react to avoid the threat, knowing that if they do not, citizen enforcement is likely to follow. An attempt by the Bush II Administration to modify ESA rules to allow agencies to "self-consult" (determining by their own BAs that further ESA compliance was unnecessary) was reversed by the Obama Administration under special statutory authorization in Public Law 111-8.

The common political impression of ESA §7 consultations is that under the Obama Administration the process halted progress on a wide range of projects, frustrating agency programs and private investment. An extensive recent statistical study published in the Proceedings of the National Academy of Sciences, however, shows a strikingly different picture. From 1979-1991 (primarily GOP administrations) there were approximately 4000 formal consultations, with 26 projects stopped or substantially modified. From January 2008 to April 2015, there were 88,290 ESA §7 consultations—81,461 informal and 6829 formal (not counting 110,850 consultations recorded as "technical assistance" consultations). Analyzing the statistical data, the Malcom-Li Report noted:

> In contrast to conventional wisdom about §7 implementation, *no project* was stopped or extensively altered as a result of FWS finding jeopardy or adverse modification during this period.... Only *one*... consultation resulted in [a BiOp finding of] jeopardy. That project, however, was still allowed to proceed by adopting RPAs (Reasonably Prudent Alternatives) to minimize and partially offset its effects.[52]

And depending on one's perspective, this history of §7 consultations could reflect an effective ESA compliance implementation process, or an abdication of meaningful regulation. The National Academy of Sciences study addressed this question:

---

52. Jacob W. Malcom and Ya-Wei Li, DATA CONTRADICT COMMON PERCEPTIONS ABOUT A CONTROVERSIAL PROVISION OF THE US ENDANGERED SPECIES ACT, 3-4 (2015) (in Proceedings of the National Academy of Sciences of the United States of America, www.pnas.org/cgi/doi/10.1073/pnas.1516938112 (2015), emphasis added).

C. "Slippage" and "Roadblock Bypasses"

> There are at least three likely reasons for the observed [low number of] jeopardy or adverse modification outcomes. First, and perhaps the one envisioned by the drafters of the Act, can be characterized as policy learning: federal agencies have now learned to plan and propose projects that minimize harm to listed species. Some agencies are proposing projects with reduced impacts because they are coordinating more closely with FWS to shape the projects well before consultations begin.
>
> A second and undesirable reason for the drop in jeopardy findings is that FWS—in the face of persistent budget cuts, increasing workload, and mounting political pressure to minimize the economic impacts of endangered species conservation—is approving more projects that should have been altered to comply with the conservation standards under the Act. One method of achieving this outcome is by reinterpreting the jeopardy and destruction/adverse modification prohibitions such that they are more difficult to trigger. . . . This second reason is a policy failure arising from insufficient resources and sociopolitical support for FWS.
>
> A third explanation is that federal agencies are now more inclined to continue negotiating the scope of their proposed projects in response to FWS issuing a draft biological opinion with a jeopardy or destruction/adverse modification conclusion. If negotiations are successful, the final biological opinion will have neither of those conclusions.[53]

It is likely that the second, less benign, explanation for why BiOp censures have been limited is indeed present in a number of cases. One very experienced observer of federal ESA implementation, however, has suggested that the actual protective function of ESA §7 consultations is a good deal greater than the actual number of final formal jeopardy findings would imply:

> One thing I would emphasize that may not be in the Malcolm-Li study is that even though FWS does not generally make jeopardy calls, there is a lot of conservation that happens because of consultation. Often times this is in the project description of BiOps [i.e. where FWS and the proponent agency reconfigure the project design, timing, or technology in order to avoid jeopardy]. It really is where the most conservation happens for species.[54]

a. Slippage, Administrative: Flex Mechanisms Added to the ESA

Starting in the Bill Clinton years, the Department of Interior, backed by some environmental groups, issued ESA regulations attempting to encourage nonfederal actors to cooperate more in species protection and thus take some heat off the Act. The three main flexibility innovations, each of which has potential pluses and minuses, are these:

- "No surprises" agreements: These guarantee landowners that when they fulfill the terms of an HCP they will face no further obligations toward any covered species. If actions under their §10 incidental take permits turn out to harm species, the landowners are immune from liability and any necessary adjustments are paid for by the agency.[55]
- "Safe harbor" agreements: These serve landowners owning species habitat who are given "baseline" estimates of the numbers of endangered animals on their land and

---

53. Id. at 4.
54. Personal communication, 28 Dec. 2015, from Noah Greenwald, endangered species director, Center for Biological Diversity.
55. 63 Fed. Reg. 8859 (Feb. 23, 1998) (codified at 50 C.F.R. pt. 222). In each of these administrative contract settings, the backdrop of the Supreme Court's *Winstar* decision means that if an agency violates its assurances, it must pay. See Bosselman, The Statutory and Constitutional Mandate for a No Surprises Policy, 24 Ecology L.Q. 707 (1997), commenting on *U.S. v. Winstar Corp.*, 518 U.S. 839 (1996).

promised that their responsibilities will not increase if the endangered population's numbers increase; future development activity is allowed to cut the number of animals back to the baseline.[56]

- "Candidate conservation" agreements (CCAs), and "candidate conservation agreements with assurances" (CCAAs): These are contracts whereby state and corporate players promise Interior that they will take various measures to protect endangered species that otherwise would be federally listed. In return, Interior agrees not to list, which means the Act is not enforceable for such species, and sometimes gives further no-restrictions assurances.[57]

The ESA has also experienced lessened species protection owing to nonenforcement,[58] non-defense of the ESA in the face of industry challenges, and support of statutory amendments like a blanket amendment exempting military facilities from various endangered species, marine mammal, and critical habitat protection requirements.

> The statute is moving away from a system of regulation by citizen enforcement toward a system of largely closed-door negotiations between agencies and regulated interests, with little meaningful public involvement. . . . HCP initiatives have seriously weakened safeguards for listed species that were a key feature of the 1982 amendments. Kostyack, Surprise, Envtl. Forum, Mar. 1998, at 19.

The realpolitik counterargument in favor of these administrative flexibility devices is that the Act has been under such brutal attack for its rigidity and harshness that some compromises had to be made. As Professor Holly Doremus has written:

> The Department undertook its flexibility initiatives with the sincere intention of maximizing conservation gains while lowering controversy to a level that would keep the ESA off the political table. It is difficult to know what the political outcome would have been in the absence of those reforms. The reformers . . . may well be right to congratulate themselves on saving the ESA from repeal or severe weakening during their tenure. . . . Perhaps the Clinton-era ESA reforms . . . increased the ESA's conservation effectiveness, although . . . that has yet to be demonstrated. If they did so, however, it was in a curious, Alice-in-Wonderland sort of fashion. The reforms rest on the assumption that the levels of protection facially mandated by the ESA are not practically and politically achievable. By stepping back from that pretense, they are supposed to achieve, in the real world, greater protection than we could expect from vigorous implementation of the ESA. They give up the possibility of strong protection for a higher probability of maintaining a reduced level of protection.[59]

---

56. See Announcement of Final Safe Harbor Policy, 64 Fed. Reg. 32706-32717 (June 17, 1999) (codified at 50 C.F.R. pts. 13 and 17).

57. Under ESA §4, it appears that listing is mandatory if the species is factually endangered and unfulfilled promises are insufficient to override biological facts.

58. The Bush II Administration was the first to fail to list even a single species or designate any critical habitat in its first two years except under court order, despite a waiting list of over 3000 candidate species, and a lack of designated critical habitat for over three-quarters of those species already listed. See Parenteau, Whatever Industry Wants . . . The Bush Environmental Record, 14 Duke Envtl. L. & Pol'y F., No. 2 (2004).

59. Doremus, Adaptive Management, the Endangered Species Act, and the Institutional Challenges of "New Age" Environmental Protection, 41 Washburn L.J. 50 (2001). It also can be argued that the main function of ESA §§7 and 9's rigidity is to leverage money out of developers to fund species-conserving compromises.

C. "Slippage" and "Roadblock Bypasses"

b. The §4(d) Polar Bear Special Rule: ESA Not to Be Used Against Global Warming

For years ESA §4(d) was a minor provision used to exempt research activities and controlled conservation actions from ESA liability. Beginning in the Bush II Administration, however, §4(d) designations were made to allow impacts on endangered wildlife desired by various states and industries.

The polar bear is the most notable use of §4(d). The ecological realities of climate-affected species like the polar bear create a politically charged clash between endangered species protection and fiercely resisted efforts to regulate greenhouse gases.

Probably no image has so captured the public's emotions and attention for climate change than the sad plight of mother polar bears no longer able to find drift ice on which to hunt for nourishment for their babies due to the drastic retreat of polar sea ice. As year by year the edge of the seasonal arctic ice pack retreats from the northern coasts of Greenland, Canada, Alaska, and Russia, polar bears, which get most of their nutrition from hunting ring seals on the ice, have less unbroken ice to hunt on, and have to swim farther and farther across open water back to land to whelp their cubs, and later to swim back to the ice pack with cubs in tow to build them all back to survival weight. The image of bears floating far out in the open sea, drowned in the attempt to make it across newly widened open water, captures a direct climate change-induced threat to the species' survival.[60]

FIGURE 10-2. *Forlorn polar bear contemplates the melting Arctic Ocean shelf ice—now reduced by half, with daunting expanses of open water—habitat conditions that prevent successful hunting for ring seals, its primary food source. Photo: NASA Earth Observatory. The official listing of the polar bear was the first to take express notice of climate change as a cause of jeopardy. The image of polar bears facing massive habitat change has served as a focal point of the debate.*

In the waning days of the Bush II Administration, under court order from multiple successful citizen suits, Interior Secretary Kempthorne finally issued a final rule under ESA §4(d), 16 U.S.C. §1533(d), designating the polar bear as threatened. Unprecedentedly, the primary cause officially stated for endangerment was climate change caused by greenhouse gases. 73 Fed. Reg. 28212 (May 15, 2008). Under ESA §§7 and 9, such a listing potentially impacted a wide range of activities, including a major restriction on polar bear hunting (the only source of monetary income for many Inuit villages) by outlawing the importation of polar bear trophies under the ESA, blocking permits for oil and gas exploration on

---

60. For excellent background on the polar bear biologically and legally, see B. Lopez, Arctic Dreams ch. 3, *Tornarssuk* (1986) and the Center for Biological Diversity, www.biologicaldiversity.org/species/mammals/polar_bear/index.html.

On April 1, 2009, representatives from Norway, Canada, Russia, Greenland, and the U.S. concluded, during an international conference dedicated to conservation of arctic species, that climate change is the most important long-term threat facing the polar bear, and all countries agreed to develop new national action plans to address bear conservation.

the coastal plains and in the Arctic and Chukchi Seas (where oil contamination has been shown to kill bears), and even more significantly to raise questions in agency issuance of operating licenses for large U.S. coal-fired electric generating plants under the ESA and NEPA, or to require §10 incidental take permissions for corporate and agency actions that produce or license greenhouse gas emissions.

To avoid the possibility that the ESA would impinge on fossil fuel issues, however, the polar bear listing included a "special rule" that the ESA could not be "used inappropriately to regulate greenhouse gas emissions." 73 Fed. Reg. 28212 (May 15, 2008); 73 Fed. Reg. 76249 (Dec. 16, 2008). After the 2008 Obama election, in Public Law 111-8, Congress authorized the new Secretary of Interior to rescind a variety of Bush Administration "midnight regulations" undercutting the ESA, but though Secretary Ken Salazar rescinded other anti-ESA provisions, he left the polar bear "special rule" on the books. "The Endangered Species Act is not the proper tool to deal with a global issue—global warming," Salazar said. "We need to move forward with a comprehensive climate change and energy plan we can be proud of."

Is it appropriate to use the polar bear and the ESA to help curb global fossil fuel emissions? On one hand, as environmental critics have said, "The special regulation prohibits the federal government from protecting the polar bear from the harmful activity that necessitated the listing in the first place." On the other hand, the linkage between the polar bear and particular sources is relatively distant, commingled, and indirect. Professor J.B. Ruhl argues that the Act shouldn't be considered a potential silver bullet to shoot down global warming. Ruhl, Keeping the Endangered Species Act Relevant, 19 Duke Envtl. L. & Pol'y F. 275 (2009). He argues that it's not an appropriate mechanism for implementing a national policy responding to climate change, and counsels against attempts to use the Act in direct action against greenhouse gas emissions:

> The Endangered Species Act . . . is not structured to provide effective greenhouse gas emission control. Applying it would require isolating and linking emissions from, say, a power plant in Florida to effects on a distant climate-threatened species—a feat beyond scientific capacity. . . . Saying that climate change globally threatens a species does not establish causal blame on any particular source of emissions; just the opposite, it lays blame on all sources. Using the Endangered Species Act to sort through that quagmire, in addition to being legally untenable and beyond the capacity of the agencies that implement the statute, would in all likelihood make the statute more of a lightning rod for controversy than it already is. Ruhl, Climate Change Adaptation & the Structural Transformation of Environmental Law, 40 Envtl. L. 363 nn.243, 244 (2010).

Professor Ruhl argues that effective and appropriate application of the ESA occurs when three conditions are met: (1) the causal mechanism of species decline is direct, (2) the cause of the species decline contains a significant federal presence, (3) and ecosystem conservation correlates strongly with species conservation. He concludes that none of the three criteria is satisfied when the Act is used to target climate change. Instead Ruhl urges that ESA enforcement efforts address climate change by conserving intact habitat. He recommends efforts consolidating habitat conservation and aggressively designating critical habitat areas, including land that threatened species can expand into for survival, thereby concurrently restricting the spread of carbon-increasing activities. He also recommends "leveraging" habitat conservation—implementing habitat protection to reinforce other carbon-reducing policies. For example, habitat conservation banks could combine carbon sequestration credits in transactions marketing ESA habitat credits. In other examples of ESA relevance and potential inter-agency synergy, Ruhl suggests the ESA can be used to combat impacts of urbanization by mandating green buildings, and to mitigate ecological

C. "Slippage" and "Roadblock Bypasses"

degradation by demanding that resource users take into account the values of natural capital and ecosystem services.

Beyond the particular case of the polar bear, the Obama Administration, expected to reject the prior administration's restricted stance on environmental protection, again disappointed environmentalists—in the case of §4(d), the Obama Administration continued to use it as a pressure release where some industries and states strongly objected to specific species protections.

c. Slippage, Judicial: the Roberts Court Takes Action: *National Association of Homebuilders*

A probably ill-considered species protection lawsuit presented the Supreme Court with an opportunity to ratchet back the scope of the ESA. Arizona had asked EPA to transfer federal water pollution authority to itself under the delegation procedures of the federal CWA. (The CWA and the CAA, two statutes reflecting the "cooperative federalism" design by which EPA delegates federal regulatory powers to the states, are examined in detail in the next two chapters.) Federal biologists raised a fear that the state's environmental protection agencies would not protect the water needs of several endangered species including a pygmy owl, threatening their survival. In 2002 the EPA approved state certification despite the ESA issue, arguing that the state had satisfied all of the specified criteria in the CWA. The Ninth Circuit granted plaintiffs' request to apply ESA §7, but the Supreme Court granted certiorari.

National Association of Home Builders (NAHB) v. Defenders of Wildlife, and U.S. E.P.A. Defenders of Wildlife

551 U.S. 644 (2007)

Alito, J. . . . The substantive statutory question raised [here] requires us to mediate a clash of seemingly categorical—and, at first glance, irreconcilable—legislative commands. Section 402(b) of the CWA provides, without qualification, that the EPA "shall approve" a transfer application unless it determines that the State lacks adequate authority to perform the nine functions specified. . . . If the nine specified criteria are satisfied, the EPA does not have the discretion to deny a transfer application. . . . Arizona satisfied each of these nine criteria.

The language of §7(a)(2) of the ESA is similarly imperative: It provides that "each Federal agency shall . . . insure that any action authorized, funded, or carried out by such agency . . . is not likely to jeopardize" endangered or threatened species or their habitats. 16 U.S.C. §1536(a)(2). . . . Applying this language literally would "add one [additional] requirement to the list of considerations under the Clean Water Act permitting transfer provision."[61] That is, it would effectively repeal the mandatory and exclusive list of criteria set forth in §402(b), and replace it with a new, expanded list that includes §7's no-jeopardy requirement. . . .

The [Reagan Administration's 1986 ESA] regulations . . . provide that "Section 7 and the requirements of this part apply to all actions *in which there is discretionary Federal involvement or control.*"[62] 50 C.F.R. §402.03. . . . EPA concluded that the mandatory nature of CWA

---

61. Quoting Berzon, J., concurring in the Ninth Circuit's denial of rehearing en banc, 450 F.3d at 404 n. 2. [EDS.]

62. Edited excerpt has emphases added. [EDS.]

§402(b)—which directs that the EPA "shall approve" a transfer request if that section's nine statutory criteria are met—stripped it of authority to disapprove a transfer based on [the ESA]....

While a later enacted statute (such as the ESA) can sometimes operate to amend or even repeal an earlier statutory provision (such as the CWA), "repeals by implication are not favored" and will not be presumed unless the "intention of the legislature to repeal [is] clear and manifest."

In *TVA v. Hill*, 437 U.S. 153 ... the Court concluded that "the ordinary meaning" of §7 of the ESA contained "no exemptions" and reflected "a conscious decision by Congress to give endangered species priority over the 'primary missions' of federal agencies." *TVA v. Hill*, however, had no occasion to answer the question presented in these cases. That case was decided almost a decade before the adoption in 1986 of the regulations contained in 50 C.F.R. §402.03. And in any event, the construction project at issue in *TVA v. Hill*, while expensive, was also discretionary. . . . That case did not speak to the question whether §7 applies to *non*-discretionary actions, like the one at issue here. The regulation set forth in 50 C.F.R. §402.03 addressed that question, and we defer to its reasonable interpretation....

Applying *Chevron*, we defer to the Agency's reasonable interpretation of ESA §7 as applying only to "actions in which there is discretionary Federal involvement or control." 50 C.F.R. §402.03. Since the transfer of NPDES permitting authority is not discretionary ... it follows that a transfer of NPDES permitting authority does not trigger ESA §7's consultation and no-jeopardy requirements.... Reversed.

[Stevens, J., filed a strong dissenting opinion joined by Justices Souter, Ginsburg, and Breyer, pointing out that Congress intended ESA §7 provisions to apply to all agency actions, even so-called nondiscretionary ones, and that in any event, the EPA had substantial "discretion" to evaluate whether a state should be delegated the CWA permitting authority.]

COMMENTARY & QUESTIONS

1. Slippage: "nondiscretionary"? To what degree does *NAHB* erode the protections of the ESA? Is *NAHB* another example of how public interest statutes are eroded over time by iron triangle resistance? The idea of the discretionary/nondiscretionary distinction provided an innovative way to limit a broad-coverage civic statutory measure like the ESA.[63] Will it substantially undercut the ESA in practice? A subsequent ESA §7 case found no reason to suspend the ESA when federal flood subsidy payments were being authorized to build subdivisions in the habitat of endangered Florida Keys deer, despite the agency's arguments of nondiscretion. *Florida Key Deer v. Pauison*, 522 F.3d 1133 (11th Cir. 2008). One scholar of the ESA expresses the wistful hope that the *NAHB* precedent will be limited or even helpful. Even before *NAHB* most legal analysts had agreed that ESA §7 does not apply to truly nondiscretionary agency actions, and "[settings] where a federal agency [is] explicitly commanded to authorize a nonfederal party to take action based on criteria that the *NAHB* Court viewed as undisputed rarely appear in the federal statutes that implicate most ESA §7 controversies. . . . Indeed, given the narrowness of the ruling, one possible outcome

---

63. In the Mexican trucking case, for example, *Department of Transp. v. Public Citizen*, 541 U.S. 752 (2004), Justice Thomas's opinion for the Court used a similar distinction to eliminate application of NEPA and the CAA.

of the *NAHB* decision is that it will cabin in some of the more over-reaching attempts by federal agencies to sweep many kinds of agency actions into the 'discretion' exemption of §7." Hasselman, *National Association of Home Builders v. Defenders of Wildlife*: The Supreme Court's Endangered Species Act Decision Should Have Limited Impacts, 22 J. Envtl. L. & Litig. 343 (2007); and see Hasselman, Holes in the Endangered Species Act Safety Net: The Role of Agency "Discretion" in §7 Consultation, 25 Stan. Envtl. L.J. (2006). An important tactical and semantic inquiry for the future will be "How elastic is the definition of 'non-discretionary' "—how much can it be stretched to circumvent protective statutes?

2. Would applying the ESA "repeal" the CWA delegation provision, or add a criterion? Why is the CWA's *shall* more powerful than the ESA's *shall*? The semantics of Justice Alito's *NAHB* opinion are interesting. Previously the premise of administrative law was that congressional mandates to federal agencies were cumulative, not preclusive. An agency building a congressionally authorized highway or airport was presumed to be concurrently subject to other statutory mandates like NEPA or the ADA. ESA §7 was considered a statutory add-on requirement for agency actions. But by seizing on the "shall" in the 1970 CWA's §402, the majority construes the *shall* in the 1973 ESA §7 as an improper "implied repeal." Congress's commands to federal agencies in the 1973 ESA, however, would act as a "repeal" of other laws only if one presumes that when Congress used the word *shall* in the prior laws it had intended their elements to be exclusive and absolute—requiring, unless expressly stated otherwise, that no subsequent additional congressional mandates would be applied to their programs—quite a novel and dangerous premise.

3. To what degree should courts defer to agency regulations that decrease constraints on their own actions? Agency rulemaking is subject to intense internal and external pressure, often resisting the imposition of unwelcome constraints on agency projects and programs. NEPA is a prime example: Agencies' own NEPA regulations sometimes tended to erode the EIS requirement,[64] so the Council on Environmental Quality's (CEQ) plenary federal regulations on NEPA are considered the authoritative NEPA rules. In *NAHB* Justice Alito gives unquestioning adherence to the Reagan Administration regulation 50 C.F.R. §402.03 that (only) limited ESA applicability. The 1986 regulation was issued by the Departments of Interior and Commerce, both of which contain subagencies deeply affected by ESA restrictions, and their rulemaking asserting the narrowing discretionary-actions-only interpretation of the statute made only a one-sentence reference to the statutory language it was interpreting. See 51 Fed. Reg. 19957 (June 3, 1986).

4. Strict rules or adaptive discretion? Democratic dilemmas in the second generation of environmental law. In the so-called second generation of environmental law, a number of commentators have suggested the need for "adaptive management" using subjective flexible performance standards. (See Chapter 9.) Looking at the original roadblock terms of the ESA—even if they made rational sense in cases such as the darters' or the spotted owls'—isn't it possible that the Act is indeed too stringent? Interior's no-surprises, safe-harbor, and CCA rules reflect the perception that a more modulated balancing is necessary. Are you at ease with the old dipolar model, trusting agencies to be guided by the public interest rather than by political pressures?

---

64. For example, a recent guidance document from the U.S. Treasury (regarding potentially large grants being given under §1603 of the American Recovery & Reinvestment Act of 2009 to applicants building major energy facilities, Office of Fiscal Assistant Secretary, July 2009, at 20) stated baldly that "[a] §1603 payment with respect to specific qualified energy property does not make the property subject to NEPA and other laws," a highly questionable declaration.

5. Endangered species in national governance. It is scarcely surprising that endangered species protection became a target of administration policies in the first years of the twenty-first century. Much of the Bush II Administration's efforts focused within the administrative process, with cutbacks on listing and enforcement (it was the first to fail to list a single species or designate any critical habitat in its first two years except under court order[65]), and in the courts where federal enforcement was lackluster.[66]

It will be interesting to see in the controversies ahead how much we have learned from the whooping crane, the snail darter, and the spotted owl. Will endangered species be listened to as early warning indicators serving to identify larger public issues at stake, or will they be trivialized in the narrowed caricature of localized tradeoffs—"What do you want, owls or jobs?" When the pumps that divert water from northern California's Sacramento River to farms and cities in California's arid south threaten to eliminate the delta smelt (*Hypomesus transpacificus*), or Klamath River water is necessary for protection of endangered salmon and suckerfish, will the question be cast as more "worthless minnows" versus jobs and progress, or an occasion to raise sensible questions about where most of the water now goes—to massive fiscal and water subsidies for inappropriate agriculture? One such basic question: "Why should we be subsidizing farmers to grow rice and other water-intensive crops in the middle of the desert?" In 2009, the industry-financed Pacific Legal Foundation petitioned the Governor of California to request a God Committee override of protections for the endangered delta smelt, and in early 2010 filed an appeal with the Ninth Circuit after losing a trial court suit against the ESA in *Delta Smelt Consolidated Cases* (No. 1:09-cv-407 OWW DLB, E.D. Cal. 2009).

6. Slippage: When is it beneficial, when is it corrosive? Like so much of environmental law, endangered species protections can serve as triggering opportunities for reviewing long-term necessities of rational social governance—which can mean thoughtful adaptive change to optimize net public values in complex settings—or can be corroded by the concentrated forces of short-term self-aggrandizement.[67] If the decisional processes ultimately turn on the merits rather than political ploys, endangered species will continue to play their socially useful role—as well as continuing to be prime symbols of a national environmental ethic.

The measure of the current ESA as a roadblock-with-bypasses will be found over time in its further evolution, including the continuing congressional debates over reauthorization. The degree to which full scientific and economic merits are brought to bear in these debates will be critical to the Act's future.

---

65. In 2010 there was a waiting list of over 3000 candidate species and a lack of designated critical habitat for over three-quarters of those species already listed.

66. The Bush II Administration hastened to accept administrative or court-approved settlements capitulating to challenges filed against its federal regulations. See 313 F.3d 1094 (9th Cir. 2002) (an agreement between Homebuilders and the Administration to nullify the majority of the 4.1 million acres in California that had been designated as critical habitat for the redlegged frog the previous year). In other cases it declined to defend the rules altogether. See Parenteau, Whatever Industry Wants . . . : The Bush Environmental Record, 14 Duke Envtl. L. & Pol'y F., No. 2 (2004). Legislative initiatives added provisions undercutting ESA protections in military reservations under its Military Readiness Act and in "fuel reduction" areas targeted for clearcutting under the Healthy Forests Restoration Act of 2003. See Pub. L. No. 108-136, §318(a), §319(b), 117 Stat. 1392 (2003), noted above, and Pub. L. No. 108-148, 117 Stat. 1887 (2003).

67. Illustrating such obstacles, a USFS-Bureau of Reclamation study indicating that management of Northwest forests to protect the spotted owl could actually create more than 15,000 new jobs for former timber workers was suppressed and recalled by the Administration. Leaked copies are available by writing to the Association of Forest Service Employees for Environmental Ethics (AFSEEE), P.O. Box 111615, Eugene, OR 97440.

C. "Slippage" and "Roadblock Bypasses"

7. An international perspective on endangered species and roadblocks. The ESA was passed by Congress pursuant to CITES, the international Convention on International Trade in Endangered Species, which has sometimes been called the world's single most effective international environmental convention.[68] CITES contains no roadblocks resembling those in the ESA.

ESA is the implementing legislation for the Convention on International Trade in Endangered Species (CITES), Mar. 3, 1973, 27 U.S.T. 1087, the principal international vehicle for conserving endangered species. CITES regulates trade in the form of both importation and exportation of endangered species and specimens. Even before the conclusion of CITES in 1973, the UK and the U.S. banned the importation of endangered species in attempt to leverage conservation policies abroad. The U.S. legislation in particular called upon the Secretary of the Interior to seek an international meeting to agree on a binding treaty regarding endangered species, an initiative that eventually matured into the CITES treaty. As of this writing, 164 states are parties to CITES, which has been in force since 1975. The agreement contains three appendices that are the analogue of listings under ESA:

1. Appendix I includes species threatened with extinction. Trade in specimens of these species requires prior permission from both the country of export and the country of import and is allowed only in exceptional circumstances. This is the highest level of protection that applies to the black rhinoceros, all sea turtles, the great apes, big cats like tigers and cheetahs, and endangered whales. It is the closest international analogue to the roadblock strategy of ESA. For instance, when the CITES parties listed the African elephant in Appendix I, the result was effectively a ban on trade in ivory.
2. Appendix II includes species not necessarily threatened with extinction, but in which trade must be controlled in order to avoid utilization incompatible with their survival. An export permit, but not an import permit, is required in advance of international commerce in the more than 25,000 species listed in Appendix II.
3. Appendix III, the lowest level of protection, contains species that are protected in at least one country, which has asked other CITES parties for assistance in controlling the trade.

Why do you think the drafters of CITES chose trade—importation and exportation—as the juncture at which the roadblock protections of the treaty would attach? What kind of incentive structure does restricting or constricting trade in endangered species create in countries of export? Of import? What would you expect to be the limitations of an approach such as CITES that focuses strictly on trade? How would you propose overcoming those limitations? While CITES has been extraordinarily successful within the scope of its operation, considerations such as these motivated a "second-generation" agreement emphasizing managerial rather than roadblock provisions, the UN Convention on Biological Diversity, May 22, 1992, 31 I.L.M. 822 (1992), which has been signed but not ratified by the U.S.

---

68. Convention on International Trade in Endangered Species of Wild Flora and Fauna, Mar. 3, 1973, 27 U.S.T. 1087, 993 U.N.T.S. 243 (entered into force July 1, 1975).

FIGURE 10-3. *An endangered northern spotted owl caught on camera in midstrike: The winged blur in the center right of this ancient forest clearing is a rare daylight image of the northern spotted owl (Strix occidentalis caurina), perhaps about to strike a red-backed vole. The background shows a fallen "nurse log" which opens a hole in the canopy for sunlight to reach the forest floor, allowing new trees to grow up from the nurse log's decomposing organic matter. The lushness of the decomposition and growth processes in the natural old-growth forests of the Pacific Northwest is supported by rhizoform fungus nodules in the forest's root systems. The fungi provide nutrients and water retention to balance forest moisture throughout the lowprecipitation summer season. Red-backed voles live in the nurse logs and specialize in eating the subsoil fungal truffles. The owls eat the voles. The fungi are then transplanted through the forests in owl pellet droppings. Without the owl, the forest's balances of life and water are disrupted. What's the First Law of Ecology?—Everything is Related to Everything Else. Photo © 1988 Gary Braasch. See* D. Kelly & G. Braasch, SECRETS OF THE OLD GROWTH FOREST (1988).

By conducting ourselves ethically toward all creatures, we enter into a spiritual relationship with the universe.

— Albert Schweitzer

11

From Harm-Based Standards to Tech-Based Standards: The Clean Air Act

A. The Clean Air Act: History and Structure
B. Harm-Based Ambient Standards Under the CAA
C. Technology-Based Standards Under the CAA
D. Technology-Forcing Under the CAA
E. Regulation of Greenhouse Gases Under the CAA

The Clean Air Act, in its basic structure as we know it today, became law in 1970, the first of the very large, complex, federal environmental "command-and-control" regulatory systems. It was the product of national politicians' response to broad public awareness of environmental problems in the wake of Rachel Carson's SILENT SPRING and vivid media coverage of the acute human health impacts of smog, smoke, and airborne lead pollution. Through years of see-sawing political and scientific battles, its development in this chapter presents students with a window into some of the most complex structures of environmental protection law and the contentious societal contexts which continue to shape its progress.

A. THE CLEAN AIR ACT: HISTORY AND STRUCTURE

The Clean Air Act (CAA), 42 U.S.C. §§7401 et seq. (1970), is arguably the most successful piece of environmental legislation ever drafted. Passed to address the sorry state of U.S. air quality, it employs a unique mix of regulatory techniques to address air quality problems. This chapter first introduces you to the history of the CAA and then delves into the principal regulatory approaches contained within the Act (except for its cap-and-trade market-enlisting program, which is analyzed in Chapter 14). Here is the basic structure of the CAA:

- **Harm-based:** Title I, §§107-110 create the basic regulatory system for control of the most commonly produced and significant air pollutants. These sections apply

> **THE CLEAN AIR ACT'S TITLES**
>
> **Title I:**
> Sections 108-110: National air quality standards (NAAQS) defined by EPA for stationary sources and applied by state or federal implementation plans (SIPs or FIPs).
>
> Section 111: Standards of performance for new and existing stationary sources.
>
> **Title II:**
> Emission standards for mobile sources of air pollution — cars, trucks, other mobile sources.
>
> **Title III:**
> Administrative details on citizen suits, judicial review, etc.
>
> **Title IV:**
> A nationwide pollution credit trading system, primarily for sulfur oxide acid precipitation control.
>
> **Title V:**
> Permit system for air pollution sources.
>
> **Title VI:**
> Protection of stratospheric ozone.

a harm-based ambient quality regulatory approach that relies on federal air quality standards designed to protect public health (NAAQS — National Ambient Air Quality Standards, see Figure 1 below) and state regulation of stationary air pollution sources that are required to achieve the federally mandated level of overall air quality. That program is covered in Section B of this chapter.

- **Best Available Technology:** Title I, §111 applies to "new [stationary] sources" of air pollution, and establishes a system of "best-technology" performance standards for the air emissions of large stationary sources. Section 112, regulating *hazardous* air pollutants such as benzene, arsenic, and many others, also employs a "tech-based" standard, but its standard is more stringent: Maximum Available Control Technology (MACT). Statutory provisions aimed at achieving and maintaining the NAAQS also include variations on Best Available Technology (BAT), such as requirements that major new and modified sources of air pollution install the Best Available Control Technology (BACT). The CAA's technology-based sections are covered in Section C of this chapter.

- **Technology-forcing:** Title II, covered in Section D of this chapter, sets strict congressional standards for reductions of automobile and truck tailpipe emissions, and authorizes EPA to continue periodically to reduce allowable emissions. Title II also mandates the use of clean-fuel vehicles in the nation's most polluted areas and requires limited production of clean-fuel vehicles by auto manufacturers.

- **Market-enlisting:** Title IV creates an innovative emissions trading program, primarily for SO_2. This program, which became the paradigm for a host of proposals for shifting environmental regulations into market-trading systems, is discussed in detail in Chapter 14.

These different regulatory techniques did not all appear at once. On the contrary, the evolution of regulatory strategies used by the CAA has occurred over a period of several decades, in four primary stages.

Stage 1—1970. The CAA as we know it today was first enacted in 1970. Although technically an amendment to the previous Air Quality Act, the 1970 Act fundamentally reshaped the federal government's approach to regulating air pollution. Whereas previous legislation had relied on essentially voluntary efforts by states to reduce air pollution to tolerable levels, the 1970 Act swept voluntarism aside by providing for nationally uniform air quality standards, and every state was ordered to implement the federal standards (notably by SIPs, State Implementation Plans) by a deadline set by Congress. The 1970 Act also set strict national standards for automobile emissions, and required new stationary sources of air pollution to meet BACT standards as determined by EPA.

A. The Clean Air Act: History and Structure

In regard to the widely emitted and harmful "criteria" pollutants, Congress in 1970 chose a "harm-based" approach to deciding how clean the air should be. The "primary" standards were to be set at a level "adequate to protect the public health" after "allowing an adequate margin of safety." These standards are the NAAQS. This central feature of the CAA thus starts from the desired endpoint, aiming to achieve air quality that could be considered "safe," i.e., sufficiently protective of human health. With this national goal, stationary sources of pollution are regulated primarily by the states.

Congress made other fundamental decisions in 1970 as well. It divided the universe of sources of pollution into two major categories, stationary sources and mobile sources, with the former more subject to state-by-state control (CAA Title I), and the latter subject mostly to direct nationwide federal regulation (CAA Title II). In some ways, the dichotomy is an obvious one. Even though there are millions of mobile sources, there are only a handful of producers of motor vehicles, and the design of a car or truck calls for an integrated pollution control system which is best built into every vehicle at the time of manufacture. Moreover, there are tremendous economies of scale in the mass production of motor vehicles and to allow each of the 50 states to set its own standards for motor vehicles threatened to wreak havoc on the auto industry. With an exception for California, where motor vehicle pollution controls already existed and where air pollution problems were recognized as requiring more stringent regulation, there was to be a single national standard for motor vehicle emissions.

Stationary sources, on the other hand, are often custom-built installations, and their variety makes a nationally uniform standard at once less necessary and potentially more inefficient. Thus, for stationary sources, the 1970 CAA made a different choice: It allowed the states, which in principle are in better touch with the economic and pollution control realities of their industries, to make many of the choices about how to get the emissions reductions needed to achieve the NAAQS. The statutory mechanism that Congress chose was to require the states to adopt state implementation plans which were, in large part, prescriptions for how each state would regulate its stationary sources. The federal EPA would review each state's SIP for each of the criteria pollutants, to determine if it would work. If EPA disapproved of a SIP, the state would have to redraft it until EPA approved. If a state refused to draft an adequate SIP, EPA could impose a federal implementation plan (FIP), a fate most of the states believed would be the worst of all possible regulatory worlds. Apart from reflexive opposition to yielding control to the national government, the states feared that EPA would be insensitive to their particular needs and desires.

Congress, however, did not leave all regulation of stationary sources completely to the states. For major new pollution sources, CAA §111 directed EPA to develop New Source Performance Standards (NSPS), which were to require new stationary sources to employ Best Available Technology (BAT) for a facility of its kind. In this way, Congress softened the potential for a race of laxity in which areas in compliance with the NAAQS would try to draw new business away from states that had not yet achieved the NAAQS.

The 1970 Act's division of authority had a profound effect on the states' efforts to attain and maintain the NAAQS. Three of the criteria pollutants—carbon monoxide (CO), nitrogen oxides (NO_x), and ozone—are major by-products of motor vehicle use. (Lead was in that category for a time, but with the elimination of lead from gasoline—accomplished through the application of the CAA provision regulating fuels—motor vehicles have ceased having an effect on lead air emissions.) If states cannot regulate mobile source pollution, their flexibility and effectiveness in attaining the NAAQS are greatly undermined. For this reason, as seen in Chapter 7's discussion of federal preemption, a number of states have taken advantage of authority given to them under the 1977 Amendments to the Act to "piggyback" onto California's strict mobile source standards. Even under the 1970 law, states could indirectly influence air pollution from mobile sources by encouraging car pooling and mass transit, insisting that the federally required pollution controls installed on mobile sources be inspected and properly maintained, and so on. These types of controls were unpopular and seldom employed voluntarily. In addition, EPA's early effort to reduce air pollution by rationing gasoline, embodied in a southern California FIP, was allowed by a federal court[1] but then rejected by Congress in a CAA amendment forbidding EPA to impose transportation controls in FIPs.

Finally, the 1970 Act also created a program, in §112, for the regulation of so-called hazardous air pollutants. (Criteria pollutants such as SO_2 and CO are themselves hazardous to human health, but §112's hazardous category included pollutants that were acutely toxic even in small amounts.) The original §112, like the NAAQS program itself, was harm-based: Congress directed EPA to set a level for hazardous air pollutants that would protect public health with an "ample margin of safety."

As with most environmental statutes, citizen organizations have played a crucial role in defining the contours of the CAA's statutory text and in creating a body of caselaw through citizen suits. To take a notable example, in the 1970s the Natural Resources Defense Council filed suit to require EPA to list lead as a criteria pollutant. The Second Circuit forced EPA to list it:

> The EPA concedes that lead meets the conditions of §108—that it has an adverse effect on public health and welfare, and that the presence of lead in the ambient air results from numerous or diverse mobile or stationary sources. The EPA maintains, however, that . . . the Administrator retains discretion whether to list a pollutant, even though the pollutant meets the criteria of §§108(a)(1)(A) and (B). . . . The Administrator argues that if he chooses to control lead . . . under §211 [regulation of fuel additives], he is not required to list the pollutant under §108 or to set air quality standards. . . . The interpretation . . . advanced by the EPA is contrary to the structure of the Act as a whole, and . . . if accepted, it would vitiate the public policy underlying the [CAA]. Section 108(a)(1) contains mandatory language . . ." the Administrator *shall* . . . publish . . . a list . . ." (emphasis added). If the EPA interpretation were accepted and listing were mandatory only for substances "for which he plans to issue air quality criteria . . ." then the mandatory language of §108(a)(1)(A) would become mere surplusage. . . . The Congress sought to eliminate, not perpetuate . . . administrative footdragging. Once the conditions of §§108(a)(1)(A) and (B) have been met, the listing of lead and the issuance of air quality standards for lead become mandatory. *NRDC v. Train*, 545 F.2d 320, at 324-325 (2d Cir. 1976).

Although this case marks the first and only time since the original 1970 Act that a pollutant has been added to the list, citizen involvement has also been instrumental in spurring Congress to amend the Act throughout its tumultuous history.

Stage 2—1977. Seven years after passage of the original Act, Congress revisited the basic questions of how clean the nation's air should be and how quickly clean air should be achieved. As for the first question, although the 1970 Act had addressed how *clean* the air in "dirty" areas—those that had not attained the NAAQS—should be, it had not addressed how *dirty* the air in "clean" areas could be allowed to become. Could states with clean air use it to attract polluting industries, keeping their air just clean enough to maintain the NAAQS, not reducing pollution overall but just spreading it around more evenly?

---

1. *City of Santa Rosa v. EPA*, 534 F.2d 150 (9th Cir. 1976).

A. The Clean Air Act: History and Structure

> At this point, note some underlying political realities of pollution regulation: the new tougher nationwide standards of the CAA were imposed by federal statute to override the tendency of states to compete for industry jobs and economic benefits by setting low standards and non-enforcement. The broad public recognition and concern rallied in the first Earth Days of the 1970s and resulting media attention motivated the politicians in Congress to pass a tough law. The economic and political forces of industry, however, naturally continue to try to minimize the effect of environmental protection rules. This tension between contending interests continues within all environmental regulatory systems today. In the case of the early tactic of "spreading around" pollution rather than reducing it overall, the original 1970 Act wasn't clear, and some states and industries hoped to use the loophole to evade the public values of nationwide air pollution reductions.

In a remarkable decision based on quite cryptic statutory language, a citizen suit in 1972 won a decision that the preamble to the 1970 Act, which declared that one purpose of the Act was "to protect and enhance the quality of the Nation's air resources," prohibited EPA from approving SIPs in relatively clean areas that would allow such areas to pollute their air to the level of the NAAQS.[2] Thus was born the Prevention of Significant Deterioration (PSD) program. In the 1977 Amendments to the Act, Congress codified and refined this judicially inspired program. The key regulatory initiative was the imposition of a lower ceiling for allowable pollution that, in effect, superseded the NAAQS as the federally mandated quality level. The new ceiling was calculated by measuring current air quality as a baseline and then allowing only a relatively small incremental amount of pollution to be added to that baseline. The 1977 Amendments also required major new (and modified) sources in PSD areas to use BACT.

As for the timing of NAAQS compliance, the 1970 Act, by today's standards, had extremely tight deadlines for compliance: "As expeditiously as practicable" but, in any event, no later than three years after having its SIP approved by EPA, a state was supposed to achieve compliance with the NAAQS. By 1977, however, it was clear that some states had missed the deadline and were not even within sight of achieving the NAAQS. For nonattainment areas, which included most of the nation's industrial centers, political influences called a retreat from the NAAQS as rigid short-term requirements and transformed the NAAQS into goals toward which only "reasonable further progress" was required. At the same time, however, Congress strengthened requirements for stationary sources and for the inspection and maintenance of automobiles in nonattainment areas. All existing sources were required to employ Reasonably Available Control Technologies (RACT). All major new sources were required to achieve the Lowest Achievable Emissions Rate (LAER) and to "offset"—by more than a 1:1 ratio—their new pollution, by arranging pollution reductions at other facilities in the area.

Stage 3—1990. For more than a decade, the CAA muddled through in its 1977 configuration, making relatively little further progress toward attainment in nonattainment areas and making virtually no progress in regulating hazardous air pollutants. Additionally, the well-known but largely unregulated problem of long-range transport of pollutants was attracting attention, particularly in regard both to ground-level ozone and to acid deposition,

---

2. *Sierra Club v. Ruckelshaus*, 344 F. Supp. 253, 255 (D.C. C. 1972), aff'd by an equally divided Court, *Fri v. Sierra Club*, 412 U.S. 541 (1973).

which was poisoning the lakes and forests of northeastern states. The statute was being criticized on all fronts: Some claimed it was too expensive in achieving the results it did obtain; others claimed it was inadequate because the air in hundreds of localities inhabited by tens of millions of people was not yet safe.

Congress took extraordinary action in 1990, making major revisions on all these fronts. As to the basic NAAQS attainment issue, Congress again set strict compliance dates and stricter requirements for SIPs, as well as tightening standards for mobile sources. The legislation spelled out specific sanctions—cutoffs of federal highway funds and other federally bestowed benefits—for states that did not comply with the new timetables and required promulgation of a FIP within two years of a state's failure to submit an adequate SIP. As to hazardous air pollutants, Congress abandoned the harm-based approach in favor of a technology-based approach that called for the installation of the MACT. As to long-range deposition, Congress created new devices to limit ozone transport and (in CAA Title IV) established an elaborate emissions trading scheme seeking to reduce SO_2 emissions by 10 million tons from 1980 levels in a decade, thereby almost halving emissions of the most significant precursor to acid rain. The statute also strengthened controls on NOx emissions.

Stage 4—Beyond 1990. Since 1990, most of the significant CAA action has been undertaken by the executive branch or the states rather than by Congress. In the late 1990s, EPA strengthened the NAAQS for ozone and particulate matter and ended up defending the new rules in the Supreme Court; developed a massive program to reduce interstate ozone pollution; for the first time required light trucks to meet the same emission standards as cars; required significant reductions in diesel emissions; and brought a series of lawsuits challenging companies that allegedly evaded the Act's technology-based permit requirements for modified sources of air pollution (the so-called New Source Review (NSR) requirements). During the same period, states began to take the opportunity to opt in to California's stringent emission rules for new automobiles.

The new millennium has seen inconsistent executive action, largely as the result of political regime change. The Bush II EPA issued rules substantially narrowing the scope of the NSR program; dropped investigations pending against some 50 power plants for violations of the former NSR rules; and issued a mercury-trading rule that was later vacated by the D.C. Circuit. The Bush II EPA also declared that greenhouse gases (GHGs), implicated in climate change, are not "air pollutants" within the meaning of the CAA and that, even if they were, EPA would decline to regulate them due to policy concerns such as the "piecemeal" nature of regulation under the Clean Air Act. The Supreme Court disagreed and ruled that the CAA does indeed give EPA the authority to regulate GHGs and that EPA may not cite policy reasons unconnected to the statute in declining to regulate them. Subsequently, the Obama EPA issued an endangerment finding for GHGs, which triggered regulation of mobile and stationary sources under the CAA. Early on, the Obama EPA also granted California a waiver to set stricter auto emissions standards, reversing another decision made by the previous administration. The Obama EPA set new efficiency standards for cars and trucks, required reporting of GHG emissions from large facilities, regulated GHGs under the NSR permitting program for stationary sources, and began to regulate sources—including, most prominently, power plants—under the SIP-like provisions of §§111(b) and (d) of the CAA. The CAA has indeed entered a new stage, one characterized by executive action (and sometimes inaction) in the face of congressional paralysis.

B. Harm-Based Ambient Standards Under the CAA

> In designing a regulatory system, the drafters of a foundational statute typically must address and define three major structural elements:—
>
> (1) what regulatory standards will be put in place: what type of standard, objective description of the specific terms to be set for each authorized standard, and the process by which each standard will be defined;
> (2) the structure by which the regulatory standards will be initially applied to the regulated target area; and
> (3) the implementation process by which the performance of the standard is monitored and enforced.
>
> CAA's NAAQS provisions are a prime example of a command-and-control system with these NAAQS standards based on *measurement of potential pollution harms*.

The NAAQS form the centerpiece of the CAA. These standards protect public health by governing the quality of the outdoor air throughout the nation. They address the pollutants that are among the best studied, most pervasive, and most diversely harmful of the byproducts of industrial society. A large part of the federal regulation that takes place under the CAA, and most of the state regulation, has as its objective the attainment of air quality consistent with the NAAQS. "Primary standards" under the Act are the nationwide levels defined by EPA for each criteria pollutant on the basis of potential harm to human health. "Secondary standards" are levels set based on potential harm to "welfare," broadly defined to include effects on soils, crops, vegetation, manmade materials, and more.

The CAA's NAAQS program is one of the signal success stories of U.S. environmental law. Emissions of most of the pollutants regulated by this program have decreased dramatically in the 45 years the program has been in place, despite substantial increases in the size of our population and in the amount of economic activity.[3] In a peer-reviewed, retrospective study of the CAA's first 20 years, EPA concluded that the Act had produced almost $22 *trillion* more in benefits than it had imposed in costs, and EPA believed that even this dazzling amount probably understated the benefits of the statute.[4] These results have been corroborated by the Office of Information and Regulatory Affairs (OIRA) within the Office of Management and Budget (OMB), an office not known as a regulatory cheerleader. OMB's 2014 report to Congress on the costs and benefits of federal regulation concluded that federal regulations from 2003 to 2013 produced from $262 billion to over $1 trillion in annual quantified benefits, while imposing from $69 to $102 billion in annual quantified costs (2010$). OMB attributed the majority of the quantified benefits to CAA regulation.[5] Nevertheless, critics remain. The ink was barely dry on the 1970 statute creating the NAAQS program when critics began charging that the program was too rigid, too strict, too expensive, and too cumbersome. These charges, and more, continue to this day.

---

3. See R.N.L. Andrews, Managing the Environment, Managing Ourselves—A History of American Environmental Policy 280 (1999) (citing U.S. Council on Environmental Quality, Environmental Quality: 25th Annual Report—1994-95, at 179, 182 (1997)).

4. EPA, Office of Air and Radiation, The Benefits and Costs of the Clean Air Act, 1970 to 1990 ES-8 (Oct. 1997). This report focused almost exclusively on the consequences of the NAAQS program.

5. OIRA, OMB, 2008 Report to Congress on the Costs and Benefits of Federal Regulations and Unfunded Mandates on State, Local, and Tribal Entities (Jan. 2009), available at www.whitehouse.gov/omb/assets/information_and_regulatory_affairs/2008_cb_final.pdf. Specifically, OIRA found the reduction of exposure to fine particulate matter created the majority of benefits under the clean air rules.

Pollutant		Primary/Secondary	Averaging Time	Level	Form
Carbon Monoxide [76 FR 54294, Aug 31, 2011]		primary	8-hour	9 ppm	Not to be exceeded more than once per year
			1-hour	35 ppm	
Lead [73 FR 66964, Nov 12, 2008]		primary and secondary	Rolling 3 month average	0.15 µg/m3 (1)	Not to be exceeded
Nitrogen Dioxide [75 FR 6474, Feb 9, 2010] [61 FR 52852, Oct 8, 1996]		primary	1-hour	100 ppb	98th percentile of 1-hour daily maximum concentrations, averaged over 3 years
		primary and secondary	Annual	53 ppb (2)	Annual Mean
Ozone [73 FR 16436, Mar 27, 2008]		primary and secondary	8-hour	0.075 ppm (3)	Annual fourth-highest daily maximum 8-hr concentration, averaged over 3 years
Particle Pollution Dec 14, 2012	PM2.5	primary	Annual	12 µg/m3	Annual mean, averaged over 3 years
		secondary	Annual	15 µg/m3	Annual mean, averaged over 3 years
	PM10	primary and secondary	24-hour	35 µg/m3	98th percentile, averaged over 3 years
		primary and secondary	24-hour	150 µg/m3	Not to be exceeded more than once per year on average over 3 years
Sulfur Dioxide [75 FR 35520, Jun 22, 2010] [38 FR 25678, Sept 14, 1973]		primary	1-hour	75 ppb (4)	99th percentile of 1-hour daily maximum concentrations, averaged over 3 years
		secondary	3-hour	0.5 ppm	Not to be exceeded more than once per year

FIGURE 11-1. *The National Ambient Air Quality Standards (NAAQS) for the officially-designated* "criteria pollutants." *Source: U.S. EPA: http://www.epa.gov/air/criteria.html.*

This chapter uses the NAAQS program as its central case study of "harm-based" pollution standards governing ambient air quality. Relying on harm-based ambient standards entails two major, foundational decisions. First, regulators must choose how, and how stringently, to set the standards for ambient environmental quality. In the case of air pollution, for example, the regulators must decide how clean the air should be. Then a choice must be made about how to allocate allowable emissions within the commons so that the end result is attainment of the ambient standard. It may sound simple, but it's not.

The NAAQS program is the leading example of this "harm-based" approach, its uniform national standards set based on scientific evidence of potential harm to human health

B. Harm-Based Ambient Standards Under the CAA

and welfare. The air pollutants currently regulated by this program are sulfur dioxide (SO_2), nitrogen dioxide (NO_2), particulate matter (PM), carbon monoxide (CO), ozone, and lead. These pollutants, called the "criteria" pollutants, are—along with GHGs—the most ubiquitous and best understood air pollutants in the U.S. Many of the regulatory requirements imposed by the CAA are aimed at achieving and maintaining compliance with the NAAQS. This chapter explains not only how regulators go about setting harm-based ambient standards under the Act, but also how they go about achieving compliance with them through a complex network of federal and state regulatory requirements.

COMMENTARY & QUESTIONS

1. Of sinks and ambient standards. Air and water are sometimes referred to as "pollution sinks," implying that airsheds and waterbodies are like large vats into which pollutants are thrown as a form of disposal. It is possible, perhaps even probable, that air and water can assimilate some man-made pollution without significant detriment to the natural systems of which they are a part. Whether exploiting this assimilative capacity is a good idea is a subject unto itself, but in the regulation of the criteria pollutants under the CAA, Congress made a pragmatic choice to "use" that assimilative capacity up to the limit of damage to human health and the environment.

The resort to ambient receiving body quality standards can be understood as a response to Hardin's tragedy of the commons (see Chapter 1). Imagine that the commons is a receiving body, such as a lake surrounded by several industrial facilities that emit effluent into the lake. To any one industrialist, the cost of avoiding pollution of the lake creates an incentive to pollute the lake. To forgo pollution might avoid costs of reduced receiving body quality, such as the need to treat water drawn from that source for industrial use, but the common pool nature of the receiving body vitiates that possible benefit of avoiding pollution. In the absence of regulatory intervention or comprehensive private agreement, there is no guarantee that the benefit of cleaner water will be obtained by any one of the firms because the other firms bordering the lake still may elect to dump their wastes into the commons. The CAA safeguards the commons of air quality by setting a national standard and then allowing the States to regulate so as to prevent private actors from polluting to such a degree that the commons would be compromised and human health would be in danger.

2. The utility of harm-based standards. Would harm-based standards be a valuable regulatory technique in fields other than air and water pollution? Harm-based standards are ubiquitous in other fields of regulation involving, for example, product safety for consumer goods and drugs, but in those settings, no commons is involved and therefore *ambient* standards are not required. Noise regulation, if it relies on setting maximum allowable levels based on avoidance of harm, is another possible example of a harm-based ambient standard.

3. The federal-state partnership under the CAA stationary source program. The principal sections of the CAA that create the harm-based NAAQS program are §§107-110, 42 U.S.C. §§7407-7410. Section 107(a) summarizes the overall concept:

> §107(a) . . . Each State shall have the primary responsibility for assuring air quality within the entire geographic area comprising such State by submitting an implementation plan for such State which will specify the manner in which national primary and secondary standards will be achieved and maintained within each air quality control region in such State.

Harm-based ambient standards and state plans for achieving them are a good example of cooperative federalism. The states have the freedom and the responsibility to make the difficult and multifaceted determinations about how to limit pollution to the allowable federal NAAQS limits, managing and accommodating the competing interests of their constituents.

4. State primacy. Why should "primary responsibility" for air quality theoretically be lodged with the states? Does the national interest in the solution of the problem of air pollution end with the attainment of acceptable ambient quality? A decision by an upwind state to require tall smokestacks and location of polluting facilities near the downwind state line might result in satisfactory ambient air quality in the upwind state, but it hardly seems consistent with sound national policy. The national interest can be protected in this sort of a case by the power of the federal government to reject such SIPs as inadequate. Section 110(a)(2)(D)—the so-called "Good Neighbor" provision of the CAA—requires states to write SIPs that

> contain adequate provisions (i) prohibiting . . . any source or other type of emissions activity within the State from emitting any air pollutant in amounts which will *(I)* contribute significantly to nonattainment in, or interfere with maintenance by, any other State with respect to any such national primary or secondary ambient air quality standard, or *(II)* interfere with . . . the applicable implementation plan for any other State . . . to prevent significant deterioration of air quality.

The federal government has used the power conferred by this section to impose substantial controls on NO_x emissions, which lead to long-range ozone transport, and on SO_2 emissions. EPA's effort, extending over almost two decades, most recently produced what the agency called the Cross-State Air Pollution Rule (also known as CSAPR or the Transport Rule). In *EPA v. EME Homer City Generation*, 134 S. Ct. 1584 (2014), discussed later in this chapter, the Supreme Court upheld the Transport Rule against a challenge to EPA's method for allocating among upwind states the emission reductions required by the Good Neighbor provision.

With so much authority reserved for EPA, even while the CAA provides for "state primacy," it is worth asking who is really in control, the states or the federal government? Recalling the concept of federal supremacy, this is a game that the states have no choice but to play. The third prong of the federal role—"FIPping," imposing FIPs on states that do not have adequate regulations—is anathema to the states. No state wants the federal bureaucracy making decisions that may have unpopular or even calamitous statewide economic repercussions, such as forcing major manufacturing facilities to shut down or relocate due to the imposition of stringent pollution control requirements. Through its power to refuse to approve SIPs and through funding cutoffs, EPA can influence how any SIP is drawn.

5. Ambient air quality standards and the race of laxity. Do harm-based ambient standards eliminate the race of laxity among the states? Areas with cleaner-than-required air can still run in the race and attract new industry with lax pollution control programs. Their race, however, will be a short one, and their victory may be Pyrrhic. The NAAQS limit how long the race can be run, and the PSD program shortens the race still further by setting ceilings on incremental increases in pollution in areas that enjoy especially clean air. Nevertheless, with a substantial percentage of air quality control regions (AQCRs) still out of compliance with at least one of the NAAQS, one might say that the race of laxity is still on; it's just not officially sanctioned.

1. What Are the Standards for Setting NAAQS?

Few regulatory judgments have as widespread economic and political ramifications as do decisions about how strict the NAAQS should be, and yet few statutory standards are

B. Harm-Based Ambient Standards Under the CAA

described quite as tersely. The CAA simply tells EPA that the primary NAAQS shall be standards "the attainment and maintenance of which in the judgment of the Administrator, based on such criteria and allowing an adequate margin of safety, are requisite to protect the public health." 42 U.S.C. §7409(b)(1). The Act requires EPA to review the existing NAAQS every five years, 42 U.S.C. §7409(d)(1), and instructs the agency to revise the standards "in the same manner as promulgated." 42 U.S.C. §7409(b)(1).

> *Lead Industries* and *American Trucking*
>
> Dirty air imposes a wide range of serious but indirect public costs. Cleaning up the air typically imposes direct economic costs on industry. Legal battles have reflected strong political tensions about where to place the public priorities—how much should *economic cost* weigh in setting environmental protection standards?

One of the most polarizing debates in the first three decades of the CAA was whether EPA was required or even allowed to consider economic costs in setting or revising the NAAQS. The issue first arose in the legal challenge to the NAAQS for lead, which was set following the addition of lead as a criteria pollutant. In *Lead Industries Ass'n v. EPA*,[6] the court upheld EPA's refusal to consider costs or technological feasibility in setting the NAAQS for lead. The court reasoned that whereas other CAA provisions expressly directed EPA to consider economic and technological feasibility in setting standards, §109(b) did not even mention costs or feasibility. The court also found support for its holding in the Act's legislative history, which the court thought demonstrated Congress's impatience with the failure to achieve progress in addressing air pollution under prior legislation.

Industry groups asked the Supreme Court to review the holdings in *Lead Industries* and three subsequent cases reaffirming it, to no avail. Then, in 1999, the D.C. Circuit set the regulatory world on fire by questioning the constitutionality of EPA's approach.

In 1997, EPA had revised the NAAQS for ozone and PM, lowering the ozone standard from 0.12 parts per million (ppm) to 0.08 ppm (while changing the averaging period from one hour to eight hours, which dampened the effect of the more stringent ozone level). The agency also set an entirely new PM standard for fine particulates of 2.5 micrometers or less in diameter; the old standard had regulated only coarser particles of 10 micrometers or less.

The inevitable legal challenge ensued. The D.C. Circuit's decision on the challenge did not overturn *Lead Industries* but instead did something even more surprising: It held that the CAA, as long interpreted by EPA to forbid consideration of costs in setting the NAAQS, violated the constitutional nondelegation doctrine. The court would have required EPA to articulate an "intelligible principle" to justify the line-drawing engaged in when setting the NAAQS. The criteria used by EPA—severity of effect, certainty of effect, and size of population affected—were not determinate enough to avoid an unlawful delegation of legislative power. The decision left EPA in a difficult position because the criterion suggested by the court, cost-benefit analysis, was unavailable to the agency under *Lead Industries*' prohibition

---

6. 647 F.2d 1130 (D.C. Cir. 1980).

against considering costs. Ultimately the case led the Supreme Court to grant review of the longstanding issue of the relevance of costs under the Act and to affirm EPA's long-held view.

Whitman v. American Trucking Associations

531 U.S. 457 (U.S. Sup. Ct. 2001)

SCALIA, J. . . . Section 109(b)(1) instructs the EPA to set primary ambient air quality standards "the attainment and maintenance of which . . . are requisite to protect the public health" with "an adequate margin of safety." 42 U.S.C. §7409(B)(1). Were it not for the hundreds of pages of briefing respondents have submitted on the issue, one would have thought it fairly clear that this text does not permit the EPA to consider costs in setting the standards. The language, as one scholar has noted, "is absolute." D. Currie, Air Pollution: Federal Law and Analysis 4-15 (1981). The EPA, "based on" the information about health effects contained in the technical "criteria" documents compiled under §108(a)(2), 42 U.S.C. §7408(a)(2), is to identify the maximum airborne concentration of a pollutant that the public health can tolerate, decrease the concentration to provide an "adequate" margin of safety, and set the standard at that level. Nowhere are the costs of achieving such a standard made part of that initial calculation.

Against this most natural of readings, respondents make a lengthy, spirited, but ultimately unsuccessful attack. They begin with the object of §109(b)(1)'s focus, the "public health." When the term first appeared in federal clean air legislation—in the Act of July 14, 1955 which expressed "recognition of the dangers to the public health" from air pollution —its ordinary meaning was "the health of the community." Webster's New International Dictionary (2d ed. 1950). Respondents argue, however, that §109(b)(1), as added by the Clean Air Amendments of 1970 (1970 Act), meant to use the term's secondary meaning: "the ways and means of conserving the health of the members of a community, as by preventive medicine, organized care of the sick, etc." Id. Words that can have more than one meaning are given content, however, by their surroundings, and in the context of §109(b)(1) this second definition makes no sense. Congress could not have meant to instruct the Administrator to set NAAQS at a level "requisite to protect" "the art and science dealing with the protection and improvement of community health." We therefore revert to the primary definition of the term: the health of the public.

Even so, respondents argue, many more factors than air pollution affect public health. In particular, the economic cost of implementing a very stringent standard might produce health losses sufficient to offset the health gains achieved in cleaning the air—for example, by closing down whole industries and thereby impoverishing the workers and consumers dependent upon those industries. That is unquestionably true, and Congress was unquestionably aware of it. Thus, Congress had commissioned in the Air Quality Act of 1967 "a detailed estimate of the cost of carrying out the provisions of this Act; a comprehensive study of the cost of program implementation by affected units of government; and a comprehensive study of the economic impact of air quality standards on the Nation's industries, communities, and other contributing sources of pollution." The 1970 Congress, armed with the results of this study, not only anticipated that compliance costs could injure the public health, but provided for that precise exigency. Section 110(f)(1) of the CAA permitted the Administrator to waive the compliance deadline for stationary sources if, inter alia, sufficient control measures were simply unavailable and "the continued operation of such sources is *essential . . . to the public health* or welfare." Other provisions explicitly permitted

B. Harm-Based Ambient Standards Under the CAA

or required economic costs to be taken into account in implementing the air quality standards. Section 111(b)(1)(B), for example, commanded the Administrator to set "standards of performance" for certain new sources of emissions that as specified in §111(a)(1) were to "reflect the degree of emission limitation achievable through the application of the best system of emission reduction which (taking into account the cost of achieving such reduction) the Administrator determines has been adequately demonstrated." Section 202(a)(2) prescribed that emissions standards for automobiles could take effect only "after such period as the Administrator finds necessary to permit the development and application of the requisite technology, giving appropriate consideration to the cost of compliance within such period." Subsequent amendments to the CAA have added many more provisions directing, in explicit language, that the Administrator consider costs in performing various duties. We have therefore refused to find implicit in ambiguous sections of the CAA an authorization to consider costs that has elsewhere, and so often, been expressly granted....

To prevail in their present challenge, respondents must show a textual commitment of authority to the EPA to consider costs in setting NAAQSs under §109(b)(1). And because §109(b)(1) and the NAAQSs for which it provides are the engine that drives nearly all of Title I of the CAA, that textual commitment must be a clear one. Congress, we have held, does not alter the fundamental details of a regulatory scheme in vague terms or ancillary provisions—it does not, one might say, hide elephants in mouseholes.

Respondents'... first claim is that §109(b)(1)'s terms "adequate margin" and "requisite" leave room to pad health effects with cost concerns.... We find it implausible that Congress would give to the EPA through these modest words the power to determine whether implementation costs should moderate national air quality standards.[7]

The same defect inheres in respondents'... arguments that... the Administrator's judgment... need not be based *solely* on those criteria, and that those criteria themselves are not necessarily *limited* to "effects on public health or welfare which may be expected from the presence of such pollutant in the ambient air."... Even if we were to concede those premises, we still would not conclude that one of the unenumerated factors that the agency can consider in developing and applying the criteria is cost of implementation. That factor is *both* so indirectly related to public health *and* so full of potential for canceling the conclusions drawn from direct health effects that it would surely have been expressly mentioned in §§108-109 had Congress meant it to be considered. Yet while those provisions describe in detail how the health effects of pollutants in the ambient air are to be calculated and given effect, they say not a word about costs.

Respondents point, finally, to a number of provisions in the CAA that *do* require attainment cost data to be generated.... Respondents argue that these provisions make no sense unless costs are to be considered in setting the NAAQS. That is not so. These provisions enable the Administrator to assist the States in carrying out their statutory role as primary *implementers* of the NAAQSs. It is to the States that the Act assigns initial and primary responsibility for deciding what emissions reductions will be required from which sources. It would be impossible to perform that task intelligently without considering which abatement technologies are most efficient, and most economically feasible—which is why we have said that "the most important forum for consideration of claims of economic and technological infeasibility is before the state agency formulating the implementation plan." *Union Elec. Co. v. EPA*, 427 U.S. 246 (1976).... That Congress chose... to assist States in

---

7. None of the sections of the CAA in which the District of Columbia Circuit has found authority for the EPA to consider costs shares §109(b)(1)'s prominence in the overall statutory scheme.

choosing the means through which they would implement the standards is perfectly sensible, and has no bearing upon whether cost considerations are to be taken into account in formulating the standards.[8] . . .

The text of §109(b), interpreted in its statutory and historical context and with appreciation for its importance to the CAA as a whole, unambiguously bars cost considerations from the NAAQS-setting process, and thus ends the matter for us as well as the EPA.[9] . . .

Section 109(b)(1) of the CAA instructs the EPA to set "ambient air quality standards the attainment and maintenance of which in the judgment of the Administrator, based on the criteria documents of §108 and allowing an adequate margin of safety, are requisite to protect the public health." The Court of Appeals held that this section as interpreted by the Administrator did not provide an "intelligible principle" to guide the EPA's exercise of authority in setting NAAQSs. "The EPA," it said, "lacked any determinate criteria for drawing lines. It has failed to state intelligibly how much is too much." The court hence found that the EPA's interpretation (but not the statute itself) violated the nondelegation doctrine. We disagree.

We agree with the Solicitor General that the text of §109(b)(1) of the CAA at a minimum requires that "for a discrete set of pollutants and based on published air quality criteria that reflect the latest scientific knowledge, the EPA must establish uniform national standards at a level that is requisite to protect public health from the adverse effects of the pollutant in the ambient air." Requisite, in turn, "means sufficient, but not more than necessary." These limits on the EPA's discretion are strikingly similar to the ones we approved in *Touby v. U.S.*, 500 U.S. 160 (1991), which permitted the Attorney General to designate a drug as a controlled substance for purposes of criminal drug enforcement if doing so was "necessary to avoid an imminent hazard to the public safety." They also resemble the Occupational Safety and Health Act provision requiring the agency to "set the standard which most adequately assures, to the extent feasible, on the basis of the best available evidence, that no employee will suffer any impairment of health"—which the Court upheld in *Industrial Union Department, AFL-CIO v. Am. Petroleum Inst.*, 448 U.S. 607, 646 (1980), and which even then Justice Rehnquist, who alone in that case thought the statute violated the nondelegation doctrine, would have upheld if, like the statute here, it did not permit economic costs to be considered.

It is true enough that the degree of agency discretion that is acceptable varies according to the scope of the power congressionally conferred. . . . We have never demanded, as the Court of Appeals did here, that statutes provide a "determinate criterion" for saying "how much of the regulated harm is too much." . . .

---

8. Respondents scarcely mention in their arguments the *secondary* NAAQS required by §109(b)(2), 42 U.S.C. §7409(b)(2). For many of the same reasons described in the body of the opinion, as well as the text of §109(b)(2), which instructs the EPA to set the standards at a level "requisite to protect the public welfare from any known or anticipated adverse effects *associated with the presence of such air pollutant in the ambient air*," we conclude that the EPA may not consider implementation costs in setting the secondary NAAQS.

9. Respondents' speculation that the EPA is secretly considering the costs of attainment without telling anyone is irrelevant to our interpretive inquiry. If such an allegation could be proved, it would be grounds for vacating the NAAQS, because the Administrator had not followed the law. It would not, however, be grounds for this Court's changing the law.

B. Harm-Based Ambient Standards Under the CAA

COMMENTARY & QUESTIONS

1. **An anticlimactic ruling?** The decision in *American Trucking* was anxiously awaited. After a long fight about the appropriate method for achieving NAAQS, spurred by private industries' opposition to the potential high costs of complying with the CAA, industrialists, environmentalists, and EPA staffers all held their breath awaiting the decision from the Supreme Court. The Court's opinion itself was arguably anticlimactic, at least on the constitutional question before it. The Court had no trouble rejecting the D.C. Circuit's renovation of the nondelegation doctrine.

On the statutory question, Justice Scalia's opinion makes clear that as a textual matter, the CAA prohibits the EPA Administrator from considering costs in setting the NAAQS. The legislative history of the Act further supports this view. Consider the comments of Senator Muskie, manager of the Senate version of the bill, explaining the purpose behind the proposed ambient air quality standards:

> The first responsibility of Congress is not the making of technological or economic judgments or even to be limited by what is or appears to be technologically or economically feasible. Our responsibility is to establish what the public interest requires to protect the health of persons. This may mean that people and industries will be asked to do what seems to be impossible at the present time. 116 Cong. Rec. 32901-32902 (1970).

2. **Cost-sensitive interpretation after *American Trucking*.** In its ruling, the Supreme Court left in place a number of lower court decisions allowing agencies to consider costs unless Congress concludes otherwise. In *Michigan v. EPA*, 135 S. Ct. 2699 (2015), the Supreme Court—with Justice Scalia again writing for the majority—characterized the statutory holding in *American Trucking* as embracing the "modest principle that where the Clean Air Act expressly directs EPA to regulate on the basis of a factor that on its face does not include cost, the Act normally should not be read as implicitly allowing the Agency to consider cost anyway." Notably, all nine Justices in *Michigan v. EPA*—including the four Justices in dissent, led by Justice Kagan—agreed that absent contrary indication from Congress "an agency must take costs into account in some manner before imposing significant regulatory burdens." We will see more of *Michigan v. EPA* later in this chapter.

3. **Justice Breyer's concurrence on risk regulation.** Justice Breyer concurred in part and concurred in the judgment. He concluded that the "legislative history, along with the statute's structure, indicates that §109's language reflects a congressional decision not to delegate to the agency the legal authority to consider economic costs of compliance." He argued:

> this interpretation of §109 does not require the EPA to eliminate every health risk, however slight, at any economic cost, however great, to the point of "hurtling" industry over "the brink of ruin," or even forcing "deindustrialization." The statute, by its express terms, does not compel the elimination of *all* risk; and it grants the Administrator sufficient flexibility to avoid setting ambient air quality standards ruinous to industry.

What does Justice Breyer's concurrence mean? Should it really be a dissent on the statutory issue—that is, is Breyer suggesting that EPA actually may look at costs in setting the NAAQS? If he's not saying that, what is he saying?

4. ***American Trucking* on remand to the D.C. Circuit.** The Supreme Court remanded the *American Trucking* case to the D.C. Circuit to determine if EPA abused its discretion in setting new NAAQS for fine PM and ozone. Employing a deferential standard, the circuit court held that the new standards implemented by EPA met the requirements prescribed by the Supreme Court. In ruling for EPA in the face of challenges to its treatment of the

scientific evidence before it, the D.C. Circuit adopted the deferential posture that has characterized most of its decisions reviewing NAAQS over the years.

5. The next stop for industry. In light of the Supreme Court's ruling and the ruling on remand, many in industry have concluded that the time to take an active role is during the state level notice-and-comment rulemaking process when states draw up implementation plans. At the state level, costs determine the appropriate implementation, and the Supreme Court itself recognized that states can and do consider the economic feasibility of implementation: "The most important forum for consideration of claims of economic and technological infeasibility is before the state agency formulating the implementation plan." *American Trucking*, 531 U.S. at 470. By interjecting itself in the state agency rulemaking process, industry will likely seek to influence how the agency assesses the feasibility of such plans. But if industry cannot convince the state agency to take feasibility into account, EPA cannot disapprove of a SIP on that basis.[10]

6. A closer look at the SIP process. When a NAAQS is first established or revised, all 50 states must revise their SIPs to ensure attainment, maintenance, and enforcement of the NAAQS. The process involves three steps. First, the state must take an inventory of the emissions of the pollution sources within its borders. Second, the state must try to predict what future emissions in the state will be, so that it can determine whether it will achieve (or maintain) compliance with the NAAQS by the deadline set by the federal government. This step involves quite complicated exercises in air quality modeling. Finally, the state must seek pollution reductions from individual sources as necessary to come into or stay in compliance with the NAAQS.

The SIP requirements usually are put in the form of a permit that dictates how a specific plant may operate in regard to emitting pollution. The stationary source permits work together with the other parts of the SIP. Those might include transportation planning, vehicle inspection and maintenance, mandatory installation of hoods or vapor recovery systems at gasoline stations, ozone action alerts recommending that citizens refrain from refueling vehicles or using lawnmowers on days having particular climatic conditions, and so on. Together, all parts of the plan must produce a net effect that allows all of the NAAQS to be met at virtually all times[11] throughout the state. If a SIP will not have that result, EPA cannot approve it. If the state is unable or unwilling to propose a SIP that EPA approves, EPA must take over the process and write a FIP. A good deal of science and art is involved in determining whether a proposed implementation plan will result in satisfactory ambient air quality.

7. Setting the NAAQS under conditions of uncertainty. Another issue that arises in setting the NAAQS concerns the role of scientific uncertainty. Standard-setting requires judgments about the causal effects of exposure to varying concentrations of pollutants. In *Lead Industries*, the D.C. Circuit recognized that EPA may act despite uncertainty:

> It may be . . . LIA's [Lead Industry Association's] view that the Administrator must show that there is a "medical consensus that [the effects on which the standards were based] are harmful. . . . " If so, LIA is seriously mistaken. This court has previously noted that some uncertainty about the health effects of air pollution is inevitable. And we pointed out that "awaiting certainty will often allow for only reactive, not preventive regulat[ory action]."*Ethyl*, 541 F.2d 1, 25 (D.C. Cir. 1976). Congress apparently shares this view; it specifically directed the Administrator to allow an adequate margin of safety to protect against effects which have not yet been uncovered by research and effects whose medical significance is a matter of disagreement. . . .

---

10. See *Union Elec. Co. v. EPA*, 427 U.S. 246 (1976) (holding that EPA may not disapprove a SIP based on the ground that it does not take technological and economic feasibility into account).

11. Some of the NAAQS do allow one or more annual exceedances.

B. Harm-Based Ambient Standards Under the CAA

Moreover, it is significant that Congress has recently acknowledged that more often than not the "margins of safety" that are incorporated into air quality standards turn out to be very modest or nonexistent, as new information reveals adverse health effects at pollution levels once thought to be harmless. See H.R. Rep. No. 95-294 at 103-117. Congress' directive to the Administrator to allow an "adequate margin of safety" alone plainly refutes any suggestion that the Administrator is only authorized to set primary air quality standards which are designed to protect against health effects that are known to be clearly harmful. . . . All that is required by the statutory scheme is evidence in the record which substantiates his conclusions about the health effects on which the standards were based. 647 F.2d at 1154-1155.

It will surprise no one to hear that the courts' long endorsement of regulating in the face of scientific uncertainty under the CAA has not silenced or even muted the critics of any new iteration of the NAAQS.

8. Protecting vulnerable subpopulations from subclinical effects. Another important issue that has dogged the NAAQS program from the start is what effects are harmful enough to justify designing a NAAQS so as to avoid them. The court in *Lead Industries* also had something to say about this issue. It rejected arguments that EPA was forbidden from considering mere "subclinical effects" from lead exposure rather than the onset of disease as the threshold of relevant harm and that EPA could not base its regulation on achieving levels that would protect the health of the most sensitive population, urban children.

9. How much harm is too much? During the 1980s and 1990s, scientific evidence that the existing NAAQS for SO_2 caused harms to sensitive populations (especially asthmatics) began to accumulate. Studies showed that short-term, "high-level bursts" of SO_2 could cause respiratory difficulties for asthmatics; these problems ranged from having to cease strenuous outdoor activity, to taking medication, to seeking medical attention. Despite considerable pressure from the American Lung Association to promulgate a "high-level burst" exposure NAAQS for SO_2, EPA long refused to do so. EPA's Clean Air Scientific Advisory Committee had concluded that the respiratory difficulties experienced by asthmatics as a consequence of these "bursts" were transitory and reversible, and that they also were within the range of adverse reactions experienced by asthmatics due to causes other than pollution. Later, however, EPA offered a different explanation for refusing to set a new short-term NAAQS for SO_2. EPA stated that while the respiratory difficulties were adverse and significant if they occurred repeatedly, and while the agency estimated that over 40,000 people would be subject to repeated instances of such effects in the absence of a stricter standard, the agency thought a new standard was not necessary because the adverse effects were "localized, infrequent, and site-specific." The D.C. Circuit failed to see a rational connection between EPA's finding that the health effects were adverse and significant and its decision not to set a new NAAQS to prevent them, and remanded the case to the agency.[12] Eventually, EPA responded to the remand by issuing revised NAAQS for SO_2, settling on a one-hour standard of 75 ppb for this pollutant. The D.C. Circuit upheld the revised standards in *National Envtl. Dev. Ass'ns Clean Air Project v. EPA*, 686 F.3d 802 (D.C. Cir. 2012), explaining: "We cannot say that the [clinical] studies necessitated a 75 ppb standard, but we also cannot say that such a standard is unreasonable or unsupported by the record before us."

A short-term standard raises special challenges for compliance monitoring. The monitoring network must be robust enough to capture the localized pollution "bursts" that were the target of the new standards. EPA struggled with this issue in the context of SO_2, offering

---

12. *American Lung Ass'n v. EPA*, 134 F.3d 388, 392 (D.C. Cir. 1998).

several different approaches in the aftermath of setting the new standards, each using different combinations of traditional, fixed monitoring equipment and computer modeling of air quality. In the end, EPA required states to monitor or model sources that emit 2000 or more tons per year of SO_2. This experience well illustrates how much analytical work is required for the NAAQS regime, beyond the "simple" step of establishing the level of air quality to be achieved.

10. Risk-risk tradeoffs. Even if EPA may not consider economic costs and technological feasibility in setting the NAAQS, may it consider potential adverse health and welfare effects arising from the standards themselves? In *American Trucking*, in a part of its decision not reviewed by the Supreme Court, the D.C. Circuit said "yes." There, EPA argued that it was not required to consider the claim that a stricter ozone standard would harm health and welfare by diluting the layer of ground-level ozone that, the argument went, helped to protect people from the adverse effects of the thinning of the stratospheric ozone layer. The court held that EPA was obliged to consider the potentially adverse health and welfare effects of the NAAQS. On remand, EPA concluded that the "protective" features of ozone pollution were too speculative to warrant basing the NAAQS on them.

In a related vein, industry groups have argued that EPA must consider the adverse health and welfare effects caused by the high economic costs of the NAAQS. High regulatory costs cause unemployment, the theory runs, and unemployment leads to adverse health consequences. The D.C. Circuit has rejected this argument, relying on the language of the CAA that directs EPA's attention to an air pollutant's adverse effects arising from the "presence of such pollutant in the ambient air," 42 U.S.C. §7408(a)(2).[13] Has Justice Breyer also rejected this argument?

11. Ozone politics. An early order of business for the Obama EPA was to consider whether to retain the revised ozone NAAQS that had been set by the Bush II EPA. The Bush II EPA had departed from the recommendation of the scientific body that advises EPA on the NAAQS—the Clean Air Scientific Advisory Committee (CASAC)—and set the primary standard at 0.075 parts per million, rather than in the 0.060 to 0.070 range preferred by CASAC. The Bush II-era ozone standard was widely regarded as among the biggest environmental defaults of the Bush II Administration relating to the environment; many thought the standard was scientifically unsound. In September 2009, the Obama EPA announced that it would reconsider the Bush II-era standard. EPA eventually forwarded a final rule package, setting the primary standard at 0.070 ppm, to the White House for approval. President Obama stunned environmentalists and, it appeared, EPA itself, by instructing the EPA Administrator, Lisa Jackson, to withdraw the revised standard. In a written statement, the President emphasized "the importance of reducing regulatory burdens and regulatory uncertainty, particularly as our economy continues to recover," and stated that given that a new review of the ozone standard was already underway, he "did not support asking state and local governments to begin implementing a new standard that will soon be reconsidered." In response, EPA left the Bush II-era standard in place. In *Mississippi v. EPA*, 744 F.3d 1334 (2013), the D.C. Circuit upheld the Bush II-era primary standard against challenges from both directions. Noting the dueling challenges, the court observed: "unlike Goldilocks, this court cannot demand that EPA get things 'just right.' Rather, for EPA's decision to survive these challenges, it need do no more than meet the statutory standards found in the Clean Air Act." Were President Obama's reasons for rejecting EPA's ozone standard lawful reasons? Does the CAA's delegation of authority to the EPA Administrator

---

13. *NRDC v. EPA*, 902 F.2d 962 (D.C. Cir. 1990).

B. Harm-Based Ambient Standards Under the CAA

to set the NAAQS presumptively imply a delegation, as well, to the President to make this decision? For the classic statement of the argument that the answer to the latter question is "yes," see Kagan, Presidential Administration, 114 Harv. L. Rev. 2245 (2001).

In 2015, EPA revised the primary ozone standard yet again, lowering it to the 0.070 ppm level EPA had tried to set four years earlier.

2. Transboundary Airflows

> One fundamental argument for federal regulation of pollution is the problem of transboundary pollution, or pollution that travels from one state to another. If, for example, Massachusetts cannot clean up its air without Ohio reducing emissions from its power plants, then federal intervention is needed to broker the dispute.

The original 1970 CAA did little to solve the problem of transboundary pollution. The statute required upwind states to give notice to downwind states of new and proposed major sources that would affect the downwind state's ability to meet the NAAQS or interfere with the downwind state's PSD program. The adversely affected state could protest to EPA, with EPA becoming the arbiter of the interstate clash of interests. The statute's language seemed to favor the downwind states. Under the 1970 CAA, an upwind state's SIP, to be approved, was required to prevent sources from emitting air pollution that would "prevent attainment or maintenance" of NAAQS by other states. In practice, however, before the 1990 Amendments to the Act downwind states won very few concessions from upwind states through appeals to EPA. They had an even worse record seeking judicial invalidation of EPA approvals of upwind activities.

Air Pollution Control Dist. v. EPA, 739 F.2d 1071 (6th Cir. 1984), an early leading case in this area, gives a flavor of the difficulty downwind states experienced. The case involved SO_2 contributions to the Louisville, Kentucky, airshed of a coal-fired power plant located just across the Ohio River in Indiana. For a few months after Indiana and Kentucky had their initial SIPs approved under the CAA of 1970, the Kentucky and Indiana SIPs required identical SO_2 control efforts for coal-fired power plants, an emission limitation of 1.2 lb of SO_2 per million British thermal units of heat input (MBTU). Indiana almost immediately won EPA approval for a revised SIP that allowed unregulated SO_2 emissions from coal-fired electric generating facilities. Kentucky, downwind on the other side of the river, held firm to the 1.2 lb./MBTU standard and forced the primary Kentucky SO_2 producer in the region, Louisville Gas & Electric (LG&E), to meet that standard. The court described the contrast in an understated way:

> It can therefore be seen that a significant disparity exists between the permissible emission limits of power plants in Jefferson County, Kentucky and the Gallagher plant in Floyd County, Indiana. LG&E, the primary producer of SO_2 in Jefferson County, spent approximately $138 million installing scrubbers to remove SO_2 from its emissions, while just across the river, Gallagher's SO_2 emissions were completely uncontrolled. 739 F.2d at 1077.

Despite Kentucky's SO_2 control efforts in the Louisville AQCR, it remained a nonattainment area even after LG&E had completed installation of all of the needed emission controls. A petition was lodged with EPA, seeking relief against the interstate effects of SO_2

pollution from the nearby Indiana plant. EPA concluded that only 3% of the Kentucky SO_2 concentrations that resulted in violations of the NAAQS were attributable to the Gallagher plant. EPA also found, however, that the Gallagher plant contributed large concentrations of SO_2 that were not part of predicted violations of the NAAQS. EPA's own study of the data observed these impacts have "a far more serious potential for limiting growth in Kentucky. . . ." EPA even stated that by 1985, when controls at the LG&E plant would be fully on line, the Gallagher plant "will be the predominate [sic] influence upon air quality in Louisville, Kentucky." Id. at 1078.

EPA denied Kentucky's petition, however, and judicial review in the federal court followed. The court held, first, that EPA had appropriately construed the Act to prohibit only interstate pollution that "significantly contributes" to present violations of the NAAQS or an already established PSD program. In defense of the court's holding, note that 42 U.S.C. §7426 requires notice to downwind states only of new sources in the upwind state that "may significantly contribute" to air quality problems in the downwind state. Also, imagine the results (political and economic) of a conclusion that the CAA forbids all transboundary air pollution.

Second, the court upheld EPA's position that interference with potential growth in the downwind state is not a ground on which relief can be granted in the absence of interference with an established PSD plan or program. The proper accommodation of interstate interests on this question presents a subtle and difficult issue. To grasp the competing positions of Kentucky and EPA more clearly, imagine what would be the course of events if the Kentucky AQCR involved in the litigation, through additional reductions in emissions, remedies the excessive concentrations of SO_2 in all locations and becomes an attainment area. At that point, Kentucky would be able to adopt a new PSD SIP that allows some new pollution to be introduced if continued compliance with the NAAQS can be maintained. As the facts set forth above showed, EPA's model of the airshed indicated that there are some parts of the AQCR where, but for the Indiana emissions from the Gallagher plant, there would be substantial room for incremental SO_2 emissions without exceeding the NAAQS. On this basis, Kentucky claims that Indiana has "stolen its PSD increment" through the failure to limit Gallagher emissions.

In the case as it was litigated, Kentucky made this argument. EPA's response was formalistic and, in light of its own findings in the case, a bit disingenuous. EPA said there could be no present stealing of a PSD increment because no PSD baseline could be set in advance of becoming an attainment area. When attainment occurred, the Kentucky concentrations attributable to the Gallagher plant would not then constitute stealing the increment because those concentrations would be part of the baseline. In this way, regardless of terminology, EPA allows Indiana to dispose of significant SO_2 emissions at Kentucky's expense.

While the EPA position seems palpably unfair to Kentucky, it has the administrative advantage of limiting the need to exercise discretion. It avoids the pitfalls of some vague equity-based approach that would inevitably embroil EPA in bitter interstate disputes involving protracted evidentiary matters concerning the precise extent of interstate pollution. The EPA approach also maintains ambient standards as its central technique, whereas an alternative rule that called for equal pollution control efforts on both sides of the state line would rely more on a mandated technology approach. Although these observations hardly amount to a ringing defense of the EPA position, they give it sufficient rationality to be sustained by a reviewing court applying a deferential standard of review.

On what principled basis can EPA determine how much pollution can cross state boundaries without constituting an injury to the downwind state? The general movement of air masses and the pollutants they carry is an uncontrollable natural event. A zero

B. Harm-Based Ambient Standards Under the CAA

transboundary emission limit is unattainable and undesirable. To meet that goal, emissions limits in the upwind state would have to be excessively restrictive. Remember that some NAAQS are measured in terms of brief sampling periods, the wind and other atmospheric conditions vary erratically, and virtually all states are both importers and exporters of pollution. These features of the air pollution problem, and the opacity of the relevant statutory provisions, continue to stalk EPA in its efforts to curb interstate air pollution.

The 1990 amendments to the CAA changed the wording of the statute's "Good Neighbor" provision from requiring states to write SIPs that forbade sources to emit pollution in amounts that would "prevent attainment or maintenance" of NAAQS, to requiring states to write SIPs that forbade sources to emit pollution in amounts that would "contribute significantly to nonattainment, or interfere with maintenance" of the NAAQS in other states. The change in wording bolstered EPA's defense of a 1998 rule—the "NO_x SIP Call"— that required some states to make significant SIP revisions for ozone control.[14] This rule required 22 states and the District of Columbia to submit SIPs that addressed the regional transport of ground-level ozone. The purpose of the action was to attempt to limit NO_x emissions in upwind states from adversely affecting ground-level ozone levels in downwind states. States that found themselves adversely affected by the rule, which included target reductions on a state-by-state basis, sued to block it. Relying in part on the 1990 changes to the Good Neighbor provision in distinguishing EPA's prior approach, reflected in the Kentucky litigation described above, the D.C. Circuit rejected the bulk of the challenges to the rule.[15]

EPA returned to the problem of interstate air pollution during the Bush II Administration, when EPA's NO_x SIP call gave way to the "Clean Air Interstate Rule" (CAIR). CAIR required steep cuts in NO_x and SO_2 emissions in 28 states and the District of Columbia. The required cuts were achieved through compliance with regionwide caps on emissions, and the rule allowed these caps to be met through interstate emissions trading. In *North Carolina v. EPA*, 531 F.3d 896 (2008), the D.C. Circuit found "more than several fatal flaws" in CAIR, including EPA's failure to link the regionwide caps and state emissions budgets to the objectives of §110 of the CAA. After initially vacating the entire rule, the court eventually left the rule in place while EPA revisited it.

In 2011, EPA finalized a new rule on interstate transport, now dubbed the "Cross-State Air Pollution Rule" (CSAPR). Like CAIR before it, CSAPR, too, allowed interstate emissions trading, but to a lesser extent. EPA relied on two analytical steps in developing CSAPR. First, EPA determined whether a state contributed more than 1% to nonattainment at a downwind site; if it did, then the upwind state was subject to the rule. Second, EPA determined the pollution reductions necessary for the states subject to CSAPR to meet their obligations under the Good Neighbor provision. In this step, EPA applied cost-effectiveness thresholds that were uniform across states but that differed depending on the pollutant and compliance setting involved. EPA allowed interstate trading, so long as states traded only with other states that had the same cost-effectiveness threshold. The D.C. Circuit ruled against EPA yet again in *EME Homer City Generation v. EPA*, 696 F.3d 7 (D.C. Cir. 2012), faulting EPA for failing to limit the pollution reductions it required in upwind states to those necessary to eliminate their "significant contributions" to nonattainment in downwind states.

---

14. Finding of Significant Contribution and Rulemaking for Certain States in the Ozone Transport Assessment Group Region for Purposes of Reducing Regional Transport of Ozone, Sept. 24, 1998, 63 Fed. Reg. 57356 (Oct. 27, 1998).

15. See *Michigan v. EPA*, 213 F.3d 663 (D.C. Cir. 2000).

In *EPA v. EME Homer City Generation v. EPA*, the Supreme Court reversed the D.C. Circuit. Writing for a six-Justice majority, Justice Ginsburg emphasized the complexity of the interstate air pollution problem addressed by EPA and leaned heavily on *Chevron* deference in endorsing the agency's chosen route through this thicket. Justice Ginsburg concluded that nothing in the CAA required the EPA (as the D.C. Circuit had held) "to provide specific metrics to States before they undertake to fulfill their good neighbor obligations" under the Act. In addition, she held, EPA was within its statutory rights in setting upwind states' air pollution budgets based on their cost-per-ton of pollution control. Using cost-effectiveness as a regulatory metric, Justice Ginsburg said "makes good sense" and "avoids [the] anomalies" of otherwise requiring states that have "already utilized lower cost pollution controls" to do still more while allowing states that have done little in this domain to "run old, dirty plants." EPA's interpretation was, Justice Ginsburg summarized, "a permissible, workable, and equitable interpretation of the Good Neighbor Provision."

Justice Scalia, joined by Justice Alito, wrote a strongly worded dissent. On EPA's use of cost-effectiveness in setting states' air pollution budgets, Justice Scalia characterized the approach (three times) as something akin to Marxism: "from each according to its ability."

In her majority opinion, Justice Ginsburg agreed with the parties challenging CSAPR to this extent: EPA could not, she concluded, require upwind states to reduce pollution more than was necessary to avoid "contribut[ing] significantly" to downwind states' nonattainment:

> If EPA requires an upwind State to reduce emissions by more than the amount necessary to achieve attainment in *every* downwind State to which it is linked, the Agency will have overstepped its authority, under the Good Neighbor Provision, to eliminate those "amounts [that] contribute . . . to nonattainment." Nor can EPA demand reductions that would drive an upwind State's contribution to every downwind State to which it is linked below one percent of the relevant NAAQS. Doing so would be counter to step one of the Agency's interpretation of the Good Neighbor Provision. See 76 Fed. Reg. 48236 ("[S]tates whose contributions are below th[e] thresholds do not significantly contribute to nonattainment . . . of the relevant NAAQS.")
>
> Neither possibility, however, justifies wholesale invalidation of the Transport Rule. First, instances of "over-control" in particular downwind locations, the D.C. Circuit acknowledged, may be incidental to reductions necessary to ensure attainment elsewhere. Because individual upwind States often "contribute significantly" to nonattainment in multiple downwind locations, the emissions reduction required to bring one linked downwind State into attainment may well be large enough to push other linked downwind States over the attainment line. As the Good Neighbor Provision seeks attainment in *every* downwind State, however, exceeding attainment in one State cannot rank as "over-control" unless unnecessary to achieving attainment in *any* downwind State. Only reductions unnecessary to downwind attainment *anywhere* fall outside the Agency's statutory authority. . . .
>
> If any upwind State concludes it has been forced to regulate emissions below the one-percent threshold or beyond the point necessary to bring all downwind States into attainment, that State may bring a particularized, as-applied challenge to the Transport Rule, along with any other as-applied challenges it may have. Satisfied that EPA's cost-based methodology, on its face, is not "arbitrary, capricious, or manifestly contrary to the statute," *Chevron*, 467 U.S., at 844, we uphold the Transport Rule. The possibility that the rule, in uncommon particular applications, might exceed EPA's statutory authority does not warrant judicial condemnation of the rule in its entirety. 134 S. Ct. at 1608-09.

Naturally, aggrieved states accepted the Court's invitation to file as-applied challenges to CSAPR. The D.C. Circuit again rejected EPA's approach. In *EME Homer City Generation, L.P. v. EPA* (2015), the court found that CSAPR's emissions budgets for several states required "over-control" of emissions insofar as they required more emissions control than was necessary to achieve attainment in downwind states. The court was untroubled by the fact that its approach would undermine uniform cost thresholds, reasoning that the Supreme Court had "explicitly authorized as-applied challenges that, when successful under the principles outlined by the Court, will *necessarily* mean a lack of uniformity in certain circumstances." Noting that vacatur of CSAPR would threaten "substantial disruption to the trading markets" that had arisen in response to the existing emissions budgets, the court declined to vacate the invalid budgets.

EPA had offered interstate trading as a cost-effective means of complying with the Good Neighbor provision. Uniform cost-effectiveness thresholds were central to its embrace of trading. Does the D.C. Circuit's latest ruling fatally undermine trading in this context? Is it consistent with the Supreme Court's general acceptance of CSAPR?

3. The Intersection of Agency Action and Environmental Justice

> Why is it that some of the very worst pollution conditions are found in low-income communities and communities of color—e.g., Cancer Alley in Louisiana, radioactive spoils dumps in western Native American regions, and inner-city neighborhoods around the nation? Low land values and political marginalization mean slacker environmental regulatory effectiveness and pollution "hot spots." This is particularly challenging for air pollution and the resulting threat to public health.

Title VI of the Civil Rights Act of 1964[16] prohibits intentional racial discrimination by recipients of federal funds. In 1994, President Clinton issued an executive order[17] and an accompanying presidential memorandum, which direct federal agencies to ensure that federal actions that substantially affect human health or the environment do not have discriminatory effects based on race, color, or national origin. In 2001, EPA issued a draft revised guidance to respond to Title VI and the Executive Order. In 2013, EPA issued a new draft revised guidance on this subject, excerpts of which follow. EPA stated that the 2013 draft guidance would supercede the 2000 draft revised guidance once the revised 2013 guidance was finalized. The 2013 guidance has not yet been finalized.

U.S. Environmental Protection Agency, Title VI of the Civil Rights Act of 1964: Adversity and Compliance with Environmental Health-Based Thresholds

78 Fed. Reg. 24739 (April 26, 2013)

. . . This paper outlines the U.S. Environmental Protection Agency's (EPA's or Agency's) current thinking about enforcement of Title VI of the Civil Rights Act of 1964 concerning how compliance with environmental health-based thresholds relates to "adversity" in the context of disparate impact claims about environmental permitting.

---

16. 42 U.S.C. §§2000d to 2000d-7 (as amended).
17. Exec. Order No. 12,898, Federal Actions to Address Environmental Justice in Minority Populations and Low-Income Populations, 59 Fed. Reg. 7629 (Feb. 16, 1994).

This paper does not address allegations about intentional discrimination, most non-permitting fact patterns, or technology- and cost-based standards; it is focused on discriminatory effects allegations that relate to the health protectiveness of pollution control permits issued by recipient agencies. In particular, this paper concerns the adversity prong of the *prima facie* case and does not address the other analytical steps necessary to determine whether a violation has occurred.... [The principles discussed here also apply compliance with health thresholds in some non-permitting settings, such as brownfields cleanups.]

BACKGROUND: The Agency has encountered a number of complex and unique issues of law and policy in the course of Title VI complaint investigations, especially allegations concerning the protectiveness of environmental permits issued by state and local agencies that receive EPA financial assistance. These challenges have been the consequence of the need to merge the objectives and requirements of Title VI with the objectives and requirements of the environmental laws that the Agency implements. The Agency's environmental regulatory mandates require complex technical assessments regarding pollution emissions, exposures, and cause-effect relationships. In addition, the cooperative federalism approach embodied in the federal environmental statutes requires that EPA accomplish its environmental protection objectives in close coordination with state and local environmental regulators. Such issues do not have ready analogues in the context of other federal agencies' Title VI programs.

The Agency's historical efforts in its Title VI program have been the subject of some criticism over the years. One particular criticism arose in response to the Agency's 1998 *Select Steel* decision – the origin of the rebuttable presumption addressed below. In *Select Steel*, EPA's Office of Civil Rights (OCR) dismissed an administrative complaint concerning a permit issued by the Michigan Department of Environmental Quality for the Select Steel facility based, in part, on the fact that the applicable National Ambient Air Quality Standards (NAAQS) were already being met, and that the facility's permitted emissions, in combination with other stressors, were not causing an adverse effect.[18] The rebuttable presumption approach was incorporated into the *Draft Revised Guidance for Investigating Title VI Administrative Complaints Challenging Permits* [2001].

The Agency has elected to reexamine the weight it accords compliance with environmental health-based thresholds because this issue, in particular, sits directly at the crossroads of environmental and civil rights law. . . .

TITLE VI LEGAL FRAMEWORK: Many Title VI investigations concern administrative complaints alleging adverse disparate impacts from the issuance of an environmental permit. Such complaints are filed pursuant to EPA's Title VI regulations. When assessing such complaints, EPA first determines whether it has jurisdiction over the complaint. If so, the

---

18. In its evaluation of the NAAQS, OCR noted that "[t]he NAAQS for ozone [and lead] is a health-based standard which has been set at a level that is presumptively sufficient to protect public health and allows for an adequate margin of safety for the population within the area." Letter from Ann E. Goode, Director, EPA/OCR, to Father Phil Schmitter and Sister Joanne Chiaverini, Co-Directors, St. Francis Prayer Center 3 (Oct. 30, 1998) [hereinafter Goode Letter]. OCR further noted that the NAAQS provides "protection for group(s) identified as being sensitive to the adverse effects of the NAAQS pollutants." Office of Civil Rights, U.S. Environmental Protection Agency, *Investigative Report for Title VI Administrative Complaint File No. 5R-98-R5 (Select Steel Complaint)* 14 (1998). As applied to the complaint, OCR found that the area around the proposed Select Steel facility would attain the NAAQS for ozone and lead, and that there was no evidence suggesting other concerns. As a result, OCR concluded that no adverse impacts occurred with respect to the state's permitting emissions of those pollutants.

B. Harm-Based Ambient Standards Under the CAA

Agency then applies the analytical framework for assessing significant adverse disparate impact claims established by the courts:

1. Is there a *prima facie* case? (The following three elements need not be established in order.)
    a. Does the alleged discriminatory act have an adverse impact?
    b. Is that adverse impact suffered disparately?
    c. Is the adverse disparate impact caused by the recipient?
2. Can the recipient offer a substantial legitimate justification for its action?
3. Is there a less discriminatory alternative?

This paper focuses only on a particular issue that may arise in the course of conducting the inquiry described in step 1.a., above. . . .

CONSIDERATION OF ENVIRONMENTAL HEALTH-BASED THRESHOLDS

In the course of investigating complaints of discrimination arising from the issuance of environmental permits, EPA may need to consider whether a permit that complies with a health-based threshold can nevertheless cause an adverse impact. Such assessments may involve analyses that are complex or, in some cases, simply infeasible with existing technical capabilities. Consequently, the Agency believes that the issue of establishing adversity warrants further consideration as described below.

Issue:

How does compliance with environmental health-based thresholds relate to whether adversity exists in Title VI investigations?

Current Position:

The *2000 Draft Guidance* addresses the question of how to analyze adversity in a case where the NAAQS – which is a health-based standard – is being met. It states that attainment of health-based NAAQS creates a rebuttable presumption that no adverse impacts are caused by the permit at issue with respect to the relevant NAAQS pollutant(s) for purposes of Title VI. As applied in an investigation involving the NAAQS, EPA would first establish whether the area in question was attaining the NAAQS for the relevant pollutant. If so, EPA would presume that the adversity component of the *prima facie* case was not satisfied (*i.e.*, there is no adversity) and then dismiss the complaint. However, if the investigation produced evidence that significant adverse impacts may be occurring with respect to the NAAQS pollutant despite attainment of the NAAQS, the presumption would be rebutted and EPA would continue to investigate the remaining prongs of the *prima facie* case. While the *2000 Draft Guidance* spoke specifically to NAAQS, EPA has considered the issue of the rebuttable presumption as it might apply to any health-based threshold and the position set forth in this paper is applicable to any complaint in which a health-based threshold is present, not just NAAQS.

Proposed Position:

While EPA has had little or no opportunity to apply the rebuttable presumption (that is, this issue has been discussed in the abstract, and has not been applied to any particular case following issuance of the *2000 Draft Guidance*), EPA now intends to eliminate application of the rebuttable presumption when investigating allegations about environmental health-based thresholds. Compliance with a health-based threshold such as a NAAQS is a serious consideration in an evaluation of whether adverse disparate impact exists. As described below, the Agency will also assess other information that may be available and appropriate when investigating whether adverse health impacts exist. While no presumption is established, compliance with a health-based threshold would be considered, along with other information, to enable the Agency to focus on the most significant cases (*i.e.*, those representing the highest environmental and public health risk) and to determine whether adversity exists.

Environmental health-based thresholds are set at levels intended to be protective of public health. While compliance with such thresholds does not guarantee no risk, such compliance strongly suggests that the remaining risks are low and at an acceptable level for the specific pollutant(s) addressed by the health-based threshold. At the same time, EPA believes that presuming compliance with civil rights laws wherever there is compliance with environmental health-based thresholds may not give sufficient consideration to other factors that could also adversely impact human health.

The approach proposed here differs from the *2000 Draft Guidance*'s rebuttable presumption. Under the latter, complying with the NAAQS created a presumption of no adversity that would stand unless affirmatively overcome. By contrast, this proposal acknowledges the relative significance of compliance with an environmental health-based threshold, while also evaluating a number of other factors, as appropriate, including the existence of hot spots, cumulative impacts, the presence of particularly sensitive populations that were not considered in the establishment of the health-based standard, misapplication of environmental standards, or the existence of site-specific data demonstrating an adverse impact despite compliance with the health-based threshold. Because EPA believes that the NAAQS (and other health-based thresholds) can be valid and appropriate, and yet not assure in all cases that no adverse impact is created, EPA will no longer presume an absence of adversity if a NAAQS (or another health-based threshold) is satisfied. Instead, EPA would consider such compliance concurrently with the type of information described above.

While EPA is eliminating the applicability of the rebuttable presumption from its analyses, nevertheless, there may be other features present that may impact EPA's ability to consider other information concurrently with compliance with health-based thresholds. Examples of such features include, but are not limited to, the Agency's existing technical capabilities and the availability of credible, reliable data (given the practical constraints of complaint investigations, EPA expects to gather pre-existing technical data rather than generating new data). . . .

[T]here will be further work necessary to develop and implement the policy issue addressed here. Thus, the analysis here does not represent the end point, but rather an important step forward in considering and evaluating these and other policy issues raised in EPA's Title VI work.

COMMENTARY & QUESTIONS

1. Is the revised standard for "adversity" too muddy? After reading the excerpts from the guidance, do you understand how compliance with health-based standards fits into the analysis of "adversity"? Was EPA's prior presumption that there is no adversity if health-based standards are met a more easily administrable standard? Has EPA retained any elements of this presumption in the current draft guidance?

2. Were the prior standards too precise? EPA's 2001 draft revised guidance has also been criticized from the opposite direction. The claim was that it relied too much on scientific evidence of risk, and other objective, quantifiable information, and too little on the

B. Harm-Based Ambient Standards Under the CAA

basic but intangible injustices of permitting decisions that have discriminatory effects.[19] EPA's emphasis on quantitative measures of harm was well illustrated by the *Select Steel* decision, discussed in the 2013 draft guidance. In *Select Steel*, EPA concluded that the claimants did not make out a case for an adverse effect (and thus did not have a meritorious case under Title VI) because the NAAQS would not be violated by the steel plant at issue there. Where health-based standards were met, EPA erected a presumption against finding an adverse impact for purposes of Title VI complaints. Knowing what you know now about NAAQS and their implementation, does EPA's presumption make sense?

3. Using this guidance document to seek enforceable legal rights and remedies. Where does the authority to promulgate the guidance come from and how much legal force should it have? President Clinton's Executive Order 12898 stated in §6-609:

> This order is intended only to improve the internal management of the executive branch and is not intended to, nor does it create any right, benefit, or trust responsibility, substantive or procedural, enforceable at law or equity by a party against the United States, its agencies, its officers, or any person. This order shall not be construed to create any right to judicial review involving the compliance or noncompliance of the United States, its agencies, its officers, or any other person with this order.

That executive order provided the predicate for EPA issuance of the guidance. As a concluding statement in the guidance, EPA reiterates the nonbinding nature of the guidance that appeared in the initial footnote. Nevertheless, the guidance states: "Recipients may be able to challenge EPA's finding in court. Moreover, those who believe they have been discriminated against in violation of Title VI or EPA's implementing regulations may challenge a recipient's alleged discriminatory act in court without exhausting their Title VI administrative remedies with EPA." Draft Title VI Guidance at 39671.

However, the Supreme Court rejected this kind of remedy in *Alexander v. Sandoval*, 532 U.S. 275 (2001). In a 5-4 decision, the Court held that private individuals may sue to enforce §601 of Title VI (the basic statement of rights), but that §601 itself prohibits only *intentional* discrimination. Although the Court acknowledged that regulations promulgated under §602 of Title VI may go beyond prohibiting intentional discrimination to interdict disparate impacts on minority groups, such disparate impact regulations cannot be enforced by private legal action, only by the agency itself. Thus only EPA can enforce its environmental justice regulations.

4. EPA's record on Title VI complaints. For years, EPA's OCR was notorious for failing to respond to administrative complaints alleging discrimination. This was a severe problem for petitioners because after *Alexander*, claims based on disparate environmental impact cannot be brought before a federal court; rather an administrative complaint must be used. Oftentimes proving intentional discrimination is very difficult if not impossible, so filing a complaint with EPA alleging disparate impact may be the sole remedy for a petitioner.

According to OCR's regulations, the office will review a complaint for acceptance or rejection within 20 days and, upon accepting a complaint, it will issue preliminary findings no later than 180 days after beginning the investigation.[20] But as illustrated by the landmark Ninth Circuit case, *Rosemere Neighborhood Ass'n v. EPA*,[21] the OCR consistently failed to follow its own timelines. In the *Rosemere* case, the Association filed a complaint with the

---

19. See Yang, The Form and Substance of Environmental Justice: The Challenge of Title VI of the Civil Rights Act of 1964 for Environmental Regulation, 29 B.C. Envtl. Aff. L. Rev. 143 (2002).
20. 40 C.F.R. §§7.120(d)(1)(i), 7.115(c)(1).
21. 581 F.3d 1169 (9th Cir. 2009).

OCR, claiming that the city of Vancouver, Washington, failed to adequately use EPA funds to address environmental burdens on low-income and minority communities in the city and retaliated against the Association by dissolving it after the complaint was filed. OCR took no action for 18 months until the Association filed suit in federal court to force the office into action. The OCR then began to investigate the complaint, and the district court dismissed the action on mootness grounds. In a remarkable opinion, the Ninth Circuit reversed, concluding the issue was not moot because EPA failed to show that it would not engage in further processing delays. As an additional, more significant reason for reversal, the court observed that "Rosemere's experience before EPA appears, sadly and unfortunately, typical of those who appeal to OCR to remedy civil rights violations. . . . EPA failed to process a *single* complaint from 2006 or 2007 in accordance with its regulatory deadlines." Why the history of foot-dragging in processing Title VI complaints? Lack of administrative resources may seem like an explanation, but this would suggest that only select complaints were processed; it would not explain a widespread pattern of failure to respond to the timelines in the regulations.

5. A new era of Title VI enforcement? In response to the *Rosemere* decision, then-Administrator Lisa Jackson promised to reform the Title VI process in order to more efficiently address environmental justice complaints. It remains to be seen whether the new initiatives Administrator Jackson endorsed, such as enhanced communications between civil right complainants and EPA, partnerships with other federal agencies to promote compliance with Title VI and including civil rights metrics in assessing EPA programs and grants, will lead to more efficient processing of environmental burden administrative complaints. Even if the OCR begins to follow the timelines, it is important to keep in mind that this will only remedy the procedural defects in the program; whether or not the OCR will find valid environmental justice claims is a substantive issue that is very much an open question.

4. Adjusting Requirements for Attainment (PSD) & Nonattainment Areas

As described in the short history of the CAA that opened the chapter, in 1977 and again in 1990, the act underwent major changes that tried to shape its application in relation to the ambient air quality as it actually existed—differentiating areas where air quality was attaining the NAAQS and areas where it was not. This section tries to briefly describe some of the details of those two programs—among the most complicated features of this complicated law.

In attainment areas, Congress imposed the PSD program that was intended to preserve air quality at levels higher than those required by the NAAQS alone, to provide additional health benefits, but more fundamentally to protect important amenity values associated with cleaner air. On another level, the PSD program was intended to limit the competitive advantage attainment areas would have in trying to attract new economic development by offering lax pollution control as an incentive to firms considering building or expanding plants in the PSD area.

The PSD program presents a complicated federal-state division of power. The PSD program backstops against excessive state backsliding on current air quality by imposing a limit on incremental pollution. This may, as a practical matter, limit a State's potential for development. The starting point for the statutory classification scheme links the highest classification (Class I) to land use, such as the presence of National Parks and wilderness areas. If these are in existence as of 1977, they may not be reclassified. All other PSD areas are initially classified as Class II. See CAA §162, 42 U.S.C. §7472. States are allowed to reclassify areas (the statutory term is *redesignate*) in accordance with CAA §164, 42 U.S.C.

B. Harm-Based Ambient Standards Under the CAA

§7474. States can upgrade areas they deem "appropriate" to Class I. Some areas, based on land use, must remain as Class I or Class II, but the states also have a power to redesignate other areas to Class III. As a practical matter, redesignation to Class III seldom allows significantly more incremental pollution because most urbanized or industrialized areas cannot "use" even the full Class II increment without exceeding the NAAQS. Complicating this arrangement, tribes are given designation powers similar to those of states, with the federal government mediating instances where tribal and state designations are in conflict.

The motivation for the nonattainment program, which is intended to bring all AQCRs into attainment for all of the criteria pollutants, was also dual in nature. Most obviously, where the NAAQS were not being met, the air was (and wherever nonattainment continues still is) "unsafe to breathe." The NAAQS primary standards are set to protect human health, and where they are not being met, the air quality is below the level at which risk of harm is controlled to an acceptable level. Also like the PSD program, the nonattainment program was keenly sensitive to the need for nonattainment areas to be able to continue to grow economically, which could be limited if absolutely no new emissions were allowed before the area came into attainment.

In the 1990 amendments, Congress took more control in setting requirements for nonattainment area SIPs. Central aspects of that legislation were the characterization of the degree of nonattainment (marginal, moderate, serious, severe, and extreme) and the imposition of more exacting requirements in areas further out of attainment, while at the same time providing a longer timeline for achieving the result. The main building blocks of the nonattainment program SIPs are summarized below. Professor Mintz addresses state and local government duties, but the requirements mentioned apply equally to all stationary sources, private and public.

Joel A. Mintz, State and Local Government Environmental Liability (2009)

§14:2. EXISTING STATIONARY SOURCE REQUIREMENTS. In preparing their nonattainment SIPs, the states must include several types of requirements with respect to existing stationary sources, including sources owned or operated by state or local governments. Among other things, the state must require existing stationary sources in nonattainment areas to apply "reasonably available control measures" through the adoption of [RACT]. This technology-based requirement is generally defined by the states in their SIPs through the application of "Control Techniques Guidelines," issued by the EPA for particular types of sources on an informal basis. The Guidelines describe reasonably available air pollution control methods and the levels of control those methods can be expected to achieve.

In addition, nonattainment area SIPs must contain control measures for existing sources that will lead to "reasonable further progress towards the attainment of NAAQS." They must include other means or techniques (including economic incentives such as fees, marketable permits, and auctions of emission rights) that may be necessary to provide for NAAQS attainment. And they must be accompanied by a state-prepared inventory of actual emissions from all sources of criteria pollutants in the nonattainment area which must be comprehensive, accurate and current.

NEW SOURCES: LOWEST ACHIEVABLE EMISSION RATE. New and modified state and local governmental sources of criteria pollutants in nonattainment areas are subject to another, more stringent, set of limitations. To the extent that such sources are "major stationary sources," as defined by the statute, they must satisfy the technology-based standards that reflect the [LAER]. This is defined as the most stringent achievable emission limit contained in the implementation plan of any state for the class or category of source in question, or any more stringent emission limitation which is achieved in practice for that source class or category.

NEW SOURCES: EMISSION OFFSET REQUIREMENTS. New major state and local stationary sources in nonattainment areas must also comply with "emission offset" requirements. These are legally enforceable reductions in emissions from other sources in the same nonattainment area, above and beyond any reductions that would otherwise be mandated for those other sources. Offsets can result from the shutdown of those other sources or from the use of very advanced control techniques at them. The 1990 Clean Air Act Amendments tightened the emission offset requirements in ozone nonattainment areas. Instead of simply requiring greater than 1 for 1 offset reductions, the Act now requires offsets of 1.1 to 1 in marginal areas, 1.15 to 1 in moderate areas, 1.2 in serious areas, 1.3 to 1 in severe areas, and 1.5 to 1 in extreme areas.

NEW SOURCES: COMPLIANCE AT OTHER FACILITIES. In addition to meeting LAER standards and emission offset requirements, state and local owners or operators of proposed new or modified sources in nonattainment areas must demonstrate that all major stationary sources that they own or operate within the same state are in compliance, or on a schedule for compliance, with all applicable [CAA] emission limitations. Moreover, they must perform an analysis of the proposed source, and of alternative sites, sizes, production processes and environmental control techniques, which must show that "the benefits of the proposed source significantly outweigh the environmental and social costs imposed as a result of its location, construction, or modification."

SANCTIONS FOR NONCOMPLYING STATES. The [CAA] authorizes the EPA to impose sanctions in instances where a state fails to make reasonable efforts to submit or carry out a SIP in a nonattainment area. In those circumstances, the agency is authorized to prohibit grants of federal highway funds and grants in support of the state's air pollution program. Additionally, the EPA may require that offset ratios for new or modified sources be increased to 2 to 1 in the nonattainment area in question.

COMMENTARY & QUESTIONS

1. **The PSD program and federalism.** Does the PSD program shift too much control over state decisionmaking about growth and development to the federal government? Should the federal sites of importance, the Yosemites and Grand Canyons, be insulated against loss of amenity value that is at times obtained at the expense of economic development in the host state? Even more generally, the PSD program restricts development in less-developed or later developing states by taking away the potential advantage of less expensive pollution control requirements.

2. **Manipulating offsets.** Offsets, in theory, are a superb tool for permitting economic growth and development without adverse air quality impacts. Indeed, if the ratio of offsets required exceeds 1:1, there will be a net reduction in pollution as a result of the entry of the new facility and the elimination of previous sources of emissions. As considered more completely in Chapter 14, trading systems, of which offsets are just one example, have many aspects that can be manipulated in ways that undercut their effectiveness. Several forms of

manipulation are on display in *Citizens Against the Refinery's Effects (CARE) v. EPA*, 643 F.2d 183 (4th Cir. 1981). In that case a large new refinery was to be introduced in Hampton Roads, Virginia, a nonattainment area for hydrocarbons (HCs), which are emitted in large quantities by refinery operations including the loading and unloading of tankers. The offsets approved by the Virginia permitting agency and upheld by EPA came from a switch by the state in its method for repaving asphalt roads. The state agreed to switch from oil-based asphalt to water-based asphalt over a region that includes the entire eastern one-third of the state and is located in parts of four different AQCRs. The amount of the reduction in emissions required choosing a baseline year for emissions from the old processes; the year chosen turned out to be a year in which the greatest amount of paving with the more polluting type of asphalt had been done. Additionally, even before Virginia had offered the change as an offset, the Highway Department had already begun switching to the water-based asphalt because it had become the less expensive option without any degradation in quality. What result would you expect in judicial review of the agency action, keeping in mind that it is reviewed on an arbitrary and capricious basis? Should EPA promulgate strict rules that would limit that sort of manipulation of the offset process?

3. Comparing the rigor of nonattainment and PSD requirements for major new or modified stationary sources. Because LAER in practice often closely resembles BAT, the primary differentiator in siting a major new stationary source or modifying an existing one is the offset requirement in nonattainment areas as it compares to the PSD increment in attainment areas. Occasionally, it will be significantly more expensive to locate in a nonattainment area, but not very often will the difference be enough to deter locating in a non-attainment area if there is any business reason to do so. Is it surprising that the CAA is so lenient with nonattainment areas, where there are ongoing unacceptable health outcomes? One answer is political: The nonattainment areas are also the areas where the vast majority of the population lives, which means that Congress, especially in the House of Representatives, is unlikely to do too much to block economic development in nonattainment areas. A less cynical explanation of the limited differentiation is that the more stubborn nonattainment problems are so deeply woven into the current urban reality and lifestyles (automobile use in particular), that improvements will be gradual.

C. Technology-Based Standards Under the CAA

1. Technology-Based Standards as a Policy Choice

Section 112 of the CAA regulates hazardous air pollutants (HAPs) and as it originally appeared in the 1970 Act was harm-based. But unlike the Act's treatment of conventional pollutants, §112 did not rely on the NAAQS process to set National Emissions Standards for Hazardous Air Pollutants (NESHAPs). Instead, EPA was required to compile a list of HAPs and promulgate emission standards directly applicable to sources that emitted the hazardous pollutants in question. Those NESHAPs were to be set at a level that in the judgment of EPA "provides an ample margin of safety to protect the public health from such hazardous air pollutant." 42 U.S.C. §7412(b)(1)(B).

Experience has shown that a harm-based standards approach is not easily applied to the problems of HAPs. By 1990, the agency, limited by the availability of adequate scientific studies on which to propose standards, and dogged by judicial challenges to those standards that it did propose, had made little progress at implementing §112. EPA had managed to promulgate standards for only seven hazardous air pollutants, had listed and was in the process of proposing standards for a handful of additional substances, and was proposing to list another ten. In 1990, Congress largely abandoned the harm-based approach to HAPs and substituted a technology-based approach that called for the employment of MACT, the "maximum achievable control technology," to be determined by examining the technology employed by the very best-controlled sources in the relevant source category. The legislation explicitly identified some 180 substances to be regulated and required EPA to regulate sources emitting more than a specified amount of these substances.

Congress made an exception, however, for power plants. Because the 1990 amendments placed a number of new requirements on these facilities, including those of the acid rain trading program, Congress instructed EPA first to study the problem of hazardous air pollution emitted by power plants and then to decide whether, considering the other requirements imposed on these facilities, regulation under §112 was "appropriate and necessary." In 2000, on the verge of surrendering the White House to the Bush II Administration, the Clinton EPA made a determination that regulation of coal- and oil-fired power plants under §112 was indeed "appropriate and necessary," focusing on the risks posed by mercury emissions from these sources.

Technology-based standards, especially when applied strictly for hazardous air pollutants, can be costly for industry to comply with and adopt. Perhaps for this reason, the Bush II EPA tried to avoid the technology-based requirements triggered by the Clinton EPA's "appropriate and necessary" determination. It established a program under CAA §111 that would have allowed power plants to trade mercury emission credits and avoid the strict MACT requirement under the CAA for mercury. In *New Jersey v. EPA*, 517 F.3d 574 (D.C. Cir. 2008), the D.C. Circuit invalidated the rule—known as the "Clean Air Mercury Rule" (CAMR)—because EPA had not followed the strict requirements of §112 in delisting power plants from the roster of sources to be regulated under that provision. The court held that once EPA listed power plants as sources to be regulated under §112, it could delist these sources only by making very narrow and strict health-based determinations, specified in §112. To the agency's argument that it had inherent authority to revisit a decision—like the 2000 determination on the appropriateness and necessity of regulating power plants under §112—which it had come to believe was incorrect, the court responded:

> An agency can normally change its position and reverse a decision, and prior to EPA's listing of EGUs under §112(c)(1), nothing in the CAA would have prevented it from reversing its determination about whether it was "appropriate and necessary" to do so. Congress, however, undoubtedly can limit an agency's discretion to reverse itself, and in §112(c)(9) Congress did just that, unambiguously limiting EPA's discretion to remove sources, including EGUs, from the §112(c)(1) list once they have been added to it. . . .
>
> EPA suggests that it would be "anomalous" for it to be forced to await a court order to correct "its own mistake" in listing coal- and oil-fired EGUs as a source under §112(c)(1). However Congress was not preoccupied with what EPA considers "anomalous," but rather with the fact that EPA had failed for decades to regulate HAPs sufficiently. In the context of this congressional concern, EPA's disbelief that it would be prevented from correcting its own listing "errors" except through §112(c)(9)'s delisting process or court-sanctioned vacatur cannot overcome the plain text enacted by Congress.

Shortly after this decision, the administration again turned over. The Obama EPA persuaded the Solicitor General's office to withdraw the petition for certiorari that had been filed by the previous administration, seeking review of the decision in *New Jersey v. EPA*. In 2012, EPA issued a final rule regulating hazardous air pollutants from power plants and made a renewed determination that regulating these sources under §112 was "appropriate

C. Technology-Based Standards Under the CAA

and necessary." The rule is arguably among the most consequential in the agency's history, taking aim at the largest single category of hazardous air pollution emissions in this country and simultaneously reducing criteria pollutants to a considerable degree. Again, litigation ensued, and again, EPA lost, this time in the Supreme Court.

Michigan v. U.S. Environmental Protection Agency
135 S. Ct. 2699 (2015)

SCALIA, J. The Clean Air Act directs the Environmental Protection Agency to regulate emissions of hazardous air pollutants from power plants if the Agency finds regulation "appropriate and necessary." We must decide whether it was reasonable for EPA to refuse to consider cost when making this finding.

The Clean Air Act establishes a series of regulatory programs to control air pollution from stationary sources (such as refineries and factories) and moving sources (such as cars and airplanes). One of these is the National Emissions Standards for Hazardous Air Pollutants Program—the hazardous-air-pollutants program, for short. Established in its current form by the Clean Air Act Amendments of 1990, 104 Stat. 2531, this program targets for regulation stationary-source emissions of more than 180 specified "hazardous air pollutants." §7412(b). . . .

Congress established a unique procedure to determine the applicability of the program to fossil-fuel-fired power plants. The Act refers to these plants as electric utility steam generating units, but we will simply call them power plants. Quite apart from the hazardous-air-pollutants program, the Clean Air Act Amendments of 1990 subjected power plants to various regulatory requirements. The parties agree that these requirements were expected to have the collateral effect of reducing power plants' emissions of hazardous air pollutants, although the extent of the reduction was unclear. Congress directed the Agency to "perform a study of the hazards to public health reasonably anticipated to occur as a result of emissions by [power plants] of [hazardous air pollutants] after imposition of the requirements of this chapter." §7412(n)(1)(A). If the Agency "finds . . . regulation is appropriate and necessary after considering the results of the study," it "shall regulate [power plants] under [§7412]." EPA has interpreted the Act to mean that power plants become subject to regulation on the same terms as ordinary major and area sources, and we assume without deciding that it was correct to do so.

And what are those terms? EPA must first divide sources covered by the program into categories and sub-categories in accordance with statutory criteria. §7412(c)(1). For each category or subcategory, the Agency must promulgate certain minimum emission regulations, known as floor standards. §7412(d)(1), (3). The statute generally calibrates the floor standards to reflect the emissions limitations already achieved by the best-performing 12% of sources within the category or subcategory. §7412(d)(3). In some circumstances, the Agency may also impose more stringent emissions regulations, known as beyond-the-floor standards. The statute expressly requires the Agency to consider cost (alongside other specified factors) when imposing beyond-the-floor standards. §7412(d)(2).

EPA completed the study required by §7412(n)(1)(A) in 1998, and concluded that regulation of coal-and oil-fired power plants was "appropriate and necessary" in 2000. In 2012, it reaffirmed the appropriate-and-necessary finding, divided power plants into subcategories, and promulgated floor standards. The Agency found regulation "appropriate" because (1) power plants' emissions of mercury and other hazardous air pollutants posed risks to human health and the environment and (2) controls were available to reduce these emissions. It found regulation "necessary" because the imposition of the Act's other requirements did not eliminate these risks. EPA concluded that "costs should not be considered" when deciding whether power plants should be regulated under §7412.

In accordance with Executive Order, the Agency issued a "Regulatory Impact Analysis" alongside its regulation. This analysis estimated that the regulation would force power plants to bear costs of $9.6 billion per year. The Agency could not fully quantify the benefits of reducing power plants' emissions of hazardous air pollutants; to the extent it could, it estimated that these benefits were worth $4 to $6 million per year. The costs to power plants were thus between 1,600 and 2,400 times as great as the quantifiable benefits from reduced emissions of hazardous air pollutants. The Agency continued that its regulation would have ancillary benefits—including cutting power plants' emissions of particulate matter and sulfur dioxide, substances that are not covered by the hazardous-air-pollutants program. Although the Agency's appropriate-and-necessary finding did not rest on these ancillary effects, the regulatory impact analysis took them into account, increasing the Agency's estimate of the quantifiable benefits of its regulation to $37 to $90 billion per year. EPA concedes that the regulatory impact analysis "played no role" in its appropriate-and-necessary finding. . . .

EPA's disregard of cost rested on its interpretation of §7412(n)(1)(A), which, to repeat, directs the Agency to regulate power plants if it "finds such regulation is appropriate and necessary." The Agency accepts that it could have interpreted this provision to mean that cost is relevant to the decision to add power plants to the program. But it chose to read the statute to mean that cost makes no difference to the initial decision to regulate.

We review this interpretation under the standard set out in *Chevron U.S.A. Inc. v. Natural Resources Defense Council, Inc.*, 467 U.S. 837 (1984). *Chevron* directs courts to accept an agency's reasonable resolution of an ambiguity in a statute that the agency administers. Even under this deferential standard, however, "agencies must operate within the bounds of reasonable interpretation." EPA strayed far beyond these bounds when it read §7412(n)(1) to mean that it could ignore cost when deciding whether to regulate power plants.

The Clean Air Act treats power plants differently from other sources for purposes of the hazardous-air-pollutants program. Elsewhere in §7412, Congress established cabined criteria for EPA to apply when deciding whether to include sources in the program. It required the Agency to regulate sources whose emissions exceed specified numerical thresholds (major sources). It also required the Agency to regulate sources whose emissions fall short of these thresholds (area sources) if they "presen[t] a threat of adverse effects to human health or the environment . . . warranting regulation." §7412(c)(3). In stark contrast, Congress instructed EPA to add power plants to the program if (but only if) the Agency finds regulation "appropriate and necessary." §7412(n)(1)(A). One does not need to open up a dictionary in order to realize the capaciousness of this phrase. In particular "appropriate" is "the classic broad and all-encompassing term that naturally and traditionally includes consideration of all the relevant factors." Although this term leaves agencies with flexibility, an agency may not "entirely fai[l] to consider an important aspect of the problem" when deciding whether regulation is appropriate. *State Farm*, at 43.

Read naturally in the present context, the phrase "appropriate and necessary" requires at least some attention to cost. One would not say that it is even rational, never mind "appropriate," to impose billions of dollars in economic costs in return for a few dollars in health or environmental benefits. In addition, "cost" includes more than the expense of complying with regulations; any disadvantage could be termed a cost. EPA's interpretation precludes the Agency from considering any type of cost—including, for instance, harms that regulation might do to human health or the environment. The Government concedes that

C. Technology-Based Standards Under the CAA

if the Agency were to find that emissions from power plants do damage to human health, but that the technologies needed to eliminate these emissions do even more damage to human health, it would still deem regulation appropriate. No regulation is "appropriate" if it does significantly more harm than good.

There are undoubtedly settings in which the phrase "appropriate and necessary" does not encompass cost. But this is not one of them. Section 7412(n)(1)(A) directs EPA to determine whether "*regulation* is appropriate and necessary." (Emphasis added.) Agencies have long treated cost as a centrally relevant factor when deciding whether to regulate. Consideration of cost reflects the understanding that reasonable regulation ordinarily requires paying attention to the advantages and the disadvantages of agency decisions. It also reflects the reality that "too much wasteful expenditure devoted to one problem may well mean considerably fewer resources available to deal effectively with other (perhaps more serious) problems." *Entergy Corp. v. Riverkeeper, Inc.*, 556 U.S. 208, 233 (2009) (Breyer, J., concurring in part and dissenting in part). Against the backdrop of this established administrative practice, it is unreasonable to read an instruction to an administrative agency to determine whether "regulation is appropriate and necessary" as an invitation to ignore cost. . . .

EPA seeks support in this Court's decision in *Whitman v. American Trucking Assns, Inc.*, 531 U.S. 457 (2001). There, the Court addressed a provision of the Clean Air Act requiring EPA to set ambient air quality standards at levels "requisite to protect the public health" with an "adequate margin of safety." 42 U.S.C. §7409(b). Read naturally, that discrete criterion does not encompass cost; it encompasses health and safety. The Court refused to read that provision as carrying with it an implicit authorization to consider cost, in part because authority to consider cost had "elsewhere, and so often, been expressly granted." *American Trucking* thus establishes the modest principle that where the Clean Air Act expressly directs EPA to regulate on the basis of a factor that on its face does not include cost, the Act normally should not be read as implicitly allowing the Agency to consider cost anyway. That principle has no application here. "Appropriate and necessary" is a far more comprehensive criterion than "requisite to protect the public health;" read fairly and in context, as we have explained, the term plainly subsumes consideration of cost. . . .

EPA argues that the Clean Air Act makes cost irrelevant to the initial decision to regulate sources other than power plants. The Agency claims that it is reasonable to interpret §7412(n)(1)(A) in a way that "harmonizes" the program's treatment of power plants with its treatment of other sources. This line of reasoning overlooks the whole point of having a separate provision about power plants: treating power plants differently from other stationary sources. Congress crafted narrow standards for EPA to apply when deciding whether to regulate other sources; in general, these standards concern the volume of pollution emitted by the source, §7412(c)(1), and the threat posed by the source "to human health or the environment." §7412(c)(3). But Congress wrote the provision before us more expansively, directing the Agency to regulate power plants if "appropriate and necessary." . . .

[T]he dissent has at most shown that some elements of the regulatory scheme mitigate cost in limited ways; it has not shown that these elements ensure cost-effectiveness. If (to take a hypothetical example) regulating power plants would yield $5 million in benefits, the prospect of mitigating cost from $11 billion to $10 billion at later stages of the program would not by itself make regulation appropriate. In all events, we need not pursue these points, because EPA did not say that the parts of the regulatory program mentioned by the dissent prevent the imposition of costs far in excess of benefits. "[EPA's] action must be measured by what [it] did, not by what it might have done." *SEC v. Chenery Corp.*, 318 U.S. 80, 93-94 (1943).

. . . The Agency must consider cost—including, most importantly, cost of compliance—before deciding whether regulation is appropriate and necessary. We need not and do not hold that the law unambiguously required the Agency, when making this preliminary estimate, to conduct a formal cost-benefit analysis in which each advantage and disadvantage is assigned a monetary value. It will be up to the Agency to decide (as always, within the limits of reasonable interpretation) how to account for cost.

Some of the respondents supporting EPA ask us to uphold EPA's action because the accompanying regulatory impact analysis shows that, once the rule's ancillary benefits are considered, benefits plainly outweigh costs. The dissent similarly relies on these ancillary benefits when insisting that "the outcome here [was] a rule whose benefits exceed its costs." As we have just explained, however, we may uphold agency action only upon the grounds on which the agency acted. Even if the Agency could have considered ancillary benefits when deciding whether regulation is appropriate and necessary—a point we need not address—it plainly did not do so here. . . .

KAGAN, J., dissenting. The Environmental Protection Agency placed emissions limits on coal and oil power plants following a lengthy regulatory process during which the Agency carefully considered costs. At the outset, EPA determined that regulating plants' emissions of hazardous air pollutants is "appropriate and necessary" given the harm they cause, and explained that it would take costs into account in developing suitable emissions standards. Next, EPA divided power plants into groups based on technological and other characteristics bearing significantly on their cost structures. It required plants in each group to match the emissions levels already achieved by the best-performing reflecting those plants' own cost analyses. EPA then adopted a host of measures designed to make compliance with its proposed emissions limits less costly for plants that needed to catch up with their cleaner peers. And with only one narrow exception, EPA decided not to impose any more stringent standards (beyond what some plants had already achieved on their own) because it found that doing so would not be cost-effective. After all that, EPA conducted a formal cost-benefit study which found that the quantifiable benefits of its regulation would exceed the costs up to nine times over – by as much as $80 billion each year. Those benefits include as many as 11,000 fewer premature deaths annually, along with a far greater number of avoided illnesses.

Despite that exhaustive consideration of costs, the Court strikes down EPA's rule on the ground that the Agency "unreasonably . . . deemed cost irrelevant." On the majority's theory, the rule is invalid because EPA did not explicitly analyze costs at the very first stage of the regulatory process, when making its "appropriate and necessary" finding. And that is so even though EPA later took costs into account again and again and . . . so on. The majority thinks entirely immaterial, and so entirely ignores, all the subsequent times and ways EPA considered costs in deciding what any regulation would look like.

That is a peculiarly blinkered way for a court to assess the lawfulness of an agency's rulemaking. I agree with the majority—let there be no doubt about this—that EPA's power plant regulation would be unreasonable if "[t]he Agency gave cost no thought at all." But that is just not what happened here. Over more than a decade, EPA took costs into account at multiple stages and through multiple means as it set emissions limits for power plants. And when making its initial "appropriate and necessary" finding, EPA knew it would do exactly that—knew it would thoroughly consider the cost-effectiveness of emissions standards later on. That context matters. The Agency acted well within its authority in declining to consider costs at the opening bell of the regulatory process given that it would do so in every round thereafter—and given that the emissions limits finally issued would depend crucially on those accountings. Indeed, EPA could not have measured costs at the process's initial stage with any accuracy. And the regulatory path EPA chose parallels the one it has trod in setting emissions limits, at Congress's explicit direction, for every other source of hazardous air pollutants over two decades. The majority's decision that EPA cannot take the same approach here—its micromanagement of EPA's rulemaking, based on little more than the word "appropriate"—runs counter to Congress's allocation of authority between the Agency and the courts. Because EPA reasonably found that it was "appropriate" to decline to analyze costs at a single stage of a regulatory proceeding otherwise imbued with cost concerns, I respectfully dissent.

. . . Cost is almost always a relevant—and usually, a highly important—factor in regulation. Unless Congress provides otherwise, an agency acts unreasonably in establishing "a standard-setting process that ignore[s] economic considerations." *Industrial Union Dept., AFL-CIO v. American Petroleum Institute*, 448 U.S. 607, 670 (1980) (Powell, J., concurring in part and concurring in judgment). At a minimum, that is because such a process would "threaten[ ] to impose massive costs far in excess of any benefit." *Entergy Corp. v. Riverkeeper, Inc.*, 556 U.S. 208, 234 (2009) (Breyer, J., concurring in part and dissenting in part). And accounting for costs is particularly important "in an age of limited resources available to deal with grave environmental problems, where too much wasteful expenditure devoted to one problem may well mean considerably fewer resources available to deal effectively with other (perhaps more serious) problems." *Id.*, at 233. As the Court notes, that does not require an agency to conduct a formal cost-benefit analysis of every administrative action. But (absent contrary indication from Congress) an agency must take into account in some manner before imposing significant regulatory burdens.

That proposition, however, does not decide the issue before us because the "appropriate and necessary" finding was only the beginning. At that stage, EPA knew that a lengthy rulemaking process lay ahead of it; the determination of emissions limits was still years away. And the Agency, in making its kick-off finding, explicitly noted that consideration of costs would follow: "As a part of developing a regulation" that would impose those limits, "the effectiveness and costs of controls will be examined." Likewise, EPA explained that, in the course of writing its regulation, it would explore regulatory approaches "allowing for least-cost solutions." That means the Agency, when making its "appropriate and necessary" finding, did not decline to consider costs as part of the regulatory process. Rather, it declined to consider costs at a single stage of that process, knowing that they would come in later on. . . .

COMMENTARY & QUESTIONS

1. What next? The Supreme Court remanded the matter to the D.C. Circuit to figure out where to go from here. Given that the legal predicate for the rule has been rejected, was the proper course vacatur? Was it likely enough that EPA would reinstate the "appropriate and necessary determination," after considering costs, that vacatur would be unreasonable? EPA has responded to *Michigan v. EPA* by proposing a new finding of the appropriateness of regulating power plants under §112, offering analyses of costs as a matter of affordability to the industry and (as a back-up) a formal cost-benefit analysis of this regulation.

2. A cost-sensitive default? Has the Court—all nine members of it—now embraced an interpretive default position holding that, unless a statute provides otherwise, an agency must consider costs before regulating? If so, is this a sensible position? Is it a sensible interpretation of Congress's general preferences? Do the majority and dissent provide good legal support for this interpretive position?

3. The special dangers of HAPs. Mercury, one of the HAPs regulated by EPA's rules on power plants, is a very potent neurotoxin. It is known to cause permanent damage to the brain, kidneys, and cardiovascular system. While it may be inhaled or absorbed through the skin, consumption of fish that have been exposed to mercury is the most common cause of mercury exposure in humans. Pregnant women are especially at risk because in utero exposure can impair an unborn child's thinking, memory, attention, language, and fine motor and visual spatial skills.

4. Coal-fired power plants and mercury emissions. Coal-fired power plants are the largest U.S. source of mercury emissions. A 2006 study of mercury deposition in Ohio, published in Environmental Science and Technology, found that local and regional combustion accounted for 70% of the mercury that comes into nearby waterbodies. In addition to their potential to concentrate locally, mercury emissions are alarming because mercury vapor has the potential to travel thousands of miles before being deposited on land or water.

5. The back story: agency politics. As noted previously, the original "appropriate and necessary finding" for regulating EGUs under §112 was issued in December 2000, shortly before the Clinton EPA turned over the keys to the Bush II EPA. The administrations' respective takes on coal plant regulation underscores the degree to which each administration had a tendency to support environmental or industrial concerns in regulatory decisions. It is important to remember that agencies like EPA are not unchanging bureaucracies. Rather, the prerogatives for executive decisions are naturally shaped by the political agendas of the administration in power. What do you think of this aspect of administrative agencies? Does it increase their popular accountability, or does it suggest that the missions of the agencies would be better served by technocrats, career specialists whose jobs do not directly depend on who is in the Oval Office?

2. Translating Statutory Obligations into Permits

Under the original text of the CAA, the Administrator of EPA was given the authority to designate air quality control regions, or AQCRs.[22] These are basically contiguous geographic areas that pose relatively similar air pollution problems and are thus treated as discrete units for purposes of determining compliance with NAAQS. Often AQCRs encompass multiple counties within a state, and some cross state borders. The rationale for creating these regions is straightforward: Pinpointing areas of homogenous air quality throughout the nation will allow EPA and the states, through their SIPs, to more easily determine which areas are meeting the NAAQS for a particular pollutant. Once a state has determined that an AQCR covering a portion of its political boundaries has or has not attained compliance with the NAAQS, its SIP for each AQCR must prescribe emission controls and other measures that will work toward reaching compliance or ensure continuing compliance. The next case arose in an area that is already in compliance with the NAAQS and is, as a result, covered by the PSD program. One of the ways in which the PSD program operates to limit increases in pollution is to apply technology requirements to new plants that seek permits in the AQCR.

---

22. See CAA §107, 42 U.S.C. §7407.

C. Technology-Based Standards Under the CAA

In re Northern Michigan University Ripley Heating Plant
Environmental Appeals Board, U.S. EPA, PSD Appeal No. 08-02 (Feb. 18, 2009)

SHEEHAN, J. On May 12, 2008, the Michigan Department of Environmental Quality ("MDEQ") issued a federal PSD permit to Northern Michigan University ("NMU"), pursuant to CAA §165. The permit authorizes NMU to construct a new circulating fluidized bed ("CFB") boiler at the Ripley Heating Plant on the University's campus in Marquette, Michigan. As permitted, the CFB boiler will function as a cogeneration unit that provides both electrical power and heat to NMU's facilities through the burning of wood, coal, and natural gas. On June 13, 2008, Sierra Club filed a petition for review of this PSD permit pursuant to 40 C.F.R. part 124, requesting on a number of grounds that the permit be remanded to MDEQ for further consideration. For the reasons set forth below, the Environmental Appeals Board ("Board") remands certain issues raised in Sierra Club's petition for review and denies review as to the remaining issues.[23]

STATUTORY AND REGULATORY BACKGROUND. In 1977, Congress enacted the PSD provisions of the CAA with a number of specific goals in mind. Among other things, Congress intended "to insure that economic growth will occur in a manner consistent with the preservation of existing clean air resources." CAA §160(3). Congress also intended "to assure that any decision to permit increased air pollution in any area to which this section applies is made only after careful evaluation of all the consequences of such a decision and after adequate procedural opportunities for informed public participation in the decisionmaking process." CAA §160(5).

Toward these ends, Congress established a PSD permitting program that is applicable in areas of the country deemed to be in "attainment" or "unclassifiable" with respect to federal air quality standards called "national ambient air quality standards," or "NAAQS." See CAA §§161, 165. Congress charged the U.S. Environmental Protection Agency with developing NAAQS for air pollutants whose presence in the atmosphere above certain concentration levels could "reasonably be anticipated to endanger public health and welfare." CAA §108(a)(1)(A). To date, EPA has promulgated NAAQS for six air contaminants: (1) sulfur oxides (measured as sulfur dioxide ("SO_2")); (2) particulate matter (measured as "PM_{10}," denoting particulates 10 micrometers or less in diameter, or as "$PM_{2.5}$," denoting particulates 2.5 micrometers or less in diameter);[24] (3) carbon monoxide ("CO"); (4) ozone (measured as volatile organic compounds ("VOCs") or as nitrogen oxides ("NO_x")); (5) nitrogen dioxide ("NO_2"); and (6) lead.

In geographical areas deemed to be in "attainment" for any of these pollutants, the ambient air quality meets the NAAQS for that pollutant. CAA §107(d)(1)(A)(ii). In areas designated "unclassifiable," air quality cannot be classified on the basis of available information as meeting or not meeting the NAAQS. CAA §107(d)(1)(A)(iii). Areas may also be designated as "nonattainment," meaning that the concentration of a pollutant in the

---

23. MDEQ is authorized to administer the PSD permitting program within the State of Michigan pursuant to a delegation agreement with Region 5 of the U.S. Environmental Protection Agency. In accordance with the delegation agreement and applicable regulations, MDEQ-issued PSD permit decisions are considered for procedural purposes to be federally issued PSD permit decisions. Consequently, appeals of MDEQ's PSD permit decisions are required to be heard by EPA's Environmental Appeals Board.

24. "Particulate matter" is "the generic term for a broad class of chemically and physically diverse substances that exist as discrete particles (liquid droplets or solids) over a wide range of sizes." . . .

ambient air does not meet the NAAQS for that pollutant. CAA §107(d)(1)(A)(i). The PSD program is not applicable, however, in nonattainment areas. See CAA §161.

Parties that wish to construct "major emitting facilities"[25] in attainment or unclassifiable areas must obtain preconstruction approval, in the form of PSD permits, to build such facilities. CAA §165. Applicants for these permits must achieve emissions limits established by the "best available control technology," or "BACT," for pollutants emitted from their facilities in amounts greater than applicable levels of significance. CAA §165(a)(4). Applicants also must demonstrate, through analyses of the anticipated air quality impacts associated with their proposed facilities, that their facilities' emissions will not cause or contribute to an exceedance of any applicable air quality standard or related criterion. See CAA §165(a)(3).

FACTUAL AND PROCEDURAL BACKGROUND. On February 5, 2007, NMU filed an application with MDEQ for permission to construct a new CFB boiler on its campus near Lake Superior in Michigan's Upper Peninsula. The boiler, which will include a steam turbine, generator, and associated equipment, is designed to serve as a cogeneration unit that provides 120,000 pounds of steam per hour and ten megawatts of electrical power to NMU's facilities. By proposing this project, NMU hopes to expand the reliability and efficiency of its existing powerhouse operations, which are conducted out of the Ripley Heating Plant on the north end of campus.

At present, the Ripley Heating Plant is comprised of three natural gas- and No. 2 fuel oil-fired boilers, the oldest of which has been in operation since 1967, along with emissions control equipment and associated infrastructure. NMU plans to construct the CFB boiler in a new building immediately adjacent to the building housing the three existing boilers. The new boiler, unlike the older ones, will be designed to burn solid fuels, including bituminous and subbituminous coals and wood. The boiler will also be designed to combust natural gas, which NMU proposes to use during boiler startup operations and as a backup fuel when neither coal nor wood is available.

NMU plans to obtain coal exclusively from two "nearby" utilities. The University also plans to obtain wood from independent suppliers and pipeline-quality natural gas from its campus natural gas supplier. NMU has arranged for shipments of the solid fuels to arrive by truck every day on average, except weekends, with a typical shipment consisting of forty tons of coal "and/or" forty tons of wood. The University plans to construct silos to hold a three-day supply of the coal and/or wood fuels, which will allow boiler operation through weekends and holidays. NMU projects that the annual maximum deliveries of solid fuels for the boiler will be in the range of "68,669 tons of bituminous coal, 95,329 tons of [Powder River Basin] coal, and 199,533 tons of wood." . . .

NMU's proposed installation of a new CFB boiler at the Ripley Heating Plant is considered a "major modification" that will result in a significant net increase in emissions of SO_2, PM_{10}, CO, and NO_x from the facility. Moreover, the University is located within Marquette County, Michigan, an area designated as attainment or unclassifiable for SO_2, CO, ozone, PM_{10}, and NO_x. Accordingly, PSD compliance is required under federal law.

MDEQ reviewed NMU's application for a PSD permit, which included BACT and air quality analyses for the CFB boiler. . . . On October 19, 2007, MDEQ issued a draft PSD

---

25. A "major emitting facility" is a stationary source in any of certain listed stationary source categories that, in new or modified form, emits or has the potential to emit 100 tons per year ("tpy") or more of any air pollutant, or any other new or modified stationary source that has the potential to emit 250 tpy or more of any air pollutant. See CAA §169(1), (2)(C).

C. Technology-Based Standards Under the CAA

permit containing proposed terms and conditions to regulate the CFB boiler. That same day, the Department published a notice inviting public comment on the draft permit and establishing a comment period, which ran through December 27, 2007. On November 27, 2007, MDEQ held a public hearing on the draft permit at the Marquette City Hall. The Department accepted numerous oral and written comments on the draft permit from interested individuals and organizations, including Sierra Club. On May 12, 2008, after reviewing the public comments on the draft permit, MDEQ issued a document responding to the comments, along with a final PSD permit authorizing NMU's construction of the CFB boiler.

On June 13, 2008, Sierra Club filed [this appeal] with this Board. . . . MDEQ submitted a response . . . [and] NMU filed a motion to intervene as a party, which the Board granted. . . . The Board heard oral argument in this dispute. The case now stands ready for decision by the Board. . . .

The question presently before the Board is whether Sierra Club has made a sufficient showing that any condition of the PSD permit is clearly erroneous or involves an important matter of policy or exercise of discretion warranting review. In its petition, Sierra Club begins by challenging MDEQ's decisions regarding BACT requirements for SO_2, $PM_{2.5}$, carbon dioxide, and nitrous oxide emissions from the CFB boiler. . . . Sierra Club then raises a series of challenges to MDEQ's air quality analysis for this permit. . . .

BACT Issues. As noted above, NMU proposes a new solid fuel-fired CFB boiler near its Ripley Heating Plant. "In support of the Governor's 21st Century Energy Plan," the boiler is "designed to allow operation on Renewable Resources (specifically wood chips) up to 100% of the total heat input." This "preference" for renewable resources, however, yields to coal and natural gas if renewable resources are unavailable or not economically feasible. The result, notwithstanding NMU's stated intention as late as its permit application addendum that wood be the "primary fuel," is a permit allowing coal burning over twenty-two days per month.

As mentioned in the decision, the Act and EPA PSD regulations make major new stationary sources and major modifications, such as the NMU facility, subject to BACT for emissions of certain pollutants. The BACT requirement is defined [in CAA §169(3)] as follows:

> [BACT] means an emissions limitation based on the maximum degree of reduction of each pollutant subject to regulation under [the Act] emitted from or which results from any major emitting facility, which the permitting authority, on a case-by-case basis, taking into account energy, environmental, and economic impacts and other costs, determines is achievable for such facility through application of production processes and available methods, systems, and techniques, including fuel cleaning, clean fuels, or treatment or innovative fuel combustion techniques for control of each such pollutant.

This high threshold demands corresponding exertions from permitting authorities. Proceeding "on a case-by-case basis," taking a "careful and detailed" look, attentive to the "technology or methods appropriate for the particular facility," they are to seek the result "tailor-made" for that facility and that pollutant.

The analytical rigor demanded by Congress has found widely adopted expression in a guidance manual issued by EPA's Office of Air Quality Planning and Standards in 1990. See generally Office of Air Quality Planning & Standards, U.S. EPA, New Source Review Workshop Manual (draft Oct. 1990) ("NSR Manual"). While not binding Agency regulation or the required vehicle for making a BACT determination, the NSR Manual offers the "careful and detailed analysis of [BACT] criteria" required by the CAA and regulations. For this reason, it has guided state and federal permitting authorities on PSD requirements and policy for many years. The Board has commonly used it as a touchstone for Agency thinking on PSD issues.

The NSR Manual's "top-down" method is simply stated: assemble all available control technologies, rank them in order of control effectiveness, and select the best. So fixed is the focus on identifying the "top," or most stringent alternative, that the analysis presumptively ends there and the top option selected—"unless" technical considerations lead to the conclusion that the top option is not "achievable" in that specific case, or energy, environmental, or economic impacts justify a conclusion that use of the top option is inappropriate. In those events, remaining options are then reranked, the several factors applied, and so on until a "best" technology emerges out of this winnowing process.

The NSR Manual thus exacts thoughtful, substantial efforts by reviewing authorities. Not merely an option-gathering exercise with casually considered choices, the NSR Manual or any BACT analysis calls for a searching review of industry practices and control options, a careful ranking of alternatives, and a final choice able to stand as first and best. If reviewing authorities let slip their rigorous look at "all" appropriate technologies, if the target ever eases from the "maximum degree of reduction" available to something less or more convenient, the result may be somewhat protective, may be superior to some pollution control elsewhere, but it will not be BACT.

MDEQ'S BACT ANALYSIS. The greater part of Sierra Club's challenge centers on particular BACT issues. We take up each in turn. But with conformity to federal standards the central question, and with NMU and MDEQ having chosen to rely on a state document purporting to guide them through their BACT responsibilities, we first briefly assess those state procedures.

The alignment between the NSR Manual and NMU's BACT analysis, as approved by MDEQ, is, at best, imperfect. The permit application itself commences with inconsistent objectives, the first paragraph assuring that NMU performed the review "in accordance with the U.S. EPA's recommended top-down procedure outlined in the [NSR Manual]," the second apparently quite the opposite—that the review follows a "more streamlined analysis by circumventing the rigorous approach set forth in the [NSR Manual]."

The "more streamlined" procedure is MDEQ's "Operational Memorandum No. 20." Even brief examination shows it to run largely against the current of EPA's NSR Manual. The latter's tenet of settling on the "top" technology—"unless" that technology's achievement is demonstrably not possible, in which case additional reviews run until an achievable "best" is identified–appears in the State Manual to transform into a four-level series of generally downward slips, away from the "top" control.

Alignment with the NSR Manual appears to occur in Level 4, which liberally paraphrases the Manual's five steps in its opening words. But the comparison fades with the State Manual's suggestion that their "best interests" usually counsel both applicant and MDEQ to "avoid" the NSR Manual, since the NSR Manual is "[h]ighly complex and quantitative," "[d]ifficult to agree upon," and "[t]ime and resource intensive."

The adequacy of MDEQ's BACT determinations turn[s] on their individual merits. The foundation beneath them, however, the State Manual, stands apart from federal standards.

SO_2 BACT: *Clean Fuels.* In its brief list of BACT production processes, methods, systems, and techniques, Congress sounds one prominent note: fuels. In addition to "fuel cleaning" and "treatment or innovative fuel combustion techniques," the remaining listed control is

C. Technology-Based Standards Under the CAA 501

"clean fuels." Congressional direction to permitting applicants and public officials is emphatic. In making BACT determinations, they are to give prominent consideration to fuels. Board cases frequently underscore this charge.

The cleanest fuel choice for the NMU facility, argues Sierra Club, is wood.[26] Its permit limits, however, allow NMU to burn coal "more than" twenty-two days per month and wood just over seven days per month. Coal will be supplied from two, and only two, sources: Marquette and Presque Isle, both "nearby" electrical generating facilities. Each facility will supply coal that is restricted, by its own PSD permit, to a specified maximum sulfur content. BACT limits were "established based on the characteristics" of the coal with the higher allowable sulfur content of the two, 1.5%. Because these fuel choices—minimal use of wood and primary use of Marquette and Presque Isle coal—form the two pillars beneath the ultimate BACT limits, we carefully examine the basis for each.

MDEQ's permit evaluation form presents three scenarios of days-of-wood-burning per month to days-of-coal-burning per month, ranging from a high of 500 hours (i.e., twenty days plus twenty hours) of wood burning to a low of 184 hours (i.e., seven days plus sixteen hours) of wood burning. The 500-hours scenario yields the lowest sulfur emission limit on a thirty-day average, 0.07 lb/MMBtu. The 184-hours option produces the highest limit, 0.15 lb/MMBtu. MDEQ selected the highest limit.

Parsing the record for the reasoning behind MDEQ's choice yields little light. As between the availability of wood and coal, the documentation is neutral, their characteristics indistinguishable. Both the fact sheet and the permit evaluation form acknowledge storage limited to "three days['] fuel supply" but do not differentiate between wood and coal such that either would be in greater supply. Likewise, both recognize inclement weather's possible disruption of "any" fuel deliveries, again without either fuel singled out as more likely to suffer the effects. Yet, at the critical point of allocating fuel proportions in the permit, wood's demonstrably lower sulfur emissions and apparent equal availability to coal seemingly have no persuasive weight and are dismissed without explanation. The result is MDEQ's decision: coal usage over wood, by a margin of nearly three to one.

Commitment to these two coal sources alone was early and, through to the latter stages of the process, unvarying. From the initial permit application to the much later permit evaluation, NMU and MDEQ settled on precisely the same expression of their wishes—that all coal "will" come from either Marquette or Presque Isle. This unwavering preference echoes elsewhere in the record, for example, in the Department's claim of "no [storage] space" beyond that set aside for coal from these "local power plants." Indeed, although the record reflects that other coal, relative to Marquette and Presque Isle coal, will produce the lowest sulfur emissions, MDEQ proceeds without explaining why these sources are unavailable or not technically feasible.[27]

In one striking instance, the Department notes that "[o]ne of the lowest [power plant] emission limits found" in its database review is 0.05 lb/MMBtu, using 0.9% sulfur coal.

---

26. The parties do not dispute that wood produces lower sulfur emissions when burned than coal.

27. MDEQ also neglects to fully analyze the possibility of natural gas as a fuel source. NMU identifies natural gas in its permit application as a fuel that "will be used primarily for boiler startup" and at "any other times when solid fuel firing may not be available" as a backup fuel source. NMU explains further that its existing natural gas supplier will provide it with "pipeline quality gas," and mentions in its own BACT analysis that "pipeline quality natural gas and wood are lower in sulfur content than coal fuels." Despite these references (which imply that natural gas is an available and technically feasible fuel for the CFB boiler), MDEQ's BACT analysis contains no evaluation of this fuel as a technological option that could potentially allow NMU to achieve very low emissions of SO_2 or other pollutants.

Although this limit is considerably less than NMU's final permitted limit, MDEQ nonetheless declined to consider it as BACT, offering not a word of explanation for not choosing it.

MDEQ roots its commitment to only some seven days of wood burning per month in its determination that winter snows impede wood delivery. This finding does not withstand the implications of its own record.

First, if snow makes uncertain the availability of "any" fuel deliveries, the Department fails to clarify why the consequences fall only on wood, and not on Marquette or Presque Isle coal deliveries.

Second, even assuming, as did the permit, disproportionate weather impacts on the order of making coal three times as available as wood, the factual predicate does not sustain the conclusion. The furthest reach of inclement weather is "winter or . . . spring," yet the permit sets a static, year-round assumption of twenty-two days of coal to seven days of wood availability per month.

Third, the record tells merely of wood provided by unidentified "independent suppliers." Whether these suppliers are nearer or more distant than Marquette or Presque Isle, and thus more or less likely to suffer delivery disruptions due to poor weather, the record does not say. In the absence of this information, the true effects of inclement weather on wood deliveries cannot be known. [The Board also concluded that MDEQ failed to present evidence of limited storage space for wood.]

Had it come after "careful and detailed" consideration, or been attentive to "[appropriate] technology or methods," MDEQ's unqualified declaration that "[c]oal will be obtained" from Marquette or Presque Isle might have withstood scrutiny. But all indications are otherwise, suggesting a fixed, preselected outcome, or at least one never subjected to serious examination.

First, the four corners of the record itself . . . belie claims of no storage space for coal other than Marquette or Presque Isle coal. Second, even were storage space limited to three days' supply, shutting out any coal but Marquette or Presque Isle coal raises an obvious question to which the record gives no answer: why even a storage-limited site is incapable of accommodating non-Marquette or non-Presque Isle coal. Third, taking MDEQ at its word of severe weather disruptions to "any" fuel supply, the argument that Marquette and Presque Isle coal deliveries will somehow—and unique among all other coals or wood—prevail over such weather, and resoundingly enough to write their use into the permit twenty-two days per month, year round, is unsustainable.

The record is silent as to why other coal sources, whether more distant or more proximate, were not considered. This gap is particularly troubling on a record that spotlights at least two coal-fired, lower sulfur-polluting facilities, both employing low sulfur coal or other low sulfur emission technological features apparently achievable but inexplicably rejected for the NMU facility.

One ambiguous sentence in the record, embellished slightly in MDEQ's brief, attempts a justification. "A different plan would redefine the source as proposed," says the Department. Yet, at best, this "plan" is opaque. The preceding sentence speaks in one breath of a broad "choice" of fuels and in another of MDEQ's decision to choose only Marquette and Presque Isle coal. At worst, MDEQ's assertion that a different coal source constitutes impermissible "redefining" is unpersuasive and not supported by the record.

MDEQ's brief also notes the difficulty of arranging transport of non-local lower sulfur coal to the Ripley Heating Plant. Such shipments, necessitating that NMU "receive," "stockpile," and "feed" the non-local coal into the boiler, would require "changes in design of the facility," thus "impermissibly redefining the source." The brief is not part of the

C. Technology-Based Standards Under the CAA

administrative record for this permit, and thus we give its factual representations no weight. We do, however, address the legal argument it raises.

"Historically, EPA has not considered the BACT requirement as a means to redefine the design of the source when considering available control alternatives." . . . As more finely rendered by the Board, "certain [design] aspects" of the proposed facility are beyond the reach of BACT; "other [design] aspects" are within it. To guide it, the Board gives central importance to "how the permit applicant defines the proposed facility's purpose or basic design," but puts the applicant's case to a "hard look."

Accordingly, the Board takes care to identify "inherent" design elements, part of the "fundamental purpose" of the proposed facility, or a design such that change to it would "call into question [the facility's] existence." This test shields from BACT review fuel choices found "integral" to the basic design. Proposed coal-fired electrical generators need not consider a natural gas turbine, for example.

On the other hand, the CAA promotes "clean fuels" with particular vigor. See CAA §169(3). Merely equating use of lower polluting fuels to impermissible redesign in the hope of paving an automatic BACT off-ramp pointedly frustrates congressional will. The U.S. Court of Appeals for the Seventh Circuit is notably dismissive of such strategies. Clean fuels may not be "read out" of the Act merely because their use requires "some adjustment" to the proposed technology. If the only required adjustment were that a dirtier fuel be "switched" to a cleaner fuel, said the court in an illustration of near perfect aptness to NMU's CFB boiler, then low sulfur coal should be the BACT choice over high sulfur coal.

Too late and on too meager a record, MDEQ attempts to inject the specter of major redesign. Its brief pushes forward entirely new theories—"transport" difficulties, "stockpile . . . and [boiler] feed" problems—that it claims amount to redesign or "redefining the source" were non-Marquette or -Presque Isle coal forced upon it. But the record before us does not sustain such claims. The documentary trail offers no basis to conclude that any fundamental design change, or any source or facility design change whatsoever, would result were NMU . . . to burn lower sulfur non-Marquette or -Presque Isle coal.

If the NSR Manual is the broad, oft-traveled thoroughfare to determining BACT, MDEQ has almost categorically declined to follow it—or any method consistently faithful to statutory and regulatory guidelines. MDEQ's SO_2 BACT analysis locks onto a combination of minimal wood burning and predominant use of Marquette or Presque Isle coal, yet offers few connecting threads of logic or data to sustain these fuel choices, justify them as enabling NMU to achieve emissions limitations clean enough to be BACT, or support the redefining-the-source claim. The Department's decision lacks a coherent, "clearly ascertainable basis," or "careful and detailed" look, and we are unable to conclude that it "meets the requirement of rationality." Therefore, under part 124, we remand the permit to MDEQ for reconsideration of the BACT limitations chosen for SO_2 emissions from the CFB boiler. . . .

COMMENTARY & QUESTIONS

1. Stationary source permit programs in a nutshell. In basic terms, the PSD program limits the incremental amount of pollution allowed in clean air areas, with smaller increments allowed in areas where there are special national or state interests served by limiting increases in pollution. PSD is part of a larger program called New Source Review (NSR), which requires preconstruction air permits for all new major stationary sources and all major modification to existing major stationary sources. The case discusses NSR as it applies to attainment and unclassifiable areas via the PSD program. For nonattainment areas, the NSR program requires that new and modified sources (1) achieve the LAER, which is the most stringent emissions limitation contained in a SIP; (2) offset new emissions; and (3) provide for the opportunity for public participation in the process. New and existing sources must also comply with any applicable New Source Performance Standards (NSPS), established by EPA pursuant to §111 of the CAA. These are emissions limitations, divided into source category, that are based on the emission limitation achievable through the use of the "best system of emission reduction which [taking costs into account] the Administrator determines has been adequately demonstrated." 42 U.S.C. §7411(a)(1). As we will see, the exact meaning of §111 is a subject of intense debate in the context of EPA's efforts to control GHGs emitted by power plants and other stationary sources.

2. Pollutants for which MDEQ's draft permit set no BACT controls. No BACT controls were set by MDEQ for $PM_{2.5}$, CO_2 and N_2O, which the Sierra Club assigned as error. As to $PM_{2.5}$, the MDEQ relied on the fact that EPA has yet to promulgate BACT for that pollutant due to "a lack of adequate tools for calculating $PM_{2.5}$ emissions," and, instead authorized interim use of PM_{10} as a "surrogate" for $PM_{2.5}$ in meeting the PSD requirements. This aspect of the MDEQ effort was approved by the EAB. CO_2 and N_2O are not "criteria" pollutants, but the Sierra Club argued that they are "subject to regulation" under the CAA and thus BACT limits must be developed for them. Is review of a single permit action the proper forum for such a challenge? The EAB remanded these arguments to the MDEQ, but in doing so cited a similar CO_2/BACT case in which there was a remand, but in which the EAB had noted:

> we recognize that this is an issue of national scope that has implications far beyond this individual permitting proceeding. The Region should consider whether interested persons, as well as the Agency, would be better served by the Agency addressing the interpretation of the phrase "subject to regulation under this Act" in the context of an action of nationwide scope, rather than through this specific permitting proceeding. *In re Deseret Power Elec. Coop.*, PSD Appeal No. 07-03, November 13, 2008, 2008 WL 5572891.

As we will see in Section E below, EPA subsequently offered a nationally applicable interpretation of the phrase "subject to regulation under this Act," with mixed results in the Supreme Court.

3. Agency review of agency decisions: the EAB. This case reflects the fact that much of modern environmental law now plays out in front of administrative bodies, which have broad delegated powers to review agency decisions before a party seeks review before a court. The EAB was created in 1992 in response to the growing number and importance of EPA adjudicatory proceedings. The EAB primarily hears appeals from permit and civil penalty decisions, but it also considers petitions for reimbursement for CERCLA cleanup costs and handles matters from all the major environmental statues that EPA administers. The body sits in panels of three judges, votes by majority, and issues opinions for noteworthy decisions, much as a federal circuit court of appeals does. EAB judges are agency personnel and are not part of the federal judiciary. A decision from the EAB constitutes the final agency decision on a case—a prerequisite for "exhausting administrative remedies" and seeking judicial review.[28] What purposes does the doctrine of exhaustion serve?

---

28. Very intricate "finality" issues can arise when the EAB action is to remand the case to the agency. In a sense, the remand does not finalize the action on the particular permit or other adjudication. Whether such cases can be reviewed by a court varies, and the availability of judicial review is affected by the terms of the delegation to the state agency.

C. Technology-Based Standards Under the CAA

Importantly, the federal regulations describing the powers of the EAB in permitting cases allow "any person who filed comments on [the] draft permit or participated in the public hearing" to petition the EAB to review "any condition of the permit decision." 40 C.F.R. §124.19. This was the mechanism by which the Sierra Club could challenge MDEQ's decision to issue the PSD permit. (Recall that Michigan has a delegated PSD program from EPA, so the EAB has authority to review MDEQ's permitting decisions.) Does the broad ability to petition the EAB show a conflict between agency review and judicial review, which is confined under both state and federal law by standing principles? Do you think Sierra Club had a sufficient stake in the case to be able to effectively challenge the permitting decision?

4. Uncertainty over "redefining the source." One argument that MDEQ and NMU unsuccessfully asserted was based on the available fuel choices. They argued that use of more wood or of coal from sources not listed in the permit application would require "redefining the source," which is not required under a BACT analysis. According to the NSR Manual, the guidance document for state and federal permitting authorities, the BACT analysis is not to be used as a means to effectively redesign the facility. See NSR Manual at B.13.[29] But the EAB emphasized the statutory preference for clean fuels and concluded that considering alternative fuels would not cause a "fundamental design change, or any source or facility design change whatsoever."

Contrast that outcome with the EAB's decision in *Prairie State Generating Co.*[30] There the proposed plant was a "mine-mouth power plant"—that is, the facility was to be located adjacent to a coal reserve. In its permitting decision, the Illinois Environmental Protection Agency (IEPA) deferred to the applicant's definition of the project, such that the local reserve of coal was interpreted as an integral part of the project. Just as in *NMU*, the *Prairie State* petitioners argued that coal from Wyoming or Montana should have been considered because of its low sulfur content. The EAB agreed with the IEPA that the 30-year reserve of on-site, Illinois coal was a part of the project. Requiring the IEPA to consider alternative fuels in the BACT analysis would "redefine the source." What explains these divergent results?

5. Making permits enforceable. Issuing a permit is, pragmatically, only the first step in obtaining real-world control of emissions from the regulated facility. After that the permit must be enforced if it is to provide a true barrier to excessive air pollution. Initially in the CWA's NPDES permits, and later in Title V of the 1990 amendments to the CAA, Congress took steps to make it reasonably likely that permits would be enforced with a reasonable degree of frequency. Subsequent EPA regulations also address these matters. Before reading on, imagine how you would design a permit system that would be easily enforceable and not exclusively reliant on agency enforcement effort (which for a variety of reasons may not be sufficiently energetic).

The basic model surrounding both CWA NPDES (33 U.S.C. §1342) and CAA Title V (42 U.S.C. §§7661-7661f) goes roughly like this:[31]

---

29. Available at http://www.epa.gov/region07/programs/artd/air/nsr/nsrmemos/1990wman.pdf.
30. Available at http://yosemite.epa.gov/oa/eab_web_docket.nsf/Decision~Date/7414685644289CEB852571D4 006785E2/$File/Denying%20Review%2047.pdf.
31. See, e.g., Reitze & Schell, Self-Monitoring and Self-Reporting of Routine Air Pollution Releases, 24 Colum. J. Envtl. L. 63 (1999); D. Wooley & E. Morss, Clean Air Handbook §8:1 (2009).

1. Impose quantified discharge (a water term of art) or emission (air) limits specified for each parameter, such as biochemical oxygen demand for water, or each of the criteria pollutants for air.
2. Require the facility to monitor its discharges/emissions on a regular basis (daily or even more frequently).
3. Ensure accurate monitoring by performing unannounced spot checks and taking independent measurements and impose heavy penalties for willful or intentional failures to monitor accurately.
4. Require the regulated facility to report its discharges/emissions on a periodic basis in a way that makes comparison of the permitted amounts and the actual amounts easy.
5. Publish the periodic reports.
6. Allow citizen suits that include the award of attorneys' fees to prevailing parties.
7. Impose penalties that exceed in cost the economic benefit of committing the violation.

As seen in subsequent chapters, this underlying strategy does not always operate quite as well in practice as might be expected. In order to allow the lead agency[32] to be the masters of their pollution control programs, citizen plaintiffs are required to give a 60-day pre-suit notice to the agency, which may take charge of the matter and thereby deprive the courts of jurisdiction over the citizen suits. Frequently, if violations are recurrent and require alteration of control equipment, the regulatory agencies will negotiate with the polluter, limit the penalty if any, and give the polluter time to come into compliance. While this may not be an unreasonable approach for the agencies to take, it can substantially slow the pace of environmental improvement.

6. An environmental victory? At first glance, Sierra Club seems to walk away from the case as a clear winner. The EAB directed MDEQ to consider alternative fuels in a BACT analysis, give more thorough documentation, consider CO_2 emissions, and (in a portion of the opinion not excerpted here) reevaluate its air quality modeling and preconstruction monitoring. Perhaps most significant is the Board's emphasis on the need to consider low-sulfur coal and increased wood use at the facility. But focusing on wood's appeal from the standpoint of air emissions does not tell the whole story. If a major power plant uses large amounts of wood in its daily operation, there is a danger of unsustainable forestry practices and deforestation, both of which may have adverse effects on air quality. It is an open question whether the decision's emphasis on sulfur content of fuels is overshadowed by the specter of increased wood demand.

This tension is indicative of the complexities in environmental policy generally. "Environmentally friendly" solutions may turn out to be otherwise upon closer inspection. Another striking example is currently unfolding in the area of renewable energy. Most policymakers now support the use of wind and photovoltaic technology to increase the country's energy independence and lessen the environmental impacts of energy production. But others have expressed concern over the adverse environmental consequences that these technologies could create. Stories of wind turbines killing migratory birds have been covered frequently in the media, but there is also the general problem of land use. Solar arrays and wind farms require enormous amounts of land, which many believe should be put to other uses or conserved in its natural state. It is important to remember when considering environmental problems that there is rarely a magic bullet.

---

32. Usually these are state environmental agencies that have taken delegation of the program.

7. Federalism and BACT. Where does the final authority to determine BACT lie? The Supreme Court answered that question in *Alaska Dep't of Envtl. Conservation (ADEC) v. EPA*.[33] ADEC issued a mining company a PSD permit for the installation of an additional generator. EPA issued an order to prevent construction after the agency concluded that the BACT required in the permit was not stringent enough. In a 5-4 decision the Court held that EPA may block construction where it determines that the state permitting authority's determination of BACT is unreasonable in light of the statutory guidelines.

D. TECHNOLOGY-FORCING UNDER THE CAA

The technology-based standards of the CAA set emissions limitations based on certain technology that EPA or the state permitting authority has determined is feasible to implement in the source under review. These are performance standards, i.e., standards that require the regulated entity to obtain a result at least as good as that obtained by the best technologies. These are not specification standards, i.e., standards that require the employment of a specifically mandated technology. This distinction preserves room for innovation in finding ways to comply with the standard. In a few instances, new technologies have developed that allow lower cost compliance with a technology-based standard than the technologies whose performance originally set the standard. More often however, compliance is obtained by employing the already proven "best" technology.

The modest amount of innovation that results under the technology-based regime poses two related, but distinct regulatory challenges. First, the lack of innovation is inefficient (results obtained at a higher cost than would otherwise be the case) and limits progress in protecting health and the environment (more effective technologies would reduce pollution more). Second, in some areas, even the application of the current best technologies is producing unacceptably bad results in terms of public health and other environmental outcomes. A third problem, less often mentioned, is deliberate technology suppression, which can occur when a better technology exists, but the persons having control of it find it more profitable to continue current production techniques. To combat those problems, Congress has occasionally employed technology-forcing. These provisions are enacted with the direct legislative intent of forcing the development of new technology, either by limiting releases of a target substance to lower amounts than can be achieved with currently available technology, or by banning some or all uses of a substance to force the creation of substitutes. Though technology-forcing is rarely used because of its potential to create economic instability, where it has been implemented, industry has been successful in developing or bringing on line innovative technology that has significantly reduced the environmental threat. In addition to the auto emissions reduction case study presented below, the following regulatory efforts are examples of effective technology-forcing: the phase-out of CFCs, EPA's prohibition of the commercial distribution and manufacture of PCBs, and EPA's phased reduction leading to a prohibition on the use of lead in gasoline.

---

33. 540 U.S. 461 (2004).

1. Reducing Auto Emissions Through CAA Title II

The most ambitious and controversial use of technology-forcing as a regulatory strategy to achieve environmental protection goals was the 1970 CAA's Title II, a remarkable example of a drastic, direct, numerical regulatory standard stipulated by the legislature itself, declaring that "emissions of carbon monoxide and hydrocarbons from light duty vehicles . . . manufactured during or after model year 1975 shall . . . require a reduction of at least 90 per centum from emissions allowable . . . in model year 1970."[34] CAA §202(b)(1)(a).

International Harvester v. Ruckelshaus
478 F.2d 615 (D.C. Cir. 1973)

LEVENTHAL, C.J. . . . These consolidated petitions of International Harvester and the three major auto companies, Ford, General Motors, and Chrysler, seek review of a decision by the Administrator [of EPA] denying petitioners' applications . . . for one-year suspensions of the 1975 emissions standards prescribed under the statute for light duty vehicles. . . .

FIGURE 11-2. *Urban pollution, originating primarily from auto emissions.*

The tension of forces presented by the controversy over automobile emission standards may be focused by two central observations: (1) the automobile is an essential pillar of the American economy. Some 28% of the nonfarm workforce draws its livelihood from the automobile and its products; (2) the automobile has had a devastating impact on the American environment. As of 1970, authoritative voices stated that "automotive pollution constitutes in excess of 60% of our national air pollution problem" and more than 80% of the air pollutants in concentrated urban areas.

---

34. The Act applied the same specific rollback to nitrogen oxides starting in the 1976 model year.

D. Technology-Forcing Under the CAA

Congressional concern over the problem of automotive emissions dates back to the 1950s, but . . . [t]he development of emission control technology proceeded haltingly. The Secretary of Health, Education, and Welfare testified in 1967 that "the state of the art has tended to meander along until some sort of regulation took it by the hand and gave it a good pull. . . . There has been a long period of waiting for it, and it hasn't worked very well."

The legislative background must also take into account the fact that in 1969 the Department of Justice brought suit against the four largest automobile manufacturers on the grounds that they had conspired to delay the development of emission control devices.

On December 31, 1970, Congress grasped the nettle and amended the Clean Air Act to set a statutory standard for required reductions in levels of HCs and CO which must be achieved for 1975 models of light duty vehicles. Section 202(b) of the Act . . . provides that, beginning with the 1975 model year, exhaust emission of HC and CO from light duty vehicles must be reduced at least 90% from the permissible emission levels in the 1970 year. In accordance with the Congressional directives, the Administrator . . . promulgated regulations limiting HC and CO emissions from 1975 model light duty vehicles to .41 and 3.4 grams per mile respectively. . . .[35]

Congress was aware that these 1975 standards were "drastic medicine" designed to "force the state of the art." There was, naturally, concern whether the manufacturers would be able to achieve this goal. Therefore, Congress provided . . . a "realistic escape hatch": the manufacturers could petition the EPA for a one-year suspension of the 1975 requirements, and Congress took the precaution of directing the National Academy of Sciences [NAS] to undertake an ongoing study of the feasibility of compliance with the emission standards. The "escape hatch" provision addressed itself to the possibility that the NAS study or other evidence might indicate that the standards would be unachievable despite all good faith efforts at compliance.[36] This provision was limited to a one-year suspension. . . .

[The EPA Administrator rejected petitioners' applications for suspensions on the ground that petitioners had not established the unavailability of control technology that could meet the stricter standards. The NAS Report concluded that the necessary control technology was not available.]

Two principal considerations compete for our attention. On the one hand, if suspension is not granted, and the prediction of the EPA that effective technology will be available is proven incorrect, grave economic consequences could ensue. . . . On the other hand, if suspension is granted, and it later is shown that the Administrator's prediction of feasibility was achievable in 1975 there may be irretrievable ecological costs. It is to this second possibility to which we first turn.

The most authoritative estimate in the record of the ecological costs of a one-year suspension is that of the NAS Report. [The NAS concluded that]

> the effect on total emissions of a one-year suspension with no additional interim standards appears to be small. The effect is not more significant because the emission reduction now required of model year 1974 vehicles, as compared with uncontrolled vehicles (80 percent for HC and 69 percent for CO), is already so substantial.

---

35. This was a default standard; some car models that were cleaner had even tougher standards. The same regulation also prescribed an interim 3.0 grams per mile 1975 standard for nitrogen oxides (NO_x). HC and NO_x combine with sunlight to produce photochemical oxidants (ozone), also known as "smog." [EDS.]

36. The suspension provision also included a criterion that the suspension must be "essential to the public interest or the public health and welfare of the United States." [EDS.]

[The court added that because the technology being tested to meet the 1975 standards would cause fuel economy, acceleration and "driveability" problems, while adding significantly to the cost of new motor vehicles, "a drop-off in purchase of 1975 cars will result in a prolonged use of older cars with *less* efficient pollution control devices.... It might even come to pass that total actual emissions (of all cars in use) would be greater under the 1975 than the 1974 standards."]

We also note that it is the belief of many experts—both in and out of the automobile industry—that air pollution cannot be effectively checked until the industry finds a substitute for the conventional automotive power plant—the reciprocating internal combustion (i.e., "piston") engine. According to this view, the conventional unit is a "dirty" engine. While emissions from such a motor can be "cleaned" by various thermal and catalytic converter devices, these devices do nothing to decrease the production of emissions in the engine's combustion chambers. The automobile industry has a multibillion-dollar investment in the conventional engine, and it has been reluctant to introduce new power plants or undertake major modifications of the conventional one. Thus the bulk of the industry's work on emission control has focused narrowly on converter devices. It is clear from the legislative history that Congress expected the Clean Air Act Amendments to force the industry to broaden the scope of its research—to study new types of engines and new control systems. Perhaps even a one-year suspension does not give the industry sufficient time to develop a new approach to emission control and still meet the absolute deadline of 1976. If so, there will be ample time for the EPA and Congress, between now and 1976 to reflect on changing the statutory approach. This kind of cooperation, a unique three-way partnership between the legislature, executive, and judiciary, was contemplated by the Congress and is apparent in the provisions of the Act....

If the automobiles of Ford, General Motors and Chrysler cannot meet the 1975 standards..., the Administrator of EPA has the theoretical authority... to shut down the auto industry, as was clearly recognized in the Congressional debate. We cannot put blinders on the facts before us so as to omit awareness of reality that this authority would undoubtedly never be exercised, in light of the fact that approximately 1 out of every 7 jobs in this country is dependent on the production of the automobile. Senator Muskie, the principal sponsor of the bill, stated quite clearly in the debate on the Act that he envisioned the Congress acting if an auto industry shutdown were in sight....

This case is haunted by the irony that what seems to be Ford's technological lead may operate to its grievous detriment, assuming the relaxation-if-necessary [of the standards]. If... any one of the three major companies cannot meet the 1975 standards, it is a likelihood that standards will be set to permit the higher level of emission control achievable by the laggard. This will be the case whether or not the leader has or has not achieved compliance with the 1975 standards. Even if the relaxation is later made industry-wide, the Government's action, in first imposing a standard not generally achievable and then relaxing it, is likely to be detrimental to the leader who has tooled up to meet a higher standard than will ultimately be required.

In some contexts high achievement bestows the advantage that rightly belongs to the leader, of high quality. In this context before us, however, the high achievement in emission control results, under systems presently available, in lessened car performance—an inverse correlation. The competitive disadvantage to the ecological leader presents a forbidding outcome... for which we see no remedy.... [The court remanded the case to EPA for reconsideration of its denial of suspension.]

D. Technology-Forcing Under the CAA

COMMENTARY & QUESTIONS

1. Was this really technology-forcing? Is technology-forcing legislation credible when the bill's sponsor assures his colleagues that the "hammer" (shutdown of large auto manufacturers) will never be allowed to fall? Is it any wonder that the auto industry did not take the threat seriously and instead continued to tinker with add-on devices that would require little modification of existing automobiles and could later be abandoned if Congress changed its mind? In fact, the "three-way partnership" among the legislature, executive branch, and judiciary acted to postpone compliance far beyond the one-year suspension. On remand, EPA granted the extension for both the HC and the CO standards, but promulgated interim standards for 1975 of 1.4 and 15 gpm (grams per mile) respectively.

EPA granted a one-year suspension of the 1976 NO_x standard of 0.2 gpm and set an interim standard of 2 gpm. Through a combination of congressional extensions and congressionally authorized EPA suspensions, the HC and CO standards, based on a 90% rollback, were not finally met until 1980 and 1983 respectively. Congress abandoned the 0.2 gpm NO_x standard in 1977 and, in its place, imposed a 1 gpm standard to be met in 1984. By the mid-1980s, the auto industry was willing to accept the standards because market demand was moving toward smaller, less-polluting, and more fuel-efficient vehicles.

Was this an example of successful technology-forcing? Or was the final attainment of the 1975 and 1976 standards merely accidental? Was attainment "too little, too late"?

2. Why the denial? Why did EPA deny the one-year suspension, knowing that its decision was in conflict with the prestigious NAS Report and sensing the lack of congressional support for strict deadlines and draconic enforcement? EPA must have realized that its denial would be overturned by a court or Congress (or both, as it turned out). Is it possible that although EPA wanted to censure the auto industry for its failure to make a genuine effort to consider new technology and its alleged conspiracy to suppress new technology, the agency believed that it would have been politically inexpedient to try to prove that the auto industry had violated the requirement of making "all good faith efforts" to meet the standards?

3. Rewarding the laggard and the risks of leading the way. Was the court correct in its assumption that a company making good faith efforts to comply with the standards would inevitably be disadvantaged by a standard relaxation dictated by the overall public interest? Whenever standards are set and then reset at different levels, parties that comply quickly may suffer unintended penalties. What if standards are tightened after a company has invested in new technology in order to meet the first change in the standard? What if a rollback approach is taken after one firm has already reduced its emissions? Both situations pose serious inter-polluter equity problems that a regulatory scheme should address. (Another approach to this problem is found in §306(d) of the CWA, which provides that a new source of water pollution that has achieved its NSPS cannot be subject to stricter standards for ten years or the depreciation or amortization period of the facility, whichever ends first.) What about using incentives such as tax deductions or preferential governmental purchasing to add inducements to early compliance?

4. The court's balancing test. Note that the court's cost-benefit analysis followed Talbot Page's recommendation in Chapter 1 that the costs of false negatives be weighed against the costs of false positives in making environmental regulatory decisions. In this case, as analyzed by the court, the cost of a false negative (not granting the suspension when it should have been granted) was relatively high in economic terms, while the cost of a false positive (granting the suspension when it should not have been) was relatively low in environmental terms. Given the broad "public interest" test articulated by Congress, balancing the costs of potential erroneous decisions appears to have been justified. But did the court conduct the balance fairly in light of the fact that the one-year extension was not a firm one, making further slippage predictable?

5. The 1990 CAA Amendments, technology-forcing, and auto pollution. By 1987, emissions of HC, CO, and lead from new cars had dropped by over 95% from uncontrolled levels, and emissions of NO_x dropped by over 75%, but increases in automobile use caused ambient air quality standards for ozone to be exceeded in many urban areas.[37] With the lessons of its 1970 technology-forcing effort firmly in mind, in 1990 Congress adopted a more sophisticated but still aggressive technology-forcing strategy to cope with ozone nonattainment problems. The 1990 amendments mandated the use of clean-fuel vehicles in the most polluted cities in the country and created demand for these vehicles by requiring certain owners of centrally fueled fleets to use clean-fuel vehicles. This helped to solve infrastructure problems because centrally fueled vehicles do not require a scattered network of fueling stations. The amendments also took a supply-side approach by requiring that vehicle manufacturers in California—the only "extreme" ozone nonattainment area—produce a certain percentage of clean-fuel vehicles in the state.

In recent years, technology-forcing in the automobile industry has revolved around increasing fuel efficiency and reducing GHG emissions. Standards jointly issued by EPA and NHTSA for light-duty vehicles and heavy trucks have appreciably enhanced the efficiency of new mobile sources. These standards are likely to force technological innovation in electric, hybrid, hydrogen, and other alternative-fuel vehicles as auto manufacturers work to meet the new regulations and consumer demand for "greener" vehicles.

E. Regulation of Greenhouse Gases Under the CAA

> While federal regulation under the CAA has largely centered on the criteria pollutants, through NAAQS and regulation of tailpipe emissions, attention has lately turned to the issue of using the CAA to regulate greenhouse gases (GHGs). Unlike the current criteria pollutants, which can cause direct physiological harm to the human body, GHGs pose a threat because of their potential to alter Earth's climate in catastrophic ways, giving new meaning to the phrase "harm to the human environment." In response to a petition that EPA regulate GHGs under the CAA, the Agency concluded in 2003 that it had no authority to do so under the statute and that even if it had the authority, it would not exercise it. Twelve states, along with several municipalities and public interest organizations, filed suit, and the case eventually reached the Supreme Court.

---

37. Nearly 50% of the U.S. population lives in areas with unhealthy levels of ozone, and approximately half of all ozone is produced by automobiles. [EDS.]

E. Regulation of Greenhouse Gases Under the CAA

Massachusetts v. U.S. Environmental Protection Agency
549 U.S. 497 (2007)

STEVENS, J. A well-documented rise in global temperatures has coincided with a significant increase in the concentration of carbon dioxide in the atmosphere. Respected scientists believe the two trends are related. For when carbon dioxide is released into the atmosphere, it acts like the ceiling of a greenhouse, trapping solar energy and retarding the escape of reflected heat. It is therefore a species—the most important species—of a "greenhouse gas."

Calling global warming "the most pressing environmental challenge of our time," a group of States, local governments, and private organizations, alleged in a petition for certiorari that the EPA has abdicated its responsibility under the CAA to regulate the emissions of four GHGs, including carbon dioxide. Specifically, petitioners asked us to answer two questions concerning the meaning of §202(a)(1) of the Act: whether EPA has the statutory authority to regulate GHG emissions from new motor vehicles; and if so, whether its stated reasons for refusing to do so are consistent with the statute. . . .

§202(a)(1) of the CAA . . . provides:

> The [EPA] Administrator shall by regulation prescribe (and from time to time revise) in accordance with the provisions of this section, standards applicable to the emission of any air pollutant from any class or classes of new motor vehicles or new motor vehicle engines, which in his judgment cause, or contribute to, air pollution which may reasonably be anticipated to endanger public health or welfare. . . .

The Act defines "air pollutant" to include "any air pollution agent or combination of such agents, including any physical, chemical, biological, radioactive . . . substance or matter which is emitted into or otherwise enters the ambient air." "Welfare" is also defined broadly: among other things, it includes "effects on . . . weather . . . and climate." . . .

On October 20, 1999, a group of 19 private organizations filed a rulemaking petition asking EPA to regulate "greenhouse gas emissions from new motor vehicles under §202 of the Clean Air Act." Petitioners maintained that 1998 was the "warmest year on record"; that carbon dioxide, methane, nitrous oxide, and hydrofluorocarbons are "heat trapping greenhouse gases"; that GHG emissions have significantly accelerated climate change; and that the IPCC's 1995 report warned that "carbon dioxide remains the most important contributor to [man-made] forcing of climate change." The petition further alleged that climate change will have serious adverse effects on human health and the environment. . . .

On September 8, 2003, EPA entered an order denying the rulemaking petition. The agency gave two reasons for its decision: (1) that contrary to the opinions of its former general counsels, the CAA does not authorize EPA to issue mandatory regulations to address global climate change; and (2) that even if the agency had the authority to set GHG emission standards, it would be unwise to do so at this time.

In concluding that it lacked statutory authority over GHGs, EPA observed that Congress "was well aware of the global climate change issue when it last comprehensively amended the [CAA] in 1990," yet it declined to adopt a proposed amendment establishing binding emissions limitations. Congress instead chose to authorize further investigation into climate change. EPA further reasoned that Congress' "specially tailored solutions to global atmospheric issues"—in particular, its 1990 enactment of a comprehensive scheme to regulate pollutants that depleted the ozone layer—counseled against reading the general authorization of §202(a)(1) to confer regulatory authority over GHGs. . . .

EPA reasoned that climate change had its own "political history": Congress designed the original CAA to address *local* air pollutants rather than a substance that "is fairly consistent in its concentration throughout the *world's* atmosphere"; declined in 1990 to enact proposed amendments to force EPA to set carbon dioxide emission standards for motor vehicles; and addressed global climate change in other legislation. . . . In essence, EPA concluded that climate change was so important that unless Congress spoke with exacting specificity, it could not have meant the agency to address it.

Having reached that conclusion, EPA believed it followed that GHGs cannot be "air pollutants" within the meaning of the Act. The agency bolstered this conclusion by explaining that if carbon dioxide were an air pollutant, the only feasible method of reducing tailpipe emissions would be to improve fuel economy. But because Congress has already created detailed mandatory fuel economy standards subject to Department of Transportation (DOT) administration, the agency concluded that EPA regulation would either conflict with those standards or be superfluous. . . .

[The Court first concluded that Massachusetts had standing to bring the action because the "rise in sea levels associated with global warming has already harmed and will continue to harm Massachusetts," and regulation of CO_2 under the CAA would reduce the risk of that harm.]

The scope of our review of the merits of the statutory issues is narrow. As we have repeated time and again, an agency has broad discretion to choose how best to marshal its limited resources and personnel to carry out its delegated responsibilities. That discretion is at its height when the agency decides not to bring an enforcement action. Therefore, in *Heckler v. Chaney*, 470 U.S. 821 (1985), we held that an agency's refusal to initiate enforcement proceedings is not ordinarily subject to judicial review. Some debate remains, however, as to the rigor with which we review an agency's denial of a petition for rulemaking.

There are key differences between a denial of a petition for rulemaking and an agency's decision not to initiate an enforcement action. In contrast to nonenforcement decisions, agency refusals to initiate rulemaking "are less frequent, more apt to involve legal as opposed to factual analysis, and subject to special formalities, including a public explanation." They moreover arise out of denials of petitions for rulemaking which (at least in the circumstances here) the affected party had an undoubted procedural right to file in the first instance. Refusals to promulgate rules are thus susceptible to judicial review, though such review is "extremely limited" and "highly deferential."

EPA concluded in its denial of the petition for rulemaking that it lacked authority under 42 U.S.C. §7521(a)(1) to regulate new vehicle emissions because carbon dioxide is not an "air pollutant" as that term is defined in §7602. In the alternative, it concluded that even if it possessed authority, it would decline to do so because regulation would conflict with other administration priorities. As discussed earlier, the Clean Air Act expressly permits review of such an action. §7607(b)(1). We therefore "may reverse any such action found to be . . . arbitrary, capricious, an abuse of discretion, or otherwise not in accordance with law." §7607(d)(9).

On the merits, the first question is whether §202(a)(1) of the CAA authorizes EPA to regulate GHG emissions from new motor vehicles in the event that it forms a "judgment" that such emissions contribute to climate change. We have little trouble concluding that it does. In relevant part, §202(a)(1) provides that EPA "shall by regulation prescribe . . . standards applicable to the emission of any air pollutant from any class or classes of new motor vehicles or new motor vehicle engines, which in [the Administrator's] judgment cause, or contribute to, air pollution which may reasonably be anticipated to endanger public health or welfare." 42 U.S.C. §7521(a)(1). Because EPA believes that Congress did not intend it to

E. Regulation of Greenhouse Gases Under the CAA

regulate substances that contribute to climate change, the agency maintains that carbon dioxide is not an "air pollutant" within the meaning of the provision.

The statutory text forecloses EPA's reading. The CAA's sweeping definition of "air pollutant" includes "*any* air pollution agent or combination of such agents, including *any* physical, chemical . . . substance or matter which is emitted into or otherwise enters the ambient air. . . ." §7602(g) (emphasis added). On its face, the definition embraces all airborne compounds of whatever stripe, and underscores that intent through the repeated use of the word "any." Carbon dioxide, methane, nitrous oxide, and hydrofluorocarbons are without a doubt "physical [and] chemical . . . substances which [are] emitted into . . . the ambient air." The statute is unambiguous. . . .

While the Congresses that drafted §202(a)(1) might not have appreciated the possibility that burning fossil fuels could lead to global warming, they did understand that without regulatory flexibility, changing circumstances and scientific developments would soon render the CAA obsolete. . . . Because GHGs fit well within the CAA's capacious definition of "air pollutant," we hold that EPA has the statutory authority to regulate the emission of such gases from new motor vehicles. . . .

The alternative basis for EPA's decision—that even if it does have statutory authority to regulate GHGs, it would be unwise to do so at this time—rests on reasoning divorced from the statutory text. While the statute does condition the exercise of EPA's authority on its formation of a "judgment," 42 U.S.C. §7521(a)(1), that judgment must relate to whether an air pollutant "causes, or contributes to, air pollution which may reasonably be anticipated to endanger public health or welfare," Put another way, the use of the word "judgment" is not a roving license to ignore the statutory text. It is but a direction to exercise discretion within defined statutory limits.

If EPA makes a finding of endangerment, the CAA requires the agency to regulate emissions of the deleterious pollutant from new motor vehicles. ("[EPA] shall by regulation prescribe . . . standards applicable to the emission of any air pollutant from any class of new motor vehicles.") EPA no doubt has significant latitude as to the manner, timing, content, and coordination of its regulations with those of other agencies. But once EPA has responded to a petition for rulemaking, its reasons for action or inaction must conform to the authorizing statute. Under the clear terms of the CAA, EPA can avoid taking further action only if it determines that GHGs do not contribute to climate change or if it provides some reasonable explanation as to why it cannot or will not exercise its discretion to determine whether they do. . . .

EPA has refused to comply with this clear statutory command. If the scientific uncertainty is so profound that it precludes EPA from making a reasoned judgment as to whether GHGs contribute to global warming, EPA must say so. That EPA would prefer not to regulate GHGs because of some residual uncertainty . . . is irrelevant. The statutory question is whether sufficient information exists to make an endangerment finding.

In short, EPA has offered no reasoned explanation for its refusal to decide whether GHGs cause or contribute to climate change. Its action was therefore "arbitrary, capricious, . . . or otherwise not in accordance with law." We need not and do not reach the question whether on remand EPA must make an endangerment finding, or whether policy concerns can inform EPA's actions in the event that it makes such a finding. We hold only that EPA must ground its reasons for action or inaction in the statute. . . .

[The dissenting opinions are omitted. Chief Justice Roberts would have dismissed the case for lack of standing. Justice Scalia argued that the Court should have deferred to EPA's interpretation that GHGs were not air pollutants and respected the agency's reasons for refusing to regulate even if it had legal authority to do so.]

COMMENTARY & QUESTIONS

1. Greenhouse gases as "air pollutants." Does it make sense to regard carbon dioxide, a colorless, odorless GHG, as an "air pollutant"? Aren't "air pollutants" supposed to be *dirty* (as Justice Scalia suggested in dissent)? Did the majority in *Massachusetts v. EPA* seem to believe it had settled, for once and for all, the status of GHGs as "air pollutants" within the meaning of the CAA? Even if so, a later decision (by Justice Scalia) rejected that broad reading of the case. In *Utility Air Regulatory Group ("UARG") v. EPA*, 134 S. Ct. 2427 (2014), the Court held that EPA had unreasonably interpreted the statutory provision triggering PSD review to include GHGs as "pollutant[s] subject to regulation" under the PSD program. Given that the numerical thresholds triggering regulation under the PSD program would bring in millions of new sources if they were applied to GHGs, the Court found it unreasonable for EPA to interpret the PSD provisions as applying to these pollutants. The Court's decision appears to require EPA to decide, on a provision-by-provision basis, whether GHGs are "air pollutants" subject to the regulatory programs of the CAA.

2. The endangerment finding. *Massachusetts v. EPA* is regarded as one of the most significant cases in environmental law history. While Congress struggled to pass comprehensive climate change legislation, the Supreme Court ruled that EPA already had the statutory authority to regulate GHGs, authority derived from one of the oldest environmental statutes on the books. Following the Court's opinion, the only way EPA could refrain from regulating GHGs under the CAA would be if the Agency found that greenhouse gases do not endanger public health or welfare, "the scientific uncertainty is so profound that it precludes EPA from making a reasoned judgment as to whether greenhouse gases contribute to global warming," or provided "some reasonable explanation" for declining to act. Given the extensive discussion of the scientific evidence for climate change in the opinion and the fact that EPA did not dispute that climate change was caused by man-made emissions, EPA had no real choice but to issue an endangerment finding and to regulate GHGs from mobile sources under CAA §202.

But theoretical clarity does not translate into tangible action, especially when an anti-regulatory administration is in control. The Bush II EPA engaged in a variety of tactics to delay issuing an endangerment finding. As a result, EPA did not issue an endangerment finding until 2009, after the administration had changed. The EPA Administrator found that six GHGs—carbon dioxide (CO_2), methane (CH_4), nitrous oxide (N_2O), hydrofluorocarbons (HFCs), perfluorocarbons (PFCs), and sulfur hexafluoride (SF_6)—endanger the public health and welfare (the "endangerment" finding). In addition, the Administrator found that four of the GHGs—CO_2, CH_4, N_2O, and HFCs—from new motor vehicles and motor vehicle engines contribute to atmospheric concentrations of these gases and therefore to climate change (the "cause or contribute" finding).

3. Mobile sources first. As a result of the positive endangerment finding, EPA was required to regulate GHG emissions from motor vehicles. EPA has now issued two rounds of rules for light-duty vehicles, together dramatically reducing GHG emissions from these sources. EPA has also issued two rounds of rules for heavy-duty trucks and trailers. In addition to the national standards, EPA granted California a waiver to regulate GHG emissions. The state originally requested the waiver in 2005 and the Bush II EPA denied the request in 2008. EPA's grant of the waiver was important for reaffirming California's historic position as a leader for experimenting with and developing emissions standards and, more broadly, signaled the role of the states in addressing climate change through emissions regulations on mobile sources.

E. Regulation of Greenhouse Gases Under the CAA

4. Stationary source permitting. The Supreme Court's decision in *UARG v. EPA*, noted above, was less a loss for EPA than it might seem. The Court rejected EPA's attempt to "tailor" the PSD program for GHGs by phasing in the permitting requirements over time, beginning with the very largest sources first. But the Court allowed EPA to regulate GHGs from sources otherwise covered by the PSD program—the so-called "anyway" sources. The combined effect of these two rulings was to leave in place PSD restrictions on the vast majority of sources EPA had sought to regulate through the "tailoring" rule.

5. NAAQS for GHGs? Recall the statutory language in CAA §202(a), central to *Massachusetts v. EPA*:

> The Administrator shall by regulation prescribe (and from time to time revise) in accordance with the provisions of this section, standards applicable to the emission of any air pollutant from any class or classes of new motor vehicles or new motor vehicle engines, which in his judgment cause, or contribute to, air pollution which may reasonably be anticipated to endanger public health or welfare. 42 U.S.C. §7521(a)(1).

The endangerment language in this section mirrors that found in the section discussing criteria pollutants in §108(a). This statutory parallel has not been lost on public interest organizations. In December 2009, the Center for Biological Diversity and 350.org petitioned EPA to designate CO_2 as a criteria pollutant and establish a NAAQS for the gas at "no greater than 350 ppm."[38] Recall that in *NRDC v. Train*, discussed in Section A, the Second Circuit concluded that where EPA has adjudged that an air pollutant endangers public health and welfare, the Administrator must list the pollutant and issue a NAAQS. The fact that the Administrator makes the endangerment finding under a section of the Act that does not deal with criteria pollutants should not matter, if one follows the Second Circuit's reasoning. A finding of endangerment is a finding of endangerment. Despite the legal arguments for a CO_2 NAAQS, we are not likely to see one anytime soon for various political and administrative reasons. As David Bookbinder, a former Sierra Club attorney, once quipped, "despite global warming, hell will freeze over before there's a NAAQS for CO_2." From what you know about the NAAQS and the structure of the CAA, what are some problems that may arise in regulating GHGs under the CAA? Should CO_2 be defined as a criteria pollutant? EPA has not responded to the Center for Biological Diversity's petition.

6. Foiling Halliburton? An amendment to the Safe Drinking Water Act—known as the "Halliburton amendment" for the company that inspired it—exempts hydraulic fracturing operations from that statute. The CAA may step in, however, where the Safe Drinking Water Act has failed. EPA has proposed regulating methane emissions from new oil and gas facilities. A recent study of the methane leakage from fracking facilities in Texas, sponsored by the Environmental Defense Fund, found that methane leaks were 90% higher than EPA had estimated—raising the climate stakes for EPA's proposal to address methane under the CAA.

7. Filling out the GHG regulatory program. EPA issued a final mandatory GHG emissions reporting rule in 2009, which requires all large domestic emitters to report their emissions annually. Included under this rule are suppliers of fossil fuels, manufacturers of vehicles and engines, as well as facilities that emit 25,000 tons of CO_2 equivalent per year.

More prominently, EPA has also issued final rules regulating GHG emissions from new and existing power plants under CAA §111. Under §111(b), applicable to new sources, EPA

---

38. Center for Biological Diversity & 350.org, Petition to Establish National Pollution Limits for Greenhouse Gases Pursuant to the Clean Air Act, available at www.biologicaldiversity.org/programs/climate_law_institute/global_warming_litigation/clean_air_act/pdfs/Petition_GHG_pollution_cap_12-2-2009.pdf.

set a New Source Performance Standard (NSPS) requiring new coal-fired power plants to install carbon capture as a means of controlling carbon pollution. Under §111(b), EPA also declined to do much of anything by way of regulating existing sources that are modified or reconstructed, resting instead with quite modest efficiency measures at these plants. Under §111(d), which creates a SIP-like process for regulating stationary sources, EPA set emissions targets for the states and offered an illustrative set of "building blocks"—including plant efficiency, fuel switching, and renewable energy—for states to choose from in developing plans to meet their emissions targets. The rules are complex, innovative, hopeful, and controversial. Legal challenges have begun and, indeed, some were filed before the rules were even finalized.

80% of pollution is caused by plants and trees.

—Ronald Reagan

We call upon the waters that rim the earth, horizon to horizon, that flow in our rivers and streams, that fall upon our gardens and fields, and we ask that they teach us and show us the way.

—Chinook Blessing Litany

I've known rivers ancient as the world and older than the flow of human blood in human veins. My soul has grown deep like the rivers. . . .

— Langston Hughes

In the world there is nothing more submissive and weak than water. Yet for attacking that which is hard and strong, there is nothing that can surpass it.

—Lao-tze, 6th century BCE

I sat by the river and forgot and forgot, until what remained was the river that went by and I who watched . . . and eventually the watcher joined the river, and there was only one of us. I believe it was the river.

—Norman MacLean

12

Technology-Based Standard Setting: The Clean Water Act

A. An Overview of the Clean Water Act
B. The Origin and Evolution of TBELs
C. Implementing TBELs Through the NPDES Process
D. Water Quality-Based Permitting and Management of Nonpoint Pollution Under the CWA
E. A Complex Hypothetical: The Average River

A. AN OVERVIEW OF THE CLEAN WATER ACT

The Clean Water Act (CWA), 33 U.S.C. §§1251 et seq., derives from the old Federal Water Pollution Control Act (FWPCA). It was given its modern form in its major amendments of 1972. Like the CAA, the CWA imposes national baseline pollution standards. For the CWA, however, Congress chose a converse approach to the standard-setting methods of the CAA. The CAA primarily employs a strategy of harm-based standard-setting, although it gradually has been moving in the direction of technology-based standard-setting. The CWA, on the other hand, is fundamentally premised on technology-based standard-setting, but in recent years increasingly has included elements of harm-based standard-setting. These tendencies are instructive.

> The legal heart of the CWA is its prohibition on the "discharge" of "pollutants" to "navigable waters" from a "point source" without a permit. Each of these key terms has been the subject of litigation, as discussed in this chapter. Consider the stakes for both water quality and regulatory costs in how this language has been interpreted and applied by the EPA and federal courts throughout the CWA's history.

The basic federal "floor" standards under the CWA are effluent limitations based on "Best Available Technology Economically Achievable" (commonly referred to as BAT), or one of its variant standards, "Best Conventional Pollutant Control Technology" (BCT) or "Best Available Demonstrated Control Technology" (BADT). Under the CWA's National Pollutant Discharge Elimination System (NPDES), all "point source" dischargers of pollutants[1] (e.g., outfall pipes from factories, municipal sewage treatment plants, vessels) are assigned EPA-promulgated performance standards based on the best water pollution control technology that has been found to be both available and economically achievable industry-by-industry among dischargers performing similar economic activities or using similar mechanical processes.[2] The resulting technology-based effluent limitations are called TBELs. In many cases, compliance with TBELs by point source dischargers located on a particular waterbody has enabled the public to return to those waters for fishing and swimming, which is one of the CWA's goals. Waterbodies that can attain the fishable-swimmable criterion through the operation of TBELs alone are called "effluent-limited" waterbodies.

However, situations arise where compliance with TBELs by point source dischargers does not produce fishable-swimmable water quality, and additional limits must be applied. These "water quality-limited" stretches (also called impaired waters) may occur where "natural pollution" levels are high (e.g., high concentrations of naturally occurring arsenic and salts in waterbodies of the western United States), intense concentrations of factories or municipal treatment plants overtax the assimilative capacities of receiving waters, past pollution ("legacy pollution") has heavily contaminated the sediments and water column, or unregulated nonpoint sources, such as large agricultural or silvicultural activities, cause heavy pollutant loadings to nearby waterbodies. Point source dischargers on water quality-limited stretches must meet, in addition to TBELs, *harm-based* effluent limitations, called water quality-based effluent limitations (WQBELs), based on achieving fishable-swimmable water quality, wherever that is attainable.

From 1972 to 1987, the major preoccupation of CWA administration was the implementation of TBELs for all point source dischargers. This stage, for the most part, has been reached. Although TBEL implementation remains a high priority for water pollution control agencies, the major focus of water pollution control programs is shifting to WQBEL-setting and implementation. This chapter first analyzes the traditional standard-setting mechanism of the CWA-TBELs and then addresses the comparatively recent developments associated with WQBELs. The chapter concludes with a discussion of nonpoint source pollution control.

The CWA's basic strategy of technology-based standard-setting has made a monumental contribution to cleaning up America's surface waterbodies. Major waterbodies that, in the 1960s, were virtual open sewers are now fit for fishing and swimming.[3] The infamous lower Cuyahoga River, which in 1969 was declared a fire hazard and actually caught fire (for the third time) as surface oil and grease was ignited by a spill of hot slag, is now sufficiently safe and attractive (although not yet fishable-swimmable, especially after heavy rains) that

---

1. The distinction between point and nonpoint source discharges is a critical one and is explored thoroughly below. In general, point source discharges are regulated by the CWA, but nonpoint source discharges are not. The CWA's regulatory mechanism applies to the "discharge of a pollutant," which is defined as "any addition of any pollutant to navigable waters from any point source." §502(12). A point source discharges through a discrete and confined conveyance, such as a pipe, ditch, or channel. A nonpoint source produces a diffuse and unconfined discharge, such as overland runoff from a farm or a paved surface.

2. "Performance standard" means that the law requires a certain *result*, without dictating *how* a person must meet it (which would be a "design standard" or a "specification standard"). Thus, although the CWA sets limits for how much of a pollutant can be discharged in a water effluent by figuring out what the best technology would achieve, it is a performance standard because it does not require the polluter to use that technology if it can reach the same result another way, say by reducing the use of polluting materials in the production process.

3. These waterbodies include major stretches of the Delaware, Connecticut, Potomac, Charles, and Tennessee Rivers, Lake Erie, New York City's East River, and Puget Sound.

A. An Overview of the Clean Water Act

the Cleveland Flats area at the river's mouth has been transformed from a fetid industrial zone into a waterside entertainment district lined with nightclubs and bistros, with tables on decks at riverside and tie-ups for pleasure boaters.[4] According to EPA estimates, about 60% of the nation's rivers, lakes, and estuaries are now fishable-swimmable, compared with approximately 36% in 1972. This nationwide improvement in water quality has resulted from the reduction of point source discharges by roughly 90%. Despite clear and often dramatic progress in cleaning up America's surface waterbodies, the bad news is that a large percentage of America's waterbodies still do not meet the CWA's fishable-swimmable goal, and nonpoint sources are still largely unregulated.

The following excerpt serves as an introduction to the range of contaminants that degrade water quality and the typical sources of those pollutants.

FIGURE 12-1. *Cuyahoga River on fire.*

U.S. Environmental Protection Agency, National Water Quality Inventory: 1994 Report to Congress

Executive Summary, 7-15

LOW DISSOLVED OXYGEN ... Dissolved oxygen is a basic requirement for a healthy aquatic ecosystem. Most fish and beneficial aquatic insects "breathe" oxygen dissolved in the water column. Some fish and aquatic organisms (such as carp and sludge worms) are adapted to

---

4. A former EPA Administrator is reputed to have quipped, "the Cuyahoga River may not be fishable and swimmable, but it is no longer flammable."

low oxygen conditions, but the most desirable fish species (such as trout and salmon) suffer if dissolved oxygen concentrations fall below 3 to 4 mg/L (3 to 4 milligrams of oxygen dissolved in 1 liter of water, or 3 to 4 parts of oxygen per million parts of water). Larvae and juvenile fish are more sensitive and require even higher concentrations of oxygen.

Many fish and other aquatic organisms can recover from short periods of low dissolved oxygen availability. However, prolonged episodes of depressed dissolved oxygen concentrations of 2 mg/L or less can result in "dead" waterbodies. Prolonged exposure to low dissolved oxygen conditions can suffocate adult fish or reduce their reproductive survival by suffocating sensitive eggs and larvae or can starve fish by killing aquatic insect larvae and other prey. Low dissolved oxygen concentrations also favor anaerobic bacteria activity that produces noxious gases or foul odors often associated with polluted waterbodies.

Oxygen concentrations in the water column fluctuate under normal conditions, but severe oxygen depletion usually results from human activities that introduce large quantities of biodegradable organic materials into surface waters [measured in terms of biochemical oxygen demand (BOD)]. Biodegradable organic materials contain plant, fish, or animal matter. Leaves, lawn clippings, sewage, manure, shellfish processing waste, milk solids, and other food processing wastes are examples of oxygen-depleting organic materials that enter our surface waters.

In both pristine and polluted waters, beneficial bacteria use oxygen to break apart (or decompose) organic materials. Pollution-containing organic wastes provide a continuous glut of food for the bacteria, which accelerates bacterial activity and population growth. In polluted waters, bacterial consumption of oxygen can rapidly outpace oxygen replenishment from the atmosphere and photosynthesis performed by algae and aquatic plants. The result is a net decline in oxygen concentrations in the water.

Toxic pollutants can indirectly lower oxygen concentrations by killing algae, aquatic weeds, or fish, which provides an abundance of food for oxygen-consuming bacteria. Oxygen depletion can also result from chemical reactions that do not involve bacteria. Some pollutants trigger chemical reactions that place a chemical oxygen demand [COD] on receiving waters.

Other factors (such as temperature and salinity) influence the amount of oxygen dissolved in water. Prolonged hot weather will depress oxygen concentrations and may cause fish kills even in clean waters because warm water cannot hold as much oxygen as cold water. Warm conditions further aggravate oxygen depletion by stimulating bacterial activity and respiration in fish, which consumes oxygen. . . .

NUTRIENTS . . . Nutrients are essential building blocks for healthy aquatic communities, but excess nutrients (especially nitrogen and phosphorus compounds) overstimulate the growth of aquatic weeds and algae.[5] Excessive growth of these organisms, in turn, can clog navigable waters, interfere with swimming and boating, outcompete submerged aquatic vegetation, and lead to oxygen depletion.

Oxygen concentrations can fluctuate daily during algal blooms, rising during the day as algae perform photosynthesis, and falling at night as algae continue to respire, which consumes oxygen. Beneficial bacteria also consume oxygen as they decompose the abundant organic food supply in dying algae cells.

---

5. This process is called eutrophication, or the premature aging of waterbodies. Excessive nutrient discharges are also suspected of creating the conditions under which the *pfisteria piscicida* bacteria has proliferated and killed hundreds of thousands of fish in Chesapeake Bay and the Pamlico River, North Carolina. [EDS.]

A. An Overview of the Clean Water Act

Lawn and crop fertilizers, sewage, manure, and detergents contain nitrogen and phosphorus, the nutrients most responsible for water quality degradation. Rural areas are vulnerable to ground water contamination from nitrates (a compound containing nitrogen) found in fertilizer and manure. Very high concentrations of nitrate (more than 10 mg/L) in drinking water cause methemoglobinemia, or blue baby syndrome, an inability to fix oxygen in the blood. . . .

SEDIMENT AND SILTATION . . . In a water quality context, sediment usually refers to soil particles that enter the water column from eroding land. Sediment consists of particles of all sizes, including fine clay particles, silt, sand, and gravel. Water quality managers use term "siltation" to describe the suspension and deposition of small particles in waterbodies.

Sediment and siltation can severely alter aquatic communities. Sediment may clog and abrade fish gills, suffocate eggs and aquatic insect larvae on the bottom, and fill in the pore spaces where fish lay eggs. Silt and sediment interfere with recreational activities and aesthetic enjoyment of waterbodies by reducing water clarity and filling in waterbodies. Nutrients and toxic chemicals may attach to sediment particles and ride the particles into surface waters where the pollutants may settle with the sediment or detach and become soluble in the water column.

Rain washes silt and other soil particles off of plowed fields, construction sites, logging sites, urban areas, and strip-mined lands into waterbodies. . . .

Five Leading Causes of Water Quality Impairment			
Rank	Rivers and Streams	Lakes	Bays and Estuaries
1	Pathogens	Mercury	Oxygen depleting-substances
2	Sediment	PCBs	PCBs
3	Nutrients	Nutrients	Pathogens
4	Oxygen-depleting substances	Oxygen-depleting substances	Mercury
5	Habitat alteration	Metals (other than mercury)	Noxious aquatic plants

BACTERIA AND PATHOGENS . . . Some waterborne bacteria, viruses, and protozoa cause human illnesses that range from typhoid and dysentery to minor respiratory and skin diseases. These organisms may enter waters through a number of routes, including inadequately treated sewage, stormwater drains, septic systems, and sewage dumped overboard from recreational boats. Because it is impossible to test waters for every possible disease-causing organism, States and other jurisdictions usually measure indicator bacteria that are found in great numbers in the stomachs and intestines of warm-blooded animals and people. The presence of indicator bacteria suggests that the waterbody may be contaminated with untreated sewage and that other, more dangerous organisms may be present. . . .[6]

---

6. The most common bacterial indicator is the *E-coli* bacteria. An overabundance of these organisms in a waterbody can trigger beach closings and shutdowns of shellfish beds to harvesting. [EDS.]

TOXIC ORGANIC CHEMICALS AND METALS . . . Toxic organic chemicals are synthetic compounds that contain carbon, such as polychlorinated biphenyls (PCBs), dioxins, and the pesticide DDT. These synthesized compounds often persist and accumulate in the environment because they do not readily break down in natural ecosystems. Many of these compounds cause cancer in people and birth defects in other predators near the top of the food chain, such as birds and fish.

Metals occur naturally in the environment, but human activities (such as industrial processes and mining) have altered the distribution of metals in the environment. In most reported cases of metals contamination, high concentrations of metals appear in fish tissues rather than the water column because the metals accumulate in greater concentrations in predators near the top of the food chain.[7]

ACIDITY/ALKALINITY pH . . . Acidity, the concentration of hydrogen ions, drives many chemical reactions in living organisms. The standard measure of acidity is pH, and a pH value of 7 represents a neutral condition. A low pH value (less than 5) indicates acidic conditions; a high pH (greater than 9) indicates alkaline conditions. Many biological processes, such as reproduction, cannot function in acidic or alkaline waters. Acidic conditions also aggravate toxic contamination problems because sediments release toxicants in acidic waters. Common sources of acidity include mine drainage, runoff from mine tailings, and atmospheric deposition.

HABITAT MODIFICATION/HYDROLOGIC MODIFICATION . . . Habitat modifications include activities in the landscape, on shore, and in waterbodies that alter the physical structure of aquatic ecosystems and have adverse impacts on aquatic life. Examples of habitat modifications include: 1) removal of streamside vegetation that stabilizes the shoreline and provides shade, which moderates instream temperatures; 2) excavation of cobbles from a stream bed that provide nesting habitat for fish; 3) stream burial or destruction; and 4) excessive suburban sprawl that alters the natural drainage patterns by increasing the intensity, magnitude, and energy of runoff waters. Hydrologic modifications alter the flow of water. Examples include channelization, dewatering, damming, and dredging.

OTHER POLLUTANTS . . . These include salts and oil and grease. Fresh waters may become unfit for aquatic life and some human uses when they become contaminated by salts. Sources of salinity include irrigation runoff, brine used in oil extraction, road deicing operations, and the intrusion of sea water into ground and surface water in coastal areas. Crude oil and processed petroleum products may be spilled during extraction, processing, or transport or leaked from underground storage tanks.[8]

                        COMMENTARY & QUESTIONS

1. **Monitoring national water quality.** In addition to the water quality inventory reports, EPA now maintains a database of state-supplied water-quality information in its Assessment TMDL Tracking and Implementation System (ATTAINS). The database incorporates the

---

7. Excessive concentrations of toxic pollutants frequently result in fish consumption advisory warnings in affected waterbodies. [EDS.]

8. Most recently, pharmaceuticals introduced as part of human and livestock waste streams have become a pollutant of concern. [EDS.]

A. An Overview of the Clean Water Act

states' biennial water-quality reports—required by CWA §305(b)—and the biennial list of impaired waters—required by CWA §303(d). The ATTAINS database allows the user to electronically access state data on individual water bodies, as well as EPA's summary of data by EPA region and for the nation as a whole. To view the database, go to http://ofmpub.epa.gov/waters10/attains_index.home.

2. Impairment percentages and sources of impairment. According to the most recent ATTAINS data, 55% of the nation's assessed rivers and streams are impaired (and less than one-third of the nation's rivers and streams have been assessed). The top three causes of impairment are pathogens, sediments, and nutrient pollution, and these pollutants are mainly the result of agricultural production. Of the assessed lakes, ponds, and reservoirs, 69% are impaired, mainly due to mercury, PCBs, and nutrient pollution. The top three probable sources of the impairment are atmospheric deposition, unknown sources, and agriculture. You can view the rest of the current national summary of water quality at the above web address, but one more figure is worth noting here. ATTAINS has collected data from 88% of the open water of the Great Lakes and 99.9% of the assessed square miles of the Great Lakes, the nation's greatest fresh water resource, is impaired.

3. A regulatory paradox. Since most point source industrial and municipal pollution has been regulated since 1972, today agriculture is a major source of water pollution in most rivers and lakes and a significant source of pollution in estuaries. Many agricultural operations are classified as nonpoint sources of pollution, however, and are thus outside the regulatory scope of the CWA. One of the most contentious issues raised during the debates on reauthorization of the CWA has been whether agriculture should finally be subject to regulation.

4. We've come a long way, but. . . . Although significant progress has been made in cleaning up America's waterways, the CWA's statutory goals have not been completely met or its policies thoroughly implemented. The CWA declares:

> The objective of this chapter is to restore and maintain the chemical, physical, and biological integrity of the Nation's waters. In order to achieve this objective it is hereby declared that, consistent with the provisions of this chapter—
>
> (1) it is the national goal that the discharge of pollutants into the navigable waters be eliminated by 1985;
> (2) it is the national goal that wherever attainable, an interim goal of water quality which provides for the protection and propagation of fish, shellfish, and wildlife and provides for recreation in and on the water be achieved by July 1, 1983;
> (3) it is the national policy that the discharge of toxic pollutants in toxic amounts be prohibited. . . .
> (7) it is the national policy that programs for the control of nonpoint sources of pollution be developed and implemented in an expeditious manner. . . . 33 U.S.C. §1251.

By "integrity of the Nation's waters" Congress meant their ecological stability, not the revival of a dehumanized state of primeval purity. The Zero-Discharge Goal of subsection (1) is not an enforceable requirement of the CWA but a rebuttable presumption that all discharges are environmentally deleterious and a declaration that pollution prevention is the most desirable form of pollution control. The CWA's enforceable requirements are derived from the "interim goal" of subsection (2).

Despite the manifest and manifold successes of the CWA, over half of our nation's waterbodies do not meet the Act's goals. Pollution in some of these waterbodies is effectively incorrigible, due to previous human perturbations and background pollutant levels. But the vast majority of these impaired waters conceivably could be restored to fishability-swimmability and ecological stability. Why are they still dirty?

Unfortunately, the CWA has not been implemented so as to adequately control certain point source discharges from industries and municipal sewerage systems as well as discharges that affect ocean water quality.[9] In addition, the CWA's provisions do not cover: (1) nonpoint sources of pollution, such as most agricultural activities, postconstruction stormwater runoff from suburban residential areas, urban stormwater runoff that is not channeled through pipes or drains, and deposition of air pollutants such as mercury and nutrients; (2) point or nonpoint sources of groundwater pollution; (3) hydrologic modifications that disrupt flows, such as dams and flood control devices; (4) water diversions for domestic, industrial, agricultural, and recreational purposes, which frequently result in desiccated waterbodies; (5) destruction of riparian zones through unwise construction, resource extraction, agricultural, silvicultural, and grazing practices; (6) resuspension, due to storms or human disturbances, of pollutants emanating from contaminated sediments; (7) introduction of exotic species of flora and fauna; (8) excessive concentrations of septic systems, which result in pollution of surface and groundwaters; and (9) the expansion of impervious surfaces, which causes not only pollution problems from runoff of sediment and toxic pollutants but also flooding and decreased groundwater recharge. Moreover, the wetlands protection provisions of the CWA, which are discussed in Chapter 9, have proven only moderately successful.

5. Navigable waters for CWA jurisdiction—*Rapanos v. United States.* In the CWA, "discharge of a pollutant" means "any addition of any pollutant to navigable waters from any point source." §502(12). "Navigable waters" is generally defined as "waters of the United States." §502(7). Many observers expected that the U.S. Supreme Court would definitively address the scope of the CWA, in particular the jurisdiction of the U.S. Army Corps of Engineers over wetlands, in *Rapanos v. United States*, 547 U.S. 715 (2006). Instead, the Court produced a fractured ruling that raised at least as much uncertainty as it resolved.

The question before the Court was whether the term "navigable waters" in the CWA extends to wetlands that do not contain and are not adjacent to waters that are navigable in fact. In two separate cases later consolidated for review by the Supreme Court, the Sixth Circuit Court of Appeals had held that the Corps of Engineers had jurisdiction pursuant to the CWA over wetlands in Michigan that were hydrologically connected to either navigable waters or tributaries of navigable waters. While five members of the Court voted to vacate the judgments of the Sixth Circuit, the Court failed to produce a majority opinion on the scope of the CWA.

Justice Scalia, writing for a four-Justice plurality, took a narrow view of the definition of "navigable waters" as "waters of the United States." Justice Scalia relied on a partial definition of "waters" from Webster's New International Dictionary to include "only relatively permanent, standing or flowing bodies of water." The plurality opinion gave no deference to the Corps of Engineers' regulations, and instead followed the reasoning of the majority in *Solid Waste Agency of Northern Cook County v. U.S. Army Corps of Engineers*, 531 U.S. 159 (2001):

> [T]he Corps' interpretation stretches the outer limits of Congress's commerce power and raises difficult questions about the ultimate scope of that power. Even if the term "the waters of the United States" were ambiguous as applied to channels that sometimes host ephemeral flows of water (which it is not), we would expect a clearer statement from Congress to authorize an agency theory of jurisdiction that presses the envelope of constitutional validity. 547 U.S. at 738.

---

9. See the discussions of nonpriority pollutants and combined sewer overflows below. With regard to ocean discharges, see Craig & Miller, Ocean Discharge Criteria and Marine Protection Areas: Ocean Water Quality Protection Under the Clean Water Act, 29 B.C. Envtl. Aff. L. Rev. 1 (2001); Pew Oceans Comm'n, America's Living Oceans: Charting a Course for Sea Change (2003), http://www.pewoceans.org.

A. An Overview of the Clean Water Act

Based on this reasoning, the plurality would require two findings to establish that wetlands are covered by the CWA:

> First, that the adjacent channel contains a "wate[r] of the United States," (i.e., a relatively permanent body of water connected to traditional interstate navigable waters); and second, that the wetland has a continuous surface connection with that water, making it difficult to determine where the "water" ends and the "wetland" begins. 547 U.S. at 742.

Justice Scalia's narrow view of CWA jurisdiction failed to attract the support of a majority of Justices. Instead, the fifth vote to vacate the Sixth Circuit judgments was provided by Justice Kennedy in a concurrence based on a very different interpretation of the CWA. Justice Kennedy was more deferential towards the Corps' regulations and offered a more broad and fact-specific test for CWA jurisdiction over wetlands:

> [T]he Corps' jurisdiction over wetlands depends upon the existence of a significant nexus between the wetlands in question and navigable waters in the traditional sense. The required nexus must be assessed in terms of the statute's goals and purposes. . . . With respect to wetlands, the rationale for Clean Water Act regulation is, as the Corps has recognized, that wetlands can perform critical functions related to the integrity of other waters—functions such as pollutant trapping, flood control, and runoff storage. 33 C.F.R. §320.4(b)(2). Accordingly, wetlands possess the requisite nexus, and thus come within the statutory phrase "navigable waters," if the wetlands, either alone or in combination with similarly situated lands in the region, significantly affect the chemical, physical, and biological integrity of other covered waters more readily understood as "navigable." When, in contrast, wetlands' effects on water quality are speculative or insubstantial, they fall outside the zone fairly encompassed by the statutory term "navigable waters." 547 U.S. at 779-780.

Because the Sixth Circuit failed to make this specific inquiry regarding "significant nexus," Justice Kennedy concurred that vacating the judgments and remanding the matter was necessary. However, in substance, Justice Kennedy's concurrence was aligned more closely with the dissent, which would have affirmed the Sixth Circuit's decisions. Justice Stevens, writing for a four-Justice dissent, viewed the case as a straightforward application of agency deference under *Chevron*:

> The Army Corps has determined that wetlands adjacent to tributaries of traditionally navigable waters preserve the quality of our Nation's waters by, among other things, providing habitat for aquatic animals, keeping excessive sediment and toxic pollutants out of adjacent waters, and reducing downstream flooding by absorbing water at times of high flow. The Corps' resulting decision to treat these wetlands as encompassed within the term "waters of the United States" is a quintessential example of the Executive's reasonable interpretation of a statutory provision. 547 U.S. at 788.

So, what is the holding of the case? As Chief Justice Roberts noted in a separate concurrence to the plurality's opinion, "[i]t is unfortunate that no opinion commands a majority of the Court on precisely how to read Congress' limits on the reach of the CWA. Lower courts and regulated entities will now have to feel their way on a case-by-case basis."

Lower courts must look for implicit agreement and common denominators between the various opinions.[10] Justice Kennedy's concurrence has little in common with Justice Scalia's plurality opinion (other than the ultimate decision to vacate the lower court rulings), but the inquiry does not end there. Instead, lower courts must look to the agreement

---

10. See M. Thurmon, Note, When the Court Divides: Reconsidering the Precedential Value of Supreme Court Plurality Decisions, 42 Duke L.J. 419, 429 (1992).

between Justice Kennedy's concurrence and Justice Stevens' dissent. The four dissenting Justices would have affirmed an application of CWA jurisdiction to any water that meets Justice Kennedy's "significant nexus" test. Thus, lower courts have used Justice Kennedy's fact-specific test to determine CWA jurisdiction disputes.[11]

6. The Clean Water Rule: Definition of "Waters of the United States." To clarify the definition of "waters of the United States" consistently with *Rapanos*, the EPA and Army Corps issued a joint rule in 2015 known as the Clean Water Rule: Definition of "Waters of the United States" (33 C.F.R. §328.3 and 40 C.F.R. §230.3; see also 80 Fed. Reg. §37054). The Clean Water Rule amends the previous definitional rules regarding "waters of the United States" through the imposition of additional qualifiers for certain types of water bodies. Under this new definition, there are four main avenues through which a water may fall under federal jurisdiction: (1) waters that impact interstate commerce, cross state boundaries, and the territorial seas (the "navigable waters"); (2) tributaries of "navigable" waters; (3) water bodies that are adjacent to the "navigable" waters; and (4) waters with a "significant nexus" to any "navigable" water body, or tributary of such. The "significant nexus" standard is one of the most significant and controversial parts of the rule.

The Clean Water Rule defines "significant nexus" as: ". . . a water, including wetlands, either alone or in combination with other similarly situated waters in the region, [that] significantly affects the chemical, physical, or biological integrity of a ["navigable" water (excluding impoundments)]." "Similarly situated waters" are those which "function alike and are sufficiently close to function together in affecting downstream waters." In order to show the water body "significantly affects" a navigable water (e.g., a water used for interstate commerce, and those waters that cross state or national borders), the effect "must be more than speculative or insubstantial." The Agency will focus on the following aquatic functions of the water in question, as they relate to the affected navigable body of water, when determining whether or not it is significantly affected:

(1) sediment trapping;
(2) nutrient recycling;
(3) pollutant trapping, transformation, filtering, and transport;
(4) retention and attenuation of flood waters;
(5) runoff storage;
(6) contribution of flow;
(7) export of organic matter;
(8) export of food resources; and
(9) provision of life cycle dependent on aquatic habitat . . . for species located in a [navigable water].

A significant nexus is present when any one of the individual aquatic functions, or any combination of those functions, performed by the water (alone or combined with similarly situated waters), "contributes significantly to the chemical, physical, or biological integrity of the nearest [navigable] water." 33 C.F.R. §328.3(c)(5).

If a significant nexus is found, the water body must meet the Clean Water Rule's additional geographic requirements to be considered a "water of the United States." It must be located within one of the following geographic boundaries: (1) waters located within the 100-year floodplain of a "navigable water" (excluding impoundments); or (2) waters

---

11. See, e.g., *N. Cal. River Watch v. City of Healdsburg*, 496 F.3d 993, 995 (9th Cir. 2007); *U.S. v. Robinson*, 505 F.3d 1208, 1222 (11th Cir. 2007).

A. An Overview of the Clean Water Act

located within 4000 feet of the "high tide line" or "ordinary high water mark" of a "navigable" water or tributary (including impoundments). 33 C.F.R. §328.3(a)(8).

In addition to creating more detailed requirements for designating a body of water a "water of the United States" based on "significant nexus," the Clean Water Rule also enumerates specific waters that are *not* "waters of the United States," "even where they otherwise meet the terms of [the rule]." 33 C.F.R. §328.3(b). These exclusions are similarly significant and controversial. The Rule excludes water treatment systems, prior converted cropland (this exclusion was also present in the previous rule), certain ditches with specific characteristics, groundwater, stormwater, and a number of wastewater recycling structures. 33 C.F.R. §328.3(b).

As expected, the Clean Water Rule has been the subject of much controversy and litigation. Numerous states have challenged the Clean Water Rule in court, opposing the federal government's expansion of jurisdiction over intrastate waters. Notably, other states have supported the Rule, as it helps bring clarity to an area of law with tremendous uncertainty. At press time, petitions challenging the Rule have been filed around the country, with some (but not all) consolidated before the Sixth Circuit. The petitions challenge the substance of the Rule and its consistency with the Supreme Court's *Rapanos* opinion. Some petitions also challenge the adequacy of notice for the final Rule, as the geographical limitation was not part of the proposed rule, and thus the public could not have anticipated the agencies' final decision as a "logical outgrowth" of its proposal. Rather than settling this area of law, the Clean Water Rule seems to have only created a new chapter in the ongoing uncertainty.

7. The CWA and groundwater. Another major unresolved question with regard to the CWA is whether its provisions apply to point source discharges to groundwater. EPA has waffled on this issue, and the courts have split as to whether "tributary groundwater" (groundwater that is hydrologically connected to surface water) is covered by the Act. Contrast *Exxon v. Train*, 554 F.2d 1310 (5th Cir. 1977) (no groundwater is covered by the CWA), with *U.S. Steel v. Train*, 556 F.2d 822 (7th Cir. 1977) (groundwater is covered if it is hydrologically connected to surface water). Relying on CWA §510's express authority for states to adopt stricter standards and limitations than those imposed by EPA, a number of states, for example California and New Jersey, require discharge permits for point source dischargers to groundwater. Cal. Water Code §10350(3); N.J. Stat. Ann. §58:10A-3.

8. Point and nonpoint sources. A "point source" is "any discernible, confined and discrete conveyance, including but not limited to any pipe, ditch, channel, tunnel, conduit, well, discrete fissure, container, rolling stock, concentrated animal feeding operation, or vessel or other floating craft from which pollutants are or may be discharged. This term does not include agricultural stormwater discharges and return flows from irrigated agriculture." §502(14). A "nonpoint source" is any man-made source, discharging to surface waters, that is not a point source. In general, a nonpoint source is a diffuse, intermittent source of pollutants that does not discharge at a single location but whose pollutants are carried over or through the soil by way of stormflow processes. Nonpoint source pollution generally results from land runoff, atmospheric deposition, drainage, or seepage of contaminants. Major sources of nonpoint pollution include agricultural and silvicultural runoff and runoff from urban areas. In contrast to the high-level technological controls that are most often used to prevent point source pollution, nonpoint sources are best controlled by low-technology Best Management Practices (BMPs) — methods, measures, or practices consisting of structural or nonstructural controls and operation-and-maintenance procedures. BMPs generally involve comparatively inexpensive land use controls and land management practices. They are selected based on site-specific conditions that reflect natural background as well as political, social, economic, and technical feasibility. For example, a set of BMPs to reduce runoff of nutrients, herbicides, and pesticides from a farm into a river might include diminished and staggered applications of these substances, contour plowing, and maintenance of vegetated stream buffers. BMPs are technology-based performance standards, rather than equipment and design specification standards, because nonpoint source control programs offer the discharger a choice from among a menu of BMPs, such as those available to the farmer in the preceding example.

The CWA regulates only point source pollution. In 1972, Congress excluded nonpoint sources from the regulatory ambit of the CWA because (1) point sources were perceived as the primary causes of water pollution, and little was then known about the deleterious impacts of nonpoint source runoff; (2) the BMPs to control nonpoint source pollution call for land use and land management restrictions that generally are implemented by local governments; and (3) nonpoint source pollution being diffuse and sporadic, it is more difficult to ascertain the dischargers and environmental effects of nonpoint source pollution than it is with regard to point sources.

The term *point source* is liberally construed and has been held to include a salmon farm, earth-moving equipment in a wetland, and ponded mine drainage that erodes a channel to a river. Dam releases, which often cause adverse water quality impacts downstream, are treated as nonpoint rather than point sources. In a criminal case involving a co-owner of a blood-testing laboratory who threw vials containing blood contaminated with hepatitis-B virus into the Hudson River, the Second Circuit Court of Appeals held that an individual human being is not a point source within the meaning of the CWA. *United States v. Plaza Health Labs*, 3 F.3d 643 (2d Cir. 1993).

The Second Circuit has also decided a case that may facilitate the regulation of some agricultural pollution under the CWA. *Concerned Area Residents for the Environment (CARE) v. Southview Farms*, 34 F.3d 114 (2d Cir. 1994), was a citizen suit contesting the unpermitted liquid manure spreading operation of a large dairy farm in western New York State. Southview Farms owned 1100 acres and a herd of over 2000 cows. Unlike on older dairy farms, the cows were not pastured but remained in their barns, except during milking. The massive quantities of manure generated by these cows were pumped first into a separator, which drained off the liquid and compressed the solids. The solids were transported to a landfill, while the liquid residue was piped to a four-acre manure storage lagoon and thence to smaller lagoons. The liquid stored in these lagoons was spread over Southview's fields by (1) a center pivot irrigation system, (2) hose systems, and (3) manure spreaders pulled by tractors. Some of the runoff from the manure spreading operations drained into a natural swale, then into a man-made tile drain leading under a stone wall, and finally into a natural ditch that drained into a river. Reversing the district court, which had found the operation to be a nonpoint source, the circuit court held that the manure runoff was a point source because (1) the swale/tile drain/ditch drainage system was a point source, (2) the manure spreading vehicles were point sources, and (3) the defendant was operating a concentrated animal feeding operation (CAFO), which is statutorily defined as a point source. In response to defendant's argument that its manure runoff fell within the CWA's "agricultural stormwater discharge" exemption, the court stated:

> . . . there can be no escape from liability for agricultural pollution simply because it occurs on rainy days. . . . We think the real issue is not whether the discharges occurred during rainfall or were mixed with rain water run-off, but rather whether the discharges were the result of precipitation. Of course, all discharges eventually mix with precipitation run-off in ditches or steams or navigable waters so the fact that the discharge might have been mixed with run-off cannot be determinative. . . . We think the jury could properly find that the run-off was primarily caused by over-saturation of the fields rather than the rain and that sufficient quantities of manure were present so that run-off could not be classified as "stormwater." 34 F.3d at 120.

A. An Overview of the Clean Water Act

The court's finding that the drainage system was a point source is potentially the most important for future cases. Pure sheet-flow runoff is comparatively rare. Most runoff over unpaved surfaces ultimately finds its way to, or creates, gullies or swales that discharge into surface waterbodies. If these are indeed point sources, then agricultural activities that do not comply with BMPs (e.g., for manure spreading or pesticide applications) may be subject to regulation under the CWA because they are not included in the "agricultural stormwater discharge" exemption. EPA and state CAFO permit programs are beginning to substantially reduce water pollution from agricultural operations (see below). The Eleventh Circuit Court of Appeals distinguished *Southview Farms* in *Fishermen Against the Destruction of the Env't, Inc. v. Closter Farms, Inc.*, 300 F.3d 1294 (11th Cir. 2002), where the court decided that the farm's operations fell within both the "agricultural stormwater discharge" and "return flow from irrigation agriculture" exceptions from CWA permitting.

Does pesticide spraying constitute a point source discharge? Originally, EPA was of the view that pesticide spraying was a point source discharge. In fact, the agency required pesticide labels to bear a notice stating that the pesticide could not be "discharge[d] into lakes, streams, ponds, or public waters unless in accordance with [a Clean Water Act] permit." Then in 2007, EPA changed course and issued a new rule that exempted pesticides, applied in accordance with the Federal Insecticide, Fungicide, and Rodenticide Act, from the CWA's permitting requirement. But in *National Cotton Council v. EPA*, 553 F.3d 927 (6th Cir. 2009), the Sixth Circuit vacated the 2007 rule. The court concluded that the agency interpretation was not entitled to *Chevron* deference because "[t]he Clean Water Act is not ambiguous" and "the EPA's Final Rule is not a reasonable interpretation of the Act." The effect of the ruling is substantial in that anyone who sprays a pesticide in or near waters of the United States will need a CWA permit. According to the EPA, this ruling will affect hundreds of thousands of applicators, including farmers, foresters, and the U.S. Coast Guard. But the court ultimately tempered the effects of its decision by staying its ruling until April 9, 2011, in response to a motion filed by EPA. The EPA argued that it needed the time to work with states and stakeholders to develop permits for pesticide applications. The agency thereafter issued the "Pesticide General Permit for Discharges from the Application of Pesticides," available at http://www3.epa.gov/npdes/pubs/final_pgp.pdf. In effect, this approach treats pesticide spraying as a point source that requires an NPDES permit, but establishes a generic process under which permits can be issued if certain conditions are met.

It appears to be settled that water withdrawals are not point source discharges, even if they might potentially increase the concentration of pollutants in waterbodies. See, e.g., *North Carolina v. Federal Energy Reg. Comm'n*, 112 F.3d 1175 (D.C. Cir. 1997).

9. "Addition" of a pollutant. EPA regulations dictate that a discharger is not legally responsible for pollutants that are present in a discharge only by reason of their presence in the discharger's intake water if the intake water is drawn from the same body of water as the receiving water and if the pollutants are not removed by the discharger as part of its normal operations. 40 C.F.R. §122.45(h) (known as the "net/gross credit"). Dam releases are not only considered nonpoint sources of pollution, but their discharges are also not additions of pollutants, even if they adversely affect the temperature or oxygen content of the receiving waters.[12] Aquaculture operations ordinarily are considered to add pollutants such as pesticides, fish feed, fish excrement, and stray fish to receiving waters; but in *Association to*

---

12. See *National Wildlife Fed'n v. Gorsuch*, 693 F.2d 156 (D.C. Cir. 1982); but also see *Committee to Save the Mokelumne River v. East Bay Mun. Util. Dist.*, 13 F.3d 305 (9th Cir. 1993) (discharges from dam used to collect acid mine drainage from abandoned mine require CWA permits).

Protect Hammersley, Eld & Totten Inlets v. Taylor Res., Inc., 299 F.3d 1007 (9th Cir. 2002), excrement from mussels suspended from rafts was not considered addition of a pollutant where the mussels had not been artificially fed or treated with pesticides.

In a related vein, EPA issued its final water-transfer rule in 2008, thereby making water transfers and conveyances exempt from regulation under the CWA as a point source of pollution into the receiving water. The rule defines a water transfer as an activity that conveys or connects waters of the United States without subjecting the transferred water to intervening industrial, municipal, or commercial use. Under this rule, if a water district transferred water from a highly polluted waterbody by pipeline to a relative clean and pristine waterbody, the water transfer would not need a CWA permit for discharging pollution into the clean waterbody. This concept is based on the EPA's "unitary waters" theory, which views the waters of the United States as indistinct. This controversial theory had been the subject of judicial skepticism and was rejected outright by the Second Circuit in *Catskills Mountain Chapter of Trout Unlimited v. City of New York*, 451 F.3d 77 (2d Cir. 2006). There the court held that transferring turbid water from one body of water to another via tunnel required a NPDES permit, as turbidity is a pollutant under the CWA. Undaunted by the judicial rebuke, EPA proceeded to formalize the policy into the 2008 water-transfer rule. This rule, in turn, attracted its own legal challenge, which the Eleventh Circuit ruled on in *Friends of the Everglades v. South Florida Water Mgmt. Dist.*, 570 F.3d 1210 (11th Cir. 2009). Because the EPA had subsequently adopted the unitary waters interpretation into a rule, the court applied *Chevron* deference and concluded that there were two reasonable interpretations of §1361(12) of the CWA: "[o]ne is that it means 'any addition . . . to[any] navigable waters;' the other is that it means 'any addition . . . to navigable waters [as a whole].'" 570 F.3d at 1227. Since the EPA's construction was consistent with the second interpretation, the court deferred. The court recognized that the EPA's reading was against the statutory goals of the Act, but stated that it is not unusual for legislation to leave permitting gaps because laws are the products of compromise. Why should a court defer to agency interpretation where it is clearly contrary to statutory goals? Does it make sense to treat all waters of the United States as a whole? In thinking about these questions, remember that the CWA focuses on the water quality of individual waters and that different water bodies have different designated uses.

10. Types of point source dischargers. Point source dischargers may be either municipal sewage treatment plants (known as Publicly Owned Treatment Works, or POTWs) or industrial or stormwater dischargers. Industrial point source dischargers are either direct dischargers, which discharge directly into waterbodies, or indirect dischargers, which discharge into sewers that lead to POTWs, which then discharge into waterbodies. As is discussed below, the technology-based effluent limitations that an industrial discharger is required to meet are determined by (1) the industrial category in which the discharger is placed, (2) the types of pollutants discharged by its operations, and (3) whether it is an existing or new source of water pollution. Stormwater point source discharges can originate from agricultural, industrial, or municipal sources.

11. The federal-state partnership. Forty-five states have been delegated primacy to administer their own counterparts of the NPDES permit program. Alaska, where the *Rybachek* placer mine was located (see below), is one of the few states that has not sought CWA primacy. EPA is authorized by CWA §518 to treat Native American tribes as states for purposes of administering the CWA, and a number of tribes have achieved primacy. In the nonprimacy states, EPA regional offices are administering the program. Nationwide, there are approximately 500,000 water discharge permittees. Do you think that the CWA's safeguards, as described in the *EPA v. California* opinion, are adequate to prevent a state from treating dischargers leniently in order to attract and retain industry? In particular, given EPA's lack of resources, can EPA effectively review draft state permits? Would an EPA threat to withdraw state program authorization be credible? Can EPA meaningfully exercise its backup enforcement authority under §309 of the CWA? Can state pollution control agencies be significantly influenced by EPA's diminishing ability to award program grants, conduct research, and perform technical assistance activities? See the critique of the purported safeguards of cooperative federalism in Chapter 5. An important aspect of CWA efficacy has been the use of citizen suits to spur state and federal enforcement, which is discussed more fully in Chapter 18.

B. THE ORIGIN AND EVOLUTION OF TBELs

U.S. Environmental Protection Agency v. California
426 U.S. 200 (1976)

[In this opinion explaining the mechanics of the CWA, the Court held that federal facilities were not required to obtain NPDES permits from states with approved programs, a decision later overridden by Congress in the CWA Amendments of 1977.]

WHITE, J. Before it was amended in 1972, the Federal Water Pollution Control Act employed ambient water quality standards specifying the acceptable levels of pollution in a State's interstate navigable waters as the primary mechanism in its program for the control of water pollution. This program based on water quality standards, which were to serve both to guide performance by polluters and to trigger legal action to abate pollution, proved ineffective. The problems stemmed from the character of the standards themselves, which focused on the tolerable effects rather than the preventable causes of water pollution, from the awkwardly shared federal and state responsibility for promulgating such standards, and from the cumbrous enforcement procedures. These combined to make it very difficult to develop and enforce standards to govern the conduct of individual polluters.

Some States developed water quality standards and plans to implement and enforce them, and some relied on discharge permit systems for enforcement. Others did not, and to strengthen the abatement system federal officials revived the Refuse Act of 1899, which prohibits the discharge of any matter into the Nation's navigable waters except with a federal permit. Although this direct approach to water pollution abatement proved helpful, it also was deficient in several respects: the goal of the discharge permit conditions was to achieve water quality standards rather than to require individual polluters to minimize effluent discharge, the permit program was applied only to industrial polluters, some dischargers were required to obtain both federal and state permits, and federal permit authority was shared by two federal agencies.

In 1972, prompted by the conclusion of the Senate Committee on Public Works that "the Federal water pollution control program . . . has been inadequate in every vital aspect," Congress enacted the Amendments, declaring "the national goal that the discharge of pollutants into the navigable waters be eliminated by 1985." For present purposes the Amendments introduced two major changes in the methods to set and enforce standards to abate and control water pollution. First, the Amendments are aimed at achieving maximum "effluent limitations on point sources," as well as achieving acceptable water quality standards. A point source is "any discernible, confined and discrete conveyance . . . from which pollutants are or may be discharged." An "effluent limitation" in turn is "any restriction established by a State or the Administrator [of EPA] on quantities, rates, and concentrations of chemical, physical, biological or other constituents which are discharged from point sources . . . including schedules of compliance." Such direct restrictions on discharges facilitate enforcement by making it unnecessary to work backward from an overpolluted body of water to determine which point sources are responsible and which must be abated. In addition, a discharger's performance is now measured against strict technology-based effluent limitations —specified levels of treatment — to which it must conform, rather than against limitations derived from water quality standards to which it and other polluters must collectively conform. Water quality standards are retained as a supplementary basis for effluent limitations, however, so that numerous point sources, despite individual compliance with [technology-based] effluent limitations, may be further regulated to prevent water quality from falling below acceptable levels.

Second, the Amendments establish the NPDES as a means of achieving and enforcing the effluent limitations. Under NPDES, it is unlawful for any person to discharge a pollutant without obtaining a permit and complying with its terms. A NPDES permit serves to transform generally applicable effluent limitations and other standards — including those based on water quality — into the obligations (including a timetable for compliance) of the individual discharger, and the Amendments provide for direct administrative and judicial enforcement of permits. With few exceptions, for enforcement purposes a discharger in compliance with the terms and conditions of an NPDES permit is deemed to be in compliance with those sections of the Amendments on which the permit conditions are based. In short, the permit defines, and facilitates compliance with and enforcement of, a preponderance of a discharger's obligations under the Amendments.

NPDES permits are secured, in the first instance, from EPA. . . . Consonant with its policy "to recognize, preserve, and protect the primary responsibilities and rights of the States to prevent, reduce, and eliminate pollution," Congress also provided that a State may issue NPDES permits "for discharges into navigable waters within its jurisdiction," but only upon EPA approval of the State's proposal to administer its own program. EPA may require modification or revision of a submitted program but when a plan is in compliance with EPA's guidelines . . . EPA shall approve the program and "suspend the issuance of permits . . . as to those navigable waters subject to such program."

The EPA retains authority to review operation of a State's permit program. Unless the EPA waives review for particular classes of point sources or for a particular permit application, a State is to forward a copy of each permit application to EPA for review, and no permit may issue if EPA objects that issuance of the permit would be "outside the guidelines and requirements" of the amendments. In addition to this review authority, after notice and opportunity to take action, EPA may withdraw approval of a state permit program which is not being administered in compliance with the [Act as amended]. . . .

COMMENTARY & QUESTIONS

1. Ineffectuality of prior law. Before 1972, under the old federal water statute, in more than two decades only one water pollution violation was successfully prosecuted, and in that case more than four years elapsed between the initial enforcement conference and the final consent decree. In those benighted days, desired uses were set by individual states, which classified waterways in categories ranging from Class A (swimming) to Class D (agricultural and industrial use). If a state was satisfied that a particular river need only be aesthetically

B. The Origin and Evolution of Tbels

tolerable and fit for commercial navigation, the law did not afford relief unless the river stank or corroded hulls of ships. The Cuyahoga River was not considered legally objectionable until it caught fire because the state-designated use of that river was waste disposal. See generally Congressional Research Service, Library of Congress, A Legislative History of the Federal Water Pollution Control Act Amendments of 1972 (1973), and Andreen, The Evolution of Water Pollution Control in the United States: State, Local, and Federal Efforts, 1789-1972: Part I, 22 Stan. Envtl. L.J. 145 (2003). See also the *Utilex* case study in Chapter 7.

If the harm-based prior law had failed so miserably, why did Congress, in the 1972 CWA, adopt both technology-based and harm-based controls, superimposing water quality-based controls on a fundamental level of technology-based controls? The answer has to do with congressional politics. The Senate favored replacing the water quality-based approach with progressively stricter technology-based effluent limitations, leading to the ultimate cessation of all discharges. The House, however, believed that a water quality-based approach was still viable. The resulting compromise entails a dual approach, with a harm-based system applicable only where necessary. Several analysts believe that the CWA's many ambiguities can be traced to this original, unsuccessful compromise.

Why did Congress move to a primarily technology-based standard-setting methodology in 1972, when it had embraced an almost totally harm-based strategy in the CAA only two years earlier? The CAA was, in effect, a statute of the 1960s because it extended and strengthened the harm-based Air Quality Act of 1967, which, ironically, followed the ambient standard approach earlier established in the 1965 FWPCA. Between late 1970, when the CAA was being finalized, and the summer of 1971, when the Senate Air and Water Pollution Subcommittee released its technology-based clean water bill (drawn from the new source performance standard section of the 1970 CAA §111), the burgeoning environmental movement had inspired dissatisfaction with the harm-based approach and its philosophy that there exists a right to discharge up to the assimilative capacity of the environment.

2. Pros and cons of technology-based controls. Critics of the technology-based approach argue that it is: (1) inadequate to protect acutely impacted waterbodies, (2) economically inefficient because it frequently demands "redundant treatment" (i.e., greater treatment than necessary to maintain desired uses for waterbodies), and (3) insufficiently technology-stimulating because it does not encourage industry to develop innovative technology (and in fact may be an example of a "perverse incentive" prompting industries to stifle innovative cleaner technology capable of achieving even greater reductions in pollution). The first charge is rebutted, at least theoretically, by the bilevel structure of the CWA, with harm-based standards becoming applicable where technology-based ones do not achieve desired water quality. As for the second objection, defenders of the CWA respond that: (1) the harm-based system has not effectively controlled pollution, having instead only exacerbated the race-to-the-bottom because of variable standards from state-to-state (see Chapter 7); (2) BAT standards are significantly simpler and less expensive to administer than harm-based standards; (3) the economic costs of BAT have been exaggerated, and its public health benefits undervalued; and (4) normatively, producers should do the best they can to protect human lives and the ecosystems upon which humans depend.

3. Frozen technology? In fact, water quality-based effluent limitations themselves freeze current technology, at least until water quality standards (WQSs) have been violated. To some extent, the charge that BAT standards create perverse incentives by freezing current technology is based on a misunderstanding of the manner in which technology-based standards are implemented in the CWA. There are two types of BAT standards: (1) equipment and design specification standards, and (2) performance standards. The former specifies the precise type of technology that a regulated party must install, whereas the latter establishes a performance standard based on the technology utilized by the best performers in a particular industrial category, but allows the regulated party to meet that standard either by installing the base technology or in any other least-cost way, including using different technology or achieving pollution prevention. As the *Rybachek* opinion excerpted later in this chapter points out, the CWA relies on BAT-based performance standards, not on equipment and design specification standards. Equipment and design specification standards typically are imposed where technology has become standardized and pollutants are difficult to measure, as in drinking water treatment. Several of the CWA's detractors, however, have not recognized the fact that the CWA relies upon performance standards rather than on equipment and design specification standards.[13]

The CWA's technology-based approach, as originally conceived, can circumvent the perverse incentive to freeze current technology and encourage the development of innovative technology by entrepreneurial ventures both inside and outside the regulated industrial sector. Although technology-based effluent limitations are based on available technology, EPA must review promulgated effluent limitations every five years, with a view toward tightening them to reflect the existence of improved pollution control devices. CWA §301(d). Improved BAT should be reflected in stricter TBELs that are included in five-year permit renewals.[14] In other words, build a better pollutant trap and the regulated dischargers must either beat a path to your door or find some other way to meet the performance standard. Unfortunately, EPA has been so preoccupied with developing its initial technology-based standards that it only recently has begun its five-year reviews of technology-based effluent limitations, partially as a result of congressional prodding through §304(m) of the CWA, added by the Water Quality Act Amendments of 1987, setting deadlines for EPA promulgation of effluent guidelines. In addition, most of EPA's water pollution control resources are currently devoted to TMDL development (see below).

There is evidence that the CWA's strategy of progressively tightening technology-based standards so as ultimately to achieve either significant pollutant reductions or zero-discharge has been realized as to some discharge categories. EPA's final effluent limitation guideline regulations for the pesticide formulating, packaging, and repackaging industry allows dischargers to choose between zero-discharge limits or a pollution prevention alternative. In 1993, EPA proposed a set of "Cluster Rules" for the pulp and paper industry (combining effluent and emissions limitations for both water and air pollution control — counteracting the inefficiencies of the media-specific approach). The water pollution control element of this proposal was based on oxygen delignification, a process that substitutes oxygen for chlorine in the bleaching of paper, thus eliminating the discharge of dioxin, a highly toxic by-product of chlorine bleaching. Goaded by the high cost of complying with this proposed BAT standard, several paper companies began substituting chlorine dioxide for chlorine, which reduced dioxin discharges by approximately 96% at substantially lower cost than oxygen delignification. In 1996, EPA reproposed these regulations and

---

13. See, e.g., Hahn, Getting More Environmental Protection for Less Money: A Practitioner's Guide, 9 Oxford Rev. Econ. Pol'y 112, 116 (1993) ("the technology-based standard, which specifies a particular technology a firm must use to comply with the law, . . . is used frequently in both air and water regulation in the United States"); Derzko, Using Intellectual Property Law and Regulatory Processes to Foster the Innovation and Diffusion of Environmental Technologies, 20 Harv. Envtl. L. Rev. 3, 18-19 ("Technology standards require polluting firms to reduce pollution using a certain prescribed technology; . . . [the CAA and CWA] still operate using technology standards.").

14. Discharge permits have a maximum duration of five years, but, once a renewal application is filed, the original permit remains in effect until renewal. The discharge permit renewal process has traditionally been plagued by severe backlogs, and many dischargers are operating under expired permits.

requested comments on both process changes as potential BAT. Finally, in 1997, EPA promulgated BAT standards based on the chlorine dioxide bleaching process. The virtually zero-discharge option was forgone in favor of a slightly less effective alternative that will be less costly to industry. Moreover, the "Cluster Rules" also include a Voluntary Advanced Technology Incentives Program (VATIP) that provides additional time for meeting effluent limitations if a company submits a viable plan for developing and implementing innovative control technology.

Nevertheless, it is clear that, in general, EPA and state administration of technology-based standard-setting systems discourage technological innovation because: (1) in practice, permissible technologies are limited to available ones that meet the standards; (2) governmental permit writers are notoriously risk-averse; (3) multimedia pollution and pollution prevention are rarely considered during the permitting process; and (4) permitting agencies disregard statutory incentives for technological innovation (e.g., CWA §301(k)'s extended compliance schedules). Environmental Law Institute, Barriers to Environmental Technological Innovation (1998). One potential solution to this problem could be allowing sales and trading of pollution control credits earned through compliance beyond minimum standards, creating an incentive to innovate and "over-comply" that could be profitably traded to another regulated discharger on the same stream segment whose costs of compliance would otherwise be higher than the cost of the purchased credit (see Chapter 14).

C. IMPLEMENTING TBELs THROUGH THE NPDES PROCESS

Because environmental issues arise from competing demands on natural resources, environmental lawyers learn to work closely with scientists, engineers, natural resource managers, planners, policy analysts, and social scientists in formulating multidisciplinary, holistic environmental protection strategies for presentation to courts, legislatures, administrative agencies, private corporations, and the general public. The following case is unusual among CWA effluent limitation cases in that it involves a relatively simple technology and is thus intelligible to readers who lack a background in environmental science or chemical engineering, while showing some of the legal complexities involved with technology-based standards under the CWA.

Rybachek v. EPA
904 F.2d 1276 (9th Cir. 1990)

O'SCANNLAIN, J. . . . Placer mining is one of the four basic methods of mining metal ores; it involves the mining of alluvial or glacial deposits of loose gravel, sand, soil, clay, or mud called "placers." These placers often contain particles of gold and other heavy minerals. Placer miners excavate the gold-bearing material (paydirt) from the placer deposit after removing the surface vegetation and non-gold-bearing gravel (overburden). The gold is then separated from the other materials in the paydirt by a gravity-separation process known as "sluicing."

In the sluicing process, a miner places the ore in an on-site washing plant (usually a sluice box) which has small submerged dams (riffles) attached to its bottom. He causes water to be run over the paydirt in the sluice box; when the heavier materials (including gold) fall, they are caught by the riffles. The lighter sand, dirt, and clay particles are left suspended in the wastewater released from the sluice box.

Placer mining typically is conducted directly in streambeds or on adjacent property. The water usually enters the sluice box through gravity, but may sometimes also enter through the use of pumping equipment. At some point after the process described above, the water in the sluice box is discharged. The discharges from placer mining can have aesthetic and water-quality impacts on waters both in the immediate vicinity and downstream. Toxic metals, including arsenic, cadmium, lead, zinc, and copper, have been found in higher concentration in streams where mining occurs than in non-mining streams.

It is the treatment of the sluice-box discharge water before it re-enters a natural water course that is at the heart of this case.

STATUTORY FRAMEWORK . . . Congress enacted the Clean Water Act to "restore and maintain the chemical, physical, and biological integrity of the Nation's waters." Under the Act, the EPA must impose and enforce technology-based effluent limitations and standards through individual NPDES permits. These permits contain specific terms and conditions as well as numerical discharge limitations, which govern the activities of pollutant dischargers. Through the Clean Water Act, Congress has directed the EPA to incorporate into the permits increasingly stringent technology-based effluent limitations.

Congress specified a number of means for the EPA to impose and to enforce these limitations in NPDES permits. For instance, it requires the Agency to establish effluent limitations requiring dischargers to use the "best practicable control technology currently available" ("BPT") within an industry. These limits are to represent "the average of the best" treatment technology performance in an industrial category. See *EPA v. National Crushed Stone Ass'n*, 449 U.S. 64 (1980). The EPA is further required to promulgate limitations both for the discharge of toxic pollutants by mandating that an industry use the "best available technology economically achievable" ("BAT") and for discharge of conventional pollutants by requiring the use of the "best conventional pollution control technology" ("BCT"); the congressionally imposed deadline for promulgation of these limitations was March 31, 1989. . . .

In addition, new pollution sources in an industry must meet a separate set of standards, called new-source performance standards ("NSPS"). These standards limit the discharge of pollutants by new sources based on the "best available demonstrated control technology" [BADT]. Finally, the EPA is authorized to establish best management practices ("BMPs") "to control plant site runoff, spillage or leaks, sludge or waste disposal, and drainage from raw material storage" in order to diminish the amount of toxic pollutants flowing into the receiving waters.

RULEMAKING HISTORY . . . On November 20, 1985, proceeding under the Clean Water Act, the EPA proposed regulations for placer mining. For most mines processing fewer than 500 cubic yards of ore per day ("yd^3/day"), the EPA proposed BPT effluent limitations of 0.2 millilitres per litre ("ml/l") of discharge for settleable solids and 2,000 milligrams per litre ("mg/l") for total suspended solids. For mines processing more than 500 yd^3/day of ore, the EPA proposed more stringent BCT and BAT limitations as well as new-source performance standards (NSPS) prohibiting the discharge of processed wastewater. Twice during the rulemaking process, the Agency published notices of new information and requested public comment on additional financial and technical data.

C. Implementing Tbels Through the NPDES Process

As a result of its studies, the comments received during the review-and-comment periods, and new studies undertaken in response to the submitted comments, the EPA promulgated final effluent-limitation guidelines and standards on May 24, 1988. The EPA established a BPT limitation, based on simple-settling technology, for settleable solids of 0.2 ml/l for virtually all mines. The final rule also established BAT limitations and NSPS based on recirculation technology, restricting the flow of processed wastewater that could be discharged. In addition, the EPA promulgated five BMPs to control discharges due to mine drainage and infiltration. These regulations were to become effective on July 7, 1988. . . .

The Alaska Miners Association ("AMA") and Stanley and Rosalie Rybachek timely petitioned this court for review of the EPA's regulations. We ordered the petitions consolidated. . . .

THE EPA'S AUTHORITY UNDER THE CLEAN WATER ACT . . . [The court first concluded that placer mines were subject to CWA regulation because they take dirt from waterways and, after extracting the gold, discharge the dirt into nearby lakes and streams, which are "waters of the United States."[15]]

On the one hand, if the material discharged is not from the streambed itself, but from the bank alongside, this is clearly the discharge into navigable waters of a pollutant under the Act. Congress defined "pollutant" as meaning, among other things, "dredged spoil . . . , rock, sand [and] cellar dirt." . . . The term "pollutant" thus encompasses the materials segregated from gold in placer mining. Congress defined "discharge" as "any addition of any pollutant to navigable waters from any point source." . . . Because, under this scenario, the material discharged is coming not from the streambed itself, but from outside it, this clearly constitutes an "addition."

And, on the other hand, even if the material discharged originally comes from the streambed itself, such resuspension may be interpreted to be an addition of a pollutant under the Act. . . .

THE FINAL RULE . . . Petitioners make a host of arguments about the content of the final rule. For instance, they attack the EPA's setting of BPT and BAT limitations. They also allege various errors by the EPA in its promulgation of BMPs and its enunciation of new-source criteria. . . .

MERITS OF THE LIMITATIONS . . . Petitioners challenge the merits of the EPA's regulations on a number of grounds; indeed, virtually every aspect of the regulations is attacked. To the extent the regulations may be divided into component parts (e.g., the BPT limitations, the BAT limitations, and new-source criteria), we address petitioner's arguments along those lines.

DETERMINATION OF BPT . . . We turn first to petitioners' argument that the EPA erred in its determination that settling ponds are the best practicable control technology currently available (BPT) within the placer mining industry. There is no dispute that settling ponds are currently available pollution control technology; in fact, the AMA concedes that they are now used by almost all miners. Rather, petitioners contend that the EPA failed to use a "cost-benefit analysis" in determining that settling ponds were BPT for placer mining. They

---

15. At least arguably, these two conclusions may have been undermined by the *Rapanos* decision, regarding "waters of the United States," and in light of the EPA's water-transfer rule, both of which are discussed earlier in the chapter. [EDs.]

also argue that the EPA failed to consider costs when it set forth BPT limitations governing settleable solids for small mines.

The Clean Water Act controls when and how the EPA should require BPT. Under 33 U.S.C. §1311(b)(1)(A), the Act requires "effluent limitations for point sources . . . which shall require the application of best practicable control technology currently available [BPT]." Under this section, the EPA is to determine whether a technology is BPT; the factors it considers "shall include . . . total cost of" the technology "in relation to effluent benefits to be achieved" from it, the age of equipment, engineering aspects, "non-water quality environmental impact . . . and such other factors as the Administrator deems appropriate."

From this statutory language, it is "plain that, as a general rule, the EPA is required to consider the costs and benefits of proposed technology in its inquiry to determine the BPT." *Association of Pacific Fisheries v. EPA*, 615 F.2d 794 (9th Cir. 1980). The EPA has broad discretion in weighing these competing factors. It may determine that a technology is not BPT on the basis of this cost-benefit analysis only when the costs are "wholly disproportionate" to the potential effluent-reduction benefits.

We look first to whether the EPA properly considered the costs of BPT and second to whether it properly weighed these costs against the benefits.

First, the record shows that the EPA properly considered costs in conducting the analysis which led to the determination that settling ponds are BPT and to the establishment of BPT effluent limitations for settleable solids. The EPA used a model-mine analysis to estimate the costs to mines of installing settling ponds. The Agency developed several model mines to represent the typical operating and compliance costs that open-cut mines and dredges of various sizes would incur. Commenters attempted to insure that the model-mine analysis reflected actual industry conditions, and the EPA accordingly modified the analysis when it thought it appropriate during the rulemaking. The EPA then determined, for each of its model mines, the incremental costs that would be incurred to construct and operate settling ponds to retain wastewater long enough to achieve a certain settleable solids level. It proceeded to conduct a detailed and complex assessment of the effect of the compliance costs on the mining industry's profits.

The EPA then properly weighed these costs against the benefits of settling ponds. Its data indicated that placer mine wastewater contained high levels of solids and metals that were reduced substantially by simple settling. The upshot of the EPA's analysis was its estimation that installation of settling ponds by open-cut mines industry-wide would remove over four million pounds of solids at a cost of approximately $2.2 million — a removal cost of less than $1 per pound of solids. We would uphold the EPA's determination of BPT.

DETERMINATION OF BAT: ANALYSIS OF COSTS . . . We next confront the AMA's challenge to the EPA's determination that recirculation of process wastewater is the best available technology economically achievable (BAT) in the placer mining industry. By definition, BAT limitations must be both technologically available and economically achievable. We conclude that the EPA's BAT limitations were both and therefore uphold them.

The technological availability of recirculating process wastewater is not in dispute; in fact, placer mines commonly practice it. It is recirculation's economic achievability that petitioner's challenge.

In determining the economic achievability of technology, the EPA must consider the "cost" of meeting BAT limitations, but need not compare such cost with the benefits of effluent reduction. The Agency measures costs on a "reasonableness standard"; it has considerable discretion in weighing the technology's costs, which are less-important factors

C. Implementing Tbels Through the NPDES Process

than in setting BPT limitations. The record demonstrates that the EPA weighed the costs that recirculation would impose on gold placer mining. . . .

TOTAL SUSPENDED SOLIDS LIMITATIONS . . . We come to petitioner's claim that the EPA has impermissibly established BAT standards to regulate the discharge of total suspended solids. Petitioners argue that total suspended solids are conventional pollutants and therefore subject to BCT (best conventional pollution control technology), rather than BAT, standards. EPA's adoption of recirculation as BAT to control total suspended solids was arbitrary, petitioners contend, because recirculation could not pass the cost-reasonableness test required in determining BCT.

The EPA declined to establish BCT for total suspended solids because test results indicated that settling technology could not consistently control the level of total suspended solids. Moreover, recirculation failed the BCT cost-reasonableness test.

Petitioners are incorrect in contending that the EPA instead adopted BAT to regulate the level of total suspended solids. The EPA's discussion of BAT in the final rule makes no reference to controlling total suspended solids. Instead, EPA set BAT standards to control the discharge of toxic pollutants — a category which, the parties agree, does not encompass total suspended solids. We therefore reject the contention that the EPA was arbitrary in establishing BAT standards.

SETTLEABLE SOLIDS LIMITATIONS . . . Petitioners also claim that settleable solids are a component of total suspended solids and that the EPA should have classified settleable solids as a conventional pollutant rather than a nonconventional pollutant. Petitioners contend that the BAT-based effluent limitations are therefore inappropriate for settleable solids. We disagree.

In the Clean Water Act, Congress classified suspended solids as a conventional pollutant. Congress did not classify settleable solids. We must determine, therefore, whether the EPA's classification of settleable solids as a nonconventional pollutant "is based on a permissible construction of the Clean Water Act." *Chevron U.S.A., Inc. v. EPA*, 467 U.S. at 843. This court may not substitute its own construction of the Act if the EPA's interpretation is reasonable.

The EPA argues that because settleable solids were not designated by Congress as either a conventional or a toxic pollutant, they should be considered a nonconventional pollutant under 33 U.S.C.A. §1311(b)(2)(F). This argument is buttressed by the fact that EPA has subjected settleable solids to BAT-level controls in other regulatory areas. And even if settleable solids should more properly be considered a conventional pollutant, we note that the EPA has determined that settleable solids in placer mining effluent are a toxic pollutant indicator and thus may be subject to BAT-level limitations. We find, therefore, that the EPA's decision to treat settleable solids as a nonconventional pollutant and thus subject to BAT standards was both reasonable and permissible. . . .

MANDATING OF TECHNOLOGY . . . The AMA next claims that by forbidding the discharge of any process wastewater, the EPA is mandating that placer miners use recirculation technology. According to the AMA, the EPA's action violates Congress' intent to avoid dictating technologies and to encourage innovation. While admitting that the wastewater flow standards are currently achievable only through certain technology, the EPA responds that the regulations only prescribe limitations reflecting actually achieved wastewater reduction. We agree with the EPA. . . .

The EPA has not mandated use of a particular technology. The Agency first determined that recirculation is BAT for the control of discharges by placer mines of toxic metals and settleable solids. Based on this determination, the EPA established that Zero discharge of process wastewater is achievable and should be the BAT limitation and new-source performance standard. That the standards and limitations are stringent and currently may be achievable only through certain technology is true. However, nothing in the EPA's regulations specifies the use of any particular technology to meet the BAT limitations and new-source performance standards achievable through recirculation. In fact, the EPA has encouraged miners to employ innovative technologies and to seek compliance extensions and alternative BAT limitations under §301(k) of the Act. We find that the EPA's setting of zero-discharge limitations based on recirculation results was within its mandate under the Clean Water Act.

AVAILABILITY OF VARIANCES . . . Petitioners claim that EPA has contravened Congress' intent by failing to allow miners to obtain variances for site-specific conditions. We first note that this assertion is flatly contradicted by the final rule's express language allowing miners to apply for fundamentally different factor ("FDF") variances for both the BPT and BAT limitations. . . .

Petitioners argue that the EPA's classification of settleable solids as a toxic pollutant indicator will prevent miners from obtaining a variance. Normally, BAT limitations for non-conventional pollutants (here, settleable solids) are subject to modification under §§301(c) and (g) of the Clean Water Act. In this instance, modifications for settleable solids under these provisions are unavailable because settleable solids are considered an indicator of toxic pollutants. This does not mean, however, that no variance in the BAT limitations for settleable solids is available; miners may still apply for an FDF variance under §301(n) of the Act. . . .

COMMENTARY & QUESTIONS

1. Evolution of categorical technology-based limitations. When the CWA was enacted in 1972, it contained two phases of technology-based limitations. In the first phase, existing industrial point source dischargers were required to meet effluent limitations based on Best Practicable Control Technology Currently Available (BPT) by 1977. During the second phase, dischargers were to meet stricter effluent limitations based on BAT by 1983. BPT was intended to be primarily "end of pipe" treatment, with process changes required only if they were normal practice within an industry. The factors to be considered in setting BAT limitations were similar to those relied upon in setting BPT-based limitations (and described in the *Rybachek* opinion), except that: (1) BAT is based on the single best performer within an industry, rather than on an average of "exemplary plants"; (2) BAT is based on process changes adopted within the industry or reasonably transferable from another industry; and (3) BAT involves a consideration only of the cost of achieving such reduction (cost effectiveness), not comparative benefits and costs, unless compliance costs are "wholly disproportionate" to water quality benefits. Congress realized that some facilities would be forced to cut back production or even close down as a result of these BAT-based limitations. As in *Rybachek,* BPT-based limitations are generally continued in effect during the three-year BAT compliance period that the CWA mandates for existing dischargers.

EPA adopted a "categorical" approach to setting technology-based effluent limitations. Industries were divided into categories, based on products manufactured, and

C. Implementing Tbels Through the NPDES Process

subcategories, based on processes or raw materials utilized in producing the products (e.g., the dredge-mining subcategory of the placer mining category). Then the BPT and BAT criteria were applied to these categories and subcategories, not to individual plants. EPA's effluent limitation regulations for each industrial subcategory contained maximum daily and monthly average limitations on relevant "parameters" (pollutants) expressed in terms of maximum volume or concentration of parameters in wastewater. These "single number" effluent limitations were uniform for existing plants in a particular subcategory, wherever they were located. EPA cannot establish a subcategory based solely on geographical location. Hundreds of lawsuits by industry and numerous divergences among circuit courts of appeals were resolved in *Dupont v. Train*, 430 U.S. 12 (1977), in which the Supreme Court upheld EPA's categorical approach but stipulated that EPA must devise a variance for plants that do not fit within an industrial subcategory. This procedure, known as the Fundamentally Different Factors (FDF) variance, was later codified as §301(n) of the CWA. For dischargers receiving an FDF variance (e.g., a placer miner that does not have adequate space for a settling pond) and dischargers for which effluent limitation regulations have not yet been promulgated, effluent limitations are set using Best Professional Judgment (BPJ) in light of the statutory criteria. The water quality of the receiving body of water cannot be considered in setting technology-based effluent limitations. Can a discharger dilute its effluent in order to meet effluent limitations? *Weyerhaeuser v. Costle*, 590 F.2d 1011 (D.C. Cir. 1978), and other cases make it clear that in-plant dilution is not an acceptable solution to pollution under the CWA. Developers of new sources possess the advantage of being able to build pollution control mechanisms into their original plant designs. Consequently, new sources are required to immediately comply with New Source Performance Standards (NSPS) based on BADT, or zero-discharge where practicable. As in *Rybachek*, NSPS are often equivalent to BAT, but EPA policy is that state-of-the-art technology may be required of new sources where it would be economically infeasible for existing sources to retrofit with such technology. However, having met the relevant NSPS, a new source cannot be required to meet stricter technology-based standards for ten years or the facility's amortization period, whichever comes first. §306.[16]

2. The midcourse corrections of 1977. Between 1972 and 1977, the installation of BPT by industry and the decrease in pollution from POTWs had significantly reduced the loadings of so-called "conventional pollutants" (BOD, TSS, pH, fecal coliform, and oil and grease) to America's waterbodies. At the same time, Congress had realized that toxic pollutants were far more of a problem than had initially been envisioned. Thus a midcourse correction was made in 1977 with regard to conventionals and toxics.

In 1977, convinced that the cost of moving to BAT for conventionals was too high, Congress devised a new standard, BCT, for them. §301(b)(2)(E). BCT includes two cost tests: (1) a comparison between the costs of reducing discharges of conventionals and the resulting water quality benefits, and (2) a comparison between industrial and municipal costs for treating conventionals. §304(b)(2)(B). The congressional supporters of BCT felt that it would produce effluent limitations falling between BPT and BAT, but in practice BCT is similar to BPT.

---

16. Stricter new source performance standards are sometimes criticized as counterproductive in that they allegedly discourage new plant construction and delay the phaseout of inefficient, polluting older facilities. There is little evidence that this has occurred in the water pollution control area. Competitive pressures militate against the perpetuation of inefficient facilities simply to save on pollution control costs. A greater danger is the offshore migration of dischargers.

The CWA's original toxic pollutant control mechanism was a cumbersome pollutant-by-pollutant, harm-based system (modeled after §112 of the CAA) that resulted in little control of toxic water pollutants. Rejecting this exercise in futility, EPA decided to regulate toxic pollutants primarily through BAT-based effluent limitations. EPA's decision was upheld by the famous "Consent Decree of 1976." *NRDC v. Train*, 8 BNA Env't Rep. Cas. 2120 (often called the "Flannery Decree" after the trial court judge). This decree established timetables for EPA to promulgate effluent limitations, based on BAT, for both direct and indirect discharges from many industrial categories, covering 65 families of compounds that EPA has broken down into 126 "priority pollutants."[17] EPA is authorized to add toxic pollutants to this list by regulation but has not done so. In 1977, Congress codified this methodology for regulating toxics. §§301(b)(2)(C) and 307(a)(1) and (2). As *Rybachek* illustrates, nontoxic pollutants that indicate the presence of toxics ("indicator" or "surrogate" parameters) may be regulated as toxics themselves. 40 C.F.R. §122.44(e)(2)(ii).

In addition to conventional and toxic pollutants, Congress in 1977 created a third class of pollutants called "nonconventional" (or nonconventional/nontoxic) pollutants. §301(b)(2)(F). Ammonia, chlorine, color, iron, and total phenols are some of the designated nonconventional pollutants. Dischargers of nonconventionals are entitled to apply for two variances, the cost-based §301(c) variance and the harm-based §301(g) variance. In *Rybachek*, petitioners unsuccessfully contested EPA's classification of settleable solids, ordinarily a nonconventional pollutant, as a toxic pollutant indicator because such classification rendered the nonconventional pollutant variances unavailable to them. Dischargers of toxics, like dischargers of conventionals, may only apply for FDF variances and §301(k) variances for innovative technology.

The table illustrates the classes of water pollutants with their appropriate technology-based effluent limitations, compliance dates, and available variances:[18]

---

17. The time limits in the consent decree were frequently delayed, and it was not until 1987 that EPA promulgated the last of the effluent limitations guidelines covered by the Flannery Decree. EPA has promulgated effluent limitations guidelines regulations for over 50 industrial categories and will, in the future, promulgate regulations applicable to additional categories. EPA estimates that BAT-based effluent limitations imposed under this program have reduced discharges of priority pollutants from point sources by 99%, but sometimes heavy discharges of toxic nonpriority pollutants from point sources and priority pollutants from nonpoint sources continue.

18. Neither EPA nor a state has the authority to regulate discharges of radioactive materials, which are within the exclusive jurisdiction of the Nuclear Regulatory Commission. *Train v. Colorado Pub. Interest Research Group*, 426 U.S. 1 (1976). States, however, can control the siting of nuclear power plants through their traditional powers over the need for, and the economic costs of, electrical power. See *Pacific Gas & Elec. v. California Energy Res. Conservation & Dev. Comm'n*, 461 U.S. 190 (1983).

C. Implementing Tbels Through the NPDES Process

Technology-Based Effluent Limitations			
Pollutant Type	**Effluent Limitation**	**Compliance Date**	**Variances?**
Conventional Pollutants (BOD, TSS, etc.)	BCT; BPT as interim standard	3 years after promulgation of standard	FDF: Fundamentally Different Factors variances
Non-Conventionals Non-Toxics (Ammonia, color, etc.)	BAT (cost-achievable best); BPT as interim standard	3 years after promulgation of standard	FDF: §301(c) and (g) variances based on economics and receiving water quality
Toxics	BAT	3 years after promulgation of standard	FDF: §301(k) 2-year extension for adoption of innovative/alternative technology
Heat	BAT	3 years after promulgation of standard	§316(a)
New Source Discharges	BADT; BPT as interim standard	3 years after promulgation of standard	None 10-year grace period
Non-Point Sources (agricultural and urban runoff, etc.)	BMP	Depends on requirements under individual state plan	Depends on requirements under individual state plan

3. Stormwater discharges. When the *Rybachek* discharge permit was issued, §304(e) was the only CWA provision that actively regulated point source stormwater discharges. That section authorizes EPA to establish BMPs "to control plant site runoff, spillage or leaks, sludge or waste disposal, and drainage from raw material storage" in order to diminish the amount of toxic pollutants flowing into receiving waters. In *Rybachek*, EPA had promulgated five BMPs to control toxic discharges due to mine drainage and infiltration. In the 1987 CWA Amendments, Congress expanded EPA's jurisdiction to regulate stormwater discharges that are associated with industrial activity and that emanate from municipal separate storm sewer systems (MS4s). CWA §402(p). Currently, there are four major CWA programs regulating stormwater discharges from (1) CAFOs, (2) industrial operations, (3) MS4s, and (4) municipal combined and sanitary sewers.

EPA's final CAFO rules (40 C.F.R. §412) became effective on April 14, 2003. A CAFO is defined as a livestock operation that raises more than a certain minimum number of animals (e.g., 1000 cattle or 125,000 chickens) where manure is disposed of by discharging it into lagoons or treating it and spraying it onto farm fields as fertilizer (as in the *Southview Farms* decision, discussed above). In the 2003 rules, EPA estimated that 15,500 CAFOs, producing some 300 million tons of manure annually, would be subject to regulation. If a CAFO is not managed properly, during storm events waste lagoons overflow and excess manure applied as fertilizer runs off into waterbodies, frequently leading to widespread nutrient and bacterial contamination.

The regulatory essence of the 2003 CAFO rules was the requirement that CAFOs develop nutrient management plans that set limits on how much manure can be applied and include BMPs for meeting those limits. Nutrient management plans (NMPs) were to be approved by states with primacy, or EPA in nonprimacy states, by 2006. States delegated primacy had the authority to design and implement, through either individual or general permits,[19] site-specific requirements containing standards that depend on the size, location, and environmental risks posed by particular CAFOs.

The EPA revised the 2003 rules in 2008, in response to the Second Circuit's decision in *Waterkeeper Alliance v. EPA*, 399 F.3d 486 (2d Cir. 2005). The court directed the EPA to require NMPs to be included as part of the permit applications, subject to public review, and included in the final permit. At the same time, the court ordered EPA to take out the requirement that all CAFOs apply for NPDES permits. In the revised rule, only those CAFOs that discharge or propose to discharge need apply for a permit.

The industrial stormwater permit program covers plant yards, material handling sites, refuse sites, shipping and receiving areas, manufacturing buildings, raw material storage areas, and other areas at industrial sites where toxic materials may be present. The program does not include stormwater from facilities engaged in wholesale, retail, service, or commercial activities. An industrial discharger of stormwater must comply with the terms of a general permit for its industrial category. Each general permit requires the development and implementation of stormwater management plans (SMPs) incorporating pollution prevention BMPs such as planning, reporting, personnel training, preventive maintenance, and good housekeeping. For example, a discharger that experiences runoff from an uncovered outdoor pile of raw materials might either build an enclosure for the pile or move it indoors. SMPs must be reviewed and certified by a registered professional engineer.

The MS4 program has been described by the U.S. General Accounting Office as follows:

> Nonpoint source pollution can result when water, such as precipitation, runs over land surfaces and into bodies of water. Significant nonpoint sources of pollution can include paved urban areas, agricultural practices, forestry, and mining. However, in urban or suburban areas, this runoff generally enters a sewer system that can be regulated as a point source of water pollution. For example, precipitation from rain or snowmelt may run into a [MS4] that eventually discharges into a body of water. The precipitation may also run into a combined sewer system, which carries a combination of storm water runoff, industrial waste, and raw sewage in a single pipe to a sewage treatment facility for discharge after treatment. Lastly, the precipitation may run off of land or paved surfaces directly into nearby receiving waters. . . . In 1987, the Congress . . . directed EPA to also control storm water discharges that enter MS4s — essentially requiring EPA to treat such storm water as a point source. MS4s are defined as those sewers that collect and convey storm water; are owned or operated by the federal, state, or local government; and are not part of a publicly owned treatment (sewage) facility.
>
> To regulate urban storm water runoff, EPA published regulations in 1990 that established the NPDES Storm Water Program and described permit application requirements. According to EPA, the program's objective . . . is to . . . reduc[e] the level of runoff pollutants to the maximum extent practicable using best management practices (BMPs).[20] . . .
>
> The [MS4] program is being implemented in two phases. . . . First, Phase I of the program requires that municipalities with a population of 100,000 or more obtain a permit for their MS4 system; second, the program requires that [private] entities obtain a permit if they discharge storm water . . . from construction activities that disturb 5 acres or more of land. Municipalities

---

19. A general permit is an overall permit that is applicable to all members of a particular class of dischargers, e.g., specific CAFOs or small wetlands developers. A general permit contains all the regulatory requirements with which members of the class must comply. A discharger within the class need not obtain an individual permit (unless required by the regulatory authority) but must file a notice of intention to be covered by the general permit and submit plans and monitoring reports as indicated in it. Violators of general permits are subject to enforcement actions in the same manner as violators of individual permits. General permits, where appropriate, conserve the resources of both administrative agencies and dischargers.

20. The "maximum extent practicable" language is the statutory standard, which is not further defined in the CWA. Typical BMPs for MS4s are street sweeping, pet litter control ordinances, and sewer grate cleaning. [EDS.]

C. Implementing Tbels Through the NPDES Process

that meet these conditions must submit a permit application to EPA or the governing regulatory state. In 1990 [when the Phase I regulations became effective], the regulations specifically identified 220 municipalities throughout the United States that were required to apply for a Phase I permit. . . . Because some permits cover more than one municipality, these permits cover about 1,000 medium and large municipalities nationwide.

The final rule for Phase II of the program was issued in December 1999. Phase II extends Phase I efforts by requiring that a storm water discharge permit must be obtained by (1) operators of all MS4s not already covered by Phase I of the program in urban areas and (2) construction sites that disturb areas equal to or greater than 1 acre and less than 5 acres of land. . . . Currently, EPA anticipates that about 5,000 municipalities may be subject to permitting requirements under Phase II of the storm water program. These municipalities are required to obtain permits no later than March 10, 2003. GAO, Better Data and Evaluation of Urban Runoff Programs Needed to Assess Effectiveness 6-8 (2001).

EPA's emphasis on BMPs in controlling stormwater discharges from MS4s was upheld in *Defenders of Wildlife v. EPA*, 197 F.3d 1035 (9th Cir. 1999) (EPA did not act arbitrarily or capriciously in issuing municipalities MS4 discharge permits that included BMPs but not numerical effluent limitations). See also *City of Abilene v. EPA*, 325 F.3d 657 (5th Cir. 2003) (Phase I regulations upheld against constitutional — including Tenth Amendment — objections). The Phase II regulations were substantially upheld in *Environmental Def. Ctr., Inc. v. EPA*, 2003 WL 22119563 (9th Cir. 2003) (constitutional objections rejected but rules remanded because notices of intent to be covered by general permits were improperly shielded from EPA review, public disclosure, and administrative hearings).

EPA also regulates combined sewer overflows (CSOs), which are a major source of urban water pollution in general and, in particular, of beach closings and swimming advisories due to high concentrations of pathogens (bacteria and viruses) from untreated municipal sewage. Combined sewer systems, in which stormwater enters pipes already carrying sewage, may overflow when rain or snowmelt entering the system exceeds the system's flow capacity. When an overflow results, the mixture of untreated sewage and runoff bypasses the POTW and is diverted directly into receiving waters. Nationwide, there are approximately 1100 combined sewer systems, serving about 43 million people. See generally *Northwest Envtl. Advocates v. Portland*, 56 F.3d 979 (9th Cir. 1995), cert. denied, 518 U.S. 1018 (1996). These combined systems generally serve the older parts of cities in the United States, whereas pipes carrying sewage and stormwater separately generally serve newer parts of cities. Although CSOs are significant point sources of pollution, the CWA does not specifically address them. Because separation of combined sewers is prohibitively expensive, EPA's CSO control requirements focus on BMPs and the development of long-term CSO control plans targeting environmentally sensitive receiving waters.

Sanitary sewer overflows (SSOs) (i.e., overflows of the sewage-carrying components of a separate sewer system) can also result from storm events. Like CSOs, SSOs are very dangerous events because they lead to pathogenic pollution in receiving waters. EPA estimates that between 25,000 and 75,000 SSOs occur in the Unites States annually. The agency issued model NPDES permit conditions in 2007 to improve regulation of these overflows by clarifying reporting and recordkeeping and proposing new requirements the collection systems that may produce SSOs.[21]

4. Municipal dischargers. POTWs must also possess NPDES permits containing technology-based effluent limitations. They were required to have met effluent limitations

---

21. For more information on sewer overflows, see EPA's 2004 Report to Congress: Impacts and Controls of CSOs and SSOs, available at http://cfpub.epa.gov/npdes/cso/cpolicy_report2004.cfm.

based on "Secondary Treatment" (generally defined as a biological process that achieves 85% removal of conventional pollutants) by 1988. §301(b)(B) and 40 C.F.R. §133. Waivers from secondary treatment are available to POTWs that discharge into deep ocean waters, §301(h), but these waivers are rarely granted. Since 1972, federal monetary subsidies have been available for the construction and upgrading of POTWs and their sewerage systems. These federal incentives were first administered as the Construction Grants Program (CWA Title II), which provided almost $60 billion to municipalities and sewerage authorities in 55 to 85% matching grants for construction and land acquisition. In 1989, the Construction Grants Program was replaced by federal capitalization grants to State Revolving Loan Funds (SRFs). CWA Title VI. Approximately another $20 billion has been granted to the states under this program. However, there is an unmet need for approximately an additional $180 billion in investment for POTWs and sewerage infrastructure upgrades. There is a growing trend toward privatization of POTWs in order to allow for badly needed improvements to municipal wastewater infrastructure that government increasingly is unable to fund.

5. Indirect dischargers and biosolids disposal. Toxic and hazardous materials discharged into sanitary and combined sewers compose a substantial percentage of toxic pollutant loadings to waterways:

> A large number of industrial facilities, ranging from pesticide manufacturers to small local electroplaters, discharge toxic wastes to the nation's sewage treatment plants. A 1986 EPA study identified approximately 160,000 industrial and commercial facilities discharging wastes with hazardous constituents to public sewers, representing about 12 percent of the total flow to POTWs.... Secondary treatment alone does not remove these pollutants. While some fraction of organic hazardous constituents is degraded incidentally in the POTW's conventional treatment process, many of these substances evaporate during the treatment (or from the sewer pipes themselves) or wind up in the water or the sludge. None of the metals that go to a treatment plant are degraded: toxic metals pass through the plant into receiving waters or into the sludge generated by the treatment process. R. Adler et al., The Clean Water Act 20 Years Later 144-145 (1993).

Section 307 of the CWA requires EPA to promulgate "pretreatment standards" for indirect discharges that interfere with POTW operations, contaminate sludge, or pass untreated through the POTW, causing the POTW to violate its discharge permit. The CWA does not compel indirect dischargers to procure discharge permits, although some states require significant industrial users (SIUs) to obtain permits.

There are two types of national pretreatment standards: "prohibited discharge standards" and "categorical pretreatment standards." 40 C.F.R. §403. Prohibited discharge standards require that pollutants introduced into a POTW not inhibit the POTW's performance. Categorical pretreatment standards set out national discharge limits based on BAT, similar to TBELs for direct dischargers. Categorical pretreatment standards may be supplemented by stricter state or local standards where necessary to enable a POTW to comply with the effluent limitations in its own discharge permit or with an element of its CSO control plan.

Pretreatment standards are primarily enforced by the POTWs themselves — through local sewer connection permits or user agreements — with the states and EPA retaining backup enforcement authority. This system creates a fox-in-the-henhouse situation because POTWs are reluctant to enforce against their own customers unless (1) the indirect discharge disrupts the plant's operations, or (2) the POTW's discharge permit contains effluent limitations for toxics, the permit is being violated, and enforcement action is being

C. Implementing Tbels Through the NPDES Process 549

taken against the POTW — a rare conjunction of circumstances. Not only has indirect discharge been a significant loophole in the CWA, but it also has been exacerbated by RCRA's exclusion of indirect discharges from its regulatory ambit. See Chapter 17. In Chapter 2, where Allied Chemical and its Life Science Products affiliate had been discharging Kepone directly into the James River, they ultimately opted for indirect discharge into the local POTW.

Biosolids (previously called "sewage sludge," but euphemistically renamed by EPA) are the final residual of the municipal sewage treatment process. Biosolids may be heavily contaminated due to inadequate pretreatment, uncontrolled flushing of household toxics (e.g., drain cleaners and pesticides), toxics entering sewers from road runoff into combined sewers or leaky sanitary sewers, and illegal hazardous waste dumping into municipal sewerage systems. Biosolids contaminated with heavy metals can preclude beneficial use as a soil conditioner on farmland, which EPA now favors as an alternative to disposal in landfills or incineration. CWA §405 establishes a permit system for biosolids disposal and requires EPA to promulgate regulations setting guidelines for biosolids disposal and reuse. EPA's biosolids disposal and reuse regulations have been highly controversial. Farmers are understandably reluctant to accept biosolids for land application because compliance with EPA standards will not insulate a farmer from common law actions brought by neighbors for abnormally dangerous activities resulting in groundwater contamination. See generally Goldfarb et al., Unsafe Sewage Sludge or Beneficial Biosolids?, 26 B.C. Envtl. Aff. L. Rev. 687 (1999).

6. Drinking water protection. Ambient water quality and tap water quality are regulated by different federal statutes. Under the Safe Drinking Water Act (SDWA), 42 U.S.C. §§300f et seq., EPA is required to promulgate national primary and secondary drinking water regulations applicable to "public water systems," defined as systems that have at least 15 service connections or regularly serve at least 25 individuals at least 60 days per year. Primary drinking water regulations identify potential toxic contaminants and, for each contaminant, set a maximum contaminant level (MCL) if the contaminant can feasibly be measured or set a treatment technique if it cannot. Secondary drinking water regulations set MCLs for nontoxic contaminants that affect other parameters, for example, color and taste.

The SDWA, like the CWA, relies on technology-based standards. EPA first promulgates Maximum Contaminant Level Goals (MCLGs), which are nonenforceable health goals for public water systems. MCLGs are to be set at levels at which "no known or anticipated adverse effects on the health of persons occur and which allows an adequate margin of safety." Then, EPA promulgates enforceable primary drinking water regulations, including MCLs and monitoring and reporting requirements for dangerous contaminants. MCLs must be set as close to MCLGs as is "feasible," which means "with the use of the best technology, treatment techniques, and other means, which the Administrator finds are generally available (taking costs into consideration)." The SDWA also authorizes federal contributions to state revolving loan funds (modeled on the State Revolving Loan Funds under the CWA) for the construction and upgrade of water purification facilities.

7. Toxics and the CWA. Although he believes that "BAT under the Clean Water Act has probably been the most effective pollution control program in the world in terms of producing identifiable abatement," Professor Oliver Houck concludes that EPA's technology-based effluent limitation program is faltering with regard to toxic pollutants. Regulation of Toxic Pollutants Under the Clean Water Act, 21 Envtl. L. Rep. 10528 (1991). EPA has not added any priority pollutants to its list since the consent decree of 1976. According to

Houck, "a greater number of individual industries remain unregulated than regulated, and a growing list of toxics have escaped scrutiny and standards."[22] Moreover, in Houck's view:

> Discharge standards have emerged unevenly, with a heavy "zero discharge" hand on such unfortunates as seafood canners and placer mine operators, and a remarkably blind eye to available closed-cycle systems for some of the nation's highest volume dischargers of broad-spectrum toxins [such as petroleum refiners and certain organic chemical producers]. The disparities in these standards reflect nothing more starkly than a disparity in clout. 21 Envtl. L. Rep. at 10539.

Skeptical of the water quality-based approach, Professor Houck recommends that Congress either (1) establish specific deadlines for EPA to promulgate new technology-based effluent limitations, with a zero-discharge "hammer" similar to RCRA's land ban (see Chapter 17); or (2) fix timetables, based on relative risk and reasonable lead times, for the elimination of toxic discharges. What are the potential disadvantages of so closely involving Congress in the intricacies of standard-setting? An argument can be made that since Congress possesses a minimum of expertise in the technical aspects of water pollution control, its decisions will be either hopelessly unrealistic or even more politically motivated than EPA's. Under some political scenarios, Professor Houck might be better off with EPA than with Congress.

The *Atlantic States* case that follows illustrates the problem of controlling nonpriority toxic pollutants in the context of administering TBELs through the discharge permit of a large, multifaceted industrial operation. The industrial discharge of Kodak and the complexity of the permit in the *Atlantic States* case is more representative of the ordinary discharge permitting context than *Rybachek*. Notice how many pieces of the puzzle that have been studied thus far (e.g., CWA regulations, discharge permits, cooperative federalism, and deferential judicial review) combine to generate the law of water pollution control. Notice also that this litigation arose by way of a citizen suit, one of the approximately 1500 CWA citizen suits that have been filed since 1972.

Atlantic States Legal Foundation, Inc. v. Eastman Kodak Co.
12 F.3d 353 (2d Cir. 1993), cert. denied, 513 U.S. 811 (1994)

WINTER, C.J.: This appeal raises the issue of whether private groups may bring a citizen suit pursuant to §505 of the Clean Water Act to stop the discharge of pollutants not listed in a valid permit issued pursuant to CWA §402. We hold that the discharge of unlisted pollutants is not unlawful under the CWA. We also hold that private groups may not bring such a suit to enforce New York State environmental regulations.

Appellee Eastman Kodak Company ("Kodak") operates an industrial facility in Rochester, New York that discharges wastewater into the Genesee River and Paddy Hill Creek under a State Pollutant Discharge Elimination System ("SPDES") permit issued pursuant to CWA §402. Appellant Atlantic States Legal Foundation, Inc. is a not-for-profit environmental group based in Syracuse, New York.

---

22. A report by the Comptroller General of the United States supports Professor Houck's conclusion. The GAO found that 77% of the discharge of all toxic pollutants across its sample (the vast majority of which were nonpriority pollutants) was uncontrolled. U.S. GAO, Poor Quality Assurance and Limited Pollutant Coverage Undermine EPA's Control of Toxic Substances (1994).

C. Implementing Tbels Through the NPDES Process

Kodak operates a wastewater treatment plant at its Rochester facility to purify waste produced in the manufacture of photographic supplies and other laboratory chemicals. The purification plant employs a variety of technical processes to filter harmful pollutants before discharge into the Genesee River at the King's Landing discharge point (designated Outfall 001) pursuant to its SPDES permit.

Kodak first received a federal permit in 1975. At that time, the pertinent regulatory scheme was the NPDES administered directly by the federal Environmental Protection Agency. Subsequently, CWA §402(b-c) delegated authority to the states to establish their own programs in place of the EPA's. As a result, Kodak applied in July 1979 to renew its permit to the New York State Department of Environmental Conservation ("DEC"). The DEC declined to act on Kodak's renewal application, and Kodak's NPDES permit remained in effect. As part of the pending application for a SPDES permit, in April 1982, Kodak provided the DEC with a Form 2C describing estimated discharges of 164 substances from each of its outfalls. Kodak also submitted an Industrial Chemical Survey ("ICS") disclosing the amounts of certain chemicals used in Kodak's facility and whether they might appear in the plant's wastewater. Although the ICS originally requested information on 144 substances, including some broad classes such as "unspecified metals," the DEC restricted the inquiry to chemicals used in excess of specified minimum levels.

On the basis of these disclosures, DEC issued Kodak a SPDES permit, number 000-1643, effective November 1, 1984, establishing specific effluent limitations for approximately 25 pollutants.[23] The permit also included "action levels"[24] for five other pollutants as well as for three of the pollutants for which it had established effluent limits. DEC further required Kodak to conduct a semi-annual scan of "EPA Volatile, Acid and Base/Neutral Fractions and PCBs priority pollutants on a 24-hr. composite sample." In May 1989, Kodak applied to renew the SPDES permit submitting a new Form 2C and ICS, but the 1984 permit will continue to remain in effect until DEC issues a final determination.

On November 14, 1991, Atlantic States filed the complaint in the instant matter. The complaint alleged that Kodak had violated CWA §§301 and 402 by discharging large quantities of pollutants not listed in its SPDES permit.[25] After discovery, Atlantic States moved for partial summary judgment as to Kodak's liability in relation to the post-April 1, 1990 discharge of one or more of 16 of the 27 pollutants listed in the complaint.[26] The 16 pollutants

---

23. UOD, TKN, Ammonia, BOD sub5, oil & grease, phosphorus, cyanide, cadmium, chromium, copper, iron, lead, nickel, silver (total and ionic), zinc, mercury, chloroform, 4-Chloro-3,5-dimethylphenol, 1,2-Dichloroethane, 1,2-Dichloropropane, N,N-Dimethylaniline, Dichloromethane, Pyridine, and Xylene. [These substances include conventional and toxic pollutants. Most of the toxic parameters are priority pollutants, but some are nonpriority pollutants. EDS.]

24. If the action level is exceeded, the permittee must undertake a "short-term, high-intensity monitoring program." If levels higher than the action levels are confirmed, the permit is reopened for consideration of revised action levels or effluent limits.

25. Specifically, the complaint alleged that Kodak had discharged "282,744 pounds of unpermitted pollutants in 1987, 308,537 pounds in 1988, 321,456 pounds in 1989, and 290,121 pounds in 1990," and that Atlantic States believed that Kodak continued to discharge such pollutants. The 27 substances Atlantic States alleged that Kodak discharged were acetonitrile, acetone, carbon tetrachloride, catechol, cyclohexane, dibutyl phthalate, diethanolamine, ethylene glycol, glycol ethers, formaldehyde, hydroquinone, manganese, methanol, methyl ethyl ketone, methyl isobutyl ketone, n-butyl alcohol, nitrobenzene, 1,1,1-trichloroethane, 1,1,2-trichloroethane, 1,4-dioxane, 2-ethoxyethanol, 2-methoxyethanol, tert-butyl alcohol, toluene, and trichloroethylene. [The great majority of these parameters are nonpriority toxic pollutants. EDS.]

26. Atlantic States' contentions regarding the number and amount of pollutants discharged are not material given our disposition of this matter. Of the 16 substances on which Atlantic States moved for partial summary judgment, seven were listed by Kodak in its permit application, Form 2C, or ICS, or were specifically mentioned in

are all listed as toxic chemicals under §313(c) of the Emergency Planning and Community Right-to-Know Act, 42 U.S.C. §11023(c). Atlantic States argued that General Provision 1(b) of the SPDES permit and §301 of the CWA prohibit absolutely the discharge of any pollutant not specifically authorized under Kodak's SPDES permit. Kodak made a cross-motion for summary judgment on the ground that neither the CWA nor the federal regulations implementing it prohibit discharge of pollutants not specifically assigned effluent limitations in an NPDES or SPDES permit.

Atlantic States argues first that the plain language of §301 of the CWA prohibits the discharge of any pollutants not expressly permitted. Section 301(a) reads: "Except as in compliance with this section and §§1312, 1316, 1317, 1328, 1342, and 1344 of this title, the discharge of any pollutant by any person shall be unlawful." This prohibition is tempered, however, by a self-referential host of exceptions that allow the discharge of many pollutants once a polluter has complied with the regulatory program of the CWA. The exception relevant to the instant matter is contained in §402, which outlines the NPDES, and specifies the requirements for suspending the national system with the submission of an approved state program, CWA §402(b-c). Section 402(k) contains the so-called "shield provision" which defines compliance with a NPDES or SPDES permit as compliance with §301 for the purposes of the CWA's enforcement provisions. The Supreme Court has noted that: "The purpose of [§402(k)] seems to be . . . to relieve [permit holders] of having to litigate in an enforcement action the question whether their permits are sufficiently strict." *E.I. du Pont de Nemours & Co. v. Train*, 430 U.S. 112, 138 n. 28 (1977).

Atlantic States' view of the regulatory framework stands that scheme on its head. Atlantic States treats permits as establishing limited permission for the discharge of identified pollutants and a prohibition on the discharge of unidentified pollutants. Viewing the regulatory scheme as a whole, however, it is clear that the permit is intended to identify and limit the most harmful pollutants while leaving the control of the vast number of other pollutants to disclosure requirements. Once within the NPDES or SPDES scheme, therefore, polluters may discharge pollutants not specifically listed in their permits so long as they comply with the appropriate reporting requirements and abide by any new limitations when imposed on such pollutants.

The EPA lists tens of thousands of different chemical substances in the Toxic Substances Control Act Chemical Substance Inventory pursuant to 15 U.S.C. §2607(b). However, the EPA does not demand even information regarding each of the many thousand chemical substances potentially present in a manufacturer's wastewater because "it is impossible to identify and rationally limit every chemical or compound present in a discharge of pollutants." Memorandum from EPA Deputy Assistant Administrator for Water Enforcement Jeffrey G. Miller to Regional Enforcement Director, Region V, at 2 (Apr. 28, 1976). "Compliance with such a permit would be impossible and anybody seeking to harass a permittee need only analyze that permittee's discharge until determining the presence of a substance not identified in the permit." Indeed, at oral argument Atlantic States could provide no principled

---

the DEC's 1988 Notice Letter: dibutyl phthalate, ethylene glycol, manganese, 1,4-dioxane, 1,1,1- trichloroethane, 1,1,2-trichloroethane, and toluene. These substances received specific regulatory inquiry. The remaining nine substances appeared on Kodak's Form R's, the source of Atlantic States' information. Kodak must file annual Form Rs, a Toxic Chemical Release Inventory Reporting Form, with both EPA and DEC, pursuant to 42 U.S.C. §11023. Although not listed in Kodak's SPDES permit, these substances were subject to DEC regulation. Even had there been no regulation of the particular substances, Atlantic States would still not have standing to sue unless it could show violations of established regulatory limits.

C. Implementing Tbels Through the NPDES Process

reason why water itself, which is conceded to be a chemical, would not be considered a "pollutant" under its view of the Act.

The EPA has never acted in any way to suggest that Atlantic States' absolutist and wholly impractical view of the legal effect of a permit is valid. In fact, the EPA's actions and policy statements have frequently contemplated discharges of pollutants not listed under a NPDES or SPDES permit. It has addressed such discharges by amending the permit to list and limit a pollutant when necessary to safeguard the environment without considering pre-amendment discharges to be violations calling for enforcement under the CWA. The EPA thus stated in its comments on proposed 40 C.F.R. §122.68(a), which applied the "application-based" limits approach to implementation of the CWA reporting scheme:

> There is still some possibility . . . that a [NPDES or SPDES] permittee may discharge a large amount of a pollutant not limited in its permit, and EPA will not be able to take enforcement action against the permittee as long as the permittee complies with the notification requirements [pursuant to the CWA]. 45 Fed. Reg. 33516, 33523 (1980).

The EPA's statement went on to note that this possibility constituted a "regulatory gap," and that, "the final regulations control discharges only of the pollutants listed in the [NPDES or SPDES] permit application, which consist primarily of the listed [priority] toxic pollutants and designated hazardous substances." [The opinion went on to uphold EPA's statutory interpretation using the deferential *Chevron v. NRDC*, 467 U.S. 837 (1984), standard of review. The decision in favor of Kodak was affirmed.]

COMMENTARY & QUESTIONS

1. CWA §402(k) and the NPDES permit shield defense. Is compliance with an NPDES permit a complete defense to *all* claims related to the discharge of pollutants through the regulated outfall? The statutory language of §402(k) links the permit compliance defense only to claims asserting violation of the CWA's effluent limitation provisions. Common law actions (primarily nuisance) survive despite permit compliance, as do state law-based statutory actions that go beyond the CWA.

2. Regulating unlisted discharges. Is it clear that the nine discharged toxic substances that Kodak did not list in its permit application will later be subjected to regulation? Federal law requires that states taking primacy, such as New York in this case, can at any time terminate or modify the permit. CWA §402(b)(1)(C)(iii). More routinely, the revision could be accomplished as part of the five-year periodic renewal process contemplated by §402(b)(1)(B). Even after a state takes primacy, EPA, under §402(i), retains residual enforcement power. Having established that DEC or EPA can force a change in Kodak's discharges, the real question is whether DEC or EPA must act to do so. General administrative law doctrines give the agency a good deal of latitude in enforcement matters (see Chapter 6).

3. The effluent limitations — BAT and BPJ. In its ongoing implementation of the CWA, EPA has identified BAT for all 65 toxic pollutants on its priority list, although it has yet to promulgate those limits for all categories of dischargers. As to nonpriority toxic pollutants, regulation of their discharge is to be based on Best Professional Judgment (BPJ).[27]

---

27. BPJ is set on the same basis as BAT but is implemented in the case-by-case context of writing specific permits. In that context, it is easy to imagine that a state permit writer could more easily be persuaded to give greater consideration to the "economically achievable" strand of the BAT standard than might EPA when it establishes its categorical BAT standards. Thus BPJ may tend to demand less stringent controls than those that would obtain if the

A slightly more comforting view of events in *Atlantic States* can be gleaned from the fact that TBELs are applied to 25 substances, including BAT-level treatments for the priority toxic chemicals, and BPJ for a number of nonpriority toxics. According to experts in the field, the treatments required (whether based on BAT or BPJ) for the toxic chemicals expressly regulated by a complex permit, such as the Kodak permit, will be identical, in some cases, to the treatments that are appropriate for some of the additional chemicals also present in the discharge but not regulated by the permit. Put differently, chemicals listed in the permits sometimes serve as regulatory surrogates for other chemicals. The matter, however, requires careful case-by-case scrutiny. The toxic combinations may require additional treatments or, worse, present treatment antagonisms rather than treatment synergies.

4. What did the permit writers know, and when did they know it? The facts of the case are a bit hard to follow: The complaint alleged unpermitted discharge of 27 pollutants, but the motion for summary judgment limited itself to 16 substances that are all on the Emergency Planning and Community Right-to-Know Act (EPCRA) list of toxic substances. The court observes in one of the reproduced footnotes that 7 of the unlisted 16 substances were included by Kodak on its permit application documents or raised for discussion by DEC. As to those substances, the court is on firm ground in saying the agency knew of them and opted not to regulate them, thereby placing them behind the "permit shield." The remaining 9 substances, however, appeared only on the EPCRA Form R. That form is a routine annual report that is filed with a different department within the state agency. The fact that the Form Rs were filed with DEC is not, without more, a very solid basis for concluding that the permit writers took cognizance of what those forms disclosed.[28]

5. CWA federalism, devolution, stricter state standards, and citizen suits. In *Atlantic States* there is a transfer from federal to state primacy, exactly as envisioned by Congress. In portions of the case that were not excerpted here, the plaintiffs argued that linguistic nuances in the New York statutes establishing the SPDES program resulted in SPDES permits having a different impact than federal NPDES permits in regard to unlisted pollutants. States indeed can regulate more stringently than the "federal floor" set by the CWA. Section 510 of the CWA, entitled "State Authority," somewhat elliptically provides that:

> ... nothing in this chapter shall (1) preclude or deny the right of any State or political subdivision thereof or interstate agency to adopt or enforce (A) any standard or limitation respecting discharges of pollutants, or (B) any requirement respecting control or abatement of pollution; except if [the state regulation] is less stringent than [the federal regulation imposed by the CWA].

In *Atlantic States*, the court, in dicta, found that the New York SPDES system was not more stringent in limiting the permit shield defense than the NPDES system in this regard. The actual holding on this point is more technical but quite important. The court ruled that a CWA §505 citizen suit cannot be used to enforce claims that are based on those stricter state laws (if the state has indeed enacted stricter-than-federal regulation). This ruling is

---

substance were a priority pollutant regulated by EPA. One favorable aspect of BPJ-based permits is that the CWA's "anti-backsliding" provisions, §402(o), prohibit, with some exceptions, the relaxation of BPJ-based effluent limitations in future permits even if subsequently promulgated effluent limitation regulations might be more lenient.

28. At the end of that footnote, Judge Winter adds an even more enigmatic limitation on Atlantic States' ability to bring suit. He asserts that there is no standing to bring suit in regard to discharges of chemicals not revealed to the agency in any fashion unless Atlantic States can also "show violations of established regulatory levels." Recalling the way in which nonpriority toxic pollutants are regulated by the ad hoc generation of BPJ standards, there are no *established* standards for those chemicals. Their discharge would be insulated from attack in a citizen suit if the footnote is correct on this point.

significant because under the CWA, in §505(d), the court "may award costs of litigation (including reasonable attorney and expert witness fees) to any prevailing, or substantially prevailing party, whenever the court determines such award is appropriate." Such fee-shifting is not generally available under state law.

However, federal citizen suits to enforce more stringent state standards may not be completely foreclosed. The permit shield defense cannot be imposed to block a citizen suit to enforce against a violation of state water quality standards, even if the discharge permit does not include specific WQBELs, as long as the permit generally requires (as most do) that the discharge must be in compliance with applicable water quality standards. See *Northwest Envtl. Advocates*, above. (In addition, most discharge permits contain the language that "discharges of toxics in toxic amounts are prohibited.")

In addition, a large, multifaceted discharger like Kodak might be required to perform expensive and complex ecological monitoring, as in *NRDC v. Texaco Ref. & Mktg., Inc.*, 182 F.3d 904 (3d Cir. 1999) (district court did not abuse its discretion by ordering defendant to implement $500,000 monitoring plan, developed by a court-appointed expert, to monitor receiving waters in order to determine the impact of noncomplying discharges on an estuarine ecosystem).

6. Who should bear the burden of proof regarding toxicity? Toxicity screening data are unavailable for approximately 90% of the high-volume chemicals utilized by industries in the United States. As for known toxics, the EPCRA list of toxic substances includes nearly 700 substances, and the State of California has listed approximately 300 substances as toxic under its Safe Drinking Water and Toxic Enforcement Act, commonly known as Proposition 65 (discussed in Chapter 10). See Roe, Ready or Not: The Coming Wave of Toxic Chemicals, 29 Ecology L.Q. 623 (2002). Clearly, the CWA's priority pollutant list is profoundly incomplete with regard to identifying toxic parameters discharged into waterbodies. The *Atlantic States* opinion places the burden on state administrative agencies to establish which substances (other than priority pollutants), in which quantities, would constitute an excessive risk when discharged into surface waterbodies. Given the paucity of toxics testing data, the large number of substances that are generally considered to be environmental toxins, and the fiscal crises facing state agencies, perhaps industries such as Kodak should be obligated to demonstrate nontoxicity of nonpriority pollutants before discharging into waterbodies. A similar precautionary approach has been unsuccessfully attempted in the ToSCA (see Chapter 15).

D. WATER QUALITY-BASED PERMITTING AND MANAGEMENT OF NONPOINT SOURCE POLLUTION UNDER THE CWA

In the first two decades since its passage, implementation of the CWA was focused on the innovative and direct technology-based effluent limitations (TBELs). This approach proved highly effective at reducing pollution from point sources, especially when coupled with the CWA's monitoring, reporting, and citizen suit provisions. Since the 1990's, the next generation of CWA implementation has focused on water quality-based effluent limitations (WQBELs), and citizen suits have again played a leading role. This shift was due in part to the diminishing returns for enforcing TBELs, a consequence of the tremendous success of that program. But despite the success of TBELs, many of the nation's waters remain polluted. A major reason is pollution from nonpoint sources, such as agriculture and logging practices, which is not subject to NPDES permits. To address nonpoint pollution, enforcement efforts have relied on the CWA's water quality provisions, notably the "total maximum daily load" (TMDLs) program. WQBELs and the TMDL program have the advantage of addressing nonpoint source pollution, but enforcement is complicated and challenging. Professor Oliver A. Houck, in TMDLs: The Resurrection of Water Quality Standards-Based Regulation Under the Clean Water Act, 27 Envtl. L. Rep. 10329, 10330-10331 (1997), summarizes the history of WQBELs and their incorporation into the CWA:

> By 1972, with reports on deteriorating water quality from every quarter, the nation was ready for a new strategy of pollution control. There was a new ethical premise, that water should simply be clean. There was a new political view, that pollution was a national problem and required federal intervention. And there was a new mechanism, technology standards. Retained in the Act, however, were the vestiges of a water quality standards-based program, codified in §303. While the initial provisions of §303 amplified on the process of establishing state water quality standards, §303(d) added a prescription for using these standards to upgrade waters that remained polluted after the application of technology-based requirements. It has become a battleground.
>
> In brief, §303(d) requires three steps. The states will:
>
> 1. identify waters that are and will remain polluted after the application of technology standards;
> 2. prioritize these waters, taking into account the severity of their pollution; and
> 3. establish "total maximum daily loads" (TMDLs) for these waters at levels necessary to meet applicable water quality standards, accounting for seasonal variations and with a margin of safety to reflect lack of certainty about discharges and water quality.
>
> States are to submit their inventories and TMDLs to EPA for approval. If EPA does not approve, the Agency is to promulgate them itself for incorporation into state planning. Under §303(e), states are to develop plans for all waters that include, inter alia, (1) discharge limitations at least as stringent as the requirements of its water quality standards and (2) TMDLs.
>
> The TMDL process represents, in the short life of environmental law, an ancient approach to pollution control. . . . From the very first hint of federal involvement in water pollution control 50 years ago, states and pollution dischargers have fought a running battle to defend and, where lost, return to the local primacy and utilitarianism of regulation by water quality standards. Whatever else might be said about the ineffectiveness and difficulties of this regulation in practice, this has been their Camelot, the land from which we were unceremoniously wrenched and to which we should return. To their dismay, we have.

Pronsolino v. Nastri

291 F.3d 1123 (9th Cir. 2002)

BERZON, J. The United States EPA required California to identify the Garcia River as a water body with insufficient pollution controls and, as required for waters so identified, to set so-called "total maximum daily loads" ("TMDL") — the significance of which we explain later — for pollution entering the river. Appellants challenge the EPA's authority under CWA §303(d), 33 U.S.C. §1313(d), to apply the pertinent identification and TMDL requirements to the Garcia River. The district court rejected this challenge, and we do as well.

CWA §303(d) requires the states to identify and compile a list of waters for which certain "effluent limitations" "are not stringent enough" to implement the applicable water quality standards for such waters. §303(d)(1)(A). Effluent limitations pertain only to point sources of pollution; point sources of pollution are those from a discrete conveyance, such as a pipe or tunnel. Nonpoint sources of pollution are non-discrete sources; sediment run-off

D. Water Quality-Based Permitting and Management of Nonpoint Source

from timber harvesting, for example, derives from a nonpoint source. The Garcia River is polluted only by nonpoint sources. Therefore, neither the effluent limitations referenced in §303(d) nor any other effluent limitations apply to the pollutants entering the Garcia River.

The precise statutory question before us is whether the phrase "are not stringent enough" triggers the identification requirement both for waters as to which effluent limitations apply but do not suffice to attain water quality standards and for waters as to which effluent limitations do not apply at all to the pollution sources impairing the water. We answer this question in the affirmative, a conclusion which triggers the application of the statutory TMDL requirement to waters such as the Garcia River.

STATUTORY BACKGROUND. . . . The Major Goals and Concepts of the CWA. Congress enacted the CWA in 1972, amending earlier federal water pollution laws that had proven ineffective. Prior to 1972, federal water pollution laws relied on water quality standards specifying the acceptable levels of pollution in a State's interstate navigable waters as the primary mechanism for the control of water pollution. The pre-1972 laws did not, however, provide concrete direction concerning how those standards were to be met in the foreseeable future.

In enacting sweeping revisions to the nation's water pollution laws in 1972, Congress began from the premise that the focus on the tolerable effects rather than the preventable causes of pollution constituted a major shortcoming in the pre 1972 laws. The 1972 Act therefore sought to target primarily the preventable causes of pollution, by emphasizing the use of technological controls.

At the same time, Congress decidedly did *not* in 1972 give up on the broader goal of attaining acceptable water quality. CWA §101(a), 33 U.S.C. §1251(a). Rather, the new statute recognized that even with the application of the mandated technological controls on point source discharges, water bodies still might not meet state-set water quality standards. The 1972 statute therefore put in place mechanisms other than direct federal regulation of point sources, designed to "restore and maintain the chemical, physical, and biological integrity of the Nation's waters." §101(a).

In so doing, the CWA uses distinctly different methods to control pollution released from point sources and that aretraceable to nonpoint sources. The Act directly mandates technological controls to limit the pollution point sources may discharge into a body of water. On the other hand, the Act provides no direct mechanism to control nonpoint source pollution but rather uses the threat and promise of federal grants to the states to accomplish this task, thereby "recogniz[ing], preserv[ing], and protect[ing] the primary responsibilities and rights of States to prevent, reduce, and eliminate pollution, [and] to plan the development and use . . . of land and water resources. . . ." §101(b).

THE STRUCTURE OF CWA §303. Section 303 is central to the Act's carrot-and-stick approach to attaining acceptable water quality without direct federal regulation of nonpoint sources of pollution. Entitled "Water Quality Standards and Implementation Plans," the provision begins by spelling out the statutory requirements for water quality standards: "Water quality standards" specify a water body's "designated uses" and "water quality criteria," taking into account the water's "use and value for public water supplies, propagation of fish and wildlife, recreational purposes, and agricultural, industrial, and other purposes. . . ." §303(c)(2). The states are required to set water quality standards for *all* waters within their boundaries regardless of the sources of the pollution entering the waters. If a state does not set water quality standards, or if the EPA determines that the state's standards do not meet the requirements of the Act, the EPA promulgates standards for the state. §§303(b), (c)(3)-(4)

Section 303(d)(1)(A) requires each state to identify as "areas with insufficient controls" "those waters within its boundaries for which the effluent limitations required by section [301(b)(1), mandating technology-based standards] are not stringent enough to implement any water quality standard applicable to such waters." *Id.* The CWA defines "effluent limitations" as restrictions on pollutants "discharged from point sources." CWA §502(11), 33 U.S.C. §1362(11). . . .

For waters identified pursuant to §303(d)(1)(A) (the "§303(d)(1) list"), the states must establish the "total maximum daily load" ("TMDL") for pollutants identified by the EPA as suitable for TMDL calculation.[29] §303(d)(1)(C). A TMDL defines the specified maximum amount of a pollutant which can be discharged or 'loaded' into the waters at issue from all combined sources."[30] The TMDL "shall be established at a level necessary to implement the applicable water quality standards. . . ." §303(d)(1)(C).

Section 303(d)(2), in turn, requires each state to submit its §303(d)(1) list and TMDLs to the EPA for its approval or disapproval. If the EPA approves the list and TMDLs, the state must incorporate the list and TMDLs into its "continuing planning process," the requirements for which are set forth in §303(e). §303(d)(2). If the EPA disapproves either the §303(d)(1) list or any TMDLs, the EPA must itself put together the missing document or documents. *Id.* The state then incorporates any EPA-set list or TMDL into the state's continuing planning process. *Id.*

The EPA in regulations has made more concrete the statutory requirements. Those regulations, in summary, define "water quality limited segment[s]"—those waters that must be included on the §303(d)(1) list—as "[a]ny segment where it is known that water quality does not meet applicable water quality standards, and/or is not expected to meet applicable water quality standards, even after the application of the technology-based effluent limitations required by sections 301(b). . . ." 40 C.F.R. §130.2(j) (2000). The regulations then divide TMDLs into two types: "load allocations," ["LA"] for nonpoint source pollution, and "wasteload allocations," ["WLA"] for point source pollution. §130.2(g)-(i). Under the regulations, states must identify those waters on the §303(d)(1) lists as "still requiring TMDLs" if any required effluent limitation or other pollution control requirement (including those for nonpoint source pollution) will not bring the water into compliance with water quality standards. §130.7(b) (2000).

The final pertinent section of §303, §303(e), requiring each state to have a "continuing planning process," gives some operational force to the prior information-gathering provisions. The EPA may approve a state's continuing planning process only if it "will result in plans for all navigable waters within such State" that include, inter alia, effluent limitations, TMDLs, areawide waste management plans for nonpoint sources of pollution, and plans for "adequate implementation, including schedules of compliance, for revised or new water quality standards." §303(e)(3).

The upshot of this intricate scheme is that the CWA leaves to the states the responsibility of developing plans to achieve water quality standards if the statutorily-mandated point source controls will not alone suffice, while providing federal funding to aid in the implementation of the state plans. As such, TMDLs serve as a link in an implementation chain

---

29. The EPA has identified all pollutants, under proper technical conditions, as suitable for TMDL calculation. 43 Fed. Reg. 60662 (Dec. 28, 1978).

30. The term "loading" refers to the addition of pollution into a body of water from either point or nonpoint sources. 40 C.F.R. §130.2(e) (2000).

D. Water Quality-Based Permitting and Management of Nonpoint Source

that includes federally-regulated point source controls, state or local plans for point and nonpoint source pollution reduction, and assessment of the impact of such measures on water quality, all to the end of attaining water quality goals for the nation's waters.

FACTUAL AND PROCEDURAL BACKGROUND—THE GARCIA RIVER TMDL. In 1992, California submitted to the EPA a list of waters pursuant to §303(d)(1)(A). Pursuant to §303(d)(2), the EPA disapproved California's 1992 list because it omitted seventeen water segments that did not meet the water quality standards set by California for those segments. Sixteen of the seventeen water segments, including the Garcia River, were impaired only by nonpoint sources of pollution. After California rejected an opportunity to amend its §303(d)(1) list to include the seventeen sub-standard segments, the EPA, again acting pursuant to §303(d)(2), established a new §303(d)(1) list for California, including those segments on it. California retained the seventeen segments on its 1994, 1996, and 1998 §303(d)(1) lists.

California did not, however, establish TMDLs for the segments added by the EPA. Environmental and fishermen's groups sued the EPA in 1995 to require the EPA to establish TMDLs for the seventeen segments, and in a March 1997 consent decree the EPA agreed to do so. According to the terms of the consent decree, the EPA set March 18, 1998, as the deadline for the establishment of a TMDL for the Garcia River. When California missed the deadline despite having initiated public comment on a draft TMDL and having prepared a draft implementation plan, the EPA established a TMDL for the Garcia River. The EPAs TMDL differed only slightly from the states draft TMDL.

The Garcia River TMDL for sediment is 552 tons per square mile per year,[31] a 60% reduction from historical loadings. The TMDL allocates portions of the total yearly load among the following categories of nonpoint source pollution: (a) "mass wasting" associated with roads; (b) "mass wasting" associated with timber-harvesting; (c) erosion related to road surfaces; and (d) erosion related to road and skid trail crossings.

The Appellants. In 1960, appellants Betty and Guido Pronsolino purchased approximately 800 acres of heavily logged timber land in the Garcia River watershed. In 1998, after re-growth of the forest, the Pronsolinos applied for a harvesting permit from the California Department of Forestry ("Forestry").

In order to comply with the Garcia River TMDL, Forestry and/or the state's Regional Water Quality Control Board required, among other things, that the Pronsolinos' harvesting permit provide for mitigation of 90% of controllable road-related sediment run-off and contain prohibitions on removing certain trees and on harvesting from mid-October until May 1. The Pronsolinos' forester estimates that the large tree restriction will cost the Pronsolinos $750,000.

---

31. TMDLs based on annual limits, such as the Garcia River TMDL, may not be permissible according to a subsequent court decision. The U.S. Court of Appeals for the District of Columbia Circuit has held that the word "daily," in the CWA §303(d) requirement regarding TMDLs for impaired waters, must be strictly interpreted to mandate that TMDLs contain actual, explicit daily loadings for point sources. *Friends of the Earth v. EPA*, 446 F.3d 140 (D.C. Cir. 2006). Thus, according to this D.C. Circuit court decision, seasonal and annual WLAs would be illegal unless they are accompanied by maximum daily loads. *Friends of the Earth v. EPA* is in direct conflict with a decision by the Second Circuit Court of Appeals (*Natural Resources Defense Council v. Muszynski*, 268 F.3d 91 (2d. Cir. 2001)) that interpreted "daily" broadly in approving seasonal WLAs for total phosphorus in the New York City reservoir system. *Muszynski* reflects the practice of many states that employ seasonal and annual water quality criteria and WLAs for pollutants, such as phosphorus, that can be expressed more effectively through long-term averaging than by daily loadings. [EDS.]

Larry Mailliard, a member of the Mendocino County Farm Bureau, submitted a draft harvesting permit on February 4, 1998, for a portion of his property in the Garcia River watershed. Forestry granted a final version of the permit after incorporation of a 60.3% reduction of sediment loading, a requirement included to comply with the Garcia River TMDL. Mr. Mailliard's forester estimates that the additional restrictions imposed to comply with the Garcia River TMDL will cost Mr. Mailliard $10,602,000.

Bill Barr, another member of the Mendocino County Farm Bureau, also applied for a harvesting permit in 1998 for his property located within the Garcia River watershed. Forestry granted the permit after incorporation of restrictions similar to those included in the Pronsolinos' permit. A forester states that these additional restrictions, included to comply with the TMDL, will cost Mr. Barr at least $962,000.

PROCEEDINGS BELOW. On August 12, 1999, the Pronsolinos, the Mendocino County Farm Bureau, the California Farm Bureau Federation, and the American Farm Bureau Federation brought this action pursuant to the Administrative Procedure Act, 5 U.S.C. §§702, 704, in the District Court for the Northern District of California against the EPA and two of its administrators. The Pronsolinos challenged the EPA's authority to impose TMDLs on rivers polluted only by nonpoint sources of pollution and sought a determination of whether the Act authorized the Garcia River TMDL. [Following cross-motions for summary judgment, the district court entered final judgment in favor of EPA, and the Pronsolinos appealed].

ANALYSIS-DEFERENCE TO THE EPA. [The court first held that it owed EPA deference in its regulations and decisions interpreting and applying CWA §303 to apply to both point and nonpoint sources of water pollution pursuant to *Chevron v. Natural Resources Defense Council*.] The EPA regulations pertinent to §303(d)(1) list[] and TMDLs focus on the attainment of water quality standards, whatever the source of any pollution. For instance, the EPA's regulations define TMDLs as the "sum of the individual WLAs for point sources and LAs for nonpoint sources and natural background." 40 C.F.R. §130.2(i). Section 130.2 also defines a "wasteload allocation" as the "portion of a receiving water's loading capacity that is allocated to one of its existing or future point sources of pollution,"§130.2(h), and a "load allocation" as the "portion of a receiving water's loading capacity that is attributed either to one of its existing or future nonpoint sources of pollution or to natural background sources,"§130.2(g). The load allocation regulation also advises that, if possible, "natural and nonpoint source loads should be distinguished." *Id.* No reason appears why, under this TMDL definition, the amount of either point source loads or nonpoint source loads cannot be zero. If the wasteload allocation is zero, then the TMDL would cover only the nonpoint sources and natural background sources. So read, the regulation provides that a TMDL can apply where there is no wasteload allocation for point source pollution.

Also consistent with application of the §303(d)(1) listing and TMDL requirements to waters impaired only by nonpoint sources is the regulation addressing water quality standards. Section 130.3 explains that "[s]uch standards serve the dual purposes of establishing the water quality goals for a specific water body and serving as the regulatory basis for establishment of water quality-based treatment controls and strategies beyond the technology-based level of treatment required. . . ." 40 C.F.R. §130.3. One purpose of water quality standards therefore—and not surprisingly—is to provide federally-approved goals to be achieved *both* by state controls and by federal strategies *other* than point-source technology-based limitations. This purpose pertains to waters impaired by both point and nonpoint source pollution. The regulations addressing states' water quality management plans, intended to attain the promulgated water quality standards, confirm this understanding. Such plans must include, among other things, TMDLs, effluent limitations, and "*nonpoint source management and control.*" 40 C.F.R. §130.6 (emphasis added).

In short, the EPA's regulations concerning §303(d)(1) lists and TMDLs apply whether a water body receives pollution from point sources only, nonpoint sources only, or a combination of the two.

The Pronsolinos nevertheless contend that the EPA's current interpretation is an invention of the early 1990s. They point out that until that time the EPA did not actively police the requirement that states include on their §303(d)(1) lists waters polluted only by nonpoint source pollution. While that is true, that agency stance reflected a more general regulatory failure to enforce the §303(d) requirements, not a failure with regard only to waters impaired by nonpoint sources. Until the early 1990s, the EPA focused its attention almost entirely on the new point source technological controls, to the exclusion of §303(d) and the TMDL program. . . .

Plain Meaning and Structural Issues—The Competing Interpretations. Section 303(d)(1)(A) requires listing and calculation of TMDLs for "those waters within [the state's] boundaries for which the effluent limitations required by [§301(b)(1)(A)] and [§301(b)(1)(B)] of this title *are not stringent enough to implement any water quality standard* applicable to such waters." §303(d) (emphasis added). The precise statutory question before us is whether, as the Pronsolinos maintain, the term "not stringent enough to implement . . . water quality standard[s]" as used in §303(d)(1)(A) must be interpreted to mean *both* that application of effluent limitations will not achieve water quality standards *and* that the waters at issue are subject to effluent limitations. As only waters with point source pollution are subject to effluent limitations, such an interpretation would exclude from the §303(d)(1) listing and TMDL requirements waters impaired only by nonpoint sources of pollution.

The EPA, as noted, interprets "not stringent enough to implement . . . water quality standard[s]" to mean "not adequate" or "not sufficient . . . to implement any water quality standard," and does not read the statute as implicitly containing a limitation to waters initially covered by effluent limitations. According to the EPA, if the use of effluent limitations will not implement applicable water quality standards, the water falls within §303(d)(1)(A) regardless of whether it is point or nonpoint sources, or a combination of the two, that continue to pollute the water.

Whether or not the appellants' suggested interpretation is entirely implausible, it is at least considerably weaker than the EPA's competing construction. The Pronsolinos' version necessarily relies upon: (1) understanding "stringent enough" to mean "strict enough" rather than "thorough going enough" or "adequate" or "sufficient"; and (2) reading the phrase "not stringent enough" in isolation, rather than with reference to the stated goal of implementing "any water quality standard applicable to such waters." Where the answer to the question "not stringent enough for what?" is "to implement any [applicable] water quality standard," the meaning of "stringent" should be determined by looking forward to the broad goal to be attained, not backwards at the inadequate effluent limitations. One might comment, for example, about a teacher that her standards requiring good spelling were not stringent enough to assure good writing, as her students still used bad grammar and poor logic. Based on the language of the contested phrase alone, then, the more sensible conclusion is that the §303(d)(1) list must contain any waters for which the particular effluent limitations will not be adequate to attain the statute's water quality goals.

Placing the phrase in its statutory context supports this conclusion. Section 303(d) begins with the requirement that each state "identify those waters within its boundaries. . . ." §303(d)(1)(A). So the statute's starting point for the listing project is a compilation of each and every navigable water within the state. Then, only those waters that will attain water quality standards after application of the new point source technology are excluded from the §303(d)(1) list, leaving all those waters for which that technology will not "implement any water quality standard applicable to such waters." §303(d)(1)(A). The alternative construction, in contrast, would begin with a subset of all the state's waterways, those that have point sources subject to effluent limitations, and would result in a list containing only a subset of that subset-those waters as to which the applicable effluent limitations are not adequate to attain water quality standards.

The Pronsolinos' contention to the contrary notwithstanding, no such odd reading of the statute is necessary in order to give meaning to the phrase "for which the effluent limitations required by [§301(b)(1)] are not stringent enough." The EPA interprets §303(d)(1)(A) to require the identification of any waters not meeting water quality standards only if specified effluent limitations would not achieve those standards. 40 C.F.R. §130.2(j). If the pertinent effluent limitations would, if implemented, achieve the water quality standards but are not in place yet, there need be no listing and no TMDL calculation. *Id.*

So construed, the meaning of the statute is different than it would be were the language recast to state only that "Each State shall identify those waters within its boundaries . . . [not meeting] any water quality standard applicable to such waters." Under the EPA's construction, the reference to effluent limitations reflects Congress' intent that the EPA focus initially on implementing effluent limitations and only later avert its attention to water quality standards. *See e.g.,* 1 *Legislative History* 171 ("The Administrator should assign secondary priority to [§303] to the extent limited manpower and funding may require a choice between a water quality standards process and early and effective implementation of the effluent limitation-permit program." (statement of Sen. Muskie, principal author of the CWA and the Chair of the Senate's Public Works Committee)).

Nothing in §303(d)(1)(A) distinguishes the treatment of point sources and nonpoint sources as such; the only reference is to the "effluent limitations required by" §301(b)(1). So if the effluent limitations required by §301(b)(1) are "as a matter of law" "not stringent enough" to achieve the applicable water quality standards for waters impaired by point sources not subject to those requirements, then they are also "not stringent enough" to achieve applicable water quality standards for other waters not subject to those requirements, in this instance because they are impacted only by nonpoint sources.

The Pronsolinos' objection to this view of §303(d) . . . is, in essence, that the CWA as a whole distinguishes between the regulatory schemes applicable to point and non-point sources, so we must assume such a distinction in applying §§303(d)(1)(A) and (C). We would hesitate in any case to read into a discrete statutory provision something that is not there because it is contained elsewhere in the statute. But here, the premise is wrong: There is no such general division throughout the CWA.

Point sources are treated differently from nonpoint sources for many purposes under the statute, but not all. In particular, there is no such distinction with regard to the basic purpose for which the §303(d) list and TMDLs are compiled, the eventual attainment of state-defined water quality standards. Water quality standards reflect a state's designated *uses* for a water body and do not depend in any way upon the source of pollution. *See* §303(a)-(c).

Additionally, §303(d) follows the subsections setting forth the requirements for water quality standards, §303(a)-(c)-which, as noted above, apply without regard to the source of pollution-and precedes the "continuing planning process" subsection, §303(e), which applies broadly as well. Thus, §303(d) is structurally part of a set of provisions governing an interrelated goal-setting, information-gathering, and planning process that, unlike many other aspects of the CWA, applies without regard to the source of pollution. True, there are,

D. Water Quality-Based Permitting and Management of Nonpoint Source

as the Pronsolinos point out, two sections of the statute as amended, §208 and §319, that set requirements exclusively for nonpoint sources of pollution. But the structural inference we are asked to draw from those specialized sections-that no *other* provisions of the Act set requirements for waters polluted by nonpoint sources-simply does not follow. Absent some irreconcilable contradiction between the requirements contained in §§208 and 319, on the one hand, and the listing and TMDL requirements of §303(d), on the other, both apply.

There is no such contradiction. Section 208 provides for federal grants to encourage the development of state "areawide waste treatment management plans" for areas with substantial water quality problems, §208(a), (f), and requires that those plans include a process for identifying and controlling nonpoint source pollution "to the extent feasible." §208(b)(2)(F). Section 319, added to the CWA in 1987, directs states to adopt "nonpoint source management programs"; provides grants for nonpoint source pollution reduction; and requires states to submit a report to the EPA that "identifies those navigable waters within the State which, without additional action to control nonpoint sources of pollution, cannot reasonably be expected to attain or maintain applicable water quality standards or the goals and requirements of this chapter." §319(a)(1)(A). This report must also describe state programs for reducing nonpoint source pollution and the process "to reduce, to the maximum extent practicable, the level of pollution" resulting from particular categories of nonpoint source pollution. §319(a)(1)(C), (D).

The CWA is replete with multiple listing and planning requirements applicable to the same waterways (quite confusingly so, indeed), so no inference can be drawn from the overlap alone. Nor are we willing to draw the more discrete inference that the §303(d) listing and TMDL requirements cannot apply to nonpoint source pollutants because the planning requirements imposed by §208 and §319 are qualified ones—"to the extent feasible" and "to the maximum extent practicable"—while the §303(d) requirements are unbending.

Essentially, §319 encourages the states to institute an approach to the elimination of nonpoint source pollution similar to the federally-mandated effluent controls contained in the CWA, while §303 encompasses a water quality based approach applicable to all sources of water pollution. As various sections of the Act encourage different, and complementary, state schemes for cleaning up nonpoint source pollution in the nation's waterways, there is no basis for reading any of those sections—including §303(d)—out of the statute.

There is one final aspect of the Act's structure that bears consideration because it supports the EPA's interpretation of §303(d): The list required by §303(d)(1)(A) requires that waters be listed if they are impaired by a combination of point sources and nonpoint sources; the language admits of no other reading. Section 303(d)(1)(C), in turn, directs that TMDLs "shall be established at a level necessary *to implement* the applicable water quality standards...." *Id.* (emphasis added). So, at least in blended waters, TMDLs must be calculated with regard to nonpoint sources of pollution; otherwise, it would be impossible "to implement the applicable water quality standards," which do not differentiate sources of pollution.

Nothing in the statutory structure—or purpose—suggests that Congress meant to distinguish, as to §303(d)(1) lists and TMDLs, between waters with one insignificant point source and substantial nonpoint source pollution and waters with only nonpoint source pollution. Such a distinction would, for no apparent reason, require the states or the EPA to monitor waters to determine whether a point source had been added or removed, and to adjust the §303(d)(1) list and establish TMDLs accordingly. There is no statutory basis for concluding that Congress intended such an irrational regime.

Looking at the statute as a whole, we conclude that the EPA's interpretation of §303(d) is not only entirely reasonable but considerably more convincing than the one offered by the plaintiffs in this case.

FEDERALISM CONCERNS. The Pronsolinos finally contend that, by establishing TMDLs for waters impaired only by nonpoint source pollution, the EPA has upset the balance of federal-state control established in the CWA by intruding into the states' traditional control over land use. That is not the case.

The Garcia River TMDL identifies the maximum load of pollutants that can enter the Garcia River from certain broad categories of nonpoint sources if the river is to attain water quality standards. It does not specify the load of pollutants that may be received from particular parcels of land or describe what measures the state should take to implement the TMDL. Instead, the TMDL expressly recognizes that "implementation and monitoring" "are state responsibilities" and notes that, for this reason, the EPA did not include implementation or monitoring plans within the TMDL.

Moreover, §303(e) requires—separately from the §303(d)(1) listing and TMDL requirements—that each state include in its continuing planning process "adequate implementation, including schedules of compliance, for revised or new water quality standards . . . for all navigable waters within such State." §303(e)(3). The Garcia River TMDL thus serves as an informational tool for the creation of the state's implementation plan, independently-and explicitly-required by Congress.

California chose both *if* and *how* it would implement the Garcia River TMDL. States must implement TMDLs only to the extent that they seek to avoid losing federal grant money; there is no pertinent statutory provision otherwise requiring implementation of §303 plans or providing for their enforcement. *See* CWA §309, 33 U.S.C. §1319; CWA §505, 33 U.S.C. §1365[32]

Finally, it is worth noting that the arguments that the Pronsolinos raise here would apply equally to nonpoint source pollution controls for blended waters. Yet, as discussed above, Congress definitely required that the states or the EPA establish TMDLs for all pollutants in waters on §303(d)(1) lists, including blended waters.

We conclude that the Pronsolinos' federalism basis for reading §303 against its own words and structure is unfounded.

CONCLUSION. For all the reasons we have surveyed, the CWA is best read to include in the §303(d)(1) listing and TMDLs requirements waters impaired only by nonpoint sources of pollution. Moreover, to the extent the statute is ambiguous—which is not very much—the substantial deference we owe the EPA's interpretation . . . requires that we uphold the agency's more than reasonable interpretation. We therefore hold that the EPA did not exceed its statutory authority in identifying the Garcia River pursuant to §303(d)(1)(A) and establishing the Garcia River TMDL, even though the river is polluted only by nonpoint sources of pollution.

---

32. The court refers here to Houck, The Clean Water Act TMDL Program at 62 for a description of the carrot and the stick: "Within the statutory scheme §319 is the carrot, funding state programs for nonpoint source abatement statewide, for all waters whether they are currently above standard or below. In keeping with its broad sweep, §319's provisions are voluntary. States may choose to participate or not. . . . Section 303(d), on the other hand, addresses a narrower and more nasty job: the chronically polluted waters of the United States. For this problem zone, enter a stick: quantified pollution load allocations. The nature of the allocations and of the implementing controls remains up to the states, but states do have to come up with them."

D. Water Quality-Based Permitting and Management of Nonpoint Source

COMMENTARY & QUESTIONS

1. A "safety net" that is now needed. The court in *Pronsolino* cites legislative history to support the rationality of the EPA's initial focus on TBELs after passage of the CWA, and relatively recent shift in focus to WQBELs. Professor Houck explains the EPA's §303(d) "avoidance years" in a slightly different way:

> Following the passage of the [CWA in] 1972, EPA was fully occupied, indeed overwhelmed, in promulgating technology standards for point sources . . . and defending them in court. The Agency had little inclination, and indeed saw little reason, to implement the "safety net" features of §303(d) before the technology requirements were in place. After all, water quality upgrading was only required when polluted waters could not be brought up to standard through best available technology requirements. And these requirements were many years away. Houck, TMDLs, Are We There Yet?: The Long Road Toward Water Quality-Based Regulation Under the Clean Water Act, 27 Envtl. L. Rep. 10391, 10392 (1997).

2. Citizen suits and the rediscovery of WQBELs. As with many other federal environmental protections, citizen suits were the catalyst for implementation of WQBELs. Professor Houck summarizes the extent and scope of these suits:

> Starting in the early 1990s, a first wave of lawsuits established that ignoring §303 was no longer possible and that continued state inaction constituted action, triggering EPA's duty to respond. [C]itizen suits . . . led to [over a dozen] consent decrees against EPA and the states in which those suits were filed. . . . Overall, litigation has challenged compliance in more than half the states of the country, and yet more is brewing. The issues in these cases have tracked the literal requirements of the statute, challenging (1) the failure to list state waters, then (2) the adequacy of these lists, and then (3) the failure to prepare TMDLs, leading to schedules for their preparation ranging from 12 years to as few as 5. Houck, TMDLs III: A New Framework for the Clean Water Act's Ambient Standards Program, 28 Envtl. L. Rep. 10415, 10416-10417 (1998).

3. The EPA shifts its focus to TMDLs. Prompted by numerous citizen suits, EPA in 1997 appeared ready to jump on the TMDL bandwagon. In an internal memorandum, Robert Perciasepe, the EPA's Assistant Administrator for Water, declared:

> Almost 25 years after the passage of the [CWA], the national water program is at a defining moment. We-meaning each of you, each of our State, local, and Tribal partners, and all of us in the Office of Water-are making the transition from a clean water program based primarily on technology-based controls to water quality-based controls implemented on a watershed basis. . . . The [TMDL] program is crucial to success because it brings rigor, accountability, and statutory authority to the process. These are the reasons the Administrator and I so strongly support the TMDL program in States, Tribes, and [EPA] Regions. New Policies for Establishing and Implementing Total Maximum Daily Loads (TMDLs), Aug. 8, 1997, http://www.epa.gov/owowwtrl/watershed/ratepace.html.

4. Two steps forward, one step back. Industry, municipal systems, and nonpoint sources of pollution such as agriculture and logging did not wait long to counterattack the new §303(d) and TMDL offensive. Professor Houck continues the saga:

> The first counterattack has come on the required biennial submissions of polluted waters under §303(d). Opposing listings as based on inadequate science ("drive-by listings," in the words of one agriculture industry attorney—a characterization that in some cases may not be far from the truth), farm and other nonpoint interests have persuaded states to reduce their submissions on impaired waters to the absolutely proven, with significant results. Incongruous as it may seem in the face of new EPA listing criteria designed to be all-inclusive, to err on the side of listing, and to facilitate the use of all relevant data, many states have actually cut their

§303(d) lists in half since 1996, relegating hundreds of waters to such categories as "further study," "insufficient information," and only "moderately impaired." [F]or years, indeed decades, the states and nonpoint industries were content with submissions that, now that they are likely to trigger compliance requirements, will be put to the bitter proof.

This said, identifying polluted waters is, from the point of view of the science involved, the easy step. The next is to identify the causes of impairment and to allocate their loads. Here is where lines get drawn deep in the sand, and among the first to draw them are the municipal sewer systems which have the not-unrealistic fear that—given the states' historic reluctance to impose serious abatement measures on nonpoint polluters—municipal systems are likely to take the hit. This anxiety has produced a remarkable document from the Association of Metropolitan Sewerage Agencies (AMSA), a self-styled "survival guide" for wastewater agencies entitled Evaluating TMDLs: Protecting the Rights of POTWs. It is a guide with a purpose; as the Executive Director of AMSA explains, "We're developing guidelines to lead our members through the TMDL process and to show them when they can challenge the state in court." Houck, TMDLs IV: The Final Frontier, 29 Envtl. L. Rep. 10469, 10476-77 (1999).

5. Still a long way to go. According to a GAO report, the vast majority of the nation's waters remain unmonitored and unassessed. Only 40% of lakes, ponds, and reservoirs and 19% of rivers and streams have been assessed to determine compliance with water quality standards, and many of these assessments were prepared without actual monitoring. Further, only 3 of 50 states reported to the GAO that they have sufficient data to develop nonpoint source TMDLs. U.S. GAO, Key EPA and State Decisions Limited by Inconsistent and Incomplete Data (2000). What incentives do states have to dedicate their limited resources to assessing waterways and developing TMDLs?

6. TMDLs and point sources. While TMDLs offer a mechanism to begin to address nonpoint sources, they can really put the screws to potential point sources subject to a NPDES permit. EPA regulations prohibit issuance of a NPDES (or SPDES) permit "to a new source or a new discharger, if the discharge from its construction or operation will cause or contribute to the violation of water quality standards." 40 C.F.R. §122.4(i). If a TMDL is in place, the permit applicant must demonstrate that (1) there are "sufficient remaining pollutant load allocations to allow for the discharge" under the TMDL, and (2) "the existing dischargers into the TMDL segment are subject to compliance schedules designed to bring the segment into compliance with applicable water quality standards." Id. For many impaired waters with a fully-allocated TMDL, this means no new NPDES permits can be issued. Does this regulation provide leverage to effectively implement a TMDL to "free-up" room for new sources of pollution? Or, does this regulation just steer new dischargers to high quality waters that are not impaired?

CONVERGING REGULATORY TECHNIQUES: THE CLEAN WATER ACT AND THE CLEAN AIR ACT

There are many variations and differences, but conceptually the Clean Water Act and Clean Air Act both rely on the two-pronged strategy of harm-based ambient standards and technology-based facility standards. Consider the parallels in the mechanisms you have now studied:
- harm-based ambient standards for water pollution under the CWA are called WQBELs and are implemented locally through TMDLs;
- harm-based ambient standards for air pollution under the CAA are called NAAQS and are implemented locally through SIPs;
- technology-based facility standards for water pollution under the CWA are called TBELs and are implemented locally through NPDES permits;
- technology-based facility standards for air pollution under the CAA are called NSPSs and are implemented locally through PSD permits.

7. Buying their way in. TMDLs essentially cap the quantity of pollution that can enter a waterway, although the cap may only be enforceable against point sources subject to NPDES permits. Where there is a cap, there is an incentive to trade. The EPA is advancing this approach through its Water Quality Trading Policy, discussed in Chapter 14.

8. Lessons from the CAA. The CWA's WQBELs and TMDL program is fundamentally similar to the CAA's NAAQS and SIP process. What lessons can be drawn from implementation of NAAQS and SIPs and applied to WQBELs and TMDLs?

9. Interstate water pollution. Interstate water pollution can be severe, especially in the Mississippi River basin. More than 40% of the phosphorous present in the waterbodies of 16 states in the Mississippi River basin originates in other states. Section 402(d) of the CWA deals with interstate water pollution in the context of issuing discharge permits. In effect, EPA acts as an arbitrator of interstate disputes. This process was described by the U.S. Supreme Court in *International Paper Co. v. Ouellette*, 479 U.S. 481, 490-491 (1987):

> While source States have a strong voice in regulating their own pollution, the CWA contemplates a much lesser role for States that share an interstate waterway with the source (the affected States). Even though it may be harmed by the discharges, an affected State only has an advisory role in regulating pollution that originates beyond its borders. Before a federal permit may be issued, each affected State is given notice and the opportunity to object to the proposed standards at a public hearing. An affected State has similar rights to be consulted before the source State issues its own permit; the source State must send notification, and must consider the objections and recommendations submitted by other States before taking action. Significantly, however, an affected State does not have the authority to block the issuance of the permit if it is dissatisfied with the proposed standards. An affected State's only recourse is to apply to the EPA Administrator, who then has the discretion to disapprove the permit if he concludes that the discharges will have an undue impact on interstate waters.... Thus the Act makes it clear that affected States occupy a subordinate position to source States in the federal regulatory program.

When an impasse develops between EPA and a source state with an approved permit program, EPA can retake jurisdiction and issue its own permit. Affected states are given additional power over discharges in source states by an EPA regulation that prohibits the issuance of a discharge permit "when the imposition of conditions cannot ensure compliance with the applicable water quality standards [including antidegradation policies] of all affected states." 40 C.F.R. §122.4(d). In *Arkansas v. Oklahoma*, 503 U.S. 91 (1992), the Supreme Court upheld this regulation on the ground that federally approved WQSs become federal law that preempts conflicting state regulations. Referring to CWA §402(d), the Court stated that "Limits on an affected State's direct participation in permitting decisions, however, do not in any way constrain the EPA's authority to require a point source to comply with downstream water quality standards." 503 U.S. at 106. Since Native American tribes are treated as states by the CWA, if a tribe has been delegated primacy and had established WQSs that have received EPA approval, upstream dischargers must comply with the tribal standards. *Albuquerque v. EPA*, 97 F.3d 415 (10th Cir. 1996), cert. denied, 522 U.S. 965 (1997). But EPA can arbitrate a dispute between a state and Native American tribe with EPA retaining the ultimate authority to approve permits and WQSs, *Wisconsin v. EPA*, 266 F.3d 741 (7th Cir. 2001), cert. denied, 535 U.S. 1121 (2002). A second attempt to curtail interstate conflicts over water pollution is CWA §118, added in 1987, which requires EPA to promulgate uniform Water Quality Guidance regulations for the Great Lakes states with regard to WQSs, antidegradation policies, and implementation procedures. It is noteworthy that the increase in litigation and legislation relating to interstate water pollution has occurred primarily because of the resurgence of water quality-based standard-setting and permitting under the CWA.

10. State water quality certification. CWA §401 provides that:

> Any applicant for a Federal license or permit to conduct any activity . . . which may result in any discharge into the navigable waters, shall provide the licensing or permitting agency a certification from the State in which the discharge originates or will originate . . . that any such discharge will comply with [applicable state WQSs]. . . . No license or permit shall be granted until the certification required by this section has been obtained or has been waived. . . . No license or permit shall be granted if certification has been denied by the State. . . . Any certification provided under this section shall . . . become a condition on any Federal license or permit subject to the provisions of this section.

Section 401 allows states to veto or place conditions on a federal permit that causes a discharge to navigable waters, such as a U.S. Army Corps of Engineers permit to discharge dredged and fill material or a Federal Energy Regulatory Commission (FERC) license to operate a hydroelectric dam under the Federal Power Act.

In *Public Util. Dist. No. 1 of Jefferson County & City of Tacoma v. Washington Dep't of Ecology*, 511 U.S. 700 (1994), petitioners wanted to build a hydroelectric project on a river possessing exceptionally high water quality. The project would have appreciably reduced the river's flow and thus would have interfered with the excellent fishery in the river. In order to protect the fishery, respondent state environmental agency included a minimum flow requirement in its §401 certification to FERC. The Supreme Court, in a 7-2 decision, affirmed the Washington Supreme Court's holding that FERC had to honor the minimum flow certification. Justice O'Connor, writing for the majority, reasoned that the state agency had a legal right to protect its WQSs, which included a strong antidegradation requirement for the particular segment involved. In response to petitioners' argument that the CWA is only concerned with water "quality," not water "quantity," Justice O'Connor responded:

> This is an artificial distinction. In many cases, water quantity is closely related to water quality; a sufficient lowering of the water quantity in a body of water could destroy all of its designated uses, be it for drinking water, recreation, navigation or, as here, as a fishery. In any event, there is recognition in the Clean Water Act itself that reduced stream flow, i.e., diminishment of water quantity, can constitute water pollution. 511 U.S. at 719.

But the state certification under CWA §401 applies only to point source discharges. In *Oregon Nat'l Desert Ass'n v. Dombeck*, 172 F.3d 1092 (9th Cir. 1998), cert. denied 528 U.S. 964 (1999), the court held that private cattle grazing on federal land, subject to a federal grazing permit, did not require a state water quality certification because grazing produces nonpoint source pollution that is not regulated by the CWA. *Jefferson County* was distinguished because although flows over dams constitute nonpoint source pollution, dam construction involved discharges of dredged and fill material and the dam's tailrace constituted a point source.

In the most recent twist, a unanimous Supreme Court rejected plaintiff power company's contention that a §401 state certification is only required where there is an addition of a pollutant to navigable waters. *S.D. Warren Co. v. Maine Bd. of Envtl. Protection*, 126 S. Ct. 1843 (2006). Section 401 was at issue because plaintiff power company was applying for a renewal of its license from FERC to operate a hydroelectric dam. Justice Souter, writing for the unanimous Court (Justice Scalia did not join in a relatively minor portion of the opinion), concluded that:

> the dispute turns on the meaning of the word "discharge," the key to the state certification requirement under §401. The Act has no definition of the term, but provides that "[t]he term

E. A Complex Hypothetical: The Average River

'discharge' when used without qualification includes a discharge of a pollutant, and a discharge of pollutants." It does define "discharge of a pollutant" and "discharge of pollutants" as meaning "any addition of any pollutant to navigable waters from any point source." But "discharge" presumably is broader, else superfluous, and since it is neither defined in the statute nor a term of art, we are left to construe it in accordance with its ordinary or natural meaning.

When it applies to water, "discharge" commonly means a "flowing or issuing out" . . . [§402] contrasts with §401 in its more specific focus. It establishes what Congress called the National Pollutant Discharge Elimination System, requiring a permit for the "discharge of any pollutant" into navigable waters of the United States. The triggering statutory term here is not the word "discharge" alone, but "discharge of a pollutant," a phrase made narrower by its specific definition requiring an "addition" of a pollutant to the water. . . . In sum, the understanding that something must be added in order to implicate §402 does not explain what suffices for a discharge under §401. 126 S.Ct. at 1847, 1850.

Thus, the holding in *S.D. Warren* is limited to applications for §401 state certifications where the dam owner requires a federal permit, not to other dam situations where only §402 is involved and plaintiff is requesting the dam owner to obtain a discharge permit.

E. A COMPLEX HYPOTHETICAL: THE AVERAGE RIVER

Here is a cumulative watershed problem, with a series of hypothetical uses named as only law professors could name them, that illustrates many of the CWA's complexities and offers a vehicle for understanding the Act's different sections:

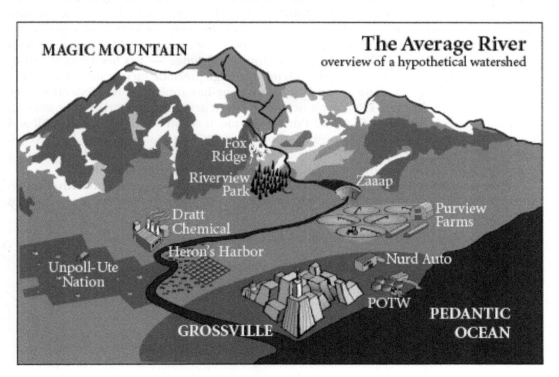

FIGURE 12-2.   *The Average River. Photo credit: Eric Abrams.*

The Average River is just that, a hypothetical typical river system. It arises on the slopes of Magic Mountain and flows into the Pedantic Ocean. As shown on the accompanying map, the Average River is also subject to typical threats to its water quality: (1) A second home development, Fox Ridge, with each home serviced by its own on-site septic system, is planned for the lower slopes of Magic Mountain, threatening to degrade the currently pristine water quality found in Riverview Park. (2) Purview Farms, downstream from the park, is a large, multifaceted agricultural enterprise that combines an extensive animal feeding operation (AFO) with irrigated field crops. Purview's operations cause animal waste, fertilizer, pesticide, and sediment residues to flow into the river and infiltrate into groundwater after storm events. In addition, Purview's irrigation water is first diverted from and then channeled back into the river. (3) The Dratt Chemical Co., Inc., discharges BOD, toxic organic chemicals, and phenols from its plant's production and sanitation facilities directly into the river, causing a violation of state-established WQSs — based on fishable-swimmable water quality — downstream of the plant. Dratt also collects its stormwater, which is contaminated by runoff from uncovered raw materials storage piles, and discharges it through a drainage ditch into the river. (4) The Tribal Council of the Unpoll-Ute Indian Nation, which owns a reservation located just below Dratt's discharge points, has approved and submitted to EPA water quality criteria based on a "None Detectable" standard for the parameters discharged by Purview and Dratt. (5) Across the river from the reservation is a wetland area, in which another residential subdivision (Heron's Harbor) is planned. (6) The City of Grossville, population 500,000, is serviced by a POTW that uses secondary treatment but is connected to a combined sewer system that contains 100 "overflow points," which discharge raw sewage mixed with stormwater into the Pedantic Ocean when storm flows exceed the capacity of the sewerage system. (7) Grossville's CSO and sewage treatment problems are exacerbated by the Nurd Auto Co., Inc.'s discharges of heavy metals into the Grossville sewers, and these heavy metals also contaminate the POTW's sewage sludge (biosolids), which is currently being stored in concrete silos at the POTW because ocean dumping — which the POTW once used to dispose of sludge — has been prohibited by federal law, and the high heavy metal levels in the sludge preclude incineration, land application or landfilling. (8) The Zaaap Power Company has applied to the Federal Energy Regulatory Commission (FERC) for a license to construct a hydroelectric power dam on the river between Riverview Park and Purview Farms; if constructed, this facility will add to existing pollution problems by raising water temperatures (depressing dissolved oxygen levels) and causing eutrophication in the reservoir behind the dam, and also by decreasing water flows (providing less dilution) and dissolved oxygen levels below the dam.

How might the CWA apply to each and all of these activities in the Average River watershed? If government does not act effectively to protect the river in these settings, what can citizens do?

13

Using Cost-Benefit Analysis in Agency Rulemaking & Review of Regulations

A. An Overview of Formal Cost-Benefit Analysis
B. The Scientific Basis: Risk Assessment
C. Open-Ended Cost-Benefit Balancing: ToSCA
D. Formal Cost-Benefit Analysis: SDWA
E. Cost-Benefit Analysis at the White House
F. Evaluating Cost-Benefit Analysis

> Cost-benefit analysis has dominated public policy discussions for decades and enjoys a large following among environmental scholars and politicians alike. Yet it is also an approach Congress has rejected as a catch-all decisionmaking framework for environmental policy and it has seldom been embraced even in discrete statutory settings. The polarization that characterizes so many environmental disputes is especially severe here. Many opponents of cost-benefit analysis argue that it should *never* be used in setting environmental policy, while ardent proponents say that it is the *only* framework that makes any sense.

Cost-benefit analysis occupies a singular position among the alternative decisionmaking frameworks for addressing environmental problems. It is the only framework that, in theory, could apply to, and guide the substantive outcome for, any environmental problem, whether it arises from industrial pollution, natural resource degradation, product hazards, or anything else. Cost-benefit analysis also offers an even more tantalizing proposition: In theory, properly applied cost-benefit analysis could collect all of the scientific and economic data concerning an environmental problem and use them to develop an economically optimal solution. In theory, therefore, cost-benefit analysis could be to policy analysis what unified field theory is to physics: a dazzling, unifying framework whose ultimate product could be, as wryly put by theoretical physicist Michio Katu, "an equation an inch long that would allow us to read the mind of God."[1]

---

1. Available from whatis.techtarget.com/definition/0,,sid9_gci554508,00.html.

After an overview of cost-benefit analysis, this chapter turns to materials that consider primarily two statutes in which Congress injected cost-benefit balancing: the Toxic Substances Control Act (ToSCA),[2] and a provision in the Safe Drinking Water Act (SDWA), as amended in 1996.[3] Cost-benefit balancing in these examples takes two different forms. Under the ToSCA form of cost-benefit balancing, items in the pro and con columns are not necessarily quantified, and many will not be translated into dollar amounts. The second form of cost-benefit balancing is more formal and restrictive; it is also the form of cost-benefit analysis most fashionable in policy circles today and is the approach reflected in the SDWA. It demands quantification and monetization of regulatory considerations wherever possible. Formal cost-benefit analysis is the approach in which tricky questions about the monetary value of human life, endangered species, and the like most frequently enter into the regulatory picture.

Following these two explorations of cost-benefit analysis, the chapter describes the executive branch's use of that tool as a cross-cutting check on regulation, a practice initiated in the Reagan Administration but also used extensively in subsequent administrations. Finally, the last part of the chapter offers commentary, for and against, on the use of cost-benefit analysis.

A. An Overview of Formal Cost-Benefit Analysis

Before turning to specific examples of cost-benefit analysis, the following excerpt provides a basic explanation of the tenets and procedures of the more formal version of this framework.

Frank Ackerman & Lisa Heinzerling, Pricing the Priceless: Cost-Benefit Analysis of Environmental Protection
150 University of Pennsylvania Law Review 1553 (2002)

. . . Cost-benefit analysis tries to mimic a basic function of markets by setting an economic standard for measuring the success of the government's projects and programs. That is, cost-benefit analysis seeks to perform, for public policy, a calculation that happens routinely in the private sector. In evaluating a proposed new initiative, how do we know if it is worth doing or not? The answer is much simpler in business than in government.

Private businesses, striving to make money, only produce things that they believe someone is willing to pay for. That is, firms only produce things for which the benefits to consumers, measured by consumers' willingness to pay for them, are expected to be greater than the costs of production. It is technologically possible to produce men's business suits in brightly colored polka dots. Successful producers suspect that no one is willing to pay for such products, and usually stick to at most minor variations on suits in somber, traditional hues. If some firm did happen to produce a polka-dotted business suit, no one would be forced to buy it; the producer would bear the entire loss resulting from the mistaken decision.

---

2. 15 U.S.C. §§2601-2695d.
3. 42 U.S.C. §300g-1(b)(3)(C)(iii).

A. An Overview of Formal Cost-Benefit Analysis

Government, in the view of many critics, is in constant danger of drifting toward producing polka dot suits—and making people pay for them. Policies, regulations, and public spending do not face the test of the marketplace; there are no consumers who can withhold their dollars from the government until it produces the regulatory equivalent of navy blue and charcoal gray. There is no single quantitative objective for the public sector comparable to profit maximization for businesses. Even with the best of intentions, critics suggest, government programs can easily go astray for lack of an objective standard by which to judge whether or not they are meeting citizens' needs.

Cost-benefit analysis sets out to do for government what the market does for business: add up the benefits of a public policy and compare them to the costs. The two sides of the ledger raise very different issues.

ESTIMATING COSTS. The first step in a cost-benefit analysis is to calculate the costs of a public policy. For example, the government may require a certain kind of pollution control equipment, which businesses must pay for. Even if a regulation only sets a ceiling on emissions, it results in costs that can be at least roughly estimated through research into available technologies and business strategies for compliance.

The costs of protecting human health and the environment through the use of pollution control devices and other approaches are, by their very nature, measured in dollars. Thus, at least in theory, the cost side of cost-benefit analysis is relatively straightforward. (In practice, as we shall see, it is not quite that simple.) . . .

MONETIZING BENEFITS. Since there are no natural prices for a healthy environment, cost-benefit analysis requires the creation of artificial ones. This is the hardest part of the process. Economists create artificial prices for health and environmental benefits by studying what people would be willing to pay for them. One popular method, called "contingent valuation," is essentially a form of opinion poll. Researchers ask a cross-section of the affected population how much they would be willing to pay to preserve or protect something that can't be bought in a store.

Many surveys of this sort have been done, producing prices for things that appear to be priceless. For example, the average American household is supposedly willing to pay $257 to prevent the extinction of bald eagles, $208 to protect humpback whales, and $80 to protect gray wolves.[4] These numbers are quite large: since there are about 100 million households in the country, the nation's total willingness to pay for the preservation of bald eagles alone is ostensibly more than $25 billion.

An alternative method of attaching prices to unpriced things infers what people are willing to pay from observation of their behavior in other markets. To assign a dollar value to risks to human life, for example, economists usually calculate the extra wage—or "wage premium"—that is paid to workers who accept more risky jobs. Suppose that two jobs are comparable, except that one is more dangerous and better paid. If workers understand the risk and voluntarily accept the more dangerous job, then they are implicitly setting a price on risk by accepting the increased risk of death in exchange for increased wages.

What does this indirect inference about wages say about the value of a life? A common estimate in recent cost-benefit analyses is that avoiding a risk that would lead, on average, to

---

4. Loomis & White, Economic Benefits of Rare and Endangered Species: Summary and Meta-Analysis, 18 Ecol. Econ. 197, 199, Table 1 (1996) (figures converted to year 2000 dollars using the consumer price index).

one death is worth roughly $6.3 million.[5] This number, in particular, is of great importance in cost-benefit analyses because avoided deaths are the most thoroughly studied benefits of environmental regulations.

DISCOUNTING THE FUTURE. One more step requires explanation to complete this quick sketch of cost-benefit analysis. Costs and benefits of a policy frequently occur at different times. Often, costs are incurred today, or in the near future, to prevent harm in the more remote future. When the analysis spans a number of years, future costs and benefits are discounted, or treated as equivalent to smaller amounts of money in today's dollars.

Discounting is a procedure developed by economists in order to evaluate investments that produce future income. The case for discounting begins with the observation that $100, say, received today is worth more than $100 received next year, even in the absence of inflation. For one thing, you could put your money in the bank today and earn a little interest by next year. Suppose that your bank account earns 3% interest. In that case, if you received the $100 today rather than next year, you would earn $3 in interest, giving you a total of $103 next year. Likewise, in order to get $100 next year you only need to deposit $97 today.[6] So, at a 3% discount rate, economists would say that $100 next year has a present value of $97 in today's dollars.

For longer periods of time, the effect is magnified: at a 3% discount rate, $100 twenty years from now has a present value of only $55. The larger the discount rate, and the longer the time intervals involved, the smaller the present value: at a 5% discount rate, for example, $100 twenty years from now has a present value of only $38.

Cost-benefit analysis routinely uses the present value of future benefits. That is, it compares current costs, not to the actual dollar value of future benefits, but to the smaller amount you would have to put into a hypothetical savings account today to obtain those benefits in the future. This application of discounting is essential, and indeed commonplace, for many practical financial decisions. If offered a choice of investment opportunities with payoffs at different times in the future, you can (and should) discount the future payoffs to the present in order to compare them to each other. The important issue for environmental policy, as we shall see, is whether this logic also applies to outcomes far in the future, and to opportunities—like long life and good health—that are not naturally stated in dollar terms. . . .

COMMENTARY & QUESTIONS

1. Estimating costs. Estimating the costs of a regulatory intervention is, in principle, the least complex of the steps required for cost-benefit analysis. In practice, however, it turns out to be very difficult to estimate these costs correctly. Empirical studies have demonstrated that costs are often substantially overestimated in advance of regulation. In part, this may be because cost estimates often originate from the regulated industries themselves, which have an incentive to overstate costs in order to defeat regulatory initiatives.

---

5. The original calculation, based on research by W. Kip Viscusi, can be found in EPA, The Benefits and Costs of the Clean Air Act, 1970 to 1990, 1997, Appendix I. For an example of a subsequent analysis citing the Clean Air Act analysis and adjusting only for inflation, see EPA, Arsenic in Drinking Water Rule: Economic Analysis, EPA Document 815-R-00-026, at 5-23 (Dec. 2000). The arsenic study used $6.1 million in 1999 dollars, which is equivalent to $6.3 million in 2000 dollars. [Editors' Note: EPA now uses a value of $8.5 million.]

6. The examples in the text are rounded off to the nearest dollar.

B. The Scientific Basis: Risk Assessment

In addition, regulation often spurs innovation and efficiencies, which in turn lead to lower actual costs than anticipated.[7] One famous example of this phenomenon is the acid rain program of the CAA (discussed in Chapter 11). The actual cost of this program turned out to be approximately one-eighth to one-quarter of industry cost estimates offered before the program was enacted.[8]

2. Describing costs. The apparent reasonableness of costs can vary greatly depending on how they are described. EPA's asbestos ban that is the subject of the next principal case, for example, was expected to cost a total of approximately $460 million—or less than 14 cents per year for each American.[9] At the insistence of the Office of Management and Budget, however, EPA represented the costs as a ratio of costs to lives saved, on an industry-by-industry basis. This decision is what led the court to find that, in some industries, the ban would cost as much as $106 million per life saved. Which is the correct way to represent costs—on a national basis, on an industry-by-industry basis, as costs per life saved? One court has held that agencies deserve deference in their decisions as to how to represent regulatory costs. *American Dental Ass'n v. Martin*, 984 F.2d 823, 827 (7th Cir. 1993) (Posner, J.).

3. "Benefits transfer"—measuring X by studying Y. Despite the explosion in recent years in economic research on willingness-to-pay for environmental improvements, there remain many gaps in the database. In few cases (perhaps none) are there data on the willingness-to-pay of the very population affected by a regulation for the very regulatory benefit conferred. Thus analysts must try to find an analogous setting in which data exist. When analysts use these data in a different setting from the one in which they arose, such as using values derived from workers' demand for wage premiums for risky work to infer the value of improvements in environmental quality for the general population, this is called "benefits transfer." Isn't it likely that the value placed on being subjected to a risk will vary based on whether the evaluator is getting paid to encounter the risk or will involuntarily be subjected to the risk?

4. Monetization and discounting. The two features of formal cost-benefit analysis that distinguish it from other decisionmaking frameworks are monetization and discounting. Are these features essential to cost-benefit analysis?

B. THE SCIENTIFIC BASIS: RISK ASSESSMENT

> Science is obviously relevant to the process of environmental regulation, but how? As the momentum behind environmental policy and law increased during the 1970s, this question arose in greater frequency and urgency. Efforts in all three branches of the federal government contributed to the subsequent emergence of quantitative risk assessment as a public policy tool, particularly for analyzing the risks of cancer from chemicals.

---

7. For a comprehensive overview and analysis, see McGarity & Ruttenberg, Counting the Cost of Health, Safety, and Environmental Regulation, 80 Tex. L. Rev. 1997 (2002).

8. Goodstein & Hodges, Polluted Data, 8 Am. Prospect (Nov.-Dec. 1997), *available at* www.prospect.org/cs/articles?articleId=4757.

9. The figure is derived by dividing $460 million by 13 (the number of years in EPA's study period) and dividing this by the approximate U.S. population at the time (250 million).

In early 1979, an interagency committee of the executive branch proposed guidelines for identifying and assessing chemical carcinogens. This early proposal on risk assessment was premised on the following principles:

- chemical exposures are a significant contribution to the overall incidence of human cancer;
- chemical-induced cancers can be prevented or reduced by identifying potential human carcinogens before exposure has occurred on the large scale necessary before a cause-and-effect relationship between exposure and disease is apparent in human populations; and
- the evaluation of potential carcinogens should be not just qualitative, but should include a numerical quantification of risks.

At around the same time, Congress began to enact legislation, such as ToSCA, that made greater demands on regulatory agencies in terms of risk balancing. The Supreme Court's 1980 opinion setting aside the Occupational Safety and Health Administration's permanent permissible exposure limit for benzene for want of a finding of "significant risk" by the agency[10] increased the momentum for quantifying risks.

The quantification of risks received still further impetus from the National Academy of Sciences' "Red Book,"[11] published in 1983. The Red Book endorsed a bifurcation of the regulatory process into two phases: "risk assessment," which in principle establishes the strictly scientific basis for regulatory action, and "risk management"—of which cost-benefit analysis is one variety—which is the multidisciplinary process of choosing regulatory measures:

> We use *risk assessment* to mean the characterization of the potential adverse health effects of human exposures to environmental hazards. Risk assessments include several elements: description of the potential adverse health effects based on an evaluation of results of epidemiologic, clinical, toxicologic, and environmental research; extrapolation from those results to predict the type and estimate the extent of health effects in humans under given conditions of exposure; judgments as to the number and characteristics of persons exposed at various intensities and durations; and summary judgments on the existence and overall magnitude of the public-health problem. Risk assessment also includes characterization of the uncertainties inherent in the process of inferring risk.
>
> The term *risk assessment* is often given narrower and broader meanings than we have adopted here. For some observers, the term is synonymous with *quantitative risk assessment* and emphasizes reliance on numerical results. Our broader definition includes quantification, but also includes qualitative expressions of risk. Quantitative estimates of risk are not always feasible, and they may be eschewed by agencies for policy reasons. Broader uses of the term than ours also embrace analysis of perceived risks, comparisons of risks associated with different regulatory strategies, and occasionally analysis of the economic and social implications of regulatory decisions—functions that we assign to risk management.
>
> *Risk management* . . . describes the process of evaluating alternative regulatory actions and selecting among them. Risk management, which is carried out by regulatory agencies under various legislative mandates, is an agency decision-making process that entails consideration of political, social, economic, and engineering information with risk-related information to

---

10. *Industrial Union Dep't, AFL-CIO v. Am. Petro. Inst.*, 448 U.S. 607 (1980). The Supreme Court held that the agency's conclusion that reduction in exposure to benzene, a demonstrated carcinogen, would decrease the risk of disease was insufficient to satisfy the statutory standard. OSHA has since proceeded under the assumption that it must quantify the risk of a hazardous workplace contaminant before regulating it.

11. National Research Council, Risk Assessment in the Federal Government: Managing the Process (1983).

B. The Scientific Basis: Risk Assessment

develop, analyze, and compare regulatory options and to select the appropriate regulatory response to a potential chronic health hazard. The selection process necessarily requires the use of value judgments on such issues as the acceptability of risk and the reasonableness of the costs of control.

In this two-stage methodology, scientific questions can supposedly be isolated and addressed in an objective matter through risk assessment methodologies at the beginning of the regulatory process. Pure policy choices are supposedly confined to the second step, risk management. At this stage, science may be relevant for such tasks as evaluating technical options. Risk management decisions, however, also engage other considerations, most notably social values. Indeed, subsequent reports by the National Research Council on quantitative risk assessment, including the 2009 "Silver Book," have moved away from the bifurcation of risk assessment into two distinct steps and have recommended that policymakers (risk managers) and scientists (risk assessors) develop a research plan together before risk assessment begins, to ensure that risk assessment answers the questions relevant to policymakers.

Even today, risk assessment is typically understood to include a four-step analysis, as described in the parenthetical quotes that follow from the Red Book: hazard identification ("the process of determining whether exposure to an agent can cause an increase in the incidence of a health condition—cancer, birth defect, etc.)"; dose-response assessment ("the process of characterizing the relation between the dose of an agent administered or received and the incidence of an adverse health effect in exposed populations and estimating the incidence of the effect as a function of human exposure to the agent"); exposure assessment ("the process of measuring or estimating the intensity, frequency, and duration of human exposure to an agent currently present in the environment or of estimating hypothetical exposures that might arise from the release of new chemicals into the environment"); and risk characterization ("the process of estimating the incidence of a health effect under the various conditions of human exposure described in exposure assessment").

Although not free from controversy, a number of generally accepted principles have since circumscribed the public policy debate over quantitative risk assessment. First, consistent with a strategy of anticipation and prevention, risk assessment could proceed in the absence of data on human response, relying when necessary on results from experimental research on animals. Because there are few human studies for many existing chemicals, and ethical considerations preclude experimentation on human beings, reliance upon non-human data is inevitable in the regulatory process. This rationale owed much to experience with the regulation of new pharmaceuticals and pesticides, in which "preclinical" or animal data could be dispositive. Second, agencies were to assess risks based on the probability of developing disease, for which a probability of developing disease, typically cancer, of one-in-a-million (10^{-6}) over a lifetime of exposure is often taken as a useful benchmark. Third, risk assessments were to be presumptively conservative, that is, protective of human health in light of scientific uncertainty, involving confidence in the actual value, and variability, ranges in the response of different individuals. In the absence of empirical data, default assumptions were to be chosen so that the actual risk from the kind of long-term, low-level doses that characterize most human and environmental exposures is likely to be no greater than that calculated using a risk assessment methodology.

Despite several rounds of evaluation of quantitative risk assessment methodologies by the National Research Council (NRC) and other advisory bodies, Congress has continued to request further refinement in scientific evaluation of the process, largely because of dissatisfaction with the results of proactive and protective public policies based on risk assessment methodologies. Politicians have hoped to find magic answers to issues in risk assessments that the regulated sector considers most troubling: principles of extrapolation from animals to human doses, models for estimating low dose risk, and handling of uncertain or incomplete data sets in assessments.[12]

COMMENTARY & QUESTIONS

1. (Nonhuman) animal studies. Risk assessment is a tool for analyzing empirical data in a manner useful for crafting regulatory policy. Those data in some situations may be produced by epidemiological studies that survey exposed human populations, but epidemiological studies of necessity survey *prior* exposures of human populations to toxins such as tobacco or asbestos. As laboratory studies involving the exposure of human subjects to potentially toxic substances that are poorly characterized or new to the market are generally considered unethical (unlike epidemiological studies involving the collection of data on previously exposed human populations such as workers), in most cases toxicological tests on laboratory animals are the only source of relevant data. This empirical information, whatever its source, must then be extrapolated to actual environmental settings, which may be very different from those under which the data were collected.

For instance, animal tests are ordinarily conducted at high doses and over a short period by comparison with the levels to which human beings typically experience long-term exposure to environmental toxins. These inferences, while necessary because of limitations on data gathering in both humans and animals, inevitably introduce uncertainty into any risk assessment: "Uncertainties in low-dose extrapolation and potency differences across species, within species, and across different routes of exposure complicate estimates of risk and make it difficult to know when enough risk research has been done." National Research Council, Science and Judgment in Risk Assessment 194 (1994). Additionally, this extrapolation necessarily requires inferences, choices, and assumptions that themselves reflect policy preferences, an area sometimes known as "science policy." How, if at all, should these factors affect regulatory decisionmaking?

2. Low-dose extrapolation. It is a truism in dealing with toxic substances (or for that matter any biologically active substances such as drugs or food additives introduced into living organisms) that response — in the case of toxic pollutants, the risk of disease — rises with increasing dose. But as discussed in the preceding note, most risk assessments rely on animal exposures at high doses, whereas regulatory measures are typically designed to address low-level, chronic human exposures, potentially over a lifetime. Consequently, the models used to estimate human risks at low doses are often the subject of great controversy.

Consider Figure 1 showing low-dose extrapolation. On the horizontal x-axis are the values for the independent variable, exposure. On the vertical y-axis are the effects associated with those exposures, an increase in risk. What do each of the alternative theories (threshold, sublinear I, etc.) posit about the action of this chemical at low doses? What public policies would be associated with each of the curves? It is increasingly clear that the timing of exposure is also important, as in the case of fetal exposure to hormone-disrupting chemicals.

---

12. The bulk of this material is taken from Wirth & Silbergeld, Risky Reform, 95 Colum. L. Rev. 1857 (1995).

B. The Scientific Basis: Risk Assessment

3. Managing uncertainty and comparative risk assessment. As should already be apparent, risk assessment involves uncertainties and assumptions, many of which may be difficult or impossible to resolve through additional research. EPA has been criticized for, and urged to discontinue, the practice of defining "point estimates" of risk, which suggest an artificially precise degree of scientific confidence, instead of quantitative ranges of uncertainty associated with an estimate of risk. These uncertainties are compounded when, as is frequently done, policymakers attempt to compare or rank hazards. Serious data gaps for even the most highly suspect bad actors can seriously affect the confidence level of individual risks assessments and undermine their "comparability." Just because we reduce an incomplete data set to a single number does not mean we understand anything more about the substance involved. Indeed, such an approach

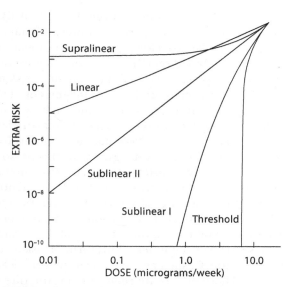

FIGURE 13-1. *Dose-Response. A typical low-dose extrapolation of risk. Results are presented for alternative low-dose models from the same experimental data, a mouse bioassay of benzopyrene. Exposure (dose) is plotted on the horizontal x-axis. The additional risk resulting from exposure to the chemical is plotted on the vertical y-axis. Note that all of the curves are based on inferences from experimental data, in this case from long-term animal tests, which would be located off the graph, far to the right. Source: National Research Council, Risk Assessment in the Federal Government: Managing the Process 24 (1983).*

may well mask significant underlying uncertainties. How would you advise regulators to present estimates of risk in a manner that appropriately captures the uncertainty associated with them? How would you advise policymakers to take uncertainty into account when setting priorities for regulatory action? How can a risk range be converted into a standard and a definition of compliance for drinking water, an effluent discharge permit level, etc.?

4. Alternatives to risk assessment: "precautionary" regulation. Regulatory interventions based on a principle of precaution have gained currency within the past two decades, particularly in the European Union. (See Chapter 22.) Precaution as a decisionmaking paradigm has its roots in such commonsense maxims as "An ounce of prevention is worth a pound of cure," "A stitch in time saves nine," "Look before you leap," and "Better to be safe than sorry." Extrapolated to the level of broad-gauge public policy, a precautionary perspective encourages prompt, vigorous governmental responses to suggestive, but perhaps inconclusive, indications of harm. The classic statement is Principle 15 of the Rio Declaration on Environment and Development:

> In order to protect the environment, the precautionary approach shall be widely applied by States according to their capabilities. Where there are threats of serious or irreversible damage, lack of full scientific certainty shall not be used as a reason for postponing cost-effective measures to prevent environmental degradation.

What would a precautionary regulation look like? Would there be a minimum amount of information required to trigger a precautionary approach, and if so what type of information would that be? How does a precautionary approach to environmental regulation differ from one based on risk assessment? Or are they perhaps complementary? If so, how? Is precaution a principle of risk assessment or risk management? Or perhaps both?

5. Risk assessment and risk management. The distinction between risk assessment, supposedly exclusively a scientific undertaking, and risk management, involving a range of policy choices, has been criticized as an artificial or a false dichotomy. Risk assessment, according to this view, like risk management involves many social values and policy preferences. To what extent do you agree with this perspective? If so, what regulatory taxonomy ought to be employed instead of the risk assessment/risk management approach?

6. Non-cancer risk assessment. U.S. regulatory agencies have been criticized for a focus on cancer-causing substances, which in turn has affected risk assessment methodologies, inviting criticisms of overzealous regulation of small risks. Risk estimates of carcinogenicity are intended to capture the probability of effects in the relatively distant future and not the severity of the illness. This form of risk assessment is unlikely to be appropriate to other toxic effects, such as non-cancer neurological effects in children from low-level lead exposure. Those effects are relatively certain, directly correlated to the level of exposure, and nondichotomous (i.e., unlike the binary "you either have the illness or not" risks from cancer).

7. Quantitative risk assessment and cost-benefit analysis. Risk assessments need not be quantitative or numerical. As stated by the WTO's Appellate Body in a seminal dispute over the EU's ban on hormone-treated beef:

> [A requirement] that a certain *magnitude* or threshold level of risk be demonstrated in a risk assessment . . . finds no basis in [WTO requirements for risk assessments]. . . . To exclude from the scope of a risk assessment . . . all matters not susceptible of quantitative analysis by the empirical or experimental laboratory methods commonly associated with the physical sciences . . . is . . . error. It is essential to bear in mind that the risk that is to be evaluated in a risk assessment . . . is not only risk ascertainable in a science laboratory operating under strictly controlled conditions, but also risk in human societies as they actually exist, in other words, the actual potential for adverse effects on human health in the real world where people live and work and die. European Community—Measures Concerning Meat and Meat Products, WT/DS26/AB/R & WT/DS48/AB/R, ¶¶186 & 187 (Jan. 16, 1998).

There has nonetheless been considerable pressure to quantify risks from human exposures to toxic substances. Associating risks from toxics with a numerical analysis quite obviously assists in the quantitative measurement of costs and benefits—which is but one of a number of taxonomic approaches to risk management. The demand for "hard" numbers in a cost-benefit analysis arguably increases the momentum toward quantification of risks. How as a scientist might you respond to that pressure? As an environmental advocate? As a government official?

8. Tallying costs of harms that would be incurred or benefits of avoidance—are they the same thing? The push toward quantification in some cases raises an apparent question of methodology: Which way are valuations properly made? It is important to note this question is one that pertains solely to the benefit of the regulation side of the ledger. The costs of regulation are not relevant here, and include things such as extra dollars spent for equipment, extra time and labor required in processing, substituting more expensive but safer materials, etc. The present approach is to focus on the positive value of a statistical life, or number of years of enhanced quality of life. These figures tend to be considerably larger (several times as large) than the narrower conceptions of viewing the same events as a sum of relatively easy to monetize detriments avoided, such as lost wages, medical expenses, sums paid for replacement services, etc. What accounts for the disparity in valuation of what might seem to be two sides of the same coin? Is it the incompleteness of the monetized itemization? Is there an environmental justice component lurking in the background having to do with the very low values that might be awarded in the case of injuries that will fall on disadvantaged populations, the less well compensated, or the aged? See generally F. Ackerman & L. Heinzerling, Priceless, On Knowing the Price of Everything and the Value of Nothing, chs. 4 & 5 (2004).

C. OPEN-ENDED COST-BENEFIT BALANCING: ToSCA

1. ToSCA's Regulatory Design

ToSCA tries to manage risks associated with the use of toxic substances by regulating the marketing of products that contain those substances, with EPA as the gatekeeper. In statutory design terms it is a "market access, front-end control" law, and is studied further in Chapter 15. In the case of asbestos, EPA acted under §6 of the statute, which applies to substances already in use that EPA finds pose unreasonable health or environmental risks.

Toxic Substances Control Act §6
(codified at 15 U.S.C. §2601ff)

§2605(a) SCOPE OF REGULATION. If the Administrator finds there is a reasonable basis to conclude that the manufacture, processing, distribution in commerce, use, or disposal of a chemical substance or mixture, or that any combination of such activities, presents or will present an unreasonable risk of injury to health or the environment, the Administrator shall by rule apply one or more of the following requirements to such substance or mixture to the extent necessary to protect adequately against such risk using the least burdensome requirements:

(1) A requirement (A) prohibiting the manufacture, processing, or distribution in commerce of such substance or mixture, or (B) limiting the amount of such substance or mixture which may be manufactured, processed, or distributed in commerce.

(2) A requirement (A) prohibiting the manufacture, processing, or distribution in commerce of such substance or mixture for (i) a particular use or (ii) a particular use in a concentration in excess of a level specified by the Administrator in the rule imposing the requirement, or (B) limiting the amount of such substance or mixture which may be manufactured, processed, or distributed in commerce for (i) a particular use or (ii) a particular use in a concentration in excess of a level specified by the Administrator in the rule imposing the requirement.

(3) A requirement that such substance or mixture or any article containing such substance or mixture be marked with or accompanied by clear and adequate warnings and instructions with respect to its use, distribution in commerce, or disposal or with respect to any combination of such activities. The form and content of such warnings and instructions shall be prescribed by the Administrator.

(4) A requirement that manufacturers and processors of such substance or mixture make and retain records of the processes used to manufacture or process such substance or mixture and monitor or conduct tests which are reasonable and

necessary to assure compliance with the requirements of any rule applicable under this subsection.

(5) A requirement prohibiting or otherwise regulating any manner or method of commercial use of such substance or mixture.

(6)(A) A requirement prohibiting or otherwise regulating any manner or method of disposal of such substance or mixture, or of any article containing such substance or mixture, by its manufacturer or processor or by any other person who uses, or disposes of, it for commercial purposes. (B) A requirement under subparagraph (A) may not require any person to take any action which would be in violation of any law or requirement of, or in effect for, a State or political subdivision, and shall require each person subject to it to notify each State and political subdivision in which a required disposal may occur of such disposal.

(7) A requirement directing manufacturers or processors of such substance or mixture (A) to give notice of such unreasonable risk of injury to distributors in commerce of such substance or mixture and, to the extent reasonably ascertainable, to other persons in possession of such substance or mixture or exposed to such substance or mixture, (B) to give public notice of such risk of injury, and (C) to replace or repurchase such substance or mixture as elected by the person to which the requirement is directed.

Any requirement (or combination of requirements) imposed under this subsection may be limited in application to specified geographic areas. . . .

(c) PROMULGATION OF SUBSECTION (a) RULES. In promulgating any rule under subsection (a) of this section with respect to a chemical substance or mixture, the Administrator shall consider and publish a statement with respect to—(A) the effects of such substance or mixture on health and the magnitude of the exposure of human beings to such substance or mixture, (B) the effects of such substance or mixture on the environment and the magnitude of the exposure of the environment to such substance or mixture, (C) the benefits of such substance or mixture for various uses and the availability of substitutes for such uses, and (D) the reasonably ascertainable economic consequences of the rule, after consideration of the effect on the national economy, small business, technological innovation, the environment, and public health.

COMMENTARY & QUESTIONS

1. What is the trigger for regulation? The subsection (a) findings that need to be made to regulate under §6 are more mud than crystals—the Administrator must have a "reasonable basis" for concluding uses of the substance will pose an "unreasonable risk of injury to health or the environment. . . ." How predictable is that? Once those findings are made, however, the statute requires ("shall") the Administrator to act by rule. Based on the materials studied in Chapter 6 covering administrative law, can the Administrator be forced to make findings, one way or another, or will that be totally discretionary?

2. How much regulation is allowed under §6? The range of the alternatives set forth in (a)(1)-(7) is broad indeed, from bans, to application and use limits, to labels and recordkeeping. What statutory language can be argued to restrict the Administrator in choosing among those options? The Administrator is authorized to protect adequately against the "unreasonable risk," but only "to the extent necessary" using the "least burdensome alternative." In an omitted portion of the case that follows, that language was interpreted to require the Administrator to make specific findings about each of the less burdensome alternatives than the one chosen and these findings would determine the choice among them. How challenging will this be?

C. Open-Ended Cost-Benefit Balancing: ToSCA

3. Standard of judicial review. Unlike most of the regulatory statutes studied in this book, ToSCA provides that EPA's decisions be reviewed under the "substantial evidence" standard of review, rather than the more deferential and more forgiving "arbitrary and capricious" standard of §706 of the APA. In the next case, the court found a difference between these standards, with substantial evidence being less forgiving than the arbitrary and capricious standard. This difference helped to embolden the court to overturn EPA's ban on asbestos.

4. Regulating new chemical substances. In addition to the §6 power to regulate toxic substances already in use, §5 of ToSCA has a proactive procedure that applies (1) to new, potentially toxic chemical substances, manufactured after ToSCA's enactment; or (2) to significantly changed uses for existing substances. Presumably, the idea of §5 is to prevent harm from such substances, rather than reacting to such harms after the toxic substance is in use. The producer must give what is called a "pre-market notice" that announces its intent to manufacture the new substance or introduce a new use for an existing substance. As part of the pre-market notice, the producer includes "*data which the person submitting the data believes show that . . . [the substance or new use] will not present an unreasonable risk of injury to health or the environment.*"[13] (Emphasis supplied.) Thereafter, the Administrator is given 90 days in which to act to block the introduction of the new product. The grounds for EPA action essentially mimic the standards for taking action under §6, and on that basis EPA can require additional testing before the substance is introduced. EPA, however, has the burden of demonstrating the need for that additional testing, which, in effect, requires EPA to prove dangerousness without necessarily having the applicant's full test data available to it. This de facto presumption of safety, like the more exacting standard of judicial review applied to ToSCA determinations, provides a sharp contrast to the other major statute that most closely parallels ToSCA. That statute, the Federal Insecticide, Fungicide, and Rodenticide Act (FIFRA), is the older of the two statutes and, as its name suggests, regulates the sale and distribution of similarly dangerous chemicals, the so-called economic poisons. FIFRA places the burden on the manufacturer to prove safety (i.e., acceptable risk) before being granted registration, which is the precondition for distribution and sale of the product. In a similar reversal of ToSCA's orientation, under FIFRA, the Administrator can act immediately to cancel a registration or suspend use of a product, with the administrative processes to follow and the burden being on the product proponent to furnish evidence of safety. Recall the Talbot Page risk management excerpt found in Chapter 1; which approach, ToSCA's or FIFRA's, seems better adapted to such potentially harmful materials? Chapter 15 provides more details.

5. Regulatory design—finding the right regulatory pressure point. To operate effectively, regulatory efforts need to be fitted into the lifecycle of the real-world activities that are being regulated. For many types of regulation, the proper place to graft them into the process is obvious. For example, CAA stationary source controls (see Chapter 11) are applied via a preconstruction or premodification permitting process that comes after the proposal is concrete enough to invest regulatory effort, but before the construction can begin. In regard to new products, both ToSCA and FIFRA make a similar choice—they regulate market access. For existing products, they allow the agency to stop their sale; for new products both statutes attach after the product or use is concrete enough to be proposed, but before investment in full-scale production and before any harm has been caused.

---

13. 15 U.S.C. §2604(b)(2)(B).

2. Regulation of Asbestos Under a ToSCA Cost-Benefit Analysis

In 1989, after ten years of study, EPA issued a final rule prohibiting the future manufacture, importation, processing, and distribution of asbestos in almost all products. EPA found that only a ban on asbestos would protect against the risks of asbestos posed by all of the stages of its lifecycle, including mining, processing, manufacturing, and disposal. EPA estimated that its rule would prevent 202 fatal cancer cases that would have occurred due to exposures occurring in the next 13 years. The agency found that it could not quantify many of the additional benefits that would be produced by the rule, including asbestosis cases avoided.

Asbestos is a naturally occurring fibrous mineral. Because it resists fire and solvents, it was used widely for insulation, building materials, fireproof clothing, and motor vehicle brake linings. Asbestos, despite its obvious utility, is harmful to human beings. Based on overwhelming epidemiological evidence, asbestos causes mesothelioma, lung cancer, and asbestosis. Thousands of private lawsuits have successfully charged asbestos manufacturers and other companies with exposing workers and others to asbestos, killing or injuring many of them, without warning those exposed of those known dangers. EPA's rulemaking occurred in the midst of the asbestos liability "crisis," which continues to this day.

The results of the EPA rulemaking were challenged in court in the case that follows. In an omitted portion of the decision, the court first ruled that EPA had erred in failing to conduct a cost-benefit analysis for every possible regulatory alternative for asbestos, beginning with the least burdensome requirements listed in §6 (such as labeling) and continuing all the way through to the most burdensome (an outright ban). The court then turned to EPA's cost-benefit methodologies, and found these wanting.

Corrosion Proof Fittings v. U.S. Environmental Protection Agency
947 F.2d 1201 (5th Cir. 1991)

SMITH, J. . . . First, we note that there was some dispute in the record regarding the appropriateness of discounting the perceived benefits of the EPA's rule. In choosing between the calculated costs and benefits, the EPA presented variations in which it discounted only the costs, and counter-variations in which it discounted both the costs and the benefits, measured in both monetary and human injury terms. As between these two variations, we choose to evaluate the EPA's work using its discounted benefits calculations.

Although various commentators dispute whether it ever is appropriate to discount benefits when they are measured in human lives, we note that it would skew the results to discount only costs without according similar treatment to the benefits side of the equation. Adopting the position of the commentators who advocate not discounting benefits would force the EPA similarly not to calculate costs in present discounted real terms, making comparisons difficult. Furthermore, in evaluating situations in which different options incur costs at varying time intervals, the EPA would not be able to take into account that soon-to-be-incurred costs are more harmful than postponable costs. Because the EPA must discount costs to perform its evaluations properly, the EPA also should discount benefits to preserve an apples-to-apples comparison, even if this entails discounting benefits of a non-monetary nature. See What Price Posterity?, The Economist, March 23, 1991, at 73 (explaining use of discount rates for non-monetary goods).

When the EPA does discount costs or benefits, however, it cannot choose an unreasonable time upon which to base its discount calculation. Instead of using the time of injury

C. Open-Ended Cost-Benefit Balancing: ToSCA

as the appropriate time from which to discount, as one might expect, the EPA instead used the time of exposure. . . .

Of more concern to us is the failure of the EPA to compute the costs and benefits of its proposed rule past the year 2000, and its double-counting of the costs of asbestos use. In performing its calculus, the EPA only included the number of lives saved over the next thirteen years, and counted any additional lives saved as simply "unquantified benefits." The EPA and intervenors now seek to use these unquantified lives saved to justify calculations as to which the benefits seem far outweighed by the astronomical costs. For example, the EPA plans to save about three lives with its ban of asbestos pipe, at a cost of $128-227 million (i.e., approximately $43-76 million per life saved). Although the EPA admits that the price tag is high, it claims that the lives saved past the year 2000 justify the price.

Such calculations not only lessen the value of the EPA's cost analysis, but also make any meaningful judicial review impossible. While TSCA contemplates a useful place for unquantified benefits beyond the EPA's calculation, unquantified benefits never were intended as a trump card allowing the EPA to justify any cost calculus, no matter how high.

The concept of unquantified benefits, rather, is intended to allow the EPA to provide a rightful place for any remaining benefits that are impossible to quantify after the EPA's best attempt, but which still are of some concern. But the allowance for unquantified costs is not intended to allow the EPA to perform its calculations over an arbitrarily short period so as to preserve a large unquantified portion.

Unquantified benefits can, at times, permissibly tip the balance in close cases. They cannot, however, be used to effect a wholesale shift on the balance beam. Such a use makes a mockery of the requirements of TSCA that the EPA weigh the costs of its actions before it chooses the least burdensome alternative.[14] . . .

The final requirement the EPA must satisfy before engaging in any TSCA rulemaking is that it only take steps designed to prevent "unreasonable" risks. In evaluating what is "unreasonable," the EPA is required to consider the costs of any proposed actions and to "carry out this chapter in a reasonable and prudent manner [after considering] the environmental, economic, and social impact of any action." 15 U.S.C. §2601(c).

As the District of Columbia Circuit stated when evaluating similar language governing the Federal Hazardous Substances Act, "the requirement that the risk be 'unreasonable' necessarily involves a balancing test like that familiar in tort law: The regulation may issue if the severity of the injury that may result from the product, factored by the likelihood of the injury, offsets the harm the regulation itself imposes upon manufacturers and consumers." *Forester v. CPSC*, 559 F.2d 774, 789 (D.C. Cir. 1977). We have quoted this language approvingly when evaluating other statutes using similar language.

---

14. We thus reject the arguments made by the Natural Resources Defense Council, Inc., and the Environmental Defense Fund, Inc., that the EPA's decision can be justified because the EPA "relied on many serious risks that were understated or not quantified in the final rule," presented figures in which the "benefits are calculated only for a limited time period," and undercounted the risks to the general population from low-level asbestos exposure. In addition, the intervenors argue that the EPA rejected using upper estimates, and that this court now should use the rejected limits as evidence to support the EPA. They thus would have us reject the upper limit concerns when they are not needed, but use them if necessary.

We agree that these all are valid concerns that the EPA legitimately should take into account when considering regulatory action. What we disagree with, however, is the manner in which the EPA incorporated these concerns. By not using such concerns in its quantitative analysis, even where doing so was not difficult, and reserving them as additional factors to buttress the ban, the EPA improperly transformed permissible considerations into determinative factors.

That the EPA must balance the costs of its regulations against their benefits further is reinforced by the requirement that it seek the least burdensome regulation. While Congress did not dictate that the EPA engage in an exhaustive, full-scale cost-benefit analysis, it did require the EPA to consider both sides of the regulatory equation, and it rejected the notion that the EPA should pursue the reduction of workplace risk at any cost. See *American Textile Mfrs. Inst.*, 452 U.S. at 510 n. 30 ("unreasonable risk" statutes require "a generalized balancing of costs and benefits").[15] Thus, "Congress also plainly intended the EPA to consider the economic impact of any actions taken by it under . . . TSCA." *Chemical Mfrs. Ass'n*, 899 F.2d at 348.

Even taking all of the EPA's figures as true, and evaluating them in the light most favorable to the agency's decision (non-discounted benefits, discounted costs, analogous exposure estimates included), the agency's analysis results in figures as high as $74 million per life saved. For example, the EPA states that its ban of asbestos pipe will save three lives over the next thirteen years, at a cost of $128-227 million ($43-76 million per life saved), depending upon the price of substitutes; that its ban of asbestos shingles will cost $23-34 million to save 0.32 statistical lives ($72-106 million per life saved); that its ban of asbestos coatings will cost $46-181 million to save 3.33 lives ($14-54 million per life saved); and that its ban of asbestos paper products will save 0.60 lives at a cost of $4-5 million ($7-8 million per life saved). See 54 Fed. Reg. at 29,484-85. Were the analogous exposure estimates not included, the cancer risks from substitutes such as ductile iron pipe factored in, and the benefits of the ban appropriately discounted from the time of the manifestation of an injury rather than the time of exposure, the costs would shift even more sharply against the EPA's position.

While we do not sit as a regulatory agency that must make the difficult decision as to what an appropriate expenditure is to prevent someone from incurring the risk of an asbestos-related death, we do note that the EPA, in its zeal to ban any and all asbestos products, basically ignored the cost side of the TSCA equation. The EPA would have this court believe that Congress, when it enacted its requirement that the EPA consider the economic impacts of its regulations, thought that spending $200-300 million to save approximately seven lives (approximately $30-40 million per life) over thirteen years is reasonable. . . .

The EPA's willingness to argue that spending $23.7 million to save less than one-third of a life reveals that its economic review of its regulations, as required by TSCA, was meaningless. As the petitioners' brief and our review of EPA caselaw reveals, such high costs are rarely, if ever, used to support a safety regulation. If we were to allow such cavalier treatment of the EPA's duty to consider the economic effects of its decisions, we would have to excise entire sections and phrases from the language of TSCA. Because we are judges, not surgeons, we decline to do so.[16]

---

15. This case is often referred to as the "Cotton Dust" case. [EDS.]

16. As the petitioners point out, the EPA regularly rejects, as unjustified, regulations that would save more lives at less cost. For example, over the next 13 years, we can expect more than a dozen deaths from ingested toothpicks—a death toll more than twice what the EPA predicts will flow from the quarter-billion-dollar bans of asbestos pipe, shingles, and roof coatings. See L. Budnick, Toothpick-Related Injuries in the U.S., 1979 Through 1982, 252 J. Am. Med. Ass'n, Aug. 10, 1984, at 796 (study showing that toothpick-related deaths average approximately one per year).

C. Open-Ended Cost-Benefit Balancing: ToSCA

COMMENTARY & QUESTIONS

1. How did the court know how much was too much to save a life? Is the toothpick comparison (see footnote 16) persuasive? Would $20 million per life have been too much to spend? $10 million? $5 million? Does the court tell us what standard it is using to judge EPA's rule? Would it be appropriate for the court to select a value for each life saved and use it to assess whether the asbestos rule is permissible? Should there be a standard figure that is used in cost-benefit analyses? This topic is considered again in the materials on the SDWA that follow this section.

2. Apples and . . . apples? Oranges? Is the court correct in requiring EPA to treat the avoidance of future cancers like an economic benefit that should be discounted to present value? Are the units equivalent, or even comparable? Consider the following critique:

> One worries about "preserv[ing] an apples-to-apples comparison" . . . only if one is dealing only with apples. In the asbestos case, the costs were dollars and the benefits were lives. These costs and benefits are the same only if dollars and lives are the same. . . . The implicit premise of an argument in favor of discounting is that lives can be measured in dollars. Far from being a "value-free and good workable rule,"[17] . . . the decision to treat future costs and benefits the same—to discount them both and to discount them at the same rate—silently resolves one of the central moral questions of the modern regulatory state. Heinzerling, Regulatory Costs of Mythic Proportions, 107 Yale L.J. 1981, 2053 (1998).

3. Does discounting miss the point? Some observers resist the very idea of applying market discount approaches to issues of planetary ecological management. Economist Peter Brown argues:

> There are some things that are not, and should not be, discounted. No one asks, "What is the optimal rate of shredding for the U.S. Constitution?" On the contrary, we assume that we should preserve the historic document for posterity. This is precisely analogous to what many people think we should do with respect to these issues; but all this response demonstrates is that [market accounting] doesn't tell us what the discount rate with respect to these issues should be, or even whether there should be one. [Moreover,] in any situation where there is a long-term asymmetry between costs and benefits, as is the case with global warming, discounting imperils the future by undervaluing it. Although the costs of averting the greenhouse effect are paid in the present, the benefits accrue in the distant future. The discounted value of harms that occur a century from now are insignificant when compared with the present costs of avoiding them. As D'Arge, Schulze, and Brookshire argue in Carbon Dioxide and Intergenerational Choice, "a complete loss of the world's GNP a hundred years from now would be worth about one million dollars today if discounted by the present prime rate." P. Brown, Greenhouse Economics: Think Before You Count, a Report from the Institute for Philosophy & Public Policy 10, 11 (1991).

4. Tilting the balance beam. The court charges that EPA performed its numerical calculations over an "arbitrarily short period so as to preserve a large unquantified portion." Might there be another, less cynical explanation for EPA's choice of a 13-year analytical horizon? EPA's predictions about the effects of its rule beyond this period become less supportable than predictions about the nearer term. Without precise information about its confidence levels in the further-out predictions, is it clear that EPA could support its resulting action with substantial evidence?

---

17. John F. Morrall III, Cotton Dust: An Economist's View, in The Scientific Basis of Health and Safety Regulation 107 (Robert W. Crandall & Lester B. Lave eds., 1981).

5. Trumping quantified costs. EPA cited substantial unquantified benefits in support of its rule, including not only benefits beyond its 13-year analytical horizon, but also including the avoidance of asbestosis and other harmful effects of asbestos. The court says unquantified benefits can play a role in close cases, but cannot be used to "effect a wholesale shift on the balance beam." Does the statute require the court's result? If important benefits are unquantified, how do we know whether it is a close case? On the other hand, if unquantified benefits were allowed to trump quantified costs without limit, would there be any meaningful limits, via judicial review or otherwise, on the agency's discretion?

6. The "least burdensome" alternative? In a portion of the opinion not excerpted here, the court criticized EPA for its analytical process. The court thought EPA should have started with the least burdensome regulatory alternative available under ToSCA, done a cost-benefit analysis of that alternative, and then continued to a more burdensome alternative (with a full-blown cost-benefit analysis there, too) only if the less onerous alternative failed to bring the risks posed by asbestos down to a reasonable level. The court found this procedural approach required by ToSCA. Do the portions of §6 excerpted above require or even support this approach to alternatives? What level of regulatory resources would have to go into each such benefit-cost analysis? What implications will such an approach have for EPA's ability to respond to toxic threats under ToSCA?

7. From asbestos to fish sinkers. The asbestos ban is EPA's first and only ban of a toxic substance under ToSCA's §6. Several years after the ban was overturned, EPA proposed banning lead fish sinkers, popular among avid anglers, due to their harmful effects on water life and on the people who made the sinkers. EPA never finalized this ban. Is it surprising that EPA has had little success using §6? In cases of widespread serious harm from a toxic substance, will tort suits deter manufacture or use sufficiently that the producer will discontinue the product? In answering, be sure to think about all the difficulties facing a toxic tort plaintiff.

8. Is ToSCA just like NEPA? Reread ToSCA's §6(c). Could you make an argument that this section, like NEPA, merely requires EPA to compile a document describing the costs, benefits, etc., of an action taken under §6 and to consider that document in coming to a decision, but does not require the benefits of the agency's action to be commensurate with the costs?

9. The sound of one hand clapping. Without a monetary value for important regulatory benefits such as saving lives, or any monetary value for avoided other diseases, how is EPA—and then the reviewing court—to decide whether an action is cost-benefit justified under §6? Where costs are stated in dollar terms but benefits are stated in lives and other values, costs take on a role rather like one hand clapping: There is nothing offered in opposition to them, yet it is hard to know what to make of their presence. For reasons like these, many people who advocate cost-benefit balancing advocate a more formal framework in which, as far as possible, both costs and benefits are reduced to monetary terms.

D. Formal Cost-Benefit Analysis: SDWA

As amended in 1996, the SDWA requires EPA to set MCLGs and MCLs for harmful pollutants in drinking water. MCLGs are nonenforceable health goals, set at levels at which "no known or anticipated adverse effects on the health of persons occur and which allow . . . an adequate margin of safety." 42 U.S.C. §300g-1(b)(4)(A). MCLs are enforceable standards for levels of contaminants in drinking water. In setting an MCL, EPA is to identify the best

D. Formal Cost-Benefit Analysis: SDWA

available control technique for removing the pollutant of concern. EPA is also required to conduct an analysis of the costs and benefits of varying MCLs. If EPA believes that an MCL less stringent than the one achieved through use of the best available control technique is warranted based on EPA's cost-benefit analysis, the agency may set a less stringent standard that "maximizes health risk reductions benefits at a cost that is justified by the benefits." 42 U.S.C. §300g-1(b)(6)(A). The statute specifically provides that "consumer willingness to pay for reductions in health risks from drinking water contaminants" is one of the approaches EPA may identify for "the measurement and valuation of benefits" under the statute. 42 U.S.C. §300g-1(b)(3)(C)(iii).

Arsenic causes cancers of the bladder, lungs, skin, kidneys, nasal passages, liver, and prostate, as well as other cardiovascular, pulmonary, neurological, immunological, and endocrine problems. In 1942, the federal government set a standard of 50 μg/L (micrograms per liter) for arsenic in drinking water. Twenty years later, the U.S. Public Health Services recommended that drinking water should contain no more than 10 μg/L. Three times in 30 years, Congress told EPA to update the 50 μg/L standard. Finally, in January 2001, the outgoing Clinton Administration EPA announced a new standard of 10 μg/L. Less than two months later, the Bush II Administration withdrew this standard—only to accept it again after eight months of further review and debate. The following excerpt is from the January 2001 preamble to the arsenic rule.

U.S. Environmental Protection Agency, National Primary Drinking Water Regulations; Arsenic & Clarifications to Compliance & New Source Contaminants Monitoring

66 Fed. Reg. 6976 (Jan. 22, 2001)

Is it appropriate to assume linearity for the dose-response assessment for arsenic at low doses given that arsenic is not directly reactive with DNA? Independent scientific panels who have considered the Taiwan study [upon which EPA based its risk assessment] have raised the caution that using the Taiwan study to estimate U.S. risk at lower levels may result in an overly conservative estimation of U.S. risk. . . . An assumption that the effects seen per dose increment remain the same from high to low levels of dose may overstate the U.S. risk. . . .

The use of a linear procedure to extrapolate from a higher, observed data range to a lower range beyond observation is a science policy approach that has been in use by Federal agencies for four decades. Its basis is both science and policy. The policy objectives are to avoid underestimating risk in order to protect public health and be consistent and clear across risk assessments. The science components include its applicability to generally available data sets (animal tests and human studies) and its basis in the fact that cancer is a consequence of genetic changes coupled with the assumption that direct reaction with DNA is a basic mode of action for chemicals causing important genetic changes.

The linear approach is intended to identify a level of risk that is an upper limit on what the risk might be. . . . There are no data on the effects of arsenic that may be precursors to cancer. Without such biological data, the exercise of blindly applying models has no anchor, in EPA's judgment. Such modeled extrapolations could take numerous shapes and there is no way to decide how shallow or steep the curve would be or where on the dose gradient the zero risk level might be, given the hundreds of possibilities. . . . Since we do not know what the mode of action of arsenic is, we cannot in fact rule out linearity. Therefore . . . the Agency cannot reasonably use anything other than a linear mode of action to estimate the upper bound of risk associated with arsenic exposure.

Today's rule, with a final MCL of 10 µg/L, reflects the application of several provisions under SDWA, the first of which generally requires that EPA set the MCL for each contaminant as close as feasible to the MCLG, based on available technology and taking costs to large systems into account. The 1996 SDWA amendments also require that the Administrator determine whether or not the quantifiable and nonquantifiable benefits of an MCL justify the quantifiable and nonquantifiable costs. This determination is to be based on the Health Risk Reduction and Cost Analysis (HRRCA) required under §1412(b)(3)(C).[18] The HRRCA must include consideration of seven analyses: (1) The quantifiable and nonquantifiable benefits from treatment to the new MCL; (2) The quantifiable and nonquantifiable benefits resulting from reductions of co-occurring contaminants; (3) The quantifiable and nonquantifiable costs resulting directly from the MCL; (4) The incremental costs and benefits at the new MCL and alternatives considered; (5) The health risks posed by the contaminant, including risks to vulnerable populations; (6) Any increased risk resulting from compliance, including risks associated with co-occurring contaminants; and (7) Any other relevant factor, including the uncertainties in the analyses and the degree and nature of risk. Finally, the 1996 SDWA amendments provide new discretionary authority for the Administrator to set an MCL less stringent than the feasible level if the benefits of an MCL set at the feasible level would not justify the costs (§1412(b)(6)) based on the HRRCA analysis.

Today's rule establishing an MCL of 10 µg/L for arsenic is the second time EPA has invoked this new authority. . . . In addition to the feasible MCL of 3 µg/L, the Agency evaluated MCL options of 5 µg/L, 10 µg/L, and 20 µg/L. . . . EPA has determined that a final MCL of 10 µg/L more appropriately meets the relevant statutory criteria referred to above. . . .

The fifth and seventh HRRCA analyses focus on the health risks to be addressed by a new MCL. Estimates of risk levels to the population remaining after the regulation is in place provide a perspective on the level of public health protection and associated benefits. SDWA clearly places a particular focus on public health protection afforded by MCLs. For instance, where EPA decides to use its discretionary authority after a determination that the benefits of an MCL would not justify the costs, §1412(b)(6) requires EPA to set the MCL at a level that "maximizes health risk reduction benefits at a cost that is justified by the benefits." (EPA does not believe the sixth HRRCA analysis, consideration of increased risk likely to result from compliance is a significant factor in connection with selection of a final MCL; rather, we believe that many of the appropriate technologies for reducing arsenic will reduce many other co-occurring inorganic contaminants as well thereby decreasing, rather than increasing risk.)

The Agency based its evaluation of the risk posed by arsenic at the MCL options of 3 µg/L, 5 µg/L, 10 µg/L and 20 µg/L on a number of considerations, including the bladder cancer risk analysis developed by the National Research Council (NRC) of the National Academy of Sciences (NRC, 1999); the NRC's qualitative assessment of other possible adverse health effects; the lung cancer risk analysis developed by Morales et al. (2000); and findings of other relevant national and international studies. . . .

The uncertainties in the analyses of costs, benefits and risks are also a factor required to be considered in the HRRCA. . . . For the arsenic risk assessment, there are several definable sources of uncertainty that were taken into account. These include, but are not limited to, the following: uncertainty about the exact exposure of individuals in the study

---

18. Codified at 42 U.S.C. §300g-1(b)(3)(C). [EDS.]

D. Formal Cost-Benefit Analysis: SDWA

population to arsenic in drinking water, water used in cooking, and food; uncertainties associated with applying data from a population in rural Taiwan to the heterogenous population of the U.S. (including differences in health status and diet between the Taiwanese and the U.S. population); and uncertainties concerning precisely how a chemical causes cancer in humans (the mode of action) that affects assessments of the extent and severity of health effects at low doses. . . .

In EPA's judgment, use of a risk range more clearly supports a qualitative consideration and recognition of the uncertainties that are inherent in any risk analysis that substantially relies upon epidemiological information. . . .

Under HRRCA analyses one and two, the Agency must consider both quantifiable and nonquantifiable health risk reduction benefits. Benefits considered in our analysis include those about which quantitative information is known and can be monetized as well as those which are more qualitative in nature (such as some of the non-cancer health effects potentially associated with arsenic) and which cannot currently be monetized. Important assumptions inherent in EPA's revised analysis of the benefits estimates include the value of a statistical life and willingness to pay to avoid illness. . . . EPA considered the relationship of the monetized benefits to the monetized costs for each the regulatory levels it considered. While strict equality of monetized benefits and costs is not a requirement under §1412(b)(6)(A), this relationship is an important consideration in the regulatory development process. . . .

EPA believes, however, that reliance on only an arithmetic analysis of whether monetized benefits outweigh monetized costs is inconsistent with the statute's instruction to consider both quantifiable and nonquantifiable costs and benefits. The Agency therefore examined and considered qualitative and non-monetized benefits in establishing the final MCL, as well as other factors discussed previously. These benefits are associated with avoiding certain adverse health impacts known to be caused by arsenic at higher concentrations, which may also be associated with low level concentrations, and include skin and prostate cancer as well as cardiovascular, pulmonary, neurological and other non-cancer effects. . . .

Other potential benefits not monetized for today's final rule include customer peace of mind from knowing drinking water has been treated for arsenic and reduced treatment costs for contaminants that may be co-treated with arsenic. (For example, increased use of coagulation and micro filtration by surface water systems will offer benefits with respect to removal of microbial contaminants and disinfection byproducts.) . . .

Both our benefits and cost estimates involve ranges, rather than point estimates, due to a variety of factors. Thus, our consideration of costs and benefits involved an examination and comparison of these ranges. . . . Both total costs and benefits increase as one examines progressively lower (i.e., more stringent) regulatory options compared to higher options. However, the benefits and costs do not increase proportionately across the range of regulatory options as shown by a comparison of net benefits (defined as costs minus benefits). Progressively more stringent regulatory options become considerably more expensive, from a cost standpoint, than the corresponding increases in benefits, as reflected in decreasing net benefits.

The MCL must be set as close as feasible to the MCLG, unless EPA invokes its discretionary authority under §1412(b)(6) of SDWA to set an alternative MCL, which must then be set at a level that maximizes health risk reduction benefits at a cost that is justified by the benefits. . . . The MCLG is zero and the feasible level is 3 µg/L. The Agency believes that there are several important considerations in examining the feasible level.

In comparing the benefits and the costs at this level, we note that it has the highest projected total national costs (relative to the other MCL options considered). In addition, while the benefits are highest at this level relative to the other MCL options, both the net benefits and the benefit/cost disparity at the feasible level are the least favorable of the regulatory options considered. For these reasons, we believe benefits of the feasible level do not justify the costs. . . .

Based on substantial public comment, EPA has reexamined the proposed MCL of 5 µg/L. In comparing this level to 10 µg/L, we note that both the net benefits and the benefit-cost relationships are less favorable for 5 µg/L as compared to 10 µg/L. Total national costs at 5 µg/L are also approximately twice the costs of an MCL of 10 µg/L. At 10 µg/L, EPA notes that the lung and bladder cancer risks to the exposed population after the rule's implementation are within the Agency's target risk range for drinking water contaminants of 1×10^{-6} to 1×10^{-4} or below. EPA recognizes that there is uncertainty in this quantification of cancer risk (as well as other health endpoints) and this risk estimate includes a number of assumptions, as discussed previously. EPA did not directly rely on the risk range in selecting the final MCL, since it is not part of the §1412(b)(6) criteria; however, it is an important consideration, because it has a direct bearing on our estimates of the benefits of the rule.

EPA does not believe an MCL less stringent than 10 µg/L is warranted from the standpoint of benefit-cost comparison. While total national costs associated with 20 µg/L are the lowest of the regulatory options considered, benefits are also the lowest of these options. Both regulatory options of 10 µg/L and 20 µg/L have relatively favorable benefit-cost relationships relative to lower regulatory options but are not significantly different from one another based on this comparison metric. However, the incremental, upper-bound benefits at 10 µg/L are more than twice those of 20 µg/L; and 10 µg/L is clearly the more protective level. Thus, we do not believe that an MCL of 20 µg/L would "maximize health risk reduction benefits" as required for an MCL established pursuant to §1412(b)(6).

Strict parity of monetized costs and monetized benefits is not required to find that the benefits of a particular MCL option are justified under the statutory provisions of §1412(b)(6) of SDWA. However, EPA believes that, based on comparisons of cost and benefits (using the various benefit-cost comparison tools discussed), the monetized benefits of a regulatory level of 10 µg/L best justify the costs. In addition, . . . our further qualitative consideration of the various sources of uncertainty in our understanding of arsenic since the proposal (e.g., such as that surrounding the mode of action), has led us to conclude that our estimate of risk (for the risks we have quantified) is most likely an upper bound of risks and that the higher MCL of 10 µg/L is appropriate. Finally, . . . EPA believes that there are a number of not yet quantified adverse health effects and potentially substantial non-monetized benefits at 10 µg/L that increase the overall benefits at this level. [EPA selected the final MCL of 10 µg/L as "the level that best maximizes health risk reduction benefits at a cost that is justified by the benefits."]

Arsenic standard (µg/L)	Compliance costs, in millions, (1999 dollars)	Health benefits, in millions, (1999 dollars)	Bladder and lung cancer cases avoided
3	$700-790	$210-490	57-140
5	$420-470	$190-360	51-100
10	$180-210	$140-200	37-56
20	$ 67-77	$ 66-75	19-20

TABLE 13-1. *EPA's estimates of the costs and benefits of different arsenic standards. Source: EPA, National Primary Drinking Water Regulations; Arsenic and Clarifications to Compliance and New Source Contaminants Monitoring; Final Rules, 66 Fed. Reg. 6976, 7009, 7017 (Jan. 22, 2001) (rounded to two significant figures).*

D. Formal Cost-Benefit Analysis: SDWA

COMMENTARY & QUESTIONS

1. What explains EPA's decision? Many scholars have promoted cost-benefit analysis on the ground that it increases objectivity and transparency in regulatory decisionmaking. In the well-known circuit court opinion in *Whitman v. American Trucking Ass'ns* (see Chapter 11), a major reason why the D.C. Circuit initially invalidated EPA's implementation of the CAA's NAAQS program was that there was no logical "stopping point" for regulation when economic costs were not taken into account. The court suggested that cost-benefit analysis, if EPA had done it in setting the CAA standards, would have provided such a stopping point. *American Trucking Ass'ns v. EPA*, 175 F.3d 1027, 1037-1038 (D.C. Cir. 1999). Does the SDWA, as applied to arsenic in drinking water, overcome this problem? Does EPA's cost-benefit analysis identify a logical stopping point for regulation, or does it still leave considerable room for discretion on the part of the agency?

2. Trumping quantified costs: reprise. At 10 µg/L, EPA thought its arsenic rule would cost about $210 million per year, while producing about $170 million in quantified benefits. The only benefit EPA could quantify was the prevention of bladder and lung cancer, although the agency concluded that many other illnesses were caused by arsenic. Is this a close case, precluding the trumping of quantified costs by unquantified benefits, as in *Corrosion Proof Fittings*? Note that drinking water standards are reviewed under the "arbitrary and capricious" standard of review. Should the arsenic rule survive judicial review? In a challenge to the arsenic rule, the D.C. Circuit upheld the SDWA and the regulation under the Tenth Amendment and Commerce Clause, but did not review EPA's specific conclusions under general principles of administrative law. *Nebraska v. EPA*, 331 F.3d 995 (D.C. Cir. 2003).

3. "The Arithmetic of Arsenic." Professor Cass Sunstein has argued that the uncertainty of important variables in EPA's analysis—such as the number of cancers prevented by the rule and the monetary value of those illnesses—was so great that EPA could have plausibly concluded that the benefits of the rule spanned a range of $0 to $560 million. Sunstein, The Arithmetic of Arsenic, 90 Geo. L.J. 2255 (2002). Nevertheless, Sunstein believes that cost-benefit analysis is a useful tool in this setting because it limits the influence of irrational perceptions of risk and makes agency decisions more transparent than other regulatory approaches do. Do you agree?

4. The value of (statistical) life. EPA's economic analysis used a value of $6.1 million for each fatal cancer case avoided by the rule. The agency arrived at this figure by considering studies of market decisions about risk. Most of these studies examine how much workers demand in extra wages in exchange for accepting extra workplace risk. EPA's regulation involved latent, passive, involuntary risks of cancer, risks faced by people who had not bargained for such risks, who owned an "entitlement" to be free from risks greater than those remaining after application of the best available control techniques unless EPA chose to depart from an MCL consistent with the best techniques, and who included men, women, and children. The studies on wage premiums for risky work, on the other hand, involved risks of immediate, active accidents among people who (in theory) were paid to take on those risks, and who were mostly men. In light of these contextual differences, was it sensible for EPA to base regulation of risks from arsenic in drinking water on such data? For an analysis and critique of the concept of "statistical life" that underlies all efforts to value human lives in monetary terms, see Heinzerling, The Rights of Statistical People, 24 Harv. Envtl. L. Rev. 189 (2000). Note that the value EPA has most recently used in its economic analyses is just over $9 million, an increase that reflects inflation, wage growth, and a somewhat different database.

5. Willingness to pay . . . for what? One limitation of the studies used to derive the value for a statistical life is the underlying assumption that workers and others making marketplace decisions about risk actually know what they are doing. These ostensibly objective measures rely on several assumptions, including that the workers are accurately informed of the extent of the risk and that the workers properly process the numerical information about the risk. The heavy reliance on wage premium studies is somewhat ironic, since many prominent advocates of monetized cost-benefit analysis, including Justice Breyer and John Graham, are among the most vociferous critics of citizens' risk perceptions.

6. Bladder cancer and chronic bronchitis: Are they the same thing? EPA's $6.1 million figure applied only to fatal cases of bladder cancer. But bladder cancer is often not fatal. "Because the suffering of persons who *survive* cancer was not incorporated into the value of statistical lives calculated from wage premiums, the EPA decided to base the value of reducing survivable cancer on the willingness of individuals to pay to avoid nonfatal cancer. Sadly, the agency lacked any economic studies of the willingness of people to pay to avoid cancer. It instead used a number that some economists had derived for the willingness to pay to avoid chronic bronchitis, which is apparently close enough to nonfatal cancer for government work. That number turned out to be $607,162." McGarity, Professor Sunstein's Fuzzy Math, 90 Geo. L.J. 2341, 2356 (2002). That monetary value for chronic bronchitis was based on responses to a survey conducted in a North Carolina shopping mall, bringing a whole new meaning to the phrase "shoppers rule." Does the need to resort to this methodology simply reflect the limits of available data? Does it suggest a more fundamental problem with using cost-benefit analysis as a key determinant of regulatory policy?

7. Risk assessment and cost-benefit analysis redux. The first three paragraphs of this excerpt from the preamble to EPA's final rule on arsenic in drinking water describe the agency's risk assessment. Can you summarize in layperson's language the justification that EPA gives in this passage? (Hint: Consult the model dose-response curve in Figure 1 and the accompanying note in Section B above.) Suppose the choice of model were challenged in a proceeding for judicial review. How would you frame your objections to the agency's reasoning? How would you react to such a challenge as a reviewing judge?

E. Cost-Benefit Analysis at the White House

The Safe Drinking Water Act is the only federal environmental statute that explicitly embraces formal cost-benefit analysis as a decisionmaking framework. Yet such analysis has, in the last several decades, become an integral part of the regulatory process. It has achieved this status through several executive orders issued by presidents of both political parties, directing agencies to send significant rules to the White House for review before they are issued and to undertake cost-benefit analysis of rules that will likely impose costs of more than $100 million per year. President Ronald Reagan's Executive Order 12291 was the first to systematize White House review and to attach formal cost-benefit analysis to it. Today, regulatory review occurs pursuant to Executive Order 12866, issued by President Bill Clinton in 1993, and Executive Order 13563, issued by President Barack Obama in 2011. Together, these executive orders continue the now decades-long tradition of requiring White House review of rules the White House deems significant and cost-benefit analysis of economically significant rules.

The process of regulatory review is run by the Office of Information and Regulatory Affairs (OIRA) within the Office of Management and Budget (OMB). The head of OIRA

E. Cost-Benefit Analysis at the White House

is known as the "regulatory czar," and with good reason, as the head of OIRA is the White House gatekeeper for regulatory actions moving through the executive agencies. Rules may be delayed or stopped altogether, or, less frequently, sped up or prompted, by the OIRA process. OIRA is, however, very reticent about the influence it has. The result is that rules may be delayed, revised, or stopped altogether and it may be impossible to understand exactly why. In a 2003 report on OIRA's regulatory activities, the GAO recommended that OIRA take steps to make its influence on agency rules more transparent. GAO, Rulemaking: OMB's Role in Reviews of Agencies' Draft Rules and the Transparency of Those Reviews (Sept. 2003). In recent years, OIRA has increased the transparency of its decisionmaking processes by making many documents available on its website, posting notices of meetings with interested parties on pending agency rulemaking proceedings, and maintaining a "dashboard" showing which rules are under review and how long they have been at OIRA. Nevertheless, many matters remain opaque. For example, OIRA does not reveal the substance of the discussions at its meetings with outside parties, nor does it post notices of meetings with parties on general regulatory matters not embraced by pending rulemaking proceedings. Even more problematically, OIRA and the agencies do not—as Executive Order 12866 would seem to require—make public the reasons for the changes that occur during regulatory review.

For a detailed account of how the process of White House review works and how it affects EPA in particular, see L. Heinzerling, Inside EPA: A Former Insider's Reflections on the Relationship Between the Obama EPA and the Obama White House, 31 Pace Envtl. L. Rev. 337 (2014).

COMMENTARY & QUESTIONS

1. OIRA's legal authority. What gives OIRA the authority to oversee agencies' regulations? Suppose a statute forbids cost-benefit balancing in standard-setting. May OIRA return a cost-blind rule to EPA on the ground that it reflects inadequate cost-benefit analysis, or that it conflicts with the President's policies or priorities? Parts of the CWA require EPA to promulgate technology-based regulation. May OIRA require EPA's technology-based rules to be justified by cost-benefit analysis? Would this change the nature of technology-based regulation?

2. Presidential administration. In a widely celebrated article, Presidential Administration, 114 Harv. L. Rev. 2245 (2001), then-professor Elena Kagan offered one theory as to the legal basis for White House review and supervision of agencies' rules. Statutes that delegate decisionmaking power to an executive agency should be presumed, she argued, to delegate power also to the president and his aides in the White House. One advantage of this idea is that it sidesteps difficult constitutional questions posed by the theory of the "unitary executive," and instead grounds presidential authority in a principle of statutory interpretation. Whatever its legal merits, Justice Kagan's theory has, in practice, been warmly embraced by presidents across political parties for decades, as each president has asserted the power ultimately to make the regulatory decisions given by statute to executive agencies. One example of a very public assertion of this power was President Barack Obama's 2011 directive to then-EPA Administrator Lisa Jackson to withdraw a revised NAAQS for ozone. In his public message explaining his decision, President Obama cited "the importance of reducing regulatory burdens and regulatory uncertainty, particularly as our economy continues to recover." Given what you learned in Chapter 11 about the factors relevant to setting the NAAQS, were President Obama's reasons for rejecting the revised ozone NAAQS legally permissible? More generally, how likely is it that presidential administration will introduce political (and perhaps extralegal) considerations into the regulatory process?

3. Is OIRA's cost-benefit analysis a one-way street? While OIRA is strict about requiring detailed cost-benefit analysis supporting major regulatory initiatives, it has not been so strict about requiring this analysis for deregulatory actions. EPA's wholesale dismantling of the CAA's NSR program (discussed in Chapter 11); EPA and the Army Corps of Engineers' reworking of the definition of "fill" material under the CWA to assert that mountaintop removal was an acceptable mining technique (noted in Chapter 12); and the Department of the Interior's decision to let the Clinton Administration's roadless area rule (protecting almost 60 million acres of public lands) go undefended by the government in federal court (see Chapter 9) — and many other decisions having a deregulatory valence were not accompanied by any cost-benefit analysis, and OIRA did not require one. Is that a fault of the methodology of cost-benefit analysis or of the performance of the people undertaking the review?

4. Does life get cheaper as you age? One of the most contentious issues OIRA has faced is how to value the lives saved by regulation. The issue received unusual public attention in 2003, when OIRA's insistence on incorporating a lower value for elderly lives in EPA analyses coincided with then-Administrator Christine Whitman's nationwide "listening tour" concerning environmental issues faced by the elderly. At every stop, Whitman was queried about her agency's so-called senior death discount. Ultimately, Whitman vowed not to use the discount anymore. John Graham, the OIRA administrator at the time, ordered agencies not to use the specific discount (37%) OIRA had previously insisted on using because he had concluded it was not empirically well-grounded. Nevertheless, at the same time, Graham continued to insist that basing regulatory policy on a consideration of the number of life-years saved by regulation made good policy sense. Does it?

5. Simpler? It's complicated. Esteemed law professor Cass Sunstein was the OIRA administrator for the first four years of the Obama Administration. In his book, SIMPLER: THE FUTURE OF GOVERNMENT (2013), Sunstein offered a revealing account of his years at OIRA. He wrote that, as OIRA Administrator, he had the power to "say no to members of the president's Cabinet"; to deposit "highly touted rules, beloved by regulators, onto the shit list"; to make sure that some rules "never saw the light of day"; and to transform cost-benefit analysis from an analytical tool into a "rule of decision," meaning that "[a]gencies could not go forward" if their rules flunked OIRA's cost-benefit test. Sunstein also reported that OIRA required cost-benefit analysis "[w]herever the law allowed." Combined, these practices mean that unless a law unambiguously forbids cost-benefit analysis, OIRA will require agencies to adopt it as a decision rule. Although Executive Orders 12866 and 13563 both state that their regulatory approach applies only to the extent "permitted by law," the very concept of what is "permitted by law" is, in a post-*Chevron* world, often up for grabs — and is now, it appears, subject to change at the behest of the White House.

F. EVALUATING COST-BENEFIT ANALYSIS

1. The Case for Cost-Benefit

In *American Trucking v. Whitman*, a group of prominent economists filed a brief asking the Court to hold that the CAA required EPA to base the NAAQS on cost-benefit analysis.

F. Evaluating Cost-Benefit Analysis

Notably, the economists explicitly declined to address the legal aspects of the case, focusing their arguments solely on policy. The brief's caption read like a Who's Who of American economists and included several Nobel laureates.

American Trucking Associations v. Browner, Brief Amici Curiae of AEI-Brookings Joint Center for Regulatory Studies, et al., in support of American Trucking Associations, et al.
1999 U.S. Briefs 1426

... Both the direct benefits and costs of environmental, health, and safety regulations are substantial—estimated to be several hundred billion dollars annually. If these resources were better allocated with the objective of reducing human health risk, scholars have predicted that tens of thousands more lives could be saved each year.[19] All presidents since Nixon—both Democratic and Republican—have attempted to make environmental, health, and safety regulations more efficient by requiring some form of oversight attempting to balance benefits and costs. President Reagan and President Clinton each crafted an executive order that required an explicit balancing of benefits and costs for major regulations to the extent permitted by law. A comprehensive regulatory impact analysis (RIA) prepared in conformance with President Clinton's Executive Order 12866 was done for the ozone and particulate matter rulemaking, but it played no official or overt part in the decision in this case because of the D.C. Circuit's view that costs must not be considered....

The concern [of amici] is how analytical methods, such as benefit-cost analysis, should be used in regulatory decisionmaking. These methods can help promote the design of better regulations by providing a sensible framework for comparing the alternatives involved in any regulatory choice. Such analysis improves the chances that regulations will be designed to achieve a particular social goal specified by legislators at a lower cost. In addition, they can make the regulatory process more transparent by providing an analytical basis for a decision. Greater transparency in the process, in turn, will help hold regulators and lawmakers more accountable for their decisions.

These analytical methods are neither anti- nor pro-regulation; they can suggest reasons why it would be desirable to have tighter or more lenient standards depending on the results of an analysis. For example, the benefit-cost analyses in the RIA on particulate matter and ozone could be interpreted as suggesting that the ozone standard should not be lowered while a new PM standard for fine particles should be introduced to protect public health....

The courts have also been receptive to the use of benefit-cost analysis in decisionmaking. Indeed, the D.C. Circuit recently held in *Michigan v. EPA*, 213 F.3d 663 (2000), that "it is only where there is 'clear congressional intent to preclude consideration of cost' that we find agencies barred from considering costs." The court went on to cite various cases and legal authorities for the "general view that preclusion of cost consideration requires a rather specific congressional direction." Id. This case and others led Professors Robert H. Frank

---

19. See Tammy O. Tengs & John D. Graham, The Opportunity Costs of Haphazard Social Investments in Life-Saving, in Risks, Costs, and Lives Saved: Getting Better Results from Regulation (Robert W. Hahn ed. 1996). (The authors, from the Harvard School of Public Health, calculated that improved priority setting across federal agencies could provide either savings of $31.1 billion from current cost levels with no additional loss of life or savings of 60,200 lives at current cost levels.)

and Cass R. Sunstein to conclude that "federal law now reflects a kind of default principle: Agencies will consider costs, and thus undertake cost-benefit analysis, if Congress has not unambiguously said that they cannot." . . . [20]

Without delving into the legal aspects of the case, we present below why we think the Court should allow the EPA to consider costs in setting standards. In particular, we believe that, as a general principle, regulators should be allowed to consider explicitly the full consequences of their regulatory decisions. These consequences include the regulation's benefits, costs, and any other relevant factors. . . .

Benefit-cost analysis is simply a tool that can aid in making decisions. Most people do a kind of informal benefit-cost analysis when considering the personal pros and cons of their actions in everyday life—more for big decisions, like choosing a college or job or house, than for little ones, like driving to the grocery store. Where decisions, such as federal environmental regulations, are by their nature public rather than private, the government, as a faithful agent of its citizens, should do something similar.

Carefully considering the social benefits and social costs of a course of action makes good sense. Economists and other students of government policy have developed ways of making those comparisons systematic. Those techniques fall under the label benefit-cost analysis. Benefit-cost analysis does not provide the policy answer, but rather defines a useful framework for debate, either by a legislature or, where the legislature has delegated to a specialized agency the responsibility of pursuing a general good, by that agency.

. . . A wide consensus exists on certain fundamental matters. In 1996, a group of distinguished economists, including Nobel laureate Kenneth Arrow, were assembled to develop principles for benefit-cost analysis in environmental, health, and safety regulation. Here, we summarize and paraphrase for the Court a number of principles that we think could be helpful in this case, which involves the review of the EPA's NAAQS standard-setting decisions.

A benefit-cost analysis is a useful way of organizing a comparison of the favorable and unfavorable effects of proposed policies. Benefit-cost analysis can help the decisionmaker better understand the implications of a decision. . . . In many cases, benefit-cost analysis cannot be used to prove that the economic benefits of a decision will exceed or fall short of the costs. Yet benefit-cost analysis should play an important role in informing the decisionmaking process, even when the information on benefits, costs, or both is highly uncertain, as is often the case with regulations involving the environment, health, and safety.

Economic analysis can be useful in designing regulatory strategies that achieve a desired goal at the lowest possible cost. Too frequently, environmental, health, and safety regulation has used a one-size-fits-all or command-and-control approach. Economic analysis can highlight the extent to which cost savings can be achieved by using alternative, more flexible approaches that reward performance.

Benefit-cost analysis should be required for all major regulatory decisions. The scale of a benefit-cost analysis should depend on both the stakes involved and the likelihood that the resulting information will affect the ultimate decision.

Agencies should not be bound by a strict benefit-cost test, but should be required to consider available benefit-cost analyses. There may be factors other than economic benefits and costs that agencies will want to weigh in decisions, such as equity within and across generations.

---

20. See Frank & Sunstein, Cost-Benefit Analysis and Relative Position, 68 U. Chi. L. Rev. 323, 330 (2001).

F. Evaluating Cost-Benefit Analysis

Not all impacts of a decision can be quantified or expressed in dollar terms. Care should be taken to ensure that quantitative factors do not dominate important qualitative factors in decisionmaking. A common critique of benefit-cost analysis is that it does not emphasize factors that are not easily quantified or monetized. That critique has merit. There are two principal ways to address it: first, quantify as many factors as are reasonable and quantify or characterize the relevant uncertainties; and second, give due consideration to factors that defy quantification but are thought to be important. . . .

COMMENTARY & QUESTIONS

1. The result in the Court. As we know from Chapter 11, in *American Trucking* the Supreme Court unanimously rejected the economists' position, choosing law over that policy argument and holding that the CAA forbids the consideration of costs in setting the harm-based NAAQS. In looking for (but not finding) an explicit directive on costs in the text of the statute itself, moreover, the Court seemed almost to create an "anti-cost-benefit default principle" — because costs loom large in any major regulatory endeavor, Congress's failure to mention them explicitly might be taken as a sign, as in *American Trucking*, that it did not want the agency to consider them. As a matter of political theory, is the proper role for cost-benefit analysis in setting regulatory standards a matter for economics policy, the courts, the executive, or the Congress?

2. Subsequent cases. Later cases have eroded, and perhaps eliminated, the default principle just described. In *Entergy Corp. v. Riverkeeper, Inc.*, 556 U.S. 208 (2009), the Court held that when EPA itself chose to consider cost and used cost-benefit analysis in determining the "best technology available" for cooling water intake structures at existing plants under §316(b) of the Clean Water Act, 33 U.S.C. §1326(b), that was a reasonable interpretation of the statute, entitled to *Chevron* deference. In *Michigan v. EPA*, 135 S. Ct. 2699 (2015), the Court went even further. Reviewing EPA's determination that it was "appropriate and necessary" to regulate power plants under §112 of the Clean Air Act and that this determination should be made without regard to cost, the Court held that it was unreasonable for the agency to refuse to take cost into account: "Read naturally in the present context, the phrase 'appropriate and necessary' requires at least some attention to cost. One would not say that it is even rational, never mind 'appropriate,' to impose billions of dollars in economic costs in return for a few dollars in health or environmental benefits." The Court declined to read *Whitman v. American Trucking Associations* as supporting EPA's decision, referring to that case's "modest principle that where the Clean Air Act expressly directs EPA to regulate on the basis of a factor that on its face does not include cost, the Act normally should not be read as implicitly allowing the Agency to consider cost anyway." Strikingly, all nine Justices—the five who joined Justice Scalia's majority opinion for the Court, and the four who joined Justice Kagan's dissent—seem to have agreed with Justice Kagan's statement that "(absent contrary indication from Congress) an agency must take costs into account in some manner before imposing significant regulatory burdens."

3. The economists' framework. How does the economists' description of what they mean by cost-benefit analysis differ from any other decisionmaking framework that takes costs into account—including even that old command-and-control standby, technology-based regulation? How will quantified and unquantified values be combined in their framework to produce a decision? The distinctions among various ways of analyzing costs and benefits has become even more pronounced in the aftermath of the Supreme Court's decision in *Michigan v. EPA*, discussed above. The Court rejected the idea that EPA must conduct "a formal cost-benefit analysis in which each advantage and disadvantage is assigned a monetary value," and instead said simply: "It will be up to the Agency to decide (as always, within the limits of reasonable interpretation) how to account for cost." Possible options for the agency include: formal cost-benefit analysis, "wholly disproportionate" analysis, and perhaps the more constrained feasibility analysis one finds in the technology-based provisions of the Clean Water Act. Which option is best? Which requires more analytical work on the part of the agency? In thinking about these questions, bear in mind that EPA had, in developing the §112 rule for power plants, undertaken a detailed cost-benefit analysis of the rule for purposes of White House review. That study showed that the benefits of regulating power plants greatly outweighed the costs—but only if the "co-benefits" of regulating non-hazardous air pollutants such as particulate matter were taken into account. May such "ancillary" benefits be taken into account in deciding whether to regulate sources under a program targeted at hazardous air pollutants? Should they be?

4. Statistical murder? John Graham, one of the authors of the study relied upon by the AEI amici economists in arguing that a failure to do cost-benefit analysis results in squandered lifesaving opportunities, has called this state of affairs "statistical murder." Anyone interested in saving lives must take notice of this argument. Most of the "tens of thousands of lives" that the Tengs-Graham study cited by the AEI amici economists said could be saved by redirecting our lifesaving resources were in the health care field, and only a very small portion of the additional lives saved was due to redirection of environmental priorities. Does the presence of good safety-improving efforts in other fields undercut the case for environmental protection? Is safety-improving regulatory action a zero-sum game, where there is a fixed amount of resources society will devote to the effort?

2. The Case Against Cost-Benefit Analysis

Frank Ackerman & Lisa Heinzerling, Pricing the Priceless: Cost-Benefit Analysis of Environmental Protection

150 University of Pennsylvania Law Review 1553 (2002)

... Cost-benefit analysis involves the creation of artificial markets for things—like good health, long life, and clean air—that are not bought and sold. It also involves the devaluation of future events through discounting.

So described, the mind-set of the cost-benefit analyst is likely to seem quite foreign. The translation of all good things into dollars and the devaluation of the future are inconsistent with the way many people view the world. Most of us believe that money doesn't buy happiness. Most religions tell us that every human life is sacred; it is obviously illegal, as well as immoral, to buy and sell human lives. Most parents tell their children to eat their vegetables and do their homework, even though the rewards of these onerous activities lie far in the future. Monetizing human lives and discounting future benefits seem at odds with these common perspectives.

The cost-benefit approach also is inconsistent with the way many of us make daily decisions. Imagine performing a new cost-benefit analysis to decide whether to get up and go to work every morning, whether to exercise or eat right on any given day, whether to wash the dishes or leave them in the sink, and so on. Inaction would win far too often—and an absurd amount of effort would be spent on analysis. Most people have long-run goals, commitments, and habits that make such daily balancing exercises either redundant or counterproductive. The same might be true of society as a whole undertaking individual steps in

F. Evaluating Cost-Benefit Analysis

the pursuit of any goal, set for the long haul, that cannot be reached overnight—including, for example, the achievement of a clean environment.

Moving beyond these intuitive responses, . . . [i]n our view, cost-benefit analysis suffers from four fundamental flaws, addressed in the next four subsections:

- The standard economic approaches to valuation are inaccurate and implausible.
- The use of discounting improperly trivializes future harms and the irreversibility of some environmental problems.
- The reliance on aggregate, monetized benefits excludes questions of fairness and morality.
- The value-laden and complex cost-benefit process is neither objective nor transparent.

DOLLARS WITHOUT SENSE. Recall that cost-benefit analysis requires the creation of artificial prices for all relevant health and environmental impacts. To weigh the benefits of regulation against the costs, we need to know the monetary value of preventing the extinction of species, preserving many different ecosystems, avoiding all manner of serious health impacts, and even saving human lives. Without such numbers, cost-benefit analysis cannot be conducted.

Artificial prices have been estimated for many, though by no means all, benefits of regulation. As discussed, preventing the extinction of bald eagles reportedly goes for somewhat more than $250 per household. Preventing retardation due to childhood lead poisoning comes in at about $9,000 per lost IQ point in the standard view, or a mere $1,500 per point in Lutter's alternative. Saving a life is ostensibly worth $6.3 million.

This quantitative precision, achieved through a variety of indirect techniques for valuation, comes at the expense of accuracy and even common sense. Though problems arise in many areas of valuation, we will focus primarily on the efforts to attach a monetary value to human life, both because of its importance in cost-benefit analysis and because of its glaring contradictions.

We note, however, that the same kind of problems we are about to discuss affect other valuation issues raised by cost-benefit analysis, such as estimating the value of clean water, biodiversity, or entire ecosystems. The upshot is that cost-benefit analysis is fundamentally incapable of delivering on its promise of more economically efficient decisions about protecting human life, health, and the environment. Absent a credible monetary metric for calculating the benefits of regulation, cost-benefit analysis is inherently unreliable.

THERE ARE NO "STATISTICAL" PEOPLE. What can it mean to say that saving one life is worth $6.3 million? Human life is the ultimate example of a value that is not a commodity, and does not have a price. You cannot buy the right to kill someone for $6.3 million, nor for any other price. Most systems of ethical and religious belief maintain that every life is sacred. If analysts calculated the value of life itself by asking people what it is worth to them (the most common method of valuation of other environmental benefits), the answer would be infinite, as "no finite amount of money could compensate a person for the loss of his life, simply because money is no good to him when he is dead."[21]

The standard response is that a value like $6.3 million is not actually a price on an individual's life or death. Rather, it is a way of expressing the value of small risks of death; for

---

21. Broome, Trying to Value a Life, 9 J. Pub. Econ. 91, 92 (1978).

example, it is one million times the value of a one in a million risk. If people are willing to pay $6.30 to avoid a one in a million increase in the risk of death, then the "value of a statistical life" is $6.3 million.

Unfortunately, this explanation fails to resolve the dilemma. It is true that risk (or "statistical life") and life itself are distinct concepts. In practice, however, analysts often ignore the distinction between valuing risk and valuing life.[22] Many regulations reduce risk for a large number of people, and avoid actual death for a much smaller number. A complete cost-benefit analysis should, therefore, include valuation of both of these benefits. However, the standard practice is to calculate a value only for "statistical" life and to ignore life itself.

The confusion between the valuation of risk and the valuation of life itself is embedded in current regulatory practice in another way as well. The Office of Management and Budget—which reviews cost-benefit analyses prepared by federal agencies pursuant to Executive Order—instructs agencies to discount the benefits of life-saving regulations from the moment of avoided death, rather than from the time when the risk of death is reduced.[23] This approach to discounting is plainly inconsistent with the claim that cost-benefit analysis seeks to evaluate risk. When a life-threatening disease—such as cancer—has a long latency period, many years may pass between the time when a risk is imposed and the time of death. If monetary valuations of statistical life represented risk, and not life, then the value of statistical life would be discounted from the date of a change in risk (typically, when a new regulation is enforced) rather than from the much later date of avoided actual death.[24]

In acknowledging the monetary value of reducing risk, economic analysts have contributed to our growing awareness that life-threatening risk itself—and not just the end result of such risk, death—is an injury. But they have blurred the line between risks and actual deaths, by calculating the value of reduced risk while pretending that they have produced a valuation of life itself. The paradox of monetizing the infinite or immeasurable value of human life has not been resolved; it has only been glossed over.

PEOPLE CARE ABOUT OTHER PEOPLE. Another large problem with the standard approach to valuation of life is that it asks individuals (either directly through surveys, or indirectly through observing wage and job choices) only about their attitudes toward risks to themselves.

A recurring theme in literature suggests that our deepest and noblest sentiments involve valuing someone else's life more highly than our own: think of parents' devotion to their children, soldiers' commitment to those whom they are protecting, lovers' concern for each other. Most spiritual beliefs call on us to value the lives of others—not only those closest to us, but also those whom we have never met. . . .

VOTING IS DIFFERENT FROM BUYING. Cost-benefit analysis, which relies on estimates of individuals' preferences as consumers, also fails to address the collective choice presented to society by most public health and environmental problems.

---

22. For further elaboration, see Heinzerling, The Rights of Statistical People, 24 Harv. Envtl. L. Rev. 189, 203-206 (2000).

23. Economic Analysis of Federal Regulations Under Executive Order 12,866, at pt. III.B.5(a) (Report of Interagency Group Chaired by a Member of the Council of Economic Advisors) (Jan. 11, 1996).

24. Heinzerling, Discounting Our Future, 34 Land & Water L. Rev. 39, 71 (1999); Heinzerling, Discounting Life, 108 Yale L.J. 1911, 1913 (1999).

F. Evaluating Cost-Benefit Analysis

Valuation of environmental benefits is based on individuals' private decisions as consumers or workers, not on their public values as citizens. However, policies that protect the environment are often public goods, and are not available for purchase in individual portions. In a classic example of this distinction, the philosopher Mark Sagoff found that his students, in their role as citizens, opposed commercial ski development in a nearby wilderness area, but, in their role as consumers, would plan to go skiing there if the development was built.[25] There is no contradiction between these two views: as individual consumers, the students would have no way to express their collective preference for wilderness preservation. Their individual willingness to pay for skiing would send a misleading signal about their views as citizens. . . .

Cost-benefit analysis turns public citizens into selfish consumers, and interconnected communities into atomized individuals. In this way, it distorts the question it sets out to answer: how much do we, as a society, value health and the environment?

NUMBERS DON'T TELL US EVERYTHING. A few simple examples illustrate that numerically equal risks are not always equally deserving of regulatory response. The death rate is roughly the same (somewhat less than one in a million) from a day of downhill skiing, from a day of working in the construction industry, or from drinking about 20 liters of water containing 50 parts per billion of arsenic, the old regulatory limit that was recently revised by EPA. This does not mean that society's responsibility to reduce risks is the same in each case.

Most people view risks imposed by others, without an individual's consent, as more worthy of government intervention than risks that an individual knowingly accepts. On that basis, the highest priority among our three examples is to reduce drinking water contamination, a hazard to which no one has consented. The acceptance of a risky occupation such as construction is at best quasi-voluntary—it involves somewhat more individual discretion than the "choice" of public drinking water supplies, but many people go to work under great economic pressure, and with little information about occupational hazards. In contrast, the choice of risky recreational pursuits such as skiing is entirely discretionary; obviously no one is forced to ski. Safety regulation in construction work is thus more urgent than regulation of skiing, despite the equality of numerical risk.

In short, even for ultimate values such as life and death, the social context is decisive in our evaluation of risks. Cost-benefit analysis assumes the existence of generic, acontextual risk, and thereby ignores the contextual information that determines how many people, in practice, think about real risks to real people.

ARTIFICIAL PRICES ARE EXPENSIVE. Finally, the economic valuation called for by cost-benefit analysis is fundamentally flawed because it demands an enormous volume of consistently updated information, which is beyond the practical capacity of our society to generate.

All attempts at valuation of the environment begin with a problem: the goal is to assign monetary prices to things that have no prices, because they are not for sale. One of the great strengths of the market is that it provides so much information about real prices. For any commodity that is actually bought and sold, prices are communicated automatically, almost costlessly, and with constant updates as needed. To create artificial prices for

---

25. Mark Sagoff, The Economy of the Earth: Philosophy, Law, and the Environment (Cambridge University Press 1990).

environmental values, economists have to find some way to mimic the operation of the market. Unfortunately the process is far from automatic, it is certainly not costless, and it has to be repeated every time an updated price is needed. . . . [T]here is constant pressure to use outdated or inappropriate valuations [and] sound economic reasons for doing so: no one can afford constant updates, and significant savings can be achieved by using valuations created for other cases.

TRIVIALIZING THE FUTURE. One of the great triumphs of environmental law is its focus on the future: it seeks to avert harms to people and to natural resources in the future, and not only within this generation, but within future generations as well. . . .

Cost-benefit analysis systematically downgrades the importance of the future in two ways: through the technique of discounting, and through predictive methodologies that take inadequate account of the possibility of catastrophic and irreversible events. . . .

DO FUTURE GENERATIONS COUNT? The first problem with the later-is-better argument for discounting is that it assumes that one person is deciding between dying or falling ill now, or dying or falling ill later. In that case, virtually everyone would prefer later. But many environmental programs protect the far future, beyond the lifetime of today's decision-makers. Thus the choice implicit in discounting is between preventing harms to the current generation and preventing similar harms to future generations. Seen in this way, discounting looks like a fancy justification for foisting our problems off onto the people who come after us.

The time periods involved in protecting the environment are often enormous—many decades for a wide range of problems, and even many centuries, in the case of climate change, radioactive waste, and other persistent toxins. With time spans this long, discounting at any positive rate will make even global catastrophes seem trivial. At a discount rate of 5 percent, for example, the death of a billion people 500 years from now becomes less serious than the death of one person today.

DOES HASTE PREVENT WASTE? The justification of discounting often assumes that environmental problems won't get any worse if we wait to address them. . . .

Too many years of delay may mean that the polar ice cap melts, the spent uranium leaks out of the containment ponds, the hazardous waste seeps into groundwater and basements and backyards—at which point we can't put the genie back in the bottle at any reasonable cost (or perhaps not at all).

Environmentalists often talk of potential "crises," of threats that problems will become suddenly and irreversibly worse. In response to such threats, environmentalists and some governments advocate the so-called "precautionary principle," which calls upon regulators to err on the side of caution and protection when risks are uncertain. Cost-benefit analysts, for the most part, do not assume the possibility of crisis. Their worldview assumes stable problems, with control costs that are stable or declining over time, and thus finds precautionary investment in environmental protection to be a needless expense. Discounting is part of this non-crisis perspective. By implying that the present cost of future environmental harms declines, lockstep, with every year that we look ahead, discounting ignores the possibility of catastrophic and irreversible harms. . . .

EXACERBATING INEQUALITY. The third fundamental defect of cost-benefit analysis is that it tends to ignore, and therefore to reinforce, patterns of economic and social inequality.

F. Evaluating Cost-Benefit Analysis

Cost-benefit analysis consists of adding up all the costs of a policy, adding up all the benefits, and comparing the totals. Implicit in this innocuous-sounding procedure is the controversial assumption that it doesn't matter who gets the benefits and who pays the costs. Both benefits and costs are measured simply as dollar totals; those totals are silent on questions of equity and distribution of resources.

Yet in our society, concerns about equity frequently do and should enter into debates over public policy....

LESS OBJECTIVITY AND TRANSPARENCY. A fourth fundamental flaw of cost-benefit analysis is that it is unable to deliver on the promise of more objective and more transparent decision-making. In fact, in most cases, the use of cost-benefit analysis is likely to deliver less objectivity and less transparency.

For the reasons we have discussed, there is nothing objective about the basic premises of cost-benefit analysis. Treating individuals solely as consumers, rather than as citizens with a sense of moral responsibility to the larger society, represents a distinct and highly contestable worldview. Likewise, the use of discounting reflects judgments about the nature of environmental risks and citizens' responsibilities toward future generations which are, at a minimum, debatable. Because value-laden premises permeate cost-benefit analysis, the claim that cost-benefit analysis offers an "objective" way to make government decisions is simply bogus.

Furthermore, as we have seen, cost-benefit analysis relies on a byzantine array of approximations, simplifications, and counterfactual hypotheses. Thus, the actual use of cost-benefit analysis inevitably involves countless judgment calls. People with strong, and clashing, partisan positions will naturally advocate that discretion in the application of this methodology be exercised in favor of their positions, further undermining the claim that cost-benefit analysis is objective....

For many of the same reasons, cost-benefit analysis also generally fails to achieve the goal of transparency. Cost-benefit analysis is a complex, resource-intensive, and expert-driven process. It requires a great deal of time and effort to attempt to unpack even the simplest cost-benefit analysis. Few community groups, for example, have access to the kind of scientific and technical expertise that would allow them to evaluate whether, intentionally or unintentionally, the authors of a cost-benefit analysis have unfairly slighted the interests of the community or some of its members. Few members of the public can meaningfully participate in the debates about the use of particular regression analyses or discount rates which are central to the cost-benefit method....

COMMENTARY & QUESTIONS

1. **Doomed, or just needs tinkering?** Are Ackerman and Heinzerling's objections to cost-benefit analysis fundamental, or would some fine-tuning refinements of cost-benefit analysis as currently practiced satisfy their concerns?

2. **What's the alternative?** What could take the place of cost-benefit analysis? In their article, Ackerman and Heinzerling suggest that regulatory approaches such as technology-based controls, emissions trading schemes, and disclosure requirements all can (and do) operate without use of cost-benefit analysis, and that they serve as proven alternatives to this analytical framework. Do you agree? Does it help to distinguish between discarding cost-benefit analysis and discarding the consideration of regulatory costs?

What is a cynic? A man who knows the price of everything and the value of nothing.

—Oscar Wilde

They were careless people. . . . They smashed up things and creatures and then retreated back into their money or their vast carelessness . . . and let other people clean up the mess they had made. . . .

— F. Scott Fitzgerald, THE GREAT GATSBY (1925)

14

Market-Enlisting Strategies: Achieving Environmental Protection Through Pollution Trading and Other Economic Incentives

A. A Survey of Market Enlistment Devices
B. Domestic Trading Experience in the U.S.
C. International Trading to Reduce GHG Emissions
D. Carbon Taxes
E. Industry Self-Regulation: The International Organization for Standardization

Using market incentives to influence polluting behavior is not a new idea in environmental regulation, but it played only a small role either internationally or domestically before 1990. This chapter begins by canvassing regulatory mechanisms that usually are thought of as economic or market-enlisting in nature; it then reviews domestic experience with those devices in the U.S.[1] The remainder of the chapter looks toward the problem of controlling GHG emissions, considering the potential superiority of a carbon tax to a cap-and-trade program and tracing the developments to date at the international level.

A. SURVEY OF MARKET ENLISTMENT DEVICES

In a report released in 1997 entitled "Evaluating Economic Instruments for Environmental Policy," the OECD labeled environmental controls "economic" in nature "[when] they affect estimates of costs and benefits of alternative actions open to economic agents."[2] The OECD distinguished four categories of controls:

---

1. In considering the design and potential of several of these market-enlisting devices, we again recommend the article by Paul Krugman, Building a Green Economy, N.Y. Times Mag., Apr. 11, 2010, at MM34, available at www.nytimes.com/2010/04/11/magazine/11Economy-t.html.
2. OECD, Evaluating Economic Instruments for Environmental Policy 15 (1997).

- charges & taxes,
- subsidies,
- tradeable emissions permits, and
- deposit refund systems.

All of these are represented in contemporary environmental law.

Effluent taxes, such as disposal fees at landfills, have a considerable history and have had the effect of reducing the flow of wastes into the landfills. Subsidies, such as grants for the construction of publicly owned [water] treatment works (POTWs), have been an effective staple of water pollution control in the U.S. for more than three-quarters of a century. More recently, the use of emissions trading systems has become the centerpiece of proposals for major shifts in regulatory policy when combating many of the world's and the U.S.'s most pressing environmental problems, particularly the emission of acid rain producing sulfur oxides and GHGs. Bottle deposit and return laws, in widespread use in the U.S., have reduced roadside litter and increased recycling of beverage containers. Still other "economic instruments," such as bounties paid for the delivery of car hulks to metal recyclers,[3] do not fit precisely into any of the categories but are "economic" influences that change behavior in ways that improve environmental quality. This chapter emphasizes trading systems, which have emerged as the economic instrument of greatest contemporary interest as an environmental regulatory strategy.

Market incentives enjoy widespread political and practical appeal. They are alluring to "free marketeers" and other opponents of traditional government regulation because direct regulation is replaced by incentives that influence the actions of "economic agents" as the means to achieve improved environmental outcomes. Proponents of market incentives claim that the favorable results will be obtained at lower total social cost than that expected with conventional command-and-control regulatory programs. Moreover, so the claim goes, those more efficient results are obtained without extensive governmental oversight and bureaucracy.

A very simple matrix of behavioral assumptions underlies virtually all of the market incentive-based approaches to environmental regulation. These behavioral assumptions posit firms and individuals as rational profit maximizers reacting to the conditions set by the relevant economic instrument. Taking as an example conventional pollution of air or water by a factory, in the absence of regulation, waste disposal into the commons is a nearly costless activity and is, therefore, the disposal method of choice. If a cost is added to disposal, firms react. The two predominant economic devices that are used to influence disposal decisions are effluent taxes and marketable trading systems.[4] The behavioral assumptions are elementary:

---

3. See, e.g., *Hughes v. Alexandria Scrap*, 426 U.S. 794 (1976).

4. After-the-fact cost internalization, as might be obtained using the common law or CERCLA, is a more attenuated form of effluent tax. The imposition of the cost (liability for damages) is less certain (suit might not be brought, a defense might succeed, etc.), but the expected results of such cases should influence polluting behavior. If the cost of controlling pollution is less than the expected cost of polluting and sometimes paying damages, firms will choose not to pollute, or to pollute less and incur fewer or smaller damage awards. Even then, an effluent tax is likely to operate more efficiently than a damage liability system due to the high transaction costs of imposing damages through a litigation-centered system.

A. Survey of Market Enlistment Devices

Characteristics of Firm:	With Effluent Taxes:	With Emissions Trading Systems:
High-cost pollution avoider	Will pay the tax and continue to pollute	Will purchase credits in the market and continue to pollute
Low-cost pollution avoider	Will reduce pollution and avoid some or all of the tax	Will reduce pollution and sell credits in the market

FIGURE 14-1. *The logic of market-enlistment taxs or trading.*

In facing the challenges posed by climate change—with atmospheric CO_2 now recognized as the GHG primarily responsible for global warming—market-enlisting regulatory approaches dominate discussions of how governments will respond. As Secretary of Energy and Nobel Laureate Steven Chu succinctly declared, "I absolutely believe a price on carbon is essential."[5] The question is how that price strategy will be delivered: by a charge or tax, by trading mechanisms, or something else.

The CAA, beginning with the 1977 Amendments and especially the 1990 Amendments, began an expansion in the use of market-enlisting regulatory regimes, particularly emissions trading, that is nothing short of revolutionary. The 1977 Amendments made possible small-scale trading: "bubbles" and netting permitted intra-firm trading, and offsets and banking allowed limited inter-firm trading. The 1990 Amendments added Title IV, an aggressive trading program intended to reduce SO_2 emission of electricity generators in the U.S. by 50% as part of the effort to combat acid rain. More broadly as canvassed later in this chapter, at least since the Kyoto conference in 1997, emissions trading had emerged as the central strategy for combating GHG emissions and global climate change. In the U.S. trading has been tried or suggested to address a host of environmental problems including regional air quality in nonattainment areas, power plant mercury emissions, nonpoint source agricultural discharges into rivers, metals deposition into POTWs (to render sewage sludge less hazardous), and even tradable quotas limiting the taking of fish stocks to prevent the tragedy of the commons problem of overfishing.

COMMENTARY & QUESTIONS

1. **Avant-garde?** For many years, trading was the rage in environmental regulation, with an avalanche of commentary on the subject. One of the most thoughtful and cross-cutting of these is Salzman & Ruhl, Currencies and the Commodification of Environmental Law, 53 Stan. L. Rev. 607 (2000). For a small sampling of the late twentieth-century legal literature on the subject, see id. at 610-611, nn.4-6. There is also a large economics literature on trading. See, e.g., Ellerman, Joskow, & Harrison, Emissions Trading in the United States: Experience, Lessons and Considerations for Greenhouse Gases (Pew Center on Global Climate Change Report, May 2003) and the sources cited there. The report is available at www.pewclimate.org. After the failure of federal legislation creating a cap-and-trade program for addressing climate change, trading lost some of its luster as the go-to strategy for dealing with environmental problems.

---

5. Zakaria, Swing for the Fences, Newsweek, April 5, 2010 at 42. Secretary Chu indicated that he favored cap-and-trade based on the incremental success of the 1990 CAA's sulfur oxide (SOx) trading precedent.

2. Fungibility. Salzman and Ruhl make a point that bears watching from the outset:

> If one compares trading programs, they all seem to share a basic feature. The CFC, fisheries, and proposed greenhouse gas environmental trading markets [ETMs], for example, all exchange commodities that appear to be fungible. One molecule of CFC, kilo of halibut, or ton of carbon dioxide seems much the same as another, both in terms of identity and impact. It is trading apples for apples (or pork bellies for pork bellies). Thus ETMs are considered a type of commodity market, where environmental credits go to the highest bidder. And for good reason, since the Chicago Board of Trade now sells rights to emit sulfur dioxide alongside pork bellies, orange juice, and grain futures.
>
> Indeed ETMs must assume fungibility—that the things exchanged are sufficiently similar in ways important to the goals of environmental protection—otherwise there would be no assurance that trading ensured environmental protection. While the precondition of fungibility may seem self-evident, this core assumption turns out to be more problematic than it first appears.
>
> As an example of why fungibility matters, consider wetlands mitigation banking. This policy permits developers, once they have taken steps to avoid and minimize wetland loss, to compensate for wetlands that will be destroyed through development by ensuring the restoration of wetlands in another location. The regulations mandate trades that ensure equivalent value and function between destroyed and restored wetlands. In practice, however, most trades are valued in units of acreage. Within very loose guidelines, trades between productive (though soon to be destroyed) wetlands and restored wetlands are approved on an acre-for-acre basis. More sophisticated banks require ratios, trading development on one acre of productive wetlands for, say, restoring four or five acres of wetlands somewhere else. Counting acres may make for easy accounting, but it is poor policy. 53 Stan. L. Rev. at 611-612 (footnotes omitted).

Are all types of emissions equally fungible and equally well suited to trading? For example, consider power plant mercury emissions, which tend to travel only a short distance once emitted. The greatest risk of this is the exposure pathway that leads to humans through the uptake of mercury in the aquatic systems culminating in bioaccumulation in fish that are then consumed by humans and other species. While units of mercury pollution emitted a half continent apart are for some purposes similar, their localized environmental impacts show they are not fungible in a trading system that is intended to protect the public health. Does that example make all trading in hazardous pollutants a dubious proposition, or does it merely call for careful scrutiny of systems that allow hazardous pollutants to be traded?

3. Will firms act "rationally"? The behavioral assumption matrix that appears in the text above relies on very simplistic assumptions regarding behavior. Given the knowledge of behavior in complex organizations such as large corporations, is it reasonable to rely on those assumptions? Timothy Malloy, in Regulating by Incentive: Myths, Models, and Micromarkets, 80 Tex. L. Rev. 531 (2002), describes the situation:

> Environmental regulation is all about using incentives to control behavior. Under direct "command and control" regulation, the government creates specific obligations and generally relies upon the negative incentives of civil and criminal penalties to motivate individuals or organizations to comply with those obligations. Alternatively, the new generation of "market-based" or "incentive-based" regulations typically creates an opportunity rather than (or in addition to) an obligation, offering the positive incentive of increased profits (or reduced costs) in the hope of eliciting the desired behavior. A regulator using either of these two regulatory approaches must identify the appropriate type and level of incentive—be it positive or negative—needed to produce the "correct" response from the target. In crafting and evaluating regulatory incentives, a regulator necessarily relies upon some basic model of how the target

A. Survey of Market Enlistment Devices

makes decisions. If that model is flawed, then the incentive will miss the mark, and the desired behavior may never occur.

Given the importance of accurately predicting responses to regulation, one might expect that regulators and legal scholars alike would carefully select the decision-making models they use. Yet surprisingly little attention is paid to how businesses make choices in the face of government regulation. Many regulators and scholars rely upon a "black-box" model in developing and evaluating environmental regulatory incentives directed at businesses. Although no single, authoritative description of the black-box model exists, most formulations include three major components. First, the model assumes that the organization is a monolithic entity that essentially makes decisions as a natural individual would. Thus, the collective nature of the firm and its internal features are largely ignored. Second, the model assumes that the unitary firm makes decisions rationally. For these purposes, a "rational" person makes decisions by collecting all relevant information, identifying and evaluating all alternatives and their likely outcomes, and selecting the alternative most likely to achieve the person's goals. Third, the traditional formulation of the black-box model assumes that the firm has one dominant goal: maximizing profits. Id. at 531-533 (footnotes omitted).

Malloy's article goes on to challenge the black-box model. He posits as more realistic a "resource allocation model" in which the firm's response to an incentive is a function of the firm's "organization and internal processes," not merely a guess based on a simplistic expected cost calculus. If Malloy is correct in his assertion that the regulator should craft a more thorough, unique model of the decisionmaking of each regulated entity, the information demands of using economic instruments (and thereby the transaction costs of this regulatory approach) increase dramatically.

4. Replacing neoclassical economics with behavioral economics—moving from simplifying assumptions to empirically derived evidence of behavior. Similar to the work that Malloy did in examining the "black-box model," the subdiscipline of behavioral economics explores the "rational maximizer" model by replacing some of its simplifying assumptions with more accurate, empirically validated descriptions of the behavior of economic actors. In the introduction to a collection of papers entitled "Behavioral Economics: Past, Present, and Future" (2002), Colin Camerer and George Loewenstein state:

> Most of the papers modify one or two assumptions in standard theory in the direction of greater psychological realism. Often these departures are not radical at all because they relax simplifying assumptions that are not central to the economic approach. For example, there is nothing in core neoclassical theory that specifies that people should not care about fairness, that they should weight risky outcomes in a linear fashion, or that they must discount the future exponentially at a constant rate.*

Behavioral economics uses empirical data about human behavior and preferences to undercut assumptions that ignore fairness, insist upon linearity of risk assessment, and discount future values exponentially. When those assumptions are undermined, how should that affect reliance on cost-benefit analysis as a decisional tool? More radically, Camerer and Loewenstein also note that they believe it likely that the neoclassical rational maximization model for making predictions of economic behavior will eventually be eclipsed because "alternative paradigms will eventually be proposed which have greater explanatory power." Id. at 2 n. 2.

5. One firm's "excess" reduction is another firm's continued pollution. Why is society better off if one company that efficiently cuts its pollution then just sells the "right" to pollute to a dirty factory somewhere else? The answers are both obvious and subtle—(1) the aggregate loadings of the receiving environmental medium are being reduced because

---

* *Source*: econ2.econ.iastate.edu/tesfatsi/CamererIntroChapter.AdvancesBE.pdf, at 2.

the combined emissions from the two sources are being reduced, and (2) for any given level of allowable loadings, trading should make it possible to obtain that reduction in pollution at a lower total social cost. Getting to the goal at lower cost makes those savings available for other socially productive uses, although initially the savings take the form of increased profits for the firms involved.

6. **Setting the cap intelligently—information demands.** By not seeking even greater levels of pollution reduction, however, the trading system entrenches a *governmentally chosen* level of emissions (the cap) and undercuts the incentives to further emissions reduction. What if it would not be very burdensome for firms to reduce their pollution even further than they would through cap-and-trade? For example, what if the application of available and economically affordable control technologies could reduce emissions by an additional 50%? This last point underscores the importance of who chooses the cap (usually the legislature, but possibly an administrative agency) and on what basis. Setting the cap at an appropriate level requires detailed knowledge of available technology, cost of compliance, and the linkage between emission levels and reduction of environmental and health damage, a calculation that belies the myth that the information demands of an optimally designed cap-and-trade program are less than those of technology-based pollution control.

B. Domestic Trading Experience in the U.S.

1. Domestic Air Pollution Trading Regimes

Emissions trading in the U.S. has been concentrated in the air pollution field. Trading regimes are utilized to a far lesser degree in regard to water pollution and even for the allocation of ocean fish harvests.[6] The following provides a catalog of the U.S. experience with its initial forays into emissions trading.

A. Denny Ellerman, Paul L. Joskow & David Harrison, Jr., Emissions Trading in the United States: Experience, Lessons and Considerations for Greenhouse Gases— the Pew Center on Global Climate Change Report

May 2003, at 4-9, 11-18[7]

Three Basic Types of Emissions Trading Programs. Three broad types of emissions trading programs have emerged: reduction credit, averaging, and cap-and-trade programs. Although all share the feature of tradability, the three differ in important respects.

Reduction credit programs provide tradable credits to facilities that reduce emissions more than required by some pre-existing regulation (or other baseline) and allow those credits to be counted towards compliance by other facilities that would face high

---

6. Extended text on trading in those other fields is available on the coursebook website in the supplementary materials for this chapter.

7. Original references and footnotes are omitted. The report is available at www.pewclimate.org.

B. Domestic Trading Experience in the U.S.

costs or other difficulties in meeting the regulatory requirements. (These programs sometimes are referred to simply as "credit-based.") Reduction credits are created through an administrative process in which the credits must be pre-certified before they can be traded.

Averaging programs also involve the offsetting of emissions from higher-emitting sources with lower emissions from other sources, so that the average emission *rate* achieves a predetermined level. Like reduction credit programs, averaging programs provide flexibility to individual sources to meet emissions constraints by allowing differences from source-specific standards to be traded between sources. The primary difference between averaging and reduction credit programs is that reduction credits are created (or "certified") through an administrative process, whereas the certification is automatic in averaging programs.

Cap-and-trade programs operate on somewhat different principles. Under a cap-and-trade program, an aggregate cap on emissions is set that defines the total number of emissions "allowances," each of which provides its holder with the right to emit a unit (typically a ton) of emissions. The permits are initially allocated in some way, typically among existing sources. Each source covered by the program must hold permits to cover its emissions, with sources free to buy and sell permits from each other. In contrast to reduction credit programs—but similar to averaging programs—cap-and-trade programs do not require pre-certification of allowances; the allowances are certified when they are distributed initially. Also, cap-and-trade programs limit *total* emissions, a contrast to reduction credit and averaging programs that are not designed to cap emissions.

A trading program might include more than one type of trading mechanism. As discussed below, both the Acid Rain trading program and RECLAIM include reduction credit supplements to the basic cap-and-trade program. In addition, a cap-and-trade program might provide for early reduction credits, which allow firms to get credits for voluntarily reducing emissions prior to the introduction of a cap-and-trade program. The credits allocated can be used to meet requirements once the cap-and-trade program goes into force.

All three types of emissions trading rely on certain factors that constitute preconditions for a successful program. First and most importantly, all three forms assume that an emissions control requirement has been put in place that requires emissions to be reduced to levels below what they otherwise would be. For credit and averaging programs, the requirement will typically be a source-specific standard (e.g., a maximum emissions rate). In a cap-and-trade program the requirement will take the form of an aggregate cap on emissions combined with the provision that each source surrender allowances equal to its emissions. Second, the cost savings achieved by all three forms of trading depend upon variability in the costs of reducing emissions among emissions sources. Differences in emission control costs across emissions sources create the opportunity to reduce costs through trading. Finally, in all three types of trading programs, the requirements must be both enforceable and enforced. A corollary to this precondition is that there must be accurate measurement of actual emissions or emissions rates—otherwise it would be impossible to enforce the requirements because it would be impossible to determine whether sources were in compliance.

OTHER FEATURES OF EMISSIONS TRADING PROGRAMS. There are many features that must be specified in an emissions trading program, some of which do not apply to all of the three basic emissions trading types. The following is a list that categorizes the major features of emissions trading programs into two major categories: design issues and implementation issues.

Design Issues. These include the decisions that arise as the program is designed and turned into a specific regulatory program.

Allocation of initial allowances. This issue is only relevant in cap-and-trade programs. Some method is required to distribute the initial allowances. Basic methods include various formulas to distribute initial allowances to participants on the basis of historical information ("grandfathering") or on the basis of updated information ("updating") as well as auctioning of the initial allowances.

Geographic or temporal flexibility or restrictions. This includes the possibility of restricting trades among different parts of the geographic range of the program. It also includes the possibility of banking (i.e., reducing emissions more than required in a given year and "banking" the surplus for future internal use or sale) or borrowing (i.e., reducing less than required in a given year and thus "borrowing," with the borrowed amount made up by reducing more than required in subsequent years).

Emission sources that are required or allowed to participate. This includes specification of the universe of sources that must participate in the trading program. It also includes the possibility of allowing additional sources to opt-in to the program.

Institutions established to facilitate trading. This includes the possibility of encouraging third parties (e.g., brokers) to participate in trading as well as the possibility of setting up an ongoing auction or other institutions to increase liquidity and establish market prices.

Implementation Issues. A number of decisions come into play as the program is implemented.

Certification of permits. This decision applies to reduction credit programs, which require that emission reductions be certified before they can be traded.

Monitoring and reporting of emissions. Methods must be designed to monitor and report emissions from each participating source.

Determining compliance and enforcing the trading program. These decisions relate to the means of determining whether sources are in compliance and enforcing the program if sources are out of compliance.

Maintaining and encouraging participation. This relates to decisions made to keep sources in the program and encourage participation of sources whose participation is optional (e.g., those given the opportunity to opt-in)....

Figure 14-2 summarizes the six major programs considered in this paper. The six programs—which represent the bulk of existing experience with emissions trading—include examples of all three basic types. The U.S. EPA has administered most of the programs, although the programs include those administered by states and local air quality agencies as well. The range of experiences represented in these programs, which span about a quarter of a century, provide important insights into the factors that affect the economic and environmental performance of emissions trading in practice....

B. Domestic Trading Experience in the U.S.

Summary of Emissions Trading Programs

Program	Agency	Type	Emissions	Source	Scope	Year
EPA Emissions Trading Program	U.S. EPA	Reduction Credit, Averaging	Various	Stationary	U.S.	1979-Present
Lead-in-Gasoline	U.S. EPA	Averaging	Lead	Gasoline	U.S.	1982-87
Acid Rain Trading	U.S. EPA	Cap-and-Trade, Reduction Credit	SO_2	Electricity Generation	U.S.	1995-Present
RECLAIM	South Coast Air Quality Management District	Cap-and-Trade	NO_x, SO_2	Stationary	Los Angeles Basin	1994-Present
Averaging, Banking, and Trading (ABT)	U.S. EPA	Averaging	Various	Mobile	U.S.	1991-Present
Northeast NOx Budget Trading	U.S. EPA, 12 states, and D.C.	Cap-and-Trade	NO_x	Stationary	Northeastern U.S.	1999-Present

FIGURE 14-2 *Summary of emissions trading programs.*

EXPERIENCE WITH EPA EMISSIONS TRADING PROGRAMS (EPA ET). Starting in the mid-1970s, the U.S. EPA and the states developed four limited emissions trading programs to increase flexibility and reduce the costs of compliance with air emissions standards for stationary sources under the Clean Air Act.

1. *Netting.* Netting allows large new sources and major modifications of existing sources to be exempted from otherwise applicable review procedures if existing emissions elsewhere in the same facility are reduced by a sufficient amount.
2. *Offsets.* The offset policy allows a major new source to locate in an area that does not attain a given National Ambient Air Quality Standard—a non-attainment area—if emissions from an existing source are reduced by at least as much as the new source would contribute (after installation of stringent controls).
3. *Bubble.* The bubble policy allows a firm to combine the limits for several different sources into one combined limit and to determine compliance based on that aggregate limit instead of from each source individually. The name alludes to an imaginary "bubble" placed over the several sources.
4. *Banking.* Under banking, firms that take actions to reduce emissions below the relevant standard can accumulate credits for future internal use or sale.

These four programs—collectively referred to as EPA Emissions Trading or EPA ET—are related by the common objective of providing sources with flexibility to comply with traditional source-specific command-and-control standards while maintaining environmental objectives focused primarily on local air quality. Reliance on these early EPA ET programs has been limited mostly as a result of implementing burdensome regulations that take up 47 pages of multi-column fine print in the *Federal Register*. In general, the regulations have restricted substantially the applicability of the programs in response to regulatory concerns that the programs would compromise environmental objectives by encouraging "paper credits" or "anyway tons"—credits for emissions reductions that would have been made without the incentives provided by the emissions trading program. Credits must meet detailed criteria to be certified as eligible for trading. Offsets can only be used in certain geographic areas and any "trades" using them are not one-for-one, since the regulations require emissions reductions at the source providing the credit to be greater than the expected increase in emissions by the source using the credit. Potential applications of the bubble policy initially faced even greater hurdles because proposed bubbles had to be approved as revisions to an applicable State Implementation Plan (SIP), a lengthy administrative process that discouraged their use. These and other EPA regulations made efforts to identify and create trading opportunities expensive and uncertain. The result of this process for creating and approving tradable credits, often called certification, is that the EPA ET programs have yielded relatively few trades and low cost savings relative to their potential. The combination of pre-approval requirements and the need to construct customized arrangements for each trade has created substantial transactions costs—often exceeding the market value of the credits. These transaction costs—in effect the result of the lack of a well-defined and standardized commodity to be traded—have been the primary obstacle to more widespread participation in these programs. . . .

LEAD-IN-GASOLINE PROGRAM. The averaging program used to regulate lead in gasoline during the mid-1980s provides an example of a much more successful trading program than the early EPA ET programs. The averaging program for lead grew out of EPA's efforts to reduce the lead content of gasoline starting in the early 1970s. . . .

ACID RAIN TRADING PROGRAM. [A remarkable feature of the Acid Rain Program] is the striking reduction of SO_2 emissions in the first year of the program. Emissions had been falling steadily throughout the 1980s, even before Title IV was enacted, and they continued to fall at about the same rate during the first half of the 1990s. But the reduction from 1994 to 1995 was far greater than anything that had been seen before, and there can be no doubt that it was caused by Title IV. The only precedent for such a rapid reduction in emissions of this magnitude in the history of the Clean Air Act is the lead phase-down program, which was also implemented by the use of emissions trading and banking.

The reason for the remarkable reduction in emissions in 1995, when the allowable emissions for that year required only a small reduction in emissions, is the availability of "inter-temporal trading" in the form of banking. The prospect of higher marginal abatement costs after 2000 made abating more than required in Phase I an appealing option for smoothing the transition to the more demanding Phase II cap. As a result, the reduction in emissions experienced in Phase I was about twice what would have been required to bring emissions below the level allowed in these years.

Inter-source or "spatial" trading also has been an important feature of the Acid Rain program. Compliance data for each year shows that about one-third of the affected units in Phase I obtained allowances from other units, either by intra-firm transfers or through purchase in the allowance market, to cover emissions in excess of the allowances allocated to those units. Spatial trading has allowed sources with high abatement costs to reduce emissions less—and those with low abatement costs to reduce emissions more—than under a command-and-control mechanism requiring uniform emissions rates, and thus has reduced the overall cost of the mandated emissions reduction.

The purchase and sale of allowances by the owners of affected units has created an active and efficient market for SO_2 allowances. This is evidenced by the single price for allowances at any one point in time regardless of the source of the price quote, by the high volume of inter-firm trades that can be deduced from the allowance registry maintained by EPA, by the low transactions costs associated with trading, and by the development of an active and diverse contract and futures market. The EPA auction has also provided a transparent mechanism to reveal prices, which was very important in the early years when few private transactions were being reported. . . .

B. Domestic Trading Experience in the U.S.

Abatement Cost and Cost Savings from Title IV Emissions Trading

	Abatement Cost With Trading	Abatement Cost Without Trading	Cost Savings from Emissions Trading				Savings as a Percentage of Cost Without Trading
			Phase I Spatial Trading	Banking	Phase II Spatial Trading	Total Cost Savings	
Average Phase I year (1995-99)	735	1,093	358			358	33%
Average Phase II year (2000-07)	1,400	3,682		167	2,115	2,282	62%
13-Year Sum	14,875	34,925	1,792	1,339	16,919	20,050	57%

Source: Adapted from Ellerman et al. (2000).

Note: All costs are in millions of present-value U.S. 1995 dollars. Estimates are based on economic reasoning assuming reasonably efficient markets based on observed allowance prices and abatement (as explained in chapter 10 of the source). A cost estimate is provided for only the first eight years of Phase II since this is the time period when most of the cost savings from banking were thought likely to be realized.

FIGURE 14-3. *Abatement cost and cost savings from Title IV emissions trading.*

The cost savings due to emissions trading in the Acid Rain Program clearly are substantial. Figure 14-3 summarizes estimates of cost savings . . . attributable to different types of trading, i.e., the savings due to spatial trading in Phase I, banking between Phases I and II, and spatial trading in the more stringent and comprehensive Phase II.

On average, spatial trading during Phase I reduced annual compliance costs by $358 million per year, a reduction of about 33 percent from the estimated cost of $1,093 million per year under a nontrading regime in which each affected unit limits emissions to the number of allowances received without any trading. During the first eight years of Phase II, the combination of spatial trading and banking is estimated to reduce annual compliance costs by about $2.3 billion per year, a reduction of over 60 percent from a total of about $3.7 billion per year. Over the first 13 years of the program, the ability to trade allowances nationwide across affected units and through time is estimated to reduce compliance costs by a total of $20 billion, a cost reduction of about 57 percent from the assumed command-and-control alternative. This percentage cost saving is similar to that developed by other researchers, although it is less than the percentage cost savings sometimes claimed for emissions trading programs, including the Title IV SO_2 cap-and-trade program.

There are several reasons why the Acid Rain Program has been successful. Of critical importance is the absence of any requirement for regulatory pre-approval of individual trades. Like the Lead Trading Program, the SO_2 program dispensed with the restrictions and cumbersome bureaucracy that characterized the EPA ET program. The lead program took the first step in avoiding the costly process of verifying credits for every transaction by allowing for an automatic crediting of differences from an agreed-upon baseline. Title IV took the further steps of explicitly recognizing the right to emit (albeit at a reduced quantity) and then determining compliance based on an account of *all* emissions, not just the differences from the agreed-upon baseline. These further steps changed the nature of the item traded from an emission reduction, which depends on an agreed upon and non-observable baseline, to emissions that are actually measured—in this case using a continuous emissions monitoring system (CEMS). As was also the case in the Lead Trading

Program, the reduced importance of location and timing of emissions facilitated the simpler procedures that made emissions trading successful. In both cases, the reduction in aggregate, cumulative emissions was more important than the precise pattern of reductions at individual sources. Both programs also built in flexibility in the timing of emissions reductions by allowing for banking. . . .

COMMENTARY & QUESTIONS

1. Which figure is more significant, $20 billion saved by Title IV over 13 years or 57%? Both figures are impressive. The percentage-based cost reduction is notable because it reflects the substantial efficiency gains that trading can deliver. The monetary savings appear less so because when parsed out to electric consumers as a measure of the change in their cost of electricity, the savings amounts to less than 2 cents per person per day. What gets obscured by minimizing the consumer savings in that way, however, is the fact that pollution control, even the more expensive, often demonized "command and control" alternative that would have cost roughly twice as much, would affect utility bills by 2 cents per person per day in the opposite direction.

2. SO_2 emissions reduction success: the virtues of an enforceable cap-and-trade program or low-hanging fruit? At the time of enactment, efforts of the electric generating industry obscured the fact—now easy to see and borne out by experience—that the Title IV cap-and-trade program was certain to work, and to do so inexpensively. The 50% rollback of 10 million tons per year reduction in SO_2 sounds like a monumental improvement, but that level of reductions is not nearly what is achievable at an economically affordable level of effort. In 1990, the known and in-use technology (including switching fuel to low-sulfur coal or the use of scrubbers for high-sulfur coal) was capable of achieving required rates (1.2 lb/mmBTU), and some plants were already operating profitably and competitively at rates four times lower than that (0.3 lb/mmBTU). As a result, Title IV required no technology improvements. All Title IV needed was a small amount of gamesmanship on the part of highly capitalized firms that could choose how best to minimize their long-term costs. Expectations of far higher costs were based on data provided by (guess who) the regulated entities that had two decades of experience fighting against air pollution regulation. Further easing the transition to lower SO_2 emissions was railroad deregulation that greatly reduced the cost of hauling low-sulfur western coal to the East where it could replace high-sulfur eastern coal. This change in the economics of the fuel supply was quite substantial, making low-sulfur fuel the favored choice on a cost per BTU basis. See, e.g., Hahn, The Impact of Economics on Environmental Policy 6 (AEI-Brookings Joint Center for Regulatory Studies, Working Paper No. 99-4, 1999); Schmalensee et al., An Interim Evaluation of Sulfur Dioxide Emissions Trading, 12 J. Econ. Persp. 53 (1998); Stavins, What Can We Learn from the Grand Policy Experiment: Positive and Normative Lessons from the SO_2 Allowance Trading, 12 J. Econ. Persp. 69 (1998).

3. Hot air credits. As in most contexts where this term is used, *hot air* is used pejoratively here. In trading regimes, *hot air credits* are credits awarded for activities that do not reduce actual emissions. Such credits not only slow progress toward environmental improvement, but they also undermine the economic incentives in the trading scheme by competing with real credits in the marketplace and, because hot air credits increase supply, they decrease the price of all credits. The lower price, in turn, sends an incorrect signal to firms that would have chosen to reduce pollution if the price of credits had been just a little bit higher. Hot air credits are introduced in a variety of ways, such as overestimating the reductions that are associated with a pollution-reducing action or setting baseline emissions and allowances at a level that exceeds actual pollution. For example, baselines are frequently set with reference to high-emission years or continuous operation capacity when reality is more accurately represented by average years and actual operations.

4. "Anyway" credits. What is the impact on a trading system that gives credit for emissions reductions that would have happened anyway? For example, in *Citizens Against the Refinery's Effects (CARE) v. EPA*, 643 F.2d 183 (4th Cir. 1981), ozone offsets were given for conduct—road paving that used less expensive and equally suitable water-based asphalt instead of oil-based asphalt—that would have happened anyway. Should reduction credits for reduced pollution be issued to a factory that is closing because it is not profitable? The answer appears to depend on the context and the underlying purposes of the trading program. In the *CARE* case, it seems that Virginia's SIP already created a general obligation to make the change because it required all sources in the state to employ RACT (reasonably available control technology). Treating that change as an offset seems like a windfall, and it also tends to retard "reasonable further progress toward attainment" (the statutory command for all nonattainment areas) by offsetting new pollution with an anyway credit. The issue for trading, however, is that delving into whether a credit is an anyway credit adds transaction costs (cost of investigation and delay) that compromise the efficiency gains of the trading system. One plausible solution to this problem when designing a cap-and-trade program is to estimate the number of anyway credits and to set the goal in a way that recognizes that some trades will involve anyway credits.

5. Accountability, measurement, and the cost of measurement. Measurement of emissions is a necessary element of a workable system. Without accurate measures of emissions, no trading system can be assured that all of the players have in hand the needed credits to cover their emissions. For large, technologically sophisticated, highly capitalized plants, the cost of monitoring is likely to be a small fraction of the cost of the operation. For example, Title IV required continuous emissions monitoring systems that added about 7% to the cost of Phase I of the program. But this requirement nevertheless overcame opposition to the program from environmental groups, which doubted the credibility of a "materials balance" method of estimating emissions based on inputs and design features. Is real-time monitoring a feasible option for small-scale emitters? What would be the cost of monitoring a wood-burning stove as a percentage of the cost of the stove and its wood? How expensive would it be to monitor the hydrocarbon emissions of a dry cleaning establishment or a farmer's on-farm gas tank? When does leaving the small entities out of the trading system undermine the overall program? Measuring credits for reductions encounters similar measurement problems.

6. Forbearance credits. Should credits be awarded for not engaging in behavior that was not previously taking place but could be pursued in the future? A prime example of this is rain forest preservation in the tropics, where slash-and-burn clearing activities would release huge amounts of GHG. Credits could be given for driving cars less than was the historical practice. Would that be sensible? Feasible? Would it be more feasible to create disincentives to driving, such as a carbon tax on fuels?

7. Initial allocation. As a matter of economic theory, building on the famous Coase Theorem, the initial allocation of allowances in the trading system should not adversely affect efficiency. Ellerman et al. address this point in relation to Title IV:

> From the perspective of the performance of the program, i.e., the cost of reducing emissions and the speed with which they were reduced, there is no credible evidence that the initial allocations had any significant effects. This is the case because the allocation process was structured so that the number of allowances a source received was independent of its future output and its future emissions.

In contrast to efficiency, welfare (wealth) effects and perceived fairness (equity) are impacted by initial allocation of allowances. The allowances are valuable, and their initial distribution enriches its holder in the event that no payment is made by those receiving the allotted allowances. An alternative charging a price would involve a sale or an auction.

8. Emissions trading and the NAAQS. What is the relationship of Title IV trading of SO_2 credits to attainment of the NAAQS harm-based ambient standard for SO_2? It may overstate the case to deny all relationship, but the two regimes are independent of one another and serve two quite distinct purposes, *both of which must be met*. There is no warrant to allow a utility to economize on its emissions control expenditures by purchasing credits and increasing its local SO_2 emissions if to do so puts the area in violation of the NAAQS (or other relevant ambient air quality standard, such as a PSD standard). Indeed, local SO_2 problems have led some utilities to invest heavily in controls, making them sellers in the emissions credits market. See Tight Limits in Wisconsin Acid Rain Program May Yield Glut of Allowances, EPA Official Says, 22 Envtl. Rep. (BNA) 2665 (Apr. 3, 1992).

9. Can downwind states add requirements that burden the trading system? Officials in New York State, home to many of the lakes and streams most affected by sulfuric acid deposition, do not believe that Title IV is stringent enough to permit the state's lakes and streams to recover. In 2000, New York enacted a statute that severely penalized in-state firms that sold emission credits to companies located in any of 14 upwind states. In *Clean Air Markets Group v. Pataki*, 194 F. Supp. 2d 147 (N.D.N.Y. 2002), the U.S. District Court held the law unconstitutional because it violated the dormant Commerce Clause by imposing a burden on interstate commerce that was not justified by its purported purpose of reducing acid deposition and thereby protecting the environment and public health. The court also applied conflict preemption as an alternative ground for invalidating the statute, finding that it conflicted with the CAA's chosen method for achieving the goal of air pollution control and acid deposition reduction.

10. Renewed Clean Air Act Trading Proposals in the GHG field. In Fall of 2015, the Obama Administration released the Clean Power Plan Final Rule. The details of the rule can be found at http://www2.epa.gov/cleanpowerplan/clean-power-plan-existing-power-plants. The eventual fate of the Rule may take many years to determine, but the Rule anticipates extensive use of trading. The Rule will operate on much the same basis as the state SIP process as to how the states meet their goals. In this instance, instead of an ambient standard, the states will start with a cap on emissions. Trading is identified as one of the means by which states can craft their compliance plans. The plan also is discussed briefly in Chapter 11.

11. Trading things other than air emissions—water pollution. There is no inherent reason to limit environmental trading systems to air emissions. Lead trading among gasoline refiners during the period in which that additive was being phased out was very efficient. EPA authorized water quality trading in areas subject to TMDLs, particularly favoring trading involving nutrients (total phosphorus and nitrogen) and sediment. See Water Quality Trading Policy, 68 Fed. Reg. 1608 (Jan. 13, 2003). In the dozen years following that regulation, utilization of water quality trading programs began very slowly but seems to be on the rise. A particular highlight that is implemented and providing positive benefits is §10 of the Chesapeake Bay TMDL which prominently features current and future nutrient and sediment trading.[8] Adapting trading to rivers can be complicated by the linear and segmented nature of rivers as a receiving body which tends to make units of pollution nonfungible. Also, smaller volume or lower flow receiving bodies are likely to encounter hot spot

---

8. See http://www2.epa.gov/sites/production/files/2014-12/documents/cbay_final_tmdl_section_10_final_0.pdf.

problems unless trading is closely monitored. Along with larger estuary plans like those for the Chesapeake Bay, one of the more promising potential uses of water pollutant trading is point source–nonpoint source trades. POTWs on water quality limited stream stretches face a very steep cost curve for improving their treatment methods, whereas nonpoint sources are subject to minimal or no requirements to reduce their pollution, and there are inexpensive practices that can reduce nutrient and sediment pollution from farms and other unregulated runoff into the streams. Although exact measurement of the reductions made by nonpoint sources is a bit problematic, trades make a great deal of sense because of the difference in cost of control.

12. Trading things other than air emissions—overharvesting of fish. Overharvesting of fish is another classic "tragedy of the commons" problem in which each user benefits by capturing as many fish as possible, but the aggregate effect reduces breeding stocks too much, and a decline toward extinction begins. Unfortunately, this is a problem for many of the world's commercially valuable aquatic species. In the U.S., the Magnuson-Stevens Fishery Conservation and Management Act (codified at 16 U.S.C. §§1801 et seq.) has authorized efforts to limit total catch since 1976 by instituting a cap-and-trade program under which a few fisheries, such as Alaskan halibut, were regulated. In 2006, P.L. 109-479 added amendments invited more trading by setting more specific guidelines for allocation of fish catch shares and limited access privilege programs (LAPPs). On December 10, 2009, NOAA released a draft policy on the use of catch share programs in fishery management plans that can be downloaded from www.nmfs.noaa.gov/sfa/domes_fish/catchshare/index.htm. What problems seem likely to attend implementation of tradable fish catch shares programs? NOAA is relying heavily on stakeholders, organized into local and regional fish management advisory councils, in formulating specific management strategies.

13. Emissions trading is already big business. By 2015 emissions trading was taking place in markets around the world. Entire businesses now provide data on emissions trades. For example, the World Carbon Market database tracks the trades being made in 13 different markets operating in locales as diverse as California, the EU, Khazakstan, and New Zealand. See, e.g., https://www.carbonmarketdata.com/en/products/world-ets-database/presentation.

2. Flawed Trading Systems and Hot Spots (Adverse Local Effects)

The South Coast Air Quality Management District (SCAQMD) is a regional state agency (with CAA authority delegated from EPA) exercising air pollution control jurisdiction cutting across several county lines in the Los Angeles area. In 1991, SCAQMD voted to institute a tradable permit system. Known as the Regional Clean Air Incentives Market (RECLAIM), the program covers the area's major stationary sources of nitrogen oxides (NO_x) and sulfur oxides (SO_x), and aims to reduce the emissions of these compounds each year by an average of 8.3% and 6.8% respectively, through 2003.[9] Thereafter, the program expanded to include trading in volatile organic compounds and other emissions linked to ozone formation. This trading system, while widely reported to have achieved significant cost savings over non-trading alternatives, has also, as reflected in the excerpt that follows, been subject to severe criticism.

---

9. See Polesetsky, Will a Market in Air Pollution Clean the Nation's Dirtiest Air? A Study of the South Coast Air Quality Management District's Regional Clean Air Incentives Market, 22 Ecology L.Q. 359, 361 (1995).

Richard Toshiyuki Drury, Michael E. Belliveau, J. Scott Kuhn & Shipra Bansal, Pollution Trading & Environmental Injustice: Los Angeles' Failed Experiment in Air Quality Policy

9 Duke Environmental Law & Policy Forum 231 (1999)

This article analyzes two of the most developed pollution trading programs in the world—Mobile Source Credits (specifically, the Rule 1610 "car scrapping" program) and RECLAIM. Both programs benefit large industrial polluters in the Los Angeles area, and have been in place for more than five years. Although industry has saved money, these air pollution trading programs have otherwise failed to deliver.

The promises of pollution trading advocates have not come to pass. Pollution trading in Los Angeles has led to concentrated toxic air emission hot-spots that have shackled low-income and minority communities with the region's air pollution. Pollution reductions have been far less than those promised by trading proponents. Furthermore, pollution trading has virtually eliminated public participation in the environmental decision-making process. . . .

LOS ANGELES: A TEST MARKET FOR AIR POLLUTION TRADING. The Los Angeles, California, region provides an ideal testing ground for environmental policies. Los Angeles' environmental problems are severe, its regulatory agencies are sophisticated, its resources are relatively ample, and the region's population is multi-racial and economically diverse. . . .

The South Coast Air Basin, which includes the metropolitan Los Angeles area, suffers the worst air quality in the nation. For example, nearly 6,000 premature deaths caused by particulate air pollution occur in the Los Angeles area each year, representing about a tenth of such fatalities nationwide. Additionally, millions of residents of the region are exposed to unhealthy levels of ground level ozone, which causes aching lungs, wheezing, coughing, headache and permanent lung tissue scarring. Levels of toxic chemicals in the air pose significant risks for causing cancer and other chronic diseases. This dangerous mix of air pollutants, which are emitted by multitudes of factories, cars, and other sources, seriously threatens public health and well-being.

A richly diverse, multi-racial and multi-ethnic population lives, works, and plays in the Los Angeles region, raising the environmental justice concern that people of color and poor people are unfairly exposed to more air pollution than others. Therefore, air pollution reduction strategies, including pollution trading programs, should be evaluated not only for their efficacy in reducing air pollution, but also for their effect on achieving environmental justice. Will such programs alleviate or worsen the environmental injustice of disproportionate exposures to air pollution already faced by the most powerless segments of society? The answer to this question is already of pressing importance in Los Angeles and will become increasingly relevant throughout the rest of the country. . . .

POLLUTION TRADING COMES OF AGE IN LOS ANGELES: FROM RULE 1610 TO RECLAIM AND BEYOND. . . . Following a pattern shaped by the policy agenda of the largest industrial polluters, a group of market-based regulations centered on pollution trading have been adopted for the South Coast Air Basin. In 1993, SCAQMD approved the first old vehicle pollution trading program in the country, known as Rule 1610 or the "car scrapping program." Rule 1610 allows stationary source polluters (such as factories and refineries) to avoid installing expensive pollution control equipment if they purchase pollution credits generated by destroying old, high-polluting cars. Ideally, an equal or greater amount of pollution can

B. Domestic Trading Experience in the U.S.

be reduced at a much lower cost by purchasing and destroying old cars than by forcing stationary sources to install expensive pollution control equipment.

Under Rule 1610, "licensed car scrappers" can purchase and destroy old cars. SCAQMD then grants the scrapper emissions credits based on the projected emissions of the car had it not been destroyed, which may then be sold to stationary source polluters (e.g. factories). The stationary sources use the pollution credits to avoid on-site emission reductions that would be required under the technology-based regulatory regime.[10] Rule 1610 requires polluters to purchase credits representing twenty percent more emission reductions than would be achieved through compliance with technology-based regulations for their plant. Although industrial plants avoid emission reductions, the scrapping of older, high polluting cars should result in greater air quality improvements at a lower cost than regulatory mandates.

SCAQMD then adopted the centerpiece of its pollution trading strategy, the Regional Clean Air Incentives Market (RECLAIM), the world's first urban smog trading program. RECLAIM replaced many of SCAQMD's technology-based regulations aimed at reducing emissions of sulfur oxides (SOx) and nitrogen oxides (NOx). RECLAIM, a "declining cap-and-trade" program, mandates annual emission reductions for industry but provides them the flexibility to achieve that goal by either purchasing emission reduction credits or by reducing their own pollution. Under RECLAIM, SCAQMD allocates pollution credits to each major source facility in the region based on its historic level of emissions. Each facility has three options: 1) it can use all of its credits and pollute up to the level they allow; 2) it can reduce its pollution and sell the excess credits to other facilities; or 3) it can increase emissions relative to its initial endowment of credits by buying credits from other facilities. Each year SCAQMD decreases the number of credits allocated by the program, forcing facilities either to decrease their pollution or purchase credits from other facilities. As the number of available credits decreases, their market price should rise, increasing the market incentive for companies to reduce pollution rather than purchase credits. According to its supporters, by 2003 RECLAIM should spur the lowest cost pollution reduction among individual industrial plants and slash aggregate emissions of NOx by seventy-five percent and SOx by sixty percent.

Toward fulfilling industry's goal of indefinitely avoiding emissions reductions at their own plants, SCAQMD aggressively expanded its emissions trading strategy. In April 1997, the SCAQMD Governing Board voted to approve Rule 2506, Area Source Credits (ASCs), which provides for the issuance of marketable credits to entities that voluntarily reduce emissions of NOx and SOx. The resulting ASCs can then be converted to RECLAIM Trading Credits or used as an alternative method of compliance with other SCAQMD regulations. The mobile source pollution trading has expanded beyond Rule 1610 to provide for the issuance of Mobile Source Emission Reduction Credits (MSERCs) for voluntary emission reductions from:

- the repair of emissions-related components in high emitting vehicles,
- the purchase of clean on-road vehicles, including new, low-emission buses, retrofitting vehicles to low-emission configurations, and purchasing zero emission vehicles,
- the electrification of truck stops and tour bus stops to prevent engine idling,
- the purchase of low or zero emission off-road vehicles,
- the purchase of clean lawn and garden equipment, such as battery-operated lawn mowers and leaf blowers, and the scrapping of old equipment. . . .

---

10. The RECLAIM Rules of SCAQMD make extensive use of technology-based measures, as well as applying the harm-based SIP regulatory standards. See, e.g., SCAQMD Rule 2005, available at www.aqmd.gov/rules/reg/reg20/r2005.pdf. [EDS.]

THE HARSH REALITY: PROBLEMS WITH POLLUTION TRADING IN LOS ANGELES. Evidence indicates that pollution trading programs in Los Angeles are plagued with problems. Although the programs have succeeded in saving money for industry, they have not effectively reduced emissions and have not promoted technology innovation or public participation. Instead, they have further concentrated the region's pollution in lower income communities and given industry a "free ride" from otherwise obligatory emissions reduction schedules.

Toxic Hot-Spots and Environmental Injustice: The Mad Science of Pollution Trading. Pollution trading programs can unfairly concentrate pollution in communities where factories purchase emissions reduction credits rather than reduce actual emissions. These localized health risks from pollution sources, or "toxic hot-spots," tend to be overlooked by policy makers focused on regional air quality concerns. However, the disproportionate burden thrust on communities surrounding major pollution emitters takes its toll in the form of increased risks of toxic exposure and damage to human health. Furthermore, it is environmentally unjust when these communities enduring localized toxic hot-spots are overwhelmingly low income and populated by people of color. Such hot-spots can be worsened when pollution trading programs ignore the differences in chemical hazards posed by the pollutants reduced to earn credits and the pollutants emitted through the purchase of credits. The problem of hot-spots is further complicated by the emission of co-pollutants and precursors, which may increase exposure to certain types of chemicals in downwind communities where pollution is concentrated.

SCAQMD's pollution trading programs have resulted in the creation of toxic hot-spots by concentrating pollution in communities surrounding major sources of pollution. Rule 1610 provides the clearest example. SCAQMD studies indicate that cars destroyed through the Rule 1610 program were registered throughout the air quality management district, a four-county region. Air pollution from these automobiles would have also been distributed throughout this region. By contrast, stationary sources in Los Angeles are densely clustered in only a few communities in this four-county region. As a result of these distribution patterns, Rule 1610 effectively takes pollution formerly distributed throughout the region by automobiles, and concentrates that pollution in the communities surrounding stationary sources.

Most of the emissions credits purchased to avoid stationary source controls have been purchased by four oil companies: Unocal, Chevron, Ultramar and GATX. Of these four companies, three are located close together in the communities of Wilmington and San Pedro; the fourth facility, Chevron, is located nearby in El Segundo. These companies have used pollution credits to avoid installing pollution control equipment that captures toxic gases released during oil tanker loading at their marine terminals. When loading oil tankers, toxic gases are forced out of the tanker and into the air, exposing workers and nearby residents to toxic vapors, including benzene, a known human carcinogen. Thus, by using pollution credits, these companies are allowed to avoid reducing local emissions of hazardous chemicals in exchange for reducing regional auto emissions. As a result of Rule 1610, the four oil companies created a toxic chemical hot-spot around their marine terminals, exposing workers and nearby residents to elevated health risks. . . .

To add insult to injury, the public health risks from the extra pollution concentrated in these neighborhoods constitutes a case of environmental injustice. The demographics of this hot-spot area starkly contrast with that of the metropolitan Los Angeles region. The residents living in San Pedro and Wilmington, which host a majority of the oil companies emitting hazardous toxic chemicals, are overwhelmingly Latino. Furthermore, the racial

B. Domestic Trading Experience in the U.S.

composition of communities living near three of the marine terminals ranges from 75 to 90 percent people of color, while the entire South Coast Air Basin has a population of only 36 percent people of color. . . .

The hazards of trading extend beyond the shifting of pollution from a dispersed region to more concentrated localized areas; inter-pollutant trading can also create toxic hotspots. Many trading programs allow facilities to trade pollution credits generated through reductions in a large variety of chemicals. For example, the Rule 1610 program allows pollution credits to be generated through reductions in VOCs. VOCs are a family of over 600 chemical compounds, some of which have high toxicity and some of which have low toxicity. VOC trading raises concerns about the difference in toxicity of VOC emissions from marine terminals compared to VOCs from automobiles. For example, benzene levels may be higher in VOC emissions from marine terminals than from cars, which leads to greater exposure and risks concentrated in the communities around the marine terminals. Benzene exposure can cause leukemia, anemia, respiratory tract irritation, dermatitis, pulmonary edema, and hemorrhaging. Therefore, the Rule 1610 program may allow continued release of highly toxic chemicals into certain communities in exchange for small area-wide reductions in much less toxic chemicals. Yet, no source testing has been required by SCAQMD to accurately characterize the differences in chemical composition and toxicity among VOC emissions subject to trading.

In addition to concerns about variable toxicity, VOCs also exhibit different degrees of reactivity related to their ability to form photochemical smog. These differences in photochemical reactivity have long been recognized in air pollution regulation and have guided priority setting in the control of VOC sources for smog control. In pollution trading programs, however, if highly reactive VOCs are emitted by purchasing credits earned for reducing low reactivity VOCs, then downwind ozone (smog) formation may be increased rather than reduced. This represents another inter-pollutant trading flaw in pollution trading programs that include VOCs. . . .

Market Incentives Run Amok: Fraud and Manipulation. Air pollution regulatory programs have been plagued with technical uncertainties in accurately accounting for the amount of emissions from different sources. Such concerns exist for both a technology-based approach and an emissions trading approach to regulation. However, for an emissions trading program, accuracy is more important than for technology-based regulations, because an accounting of pollution forms the basis for the number of emissions reduction credits required by each facility. Furthermore, when an emissions trading approach is employed, the incidence of fraud may be greater. Pollution trading programs create stronger incentives to manipulate the numbers and cheat, because credits that are fraudulently created are still worth money. The Los Angeles pollution trading experience with car scrapping has been plagued by a history of under-reporting of actual emissions from industry and an over-reporting of claimed emission reductions from cars. . . .

Rather than measure actual emissions released, companies estimate emissions using emission factors developed by the Western States Petroleum Association. Emissions factors are surrogate estimates of emissions based on activity level. For example, engineers may estimate that a small industrial boiler will release so many pounds of NOx for every barrel of fuel oil burned. Emission factors are hotly argued among technical specialists from different fields and change as new information becomes available. Emissions factors are poor surrogates for actual measurements. With margins of error ranging from fifty percent to one hundred percent, emissions factors are highly uncertain, making claimed emission reduction difficult to verify. They can readily be adjusted to report emissions as being higher or lower, since at best they represent educated guesses of actual emissions. Source testing, which measures actual emissions, was required to ensure compliance with the technology-based emission limits set under Rule 1142 for marine terminals.

Information recently obtained through the Freedom of Information Act reveals that the oil companies did, in fact, measure their emissions. When the actual measurements were compared to reported emissions based on industry emissions factors, striking differences were revealed. Oil companies under-reported their oil tanker emissions by factors between 10 and 1000. As a result, the oil companies purchased between 10 and 1000 times too few credits from scrapping old, high-polluting cars to offset their tanker pollution. This persistent problem was completely overlooked by SCAQMD and was only detected through a time-consuming investigation by Communities for a Better Environment. However, despite this under-reporting, SCAQMD continues to allow the use of emissions factors to underestimate emissions.

Exacerbating the huge gap between actual emissions and credits purchased by polluters, credit generators—the car scrappers—have abused the system. Many of the cars allegedly destroyed through the Rule 1610 program were not, in fact, destroyed, according to Bruce Lohmann, SCAQMD's Chief Inspector for the Rule 1610 program. While the car bodies were crushed, many of the engines which produce the pollution were not. Instead, many of those engines were sold for re-use, despite the fact that pollution credits for destroying the car had been granted by SCAQMD. EPA has refused to approve the Rule 1610 program precisely because car engines are not always destroyed. . . .

Distortion of the Market: Hot Air and Phantom Reductions. In addition to fraud by market participants, "cap-and-trade" strategies, like Los Angeles' RECLAIM program, are plagued by a broader form of institutional manipulation. This manipulation takes the form of "phantom reductions" in air emissions—reductions that exist on paper only. Under RECLAIM, allowable emissions have declined each year as required by regulation. However, because emissions reduction credits were initially allocated in an amount significantly inflated above actual emissions, early "reductions" in emissions were illusory. In the first three years of the RECLAIM program, actual industrial NOx emissions have declined by at most three percent, while allowable emissions have been reduced on paper by about thirty percent. In the global context, the term "hot air" has been used to describe the vesting of certain countries like Russia with excess credits. Not only does the trading in hot air credits represent illusory environmental gains, the excess allocation drives down the price of credits, reducing the motivation to invest in actual emission reductions or technological innovation. . . .

According to a SCAQMD audit, over the first three years, RECLAIM has produced barely discernible pollution reductions. In fact, during the first two years of RECLAIM, 1994 and 1995, NOx and SOx emissions reportedly increased compared to 1993. Only in 1996 were emissions reduced, and then by at most three percent from 1993 NOx levels and by less than ten percent from 1993 SOx levels. This pattern contrasts sharply with the time period 1989-1993 when NOx emissions from industrial facilities declined steeply, by approximately thirty-seven percent, as a result of technology-based control regulations. . . .

COMMENTARY & QUESTIONS

1. The moral trouble with trading. In a portion of the article that was not excerpted here, its authors take trading to task on several fronts, one of them being moral: "What once was a wrong—polluting—is now a 'right.'" Id. at 269. Is that criticism warranted

B. Domestic Trading Experience in the U.S.

any more than saying that an NPDES or CAA permit creates rights to pollute? The other moral failing attributed to trading is that of environmental injustice. Most emissions trading systems, especially to the extent that hot spots are not scrupulously avoided, may tend to concentrate pollution in industrialized areas that are home to low-income communities of color. Is that a reason to refuse to permit trading systems? Are there forms of compensation to adversely affected communities that could be melded into trading systems, particularly if a charge were made for initial allocations?

2. The practical trouble with trading. Going beyond hot spots, can you construct a list of practical problems that are likely to arise in most trading systems? RECLAIM seems to have failed to obtain substantial reductions, whereas Title IV had a major effect. Several RECLAIM-specific failings were detailed in the excerpt. There were others, such as "co-pollutant" problems, where the traded pollutant is also an indicator of the presence of numerous other pollutants that are not necessarily eliminated in the trades. In RECLAIM, for example, the off-gassing of tankers unloading emits a host of pollutants that would be captured by hoods that are not in place because of VOC trades for reductions derived from activities such as car scrapping that do not eliminate equivalent amounts of the co-pollutants. Air chemistry also complicates the issue of trading flexibility. RECLAIM allows industrial sources separately to trade two combustion by-products, NO_x and SO_x. Allowing extra SO_x emissions and less NO_x emissions may reduce smog, but simultaneously it may introduce fine particulates that are formaldehyde precursors. Is that a safety-improving trade?

Credit modeling is a more general problem. Try to identify all the variables that have to be assumed or measured to determine how much of an emission reduction accompanies the destruction of an older automobile. Should the program try to validate assumptions in trades? That would drive up transaction costs, but investigations of Rule 1610 showed numerous cases of repair to cars that were inoperable solely to prepare them for service as a trading credit and the bounty that would be paid. Another generic criticism of trading is that it tends to stifle innovation. See Driesen, Free Lunch or Cheap Fix? The Emissions Trading Idea and the Climate Change Convention, 26 B.C. Envtl. Aff. L. Rev. 1, 18-35 (1998). Likewise, public participation diminishes in a market system, and monitoring and enforcement seem likely to be less effective than under a typical modern permit system.

3. Hot spots. The excerpted article is not alone in decrying hot spots as a major problem in trading schemes. Interestingly, that critique is made by commentators who are associated with more conservative views. For example, in December 2002, Curtis Moore (formerly Republican Counsel to the Senate Environment & Public Works Committee when it was chaired by Senator Robert Stafford (R-Vt.), on behalf of the Clean Air Trust, stated, "Trading is a policy that ought to be avoided altogether, except in the most narrow and carefully monitored circumstances." Marketing Failure: The Experience with Air Pollution Trading in the U.S., 34 Envtl. Rep. (BNA) 9 (Jan. 3, 2003). The study focused on SO_2 trading and RECLAIM.[11] Jonathan Nash and Richard Revesz suggest building a computer model of the airshed that predicts the geographic impact of sources and allows trades only when they do not create hot spots.[12] Unfortunately for the practicality of the Nash and Revesz proposal, airshed dispersion modeling remains an inexact art, not a science. Would trading that focuses on effects rather than emissions work any better? For an attempt to describe such a

---

11. Press Release, Clean Air Trust, Debunking the Myth of Emission Trading (Dec. 19, 2002), available at http://www.cleanairtrust.org/release.121902.html.

12. Jonathan Remy Nash & Richard L. Revesz, Markets and Geography: Designing Marketable Permit Schemes to Control Local and Regional Pollutants, 28 Ecol. L.Q. 569, 572-573 (2001).

system, see Akers, New Tools for Environmental Justice: Articulating a Net Health Effects Challenge to Emissions Trading Markets, 7 Hastings W.-Nw. J. Envtl. L. & Pol'y 203 (2001).

4. A favorable view of RECLAIM: trading for efficiency's sake when hot spots don't matter. In Ellerman et al., Emissions Trading in the United States: Experience, Lessons and Considerations for Greenhouse Gases (Pew Center on Global Climate Change Report, May 2003), from which excerpts were reproduced previously, the authors give a far more favorable view of RECLAIM. The empirical data they developed depict RECLAIM as an economic instrument that reduced the cost of pollution reduction through active trading, thus making it another "success" story for cap-and-trade. "That study asserted the high volume of trading in the RECLAIM program implies significant cost savings relative to command-and-control alternative that it replaced. . . ." Id. at 24. The focus of that report, on trading as a mechanism for GHG reduction, allows it to have little concern for hot spots effects and the potential adverse public health consequences of cross-pollutant trades. GHG issues are uniquely ones of long-term global dispersion, while hot spots are not a major concern. Thus, for example, that report was more concerned with limits on trading than with hot spots, noting that "[RECLAIM] does not allow banking because of concerns that the ability to use banked emissions might lead to substantial increases of actual emissions in some future year, and thus delay compliance with ambient air quality standards." Id. at 21.

5. Can the cost of credits ever get too high and stifle the entire economy? In 2000, due to a combination of deregulation of energy prices, poor planning, and illegal and collusive behavior by energy suppliers and energy traders, California was subjected to months of rolling brownouts and blackouts to conserve the available power. During that period, the price of RECLAIM NO_x credits experienced massive spikes. Companies that wanted to increase generation by bringing additional fossil fuel burning facilities on line, including a number of old gas-fired plants for which NO_x controls had not been upgraded, found that the cost of the needed emissions credits were being driven up to prohibitively high prices. Previous to that year, prices for all vintages of RECLAIM NO_x credits had ranged in a band between $1500 and $3000 per ton. In 2000, the spike in demand for vintage 2000 NO_x credits drove the price up from its previous record high of $4,284 in 1999, to an average price of $45,000 per credit in 2000, with the highest single price reported to be in excess of $90,000 per credit. With prices at those levels, the RECLAIM NO_x cap was perceived as a major contributing reason that prevented California from being able to respond effectively to the electricity shortage. Rather than taking the heat (figuratively and literally due to the lack of air conditioning), RECLAIM temporarily suspended its requirements for electricity generators. Is this example of unwillingness to stay the course, when a trading system comes under political and economic pressure, a cause for concern when opting for trading as opposed to more traditional emissions limitations?

6. Conclusions? The Drury et al. excerpt lists eight recommendations for urban air quality trading programs:

1. prohibit toxic trading,
2. prohibit trading into overburdened communities,
3. assess and prevent toxic hot spots and discriminatory impacts,
4. prohibit trading out of RACT requirements,
5. prohibit cross-pollutant trading,
6. allow affected communities to review and comment on proposed trades,
7. ban inter-source trading between mobile, stationary, and area sources, and
8. prohibit hot air credits that result from overallocating the baseline.[13]

---

13. 9 Duke Envtl. L. & Pol'y F. at 283-286.

Are there other recommendations that should be included? Has trading really improved the situation or simply obfuscated the problem by making a complex undertaking wrongly appear simple? The failure of RECLAIM to reduce loadings significantly is troubling. The likelihood that it has increased the level of hazard for identifiable groups of citizens is an indictment. In this regard, RECLAIM is not alone. Other trading programs have similar implementation stories that chronicle their adverse effects on discrete populations. See EPA Ignored Employees' Objections on Louisiana Program, Group Charges, 33 Envtl. Rep. (BNA) 2401 (Nov. 8, 2002), citing materials marshaled by Public Employees for Environmental Responsibility (PEER). See also EPA Office of the Inspector General, Open Market Trading Program for Air Emissions Needs Strengthening, Rep. No. 2002-P-00019 (Sept. 30, 2002).

C. INTERNATIONAL TRADING TO REDUCE GHG EMISSIONS

> "We need to reject a magical conception of the market, which would suggest that problems can be solved simply by an increase in the profits of companies or individuals. Is it realistic to hope that those who are obsessed with maximizing profits will stop to reflect on the environmental damage which they will leave behind for future generations? Where profits alone count, there can be no thinking about the rhythms of nature, its phases of decay and regeneration, or the complexity of ecosystems which may be gravely upset by human intervention." Pope Francis, Laudato si´ (Encyclical on Care for Our Common Home 2015).

Based in part on the U.S. experience with emissions trading to address acid rain, the nations of the world decided to proceed with a cap-and-trade approach to addressing GHG emissions multilaterally, an undertaking of unprecedented scale on the international level. As described in Chapter 22, the Third Conference of the Parties (COP-3) of the UN Framework Convention on Climate Change adopted the Kyoto Protocol, an ancillary instrument to the Convention, in 1997. The Protocol sets out commitments by 38 enumerated industrialized countries and economies in transition (former Communist bloc states) to limit or reduce their emissions of GHGs—CO_2, methane, NO_x, and others. During the first commitment period, from 2008 to 2012, the required reductions averaged about 5% and range as high as 8% for particular countries, measured by reference to 1990 levels.

The Protocol also anticipated additional reductions in a second and subsequent commitment periods, which were partially implemented through an amendment adopted in Doha, Qatar, intended to cover the period 2012-2020. By then, Canada had withdrawn from Kyoto, and the United States—ironically, a principal architect of the Protocol's signature international trading scheme—had never become party to the instrument. Japan and the Russian Federation declined to accept new obligations in the instrument, leaving basically only the 28-member EU as a partisan of Kyoto. As of this writing, the Doha Amendment has not formally entered into force, but is being applied by the EU on a voluntary basis.

Among the novel features of the Kyoto Protocol are its "flexible mechanisms" designed to reduce the cost of implementation by expanding the range of options available to states in fulfilling their obligations under the agreement. The Kyoto Protocol establishes that rights to emit may be traded among parties to the Protocol with substantive reduction obligations, under a system of international emissions trading (IET). Second, the Protocol permits Annex I parties to undertake cooperative projects that reduce emissions of GHGs in other Annex I parties and to obtain credit for those reductions, an option known as "joint implementation." Like "assigned amount units" (AAUs), the resulting "emissions reduction units" are tradable.

Third, the Protocol establishes a "clean development mechanism" (CDM), which provides a basis for Annex I parties to implement their reduction commitments by undertaking projects in developing countries. As suggested by the name, one purpose of the CDM was to establish environmentally beneficial demonstration projects designed to sequester or reduce carbon emissions in developing countries, which do not have substantive emissions reductions obligations under the Protocol. "Certified emissions reductions units" (CERs) generated by such project may also be traded. CDM projects must meet a requirement of "additionality," which is satisfied "if anthropogenic emissions of greenhouse gases by sources are reduced below those that would have occurred in the absence of the registered CDM project activity," as determined by an Executive Board reporting to the Conference of the Parties.

The implementation of the trading mechanisms under the Protocol, like that of any trading scheme, is largely a question of accounting for emissions, the equivalent of bean-counting. Without reliable accounting, one can imagine many undesirable consequences, as in any accounting scheme. Inadequate implementation, lack of confidence in the accuracy of reported emissions, and adverse effects on price are but a few. The structural problems are not dissimilar to many of the financial accounting scandals of recent years. The CDM—all of whose projects generate credits in countries with no reduction obligations—has been criticized for failing to demonstrate reductions from a business-as-usual scenario, and for a concentration on China in what appears to be a subsidy for foreign investment.

The Protocol requires states with quantified emissions targets to establish systems for calculating their GHG emissions and to report them annually. The Marrakesh Accords, a 200-page subsidiary instrument to the Protocol, consequently contain standards for accounting and reporting of emission units in accordance with the flexible mechanisms. To implement these obligations as well as the accord's substantive requirements, the Protocol anticipates an initial allocation of what have since come to be identified as AAUs corresponding to each state party's legally binding cap.

The Kyoto Protocol allows regional economic-integration organizations to reapportion their obligations among their member states. This provision was drafted in anticipation of its utilization by the EU, which has adopted an internal agreement redistributing the EU member states' uniform reduction target of 8%. While non-EU states have raised questions concerning the terms of access to this provision, the Marrakesh Rules do not treat the EU "bubble" as a mechanism subject to potential restrictions.[14]

In 2000, the EU implemented its "European Climate Change Programme" (ECCP) to meet its 8% reduction target under Kyoto, including provisions establishing an emissions trading scheme (ETS) to implement the flexible mechanisms of the Protocol. European markets for GHG emissions credits experienced a disruption in May 2006 due to overallocation of initial allowances, although the extent of the problem seems to have been overstated in the press. Nonetheless, as underscored by the other examples in this chapter, the incident demonstrates the need for rigor in the initial allocation of allowances for GHGs and in other analogous trading settings.

---

14. The bulk of this material is taken from Wirth, The Sixth Session, Part Two, and Seventh Session of the Conference of the Parties to the Framework Convention on Climate Change, 96 Am. J. Int'l L. 648 (2002).

C. International Trading to Reduce GHG Emissions

Beginning in 2012, in Directive 2008/101, the EU emissions trading scheme was extended from industries and utilities to cover aviation, by requiring all airlines—including those of non-EU Member States—to acquire emissions allowances for their flights which depart from and arrive at European airports. A number of American and Canadian airlines and airline associations contested the measures implementing that portion of the ETS in the United Kingdom, which they asserted contravened principles of customary international law, as well as international agreements governing civil aviation, including the Chicago Convention. The European Court of Justice in 2011 rendered the following opinion.

Air Transport Association of America et al. v. Secretary of State for Energy and Climate Change

European Court of Justice, Case C-366/10, 2011 E.C.R. I-13755.

101. Under [its governing treaties], the European Union is to contribute to the strict observance and the development of international law. Consequently, when it adopts an act, it is bound to observe international law in its entirety, including customary international law, which is binding upon the institutions of the European Union. . . .

103. The referring court mentions a principle that each State has complete and exclusive sovereignty over its airspace and another principle that no State may validly purport to subject any part of the high seas to its sovereignty. It also mentions the principle of freedom to fly over the high seas.

104. These three principles are regarded as embodying the current state of customary international maritime and air law and, moreover, they have been respectively codified in Article 1 of the Chicago Convention [on International Civil Aviation, which established the International Civil Aviation Organization].

105. Nor has the existence of those principles of international law been contested by the Member States, the institutions of the European Union, the Republic of Iceland or the Kingdom of Norway in their written observations or at the hearing.

106. As regards the . . . principle set out by the referring court, namely the principle that aircraft overflying the high seas are subject to the exclusive jurisdiction of the State in which they are registered, it must be found by contrast that, apart from the fact that the United Kingdom Government and, to a certain extent, the German Government dispute the existence of such a principle, insufficient evidence exists to establish that the principle of customary international law, recognised as such, that a vessel on the high seas is in principle governed only by the law of its flag would apply by analogy to aircraft overflying the high seas.

107. The principles of customary international law mentioned in paragraph 103 of the present judgment may be relied upon by an individual for the purpose of the Court's examination of the validity of an act of the European Union in so far as, first, those principles are capable of calling into question the competence of the European Union to adopt that act. . . .

110. Since a principle of customary international law does not have the same degree of precision as a provision of an international agreement, judicial review must necessarily be limited to the question whether, in adopting the act in question, the institutions of the European Union made manifest errors of assessment concerning the conditions for applying those principles.

111. Having regard to all the foregoing considerations, the answer to the first question is that the only principles and provisions of international law, from among those mentioned

by the referring court, that can be relied upon, in circumstances such as those of the main proceedings and for the purpose of assessing the validity of Directive 2008/101, are:

– first, within the limits of review as to a manifest error of assessment attributable to the European Union regarding its competence, in the light of those principles, to adopt that directive:
– the principle that each State has complete and exclusive sovereignty over its airspace,
– the principle that no State may validly purport to subject any part of the high seas to its sovereignty, and
– the principle which guarantees freedom to fly over the high seas. . . .

112. The referring court asks in essence, if and in so far as Directive 2008/101 is intended to apply the allowance trading scheme to those parts of flights which take place outside the airspace of the Member States, including to flights by aircraft registered in third States, whether that directive is valid in the light of the principles of customary international law. . . .

113. Having regard to the wording of these questions and the fact that the claimants in the main proceedings are airlines registered in a third State, it should first be determined whether and to what extent Directive 2008/101 applies to those parts of international flights that are performed outside the airspace of the Member States by such airlines. Second, the directive's validity should be examined in that context. . . .

122. It is to be noted at the outset that European Union law and, in particular, Directive 2008/101 cannot render Directive 2003/87 establishing the ETS applicable as such to aircraft registered in third States that are flying over third States or the high seas.

123. The European Union must respect international law in the exercise of its powers, and therefore Directive 2008/101 must be interpreted, and its scope delimited, in the light of the relevant rules of the international law of the sea and international law of the air.

124. On the other hand, European Union legislation may be applied to an aircraft operator when its aircraft is in the territory of one of the Member States and, more specifically, on an aerodrome situated in such territory, since, in such a case, that aircraft is subject to the unlimited jurisdiction of that Member State and the European Union.

125. In laying down a criterion for Directive 2008/101 to be applicable to operators of aircraft registered in a Member State or in a third State that is founded on the fact that those aircraft perform a flight which departs from or arrives at an aerodrome situated in the territory of one of the Member States, Directive 2008/101, inasmuch as it extends application of the scheme laid down by Directive 2003/87 to aviation, does not infringe the principle of territoriality or the sovereignty which the third States from or to which such flights are performed have over the airspace above their territory, since those aircraft are physically in the territory of one of the Member States of the European Union and are thus subject on that basis to the unlimited jurisdiction of the European Union.

126. Nor can such application of European Union law affect the principle of freedom to fly over the high seas since an aircraft flying over the high seas is not subject, in so far as it does so, to the allowance trading scheme. Moreover, such an aircraft can, in certain circumstances, cross the airspace of one of the Member States without its operator thereby being subject to that scheme.

127. It is only if the operator of such an aircraft has chosen to operate a commercial air route arriving at or departing from an aerodrome situated in the territory of a Member State that the operator, because its aircraft is in the territory of that Member State, will be subject to the allowance trading scheme.

128. As for the fact that the operator of an aircraft in such a situation is required to surrender allowances calculated in the light of the whole of the international flight that its aircraft has performed or is going to perform from or to such an aerodrome, it must be pointed out that, as European Union policy on the environment seeks to ensure a high level of protection in accordance with [the EU's governing treaties], the European Union legislature may in principle choose to permit a commercial activity, in this instance air transport, to be carried out in the territory of the European Union only on condition that operators comply with the criteria that have been established by the European Union and are designed to fulfill the environmental protection objectives which it has set for itself, in particular where those objectives follow on from an international agreement to which the European Union is a signatory, such as the Framework Convention and the Kyoto Protocol.

129. Furthermore, the fact that, in the context of applying European Union environmental legislation, certain matters contributing to the pollution of the air, sea or land territory of the Member States originate in an event which occurs partly outside that territory is not such as to call into question, in the light of the principles of customary international law capable of being relied upon in the main proceedings, the full applicability of European Union law in that territory.

130. It follows that the European Union had competence, in the light of the principles of customary international law capable of being relied upon in the context of the main proceedings, to adopt Directive 2008/101, in so far as the latter extends the allowance trading scheme laid down by Directive 2003/87 to all flights which arrive at or depart from an aerodrome situated in the territory of a Member State.

[The Court also upheld the Directive by reference to the multilateral agreements identified by the parties].

The 2015 Paris Agreement. The 21st Conference of Parties to the Framework Convention addressed the "original sin" of the Kyoto Protocol—a division of the world into states that have substantive emissions reduction obligations and those that do not—by adopting the 2015 Paris Agreement (further explored in Chapter 22), a universal instrument potentially applicable to all states. As would have been expected given it history, the Paris Agreement addresses emissions trading, in the following passage:

Paris Agreement

Dec. 12, 2015, http://unfccc.int/resource/docs/2015/cop21/eng/l09r01.pdf

Article 6

1. Parties recognize that some Parties choose to pursue voluntary cooperation in the implementation of their nationally determined contributions to allow for higher ambition in their mitigation and adaptation actions and to promote sustainable development and environmental integrity.

2. Parties shall, where engaging on a voluntary basis in cooperative approaches that involve the use of internationally transferred mitigation outcomes towards nationally determined contributions, promote sustainable development and ensure environmental integrity and transparency, including in governance, and shall apply robust accounting to ensure, inter alia, the avoidance of double counting, consistent with guidance adopted by the Conference of the Parties serving as the meeting of the Parties to the Paris Agreement.

3. The use of internationally transferred mitigation outcomes to achieve nationally determined contributions under this Agreement shall be voluntary and authorized by participating Parties.

4. A mechanism to contribute to the mitigation of greenhouse gas emissions and support sustainable development is hereby established under the authority and guidance of the Conference of the Parties serving as the meeting of the Parties to the Paris Agreement for use by Parties on a voluntary basis. It shall be supervised by a body designated by the Conference of the Parties serving as the meeting of the Parties to the Paris Agreement, and shall aim:

(a) To promote the mitigation of greenhouse gas emissions while fostering sustainable development;
(b) To incentivize and facilitate participation in the mitigation of greenhouse gas emissions by public and private entities authorized by a Party;
(c) To contribute to the reduction of emission levels in the host Party, which will benefit from mitigation activities resulting in emission reductions that can also be used by another Party to fulfil its nationally determined contribution; and
(d) To deliver an overall mitigation in global emissions.

5. Emission reductions resulting from the mechanism referred to in paragraph 4 of this Article shall not be used to demonstrate achievement of the host Party's nationally determined contribution if used by another Party to demonstrate achievement of its nationally determined contribution.

6. The Conference of the Parties serving as the meeting of the Parties to the Paris Agreement shall ensure that a share of the proceeds from activities under the mechanism referred to in paragraph 4 of this Article is used to cover administrative expenses as well as to assist developing country Parties that are particularly vulnerable to the adverse effects of climate change to meet the costs of adaptation.

7. The Conference of the Parties serving as the meeting of the Parties to the Paris Agreement shall adopt rules, modalities and procedures for the mechanism referred to in paragraph 4 of this Article at its first session.

COMMENTARY & QUESTIONS

1. EU limitations on aviation emissions take a nosedive. The aviation emissions directive upheld in *Air Transport Association of America* against challenges alleging inconsistencies with international law can be understood as a means of dealing with competitive disadvantages resulting from the laggard or free rider problem described more fully in Chapter 22. The directive was immensely controversial among non-EU countries, resulting in threats of trade-based challenges and other forms of retaliation. As a result, the requirements were suspended for flights to and from non-European countries for 2012, and the legislation was subsequently amended similarly for the period 2013-2016. According to the EU, the reason for this action was "to allow time for negotiations on a global market-based measure applying to aviation emissions" to be considered in ICAO, a UN specialized agency. In February 2016, ICAO with U.S. support adopted the first-ever global carbon emissions standards for commercial airplanes.

2. Safeguards for international trading. International emissions trading of the scale anticipated by the Kyoto Protocol and the Marrakesh Accords had never been attempted before. The Kyoto parties decided to create a two-track Compliance Committee, composed of a Facilitative Branch and an Enforcement Branch. The Facilitative Branch is intended to help parties comply with the Protocol. Why might a party self-identify as benefiting from the services of the Facilitative Branch? In April 2008, the Enforcement Branch found that Greece had breached its obligations under the Protocol because it does not have a reliable national system for measuring and recording GHG emissions, and it briefly suspended Greece from the trading scheme. Article 15 of the Paris Agreement sets up a compliance mechanism that is to be strictly "facilitative in nature . . . non-adversarial and non-punitive."

3. Giving credit for the road that would not have been taken. In several places in the Marrakesh Accords, credits are limited to those "emission reductions or removals that are additional to any that would have occurred without the project." Why is that an important concept? In *Citizens Against the Refinery's Effects*, noted in Chapter 11, the plaintiffs objected to granting offsets for a pollution reducing change in road paving practice that involved a cost saving rather than a cost increase. Will it be easy to ascertain what steps would have been taken without the incentive provided by the emissions trading mechanisms? This is one of the principal criticisms that was leveled at the Clean Development Mechanism.

4. Baseline choices and the overcreation of credits. The choice of 1990 as the date for baseline emissions in the Kyoto Protocol created a vast oversupply of AAUs—colloquially known as "hot air"—for some countries, notably Russia, as a result of substantially decreased economic activity following the end of the Cold War. Trading of "hot air" was not subject to the "would not have happened anyway" limitation. Was the grant of these seemingly excess AAUs a political imperative needed to "buy" the participation of these states? As noted in the text, even the EU's ETS system was dogged by assertions of the overcreation of credits at its launch. Is that simply part of the political price to be paid for trading schemes? The initial distribution of allowances is always a source of political wrangling. Although economists would generally favor an auction as reflecting the true price of the good (emissions), note the generous give-aways in the ETS even into the first commitment period under Kyoto.

5. How effective is cap-and-trade? In CARBON SHOCK: A TALE OF RISK AND CALCULUS ON THE FRONT LINES OF THE DISRUPTED GLOBAL ECONOMY (2014), journalist Mark Schapiro offers a devastating critique of the failure of carbon markets. In early 2013, the price of a ton of carbon emissions fell to a record low of 2.81 Euros ($3.74) when the European Parliament declined to intervene to prop up prices by limiting the future availability of future allowances. What are the policy consequences of a carbon price that is too low? Economists disagree on the precise figure, but generally agree that a price of at least $60 per ton is necessary to influence the private sector's behavior with respect to alternative fuel choices, efficiency improvements, and other micro-level choices that contribute to overall carbon emissions reductions.

6. Paris is a long way from Kyoto. The Paris Agreement and its accompanying non-binding decision address non-market approaches to mitigation, but make no reference whatsoever to market-based strategies or emissions trading. While it certainly does not preclude emissions trading, Article 6 of the Paris Agreement, set out above, gives at best lukewarm endorsement to the notion. In adopting this provision, what signal do you think the signatories to the Paris Agreement are sending to what is left of the Kyoto flexible mechanisms, and particularly the Clean Development Mechanism? What would you expect the "mechanism" referred to in Article 6, paragraph 4, to look like, and how would it likely be similar to or different from the Kyoto mechanisms?

D. Carbon Taxes

A tax or fee is an alternative market-enlisting strategy that puts a price on pollutants such as climate-disrupting GHGs, and the preferred choice of many economists. To understand why, it is helpful to begin with the concept of "public goods," such as clean air and water, the stratospheric ozone layer, the global climate, the high seas, and common grazing areas described by Garrett Hardin in Chapter 1. Public goods share the characteristic that others may not be excluded from their use—whether as in the case of the ozone layer and climate by their inherent nature, or, as in the case of the high seas or shared pastureland, through rules constructed by human interactions. Hardin's "tragedy" results from overuse or overconsumption of the resource by individuals' engaging in their own self-interest, lacking incentives for restraint out of regard for the common good.

One can imagine a number of strategies in response to the tragedy of the commons. Prescriptive regulation—often pejoratively described as a "command and control" approach—is the approach taken in much of U.S. environmental regulation as described in the remainder of this book. Effluent limitations for point sources promulgated under the CWA are a classic example of such a strategy. Privatization, a second, is one of the policy responses considered by Hardin, designed to encourage the identification of pastoralists with particular pieces of land and to conserve their own resources. On a broader scale, this is the approach taken in cap-and-trade schemes, which establish a limit on the degradation of the resource (the cap) and apportion out rights to use the resource, which can then be bought and sold on a market (trading).

A tax as a third public policy response follows from conceptualizing the tragedy of the commons as a market failure—the lack of a price on a collective resource as a result of its accessibility to all without charge. For example, a utility must invest in fuel in the form of coal or natural gas, along with the infrastructure of a power plant and transmission lines, to produce a saleable good in the form of electricity. But the firm's emissions of GHGs also utilize the global climate as an input for free. The adverse effects on the resource from carbon pollution consequently are not reflected in the price of the finished product. In consuming a public good—the climate—without paying, the utility is externalizing environmental costs, shifting them onto the public as a whole.

One can identify these negative externalities[15] as the source of much environmental pollution, and the failure to require a polluter to pay for its use of common resources as the source of excess environmental degradation.[16] Understanding the problem of environmental pollution in this manner, public policy should require the internalization of environmental costs. A fee levied by a governmental authority, known as a Pigouvian tax after the British economist generally credited with identifying the concept, is the most obvious regulatory vehicle for accomplishing this goal. In the absence of a means for assuring payment for the consumption of clean air or water, or the climate—a market failure—the fee

---

15. Environmental externalities are generally "negative" in that they impose costs on society. One can also imagine positive externalities, in which private behavior generates larger social benefits, such as a parent's decision to inoculate her child, who then is less likely to transmit disease to others.

16. This insight is the motivation for the famous "polluter pays principle," for example as codified in Principle 16 the 1992 Rio Declaration in Chapter 22.

D. Carbon Taxes

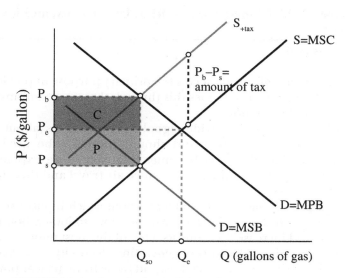

FIGURE 14-4 *A tax in the gasoline market.*
Source: http://welkerswilkinomics.com/blog/2008/01/14/when-more-tax-is-a-good-tax/

operates as a surrogate price, requiring the polluter to pay for the consumption of common resources as it would any other input.

To understand the operation of an environmental fee, consider the above diagram analyzing the effect of a gasoline tax, essentially a form of carbon tax.

The horizontal axis, labelled "Q," quantifies inputs consumed, in this case gasoline. The vertical axis correlates price "P" with quantity. The supply curve "S" reflects suppliers' incentives to produce more gasoline as the price increases. The demand curve "D" describes consumers' tendency to consume less of the commodity as the price increases. The equilibrium price and quantity at P_e and Q_e, where the two curves cross, is a graphical depiction of the familiar law of supply and demand, where the two are equal. But from the point of view of socially optimal levels of gasoline consumption, at P_e and Q_e the price is too low and the quantity too high because environmental costs have not been reflected in the respective supply and demand curves.

The imposition of a tax causes the demand curve D to shift down, as consumers respond to the price signal of the fee by consuming less gasoline. Suppliers also respond to market signals in the form of the potential for increased revenue, as indicated by higher prices, which causes the supply curve to shift upward (S_{+tax}). As expected, the resulting equilibrium quantity is lower (Q_{so}) and the price (P_b) higher than would be the case without the governmental intervention in the form of the tax. Because they take into account the environmental costs of the consumption of a unit of gasoline, Q_{so} and P_b reflect a socially optimal outcome that maximizes economic efficiency.

The following excerpt by a prominent Yale economist known particularly for his work on the economics of climate change describes the benefits of carbon pricing, focusing on a carbon tax.

William Nordhaus, The Climate Casino: Risk, Uncertainty, and Economics for a Warming World

Yale University Press (2013)

Putting a price on the use of carbon serves the primary purpose of providing strong incentives to reduce carbon emissions. It does this through three mechanisms: by affecting consumers, producers, and innovators.

First, a carbon price will provide signals to consumers about what goods and services have high carbon content and should therefore be used more sparingly. Consumers will find that air travel becomes relatively more expensive than visiting local sights or taking the train, which will reduce air travel and therefore the emissions from air travel.

Second, it will provide signals to producers about which inputs use more carbon and which use less or none. It thereby induces firms to move to low-carbon technologies so as to lower their costs and increase their profits. One of the most important signals will come in electric power generation. The costs of generating electricity from coal will rise sharply; costs from natural gas will rise somewhat less; and those from nuclear power and renewable sources like wind will rise not at all. Of all the adjustments, reducing CO_2 emissions from coal is probably the most important step for the United States.

A high carbon price will get the attention of electricity generators. Indeed, many companies already build the possibility of high carbon prices into their long-term plans, even though the current price in the United States is zero. For example, a survey of twenty-one electric utilities in 2012 in the United States found that sixteen had built a positive CO_2 price into their planning, with the average price for 2020 being slightly below $25 per ton of CO_2.

A third and more subtle effect is that carbon prices will give market incentives for inventors and innovators to develop and introduce low-carbon products and processes to replace current technologies. Suppose you are the executive in charge of research and development (R&D) at a large company like GE, which had an R&D budget of $5 billion in 2012. You make equipment for generating electricity from different sources — coal, nuclear energy, and wind. Most generating facilities will last for decades. If carbon prices are going to be zero or very low, then coal-burning plants will continue to be an important source of profits, and you will continue to do substantial R&D for coal technologies.

On the other hand, if you expect carbon prices to rise sharply, few conventional coal stations will be built, and zero-carbon technologies like wind and nuclear power will be the areas on which to place your bets. In other areas where consumer or producer demand is sensitive to carbon prices — air travel, consumer appliances, and automobiles being good examples — companies with big R&D budgets will be sensitive to the signals given by carbon prices and redirect their investments accordingly. . . .

There are two ways to raise the price of carbon:

- The easiest way is simply to tax CO_2 emissions: a "carbon tax." It would require firms and people to pay a tax on their emissions much the same way as they do when buying gasoline.
- A second and more indirect method requires firms to have permits to emit CO_2, and to allow them to be bought and sold. This is called "cap and trade" because

D. Carbon Taxes

the quantity of emissions is capped, but the rights to emit can be traded for a price among firms. . . .

In the second approach to raising the carbon price, known as carbon taxation, governments directly tax CO_2 emissions. The basic idea is simple. When a firm burns fossil fuels, the combustion leads to a certain quantity of CO_2 entering the atmosphere. The tax would be levied on the CO_2 content of each fuel. The definitional issues are the same for carbon taxes and emissions caps. The only difference is that one taxes a quantity while the other limits the quantity. The definitions of the quantities are the same.

Let's take an example. Suppose a company generates electricity using coal. A large plant might burn 500 million tons of coal each year. At a tax of $25 per ton of CO_2, the plant would pay almost $400 million per year in carbon taxes. This would be the single most important component of costs and would definitely get the attention of management.

A universal carbon tax would be similar to this example but would apply to all sources of CO_2 (and other GHGs as well). Coal, oil, and petroleum are the major sources of CO_2, but other areas such as cement production and deforestation would also come under a universal tax. As in any tax system, there are many lawyerly details.

Carbon taxes (or more frequently their relatives such as energy taxes) featured in the early discussions of climate-change policy. They were shunted aside in the late 1990s because the political negotiators at international meetings believed that quantitative restrictions were more familiar and more likely to be acceptable to the public and national governments. Since 1997 [when the Kyoto Protocol was adopted], as a consequence, quantitative restrictions such as cap and trade along with regulations have been the norm in international negotiations. . . .

Generally, economists lean toward carbon taxation as preferable, while negotiators and environmental specialists lean toward the cap-and-trade approach. The following are some of the major considerations.

Carbon tax advocates point out that tax systems are mature and universal institutions of policy. Every country uses taxes. Countries have administrative tax systems, tax collectors, tax lawyers, and tax courts. Countries need revenues, and indeed many countries face large fiscal deficits today. By contrast, there is limited experience with cap-and-trade systems in most countries and virtually no international experience.

A related point is that quantitative limits produce severe volatility in the market price of carbon under an emissions-targeting approach. . . . The volatility arises because both supply and demand for permits are insensitive to the permit price. The high level of volatility is economically costly and sends inconsistent signals to private sector decision makers. Clearly, a carbon tax would provide consistent price signals and would not vary so widely from year to year, or even day to day.

COMMENTARY & QUESTIONS

1. The carbon tax debate. Surveying the carbon landscape, the Economist magazine stated flatly that "economists prefer carbon prices, especially those set by taxes rather than cap-and-trade systems, which are more vulnerable to capture by the polluters." Stopping Climate Change, Economist, Dec. 5, 2009. See Avi-Yonah & Uhlmann, Why a Carbon Tax Is a Better Response to Global Warming than Cap-and-Trade, 28 Stan. Envtl. L.J. 3

(2009). Commentators as diverse as Yale's William Nordhaus, quoted above, and the New York Times' Paul Krugman have argued forcefully that a carbon charge or tax is far more likely to achieve the desired kinds of carbon controls than is Kyoto's quantitative trading approach.[17] A carbon charge or tax arguably is much less skewable and much more easily implemented than a cap-and-trade system.

On the other hand, beyond the visceral repugnance of the word *tax*, expert voices have argued against carbon charges on the merits:

> First, a "one size fits all" tax requires an impossible calculation of the average cost of reducing emissions over a given period of time. Compare this with an emissions-trading system that works on the free-floating marginal cost of abating emissions. Second, carbon taxes would be levied locally and so impossible to properly administer on a global scale. A global carbon-market price is perfectly pervasive. And third, taxation cannot guarantee a reduction in greenhouse-gas emissions; emitters could opt to pay the tax and continue emitting at will. Conversely, a cap-and-trade solution introduces a carbon ceiling and the price acts as no more than a useful barometer of how close we are to achieving that goal; prices will tend to zero as the requisite level of emission reductions is achieved. James Emanuel, Letter to the Editor, Economist, Jan. 2, 2010.

Despite the complexities of the policy discourse and political difficulties, a number of jurisdictions, including Sweden, Ireland, and the Canadian provinces of Québec and British Columbia, have adopted some form of carbon tax. For a compendium of carbon taxes internationally, see Carbon Tax Center, Where Carbon is Taxed at http://www.carbontax.org/where-carbon-is-taxed.

2. Setting the level of a carbon tax—the great danger of setting it too low. "Getting the price right," in terms of establishing the amount of the tax, is not only a significant political challenge, but also a technical one that is frequently glossed over in the carbon tax debate. The political difficulty of enacting a carbon tax in the U.S. is already daunting. Imagine how much harder it would be politically to adjust the tax upward if the level of reductions obtained at the original level of tax is insufficient to obtain the necessary level of GHG reductions. Not only would political capital have been spent on the initial tax, the impact of the tax would have been to raise prices of almost everything that relies on energy inputs to almost everyone. In that political environment, it is hard to imagine passing a significant increase in the tax. How does one value the social cost of the emission of a ton of carbon equivalents of GHGs? Through a cost benefit analysis, the likely answer from economists? The social costs, in the form of the tax, are readily identifiable. But how does one value the benefits to the climate system, especially far into the future, including the value of avoided climate degradation to future generations (an issue explored in the previous chapter)? What knowledge is required to accurately predict how firms will react to a carbon tax—i.e., reduce emissions to avoid the tax, or simply pay it and pass on the cost to users of the carbon-producing activity? Does the difficulty of obtaining reliable answers to these questions argue in favor of a cap-and-trade system, where the environmental results are the one thing that is known in advance? Note, not-so-incidentally, that according to this theory of environmental economics, it is possible for the collective public welfare to suffer from levels of environmental pollution that are not only too high, but also too low. Do you see why? Translated into the nomenclature of carbon taxes, it is possible to overcompensate by setting a fee at too high a level, in effect overvaluing environmental benefits.

---

[17]. The debate is nicely analyzed in Wolf, Taxation Can Give the Earth a Chance, Fin. Times, July 19, 2006, at 19.

D. Carbon Taxes

3. The bigger picture, including revenue. Generating revenue is not the principal public policy purpose of a Pigouvian tax. But in the real world, there is likely to be considerable dickering over what to do with the revenue generated. An analogous problem in a cap-and-trade system concerns the initial allocation of allowances. Giving them away to existing polluters in effect means a windfall in the form of a free right to pollute. The alternative, much preferred by economists, is to auction off allowances rather than distributing them gratis. In any event, whether by tax or by cap-and-trade based on an auction as the allocation method, government becomes the beneficiary of a considerable sum of money. Could that money be selectively rebated to individuals, small businesses, and industries where the cost of the tax or purchasing credits is unusually burdensome? Could the money be used to subsidize investment in pollution control equipment or research and development of less polluting alternative energy sources? As another alternative, the government revenue could be applied to reducing the deficit being passed on to future generations that still will be facing considerable environmental burdens related to global warming.

4. The counter-case claiming cap-and-trade is better. The virtues of cap-and-trade versus a carbon tax have been debated at great length. The generally favorable experience with Title IV of the CAA of 1990 is regularly trotted out as the example that proves the efficacy of cap-and-trade systems as a means of pollution control. Is global GHG pollution in any way similar in regard to, for example, the number of sources to be controlled, the variety of emissions and credits to be traded, or the ease of monitoring? Recall the matrix describing expected polluter behavior in the face of a pollution tax or a cap-and-trade system. The principal efficiency gains of market instruments over command-and-control regulation, at least in theory, are achieved under both systems—individual firms will make the least cost choice rather than having some high cost choices forced on regulated firms.

One more entertaining entry in the debate was a web-video cartoon produced by Annie Leonard lambasting cap-and-trade. See www.storyofstuff.com/capandtrade. Academic bloggers found both accuracies and inaccuracies in the lampoon, and also raised serious points favoring cap-and-trade. One key point about cap-and-trade, properly designed, is that there is a cap that ensures reductions. In commenting on the distortions of cap-and-trade to favor polluters that was prominent in video, Professor Shi-Ling Hsu wrote: "politics will distort both a cap & trade system and a tax, but such distortions will undermine the environmental effectiveness of a tax (loopholes in the tax code to favor special interests will reduce the effective tax rate), whereas such distortions will generally not undermine the environmental effectiveness of cap & trade (special interest wrangling over allowance allocation will change the distribution of allowances, but not the aggregate cap)." Hsu also found cap-and-trade to be more attractive for international adoption and more enforceable because once implemented, "the political economy of implementation also favors cap & trade: after adoption, a tax will engender resistance by all taxpayers, whereas a cap & trade system will create a new constituency (allowance holders) who lobby in favor of monitoring and enforcing the cap."

Not long after that, Professor Hsu jumped squarely into the carbon tax camp, publishing a book entitled, THE CASE FOR A CARBON TAX: GETTING PAST OUR HANG-UPS TO EFFECTIVE CLIMATE POLICY (2011). In a precis of the book, Professor Hsu listed ten separate reasons for favoring a carbon tax.

- Government is bad at picking winners, and losers are good at picking governments;
- economic efficiency;
- broader incentive to innovate;
- deeper and steadier incentives to innovate;

- carbon taxes to not subsidize the formation of capital;
- respect for federalism;
- carbon taxes are administratively simpler;
- revenue raising;
- international coordination;
- economic efficiency again.

The Precis is available at http://myweb.fsu.edu/shsu/HSU_carbon_tax_precis4.pdf.

5. Two Nobel Laureate economists weigh in — Ronald Coase and Paul Krugman. In evaluating the choice between a carbon tax and cap-and-trade proposals, Robert H. Frank decided that it would be useful to talk with the "patron saint" himself (namely, Professor Coase), several years before the Nobel laureate's death in 2013 at age 102. Frank writes:

> Climate scientists agree that the cheapest way to combat global warming is to curb carbon dioxide emissions. And economists agree that the cheapest way to do that is by changing emitters' incentives, either by taxing emissions or requiring emission permits.
>
> I chatted with Mr. Coase briefly last week, and he is still following these issues. He agreed that both taxes and tradable permits satisfy his criterion of concentrating damage abatement with those who can accomplish it at least cost. Those with inexpensive ways of reducing emissions will find it attractive to adopt them, thus avoiding carbon dioxide taxes or the need to purchase costly permits. Others will find it cheaper to pay taxes or buy permits. . . . Robert H. Frank, Of Individual Liberty and Cap-and-Trade, N.Y. Times, Jan. 10, 2010, at 7.

If, as Frank concludes, both carbon taxes and cap-and-trade pass muster within the Coase framework, then what is the ongoing political debate over reducing carbon emissions really about? Frank posits that the debate is actually premised on differing views about the value of "social engineering" through government intervention in the economy. However, social engineering, according to Frank, has little to do with Professor Coase's views. "But while Mr. Coase has often been skeptical of government intervention, he is no ideologue." Under the Coase approach, according to Frank, the key is to achieve damage abatement at least cost, regardless of political ideology. Nonetheless, political ideology will certainly play a meaningful role in the ultimate choice between a carbon tax and cap-and-trade.

As noted before, Professor Paul Krugman has expressed a preference for a tax over cap-and-trade, but he eventually concludes cap-and-trade is more readily achievable in the United States.

> There is widespread agreement among environmental economists that a market-based program to deal with the threat of climate change — one that limits carbon emissions by putting a price on them — can achieve large results at modest, though not trivial, cost. There is, however, much less agreement on how fast we should move, whether major conservation efforts should start almost immediately or be gradually increased over the course of many decades. . . .
>
> In practice there are a couple of important differences between cap-and-trade and a pollution tax. One is that the two systems produce different types of uncertainty. If the government imposes a pollution tax, polluters know what price they will have to pay, but the government does not know how much pollution they will generate. If the government imposes a cap, it knows the amount of pollution, but polluters do not know what the price of emissions will be. Another important difference has to do with government revenue. A pollution tax is, well, a tax, which imposes costs on the private sector while generating revenue for the government. Cap-and-trade is a bit more complicated. If the government simply auctions off licenses and collects the revenue, then it is just like a tax. Cap-and-trade, however, often involves handing out licenses to existing players, so the potential revenue goes to industry instead of the government. . . .

E. Industry Self-Regulation 643

> There is a rough consensus among economic modelers about the costs of action. That general opinion may be summed up as follows: Restricting emissions would slow economic growth—but not by much. The Congressional Budget Office, relying on a survey of models, has concluded that [cap-and-trade legislation introduced by Congressmen Waxman and Markey, the only bill to pass either chamber of the Congress] "would reduce the projected average annual rate of growth of gross domestic product between 2010 and 2050 by 0.03 to 0.09 percentage points." That is, it would trim average annual growth to 2.31 percent, at worst, from 2.4 percent. Over all, the Budget Office concludes, strong climate-change policy would leave the American economy between 1.1 percent and 3.4 percent smaller in 2050 than it would be otherwise.[18] We know how to limit greenhouse-gas emissions. We have a good sense of the costs—and they're manageable. All we need now is the political will. Paul Krugman, Building a Green Economy, N.Y. Times, Apr. 11, 2010, at MM34.

6. Carbon taxes in the Paris Agreement. Taxes and fees are conspicuous by their absence in the text of the Paris Agreement and the accompanying non-binding decision adopted at COP-21 in Paris in late 2015. Nonetheless, there is widespread agreement that states parties may utilize carbon taxes to fulfill their individual nationally determined contributions under the Agreement. Compare this result with the Paris Agreement's ambivalent approach toward cap-and-trade (noted above). The question of preferred approaches to national efforts is likely to become a consideration in the case of developing countries seeking international financial support for their domestic mitigation programs. Is this agnosticism toward market-based approaches desirable from a public policy point of view? On the one hand, the Paris Agreement leaves states free to implement their national undertakings flexibly, avoiding the prescriptive approach of the Kyoto Protocol. On the other, perhaps a thumb—or, in the case of taxes or fees, a pinkie—on the scale might nudge the states parties to the Agreement in a useful direction.

E. INDUSTRY SELF-REGULATION: THE INTERNATIONAL ORGANIZATION FOR STANDARDIZATION

The bulk of this coursebook is devoted to mandatory performance requirements transmitted from government to the private sector. This regulatory model, however, is not the only approach for promoting environmental progress and sustainability. Standards crafted by and for the private sector—typically, although not exclusively, businesses—also play a role. Since privately generated standards do not have the authority of government behind them, they are nonbinding and voluntary. One prominent set of such standards is adopted and implemented by the International Organization for Standardization (ISO).

ISO is an international federation of 162 standardizing bodies from a similarly wide variety of countries. ISO is not an intergovernmental organization such as the UN, constituted by multilateral agreement whose members are states represented by governments. Although the ISO members from some countries are governmental entities, most are not. The U.S. member of ISO is the American National Standards Institute (ANSI), a private

---

18. Krugman asserts the outcry of some conservative groups against those reports (e.g., the Heritage Foundation, which usually champions market approaches) is premised on their antipathy to government intervention because, in Krugman's view, those criticisms of the CBO and other supporting research are bad faith distortions of the research and the data. [EDS.]

entity. The primary U.S. participants in ISO processes are representatives from private industry.

ISO's principal work product consists of voluntary standards adopted by consensus. In contrast to some of the output of intergovernmental organizations, ISO standards are strictly hortatory and are not binding under international law. Nevertheless, ISO standards often have considerable influence. Probably the best-known ISO standards are those adopted for film speeds. As a result of harmonization through ISO, film with standardized speeds of 100, 200, or 400, is compatible with virtually all cameras of whatever brand are available throughout the world.

In the mid-1990s, ISO's Technical Committee (TC) 207 on environmental management began to issue its 14000 series of environmental management standards, a process that continues today. The centerpiece of the program is ISO 14001 on environmental management systems (EMSs). Unlike product standards such as film speeds, EMS is a process-oriented approach designed to help an organization "develop and implement its environmental policy and manage its environmental aspects," including "organizational structure, planning activities, responsibilities, practices, procedures, processes and resources." Also included in the 14000 series are standards for environmental assessments, product labeling and declarations, lifecycle assessment, environmental communication, and GHG emissions reporting.

Although the standard is intended to have societal benefits as well, the principal purpose of ISO 14001 is to assist businesses in developing and implementing their own environmental policies and programs. Apart from its voluntary character, the standard is strictly procedural in nature and does not specify particular outcomes. The program also includes a private third party auditing and certification scheme to verify compliance and implementation. The ISO 14000 series of standards is therefore fundamentally different in kind from mandatory governmentally adopted requirements such as effluent limitations adopted under the CWA.

In 2008, just over ten years after the issuance of ISO 14001, a concerted process for reviewing and revising that standard has now begun. ISO has since released a new standard, ISO 14005, containing guidance for all organizations, but particularly small- and medium-sized enterprises, on the phased development, implementation, maintenance and improvement of an environmental management system. Environmentally related efforts are taking place in other technical committees besides TC 207. In 2010 ISO released a new standard 26000 containing guidance with respect to social responsibility, which also has an environmental component.

ISO standards, including the 14000 series, potentially have a global reach. A large proportion of the countries on the planet participate in ISO activities, and ISO standards have a high profile within multinational corporations. There have nonetheless been concerns about "representativeness" in drafting ISO standards, and until ISO 26000 there had been little or no multistakeholder engagement.

One salient feature of ISO 14001, often cited, is the effect of elevating environmental issues within an enterprise. Because an EMS is addressed to the entirety of the production process, at least in principle the exercise of preparing and adopting an EMS engages the entire corporation, including top management.

Although EMS is a process-oriented approach that in principle is distinct from substantive, governmentally established regulatory requirements, the two are strongly interrelated. That is, an ISO-conforming EMS ought to assist a firm in meeting performance-based standards such as emissions limitations promulgated under the major environmental regulatory statutes. Among other benefits of ISO 14001 are "reduced environmental footprint in terms of environmental emissions, discharges and waste; improved internal communications and

E. Industry Self-Regulation

external partnerships; [and] continual system improvements resulting from EMS objectives, targets, programs, periodic audits and management reviews."

ISO standards set out uniform expectations from one country to another. To that extent, the meaning of an ISO-conforming EMS is similar or identical regardless of location. One frequently identified corollary benefit of uniformity is the salutary effect on international trade. Although this attribute is not immediately obvious in the case of ISO 14001, which adopts a process-oriented approach, other standards in the ISO 14000 series demonstrate the utility of homogeneity. Two motivations for standards on environmental labeling, for instance, are to assure consistency for environmental claims and to assure that environmental labels do not operate as disguised barriers to trade. ISO standards on reporting GHG emissions or removals are designed to assure consistency in metrics from one country to another so as to facilitate comparability of data.

Although perhaps easily overlooked from a U.S. perspective, ISO standards also elevate environmental protection to an international plane. Although voluntary and adopted primarily by industry representatives for the benefit of industry, ISO standards are indeed standards. If nothing else, the mere existence of environmental ISO standards signals that this subject matter is an issue of transnational importance. The process of developing ISO standards, moreover, encourages an international dialogue that lifts the topics addressed by the standards above the domestic level.

Some governments, particularly those of developing countries, may have limited or inadequate regulatory infrastructure. In such a setting, ISO standards can create a template for national laws and regulations. Because they are addressed directly to private parties, including multinational corporations, ISO standards in those countries with limited regulatory infrastructure can also operate as something of a default safety net. In situations where governments may be less than effective in assuring environmental quality, ISO requirements may serve literally as a standard for governments and the public to hold private entities accountable.

One of the principal features of ISO 14001 is the availability of third party certification. Although firms may implement an ISO 14001-like environmental management system without seeking certification, the availability of third party certification is an additional factor that encourages consistency, as well as improved market share and institutional reputation. Some customers may demand ISO 14001 certification from their suppliers.

ISO 14001 consequently is written to be "auditable" or verifiable. The third party certification scheme is designed to increase public confidence in a corporation's accountability and its products or services. Certification also promotes positive relationships with local communities, which may be concerned about the environmental performance of a nearby facility. Moreover, the prospect of certification creates incentives for industry to adopt EMSs. More than 21,000 entities in North America are now certified under ISO 14001.

Because entities may self-declare or self-certify, under ISO 14001 the number of facilities implementing ISO 14001 is higher than the number of certifications. Although the obvious value of third party certification is credibility, the standard itself anticipates that this is not necessary to obtain the benefits of ISO 14001. For instance, local governments or utilities may wish to improve their environmental performance by using ISO standards, but they may believe that other forms of political accountability render certification redundant or unnecessary.

In the U.S., ISO 14001 has had particular utility in the public sector, where it has served as a basis for the adoption of EMSs for public buildings and undertakings. The Clinton Administration promulgated an executive order that specifically required the implementation of EMSs by federal agencies and facilities by the end of 2005. While not mentioning

ISO 14001 by name, the ISO standard has been the typical model for implementing the Executive Order, an important instrument for reducing the federal government's environmental footprint. Presidents Bush and Obama have both also issued executive orders directing federal agencies to utilize EMSs. Governmental entities at the state and local level have also successfully employed EMSs, including those that conform to ISO 14001.[19]

COMMENTARY & QUESTIONS

1. **Private voluntary standards and public regulation.** The relationship between private voluntary standards and domestic regulatory requirements is frequently an uncomfortable one. U.S. federal law (the National Technology Transfer and Advancement Act of 1995) and executive order (OMB Circular No. A-119; Federal Participation in the Development and Use of Voluntary Consensus Standards and in Conformity Assessment Activities) direct federal agencies to consider private voluntary standards, such as those adopted by ISO, in their regulatory processes like rulemakings. There are benefits to such an approach. A voluntary consensus standard may generate better data than the regulatory process, may be an efficacious vehicle for educating regulatory officials as to the practical needs of industry, and, if effective, may obviate the need for regulatory intervention altogether. On the other hand, more or less by definition, the public interest is poorly represented in a private standard-setting context, and there is a potential for self-interested behavior by industry to distort or derail needed public action. How do you think this tension should be resolved? What should be the role, if any, of private voluntary standards in, for example, EPA rulemakings? What about the role of EPA in ISO processes?

2. **Representation and transparency.** ISO standards are adopted by consensus, involving a complex procedure of drafts and commenting. *Consensus* is defined as "general agreement, characterized by the absence of sustained opposition to substantial issues by any important part of the concerned interests and by a process that involves seeking to take into account the views of all parties concerned and to reconcile any conflicting arguments," qualified by a note observing that "consensus need not imply unanimity." One concern about the adoption of essentially global standards is the potential for a disappointing least-common-denominator result in which objections to excessive stringency can be expected to dominate over initiatives that might push for greater rigor. Second, ISO, whose members are representatives of affected industries, does not necessarily represent the public interest more broadly. Although environmental organizations and academics have been invited to participate in the ISO process in the U.S., it would be difficult to say that ISO as a forum reflects a balanced representation of stakeholders on environmental issues. The prevailing tone is still very much industry-oriented. Because of the voluntary nature of ISO standards, the perception of industry domination of the forum, the lengthy and complicated process for adoption of ISO standards, and the expense of attending frequent overseas meetings, few U.S. nonprofit environmental organizations have made a significant commitment to the ISO process. How, if at all, would you go about restructuring ISO processes so as to make them more broadly representative? Or would that defeat the purpose of the undertaking?

3. **ISO 14001's process orientation.** ISO 14001, unlike a product standard such as film speed, is fundamentally procedural in nature. An ISO 14001-conforming EMS is designed

---

19. The bulk of this material is taken from Wirth, The International Organization for Standardization: Private Voluntary Standards as Swords and Shields, 36 B.C. Envtl. Aff. L. Rev. 79 (2009).

E. Industry Self-Regulation

to help a company achieve its own environmental goals through an iterative process of "continual improvement." ISO 14001 has been criticized for its failure to engage with substantive regulatory requirements. Consistent with ISO 14001's process—as opposed to a performance approach—a company may receive ISO 14001 certification even with outstanding regulatory violations—an attribute that has been the subject of much public criticism. Given that an ISO-conforming EMS is produced by industry for its own use in improving its own performance, do you think that criticism is fair? Some companies have used ISO 14001 certification as a marketing tool that implies high environmental performance, at least potentially in situations of uncorrected violations of substantive regulatory laws. Given that the public is largely unfamiliar with ISO 14001's requirements, is this an appropriate use of ISO certification?

4. ISO and trade. Multinational corporations tend to support private voluntary standards like those adopted by ISO because regulatory convergence or "harmonization" of domestic health, safety, and environmental requirements promotes a more predictable trade climate. One study examined the efficacy of ISO 14001 from this point of view, noting that Germany, with 1260 ISO certifications, has among the most stringent environmental regulations, relatively little environmental litigation, and a high participation rate in international organizations. Nicaragua, by contrast, which had only one ISO 14001 certification, has the least stringent environmental regulations of the countries surveyed and a low rate of participation in international efforts. The authors conclude that "countries have more ISO 14001 certifications when they are more heavily embedded in the international context via strong export ties with heavily ISO 14001 countries. . . ." Potoski & Prakash, Regulatory Convergence in Nongovernmental Regimes? Cross-National Adoptions of ISO 14001 Certifications, 66 J. Politics 885, 899 (2004). Does this result suggest that trade, private voluntary standards, and environmental protection may be mutually reinforcing goals?

5. ISO standards as swords and shields. The utility of private voluntary standards in encouraging trade has not gone unnoticed by the negotiators of trade agreements. In 1994 the WTO adopted a new agreement on Technical Barriers to Trade (TBT). The TBT agreement takes aim at national standards for a variety of products, including safety standards for children's toys, appliance efficiency criteria, and vehicle fuel efficiency standards. Under the WTO's dispute settlement system, states can challenge each other's technical barriers by reference to ISO standards. Domestic requirements that are more rigorous than ISO standards are vulnerable to attack, while those that conform are entitled to considerable deference. For example, the WTO's Appellate Body is—its highest judicial organ—held that the EU's labeling requirements for sardines violated the TBT Agreement because they failed to conform to international standards. Appellate Body Report, European Communities —Trade Description of Sardines, WT/DS231/AB/R (Sept. 26, 2002). ISO's 14000 series also includes standards for eco-labeling, GHG reporting, and lifecycle analysis. How might the existence of these standards, and the availability of the trade agreement dispute settlement system, affect national decisionmaking? For the better or the worse?

6. EMSs in the courts. The ISO 14001 standard for EMSs and other similar requirements are beginning to work their way into the court system. For example, the Provincial Court of Alberta (Canada) ordered a chemical company to obtain ISO certification as part of its sentence in a criminal case for violation of the Environmental Protection and Enhancement Act. *R. v. Prospec Chems.*, 19 C.E.L.R. (N.S.) 178 (Alta. 1996). What do you think of the application of private voluntary standards in a judicial setting? How else could you imagine ISO standards being used by a court? Potentially abused by litigants?

7. Combining voluntary standards and mandatory regulation. The perception of diminishing returns from command and control regulation has led to the establishment of optional "excellence" programs that require or encourage the use of voluntary standards. The most recent iteration at EPA was known as the "National Environmental Performance Track." The concept attracted negative attention during the Bush administration as a perceived alternative to compulsory regulatory standards, and the Obama administration terminated the program in 2009. Can private voluntary standards complement mandated regulatory requirements? If so, how?

15

Front-End Strategies: Market Entry Controls, Pollution Prevention, and Toxic Use Reduction

A. Pesticides—FIFRA
B. Toxics—Market Access Regulation: U.S. & Europe, ToSCA & REACH

Environmental regulatory strategies in the United States were originally dominated by a desire to clean up conventional pollution. These strategies focused on the minimization of "false positives"—by regulating only after environmental problems had already occurred. Operating at the "back-end" of the regulatory continuum, these strategies emphasized control of polluting products after their introduction and use in the marketplace. The major drawback of these back-end strategies was the risk of serious and widespread damage to human health and the environment, because these strategies were designed to control, but not to prevent, pollution. Perhaps the best examples of the damage that can be caused by back-end strategies are our abandoned hazardous waste sites, which collectively can be cleaned up only at a cost running into many billions of dollars.

Given the limitations of back-end strategies, an alternative set of environmental regulatory strategies soon developed in the United States, which focused primarily on the minimization of "false negatives"—by regulating in anticipation of environmental problems that had not yet occurred. Operating at the front-end of the regulatory continuum, these strategies emphasized precautionary control of market access and pollution prevention. Their goal was to prohibit the introduction of new products, or the further sales of existing products, when such products might conceivably be hazardous to human health or the environment. The major drawback of these front-end strategies was the risk of imposing a disabling impact on our system of market enterprise, particularly if a product's environmental damage was uncertain or its environmental benefits outweighed its economic costs.

With one exception, federal environmental protection statutes adopting a front-end regulatory strategy have attempted to achieve a balance between the environmental benefits and economic costs of denying market access to a particular product. That single exception was the ban in the Delaney Clause of the Federal Food, Drug, and Cosmetic Act (FFDCA), which banned any food additive that had been found to induce cancer in humans or animals in any dosage. In the Food Quality Protection Act of 1996 (FQPA),[1] however, Congress removed pesticide residues from the Delaney Clause's ban, by amending the FFDCA's definition of "food additive" to exclude pesticide chemical residues on raw or processed foods. (The Delaney Clause remains in effect regarding other food additives.) In particular, Congress determined that a pesticide residue on such foods is to be considered unsafe only if (i) the EPA has set a tolerance level for the substance and (ii) the residue fails to satisfy that level. As a result, the EPA is now allowed to grant a tolerance and register a pesticide upon a finding of safety. Under FQPA §405, "safe" means that "there is a reasonable certainty that no harm will result from aggregate exposure to the pesticide chemical residue,"[2] including both dietary and nondietary total exposure. Thus, the original "zero risk" approach of the Delaney Clause has now been repealed insofar as pesticide residues are concerned, in favor of a standard of "reasonable certainty" that no harm will come from aggregate exposure.[3]

Today, the two most important front-end federal environmental product regulation statutes in the United States are the Federal Insecticide, Fungicide, and Rodenticide Act (FIFRA)[4] and the Toxic Substances Control Act (ToSCA).[5] Although both statutes involve the regulation of toxics, they take disparate approaches to the triggering mechanisms for regulation and enforcement. Under FIFRA, Congress established the basic framework for pesticide regulation, including the registration of pesticides and the process by which EPA may ban unreasonably dangerous pesticides. Under ToSCA, Congress provided EPA with authority to regulate or prohibit the manufacture, distribution, or use of chemicals that pose unreasonable risks, including the authority to require pre-manufacture notification to EPA for new chemicals or significant new uses of existing chemicals.

To a great extent, FIFRA places the burden of going forward—collecting data, establishing testing protocols, testing, and proving safety—on the manufacturer itself under threat of potentially severe legal sanctions. By placing the burden of going forward and proving safety on the manufacturer, FIFRA attempts to provide a comprehensive approach to the pesticide regulation process that regulates environmental toxics from the very outset. By contrast, ToSCA primarily places the burden of going forward on EPA, not on the manufacturer. ToSCA requires the EPA to establish, by substantial evidence, that chemical testing is necessary and then to set testing protocols.

---

1. 21 U.S.C. §346a.
2. 21 U.S.C. §346a(b)(2)(A)(ii).
3. As a result of the 1996 Amendments, there has been a substantial debate over the extent to which the Delaney Clause was rendered obsolete by Congress's action. See Turner, Delaney Lives! Reports of Delaney's Death Are Greatly Exaggerated, 28 Envtl. L. Rep. 10003 (1998) (concluding that the 1996 Amendments neither remove the protections provided by the Delaney Clause prohibition against adding cancer-causing additives to food nor reflect a public policy rationale or political consensus to do so). For a thorough discussion of the history of the FQPA, see McGarity, Politics by Other Means: Law, Science, and Policy in EPA's Implementation of the Food Quality Protection Act, 53 Admin. L. Rev. 103 (2001).
4. 7 U.S.C. §§135 et seq.
5. 15 U.S.C. §§2601 et seq.

> **Contrasting FIFRA and ToSCA**
>
> In considering the differing approaches taken by FIFRA and ToSCA, assume that a manufacturer has invented a potentially useful chemical that can serve as an effective pesticide but that has never been used before. In connection with bringing this new chemical to market, the manufacturer would need to consider the regulatory effect of both FIFRA and ToSCA. Which statutory approach is more effective in regulating the new chemical the manufacturer seeks to bring to market? Is it more efficient, or more beneficial for public health, for the government to regulate a product during the manufacturing process, or to wait until the product has reached the market? Is it the government, or the manufacturer, which is in the best position to collect data, engage in medical testing, or establish testing protocols?

As you review these statutory schemes and their differing approaches, also consider whether a major overhaul to chemical regulation may be preferable. In fact, significant proposed changes to ToSCA are now pending before Congress. While these changes have not yet become law at press time, they do represent a major bipartisan effort designed to strengthen the EPA's authority over chemical regulation in a material way, as detailed further later in this chapter.

With respect to alternative statutory approaches to chemical regulation, developments in the European Union, as reflected in the chemical regulation known as REACH (the Registration, Evaluation, Authorisation, and Restriction of Chemicals), are also instructive. REACH provides an extremely demanding set of regulatory requirements for chemicals, by imposing requirements which are much more comprehensive than those presently established in ToSCA. A key question going forward is whether there will be any impact from REACH upon ToSCA reform, a topic we address later in this chapter.

A. PESTICIDES—FIFRA

Marshall Miller, Federal Regulation of Pesticides, Environmental Law Handbook

284-301 (14th ed. 1997)

The benefits of pesticides, herbicides, rodenticides, and other economic poisons[6] are well known. They have done much to spare us from the ravages of disease, crop infestations, noxious animals, and choking weeds. Over the past two decades, however, beginning with Rachel Carson's *Silent Spring* in 1962, there has been a growing awareness of the hazards,

---

6. The term "economic poisons" has been applied to pesticides since the 1940s. It reflects the "necessary evil" character of these substances, which FIFRA expresses in its weighing of benefits against costs. As "economic poisons," pesticides can cause adverse effects beyond their target species, thereby resulting in "collateral damage" that must be weighed against the benefits of pesticide use. Rachel Carson's SILENT SPRING was among the first books to recognize the toxics problems caused by pesticide use. [EDS.]

as well as the benefits of these chemicals, which may be harmful to man and the balance of nature.

The ability to balance these often conflicting effects is hampered by continuing scientific uncertainties. We still lack full understanding of environmental side effects, the sub-cellular mechanism of human carcinogens, and a host of other factors that are important for a proper evaluation of pesticide suitability. Yet scientific progress, especially in the genetic area, has been so rapid over the past decade or two that we are now realizing that many of our previous assumptions have been wrong, or at least over simplified. The best scientific knowledge is now critical for the agency as it attempts to conduct accelerated reviews of hundreds of chemicals that had been registered earlier under less strict standards.

Public concern regarding pesticides was a principal cause for the rise of the environmental movement in the United States in the late sixties and early seventies, and therefore was probably the single most important reason for the creation of the EPA. While public attention since then has shifted to various other environmental media, the pesticide issue—with its implications for the safety of food supply and of people in the agricultural area—is still central to the public's notion of environmental protection. Indeed, the fluctuation of interest in this topic is often an accurate barometer of public distrust in the official environmental agencies.

In the last few years this distrust has taken a new and different form. EPA is now being criticized not only by the environmentalists for not doing enough, but also by others for ordering unnecessarily costly or extreme measures. At the heart of both views is the belief that the agency's actions are not always firmly based on good science—a skepticism that is of course by no means limited to EPA's pesticide program.

Chemical pesticides have been subject to some degree of federal control since the Insecticide Act of 1910. This Act was primarily concerned with protecting consumers, usually farmers, from ineffective products and deceptive labeling, and it contained neither a federal registration requirement nor any significant safety standards. The relatively insignificant usage of pesticides before World War II made regulation a matter of low priority.

The resulting effects on public health and farm production made pesticides a virtual necessity. The agricultural chemical industry became an influential sector of the economy. In 1947, Congress enacted a more comprehensive statute, the Federal Insecticide, Fungicide, and Rodenticide Act ("FIFRA"). This law required that pesticides distributed in interstate commerce be registered with the United States Department of Agriculture ("USDA"). It also established rudimentary labeling requirements. This Act, like its predecessor, was mostly concerned with product effectiveness; the statute did, however, declare pesticides "misbranded" if they were necessarily harmful to man, animals, or vegetation (except weeds) even when properly used.

Three major defects in the new law soon became evident. First, the registration process was largely an empty formality since the Secretary of Agriculture could not refuse registration even to a chemical he deemed highly dangerous. He could register "under protest," but this had no legal effect on the registrant's ability to manufacture or distribute the product. Second, there was no regulatory control over the use of a pesticide contrary to its label, as long as the label itself complied with statutory requirements. Third, the Secretary's only remedy against a hazardous product was a legal action for misbranding or adulteration, and—this was crucial—the difficult burden of proof was on the government. . . .

In 1964 the USDA persuaded Congress to remedy two of these three defects: the registration system was revised to permit the secretary to refuse to register a new product or to cancel an existing registration, and the burden of proof for safety and effectiveness was placed on the registrant. Those changes considerably strengthened the act, in theory, but

A. Pesticides—FIFRA

made little difference in practice. The Pesticide Registration Division, a section of USDA's Agricultural Research Service, was understaffed . . . and the division was buried deep in a bureaucracy primarily concerned with promoting agriculture and facilitating the registration of pesticides. The cancellation procedure was seldom if ever used, and there was still no legal sanction against a consumer's applying the chemical for a delisted use.

The growth of the environmental movement in the late 1960s, with its concern about the widespread use of agricultural chemicals, overwhelmed the meager resources of the Pesticide Division. Environmental groups filed a barrage of lawsuits demanding the cancellation or suspension of a host of major pesticides such as DDT, Aldrin-Dieldrin, Mirex and the herbicide 2,4,5-T. This demanding situation demanded a new approach to pesticide regulations.

On December 2, 1970, President Nixon signed Reorganization Order No. 3 creating the Environmental Protection Agency. This Order assigned to EPA the functions and many of the personnel previously under Interior, Agriculture, and other government departments. EPA inherited from USDA not only the Pesticides Division but also the environmental lawsuits against the Secretary of Agriculture. . . .

The Federal Insecticide, Fungicide, and Rodenticide Act (FIFRA), as amended by the Federal Environmental Pesticide Control Act (FEPCA) of October 1972 and the FIFRA amendments of 1975, 1978, 1980, 1988, and 1996, is a complex statute. Terms sometimes have a meaning different from, or even directly contrary to, normal English usage. For example, the term "suspension" really means an immediate ban on a pesticide, while the harsher-sounding term "cancellation" indicates only the initiation of administrative proceedings which can drag on for many years. . . .

All new pesticide products used in the United States, with minor exceptions, must first be registered with EPA. This involves the submittal of the complete formula, a proposed label, and "full description of the tests made and the results thereof upon which the claims are based." The registration is very specific; it is not valid for all formulations or uses of a particular chemical. That is, separate registrations are required for [the] specific crops and insects on which the pesticide product may be applied, and each use must be supported by research data on safety and efficacy. . . .

The Administrator must approve the registration if the following conditions are met:

- Its composition is such as to warrant the proposed claim for it;
- Its labeling and other materials required to be submitted comply with the requirements of this act;
- It will perform its intended function without unreasonable adverse effects on the environment; and
- When used in accordance with widespread and commonly recognized practice it will not generally cause unreasonable adverse effects on the environment.

The operative phrase in the above criteria is "unreasonable adverse effects on the environment," which was added to the act in 1972. This phrase is defined elsewhere in FIFRA as meaning "any unreasonable risk to man or the environment, taking into account the economic, social, and environmental costs and benefits of the use of the pesticide." . . .

Registrations are for a limited, five-year period; thereafter, they automatically expire unless an interested party petitions for renewal and, if requested by EPA, provides additional data indicating the safety of the product. For the past few years, pre-EPA registrations have been coming up for renewal under much stricter standards than when originally issued. . . .

Until the 1972 reforms, the government had no control over the actual use of a pesticide once it had left a manufacturer or distributor properly labeled. Thus, for example, a chemical which would be perfectly safe for use on a dry field might be environmentally hazardous if applied in a marshy area, and a chemical acceptable for use on one crop might leave dangerous residues on another. EPA's only recourse . . . was to cancel the entire registration — obviously too unwieldy a weapon to constitute a normal means of enforcement. A second problem was that a . . . chemical might be too dangerous for general use but could be used safely by trained personnel. There was, however, no legal mechanism for limiting its use only to qualified individuals.

Because of these problems, both environmentalists and the industry agreed that EPA should be given more flexibility than merely the choice between cancelling or approving a pesticide. Congress therefore provided for the classification of pesticides into general and restricted categories, with the latter group available only to Certified Applicators. . . .

While the registration process may be the heart of FIFRA, cancellation represents the cutting edge of the law and attracts the most public attention. Cancellation is used to initiate review of a substance suspected of posing a "substantial question of safety" to man or the environment.

Contrary to the public assumptions, during the pendency of the proceedings the product may be freely manufactured and shipped in commerce. A cancellation order, although final if not challenged within thirty days, usually leads to a public hearing or scientific review committee, or both, and can be quite protracted; this can last a matter of months or years. A recommended decision from the agency hearing examiner (now called the administrative law judge) goes to the Administrator or his delegated representative, the chief agency judicial officer, for a final determination on the cancellation. . . .

A suspension order, despite its misleading name, is an immediate ban on the production and distribution of a pesticide. It is mandated when a product constitutes an "imminent hazard" to man or the environment, and may be invoked at any stage of the cancellation proceeding or even before a cancellation procedure has been initiated. . . .

The purpose of an ordinary suspension is to prevent an imminent hazard during the time required for cancellation or change in classification proceedings. An ordinary suspension proceeding is initiated when the Administrator issues notice to the registrant that he is suspending use of the pesticide and includes the requisite findings as to imminent hazard. The registrant may request an expedited hearing within five days of receipt of the Administrator's notice. If no hearing is requested, the suspension order can take effect immediately thereafter and the order is not reviewable by a court. . . .

The emergency suspension is the strongest action EPA can take under FIFRA. It immediately halts all uses, sales, and distribution of the pesticide. An emergency suspension differs from an ordinary suspension in that it is ex parte. The registrant is not given notice or the opportunity for an expedited hearing prior to the suspension order taking effect. The registrant is, however, entitled to an expedited hearing to determine the propriety of the emergency suspension. The Administrator can only use this procedure when he determines that an emergency exists which does not allow him to hold a hearing before suspending use of a pesticide. This authority has only rarely been invoked. . . .

Environmental Defense Fund, Inc. v.
U.S. Environmental Protection Agency

465 F.2d 528 (D.C. Cir. 1972)

LEVENTHAL, C.J. On December 3, 1970, petitioner Environmental Defense Fund (EDF), a non-profit New York Corporation, petitioned the Environmental Protection Agency under

A. Pesticides — FIFRA

the Federal Insecticide, Fungicide, and Rodenticide Act, for the immediate suspension and ultimate cancellation of all registered uses of aldrin and dieldrin, two chemically similar chlorinated hydrocarbon pesticides. On March 18, 1971, the Administrator of the EPA announced the issuance of "notices of cancellation" for aldrin and dieldrin because of "a substantial question as to the safety of the registered products which has not been effectively countered by the registrant." He declined to order the interim remedy of suspension, pending final decision on cancellation after completion of the pertinent administrative procedure, in light of his decision that "present uses [of aldrin and dieldrin] do not pose an imminent threat to the public such as to require immediate action." EDF filed this petition to review the EPA's failure to suspend the registration. . . .

The EPA's Statement points out that whereas a notice of cancellation is appropriate whenever there is "a substantial question as to the safety of a product," immediate suspension is authorized only in order to prevent an "imminent hazard to the public," and to protect the public by prohibiting shipment of an economic poison "so dangerous that its continued use should not be tolerated during the pendency of the administrative process." The EPA describes its general criteria for suspension as follows:

> This agency will find that an imminent hazard to the public exists when the evidence is sufficient to show that continued registration of an economic poison poses a significant threat of danger to health, or otherwise creates a hazardous situation to the public, that should be corrected immediately to prevent serious injury, and which cannot be permitted to continue during the pendency of administrative proceedings. An "imminent hazard" may be declared at any point in a chain of events which may ultimately result in harm to the public. It is not necessary that the final anticipated injury actually have occurred prior to a determination that an "imminent hazard" exists. In this connection, significant injury or potential injury to plants or animals alone could justify a finding of imminent hazard to the public from the use of an economic poison. The type, extent, probability and duration of potential or actual injury to man, plants, and animals will be measured in light of the positive benefits accruing from, for example, use of the responsible economic poison in human or animal disease control or food production.

Part II of the Statement of Reasons, captioned "Formulation of Standards," begins with the general standards deemed pertinent to the administration of FIFRA.

EPA points out that, in general, economic poisons, including those under present consideration, are "ecologically crude" — that is, by reason of technology limitations, [they] are toxic to non-target organisms as well as to pest life. Thus continued registration for particular ecologically crude pesticides "are acceptable only to the extent that the benefits accruing from use of a particular economic poison outweigh" the adverse results of effects on non-target species. EPA cites "dramatic steps in disease control" and the gradual amelioration of "the chronic problem of world hunger" as examples of the kind of beneficial effect to be looked for in balancing benefits against harm for specific substances. But it cautions that "triumphs of public health achieved in the past" will not be permitted to justify future registrations, recognizing that fundamentally different considerations are at work in evaluating use of a dangerous pesticide in a developed country such as the United States rather than in a developing non-industrial nation. . . .

Laboratory tests with some substances have raised serious questions regarding carcinogenicity that "deserve particular searching" because carcinogenic effects are generally cumulative and irreversible when discovered. Threats presented by individual substances vary not only as to observed persistence in the environment but also as to environmental mobility—which in turn depends in part on how a particular pesticide is introduced into the environment either by ground insertion or by dispersal directly into the ambient air or water.

Based on the discussion of these general considerations, the EPA concludes that individual decisions on initial or continued registration must depend on a complex administrative calculus, in which the "nature and magnitude of the foreseeable hazards associated with use of a particular product" is weighed against the "nature of the benefit conferred" by its use. . . .

The EDF's main argument [is that] while the Statement of Reasons sets forth, as a matter of EPA policy, that suspension decisions would be made only after the Administrator makes a preliminary assessment of immanency of hazard that includes a balancing of benefit and harm, yet when the EPA discussed aldrin and dieldrin, it inconsistently failed to identify any offsetting benefits, and limited itself to the reference to certain hazards.

The EPA concedes that the "thrust" of the Administrator's analysis related to the absence of any short run major hazards. But it parries that he "did refer to the purposes for which aldrin and dieldrin are used."

In light of his findings with respect to the absence of any foreseeable hazard, there was little need for the Administrator to go into detail in considering—as he had indicated he would do in suspension decisions . . . —"the positive benefits."

We are not clear that the FIFRA requires separate analysis of benefits at the suspension stage. We are clear that the statute empowers the Administrator to take account of benefits or their absence as affecting imminency of hazard. The Administrator's general decision to follow that course cannot be assailed as unreasonable. The suspension procedures of this agency, though in the abstract designed for emergency situations, seem to us to resemble more closely the judicial proceedings on a contested motion for a preliminary injunction, to prevail during the pendency of the litigation on the merits, rather than proceedings on an ex parte application for an emergency temporary restraining order. The suspension decision is not ordinarily one to be made in a matter of moments, or even hours or days. The statute contemplates at least the kind of ventilation of issues commonly had prior to decisions by courts that govern the relationships of parties pendente lite, during trial on the merits.

Judicial doctrine teaches that a court must consider possibility of success on the merits, the nature and extent of the damage to each of the parties from the granting or denial of the injunction, and where the public interest lies. It was not inappropriate for the Administrator to have chosen a general approach to suspension that permits analysis of similar factors. By definition, a substantial question of safety exists when notices of cancellation issue. If there is no offsetting claim of any benefit to the public, then the EPA has the burden of showing that the substantial safety question does not pose an "imminent hazard" to the public.

EDF is on sound ground in noting that while the EPA's general approach contemplates a decision as to suspension based on a balance of benefit and harm, the later discussion of aldrin and dieldrin relates only to harm.

The Administrator's mere mention of these products' major uses, emphasized by the EPA, cannot suffice as a discussion of benefits, even though the data before him . . . reflected the view that aldrin-dieldrin pesticides are the only control presently available for some twenty insects which attack corn and for one pest which poses a real danger to citrus orchards. . . .

The interests at stake here are too important to permit the decision to be sustained on the basis of speculative inference as to what the Administrator's findings and conclusions might have been regarding benefits. . . .

Our conclusion that a mere recitation of a pesticide's uses does not suffice as an analysis of benefits is fortified where, as here, there was a submission, by EDF, that alternative pest control mechanisms are available for such use. The analysis of benefit requires some

A. Pesticides — FIFRA

consideration of whether such proposed alternatives are available or feasible, or whether such availability is in doubt.

The importance of an EPA analysis of benefits is underscored by the Administrator's flexibility, in both final decisions and suspension orders, to differentiate between uses of the product. Aldrin and dieldrin are apparently not viewed by the EPA as uniform in their benefit characteristics for all their uses. The Administrator had previously stopped certain uses of the pesticides in question in house paints, and in water use. These actions presumably reflected some evaluation of comparative benefits and hazards. The Administrator's reliance on the "pattern of declining gross use" itself indicates that for some purposes aldrin and dieldrin are or will soon become non-essential. Even assuming the essentiality of aldrin and dieldrin, and of the lack of feasible alternative control mechanisms for certain uses, there may be no corresponding benefit for other uses, which may be curtailed during the suspension period. . . .

We do not say there is an absolute need for analysis of benefits. It might have been possible for EPA to say that although there were no significant benefits from aldrin-dieldrin, the possibility of harm — though substantial enough to present a long-run danger to the public warranting cancellation proceedings — did not present a serious short-run danger that constituted an imminent hazard. EPA's counsel offers this as a justification for its action.

If this is to be said, it must be said clearly, so that it may be reviewed carefully. Logically, there is room for the concept. But we must caution against any approach to the [statutory] term "imminent hazard" . . . that restricts it to a concept of crisis. It is enough if there is substantial likelihood that serious harm will be experienced during the year or two required in any realistic projection of the administrative process. It is not good practice for an agency to defend an order on the hypothesis that it is valid even assuming there are no benefits, when the reality is that some conclusion of benefits was visualized by the agency. This kind of abstraction pushes argument — and judicial review — to the wall of extremes, when realism calls for an awareness of middle ground.

COMMENTARY & QUESTIONS

1. The subsequent suspension of aldrin and dieldrin. The court remanded the matter to EPA for further study. After considering the Advisory Committee Report and further public comments, EPA affirmed its previous decisions to cancel without interim suspension. Twelve months into the cancellation proceeding, the Administrator issued a notice of intent to suspend, and the suspension became final on October 1, 1974. EPA's suspension decision was substantially upheld in *EDF v. EPA*, 510 F.2d 1292, 1302 (D.C. Cir. 1975), where Judge Leventhal, emphasizing that "the responsibility to demonstrate that the benefits outweigh the risks is upon the proponents of continued registration," upheld EPA's finding that alternatives to aldrin-dieldrin were currently available. See also *EDF v. EPA*, 548 F.2d 998, 1005 (D.C. Cir. 1976) (heptachlor and chlordane). For further insight into Judge Leventhal's views, see .Leventhal, Environmental Decisionmaking and the Role of the Courts, 122 U. Pa. L. Rev. 509 (1974); Rodgers,, Benefits, Costs and Risks: Oversight of Health and Environmental Decisionmaking, 4 Harv. Envtl. L. Rev. 191 (1980).

2. Emergency suspension. The aldrin-dieldrin case was an ordinary suspension rather than an emergency suspension. EPA first used the emergency suspension procedure in 1979, when it suspended many uses of 2,4,5-T and Silvex. Emergency suspension is the most potent action available to EPA under FIFRA because it immediately stops all uses, sales, and distribution of the pesticide. In *Dow Chemical Co. v. Blum*, 469 F. Supp. 892 (E.D. Mich.

1979), a federal district court, upholding EPA's emergency suspension, concluded that whereas an ordinary suspension proceeding is similar to a motion for a preliminary injunction during a lawsuit, the emergency suspension proceeding is similar to an application for a temporary restraining order. An emergency suspension order will be upheld if there is "minimal evidence in the record to support EPA's decision." Id. at 906. Should a reviewing court be more or less deferential to an EPA decision on an ordinary suspension because of the existence of the emergency suspension device? Does the emergency suspension device provide reassurance to courts that EPA can act quickly if further information indicates that suspension is desirable? If so, does the existence of the emergency suspension device affect judges' views pertaining to whether to overturn an ordinary suspension?

Section 102 of the FQPA amended FIFRA to make a material change in the emergency suspension process by allowing a suspension for no more than 90 days without a simultaneous notice of intent to cancel. What concerns was Congress addressing in making this change?

3. Imminent hazards. FIFRA operates as a threshold preventative in that it applies "up front" before a potentially dangerous pesticide is introduced into commerce. On the other hand, FIFRA's standards are not pure safety criteria, because the economic benefits and costs of regulation are weighed at the registration, cancellation, and suspension stages. Does the "imminent hazard" standard serve as a margin of safety where economic benefits are tangible and potential environmental harms are uncertain? EPA's interpretive statement on "imminent hazard" is highly precautionary, justifying action whenever there is "significant injury or potential injury to plants or animals alone. . . ." Another administrative mechanism for erring on the side of safety is EPA's Special Review process (formerly called Rebuttable Presumption Against Registration, or RPAR), in which evidence developed by EPA or a third party that a pesticide exceeds specified "risk criteria" will raise a presumption against registration or in favor of cancellation or suspension. 40 C.F.R. pt. 154. Moreover, the *EDF v. EPA* court adds that once a notice of cancellation is issued—if there is no offsetting claim of benefits—then "EPA has the burden of showing that the substantial safety question does not pose an 'imminent hazard' to the public." It seems, as the court points out, that "imminent hazard" does not mean "crisis." Operationally it means that the greater the amount of credible evidence EPA has about potential dangers posed by a registered pesticide, the more quickly and easily its use can be discontinued, and the more pronounced benefits must be in order to justify its continued use. How effective is a regulatory scheme that allows a product to be marketed but that makes quick protective withdrawal possible once negative evidence appears? How is negative evidence to be measured or quantified, particularly when scientific uncertainty factors affect benefit-cost analysis? Is it easier for EPA to suspend a pesticide under a "significant threat" standard then under a "crisis" standard of "imminence"?

"Imminent hazard" is one of those all-important statutory terms that defies precise analysis but facilitates administrative and judicial determinations regarding uncertainty and burdens of proof, creating the "common law" of particular statutes. The "imminent hazard" phrase serves a similar function in RCRA (see Chapter 17) and CERCLA (see Chapter 16). Another such term is "endanger." See *Ethyl Corp. v. EPA*, 541 F.2d 1 (D.C. Cir. 1976).

4. The role of benefits in a suspension proceeding. Must benefits be analyzed in a suspension proceeding? Judge Leventhal's opinion is not consistent on this point. Does it depend on whether evidence of available alternatives has been introduced? If there is no short-term danger, why bother analyzing benefits at all? In order to analyze benefits, must they be quantifiable? If not, how do we measure them? Is it possible to distinguish clearly between short- and long-term hazards?

A. Pesticides—FIFRA

5. Nonregistration of exports. Although imported pesticides are subject to FIFRA registration requirements, exports are excluded from the regulatory provisions of the Act. Should the federal government permit DDT to be exported to a developing nation where malaria is a serious problem if the pesticide is the only affordable malaria-control alternative? To what extent should the transboundary character of pollution from persistent pesticides be considered in such judgments? Are risk-benefit calculations, as applied to challenged pesticides in the United States, applicable to conditions faced abroad? If the United States unilaterally regulates pesticide exportation, will other pesticide producing nations gain an unfair competitive advantage?

6. Paying for suspension. A controversial provision of the 1972 Amendments required EPA to indemnify registrants, formulators, and end users of cancelled or suspended pesticides for remaining stocks that were not permitted to be exhausted. Needless to say, this provision had a chilling effect on cancellations and suspensions. In the 1988 FIFRA Amendments, the indemnity requirement was deleted except for end users (farmers and applicators).[7]

7. FIFRA and preemption. There are several questions involved here. First, do FIFRA's labeling requirements preempt private common law tort suits filed in state court based on inadequate labeling ("failure to warn")? Second, can states impose labeling and packaging requirements stricter than those imposed by EPA under FIFRA?

The issue of preemption under FIFRA reached the Supreme Court in *Bates v. Dow Agrosciences LLC*, 544 U.S. 431 (2005). In that case, the Court ruled that farmers' state common law claims against a herbicide manufacturer for defective design, defective manufacture, negligent testing, and breach of express warranty did not impose "requirements for labeling or packaging" and thus were not preempted by FIFRA; however, the Court also ruled that the farmers' state law fraud and negligent failure to warn claims may be preempted if the particular common law duties imposed by state law are equivalent to FIFRA's misbranding standards.

The case involved the claims of Texas peanut farmers, who alleged that their crops were severely damaged by the application of Dow's pesticide, which the EPA had registered under FIFRA. The farmers gave Dow notice of their intent to sue, claiming that the label on Dow's pesticide recommended its use in all peanut growing areas when Dow knew or should have known that the pesticides would stunt peanut growth. Dow in response sought a declaratory judgment that FIFRA preempted the farmers' claims.

Vacating and remanding the Fifth Circuit's holding that preemption applied, the Supreme Court held that FIFRA's preemption provision (7 U.S.C. §136v(b)) applies only to state law "requirements for labeling or packaging." The Supreme Court ruled that no such requirements were involved in the farmers' defective design, manufacture, negligent testing, or breach of express warranty claims, because none of the common law rules upon which those claims were based required that manufacturers label or package their products in any particular way. In addition, the Supreme Court further concluded that the farmers' fraud and negligent-failure-to-warn claims were based on common law rules that qualify as "requirements for labeling and packaging," since those rules set a standard for a product's labeling that Dow was alleged to have violated. Nonetheless, the Court found that while these common law rules are subject to §136v(b), it does not automatically follow that they are preempted. Section 136v(b) prohibits only state law labeling requirements that are "in addition to or different from" FIFRA's labeling requirements. Accordingly, the Court

---

7. Pub. L. No. 100-532, §501.

determined that §136v(b) preempts any statutory or common law rule that would impose a labeling requirement that diverges from those set out in FIFRA and its implementing regulations. It does not preempt a state law requirement that is equivalent to, and fully consistent with, FIFRA's labeling standards.

Since *Bates*, several federal appellate decisions have found that tort claims regarding pesticides, including defective design, defective manufacture, negligent testing, and breach of warranty, do not implicate labeling requirements and therefore are not preempted. See, e.g., *Mortellite v. Novartis Crop. Prot., Inc.*, 460 F.3d 483 (3d Cir. 2006) (holding, in part, that strict liability, negligent testing, and breach of express warranty claims did not impose liability requirements and thus did not conflict with FIFRA); *Wuebker v. Wilber-Ellis Co.*, 418 F.3d 883 (8th Cir. 2005) (holding that state law product liability claims were neither expressly nor impliedly preempted by FIFRA).

Another issue involving preemption is whether municipalities can ban or limit the use of pesticides registered under FIFRA. The Supreme Court resolved a conflict among the federal circuits by unanimously holding, in *Wisconsin Public Intervenor v. Mortier*, 501 U.S. 597 (1991), that municipalities are not preempted by FIFRA from controlling pesticide use:

> FIFRA nowhere seeks to establish an affirmative permit scheme for the actual use of pesticides. It certainly does not equate registration and labeling requirements with a general approval to apply pesticides throughout the Nation without regard to regional and local factors like climate, population, geography, and water supply. Whatever else FIFRA may supplant, it does not occupy the field of pesticide regulation in general or the area of local use permitting in particular. 501 U.S. at 613-614.

Although the local ordinance upheld in the *Mortier* case involved the legality of a permit requirement for aerial spraying on private lands, the opinion appears to condone local pesticide bans as well.

8. FIFRA as a licensing statute. As commentators have noted, FIFRA creates a unique form of licensing system. See Applegate, The Perils of Unreasonable Risk: Information, Regulatory Policy, and Toxic Substances Control, 91 Colum. L. Rev. 261 (1991) (hereafter "Applegate"). Professor Applegate has written:

> If as a general rule manufacturers can develop toxicology information more cheaply than EPA, or if the cost is more efficiently or equitably borne by them and their customers, then it makes sense to assign the burden of proof to the manufacturer. In regulatory systems, shifting the burden of proof from the government to industry is typically accomplished by enacting a licensing or screening system. In the case of toxic substances, chemical producers would have to demonstrate the safety of their products before these products could be introduced into commerce. Licensing, therefore, not only provides an incentive to development of new information; it also shifts the cost of development away from government to a group that in theory has the capacity to absorb and spread the [loss].
>
> Of the toxics statutes, only FIFRA has a true licensing scheme. Before pesticides can be sold, they must be registered and EPA must determine that they do not present an unreasonable risk. The registrant has the initial and continuing burden of demonstrating safety, though EPA has an initial burden of production in a cancellation proceeding and must ultimately be able to support its conclusions by substantial evidence. By placing the burden on the registrant, EPA is able to obtain whatever information it deems necessary to assess whether the chemical poses an unreasonable risk through the simple expedient of specifying data requirements for registration. EPA needs only the most general justification for these requirements, given the breadth of factors relevant to the unreasonable risk determination. Furthermore, the data requirements apply to all pesticides, eliminating the need to demand data on a chemical-by-chemical basis. This technique obviously brings the full profit motive to bear in developing adequate data in an expeditious manner. Applegate, supra, at 308-309 (footnote omitted).

A. Pesticides—FIFRA

Nevertheless, FIFRA, like all licensing statutes, has two major disadvantages:

First, the premarket phase of product development is the time when the least information is known about a chemical's long-term effects. Without indications of chronic toxicity, it is hard to justify lengthy, expensive bioassays. Second, a licensing scheme intercepts only new or prospective risks. Since older chemicals are likely to be less well-tested relative to more recently licensed chemicals, the lack of data on existing chemicals constitutes a major gap in an information generation system. This problem can be resolved by a retroactive licensing arrangement like FIFRA's re-registration process. . . . Recognizing that licensing fails to generate any information for existing chemicals or post-license information for new ones, FIFRA established a five-year registration period after which reconsideration is necessary. This provision has not generated large amounts of data, however, because EPA has never used the five-year period aggressively for this purpose. Indeed, EPA has lacked sufficient resources to do much more than keep current on new registrations and cancellations. Applegate, supra, at 312-313 (footnote omitted).

These drawbacks in the FIFRA licensing system further emphasize the importance of the cancellation and suspension mechanisms. Ultimately, the best way to prevent pesticide pollution may be Integrated Pest Management (IPM)—placing primary reliance on biological and management controls, with limited applications of pesticides permitted only when absolutely necessary and where least likely to cause environmental damage. Genetic engineering also shows promise in redesigning plants for immunity to traditional pests.

9. The trouble with FIFRA. Although FIFRA creates a unique form of licensing, FIFRA nonetheless has come under attack for not effectively protecting public health and the environment against the adverse effects of toxic pesticides. The underlying problem of pesticide policy, manifested in FIFRA, has been to implement a defensible standard of "reasonable risk" that effectively places the burden of proof on pesticide registrants to show that their products' risks are acceptable under FIFRA's cost-benefit framework.

Well over one billion pounds of pesticides are applied annually in the United States. Pesticides have been shown to cause significant environmental impacts, such as acute or chronic health effects among workers in the manufacturing process, on third parties due to accidents in manufacturing or transport, among applicators and farm workers, and among consumers due to residues on food; contamination of groundwater due to leaching; contamination of surface waters from farm run-off; poisoning of bees and other wildlife; and contamination of the environment due to improper disposal of unused pesticides and their containers. Hornstein, Lessons from Federal Pesticide Regulation on the Paradigms and Politics of Environmental Law Reform, 10 Yale J. Reg. 369, 394-395 (1993) (hereinafter "Hornstein"). Pesticide contamination of groundwater, for example, is a potent threat to human health because nearly 50% of all Americans derive their potable water from groundwater. Many of these are homeowners on private wells who drink untreated groundwater directly from aquifers.

In 1991, the U.S. General Accounting Office evaluated EPA's efforts to deal with the problem of groundwater contamination by pesticides. Pesticides: EPA Could Do More to Minimize Groundwater Contamination (April 1991). In testimony based on that study, a GAO official concluded that

EPA needs to take more initiative in ensuring that groundwater contamination by pesticides is minimized. Efforts are needed in three areas. First, EPA has been slow in reviewing the scientific studies needed to assess pesticides' potential to leach into groundwater. Therefore, detailed information on the factors that contribute to leaching is not available to pesticide applicators and the pace of reassessing older pesticides has been slowed. Second, while EPA has used the regulatory tools available[8] in some cases, the agency could do more to help prevent groundwater contamination from worsening. Third, when EPA assesses risks from pesticide residues in food—in order to set residue limits known as tolerances—the agency is not routinely considering the additional exposure that can result from pesticide-contaminated groundwater. As a result, the agency lacks assurance that tolerances for pesticides that leach into groundwater are set low enough to protect public health.

Professor Hornstein attributes these problems, in great measure, to the centrality of risk assessment under FIFRA:

> Risk analysis . . . serves as a procedural device that favors pesticide-using political constituencies in three ways. First, because EPA has no independent method of developing data, risk analysis makes EPA dependent on the data generated by pesticide manufacturers—raising opportunities for various types of bias. Information bias is not limited to cases of data falsification. . . . The more intractable problems are foot-dragging in submitting data to [EPA] and the ability of industry to shade the way data is presented (without falsification) simply by emphasizing the subtle but genuinely contestable "inference options" on which risk assessments depend. In the mid-70s, an internal EPA audit on the data underlying twenty-three randomly selected pesticides found that "all but one of the tests reviewed were unreliable and inadequate to demonstrate safety"—a level of unreliability that, by 1992, continued for at least some pesticides. . . . In short, the risk assessment enterprise is so information intensive that it creates strategic incentives to avoid a serious scientific examination of "true" levels of public health and environmental risk.
>
> Second, despite the burden of proof ostensibly shouldered by pesticide manufacturers under FIFRA, the informational demands of risk analysis doom the regulatory process to a perpetual state of slow motion. The [GAO] reported in March 1992 that, "After some 20 years collecting data to reevaluate the health and environmental effects of 19,000 older pesticides, EPA . . . had reregistered only 2 products." Despite a congressional deadline of 1997 recently set for reregistration, GAO confirms EPA's own projections that the reregistration effort will extend "until early in the next century." Even when EPA chooses to act, the risk analyses required for Special Reviews or cancellation proceedings effectively innoculate pesticide manufacturers against timely action. Special Reviews, which were introduced in the mid-1970s to accelerate the cancellation process which then took an average of two years, now themselves average over seven years. . . . As a practical matter, the burdensomeness of risk analysis has tempered FIFRA's success in shifting the burden of proof to manufacturers.
>
> Third, risk analysis offers the conceptual umbrella of "science" under which numerous nonscientific values can take shelter from public scrutiny and yet prolong the longevity of pesticides that may be neither desirable nor needed. . . . Hornstein, supra, at 437-438.

Thus FIFRA, although it facially requires a manufacturer to bear a more demanding burden of proof than ToSCA, has failed because, in practice, political pressures have caused the same "information bias" in FIFRA that has virtually disabled ToSCA.[9]

---

8. Such as prominent advisories on pesticide labels, prohibitions on use within a specified distance of wells (i.e., well setbacks), prohibitions on use in designated geographic areas, and restricting pesticides' use to certified applicators. [EDS.]

9. Of particular interest to the observation that market access statutes are handicapped by a persistent "information bias" is a line of cases holding that a manufacturer that withholds information from a federal agency is estopped from asserting preemption of packaging and labeling claims. See, e.g., *Roberson v. E.I. DuPont De Nemours & Co.*, 863 F. Supp. 929 (W.D. Ark. 1994); *Burke v. Dow Chem. Co.*, 797 F. Supp. 1128, 1141 (E.D.N.Y. 1992) (recognizing that allowing preemption would "permit a manufacturer that was . . . aware of dangers to refrain from informing EPA of needed changes in its product's label and then to hide behind the very label it knew to be inadequate"); and *Hurley v. Lederle Lab. Div. of Am. Cyanamid*, 863 F.2d 1173 (5th Cir. 1988).

Are proactive market access statutes inherently ineffectual in a nation that presumes the beneficence of an unregulated market system? Professor Hornstein does not directly ask this question, but he appears to imply a positive answer to it when he argues that FIFRA has "[been] one of the most colossal regulatory failures in Washington" because it does not get at the root causes of excessive pesticide use. Hornstein, supra, at 371. American pesticide law "is not a body of law that addresses in any strategic way the underlying prevalence of pesticides in American agriculture, nor is it a body of law designed to minimize pesticide use." Id. at 392. He recommends a cause-based approach to pesticide regulation that would emphasize pest control technologies to limit pesticide use without significantly decreasing crop yields or growers' profitability and that would address existing economic incentive structures that lead growers to bypass improved technologies in favor of pesticide use that exceeds economically optimal levels.

B. Toxics — Market Access Regulation: U.S. & Europe, ToSCA & REACH

1. ToSCA

ToSCA extended the product regulation concept in the United States to most new and existing chemicals. Environmental and industry groups lobbied heavily during congressional deliberations over ToSCA. The result is perhaps the most complex, confusing, and ineffective of all our federal environmental protection statutes.

Ray M. Druley and Girard L. Ordway, The Toxic Substances Control Act

1-4 (1977)

As summarized by the House Interstate and Foreign Commerce Committee Report, the major provisions of the Act:

- Require manufacturers and processors of potentially harmful chemical substances and mixtures to test the substances or mixtures, as required by rules issued by the Administrator of [EPA], so that their effect on health and the environment may be evaluated.
- Require manufacturers of new chemical substances and manufacturers and processors of existing chemical substances for significant new uses to notify the Administrator ninety days in advance of commercial production.
- Authorize delays or restrictions on the manufacture of a new chemical substance if there is inadequate information to evaluate the health or environmental effects of the substance and if in the absence of such information, the substance may cause or significantly contribute to an unreasonable risk to health or the environment.
- Authorize the Administrator to adopt rules to prohibit the manufacture, processing, or distribution of a chemical substance or mixture, to require labeling, or to regulate the manner of disposal of a chemical substance or mixture for which there is a reasonable basis to conclude that it causes or significantly contributes to an unreasonable risk to health or the environment.

- Authorize the Administrator to obtain injunctive relief from a United States district court to protect the public and the environment from an imminently hazardous chemical substance or mixture.
- Authorize the Administrator to require manufacturers and processors to submit reports and maintain records respecting their commercially produced chemical substances and mixtures, to maintain records respecting adverse health or environmental effects of such substances and mixtures, and to provide available health and safety data on them.
- Require manufacturers and processors of chemical substances and mixtures to immediately notify the Administrator of information indicating that one of their substances or mixtures causes or contributes to a substantial risk to health or the environment.
- Permit administrative inspections to enforce the bill and authorize court actions for seizures of chemical substances and mixtures which have been manufactured or distributed in violation of the requirements of the bill or of rules and orders promulgated under it.
- Permit citizens to bring suits to obtain compliance with the bill.
- Permit federal district courts to order the Administrator to initiate rulemaking proceedings in response to citizen petitions.
- Set up procedural mechanisms to insure that all interested persons have an opportunity to participate in the agency rulemaking proceedings.
- Provide protection for employees who cooperate in the enforcement of the bill.
- Provide for evaluation on a continuing basis of the effects on employment of actions taken under the bill. . . .

TESTING AND PRE-MARKET NOTIFICATION . . . Under the Act, EPA cannot require testing of every chemical. The Act does not regulate all chemicals which pose a risk, but only those which the EPA finds present an "unreasonable" risk of harm to human health or the environment. Accordingly, EPA must first find that there may be a risk or that there may be extensive human or environmental exposure and that information is lacking and testing is necessary. Given these findings, EPA must issue a rule requiring a manufacturer to perform testing and specifying the actual form of testing.

EPA is to issue its testing rules with the advice of an inter-agency committee, which will recommend testing priorities. Although the committee's advice is not binding, EPA is required to publish reasons for not requiring testing of certain specially designated compounds given high priority by the committee.

One of the key provisions of the Act is the section requiring manufacturers to provide EPA with data in advance of marketing. Chemical manufacturers must provide at least a 90-day notice before starting the manufacture of a new chemical or marketing a chemical for a new use as prescribed by EPA.

In order to determine what constitutes a new chemical that must be reported to EPA, EPA must publish an inventory list of chemicals known to be manufactured in the U.S. If a substance is not listed, it is to be considered a new chemical, and its planned production must be reported.

Under certain circumstances EPA can block the marketing of a chemical product pending the completion of testing. If a test order has been issued, test data must be submitted at the same time as the pre-market notification. Because testing may often require several years, this is a much more stringent requirement than simple 90-day notification.

B. Toxics—Market Access Regulation, ToSCA & REACH

EPA may also publish a hazardous substance list and can even do so by generic names. A manufacturer planning to market a substance included in the list must submit data to show that it is not a hazard for health or the environment.

Finally, if EPA determines upon notification that it has insufficient data on which to base a safety judgment, it may issue a proposed order to block production until testing is completed. The manufacturer may protest this order, and in this case EPA must apply to a federal district court for an injunction in order to block production.

Experimental and research chemicals produced in small quantities are exempt from the premarket notification requirements of the Act.

[ToSCA also does not apply to the following products regulated under other federal laws: firearms and ammunition; food, food additives, and drugs and cosmetics; meat and meat products; eggs and egg products; poultry and poultry products; pesticides; tobacco or tobacco products; and nuclear materials.]

Chemical Manufacturers Association v. U.S. Environmental Protection Agency

859 F.2d 977 (D.C. Cir. 1988)

WALD, C.J. Petitioners, Chemical Manufacturers Association and four companies that manufacture chemicals (collectively "CMA"), seek to set aside a rule promulgated by the Environmental Protection Agency. This Final Test Rule was promulgated under §4 of the Toxic Substances Control Act. The final test rule required toxicological testing to determine the health effects of the chemical 2-ethylhexanoic acid ("EHA")....

We uphold EPA's interpretation of ToSCA as empowering the Agency to issue a test rule on health grounds where it finds a more-than-theoretical basis for suspecting that the chemical substance in question presents an "unreasonable risk of injury to health." This, in turn, requires the Agency to find a more-than-theoretical basis for concluding that the substance is sufficiently toxic, and human exposure to it is sufficient in amount, to generate an "unreasonable risk of injury to health." We hold, further, that EPA can establish the existence and amount of human exposure on the basis of inferences drawn from the circumstances under which the substance is manufactured and used. EPA must rebut industry-supplied evidence attacking those inferences only if the industry evidence succeeds in rendering the probability of exposure in the amount found by EPA no more than theoretical or speculative. The probability of infrequent or even one-time exposure to individuals can warrant a test rule, so long as there is a more-than-theoretical basis for determining that exposure in such doses presents an "unreasonable risk of injury to health." Finally, we hold that the Agency correctly applied these standards in this case and that its findings are supported by substantial evidence. Consequently, we affirm the Final Test Rule.

ToSCA provides for a two-tier system for evaluating and regulating chemical substances to protect against unreasonable risks to human health and the environment. Section 6 of the Act permits EPA to regulate a substance that the Agency has found "presents or will present an unreasonable risk of injury to health or the environment." Section 4 of the Act empowers EPA to require testing of a suspect substance in order to obtain the toxicological data necessary to make a decision whether or not to regulate the substance under §6. The Act provides, not surprisingly, that the level of certainty of risk warranting a §4 test rule is lower than that warranting a §6 regulatory rule. EPA is empowered to require testing where it finds that the manufacture, distribution, processing, use or disposal of a particular chemical substance "may present an unreasonable risk of injury to human health or the environment." The Agency's interpretation of this statutory standard for testing is the central issue in this case.

One of the chief policies underlying the Act is that adequate data should be developed with respect to the effect of chemical substances and mixtures on health and the environment and that the development of such data should be the responsibility of those who manufacture and those who process such chemical substances and mixtures.

The statute establishes an Interagency Testing Committee, comprised of scientists from various federal agencies, to recommend that EPA give certain chemicals "priority consideration" for testing. Under §4, the Agency "shall by rule require that testing [of a particular chemical] be conducted" if three factors are present: (i) activities involving the chemical "may present an unreasonable risk of injury to health or the environment"; (ii) "insufficient data and experience" exist upon which to determine the effects of the chemical on health or environment; and (iii) testing is necessary to develop such data. The companies that manufacture and process the substance are to conduct the tests and submit the data to the Agency. Costs of the testing are to be shared among the companies, either by agreement or by EPA order in the absence of agreement.

A test rule promulgated under §4 is subject to judicial review in a court of appeals. . . . A test rule may be set aside if it is not "supported by substantial evidence in the rulemaking record . . . taken as a whole."

EHA is a colorless liquid with a mild odor. It is used exclusively as a chemical intermediate or reactant in the production of metal soaps, peroxyesters and other products used in industrial settings. EHA itself is totally consumed during the manufacture of these products; as a result, no products offered for sale to industry or to consumers contain EHA.

The Interagency Testing Committee first designated EHA for priority consideration for health effects tests on May 29, 1984. The Committee based its recommendation in part on the structural similarity of EHA to chemicals known to cause cancer in test animals and on its finding that insufficient information existed concerning the chronic health effects of EHA. Subsequently, EPA held two public meetings on EHA. During these meetings, in which persons representing the petitioners made appearances, EPA sought information on a variety of issues relating to EHA uses, production and human exposure.

EPA issued a proposed test rule on May 17, 1985. The rule proposed a series of tests to ascertain the health risks of EHA, and it set out proposed standards for the conduct of those tests. EPA based the Proposed Test Rule on a finding that EHA "may present an unreasonable risk" of subchronic toxicity (harm to bodily organs from repeated exposure over a limited period of time), oncogenicity (tumor formation) and developmental toxicity (harm to the fetus.) As to subchronic toxicity, EPA cited studies suggesting that both EHA and chemicals structurally similar to it cause harm to the livers of test animals. As to oncogenicity, EPA cited studies suggesting that chemicals structurally analogous to EHA cause cancer in laboratory animals. As to developmental toxicity, EPA cited studies indicating that both EHA and its chemical analogues have produced fetal malformations in test animals.

The Proposed Test Rule also addressed the question of whether humans are exposed to EHA, a question of critical importance to this case. The Agency acknowledged that, since no finished products contain EHA, consumer exposure is not a concern. It likewise discounted the dangers of worker exposure to EHA vapors. The Agency based its Proposed Test Rule solely on the potential danger that EHA will come in contact with the skin of workers. As evidence of potential dermal exposure, the Agency noted that approximately 400 workers are engaged in the manufacture, transfer, storage and processing of 20 to 25 million pounds of EHA per year. Further, rebutting claims by industry representatives that gloves are routinely worn during these activities, EPA noted that worker hygiene procedures "can vary widely throughout the industry," that workers are not required by existing federal regulations to wear gloves, and that the industry had not monitored work sites for exposure to EHA.

A public comment period commenced with the publication of the Proposed Test Rule and ended on July 16, 1985. EPA held a public meeting on October 8, 1985, to discuss issues related to the Proposed Test Rule. Industry representatives submitted extensive comments on July 15, 1985, and January 17, 1986. Before publication of the Final Test Rule, EPA received notice of a new study purporting to present further evidence of the potential developmental toxicity of EHA. . . .

EPA published the Final Test Rule for EHA on November 6, 1986. The Rule required a 90-day subchronic toxicity test, a developmental toxicity test, and a pharmacokinetics test. . . . The pharmacokinetics study required by the rule entailed the oral and dermal administration of EHA to experimental animals at low and high doses. The subchronic toxicity study involved administering EHA to animals in graduated daily doses over a period of 90 days. The developmental toxicity tests entailed administering EHA orally in various doses during the pregnancy of experimental animals. All studies were to be conducted in accordance with EPA standards. Results were to be submitted by certain deadlines, the last of which was 18 months after the effective date of the Final Test Rule. . . .

The [ToSCA] requires EPA to promulgate a test rule under §4 if a chemical substance, inter alia, "may present an unreasonable risk of injury to health or the environment." The parties both accept the proposition that the degree to which a particular substance presents a risk to health is a function of two factors: (a) human exposure to the substance, and (b) the toxicity of the substance. See *Ausimont U.S.A., Inc. v. EPA*, 838 F.2d 93, 96 (3d Cir. 1988). They also agree that EPA must make some sort of threshold finding as to the existence of an "unreasonable risk of injury to health." The parties differ, however, as to the manner in which this finding must be made. Specifically, three issues are presented.

The first issue is whether, under §4 of ToSCA, EPA must first find that the existence of an "unreasonable risk of injury to health" is more probable than not in order to issue a test rule. CMA argues that the statute requires a more-probable-than-not finding. EPA disagrees, contending that the statute is satisfied where the existence of an "unreasonable risk of injury to health" is a substantial probability—that is, a probability that is more than merely theoretical, speculative, or conjectural.

The second issue is whether, once industry has presented evidence tending to show an absence of human exposure, EPA must rebut it by producing direct evidence of exposure. CMA claims that, when industry evidence casts doubt on the existence of exposure, the burden of production shifts back to EPA, which must produce direct evidence documenting actual instances in which exposure has taken place. EPA, on the other hand, argues that it can make the requisite finding of exposure based solely on inferences drawn from the circumstances under which a chemical substance is manufactured and used.

The third issue is whether the Agency has authority to issue a test rule where any individual's exposure to a substance is an isolated, non-recurrent event. CMA argues that, even if EPA presents direct evidence of exposure, the Act precludes issuance of a test rule where exposure consists only of rare instances involving brief exposure. EPA contends, on the other hand, that the Act does not require in all circumstances a risk of recurrent exposure. . . .

As to the first issue in this case, . . . both the wording and structure of ToSCA reveal that Congress did not expect that EPA would have to document to a certainty the existence of an "unreasonable risk" before it could require testing. This is evident from the two-tier structure of the Act. In order for EPA to be empowered to regulate a chemical substance, the

Agency must find that the substance "presents or will present an unreasonable risk of injury to health or the environment." The testing provision at issue here, by contrast, empowers EPA to act at a lower threshold of certainty than that required for regulation. Specifically, testing is warranted if the substance "*may* present an unreasonable risk of injury to health or the environment." Thus, the language of §4 signals that EPA is to make a probabilistic determination of the presence of "unreasonable risk."

The legislative history of ToSCA compels a further conclusion. It not only shows that "unreasonable risk" need not be a matter of absolute certainty; it shows the reasonableness of EPA's conclusion that "unreasonable risk" need not be established to a more-probable-than-not degree.

A House Report on the version of the bill that eventually became ToSCA underscores the distinction between the §6 standard and the §4 standard. To issue a test rule, EPA need not find that a substance actually does cause or present an "unreasonable risk."

> Such a finding requirement would defeat the purpose of the section, for if the Administrator is able to make such a determination, regulatory action to protect against the risk, not additional testing, is called for. H.R. Rep. No. 1341, 94th Cong., 2d Sess.

The House Report also contains signals indicating that Congress expected EPA to act even when evidence of "unreasonable risk" was less than conclusive. According to that report, the word "may" in §4 was intended to focus the Agency's attention on chemical substances "*about which there is a basis for concern, but about which there is inadequate* information to reasonably predict or determine the effects of the substance or mixture on health or the environment." Id. at 17 (emphasis added). The Conference Committee Report re-emphasized that the statutory language focused the Agency's attention on substances "about which there is a basis for concern." H.R. Conf. Rep. No. 1679, 94th Cong., 2d Sess. 61 (1976).

These indications of congressional intent illustrate that EPA's reading of ToSCA is a permissible one. Congress intended to authorize testing where the existence of an "unreasonable risk" could not yet be "reasonably predicted." The Agency's determination that it is empowered to act where the existence of an "unreasonable risk" cannot yet be said to be more probable than not is entirely consistent with that expression of intent. The EPA interpretation is likewise consistent with the level of certainty suggested by the phrase "basis for concern." To accept the CMA's position would require the Agency to gather "adequate" information to make a reasonable prediction or determination of risk before issuing a test rule. To say the least, this is not mandated by the statutory history, which indicates Congress's desire that EPA act on the basis of rational concern even in the absence of "adequate" information that an unreasonable risk existed. Section 4 may permissibly be read to authorize issuance of a test rule on the basis of less than more-probable-than-not evidence about a potentially unreasonable risk to health.

This conclusion is further bolstered by the legislative history underlying §6. If CMA were correct that EPA must make a more-probable-than-not finding of risk under §4's "may present" language, then it would logically follow that §6—which contains the term "presents or will present an unreasonable risk"—must require an even stronger than more-probable-than-not demonstration of "unreasonable risk." Yet neither §6 nor its legislative history indicate any such super-requirement of certainty. Indeed, §6 states expressly that the Agency need only find a "reasonable basis" to conclude that an "unreasonable risk" exists. A "reasonable basis" requirement is certainly no more demanding than a more-probable-than-not requirement; indeed the phrase suggests a less demanding standard. This interpretation is confirmed by the House Report, which states that an EPA finding of "unreasonable risk" under §6 is not expected to be supported by the same quantum of

B. Toxics—Market Access Regulation, ToSCA & REACH

evidence as is customary in administrative proceedings. . . . In sum, the standard Congress set for §6 regulation, that the chemical "will present an unreasonable risk," is no more rigorous (and arguably is less rigorous) than a more-probable-than-not finding. It follows as a matter of course that §4's "may present" language demands even less.

Of course, it is also evident from the legislative history that Congress did not intend to authorize EPA to issue test rules on the basis of mere hunches. The House Report states:

> The term "may" . . . does not permit the Administrator to make a finding respecting probability of a risk on the basis of mere conjecture or speculation, i.e., [that] it may or may not cause a risk. H.R. Rep. No. 1341, at 18.

Congress obviously intended §4 to empower EPA to issue a test rule only after it had found a solid "basis for concern" by accumulating enough information to demonstrate a more-than-theoretical basis for suspecting that an "unreasonable risk" was involved in the use of the chemical. . . .

[Relying on the "more-than-theoretical-basis" test, the court then rejected CMA's other two arguments regarding use of inferences versus direct evidence of exposure and rare versus recurrent exposure. Finally, the court analyzed the evidence submitted by EPA for the Final Test Rule and held that the Agency had produced substantial evidence "to demonstrate not fact, but doubt and uncertainty."]

COMMENTARY & QUESTIONS

1. An exceptional case. *Chemical Manufacturers* is an unusual example of ToSCA working smoothly with regard to the promulgation of test rules for existing chemicals. When ToSCA was enacted, some commentators predicted that the statute would be unenforceable because it had been so compromised during the legislative process. Unfortunately, these dire predictions have often been borne out. ToSCA's requirements that EPA promulgate test rules through notice-and-comment rulemaking and support them by substantial evidence, combined with the historical inadequacy of EPA's budget for ToSCA implementation and intense lobbying by industry, have militated against EPA promulgation of test rules. For example, "[b]y the end of fiscal year 1989, EPA had received full test data for only six chemicals and had not completed review of the data for any." Applegate, supra, at 319 n. 312, citing U.S. GAO, EPA's Chemical Testing Program Has Made Little Progress (April 1990). EPA did not perform its mandatory duty to respond to Interagency Testing Committee (ITC) recommendations until compelled to do so by court order. *Natural Resource Defense Council v. Costle*, 14 Env't Rep. Cas. (BNA) 1858 (1980). Moreover:

> EPA has historically rarely imposed a testing rule. . . . The agency has more often found reasons for declining to follow the ITC's testing recommendations. In addition, EPA has followed an administrative practice of entering into Negotiated Testing Agreements (NTAs) with industry trade associations in lieu of issuing test rules, wherever possible. D.W. Stever, The Law of Chemical Regulation and Hazardous Waste 2-8 (1991).

The NTA program was struck down in *Natural Resources Defense Council, Inc. v. EPA*, 595 F. Supp. 1255 (S.D.N.Y. 1984), partly because it excluded public interest groups. But ToSCA's cumbersome test rule procedures give EPA and the public little leverage in negotiations with industry.

2. ToSCA and new chemicals. ToSCA has largely been no more effective with regard to the introduction of new chemicals into commerce. EPA cannot require the testing of all new chemicals under ToSCA. Unless a test rule is in effect for a component of a new chemical compound, or that component is included on EPA's §5(b)(4) "suspect list," a manufacturer need not submit health and environmental test data unless it has independently developed these data or they are generally available elsewhere. Thus, ToSCA does not require a set of pre-market data on a new chemical. Does ToSCA actually discourage pre-market testing and encourage concealment of information? Or would a manufacturer most likely test a substance prior to manufacture in order to forestall tort liability? For a negative answer to the latter question, see Applegate, supra, at 299 ("industry has real incentives to avoid either creating toxic risk data or disclosing the data it already has"), and Lyndon, Information Economics and Chemical Toxicity: Designing Laws to Produce and Use Data, 87 Mich. L. Rev. 1795 (1989).

If EPA does not act to require testing before the expiration of the 90-day PMN period plus an optional additional 90 days, the manufacturer may commence manufacture or distribution. On the other hand, if after receipt of a PMN EPA finds that it has insufficient information on which to base an evaluation of the chemical substance, it may propose a test rule or, after making findings similar to those in §4, may issue a proposed order to prohibit or limit the production of the substance. If the manufacturer formally objects to the proposed order, EPA must seek an injunction in federal district court under §5(e). The strictness of these time constraints and the necessity of resorting to judicial action if a test rule cannot be proposed in time has, in the past, virtually guaranteed agency inaction.

3. FIFRA and ToSCA. In the congressional proceedings leading to the passage of ToSCA, the Senate preferred a licensing system similar to FIFRA, while the House favored allowing new chemicals to be marketed without notification or registration unless the chemicals or their components appeared on EPA's "suspect list." The emergent ToSCA compromise was based on notification and discretionary intervention by EPA. According to Professor Lyndon, the FIFRA presumption that a substance is unsafe unless the manufacturer proves safety has, in ToSCA, been transformed into a presumption that a substance is safe unless EPA can prove that it is unsafe:

> ToSCA's requirement that the EPA issue a rule before requiring testing distinguishes it from food, drug, and pesticide regulations, which mandate production of safety data prior to marketing. The ToSCA standard essentially establishes a presumption of safety, which the agency must overcome before it may require further testing of a chemical. Thus, the ToSCA's use of strict rulemaking standards inhibits the very information production the statute was written to encourage. 87 Mich. L. Rev. at 1824.

There is a fundamental ToSCA paradox (or Catch-22) in regulatory information gathering. Where is EPA to procure the information that it needs to require manufacturers—who have every incentive not to disclose negative information—to produce health and safety data regarding new and existing chemicals? Does EPA have to know already what it needs to know in order to ask for information about it? Is the necessary information even obtainable, or are there data gaps? See Dernbach, The Unfocused Regulation of Toxic and Hazardous Pollutants, 21 Harv. Envtl. L. Rev. 1, 28 (1997) (noting that no toxicity information was then available for 78% of the 12,860 chemicals then used in commerce in quantities of more than 1 million pounds per year, and that only minimal toxicity information was available concerning the rest).

4. Regulation and the common law. CMA's arguments in opposition to the Final Test Rule were based on common law analogues: (1) the more-probable-than-not test is similar to the "preponderance of the evidence" standard in common law civil litigation, (2) the criticism of EPA's inferences regarding modes of EHA use reflects the burden placed on a common law plaintiff to prove causation-in-fact by a preponderance of the evidence, and (3) the objection to EPA's regulating nonrecurrent exposures echoes a common law defendant's argument that an injunction should not be granted because there is an adequate remedy at law (damages) if the event is unlikely to recur. Administrative agencies, however, are not limited by these common law constraints, as the court reaffirmed in its rejection of CMA's arguments.

5. The more-than-theoretical-basis test. Could this standard be used to support a test rule where EPA has not yet explored the toxicity of a chemical but suspects, based on an educated guess, that the substance may be toxic? The more-than-theoretical-basis test probably could not be extended this far, but another section of ToSCA might cover such a situation. Section 4(a)(1)(B) (15 U.S.C. §2603(a)(1)(B)) provides that EPA may require testing where:

> a chemical substance or mixture is or will be produced in substantial quantities, and (I) it enters or may reasonably be anticipated to enter the environment in substantial quantities or (II) there is or may be significant or substantial human exposure to such substance or mixture.

In *Chemical Manufacturers Ass'n v. EPA*, 899 F.2d 344 (5th Cir. 1990) (frequently referred to as *Chemical Manufacturers II*), EPA contended:

> While there is a need to show a potential for exposure in order to make a §4(a)(1)(A) finding ["may present an unreasonable risk of injury to health or the environment"], the exposure threshold is much lower than that under §4(a)(1)(B). This is because the former ... finding was intended to focus on those instances where EPA has a scientific basis for suspecting potential toxicity and reflects that the potential for risk to humans may be significant even when the potential for exposure seems small as, for example, when the chemical is discovered to be hazardous at very low levels. In contrast, the §4(a)(1)(B) finding was intended to allow EPA to require testing, not because of suspicions about the chemical's safety, but because there may be a substantial or significant human exposure to a chemical whose hazards have not been explored. 899 F.2d at 358 n. 20.

The language of §4(a)(1)(B), however, is arguably so ambiguous that this section is of doubtful utility. In *Chemical Manufacturers II,* the Court remanded the test rule to EPA to explain what it meant by "substantial" quantities and human exposure.

6. The role of economics. All ToSCA regulatory decisionmaking must balance economic costs against environmental benefits under the "unreasonable risk" standard imported from FIFRA. In addition, §2(c) provides that EPA "shall consider the environmental, economic, and social impact of any action" taken by it under ToSCA. Section 2(b) declares a policy that "authority over chemical substances ... be exercised ... so as not to impede unduly or create unnecessary economic barriers to technological innovation." Pursuant to §4(b), in specifying tests to be carried out, the EPA shall consider "the relative costs of the various test protocols and the methodologies which may be required." Is it fair to balance tangible and predictable economic costs against intangible and uncertain environmental benefits? The human mind naturally prefers the certain to the uncertain, leading to a "fallacy of numeration." Should the "unreasonable risk" balance be weighted on the side of the environment? Going even further, Professor Applegate recommended that the "unreasonable risk" standard be eliminated from §4:

> Unreasonable risk should be replaced in the §4 context by a more readily satisfied, less complex standard—something, in short, with less baggage. The term "unreasonable" should be dropped. The appropriate level (as opposed to existence) of risk is a policy question and more suitable in the standard-setting stage than in data collection. Under §4, EPA should be exploring policy options, not setting policy. Reasonable restraint by EPA can be assured by the

existing provision requiring cost-effective testing and by the usual understanding that the term "risk" standing alone does not include de minimis risks. Applegate, supra, at 320.

But is it likely that Congress will repudiate "unreasonable risk," even as to data collection? Congress often prefers standards such as "unreasonable risk," which leave the difficult policy decisions to administrative agencies and courts. Although many critics have recommended that Congress allow agencies flexibility in areas of technical expertise and administrative procedure, and the Supreme Court has acknowledged that agencies should be allowed flexibility in setting their own procedures, the trend in Congress is often towards selective micromanagement of deadlines and other goals. In many cases, the result has been agency paralysis, missed deadlines, and bureaucratic frustration.

7. ToSCA §6. Under §6 of ToSCA, EPA has authority to regulate existing chemicals that present unreasonable risks to health or the environment. EPA may place controls and restrictions, including outright bans if necessary, upon the manufacture, use, processing, disposal, or distribution of such chemicals. As discussed in *Chemical Manufacturers*, "if the Administrator finds that there is a reasonable basis to conclude that the manufacture, processing, distribution in commerce, use, or disposal of a chemical substance or mixture, or that any combination of such activities, presents or will present an unreasonable risk of injury to health or the environment, the Administrator shall by rule" impose one of the following measures: a prohibition or limitation on the manufacture, processing, or distribution of a substance in general or for specific uses, or an imposition of concentration limits; a requirement as to labeling, public warning, recall, or recordkeeping; or a ban or limitation on a particular form of use or disposal. All other things being equal, however, EPA must regulate under another statute rather than ToSCA §9(b). Although §6, like §4, has not been utilized very often, it does represent a "catchall" or residuary pollution control statute, providing authority to regulate substances or uses that cannot be controlled under other federal pollution control statutes. EPA, for example, initially moved to regulate leaking underground storage tanks under ToSCA §6 until Congress enacted the 1984 RCRA Amendments. See Chapter 17. EPA has also relied on §6 to set soil concentration limits for land application of dioxin-containing pulp and paper sludge. See Proposed Regulation of Land Application of Sludge from Pulp and Paper Mills Using Chlorine and Chlorine Derivative Bleaching Processes, 56 Fed. Reg. 21,802 (May 10, 1991).

8. The EPA's attempted asbestos ban. Asbestos is a naturally occurring fibrous material that resists fire and most solvents. For years, it was used as a heat resistant insulator in building materials, in fireproof gloves and clothing, and in motor vehicle brake linings. Asbestos, however, is also a toxic material. Occupational exposure to asbestos dust can cause cancer.

In 1989, after years of review of scientific evidence of asbestos carcinogenity, EPA promulgated a final rule imposing a staged ban on most commercial uses of asbestos. Invoking ToSCA §6, EPA concluded that asbestos exposure "poses an unreasonable risk to human health." This asbestos ban was EPA's first and, to date, only national ban of a toxic substance under ToSCA §6. EPA implemented this ban after it concluded that the ban would, over a 13-year period, save approximately 200 lives otherwise lost to cancer, plus other lives in the future. EPA also estimated that the ban would cost between $450 million to $800 million. EPA estimated that the costs per life saved of the rule ranged between $7 to $8 million (in the asbestos paper product industry) and $72 to $106 million (in the asbestos shingle community).

In its 1991 decision in *Corrosion Proof Fittings v. EPA*, 947 F.2d 1201 (5th Cir. 1991), the Fifth Circuit held that EPA had presented insufficient evidence to justify the asbestos ban.

B. Toxics—Market Access Regulation, ToSCA & REACH

The Fifth Circuit concluded that EPA had failed to consider all necessary evidence and had failed to give adequate weight to the statutory language in §6, which requires EPA to promulgate the least burdensome, reasonable regulation necessary to protect the environment adequately. In reaching this result, the Fifth Circuit emphasized that, in providing for the regulation of "unreasonable risk" under ToSCA, Congress could not have meant to spend so much money in saving so few lives:

> While we do not sit as a regulatory agency that must make the difficult decision as to what an appropriate expenditure is to prevent someone from incurring the risk of an asbestos-related death, we do note that the EPA, in its zeal to ban any and all asbestos products, basically ignored the cost side of the ToSCA equation. The EPA would have this court believe that Congress, when it enacted its requirement that the EPA consider the economic impacts of its regulations, thought that spending $200-300 million to save approximately seven lives (approximately $30-40 million per life) over thirteen years is reasonable....
>
> The EPA's willingness to argue that spending $23.7 million to save less than one-third of a life reveals that its economic review of its regulations, as required by ToSCA, was meaningless.... If we were to allow such cavalier treatment of the EPA's duty to consider the economic effects of its decisions, we would have to excise entire sections and phrases from the language of ToSCA. Because we are judges, not surgeons, we decline to do so. 947 F.2d at 1222-1223.

Corrosion Proof Fittings highlights the constraints on EPA in assessing risk and in engaging in risk management under §6 of ToSCA. Although EPA has the duty under ToSCA to assess and manage the risk posed by products like asbestos, Congress has imposed statutory limitations upon EPA in carrying out those functions. How is EPA to determine what is the least burdensome, reasonable regulation necessary to protect the environment? How should EPA engage in a cost-benefit risk balancing under §6? Would EPA's attempted asbestos ban have had more likelihood of success if §6 were more like the stark prohibition provisions of the former Delaney Clause? Alternatively, would EPA have been more successful if, rather than an asbestos ban, EPA had focused instead on regulating uses of asbestos releasing the highest concentrations of fibers and considered alternatives other than a ban? Does the decision in *Corrosion Proof Fittings* demonstrate that ToSCA is a "broken statute"?

Is it appropriate for EPA to attempt to justify proposed action under §6 by estimating costs per life saved? The Fifth Circuit in *Corrosion Proof Fittings* seems to suggest that the estimated costs per life saved under EPA's proposed asbestos ban were patently unreasonable. A subsequent study reviewed the economic data relied upon by EPA in support of its asbestos, pesticide, and carcinogenic air pollution regulations, finding that EPA, in effect, had attached a value of $15 million to $45 million to the prevention of one case of cancer. See Van Houtven & Cropper, When Is a Life Too Costly to Save? The Evidence from Environmental Regulations, Resources, Winter 1994, at 6. Recent analysis of the regulatory costs of lives saved, however, raises significant questions as to the validity of the high estimates relied upon by EPA in *Corrosion Proof Fittings* and subsequent studies. See Heinzerling, Regulatory Costs of Mythic Proportions, 107 Yale L.J. 1981, 2038-2040 (1998) (reviewing the data relied upon in numerous studies but concluding that such data indicates a cost per life saved of less than $5 million in most cases). The same analysis also challenges the propriety of "discounting lives" in seeking to estimate the benefits of environmental regulation. Id. at 2043-2056.

9. The PCB Mega Rule. Polychlorinated biphenyls (PCBs) are a class of compounds that were widely used in electrical equipment because of their low flammability, heat capacity, and dielectric properties. Transformers, cooling systems, hydraulic systems, electromagnets, switches, and voltage regulators were the primary types of equipment that contained PCBs.

When Congress enacted ToSCA, it was aware that PCBs were potentially carcinogenic and very persistent in the environment (that is, they decompose slowly). Congress also was aware that PCBs can accumulate in plants, animals, and human tissue and that PCBs have adverse effects on fish and wildlife. As a result, in ToSCA §6(e), Congress determined that PCBs presented an unreasonable risk to human health and the environment and directed EPA to promulgate regulations concerning the use, storage, and disposal of PCBs. EPA issued its first PCB regulations in 1979. See *EDF v. EPA*, 636 F.2d 1267 (D.C. Cir. 1980) (EPA's PCB regulations overturned and remanded).

In the years since EPA began regulating PCBs, a number of issues arose pertaining to the means and methods of PCB regulation. Rather than address these issues on a piecemeal basis, EPA proposed and subsequently adopted a comprehensive overhaul of its PCB regulations, commonly known as the "PCB Mega Rule." The rule became effective on August 28, 1998. See Disposal of Polychlorinated Biphenyls (PCBs), 63 Fed. Reg. 35,384 (June 29, 1998).

One of the most important changes in the Mega Rule pertains to EPA's reinterpretation of its so-called anti-dilution provision. The anti-dilution provision states that no PCB regulation specifying a concentration can be avoided through dilution. In the past, EPA applied the provision to all cases where dilution has occurred, even if the dilution was accidental. EPA now regulates whether PCBs can be disposed of according to the actual PCB concentration at the time of disposal, thereby reducing disposal costs for large volumes of soil contaminated with low concentrations of PCBs.

EPA also revised its PCB Spill Cleanup Policy, which requires the cleanup of PCBs to certain levels depending upon the spill location, the potential for exposure to residual PCBs remaining after cleanup, the concentration of PCBs initially spilled (high concentration or low), and the nature and size of the population at risk of exposure to residual PCBs. Under the Mega Rule, the EPA now addresses the problem of PCBs in the environment through a single, flexible process. PCBs released into the environment prior to April 18, 1978, will generally be considered disposed of in a manner that does not present a risk of exposure. No further disposal of non-landfilled material will be required unless EPA makes a finding that the released material presents a risk of exposure. If such a finding is made, EPA will then require remediation based on the degree of risk posed by the spill. For spills or releases occurring after April 18, 1978, the PCB Mega Rule provides different methods for remediating the PCB-contamination: (1) remediation in accordance with specific parameters identified in the PCB Mega Rule itself; (2) remediation under a work plan meeting specified performance criteria approved by EPA; and (3) remediation utilizing a risk assessment, under which EPA approves a cleanup consistent with the specific risks posed to the human health and the environment.

EPA also revised cleanup standards and procedures for PCB bulk product waste. Such PCB waste includes nonliquid bulk wastes such as debris from the demolition of buildings and "fluff" from the shredding of automobiles and household and industrial appliances. PCB bulk product wastes must be disposed of in a ToSCA-approved incinerator or chemical waste landfill if the PCB concentration in the waste is above 50 ppm or in a municipal or industrial solid waste facility if the concentration is less than 50 ppm. Is the Rule a form of deregulation for high-volume, low PCB-concentration wastes?

10. EPA's proposed rulemaking concerning the disclosure of the chemicals and mixtures used in hydraulic fracking. On May 9, 2014, the U.S. EPA initiated a process that may

B. Toxics — Market Access Regulation, ToSCA & REACH

result in the first federal regulation of chemicals used in fracking, a drilling technique that has significantly enhanced energy production and development in the United States.

In a response to a citizen petition under §21 of ToSCA submitted by environmental groups in 2011 seeking the disclosure of the chemicals used in fracking, the EPA issued an advance notice of proposed rulemaking on May 9, 2014. Pursuant to that notice, the EPA announced that it will be considering rules requiring oilfield service companies and others to provide disclosure concerning the health and safety of the chemicals used in fracking. At the same time, the EPA indicated that it may stop short of issuing final rules, by instead developing incentives to induce voluntary disclosure.

Since fracking was first initiated in the United States, environmental groups have been demanding that EPA collect information on the fluids that are injected with water and sand in the fracking process. The mixture of those fluids with water and sand breaks apart underground rocks to release oil and natural gas. In particular, fracking activities include the injection of water, chemicals, proppant, and/or tracers to: (1) prepare geologic formations for hydraulic fracturing, (2) complete a hydraulic fracturing stimulation stage, (3) evaluate the extent of resulting fractures, and (4) ensure the future ability to continue enhancement of production through stimulation by hydraulic fracturing. During each hydraulic fracturing stimulation stage, pressurized fluids containing carrier fluids such as water or gas and any combination of proppant and chemicals are injected into wells, to fracture portions of the formation surrounding a selected well section.

As part of its rulemaking, EPA has requested comment on the information that should be obtained or disclosed and the mechanism for obtaining or disclosing information about chemicals and mixtures used in hydraulic fracturing. EPA is also seeking comment on best management practices for the generation, collection, reporting, and/or disclosure of public health and environmental information from or by companies that manufacture, process, or use chemical substances or mixtures in hydraulic fracturing activities — that is, practices or operations that can be implemented and verified in order to achieve protection of public health and the environment — and whether voluntary third-party certification and incentives for disclosure could be valuable tools for improving chemical safety. In addition, the EPA is seeking comment on ways to minimize reporting burdens and costs, avoid duplication of efforts, and maximize transparency and public understanding. Finally, EPA is soliciting comments on incentives and recognition programs that could be used to support the development and use of safer chemicals in hydraulic fracturing.

As authority for its rulemaking, EPA has invoked ToSCA §8(d) (15 U.S.C. §2007(d)), which authorizes EPA to require the submission of lists of health and safety studies conducted or initiated by or for, or known to or reasonably ascertainable by manufacturers, processors, and distributors of (and any person who proposes to manufacture, process, or distribute) any chemical substance or mixture. ToSCA §8(d) also authorizes EPA to require the submission of copies of studies that are otherwise known by the person submitting the list.

EPA has also invoked the Pollution Prevention Act (PPA) (42 U.S.C. §§13101 et seq.), which makes pollution prevention the national policy of the United States. The PPA identifies an environmental management hierarchy in which pollution "should be prevented or reduced whenever feasible; pollution that cannot be prevented or recycled should be treated in an environmentally safe manner whenever feasible; and disposal or release into the environment should be employed only a last resort . . ." (42 U.S.C. §13103). Among other requirements, the PPA directs EPA to develop improved methods of coordinating, streamlining, and assuring public access to data collected under federal environmental statutes; to facilitate the adoption of source-reduction techniques by businesses; and to establish an annual awards program to recognize a company or companies that operate outstanding or innovative source reduction programs.

In June 2015, EPA also released for public comment and peer review a draft assessment of fracking activities on the quality and quantity of drinking water. This draft assessment is based upon extensive review of literature, results from EPA research, and technical input received from state, industry, and other stakeholders.

While EPA has labeled its proposed rulemaking as a major first step in considering whether fracking should be a more transparent process, the oil and gas community is wary of any regulation that would undercut the growth and development of fracking. As an alternative, oil and gas producers have typically advocated for regulation on a state-by-state basis, which they believe will be more effective as well as more compatible with their business interests. At the same time, environmentalists have already criticized the EPA's proposed rulemaking as merely a "baby" step, because there is no guarantee that EPA will issue rules mandating the disclosure of chemicals and mixtures used in fracking.

The controversy over disclosure will likely continue to grow. Fracking has already led to a natural gas boom in a number of states, including, in particular, North Dakota, Pennsylvania, Ohio, and Texas. Although drilling companies have been disclosing chemical information on an industry website (www.FracFocus.org), critics contend that the website allows too many exemptions that keep ingredients secret and precludes ready aggregation of information concerning the specific chemicals used in fracking. Given the fracking boom, whether and to what extent the chemicals used in fracking are disclosed will undoubtedly remain a hot topic, both on the state and federal levels.

11. Market access statutes and confidentiality. Given industry's desire to protect trade secrets from competitors, and potential tort plaintiffs' eagerness for access to health and safety testing data, both FIFRA and ToSCA contain extensive provisions regarding confidentiality of information disclosed to EPA. With regard to FIFRA, see *Ruckleshaus v. Monsanto Co.*, 467 U.S. 986 (1984); as to ToSCA, see McGarity & Shapiro, The Trade Secret Status of Health and Safety Testing Information: Reforming Agency Disclosure Policies, 93 Harv. L. Rev. 837 (1980), and *Chevron Chemical Co. v. Costle*, 443 F. Supp. 1024 (N.D. Cal. 1978.) Historically, EPA has rarely challenged a manufacturer's assertions that its chemical identities and other data should be protected. But do these provisions on confidentiality of information disclosed to EPA need modification? For example, should EPA be allowed to share data with state regulators and other countries? Alternatively, should confidentiality protection "sunset" after a certain number of years?

12. The future of ToSCA. Congress has long discussed, but not enacted, potential reforms to ToSCA, which has not been significantly amended since it was first adopted in 1976.

> Criticisms of ToSCA have largely focused on the statute's failure to ensure chemical safety. These criticisms primarily concern the contentions that ToSCA:
>
> - has failed to deliver information necessary to identify unsafe, as well as safer, chemicals;
> - prevents the federal government from sharing much of the limited information it does obtain;
> - imposes a significant burden on government to prove actual harm in order to control or replace a dangerous chemical; and
> - perpetuates the failure of the chemical industry to develop safer chemicals and product design.

B. Toxics—Market Access Regulation, ToSCA & REACH

As noted earlier in this chapter, however, recently there has been significant movement in Congress towards the reform of ToSCA. On June 23, 2015, by a 398 to 1 vote, the House of Representatives approved legislation to reform ToSCA (known as the ToSCA Modernization Act (H.R. 2576)). On December 17, 2015, the Senate approved a proposed companion bill (also known as the Frank R. Lautenberg Chemical Safety for the 21st Century Act Senate (S. 697)), which is also designed to strengthen EPA's hand in regulating chemicals.

The House bill (H.R. 2576), for the first time, would require EPA to evaluate the risks of chemicals in commerce, make it easier for EPA to obtain toxicity and other data from chemical manufacturers, and impose fees on chemical manufacturers for certain services EPA provides as it reviews new or existing chemicals. The House bill also seeks to get rid of the requirement under ToSCA that EPA choose the "least burdensome" means of addressing the risks posed by a chemical found by EPA to cause an unreasonable health or environmental risk. The House bill takes a narrower approach to preemption of state toxics programs than the Senate bill. It would "grandfather," or preserve existing state chemical safety laws that have taken effect before August 1, 2015, and preserve state toxic tort claims, after EPA takes final action on a chemical, unless they "actually conflict" with new federal mandates. New state chemical laws, however, would be preempted once EPA finishes a restriction under ToSCA.

The Senate bill (S. 697) also contains grandfathering provisions to preserve existing laws, but preemption for new chemical rules and laws would occur when EPA launches a review of a chemical. In addition, under the Senate bill—which passed the Senate by voice vote on December 17, 2015—EPA is required to consider only the health and safety impact of a chemical when assessing its safety. In addition, the bill would: (1) ensure special protections for those most vulnerable to chemicals (e.g., pregnant women, infants, the elderly, and chemical workers); (2) establish a new user fee requiring chemical companies to bear a larger share of the cost of evaluating and regulating chemicals; (3) provide increased funding for EPA resources through industry fees; (4) ensure faster industry compliance with EPA regulations; (5) simplify the preemption waiver process for states; and (6) expedite action on EPA work on chemicals known to be dangerous.

To become law, the Senate and House bills must now be reconciled and, once reconciliation is completed, presented to the President for signature. Nonetheless, despite the action in both Houses and now almost universal interest in ToSCA reform, these proposed bills have been criticized by some as a "step backward." For example, Professor Noah Sachs of the University of Richmond School of Law recently made the following insightful comments regarding the House vote on January 23, 2015:

> Given an overwhelming bipartisan House vote in favor, and given that a companion Senate Bill, S. 697, has forty co-sponsors, including 19 Democrats, there's a strong chance that a ToSCA reform bill will pass . . . and be signed by the President. Both bills are heavily supported by the chemical industry, and the environmental community is somewhat divided. The Environmental Working Group opposes both bills, while EDF supports the Senate bill as an improvement over existing law.
>
> This could be the biggest piece of environmental legislation since the 1990 Clean Air Act amendments, but it's not getting much attention outside chemical policy circles.
>
> I've been calling for ToSCA reform for many years (as have others on this list), but I think the House bill is a step backward.
>
> —For the first time, it requires EPA to move through the huge backlog of chemicals that have never been tested for health effects (estimated at more than 80,000), but it moves at a snail's pace: a minimum of 10 chemicals per year. This essentially ratifies the status quo. We'll still wait decades before the most commonly used chemicals are tested.

—It allows manufacturers to propose chemicals for testing and requires EPA to test the chemicals that manufacturers want (manufacturers pay a fee). So I fear manufacturers will set the priorities for the agency, stretching the capabilities of the tiny Office of Pollution Prevention and Toxics and driving its agenda.

—It gets rid of the old requirement that EPA choose the "least burdensome" regulatory option when it wants to restrict a chemical, but it replaces it with something at least as damaging: a requirement that if EPA wants to ban a particular chemical or use, it must "determine whether technically and economically feasible alternatives that [are more beneficial to] health or the environment . . . will be available as a substitute."

This last item seems to provide the wide "viewscreen" that regulation scholars have called for. It makes sense at first glance to focus not just on one risk, but also on a comparison of the risks of substitutes. But it sets up yet another procedural hurdle to regulation, and it puts the task of an evaluation of substitutes on the agency rather than on the manufacturer. Not every chemical use is essential. As Richard Denison at EDF has pointed out, if a manufacturer wants some new scent of air freshener, and EPA determines the scent is a carcinogen, why is it EPA's job to evaluate the technical and economic feasibility of substitutes? This will just cause delay and raise the bar to sensible regulation of the chemical that has been identified as a risk to the public. . . .

As this edition of the coursebook goes to press, the new ToSCA has not been enacted into law. If, and when, enacted, the new ToSCA will be analyzed further on the new coursebook website.

13. Market access beyond toxics: mad cows! A single picture (of a single cow) may be worth many thousands of (previously futile) words. This is especially true when the picture is broadcast on network news, and its subject is a cow in Washington—Washington State, of course, not Washington, D.C.—suffering from bovine spongiform encephalitis (BSE or "mad cow" disease). Meat from BSE animals can cause Creutzfeldt-Jacob disease in humans, an untreatable and fatal nervous system wasting disease. The U.S. Department of Agriculture (USDA) oversees many facets of the food supply marketing stream, controlling production and market access of food products to ensure public safety. Not much U.S. regulation was specifically directed at BSE prior to the 1986 BSE outbreak in England that led to destruction of herds and loss of market for English beef. In 1997, regulators sought to avoid similar problems in the U.S. livestock industry by banning animal parts from feed, thereby narrowing BSE's principal exposure pathway into the herds. Additional and more extensive measures, including a ban on meat from "downer cows" (cows unable to walk at the time of arrival at the slaughterhouse but nevertheless processed into food products) were proposed by USDA but were not implemented due to opposition by cattle industry lobbyists. In a most unusual sequence of events, as part of the 2002 Farm Bill, both houses of Congress passed a ban on downer cows, but when the legislation emerged from conference committee, without explanation the downer cow ban had been removed.[10]

Reaction to the discovery of the Washington BSE cow was swift and economically disruptive. Numerous countries, including Japan, a particularly lucrative market for U.S. cattle, placed an immediate ban on imports of beef from this country. Within days, to the applause of the American Beef Council, the USDA's Food Safety and Inspection Service, pursuant to the Federal Meat Inspection Act, 21 U.S.C. §§601 et seq., announced new emergency measures and quickly promulgated an array of new rules. Antidrug and Alcohol

---

10. Allison Aubrey, Analysis: Ban on Downer Cows, NPR Morning Edition (Jan. 12, 2004). See Downed Animal Protection Act, S. 1298 and H.R. 2519, 108th Cong. (2003). See also *Baur v. Veneman*, 352 F.3d 625 (2d Cir. 2003) (plaintiff who petitioned USDA to pass ban on use of downed cows for food has standing to seek review of agency's refusal to do so).

Misuse Prevention Programs for Personnel Engaged in Specified Aviation Activities, 69 Fed. Reg. 1861-1874 (Jan. 12, 2004). Interestingly, however, the new market access administrative rules do not ban downer cows. Instead they require product-holding procedures (forbidding cattle products to be marketed as "inspected and passed" until after test results are received). The rules also expand a "Specified Risk Material" category for body parts in cattle more than 30-months-old that are banned from entering the human food supply. The mad cow issue provides an interesting case study of how risk-regulating market access rules are shaped and implemented in the real world. If there are no more mad cow cases that prolong public attention, will the BSE regulatory issue have temporal staying power? Will the jury of U.S. public opinion, which did not react fearfully to beef in the marketplace, nevertheless prompt Congress to enact downer cow legislation despite continuing industry opposition? What motivates the beef industry, the USDA, and the eating and voting public? Are their positions driven by objective risk management calculations?

2. Regulation in the European Union: REACH

In late 2006, the EU, after several years of proposals and debate, formally adopted a new comprehensive chemical management regulation known as REACH (Registration, Evaluation, Authorisation and Restriction of Chemicals), designed to systematize and strengthen chemical regulation by requiring the registration of existing and new chemicals. REACH, which operates as domestic law in the 28 EU Member States, contains easily the most demanding regulatory requirements for chemicals on the planet.

REACH requires registration of all existing and new chemicals produced or imported in volumes of a ton or more per year per manufacturer or importer. Contrary to the approach of ToSCA, which presumes market access in the absence of regulatory restrictions promulgated by U.S. EPA, REACH embodies a regulatory philosophy of "no data, no market." Failure to register means that the substance or chemical will not be commercially available. REACH covers approximately 30,0000 chemicals and is designed to identify those which might be carcinogenic (causing cancer), mutagenic (causing genetic mutations), or teratogenic (causing adverse reproductive effects); which are persistent and bioaccumulate (such as polychlorinated biphenyls (PCBs)); and, in certain cases, chemicals which might be endocrine (hormone) disrupters. The registration process requires the production of basic toxicological data, including studies of environmental toxicity, if they are not already available. Chemical safety reports are required which describe exposure and measures to reduce risks.

REACH not only concerns chemical substances, but also applies to certain "articles." An article includes all objects whose special shape, surface, or design determine their function to a greater degree than does their chemical composition — virtually everything except for specifically mentioned substances or preparations. Generally, specific REACH requirements apply to articles acting as containers

> The European Union (EU) is a regional economic integration organization, to which — in contrast to the other international organizations discussed in this coursebook — the 28 Member States have ceded a portion of their sovereign legislative authority. EU legislation comes in two principal forms: (1) regulations, which are immediately binding in the Member States; and (2) directives, which are instructions to the Member States to take action consistent with principles outlined in the instrument. EU legislation is made by its principal political institutions: the European Commission (roughly the equivalent of an executive representing the entire EU); the Council of the European Union (in which the Member States are represented by ministers, and which takes decisions by weighted majority voting in most cases); and the European Parliament. The European Court of Justice, located in Luxembourg, has the power authoritatively to

> interpret EU law and its governing constitutional instruments, in particular the Treaty on European Union. Compare this understanding of sovereignty to those presented in Chapter 7.

for substances (or whose release is reasonably foreseeable), and to articles containing substances of very high concern.

The testing regime is graduated by volume, with progressively more rigorous requirements for higher-volume chemicals. In response to concerns about the potential impact on small businesses, the final compromise version of REACH imposes only very modest demands on chemicals produced in amounts of less than 100 tons per year. More information is required for chemicals produced in amounts above 100 tons per year. Firms are encouraged to form consortia and to collaborate, reducing testing costs in registration and testing, when they are registering the same chemical. The use of information on tests already performed is encouraged. One of the chief issues in the final stages of negotiation on the proposal concerned the "substitution principle," addressing the conditions under which the most toxic substances are to be replaced.

A new European Chemicals Agency (ECHA) located in Helsinki, Finland grants the required registration. A preliminary evaluation of the registration dossier is performed by this agency, which can request more information or enforce testing requirements. A more comprehensive evaluation procedure can be initiated if it is suspected that a substance may present a risk to human health or to the environment. The requirement for registration will be phased in, with the chemicals of greatest toxicological concern produced in or imported into the EU in the greatest quantities subject first to the registration process. For substances of very high concern — and which will be identified through a decisionmaking procedure involving the Agency, the Member States, and the European Commission — prior approval in the form of authorization by the Commission is required. The regulation also provides for public access to basic toxicological information, a public policy strategy that complements the remainder of the measure's regulatory architecture.

REACH affects not only manufacturers and importers of chemical substances, but also virtually all manufacturing businesses that are active on the EU market and use substances in their products. Because REACH applies to chemicals manufactured or imported into Europe, U.S. companies doing business in Europe have been required to make public their basic health and safety data on those chemicals used in production that are subject to the EU authorization process. Formally, the requirements of REACH apply only to the natural or juridical person placing a substance on the market there. Consequently, only European entities can register substances with the ECHA, and foreign manufacturers and exporters must identify an "only representative" within Europe for purposes of REACH through which the registration and data transmission requirements can be met.[11]

December 1, 2008 was a major juncture for the implementation of REACH. From June 1, 2008, the effective date of the registration requirement, until December 1, chemical manufacturers and importers could submit a "preregistration," assuring continued access to the European market during a phase-in period pending completion of a full registration dossier. Those companies and chemicals which had not been preregistered, and which required registration, were banned from sale in the EU pending preparation of a full registration dossier. As a result of this incentive for early registration, the European

---

11. This bulk of this material is taken from Wirth, The EU's New Impact on American Environmental Regulation, 31 Fletcher F. World Aff. 91 (2007).

B. Toxics—Market Access Regulation, ToSCA & REACH

Chemicals Agency in Helsinki received 2.75 million preregistration notifications, considerably more than expected, from 65,000 companies identifying 150,000 chemicals. The ECHA has already adopted a candidate list of "substances of very high concern," numbering 168 as of early 2016, which are subject to a system of prior approval or "authorization" under REACH. Those substances also require a "substitution plan," designed to identify alternatives.

REACH is far more comprehensive than ToSCA. While opposing the proposal and attempting to weaken it through the U.S. Government and its own efforts, U.S. industry also realizes that it is going to have to adapt to those aspects that cannot be changed. U.S. exports subject to REACH amount to $14 billion per year and are responsible for 54,000 jobs in the United States. Many firms that operate in the United States that would be affected by REACH are, moreover, multinationals whose activities in Europe will be directly regulated. REACH's requirements consequently apply to every major consumer product manufacturer in the world. As agreed at the U.S.-EU summit held in April 2007, EPA and the EU have undertaken a joint program to work toward regulatory convergence on scientific, technical, and chemicals management issues, including those relating to REACH implementation projects (RIPs). The U.S. Department of Commerce is even said to be assisting U.S. firms in complying with the requirements of REACH.

The European Court of Justice (ECJ), the EU's highest judicial organ, in September 2015 delivered an important opinion concerning the scope of REACH. At stake was the interpretation of the term "article." The scope of the term is critical to the implementation of the scheme, especially with respect to articles containing chemicals on the Candidate List of Substances of Very High Concern. Article 7(2) of the REACH regulation requires producers and importers of articles to notify the ECHA of the presence of Candidate List substances in an "article" if the concentration of that substance exceeds the threshold of 0.1% in the article. Article 33 of the Regulation further requires suppliers of articles that contain Candidate List substances over the 0.1% threshold to provide consumers with sufficient information, including the name of the substance, to allow the safe use of the article.

> **REACH:**
> - Constitutes domestic law in the EU states.
> - Requires registration by the European Chemical Agency (ECHA) of all new and existing chemicals produced in the EU.
> - Has a "no data, no market" regulatory philosophy.
> - Concerns both chemical substances and "articles."
> - Also applies to all chemicals imported into Europe, thereby requiring compliance by U.S. and other companies doing business in Europe.
> - Is far more comprehensive than ToSCA.

The definition of an "article" is consequently crucial with respect to products like desktop computers, which can contain on the order of 10 subparts, comprising hundreds of components, themselves containing more than 1000 substances. Many of those components are sourced from numerous suppliers all over the world. The Commission, the ECHA, and a majority of EU Member States took the position that the 0.1% concentration threshold should be measured on the basis of the whole article—for example, a finished computer as an article in commerce, which would probably not trigger the 0.1% threshold. Other Member States, including France, Belgium and Germany, and the Advocate General argued that an "article" consists of each of the individual components, the "once an article, always an article" theory. The ECJ, in response to a reference for a preliminary ruling from the French *Conseil d'État* (highest administrative court), rendered the following opinion.

Fédération des entreprises du commerce et de la distribution (FCD) & Fédération des magasins de bricolage et de l'aménagement de la maison (FMB) v. Ministry of Ecology, Sustainable Development, and Energy

European Court of Justice, 2015, Case C-106/14

44. . . . . FCD and FMB submit that the classification as "article" within the meaning of Article 3(3) of the REACH Regulation applies only to the final product the composition of which includes articles. An interpretation to the contrary would involve considerable burdens, in particular:

- an obligation for suppliers and importers to determine the concentration of substances of very high concern in the final product manufactured, imported or placed on the market, using tests or on the basis of information provided by their own suppliers, entailing a complex and costly process;
- substantial difficulties for importers in obtaining detailed information on substances of very high concern present in each of the components making up complex products from producers established outside the European Union.

45. The French Government submits that Article 3(3) of the REACH Regulation defines an article as a manufactured object the shape of which is more important than the chemical composition for determining its function. No object is outside the scope of that definition once it is given a special shape, surface or design during production, which—more than its chemical composition—determines its function. Articles 7(2) and 33 of that regulation do not provide that the term 'article' must be interpreted more restrictively than under Article 3(3) thereof.

46. It should be observed in that regard that Article 3(3) defines "article" as "an object which during production is given a special shape, surface or design which determines its function to a greater degree than does its chemical composition."

47. It is clear from that definition that the classification of an object as an article within the meaning of the REACH Regulation turns on three factors. Firstly, the term "article" refers only to objects which have undergone "production." It therefore pertains only to manufactured objects, in contrast to objects in their natural state. Secondly, the production process must give the object in question "a special shape, surface or design," except for inter alia physical or chemical properties. Thirdly, that shape, surface or design resulting from the manufacturing process must be more decisive for the function of the object in question than its chemical composition.

48. The situation referred to by the referring court concerns a so-called "complex" product because it is made up of a number of manufactured objects meeting the criteria laid down in Article 3(3) of the REACH Regulation. Such a situation raises the question whether the classification as an article must be applied both to the product as a whole and simultaneously to each of the articles forming part of its composition.

49. It should be noted that the REACH Regulation does not contain any provisions governing specifically the situation of a complex product containing more than one article. That legislative silence must be construed in the light of the principal objective pursued by the regulation, which is not to regulate all manufactured products, but to monitor the chemical substances present by themselves or in a mixture as well as, in certain cases, particularly those listed restrictively in Article 7 thereof, when they are contained in articles.

B. Toxics—Market Access Regulation, ToSCA & REACH

50. Consequently, in the absence of any specific provision, there is no need to draw a distinction not provided for by the REACH Regulation between the situation of articles incorporated as a component of a complex product and that of articles present in an isolated manner. The question whether a complex product itself may be classified as an article therefore turns solely on a determination according to the criteria laid down in Article 3(3) of that regulation.

51. It is therefore only if the production of an object using a combination of more than one article gives that object a special shape, surface or design which is more decisive for its function than its chemical composition that that object may be classified as an article. Accordingly, unlike a simple assembly process, that production process must alter the shape, surface or design of the articles used as components.

COMMENTARY & QUESTIONS

1. Competing considerations. According to one commentator, the ECJ's opinion in this case "does not give much weight to proportionality and international trade concerns." A requirement of "proportionality"—the relationship between the seriousness of an issue to be addressed and the rigor of the governmental means employed to respond—is the equivalent of a constitutional principle found in the Treaty Establishing the European Union, by reference to which the ECJ can subject EU legislation to judicial review. Why do you think the Court nonetheless decided as it did?

2. Extraterritorial application of EU law. States in the international legal sense, including the United States, sometimes regulate in ways that have impacts on public policy in other jurisdictions. For instance, after the Enron scandal, the U.S. Congress adopted securities reform legislation, the Sarbanes-Oxley Act, that had impacts well beyond U.S. borders. Although REACH is similarly likely to have a global impact, as a technical matter its application is confined to the territory of the European Union and to EU entities. If you were drafting the legislation, why might you make this choice? To what extent, if any, are legal considerations relevant?

3. Upward harmonization: the "California effect." A jurisdiction adopting a strict regulatory measure may have such a large share of a particular market that industry finds it impractical or excessively costly to produce an alternative product for other markets. This phenomenon is familiar in the U.S. federal system, and is sometimes known as the "California effect." California is itself one of the ten largest markets in the world, with a total GDP greater than that of Canada, Spain, or South Korea. When California regulates a particular product or activity, a firm doing business there has a number of choices: It may decide (1) to undertake special modifications to its business practices just for the California market; (2) to forego sales in California; or, as is frequently the case, (3) to alter its products or services offered for sale in all markets to conform to the California standards, especially if creating two product streams would be impracticable or excessively costly. With its recent expansion to 28 Member States, the EU now has a population more than one and a half times as large as that of the United States and an economy of roughly equivalent size. To what extent can the impact of REACH be equated with the "California effect"? What are the similarities in structural context? The differences? What is the operative significance of those similarities or differences?

4. Borrowing from other jurisdictions. At the sub-national level, states in the United States are beginning to respond to legislation originating from the European Union. California's Electronic Waste Recycling Act of 2003 references the EU's Restriction of Hazardous

Substances (RoHS) directive by name, incorporating its standards by reference for the purpose of establishing regulatory requirements for electronic devices containing certain heavy metals. In a multiple-tiered "California effect," this state-level statute relying on an EU directive could have the practical effect of leveraging the application of European standards for the entire U.S. market, all without any formal policy input from the U.S. federal government. A similar phenomenon can operate internationally. For instance, China has adopted its own version of the EU RoHS directive. What would be the incentives for California or China to copy EU regulatory legislation in the field of environment and public health?

5. Negative harmonization: regulatory disparities as trade disputes. Differences in national regulatory approaches can lead to trade disputes, the resolution of which is one of the principal purposes of the World Trade Organization, as discussed in chapters 7.B.3 and 22.E.2. If exporters from one country claim that another's higher standards are impeding market access, the question is then whether the higher standard is a non-tariff barrier to trade whose principal purpose is to protect domestic industry and foreign competition or, alternatively, a legitimate exercise of a state's sovereign police power to protect consumer welfare and the environment. Assuming a dispute reaches a sufficiently high level, the state with the lower standard may seek recourse through litigation initiated through a trade agreement's dispute settlement mechanism, typically among the more efficacious in the international system. The mere threat of a conflict, as opposed to an actual dispute, may also act to dampen national regulatory efforts—a "raised eyebrow," biased toward inaction and against regulatory intervention. Because they encourage this kind of "negative" harmonization toward a least-common-denominator, the operation of trade agreements has frequently been compared with that of the Dormant Commerce Clause, as discussed in chapter 7.A.2. To what extent is that a good comparison?

6. The EU as alternative policy center. According to some, the European Union, due to its increasing size and growing regulatory momentum, is becoming an alternative power center to the United States in the field of environmental policy. For example, major multilateral mergers now often require not only approval from the Antitrust Division of the U.S. Department of Justice, but also by the European Commission's competition authorities. This accounts for an emerging and discernible impact of EU policy and law on the environmental laws and policy of United States, with REACH one of the principal examples. See, e.g., Schapiro, Exposed: The Toxic Chemistry of Everyday Products and What's at Stake for American Power (White River Junction, Vermont: Chelsea Green 2008). What are the implications for the United States if, in some meaningful sense, our laws are being made not in Washington, but Brussels (the seat of the European Union)?

7. EU law creates international practice opportunities. Described by one online publication as a "ticking time bomb," REACH's effectively global coverage has created the need for legal services outside the EU. A number of law firms with regulatory practices have offered comprehensive services to their clients, including identification of an "only representative" for exporters to the EU, supply chain communication obligations for potential substances of very high concern (SVHCs), and the registration and notification obligations applicable to "articles." Concrete practice opportunities such as these can—or at least should—affect how we train the lawyers of tomorrow. The demand for international perspectives and practice experience is likely to increase as the practitioners of the future are trained and hired. In addition to the toolbox applicable to U.S. regulatory actions by agencies like EPA, what skill set(s) would you want to access to feel comfortable advising a client about the requirements of REACH?

8. Judicial review in the EU. The ECJ judgment reproduced in the text has been lauded as a victory for both the integrity of REACH and for the environment and public health.

It also reflects, at least in one view, an appropriate role both for the Court and the expert agency in judicial review of policy-relevant science. The Advocate General, an advisor to the ECJ in a role in some respects similar to the U.S. Solicitor General, in this case referred to

> the broad discretion enjoyed by the European Union authorities in the assessment of highly complex scientific and technical facts. . . . That discretion is also accorded to ECHA, for example in connection with the inclusion of substances in the candidate list under Article 59 of the REACH Regulation. However, the point at issue is not an assessment of facts, but the interpretation of EU law. This is reserved for the Court even in the case of complex legal matters.

Which do you think the question presented by this case is—a question of science or a question of law? What principle(s) would you employ to distinguish between them? What are the policy implications for each of the two choices? How does the Advocate General's treatment of the distinction between the application of legal and scientific expertise compare to that of courts in the United States? Compare *International Harvester v. Ruckelshaus*, Chapter 11.

9. Extending the REACH of toxic torts. The studies required by REACH, and made public pursuant to its requirements, may document previously unknown health effects. Given relatively vigorous toxic tort litigation activity in the United States, information generated or released in Europe may fuel lawsuits brought in the United States. (See Chapter 4.) To what extent can or should American courts allow tort litigation based on the data generated by REACH? How would those data likely be treated under *Daubert*? Is REACH likely to emerge as a target for twenty-first century ambulance chasers?

10. Diplomacy and U.S. law. While the legislation that eventually became REACH was being debated in the European Parliament, the Executive Branch was actively opposing the directive, in effect adopting the position of the American chemicals industry on REACH as U.S. Government policy. Anecdotal accounts describe lobbying EU institutions in Brussels and elsewhere, démarches (diplomatic communications) in EU Member State capitals, and appeals to weaken REACH in non-EU countries including South Africa and Asian countries like Malaysia, Korea, Thailand, and the Philippines. Diplomatic pressure of this kind is frequently exerted by the Executive Branch, often with little or no public or Congressional input. Should the U.S. government's lobbying activities on foreign legislation be controlled, prohibited, or regulated? If so, how? In Washington? By foreign states in Brussels and other capitals? Are there any legal, and in particular constitutional, limitations on attempts to control diplomatic interactions of this sort?

11. REACH and ToSCA reform. According to Mark Schapiro, the new information generated by REACH will force a thorough reevaluation or replacement of ToSCA, the principal U.S. statutory authority, within the next three to five years. Recent proposals to reform ToSCA are discussed in the Commentary & Questions, at ¶12 in the previous section (see pages 676-678, *supra*). To what extent do you see the influence of REACH reflected in those proposals? In what settings could you imagine efforts at regulatory convergence between the U.S. system and REACH to be undertaken?

16

Remedial Liability Regulatory Strategies: CERCLA

A. CERCLA's Liability Rules as Developed Through the Judicial Process of Statutory Interpretation
B. EPA's CERCLA Administrative Order Process
C. Identifying Sites, Funding, and Setting the Standards for Cleanups
D. EPA's Strategy for Cost Recovery and Loss Allocation

The environmental events that have most galvanized public opinion over the years have been high-profile cases involving the release of hazardous substances into the environment and the resulting threats to public health. Few symbols are as potent as the homes and schools at Love Canal virtually afloat on a toxic stew, or working families suffering "the shakes" from Kepone in Hopewell, Virginia, or workers in space suit-like outfits removing PCBs from the newly abandoned ghost town at Times Beach, Missouri. In the face of that degree of public outrage, an almost certain political reaction is to pass laws addressing the subject, not only laws that seek to avert repetition of the calamity, as with Subtitle C of the Resource Conservation and Recovery Act (RCRA) (see Chapter 17), but also laws that seek to assuage public anger at the parties responsible for the events by making those parties accountable for the results of their actions.

Enacting into law the public desire for an accounting from responsible parties is a natural enough sentiment, but to do so within the constraints imposed by the U.S. Constitution, and to do so effectively, is a more sophisticated proposition. Newly enacted laws that attempt to attach present consequences for past actions have some hurdles to overcome. Not only does Article I §9 of the Constitution state that "No bill of Attainder or ex post facto law shall be passed," but that provision is also complemented by the more general notion that constitutionally guaranteed due process of law requires fair advance notice of what the law requires before sanctions can be imposed for disobedience of the legal command. Beyond the retroactive application of law, crafting a law that holds the "right" actors accountable for acts that have occurred in the distant past raises a host of additional complexities.

In enacting the Comprehensive Environmental Response, Compensation, and Liability Act (CERCLA, popularly named "Superfund"), Congress took on those challenges and more—it imposed retroactive liability on a broad group of actors whom it deemed to be the responsible parties, and it created a system that was intended to secure prompt environmental cleanups of releases of hazardous substances into the environment. CERCLA makes a very serious effort to effectuate the polluter-pays principle (PPP)—that is, re-internalizing the costs of environmental harm, by imposing an accounting upon those whose actions caused the harm. Its principal method of doing so is to insist on cleanup of the environment in conjunction with a liability scheme that passes the costs of cleanup on to those responsible for the release of the hazardous material into the environment. In effectuating that scheme, CERCLA incorporates devices that ensure that most sites of contamination will be discovered and, thereafter, orchestrates their cleanup and the eventual shifting of the cost to the responsible parties.

CERCLA embodies a particular implementation strategy, that of remedial cost internalization. CERCLA seeks to remediate contamination and to establish liability for past contamination practices that have ongoing environmental consequences. In reviewing CERCLA's remedial implementation strategy, several rather distinct features immediately stand out: (1) the extent to which traditional norms of tort liability are inadequate to obtain remedial cost internalization, (2) the difficulties in equitably applying the PPP to past occurrences that were not monitored with the PPP in mind, and (3) the whole panoply of powers that must be granted to the administering agency to allow for the development of a coherent implementation strategy. Beyond those implementation-based observations, CERCLA's operation and implementation also provide a most instructive case study of statutory evolution.

One of the key and most well-known statutory mechanisms created by Congress in CERCLA is the Superfund itself. After the amendment and reauthorization of CERCLA in 1986,[1] the Superfund operated as a mechanism to ensure that funding would be available to pay for cleanups at the most seriously contaminated sites. The need for the fund part of a Superfund law, however, may not be immediately obvious. After all, if state common law is inadequate to fix liability on the industries that generate, transport, and dispose of hazardous wastes, a federal law imposing liability on a somewhat broader range of potentially responsible parties would seem to be all that is needed. Under such a law, those responsible for hazardous releases could be ordered to undertake a cleanup and to compensate others damaged by their releases. This latter damage calculation would include any cleanup expenses incurred by third parties or government.

The major reasons for the "fund" component of Superfund are that the responsible parties cannot always be identified—as in the notorious practice of "midnight dumping"—and that responsible parties may be unable to pay the amount of the cleanup costs. The reason that the fund must be "super" is a function of cost. Purging a hazardous waste site of contaminants has typically been a multimillion dollar undertaking.

---

1. Superfund Amendments and Reauthorization Act of 1986 (SARA), Pub. L. No. 99-499, 100 Stat. 1613.

> **But just who is paying today?**
>
> The staggering amounts of money needed for CERCLA cleanups have to come from somewhere, but where? The answer originally was that the polluter-pays-principle was going to be invoked with a vengeance. Consequently, Congress created a Superfund trust fund, established to pay only in those cases where no financially solvent, jointly, or severally liable potentially responsible parties (PRPs) could be identified.
>
> In earlier years, revenues for the Superfund trust fund came from dedicated excise taxes and an environmental corporate income tax. These taxes included: (1) an excise tax of 9.7 cents per barrel on crude oil or oil refined products; (2) an excise tax on imported substances that use one or more of the hazardous chemicals subject to excise tax in their manufacture; and (3) an environmental income tax of 0.12% on the amount of a corporation's modified alternative minimum taxable income that exceeded $2 million. Through these taxes, the chemical industry took a hit beyond its PRP share, and the public at large escaped the cost.
>
> But these taxes expired in 1995, and as a result, the amount of available unobligated money in the fund gradually declined to zero by the end of fiscal year 2003. Ever since, the Superfund trust fund has been supported almost entirely by general funds from the U.S. Treasury. Consequently, it is taxpayers who now foot the bill when polluters do not pay.

The primary statutory mechanisms of CERCLA were succinctly described at the time of its enactment:

> Essentially, CERCLA authorizes governmental responses to actual and threatened releases of a wide range of harmful substances. Parties causing releases of such substances may then be held liable without regard to fault for certain damages resulting from the release, which primarily include government incurred costs for cleanup, removal, and resources restoration. To ensure that such injuries are redressed, the law establishes a [multi-billion dollar] Hazardous Substances Response Fund, financed jointly by industry and the federal government.... When polluters are unknown, or are unable or unwilling to provide recompense, a claim for specified damages may be filed against the fund. Payment of claims by the fund then subrogates the fund to the rights of the claimant.[2]

Focusing on specific remedial provisions, CERCLA's provisions retrace the imminent hazard provisions of RCRA[3] and add provisions that relate to recoupment and allocation of cleanup costs already incurred in response to hazardous waste releases.[4]

Although CERCLA's remedial implementation strategy was designed to force cleanups of contaminated sites, that strategy has not always functioned as intended. Perhaps the best example of CERCLA's unintended consequences concerns sites known as "brownfields"—abandoned, idled, or underutilized industrial or commercial sites suffering from

---

2. Comment, Superfund at Square One: Promising Statutory Framework Requires Forceful EPA Implementation, 11 Envtl. L. Rep. 10101 (1981).

3. See CERCLA §106, codified at 42 U.S.C. §9606.

4. See CERCLA §107, codified at 42 U.S.C. §9607. The 1986 Amendments to §107, while adding some material, did not make major changes in the scope and coverage of §107. Its impact with regard to the liability of "innocent purchasers" of realty that is discovered to be contaminated is significantly affected by the amendments to §101(35), wherein the obligations of purchasers to use due diligence to discover the presence of contaminants are spelled out.

environmental contamination. Fearing the broad liability provisions of CERCLA, many prospective purchasers, developers, and lenders historically chose to avoid brownfields redevelopment altogether, with the result that a number of brownfields sites became major community and taxpayer burdens. Recognizing that CERCLA's remedial implementation strategy unfortunately has contributed to the perpetuation of brownfields rather than their remediation, EPA and the states have developed strategies to work more closely with regulated communities to encourage the redevelopment of brownfields. This shift in focus, towards a more cooperative approach in partnership with the regulated community, signals a more flexible trend in environmental cleanup policies and programs.

A. CERCLA's Liability Rules as Developed Through the Judicial Process of Statutory Interpretation

Congress expended considerable effort filling in the details of the remedial side of CERCLA but also left many areas in need of judicial interpretation and clarification. Consequently, CERCLA, like RCRA, has become one of the most actively litigated statutes in environmental law. Together, supplemented by state common law tort theories studied in prior chapters, they form the legal basis for determining who will bear the costs associated with the release of hazardous materials on land and into groundwater.[5]

1. The Basics of Statutory Remedial Liability for Cleanup of Hazardous Materials

42 U.S.C. §9607.[6] **Liability**

(a) Covered persons; scope; recoverable costs and damages. . . . Notwithstanding any other provision or rule of law, and subject only to the defenses set forth in subsection (b) of this section —
    (1) the owner and operator of a vessel or a facility,
    (2) any person who at the time of disposal of any hazardous substance owned or operated any facility at which such hazardous substances were disposed of,
    (3) any person who by contract, agreement, or otherwise arranged for disposal or treatment, or arranged with a transporter for transport for disposal or treatment, of hazardous substances owned or possessed by such person, by any other party or entity, at any facility or incineration vessel owned or operated by another party or entity and containing such hazardous substances, and
    (4) any person who accepts or accepted any hazardous substances for transport to disposal or treatment facilities, incineration vessels or sites selected by such person, from which there is a release, or a threatened release which causes the incurrence of response costs, of a hazardous substance, shall be liable for —
        (A) all costs of removal or remedial action incurred by the United States Government or a State or an Indian tribe not inconsistent with the national contingency plan;

---

5. The release of hazardous materials into the navigable waters (i.e., surface waters) of the U.S. is governed by the Clean Water Act (CWA), 33 U.S.C. §§1251 et seq.
6. Section 107 in the original Act.

A. CERCLA: Judicial Process Interpretation

(B) any other necessary costs of response incurred by any other person consistent with the national contingency plan;

(C) damages for injury to, destruction of, or loss of natural resources, including the reasonable costs of assessing such injury, destruction, or loss resulting from such a release; and

(D) the costs of any health assessment or health effects study carried out under section 9604(i) of this title. . . .

(b) Defenses . . . There shall be no liability under subsection (a) of this section for a person otherwise liable who can establish by a preponderance of the evidence that the release or threat of release of a hazardous substance and the damages resulting therefrom were caused solely by—

(1) an act of God;

(2) an act of war;

(3) an act or omission of a third party other than an employee or agent of the defendant, or than one whose act or omission occurs in connection with a contractual relationship, existing directly or indirectly, with the defendant (except where the sole contractual arrangement arises from a published tariff and acceptance for carriage by a common carrier by rail), if the defendant establishes by a preponderance of the evidence that (a) he exercised due care with respect to the hazardous substance concerned, taking into consideration the characteristics of such hazardous substance, in light of all relevant facts and circumstances, and (b) he took precautions against foreseeable acts or omissions of any such third party and the consequences that could foreseeably result from such acts or omissions; or

(4) any combination of the foregoing paragraphs. . . .

(5) Actions involving natural resources; maintenance, scope, etc . . . (1) Natural resources liability—In the case of an injury to, destruction of, or loss of natural resources under subparagraph (C) of subsection (a) of this section liability shall be to the United States Government and to any State for natural resources within the State or belonging to, managed by, controlled by, or appertaining to such State and to any Indian tribe for natural resources belonging to, managed by, controlled by, or appertaining such tribe . . . .

A review of CERCLA's definition sections demonstrates that the universe of conduct that might fall within §107 is quite broad and does not explicitly describe the standards of liability that define what conduct is actionable and what is not. This void has been largely filled by the courts. The following excerpt provides a roadmap to some of the early rulings that started to define the operation of CERCLA.

David A. Rich, Personal Liability for Hazardous Waste Cleanup: An Examination of CERCLA §107

13 B.C. Envtl. Aff. L. Rev. 643, 653-658 (1986)

Section 107 of CERCLA designates certain parties who may be liable for the cleanup costs of a hazardous waste site. Section 107 imposes liability for cleanup costs and damage to natural resources[7] on: (1) past and present owners and operators of hazardous waste facilities; (2) persons who arrange for disposal of hazardous substances to facilities (usually

---

[7]. "Natural resources" under CERCLA means "fish, wildlife, biota, air, water, groundwater, drinking water supplies, and other such resources belonging to, managed by, held in trust by, appertaining to, or otherwise controlled by the United States—any state or local government, or any foreign government." 42 U.S.C. §9601(16).

generators); and (3) persons who transport hazardous substances to facilities from which there is a release or a threatened release of toxic chemicals that results in response costs. These responsible parties are liable for three types of costs incurred as a result of a release or a threatened release of hazardous waste: (1) governmental response costs (costs incurred by the federal government to clean up hazardous waste sites); (2) private response costs (costs incurred by other parties consistent with the National Contingency Plan), and (3) damages to natural resources.

Section 107 provides limited defenses. Parties otherwise liable under §107 may escape liability if they can establish that the release or threat of release of hazardous substances and resulting damages were caused by an act of God, an act of war, or an act or omission of a third party other than an employee or agent of the defendants, or one whose act or omission occurs in connection with a contractual relationship with the defendants. The third party exception applies only if defendants both exercised due care with respect to the hazardous substance, and took necessary precautions against acts or omissions by the third party.

STRICT LIABILITY . . . In spite of the comprehensive nature of its hazardous waste cleanup provisions, CERCLA's standards of liability are vague. Congress removed references to strict liability and joint and several liability before the bill's final passage, leaving these matters for judicial interpretation.

The standard of liability under CERCLA is strict liability. Although it does not specifically mention strict liability, §101, CERCLA's definitional section, states that liability under CERCLA "shall be construed to be the standard of liability which obtains under §311 of the Federal Water Pollution Control Act." Although §311 of the Federal Water Pollution Control Act (FWCPA) [which was passed to impose liability on owners and operators of vessels or facilities causing spills of oil or hazardous substances on navigable waters, which required owners and operators to pay the government's response costs, and which established a fund for EPA and the Coast Guard to respond to such spills] does not explicitly mention strict liability, courts have inferred such liability from the language of that Act, which subjects certain parties to liability unless they can successfully assert one of the limited defenses specified. Congress' reference to FWCPA §311 in CERCLA is logical, because the same defenses to liability found in FWCPA §311 also appear in §107 of CERCLA. Courts construing CERCLA have therefore held parties strictly liable for statutory violations.

JOINT AND SEVERAL LIABILITY . . . Congress also deleted references to joint and several liability from the final version of CERCLA. The original Senate proposal specifically imposed joint and several liability, but this language was deleted from the final version of the bill as part of the "hastily drawn compromise which resulted in the enactment of CERCLA." Federal courts construing liability under CERCLA, however, uniformly have held that CERCLA permits, but does not mandate, joint and several liability. It is therefore within the discretion of the court to impose joint and several liability. Furthermore, some courts have held that joint and several liability should be imposed under CERCLA, unless the defendants can establish that a reasonable basis exists for apportioning the harm against them.[8]

---

8. *United States v. Northeastern Pharm. & Chem. Co.* (NEPACCO), 579 F. Supp. 823, 844 (W.D. Mo. 1984).

A. CERCLA: Judicial Process Interpretation

FIGURE 16-1. *An EPA aerial survey photograph of a New England toxic waste storage site. Many drums at this and similar sites are unmarked and leaking; some of the semi-trailers are filled with materials too unstable to be unloaded; site owners lack the resources required to maintain storage integrity or to clean up toxic contamination on the site.*

CERCLA's standard of strict liability, coupled with the possibility of joint and several liability, places a heavy burden on defendants. CERCLA does, however, place some constraints on the amount of liability that courts may impose under §107. Section 107 liability is premised upon a governmental response pursuant to §104 and the National Contingency Plan, or a response by another party in accordance with the National Contingency Plan. Both §104 and the National Contingency Plan impose practical limitations on the extent and cost of hazardous waste cleanup operations . . . .

The National Contingency Plan establishes procedures and standards for responding to releases of hazardous substances, pollutants, and contaminants. These procedures include methods for discovering and investigating hazardous substance disposal facilities, for determining the appropriate extent of removal of the substances, for assuring that remedial actions are cost-effective, and for determining priorities among releases or threatened releases. The statute and the National Contingency Plan thus limit the extent of liability under CERCLA §107.

PERSONAL LIABILITY UNDER CERCLA §107 . . . As discussed earlier, CERCLA imposes liability on: (1) past and present owners and operators of hazardous waste facilities; (2) persons who arrange for the transport of hazardous waste; and (3) persons who transport hazardous waste. These parties include individuals as well as corporations. The federal government has sought to hold both corporations and their corporate officers and employees responsible for the costs of hazardous waste cleanup under CERCLA. Although individual defendants have argued that their actions were the actions of the corporation, thereby shielding them from liability under the doctrine of limited liability, this argument has not succeeded. The few district courts to consider this issue have uniformly held that the corporate form does not shield individuals from personal liability where such individuals have exercised personal control over, or have actually been involved in, the disposal of hazardous waste.

COMMENTARY & QUESTIONS

1. A common law substitute for Superfund? What does CERCLA §107 accomplish that the common law could not?[9] The common law can do some of the things that §107 provides. It is quite possible that a common law court would be willing to hold defendants who release hazardous materials into the environment strictly, jointly, and severally liable even in the absence of a statute allowing it. Perhaps the common law might also adopt a relaxed standard of proof of causation similar to that of CERCLA in cases involving concurrent actions of multiple tortfeasors. (In the CERCLA cases, however, the furtherance of legislative policy is a key element underlying judicial willingness to relax traditional tort law standards of proof.) Going further, §107 allows for remedies that would be very difficult to fashion under the common law. The damage assessment of §107(a)(4)(A) is not a traditional damage measure — it assesses the actual costs of environmental remediation (i.e., response costs), not the amount of plaintiffs' loss. Compare, for example, the award of damages paid in *Boomer*. By providing damages for natural resources, §107(a)(4)(C) also moves a step

---

9. CERCLA as a whole does many things that are far beyond the realm of common law possibility. Most obviously, its creation of a national fund from which cleanup expenses can be paid is a mechanism that the common law does not provide. Similarly, the creation of a National Priorities List that identifies and ranks sites as to the need for cleanup action is unthinkable without the intervention of a public law mandate.

A. CERCLA: Judicial Process Interpretation

beyond traditional tort law, and §107(a)(4)(D) identifies health studies as an item of recoverable damage, hardly a regular feature of damage awards under the common law.

2. Joint and several liability in CERCLA cases. Joint and several liability is the concept (imported from common law) that makes CERCLA so strategically potent. Courts uniformly interpret CERCLA as manifesting an intent on the part of Congress to allow joint and several liability among potentially responsible parties (PRPs). The consequence of imposing joint and several liability is potentially to shift the entire burden of cleanup onto any identifiable PRP. Although CERCLA imposes a strict liability standard, does it mandate "joint and several" liability in every case? Or did Congress intend that the scope of liability be determined from traditional and evolving principles based on the common law?

In the early years after the passage of CERCLA, there was, for the most part, an unrelenting stream of decisions by the federal district courts imposing strict joint and several liability on PRPs. But starting with Chief Judge Carl Rubin of the United States District Court for the Southern District of Ohio, the lower federal courts began to question whether, in light of CERCLA's history, CERCLA necessarily required "joint and several" liability in each case. See, e.g., *United States v. Chem-Dyne Corp.*, 572 F. Supp. 802 (S.D. Ohio 1983). The approach originated by Judge Rubin in *Chem-Dyne* was later followed by a number of federal courts of appeal. See, e.g., *In re Bell Petroleum Services, Inc.*, 3 F.3d 889, 901-902 (5th Cir. 1993); *United States v. Alcan Aluminum Corp.*, 964 F.2d 252, 268 (3d Cir. 1992); *O'Neil v. Picillo*, 883 F.2d 176, 178 (1st Cir. 1989); *United States v. Monsanto Co.*, 858 F.2d 160, 171-173 (4th Cir. 1988).

United States v. Monsanto, 858 F.2d 160 (4th Cir. 1988) is illustrative. In that case, the Fourth Circuit held that site-owners and generator defendants were jointly and severally liable under §107(a) of CERCLA for the response costs expended by the United States and by South Carolina in removing hazardous wastes from a disposal facility. As to the site-owners' liability, the court found sufficient that they owned the site at the time that the hazardous substances were deposited there. As to the generator defendants' liability, the court found them liable because it was undisputed that (1) they shipped hazardous substances to the facility, (2) hazardous substances "like" those present in the generation defendants' waste were found at the facility, and (3) there had been a release of hazardous substances at the site.

Turning next to the issue of apportionment of liability, the Fourth Circuit concluded that CERCLA permits the imposition of joint and several liability in cases of indivisible harm. The court clarified the applicable legal principles by referencing the common law:

> Under common law rules, when two or more persons act independently to cause a single harm for which there is a reasonable basis of apportionment according to the contribution of each, each is held liable only for the portion of harm that he causes. When such persons cause a single and indivisible harm, however, they are held liable jointly and severally for the entire harm. We think these principles, as reflected in the Restatement (Second) of Torts, represent the correct and uniform federal rules applicable to CERCLA cases. 858 F.2d at 171-172.

Applying these principles, the Fourth Circuit rejected the generator defendants' argument that there was a reasonable basis for apportioning the harm. In particular, the court found that the generator defendants presented no evidence showing a relationship between waste volume, the release of hazardous substances, and the harm at the site. Because hazardous substances at the site were commingled, there could be no reasonable apportionment "without some evidence disclosing the individual and interactive qualities of the substances deposited there. Common sense counsels that a million gallons of certain substances could be mixed together without significant consequences, whereas a few pints of others improperly mixed could result in disastrous consequences." 858 F.2d at 172. Because volumetric allocation could not establish the effective contribution of each waste generator to the harm at the site, the court affirmed the imposition of joint and several liability.

3. The unfairness of joint and several liability. Is it patently unfair to make a deep-pocket responsible party, such as Monsanto, liable for an entire cleanup when it is demonstrable that it is but one of several causes of the problem? Is it fair to tap the assets of only one of the responsible parties for the entire cost of the cleanup? The Fourth Circuit in its *Monsanto* decision rationalized the initial imposition of potentially unfair allocations in reliance on the later ability of the unfairly burdened party to reallocate some part of the loss by obtaining contribution from fellow joint tortfeasors. Specifically, the court concluded that "the defendants still have the right to sue responsible parties for contribution, and in that action they may assert both legal and equitable theories of cost allocation." 858 F.2d at 173. Although the topic of contribution is considered at length later in this chapter, can you predict why it may prove difficult for parties who pay more than their fair share in a government cleanup action to recover an appropriate amount via contribution?

4. Divisibility of harm or of costs? In cases like *Monsanto*, the indivisibility of the environmental harm is the predicate for application of joint and several liability. In *United States v. Kramer*, 757 F. Supp. 397 (D.N.J. 1991), the generator defendants at a landfill site argued as a defense that the bulk of the anticipated $60 million cleanup cost was attributable to the quantitatively large volume of municipal solid waste and sludge deposited at the site. More narrowly, the nonmunicipal generator defendants sought to limit their liability to an amount that could be calculated arithmetically as the difference between the cleanup cost with, and without, their waste being present at the site. Why might this approach prove less costly to the nonmunicipal defendants?

Given the limited ability of municipalities to raise large sums of money, an apportionment that left the lion's share of the liability with the municipalities posed a collectability problem for EPA. Historically, EPA limited its efforts to recover a "fair" share from municipalities at sites where other PRPs can be identified and pursued. See EPA's 1989 Interim Policy on CERCLA Settlements Involving Municipalities and Municipal Wastes, 54 Fed. Reg. 51,071 (Dec. 12, 1989) (and see the supplemental EPA guidance, reprinted at 28 BNA Env't Rep. 2136 (1998)). As an example, at the Kramer site, EPA did not name the municipalities as defendants in its original complaint, but they remained vulnerable to contribution claims from the named defendants. The federal courts, however, have consistently ruled that municipalities, which unlike the states are not protected by the Eleventh Amendment, may be liable as owners, operators, transporters, and generators of hazardous waste. See Manko & Cozine, The Battle over Municipal Liability under CERCLA Heats Up: An Analysis of Proposed Congressional Amendments to Superfund, 5 Vill. Envtl. L.J. 23 (1994).

2. Apportionment in CERCLA Actions

As noted above, the federal appellate courts have repeatedly recognized that, in deciding whether to impose joint and several liability or to divide "the harm" in CERCLA cases among PRPs, the starting point is the Restatement (Second) of Torts.

Thus, under the Restatement, apportionment is proper when "there is a reasonable basis for determining the contribution of each cause to a single harm." Restatement (Second) of Torts §433A(1)(b), at 434 (1965).

> **Under the Restatement (Second) of Torts:**
>
> When two or more persons acting independently caus[e] a distinct or single harm for which there is a reasonable basis for division according to the contribution of each, each is subject to liability only for the portion of the total harm

A. CERCLA: Judicial Process Interpretation

But when are harms capable of apportionment? And when will the courts allow apportionment, if each PRP is charged with responsibility for the entire harm? And do CERCLA defendants have the burden to prove that a reasonable basis for apportionment exists? And, if so, what type of evidence will satisfy that burden of proof?

The legal debate over the nature, extent, and degree of proof necessary to establish joint and several liability in CERCLA cases has continued to percolate in the federal courts. But in an 8-1 decision rendered on May 4, 2009, the U.S. Supreme Court addressed, and clarified, the interpretation and application of the joint and several liability provisions of CERCLA, in the decision which follows.

> that he has himself caused. Restatement (Second) of Torts, §§433A, 881 (1967); Prosser, Law of Torts, pp. 313-314 (4th ed. 1971) . . . . But where two or more persons cause a single and indivisible harm, each is subject to liability for the entire harm. Restatement (Second) of Torts, §875; Prosser, at 315-316. *Chem-Dyne Corp.*, 572 F. Supp. at 810.

Burlington Northern and Santa Fe Railway Co. v. United States
129 S. Ct. 1870 (2009)

[The facts giving rise to this controversy began in 1960. At that time, Brown & Bryant, Inc. (B&B), a chemical distributor, began operating a chemical distribution facility on a parcel (the original Arvin site) next to land owned by predecessors to the Burlington Northern & Santa Fe and the Union Pacific railroads (the Railroads). In 1975, B&B leased part of the Railroads' property to expand its operations. B&B distributed chemicals which were also classified as hazardous substances: dinoseb, D-D, and Nemagon, the latter two of which were manufactured by Shell. In the 1960s, Shell required its distributors to use bulk distribution for D-D. Shell sent the chemicals to B&B by common carrier, with the shipping term "free on board destination." During the transfer from the common carrier to B&B's bulk operation, leaks and spills could—and often did—occur. Aware that spills of D-D were commonplace among its distributors, Shell took several steps to encourage safe handling of its products, including site inspections and a program that provided discounts for safety improvements.

Over the course of B&B's operations, dinoseb, D-D and Nemagon were allowed to seep into the soil and upper levels of groundwater at the B&B facility. California's Department of Toxic Substances Control (DTSC) and U.S. EPA both investigated the site. B&B undertook some efforts at remediation, but it became insolvent in 1989. The facility was added to the National Priorities List and U.S. EPA issued an administrative order forcing the Railroads, as the landlord of a portion of the B&B facility, to undertake certain remedial tasks at the facility. Two CERCLA actions ensued: the Railroads sought cost recovery from B&B; and U.S. EPA and DTSC sought cost recovery from the Railroads and Shell, who, the agencies contended, "arranged" to dispose of hazardous substances at the B&B facility. Shell, in response, argued (and the Supreme Court in its opinion agreed, as discussed later in this chapter) that Shell was not an "arranger," as defined in CERCLA, 42 U.S.C. §9607(a)(3), but instead was the seller of a useful product that B&B mishandled. In the excerpt from the Supreme Court's opinion below, the Court addresses whether the Railroads were jointly and severally liable for the full cost of the Government's response efforts.]

STEVENS, J. In 1980, Congress enacted the Comprehensive Environmental Response, Compensation, and Liability Act (CERCLA), 94 Stat. 2767, as amended, 42 U.S.C. §§9601-9675, in response to the serious environmental and health risks posed by industrial pollution. See *United States v. Bestfoods*, 524 U.S. 51, 55, 118 S. Ct. 1876, 141 L. Ed. 2d 43 (1998). The Act was designed to promote the "'timely cleanup of hazardous waste sites'" and to ensure that the costs of such cleanup efforts were borne by those responsible for the contamination. *Consolidated Edison Co. of N.Y. v. UGI Util., Inc.*, 423 F.3d 90, 94 (C.A.2 2005); see also *Meghrig v. KFC Western, Inc.*, 516 U.S. 479, 483, 116 S. Ct. 1251, 134 L. Ed. 2d 121 (1996); *Dedham Water Co. v. Cumberland Farms Dairy, Inc.*, 805 F.2d 1074, 1081 (C.A.1 1986). These cases raise the questions whether and to what extent a party associated with a contaminated site may be held responsible for the full costs of remediation. . . .

Not all harms are capable of apportionment . . . and CERCLA defendants seeking to avoid joint and several liability bear the burden of proving that a reasonable basis for apportionment exists. See *Chem-Dyne Corp.*, 572 F. Supp., at 810 (citing Restatement (Second) of Torts §433B (1976)) (placing burden of proof on party seeking apportionment). When two or more causes produce a single, indivisible harm, "courts have refused to make an arbitrary apportionment for its own sake, and each of the causes is charged with responsibility for the entire harm." Restatement (Second) of Torts §433A, Comment *i*, p. 440 (1963-1964).

Neither the parties nor the lower courts dispute the principles that govern apportionment in CERCLA cases, and both the District Court and Court of Appeals agreed that the harm created by the contamination of the Arvin site, although singular, was theoretically capable of apportionment. The question then is whether the record provided a reasonable basis for the District Court's conclusion that the Railroads were liable for only 9% of the harm caused by contamination at the Arvin facility.

The District Court criticized the Railroads for taking a "'scorched earth,' all-or-nothing approach to liability," failing to acknowledge any responsibility for the release of hazardous substances that occurred on their parcel throughout the 13-year period of B & B's lease. According to the District Court, the Railroads' position on liability, combined with the Governments' refusal to acknowledge the potential divisibility of the harm, complicated the apportioning of liability. . . . Yet despite the parties' failure to assist the court in linking the evidence supporting apportionment to the proper allocation of liability, the District Court ultimately concluded that this was "a classic 'divisible in terms of degree' case, both as to the time period in which defendants' conduct occurred, and ownership existed, and as to the estimated maximum contribution of each party's activities that released hazardous substances that caused Site contamination." *Id.*, at 239a. Consequently, the District Court apportioned liability, assigning the Railroads 9% of the total remediation costs.

The District Court calculated the Railroads' liability based on three figures. First, the court noted that the Railroad parcel constituted only 19% of the surface area of the Arvin site. Second, the court observed that the Railroads had leased their parcel to B & B for 13 years, which was only 45% of the time B & B operated the Arvin facility. Finally, the court found that the volume of hazardous-substance-releasing activities on the B & B property was at least 10 times greater than the releases that occurred on the Railroad parcel, and it concluded that only spills of two chemicals, Nemagon and dinoseb (not D-D), substantially contributed to the contamination that had originated on the Railroad parcel and that those two chemicals had contributed to two-thirds of the overall site contamination requiring remediation. The court then multiplied .19 by .45 by .66 (two-thirds) and rounded up to determine that the Railroads were responsible for approximately 6% of the remediation costs. "Allowing for calculation errors up to 50%," the court concluded that the Railroads could be held responsible for 9% of the total CERCLA response cost for the Arvin site. . . . .

The Court of Appeals criticized the evidence on which the District Court's conclusions rested, finding a lack of sufficient data to establish the precise proportion of contamination that occurred on the relative portions of the Arvin facility and the rate of contamination

A. CERCLA: Judicial Process Interpretation

in the years prior to B & B's addition of the Railroad parcel. The court noted that neither the duration of the lease nor the size of the leased area alone was a reliable measure of the harm caused by activities on the property owned by the Railroads, and-as the court's upward adjustment confirmed-the court had relied on estimates rather than specific and detailed records as a basis for its conclusions.

Despite these criticisms, we conclude that the facts contained in the record reasonably supported the apportionment of liability. The District Court's detailed findings make it abundantly clear that the primary pollution at the Arvin facility was contained in an unlined sump and an unlined pond in the southeastern portion of the facility most distant from the Railroads' parcel and that the spills of hazardous chemicals that occurred on the Railroad parcel contributed to no more than 10% of the total site contamination . . . some of which did not require remediation. With those background facts in mind, we are persuaded that it was reasonable for the court to use the size of the leased parcel and the duration of the lease as the starting point for its analysis. Although the Court of Appeals faulted the District Court for relying on the "simplest of considerations: percentages of land area, time of ownership, and types of hazardous products," 520 F.3d, at 943, these were the same factors the court had earlier acknowledged were *relevant* to the apportionment analysis. See *id.*, at 936, n. 18 ("We of course agree with our sister circuits that, if adequate information is available, divisibility may be established by 'volumetric, chronological, or other types of evidence,' including appropriate geographic considerations" (citations omitted)).

The Court of Appeals also criticized the District Court's assumption that spills of Nemagon and dinoseb were responsible for only two-thirds of the chemical spills requiring remediation, observing that each PRP's share of the total harm was not necessarily equal to the quantity of pollutants that were deposited on its portion of the total facility. Although the evidence adduced by the parties did not allow the court to calculate precisely the amount of hazardous chemicals contributed by the Railroad parcel to the total site contamination or the exact percentage of harm caused by each chemical, the evidence did show that fewer spills occurred on the Railroad parcel and that of those spills that occurred, not all were carried across the Railroad parcel to the B & B sump and pond from which most of the contamination originated. The fact that no D-D spills on the Railroad parcel required remediation lends strength to the District Court's conclusion that the Railroad parcel contributed only Nemagon and dinoseb in quantities requiring remediation.

The District Court's conclusion that those two chemicals accounted for only two-thirds of the contamination requiring remediation finds less support in the record; however, any miscalculation on that point is harmless in light of the District Court's ultimate allocation of liability, which included a 50% margin of error equal to the 3% reduction in liability the District Court provided based on its assessment of the effect of the Nemagon and dinoseb spills. Had the District Court limited its apportionment calculations to the amount of time the Railroad parcel was in use and the percentage of the facility located on that parcel, it would have assigned the Railroads 9% of the response cost. By including a two-thirds reduction in liability for the Nemagon and dinoseb with a 50% "margin of error," the District Court reached the same result. Because the District Court's ultimate allocation of liability is supported by the evidence and comports with the apportionment principles outlined above, we reverse the Court of Appeals' conclusion that the Railroads are subject to joint and several liability for all response costs arising out of the contamination of the Arvin facility.

For the foregoing reasons . . . we conclude that the District Court reasonably apportioned the Railroads' share of the site remediation costs at 9%. The judgment is reversed, and the cases are remanded for further proceedings consistent with this opinion.

COMMENTARY & QUESTIONS

1. Arguments for apportionment. By addressing the issue of whether Superfund liability is joint and several where a "reasonable" basis for apportionment exists, does the Supreme Court's ruling now provide virtually all potentially responsible parties with a basis to argue that they are entitled to an apportioned amount of liability in Superfund cases?

The district court found that the trial evidence demonstrated that the harm was capable of apportionment and, based on that evidence, allocated the Railroads a 9% overall share and Shell a 6% overall share of the governments' cleanup cost (a determination that the Supreme Court later reversed as to Shell on the grounds that Shell was not liable as an "arranger" under CERCLA), leaving 85% of the government's costs unreimbursed. While it agreed with the government that the defendants' burden to show an appropriate basis for apportionment "is heavy," and that "[t]he evidence supporting divisibility must be concrete and specific," the district court concluded that defendants had met that burden. The apportionment showing was based on years of ownership, the relative amount of property owned, and the estimated maximum contribution of the contaminants released by each party. After reviewing the evidence, the district court apportioned the Railroads' share of liability by multiplying the percentage of the overall land owned by the Railroads (19.1%), the percentage of time the Railroads leased land to B&B during its operations (45%), and the percentage of overall site contamination attributable to the two chemicals that had contaminated the Railroad's land (66%), generating an initial allocation of 6% for the Railroads. Then, allowing for "errors in calculation," the district court applied a 50% premium to that figure, and came up with a 9% overall share for the Railroads. A similar type of analysis was used to come up with Shell's 6% share. What was the basis for the 50% premium? Was the use of the 50% premium within the sound discretion of the district court?

2. Apportionment and administrative orders. CERCLA §106 and RCRA §7003 both grant EPA power to issue orders requiring cleanups that address imminent threats to health and the environment caused by the release of hazardous substances into the environment. These sections complement CERCLA §107, by providing additional remedial options for the EPA. If the Supreme Court's decision allows PRPs to seek apportionment of an amount which, in their view, is closer to their "fair share," will that possibility incentivize PRPs to refuse to settle allocation issues? Will the lowering of the bar for avoiding joint and several liability provide arrangers and landowners with a strong argument to minimize liability in negotiations and litigation with the government? For example, will PRPs refuse to comply with administrative orders, in order to focus the EPA earlier in the process on what constitutes a fair apportionment? Or do the risks of defying administrative orders still remain too great? The extraordinary nature of administrative orders is addressed later in this chapter.

3. The role of orphan shares. Consider the role of orphan shares in apportioning liability. The United States argued that, if the Railroads effectively won by limiting their liability to only 9% of the cleanup costs, that result would leave the federal government with responsibility for the great majority of the costs—the orphan share—because the primary liable party (B&B) was bankrupt. Does the Supreme Court's decision implicitly reject the federal government's argument that it would be unfair to hold the United States liable for the orphan share? If so, will the United States have added incentive to design

A. CERCLA: Judicial Process Interpretation

and implement more cost-effective remedies, in order to mitigate its own potential liability exposure? Will lower remedial costs lead to faster settlements?

4. Voluntary cleanups. Will voluntary cleanups now pose more of a risk? If it will be more difficult for PRPs to recover any orphan share they pay up front, will that create a disincentive to settle liability issues early?

3. The Government's Relaxed Burden of Proof of Causation in CERCLA Cases

The material in earlier chapters on toxic tort litigation emphasized the difficulty that plaintiffs encounter in proving that the defendant's activities are the cause in fact of plaintiffs' injuries. Even in a strict liability regime, that same difficulty could scuttle much of CERCLA's effectiveness if the government in every case had to trace each facet of cleanup costs to the actions of a particular PRP. Tracking the actions of a particular PRP in older sites or midnight dumping sites is especially problematic, where the records of what wastes were deposited by whom are sketchy or nonexistent. The courts began to confront this problem within the first years following CERCLA's enactment.

United States v. Wade (*Wade II*)
577 F. Supp. 1326 (U.S. Dist. Ct., E.D. Pa., 1983)

[The *Wade* litigation involved a large disposal site in Chester, Pennsylvania. The site was an extraordinarily high-visibility one, having been the scene of a major fire in 1978 that damaged many of the several thousand tank cars and drums stored on the property. After testing discovered the presence of more than 50 hazardous substances at the site, many of which were leaking into the groundwater and from there into the Delaware River, legal action was instituted.

The Wade site was among the first sites for which the U.S. EPA sought remedies under RCRA and CERCLA. The litigation began in 1979 with the filing of a RCRA §7003 complaint. Shortly after the enactment of CERCLA in 1980, an amended complaint added counts under CERCLA §106 and §107. The United States sought both injunctive relief as to the cleanup of the site and monetary relief for the response costs incurred by the government and others who had already undertaken steps to begin to seal the site and remove additional wastes still stored there. The parties sued by the United States included the site's owner (Wade), several off-site generators, and some of the transporters who had deposited materials at the site. Earlier litigation had focused on the scope and retroactivity of the major statutes; the excerpted portion of this decision addresses only the issue of proof of causation.]

NEWCOMER, J. This is a civil action brought by the United States against several parties allegedly responsible for the creation of a hazardous waste dump in Chester, Pennsylvania. The government seeks injunctive relief against Melvin R. Wade, the owner of the dump site, ABM Disposal Service, the company which transported the hazardous substances to the site, and Ellis Barnhouse and Franklin P. Tyson, the owners of ABM during the time period at issue ("non-generator defendants"). The government also seeks reimbursement of the costs incurred and to be incurred in cleaning up the site from the non-generator defendants as well as from Apollo Metals, Inc., Congoleum Corporation, Gould, Inc., and Sandvik, Inc. ("generator defendants").

The claims for injunctive relief are brought pursuant to §7003 of the Resource Conservation and Recovery Act of 1976 ("RCRA"), 42 U.S.C. §6973, and §106 of CERCLA, 42 U.S.C. §9606. The claims for monetary relief are based on §107(a) of CERCLA, 42 U.S.C. §9607(a), as well as a common law theory of restitution. Presently before the Court are the government's motions for partial summary judgment on the issue of joint and several liability under §107(a) against each of the defendants. . . .

The generator defendants' motions for summary judgment on the CERCLA claims generally advance two arguments. First, they argue that the government has not and cannot establish the requisite causal relationship between their wastes and the costs incurred by the government in cleaning up the site. . . .

THE CAUSATION ARGUMENT . . . Even assuming the government proves that a given defendant's waste was in fact disposed of at the Wade site, the generator defendants argue it must also prove that a particular defendant's actual waste is presently at the site and has been the subject of a removal or remedial measure before that defendant can be held liable. In the alternative, the generator defendants argue that at a minimum the government must link its costs incurred to waste of the sort created by a generator before that generator may be held liable. . . .

Part of the generator defendants' argument revolves around the use of the word "such" in referring to the "hazardous substances" [in CERCLA §107(a)(3)] contained at the dump site or "facility." It could be read to require that the facility contain a particular defendant's waste. On the other hand it could be read merely to require that hazardous substances like those found in a defendant's waste must be present at the site. The legislative history provides no enlightenment on this point. I believe that the less stringent requirement was the one intended by Congress.

The government's experts have admitted that scientific technique has not advanced to a point that the identity of the generator of a specific quantity of waste can be stated with certainty. All that can be said is that a site contains the same kind of hazardous substances as are found in a generator's waste. Thus, to require a plaintiff under CERCLA to "fingerprint" wastes is to eviscerate the statute. Given two possible constructions of a statute, one which renders it useless should be rejected. Generators are adequately protected by requiring a plaintiff to prove that a defendant's waste was disposed of at a site and that the substances that make the defendant's waste hazardous are also present at the site. . . .

I turn now to the generator defendants' contention that the government must link its costs incurred to wastes of the sort created by them.

A reading of the literal language of the statute suggests that the generator defendants read too much into this portion of its causation requirement. Stripping away the excess language, the statute appears to impose liability on a generator who has (1) disposed of its hazardous substances (2) at a facility which now contains hazardous substances of the sort disposed of by the generator (3) if there is a release of that or some other type of hazardous substance (4) which causes the incurrence of response costs. Thus, the release which results in the incurrence of response costs and liability need only be of "a" hazardous substance [the language of CERCLA §107(a)(4)] and not necessarily one contained in the defendant's waste. The only required nexus between the defendant and the site is that the defendant has dumped his waste there and that the hazardous substances found in the defendant's waste are also found at the site. I base my disagreement with defendants' reading in part on the Act's use of "such" to modify "hazardous substance" in paragraph three and the switch to "a" in paragraph four. . . .

A. CERCLA: Judicial Process Interpretation

Deletion of the causation language contained in the House-passed bill and the Senate draft is not dispositive of the causation issue. Nevertheless, the substitution of the present language for the prior causation requirement evidences a legislative intent which is in accordance with my reading of the Act.

COMMENTARY & QUESTION

Comparison to toxic tort cases. How does the relaxation of the government's burdens in proving causation in CERCLA cases compare with the handling of burden of proof issues in traditional and toxic tort cases that were studied in earlier chapters?

4. The Individual Liability of Managerial Officers

The focus of the Rich excerpt is personal individual liability for §107 recoveries. The typical cases in which this issue arises are those in which a hazardous waste generator, transporter, or disposer is a corporation, and a §107 action seeks to hold individual corporate officers or employees liable (for fiscal or punitive reasons). Their classic defense is to argue limited liability for corporate acts, the protective doctrine that provides such an important incentive to corporate entrepreneurialism. But courts increasingly have allowed application of individual personal liability for corporate officers under CERCLA and other statutes. Analytically the cases fall into three categories.

The first category, occurring most often in small, closely held corporations, involves piercing the corporate veil when corporate structure stands as an impediment to reaching the assets of individuals who have directly profited from the corporation's activities, even though they may not have been personally involved in day-to-day operations. These cases require the sorts of rigorous showings that are required in non-CERCLA veil-piercing cases.

The second category of cases involves officers held liable for their own wrongful personal actions, as, for example, where they themselves personally dumped toxics or directly ordered the illegal act. This is perhaps the simplest predicate for individual liability, based on the combination of §107(a) (which sets out the categories of "persons" who can be responsible parties) and §101(2) (which defines "person" to include an individual).

The third category of cases involves individuals held liable because of their role as managerial officers, responsible for directing the corporate activity with respect to which violations occurred.

Several of these liability theories are explored further in the criminal law materials in Chapter 19, and in the following case arising under CERCLA and RCRA.

United States v. Northeastern Pharmaceutical & Chemical Co. (NEPACCO)

810 F.2d 726 (8th Cir. 1986), cert. denied, 484 U.S. 848 (1988)

MCMILLIAN, J. Northeastern Pharmaceutical & Chemical Co. (NEPACCO), Edwin Michaels, and John W. Lee appeal from a final judgment entered in the District Court for the Western District of Missouri finding them and Ronald Mills jointly and severally liable for response costs incurred by the government after December 11, 1980, and all future response costs relative to the cleanup of the Denney farm site that are not inconsistent with the national contingency plan (NCP) pursuant to §§104 and 107 of the Comprehensive Environmental Response, Compensation, and Liability Act of 1980 (CERCLA), 42 U.S.C. §§9604, 9607. . . .

The following statement of facts is taken in large part from the district court's excellent memorandum opinion, 579 F. Supp. 823 (W.D. Mo. 1984). NEPACCO was incorporated in 1966. . . . Although NEPACCO's corporate charter was forfeited in 1976 for failure to maintain an agent for service of process, NEPACCO did not file a certificate of voluntary dissolution with the secretary of state of Delaware. In 1974 its corporate assets were liquidated, and the proceeds were used to pay corporate debts and then distributed to the shareholders. Michaels [had] formed NEPACCO, was a major shareholder, and was its president. Lee was NEPACCO's vice-president, the supervisor of its manufacturing plant located in Verona, Missouri, and also a shareholder. Mills was employed as shift supervisor at NEPACCO's Verona plant.

From April 1970 to January 1972, NEPACCO manufactured the disinfectant hexachlorophene at its Verona plant. NEPACCO leased the plant from Syntex Agribusiness, Inc. (Syntex). . . . Michaels and Lee knew that NEPACCO's manufacturing process produced various hazardous and toxic byproducts, including 2,4,5-trichlorophenol (TCP), 2,3,7,8-tetra-chlorodibenzo-p-dioxin (TCDD or dioxin), and toluene. The waste byproducts were pumped into a holding tank which was periodically emptied by waste haulers. Occasionally, however, excess waste byproducts were sealed in 55-gallon drums and then stored at the plant.

In July 1971 Mills approached NEPACCO plant manager Bill Ray with a proposal to dispose of the waste-filled 55-gallon drums on a farm owned by James Denney located about seven miles south of Verona. Ray visited the Denney farm and discussed the proposal with Lee; Lee approved the use of Mills' services and the Denney farm as a disposal site. In mid-July 1971 Mills and Gerald Lechner dumped approximately 85 of the 55-gallon drums into a large trench on the Denney farm (Denney farm site) that had been excavated by Leon Vaughn. Vaughn then filled in the trench. Only NEPACCO drums were disposed of at the Denney farm site.

In October 1979 the Environmental Protection Agency (EPA) received an anonymous tip that hazardous wastes had been disposed of at the Denney farm. Subsequent EPA investigation confirmed that hazardous wastes had in fact been disposed of at the Denney farm and that the site was not geologically suitable for the disposal of hazardous wastes. Between January and April 1980 the EPA prepared a plan for the cleanup of the Denney farm site and constructed an access road and a security fence. During April 1980 the EPA conducted an on-site investigation, exposed and sampled 13 of the 55-gallon drums, which were found to be badly deteriorated, and took water and soil samples. The samples were found to contain "alarmingly" high concentrations of dioxin, TCP and toluene.

In July 1980 the EPA installed a temporary cap over the trench to prevent the run-off of surface water and to minimize contamination of the surrounding soil and groundwater. . . . The 55-gallon drums are now stored [utilizing] a specially constructed concrete bunker on the Denney farm. The drums as stored do not present an imminent and substantial endangerment to health or the environment; however, no plan for permanent disposal has been developed, and the site will continue to require testing and monitoring in the future.

In August 1980 the government filed its initial complaint against NEPACCO, the generator of the hazardous substances; Michaels and Lee, the corporate officers responsible for arranging for the disposal of the hazardous substances; Mills, the transporter of the hazardous substances; and Syntex, the owner and lessor of the Verona plant, seeking injunctive relief and reimbursement of response costs pursuant to RCRA §7003. In August 1982 the

A. CERCLA: Judicial Process Interpretation

government filed an amended complaint adding counts for relief pursuant to CERCLA [which] was enacted after the filing of the initial complaint. . . .

SCOPE OF LIABILITY . . . The district court found NEPACCO liable as the "owner or operator" of a "facility" (the NEPACCO plant) under CERCLA §107(a)(1) and as a "person" who arranged for the transportation and disposal of hazardous substances under CERCLA §107(a)(3). The district court found Lee liable as a "person" who arranged for the disposal of hazardous substances under CERCLA §107(a)(3) and as an "owner or operator" of the NEPACCO plant under CERCLA §107(a)(1) by "piercing the corporate veil." Id. at 848-849. The district court also found Michaels liable as an "owner or operator" of the NEPACCO plant under CERCLA §107(a)(1).

Appellants concede NEPACCO is liable under CERCLA §107(a)(3) for arranging for the transportation and disposal of hazardous substances at the Denney farm site. Because NEPACCO's assets have already been liquidated and distributed to its shareholders, however, it is unlikely that the government will be able to recover anything from NEPACCO.

Appellants argue (1) they cannot be held liable as "owners or operators" of a "facility" because "facility" refers to the place where hazardous substances are located and they did not own or operate the Denney farm site, (2) Lee cannot be held individually liable for arranging for the transportation and disposal of hazardous substances because he did not "own or possess" the hazardous substances and because he made those arrangements as a corporate officer or employee acting on behalf of NEPACCO, and (3) the district court erred in finding Lee and Michaels individually liable by "piercing the corporate veil." Appellants have not claimed that any of CERCLA's limited affirmative defenses apply to them.

The government argues Lee can be held individually liable without "piercing the corporate veil," under CERCLA §107(a)(3), and that Lee and Michaels can be held individually liable as "contributors" under RCRA §7003(a). For the reasons discussed below, we agree with the government's liability arguments.

LIABILITY UNDER CERCLA §107(a)(1) . . . First, appellants argue the district court erred in finding them liable under CERCLA §107(a)(1) as the "owners and operators" of a "facility" where hazardous substances are located. Appellants argue that, regardless of their relationship to the NEPACCO plant, they neither owned nor operated the Denney farm site, and that it is the Denney farm site, not the NEPACCO plant, that is a "facility" for purposes of "owner and operator" liability under CERCLA §107(a)(1). We agree.

CERCLA defines the term "facility" in part as "any site or area where a hazardous substance has been deposited, stored, disposed of, or placed, or otherwise come to be located." CERCLA §101(9)(B); see *New York v. Shore Realty Corp.*, 759 F.2d 1032, 1043 n. 15 (2d Cir. 1985). The term "facility" should be construed very broadly to include "virtually any place at which hazardous wastes have been dumped, or otherwise disposed of." *United States v. Ward*, 618 F. Supp. at 895. In the present case, however, the place where the hazardous substances were disposed of and where the government has concentrated its cleanup efforts is the Denney farm site, not the NEPACCO plant. The Denney farm site is the "facility." Because NEPACCO, Lee and Michaels did not own or operate the Denney farm site, they cannot be held liable as the "owners or operators" of a "facility" where hazardous substances are located under CERCLA §107(a)(1).

INDIVIDUAL LIABILITY UNDER CERCLA §107(a)(3) . . . CERCLA §107(a)(3) imposes strict liability upon "any person" who arranged for the disposal or transportation for disposal of hazardous substances. As defined by statute, the term "person" includes both individuals and corporations and does not exclude corporate officers or employees. Congress could have limited the statutory definition of "person" but chose not to do so. Compare CERCLA §101(20)(A) (limiting definition of "owner or operator"). Moreover, construction of CERCLA to impose liability upon only the corporation and not the individual corporate officers and employees who are responsible for making corporate decisions about the handling and disposal of hazardous substances would open an enormous, and clearly unintended, loophole in the statutory scheme.

First, Lee argues he cannot be held individually liable for having arranged for the transportation and disposal of hazardous substances under CERCLA §107(a)(3) because he did not personally own or possess the hazardous substances. Lee argues NEPACCO owned or possessed the hazardous substances.

The government argues Lee "possessed" the hazardous substances within the meaning of CERCLA §107(a)(3) because, as NEPACCO's plant supervisor, Lee had actual "control" over the NEPACCO plant's hazardous substances. We agree. It is the authority to control the handling and disposal of hazardous substances that is critical under the statutory scheme. The district court found that Lee, as plant supervisor, actually knew about, had immediate supervision over, and was directly responsible for arranging for the transportation and disposal of the NEPACCO plant's hazardous substances at the Denney farm site. We believe requiring proof of personal ownership or actual physical possession of hazardous substances as a precondition for liability under CERCLA §107(a)(3) would be inconsistent with the broad remedial purposes of CERCLA.

Next, Lee argues that because he arranged for the transportation and disposal of the hazardous substances as a corporate officer or employee acting on behalf of NEPACCO, he cannot be held individually liable for NEPACCO's violations. Lee also argues the district court erred in disregarding the corporate entity by "piercing the corporate veil" because there was no evidence that NEPACCO was inadequately capitalized, the corporate formalities were not observed, individual and corporate interests were not separate, personal and corporate funds were commingled or corporate property was diverted, or the corporate form was used unjustly or fraudulently.

The government argues Lee can be held individually liable, without "piercing the corporate veil," because Lee personally arranged for the disposal of hazardous substances in violation of CERCLA §107(a)(3). We agree. As discussed below, Lee can be held individually liable because he personally participated in conduct that violated CERCLA; this personal liability is distinct from the derivative liability that results from "piercing the corporate veil." "The effect of piercing a corporate veil is to hold the owner [of the corporation] liable. The rationale for piercing the corporate veil is that the corporation is something less than a bona fide independent entity." *Donsco, Inc. v. Casper Corp.*, 587 F.2d 602, 606 (3d Cir. 1978). Here, Lee is liable because he personally participated in the wrongful conduct and not because he is one of the owners of what may have been a less than bona fide corporation. For this reason, we need not decide whether the district court erred [by] piercing the corporate veil under these circumstances.

We now turn to Lee's basic argument. Lee argues that he cannot be held individually liable for NEPACCO's wrongful conduct because he acted solely as a corporate officer or employee on behalf of NEPACCO. The liability imposed upon Lee, however, was not derivative but personal. Liability was not premised solely upon Lee's status as a corporate officer or employee. Rather, Lee is individually liable under CERCLA §107(a)(3) because he personally arranged for the transportation and disposal of hazardous substances on behalf of NEPACCO and thus actually participated in NEPACCO's CERCLA violations.

A. CERCLA: Judicial Process Interpretation

A corporate officer is individually liable for the torts he [or she] personally commits [on behalf of the corporation] and cannot shield himself [or herself] behind a corporation when he [or she] is an actual participant in the tort. The fact that an officer is acting for a corporation also may make the corporation vicariously or secondarily liable under the doctrine of respondeat superior; it does not however relieve the individual of his [or her] responsibility. *Donsco, Inc. v. Casper Corp.*, 587 F.2d at 606.

Thus, Lee's personal involvement in NEPACCO's CERCLA violations made him individually liable.

INDIVIDUAL LIABILITY UNDER RCRA §7003(a) . . . The district court did not reach the question of individual liability under RCRA because it concluded that RCRA did not impose liability upon past non-negligent off-site generators like NEPACCO. . . . RCRA is applicable to past non-negligent off-site generators. The government argues Lee and Michaels are individually liable as "contributors" under RCRA §7003(a). We agree.

RCRA §7003(a) imposes strict liability upon "any person" who is contributing or who has contributed to the disposal of hazardous substances that may present an imminent and substantial endangerment to health or the environment. As defined by statute, the term "person" includes both individuals and corporations and does not exclude corporate officers and employees. As with the CERCLA definition of "person," Congress could have limited the RCRA definition of "person" but did not do so. [Again] compare CERCLA §101(20)(A) (limiting definition of "owner and operator"). More importantly, imposing liability upon only the corporation, but not those corporate officers and employees who actually make corporate decisions, would be inconsistent with Congress' intent to impose liability upon the persons who are involved in the handling and disposal of hazardous substances.

Our analysis of the scope of individual liability under the RCRA is similar to our analysis of the scope of individual liability under CERCLA. NEPACCO violated RCRA §7003(a) by "contributing to" the disposal of hazardous substances at the Denney farm site that presented an imminent and substantial endangerment to health and the environment. Thus, Lee and Michaels can be held individually liable if they were personally involved in or directly responsible for corporate acts in violation of RCRA.

We hold Lee and Michaels are individually liable as "contributors" under RCRA §7003(a). Lee actually participated in the conduct that violated RCRA; he personally arranged for the transportation and disposal of hazardous substances that presented an imminent and substantial endangerment to health and the environment. Unlike Lee, Michaels was not personally involved in the actual decision to transport and dispose of the hazardous substances. As NEPACCO's corporate president and as a major NEPACCO shareholder, however, Michaels was the individual in charge of and directly responsible for all of NEPACCO's operations, including those at the Verona plant, and he had the ultimate authority to control the disposal of NEPACCO's hazardous substances. Cf. *New York v. Shore Realty Corp.*, 759 F.2d at 1052-1053 (shareholder-manager held liable under CERCLA).

In summary, we hold Lee individually liable for arranging for the transportation and disposal of hazardous substances in violation of CERCLA §107(a)(3), and Lee and Michaels individually liable for contributing to an imminent and substantial endangerment to health and the environment in violation of RCRA §7003(a). . . .

COMMENTARY & QUESTIONS

1. Private plaintiffs and cleanup legislation. *NEPACCO*, like many other cases brought under RCRA and CERCLA, features the United States as plaintiff. Private plaintiffs may also sue to enforce those statutes. For example, a subsection of the citizen suit provision of RCRA, 42 U.S.C. §6972(a)(1), authorizes private suits to enforce violation of any of RCRA's regulatory mechanisms, or the imminent hazard provision (see Chapter 17). Still, even with the presence of a citizen suit provision allowing its enforcement, RCRA has been held to create no private cause of action for damages. See, e.g., *Walls v. Waste Res. Corp.*, 761 F.2d 311 (6th Cir. 1985). CERCLA does allow private recovery of response costs, a matter that is considered more fully later in this chapter.

2. The strategy of avoiding §107 recoveries. In *Wade*, the government sought an injunctive order requiring the defendant generators to clean up the site under CERCLA §106. As noted previously, CERCLA provides for creation of a Superfund from which the government may draw to pay for the cleanup of hazardous waste contamination. The government, when it uses the fund to pay for cleanups, may then sue responsible parties to recoup sums spent and thereby replenish the fund. Given the existence of Superfund cleanup funding and recoupment provisions under §107 and of state law damage remedies, why would EPA seek such an order? Few, if any, of the parties ordered to clean a site are in a position to do the work themselves. Viewed in this light, the order to clean a site looks like an order to pay a contractor to clean the site, which looks like a damage remedy. When first authorized, Superfund had only $1.6 billion available under §107, and the pace of efforts that would have replenished the fund was slow. By obtaining relief under the imminent hazard prongs of RCRA §7003 and CERCLA §106, EPA could bypass the potential cash flow problem facing Superfund cleanups. EPA's position was validated by the fact that CERCLA reimbursement has been very problematic, with only a fraction of the money expended on Superfund cleanups having been recovered and put back into the fund.

3. Arranging for disposal under CERCLA §107(a)(3). The most far-reaching development in the *NEPACCO* case is its ruling that holds Michaels personally liable under RCRA §7003 as a person who "contributed" to the disposal of hazardous waste, even though Michaels was not involved in the day-to-day operations of the plant in Verona, Missouri. The key phrases in the court's holding on this point cast a broad net — Michaels was "the individual in charge of and directly responsible . . . and he had ultimate authority to control the disposal of NEPACCO's hazardous substances." 810 F.2d at 745. But that description fits almost all chief operating officers of corporations. Looking at CERCLA §107(a)(3), can the "arranging for disposal" language of that liability section be read as broadly? One court has proposed a liability standard based on ability to prevent improper disposal:

> This standard is different, but more stringent on the whole than traditional corporate tort liability, yet it requires more than mere status as a corporate officer or director. . . . The test — whether the individual in a close corporation could have prevented or significantly abated the release of hazardous substances — allows the fact-finder to impose liability on a case-by-case basis. . . . *Kelley ex rel. Michigan Natural Resources Comm'n v. ARCO Indus. Corp.*, 723 F. Supp. 1214, 1220 (W.D. Mich. 1989).

As discussed later in this chapter, setting appropriate limits on the scope of liability in "ability to control" situations has become an even hotter issue in other contexts. The ARCO Industries standard applies to close corporations, that is, corporations owned and controlled by just a few shareholders. Is there any reason why the same standard would not be equally well suited to determining liability of corporate officers in large publicly held

A. CERCLA: Judicial Process Interpretation

corporations? See also *United States v. TIC Inv. Corp.*, 68 F.3d 1082 (8th Cir. 1995) (holding an officer in a subsidiary corporation liable as an arranger for disposal of hazardous waste as a matter of law, where the officer did not delegate authority and left no room for others to exercise decisionmaking authority or judgment).

4. Selling hazardous materials as a form of disposal. Given the breadth of RCRA and CERCLA liability, is it possible that the sale of products that contain hazardous materials can be considered "arranging for disposal" of those materials under §107(a)(3) of CERCLA? Congress did not define the term "arranged" in the statute, and the courts have had to supply a definition. In general, the courts have been quick to reject liability, protecting the sellers of useful products from liability.

The Supreme Court addressed the issue of the potential liability of sellers of useful products in the *Burlington Northern* case, discussed above. In its certiorari petition to the Supreme Court in *Burlington Northern,* Shell argued that the Ninth Circuit's application of arranger liability was overbroad, in that:

> no other circuit has found a manufacturer liable under CERCLA as an arranger of hazardous substance disposal where, as here, that manufacturer sells (1) a new useful product manufactured for sale (2) that is shipped by common carrier with delivery FOB destination, so that (3) title, possession and ownership are transferred to the purchaser when the common carrier arrives, and thus (4) the manufacturer lacks ownership or actual control of the product that is spilled or leaked into the environment.

On appeal to the Supreme Court, Justice Stevens, writing for the majority of the Court, held in *Burlington Northern* that Shell was not liable as an arranger within the ordinary meaning of the term. Analyzing the statutory language, the Court noted that CERCLA does not define "arranger," but, under its common definition, "the word 'arrange' implies action directed to a specific purpose." 129 S. Ct. at 1879. The Court held that, although "disposal" could be unintentional, the specific intent required by "arrange" showed that Congress sought to apply arranger liability only to entities that expressly intended to dispose of hazardous substances. Id. at 1879-1880. Thus, knowledge that a disposal may occur may be evidence of the requisite intent, but it is not alone sufficient. Id. at 1880. The Supreme Court noted that although Shell was aware of "minor, accidental spills . . . during the transfer of D-D," Shell's extensive product stewardship efforts showed that Shell did not intend for disposal of its product, regardless of the level of success of its stewardship efforts. Id.

Does the Supreme Court's treatment of arranger liability mean that such liability is a fact intensive inquiry, in which a CERCLA plaintiff will have to show that the seller of an otherwise useful product actually intended the product, or some portion of it, to be disposed of pursuant to the normal course of dealing? Several cases decided by the lower courts since *Burlington Northern* have reinforced the view that the inquiry into arranger liability is "fact intensive." See, e.g., *Appleton Papers Inc. v. George A. Whiting Paper Co.*, No. 08-C-16, 2009 WL 5064049 (E.D. Wis. Dec. 16, 2009); *United States v. Wash. State Dep't of Transp.*, 665 F. Supp. 2d 1233 (W.D. Wash. Sept. 15, 2009); *Frontier Communications Corp. v. Barrett Paving Materials, Inc.*, No. Civ. 07-113-B-S (D. Me.); and *United States v. General Elec. Co.*, No. 06-354, Def's Supp. Mem. on the Evidence of Intent or Knowledge Required to Prove that a CERCLA Def. has "Arranged For" Disposal or Treatment of Hazardous Waste (D.N.H. Nov. 5, 2008) (Dkt. #89). See also *Consolidated Coal Co. v. Georgia Power Co.*, 2015 BL 76552, 4th Cir., No. 13-1603, 3/20/15; *PCS Phosphate Co. v. Georgia Power Co.*, 4th Cir., No. 13-1664, 3/20/15; *Consolidated Coal Co. v. Georgia Power Co.*, 4th Cir. No. 13-1617, 3/20/15; *Consolidated Coal Co. v. Georgia Power Co.*, 4th Cir., No. 13-1666, 3/20/15 (holding that a public utility's sale of useful, but PCB-tainted, electrical transformers for reconditioning and resale is not alone sufficient to establish its liability as a Superfund "arranger," based on the conclusion that intent to sell a product that happens to contain a hazardous substance is not equivalent to intent to dispose of a hazardous substance under CERCLA). If a fact intensive inquiry is in order, consider the types of evidence that may prove dispositive. Is it enough to show that the product is manufactured for sale, shipped by common carrier with delivery FOB destination, or that the manufacturer had no legal ownership or control when the product was released into the environment? Or is more evidence required? For example, will sellers of "useful products," going forward, also seek to mitigate their potential status as "arrangers" by establishing good product stewardship programs? Would such action be probative evidence that useful products are not intended for disposal?

5. Processing hazardous materials through third parties as a form of disposal. Another important issue under §107(a)(3) of CERCLA is whether companies owning a particular substance may be liable for disposal that occurs when a third party is processing or refining that substance. The decision by the Eighth Circuit in *United States v. Aceto Agric. Chems. Corp.*, 872 F.2d 1373 (8th Cir. 1989) is instructive as to the approach taken by the federal appellate courts before *Burlington Northern*. In *Aceto*, the Eighth Circuit broadly construed the phase "arranged for disposal" in §107(a)(3) to include manufacturers who sent their pesticide ingredients to a formulator under a tolling agreement, where the formulation activities gave rise to contamination. The manufacturers argued that they could not be said to have "arranged for disposal" of any hazardous substances because they provided only base materials that were to be processed into a valuable product. Nonetheless, in denying a motion to dismiss, the court ruled that the manufacturers were potentially liable as "arrangers" for disposal:

> Defendants nonetheless contend they should escape liability because they had no authority to control Aidex's operations, and our *NEPACCO* decision states " [i]t is the authority to control the handling and disposal of hazardous substances that is critical under the statutory scheme." . . . In *NEPACCO,* we were confronted with the argument that only individuals who owned or possessed hazardous substances could be liable under CERCLA. We rejected that notion and imposed liability, in addition, on those who had the authority to control the disposal, even without ownership or possession. . . . Defendants in this case, of course, actually owned the hazardous substances, as well as the work in process. *NEPACCO* does not mandate dismissal of plaintiffs' complaint under these circumstances. 872 F.2d at 1381-1382.

Aceto led to further analysis of the nature of "arranger" liability. Of particular note, in *Morton Int'l, Inc. v. A.E. Staley Mfg.*, 343 F.3d 669 (3d Cir. 2003), the Third Circuit dealt with a claim by the owner of a site previously used as a mercury processing plant for contribution from a pipeline company. The owner contended that the pipeline company was responsible for some of the cleanup costs at the site because the pipeline company allegedly "arranged for" the processing of mercury at the facility for many years, resulting in the release of hazardous wastes into the environment. At the outset of its analysis, the Third Circuit recognized that not only did Congress not define the term "arranged for" in CERCLA, but also that the standards adopted for "arranger liability" among the federal circuit courts vary. After reviewing these varying standards, the Third Circuit identified the principal factors necessary, in its view, to establishing the baseline for determining "arranger liability":

> In sum, we conclude that the analysis of "arranger liability" under Section 107(a)(3) should focus on these principal factors: (1) the ownership or possession of a material by the defendant; and (2) the defendant's knowledge that the processing of that material can or will result in the release of hazardous waste; or (3) the defendant's control over the production process. A plaintiff is required to demonstrate ownership or possession, but liability cannot be imposed on that basis alone. A plaintiff is also required to demonstrate either knowledge or control. . . .

A. CERCLA: Judicial Process Interpretation

It is certainly possible that other factors could be relevant to the analysis in a given case, and we encourage consideration of those as well. 343 F.3d at 679.

Applying this baseline analysis, the Third Circuit remanded for further proceedings because material factual issues remained with respect to the pipeline company's (1) ownership or possession of mercury, (2) knowledge of the environmental hazards of mercury processing at the plant, (3) control over the waste disposal practices at the plant, and (4) shipment of its own "dirty mercury" to the plant.

To review the approaches of other federal circuits on "arranger liability" prior to the decision in *Burlington Northern*, see *Geraghty & Miller, Inc. v. Conoco Inc.*, 234 F.3d 917, 929 (5th Cir. 2001); *Freeman v. Glaxo Wellcome, Inc.*, 189 F.3d 160, 164 (2d Cir. 1999); *Pneumo Abex Corp. v. High Point, Thomasville & Denton R.R.*, 142 F.3d 769, 775 (4th Cir. 1998); *United States v. Cello-Foil Prods., Inc.*, 100 F.3d 1227, 1231-1232 (6th Cir. 1996); *South Fla. Water Mgmt. Dist. v. Montalvo*, 84 F.3d 402, 407 (11th Cir. 1996); *Amcast Indus. Corp. v. Detrex Corp.*, 2 F.3d 746, 751 (7th Cir. 1993); and *Jones-Hamilton Co. v. Beazer Materials & Servs., Inc.*, 973 F.2d 688, 695, 694-95 (9th Cir. 1992).

6. Recycling. Where on the continuum between sale of a useful product and arranging for disposal does recycling fall? In early cases construing CERCLA, most courts ruled that conventional recycling, even where the recycler paid for the used product, rendered the seller of the used product liable as an "arranger." See, e.g., *Chesapeake & Potomac Tel. Co. of Va. v. Peck Iron & Metal Co.*, 814 F. Supp. 1269 (E.D. Va. 1992); but see *Catellus Dev. Corp. v. U.S.*, 828 F. Supp. 764 (N.D. Cal. 1993) (holding auto parts company not liable for sale of spent batteries to lead reclamation firm that caused release), rev'd 34, F.3d 748 (9th Cir. 1994). As a result of these decisions, Congress became concerned that the imposition of arranger liability in the recycling context was working at cross purposes with the desirability of recycling when compared to the use of virgin raw materials. Congress responded with the Superfund Recycling Equity Act (SREA), 42 U.S.C. §9627, signed into law by President Clinton in November 1999. SREA exempts from liability under §107(a)(3) and §107(a)(4) of CERCLA those persons who "arranged" for the recycling of a "recyclable material." SREA defines "recyclable material" to include scrap paper, plastic, glass, textiles, rubber, metal, and spent batteries. See §127(b), codified at 42 U.S.C. §9627(b) (defining recyclable material).

5. The Classes of Parties Who May Be Held Liable Under CERCLA

CERCLA holds liable all persons or entities classified as "owners or operators" of treatment, storage, or disposal (TSD) facilities and as "generators"[10] and "transporters" of hazardous waste. These latter two terms are easily understood. "Owners or operators" is a more specialized term and is defined as follows by §101(20) of CERCLA, 42 U.S.C. §9601(20):

> **Potentially Responsible Parties Under CERCLA:**
> - Owners or operators
> - Generators
> - Transporters

(A) The term "owner or operator" means (i) in the case of a vessel, any person owning, operating, or chartering by demise, such vessel, (ii) in the case of an onshore facility or an offshore facility, any person owning or operating such facility, and (iii) in the case of any facility, title or control of which was conveyed due to bankruptcy,

---

10. Generator liability is traceable to the previously reproduced provision in §107(a)(3) holding liable persons who arranged for disposal of hazardous materials that later are the subject of a removal or remedial action.

foreclosure, tax delinquency, abandonment, or similar means to a unit of State or local government, any person who owned, operated or otherwise controlled activities at such facility immediately beforehand. Such term does not include a person, who, without participating in the management of a vessel or facility, holds indicia of ownership primarily to protect his security interest in the vessel or facility. . . .

(D) The term "owner or operator" does not include a unit of State or local government which acquired ownership or control involuntarily through bankruptcy, tax delinquency, abandonment, or other circumstances in which the government involuntarily acquires title by virtue of its function as sovereign. The exclusion provided under this paragraph shall not apply to any State or local government which has caused or contributed to the release or threatened release of a hazardous substance from the facility, and such a State or local government shall be subject to the provisions of this chapter in the same manner and to the same extent, both procedurally and substantively, as any nongovernmental entity, including liability under section 9607 of this title.

Despite the presence of an explicit statutory definition, the scope of the "owner or operator" provisions of CERCLA has proved particularly troublesome. The courts have played an important role in delineating the contours of hazardous waste liability through case law interpreting the statutory terms. Three major areas of litigation have emerged.

The first line of cases focuses on attempts to expand the class of operators. Many of these cases initially concerned the potential liability of lenders who made loans to operators of TSD facilities or to generators. Frequently, when the borrower encountered financial difficulty, the lender attempted to salvage its loan by becoming involved in the operation of the debtor's business. Not surprisingly, the presence of a solvent entity (the lender) participating in the affairs of a financially troubled TSD facility or generator has typically made an inviting target for a CERCLA plaintiff. After years of litigation, as detailed below, EPA sought and obtained a "legislative fix" in the form of an amendment to CERCLA that clarifies the scope of lender liability under the secured creditor exemption of CERCLA, §101(20)(A).[11]

The second line of cases concerns efforts to exonerate innocent purchasers of contaminated parcels from liability. As previously noted, current owners of contaminated property are liable under §107(a) unless they can establish an affirmative defense under §107(b). The first two of the defenses under §107(b) apply only when either an act of God (e.g., pollution caused by an earthquake and a subsequent flood) or an act of war (e.g., pollution caused by wartime bombing) is the sole cause of the release or threatened release and the resulting harm. See §107(b)(1) and (2). To date, these provisions have resulted in little relief for CERCLA defendants.[12] The third affirmative defense, §107(b)(3), applies if a party not in contractual privity with the person asserting the defense is the sole cause of the release or threatened release and the resulting harm. This defense protects property owners against unauthorized "midnight dumping." But under what circumstance does the defense protect predecessors in the chain of title, with whom there will often be a contractual relationship? Congress tried to clarify the third affirmative defense by amendments now codified in §101(35), as discussed more fully below.

---

11. That part of CERCLA §101(20)(A) known as the "secured creditor exemption" provides: "Owner" or "operator" "does not include a person, who, without participating in the management of a vessel or facility, holds indicia of ownership primarily to protect his security interest in the vessel or facility."

12. See, e.g., *United States v. Stringfellow*, 661 F. Supp. 1053, 1061 (C.D. Cal. 1987) (heavy but foreseeable rains do not constitute an act of God).

A. CERCLA: Judicial Process Interpretation

The third line of cases focuses less on expanding the class of operators and more on expanding the class of owners. For the most part, these cases concern pinning down who really owns the facility. Here the issues involve corporate structures involving either the relationship of a parent corporation to a subsidiary or corporate succession.[13] These cases, as explained below, initially resulted in substantial disagreement among the federal circuit courts over (1) the circumstances under which a parent corporation will be found liable for environmental conditions caused by its subsidiary or (2) the circumstances under which a successor corporation is responsible for the liabilities of an entity it has taken over.

COMMENTARY & QUESTIONS

1. **The Superfund Amendments and Reauthorization Act of 1986 (SARA).** In 1986, Congress revisited a number of areas of CERCLA in a far-reaching set of amendments that also reauthorized the continuing operation of the Superfund system. Pub. L. No. 99-499, 100 Stat. 1613. SARA, as the 1986 legislation is known, addressed a number of liability issues, usually in ways that confirmed broad judicial interpretations of the liability provisions. As in §101(35), Congress clarified a variety of questions about the scope of the statute. SARA did not cut back on the scope of CERCLA liability. To the contrary, the generally pro-liability posture of SARA led some experts in the field to suggest that its acronym ought to be changed to RACHEL, because the Reauthorization Act Confirms How Everyone's Liable. See, e.g., *United States v. Kramer*, 757 F. Supp. 397 (D.N.J. 1991); Glass, Superfund and SARA: Are There Any Defenses Left?, 12 Harv. Envtl. L. Rev. 385 (1988). In the same vein, one commentator wrote, "With only slight exaggeration, one government lawyer has described a [CERCLA] trial as requiring only that the Justice Department lawyer stand up and recite: 'May it please the Court, I represent the government and therefore I win.'" Marzulla, Superfund 1991: How Insurance Firms Can Help Clean Up the Nation's Hazardous Waste, 4 Toxics L. Rep. (BNA) 685 (Nov. 8, 1989).

2. **Lender liability and the 1996 Superfund Amendments.** Although CERCLA's secured creditor exemption, §101(20)(A), was designed to protect lenders from strict CERCLA liability, for years there was vigorous litigation over the exemption's proper scope. The chief difficulty concerned the phrase "participating in the management." Some courts held that a lender did not participate in management unless it actually ran the vessel's or facility's operations. See, e.g., *In re Bergsoe Metal Corp.*, 910 F.2d 668 (9th Cir. 1990). In contrast, other courts found creditors liable based simply on their capacity to control a vessel or facility's operations. See, e.g., *United States v. Fleet Factors Corp.*, 901 F.2d 1550 (11th Cir. 1990). In light of these conflicting judicial interpretations, lenders faced great uncertainty concerning their potential exposure.

In attempting to alleviate this confusion, EPA promulgated regulations to define the secured creditor exemption's scope. EPA's lender liability rule, which was issued in April 1992 and codified at 40 C.F.R. §300.1100(c), was short-lived. In response to industry challenges, the D.C. Circuit vacated the rule, holding its promulgation to be beyond EPA's statutory authority. *Kelley v. EPA*, 15 F.3d 1100 (D.C. Cir. 1994). Two years later, in response to the *Kelley* decision and the continuing uncertainty surrounding the secured creditor

---

13. These issues are not limited to the ownership of TSD facilities but can also arise in the context of deciding who is a generator or transporter.

exemption, Congress amended CERCLA in the Asset Conservation, Lender Liability, and Deposit Insurance Protection Act of 1996, Pub. L. No. 104-208 (the 1996 Act).

The 1996 Act effectively overruled the *Kelley* decision by statutorily reinstating EPA's lender liability rule. The 1996 Act amended CERCLA's definition of "owner or operator" to clarify that most routine lending activities do not constitute "participating in the management" of a vessel or facility. Instead, CERCLA now provides that a lender cannot be liable as an owner or operator unless the lender "actually participates in the management or operational affairs of a vessel or facility." See 42 U.S.C. §9601, §101(20)(E)-(G). In addition, the 1996 Act specified that the following activities, routinely performed by lenders in administering a loan, do not amount to "participating in the management" of a vessel or facility: holding, abandoning, or releasing a security interest; including a covenant or warranty of environmental compliance in a loan or security instrument; monitoring or enforcing the terms and conditions of a loan instrument; monitoring or inspecting a facility or vessel; requiring the borrower to address a release or threatened release of hazardous substances; providing financial advice to the borrower or otherwise taking steps to prevent diminution of value of collateral; restructuring or renegotiating the terms of a loan or security interest; exercising available remedies for breach of a condition of the loan; and conducting a response action under the direction of state or federal on-site officials. Id. Perhaps most significantly, the 1996 Act attempted to clarify when creditors may foreclose on property without risking liability. The 1996 Act allows a lender to foreclose and wind up operations as long as it subsequently divests the property at the "earliest practicable, commercially reasonable time, on commercially reasonable terms, taking into account market conditions and legal and regulatory requirements." See 42 U.S.C. §9601, §101(20)(E)(ii)(II). For further details on the events leading to the promulgation of the 1996 Act, see EPA Policy on Interpreting CERCLA Provisions, Addressing Lenders and Involuntary Acquisitions by Government Entities, 28 Env't Rep. (BNA) 35,656 (1997).

3. How the courts make CERCLA liability policy. After reviewing the preceding notes' forays into the nuts and bolts of CERCLA liability, the prominent role of courts in framing the contours of CERCLA as part of a case-by-case development should be apparent. What is less clear is whether the courts are interpreting statutes or "making law." In any event, the courts are not merely engaged in a rote process of statutory interpretation that deduces the intent of Congress through a series of simple logical steps. The process of judicial interpretation frequently calls upon courts to weigh and balance competing policy concerns, giving the process of statutory interpretation much of the same dynamism as the common law. The Sixth Circuit, in a successor liability case, reflected on the role of courts in these terms:

> The Supreme Court has stated that "the authority to construe a statute is fundamentally different from the authority to fashion a new rule or to provide a new remedy which Congress has decided not to adopt." *Northwest Airlines, Inc. v. Transport Workers Union of America*, 451 U.S. 77, 97 (1981). As Justice Stevens wrote in *Northwest Airlines*, "Broadly worded constitutional and statutory provisions necessarily have been given concrete meaning and application by a process of case-by-case judicial decisions in the common-law tradition." Id. at 95.
>
> Of course, the line separating statutory interpretation and judicial lawmaking is not always clear and sharp. If a statute is found to be abundantly clear and well defined, a judicial decision that expands or contracts its reach or adds or deletes remedies fashions federal common law. On the other hand, if the court detects only gaps in definitions or descriptions, it may fill these interstices of the statute by exercising its authority to interpret or construe the statute. As the Supreme Court has stated, these two exercises of judicial authority are fundamentally different, and they are subject to different standards. The authority to construe a statute lies at the very heart of judicial power and is not subject to rigorous scrutiny. The rule is otherwise with respect to outright judicial lawmaking, however. Before a federal court may fashion a body

A. CERCLA: Judicial Process Interpretation

of federal common law, it must find either (1) that Congress painted with a broad brush and left it to the courts to "flesh out" the statute by fashioning a body of substantive federal law, or (2) that a federal rule of decision is necessary to protect uniquely federal interests. *Anspec Co. v. Johnson Controls, Inc.*, 922 F.2d 1240, 1245 (6th Cir. 1991).

4. Would you buy this land? Assume that you are a commercial investor and are aware of a contaminated parcel that is otherwise well suited for investment. Should you purchase the property? Under CERCLA §101(35), as a purchaser of the property with knowledge of its contamination, you would be liable for cleanup costs as a responsible party. If the sum of the purchase price plus the cost of cleanup is sufficiently low that the parcel freed of contamination is worth more than that sum, the purchase should be consummated. In the case of badly contaminated parcels, however, the cleanup costs alone often dwarf the "clean" market value of the parcel. Those are problem cases for society because one important goal of CERCLA is (or ought to be) the return of contaminated sites to productive use. In recent years, there has been legislative action seeking to encourage the redevelopment of contaminated brownfields on both the federal and state levels. In late 2001, for example, Congress passed the Small Business Liability Relief and Brownfields Revitalization Act, which was designed to encourage the development and reuse of brownfields, especially where the level of pollution is not so severe that the brownfields are designated as cleanup "priorities" by the EPA or by state environmental agencies. This Act, which signifies a policy of greater regulatory flexibility and cooperation by EPA and the states in the enforcement of the environmental laws, is detailed more fully in Chapter 18.

5. The "act of a third party" defense. CERCLA §107(b)(3), set forth in the first section of this chapter, permits a defense when the hazardous release or threatened release is caused solely by the act of a third party with whom the defendant has little or no relation. Section 101(35) in relevant part reads as follows:

(A) The term "contractual relationship," for the purpose of §9607(b)(3) of this title includes, but is not limited to, land contracts, deeds or other instruments transferring title or possession, unless the real property on which the facility concerned is located was acquired by the defendant after the disposal or placement of the hazardous substance on, in, or at the facility, and one or more of the circumstances described in clause (i), (ii), or (iii) is also established by the defendant by a preponderance of the evidence:

(i) At the time the defendant acquired the facility the defendant did not know and had no reason to know that any hazardous substance which is the subject of the release or threatened release was disposed of on, in, or at the facility.

(ii) The defendant is a government entity which acquired the facility by escheat, or through any other involuntary transfer or acquisition, or through the exercise of eminent domain authority by purchase or condemnation.

(iii) The defendant acquired the facility by inheritance or bequest. In addition to establishing the foregoing, the defendant must establish that he has satisfied the requirements of §9607(b)(3)(a) and (b) of this title.

(B) . . . To establish that the defendant had no reason to know, as provided in clause (i) of subparagraph (A) of this paragraph, the defendant must have undertaken, at the time of acquisition, all appropriate inquiry into the previous ownership and uses of the property consistent with good commercial or customary practice in an effort to minimize liability. For purposes of the preceding sentence the court shall take into account any specialized knowledge or experience on the part of the defendant, the relationship of the purchase price to the value of the property if uncontaminated, commonly known or reasonably ascertainable information about the property, the obviousness of the presence or likely presence of contamination at the property, and the ability to detect such contamination by appropriate inspection. . . .

Consider whether that defense is available in the following hypothetical situation: Buyer is considering acquiring a piece of commercial property that shows no obvious signs of contamination. Under what circumstances, if any, will Buyer be free from §107(a)(1) owner's liability if, in the future, it is discovered that previously disposed of hazardous substances are buried under the surface and are releasing toxic contaminants into the groundwater? Does being in the chain of title, without more, vitiate the defense? Or to vitiate the defense, must the contractual relationship relate to the hazardous substances being released? See *New York v. Lashins Arcade Co.*, 91 F.3d 353 (2d Cir. 1996) (holding that a purchaser established a defense to CERCLA liability under §107(b)(3), where the purchase contract did not relate to the hazardous substances or allow the purchaser to exert control over the seller's activities). In this connection, does it matter if a "release" of contaminants is active or, in the alternative, simply the result of prolonged passive migration? See *Nurad, Inc. v. William E. Hooper & Sons Co.*, 966 F.2d 837 (4th Cir. 1992); *United States v. CDMG Realty Co.*, 96 F.3d 706 (3d Cir. 1996). For more on the issue of the "due care" required of "innocent" landowners, see Hernan, Due and Don't Care Under CERCLA: An Emerging Standard for Current Owners, 27 Envtl. L. Rep. 10,064 (1997); see also Caplan, Escaping CERCLA Liability: The Interim Owner Passive Migration Defense Gains Circuit Recognition, 28 Envtl. L. Rep. 10,121 (1998).

6. Insurance. CERCLA has created a high-stakes specialized cottage industry in the litigation of defense against claims and the pollution exclusion clause sections of insurance policies. The most readily understood of these cases arise initially when a facility owner PRP receives a PRP letter and looks to its insurer to provide (and pay for) the costs of defending the claim. Later, after being held liable, the PRP seeks indemnification from the insurer. The cases, in the main, involve comprehensive general liability policies (CGL), many of which included a "pollution exclusion" clause that exempted ordinary pollution but covered "sudden and accidental" events. See, e.g., *Allstate Ins. Co. v. Klock Oil Co.*, 426 N.Y.S.2d 603, 604 (N.Y. App. Div. 1980). Pollutants leaching into groundwater over many years, a typical CERCLA scenario, have proven hard to classify. Intra-insurer conflicts arise because of the durational aspect of the cases — CGL policies cover specific periods of time, but the leaking may have occurred over a period of years, implicating a whole series of insurance policies that may have been issued by different insurers and leading as well to litigation over whether such releases are "sudden and accidental."

7. Insolvency. Insolvency issues have led the development of CERCLA into another area of law, that of bankruptcy. A fundamental tension exists between the remedial goals and aspirations of CERCLA and the objectives of bankruptcy law. One goal of bankruptcy law is to distribute the bankrupt's assets fairly among all of the creditors. A second objective is to provide the bankrupt with a fresh start, freed of the previous debts. In contrast, a central concern animating CERCLA is assuring the availability of sufficient resources for the cleanup of hazardous release sites. Accordingly, CERCLA has a strong interest in making all the bankrupt's assets, both present and future, available to remediate the hazards that the PRP bankrupt has helped to create. This CERCLA-based interest collides with bankruptcy law, when bankruptcy law seeks to protect co-creditors through a fair division of the available assets. Specifically, bankruptcy law preferences secured creditors over unsecured creditors, as the government would be in regard to a CERCLA recovery. As a second matter, under normal bankruptcy law, the debtor can expect to be absolved from personal post-bankruptcy obligations relating to CERCLA liabilities. Congress did nothing to broker the competition between these two statutory children, CERCLA and the bankruptcy act, so that task has fallen by default to the courts. This seemingly specialized area of intersection has its

A. CERCLA: Judicial Process Interpretation

own treatise. See Lawrence R. Ahern, III & Darlene T. Marsh, Environmental Obligations in Bankruptcy (2010).

6. Corporate Liabilities Under CERCLA

"The time has come," the walrus said, "to talk of many things . . . of 'subsids,' parents, shareholders, of cabbages and kings." The courts consistently have construed CERCLA's scope of liability broadly in a variety of contexts that involve scrutinizing a corporation's form. For a number of years, various federal circuits went beyond the traditional common law doctrine that allows for piercing the corporate veil when corporate form is being used as a sham to defraud creditors. To go beyond traditional rules of corporate law in imposing liability on owners of corporations is a very delicate matter, because one of the principal assurances of corporate form is that only corporate assets are put at risk by corporate activities; personal assets of a corporation's owners are not supposed to be put at risk. As a matter of policy, adherence to this general principle is quite important. Limited liability invites the formation of new companies that may or may not survive, and is thus vital to economic innovation and dynamism. Shareholder immunity from liability is likewise a vital element in capital formation. Without it, shareholders would be inhibited from purchasing stock as a form of investment in corporations.

Despite these dangers, CERCLA liability was initially extended by certain federal courts beyond the traditional limits of corporate law in a number of disparate settings, as the courts struggled with whether a parent company could be liable under CERCLA by exercising control over its subsidiaries. In June 1998, this issue reached the Supreme Court.

United States v. BestFoods Corp.
524 U.S. 51 (1998)

[In this case, the U.S. Supreme Court addressed whether a parent corporation that actively participated in and exercised control over the operations of a polluting subsidiary may be held liable. The United States brought the action under §107(a)(2) for the costs of cleaning up industrial waste. The BestFoods Corporation just happened to be the case's first-named defendant; it was an "arranger"; the issue in the case, however, dealt with whether a parent corporation, CPC International (which spun off the subsidiary Ott II that "operated" a CERCLA-liable facility in Muskegon, Michigan), was itself an "operator."

The chemical plant involved in the case had been owned by different companies over a 30-year period and had caused substantial contamination. The federal government sued several defendants to recover the money it had spent cleaning up the site. The district court found the parent corporation liable under CERCLA as a former "owner or operator" of the subsidiary's plant because, in part, the parent had appointed its employees as officers and directors of the subsidiary. On appeal, the Sixth Circuit reversed in a 7-6 en banc decision, concluding that where a parent corporation was not directly involved in the operations of a subsidiary's facility as a joint venturer or co-operator, it could not be held liable under CERCLA as an "owner or operator" simply because it exercised corporate oversight of a subsidiary's affairs, except when the requirements of piercing the corporate veil could be met under state law. Thereafter, the Supreme Court granted certiorari.]

SOUTER, J. The United States brought this action for the costs of cleaning up industrial waste generated by a chemical plant. The issue before us, under CERCLA, is whether a parent corporation that actively participated in, and exercised control over, the operations of a subsidiary may, without more, be held liable as an operator of a polluting facility owned or operated by the subsidiary. We answer no, unless the corporate veil may be pierced. But a corporate parent that actively participated in, and exercised control over, the operations of the facility itself may be held directly liable in its own right as an operator of the facility....

[III.] It is a general principle of corporate law deeply "ingrained in our economic and legal systems" that a parent corporation (so-called because of control through ownership of another corporation's stock) is not liable for the acts of its subsidiaries.... Thus it is hornbook law that "the exercise of the 'control' which stock ownership gives to the stockholders ... will not create liability beyond the assets of the subsidiary. That 'control' includes the election of directors, the making of by-laws ... and the doing of all other acts incident to the legal status of stockholders. Nor will a duplication of some or all of the directors or executive officers be fatal." Although this respect for corporate distinctions when the subsidiary is a polluter has been severely criticized in the literature, ... nothing in CERCLA purports to reject this bedrock principle, and against this venerable common-law backdrop, the congressional silence is audible.... The Government has indeed made no claim that a corporate parent is liable as an owner or an operator under §107 simply because its subsidiary is subject to liability for owning or operating a polluting facility.

But there is an equally fundamental principle of corporate law, applicable to the parent-subsidiary relationship as well as generally, that the corporate veil may be pierced and the shareholder held liable for the corporation's conduct when, inter alia, the corporate form would otherwise be misused to accomplish certain wrongful purposes, most notably fraud, on the shareholder's behalf.... Nothing in CERCLA purports to rewrite this well-settled rule, either. CERCLA is thus like many another congressional enactment in giving no indication "that the entire corpus of state corporation law is to be replaced simply because a plaintiff's cause of action is based upon a federal statute," and the failure of the statute to speak to a matter as fundamental as the liability implications of corporate ownership demands application of the rule that" [i]n order to abrogate a common-law principle, the statute must speak directly to the question addressed by the common law."... The Court of Appeals was accordingly correct in holding that when (but only when) the corporate veil may be pierced, may a parent corporation be charged with derivative CERCLA liability for its subsidiary's actions.

[IV. A.] If the act rested liability entirely on ownership of a polluting facility, this opinion might end here; but CERCLA liability may turn on operation as well as ownership, and nothing in the statute's terms bars a parent corporation from direct liability for its own actions in operating a facility owned by its subsidiary. As Justice (then-Professor) Douglas noted almost 70 years ago, derivative liability cases are to be distinguished from those in which "the alleged wrong can seemingly be traced to the parent through the conduit of its own personnel and management" and "the parent is directly a participant in the wrong complained of."... In such instances, the parent is directly liable for its own actions.... The fact that a corporate subsidiary happens to own a polluting facility operated by its parent does nothing, then, to displace the rule that the parent "corporation is [itself] responsible for the wrongs committed by its agents in the course of its business,"... and whereas the rules of veil-piercing limit derivative liability for the actions of another corporation, CERCLA's "operator" provision is concerned primarily with direct liability for one's own actions.... It is this direct liability that is properly seen as being at issue here.

Under the plain language of the statute, any person who operates a polluting facility is directly liable for the costs of cleaning up the pollution. See 42 U.S.C. §9607(a)(2). This is

A. CERCLA: Judicial Process Interpretation

so regardless of whether that person is the facility's owner, the owner's parent corporation or business partner, or even a saboteur who sneaks into the facility at night to discharge its poisons out of malice. If any such act of operating a corporate subsidiary's facility is done on behalf of a parent corporation, the existence of the parent-subsidiary relationship under state corporate law is simply irrelevant to the issue of direct liability. . . .

This much is easy to say; the difficulty comes in defining actions sufficient to constitute direct parental "operation." Here of course we may again rue the uselessness of CERCLA's definition of a facility's "operator" as "any person-operating" a facility, 42 U.S.C. §9601(20)(A)(ii), which leaves us to do the best we can to give the term its "ordinary or natural meaning. . . ." So, under CERCLA, an operator is simply someone who directs the workings of, manages, or conducts the affairs of a facility. To sharpen the definition for purposes of CERCLA's concern with environmental contamination, an operator must manage, direct, or conduct operations specifically related to pollution, that is, operations having to do with the leakage or disposal of hazardous waste, or decisions about compliance with environmental regulations.

[IV. B.] With this understanding, we are satisfied that the Court of Appeals correctly rejected the District Court's analysis of direct liability. But we also think that the appeals court erred in limiting direct liability under the statute to a parent's sole or joint venture operation, so as to eliminate any possible finding that CPC is liable as an operator on the facts of this case.

By emphasizing that "CPC is directly liable under §107(a)(2) as an operator because CPC actively participated in and exerted significant control over Ott II's business and decision-making," 777 F. Supp., at 574, the District Court applied the "actual control" test of whether the parent "actually operated the business of its subsidiary," id., at 573, as several Circuits have employed it. . . .

The well-taken objection to the actual control test, however, is its fusion of direct and indirect liability; the test is administered by asking a question about the relationship between the two corporations (an issue going to indirect liability) instead of a question about the parent's interaction with the subsidiary's facility (the source of any direct liability). If, however, direct liability for the parent's operation of the facility is to be kept distinct from derivative liability for the subsidiary's own operation, the focus of the inquiry must necessarily be different under the two tests. "The question is not whether the parent operates the subsidiary, but rather whether it operates the facility, and that operation is evidenced by participation in the activities of the facility, not the subsidiary. Control of the subsidiary, if extensive enough, gives rise to indirect liability under piercing doctrine, not direct liability under the statutory language. . . . The District Court was therefore mistaken to rest its analysis on CPC's relationship with Ott II, premising liability on little more than "CPC's 100-percent ownership of Ott II" and "CPC's active participation in, and at times majority control over, Ott II's board of directors." 777 F. Supp., at 575. The analysis should instead have rested on the relationship between CPC and the Muskegon facility itself. . . .

In imposing direct liability. . . , the District Court failed to recognize that . . . it is entirely appropriate for directors of a parent corporation to serve as directors of its subsidiary, and that fact alone may not serve to expose the parent corporation to liability for its subsidiary's acts. . . . This recognition that the corporate personalities remain distinct has its corollary in the "well established principle [of corporate law] that directors and officers holding positions with a parent and its subsidiary can and do 'change hats' to represent the two corporations separately, despite their common ownership." *Lusk v. Foxmeyer Health*

Corp., 129 F.3d 773, 779 (5th Cir. 1997); see also *Fisser v. International Bank*, 282 F.2d 231, 238 (2d Cir. 1960). Since courts generally presume "that the directors are wearing their 'subsidiary hats' and not their 'parent hats' when acting for the subsidiary" . . . it cannot be enough to establish liability here that dual officers and directors made policy decisions and supervised activities at the facility. The Government would have to show that, despite the general presumption to the contrary, the officers and directors were acting in their capacities as CPC officers and directors, and not as Ott II officers and directors, when they committed those acts. The District Court made no such inquiry here, however, disregarding entirely this time-honored common law rule.

In sum, the District Court's focus on the relationship between parent and subsidiary (rather than parent and facility), combined with its automatic attribution of the actions of dual officers and directors to the corporate parent, erroneously, even if unintentionally, treated CERCLA as though it displaced or fundamentally altered common law standards of limited liability. Indeed, if the evidence of common corporate personnel acting at management and directorial levels were enough to support a finding of a parent corporation's direct operator liability under CERCLA, then the possibility of resort to veil piercing to establish indirect, derivative liability for the subsidiary's violations would be academic. There would in essence be a relaxed, CERCLA-specific rule of derivative liability that would banish traditional standards and expectations from the law of CERCLA liability. But, as we have said, such a rule does not arise from congressional silence, and CERCLA's silence is dispositive.

We accordingly agree with the Court of Appeals that a participation-and-control test looking to the parent's supervision over the subsidiary, especially one that assumes that dual officers always act on behalf of the parent, cannot be used to identify operation of a facility resulting in direct parental liability. Nonetheless, a return to the ordinary meaning of the word "operate" in the organizational sense will indicate why we think that the Sixth Circuit stopped short when it confined its examples of direct parental operation to exclusive or joint ventures, and declined to find at least the possibility of direct operation by CPC in this case. . . .

Again norms of corporate behavior (undisturbed by any CERCLA provision) are crucial reference points. Just as we may look to such norms in identifying the limits of the presumption that a dual officeholder acts in his ostensible capacity, so here we may refer to them in distinguishing a parental officer's oversight of a subsidiary from such an officer's control over the operation of the subsidiary's facility." [A]ctivities that involve the facility but which are consistent with the parent's investor status, such as monitoring of the subsidiary's performance, supervision of the subsidiary's finance and capital budget decisions, and articulation of general policies and procedures, should not give rise to direct liability. . . ." The critical question is whether, in degree and detail, actions directed to the facility by an agent of the parent alone are eccentric under accepted norms of parental oversight of a subsidiary's facility.

There is, in fact, some evidence that CPC engaged in just this type and degree of activity at the Muskegon plant. The District Court's opinion speaks of an agent of CPC alone who played a conspicuous part in dealing with the toxic risks emanating from the operation of the plant. G.R.D. Williams worked only for CPC; he was not an employee, officer, or director of Ott II . . . , and thus, his actions were of necessity taken only on behalf of CPC. The District Court found that "CPC became directly involved in environmental and regulatory matters through the work of . . . Williams, CPC's governmental and environmental affairs director. Williams . . . became heavily involved in environmental issues at Ott II." 777 F. Supp., at 561. He "actively participated in and exerted control over a variety of Ott

A. CERCLA: Judicial Process Interpretation

II environmental matters," ibid., and he "issued directives regarding Ott II's responses to regulatory inquiries," id., at 575.

We think that these findings are enough to raise an issue of CPC's operation of the facility through Williams's actions, though we would draw no ultimate conclusion from these findings at this point. Not only would we be deciding in the first instance an issue on which the trial and appellate courts did not focus, but the very fact that the District Court did not see the case as we do suggests that there may be still more to be known about Williams's activities. Indeed, even as the factual findings stand, the trial court offered little in the way of concrete detail for its conclusions about Williams's role in Ott II's environmental affairs, and the parties vigorously dispute the extent of Williams's involvement. Prudence thus counsels us to remand, on the theory of direct operation set out here, for reevaluation of Williams's role, and of the role of any other CPC agent who might be said to have had a part in operating the Muskegon facility. . . .

COMMENTARY & QUESTIONS

1. Piercing the corporate veil. Does the *BestFoods* decision simply involve the application of traditional corporate law principles? Justice Souter, writing for a unanimous Supreme Court, began his analysis by emphasizing the general corporate principle of law that a parent corporation is not liable for the acts of its subsidiary simply by virtue of stock ownership or because it exercised supervision over its subsidiary. Justice Souter went on to declare that the CERCLA statute, despite its public purpose of furthering cleanups, did not alter this "bedrock principle." The Supreme Court upheld the Sixth Circuit's ruling that a parent corporation could be held derivatively liable for the acts of its subsidiary only where the corporate veil could be pierced under common law. The common law exceptions to the limited liability principle include the failure of the subsidiary to maintain the corporate formalities and the use of the subsidiary for a fraudulent purpose. Absent proof of one of these traditional exceptions, the common law principle that parent corporations could not be held derivatively liable would control in a CERCLA case.

2. Operator liability of the parent corporation. Does the *BestFoods* decision simply involve the application of standard "operator" liability concepts under CERCLA? After analyzing parent corporation liability under corporate law principles, Justice Souter turned to the question of whether CERCLA's creation of "operator" liability expanded the circumstances under which parent corporations may be held liable. Here, the Court began the analysis by focusing on the distinction between "operating" a facility or site and "operating" a subsidiary. In the Supreme Court's analysis, "operator" liability under CERCLA is predicated on the actions that a person or corporation performs directly to operate a facility, not on its control of another company that owns the site. Thus, the Court acknowledged that a parent corporation may be held directly liable under CERCLA where its own employees direct or control environmental activities at a facility, but not where it simply exercises control of the subsidiary that owns the site through the normal mechanisms of corporate governance. In this respect, the Supreme Court was careful to clarify that a parent corporation does not become an "operator" of a subsidiary's facility through the routine practice of supervising the subsidiary's business. A parent corporation's routine supervision of a subsidiary could include appointing a subsidiary's officers and directors, monitoring its performance, supervising the subsidiary's finances, approving budgets and capital expenditures, and even articulating general policies and procedures for the subsidiary. All of these practices fall within the normal scope of the parent-subsidiary relationship and do not give rise to operator liability under CERCLA. Instead, to incur liability, a parent or its representatives must engage in actions that "are eccentric under the accepted norms of parental oversight of a subsidiary's facility."

3. Parent corporation liability through the acts of officers and directors. In assessing the liability arising from actions of officers and directors, does the *BestFoods* decision again simply apply established principles? Justice Souter specifically addressed the question of whether the parent corporation may incur liability through the acts of officers and directors who hold positions in both the parent corporation and its subsidiary. Justice Souter reasoned that it is typical corporate practice for the same individual to hold positions in both companies, and that the general rule is that where a dual officeholder acts in the capacity of an officer or director of the subsidiary, the law presumes that the officeholder is acting on behalf of the subsidiary and not the parent. The presumption can be overcome, however, where the dual officeholder acts contrary to the interest of the subsidiary and to the advantage of the parent.

4. What types of acts are enough for "operator" liability to attach for parent corporations? The Court indicated that for a parent corporation to be held liable as an operator, it must have acted directly to control the operations of the facility, not to have simply supervised the business of its subsidiary. The Supreme Court identified four situations in which the parent company may be directly liable under CERCLA:

1. where the parent company actually directed operations at a site owned by one of its subsidiaries, such as when a parent had leased property from its subsidiary to conduct its own operations;
2. where a parent corporation participated in a joint venture with its subsidiary;
3. where an officer or director who holds positions in both the parent and the subsidiary abuses his or her position in the subsidiary by making decisions concerning hazardous waste or environmental compliance that, under the norms of corporate behavior, are not in the interest of the subsidiary and are to the advantage of the parent; and
4. where an employee of the parent, who holds no position in the subsidiary, directly controls those operations at the site that involve hazardous substances or environmental compliance.

Are there any other situations in which the parent company may itself be directly liable? What specific type of evidence would be required to establish parental liability?

5. After *BestFoods*, will it be more difficult to hold parent corporations liable under CERCLA for contamination at their subsidiary's sites? Much of the evidence upon which the government has traditionally relied in suing parent corporations is likely insufficient to establish CERCLA liability after *BestFoods*. In the past, the government built many of its cases against parent corporations by showing that the same individuals were officers or directors of both the parent and the subsidiary, that the parent established general policies and practices for the subsidiary to follow, and that the parent's approval was necessary before the subsidiary could make substantial expenditures. Now this evidence will be viewed as indicative of normal parent-subsidiary relationships and, without additional facts, not proof of CERCLA liability. To hold a parent company liable, the government will have to meet either the common law standards of piercing the corporate veil or show that the parent directly controlled environmental activities at the subsidiary's site.

6. After *BestFoods*, may a parent corporation rely on its own environmental management staff to supervise its subsidiary's compliance without risk of Superfund liability?

A. CERCLA: Judicial Process Interpretation

The *BestFoods* decision indicates that a parent company may risk CERCLA liability if it assigns its own environmental affairs manager to supervise its subsidiary's compliance, unless that manager also holds a position in the subsidiary. Does this suggest that a parent company should be cautious to make sure that its subsidiary has its own environmental management staff, even if that staff includes individuals who hold dual positions with the parent and the subsidiary?

7. Successor corporations. Often one corporation will purchase the productive assets of another, either via merger, through the purchase of stock, or through the purchase of the assets themselves. Corporate law has developed general principles that establish when successor corporations will be held to have purchased the liabilities of their predecessors. EPA has issued the following guidance document that sets forth its general approach to issues of corporate succession:

> In establishing successor liability under CERCLA, the Agency should initially utilize the "continuity of business operation" approach of federal law. However, to provide additional support or an alternative basis for successor corporation liability, the Agency should be prepared to apply the traditional exemptions to the general rule of non-liability in asset acquisitions. EPA Memorandum of Courtney Price, Liability of Corporate Shareholders and Successor Corporations for Abandoned Sites Under [CERCLA] 15-16 (June 13, 1984).

At least one commentator has argued that this position marks a substantial expansion of successor liability because the continuation of the business entity test ignores the nuances of asset transfer that are often a key to determining successor liability under traditional state corporation law. See Wallace, Liability of Corporations and Corporate Officers, Directors, and Shareholders Under Superfund: Should Corporate and Agency Law Concepts Apply?, 14 J. Corp. L. 839, 879-884 (1989). The business continuation standard, instead, has its roots in the modern products liability revolution that has so greatly expanded liability in that realm.

In general, the courts have been receptive to imposing successor liability in CERCLA cases, particularly where the predecessor corporation would have been a PRP at the site. See, e.g., *Smith Land & Improvement Corp. v. Celotex Corp.*, 851 F.2d 86 (3d Cir. 1988); *Louisiana-Pacific Corp. v. Asarco, Inc.*, 909 F.2d 1260 (9th Cir. 1990); *United States v. Mexico Feed & Seed Co.*, 980 F.2d 478 (8th Cir. 1992); *City Envtl. Inc. v. U.S. Chem. Co.*, 814 F. Supp. 624 (E.D. Mich. 1993) aff'd on other grounds, 43 F.3d 244 (6th Cir. 1994); see also *Atchison, Topeka & Santa Fe Ry. v. Brown & Bryant Inc.*, 159 F.3d 358 (9th Cir. 1998) (questioning whether federal rather than state common law should govern successor liability under CERCLA). The traditional corporate law dividing line for liability in these cases is often linked to whether the entity is a mere asset purchaser (nonliability) or a corporate successor through a stock purchase (liability). CERCLA has pushed the precedents that are used to recognize corporate successorship to where liability can, at times, be found in cases where it would not have in the past. These areas are usually referred to as "continuing business enterprise" cases and "product line" cases. For an overview of the general distinction between successorship and asset purchases, see Janke & Kuryla, Environmental Liability Risks for Asset Purchasers, 24 Env't Rep. (BNA) 2237 (1994). The courts generally have also been receptive to efforts by parties to modify successor liability by contract, typically through the use of indemnification agreements. See, e.g., *Mardan Corp. v. C.G.C. Music, Ltd.*, 804 F.2d 1454 (9th Cir. 1986) (upholding claim by purchaser against seller under indemnity agreement); *AM Int'l, Inc. v. Int'l Forging Equip. Corp.*, 982 F.2d 989 (6th Cir. 1993) (ruling that §107(e) of CERCLA does not bar indemnification agreements).

7. Private Litigation Under CERCLA §107

Under §107(a)(2)(B), even nongovernmental entities are accorded a remedy to recover for costs that are consistent with the National Contingency Plan (NCP).[14] In this way, CERCLA expressly authorizes private litigants to seek recoveries from PRPs. This cause of action is complementary to causes of action that may exist under the common law, for the allowable scope of recovery relates exclusively to costs that are incurred in the cleanup of a contaminated site. Items such as recovery for personal injuries, or loss of amenity value, remain the province of traditional actions in tort.

The typical scenarios of private §107 actions involve current owners of contaminated property as plaintiffs suing either former occupiers of the property, parties whose wastes were disposed of there, or parties whose wastes have migrated there.[15] In some cases, the current owner will already have been ordered to clean the site by the government; in other cases, the cleanup effort may have preceded governmental involvement. For some time, there was ambiguity about whether costs could be incurred consistent with the NCP in advance of a governmentally initiated investigation or cleanup order and still be recoverable. That issue has been the subject of ongoing debate, as detailed more fully below.

The private cause of action under §107 has four basic elements: the plaintiff must prove that (1) the site in question is a "facility," (2) the defendant is a liable party under CERCLA §107(a), (3) a release or threatened release of a hazardous substance has occurred at the facility, and (4) the plaintiff has incurred response costs consistent with the NCP in responding to the release or threatened release. In light of the broad readings given to CERCLA liability issues, the consistency (with the NCP) requirement has been one of the most ardently litigated issues in private §107 suits.[16]

Another vigorously litigated issue in recent years has dealt with which costs constitute recoverable "response costs" in Section 107 cost recovery actions. In *Key Tronic Corp v. United States*, 511 U.S. 809, 818 (1994), all nine Justices agreed that §107 "unquestionably provides a cause of action for private parties to seek recovery of cleanup costs," although the court disallowed certain attorneys' fees as being recoverable costs. Nonetheless, the Supreme Court's subsequent decision in *Cooper Industries v. Aviall Services, Inc.*, 543 U.S. 157 (2004) raised serious questions about the breadth of the Court's statement in *KeyTronic*.

In *Cooper Industries*, the Supreme Court ruled that the current owner of certain contaminated sites (namely, Aviall Services), which had voluntarily incurred cleanup costs (to clean up releases of hazardous substances into soil and groundwater) after purchasing the sites from their former owner, Cooper Industries, could not bring a contribution action under §113(f), because §113(f) only allows contribution "during or following" a civil action under §106 or §107(a). The majority opinion, written by Justice Thomas, recognized that the cost recovery remedy of §107(a)(4)(B) and the contribution remedy of §113(f) are similar, in that both allow private parties to recoup costs from other private parties. But Justice Thomas also recognized that the two remedies are clearly distinct, stating (i) that in order to decide whether Aviall services could pursue an action under §107, the Court would have to consider the unbriefed question of whether a private party which is itself a PRP could

---

14. The NCP is discussed more fully below. For present purposes, the NCP can be understood as a set of guidelines framed by the United States that delineate the proper procedures and actions that are to be taken in cleaning up a Superfund site.

15. Adversely affected adjacent landowners are also allowed to sue. See, e.g., *Standard Equip., Inc. v. Boeing Co.*, No. C84-1129 (W.D. Wash. 1986).

16. See Steinway, Private Cost Recovery Actions Under CERCLA: The Impact of the Consistency Requirements, 4 Toxics L. Rep. (BNA) 1364 (May 2, 1990).

A. CERCLA: Judicial Process Interpretation

seek joint and several liability against other PRPs, and (ii) that it was prudent to withhold judgment on these matters in *Cooper Industries*, particularly given numerous circuit court decisions to the contrary.[17] Justice Thomas also seriously questioned whether there was an implied right of recovery under §107. The dissenting opinion, by contrast, urged, among other things, that, if Aviall could not bring an action for contribution under §113(f), Aviall ought to be allowed to proceed under §107(a).

Following the *Cooper Industries* decision, a split developed among the federal courts of appeal over whether a liable party could bring a cost recovery action under §107(a) (or had an implied right of action under §107(a)) after voluntarily cleaning up a contaminated site, even when an action for contribution under §113(f) could not be brought because the cleanup was a voluntary one. In 2007, the Supreme Court addressed this split in the unanimous decision also written by Justice Thomas which follows.

United States v. Atlantic Research Corp.

551 U.S. 128 (2007)

[This case involved an action by Atlantic Research Corporation to recover costs it incurred in voluntarily cleaning up a site on which it had previously retrofitted rocket motors for the United States. Atlantic Research sued the United States under §107, claiming that the United States was a PRP obligated to share in the costs of cleaning up the contamination resulting from retrofitting the rocket motors. In response, the United States argued that Atlantic Research was barred from bringing a §107 action because Atlantic Research was itself a PRP at the site. Rejecting the position of the United States, the Eighth Circuit held that Atlantic Research could recover its cleanup costs under §107(a). In a unanimous opinion written by Justice Thomas, the U.S. Supreme Court affirmed.

In its decision, the Supreme Court chiefly relied on the plain language of §107(a). The Court determined that the "any other person" language in subparagraph (B) of §107(a)(4) means that any person [other than the persons listed in subparagraph (A), which include the United States, states, or Indian tribes] may bring an action under §107 for cost recovery. Rather than render §107(a)(4)(B) superfluous, the Court found that the "any other person" language clarifies that §107(a)(4)(B) merely excludes those persons enumerated in the language of §107(a)(4)(A), rather than barring suit for cost recovery by PRPs generally.

The seeming tension between §107(a) and §113(f) of the Superfund Law was another point of contention before the Supreme Court. In its brief, and during oral argument, the United States argued that allowing a PRP which had voluntarily cleaned up a site to bring an action under §107(a) would have unintended consequences. Specifically, the United States argued that, if allowed to proceed under §107(a), PRPs could (1) evade the shorter statute of limitations for certain contribution actions, (2) seek joint and several liability rather than be limited to the equitable apportionment allowed in contribution actions, and (3) avoid the settlement bar that protects parties settling their liabilities with the government from

---

17. Compare *E.I. DuPont de Nemours & Co. v. U.S.*, 460 F.3d 515 (3d Cir. 2006), vacated, 551 U.S. 1129 (2007), with *Consolidated Edison of N.Y., Inc. v. UGI Utilities, Inc.*, 423 F.3d 90, 103 (2d Cir. 2005), *Atlantic Research Corp. v. U.S.*, 459 F.3d 827 (8th Cir. 2006), aff'd, 551 U.S. 128 (2007), and *Metropolitan Water Reclamation Dist. of Greater Chicago v. N. Am. Galvanizing & Coatings, Inc.*, 473 F.3d 824 (7th Cir. 2007). A great majority of the circuit courts prior to the Supreme Court's decision in *Cooper Industries* (and after the 1986 CERCLA Amendments that added the §113(f) contribution provision) had precluded joint and several cost recovery for response costs under §107(a).

further claims in contribution. In the excerpt that follows, the Court addresses these arguments by the United States.]

THOMAS, J. Two provisions of the Comprehensive Environmental Response, Compensation, and Liability Act of 1980 (CERCLA) — §§107(a) and 113(f) — allow private parties to recover expenses associated with cleaning up contaminated sites. 42 U.S.C. §§9607(a), 9613(f). In this case, we must decide a question left open in *Cooper Industries, Inc. v. Aviall Services, Inc.*, 543 U.S. 156, 161, 125 S. Ct. 577, 160 L. Ed. 2d 548 (2004): whether §107(a) provides so-called potentially responsible parties (PRPs), 42 U.S.C. §§9607(a)(1)-(4), with a cause of action to recover costs from other PRPs. We hold that it does....

Section 113(f) explicitly grants PRPs a right to contribution. Contribution is defined as the "tortfeasor's right to collect from others responsible for the same tort after the tortfeasor has paid more than his or her proportionate share, the shares being determined as a percentage of fault." Black's Law Dictionary 353 (8th ed. 2004). Nothing in §113(f) suggests that Congress used the term "contribution" in anything other than this traditional sense. The statute authorizes a PRP to seek contribution "during or following" a suit under §106 or §107(a). 42 U.S.C. §9613(f)(1). Thus, §113(f)(1) permits suit before or after the establishment of common liability. In either case, a PRP's right to contribution under §113(f)(1) is contingent upon an inequitable distribution of common liability among liable parties.

By contrast, §107(a) permits recovery of cleanup costs but does not create a right to contribution. A private party may recover under §107(a) without any establishment of liability to a third party. Moreover, §107(a) permits a PRP to recover only the costs it has "incurred" in cleaning up a site. 42 U.S.C. §9607(a)(4)(B). When a party pays to satisfy a settlement agreement or a court judgment, it does not incur its own costs of response. Rather, it reimburses other parties for costs that those parties incurred.

Accordingly, the remedies available in §§107(a) and 113(f) complement each other by providing causes of action "to persons in different procedural circumstances." *Consolidated Edison*, 423 F.3d, at 99; see also *E.I. DuPont de Nemours*, 460 F.3d, at 548 (Sloviter, J., dissenting). Section 113(f)(1) authorizes a contribution action to PRPs with common liability stemming from an action instituted under §106 or §107(a). And §107(a) permits cost recovery (as distinct from contribution) by a private party that has itself incurred cleanup costs. Hence, a PRP that pays money to satisfy a settlement agreement or a court judgment may pursue §113(f) contribution. But by reimbursing response costs paid by other parties, the PRP has not incurred its own costs of response and therefore cannot recover under §107(a). As a result, though eligible to seek contribution under §113(f)(1), the PRP cannot simultaneously seek to recover the same expenses under §107(a). Thus, at least in the case of reimbursement, the PRP cannot choose the 6-year statute of limitations for cost-recovery actions over the shorter limitations period for §113(f) contribution claims.

For similar reasons, a PRP could not avoid §113(f)'s equitable distribution of reimbursement costs among PRPs by instead choosing to impose joint and several liability on another PRP in an action under §107(a). The choice of remedies simply does not exist. In any event, a defendant PRP in such a §107(a) suit could blunt any inequitable distribution of costs by filing a §113(f) counterclaim. 459 F.3d, at 835; see also *Consolidated Edison*, supra, at 100, n. 9 (collecting cases). Resolution of a §113(f) counter-claim would necessitate the equitable apportionment of costs among the liable parties, including the PRP that filed the §107(a) action. 42 U.S.C. §9613(f)(a) ("In resolving contribution claims, the court may allocate response costs among liable parties using such equitable factors as the court determines are appropriate").

Finally, permitting PRPs to seek recovery under §107(a) will not eviscerate the settlement bar set forth in §113(f)(2). That provision prohibits §113(f) contribution claims against "[a] person who has resolved its liability to the United States or a State in an administrative

A. CERCLA: Judicial Process Interpretation

or judicially approved settlement. . . ." 42 U.S.C. §9613(f)(2). The settlement bar does not by its terms protect against cost-recovery liability under §107(a). For several reasons, we doubt this supposed loophole would discourage settlement. First, as stated above, a defendant PRP may trigger equitable apportionment by filing a §113(f) counterclaim. A district court applying traditional rules of equity would undoubtedly consider any prior settlement as part of the liability calculus. Cf. 4 Restatement (Second) of Torts §886A(2), p. 337 (1977) ("No tortfeasor can be required to make contribution beyond his own equitable share of the liability"). Second, the settlement bar continues to provide significant protection from contribution suits by PRPs that have inequitably reimbursed the costs incurred by another party. Third, settlement carries the inherent benefit of finally resolving liability as to the United States or a State.

Because the plain terms of §107(a)(4)(B) allow a PRP to recover costs from other PRPs, the statute provides Atlantic Research with a cause of action. We therefore affirm the judgment of the Court of Appeals.

COMMENTARY & QUESTIONS

1. The purpose of the consistency requirement. Why must cleanups be consistent with the NCP to allow recovery in a §107 action? Why should not the key issue only be whether the response action was effective? One answer was suggested by counsel for Litton in an oral argument in the Eighth Circuit, when he indicated that defendants in private cost recovery suits need protection from parties that voluntarily perform "a Rolls-Royce cleanup when a Volkswagen one would do." See Need Protection from Rolls-Royce Cleanup, Eighth Circuit Told in Suit to Recover Costs, 5 Toxics L. Rep. (BNA) 651 (Oct. 17, 1990). (The issue of "Cadillac cleanups" is discussed below.) On the other end of the scale, NCP-consistent cleanups are a means of guaranteeing that the effort is effective. Particularly under the revised NCP, satisfying its requirements would help to ensure an effective cleanup and also involve community sentiment as a factor in the cleanup process.

But what does compliance with the NCP entail? *General Elec. Co. v. Litton Indus. Automation Sys., Inc.*, 920 F.2d 1415 (8th Cir. 1990), a leading case on consistency with the NCP, concerned the merger by Litton with a former owner and occupant of land now owned by GE. From 1959 to 1962, during the occupancy of the company taken over by Litton, improper disposal of cyanide-based electroplating wastes, sludges, and other pollutants had occurred on the parcel. In the early 1980s, GE and the Missouri Department of Natural Resources (MDNR) investigated the site and decided that no cleanup was necessary. In 1984, GE sold the site to a commercial real estate developer. Shortly thereafter, the MDNR changed its position on the need for a cleanup, at which point GE was threatened with CERCLA lawsuits by both its vendee and MDNR. Negotiations followed in which GE agreed to clean up the site and did so to the satisfaction of MDNR.

Thereafter GE sued Litton under §107. Litton's most vigorous defense was that the cleanup was not consistent with the NCP. The district court ruled in favor of GE, awarding $940,000 as reimbursement for response costs and an additional $419,000 in attorneys' fees. See *General Elec. Co. v. Litton Bus. Sys.*, 715 F. Supp. 949 (W.D. Mo. 1989), aff'd, 920 F.2d 1415 (8th Cir. 1990). In reviewing the critical finding that the costs incurred were consistent with the NCP despite having omitted some detailed requirements mentioned in the NCP, the court wrote:

> We are satisfied that the thorough evaluation that was performed here is consistent with the NCP, specifically with 40 C.F.R. §300.65(b)(2). The site evaluation does not have to comply

strictly with the letter of the NCP, but only must be consistent with its requirements. It is not necessary that every factor mentioned by the NCP be dealt with explicitly; thus, for instance, a failure to consider explicitly the weather conditions factor is not fatal to an evaluation's consistency with the NCP. 920 F.2d at 1420.

2. Standing in the shoes of the government. In a private §107 action, should the plaintiff enjoy all of the same advantages (joint and several strict liability with a relaxed standard of causation) as the government does when it sues PRPs? In *Dedham Water Co. v. Cumberland Farms Dairy, Inc.*, 889 F.2d 1146 (1st Cir. 1989), clarified, 901 F.2d 3 (1st Cir. 1990), the appeals court reversed a ruling that had required the plaintiff to prove which of two possible sources had caused the contamination of its well that had given rise to CERCLA response costs. The court drew heavily on the liberal liability provisions of CERCLA to find that "a literal reading of the statute imposes liability if releases or threatened releases from defendant's facility cause the plaintiff to incur response costs; it does not say that liability is imposed only if the defendant causes actual contamination of the plaintiff's property." Does it seem odd to hold a party like Cumberland Farms liable, when the facts as found by the trial court (and not overturned on appeal) were that two other nearby operations "were 'probable' causes" of the contamination of plaintiff's wells? Is this like the *Wade II* relaxed standard of causation that, in effect, treats all parties whose acts are potential causes of the pollution as being actual causes of the problem?

3. Cost recovery versus contribution. As noted in *Atlantic Research*, private cost recovery suits filed under §107(a) are different in material ways from contribution actions filed under §113(f)(1). Before *Atlantic Research*, the principal reason to characterize a suit as one or the other was the posture of the party bringing the suit — is the party an innocent victim of the contamination (§107 available) or a member of the PRP class (only §113 available)? See, e.g., *Pinal Creek Group v. Newmont Mining Corp.*, 118 F.3d 1298 (9th Cir. 1997); *Rumpke of Ind., Inc. v. Cummins Engine Co.*, 107 F.3d 1235 (7th Cir. 1997); *United Techs. Corp. v. Browning-Ferris Indus.*, 33 F.3d 96 (1st Cir. 1994); *Akzo Coatings, Inc. v. Aigner Corp.*, 30 F.3d 761 (7th Cir. 1994); *In re Dant & Russell, Inc.*, 951 F.2d 246 (9th Cir. 1991). Accompanying a loss of cost recovery under §107 would be a loss of joint and several liability and a shift to an equitable contribution action in which the plaintiff (and all of the other parties) have to try to persuade the trier of fact of how responsibility ought to be apportioned. But there are other differences as well, including a different and shorter (three years rather than six) statute of limitations in contribution claims. See Araiza, Text, Purpose, and Facts: The Relationship Between CERCLA Sections 107 and 113, 72 Notre Dame L. Rev. 193 (1996); Evans, The Phantom PRP in CERCLA Contribution Litigation: EPA to the Rescue?, 26 Env't Rep. (BNA) 2109 (1996).

4. The questions left open by *Atlantic Research*. The Supreme Court's decision in *Atlantic Research* leaves several key questions open for further consideration. The Court did not address the question of what remedy (under §107(a), §113(f), or both) would be available to a PRP that incurred expenses pursuant to a consent decree following suit under §106 or §107(a). In addition, it did not address the question of whether §107(a) also provided an implied right of contribution for PRPs ineligible for relief under §113(f). Furthermore, it assumed but did not decide that §107(a) provides for joint and several liability.

And what about settlement? The United States argued in *Atlantic Research* that allowing suits under §107(a) after voluntary cleanups will undermine the ability to achieve settlement with PRPs. The Supreme Court was not impressed by this argument. According to the Court, allowing PRPs to bring §107(a) claims will have only a minimal impact on whether parties ultimately decide to settle with the government.

Is the Supreme Court's lack of concern well-founded? Although it is true that, after *Atlantic Research*, PRPs may bring §107(a) claims against other PRPs that have negotiated settlements with the government, this should not meaningfully deter settlements. Rather, to

A. CERCLA: Judicial Process Interpretation

achieve fairness in cost allocations among PRPs, won't settling PRPs still be entitled to bring §113(f) claims against the non-settling PRPs? In a real world scenario, as the Court noted, equitable factors will still play a key role in evaluating the importance of any prior settlements with the government. In fact, it is likely that, even though they may bring a §107(a) claim, non-settling parties will factor in the expense of litigation along with the likelihood of having to defend a §113 claim prior to bringing claims against parties that have settled with the government. In addition, as recognized by the Supreme Court, settling with the government inherently brings liable parties the resolution of the government's action against them, no small benefit indeed. Although it may not be as formidable as it was prior to the *Atlantic Research* decision, the settlement bar is still an incentive to settle with the government.

The Supreme Court acknowledged in the *Atlantic Research* opinion that there may be some overlap between §107(a) claims and §113(f) claims. However, the Court declined to address how parties and courts should address that overlap. For example, it is unclear what type of action would be appropriate if a party incurs response costs pursuant to a government consent decree, administrative order, or a settlement. Following *Aviall*, such parties may have believed that they were limited solely to a §113 action and then only if they had been subject to a §106 or §107 "civil action." Now, after *Atlantic Research*, parties must reassess their options and reconsider whether and to what extent both §107(a) and §113(f) claims are available. PRPs are likely to be more interested in pursuing §107 claims because of the opportunity to impose joint and several liability, although the Court only "assumed" but did not decide that §107 imposed joint and several liability.

Going forward, we can anticipate that parties will likely bring claims under both provisions of the Superfund Law, to maximize the likelihood of obtaining the broadest possible remedy. Bringing claims under both provisions increases the possibility that the defending party will file a motion to dismiss or for summary judgment, arguing that one or the other provision is an inappropriate basis for recovery. We can, therefore, expect future judicial clarification on the scope of Superfund claims available to a party subject to a consent decree, administrative order, or settlement. To that end, the Eleventh Circuit, in *Solutia, Inc. Pharmacia Corp. v. McWane, Inc.* 672 F.3d 1230 (11th Cir. 2012) held that a party seeking contribution under §113 for response costs incurred pursuant to an administrative or judicially approved settlement may not simultaneously seek cost recovery under §107. In reaching this result, the Eleventh Circuit followed decisions already issued by the Eighth Circuit (*Morrison Enters., LLC v. Dravo Corp.*, 638 F.3d 594, 603 (8th Cir. 2011)); the Third Circuit (*Agere Sys., Inc. v. Advanced Envtl. Tech. Corp.*, 602 F.3d 204, 229 (3d Cir. 2010) (holding that parties subject to a consent decree cannot bring a claim under §107(a))); the Second Circuit (*Niagara Mohawk Power Corp. v. Chevron U.S.A., Inc.*, 596 F.3d 112 (2d Cir. 2010) (holding that parties that settle CERCLA liability with government agencies can only bring §113(f) contribution claims)); and the Sixth Circuit (*IIT Indus., Inc. v. BorgWarner, Inc.*, 506 F.3d 452, 458 (6th Cir. 2007)). In each of these decisions, the Courts of Appeal ruled that §113(f) provides the exclusive remedy for a liable party compelled to incur response costs pursuant to an administrative or judicially approved settlement under §107.

Consider the consequences of this result of barring claims under §107 and limiting liable parties to contribution under §113. Unlike §107(a), §113(f)'s right of contribution only allows allocation of responsibility between the contribution plaintiff and the defendants. Furthermore, §113(f)(2) does not allow a plaintiff to seek contribution from parties who have previously settled their liability to the United States or a state. This was the basis for the settling defendants' motion in *Solutia*. Finally, the statutes of limitation differ, depending on whether a plaintiff is proceeding under §107 or §113. See 42 U.S.C. §9613(g)(2)-(3).

5. The "big gorilla" of Defense Department Superfund liability. Private parties who voluntarily remediate contaminated sites can now (after *Atlantic Research*) bring cost recovery actions under §107(a) of the Superfund Law, even though (after *Aviall*) they are not entitled to bring contribution actions under §113(f). Although the Supreme Court grounded its analyses in *Atlantic Research* and in *Aviall* on the plain language of the Superfund statute, the Court's decision in *Atlantic Research* appears to serve one of the Superfund law's primary purposes—encouraging private parties to clean up contaminated sites, rather than waiting until they are forced to do so by the government.

In light of these seeming benefits to the position adopted by the Supreme Court in *Atlantic Research*, why was the United States so adamantly opposed to expanding the reach of §107? The United States argued that §107—which the government generally uses to impose liability—does not also give PRPs engaged in voluntary cleanup the right to sue other polluters. The underlying basis for the government's determined advocacy may be, in part, the fact that the United States faces many millions of dollars in potential liability at former U.S. Defense Department owned and/or operated sites, including the one at issue in *Atlantic Research*. As one of the "biggest gorillas" potentially responsible for the cleanup of these sites, the United States was undoubtedly concerned that expanding the right to bring §107 suits would increase its own potential liabilities. But the United States—like other PRPs—is still not without its other defenses. We can expect, for example, that the focus of much contentious cost recovery litigation going forward will now focus on whether voluntary cleanups for which PRPs seek reimbursement were conducted consistent with the EPA's National Contingency Plan (NCP).

6. A reminder about state law remedies. Even if it borders on redundancy, it is important to keep in mind the continuing availability of state statutory and common law remedies for environmental harms caused by hazardous materials. Despite the broad federal efforts to govern hazardous groundwater contamination, reflected in both RCRA and CERCLA, Congress was well aware that it was entering a field having a strong tradition of state regulatory and remedial primacy. Both RCRA and CERCLA contain provisions extending authority to states to enact additional more stringent measures.[18] Beyond that, §114(a) of CERCLA provides:

> Nothing in this chapter shall be construed or interpreted as pre-empting any State from imposing any additional liability or requirements with respect to the release of hazardous substances within such State.[19]

7. CERCLA and the time in which to bring state-law based claims involving hazardous substance contamination. CERCLA §9658 expressly preempts state statutes of *limitations* in "any action brought under State law for personal injury, or property damages, which are caused or contributed to by exposure to any hazardous substance, or pollutant or contaminant, released into the environment from a facility. . . ." In *CTS Corp. v. Waldburger*, 134 S. Ct. 2175 (2014), however, the Supreme Court held that statutes of *repose* are not preempted by CERCLA §9658.

The basic facts of the case are straightforward. From 1959-1985, CTS Corporation operated an electronics plant in North Carolina. In 2011, the owners of the former CTS

---

18. RCRA §3009, codified at 42 U.S.C. §6929; CERCLA §114(a), codified at 42 U.S.C. §9614(a).

19. Despite this expressly nonpreemptive character, there are narrow areas of state legislative authority that are preempted by CERCLA and RCRA. These cases arise when states enact their own mini-Superfund laws and fund them via a tax like that used to fund CERCLA. See *Exxon Corp. v. Hunt*, 475 U.S. 355 (1986). There have also been cases preempting local regulation of RCRA-regulated waste handling facilities. See *ENSCO, Inc. v. Dumas*, 807 F.2d 743 (8th Cir. 1986) (preempting local waste handling regulations that bar methods encouraged by RCRA). The preemption of common law by statutes is generally disfavored; the canon of statutory construction cautions that statutes in derogation of common law are to be narrowly construed.

property and adjacent properties filed a state law nuisance case in federal district court, seeking to hold CTS responsible for contaminants on the property. The district court ruled that, because CTS had sold the property in 1987, the suit was barred by the North Carolina statute of repose, which prohibits tort suits for personal injury or physical damage to property filed more than ten years after the defendant's last culpable act. (See N.C. Gen. Stat. Ann. §1-52(16) (Lexis 2013) ("[N]o cause of action shall accrue more than 10 years from the last act or omission of the defendant giving rise to the cause of action.")) On appeal, the Fourth Circuit reinstated the landowners' lawsuit, on the grounds that the North Carolina statute of repose was preempted by CERCLA §9658, but the Supreme Court—by a vote of seven to two—reversed the Fourth Circuit.

In an opinion by Justice Kennedy, the Court explained that, although there is considerable common ground between a statute of limitations and a statute of repose, the two nonetheless serve different purposes. In particular, a statute of repose reflects a judgment that a defendant should not be held liable for his actions at all after a specific amount of time has passed, embodying the idea that, at some point, a defendant should be able to put past events behind him. The Court observed that CERCLA §9658 repeatedly refers to a "statute of limitations," and the Court placed particular emphasis on a 1982 report commissioned by Congress in connection with CERCLA that specifically referred to "statutes of repose as a distinct category" and urged Congress to preempt statutes of repose as well. Congress's failure to make that same distinction, along with other aspects of §9658, the Court concluded, indicated that although CERCLA §9658 does preempt and was designed to preempt state statutes of limitation, Congress did not intend for §9658 also to preempt state statutes of repose.

A number of questions are raised by this decision. First, does the decision incentivize states to restrict toxic tort suits, by empowering additional states to pass statutes of repose like the one upheld in North Carolina? The landowners tried to convince the Supreme Court that CERCLA §9658 can be interpreted to include statutes of repose (as well as statutes of limitation), by arguing that statutes of repose were used interchangeably with statutes of limitation when Congress passed CERCLA §9658. Now that the Supreme Court has disagreed, other states may well consider whether they should have a statute of repose as well. The Supreme Court's decision appears to ensure that the nation's highest court will not be upending whatever policy decision states decide to make concerning statutes of repose. Second, many scientists would concur that the latency period of certain cancers after toxic exposure can be many years or even decades. If so, does the Court's decision mean that victims will not be able to sue for wrongful pollution if a statute of repose applies and the cancer or health condition at issue does not manifest itself until years later? Third, is the decision at odds with the remedial purpose of CERCLA and CERCLA's historical adherence to the polluter-pays principle (PPP)? In states having statutes of repose like the one in North Carolina, will such statutes disincentivize polluters from internalizing the costs of environmental harm, by eliminating their accountability for that harm?

B. EPA's CERCLA Administrative Order Process

In creating CERCLA's liability rules, Congress empowered EPA to remediate contaminated sites itself, using federal money, and also allowed EPA to recover its expenditures from persons responsible for the contamination. In passing CERCLA, however, Congress also established another powerful mechanism for use by EPA in seeking to remediate contaminated sites. In CERCLA §106, Congress empowered EPA to bring administrative or judicial enforcement actions against responsible parties to force them to perform the remediation. EPA's administrative order authority provides EPA with perhaps its most potent enforcement tool (see Chapter 18). By its terms, §106 authorizes EPA to seek relief whenever it determines that a site "may" present "an imminent and substantial endangerment to public health or . . . the environment." It authorizes EPA to issue "such orders as may be necessary to protect public health and welfare and the environment." The key text is as follows:

42 U.S.C. §9606.[20] Abatement Actions

(a) Maintenance, jurisdiction, etc. In addition to any other action taken by a State or local government, when the President determines that there may be an imminent and substantial endangerment to the public health or welfare or the environment because of an actual or threatened release of a hazardous substance from a facility, he may require the Attorney General of the United States to secure such relief as may be necessary to abate such danger or threat, and the district court of the United States in the district in which the threat occurs shall have jurisdiction to grant such relief as the public interest and the equities of the case may require. The President may also, after notice to the affected State, take other action under this section including, but not limited to, issuing such orders as maybe necessary to protect public health and welfare and the environment. . . .

(b) Fines; reimbursement. (1) Any person who, without sufficient cause, willfully violates, or fails or refuses to comply with, any order of the President under subsection (a) of this section may . . . be fined not more than $25,000 for each day in which such violation occurs or such failure to comply continues. . . .

Section 106 is often invoked by EPA to encourage PRPs to do more of the removal and remedial work at sites themselves. When a voluntary agreement to do so cannot be reached (or when a previous agreement is breached), EPA may require PRPs to respond. EPA states its policy as follows:

EPA prefers to obtain private-party response action through the negotiation of settlement agreements with parties willing to do the work. When viable private parties exist and are not willing to reach a timely settlement to undertake work under a consent order or decree, or prior to settlement discussions in appropriate circumstances, the Agency typically will compel private-party response through unilateral orders. If PRPs do not comply with the order, EPA may fund the response or may refer the case for judicial action to compel performance and recover penalties. EPA, Guidance on CERCLA Section 106(a) Unilateral Administrative Orders for Remedial Designs and Remedial Actions, OSWER Directive No. 9833.0-la, at 3 (Mar. 7, 1990).

Section 106(a) administrative orders cannot be disobeyed without substantial risk. Section 106(b)(1) allows EPA to seek a fine in court of up to $25,000 per day against "[a]ny person who, without sufficient cause, willfully violates, or fails or refuses to comply with, any order. . . ." Most courts have concluded that, in connection with whether the defendant in a §106 order is a proper PRP, the relevant liability principles, both with respect to the identity of the parties and the applicable standards of liability, are established by §107. See, e.g., *United States v. A&F Materials Co.*, 578 F. Supp. 1249, 1257-1258 (S.D. Ill. 1984).

Alternatively, pursuant to CERCLA §107(c)(3), EPA can undertake the abatement action itself and then sue for reimbursement and statutory punitive damages "in an amount at least equal to, and not more than three times" the amount of the cost of the government action!

---

20. Section 106 in the original Act.

B. EPA's CERCLA Administrative Order Process

There is nothing in the statutory language to suggest that EPA cannot seek both the daily penalties and the punitive damages in cases where EPA eventually undertakes the work.

Administrative orders are even more powerful because they are not subject to pre-enforcement review. CERCLA §113(h) explicitly provides that no federal court has jurisdiction "to review any challenges to . . . any order issued under 9606(a) [CERCLA §106(a)] . . . ." The jurisdictional proviso lists a number of exceptions, only one of which can take place before the required action has been performed. That one exception is a suit brought by EPA to compel a remedial action. See CERCLA §113(h)(5). Courts interpret the law to preclude pre-enforcement review. In so doing, the courts have repeatedly rejected constitutional attacks that challenge the Hobson's choice (take expensive action pursuant to an administrative order that you allege to be illegal, or risk a far more costly array of punitive sanctions if your post-cleanup attack on the order fails) as being a denial of due process. See, e.g., *North Shore Gas Co. v. U.S. EPA*, 753 F. Supp. 1413 (N.D. Ill. 1990), aff'd, 930 F.2d 1239 (7th Cir. 1991); *Aminoil, Inc. v. U.S. EPA*, 599 F. Supp. 69 (C.D. Cal. 1984).

Defense of subsequent suits seeking sanctions for noncompliance with §106(a) orders is also difficult. The defendant-violator has the burden of proving that there was "sufficient cause" for noncompliance. This amounts to proving that either (1) the defendant was not a person to whom the order could have been issued (i.e., was not a PRP), or (2) the actions ordered were inconsistent with the NCP. Making the sufficient cause defense even harder to establish, most courts require that the defendant, by objective evidence, prove that its belief in the invalidity of the order was held reasonably and in good faith. See Donald, Defending Against Daily Fines and Punitive Damages Under CERCLA: The Meaning of "Without Sufficient Cause," 19 Colum. J. Envtl. L. 185 (1994).

Wary of EPA's enforcement priorities and unhappy with the Hobson's choice posed by §106, the regulated community has continued to seek ways to thwart the formidable §106 power. The latest significant challenge came from General Electric, which sought a declaratory judgment that §106, in tandem with §107(c)(3) and §113(h) of CERCLA, together create a regime that violates due process. GE argued that these sections fail to provide any hearing or other procedural safeguards before EPA issues a §106 order, contrary to fundamental due process requirements. But, after years of litigation, GE did not prevail. In 2010, the D.C. Circuit ruled that a §106 Unilateral Administrative Order's (UAO) imposition of financial consequences (i.e., treble damages, plus penalties of up to $37,500 per day for noncompliance) did not deprive PRPs like GE of property under the Fifth Amendment's due process clause. *G.E. v. Jackson*, 610 F.3d 110 (D.C. Cir. 2010) (affirming the grant of summary judgment to the EPA, in concluding that CERCLA §106, both on its face and as applied, does not violate the due process clause).

GE's certiorari petition raised two questions for Supreme Court review:

(1) whether a UAO's imposition of response costs, or decreases in a PRP's stock price and credit rating, amounts to a deprivation of property under the due process clause; and
(2) whether CERCLA's UAO scheme violates the due process clause by impermissibly coercing compliance in making judicial review of a UAO contingent on the threat of treble damages and fines that accumulate at the EPA's discretion.

In its brief in opposition, the United States argued that certiorari should be denied, citing several "procedural protections" available to parties targeted by a UAO. The United States pointed out that, before a UAO is issued, EPA provides a notice to the PRP allowing it to submit information disputing liability. If EPA decides to move forward with the enforcement action, it has to file a civil suit in federal district court to compel compliance. A

PRP can also comply with the UAO and then seek reimbursement of the cleanup costs it has incurred. The United States also argued that, contrary to GE's contentions, CERCLA itself does not impose treble damages plus penalties for noncompliance; only a federal court can do so, and then only after the PRP has had an opportunity to present its case.

When the Supreme Court declined to grant certiorari on June 6, 2011, it ended a decade of unsuccessful litigation by GE over the constitutionality of CERCLA §106. While it is never a good idea to read too much into a denial of certiorari, it seems reasonable to infer that the Court did not believe that its recent decision in *Sackett v. EPA*, 132 S. Ct. 1367 (2012) was controlling. In *Sackett*, the Court invalidated, as an unconstitutional denial of due process, an EPA Clean Water Act compliance order that required restoration of a parcel that EPA had determined to be wetlands and that was entered without a hearing in which the landowner could oppose the designation of the parcel as wetlands. *Sackett* had drawn a distinction between its statutory setting and that of some other statutes (but not mentioning CERCLA among them), in which Congress had set out the procedural process in a manner that did not allow pre-enforcement review of the initial agency determination.

COMMENTARY & QUESTIONS

1. EPA's use of its §106 power. Given the formidable §106 power, it might seem strange that EPA does not always make administrative cleanup orders its remedial method of choice. There are at least six reasons why EPA would still prefer to negotiate consent decrees for remedial (as opposed to removal) actions. These include: (1) setting the proper tone for the long-term relationship that is entailed in EPA supervision of a PRP-conducted cleanup, (2) rewarding volunteers (by working out fair agreements), (3) punishing recalcitrants, (4) the congressional policy favoring settlements, (5) judicial supervision of court orders, and (6) the availability of CERCLA §122(l) civil penalties, and the availability of CERCLA §122(e)(3)(B) administrative subpoenas to compel testimony and the production of information. See Mugdan, The Use of CERCLA Section 106 Administrative Orders to Secure Remedial Action, in ALI-ABA, Study Materials on Hazardous Wastes, Superfund, and Toxic Substances 601-603 (Oct. 25-27, 1990).

2. Punitive treble damages. Despite its presence in CERCLA since original enactment in 1980, the treble damage remedy has not been frequently used. *United States v. Parsons*, 723 F. Supp. 757 (N.D. Ga. 1989), marked the first time that treble damages were awarded for noncompliance with a CERCLA §106(a) order.[21] After subsequent litigation over the issue of whether one of the Parsons defendants had made a good faith effort at compliance with the order, the court entered judgment for EPA in the amount of $2,260,173.72, based on trebling proven EPA response costs of $753,391.24. EPA sought reconsideration of the award, arguing that it was entitled to both the response costs and the penalty. The district court ruled against awarding EPA "quadruple" damages. *United States v. Parsons*, 738 F. Supp. 1436 (N.D. Ga. 1990), but was reversed on appeal, 936 F.2d 526 (11th Cir. 1991) (holding that the federal government could recover four times the amount that EPA spent to clean up a site).

3. Agency leverage or abuse of power? The power to seek treble damages is, obviously, a significant tool. How much confidence do you have that EPA will use its §106 leverage prudently, without abusing the power that such leverage provides?

---

21. See EPA Granted Damages for Company's Failure to Obey 106 Order to Perform Response Action, 4 Toxics L. Rep. 515 (1989).

4. Chasing recalcitrant parties. Does EPA have the power under §106 to pursue recalcitrant parties when other PRPs have previously agreed to perform the necessary response actions? Is EPA entitled to seek "duplicate recovery" on the grounds that recalcitrant parties are also jointly and severally liable? If EPA lacks this power, will recalcitrants be even less willing to join a settling group if the threat of sanctions under §106 no longer looms over them?

5. The common law, §106, and RCRA corrective action. What does CERCLA §106 accomplish that the common law does not? Section 106 makes prospective relief routinely available. Under the common law, it is only the extraordinary case that prevents a harm before it happens. Section 106 offers an extrajudicial remedy: EPA can go to court, but it can also issue its own administrative orders against polluters. RCRA §7003 also offers EPA an extrajudicial remedy. Under RCRA §7003, EPA can go to court (as in *NEPACCO*), but EPA can also issue "such orders as may be necessary to protect public health and the environment." 42 U.S.C. §6973. However, RCRA corrective action is not governed by the same set of liability rules as CERCLA §106. For example, under RCRA, a party may, in connection with corrective action, move or excavate soil within a corrective action management unit (CAMU) without liability attaching. Movement of waste within a CAMU does not constitute treatment, storage, or disposal of hazardous waste under RCRA, does not constitute "land disposal" triggering RCRA hazardous waste disposal requirements, and does not "produce" hazardous waste implicating RCRA generator requirements. Under CERCLA, by contrast, a party that moves or excavates soils causing a release of hazardous substances, even if in connection with a required cleanup under §106, may nonetheless be held liable either as an operator (under CERCLA §107(a)(2)) or for accepting hazardous substances for transport to sites that it has selected (under CERCLA §107(a)(4)). See, e.g., *Kaiser Aluminum & Chem. Corp. v. Catellus Dev. Corp.*, 976 F.2d 1338 (9th Cir. 1992) (holding liable under CERCLA contractor hired to excavate land who spread contaminated soil over uncontaminated soil in the process).

C. IDENTIFYING SITES, FUNDING, AND SETTING THE STANDARDS FOR CLEANUPS

CERCLA not only sets up liability rules enforceable under §106 and §107 but also creates an administrative system for environmental remediation—removing harmful materials improperly dumped into the environment over past years. In this context, what is important are matters of process and execution: identifying sites in need of environmental cleanups, setting priorities among the needed cleanup efforts, planning what actions are needed on a site-by-site basis, and ensuring that planned responses are properly executed. This process begins with a procedure for identifying and ranking the hazards posed by sites of hazardous materials contamination. On the basis of that hazard ranking system (HRS), CERCLA establishes a national priorities list (NPL) that then functions to ensure that the most dangerous sites are remediated first. CERCLA requires EPA to establish a National Contingency Plan (NCP), which is, in essence, a compendium of the standards and procedures for cleanups that will ensure an acceptable

> **CERCLA's Administrative System for Remediation:**
> - Hazard Ranking System (HRS)
> - National Priorities List (NPL)
> - National Contingency Plan (NCP)
> - Removal Actions
> - Remedial Actions

result. Cleanups are of two kinds: Removals are short-term measures taken to minimize the dangers to health and the environment from emergency situations, whereas remedial actions are long-term efforts that attempt to rid the site of dangers on a permanent basis.

Generally, CERCLA's cleanup process has worked as expected.[22] The HRS has been used to identify sites and subsequently generate the NPL that serves as the principal means of dictating EPA's cleanup priorities. EPA, through a combination of Superfund money and PRP-funded response and remedial actions, has made progress in the remediation of numerous sites throughout the nation. Nevertheless, the cost and complexity of cleanups has made CERCLA an exciting and intensely fought aspect of hazardous materials regulation. There are literally billions of dollars to be paid by PRPs, as thousands of sites of hazardous material releases are remediated. For many lawyers representing PRPs, the problem is less one of environmental law than it is one of engaging in strategic behavior to minimize both the amount spent on cleanups and the share of the cleanup cost allocated to their clients. EPA, too, is engaged in a strategic process, whereby it seeks to accomplish as much of the massive cleanup job as it can with limited human and material resources.

Cleanup procedures are governed by the NCP. According to CERCLA §105, in the NCP, EPA is to "establish procedures and standards for responding to releases of hazardous substances, pollutants, and contaminants. . . ." The statutorily mandated scope of the NCP includes methodologies that will identify sites in need of remediation, analyze the danger to health and the environment posed by releases and threatened releases, determine the scope and extent of needed remedial measures, and ensure that remedial actions are cost-effective.[23] The NCP must address such mundane matters as the procurement and maintenance of response equipment and the qualifications of private cleanup firms that will be engaged to do the cleanup work on Superfund projects. More politically sensitive matters must also be covered by the NCP. These include the division of authority between the federal, state, and local governments in effectuating the plan and the standards by which innovative cleanup technologies will be judged.[24]

The required priority ranking of sites in order of hazard (i.e., the HRS/NPL process) is also a part of the NCP. In this area, Congress has provided some general directions for EPA. EPA, for example, is required to revise the NPL to reflect new information about existing and additional sites.[25] Similarly, CERCLA specifies that the relative risk assessment under the HRS should include the extent of the population put at risk by the site, the hazard potential of the substances found at the site, the potential to contaminate groundwater or surface water that is used for either drinking water supply or recreation, the potential for direct human contact, the potential for the destruction of natural resources that affect the human food chain, state preparedness, and "other appropriate factors."[26]

---

22. CERCLA's major miscalculation has been its gross underestimation of cleanup costs and recoupment rates.
23. CERCLA §105(a)(1)-(3), (7), 42 U.S.C. §9605(a)(1)-(3), (7).
24. CERCLA §105(a)(5)-(6), (9)-(10), 42 U.S.C. §9605(a)(5)-(6), (9)-(10).
25. CERCLA §105(a)(8), 42 U.S.C. §9605(a)(8).
26. CERCLA §105(a)(8)(A), (c)(2), 42 U.S.C. §9605(a)(8)(A), (c)(2).

C. Identifying Sites, Funding, and Setting the Standards for Cleanups

Finally, the statute puts EPA in charge of obtaining the needed cleanups of sites on the NPL in ways that are consistent with the NCP. In this regard, EPA is empowered to: (1) undertake cleanups itself, using Superfund monies, and to seek reimbursement from PRPs; (2) issue administrative orders to PRPs directing them to undertake cleanups; (3) seek court orders directing PRPs to undertake cleanups; or (4) use a combination of approaches.

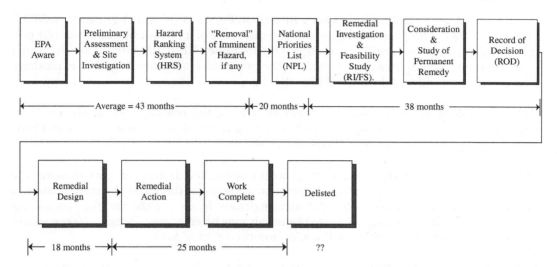

FIGURE 16-2. *Average Time Between Principal Steps in the Superfund Process. Source: P. Acton, Understanding Superfund: A Progress Report 16 (Rand Corporation Institute for Civil Justice, 1989) (modified by Authors).*

After an uneven start,[27] EPA made extensive efforts to regularize Superfund procedures to ensure that all sites receive a thorough investigation and that decisions about remedial actions at each site are made by reference to consistent principles — focusing in each case on a site study document known as a Remedial Investigation/Feasibility Study (RI/FS). After the study and analysis is complete, EPA issues a record of decision (ROD) that selects the principal remedial actions to be taken. An even more detailed remedial design (RD) is prepared and, finally, remedial activity begins. The diagram above shows the major steps in the CERCLA process and the average duration of each of those steps.

---

27. During the Reagan presidency, when extensive government regulation and intervention was ideological anathema, EPA was not allowed to take an active role under Superfund. In fact, Superfund's misadministration by EPA in the early 1980s was a source of scandal, and several EPA officials were criminally prosecuted and convicted. This period in EPA's CERCLA history is recounted in detail in Mintz, Agencies, Congress, and Regulatory Enforcement: A Review of EPA Hazardous Waste Enforcement Effort, 1970-1987, 18 Envtl. L. 683, 715-743 (1988).

Lawrence Starfield, The 1990 National Contingency Plan—More Detail and More Structure, But Still a Balancing Act

20 Environmental Law Reporter 10222, 10228-10229, 10236-10241 (1990)

... A ROAD MAP TO THE CERCLA SITE RESPONSE PROCESS [SUBPART (E) OF THE NCP]: SITE DISCOVERY. The process begins with the discovery of a release by one of several possible mechanisms (e.g., notification requirements under CERCLA §103(a) or (b) under other laws, a petition from a citizen, etc.). In the case of an emergency (e.g., fire, explosion), a removal action will be taken to stabilize the site.

REMOVAL ASSESSMENT. In non-emergency situations, the release is evaluated to determine if a removal action is appropriate based on a removal preliminary assessment (PA) and, if appropriate, a removal site inspection (SI).

REMOVAL ACTION. Where necessary to protect human health and the environment, the Agency may initiate a removal action to prevent, mitigate, or minimize the threat posed by the release. This may involve removal of surface drums, fencing of the site, the provision of temporary drinking water supplies, etc. Removals may be emergency actions (taken within hours of discovery), time-critical actions, or non-time-critical actions.

REMEDIAL SITE EVALUATION. A remedial PA (and SI, where appropriate) is conducted on all sites in the CERCLA Information System database (CERCLIS), to see if the site is a priority for long-term remedial response. These evaluations involve the collection of data for scoring the site under the hazard ranking system (HRS) model; sites scoring above the threshold in the HRS are placed on the national priorities list (NPL) for further evaluation and possible remedial action.

REMEDIAL PRIORITIES. The Agency evaluates releases for inclusion on the NPL based on the HRS score or one of the other methods for listing outlined in the NCP. The Agency may spend Fund monies for remedial action only at those sites that are on the NPL. ("Fund-financed remedial action" does not include removal action or enforcement action.)

REMEDIAL INVESTIGATION/FEASIBILITY STUDY. The Agency will undertake a remedial investigation and feasibility study (RI/FS) at sites that are, or appear to be, priorities for action (i.e., that are on, or are proposed for listing on, the NPL). The RI/FS, like any other investigation conducted pursuant to CERCLA §104(b), is a removal action under CERCLA §101(23), despite the word remedial in its name.

During the RI, the nature and extent of the threat posed by the contamination is studied; concurrently, alternative approaches are developed as part of the FS for responding to and managing the site problem.

PRELIMINARY REMEDIATION GOAL. The first step in developing alternatives during the FS is the establishment of a preliminary goal for the remediation of the site. This goal is initially based on readily available information, such as chemical-specific applicable, relevant and appropriate requirements of other environmental laws (ARARs), or the "point of departure" in the range of acceptable risk. Alternatives are then developed that are capable of attaining the preliminary remediation goal. (The goal maybe modified as additional information is developed.)

C. Identifying Sites, Funding, and Setting the Standards for Cleanups

SCREENING OF REMEDIAL ALTERNATIVES. A broad list of alternatives is then reviewed and screened, with the more extreme, impracticable options being eliminated before the detailed analysis of alternatives begins. Alternatives may be eliminated during screening based on effectiveness, implementability, or "grossly excessive" cost.

ANALYSIS OF ALTERNATIVES USING THE NINE CRITERIA. The Agency then conducts a detailed analysis of the remaining alternatives (usually three to nine [of them], depending on the complexity of the problem). The advantages and disadvantages of the alternatives are studied and compared using the following nine remedy selection criteria:[28]

- Overall protection of human health and the environment,
- Compliance with (or waiver of) the ARARs of other laws,
- Long-term effectiveness and permanence,
- Reduction of toxicity, mobility, or volume through treatment,
- Short-term effectiveness,
- Implementability,
- Cost,
- State acceptance, and
- Community acceptance.

SELECTION OF REMEDY. The nine criteria are then used to select the remedy by evaluating them in three functional categories (threshold, balancing, and modifying criteria), in order to reflect the nature and/or timing of their application. The first two criteria — protectiveness and compliance with ARARs — are identified as threshold criteria; only the alternatives that meet those criteria may be carried forward.

Protective, ARAR-compliant alternatives are then "balanced" (i.e., used to evaluate tradeoffs) based on the middle five criteria (and the two modifying criteria, to the extent they are known). The Agency then attempts to select the remedial alternative that "utilizes permanent solutions and treatment . . . to the maximum extent practicable," and is "cost-effective" based on a comparison of the appropriate balancing or modifying criteria. Alternatives are judged cost-effective if their costs are "in proportion" to their overall effectiveness; an alternative is found to achieve the maximum permanence and treatment practicable based on a balancing of the seven nonthreshold criteria, with an emphasis on the factors of "long-term effectiveness and permanence" and "reduction in mobility, toxicity or volume through treatment."

ERA and the state then discuss the remedial options and issue a proposed plan, which sets out the lead agency's recommended alternative. Consistent with CERCLA §117, the public is afforded an opportunity to review and comment on the alternatives studied in the FS and the proposed plan. After review of and response to public comments, and formal consideration of the two modifying criteria (state and community acceptance), the final remedy selection is documented in a record of decision (ROD).

REMEDIAL DESIGN/REMEDIAL ACTION AND OPERATION AND MAINTENANCE. The lead agency then sets about designing, constructing, and implementing the selected remedy. Often, the remedial action plan set out in the ROD will need to be modified in light of information developed during the design phase (e.g., the Agency may learn that more

---

28. NCP §300.430(e)(9) [40 C.F.R. §300.430(e)(9)].

soil is contaminated and needs to be excavated). If the remedial action to be taken differs "significantly" from the remedy selected in the ROD with respect to scope, performance, or cost, the lead agency will issue an explanation of significant differences (BSD). If the action to be taken "fundamentally alters" the basic features of the remedy selected in the ROD, the lead agency will propose and take comment on a ROD amendment.

Once the remedy is operational and functional (or later, for groundwater restoration remedies), the state undertakes responsibility for funding and carrying out operation and maintenance (O&M) of the remedy.

DELETION FROM THE NPL, FIVE-YEAR REVIEW. Once EPA has determined that no further response action is appropriate, the site may be proposed for deletion, or recategorized on the NPL, even where O&M is continuing. Sites at which hazardous substances remain above levels that allow for unlimited use and unrestricted exposure must be reviewed at least every five years after the initiation of the remedy (not merely after completion), consistent with CERCLA §121(c)....

RISK ASSESSMENT AND RISK RANGE. ... The NCP contemplates the use of risk assessments as an integral part of the process for developing remedial alternatives that are protective of human health and the environment.

Risk analysis begins during the early stages of the RI, when a "baseline risk assessment" is performed to evaluate the risk posed by a site in the absence of any remedial action. It is based on a comparison with this no-action risk level that the lead agency will target levels of risk that will be adequately protective of human health for a particular site. The baseline risk assessment also helps to provide justification for performing remedial action at the site.

Concurrently, the lead agency would begin to set a "preliminary remediation goal" as part of the FS. The preliminary remediation goal is an initial statement of the desired endpoint concentration or risk level, and alternatives are developed that are capable of meeting that goal. It is based on readily available information, such as chemical-specific ARARs (e.g., a drinking water standard), concentrations associated with the reference doses or cancer potency factors, or the point of departure for the Agency's acceptable risk range, discussed below....

Where environmental effects are observed, EPA sets remediation goals based on environmental ARARs (where they exist) and levels based on a site-specific assessment of what is protective of the environment....

The use of a range of acceptable risk is general practice for most government programs. As discussed below in the section on role of cost, it affords the Agency the flexibility to take into account different situations, different kinds of threats, and different kinds of technical remedies. If a single risk level had been adopted (e.g., at the more stringent end of the risk range), fewer alternatives would be expected to pass the protectiveness threshold and qualify for consideration in the balancing phase of the remedy selection process....

ROLE OF COST. The role of cost in remedy selection has been one of the most hotly disputed issues in the Superfund program. Many PRP groups argue that cost must be a major factor in deciding on an appropriate remedy and note that the requirement to select "cost-effective" remedies appears in CERCLA §121(a) and (b). Many environmentalists and some legislators have argued that cost is given too much emphasis in remedy selection and have posited that cost should be considered only in determining the cost-efficient method for implementing a selected remedy. In effect, they argue that the proper cleanup level for a site should be set, and then a remedy should be selected to attain that level, without consideration of cost. Cost is specifically considered during the final balancing process, as the Agency attempts to satisfy two statutory mandates of CERCLA §121(b)(1) by identifying the remedial alternative that utilizes "permanent solutions and treatment . . . to the maximum extent practicable" while being cost-effective. These determinations are intended to be made simultaneously; however, for ease of analysis, they are discussed separately in the NCR

COST-EFFECTIVENESS. The determination whether a proposed remedial alternative is cost-effective is based on an evaluation of several of the nine criteria. First, overall effectiveness is assessed based on: long-term effectiveness and permanence; reduction of mobility, toxicity, or volume through treatment; and short-term effectiveness. The overall effectiveness is then compared to the cost of the alternative to determine if they are "in proportion" to one another (i.e., does the approach represent a reasonable value for the money?). In making this comparison, the decisionmaker is not directed by the NCP to place special emphasis on the factors of "reduction of toxicity, mobility or volume through treatment" and "long-term effectiveness and permanence," as is required during the assessment of permanence and treatment to the maximum extent practicable (as provided in NCP §300.430(f)(l)(ii)(E)). However, because "effectiveness" is measured based on those two factors (plus short-term effectiveness), an alternative that is high in treatment and permanence will be considered more effective and thus can justify a relatively higher cost (high effectiveness and high cost would be in proportion). The comparison of cost to effectiveness is performed for each alternative individually and for all the alternatives in relation to one another. This latter analysis allows the Agency to identify alternatives that produce an incremental increase in effectiveness for a reasonable increase in cost, based on a comparison of corresponding increases for other alternatives. Several alternatives may be found to be cost-effective. . . .

COST AND PRACTICABILITY. The statutory requirement to select the alternative (there is only one) that utilizes permanence and treatment to the maximum extent practicable is fulfilled by selecting the protective, ARAR-compliant alternative that provides the best balance of tradeoffs among alternatives based on a review of all the balancing and modifying criteria (if the latter are known). It is a subjective judgment, but the NCP sets out some parameters to help assure consistency in its application. Specifically, the NCP requires that during the balancing process, the factors of long-term effectiveness and permanence and reduction in toxicity, mobility, or volume should be emphasized, and that the "preference for treatment as a principal element" and the "bias against off-site land disposal of untreated wastes" must be considered. This statutory determination is the final step in the process before a remedy is recommended in the proposed plan.

Although cost, as one of the nine criteria, is considered in making this determination, it is not expected to play a major role. The importance of almost every other criterion to this determination is emphasized by the NCR. . . .

COST AS A SCREEN. Cost may also be considered during one other aspect of the remedy selection process: screening, when alternatives that are deemed not to be viable are eliminated from more thorough consideration. The use of cost at this early stage has also been the subject of considerable comment. Many were concerned that cost would be used to screen out appropriate remedial technologies early in the process before they were given a fair evaluation and without the benefit of public review and comment.

The final NCP has been revised to narrow the circumstances under which cost may be considered when screening alternatives at the start of the evaluation process. Specifically, the final rule provides that a given alternative maybe eliminated during screening if it is determined that the cost of the alternative is "grossly excessive" compared with its effectiveness. This provision will allow the Agency to avoid the need to conduct resource-intensive analyses of extreme and unrealistic options, while at the same time not allowing cost to compromise consideration of viable options that may simply be more expensive than other alternatives. . . .

COMMENTARY & QUESTIONS

1. The slow pace of CERCLA remediation. Do you find it surprising that the overall average time elapsed between EPA's initial discovery of a potential site's existence and completion of cleanup is 10+ years? With the exception of the period of time needed to do the site remediation, all of the stages seem to be longer than necessary, especially the five years that go by at the front end of the process in which the only real activity is making preliminary assessments and obtaining a hazard ranking score. A number of factors that may combine to explain the slow pace. These include a lack of aggressiveness by EPA, the complexity of the Superfund program, delays caused while legal interpretations of various portions of the law are obtained, program rigidity, the litigious atmosphere surrounding the program, uncertainty about the efficacy of remedies, and shortages of critical personnel.

2. Lead agencies and PRP-led activities. The NCP allows EPA to delegate "lead agency" status to a state, political subdivision of a state, or Indian tribe that EPA finds to have adequate ability and enforcement authority (under state or tribal law) to carry out a NCP-consistent removal or remedial action. EPA is also authorized to allow PRPs to conduct many of the phases of the CERCLA process, including, for example, performing the RI/FS,[29] or doing the actual site remediation work. In instances where PRPs take the lead role, EPA remains the official lead agency. The work is done by the PRPs pursuant to a court or administrative order, or in accordance with an express agreement with EPA.

3. The vital points in the process. While it is probably fair to say that all of the steps in the remediation process are important, the RI/FS and ROD stages stand out as the points at which the site-specific remedy is selected. Remedy selection determines many of the key issues. For the affected community, the remedy selection determines the extent to which the hazard will be eliminated. For the PRPs, the remedy selection commits the EPA to having a particular type and amount of work done, the cost of which will be borne by the PRPs. By statute, the RI/FS and ROD process is designed to allow input from states and affected communities as well as from PRPs and the EPA itself. Toward that end, the statute authorizes EPA to make grants to affected communities for hiring experts to make community participation in the RI/FS and ROD process more effectual.[30]

4. Challenging EPA's decisions. Congress provided for judicial review of EPA's remedy selection process. The key provisos governing judicial review are a limitation on the scope of review to the administrative record[31] and setting "arbitrary and capricious" as the standard of review.[32] Interested parties can participate in the building of the administrative record,[33] and EPA must give reasonable notice of the proceeding to identifiable interested

---

29. See CERCLA §104(a), 42 U.S.C. §9604(a).
30. See CERCLA §§104(c)(2), 113(k)(2), 117,121(f); 42 U.S.C. §§9604(c)(2), 9613(k)(2), 9617, 9621(f).
31. CERCLA §113(j)(l), 42 U.S.C. §9613(j)(l).
32. CERCLA §113(j)(2), 42 U.S.C. §9613(j)(2).
33. CERCLA §113(k), 42 U.S.C. §9613(k).

parties, including PRPs and the affected community. Do these procedures allow a meaningful opportunity to participate in the remedy selection process?

5. ARARs as cleanup standards. ARARs function in a very real sense as cleanup standards, defining how thorough the remedial action must be in its efforts to eliminate environmental hazards at the site. Why does the NCP place so heavy a reliance on ARARs? At a minimum, the borrowing of environmental standards from other areas of the law relieves EPA and the NCP of redundant proceedings concerning contaminant issues that have already been fully determined in other environmental regulatory processes. Simultaneously, by employing the ARARs concept, issues of competing applicability of parallel standards do not arise because there is only one standard to apply.

One of the more perplexing ARARs problems has been whether the exceedingly stringent land disposal regulations of RCRA, the hazardous wastes management statute, are applicable as ARARs at CERCLA sites. Paradoxically, RCRA's treatment standards, if applicable as ARARs, can require EPA to elect a less complete remedial action due to the great cost associated with treatment in accordance with RCRA standards. See Chapter 17.

6. The staggering cost of "Cadillac" cleanups. In a provocative article, Peter Passell quotes a noted economist as saying, in reference to how thorough hazardous waste cleanups should be, "Everybody wants a Cadillac as long as someone else is paying."[34] To illustrate the impact of that attitude on CERCLA cleanups, Passell gives the example of the options available for remediating one small (in area) Missouri Superfund site. An expenditure of $71,000 could permanently isolate the contaminants at the site and prevent any exposure from ever reaching the community; an expenditure of $3.6 million could clean up virtually all hazardous material residues and bury any remaining traces under a blanket of clay; an expenditure of $41.5 million could remove and incinerate the 14,000 tons of contaminated soil and building materials at the site. EPA selected a mix — incineration of the most severely contaminated materials, and clay-lined on-site disposal of the remainder, at a cost of $13.6 million.

Under the NCP, is each of these options sufficiently protective of health and environment? What are the advantages of the more expensive approaches? The most obvious difference between the low-end and high-end choices is that the high-end choices return the site to suitability for renewed use. As a matter of social policy, is spending $10 million to reclaim a few acres in Missouri a wise investment of resources? Can the predictable local opposition to anything less than a total cleanup be ignored? Two possibilities raised by economists are to make local citizens help pay for "Cadillac" cleanups, or rebate to local communities a percentage of the difference between such a cleanup and a "merely" functional one.

7. Natural resource damages. CERCLA treats liability for "damages" to natural resources differently from liability for "response costs." CERCLA §107(a)(4)(C) provides for the recovery of natural resource damages caused by the release of hazardous materials. The federal government, the states (and their subdivisions), and Indian tribal governments are designated as trustees empowered to sue for those damages by §107(f). While natural resource damage claims have, to date, been secondary to those involving cost recovery, they represent a "sleeping giant" because the potential liability can be enormous.

Section 301(c) of CERCLA authorized the Department of Interior to promulgate regulations for the assessment of natural resource damages, although trustees may seek to

---

34. See Passell, Experts Question Staggering Costs of Toxic Cleanups, N.Y. Times, Sept. 1, 1991, at 1.

establish an alternative measure of damages in any particular case. See 43 C.F.R. §11.10.[35] However, a rebuttable presumption of validity attaches to those assessments conducted in accordance with Interior's regulations, and, accordingly, trustees have a significant incentive to conduct their assessments pursuant to Interior's rules.

The most significant issue in the natural resource damages context involves the appropriate measure of damages. In *Ohio v. U.S. Dep't of Interior*, 880 F.2d 432 (D.C. Cir. 1989), Ohio challenged Interior's regulation providing that natural resource damages shall be the "lesser of" (1) restoration or replacement costs, or (2) lost-use-value. The court invalidated the "lesser of" rule, holding that Congress established a distinct preference for restoration cost as the measure of recovery in natural resource damage cases. The court also concluded, however, that there might be some cases where other considerations—such as infeasibility of restoration or grossly disproportionate cost to use value—might warrant a different standard. Thereafter, in March 1994, Interior issued revisions to its rules, eliminating the "lesser of" rule and replacing it with a requirement that the trustee consider a wide array of "restoration" alternatives and select the most appropriate one. See 43 C.F.R. §11.82. Interior stopped short of requiring significant active restoration in every case. The rule specifically contemplated that included among the "restoration" alternatives to be considered must be one that relies on "natural recovery with minimal management actions." 43 C.F.R. §11.82(c).

The rule listed ten factors to be considered in selecting from among restoration alternatives:

(1) Technical feasibility; (2) the relationship of the expected costs of the proposed actions to the expected benefits from the restoration, rehabilitation, replacement, and/or acquisition of equivalent resources; (3) cost-effectiveness; (4) the results of any actual or planned response actions; (5) the potential for additional injury resulting from the proposed actions, including long-term and indirect impacts, to the . . . injured resource or other resources; (6) the natural recovery period; (7) the ability of the resource to recover with or without alternative actions; (8) any potential effects of the action on human health and safety; (9) consistency with applicable Federal and State and tribal policies; and (10) compliance with applicable Federal, State and tribal laws. 43 C.F.R. §11.82(d).

The D.C. Circuit later upheld most elements of Interior's regulations, specifying the procedures that are sufficiently reliable and valid for trustees to use in calculating their damage assessments. See *Kennecott Utah Copper Corp. v. U.S. Dep't of the Interior*, 88 F.3d 1191, 1217 (D.C. Cir. 1996) (upholding Interior's natural resource damage assessment regulations to allow public trustees to consider acquisition of equivalent resources equally with strategies for restoration or replacement of natural resources); *General Elec. Co. v. U.S. Dep't of Commerce*, 128 F.3d 767 (D.C. Cir. 1997) (upholding NOAA final rule concerning liability for natural resource damages arising from oil spills under OPA).

8. Superfund's scorecard. The impact of Superfund can be evaluated both quantitatively and qualitatively. For example, using a quantitative approach, EPA calculated that by 2003 its program has assessed over 44,000 sites; that over 33,000 sites have been removed from the Superfund inventory (i.e., 75%); and that over 11,000 sites remain active with the state assessment program or are on the NPL. In addition, EPA concluded that its removal program has conducted over 7399 removals at over 5000 sites; that 1560 sites were either proposed, final, or deleted from the NPL; that the cumulative value of private party

---

35. Congress authorized recovery of natural resource damages under both CERCLA and OPA, 42 U.S.C. §9651(c). Under OPA, the National Oceanic and Atmospheric Administration (NOAA) promulgates regulations for natural resource damage assessments.

settlements approximated $20.6 billion; and that responsible parties have performed over 70% of nonfederal remedial actions. Although these statistics are impressive, a key question remains: Do the statistics truly reflect progress in cleaning up the environment or are they mere "beancounting" by the EPA without material improvement in environmental quality?

That brings us to the issue of the qualitative assessment of Superfund. In an article by John Quarles and Michael W. Steinberg entitled "The Superfund Program at its 25th Anniversary," 36 Envtl. L. Rep. 10,364 (2006), the authors take "time to reflect upon the extraordinary history of this singular environmental law" and examine "some of the many challenges that still confront Superfund as it moves into its second quarter-century." The authors conclude that in the future, attention will shift in the Superfund Program from a focus on the hundreds of huge multiparty sites with severe contamination to a focus on the many thousands of sites with significant but not severe contamination. They also conclude that the opportunities for cost effective source removal and treatment may be limited at sites with significant but not severe contamination, thereby requiring more ingenuity going forward in effectuating cost-effective cleanups. The authors further state that, without question, the role of the states in connection with Superfund will continue to grow; they predict that, for EPA, the challenge in the future will be to provide wise and effective leadership, particularly if sites are increasingly handled at the state rather than at the federal level.

D. EPA's Strategy for Cost Recovery and Loss Allocation

EPA is charged with many responsibilities in the hazardous waste arena, including its responsibility not only to obtain cleanups at NPL sites but also to ensure that the burden of paying for those cleanups falls primarily on PRPs rather than the Superfund itself. Although it was understood that the Superfund would have to absorb the costs of cleanups of orphan sites where no solvent PRPs could be identified, the mandate to assign the cost of cleanups to the PRPs is a central feature in CERCLA's structure.

The problems facing EPA in husbanding the monies of the Superfund and running the cost recovery program can be divided into three distinct categories. Perhaps the most rudimentary problem is cash flow. If the average cleanup spans a ten-year period, and EPA is expending funds at a large number of NPL sites from the investigatory stages onward, the fund may get depleted before §107 cost recovery actions can replenish it. Second, years of experience with the cost recovery program have revealed that the program has a surprisingly low rate of recovery. Third, EPA has historically had a staffing problem in both the site management and cost recovery aspects of its operations. The site management staffing problem is simply a lack of sufficient trained and experienced personnel to ensure that sites are cleaned up in the proper manner.

The cost recovery staffing problem arises in large part as a result of the nature of CERCLA cases. In most instances, NPL sites involve numerous PRPs with substantial liabilities. The high stakes create a sufficient incentive for PRPs to fight hard to limit their losses on many fronts. They will also be inclined to challenge EPA decisions regarding selection of expensive cleanup measures. PRPs try to minimize EPA's assessment of their contribution to the site, contesting the accuracy of EPA's particular "waste-in" lists,[36] and the

---

36. A "waste-in" list is a computer printout generated by EPA after extensive detective work on each site, collecting much data on who dumped what, based on identifiable barrels, trucking invoices, interviews with

identification of materials found at the site as belonging to them rather than some other PRP. The effort to sort out comparative responsibility also has the potential to make each of the cost recovery suits a quagmire for all involved. Finally, even when the cost allocation issue is absent, experience in all fields of law has shown that complex multiparty litigation invariably imposes massive burdens on all of the parties involved.

Lawsuits prosecuted under RCRA §7003 and CERCLA §§106 and 107 have proven particularly burdensome and expensive to litigate, to the extent that litigation at times proves to be counterproductive. A great deal of money is often spent that might otherwise be directed toward remediation of toxic contamination.

COMMENTARY & QUESTIONS

1. **The likelihood of settlement.** Assume that a site presents a complex groundwater remediation problem. How often will a settlement be achieved? The key factors will include the cost of the cleanup, the sheer number of PRPs, their solvency, the accuracy of the "waste-in" list, and, perhaps, the negotiating strategy of the parties. The high costs of litigation can act as an inducement to settlement. Lowering the total cost, such as by obtaining EPA approval of a PRP-managed cleanup, can also improve the chances of settlement, as noted more fully below. Settling PRPs are protected against additional liability and may seek contribution from nonsettling PRPs.

2. **Settlements and administrative orders as cures for Superfund solvency issues and litigation burdens.** In order to preclude the cash flow and low recovery rate problems, EPA has tried to reduce outlays of monies from the Superfund by increasing the amount of the cleanup work done by the PRPs (or their contractors) rather than by contractors hired by EPA. One means for shifting the costs to PRPs has been to enter into settlements with PRPs in advance of cleanup that place the full anticipated present and future costs on the PRPs. This method of proceeding has the additional advantage of avoiding two types of staffing problems. PRP-led cleanups require EPA oversight, but that is a far more modest task than managing the cleanup. Similarly, by settling in advance of litigation, the burdens of complex litigation are greatly reduced.[37] A second avenue toward increasing the amount of cleanup work done by PRPs is to require that PRPs do the work pursuant to administrative order, a power expressly granted to EPA by Congress. This power is limited to cases where a release or threatened release of hazardous material poses "an imminent and substantial endangerment to public health or welfare or the environment. . . ."[38] Given the nature of Superfund sites, few, if any, do not pose such a danger.

3. **Congressional guidelines for EPA settlements.** Owing to the abuses of the Superfund program in the early years of the Reagan Administration, Congress added extremely detailed provisions when it reauthorized CERCLA in 1986 that were intended to support EPA's pursuit of settlements while keeping a check on EPA to be sure that the settlement process was administered in an evenhanded way. See CERCLA §122. EPA has fully

---

workers, corporate records, etc. Based on the list, EPA sends out PRP liability notices, sometimes to hundreds of potentially liable addressees.

37. Litigation is not wholly avoided. At times, settlements will be reached after litigation is initiated but before it has matured. At other times, settlements will be reached with less than all of the PRPs, leaving EPA to litigate with the remaining PRPs. See, e.g., *O'Neil v. Picillo*.

38. See CERCLA §106(a), 42 U.S.C. §9606(a). That same subsection authorizes EPA to initiate litigation seeking injunctive relief to the same effect, as discussed in Part B of this chapter.

D. CERCLA Cost Recovery and Loss Allocation

complied with the directive and has promulgated a whole series of guidance documents that announce EPA settlement policies and procedures.

4. PRP letters—the invitation to the dance. One of the rituals of Superfund enforcement is the way in which many of EPA's actions are begun. After identifying a site and compiling a list of PRPs, EPA mails letters informing PRPs of their (unhappy) status and inviting them to a forthcoming meeting, usually at a large meeting hall or hotel ballroom near the site. At that meeting, EPA typically presents its waste-in list and a summary of what the agency knows about the site, and then tells the assemblage that they have a few hours to organize themselves into groups for the purpose of negotiating settlements with EPA. The EPA representatives may then depart, returning after a few hours to begin discussions with the various newly formed PRP groups. If settlements are not reached within 60 days, the period for negotiation (unless extended for an additional 60 days by EPA) is over, and EPA will file suit or issue administrative orders. Is this reliance on PRPs to organize themselves on such short notice an effective procedure to follow in complex Superfund cases? Are brutally short deadlines appropriate and necessary?

Of course, if EPA or its state counterpart do not reach settlement and ultimately file suit after undertaking cleanup, recalcitrant PRPs rejecting "the invitation to the dance" may find themselves liable under §107 both for past cleanup costs and for all future costs associated with the site. In the following case, the First Circuit Court of Appeals examined one such situation, where the nonsettling parties fought aggressively, but unsuccessfully, to avoid the onus of joint and several liability.

O'Neil v. Picillo

883 F.2d 176 (1st Cir. 1989), cert. denied, 493 U.S. 1071 (1990)

COFFIN, J. In July of 1977, the Picillos agreed to allow part of their pig farm in Coventry, Rhode Island to be used as a disposal site for drummed and bulk waste. That decision proved to be disastrous. Thousands of barrels of hazardous waste were dumped on the farm, culminating later that year in a monstrous fire ripping through the site. In 1979, the state and the Environmental Protection Agency (EPA) jointly undertook to clean up the area. What they found, in the words of the district court, were massive trenches and pits "filled with free-flowing, multi-colored, pungent liquid wastes" and thousands of "dented and corroded drums containing a veritable potpourri of toxic fluids." *O'Neil v. Picillo*, 682 F. Supp. 706, 709, 725 (D.R.I. 1988).

This case involves the State of Rhode Island's attempt to recover the clean-up costs it incurred between 1979 and 1982 and to hold responsible parties liable for all future costs associated with the site. The state's complaint originally named thirty-five defendants, all but five of whom eventually entered into settlements totaling $5.8 million, the money to be shared by the state and EPA. After a month-long bench trial, the district court, in a thorough and well reasoned opinion, found three of the remaining five companies jointly and severally liable under §107 of CERCLA for all of the State's past clean-up costs not covered by settlement agreements, as well as for all costs that may become necessary in the future. The other two defendants obtained judgments in their favor, the court concluding that the state had failed to prove that the waste attributed to those companies was "hazardous," as that term is defined under the Act.

Two of the three companies held liable at trial, American Cyanamid and Rohm & Haas, have taken this appeal. Both are so called "generators" of waste, as opposed to transporters or site owners. See §107(a)(3), 42 U.S.C. §9607. Neither takes issue with the district court's finding that some of their waste made its way to the Picillo site. Rather, they contend that their contribution to the disaster was insubstantial and that it was, therefore, unfair to hold them jointly and severally liable for all of the state's past expenses not covered by settlements. . . .

JOINT AND SEVERAL LIABILITY: STATUTORY BACKGROUND . . . It is by now well settled that Congress intended the federal courts to develop a uniform approach governing the use of joint and several liability in CERCLA actions. The rule adopted by the majority of courts, and the one we adopt, is based on the Restatement 2d of Torts: damages should be apportioned only if the defendant can demonstrate that the harm is divisible.

The practical effect of placing the burden on defendants has been that responsible parties rarely escape joint and several liability, courts regularly finding that where wastes of varying (and unknown) degrees of toxicity and migratory potential commingle, it simply is impossible to determine the amount of environmental harm caused by each party. It has not gone unnoticed that holding defendants jointly and severally liable in such situations may often result in defendants paying for more than their share of the harm. Nevertheless, courts have continued to impose joint and several liability on a regular basis, reasoning that where all of the contributing causes cannot fairly be traced, Congress intended for those proven at least partially culpable to bear the cost of the uncertainty.

In enacting the Superfund Amendments and Reauthorization Act of 1986 (SARA), Congress had occasion to examine this case law. Rather than add a provision dealing explicitly with joint and several liability, it chose to leave the issue with the courts, to be resolved as it had been — on a case by case basis according to the predominant "divisibility" rule first enunciated by the *Chem-Dyne* court [572 F. Supp. 802 (S.D. Ohio 1983)]. Congress did, however, add two important provisions designed to mitigate the harshness of joint and several liability. First, the 1986 Amendments direct the EPA to offer early settlements to defendants who the Agency believes are responsible for only a small portion of the harm, so-called de minimis settlements. See §122(g). Second, the Amendments provide for a statutory cause of action in contribution, codifying what most courts had concluded was implicit in the 1980 Act. See §113(f)(1). Under this section, courts "may allocate response costs among liable parties using such equitable factors as the court determines are appropriate." We note that appellants already have initiated a contribution action against seven parties before the same district court judge who heard this case.

While a right of contribution undoubtedly softens the blow where parties cannot prove that the harm is divisible, it is not a complete panacea since it frequently will be difficult for defendants to locate a sufficient number of additional, solvent parties. Moreover, there are significant transaction costs involved in bringing other responsible parties to court. If it were possible to locate all responsible parties and to do so with little cost, the issue of joint and several liability obviously would be of only marginal significance. We, therefore, must examine carefully appellants' claim that they have met their burden of showing that the harm in this case is divisible. . . .

REMOVAL COSTS . . . The state's removal efforts proceeded in four phases, each phase corresponding roughly to the cleanup of a different trench. The trenches were located in different areas of the site, but neither party has told us the distance between trenches. Appellants contend that it is possible to apportion the state's removal costs because there was evidence detailing (1) the total number of barrels excavated in each phase, (2) the number of barrels in each phase attributable to them, and (3) the total cost associated with each phase. In support of their argument, they point us to a few portions of the record, but for

D. CERCLA Cost Recovery and Loss Allocation

the most part are content to rest on statements in the district court's opinion. Specifically, appellants point to the following two sentences in the opinion: (1) "I find that [American Cyanamid] is responsible for ten drums of toxic hazardous material found at the site"; and (2) as to Rohm & Haas, "I accept the state's estimate [of 49 drums and 303 five-gallon pails]. "Appellants then add, without opposition from the government, that the ten barrels of American Cyanamid waste discussed by the district court were found exclusively in Phase II, and that the 303 pails and 49 drums of Rohm & Haas waste mentioned by the court were found exclusively in Phase III. They conclude, therefore, that American Cyanamid should bear only a minute percentage of the $995,697.30 expended by the state during Phase II in excavating approximately 4,500 barrels and no share of the other phases, and that Rohm & Haas should be accountable for only a small portion of the $58,237 spent during Phase III in removing roughly 3,300 barrels and no share of the other phases. We disagree.

The district court's statements concerning the waste attributable to each appellant were based on the testimony of John Leo, an engineer hired by the state to oversee the cleanup. We have reviewed Mr. Leo's testimony carefully. Having done so, we think it inescapably clear that the district court did not mean to suggest that appellants had contributed only 49 and 10 barrels respectively, but rather that those amounts were all that could be positively attributed to appellants.

Mr. Leo testified that out of the approximately 10,000 barrels that were excavated during the four phases, only "three to four hundred of the drums contained markings which could potentially be traced." This is not surprising considering that there had been an enormous fire at the site, that the barrels had been exposed to the elements for a number of years, and that a substantial amount of liquid waste had leaked and eaten away at the outsides of the barrels. Mr. Leo also testified that it was not simply the absence of legible markings that prevented the state from identifying the overwhelming majority of barrels, but also the danger involved in handling the barrels. Ironically, it was appellants themselves who, in an effort to induce Mr. Leo to lower his estimate of the number of barrels attributable to each defendant, elicited much of the testimony concerning the impossibility of accurately identifying all of the waste.[39]

In light of the fact that most of the waste could not be identified, and that the appellants, and not the government, had the burden to account for all of this uncertainty, we think it plain that the district court did not err in holding them jointly and severally liable for the state's past removal costs. Perhaps in this situation the only way appellants could have demonstrated that they were limited contributors would have been to present specific evidence documenting the whereabouts of their waste at all times after it left their facilities. But far from doing so, appellants deny all knowledge of how their waste made its way to the site. Moreover, the government presented evidence that much of Rohm & Haas' waste found at the site came from its laboratory in Spring House, Pennsylvania and that during the relevant years, this lab generated over two thousand drums of waste, all of which were consigned to a single transporter. Under these circumstances, where Rohm & Haas was entrusting substantial amounts of waste to a single transporter who ultimately proved unreliable, we simply cannot conclude, absent evidence to the contrary, that only a handful of the 2,000 or more barrels reached the site.[40]

---

39. Appellants contend that the state's record keeping was subpar.... In the context of this case, the state's failure to document its work during Phase I was harmless error since Mr. Leo testified that even when the state made an effort to identify the barrels, it could rarely do so.

40. Even if it were possible to determine how many barrels each appellant contributed to the site, we still would have difficulty concluding that the state's removal costs were capable of apportionment.... Appellants

Appellants have argued ably that they should not have been held jointly and severally liable. In the end, however, we think they have not satisfied the stringent burden placed on them by Congress. As to all other issues, we affirm substantially for the reasons set out by the district court. Appellants should now move on to their contribution action where their burden will be reduced and the district court will be free to allocate responsibility according to any combination of equitable factors it deems appropriate. Indeed, there might be no reason for the district court to place any burden on appellants. If the defendants in that action also cannot demonstrate that they were limited contributors, it is not apparent why all of the parties could not be held jointly and severally liable. However, we leave this judgment to the district court. See, e.g., Developments, Toxic Waste Litigation, 99 Harv. L. Rev. 1458,1535-1543 (1986). Affirmed.

COMMENTARY & QUESTIONS

1. The impact of joint and several liability. Although the proofs in the case are riddled with uncertainty, assume for a moment that the amounts actually contributed to the Picillo site by Cyanamid and Rohm & Haas were little more than the 59 identifiable barrels, and that they were present in only one of the four trenches. Those companies are now liable for all past and future costs at the site not paid by other PRPs. Although the court does not make the point explicitly, the unpaid past costs plus all future costs could amount to millions of dollars beyond the $5.8 million already recovered through settlement with other PRPs. (In fact, Cyanamid and Rohm & Haas were subsequently found liable for $3.5 million in addition to $1.5 million they had already paid.) Both Cyanamid and Rohm & Haas are large, well-financed companies and can pay the amount due. To whatever extent that amount (under the present assumptions of limited contribution of materials to the site) is grossly disproportionate to their responsibility for causing the problems at the site, the operation of joint and several liability appears harsh.

The court refers on several occasions to the possibility that subsequent contribution actions by Cyanamid and Rohm & Haas will remedy the unfairness of being held liable for an overly large share of cleanup costs. But the possibility of obtaining contribution in this case was limited because the other parties whom EPA identified as PRPs had settled with the government, and these settlements act as a defense to contribution actions.

2. Problems of uncertainty. The unfairness in this case appears to be exacerbated by the actions taken by Rhode Island in cleaning up the site in a way that leaves so much uncertainty about whose wastes were actually present at the site. The court, in essence, answers this complaint by claiming that Congress intended PRPs — as the ones who had benefitted from inadequate disposal practices — to bear the risk of occasionally unfair allocations rather than thrusting that risk onto the Superfund. Does the potential unfairness to PRPs of poorly managed cleanups help to explain why the NCP standards for cleanups are so elaborate?

3. Seeking fairer alternatives. Even if Cyanamid and Rohm & Haas can justly claim unfairness, are there better alternatives to arming EPA with joint and several liability and

---

have proceeded on the assumption that the cost of removing barrels did not vary depending on their content. This assumption appears untenable given the fact that the state had to take added precautions in dealing with certain particularly dangerous substances.... Moreover... because there was substantial commingling of wastes, we think that any attempt to apportion the costs incurred by the state in removing the contaminated soil would necessarily be arbitrary.

placing the burden on PRPs to show divisibility of harm? One family of alternatives, the insistence on the traditional rules of liability, seems to leave EPA and the Superfund without any means by which to shift the loss to PRPs. Forcing EPA to meet traditional cause-in-fact standards, for example, would result in minimal cost recoveries whenever a highly accurate waste-in list doesn't exist. In the end, this burdens the taxpayers who, comparatively speaking, are surely more "innocent" than any of the PRPs. A more promising avenue is to consider ways in which costs that cannot be attributed to any particular PRP might be shared among the PRP group, rather than thrust upon a single PRP using joint and several liability. The law has generally made this attempt in regard to contribution actions.

4. Contribution among PRPs. In light of strict liability and the difficulty of proving that the toxic cleanup harm can be apportioned, PRPs potentially may be faced with the possibility that, if sued under CERCLA, they may lose and be held jointly and severally liable for all recoverable costs. In the event that a party pays the loss and a claim for contribution is available, the appropriate course of action may be to seek to shift all or part of the loss to other PRPs via contribution.[41]

Congress directs the courts to apply a federal law of contribution under §113(f)(1) of CERCLA "using such equitable factors as the court determines are appropriate." One of numerous commentators who have addressed this subject summarized federal practice:

> Recent cases suggest that federal courts are creating a federal common law of contribution that follows the Restatement [(Second) of Torts], §886A, and apportions liability according to a modified comparative fault approach that incorporates equitable defenses as to mitigation of damages, and the multi-factor approach suggested by the [unenacted] Gore Amendment [to CERCLA].[42]

The Restatement (Second) of Torts §886A provides generally that in actions for contribution joint tortfeasors cannot be held liable for more than their equitable share. Its key language provides:

> (2) The right of contribution exists only in favor of a tortfeasor who has discharged the entire claim for the harm by paying more than his equitable share of the common liability, and is limited to the amount paid by him in excess of his share. No tortfeasor can be required to make contribution beyond his own equitable share of the liability.

In its commentary on the "method of apportionment," the Restatement identifies two approaches, either pro rata contribution or by means of a comparative fault determination.

---

41. Indemnity may also be a possibility. CERCLA itself creates no general right of indemnification in favor of one responsible party against another. Indemnity is available under traditional common law doctrines, such as granting indemnity pursuant to contractual indemnity agreements or permitting a party that is only passively responsible to seek indemnity from parties that are actively responsible for harm or loss.

42. Russo, Contribution Under CERCLA: Judicial Treatment After SARA, 14 Colum. J. Envtl. L. 267, 278 (1989). [The Gore Amendment, though never enacted, has nevertheless been applied as persuasive analysis by the courts. EDS.] The factors in the Gore Amendment that facilitate a comparative approach include (1) the extent to which the defendant's level of contribution to the problem can be distinguished, (2) the amount of hazardous waste involved, (3) the degree of toxicity of the hazardous waste involved, (4) the degree of involvement by the parties in the generation, transportation, treatment, storage or disposal of the hazardous waste, (5) the degree of care exercised, taking into account the characteristics of the hazardous materials involved, and (6) the degree of cooperation of the party with public officials in working to prevent harm to public health or the environment. See 126 Cong. Rec. 26,781 (1980); see also Garber, Federal Common Law of Contribution under the 1986 CERCLA Amendments, 14 Ecology L.J.Q. 365 (1987); Dubuc & Evans, Recent Developments Under CERCLA: Toward a More Equitable Distribution of Liability, 17 Envtl. L. Rep. 10197 (1987).

The pro rata (equal shares) approach has its roots in the equitable maxim that, "Equality is equity." A pro rata share, moreover, is easy to calculate. The total amount paid in the CERCLA case is divided by the number of parties who were found jointly and severally liable. An equal sharing of costs may be fair in some cases, but the typical CERCLA case involves PRPs having markedly different degrees of responsibility for conditions at the site. Some may have minimal volumes of relatively benign wastes at the site while others have been major contributors to the problem. If the PRP selected by EPA to pay the judgment is in the former category, a pro rata recovery on the contribution claim is unsatisfactory.

To obtain a non-pro rata basis for contribution the party seeking that result has to provide the court with a reasonable alternative basis on which to apportion responsibility. Even using the Gore Amendment factors, that task has a Catch-22 quality about it. Recalling that joint and several liability was imposed initially because of the great difficulty of apportioning responsibility among PRPs, PRPs with only a small share of the responsibility face an unpleasant paradox: They could get contribution (on other than a pro rata basis) if the harm could be apportioned, but they are being held jointly liable precisely because the harm cannot be apportioned.

The availability of contribution, even properly apportioned, is not a panacea for PRPs who have paid more than their "fair share." The PRP who pays the judgment to the government will find that co-PRPs who settled with EPA or the state are immune to suits for contribution, an immunity often referred to as "contribution protection." In 1986, Congress added §113(f)(2) to CERCLA establishing the effect of settlement on settling parties' subsequent liability for contribution:

> A person who has resolved its liability to the United States or a State in an administrative or judicially approved settlement shall not be liable for claims for contribution regarding matters addressed in the settlement. Such settlement does not discharge any of the other potentially liable persons unless its terms so provide, but it reduces the potential liability of the others by the amount of the settlement.

5. Catch-22 revisited. The seemingly empty promise of non-pro rata contribution described in the text overstates to some extent the problem of apportionment among the PRPs in contribution suits. The rationale for creating a de facto presumption that CERCLA site harms are not divisible in government suits for cost recovery is the congressional policy of imposing the cost of cleanups on PRPs rather than on the Superfund. In the contribution suit, no party comes to the court with a preferred position. All of the PRPs are partly responsible for the harm and none is entitled to preferential treatment as a matter of statutory policy; thus the court in the contribution suit will seek to do whatever is most equitable. In that apportionment setting, it is as if no party has the burden of proof on the apportionment issue.

6. Congressional intent on encouraging settlements. Why did Congress grant "contribution protection" to settling PRPs? The answer has almost nothing to do with contribution and a great deal to do with encouraging settlement. In a settlement, a settling PRP pays only once, an amount that both the PRP and the government think fairly represents the settlor's liability. Absent contribution protection, the settling PRP is at risk of later being held liable for contribution in judgments arising in other subsequent cases, which would reduce the benefits of settling. Settlement without contribution protection would not fix for all time the amount of liability, would not preclude the expense of litigation (e.g., for defense on the merits in contribution actions), and would not offer any respite from the possibility of greater liability that inheres in litigation.

D. CERCLA Cost Recovery and Loss Allocation

7. EPA's use of contribution protection as a sword. Does EPA use §113(f)(2) to coerce parties into settlements? Settling PRPs are free of any contribution responsibility, so if EPA enters into "sweetheart" settlements (i.e., settlements that do not recover a fair proportion of the total liability in relation to the responsibility of settling PRPs for expenses at the site), nonsettling PRPs will inevitably end up paying a disproportionate share. EPA generally does not want to act in ways that are arbitrary and unfair, but making strategic use of legal rules in furtherance of the legitimate policy of seeking to promote settlement is not arbitrary. As discussed below, EPA has been able to make settlements attractive even without offering overlenient terms.

8. State law analogies, and pitfalls in obtaining contribution. Although relatively little has been said in this chapter about parallel state cleanup laws — often called spill laws or polluter-pay laws — at times they impose even harsher consequences than CERCLA on parties who pay for cleanups. For example, a New Jersey Supreme Court decision dismissed the appeal of the present owner of a parcel who had cleaned up a toluene contamination site under the New Jersey Environmental Cleanup Responsibility Act (13 N.J. Stat. Ann. §13:1K-6 (1983)), a strict liability statute that requires owners to remedy contamination before they can transfer the parcel. The present owner sought contribution from other parties, including the former owner of the parcel who had contributed to the toluene pollution. The owner was not able to invoke the benefits of strict and joint and several liability in its contribution suit against the past owner. Instead, it had to carry the ordinary common law burdens of proof on the issues of causation and severability of harm in order to recover against the former owner. See *Superior Air Prods Co. v. NL Indus.*, 522 A.2d 1025 (N.J. Super. Ct. App. Div. 1987); see also High Court Dismisses Suit by Superior Air; Appeal "Improvidently Granted," Justices Say, 5 Toxics L. Rep. (BNA) 1455 (Apr. 17, 1991).

9. Strategic EPA behavior in seeking settlements. EPA can do a great deal to encourage settlement. Consider its tool set: §106 orders, contribution protection, control of the remedy selection process, and, of course, the ability to use Superfund monies to remediate the site and to seek to impose §107 liability. Are there policies EPA could adopt that would reward settling PRPs and punish "recalcitrants"? Could EPA manipulate the way it accounts for the possibility of undiscovered pollution or cleanup cost overruns? The short answer to both of these questions is in the affirmative. In fact, EPA has developed explicit policies in this area. PRPs who find these policies unfair to them are most often left with futile lawsuits in which they are challenging a consent decree being entered into by EPA and the settling PRPs. See, e.g., *United States v. Cannons Eng'g Corp.*, 720 F. Supp. 1027 (D. Mass. 1989); aff'd, 899 F.2d 79 (1st Cir. 1990).

17

Life Cycle Regulatory Strategies: RCRA

A. Tracking and Controlling the Life Cycle of Hazardous Waste Materials
B. The "Land Ban" and the Use of "Hammers" to Control Agency Action
C. RCRA Citizen Suits to Obtain Cleanup

Dangerous substances—including PCBs, mercury, arsenic, various petroleum distillates, and a host of others—play vital, even indispensable, roles in producing the material benefits of modern life. They aid in the production of paper, plastics, and other goods; the transmission of electricity; and the powering of motor vehicles. When properly confined, these materials cause little mischief. If released into the environment, however, they pose threats of serious harm to humans, as well as to plants, animals, and natural systems that make up the ecosphere.

As noted in prior chapters, a number of significant statutes play a role in regulating various aspects of the production, use, and disposal of hazardous materials. In connection with hazardous waste contamination and control, however, two federal statutes are key—CERCLA, studied in the preceding chapter, 42 U.S.C. §§9601 et seq., and RCRA, the Resource Conservation and Recovery Act, 42 U.S.C. §§6901 et seq. Although these statutes both address the handling and disposal of wastes, they represent disparate, albeit complementary, approaches. CERCLA establishes the authority to remediate contamination from past waste disposal practices that now endanger, or threaten to endanger, public health or the environment. It does so primarily by imposing strict liability on those parties responsible for the release of "hazardous substances" and by creating a "Superfund" to finance actions to clean up such releases. By contrast, RCRA establishes a regulatory program designed to track and control the life cycle of hazardous wastes "from cradle to grave"—from the time of their initial generation (i.e., the "cradle") to the time of their ultimate disposal (i.e., the "grave"). Rather than focus on past disposal practices, RCRA's life cycle regulation seeks to eliminate the threats of harm from present and future waste disposal.[1] The principal goal of RCRA is to prevent future Superfund sites.

---

1. Note that the standard "cradle-to-grave" metaphor for RCRA does not mean that RCRA tracks all hazardous *materials* from creation to disposal. It means only that covered chemical and other waste materials are tracked

Because monumental difficulties surround the cleanup of hazardous materials once they have already been released into the environment, the life cycle waste control strategies of RCRA—focusing on preventing or limiting the release of hazardous wastes in the first instance—deserve a very high regulatory priority. RCRA establishes a comprehensive, complex, and detailed scheme for regulating hazardous waste management activities that governs the day-to-day operations and waste handling activities of literally hundreds of thousands of corporations and individuals. By regulating all those who (1) generate, (2) transport, or (3) treat, store, or dispose of hazardous wastes, RCRA creates a three-stage regulatory approach that is pervasive and comprehensive. RCRA's broad scope, in fact, was a major factor in the growth of the environmental regulatory community beginning in the early 1980s, as the requirements of RCRA created a demand for environmental consultants, engineers, and lawyers. In its comprehensive approach, RCRA utilizes a variety of regulatory devices to meet its specific regulatory needs.

It is important to note that this perspective on RCRA inevitably deemphasizes two important matters. First, although this chapter focuses on hazardous wastes, RCRA as a statute covers much more, including regulation of solid waste generally (a category dominated by nonhazardous industrial waste and municipal waste), underground storage tanks, medical waste, and other categories. Second, although the focus here concerns the requirements set by federal law, much RCRA enforcement and regulation takes place at the state level. RCRA, like many federal environmental statutes, encourages the states to take primary authority.[2]

A. Tracking and Controlling the Life Cycle of Hazardous Waste Materials

RCRA's Subtitle C, regulating hazardous waste, 42 U.S.C. §§6926 et seq., is organized around a pragmatic strategy that can be reduced to the simplest of terms: "If I know where hazardous waste material is, and I know the place is secure, I also know that the material is not loose in the environment causing problems."[2]

In addition to tracking wastes, RCRA and its implementing regulations prescribe waste handling and treatment standards and practices intended to reduce the possibility of escape. This involves equipment, procedure, and design specifications for all parties that play a role in the life cycle of hazardous wastes. In this fashion, generators of waste are regulated, as are transporters and operators of treatment, storage, and disposal (TSD) facilities. RCRA even tries to assure that waste handlers are responsible people who can be trusted with a dangerous assignment, and whose long-term stability can be demonstrated. Administrative effort under RCRA, moreover, has increasingly encouraged policies

---

from the time they become wastes. Other statutes (such as ToSCA) regulate commercial chemicals and other hazardous materials at the stages of manufacture and use (i.e., before they become waste). Still other statutes (such as the CWA, the CAA, OSHA, and EPCRA) regulate the release of hazardous and toxic pollutants from and within industrial facilities.

2. RCRA §3009, 42 U.S.C. §6929. The statute also directs the EPA Administrator to "give a high priority to assisting and cooperating with States in obtaining full authorization of State programs" under Subtitle C. 42 U.S.C. §6902(a)(7).

A. Tracking the Lifecycle of Hazardous Waste

of "waste minimization," under the assumption that there will be fewer releases if there is less hazardous waste to control.[3]

1. RCRA's Enactment and Initial Implementation

RCRA was described by one judge called upon to interpret it as a statute of "mind-numbing" complexity.[4] Many forces contributed to RCRA's complexity, but EPA's early failure to implement RCRA is surely among the most prominent.

In the years shortly before RCRA's appearance in 1976 (in the form of amendments to the ineffectual Solid Waste Disposal Act), both the CAA and the CWA established major new programs that protected the nation's air and water by mandating the capture and removal of hazardous materials before they were released and thus allowed to pollute these two environmental media. However, the new air and water programs also served to exacerbate an already existing problem—the improper disposal of the hazardous materials extracted from industrial smokestacks and wastewater systems. The disposal and extraction of these hazardous materials was soon determined to be an increasing cause of pollution to other environmental media, in particular the soil and groundwater. Reacting to the need to protect these other environmental media, Congress passed RCRA in an effort to close the circle of environmental regulation.[5]

Although Congress instructed EPA to promulgate regulations promptly, the Carter Administration treated RCRA as a low EPA priority, channeling funds and energy into other issues. Successful citizen suits eventually forced EPA to issue regulations just as the Reagan Administration was taking office. That incoming Administration, however, made the environmental area one of the prime targets of its deregulation philosophy and further delayed the promulgation of implementing regulations and the creation of an effective enforcement program. The foot-dragging of EPA in regard to RCRA, coupled with scandals regarding the administration of CERCLA, eroded congressional confidence in EPA. This led, in 1984, to a major legislative effort requiring more vigorous administration of hazardous waste law, under the Hazardous and Solid Waste Amendments of 1984 (HSWA), Pub. L. No. 98-616, 98 Stat. 3221 (1984). HSWA represented a key turning point in the congressional relationship with EPA. Rather than relying on the EPA to set regulatory parameters and to exercise its discretion in setting and enforcing requirements, Congress became extraordinarily prescriptive and detailed in HSWA, utilizing statutory "hammers" (i.e., the land ban considered later in this chapter) to establish deadlines and limit EPA's discretion. The following article recounts the political climate that surrounded the initial implementation of RCRA.

---

3. The waste reduction strategy also seeks to limit the need for (1) long-term storage of materials for which treatment methods are not yet available, and (2) disposal of the by-products of treatment that may themselves be hazardous materials (such as ash from incineration.) See 42 U.S.C. §6902(a)(6) & (b). The Pollution Prevention Act of 1990, 42 U.S.C. §§13101 et seq., confirms and generalizes the waste minimization strategy, applying it to all types of pollution. RCRA also contributes to hazardous waste minimization by making the treatment, storage and disposal of such wastes far more costly, creating a market incentive to waste reduction.

4. *American Min. Congress v. U.S. EPA*, 824 F.2d 1177, 1189 (D.C. Cir. 1987) (Starr, J., writing for the majority).

5. The environmentalist Barry Commoner has admonished that "Everything goes somewhere" in recognition of the fact that every waste treatment process creates a residual that, because it is more concentrated, may be more toxic than the corresponding waste inputs. In passing RCRA, Congress was concerned with the residual hazardous wastes left over from waste treatment under the CAA and the CWA.

James J. Florio, Congress as Reluctant Regulator: Hazardous Waste Policy in the 1980s

Yale J. on Reg. 351, 353-376 (1986)[6]

Congress passed the Resource Conservation and Recovery Act, the first federal effort to control the disposal of hazardous waste, in 1976, before the extent and danger of hazardous waste disposal problems became widely known. RCRA created a "cradle to grave" regulatory system for hazardous waste, requiring generators, transporters, and disposers to maintain written records of waste transfers, and establishing standards, procedures, and permit requirements for disposal.

As in most other federal regulatory statutes, including other environmental laws, Congress (in 1976) prescribed goals in broad terms only: what was to be achieved by EPA and when. For example, EPA was directed to develop standards within eighteen months for facilities disposing of hazardous waste and to include provisions for record-keeping; treatment, storage, and disposal methods; requirements for location, design, and construction; contingency plans for accidents; and financial responsibility requirements. The only substantive direction was a requirement that the EPA regulations protect "health and the environment."

Although the task given to EPA was enormously complex—perhaps more complex than anyone, including Congress, understood at the time—the delegation of enormous discretion to EPA was sensible. Prescribing standards for hazardous waste disposal required careful analysis of scientific and economic data and a thorough understanding of the commercial system for hazardous waste disposal. In 1976, the information and analysis necessary for sound formulation of the regulatory details were simply not available to Congress, although enough was known to indicate that considerable hazards did exist.

In our scheme of government, the role of an environmental regulatory agency is to act as the scientific and technical expert in filling in the details of the environmental protection policy enunciated by Congress. Only an executive branch agency possessing sufficient technical expertise, administrative skills, and bureaucratic resources can administer a nationwide regimen for controlling the disposal of hazardous waste. Soon after the enactment of RCRA, EPA learned that the development of hazardous waste regulations would be an enormously difficult task. The complexity of the technical issues involved in determining disposal methods appropriate to the thousands of different chemicals and other wastes, each presenting different dangers, was compounded by the enormous economic impact of controlling the high volume of hazardous waste produced in this country. In the developmental stage of this regulatory system, EPA, like any bureaucracy in a similar situation, moved slowly. . . .

Implementation of the RCRA program began during the Carter Administration. The delays and false starts inherent in the initial implementation of most regulatory efforts were commonplace: EPA quickly fell behind schedule in efforts to issue regulations for permits and standards by the statutory deadlines as it discovered the complexity of the problem and

---

6. In 1986, when Mr. Florio authored this article, he was a member of the House of Representatives from New Jersey and Chairman of the House Subcommittee on Commerce, Transportation, and Tourism, which had jurisdiction over hazardous waste issues.

A. Tracking the Lifecycle of Hazardous Waste

the decisions it faced. EPA's pace under Carter prompted criticism, but its underlying commitment to implementing the statute was not challenged.

In 1981, the situation changed. EPA's nominal efforts to implement the protective provisions of RCRA clearly reflected the Reagan Administration's antipathy for regulation by the federal government and its concern for selection of the least expensive means to dispose of hazardous waste. Indeed, the test at EPA was not whether a regulatory system met the statutory prescription to protect the environment, but rather whether it met the Administration's ideological regulatory standard. Congress fully expects agencies to exercise delegated discretion in a manner consistent with the Executive's political ideology. Tension between legislative intent and regulatory implementation is inevitable and expected. This tension is usually resolved through a series of small compromises and skirmishes between the legislative and executive branches, often effectuated through Congressional oversight. In the case of EPA and RCRA, however, the Administration's philosophy was more fundamentally at odds with the statute. EPA's implementation of the Administration's philosophy actually subverted the statutory goals by delaying statutorily required action and ignoring technical and scientific information that indicated a need for additional requirements.

In the early 1980's, evidence of the seriousness and scope of the hazardous waste problem mounted while EPA stalled. Congress grew increasingly frustrated with the obvious manipulation practiced by the political appointees at the Agency, as well as with the substantive environmental policy the Agency pursued.

In 1983, five and one-half years after the mandatory deadline for promulgation of RCRA standards and permits, the 98th Congress began a reauthorization process for RCRA. There was still no enforceable system for regulating the disposal of hazardous waste and little prospect for one soon. The problems recognized in 1976 had become common knowledge and, by 1983, evidence of the dangers was even more compelling. Not surprisingly, Congress made clear that it would not allow the delays to continue. Any confidence that EPA could be trusted to act expeditiously had long since evaporated. Witnesses at Congressional hearings urged a legislative solution requiring that disposal firms obtain a permit and meet the federal operating standards.

Congress responded by reauthorizing RCRA with a maze of new deadlines and statutory requirements. . . . Congressional reluctance to rely on EPA judgments was not limited to technological standards, but extended into all areas of the RCRA program. . . .

In the area of hazardous waste regulation during the 1980's, . . . the traditional reliance on delegated responsibility . . . collapsed, with profound implications for the overall regulatory structure. The wide discrepancy between the public's desire for vigorous environmental protection and the Reagan Administration's ideological preference for regulatory relief . . . forced Congress to produce a new regulatory system that significantly reduces agency discretion.

> **The Tension Between Congress and the Executive Branch**
>
> One axiom of regulatory design is that the implementing agency should not distort or disrupt the policy established by Congress in its enabling legislation. This axiom was apparently violated by EPA in its early approach toward implementing RCRA. Congress's response was to attempt to micromanage RCRA implementation. The advantages and disadvantages of legislative micromanagement are discussed below.

2. RCRA's Administrative Thicket: Defining Hazardous Wastes

A significant threshold issue under RCRA is defining what materials are to be statutorily regulated as "solid waste" and, further, what solid waste is to be considered "hazardous waste." The process of defining materials (1) as "solid wastes" and (2) as a subset of solid wastes, known as "hazardous wastes," is described below.

First, Congress defined "solid waste" as

> any garbage, refuse, sludge from a waste treatment plant, water supply treatment plant, or air pollution control facility and other discarded material, including solid, liquid, semisolid, or contained gaseous material resulting from industrial, commercial, mining, and agricultural operations, and from community activities, but does not include solid or dissolved material in domestic sewage, or solid or dissolved materials in irrigation return flows or industrial

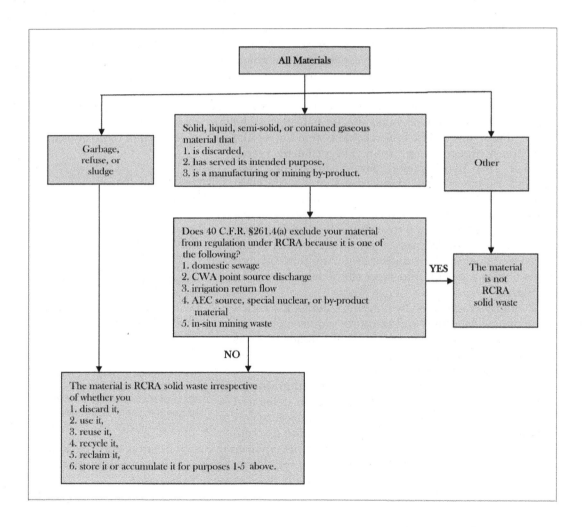

FIGURE 17-1. *Definition of a Solid Waste.*

A. Tracking the Lifecycle of Hazardous Waste

discharges which are point sources subject to permits under §402 of the Federal Water Pollution Control Act [33 U.S.C. §1342], or source, special nuclear, or byproduct material as defined by the Atomic Energy Act of 1954 as amended (68 Stat. 923) [42 U.S.C. §§2011 et seq.]. 42 U.S.C. §6903(27).

Under this portion of the statute, as illustrated in Figure 1, EPA has promulgated a definition of solid waste that includes abandoned, recycled, and inherently waste-like materials. See 40 C.F.R. §261.2(a)(2). Abandoned materials are those that have been disposed of, burned, incinerated, or accumulated or stored in lieu of being disposed of, burned, or incinerated. See 40 C.F.R. §261.2(b). Recycled materials include sludges, by-products, some commercial chemicals, and scrap metals that have been recycled in various ways. See 40 C.F.R. §261(c). The "inherently waste-like" category is a catch-all that includes materials that are usually treated like waste in that they are usually disposed of, burned, or incinerated. Materials are also classified as inherently waste-like if they contain EPA-listed toxic constituents (see 40 C.F.R. §261, Appendix VIII) that are not ordinarily found in the raw materials for which the toxic-bearing materials are being used as a substitute. See 40 C.F.R. §261.2(d)(2). Further, materials such as dioxin that may pose a substantial hazard to human health and the environment when recycled are likewise defined as inherently waste-like. Id.

By their exclusion from the definition of "solid waste," certain categories of waste are exempted from RCRA by Congress or EPA. These exclusions can have significant environmental consequences because the wastes removed from the RCRA regulatory program include whole categories of hazardous materials whose disposal is largely unregulated. As Figure 1 shows, the most important exclusions from the solid waste definition[7] include domestic sewage—alone or in combination with other waste material—that passes through publicly owned treatment works; legal point source discharges; irrigation return flows; and material regulated by the Atomic Energy Act of 1954.[8] In addition, EPA regulations also exempt a number of solid wastes from being considered hazardous wastes. The principal

---

7. As reflected in Figure 1, the exclusions are listed in 40 C.F.R. §261.4(a).
8. On October 30, 2008, EPA also issued a final rule, effective December 29, 2008, excluding from the definition of solid waste the following categories of secondary hazardous materials: (1) materials that are legitimately reclaimed at the site of generation under specific management and notification requirements; and (2) materials that are transferred offsite for legitimate reclamation in compliance with more detailed management and notification requirements. 40 C.F.R. §261.1(c)(4). According to the Federal Register notice published on October 30, 2008, "the purpose of this final rule is to encourage safe, environmentally sound recycling and resource conservation and to respond to several court decisions concerning the definition of solid waste." (73 Fed. Reg. 64,668 (Oct. 30, 2008)). Thereafter, on January 13, 2015, EPA published a new rule revising the Definition of Solid Waste under RCRA. 80 Fed. Reg. 1693. The most significant change made in the 2015 revision was EPA's withdrawal of the transfer-based exclusion codified in the 2008 rule. In its place, EPA created the "verified recycler exclusion." This new provision requires that all recyclers have RCRA permits or obtain variances prior to reclaiming hazardous secondary materials. The rule retains the exclusion for hazardous secondary materials that are legitimately reclaimed under the control of the generator (generator-controlled exclusion), but adds several conditions to the exclusion, including notification, recordkeeping, and emergency preparedness and response conditions. EPA has also modified the transfer-based exclusion by adding several conditions, including that recyclers have financial assurance in place to manage the materials left behind when the facility closes. The revised rule became effective July 13, 2015. However, because most states are authorized by EPA to administer the RCRA hazardous waste program, the revisions will not become effective in RCRA-authorized states until those states revise their programs to adopt the changes and EPA approves the states' revised programs.

exemptions of this type are household wastes (i.e., the garbage generated at home) and fertilizer used in agricultural operations.[9]

Once material is found to be solid waste, it must further be defined as hazardous waste before the more stringent segments of RCRA Subtitle C are applicable. The statute defines "hazardous waste" as:

> a solid waste, or combination of solid wastes, which because of its quantity, concentration, or physical, chemical, or infectious characteristics may—
>
> (A) cause, or significantly contribute to an increase in mortality or an increase in serious irreversible, or incapacitating reversible, illness; or
>
> (B) pose a substantial present or potential hazard to human health or the environment when improperly treated, stored, transported, or disposed of, or otherwise managed. 42 U.S.C. §6903(5)(A) & (B).

A separate section of RCRA, 42 U.S.C. §6921(a), directs that EPA promulgate regulations for hazardous wastes taking into account (1) toxicity, persistence, and degradability, (2) the potential of the material to bioaccumulate in plants and animals, and (3) flammability, corrosiveness, and other hazardous characteristics. EPA responded with a dual approach, one that defined material as hazardous waste due to its generic characteristics, and the other listing specifically identified materials or waste streams as hazardous. The characteristics approach relies on four criteria: ignitability, corrosivity, reactivity, and toxicity.[10] See 40 C.F.R. §§261.21-261.24. Under the specific listing approach, EPA produced three lists, one identifying specific materials that are hazardous without regard to source (see 40 C.F.R. §261.31), another listing materials that are hazardous due to their generation as part of a particular waste stream (e.g., waste from the inorganic chemical industry) (see 40 C.F.R. §261.32), and a third for a variety of discarded materials that are acutely hazardous or toxic (see 40 C.F.R. §261.33).

---

9. Still further exemptions from Subtitle C were established by Congress with regard to five categories of "special wastes." In general, these wastes are high-volume, low-toxicity material, including certain mining materials that remain largely in place throughout the mining process, cement kiln dust, and certain coal and fuel combustion by-products such as fly ash. For each category of special waste, EPA is required to study the matter and determine whether the exemption from Subtitle C should be made permanent. Pending that determination, special wastes are subject to RCRA regulation on the same basis as most nonhazardous solid waste. RCRA §3001(b)(2)-(3), 42 U.S.C. §6921(b)(2)-(3).

10. To assess toxicity, EPA historically utilized a test method called the TCLP (Toxicity Characteristic Leaching Procedure). TCLP is a testing procedure that extracts the toxic constituents from a waste in a manner that EPA believed simulated the leaching action that occurs in landfills. See 40 C.F.R. §261.24, as amended, 55 Fed. Reg. 11,862 (Mar. 29, 1990). However, in 1998, the D.C. Circuit held that EPA's use of the TCLP to determine compliance with its treatment standard was arbitrary and capricious because the TCLP failed accurately to predict the actual behavior of hazardous constituents in leachate, in a situation where aluminum waste was treated and disposed of in a landfill. *Columbia Falls Aluminum Co. v. EPA*, 139 F.3d 914 (D.C. Cir. 1998).

A. Tracking the Lifecycle of Hazardous Waste

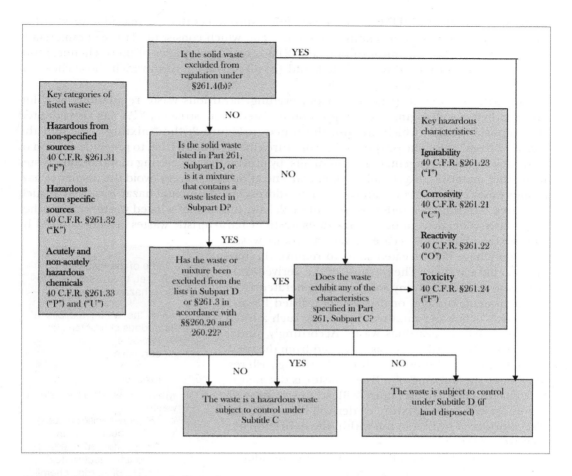

FIGURE 17-2. *Definition of a Hazardous Waste.*

Figure 2 illustrates graphically the dual approach undertaken by EPA in determining whether solid waste is "hazardous." If a solid waste is not exempted or excluded from Subtitle C regulation,[11] a determination as to whether a solid waste is hazardous depends upon whether it exhibits one of the four hazardous characteristics ("characteristic wastes") or is specifically listed as a hazardous waste in EPA regulations ("listed wastes").[12]

As Figure 2 indicates, waste streams can be specifically listed as hazardous if EPA determines that they routinely contain hazardous constituents or exhibit hazardous characteristics. As further specified in Figure 2, EPA has established four general categories of listed wastes (e.g., the "F," "K," "P," and "U" lists).[13] The "F" list includes wastes from certain common industrial and manufacturing processes. The "K" list includes wastes from specific

---

11. The disposal of exempted materials is subject to the much more lenient provisions of RCRA Subtitle D, 40 C.F.R. §261.4(b).

12 EPA developed a hazardous waste definition that relies on both "listings" and "characteristics," after EPA determined that it was not able to define and select test methods for identifying all hazardous charcteristics, including organic toxicity, mutagenicity, teratogenicity, bioaccumulation potential, and phototoxicity.

13. The key categories of "listed wastes" list wastes that are (1) hazardous from nonspecific sources (40 C.F.R. §261.31) ("F"), (2) hazardous from specific sources (40 C.F.R. §261.32) ("K"), (3) acutely hazardous chemical products (40 C.F.R. §261.33) ("P"), or (4) nonacutely hazardous chemical products (40 C.F.R. §261.33(f)) ("U"). EPA has listed hundreds of types of wastes as hazardous by placing them in one of these four categories.

industries. The "P" and "U" lists include chemical substances that are manufactured or formulated for commercial or manufacturing use and which consist of (1) the commercially pure grades of those chemical substances, (2) any technical grades of those chemical substances that are produced or marketed, and (3) all formulations in which those chemical substances are the sole active ingredients.

In order to prevent generators from evading hazardous waste regulations by diluting or otherwise changing the composition of listed waste streams, EPA has also adopted two important rules, which are also illustrated in Figure 2: the "mixture" rule and the "derived-from" rule. The purpose of the mixture rule is twofold: first, to preclude evasion of hazardous waste management requirements, by preventing the mixing of hazardous wastes with other materials so as to dilute their concentration and thereby avoid the display of hazardous waste characteristics; and second, to address environmental hazards caused by such mixtures. Accordingly, under the mixture rule, any mixture of a listed waste with another solid waste is deemed to be a "hazardous waste." Characteristic wastes are not covered by the mixture rule; they cease to be hazardous wastes once they have been treated so as to remove the hazardous characteristic. The purpose of the derived-from rule is to ensure that any solid waste generated from the treatment, storage, or disposal of a listed hazardous waste, or a waste mixture containing such a listed waste, is itself a hazardous waste. Accordingly, under the derived-from rule, any waste derived-from the treatment, storage, or disposal of a listed waste (e.g., ash residue from the burning of a listed waste) is deemed to be a hazardous waste. As Figure 2 illustrates, wastes falling under either the mixture or derived-from rules are also considered by EPA to fall within the definition of a "hazardous waste."

In summary, as Figure 2 shows, EPA considers a solid waste to be "hazardous" when:

- the waste exhibits a hazardous characteristic,
- the waste meets the description of a listed waste,
- the waste is mixed with a listed waste, or
- the waste is derived from the storage, treatment, or disposal of a hazardous waste.

> If any one of the following criteria is met, then a solid waste is also a hazardous waste:
>
> - when the waste exhibits a hazardous characteristic:
>   - ignitable
>   - corrosive
>   - reactive
>   - toxic, or
> - when the waste is a listed waste:
>   - "F" (nonspecific sources), "K" (specific sources), "P" (discarded chemical products, acutely toxic), or "U" (discarded chemical products) lists
>   - supplemental state lists, if any, or
> - when the waste is mixed with a listed waste, or
> - when the waste constitutes derived-from waste.

To avoid the hazardous waste regulatory system, a waste must be wholly or partially exempted or the hazardous waste status must be terminated.[14]

3. Regulating Participants in the Hazardous Waste Life Cycle

As noted previously, RCRA divides the universe of persons in the hazardous waste life cycle into three categories: (1) generators of waste, (2) transporters of waste, and (3) owners and operators of TSD facilities. Of the three groups, only TSD facilities require RCRA

---

14. Wastes that have been listed as hazardous must be managed under Subtitle C, unless EPA grants a petition to delist a waste generated at a particular site under RCRA §3001(f).

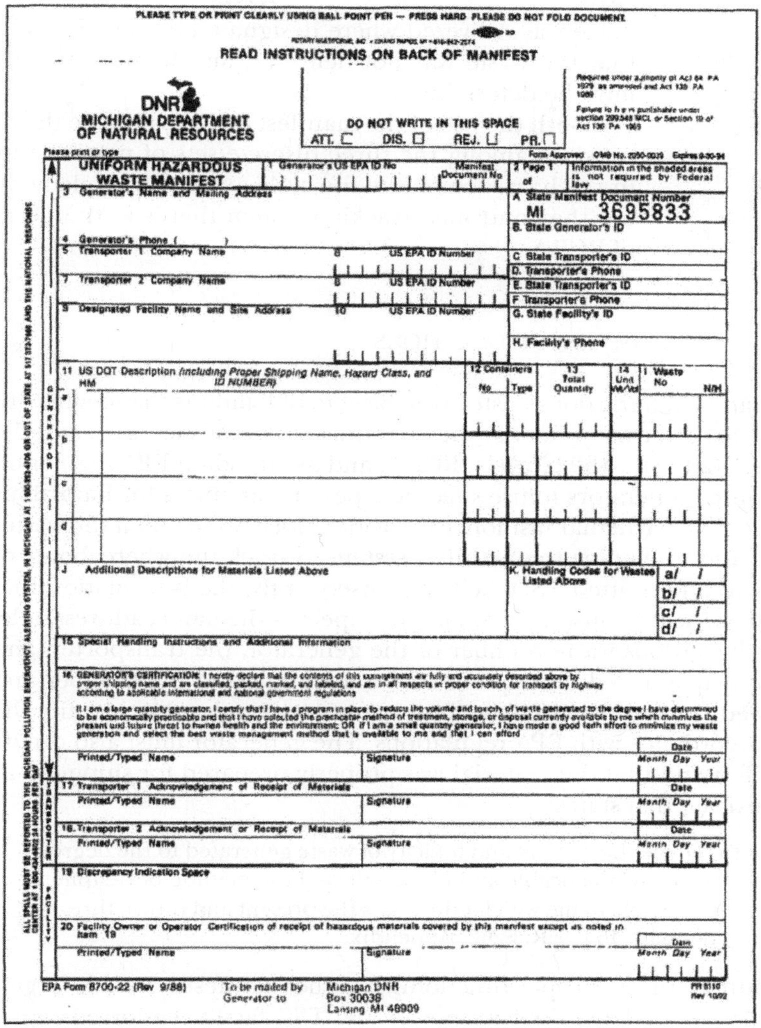

A. Tracking the Lifecycle of Hazardous Waste

FIGURE 17-3. *A State of Michigan Uniform Hazardous Waste Manifest*

permits to operate, but for each of these groups RCRA sets statutory duties that are liberally supplemented by administrative regulation. In general, the very demanding requirements for TSD licensure have limited the number of TSD sites and greatly increased the cost of lawful disposal of hazardous waste.[15]

Although RCRA divides the universe of persons into these three categories, RCRA also links these categories together through the use of a manifest system. The Uniform Hazardous Waste Manifest (the manifest) is the paper trail linking the generator, the transporter, and the TSD for every shipment of hazardous waste from the point of its generation to the point of its ultimate treatment, storage, or disposal. Each time the waste is transferred (e.g., from one transporter to another or from a transporter to a designated facility), the manifest must be signed to acknowledge the receipt of the waste. A copy of the manifest is retained by each link in the transportation chain and provides verification that

---

15. To avoid the possibility that generators will seek to avoid the cost of disposal by storing waste on-site, EPA requires that all but a small portion of a generator's hazardous waste must be consigned for delivery to a TSD facility within 90 days after the date of generation. 40 C.F.R. §262.34 (the "90-day accumulation rule") – some generators have obtained on-site RCRA permits, but the burdens of RCRA regulation and economies of scale have made off-site treatment, storage, and disposal the norm. Small-quantity generators of between 100 kilograms per month and 1000 kilograms per month may store hazardous wastes on site for longer periods than prescribed in the 90-day accumulation rule but must comply with RCRA in virtually all other respects. See 40 C.F.R. §262.34(d)(i).

> **The Three Participants in the Hazardous Waste Life Cycle:**
>
> 1. Generators
> 2. Transporters
> 3. TSD Facility Owners or Operators

waste was delivered where designated or, alternatively, that the waste was not delivered and its whereabouts must be determined.

Both the use of the manifest and the linkage that it provides among the three discrete sets of participants in the hazardous waste life cycle are key to implementing the controlled tracking system that is at the heart of RCRA.

COMMENTS & QUESTIONS

1. Generators. Generators of hazardous waste are subject to obligations that begin with "recordkeeping practices that accurately identify the quantities . . . constituents . . . and the disposition of such wastes." 42 U.S.C. §6922(a)(1). RCRA, and its attendant EPA regulation (40 C.F.R. §262), also require generators to use specific types of containers for hazardous wastes, to label those wastes in a particular fashion, to provide information about the wastes and their characteristics, and to employ the manifest system to track the whereabouts of material until its delivery to a permitted TSD facility. Consequently, the information that must appear on the manifest includes just what you might expect—the name, address, telephone number, and EPA hazardous waste number of the generator, the transporter, and the TSD facility; a carefully quantified description of the materials and the number and types of containers involved; and a series of descriptive names and codes that identify the waste and its hazards in accordance with EPA regulations. The generator must also certify the accuracy of the manifest and that the material was properly prepared for shipment in addition to signing a certificate that states:

> I have a program in place to reduce the volume and toxicity of waste generated to the degree I have determined to be economically practicable and I have selected the method of treatment, storage, or disposal currently available to me which minimizes the present and future threat to human health and the environment. 40 C.F.R. §262, Appendix.

The administrative burden of the proper functioning of the manifest system is largely on the generator, who must obtain from the transporter and TSD facility endorsed copies of the manifest that document proper delivery of the material to the TSD facility within 35 days of the time that the material was consigned for delivery. If successful delivery is not documented within 45 days, the generator must file a report with EPA (or the state where the state program is authorized) advising it of that failure and detailing the generator's efforts to locate the waste. See 40 C.F.R. §262.42.

2. Transporters. Transporters are the least heavily regulated actors in the RCRA hazardous waste life cycle.[16] Their basic obligations under RCRA are to facilitate the operation of the manifest system by making sure (as far as possible) that the manifests are accurate and by delivering the material in accordance with the manifests. In the event of a spill, transporters come under additional obligations to minimize the spill's effects and to notify local and federal spill response authorities. Transporters, if they mix dissimilar wastes for shipment in a single container or accept wastes from sources outside of the country, can

---

16. Transporters, however, are regulated separately by the U.S. Department of Transportation (DOT) pursuant to the Hazardous Materials Transportation Act, 49 U.S.C. §§5101-5128. DOT has promulgated extensive equipment and materials handling specifications under this statute.

A. Tracking the Lifecycle of Hazardous Waste

become liable as generators of wastes for RCRA purposes. Likewise, transporters who store wastes beyond regulatory limits or alter the characteristics of the wastes can become subject to regulation as TSD facilities.

3. TSD facility owners or operators. TSD facilities are the most extensively regulated parties in the RCRA hazardous waste life cycle. The three components of TSD are denned broadly. Treatment includes:

> any method, technique, or process, including neutralization, designed to change the physical, chemical, or biological character or composition of any hazardous waste so as to neutralize such waste, or so as to recover energy or material resources from the waste, or so as to render such waste non-hazardous, or less hazardous, safer to transport, store, or dispose of, or amenable for recovery, amenable for storage, or reduced in volume. 40 C.F.R. §260.10.

Storage includes:

> the holding of hazardous waste for a temporary period, at the end of which the hazardous waste is treated, disposed of, or stored elsewhere. Id.

Disposal includes:

> the discharge, deposit, injection, dumping, spilling, leaking, or placing of any solid waste or hazardous waste into or on any land or water so that such solid waste or hazardous waste or any constituent thereof may enter the environment or be emitted into the air or discharged into any waters, including ground waters. Id.

The obligations of TSD facilities are again predictable. RCRA requires that TSD facilities:

> (1) treat, store, and dispose of wastes in a manner consistent with EPA directives and standards; (2) maintain records of the wastes treated, stored, or disposed of; (3) comply with the requirements of the manifest system; (4) be built to meet certain EPA specified design and siting requirements that seek to ensure safety, such as not being located in flood plains or along earthquake faults; (5) monitor the site for releases of hazardous materials; and (6) take corrective action in the event of a release or threatened release of hazardous materials.[17]

Going further, EPA has set standards for continuity of operations, training personnel, and eventual closure of the facility.

RCRA also requires that TSD operators meet qualifications that touch on issues of financial responsibility, past record of regulatory compliance, and freedom from criminal activity. The financial responsibility standards are intended to avoid the dangers associated with "orphan" sites that have been a major problem in the past. The worry is that a presently solvent and viable TSD operation may become insolvent, leaving behind a potential toxic time bomb that becomes a burden on public resources. The good character and compliance record requirements are aimed at excluding organized crime organizations from the industry and also limiting the class of TSD operators to persons and companies having a sound history of regulatory compliance.

EPA labels the phases of the TSD facility life cycle as operational, closure, and postclosure. In the operational stage, the site is able to accept wastes, for which fees are charged and from which an income stream is generated. Closure is typically a six-month period that

---

17. See generally RCRA §3004, 42 U.S.C. §6924. Especially in the early years of RCRA operation, TSD licensing proceeded on a dual track that allowed facilities to obtain "interim" licenses by meeting less stringent standards and to obtain "permanent" status by meeting the full array of Subtitle C regulation. In the 1984 HSWA, Congress set firm deadlines to retire all interim status facilities, the last of which fell due in 1992.

begins when wastes are no longer accepted at the facility, during which time treatment and disposal operations are completed on all wastes that are not going to be relocated to other operating TSD facilities. Closure also includes dismantling and decontaminating equipment and making needed site improvements, such as applying clay capping over hazardous materials that are to be disposed of on-site. Postclosure is typically a 30-year period following closure during which the TSD facility operator has continuing monitoring, maintenance, and remediation responsibilities.

Both closure and postclosure costs, including costs for relocation of waste, are substantial and pose a special problem that must be addressed by the financial responsibility regulations. By definition, those costs occur at a time when no additional waste is being accepted at the site, and, hence, there is no longer a positive income stream available to meet expenses. Anticipating this situation, as part of licensure, a facility-specific closure plan is required, and its cost is estimated using a "worst case scenario." This figure is adjusted annually to reflect revisions (if any) in the plan itself, and changes in plan costs due to inflation or other factors. The law requires that the TSD operator provide a financial assurance in that amount by establishing a closure trust fund during the operational life of the facility, obtaining a surety bond or irrevocable letter of credit, purchasing closure insurance, or, under certain corporate solvency conditions, giving a corporate guarantee. To alleviate problems of TSD operator insolvency that may occur before closure, a second prong of the financial responsibility regulation requires the purchase of liability insurance, or its equivalent, for both sudden and nonsudden accidental releases of hazardous materials.

COMMENTARY & QUESTIONS

1. RCRA's regulatory scheme as a series of statutory types. Recall the variety of statutory types studied in preceding chapters. As discussed so far, what kind of statute is RCRA? Although several facets of RCRA have been mentioned only briefly so far in this chapter, RCRA can already be seen to be a composite statute that integrates many taxonomic regulatory mechanisms into a comprehensive, although not complete, hazardous waste management system. The wonder is that this spectrum of approaches has evolved into a coherent overall program.

RCRA as a Composite Statute

- The manifest system is a form of mandatory disclosure.
- The hammer clauses (i.e., the "land ban" considered later in this chapter) are a form of roadblock statute.
- The TSD licensing procedure is, in part, a form of a traditional review-and-permit statute.
- The financial responsibility requirements are a form of control of market access.
- A number of the congressionally fixed TSD facility design requirements are a form of specific, directly legislated standards.
- The limitation on land-based disposal, making necessary the development of alternative disposal methods, is a form of technology-forcing.
- The TCLP (Toxicity Characteristic Leaching Procedure) test used to define some wastes as hazardous is a form of harm-based ambient standard.
- EPA's land disposal waste treatment regulations are based, in part, on BDAT (Best Demonstrated Available Technology, considered later in this chapter), a form of technology-based regulation.

A. Tracking the Lifecycle of Hazardous Waste

> - In an indirect way, due to the high cost of dealing with hazardous solid waste under Subtitle C, RCRA rewards and encourages waste reduction, thereby serving as a market incentives statute.
> - The power of EPA to order corrective action is a form of cleanup statute.
> - And, finally, the siting requirements for TSD facilities are a form of land-use control.

2. RCRA's impact. Estimates of the amount of hazardous waste generated in the U.S. vary considerably. According to EPA estimates, of the over 13 billion tons of industrial, agricultural, commercial, and household wastes generated annually, over 300 million tons are "hazardous" as defined by RCRA regulations. EPA has also estimated that there has been a historical reduction in the number of facilities where hazardous waste disposal takes place. A 1982 EPA study found that there were in excess of 180,000 facilities at which hazardous waste disposal was occurring prior to RCRA's enactment.[18] By four years later, however, the number of sites, at which legal (RCRA-permitted) disposal of hazardous waste was occurring, had dropped below 2000 facilities.[19]

What was so impressive about this rapid reduction in the number of facilities at which hazardous waste disposal was occurring in the period following RCRA's enactment? Recalling the "if I know where it is, I know that it's not somewhere else that's worse" aspect of the RCRA system, it should be clear that herding a substantial portion of the nation's hazardous wastes into RCRA Subtitle C facilities was a vast improvement over past practices. Previously, most generators either kept hazardous waste on-site in slag piles, pits, ponds, and lagoons, or shipped it away for disposal at sites that employed the same unsophisticated disposal practices.

Another key element in evaluating RCRA's impact concerns the expense involved in the lawful disposal of hazardous waste. Estimates of the cost of building a RCRA-compliant hazardous waste TSD facility range in the tens of millions of dollars for a moderate- to large-sized facility. The process of obtaining a permit alone may cost well in excess of $1 million. These costs, of course, are typically passed through, in whole or in part, to firms that send their wastes to TSD facilities.

Another issue involved in evaluating RCRA's impact is the effect upon the number of TSD facilities in use. One of the avowed aims of RCRA was to drive undercapitalized firms from the TSD industry, and RCRA seems to have succeeded in this area. For example, even as early as 1989, a GAO survey of all nonfederal RCRA-permitted land disposal, land treatment, and surface impoundment facilities indicated that the industry had become the province of large firms.[20] Why are properly capitalized firms central to the effective implementation of RCRA?

3. Criticizing RCRA: under-regulation. More than half of the nation's hazardous waste is outside of the RCRA system. The most significant legal reason for this under-regulation is that Congress and EPA have excluded whole categories of waste from regulation. Why should those categories be exempt from RCRA regulation? Although cost is alleged by some to be the answer, the cost of safe (or at least far safer) disposal is not large in comparison to the value of the finished products of which the wastes are a by-product.

---

18. See EPA, Surface Impoundment Assessment: National Report (Dec. 29, 1982).
19. See U.S. GAO, Report to the Chairman, Subcommittee on Environment, Energy, and Natural Resources, Committee on Government Operations, House of Representatives, Hazardous Waste - The Cost and Availability of Pollution Insurance 12 (Oct. 1989).
20. U.S. GAO, Hazardous Waste: The Cost and Availability of Pollution Insurance 15 (Oct. 1989).

The largest RCRA loophole involves industrial waste[21] not legally defined as "hazardous":

> There exists a widespread perception that Subtitle D, or nonhazardous waste, is mostly municipal waste. This perception is reinforced by news reports highlighting disposal capacity, ash barges, recycling, and the anticipated publication of EPA's final municipal waste regulations. However, this perception is wrong. Between hazardous waste and municipal waste is a kind of waste that is generated in vastly greater volumes than the other two combined—nonhazardous industrial waste, or simply industrial waste.
>
> The magnitude of the industrial waste problem is overwhelming when it is stated in figures. Nationally, about 211 million tons of municipal waste and approximately 300 million tons of hazardous waste are generated annually. These numbers seem small compared with the 7,600 million tons of industrial waste that are generated and disposed of on-site annually. . . .

Waste that does not meet the legal definition of "hazardous," however, is subject only to EPA's open dump criteria. These criteria apply to only a limited number of waste disposal problems, address many of these problems rather vaguely, and do not apply to treatment, storage, or transportation. 40 C.F.R. §257. RCRA does not expressly require that nonhazardous waste TSD facilities be permitted. Generally, Subtitle D treats all nonhazardous waste the same and only includes specific provisions for municipal waste, household hazardous waste, small-quantity generator hazardous waste, and recycled oil. Industrial waste is not given separate attention. The disparity in regulatory control between hazardous and nonhazardous waste is so great that delisting of a hazardous waste means virtual federal regulatory abandonment.

4. Criticizing RCRA: over-regulation. Without question, RCRA is a giant step forward from unregulated hazardous waste disposal practices, but RCRA inevitably over-regulates in a way that has unintended results. Dr. Robert Powitz, when he was the Director of Environmental Health and Safety at Wayne State University, posed the following examples in a lecture to law students.

> Waste acids can often be combined in a chemical reaction with waste bases to form salt and water. If performed, this reaction would eliminate the need for transport of two hazardous substances (the acid and the base), having changed them to nonhazardous materials. To do so, however, is to perform treatment under RCRA which requires the treater to obtain a TSD license that the University cannot afford to obtain. The University estimates that the cost of mere application for a license is in excess of $1 million. The University's annual disposal costs attributable to materials that could be treated safely on campus without major capital investments is in the $50,000 per year range. The alternative is to ship the hazardous material 80 miles through several heavily populated areas to a licensed TSD facility.
>
> A major chemical facility in the suburbs of Detroit, Michigan, produces isocyanate (of Bhopal infamy) as a by-product of plastics production. Isocyanates react readily with water to produce nontoxic by-products. Again, however, to combine them with the water is to engage in treatment and requires a TSD license that the chemical company does not wish to obtain. (Here the hesitancy to seek licensure is less the cost than the desire to avoid being a TSD facility with all of the regulatory burdens that entails.) The lawful disposal requires shipment of isocyanate through residential areas in the vicinity of the plant and highway travel to a facility some 60 miles away.

---

21. Industrial waste is not specifically defined by RCRA. The category includes more than 90% of the waste streams of factories, foundries, mills, processing plants, refineries, and slaughterhouses. It also includes sludges and other by-products of in-plant waste treatment and those generated by water pollution control facilities. Many of the compounds that are included in this waste stream have chemical constituents similar to hazardous wastes. As an example, off-specification pesticides containing multiple active ingredients fall into the industrial waste category, as does waste containing concentrations of hazardous materials that fall below the EPA thresholds for hazardousness.

A. Tracking the Lifecycle of Hazardous Waste

Do the examples demonstrate that RCRA thwarts its own objectives of increased safety and waste minimization? Should EPA write a blanket exception for safety-enhancing treatment at generators' sites or promulgate certain categorical exceptions from TSD licensure requirements?

5. Criticizing RCRA: definitional nightmares concerning "hazardous" wastes. One of RCRA's most obvious problems lies in the complex set of definitions and rules that combine to identify what materials qualify as hazardous wastes subject to its stringent regulatory provisions. Some of the complexity is attributable to what wastes are "characteristic" or what wastes are properly "listed" by EPA. Other cases construing RCRA's definition of "hazardous waste" include *American Min. Congress v. U.S. EPA*, 824 F.2d 1177 (D.C. Cir. 1987) (EPA is not authorized to regulate in-process recycled materials because they are not "discarded materials"); *Horsehead Res. Dev. Co. Inc. v. Browner*, 16 F.3d 1246 (D.C. Cir. 1994) (EPA can regulate cement kiln dust and combustion residues when they are produced by boilers and industrial furnaces that burn fuel containing hazardous waste); and *NRDC v. U.S. EPA*, 25 F.3d 1063 (D.C. Cir. 1994) (used oil need not be listed as a hazardous waste in all circumstances).

Still greater complexity is added by the "mixture" and "derived-from" rules. In 1991, a major blow to EPA's RCRA administration occurred when the D.C. Circuit vacated EPA's mixture and derived-from rules in *Shell Oil Co. v. EPA*, 950 F.2d 741 (D.C. Cir. 1991). The ground for vacating the rules was a failure by EPA to allow properly for notice and comment, a defect that could be overcome by repeating the process with adequate procedural steps. Pursuant to §553(b)(3)(B) of the Administrative Procedure Act, EPA then re-enacted the rules on an interim basis until new rules could be promulgated with full notice and comment. The interim rules were also challenged in the D.C. Circuit. In response to this challenge, Congress enacted legislation stating that the interim mixture and derived-from rules "shall not be terminated or withdrawn until revisions are promulgated and become effective." Congress also set a deadline of October 1994, for promulgation of the new rules, but EPA missed the deadline. Faced with lawsuits over failing to meet the deadline, EPA signed a consent decree requiring it to propose a new Hazardous Waste Identification Rule (HWIR).

After a number of iterations (undertaken in light of criticisms by industry groups and others contending that EPA's approach was technically challenging, overly complicated, and costly to implement), EPA ultimately revised, and then issued in May 2001, the mixture and derived-from rules that became effective on August 14, 2001. In June 2001, the American Chemistry Council filed suit in the U.S. Court of Appeals for the District of Columbia challenging the final HWIR as it relates to the mixture and derived-from rules. But the D.C. Circuit upheld the rules and denied the petition in 2003. See *American Chemistry Council v. EPA*, 337 F.3d 1060 (D.C. Cir. 2003) (concluding that Congress wanted the EPA, in deciding what substances to regulate as "hazardous" under RCRA, to err on the side of caution, and that the HWIR is a reasonable exercise of such caution).

6. When exempt household waste is incinerated, is its hazardous ash exempt too? According to EPA estimates, almost 300 facilities burn almost 4 million tons of hazardous wastes in incinerators each year. In 1994, the U.S. Supreme Court resolved a split between two of the nation's circuit courts of appeal with regard to whether ash created by the incineration of municipal solid waste can be regulated as hazardous waste under RCRA Subtitle C. Items that would normally qualify as hazardous solid waste, such as discarded batteries, paint, garden care products, and many others, are mixed with other refuse in municipal garbage. Congress foresaw the burden municipalities would face if their entire waste streams had to be disposed of at Subtitle C facilities, and Congress therefore exempted municipal solid waste (MSW) from Subtitle C.

However, when burned, as is common in trash-to-energy incinerators, the ash left after the combustion of MSW would often, depending on its characteristics, be considered a hazardous waste that required RCRA Subtitle C disposal. Perhaps displaying insufficient foresight, Congress did not specify if ash from incineration of MSW is also Subtitle C exempt. The Supreme Court held that the generation of toxic ash is not included within the activities covered by the exemption and thus must be regulated under Subtitle C if the ash possesses the characteristics of hazardous waste. *City of Chicago v. Environmental Defense Fund*, 511 U.S. 328 (1994). As a result, Chicago was no longer able to claim that it was entitled to a cost-saving waste stream exemption. After the Supreme Court's ruling, EPA announced new RCRA permit procedures for "facilities managing ash from waste-to-energy facilities." 59 Fed. Reg. 29,372 (Feb. 3, 1995).

7. Rethinking RCRA. In their dialogue entitled Rethinking the Resource Conservation and Recovery Act for the 1990s, 21 Envtl. L. Rep. 10,063 (1991), Marcia E. Williams and Jonathan Z. Cannon made a series of very technical but very telling criticisms of RCRA that remain pertinent today. One of their most fundamental attacks on RCRA can be stated in simplified form—RCRA makes a great deal turn on the division of wastes into the categories of hazardous and nonhazardous, and then draws that line in a fiendishly complicated way. This leads to a multitude of untoward results. First, because the cost of disposal of hazardous waste is vastly greater than the cost of disposal of nonhazardous waste, generators have immense incentives to contest the categorization decisions. In conjunction with the byzantine definitional rules that are currently in force, a disproportionate amount of both regulatory and enforcement effort is directed to issues of coverage that result in little or no environmental benefit.

A related criticism is that the definitional distinctions drawn between hazardous and nonhazardous are too often irrational if one keeps in mind RCRA's goal of reducing the release of dangerous substances. Here, the principal examples are the listing of some compounds as hazardous and the nonlisting of chemically similar compounds having much the same potential for damaging human health and the environment. Moving from the definitional into the regulatory sphere, Williams and Cannon accuse RCRA of severe under- and over-regulation. The under-regulation occurs in regard to the laxity with which nonhazardous wastes are treated. Their point is that many waste streams that are designated as nonhazardous contain substantial quantities of hazardous materials that find their way into the environment. The over-regulation occurs in practices that overestimate risks (such as assuming that all wastes will be totally mismanaged), or in the adoption of anti-dilution rules that are inflexibly applied as rigid "tracking" rules so that wastes remain legally hazardous, even after treatment that produces a by-product that is nonhazardous according to EPA standards.

A somewhat different perspective on RCRA's future focuses on the failure of Subtitle C to address the larger issues of the solid waste problem posed by the need to dispose safely of such vast quantities of material. Taken together, the severity of regulation under Subtitle C, the expense entailed by detoxification of materials under that portion of RCRA, and the laxity of regulation under Subtitle D form an unsatisfactory whole. Too little waste is required to be treated, and the waste that is treated is handled in ways that are often too expensive to be used for substantial additional quantities of waste. In the end, long-term land disposal of Subtitle D solid waste imposes risks that new environmental problems will be created should there be a breach in containment.

8. International shipments. RCRA is not limited to domestic hazardous wastes. RCRA directs exporters to notify the EPA of the nature of international shipments (e.g., dates, quantity, and description of wastes) at least four weeks prior to shipment. Within 30 days of the receipt of the notification, the State Department, on behalf of the EPA Administrator,

A. Tracking the Lifecycle of Hazardous Waste

must inform the receiving country about the export. The importing country, in turn, must consent (in writing) to accept the waste unless an existing international agreement provides otherwise.

The three North American countries (U.S., Canada, and Mexico) have traditionally shipped waste across borders for cheaper and more convenient disposal. The U.S. ratified the Basel Convention, which sharply limits international shipments of hazardous waste. Historically, the U.S. has exported less than one percent of its hazardous wastes.

9. Underground storage tank regulation. Subtitle I of RCRA, 42 U.S.C. §§6991 et seq., establishes a comprehensive regulatory program for Underground Storage Tanks (USTs).[22] RCRA defines a UST as:

> Any one or combination of tanks (including underground pipes connected thereto) which is used to contain an accumulation of regulated substances [hazardous substances and petroleum, except for RCRA Subtitle C hazardous wastes], and the volume of which (including the volume of underground pipes connected thereto) is 10 percent or more beneath the surface of the ground. 42 U.S.C. §6991(10).

The UST Program contains the following elements:

- standards for design, construction, and installation of new tanks;
- requirements for retrofitting existing tanks with anti-corrosion, overfill prevention, and release detection systems;
- operation, maintenance, and inspection requirements;
- release detection, investigation, and reporting requirements;
- corrective action obligations;
- tank closure procedures;
- financial responsibility requirements.

A miniature Superfund (the Leaking Underground Storage Tank Trust Fund, financed by a tax on motor fuels) has been created to fund EPA or state cleanups of UST releases.

10. Life cycle assessment in the private sector. As the following excerpt indicates, life cycle assessment, which underlies RCRA's regulatory strategy, has also been popular in the private sector for a number of years:

> Life cycle assessment ("LCA") is intended to evaluate as comprehensively as possible "cradle-to-grave" environmental consequences of a product, package, process, or practice. It is supposed to account for energy and material inputs and outputs associated with making, using, and retiring a product, including the environmental risk associated with the life cycle of the product. It could similarly be applied to evaluate processes and practices in manufacturing to account for every resource and environmental risk encountered in making, using, and disposing of a product. LCA is thus a tool for identifying material and energy use and the waste released during production, formulation, distribution, consumer use, recycling, and disposal. . . .
>
> [The current technical framework for LCA consists of three distinct but interrelated components:]

---

22. This program is now called the UST Program. It was originally referred to as the LUST (Leaking Underground Storage Tank) Program. The principal focus of the UST program is the roughly 800,000 petroleum tanks at gasoline stations and other fuel and automotive distribution centers around the country. Designed to protect groundwater from contamination, EPA's regulations govern construction, operation, and closure of tanks to minimize the cause of leaks. One of the more problematical issues arising with problem tanks has been the leaking of MTBE, a toxic additive that travels exceedingly fast through groundwater. Significant toxic tort and insurance coverage litigation in recent years has concerned the contamination of groundwater supplies by gasoline with MTBE leaking from problem tanks.

- *Life cycle inventory:* An objective, data-based process of quantifying energy and raw material requirements, air emissions, waterborne effluents, solid waste, and other environmental releases incurred throughout the life cycle of a product, process, or activity.
- *Life cycle impact analysis:* A technical, quantitative, or qualitative process to characterize and assess the effects of the environmental loadings identified in the inventory component. The assessment should address both ecological and human health considerations as well as other effects such as habitat modification and noise pollution.
- *Life cycle improvement analysis:* A systematic evaluation of the needs and opportunities to reduce the environmental burden associated with energy and raw materials use and waste emissions throughout the life cycle of a product, process, or activity. This analysis may include both quantitative and qualitative measures of improvements, such as changes in product design, raw materials use, industrial processing, consumer use, and waste management.

Environmental benefits can be realized at each step in the LCA process. For example, the inventory alone maybe used to identify opportunities for reducing emissions or the use of energy and materials. The impact analysis and improvement analysis tools, meanwhile, can help ensure optimization of potential reduction strategies and avoidance of unanticipated impacts in improvement programs. Denison, Evaluating Environmental Impacts, in National Academy of Engineering, Industrial Ecology: U.S.-Japan Perspectives 29 (1993).

In the light of subsequent paradigm shifts in private-sector thinking, such as LCA, RCRA's life cycle approach was far ahead of its time. RCRA's conceptual framework may ultimately prove as important as its regulatory provisions in stimulating pollution prevention.

11. Sustainable Materials Management. In 2002, EPA initiated a program known as the Resource Conservation Challenge (RCC), which was an early effort to place renewed emphasis on RCRA mandates to prevent pollution and to conserve natural resources and energy, through more efficient materials management. Since that time, the RCC has evolved to encompass four major resource areas:

(1) municipal solid waste reuse and recycling;
(2) green initiatives, such as reducing the life-cycle environmental impacts of electronics, promoting green building construction, and the retrofitting of existing buildings;
(3) the reuse of industrial materials and their recycling; and
(4) the reduction of toxic chemicals in products and waste.

The RCC initiatives launched by EPA focus primarily on the affirmative use of materials (that would otherwise be disposed of) as an important element in what has come to be known as "sustainable materials management." To that end, the RCC also includes initiatives seeking to reduce the use of toxic chemicals, challenging electronics manufacturers to remove toxics, encouraging the use of recycled materials, and endeavoring to encourage a sustainable flow of materials through design guidance by emphasizing the selection of more sustainable materials in packaging and construction.

The RCC has led to questions different from those historically considered in managing solid and hazardous wastes. For example, those seeking to manage such wastes might ask: "What should we do with scrap tires, or electronics, or fluorescent lights when we need to dispose of them?" However, in the future, the question may be rephrased as: "Is there a way to eliminate this waste completely, to provide the same or similar services with fewer resources, or to eliminate adverse environmental impacts?" In other words, can we substitute materials that do not wear out as quickly, or that can be reused, or that can be fully recovered, or that can be repurposed so that they never become waste? For further insight into EPA's RCC initiatives, see the Sep. 2009 EPA report entitled "Sustainable Materials Management: The Road Ahead."

B. THE "LAND BAN" AND THE USE OF "HAMMERS" TO CONTROL AGENCY ACTION

The HSWA of 1984[23] made important changes that greatly expanded the reach of federal hazardous waste law. In what may be its most significant feature, the HSWA added stringent regulation of land disposal of hazardous wastes,[24] often referred to as the land ban. In Congress's own words:

> reliance on land disposal should be minimized or eliminated and land disposal, particularly landfill and surface impoundment, should be the least favored method for managing hazardous wastes.... 42 U.S.C. §6901(b)(7).

As the Florio article above points out in reviewing RCRA's history, Congress feared undue delay if the implementation of its objectives was left to EPA's discretion. Thus Congress placed stringent time deadlines on EPA for the issuance of regulations. To make sure EPA acted promptly, Congress included "hammer clauses" that amounted to direct congressional regulation if EPA failed to act in a timely fashion. Congress took a three-pronged approach to land disposal: (1) it made liquids a particular focus of regulation because of their role in facilitating the migration of hazardous wastes away from disposal sites,[25] (2) it overhauled the means by which solid wastes could be defined as hazardous for purposes of land disposal, and (3) it set specific standards for landfills and surface impoundments that stressed multiple leachate control mechanisms.[26]

To ensure that EPA did not dally in its assigned regulatory tasks, Congress used the threat of a total nationwide ban on land disposal of hazardous waste as a hammer—EPA could avoid the land ban only by promulgating rigorous disposal standards within the allotted time periods. The lists of hazardous wastes were developed in part by Congress and in part by EPA.[27] Before authorizing the land disposal of any listed waste, EPA first had to conclude that a ban on the land disposal of that particular hazardous waste was "not

---

23. Pub. L. No. 98-616 (1984). For a discussion of the amendments, see Rosbe & Gulley, The Hazardous and Solid Waste Amendments of 1984: A Dramatic Overhaul of the Way America Manages Its Hazardous Wastes, 14 Envtl. L. Rep. 10458, 10459 (Dec. 1984) (hereinafter cited as Rosbe & Gulley).

24. The term *land disposal* as defined by RCRA includes, but is not limited to, "Any placement of . . . hazardous waste in a landfill, surface impoundment, waste pile, injection well, land treatment facility, salt dome formation, salt bed formation, or underground mine or cave." RCRA §3004(k), 42 U.S.C. §6924(k).

25. RCRA §3004(c), 42 U.S.C. §6924(c). Uncontainerized liquid hazardous waste was banned from landfills as of May 1985; the placement of nonhazardous liquids in landfills containing hazardous waste was banned as of November 1985; and containerized liquid hazardous waste and free liquid in containers containing other hazardous wastes were minimized as of February 1986.

26. Congress required all systems to have at least two liners, a leachate collection system above and between liners in landfills, and groundwater monitoring. RCRA §3004(o)(1), 42 U.S.C. §6924(o)(1). EPA was also required to promulgate additional design standards that would require leak detection systems to be present in all types of new facilities.

27. Congress adopted the so-called "California list" that identified a number of specific materials at varying concentrations as hazardous. See RCRA §3004(d)(2), 42 U.S.C. §6924(d)(2). In addition, Congress required regulation of certain solvents and dioxins. See RCRA §3004(e), 42 U.S.C. §6924(e). Finally, EPA was to develop a schedule for reviewing all other hazardous wastes. See RCRA §3001, 42 U.S.C. §6921. EPA was given a triparte deadline

required . . . to protect human health and the environment for as long as the waste remains hazardous." In making that determination, EPA had to consider "(A) the long-term uncertainties associated with land disposal, (B) the goal of managing hazardous waste in an appropriate manner in the first instance, and (C) the persistence, toxicity, mobility, and propensity to bioaccumulate of such hazardous wastes and their hazardous constituents." 42 U.S.C. §6924(d)(1). Congress also circumscribed EPA's discretion by stating that land disposal could not be allowed unless EPA found that wastes had been treated to levels that "substantially diminish the toxicity of the waste or substantially reduce the likelihood of migration of hazardous constituents from the waste so that short-term and long-term threats to human health and the environment are minimized." 42 U.S.C. §6924(m)(1).

The land ban portended far-reaching changes.

But to the surprise of many, EPA met many of the HSWA land ban deadlines.[28] What emerged, though, was not a set of substance-specific treatment standards. Instead, EPA relied on a general treatment standard for hazardous waste that requires treatment using Best Demonstrated Available Technology (BDAT) prior to landfilling of the waste.

The BDAT approach created a problem of inadequate treatment capacity. Especially in the shorter term, there was insufficient capacity nationwide to treat all of the waste that was in need of land-based disposal. As a result, EPA was forced to issue variances, because disposal of untreated hazardous wastes in permitted Subtitle C facilities was preferable to storing the materials in other locations until treatment capacity is increased. Over time the supply of BDAT treatment capacity has grown, although that growth has been severely inhibited by the NIMBY phenomenon and the obstacles it presents to siting hazardous waste treatment facilities.

EPA's move to select BDAT treatment as a precondition for land disposal provoked a legal challenge. Generators feared that they would now be faced with the costly prospect of incineration, even in circumstances where putting untreated waste in landfills would arguably provide adequate protection of human health and the environment.

Hazardous Waste Treatment Council v. U.S. Environmental Protection Agency

886 F.2d 355 (D.C. Cir. 1989)

Before WALD, C.J., SILBERMAN and D.H. GINSBURG, JJ.

PER CURIAM: RCRA requires EPA to implement the land disposal prohibition in three phases, addressing the most hazardous "listed" wastes first. In accordance with strict statutory deadlines, the Administrator is obligated to specify those methods of land disposal of each listed hazardous waste which "will be protective of human health and the environment." In addition, "[s]imultaneously with the promulgation of regulations . . . prohibiting . . . land disposal of a particular hazardous waste, the Administrator" is required to promulgate regulations specifying those levels or methods of treatment, if any, which substantially diminish the toxicity of the waste or substantially reduce the likelihood of migration of

---

for completing this process, which led to the description of the EPA regulations as being first third, second third, and third third. See RCRA §3004(g), 42 U.S.C. §6924(g).

28. See generally Note, An Analysis of the Land Disposal Ban in the 1984 Amendments to the Resource Conservation and Recovery Act, 76 Geo. L.J. 1563 (Apr. 1988); Williams & Cannon, Rethinking the Resource Recovery and Conservation Act for the 1990s, 21 Envtl. L. Rep. 10063 (1991).

B. The "Land Ban" and "Hammers"

hazardous constituents from the waste so that short-term and long-term threats to human health and the environment are minimized. §6924(m).

SECTION 3004(M) TREATMENT STANDARDS. In the Proposed Rule, EPA announced its tentative support for a treatment regime embodying both risk-based and technology-based standards. The technology-based standards would be founded upon what EPA determined to be the Best Demonstrated Available Technology ("BDAT"); parallel risk-based or "screening" levels were to reflect "the maximum concentration [of a hazardous constituent] below which the Agency believes there is no regulatory concern for the land disposal program and which is protective of human health and the environment." The Proposed Rule provided that these two sets of standards would be melded in the following manner:

> First, if BDAT standards were more rigorous than the relevant health-screening levels, the latter would be used to "cap the reductions in toxicity and/or mobility that otherwise would result from the application of BDAT treatment [.]" Thus, "treatment for treatment's sake" would be avoided. Second, if BDAT standards were less rigorous than health-screening levels, BDAT standards would govern and the screening level would be used as "a goal for future changes to the treatment standards as new and more efficient treatment technologies become available." Finally, when EPA determined that the use of BDAT would pose a greater risk to human health and the environment than land disposal, or would provide insufficient safeguards against the threats produced by land disposal, the screening level would actually become the 3004(m) treatment standard.

EPA invited public comment on alternative approaches as well. The first alternative identified in the Proposed Rule (and the one ultimately selected by EPA) was based purely on the capabilities of the "best demonstrated available technology."

The Agency received comments supporting both approaches, but ultimately settled on the pure-technology alternative. Of particular importance to EPA's decision were the comments filed by eleven members of Congress, all of whom served as conferees on the 1984 RCRA amendments. As EPA recorded in the preamble to the Final Rule:

> [these] members of Congress argue strongly that [the health screening] approach did not fulfill the intent of the law. They asserted that because of the scientific uncertainty inherent in risk-based decisions, Congress expressly directed the Agency to set treatment standards based on the capabilities of existing technology.
>
> The Agency believes that the technology-based approach adopted in [the] final rule, although not the only approach allowable under the law, best responds to the above stated comments.

EPA also relied on passages in the legislative history supporting an approach under which owners and operators of hazardous waste facilities would be required to use "the best [technology] that has been demonstrated to be achievable." And the agency reiterated that the chief advantage offered by the health-screening approach—avoiding "treatment for treatment's sake"—could "be better addressed through changes in other aspects of its regulatory program." As an example of what parts of the program might be altered, EPA announced that it was "considering the use of its risk-based methodologies to characterize wastes as hazardous pursuant to §3001 [of RCRA]...."[29]

---

29. EPA's announcement foreshadowed its subsequent proposed Hazardous Waste Identification Rule, discussed above. [EDS.]

CMA challenges EPA's adoption of BDAT treatment standards in preference to the approach it proposed initially primarily on the ground that the regulation is not a reasonable interpretation of the statute. CMA obliquely, and Intervenors Edison Electric and the American Petroleum Institute explicitly, argues in the alternative that the agency did not adequately explain its decision to take the course that it did. We conclude, as to CMA's primary challenge, that EPA's decision to reject the use of screening levels is a reasonable interpretation of the statute. We also find, however, that EPA's justification of its choice is so fatally flawed that we cannot, in conscience, affirm it. We therefore grant the petitions for review to the extent of remanding this issue to the agency for a fuller explanation.

CONSISTENCY OF EPA'S INTERPRETATION WITH RCRA. Our role in evaluating an agency's interpretation of its enabling statute is as strictly circumscribed as it is simply stated: We first examine the statute to ascertain whether it clearly forecloses the course that the agency has taken; if it is ambiguous with respect to that question, we go on to determine whether the agency's interpretation is a reasonable resolution of the ambiguity.

CHEVRON **STEP 1: IS THE STATUTE CLEAR?** CMA reads the statute as requiring EPA to determine the levels of concentration in waste at which the various solvents here at issue are "safe" and to use those "screening levels" as floors below which treatment would not be required. CMA supports its interpretation with the observation that the statute directs EPA to set standards only to the extent that "threats to human health and the environment are minimized." We are unpersuaded, however, that Congress intended to compel EPA to rely upon screening levels in preference to the levels achievable by BDAT.

The statute directs EPA to set treatment standards based upon either "levels or methods" of treatment. Such a mandate makes clear that the choice whether to use "levels" (screening levels) or "methods" (BDAT) lies within the informed discretion of the agency, as long as the result is "that short-term and long-term threats to human health and the environment are minimized." To "minimize" something is, to quote the *Oxford English Dictionary*, to "reduce [it] to the smallest possible amount, extent, or degree." But Congress recognized, in the very amendments here at issue, that there are "long-term uncertainties associated with land disposal," 42 U.S.C. §6924(d)(1)(A). In the face of such uncertainties, it cannot be said that a statute that requires that threats be minimized unambiguously requires EPA to set levels at which it is conclusively presumed that no threat to health or the environment exists.

This is not to say that EPA is free, under §3004(m), to require generators to treat their waste beyond the point at which there is no "threat" to human health or to the environment. That Congress's concern in adopting §3004(m) was with health and the environment would necessarily make it unreasonable for EPA to promulgate treatment standards wholly without regard to whether there might be a threat to man or nature. That concern is better dealt with, however, at *Chevron's* second step; for, having concluded that the statute does not unambiguously and in all circumstances foreclose EPA from adopting treatment levels based upon the levels achievable by BDAT, we must now explore whether the particular levels established by the regulations supply a reasonable resolution of the statutory ambiguity.

CHEVRON **STEP II: IS EPA'S INTERPRETATION REASONABLE?** The screening levels that EPA initially proposed were not those at which the wastes were thought to be entirely safe. Rather, EPA set the levels to reduce risks from the solvents to an "acceptable" level, and it explored, at great length, the manifest (and manifold) uncertainties inherent in any attempt to specify "safe" concentration levels. The agency discussed, for example, the lack

B. The "LandBan" and "Hammers"

of any safe level of exposure to carcinogenic solvents, the extent to which reference dose levels (from which it derived its screening levels) understate the dangers that hazardous solvents pose to particularly sensitive members of the population, the necessarily artificial assumptions that accompany any attempt to model the migration of hazardous wastes from a disposal site, and the lack of dependable data on the effects that solvents have on the liners that bound disposal facilities for the purpose of ensuring that the wastes disposed in a facility stay there. Indeed, several parties made voluminous comments on the Proposed Rule to the effect that EPA's estimates of the various probabilities were far more problematic than even EPA recognized.

CMA suggests, despite these uncertainties, that the adoption of a BDAT treatment regime would result in treatment to "below established levels of hazard." It relies for this proposition almost entirely upon a chart in which it contrasts the BDAT levels with (1) levels EPA has defined as "Maximum Contaminant Levels" (MCLs) under the Safe Drinking Water Act; (2) EPA's proposed "Organic Toxicity Characteristics," threshold levels below which EPA will not list a waste as hazardous by reason of its having in it a particular toxin; and (3) levels at which EPA has recently granted petitions by waste generators to "delist" a particular waste, that is, to remove it from the list of wastes that are deemed hazardous. CMA points out that the BDAT standards would require treatment to levels that are, in many cases, significantly below these "established levels of hazard."

If indeed EPA had determined that wastes at any of the three levels pointed to by CMA posed no threat to human health or the environment, we would have little hesitation in concluding that it was unreasonable for EPA to mandate treatment to substantially lower levels. In fact, however, none of the levels to which CMA compares the BDAT standards purports to establish a level at which safety is assured or "threats to human health and the environment are minimized." Each is a level established for a different purpose and under a different set of statutory criteria than concern us here; each is therefore irrelevant to the inquiry we undertake today. . . .

In sum, EPA's catalog of the uncertainties inherent in the alternative approach using screening levels supports the reasonableness of its reliance upon BDAT instead. Accordingly, finding no merit in CMA's contention that EPA has required treatment to "below established levels of hazard," we find that EPA's interpretation of §3004(m) is reasonable.

To summarize [EPA's explanation for abandoning the combination of using BDAT and screening levels in favor of BDAT alone]: after EPA issued the Proposed Rule, some commenters, including eleven members of Congress, chastised the agency on the ground that the use of screening levels was inconsistent with the intent of the statute. They stated that because of the uncertainties involved, Congress had mandated that BDAT alone be used to set treatment standards. EPA determined that the "best response]" to those comments was to adopt a BDAT standard. It emphasized, however, that either course was consistent with the statute (and that it was therefore not required to use BDAT alone). Finally, it asserted, without explanation, that its major purpose in initially proposing screening levels "may be better addressed through changes in other aspects of its regulatory program," and gave an example of one such aspect that might be changed.

This explanation is inadequate. It should go without saying that members of Congress have no power, once a statute has been passed, to alter its interpretation by post-hoc "explanations" of what it means; there maybe societies where "history" belongs to those in power, but ours is not among them. In our scheme of things, we consider legislative history because it is just that: history. It forms the background against which Congress adopted the relevant statute. Post-enactment statements are a different matter, and they are not to be considered by an agency or by a court as legislative history. An agency has an obligation to consider the comments of legislators, of course, but on the same footing as it would those of other commenters; such comments may have, as Justice Frankfurter said in a different context, "power to persuade, if lacking power to control."

It is unclear whether EPA recognized this fundamental point. On the one hand, it suggested that the adoption of a BDAT-only regime "best-respond [ed]" to the comments suggesting that the statute required such a rule. On the other hand, EPA went on at some length to establish that the comments were in error, in that screening levels are permissible under the statute. EPA's "rationale," in other words, is that several members of Congress (among others) urged upon it the claim that Proposition X ("Congress mandated BDAT") requires Result A ("EPA adopts BDAT"), and that although Proposition X is inaccurate, the best response to the commenters is to adopt Result A.

Nor is anything added by EPA's bald assertion that its reason for initially preferring Result B (screening levels) "may be" better served by other changes in the statutory scheme. In its Proposed Rule, EPA had, after extensive analysis of the various alternatives, come to the opposite conclusion. It is insufficient, in that context, for EPA to proceed in a different direction simply on the basis of an unexplained and unelaborated statement that it might have been wrong when it earlier concluded otherwise. . . . Accordingly, we grant the petitions for review in this respect.

COMMENTARY & QUESTIONS

1. Politics and judicial review. In the *HWTC* case, we catch a glimpse of an administrative agency caught in the middle between a Congress and an executive branch with widely different political agendas. An agency must simultaneously attempt to placate both its titular "boss," the Chief Executive, who appoints its leaders and filters its requests for funding, legislative authority, and clearance of proposed regulations, and the legislature that provides its funding and legislative authority, in addition to holding potentially embarrassing oversight hearings. Faced with a Congress enthusiastic about RCRA and an executive branch intent upon turning the statute into symbolic assurance by nonenforcement, EPA, perhaps wisely, decided to procrastinate. The result was congressional frustration and the legislative micromanagement encountered in the HSWA of 1984. EPA's delicate political position was exemplified by its painfully ambiguous and inconsistent explanation of its change in strategy from the Proposed to the Final §3004(m) Rule. The court, although operating under a highly deferential standard of judicial review, forced EPA to take a definite stand on this issue by remanding for the production of a rational and consistent explanation of EPA's position. As in this case, the requirement that an agency produce an adequate record for judicial review raises the visibility of politicized issues and compels an agency to adopt clear, if not universally popular, positions.

2. Legislative micromanagement, pro and con. In this situation, legislative micromanagement appears to have been successful in breaking the political logjam and pushing a reluctant EPA to implement RCRA. But there are possible disadvantages to legislative control of agency regulatory agendas in highly technical areas such as hazardous waste management. In 1986, Congress attempted to goad the Reagan Administration into increasing its sluggish pace of CERCLA cleanups by enacting §116 of CERCLA, 42 U.S.C. §9616, which required EPA to commence specified numbers of remedial investigations/feasibility studies by definite dates, and also to begin remedial actions at the rate of 175 during the first three years after enactment and an additional 200 during the following two years. Given EPA's level of funding and the complexity of the cleanup determinations involved, these

B. The "LandBan" and "Hammers"

timetables proved to have been wildly unrealistic. A similar result occurred when Congress amended the SDWA in 1986 to place EPA on a mandatory timetable for promulgating maximum contaminant goals and maximum contaminant levels for toxic contaminants in drinking water. 42 U.S.C. §300g-1. It appears that legislative micromanagement works best where Congress resorts to a technically crude device such as a hammer clause.

3. Hammer clauses. The generally accepted explanation for the presence of hammer clauses in the HSWA is congressional displeasure with the dilatory performance of EPA in the early years of RCRA. Have the hammer clauses proved effective? The short answer is that the hammer clauses and the threat of a true land ban[30] did force EPA into prompt action to provide an alternative that was less disruptive of on-going economic activity. If the RCRA scenario is to serve as a basis for generalization, it seems that hammer clauses work well as long as the contingent legislative regulation (the hammer) is so stringent that the outcome of administrative process is likely to be more favorable to the regulated community.

4. Is BDAT bad? In opting for treatment standards founded on BDAT, EPA seemed to be locking in existing treatment methods as the future norm, thereby deterring, rather than spurring, advances in the field. A second major criticism of BDAT as the treatment standard is that it trades a land disposal problem for an air pollution problem. This criticism arises because incineration traditionally constituted BDAT for most types of hazardous waste, and even in the best incinerators many hazardous constituents are not fully destroyed. Beyond that, incineration is not a complete treatment insofar as the ash that remains is itself usually a hazardous material in need of subsequent disposal. Still, BDAT is not without some redeeming features, one of which is its clarity. Once a technology is determined to be the BDAT for the treatment of a hazardous substance, generators and TSD facilities alike know what they must do to comply with the law.

5. The "no migration" variance. RCRA authorizes variances to the land ban based on a harm-based review. In order to obtain a variance from BDAT standards, a petitioner must show "to a reasonable degree of certainty, that there will be no migration of hazardous constituents from the disposal unit or injection zone for as long as the wastes remain hazardous." 42 U.S.C. §6924(d)(l). EPA interprets this statutory language to mean that concentrations of hazardous constituents shall not exceed Agency-approved health-based or ecosystem-based levels, in any environmental medium, at the boundary of the unit or injection zone. EPA set strict ambient standards for granting a "no migration" variance, and only a limited number of variances have been granted. The "no migration" variance is an interesting taxonomic device in that it places the burden of overcoming uncertainty on the applicant, who must show that the fundamental technology-based standard is unnecessary. This approach remedies one of the shortcomings of the pure harm-based approach — the heavy regulatory burden placed on a standard-setting agency to establish harm-based standards under conditions of pervasive scientific uncertainty and political rancor.

6. Underground injection. The underground injection of hazardous waste through wells is a form of land disposal that is covered by RCRA and by the Underground Injection Control (UIC) program under Part C of the SDWA, 42 U.S.C. §§300(h) et seq. The UIC regulations (40 C.F.R. pts. 144-148) are primarily concerned with the protection of underground sources of drinking water. The UIC program categorizes hazardous waste injection wells as Class I wells, which receive the highest level of UIC regulation. See 40 C.F.R. §146.61. Although the surface storage and management of hazardous wastes are still subject

---

30. See, e.g., RCRA §3004(g)(6)(C), 42 U.S.C. §6924(g)(6)(C) (total prohibition on land disposal unless EPA promulgates adequate standards).

to RCRA, and although certain closure, corrective action, land disposal, and general RCRA requirements apply to Class I wells, generally the RCRA regulations defer to the UIC regulations for the actual injection process. 40 C.F.R. §264.1(d).

7. Undersupply of TSD capacity. Does the combination of a growing universe of generators and the comprehensive regulation of TSD facilities threaten a supply-and-demand imbalance, in which more hazardous waste needs to be processed than can be handled by permitted facilities? Initially, the problem was finessed by allowing variances to TSD facilities by which they could obtain interim permits even though they were not yet employing BDAT treatment of waste prior to land disposal. Is the variance expedient an effective way to manage the RCRA program? Another factor in the TSD supply equation is, of course, the NIMBY phenomenon. Is there any guarantee that there will be adequate disposal capacity? The answer to that question may lie in CERCLA §104(c)(9)(A), 42 U.S.C. §9604(c)(9)(A), which threatens to withhold Superfund remedial actions in states that do not provide disposal capacity for wastes generated within their borders.

8. The RCRA Subtitle C universe. In a probing review, EPA years ago identified many trends and problems with its RCRA program. See generally EPA, The Nation's Hazardous Waste Management Program at a Crossroads: The RCRA Implementation Study (July 1990). EPA described the impact of the HSWA as follows:

> HWSA Greatly Expanded the Regulated Universe.... To strengthen the nation's shield against hazardous wastes, HWSA established over 70 statutory requirements (often with very tight deadlines) for EPA's action. They can generally be summarized as follows:

- Move away from land disposal as the primary means of hazardous waste management by requiring the treatment of wastes before their final disposal.
- Reduce the environmental and health risks posed by hazardous waste still managed at land disposal facilities by establishing minimum technology requirements.
- Close down facilities that cannot safely manage wastes.
- Decrease and clean up releases to the environment from waste management units by requiring facilities to take corrective action.
- Issue permits for all treatment, storage, and disposal facilities within prescribed time frames.
- Close loopholes in the types of wastes and waste management facilities not covered under RCRA.
- Expand the universe of regulated sources by including generators of small quantities of hazardous wastes.
- Minimize the amount of wastes being produced.

With this comprehensive sweep of hazardous waste issues, HWSA greatly expanded the magnitude of waste types and waste management facilities requiring regulation.

The same part of the report also predicted that the continuing expansion of the list of hazardous wastes due to the operation of the TCLP would lead to a further increase in the size of the Subtitle C universe. In fact, that prediction has come to pass. With more substances considered hazardous, some existing facilities that in the past were not considered to be within RCRA's reach are now within RCRA's scope.

C. RCRA Citizen Suits to Obtain Cleanup

CERCLA, studied in Chapter 16, is the traditional vehicle by which cleanups and cost recoveries are obtained. Historically, however, RCRA came first, having been enacted in 1976,

C. RCRA Citizen Suits

followed by CERCLA in 1980. For a time, then, RCRA was the only federal law available for obtaining cleanups, and it was utilized, especially by the federal government, as the basis for seeking the cleanup of contaminated sites.[31]

With the passage of CERCLA, Congress made plain its intent that CERCLA, not RCRA, was the primary vehicle for not only the federal government but also for private parties to obtain cleanups and cost recoveries. RCRA §7002 (citizen suits) was amended to include provisions that forbade suit if CERCLA processes had been invoked. See 42 U.S.C. §6972(b)(2)(B); see also Chapter 16. However, CERCLA processes cannot always be invoked. This is especially important with respect to releases of petroleum products. Petroleum products are not covered by CERCLA, having been excluded by Congress from CERCLA's definition of "hazardous substances." See 42 U.S.C. §9601(14)(F) (specifically excluding "petroleum" from the "hazardous substance" definition). RCRA does not have the same limitation, which has led to efforts by parties whose land was contaminated by petroleum releases to seek a remedy under RCRA utilizing its citizen suit provision.

For many years, it appeared that the citizen suit remedy provided by RCRA was limited to abatement of the contamination, not reimbursement for cleanup costs incurred by the RCRA plaintiff. In *KFC Western, Inc. v. Meghrig*, 49 F.3d 518 (9th Cir. 1995), a private cost recovery action against former service station operators was successfully maintained by a party who had cleaned up a petroleum release on that parcel. Other circuits, however, held that no such cause of action existed under RCRA. The Ninth Circuit's decision in *Meghrig* was reviewed and reversed by the Supreme Court in the opinion that follows.

Meghrig v. KFC Western, Inc.
516 U.S. 479 (1986)

O'CONNOR, J. We consider whether §7002 of the Resource Conservation and Recovery Act of 1976 (RCRA), 42 U.S.C. §6972, authorizes a private cause of action to recover the prior cost of cleaning up toxic waste that does not, at the time of suit, continue to pose an endangerment to health or environment. We conclude that it does not.

Respondent KFC Western, Inc. (KFC), owns and operates a "Kentucky Fried Chicken" restaurant on a parcel of property in Los Angeles. In 1988, KFC discovered during the course of a construction project that the property was contaminated with petroleum. The County of Los Angeles Department of Health Services ordered KFC to attend to the problem, and KFC spent $211,000 removing and disposing of the oil-tainted soil.

Three years later, KFC brought suit under the citizen suit provision of RCRA . . . seeking to recover these cleanup costs from petitioners Alan and Margaret Meghrig. KFC claimed that the contaminated soil was a "solid waste" covered by RCRA . . . that it had previously posed an "imminent and substantial endangerment to health or the environment," . . . and that the Meghrigs were responsible for "equitable restitution" of KFC's cleanup costs under [the citizen suit provision, 42 U.S.C.] §6972(a) because, as prior owners of the property, they had contributed to the waste's "past or present handling, storage, treatment, transportation, or disposal." . . .

---

31. An early example of the use of RCRA was *U.S. v. Northeastern Pharm. & Chem. Co. (NEPACCO)*, 810 F.2d 726 (8th Cir. 1986) (see Chapter 16), initially filed by the federal government under RCRA §7003 and then amended to include counts under the then newly passed CERCLA legislation.

RCRA is a comprehensive environmental statute that governs the treatment, storage, and disposal of solid and hazardous waste. Unlike the Comprehensive Environmental Response, Compensation and Liability Act of 1980 (CERCLA), RCRA is not principally designed to effectuate the cleanup of toxic waste sites or to compensate those who have attended to the remediation of environmental hazards. RCRA's primary purpose, rather, is to reduce the generation of hazardous waste and to ensure the proper treatment, storage, and disposal of that waste which is nonetheless generated, "so as to minimize the present and future threat to human health and the environment." 42 U.S.C. §6902(b)....

Two requirements . . . defeat KFC's suit against the Meghrigs. The first concerns the necessary timing of a citizen suit brought under §6972(a)(l)(B): That section permits a private party to bring suit against certain responsible persons, including former owners, "who ha[ve] contributed or who [are] contributing to the past or present handling, storage, treatment, transportation, or disposal of any solid or hazardous waste which may present an *imminent* and substantial endangerment to health or the environment." (Emphasis added by the Court.) The second defines the remedies a district court can award in a suit brought under §6972(a)(l)(B): §6972(a) authorizes district courts "to restrain any person who has contributed or who is contributing to the past or present handling, storage, treatment, transportation, or disposal of any solid or hazardous waste, . . . to *order such person to take such other action as may be necessary*, or both." (emphasis added by the Court).

It is apparent from the two remedies described in §6972(a) that RCRA's citizen suit provision is not directed at providing compensation for past cleanup efforts. Under a plain reading of this remedial scheme, a private citizen suing under §6972(a)(1)(B) could seek a mandatory injunction, i.e., one that orders a responsible party to "take action" by attending to the cleanup and proper disposal of toxic waste, or a prohibitory injunction, i.e., one that "restrains" a responsible party from further violating RCRA. Neither remedy, however, is susceptible of the interpretation adopted by the Ninth Circuit, as neither contemplates the award of past cleanup costs, whether these are denominated "damages" or "equitable restitution."

In this regard, a comparison between the relief available under RCRA's citizen suit provision and that which Congress has provided in the analogous, but not parallel, provisions of CERCLA is telling. CERCLA was passed several years after RCRA went into effect, and it is designed to address many of the same toxic waste problems that inspired the passage of RCRA. Compare 42 U.S.C. §6903(5) . . . (RCRA definition of "hazardous waste") and §6903(27) (RCRA definition of "solid waste") with §9601(14) (CERCLA provision incorporating certain "hazardous substance[s]," but not the hazardous and solid wastes defined in RCRA, and specifically not petroleum). CERCLA differs markedly from RCRA, however, in the remedies it provides. CERCLA's citizen suit provision mimics §6972(a) in providing district courts with the authority "to order such action as may be necessary to correct the violation" of any CERCLA standard of regulation. 42 U.S.C. §9659 (1988 ed.). But CERCLA expressly permits the Government to recover "all costs of removal or remedial action," §9607(a)(4)(A), and it expressly permits the recovery of any "necessary costs of response, incurred by any . . . person consistent with the national contingency plan," §9607(a)(4)(B). CERCLA also provides that "[a]ny person may seek contribution from any other person who is liable or potentially liable" for these responses costs. See §9613(f)(1). Congress thus demonstrated in CERCLA that it knew how to provide for the recovery of cleanup costs, and that the language used to define the remedies under RCRA does not provide that remedy.

That RCRA's citizen suit provision was not intended to provide a remedy for past cleanup costs is further apparent from the harm at which it is directed. Section 6972(a)(l)(B)

C. RCRA Citizen Suits

permits a private party to bring suit only upon a showing that the solid or hazardous waste at issue "may present an imminent and substantial endangerment to health or the environment." The meaning of this timing restriction is plain: An endangerment can only be "imminent" if it "threaten[s] to occur immediately," Webster's New International Dictionary of English Language 1245 (2d ed. 1934), and the reference to waste which "may present" imminent harm quite clearly excludes waste that no longer presents such a danger. As the Ninth Circuit itself intimated in *Price v. U.S. Navy*, 39 F.3d 1011, 1019 (1994), this language "implies that there must be a threat which is present now, although the impact of the threat may not be felt until later." It follows that §6972(a) was designed to provide a remedy that ameliorates present or obviates the risk of future "imminent" harms, not a remedy that compensates for past cleanup efforts. Cf. §6902(b) (national policy behind RCRA is "to minimize the present and future threat to human health and the environment").

Other aspects of RCRA's enforcement scheme strongly support this conclusion. Unlike CERCLA, RCRA contains no statute of limitations, compare §9613(g)(2) (limitations period in suits under CERCLA §9607), and it does not require a showing that the response costs being sought are reasonable, compare §9607(a)(4)(A) and (B) (costs recovered under CERCLA must be "consistent with the national contingency plan"). If Congress had intended §6972(a) to function as a cost-recovery mechanism, the absence of these provisions would be striking. Moreover, with one limited exception, . . . (noting exception to notice requirement "when there is a danger that hazardous waste will be discharged"), a private party may not bring suit under §6972 (a)(1)(B) without first giving 90 days' notice to the Administrator of the EPA, to "the State in which the alleged endangerment may occur," and to potential defendants, see §6972(b)(2)(A)(I)-(iii). And no citizen suit can proceed if either the EPA or the State has commenced, and is diligently prosecuting, a separate enforcement action, see §6972(b)(2)(B) and (C). Therefore, if RCRA were designed to compensate private parties for their past cleanup efforts, it would be a wholly irrational mechanism for doing so. Those parties with insubstantial problems, problems that neither the State nor the Federal Government feel compelled to address, could recover their response costs, whereas those parties whose waste problems were sufficiently severe as to attract the attention of Government officials would be left without a recovery. . . .

RCRA does not prevent a private party from recovering its cleanup costs under other federal or state laws, see §6972(f) (preserving remedies under statutory and common law), but the limited remedies described in §6972(a), along with the stark differences between the language of that section and the cost recovery provisions of CERCLA, amply demonstrate that Congress did not intend for a private citizen to be able to undertake a clean up and then proceed to recover its costs under RCRA. . . .

Without considering whether a private party could seek to obtain an injunction requiring another party to pay cleanup costs which arise after a RCRA citizen suit has been properly commenced, . . . or otherwise recover cleanup costs paid out after the invocation of RCRA's statutory process, we agree with the Meghrigs that a private party cannot recover the cost of a past cleanup effort under RCRA, and that KFC's complaint is defective for the reasons stated by the District Court. Section 6972(a) does not contemplate the award of past cleanup costs, and §6972(a)(1)(B) permits a private party to bring suit only upon an allegation that the contaminated site presently poses an "imminent and substantial endangerment to health or the environment," and not upon an allegation that it posed such an endangerment at some time in the past. The judgment of the Ninth Circuit is reversed.

COMMENTARY & QUESTIONS

1. Remaining questions regarding the scope of 42 U.S.C. §6972. Can a private party sue under 42 U.S.C. §6972(a)(1)(B) while an imminent endangerment still exists and obtain an injunction to require the payment of cleanup costs arising after commencement of the citizen suit? *Meghrig* expressly avoids answering that question. Would the Supreme Court be reluctant to provide such a remedy given Congress's failure to do so expressly? How could such a remedy be implied, if, as Justice O'Connor concluded, "Congress thus demonstrated in CERCLA that it knew how to provide for the recovery of cleanup costs, and that the language used to define the remedies under RCRA does not provide that remedy?"

2. The importance of *Meghrig*. In advance of the Supreme Court's decision in *Meghrig*, one commentator wrote, "The implications of the Ninth Circuit ruling in *KFC Western* are significant. Private parties can now obtain more complete relief under §6972(a)(1)(B) than they can obtain under [CERCLA]." Robertson, Restitution Under RCRA §6972(a)(l)(B): The Courts Finally Grant What Congress Authorized, 25 Envtl. L. Rep. 10491 (1995). Does the *Meghrig* decision leave a gap in which no remedies are available to recover costs paid to remediate petroleum spills? Probably not. Up until the Ninth Circuit's *Meghrig* decision, RCRA had been on the books for almost 15 years without great fanfare surrounding the lack of a restitutionary remedy. While CERCLA had lacked jurisdiction over petroleum releases and was far too cumbersome in many ways, state common law and statutory remedies for contamination were still available, although sometimes open to criticism. See Lopez, Cost Recovery for Petroleum Contamination: Will *RCRA* Citizen Plaintiffs Be Cookin' with KFC or Relegated to a State Law Jungle?, 10 Toxics L. Rep. 946 (1996).

3. Strategic considerations after *Meghrig*. After the Supreme Court's decision in *Meghrig*, does a party faced with petroleum contamination on its property have an incentive to sue those responsible for the contamination before undertaking the cleanup? If a party defers cleanup and instead seeks relief from those contributing to an imminent and substantial endangerment, that party may still seek an injunction to require those responsible to participate in the cleanup. May that party also seek restitution of its prospective cleanup costs? Is the *Meghrig* decision one that provides a strategic incentive to sue first and clean up later, in hopes of recouping cleanup costs? Could such an incentive—to defer cleanups rather than to expedite them—be one that Congress had intended? Attempting to answer these questions, the Seventh Circuit has responded with a resounding "no," holding that a property owner may not recover its cleanup costs under 42 U.S.C. §6972 from the party responsible for the contamination, a decision that the Supreme Court declined to review. See *Avondale Fed. Sav. Bank v. Amoco Oil Co.*, 170 F.3d 692 (7th Cir. 1999), cert. denied, 528 U.S. 922 (1999).[32] Most lower court decisions have similarly concluded that private parties cannot obtain an injunction to obtain, or assert claims under 42 U.S.C. §6972(a)(1)(8) for, the payment of future cleanup costs.[33]

---

32. See also *Albany Bank & Trust Co. v. Exxon Mobil Corp.*, 310 F.3d 969 (7th Cir. 2002) (holding that investigatory costs are no more recoverable than cleanup costs would be); *Abreu v. U.S.*, 468 F.3d 20, 31 (1st Cir. 2006); *South Carolina Dept. of Health & Envtl. Control v. Commerce & Indus. Ins. Co.*, 372 F.3d 245, 256 (4th Cir. 2004).

33. See, e.g., *U.S. v. Domestic Indus., Inc.*, 32 F. Supp. 2d 855, 871 (E.D. Va. 1999); *Davenport v. Neely*, 7 F. Supp. 2d 1219, 1229 (M.D. Ala. 1998); *Express Car Wash Corp. v. Irinaga Bros., Inc.*, 967 F. Supp. 1188, 1194 (D. Or. 1997); *Audritz Sprout-Bauer v. Beazer East, Inc.* 174 F.R.D. 609 (M.D. Pa. 1997); *Cross Oil Co. v. Phillips Petroleum Co.*, 944 F. Supp. 787, 789 (E.D. Mo. 1996). But see *Briggs & Stanton Corp. v. Concrete Sales & Servs.*, 20 F. Supp. 2d 1356 (M.D. Ga. 1998) (court allowed a potentially responsible party to pursue RCRA citizen suit claim against former owners of the site, along with its CERCLA cost recovery and other state law claims, where the presence of contaminated soil and groundwater represented a continuing violation of RCRA).

4. The dischargeability in bankruptcy of RCRA cleanup injunctions. A critical issue at the intersection of environmental law and bankruptcy law is whether the government's right to an injunction ordering a party to engage in an environmental cleanup constitutes a "claim" that can be discharged in bankruptcy. The resolution of this question largely turns on whether the statutory basis for suit allows the government to sue solely for injunctive relief or, alternatively, allows the government to seek cost recovery, damages, or some other "right to payment" dischargeable under the Bankruptcy Code. If a right to payment is available, then there is a strong possibility that a bankruptcy court will discharge the environmental claims involved.

The issue of dischargeability was raised directly in *United States v. Apex Oil*, 579 F.3d 734 (7th Cir. 2009). In that case, the United States brought suit under RCRA §7003, seeking injunctive relief to require Apex Oil, among other things, to abate a petroleum plume at an oil refinery previously owned by Apex Oil's predecessor. After Apex Oil interposed its prior bankruptcy discharge as a defense and argued that its environmental liabilities under RCRA were discharged in bankruptcy, the Seventh Circuit held that the government's claims to injunctive relief under RCRA §7003 were not discharged by Apex Oil's prior bankruptcy. Recognizing that the relief available under RCRA §7003 is equitable only, the Seventh Circuit determined that a reorganized debtor's obligation under RCRA to pay for an environmental cleanup of property that it no longer owned is not dischargeable.

In reaching this result, the Seventh Circuit focused on the statutory basis for the government's claims. Because the government brought suit under RCRA § 7003(a) (42 U.S.C. §6973(a)), the Seventh Circuit analyzed whether the government's right to an injunction under RCRA §7003(a) was a dischargeable "claim" under the Bankruptcy Code. In its analysis, the Seventh Circuit placed heavy emphasis on the fact that RCRA §7003 claims have a unique feature: they do not authorize any form of monetary relief and seek purely injunctive relief. Finding that the right to a RCRA injunction "was not a right to an equitable remedy . . . the breach of which gave rise to a right to payment" under §101(5) of the Bankruptcy Code, the Seventh Circuit concluded that RCRA does not provide for a monetary recovery. Consequently, the Seventh Circuit reasoned that there was no "right to payment" under RCRA, even though the cleanup would ultimately cost the debtor money to hire a contractor to perform the work required under the injunction.

The statutory basis for the government's claims was central to the Seventh Circuit's analysis. In light of the petroleum contamination involved, the government brought its claims against Apex Oil under RCRA rather than CERCLA, thereby avoiding the petroleum exclusion under CERCLA §101(14)(F). Furthermore, the government sued solely under RCRA, recognizing that, in contrast to CERCLA, RCRA provides solely for injunctive relief and does not concern the recovery of cleanup costs or damages. By contrast, in a CERCLA action, a debtor seeking a discharge of environmental claims can argue that because CERCLA creates an alternative right to monetary relief (e.g., cost recovery), CERCLA claims can give rise to a right to payment and are therefore dischargeable under the Bankruptcy Code. See 42 U.S.C. §§9606(a) and 9607(a), and U.S.C. §1105; see also Chapter 16, Sections A and D. But in *Apex Oil*, the government's suit relied solely on RCRA §7003(a) and sought injunctive relief alone.

V
OVERARCHING LEGAL PERSPECTIVES

Only a crisis—actual or perceived—produces real change. When that crisis occurs, the actions that are taken depend on the ideas that are lying around. That, I believe, is our basic function: to develop alternatives to existing policies, to keep them alive and available until the politically impossible becomes politically inevitable.

—Milton Friedman

18

Evolving Patterns of Enforcement and Compliance

A. The Continuing Debate over Environmental Enforcement Strategies
B. The Governmental Enforcement Process
C. Citizen Enforcement to Complement Governmental Efforts
D. Alternative Dispute Resolution Processes
E. The Impetus to Self-Generated Corporate Compliance

A. The Continuing Debate over Environmental Enforcement Strategies

The effectiveness of environmental enforcement in the United States has long been the subject of serious debate. After the passage in the early 1970s of the Clean Air Act (CAA) and Clean Water Act (CWA), EPA's enforcement strategies initially focused on educating the regulated community, providing technical support, and encouraging compliance. EPA's programs were new, and most of EPA's early initiatives involved assisting the regulated community in developing the training, the expertise, and the tools necessary to achieve compliance with EPA's newly promulgated regulatory schemes. Although Congress armed the EPA with the ability to seek significant sanctions, most penalties sought by the EPA in its early years were modest (in the five-figure range), and the EPA's focus was on negotiated settlements with the regulated community.

This paradigm began to shift by the mid-1970s. By that time, criticism of EPA's effectiveness in enforcement was growing, both in Congress and from an increasingly assertive array of environmental citizen groups. At the same time, EPA was becoming increasingly concerned that, absent meaningful accountability for noncompliance, the regulated community would not, on its own, modify its behavior or practices to comply with the growing body of environmental regulations and requirements. Acting on that concern, EPA concluded that there was a need for more demonstrable environmental progress, and, accordingly, EPA adopted a revised enforcement ideology based on the premise that deterrence must be at the heart of an effective regulatory program.

By the late 1970s, as the emphasis on deterrence continued to grow, EPA embraced civil and criminal command-and-control requirements, which were designed to maintain accountability for noncompliance by systematically identifying, prosecuting, and penalizing violators. As environmental enforcement continued through the 1980s, EPA honed its deterrence approach. Armed with tough laws and operating under the watchful eyes of Congress and citizen groups, EPA developed programs involving rigorous inspections of the regulated community coupled with mandatory self-reporting required of violators. Rather than seek out partnerships with the regulated community, EPA's strategy was to maintain an arm's-length approach, which emphasized sanctioning violators and deterring other parties from committing violations. EPA assumed that the greater its resources, the higher would be the likelihood that violations would be deterred and that compliance would be achieved. Accordingly, EPA sought, and obtained, more lawyers, investigators, and enforcement personnel. The U.S. Department of Justice (DOJ) was also enlisted to initiate and enforce the growing body of environmental laws.

By the early 1990s, the federal environmental statutes alone exceeded 1300 pages, and the regulations promulgated to implement those statutes were already over 12,000 pages in length. As hundreds of thousands of regulated entities attempted to deal with an increasingly complicated set of federal, state, and local environmental requirements, the nation spent over $700 billion on environmental cleanup efforts. At the same time, approximately 2% of the gross national product was now devoted to pollution control and regulation. The magnitude of these expenditures reflected a major shift in U.S. business priorities. Environmental issues had become central to virtually every significant business decision or transaction. No sale of a business, transfer of real estate, or use of hazardous chemicals could proceed prudently without consideration of the environmental risks, costs, or effects.

What triggered this realignment of U.S. business priorities? Under the traditional enforcement yardsticks employed by EPA—measured in the "bean counting" terms of cases brought and total dollar penalties imposed—EPA contended that its deterrence strategy had caused this shift. EPA touted its enforcement record to Congress and the public as the measure of its success. During fiscal year 1994, for example, EPA reported the initiation of 2249 federal enforcement actions; a total of 430 civil and 200 criminal cases referred to the DOJ for prosecution; criminal charges brought against 250 individuals and corporations; and over $165 million in administrative, civil, and criminal fines.[1]

Despite regularly setting records for the number of new enforcement actions filed, penalties imposed, and sanctions levied, EPA's enforcement efforts continued to be questioned. By the mid-1990s, there emerged a growing recognition at EPA, and elsewhere, that EPA's singular focus on deterrence had major limitations. In particular, critics argued that EPA's deterrence approach focused on punishing violations after they occurred, rather than encouraging systems to prevent violations; relied on governmental enforcement actions rather than enhancing or rewarding private sector compliance; necessarily depended on the limitations of politically influenced enforcement budgets and priorities; and perversely preferred actions yielding high penalties over actions yielding greater impact on environmental quality, thereby confusing means with ends.[2]

Even more significantly, EPA was stung by the criticism that, although its actions in the 1970s and 1980s may have contributed to the shift in U.S. business priorities, by the 1990s EPA's enforcement strategies were actually a drag on environmental progress in the corporate community. By then, many U.S. corporations were reducing emissions and achieving compliance arguably on their own initiative. Critics pointed out that, at a time when corporate environmental focus had progressed to implementing management systems,

---

1. See New Records for Actions, Fines Set by EPA Despite Restructuring Program, 25 BNA Env't Rep. 1501 (Dec. 2, 1994).
2. See Diamond, Confessions of an Environmental Enforcer, 26 Envtl. L. Rep. 10,252 (1996); Garrett, Reinventing EPA Enforcement, 12 Nat. Res. & Env't. 180 (Winter 1998).

A. Environmental Enforcement Strategies

sustainable development, reuse/recycling, pollution prevention, industry responsible care programs, and international environmental standards, EPA's deterrence approach was still focused on bringing an increasing number of lawsuits in order to collect higher fines. The debate centered on whether EPA was so preoccupied with justifying its budget and proving its enforcement record to Congress that it failed in its central mission to improve environmental quality.

By the mid-1990s, EPA began to reassess its enforcement paradigm and to evaluate whether its approach should be modified once again. To that end, EPA began to consider new initiatives emphasizing compliance assurance and noncompliance prevention. These initiatives were designed to prevent pollution as well as to punish violations after they occurred, to harness market forces proactively (rather than relying solely on command and control), and to seek more partnerships with U.S. business that advance designated environmental priorities. EPA also began a period of greater cooperation with the states. This changing emphasis was most apparent in EPA's increasing efforts to work with the states and the regulated community to redevelop brownfields.

By the year 2000, the Bush II Administration promised a new era of environmental enforcement protection, claiming that it would seek to tie environmental issues to economic growth, to protection from undue regulation, and to increased energy production.[3] But critics responded that environmental enforcement was in retreat, as exemplified by the Administration's rejection of a treaty on global warming, questioning of rules concerning forest protection, and apparent lack of enthusiasm for strict environmental enforcement.[4] The election of the Obama Administration in 2008 and again in 2012 promised a reawakening of environmental enforcement initiatives and a renewed emphasis on regulating climate change, including international cooperation to redress the continued growth of carbon dioxide emissions.[5] But, again, critics have questioned whether that Administration's promises have translated into effective action. Meanwhile, on the state level, and in light of seeming Congressional inaction on a variety of issues, including climate change, a number of states have taken the initiative, both individually and regionally, to step up their own environmental enforcement, to encourage energy efficiency and the development of alternative energy sources (such as wind power and solar power), and to regulate more aggressively facilities which emit carbon dioxide and thereby contribute to climate change.

---

3. "Our approach is to maximize the quality of life in America," said James L. Connaughton, Chairman of the Council on Environmental Quality, "and that means balancing the environmental equation with the natural resource equation, the social equation, and the economic equation." Jehl, On Environmental Rules, Bush Sees a Balance, Critics a Threat, N.Y. Times, Feb. 23, 2003, at 1.

4. "Across the board," said Senator James M. Jeffords, the Vermont independent who served for a period as the chairman of the Senate Committee on Environmental and Public Works, "we would be better off doing nothing than doing what the administration wants to do, which will make things worse than they already are." Id. at 1, 22.

5. The Obama Administration's $10.5 billion budget for EPA for fiscal year 2010 was the largest in EPA's history. Of that total, $600 million was proposed for enforcement, also the largest in EPA's history. The Obama Administration also planned to keep all of the enforcement priorities of the Bush EPA ((i) air toxics; (ii) new source review; (iii) prevention of significant deterioration; (iv) concentrated annual feeding operations; (v) municipal combined sewer and sanitary sewer overflows; (vi) storm water; (vii) mineral processing; (viii) financial responsibility; and (ix) Indian country), while adding eight new ones ((i) environmental justice; (ii) pesticides at day care facilities; (iii) worker protection standards; (iv) resource extraction; (v) RCRA enforcement; (vi) surface impoundments; (vii) marine debris; and (viii) wetlands).

> **The Ongoing Environmental Enforcement Debate**
>
> The continuing debate over enforcement strategies, as exemplified by shifting patterns of enforcement, raises important issues pertaining to environmental enforcement, environmental compliance, and their interrelationship:
>
> - How does the existing governmental enforcement process work? What are the key steps in the enforcement process, and what enforcement tools are available and effective?
> - What is the significance of citizen involvement in environmental enforcement? Do citizen suits prod government to act or provide a credible enforcement alternative when government fails to act?
> - If environmental compliance is now a major priority of most companies, what factors caused this shift in business goals? Are there major business events that trigger the need for environmental compliance? What compliance tools are available to U.S. business, and how effective are they? Is U.S. business engaged today in self-generated compliance independent of environmental enforcement, or does business now seek compliance primarily due to the credible threat of continuing environmental enforcement?
> - What is the future of enforcement and compliance? What patterns of enforcement and compliance exist, and what changes are likely to occur?

This chapter explores the scope and effectiveness of environmental enforcement. Since the early, formative days of the 1970s, when EPA and the states first began enforcing the environmental laws, layers of new environmental requirements have complicated the regulatory structure. Amidst these changes, however, one key constant remains: For environmental regulation to achieve its goals, it must induce compliance. Thus the interplay between environmental enforcement and compliance remains the key inquiry.

B. THE GOVERNMENTAL ENFORCEMENT PROCESS

Governmental enforcement of the environmental laws cuts across all of the environmental statutes. Although the particular means of enforcement varies from statute to statute, or may be modified as a statute is amended or reauthorized,[6] the governmental enforcement process typically moves violators along toward an inevitable day of reckoning.

> **Three Phases of EPA Enforcement:**
>
> 1. inspection and information gathering;
> 2. administrative case development; and
> 3. formal litigation.

---

6. On a variety of occasions, Congress has revised federal statutory enforcement mechanisms. For example, when amending the CAA in 1990, Congress sought to improve the reporting of violations and compliance monitoring. In §113(f) of the CAA (42 U.S.C. §7413(f)), Congress added a bounty provision authorizing EPA to pay up to $10,000 as a reward to anyone providing information leading to a civil penalty or criminal conviction under the Act. 42 U.S.C. §7413(f). To improve monitoring, Congress amended the Act to add the requirement that major sources of air pollution conduct "enhanced monitoring" of their emissions and their pollution control equipment (see CAA §114(a)(3), 42 U.S.C. §7414(a)(3)), a phrase interpreted by EPA to require facilities to develop monitoring protocols that would be incorporated into their Title V permits.

B. The Governmental Enforcement Process

1. Phases in the Enforcement Process

<u>Joel A. Mintz, Enforcement at the EPA: High Stakes and Hard Choices</u>
11-16 (1995)

At EPA, enforcement cases typically go through three phases; inspection and information gathering, administrative case development, and (if the matter has not yet been resolved) formal litigation. In noncriminal cases, the agency has several primary sources of compliance information: self-monitoring, record keeping and reporting by individual sources of pollution, inspections by government personnel, and the specific complaints of concerned citizens.

Most EPA inspections are announced to the pollution source ahead of time to ensure the presence of vital plant personnel. Inspections may be either "for cause," that is, based on a reasonable suspicion that the inspected source is in violation, or else routinely conducted pursuant to a "neutral inspection scheme." Perhaps surprisingly, of the approximately 1,600 individuals who perform EPA inspections, more than 75 percent do so less than 20 percent of the time.

When the agency conducts an investigation on the basis of citizen information, that information may have come from a variety of individuals. Citizen informants often include, for example, disgruntled employees of suspected violators, neighbors, state or local inspectors, environmental citizens organizations, and suspected violators' economic competitors. In potential criminal matters, these sources of information may be replaced—or supplemented—by targeted inspections, conducted under color of search warrant, by EPA criminal investigators and/or special agents of the Federal Bureau of Investigation (FBI), as well as by grand jury proceedings under the auspices of the DOJ.

Once EPA (and/or DOJ) investigators have completed their information gathering, they must determine whether the source in question is in violation of applicable standards and, if so, what type of enforcement response the agency will make. Under most of the relevant federal environmental statutes, EPA has a range of options available to it. It may begin enforcement by issuing a notice of violation to the allegedly violating source, describing the violation and inviting the source to confer informally with agency enforcement personnel. Alternatively, EPA may issue the source an administrative order requiring compliance with applicable requirements and, in some cases, an assessed civil penalty. In addition, EPA is generally authorized to refer enforcement matters to the DOJ for civil action or criminal prosecution. If it deems the circumstances appropriate, the agency may defer to a planned or ongoing enforcement action by state or local environmental officials.

EPA decisions as to which of these various enforcement options to pursue are generally made at the regional level by technically trained personnel working in cooperation with enforcement attorneys. These determinations frequently take account of a number of factors. Regional officials typically consider, among other things, the degree to which the source's discharge or emission exceeds applicable legal requirements, the duration of the violation, the number of previous enforcement actions that have been taken successfully against the same source, any relevant national EPA enforcement policies, the potential deterrence value of the case, the resources available to the agency and DOJ at the time of the decision, EPA's working relationship with interested state and local officials, and the agency's estimation of the enforcement capability of those same officials. These calculations, which are usually made with little public knowledge or participation, have great administrative significance. . . .

At EPA, as at many regulatory agencies and departments, enforcement work involves considerable bargaining. In most instances, bargaining serves the interests and goals of both the agency itself and the regulated enterprises that are subject to enforcement action. From EPA's point of view, the time and energy of its enforcement staff is limited. To accomplish its objectives, it is usually to the agency's advantage to resolve acceptably as many enforcement matters as possible, without resorting to expensive and resource-intensive litigation. Another consideration for agency officials is the bureaucratic wish to retain control over decisions within one's area of responsibility. When compromise is not possible and EPA refers a matter to the DOJ for litigation, some of that control is inevitably relinquished to judges and DOJ attorneys and managers.

Although a number of EPA enforcement cases implicate minor, routine violations that are amenable to prompt resolution, in other matters the enforcement process is laborious and time consuming. For all concerned, these more complex cases involve high stakes and hard choices.

For regulated enterprises, the risks of enforcement sanctions—including the possibility of monetary penalties, mandatory pollution control measures that may be expensive to install and maintain, and even, in some criminal cases, jail time for responsible corporate officials—are very great. . . .

Beyond avoiding or minimizing sanctions, regulated industries have an interest in dispelling uncertainties about their future environmental responsibilities and the costs those responsibilities will entail. In many cases, they are also concerned with preserving (or repairing) their public image as responsible corporate citizens and in reassuring lenders, shareholders, and potential investors of their good faith and freedom from impending open-ended liability. At the same time, regulated enterprises must take care that any settlement they enter into with EPA enforcement officials not harm their firm's competitive standing within its industry. Monies expended on pollution control measures and environmental penalties will not be available for investment in productive manufacturing equipment that can increase corporate profits. As they negotiate with regulators, representatives of industrial firms are thus often mindful of individuals within their companies who focus mostly on the bottom line and see little need for or benefit from corporate environmental expenditure.

For EPA's representatives there are difficult choices as well in enforcement negotiations. Any attempt at standardized decision-making by EPA is confounded by the enormous variety of conditions and circumstances that individual cases involve. The agency's enforcement engineers and attorneys frequently face sensitive decisions with respect to the pollution control measures they will accept, the penalties they will assess, the amount of time they will allow a violator to come into compliance, the legal prerogatives and safeguards they will insist upon, and the appropriateness of avoiding, or terminating, negotiations and referring a matter to the Justice Department for civil or criminal action. These judgments are complex and demanding. . . .

2. The Flow of the Enforcement Process

Successful enforcement typically occurs in a setting that balances the formality of the enforcement bureaucracy with the informality that necessarily affects and informs the prosecutorial discretion of environmental authorities. Although a certain degree of flexibility is inherent in the governmental enforcement process, for the most part the steps in the process follow a prescribed sequence.

As the flow chart in Figure 1 shows, the three phases of enforcement at EPA—(1) inspection and information gathering, (2) administrative case development, and (3) formal

B. The Governmental Enforcement Process

litigation—can be illustrated as a series of sequential steps moving violators along a path that, if uninterrupted, will inevitably result in civil or criminal adjudication.

Inspection and information gathering usually begins the enforcement process. As Figure 1 illustrates, the goal of this first phase is for EPA, as the prime enforcer of the federal environmental statutes, to make a decision concerning whether to proceed with enforcement. Typically, EPA's enforcement decision will be informed by the quality and quantity of information gathered by EPA investigators and technical personnel (or by information supplied by third parties) through site observations, sampling, lab analysis, and other investigative techniques. EPA's ability to gather the information essential to sound enforcement judgments, in part, relies on the mandatory self-monitoring, record keeping, and reporting requirements of various environmental statutes that enable EPA to obtain information on regulatory targets.

As part of its enforcement decision, EPA must consider whether EPA or the applicable state should take the enforcement lead. Under many federal environmental statutes, EPA may delegate implementation and enforcement authority to those states that demonstrate the capability to enforce adequate environmental programs. Generally, delegation under applicable statutes is only allowable when a state has developed a program that is substantially equivalent to, or no less stringent than, the federal program developed by EPA. Where a federal statute does not allow delegation to a state, EPA may alternatively enter into "cooperative agreements" allowing state involvement. EPA also claims the authority to initiate enforcement actions concurrent with that of a state taking the enforcement lead (an enforcement technique known as "overfiling").[7] Even when a state has already taken the enforcement lead, EPA claims the authority to take its own enforcement action if EPA concludes that the state action is not timely or sufficient.

Phase two of the enforcement process, administrative case development, proceeds from the decision to enforce. If the state takes the enforcement lead, then the state may invoke its own administrative process, as Figure 1 illustrates. Alternatively, if EPA takes the lead, then EPA typically will initiate an administrative process commencing with the issuance of a warning letter or notice of violation (NOV). This administrative process can result in administrative orders and penalties, negotiated penalties with noncomplying entities or individuals, and compliance agreements with continuing EPA oversight and supervision. If EPA assesses administrative civil penalties that are contested, then an alleged violator can seek relief from an administrative law judge (ALJ), whose decisions are subject to judicial review based on the administrative record. Although ALJs are EPA employees, they are full-time judges. Proceedings before an ALJ involve trial-type procedures, although typically they are less formal than civil trial proceedings in federal court. To hear appeals of administrative enforcement decisions, EPA has created a permanent Environmental Appeals Board.

---

7. Overfiling has been called into question by conflicting decisions of the federal courts of appeal. See *Harmon Indus., Inc. v. Browner*, 191 F.3d 894 (8th Cir. 1999) (holding that RCRA precludes the EPA from overfiling for a violation of a state's hazardous waste laws against a facility, when an authorized state has already instituted an enforcement action for the same violations); and *United States v. Power Eng'g Co.*, 303 F.3d 1232 (10th Cir. 2002) (holding that EPA may overfile under RCRA, even after a state has agreed to settle its enforcement action against the regulated entity).

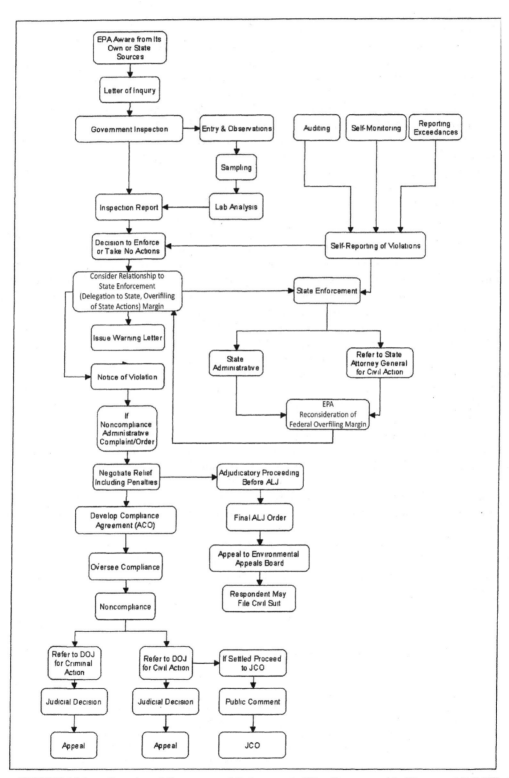

FIGURE 18-1. *Overview of Governmental Enforcement of Non-Emergency Air, Water, and Solid Waste Violations.*

B. The Governmental Enforcement Process

If the EPA, or a state taking the enforcement lead, cannot or will not resolve a matter administratively, or if an action ordered by EPA in an administrative proceeding is not obeyed, then the third phase of enforcement, formal litigation, can result. On the federal level, as Figure 18-1 shows, EPA can refer cases to the DOJ and assist DOJ with civil and criminal environmental investigations and proceedings. On the state level, a state can refer cases to its attorney general or other enforcement arm for civil or criminal litigation if a matter cannot be resolved administratively. Because litigation is expensive and time-consuming, federal and state enforcement authorities typically reserve this third phase of enforcement for only the most significant violations.

3. Enforcement Tools

Administrative Orders. EPA has increasingly used administrative orders to achieve its enforcement agenda. Administrative orders typically require fewer resources than litigation, can be issued unilaterally, do not require the consent of the alleged violator, and allow EPA to control the direction and outcome of enforcement without DOJ involvement.

Administrative orders have a variety of purposes. They may be issued to gather information, to require compliance, to require remedial action, to suspend or revoke permits, or to assess penalties. Administrative orders also have significant force. Normally, such orders are not subject to pre-enforcement review and accordingly place considerable pressure on alleged violators to comply or suffer significant consequences. Only when EPA attempts to enforce administrative orders are they subject to judicial review.

> **EPA's Four Primary Enforcement Tools**
>
> As a case moves along in the enforcement process, EPA utilizes an arsenal of enforcement tools to implement its goals, prerogatives, and strategies. Four sets of tools are most prominent:
>
> 1. administrative orders;
> 2. civil actions for injunctions, penalties, and other relief;
> 3. criminal prosecutions; and
> 4. suspension, debarment, and listing.

By their terms, administrative orders can be elaborate and detailed.[8] Violations of administrative orders may result in assessments of civil penalties, typically up to $37,500 for each day of noncompliance for each violation. In determining the amount of the penalty to be assessed, EPA is guided by civil penalty policies. Under its primary policy on civil penalties, EPA calculates the size of the penalty for which it will settle by first considering the gravity of the violation and the economic benefit derived from the violation. Under the gravity component, EPA reviews the seriousness of the violation and the extent to which the violation varies from specified requirements. Under the economic benefit component, EPA determines the gains derived from failure to comply. In calculating the benefits received by the violator from noncompliance, EPA has utilized computer models and encouraged state

---

8. A typical CERCLA §106 order issued under CERCLA (specifically under 42 U.S.C. §9606), for example, may be lengthy and exacting in ordering remedial action activities at a facility to abate an alleged imminent and substantial endangerment presented by the release or threatened release of hazardous substances. Such an order may contain multiple parts and pages, including: (1) identification of the parties bound; (2) detailed findings of fact and determinations by EPA pertaining to the conditions at the facility, the responsible parties, and the actions or factors resulting in liability; (3) ordering provisions specifying the work to be performed, requiring EPA approval of engineers and contractors, and further requiring EPA approval of the remedial plan and design; (4) requirements allowing further EPA periodic review; (5) quality assurance provisions imposed by EPA requiring that remedial action be performed to specified standards; (6) provisions allowing EPA future facility access, sampling, and document availability; (7) requirements for periodic progress reports to be made to EPA; and (8) notice outlining penalties for noncompliance.

and local agencies to use such models as well, especially in cases where EPA has delegated federal enforcement responsibilities. After calculating the base penalty, EPA may make adjustments in light of willfulness, cooperation, history of noncompliance, and mitigating factors demonstrated by the violator including the violator's ability to pay.

Another EPA civil penalty policy is its Supplemental Environmental Project (SEP) Policy, pursuant to which EPA may mitigate a portion of the penalty as a quid pro quo for the violator's undertaking an environmental improvement not otherwise required. SEPs typically are part of a negotiated settlement, utilized as partial offsets to penalties. A SEP precludes the competitive advantage of noncompliance by causing the violator to expend funds on environmental improvements. In negotiating SEPs, EPA will consider whether a penalty should be mitigated by benefits to the environment or the public from a supplemental project, innovation caused by the project, risk reduction to minority or low-income communities, multimedia impacts, and pollution prevention. By encouraging supplemental environmental projects, EPA seeks to produce more environmentally beneficial enforcement settlements. However, qualifying SEPs must maintain a nexus between the original violation and the supplemental project and are not intended to reward the violator for undertaking activities in its economic self-interest.

An additional enforcement mechanism closely related to SEPs are Environmentally Beneficial Expenditures (EBEs). Enforcement actions frequently result in pretrial consent decrees, which can include polluter-financed EBEs such as donations to purchase critical lands in watersheds where violations have taken place or donations to universities to perform studies.

Civil Actions for Injunctions, Penalties, and Other Relief. In addition to issuing administrative orders to achieve its enforcement goals, EPA, alternatively, can seek a judicial order by requesting DOJ to initiate a civil action in federal court. Because this alternative requires coordination with DOJ, involves the commitment of resources in litigation, and does not allow EPA directly to control the outcome of enforcement, judicial enforcement is used less frequently than administrative enforcement.

If EPA issues an administrative order that is not obeyed, EPA must proceed in federal court to secure compliance. Of course, when EPA attempts to enforce administrative orders, such orders are then subject to judicial review, and the statutory provisions prohibiting pre-enforcement review are inapposite.

Once suit is filed in federal court, it may be resolved by settlement in lieu of trial. Normally, DOJ files actions only when DOJ believes, and when the likelihood is, that DOJ will prevail. Consequently, few enforcement cases are tried because most defendants find it advantageous to settle such cases. Settlement often reflects the reality that violations may be straightforward or readily proved, using the violator's own discharge monitoring or other reports. Settlements typically are embodied in consent decrees, in which the parties agree on a penalty amount and a compliance schedule. DOJ policy requires that all proposed consent decrees be available for public comment prior to entry. In reviewing consent decrees or otherwise deciding whether to impose penalties, courts are not bound by EPA's penalty policies, although such policies may provide useful guidance and receive substantial deference in court. If a consent decree is approved, the court will typically enter it as an enforceable court order.

Criminal Prosecutions. Environmental criminal prosecution has increased over the years. The federal environmental statutes provide for criminal liability for violators and, in certain cases, do not include a specific requirement of knowledge or other evidence of criminal intent (see Chapter 19). When determining whether to proceed criminally against an individual or corporation, EPA considers the degree of actual or threatened harm as well as the type and nature of the culpable conduct. On the basis of this review, EPA decides whether to make a referral to DOJ for criminal prosecution. In deciding whether to

B. The Governmental Enforcement Process

proceed criminally, DOJ considers, among other factors, voluntary compliance and voluntary disclosure of noncompliance to prosecuting authorities.

Fines as well as incarceration for individuals are available to sanction criminal violators. Statutory provisions as well as U.S. Sentencing Commission Guidelines provide guidance as to the range of punishment generally available for criminal environmental violations. Although criminal sanctions do not include injunctive orders for compliance or to remedy environmental harm, such requirements may be imposed in connection with fashioning an appropriate penalty under the Sentencing Guidelines. To remedy environmental problems and punish violators, the government can also seek to pursue "parallel" civil and criminal proceedings at the same time, as long as doing so is consistent with due process and other constitutional and statutory protections.

Suspension, Debarment, and Listing. With the increase in civil and criminal enforcement, EPA is now making more use of its contractor listing programs under CWA §508 and CAA §306. Under these programs, EPA may suspend (an interim period of probation), debar (a prohibition from contracting for a denned period), or list facilities that are guilty of criminal violations. Being named on the list disqualifies the facility from receiving federal grants or contracts. Such action can be crippling to a violator heavily dependent on such contracts.

COMMENTARY & QUESTIONS

1. Counting enforcement "beans." EPA has traditionally measured its enforcement success by bean counting—toting up the number of enforcement cases initiated and resolved each fiscal year. Using bean counting to measure success has serious implications for enforcement. Merely counting beans gives as much credit for enforcement based on mandatory self-reporting as for enforcement based on extensive investigation. Counting beans focuses on quantity, not quality, giving as much credit for initiating a case with little hope of improving environmental quality as one that seeks to redress serious environmental harm. Counting beans also favors actions yielding high penalties over actions yielding greater impact on environmental quality.

> Budgetary constraints encourage EPA to put resources into activities that have a measurable payoff. Since current measures of enforcement success place almost exclusive reliance on initiation (and, to a lesser extent, the resolution) of enforcement cases, funding tends to go to activities that will result in production of the much-craved, commodity—the enforcement "bean." [Perversely, compliance] can become a hindrance to the bean harvest, rather than a welcome sign of progress. This doesn't mean that EPA officials encourage violations, but bean counting does tend to isolate enforcement personnel from larger issues of environmental progress. Diamond, Confessions of an Environmental Enforcer, 26 Envtl. L. Rep. 10,252 (1996).

Is there any way to measure enforcement progress other than by utilizing the enforcement bean? Because for so many years EPA has reported its enforcement activity as an accomplishment, Congress has grown accustomed to measuring EPA's success by relying on the number of enforcement cases filed. Declining numbers are interpreted as evidence of a less vigilant EPA.

A related and equally important question is whether bean counting is a real measure of success. By relying for so long on the enforcement bean, EPA "has no comparative basis for evaluating whether this is the best approach to improving environmental protection. Indeed, the Agency cannot say with any level of precision what impact its enforcement cases have had, either on compliance with environmental requirements or on the environment itself. EPA has simply filed its cases, counted up its penalties, and assumed it was making progress." Id.

2. The increasing use of SEPs. EPA has long encouraged the use of Supplemental Environmental Projects (SEPs). Under EPA's SEP Policy, seven specific categories of projects may qualify: (1) public health projects; (2) pollution prevention projects; (3) pollution redirection projects; (4) environmental restoration and protection projects; (5) assessment and audit projects; (6) environmental compliance promotion projects; and (7) emergency planning and preparedness projects. By negotiating SEP with EPA, a violator may obtain a significant reduction in a proposed penalty by committing voluntarily to perform an environmentally beneficial project. The SEP Policy, however, requires that the final penalty must still equal or exceed either: (a) the economic benefit of noncompliance plus 10% of the gravity component, or (b) 25% of the gravity component only, whichever is greater.

How effective are SEPs? By utilizing SEPs, EPA furthers its goals of securing significant environmental or public health improvements while promoting pollution prevention and, where appropriate, environmental justice. From the violator's perspective, SEPs may also present an attractive option. Rather than simply paying a civil fine or penalty to the federal treasury, a violator instead can dedicate penalty dollars to local public health or environmental concerns or to improving facility efficiency or operation. Incorporating an SEP into a settlement agreement with EPA can also reduce a violator's civil penalty significantly, even though the guidelines provide for certain thresholds of penalty. Violators can also be creative in proposing SEPs, because the SEP Policy provides for flexibility to incorporate worthwhile projects beyond the seven categories of projects typically allowable.

3. Calculating civil penalties. EPA's civil penalty policies, on their face, appear to provide a rational basis for establishing settlement amounts by utilizing what EPA claims are fair and equitable formulas. Those facing civil penalties, however, often encounter a world unto itself, consisting of statute-specific civil penalty policies; gravity of environmental harm calculations; and computer models designed to determine the economic benefit of noncompliance (BEN), the present value of SEPs, and the "ability to pay for environmental liability" (ABEL). See Fuhrman, Almost Always ABEL: How EPA Deals with Ability-to-Pay Issues in Civil Penalty Cases, Toxics L. Rep. 1125 (Mar. 12, 1997).

As an example, consider the application of the CWA's civil penalty policy. That policy is summarized in the following formula:

Settlement Penalty = Economic Benefit + Gravity Component ± Adjustments

Although the policy provides the appearance of objectivity, consider the following commentary:

> Under the CWA civil penalty policy, a monetary value is placed on gravity through the use of a scoring system in which each point adds $1,000 to the penalty. . . . EPA personnel are instructed to assign points based on four criteria: the significance of the violation, harm to health and the environment, the number of violations, and the duration of non-compliance. Points are to be assigned for each month in which a violation occurred, and one additional point is to be added for each such month.
>
> The methodology for quantifying the "significance of the violation" is based on the most significant effluent violation in each month and appears quite quantitative. The CWA policy contains a table that translates the percentage of the exceedance over the allowable level of effluence into a number of points. The point system ranges from zero to 15 points for non-toxic and from zero to 20 for toxic pollutants. Harm to health and the environment is much more difficult to quantify. Nonetheless, the CWA policy allows the attribution of between 10 points and 25 points per month for violations that affect human health. Alternatively, between one point and 10 points maybe assigned for impacts on the aquatic environment.
>
> This aspect of the methodology is highly arbitrary, overlaps with the significance of the violation criterion, and avoids the difficult task of identifying and quantifying the harm to human health and natural resources caused by a release of pollutants. It also provides EPA with great flexibility to increase or decrease the monetary value attributed to the gravity component, depending on the attitudes of the litigation team. The guidance for assessing the number of violations is vague. It allows for assigning between zero and five points based on the total

number of violations each month, but provides very superficial guidance on how many points should be assigned in a given situation. The discussion of how to assign points for the duration of non-compliance is even more vague. This factor is intended to punish the violator of continuing, long-term violations of an effluent limitation or permit conditions, generally defined as violations continuing for three or more consecutive months. The plaintiffs may identify between zero and five points per month for this category. Given the subjective nature of some of these criteria, two entities in identical situations may receive quite different assessments.

According to the CWA civil penalty policy, after calculating the initial penalty amount (i.e., after adding together the economic benefit and monthly gravity components), this total may be modified by three adjustment factors: the history of non-compliance (which can increase the penalty up to 1.5 times the initial amount), the violator's ability to pay (which may lead to a decrease in the penalty), and litigation considerations (which may also lead to a decrease). . . .

The penalty policy's discussion of how to treat recalcitrance is so lacking in specifics that almost any outcome can be rationalized within its guidance. The discussion also tells the EPA staff that they may increase the recalcitrance factor during the negotiations if the alleged violator continues to be recalcitrant "with the remedy or with settlement efforts." Clearly, the policy provides leverage for plaintiffs. While recognizing that recalcitrance is an explicit consideration in assessing penalties under most environmental statutes, one can easily criticize the amorphous nature of this part of the guidance. Although it is unlikely that recalcitrance is a factor in all environmental violations, when EPA starts negotiating with an alleged CWA violator, it typically increases the initial penalty at least 50 percent due to alleged recalcitrance. The guidance provides no benchmark for analyzing the appropriate adjustment factor for recalcitrance in a case with a given fact pattern. Fuhrman, Improving EPA's Civil Penalty Policies—And Its Not-So-Gentle BEN Model, 23 Envtl. L. Rep. 874, 876-878 (Sep. 9, 1994).

In light of questions that can be raised about EPA's economic benefit methodology, does it seem unfair to increase the recalcitrance factor when both parties are negotiating in good faith? In certain cases. EPA has chosen not to share the basis for its gravity calculations with defendants. This practice preserves the government's flexibility to raise or lower the monetary amount attributed to this factor in settlement negotiations. But does the failure to disclose fuel the perception that the government has not treated the alleged violator objectively and evenhandedly?

4. Regulatory creep: The enforceability of EPA informal guidance documents. Many in the regulated community have experienced firsthand EPA's practice of using informal agency interpretations to broaden the scope of federal regulations. The ever-widening scope of regulation that follows often is referred to as "regulatory creep." However, the D.C. Circuit has raised significant questions concerning EPA's longstanding practice of expanding the reach of existing rules through informal guidance documents. In *Appalachian Power Co. v. EPA*, 208 F.3d 1015 (D.C. Cir. 2000), several electric power companies and chemical and petroleum trade associations (the Petitioners) challenged the validity of portions of a 1998 EPA guidance document entitled "Periodic Monitoring Guidance" (the Guidance). The Guidance included the agency's interpretation of 40 C.F.R. §70.6(a)(3)(i)(B) (the Rule), one of the implementing regulations for the Title V air permit program. The Rule states that where the applicable air emissions requirement for a facility does not require periodic testing or monitoring, state-issued Title V permits must contain "periodic monitoring sufficient to yield reliable data from the relevant time period that are representative of the source's compliance with the permit." The Petitioners argued that the only purpose of this Rule is to fill the gap when an applicable emissions requirement does not contain any testing or monitoring requirements.

However, the EPA's Guidance interpreted this provision more broadly to allow the state agencies to evaluate applicable requirements and impose a periodic monitoring requirement if the state determines that the monitoring provision in the applicable requirement "does not provide the necessary assurance of compliance." State authorities had invoked this EPA Guidance to require continuous opacity monitors (i.e., 24-hour automated monitoring) of Title V applicants even when the applicable standard specified only a simple visual observation method for ensuring compliance.

The D.C. Circuit agreed with the Petitioners that the plain language of the Rule creates only a gap-filling function and concluded that, as a result, the Guidance necessarily assigns broader authority to state agencies than granted to them in the Rule. In reaching this result, the D.C. Circuit also cited the inconsistency of the Guidance with the 1992 preamble to the Rule. In the preamble, EPA stated that if there is "any federally promulgated requirement with insufficient monitoring, EPA will issue a rulemaking to revise such requirement." 57 Fed. Reg. 32,278 (July 21, 1992). As the Court pointed out, the Guidance provides for an altogether different procedure. Under the Guidance, "it is initially up to the States to identify federal standards with deficient monitoring, doubtless with EPA's input, formal or informal. And it is the state and local agencies that must alter the standards by requiring permittees . . . to comply with more stringent monitoring requirements. Needless to say, EPA's approach . . . raises serious issues, not the least of which is whether EPA possesses the authority it now purports to delegate." 208 F.3d at 1026. The D.C. Circuit accordingly held that the Guidance's more expansive reading of the Rule could not stand: "[i]n directing state permitting authorities to conduct wide-ranging sufficiency reviews and to enhance the monitoring required in individual permits beyond that contained in State or federal emissions standards . . . EPA has in effect amended §70.6(a)(3)(i)(B). This it cannot legally do without complying with the rulemaking procedures required by 42 U.S.C. §7607(d) [the APA]." Id. at 1028.

Will this decision aid in challenges to guidance documents related to implementing rules for the CWA, RCRA, CERCLA, and other major federal environmental laws? What steps could EPA undertake to eliminate challenges to its guidance documents?

5. Environmental enforcement after the BP *Deepwater Horizon* oil spill. The largest oil spill in U.S. history began in April 2010 with the blowout of the Macondo Well off the coast of Louisiana, resulting in the release of millions of barrels of oil into the Gulf of Mexico. The well was drilled in 5000 feet of water and reached from the seabed floor to an oil and gas reservoir 13,000 feet below.

The Macondo Well was drilled by a mobile offshore drilling unit—commonly known as a "rig"—called the *Deepwater Horizon*. The *Deepwater Horizon* was owned by a group of entities known as Transocean, which had been hired by BP Exploration and Production, Inc. ("BP") to drill the well under BP's direction. The *Deepwater Horizon* was connected to the well by a "riser" and a "blowout preventer." The riser was a 5,000-foot pipe extending down from the rig, and the blowout preventer was a 50-foot-tall device connecting the riser to the well on the seabed floor. The blowout preventer functioned both as a drilling tool and as an emergency safety mechanism. It was designed to seal the well and halt the upward flow of oil into the riser if control of the well was lost. Both the riser and the blowout preventer were appurtenances of the *Deepwater Horizon*.

On April 20, 2010, the Macondo Well blew out and began a massive, uncontrolled discharge of oil into the Gulf of Mexico. The blowout occurred as the *Deepwater Horizon* was preparing to abandon the well temporarily so that a different rig could be brought in to complete the development of the well for oil production. In part because the abandonment procedure included the removal of the blowout preventer and riser, the well itself had to contain barriers sufficient to prevent oil from escaping.

As part of the abandonment process, cement was pumped into the bottom of the wellbore to prevent oil from moving from the reservoir into the well. The cement failed to seal the well, however, resulting in the high-pressure release of gas, oil and other fluids, while the *Deepwater Horizon* was still in place. The blowout preventer also failed, allowing the oil and gas surging up from the well to continue through the riser and onto the deck of the *Deepwater Horizon*. The escaping oil and gas exploded, killing 11 workers and setting the rig on fire.

B. The Governmental Enforcement Process

After burning for two days, the *Deepwater Horizon* sank. The riser was severed far below the water's surface, and for the next three months, oil gushed from the well into the Gulf. Initially, the oil flowed through the blowout preventer. The flow of oil was finally halted in July 2010, after a cap was installed on the blowout preventer.

The Macondo Well blowout caused enormous damage and has spawned numerous civil and criminal proceedings. (See also Chapter 19.) Since the spill, the U.S. Court of Appeals for the Fifth Circuit, on repeated occasions, affirmed that BP and Anadarko Petroleum Corp. were liable under CWA §311 (33 U.S.C. §1321), because they co-owned the Macondo Well, where the uncontrolled movement of oil originated.

After the conclusion of the proceedings in the Fifth Circuit, the oil companies filed petitions for certiorari from the Fifth Circuit's 2014 ruling upholding a 2012 federal district court decision that the oil companies were responsible for the underwater spill as the owners of the Macondo Well. The oil companies (namely, BP and Anadarko) argued in their petitions that the oil had flowed not from the well itself but from equipment owned by the rig owner (Transocean) and that the CWA does not clearly define "discharge."

In his 2012 ruling that formed the foundation for the proceedings on liability for the oil spill, U.S. District Judge Carl Barbier rejected Anadarko's argument that the oil spilled out of a blowout preventer owned by Transocean, finding that there was abundant proof that the uncontrollable flow of oil began in the Macondo Well and not the blowout preventer, which he called a "passive conduit" through which the oil had flowed. *In re Oil Spill by the Oil Rig Deepwater Horizon*, 844 F. Supp. 2d 758 (E.D. La. 2012).

The Fifth Circuit agreed in its June 2014 ruling, finding that the language of the law and the facts of the case clearly pointed to liability for the oil companies. *United States v. BP Exploration & Prod. Inc.*, 753 F.2d 570 (5th Cir. 2014); see also *In re Deepwater Horizon, United States v. BP Exploration & Prod. Inc., et al.*, 772 F.3d 350 (5th Cir. 2014). In January 2015, the Fifth Circuit declined 7-6 to review the decision en banc.

Anadarko petitioned for certiorari in March 2015, arguing that while other courts have interpreted "discharge" to mean a "flow or issuing out" of containment, the Fifth Circuit found it to be a "'loss' or 'absence' of controlled confinement." Anadarko contended that the Fifth Court's ruling was an entirely new and expansive interpretation of discharge that contradicts numerous requirements of the CWA, and that the ruling unlawfully empowered the government to prosecute any party with a facility or vessel associated with a spill, whether or not that party had released pollutants.

Then, in April 2015, BP also asked the Supreme Court to review the Fifth Circuit's 2014 decision, arguing that the federal government, the district court below, and the Fifth Circuit panel had imposed liability on BP by invoking different shifting interpretations of the CWA's phrase "from which oil or hazardous substance is discharged."

In opposing the petitions for certiorari, the federal government argued that the Fifth Circuit ruling should stand, because otherwise polluters would be able to avoid liability in cases where the released substances flowed through a facility owned by someone else. Citing Section CWA §1321(b)(7) (which imposes liability on the owners of any vessel or facility from which oil is discharged), the federal government argued that: (1) the CWA does not require oil to be discharged directly into the water, and (2) the well itself is a facility from which oil was "discharged" in this case, as defined under the CWA.

On June 29, 2015, the Supreme Court denied the petitions for certiorari. On June 30, 2015, following on the heels of the denial of certiorari by the Supreme Court, BP, and five Gulf states announced an $18.7 billion settlement over BP's role in the *Deepwater Horizon* spill.

The settlement money will be used to: resolve the CWA penalties; resolve natural resources damage claims; settle economic claims; and resolve economic damage claims of local governments, according to pleadings filed in federal court. In addition to the federal government, the settlement involves Florida, Alabama, Mississippi, Louisiana, and Texas.

The settlement announcement came just as the district court was preparing to rule on how much BP owed in federal CWA penalties. The district court had already found that 3.19 million barrels of oil—nearly 134 million gallons—spewed into the Gulf. Individual states also were pursuing litigation.

Costs incurred by BP so far include an estimated $14 billion for response and cleanup and $4.5 billion in penalties announced after a settlement of a criminal case with the government.

In 2012, BP reached a settlement over economic and property damage claims arising from the spill. In its first-quarter earnings report for 2015, BP stated that it could estimate at least a $10.3 billion cost. But it also stressed that the cost could be higher, depending on how many legitimate claims were filed by a recently passed deadline.

4. Brownfields Federalism and Its Policy of Greater Flexibility and Cooperation

As patterns of environmental enforcement have evolved, an area in which the greatest changes have been made is in relation to regulatory developments pertaining to brownfields. As defined by EPA, brownfields are "abandoned, idled, or underused industrial and commercial sites where expansion or redevelopment is complicated by real or perceived environmental contamination that can add cost, time or uncertainty to a redevelopment project."[9]

In the past, redevelopment of brownfields was often avoided for fear of environmental liabilities arising primarily under CERCLA (see Chapter 16), its state equivalents, and RCRA (see Chapter 17). The extensive jurisdictional reach of these statutes, their broad liability provisions, and the fear of federal and state enforcement were all blamed for impeding the redevelopment of many brownfields sites. Historically, prospective purchasers, who often desired to quantify cleanup costs before purchasing a contaminated site, found that governmental entities were unwilling or unable to provide assistance in determining what constitutes an acceptable cleanup. In large part, therefore, brownfields sites often sat idle and undeveloped, even if such development was in the public interest. Potential investors, faced with uncertain costs and potential associated legal liabilities, sought development elsewhere, often at pristine rural sites (labeled "greenfields"). Brownfields sites, in turn, became major burdens on the community and taxpayers.

In the 1990s, EPA and the states began to recognize that, rather than encouraging brownfields redevelopment, their deterrent enforcement strategies were actually having the opposite effect by discouraging prospective purchasers. In response, federal and state regulatory reforms were announced with the express purpose of spurring brownfields redevelopment. These reforms reflected: (1) a shift from historical reliance on a deterrent and penalty-based enforcement ideology to more flexible initiatives, seeking to induce brownfields development through partnering with the regulated community; and (2) a shift towards increasing cooperation between federal and state enforcement authorities, seeking to harmonize enforcement priorities to allow brownfields development to move forward.

U.S. Environmental Protection Agency, Brownfields Action Agenda

(1995)

[This agenda had six key reforms, each designed to deal with particular obstacles to brownfields redevelopment.]

---

9. EPA Region 5, Office of Pub. Affairs, Basic Brownfields Fact Sheet (1996). There are an estimated 130,000 to 450,000 contaminated brownfield sites around the country. Current cleanup estimates range up to $650 billion.

B. The Governmental Enforcement Process

1. **PROSPECTIVE PURCHASER AGREEMENTS.** This reform represents EPA's effort to provide a liability waiver to prospective buyers of brownfields sites. A prospective purchaser agreement is a binding contract entered into between EPA, the owner of a contaminated property, and a prospective purchaser, exonerating the purchaser from any future environmental liability at the site and obligating the EPA not to sue the purchaser for any existing contamination. . . . Only 16 prospective purchaser agreements were made between 1989 and 1995. In response to pressure for a more flexible, compliance oriented policy, EPA revised its prospective purchaser guidelines in 1995, specifically clarifying and encouraging the use of prospective purchaser agreements. EPA, Announcement and Publication of Guidance on Agreements With Prospective Purchasers of Contaminated Property and Model Prospective Purchaser Agreement, 60 Fed. Reg. 34, 792-98 (1995).

2. **DELISTING SITES FROM THE CERCLIS DATABASE.** To remove the stigma from listing a site on CERCLIS, the national list of CERCLA sites, EPA voluntarily delisted 25,000 (of a total of 38,000) sites for which it plans no further remediation. See CERCLIS Definition Change, 60 Fed. Reg. 16,053 (1995).

3. **OTHER PURCHASER PROTECTIONS.** EPA also issued a guidance document pledging not to pursue innocent landowners with contaminated aquifers and pledging to issue "comfort letters" to those engaged in voluntary cleanups. See U.S. EPA Policy Toward Owners of Property Containing Contaminated Aquifers (Nov. 1995).

4. **LAND USE POLICY.** EPA also promulgated a directive allowing future land uses to be considered in selecting the appropriate remedial action at sites on the National Priorities List. See U.S. EPA, Land Use in the CERCLA Remedy Selection Process, OSWER Directive No. 9355.7-04 (May 25, 1995).

5. **PILOT PROJECT GRANTS.** EPA agreed to fund economic redevelopment projects at brown-field sites, in an effort to develop new and more cost-effective cleanup standards. See Superfund: Reports Cite Savings in Remedy Selection Resulting from Superfund Reform at EPA, 27 BNA Env't Rep. 1874 (1997); and

6. **MEMORANDUMS OF AGREEMENT REGARDING STATE VOLUNTARY CLEANUPS.** Certain EPA Regions entered into Memorandums of Agreement (MOAs) with state environmental agencies, providing that EPA will not take enforcement action at sites where private parties have conducted cleanups under the state's direction or under state voluntary cleanup statutes. See ABA, Brownfields Redevelopment: Cleaning Up the Urban Environment 117-25 (Mar. 7, 1996).

COMMENTARY & QUESTIONS

1. **The old horrors of Superfund cleanups.** Chapter 16 reviews how Superfund works or, in the eyes of some critics, how Superfund fails to work. Why was EPA so insistent on rigid, dictatorial cleanups and on harsh bargaining positions in Superfund's earlier years? Many answers are possible. Some relate to the backlash against the Gorsuch-era Superfund nonenforcement in the early Reagan Administration; others relate to the unthinking attitude of EPA as an overzealous agency taking itself too seriously in the exercise of the enormous powers granted by CERCLA §§106 and 107. There are more benign answers as well; for example, the change could have been part of a natural agency learning process, through which the agency was able to recognize that a different approach better served the public interest. Most flattering to EPA, it is also possible that the change in course coincided with a change in the nature of the underlying

problem and the behavior of the regulated community that had been brought about by EPA's past practices. As to the problem itself, EPA has listed the worst sites on the national priorities list (NPL) and has cleanups well underway at most of them. Sites not on the NPL tend to pose fewer public health hazards and exhibit problems of a more localized nature that do not waken the Love Canal and Times Beach hysteria. Remediation techniques and cleanup methods are now better understood and more efficacious as a result of past experience. Moreover, the regulated entities understand the CERCLA liability scheme better. They are far more adept at estimating their own liabilities under the law, and far more wary of protracted litigation, or strategies of recalcitrance. The combination of less seriously polluted sites and regulated parties ready to negotiate allows EPA the leeway to adopt more flexible approaches.

2. State law and policy changes affecting enforcement. Along with federal policy changes, state agencies and state cleanup laws have also changed, perhaps to an even greater degree. Many state laws that mimicked CERCLA were at least as draconian. See Elizabeth Glass Geltman, Recycling Land: Encouraging the Redevelopment of Contaminated Property, 10 Nat. Res. & Env't 3 (Spring 1996). In particular, a majority of the states implemented voluntary cleanup programs or enacted brownfields legislation. These state developments are illustrated in the pie chart set forth in Figure 2.

State brownfields legislation generally has four basic components: (1) risk-based, end-use cleanup standards and voluntary programs; (2) implementation of liability control, comfort, and protection through the use of covenants not to sue; (3) an accelerated program for cleaning up contaminated sites to standards pegged to future property use (so called tiered action objectives); and (4) economic and employment opportunities, particularly for disadvantaged

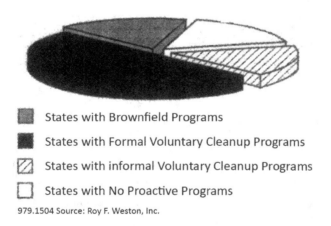

- States with Brownfield Programs
- States with Formal Voluntary Cleanup Programs
- States with informal Voluntary Cleanup Programs
- States with No Proactive Programs

979.1504 Source: Roy F. Weston, Inc.

FIGURE 18-2. *State Brownfields and Voluntary Cleanup Programs.*

areas, through the cleanup and redevelopment of contaminated sites. Many states have also added unique and potentially important components to their legislative efforts, including tax breaks or incentives for the cost of investigation and remediation associated with an individual site, and financial lender liability protection. This protection often provides for a definition of "owner" that eliminates the lender as a potentially responsible party (PRP).

Looking more closely at examples of how these individual states are tackling the brownfields problem provides insight into the impact of economic development on enforcement strategies. Figure 18-3 shows selected states and the legislative status and important features of their programs. An interesting aspect of many state initiatives is the impact of neighboring state

B. The Governmental Enforcement Process

STATE	BROWNFIELD LEGISLATION	VOLUNTARY PROGRAM	RISK BASED/ END-USE CLEANUP STANDARDS	BUYER LIABILITY PROTECTION	LENDER LIABILITY PROTECTION	TAX INCENTIVES
Pennsylvania	Yes	Yes	Yes	Yes	Yes	Yes
Delaware	Yes	Yes	Yes	Yes	No	Yes
New Jersey	Yes	Yes	Yes	Yes	No	No
Massachusetts	Yes	Yes	Yes	Yes	Yes	Yes
Georgia	Yes	Yes	Partial	No	No	No
Illinois	Yes	Yes	Yes	Yes	Yes	No
Minnesota	Yes	Yes	Yes	Yes	No	No
New York	Yes	Yes	Yes	Yes	No	No
Michigan	Yes	Yes	Yes	Yes	Yes	No
Ohio	Yes	Yes	Yes	Yes	No	No

FIGURE 18-3. *Status of Selected State Brownsfields Programs.*

legislation on their programs, and the "competing" economic development and environmental programs developed in efforts by certain states to become more user-friendly to business.

3. Cooperative federalism in enforcement: federal and state memoranda of agreement. EPA Region V was one of the first EPA regional offices to organize a Brownfields Task Force. This task force first issued a proposed enforcement strategy 20 years ago. According to this strategy, Region V would seek to encourage brownfields redevelopment based on four basic principles: (1) promote cleanups by encouraging participation in state voluntary cleanup programs; (2) provide information to promote informed decisionmaking by prospective purchasers and lenders; (3) encourage community participation in the cleanup process; and (4) develop partnerships among Region V states, local governments, and stakeholders. The strategy also delineated specific initiatives, including issuing generic "comfort letters," developing site-specific covenants not to sue, and developing consensus on risk-based cleanup protocols linked to future land use scenarios.

To accomplish these goals, Region V developed a Memorandum of Agreement (MOA) with each of the midwestern states to include language that releases sites remediated successfully under state authority from further attention by Region V. Region V's MOA with the State of Illinois, executed on April 6, 1995, is set forth below.

Superfund Memorandum of Agreement
Illinois Environmental Protection Agency, U.S.
Environmental Protection Agency, Region V

(1995)

I. BACKGROUND. The Illinois Environmental Protection Agency ("IEPA") and the United States Environmental Protection Agency, Region V ("Region V") entered a Superfund Memorandum of Agreement (SMOA) effective December 18, 1991. Among other things, the SMOA established operating procedures for general Superfund program coordination and communication between IEPA and Region V.

II. BROWNFIELDS. In 1993 IEPA and Region V began developing strategies to promote the remediation and redevelopment of "Brownfield" sites. Both agencies recognize that a key factor to the Brownfields program in Illinois is for both agencies to exercise their authorities and use their resources in ways that are mutually complementary and are not duplicative. Two operational factors are important in this regard. First, the IEPA has successfully operated a voluntary cleanup program since the late 1980s. This program, more formally known as the Pre-Notice Site Cleanup Program ("PNSCP"), provides guidance assistance and oversight by IEPA to owners and operators of sites in Illinois who perform site assessment and remediation in accordance with the practices, and under the approval, of the IEPA. In addition, IEPA has established a consistent cleanup objectives process across all its remediation programs (PWSCP, CERCLA, RCRA, and LUST) which is protective of human health and the environment. Second, USEPA has administered a national site assessment program to assess sites listed on the federal CERCLIS list. This assessment process identifies and prioritizes sites for remediation needs and also establishes a "no further remedial action planned" or NFRAP category of sites. As a result of the success of these two programs, IEPA and Region V have concluded that the principles and procedures set forth in this Addendum will meaningfully assist in the remediation and development of Brownfield sites.

III. PRINCIPLES. If a site in Illinois has been remediated or investigated under the practices and procedures of the Illinois PNSCP and IEPA has approved the remediation as complete or made a no-action determination upon review of an investigation, consistent with existing information the site will not be expected to require further response actions. Accordingly, Region 5 will not plan or anticipate any federal action under Superfund law unless, in exceptional circumstances, the site poses an imminent threat or emergency situation. Region 5 will also continue to work with Illinois to remove any concerns about federal activity under Superfund so as to encourage appropriate redevelopment.

This Principle does not apply to sites which have been listed on the National Priorities List or sites subject to an order or other enforcement action under Superfund law or sites imminently threatening public health or the environment. Future IEPA activities at the site will be based on the conditions of the remediation approval and whether any imminent threat subsequently arises.

IV. REPORTING. On an annual basis IEPA will report to Region V on the number of . . . sites in the PNSCP, sites entering the PNSCP the previous year, and sites having received approvals by IEPA of full or partial completions in the previous year. . . .

COMMENTARY & QUESTIONS

1. How much assurance? EPA has negotiated agreements on a case-by-case basis with PRPs that include express promises not to go to court and commence enforcement proceedings (covenants not to sue). The MOA does not rise to the level of a covenant not to sue. The MOA does provide prospective purchasers with assurance that, by participating in the Illinois Cleanup Program, they are unlikely to face federal enforcement action. Is that enough assurance to satisfy the PRP's desire to put an upper bound on liability? Also note that the MOA contains exceptions for sites listed on the NPL, for sites already subject to enforcement action under Superfund, and for sites imminently threatening the public health or the environment. Why were these exceptions made? Do the exceptions create

B. The Governmental Enforcement Process

"pariah parcels" in the sense that no prospective purchasers will buy such parcels when there are MOA-eligible parcels also available? At a minimum, Region V's MOA encourages prospective purchasers to work more closely with Illinois environmental officials to remediate properties under Illinois law. Does the MOA represent evidence that cooperative federalism is maturing, at least where brownfields are concerned?

2. Enforcing promises of regulatory forbearance. As suggested above, a covenant not to sue represents a form of promise by the regulator to exercise its authority in a particular fashion. It is akin to a contract, but is it (or any other promise of regulatory forbearance) enforceable against the government if the government changes its mind? Consent decrees that extinguish liabilities bind government to its promises. See *Frew ex rel. Frew v. Hawkins*, 540 U.S. 431 (2004) (holding unanimously that the enforcement of a federal consent decree designed to implement a federal statute against state agencies did not violate the Eleventh Amendment, when state officials waived the Eleventh Amendment when they asked the court to approve the consent decree). But mere promises of the regulator are seldom enforceable. See Toscano, Note, Forbearance Agreements: Invalid Contracts for the Surrender of Sovereignty, 92 Colum. L. Rev. 426 (1992). See also Abrams, Binding Agreements with Governmental Entities, ABA Water L. Conf. Proceedings, Feb. 20, 1998. The reasons that government is free to "change its regulatory mind," even after promising not to do so, have to do with the preservation of sovereignty. Is the enforceability of promises of regulatory forbearance critical to EPA's policies of more cooperative relations with the regulated community?

3. EPA's rule on brownfield property assessments to avoid liability. A final rule, clarifying how certain owners or purchasers of potentially contaminated property should conduct assessments to avoid Superfund liability, was adopted by the EPA effective June 9, 2003. Under the rule, EPA detailed the standards to be used by prospective purchasers of brownfields and owners of land contiguous to contaminated sites to assess contamination and identify all prior uses, so that prospective purchasers are not held liable for the pollution.

The EPA developed the rule in response to the Small Business Liability Relief and Brownfields Revitalization Act, 42 U.S.C. §9601 (2000), enacted in January 2002. The Act established new defenses for property owners, provided liability relief to certain kinds of generators, and created a statutory brownfields funding program. The Act also extended financial assistance to states to help establish or administer brownfields or voluntary cleanup programs, and established standards for conducting due diligence. In particular, under the Act, bona fide prospective purchasers and contiguous landowners are protected from Superfund liability as long as they conduct "all appropriate inquiry" into former uses of the land and take other required steps.

The EPA's final rule, and the Act itself, continue the trend toward brownfields federalism by emphasizing the need for increased cooperation between federal and state enforcement authorities. With certain exceptions identified in the Act, EPA may not bring CERCLA enforcement actions when a cleanup is performed at an "eligible response site" and the state response program meets the minimum standards. An "eligible response site," under §129 of the Act, includes (1) sites that fall within the definition of a brownfield site, and (2) those sites that EPA determines are eligible for brownfields assistance on a case-by-case basis. Sites specifically excluded from the definition are NPL sites, and sites where the EPA has conducted or is conducting a preliminary assessment and site inspection whereby it determines, after consultation with the state, that the site is eligible for inclusion on the NPL.

5. Administrative Reforms in Environmental Enforcement

Administrative Reforms:

1. Project XL: "Multimedia" Permitting
2. "Common Sense Initiative"
3. Negotiated Rulemaking

Regulatory reforms pertaining to environmental enforcement have repeatedly been proposed from all corners of the political compass and from government itself. In the 1990s, environmental regulation faced frontal assaults by marketplace forces in the 104th Congress, via a Clinton Administration program of "Reinventing Government" that continued experiments in negotiated rulemaking, market-enlisting economic incentive programs to change the traditional command-and-control regulatory model, and a number of agency initiatives to simplify regulatory procedures.

The 104th Congress produced a flurry of industry-inspired assaults on environmental regulation. Some, targeting the CWA and ESA, were quite specific; others were quite generic. The House of Representatives, for instance, passed a "regulatory moratorium" drafted by Gordon Gooch, a Project Relief lobbyist for the petrochemical industry, which included as its major provision a freeze and rollback of almost all federal regulations proposed after November 1994. The moratorium was an example of a crude blunt "reform" initiative. Its scope was breathtaking; in fact it suspended a host of rules without knowing what they were. "Regulatory Reform Act" bills were proposed to set up an intricate series of procedural and analytical roadblocks before agencies could put forward environmentally protective regulations, although the 104th Congress bills had fast-track exemptions for pesticide approvals and similar market-permissive rules. The intent of these bills was regulatory "paralysis by analysis." "Property rights" bills provided that regulatory agencies would have to compensate regulated interests if any portion of their property was reduced in value by 20% or more; if the agency did not pay, regulations would be unenforceable. The Unfunded Mandates Reform Act burdened federal-state regulatory systems of "cooperative federalism" by placing procedural hurdles before Congress could delegate regulatory roles to the states.

These political initiatives to change regulatory practices have come to very little, as legislators have discovered that attacks on environmental regulation, once the media covers them, became political hot potatoes, ready to burn anyone who picks them up. With the exception of the unfunded mandates law, marketplace attempts to undercut the regulatory process are either in remission or keeping a lower profile.

Other reform attempts have come from within the executive branch itself—the "Reinventing Government" Executive Order on Regulatory Planning and Review; the EPA's Regulatory Unified Agenda implementations of the Reinventing Government Executive Order; EPA's Project XL Multimedia Permitting; and various Advisory Councils established by EPA under the Federal Advisory Committee Act,[10] including the Common Sense Initiative program, the National Environmental Justice Advisory Council, the Federal Facilities Environmental Restoration Dialogue Committee, and the National Advisory Council for Environmental Policy and Technology (NACEPT).

Project XL: "Multimedia" Permitting. In an attempt to reduce the expensive and lengthy permit process, EPA initiated the program known as "Project XL"—a multipurpose environmental permit designed to replace the extreme complexities of some existing procedures. Under the program, the agency issues a single master permit—simplifying the

---

10. Federal Advisory Committee Act, Pub. L. No. 92-463, 86 Stat. 770 (1972).

regulatory process by combining or eliminating the need for separate permits in areas such as air, water, and hazardous wastes. The purpose of Project XL is to allow companies freedom to take innovative approaches to pollution control by allowing them to skirt certain regulatory requirements in exchange for setting up an alternative plan that will produce superior overall environmental results. The "multimedia" permit is a single, performance-based plan that considers a facility's total net impact on the environment rather than attempting to regulate individual technologies used. The danger, of course, is that, in such master permit processes, some of the substantive requirements of public and environmental health and safety get compromised. If erosion of norms can be avoided, however, the rationality of the approach militates in favor of the experiment.

EPA's Industry-Specific "Common Sense Initiative." EPA announced in 1994 that it would begin an experiment in cooperation with industry groups to rationalize regulatory approaches where it appeared that equal or greater pollution abatements could be achieved by alternative lower-cost abatement strategies. Targeting the auto, petroleum refining, iron and steel, metal finishing and plating, computer and electronics, and printing industries, the approach presumes that in many cases industry expertise and self-interest will identify protective measures of greater efficiency and oversell net savings. One example is benzene emissions at oil refining facilities. The industry identified the loading stage — the point at which refined petroleum products were being nozzled into tankers or other transport facilities — as generating more ambient benzene emissions than the refining facilities themselves, and these emissions from loading were abatable at far lower cost. EPA proposed to allow that industry to comply with benzene standards by rolling back loading stage emissions rather than requiring the far more difficult and expensive refining process emission cutbacks.

This "common sense initiative" has the potential to improve both the tone and the overall results of our massive command-and-control regulatory systems, but obviously it must take account of the opposing tensions inherent in regulation of economic forces. EPA acceptance of such tradeoffs requires full, comparative, accurate information before and after each tradeoff, and careful implementation and monitoring. A fear on the industry side is that there is no EPA estoppel: The accomplishment of net gains by an industry-suggested alternative does not prevent EPA from coming back later for further incremental improvements under the bypassed restrictions.

Negotiated Rulemaking. A number of regulatory experiments with negotiated rulemaking — "reg-neg" — have taken place in the environmental setting, particularly in EPA and the Department of Interior, under the terms of the Administrative Dispute Resolution Act[11] and the Negotiated Rulemaking Act,[12] passed as amendments to the adjudication section of the APA. See Subchapter D below.

COMMENTARY & QUESTIONS

1. The quest for efficiency. EPA's Project XL and Common Sense Initiative have faced problems with the battleground setting of interest-representation regulatory politics. OSHA's attempt to cope with the vast number of rulemakings Congress had required of

---

11. Administrative Dispute Resolution Act, Pub. L. No. 101-552, 104 Stat. 2736 (1990).
12. Negotiated Rule Making Act, Pub. L. No. 101-648, 104 Stat. 4,969 (1990).

it floundered on the rocks of judicial review, when the court's requirement of voluminous individual databases for each proposed new standard proved quite simply to be impossible.

One of the secrets of U.S. government is that legislatures do not provide agencies with the economic or political capital needed to enforce all the laws on the books. But a will to enforce, coupled with innovative administrative planning, can improve upon the situation. EPA continues to try to make the administrative process "more transparent" so that citizen participation can enter into the bargaining process of regulation. Based on informal communications with OSHA, the agency has foregone a prior attempt to do consolidated "omnibus" rulemaking. See *AFL-CIO v. OSHA*, 965 F.2d 962 (11th Cir. 1992). EPA, on the other hand, has proceeded with major new "cluster rule-making" under the CWA, treating classes of industry in the same business in an omnibus process. (EPA's job is easier than OSHA's because its statutory standards under the CWA are based on industrywide BAT rather than the individual safety of each substance standard as with OSHA.)

2. Other reforms: citizen oversight councils. Citizen councils, built into governmental regulatory processes, offer interesting innovations for environmental administrative law. Notable examples of citizen councils were created in the aftermath of the *Exxon-Valdez* oil spill. RCACs, Regional Citizens Advisory Councils, generally vested with subpoena powers, bring citizens most directly threatened by environmental hazards into the official public law regulatory process. Faced with the conclusion that official regulatory oversight and enforcement before the Alaska oil spill had been lax and complacent in the face of industry corner-cutting, three models of citizen oversight councils were initiated — a council formed in citizen negotiations with industry; a state-legislated citizens council, chaired by Professor Harry Bader who had helped conceptualize it; and a federal model of citizens council written into law in the Oil Pollution Act of 1990. The first model was incorporated into the third. The state council, after its research began to produce embarrassing evidence of state nonenforcement of pollution laws, was defunded and shut down through the efforts of industry lobbyists. The terms of these innovative administrative experiments are interesting and potentially important far beyond the waters of the Gulf of Alaska. See Oil Pollution Act of 1994, 33 U.S.C. §2732; Alaska Stat. §§24.20.160 et seq. (1990). Citizen councils offer valuable advantages in quality control efforts of both private and governmental resource protection activities, and are designed to be relatively immune from cooptation. These experiments bear continuing study as examples of utilitarian pluralism in government.

3. "Collaborative governance." From her study of environmental regulation at OSHA and EPA, Professor Jody Freeman has long advocated experiments with "collaborative governance" to respond to the litany of criticisms about the quality, implementability, and legitimacy of rulemaking by agency establishments and cohorts of lobbyists. Collaborative governance would reorient regulatory reform toward joint problem solving and away from controlling discretion. Collaborative governance requires improved mechanisms for problem solving, broad participation, provisional solutions, the sharing of regulatory responsibility across the public-private divide, and flexible, engaged agencies:

> Recent experiments with multi-stakeholder decision-making processes, such as regulatory negotiation and Project XL, which offer parties more direct access to, and responsibility for, all stages of the administrative process are promising alternatives to discretion-constraining instruments. They have some potential to facilitate problem solving, produce better-quality rules, and create mechanisms of accountability that take advantage of the capacities of nongovernmental groups. They are not, however, without limitations. . . . All administrative law reform proposals must cope with the "structural embeddedness" of agencies. . . . It is still unclear whether a collaborative model that remains dependent upon interest groups can overcome the pathologies of interest-representation, including its strategic-bargaining orientation

and its tendency to exclude less-organized interests. Moreover, the potential for a problem-oriented, deliberative dynamic to emerge in the administrative process may be undermined by the reality that "repeat players" . . . pursue their interests in a wide variety of settings beyond rule making and implementation. . . . Parties' interactions in the legislative process, litigation, election campaigns, and state and local regulation can hinder collaboration. . . . Freeman, Collaborative Governance in the Administrative State, 45 UCLA L. Rev. 1 (1997).

Nevertheless Professor Freeman concludes that the destructive and convoluted process of modern lobbyist-dominated interest-representation regulatory politics deserves to be rethought in a more transparent and articulated participatory decisionmaking system.

4. Sunsets. Sunsetting provisions are a regulatory reform device with mixed reviews. Much recent public interest legislation has been freighted with a provision suspending funds, authority, or both after a period of years, often five years, thereafter requiring renewal. This approach was touted as making agencies justify their work periodically in a democratic forum. In practice, it typically has been attached to laws such as ESA that do not have sustained marketplace political momentum. This effectively guarantees that environmental protections passed into law have to be defended against assault every five years. Mining, lumbering, and grazing programs on public lands, U.S. Army Corps of Engineers draining and damming programs, and the like never seem to have sunsets attached to them. Administrative law, like the rest of life, is not consistently dominated by civic values or neutral principles, but rather is a continuing reflection of the convoluted tendencies of power coupled with human nature.

C. Citizen Enforcement to Complement Governmental Efforts

In the mid-1970s, as chronicled in Chapter 6, private environmental organizations seized the opportunity to enforce major environmental statutes against polluters by invoking the statutes' citizen suit provisions. Beginning in 1970 with the CAA, Congress included citizen suit provisions in virtually all of the major environmental laws.[13] Although the use of citizen suit provisions in federal environmental statutes was new at the time, citizen enforcement was not a new concept. Stockholder derivative suits under the securities laws, various private rights of action via statutes such as the civil rights acts, and statutory torts provided precedents for private enforcement of federal environmental statutes.

In enacting the citizen suit provisions of the environmental laws, Congress viewed the citizen suit both as an efficient policy instrument and as a participatory mechanism, based on democratic ideals that would allow concerned citizens to redress environmental pollution.[14] Citizen suits thus were designed to serve as adjuncts to federal, state, and local enforcement efforts. In a time of limited resources, when governmental enforcers cannot always seek compliance from polluters, citizen suits represent an enforcement safety valve, essentially conferring "private attorney general status" on the citizenry to sue on behalf of the community at large rather than merely to redress individual rights involving economic

---

13. Citizen suit provisions, for example, appear in CAA §304, CWA §505, ESA §11 (g), RCRA §7002, ToSCA §18, and CERCLA §310, and others noted in Chapter 6. There is no citizen suit provision in FIFRA or in MMPA.

14. Although this assessment is shared by a large majority of legal scholars, not all agree. See Greve, The Private Enforcement of Environmental Law, 65 Tul. L. Rev. 339 (1990) (arguing that congressional support for private environmental law enforcement is an outgrowth of interest group politics and contending that citizen suit provisions are an off-budget entitlement program for the environmental movement).

loss. In addition to conferring statutory authority to prosecute members of the regulated community for certain violations of the environmental laws, Congress also suspected that there would be occasions when the executive branch would not perform its responsibilities diligently under the environmental laws. Accordingly, citizen suit provisions were also enacted to address the further concern that citizen action might be necessary to force government agencies to perform their civic duties. For these reasons, Congress provided the authority to undertake citizen suits against public officials (like the Administrator of EPA) based upon the alleged failure to perform nondiscretionary duties under the environmental laws.

Neither governmental enforcement nor citizen enforcement of the environmental laws occurs in a vacuum. Citizen enforcement historically has acted as a check on government, provoking enforcement action or providing an alternative when government fails to act. When business fails to comply with environmental requirements, governmental and citizen enforcement together can create an impressive threat to business in the marketplace economy.

COMMENTARY & QUESTIONS

1. Citizen suits and the command-and-control model. Citizen suits typically do not interfere with the formal processes by which government sets enforcement priorities and balances costs and benefits. Instead, citizen suits implement those decisions by enforcing them. Generally, the government remains the party charged with the policy assessment. The citizen suit, in turn, concerns whether the alleged violator has met the governmental standards, or whether the governmental administrator has carried out the mandatory duties that Congress has prescribed. Nonetheless, citizen suits can affect the command-and-control model. By allowing private enforcement of the goals defined, citizen suits can affect enforcement priorities. Citizen suits can also have the beneficial effect of exposing those priorities to public scrutiny and comment. For example, in the early 1980s, when EPA (during the Reagan Administration) virtually stopped enforcing the environmental laws, citizen groups filed hundreds of suits that not only enforced the environmental laws (primarily the CWA at the time) but also highlighted EPA's abdication of its enforcement responsibilities.

2. How much is accomplished by citizen suits? Quantitatively, it is tempting to give a bean counter's answer based on the number of filings, but the more probing answer lies in estimating the impact of citizen suits and their availability on governmental enforcement performance and voluntary compliance by regulated entities. Such estimates generally agree that citizen suits can have a material impact on both governmental and regulated entity performance. See, e.g., Maples, Reforming Judicial Interpretation of the Diligent Prosecution Bar: Ensuring an Effective Citizen Role in Achieving the Goals of the Clean Water Act, 16 Va. Envtl. L.J. 195, 203-204 (1996) ("Citizen suits have become so effective that now industry fears them more than negotiation and settlement with the enforcing agency"); Miller, Private Enforcement of Federal Pollution Control Laws Part 1, 13 Envtl. L. Rep. 10309 (1983) (concluding that the most celebrated uses of citizen suits have been against EPA for its failures to implement environmental statutes in a timely and complete manner, and that the significance of citizen suits can hardly be doubted); Mann, Polluter-Financed Environmentally Beneficial Expenditures: Effective Use or Improper Abuse of Citizen Suits Under the Clean Water Act?, 21 Envtl. L. 175, 182-185 (1991) (concluding that citizen suits seeking relief against EPA for failing to

C. Citizen Enforcement

perform mandatory duties have had a major impact on shaping implementation of the environmental statutes).

3. Forms of relief available in citizen suits. Under the citizen suit provisions of the environmental laws, private citizens can enforce statutory, regulatory, or permit requirements through suits seeking compliance orders and penalties. In addition to this enforcement type of citizen suit, a mandamus type of action is also available for citizens seeking to require a regulator to comply with his duties under the environmental laws. For example, under the CWA, the EPA Administrator may be sued by citizens "where there is alleged a failure of the Administrator to perform any act or duty—which is not discretionary." CWA §505(a)(1)(2), 33 U.S.C. §1365(a)(l)(2). Significantly, mandamus is not available to require EPA to take enforcement action when a citizen provides EPA with notice of an alleged violation. This point had been the subject of a split in the early cases, particularly because CWA §309(a)(3) provides in pertinent part:

> Whenever on the basis of any information available to him, the Administrator finds that any person is in violation of §1311 [relating to unpermitted discharges] . . . he *shall* issue an order requiring such person to comply with such section . . . , or he shall bring a civil action in accordance with subsection (b) of this section. [Emphasis added.]

In what has become a leading case on the issue, *Dubois v. Thomas (Administrator of EPA)*, 820 F.2d 943 (8th Cir. 1987), the Eighth Circuit invoked *Chevron* and deferred to EPA's interpretation that claimed discretion not to enforce despite the presence of the usually obligatory word "shall." To buttress its position, the Court relied on *Heckler v. Chaney*, 470 U.S. 821, 831 (1985), which concluded:

> An agency decision not to enforce often involves a complicated balancing of a number of factors which are peculiarly within its expertise. Thus, the agency must not only assess whether a violation has occurred, but whether agency resources are best spent on this violation or another, whether the agency is likely to succeed if it acts, whether the particular enforcement action requested best fits the agency's overall policies, and indeed, whether the agency has enough resources to undertake the action at all. An agency generally cannot act against each technical violation of the statute it is charged with enforcing.

4. Prerequisites to citizen enforcement. Before a citizen suit can proceed, several key statutory and jurisprudential hurdles must be overcome. This should be a familiar topic, having appeared earlier in reviewing the concept of standing (Chapter 6). Beyond standing, additional barriers to citizen suits seek to integrate citizen enforcement with the regulatory regime as administered by governmental officials. First, in order to initiate suit, the citizen must give notice to EPA, the state where the violation occurred, and the alleged violator. Generally, 60 days' notice is required, although the amount of notice can vary for certain kinds of violations. The purpose of notice is to allow the federal government the opportunity to initiate its own suit, precluding the citizen's suit, or to allow the violator to comply and correct its violation. Second, suit must be brought within the applicable statute of limitations, generally viewed, in most citizen suit actions, to be five years. See, e.g. *Atlantic States Legal Found., Inc. v. Tyson Foods, Inc.*, 897 F.2d 1128 (11th Cir. 1990); *Sierra Club v. Chevron U.S.A., Inc.*, 834 F.2d 1517 (9th Cir. 1987). Third, the citizen suit provisions generally specify that if federal or state authorities are diligently prosecuting an action to require compliance, filing of a citizen suit is barred, although citizens may still intervene in federal enforcement actions as of right. This hurdle is designed to prevent citizen suits from infringing on the exercise of enforcement discretion by federal and state authorities. Although a citizen suit is precluded if there is a pending judicial action by a regulatory authority that is being diligently prosecuted, does an administrative action by a regulatory authority also have a preclusive effect on a citizen suit? One court summarized the case law as follows:

> A number of courts have interpreted the statutory language concerning citizen suits when the state has already begun an administrative action. In *Baughman v. Bradford Coal Co. Inc.*, 592 F.2d 215 (3d Cir. 1979), the court first held that in certain circumstances an administrative hearing can be the equivalent of a court action. It then held that the court should measure the power of the administrative agency against that of the court to determine whether the administrative action was similar enough to a court action to fall within the statutory language. In *Friends of the Earth v. Consolidated Rail Corp.*, 768 F.2d 57 (2d Cir. 1985), the Second Circuit rejected this rationale, stating it would be inappropriate to expand the statutory language to include administrative enforcement actions. The Ninth Circuit adopted the *Friends of the Earth* rationale, and held that the plain language of the statute provided that only an ongoing action in a court, rather than an administrative agency, would preclude a citizen suit. *Sierra Club v. Chevron U.S.A., Inc.*, 834 F.2d 1517, 1525 (9th Cir. 1987). At least one District Court outside these circuits has followed the *Friends of the Earth* interpretation in *Maryland Waste Coalition v. SCM Corp.*, 616 F. Supp. 1474, 1478-1481 (D. Md. 1985). This Court also adopts the *Friends of the Earth* rationale. *Lykins v. Westinghouse Elec. Corp.*, 715 F. Supp. 1357, 1358-1359 (E.D. Ky 1989).

5. Citizen suit notice. One of the most frequently litigated issues under the citizen suit provisions of the environmental laws is whether to dismiss cases filed by plaintiffs who "jump the gun" and either file suit before passage of the requisite notice period or file a defective notice. In *Hallstrom v. Tillamook County*, 493 U.S. 20 (1989), the Supreme Court considered whether a case should be dismissed for the complete failure to give notice. Although affirming dismissal, the Court left open whether notice is a jurisdictional prerequisite to suit and how to treat issues of incomplete or defective notice. Should defects in the content and form of notice (as opposed to the timing) result in dismissal? In her article, Notice Letters and Notice Pleading, 78 Or. L. Rev. 105 (1999), Robin Craig describes a conflict between the Supreme Court's interpretation of environmental citizen suit notice requirements and the notice pleading standard in Rule 8 of the Federal Rules of Civil Procedure. Whereas under Rule 8 defendants are deemed to have notice of those allegations that a reasonable person would understand the complaint to contain, the Supreme Court's interpretation of citizen suit notice, since *Hallstrom v. Tillamook* County, has tended to narrow the scope of environmental plaintiffs' claims through requirements such as notice letters, in which plaintiffs must detail every allegation 60 or 90 days prior to filing a complaint. Craig argues that such citizen suit notice standards impermissibly undermine the Federal Rules.

6. Cessation of violation in a post-*Gwaltney* world. *Gwaltney of Smithfield, Ltd. v. Chesapeake Bay Found.*, 484 U.S. 49 (1987), the case in which the Supreme Court held that citizen suits under the CWA would not lie for wholly past violations, has become standard fare in the interpretation of citizen suit provisions. Courts now carefully inspect the language of the specific provision being considered to see if it refers to past or to current violations, and rule accordingly. After *Gwaltney*, where the relevant citizen suit provision speaks of violation in the present tense, citizens must be prepared to prove at least the likelihood of ongoing violations in order to prevail. See, e.g., *Coburn v. Sun Chem. Co.*, 19 Envtl. L. Rep. 20256 (E.D. Pa. Nov. 9, 1988) (construing "to be in violation" language of RCRA §7002(a)(1)(A) to prevent suit against past owners of parcel allegedly presenting an imminent endangerment while permitting suit against present owner).

The cases in this area tend to be somewhat technical and formalistic in deciding what suffices to constitute allegation of an ongoing violation. First, judgments concerning whether a violation is ongoing are to be made as of the time the complaint is filed. See

C. Citizen Enforcement 819

Atlantic States Legal Found., Inc. v. Tyson Foods, Inc., 897 F.2d 1128 (11th Cir. 1990). Second, a violation will not be considered to be ongoing if remedial measures establish that there is no reasonable prospect for recurrence. See *Chesapeake Bay Found., v. Gwaltney of Smithfield, Ltd.*, 844 F.2d 170 (4th Cir. 1988). Third, plaintiffs, as a pleading matter, need only make a good faith allegation of an ongoing or repeat violation in order to be able to file suit, see *Sierra Club v. Union Oil Co. of Cal.*, 853 F.2d 667 (9th Cir. 1988). Finally, ongoing violations can be established by showing that violations continued on or after the filing of a complaint or by producing evidence from which a reasonable trier of fact could find a continuing likelihood that intermittent or sporadic violations would occur. See *Connecticut Coastal Fishermen's Ass'n v. Remington Arms Co. Inc.*, 989 F.2d 1305 (2d Cir. 1993).

Of what significance are these technical post-*Gwaltney* decisions? In part, they reflect an attempt by the federal courts to avoid cluttering their dockets with citizen suits. Consider, for example, the following comment on the proliferation of citizen suits under CWA §505:

> The primary reason for the predominance of citizen suits under §505 is the relative ease of uncovering and proving a violation under CWA §402's NPDES program. . . . [D]ischargers under the program must routinely file discharge monitoring reports [DMRs] with both state regulatory agencies and the EPA. The discharger must certify the accuracy of each DMR and the CWA imposes substantial penalties for false reports. Each DMR must list the actual quantity of waste discharged, as well as the permitted amount that may be discharged. As a consequence, in many instances spotting permit violations is as easy as comparing two numbers on a printout. . . . The majority of courts have held that DMRs are admissible as evidence of the violations, and have granted summary judgment to citizen plaintiffs based solely on DMRs. . . . Mann, Polluter-Financed Environmentally Beneficial Expenditures: Effective Use or Improper Abuse of Citizen Suits Under the Clean Water Act?, 21 Envtl. L. 175, 183-184 (1991).

In these circumstances, judicial reliance on jurisprudential mechanisms to limit the number and scope of citizen suits can be seen as a form of judicial administration. In such cases, courts may seek to minimize litigation based on citizens' spotting technical permit violations simply by "comparing two numbers on a printout." Id.

7. The *Steel Company* case. Another post-*Gwaltney* question was resolved by the Supreme Court itself, as noted in Chapter 6, in addressing whether a violator may escape liability by completing remedial action after receiving notice of a citizens group's intent to file a suit but before the citizen suit is filed. In *Steel Co. v. Citizens for a Better Environment (CBE)*, 523 U.S. 83 (1998), the Steel Company was charged by a citizens group with violating the Emergency Planning and Community Right-to-Know Act (EPCRA), 42 U.S.C. §§11001 et seq., by failing to file timely toxic and hazardous chemical storage and emission reports for past years. By the time the complaint was filed, after the requisite statutory notice period, the Steel Company had brought its filings up to date. The Supreme Court held that because none of the relief sought would remedy the citizen group's alleged injury in fact, there was no standing to maintain the suit, and the complaint should be dismissed. In particular, the Supreme Court found that none of the specific items of relief sought—a declaratory judgment that the Steel Company violated EPCRA; injunctive relief authorizing CBE to make periodic inspections of the Steel Company's facility and records, and requiring the Steel Company to give CBE copies of its compliance reports; and orders requiring the Steel Company to pay EPCRA civil penalties to the Treasury and to reimburse CBE's litigation expenses—and no conceivable relief under the complaint's final general request—would serve to reimburse CBE for losses caused by the Steel Company's late reporting, or eliminate any effects of that late reporting upon CBE.

Faced with the prospect of enforcement through citizen efforts, can a company, after the decision in *Steel Company*, target its compliance to eliminate identified sources prior to the filing of a citizen suit? If so, citizen enforcement efforts are thereby chilled; citizens, moreover, then get no reimbursement fees for performing this enforcement compliance function, because the case cannot survive in court. There is a special sense in which this is a particular problem with EPCRA, where compliance can take the form of filing reports, rather than installing complex pollution control equipment that may or may not adequately reduce discharges or emissions. In the EPCRA context, as the Seventh Circuit noted below in *Steel Company*, to say that industries cannot be sued when they withhold information from the public about use and release of toxic chemicals until citizens file enforcement notices, if they just provide the overdue information prior to the lawsuit, raises important questions concerning the significance of citizen enforcement provisions.

> If citizen suits could be fully prevented by 'completing and submitting' forms, however late, citizens would have no real incentive to incur the costs of learning about EPCRA, investigating suspected violators, and analyzing information. [If] citizen suits could only proceed when a violator received notice of intent to sue and still fails to spend the minimal effort required to fill out the forms and turn them in, . . . private citizens would have to absorb much of the cost of [enforcement], with little or no hope of recovering those costs through awards of litigation expenses . . . *Citizens for a Better Env't v. Steel Co.*, 90 F. 3d 1237, 1244-1245 (7th Cir. 1996).

After the *Steel Company* case, when again addressing redressibility, the Supreme Court held that civil penalties for ongoing violations (that have not abated by the time of suit) provide sufficient deterrence to support redressibility. *Friends of the Earth, Inc. v. Laidlaw Envtl. Servs., Inc.*, 528 U.S. 167 (2000).

8. Defining agency enforcement diligence. Citizens affected by a polluter's actions often suffer real and immediate consequences as a result of the pollution. Governmental regulators have a different perspective that is shaped by their need to administer the program to achieve its regulatory ends within the constraints of a limited agency budget and under the realities of having to work with the regulated entities on an ongoing basis. Given these differences, cases arise in which the citizens assert that the governmental agency is not prosecuting diligently. Some of these citizen suits allege, or at least imply, that the governmental filing is collusive and is intended to shield the polluter from enforcement rather than to seek enforcement. Courts have already had to decide cases, for example, where defendants sought to ensure diligent prosecution for the sole purpose of avoiding a citizen suit. In *Friends of the Earth, Inc. v. Laidlaw Envtl. Servs., Inc.*, 890 F. Supp. 470 (D.S.C. 1995), the defendant requested that its settlement with the state environmental agency and EPA be filed as a lawsuit, so as to avoid the looming citizen suit. The agencies accepted the request on the condition that the defendant cover the expenses. The defendant thereafter funded the filing of a complaint against itself on behalf of the state environmental agency. When the citizen suit was filed two days later, the defendant filed a motion to dismiss based on the diligent prosecution bar. Although the motion was denied, the case warns of the potential misuse of the diligent prosecution bar.

9. Attorneys' fees and costs under citizen suit provisions. When citizens embark as "private attorneys general" attempting to enforce existing law in agencies and courts, they often face substantial administrative and financial burdens, and opponents who are either public officials or well-financed corporate entities writing off expenses against revenues. Expert witnesses and attorneys cost money. For plaintiff groups like the citizens in *Overton Park*, this often means having to raise funds through bake sales, raffles, logo t-shirt sales, or hat passing. The larger national environmental groups have substantially greater resources

D. Alternative Dispute Resolution

but are confronted with a proportionally broader range of advocacy commitments, and likewise depend upon volunteer contributions.

Environmentalists have turned to both the courts and Congress in attempts to win financial recognition of the role played by private attorneys general. In court, environmentalists face the American rule of fee-shifting; unlike their counterparts under the English rule, prevailing plaintiffs in American courts generally are unable to recover the costs of litigation from defendants. (In part, this explains why punitive damages are often sought in common law litigation.)

The opportunity to recover attorneys' fees and costs can be vital to citizen suit enforcement and is often a vigorously contested issue. The citizen suit provisions of the CAA allow an award of attorneys' fees and costs where appropriate. See CAA §304(d), 42 U.S.C. §7604(d). Citizen suit provisions of the CWA, RCRA, and CERCLA provide for an award of attorneys' fees and costs to prevailing parties or substantially prevailing parties. See CWA §505(d), 33 U.S.C. §1365(d); RCRA §7002(e), 42 U.S.C. §6972(e); CERCLA §310(f), 42 U.S.C. §9659(f).[15] Environmental fee-shifting provisions are viewed typically as a necessary incentive to environmental enforcement because few private plaintiffs can afford to finance expensive environmental litigation that usually results in nonmonetary benefits to the public at large (rather than damage awards to the individual plaintiffs). Congress accordingly included fee-shifting incentives in various environmental statutes as an incentive to spur enforcement of meritorious claims.

D. ALTERNATIVE DISPUTE RESOLUTION PROCESSES

1. Why Alternative Dispute Resolution?

Environmental law was born and raised in the arena of adversarial combat—the traditional litigation mode in court and agency proceedings. Few argue, however, that the adversarial litigation process is ideal. Environmental enforcement through litigation often proves to be a crude mechanism for achieving resolutions, results in antagonistic relationships, and drains scarce resources in terms of time, money, and energy. Because of its obstacles and inefficiencies, ultimately many disputes never get resolved within the formal mechanisms of the legal system. Because of its practical burdens, the traditional model is often unavailable to those who lack financial and political resources.

Even within traditional adversarial litigation, of course, most disputes are settled out of court through a process of negotiation prior to final judgment. But other options for conflict resolution are increasingly available. A growing movement both within and outside the legal profession is calling for a shift to alternative dispute resolution (ADR) mechanisms such as mediation, arbitration, mini-trials, and other procedures. Whether by

---

15. In a variety of federal statutes authorizing citizen suits, as in CWA §505, Congress consistently inserted a fee recovery provision in terms similar to the following:

> §505(d) Litigation costs. The court, in issuing any final order in any action brought pursuant to this section, may award costs of litigation (including reasonable attorney and expert witness fees) to any prevailing or substantially prevailing party, whenever the court determines such award is appropriate. 33 U.S.C. §1365(d).

Note that the language "prevailing party," on its face, includes prevailing defendants as well as prevailing plaintiffs.

statutory mandate or pragmatic decision of the parties, many issues that previously would have been handled by litigation or agency enforcement now are resolved through ADR. The trend reemphasizes that the practice of law need not be what many laypersons consider it—an unproductive, insulated mechanism for implementing the more negative elements of human nature—but rather can be a profession that tries to make social relationships and civic mechanisms work.

ADR was first used in the environmental setting (where it is often referred to as EDR) in the late 1970s.[16] Unlike most litigation models, which are only retrospective or reactive to existing disputes, the ADR approach is forward-looking—designed to anticipate future policy or practical conflicts.[17]

The viability of ADR as an alternative to litigation has caused fierce debate in academic and practice communities. Richard Mays, arguing for expanded environmental use of ADR, notes that in standard EPA enforcement cases, "the average time between discovery of a violation and settlement might easily be three to five years or more. Even after this delay, [all but 5%] of EPA's judicial cases are settled rather than tried."[18] Enormous amounts of time and resources spent on such cases could be reduced dramatically if resolutions were reached through negotiation rather than through the process or threat of litigation.

Not all cases can or should be settled through ADR. Even proponents like Mays agree that adversarial litigation is necessary and appropriate in some cases—for example, if important precedential legal issues need resolution, if injunctions or other court-supervised remedies are necessary and parties lack the time or interest required for negotiating settlements, or if, in light of a party's egregious conduct, the public interest requires an open public trial and punishment. These exceptional cases, they argue, however, make up only a small percentage of the total number of environmental suits filed each year.

Some opponents of alternative remedies claim that ADR's purported savings in time and expense are bought at the cost of accuracy, justice, and democratic process. Edward Brunei, a staunch opponent of ADR, claims that "only formal litigation and adjudication provide a mechanism for accurate determination of facts."[19] Brunet maintains that the informality of ADR procedures makes them "weak since they rely on voluntary party exchange of data and do not have an authority figure equivalent to a judge to prevent discovery abuse." In environmental disputes, Brunet claims, the informality of ADR is particularly dangerous. Given the complexity of environmental disputes, "the 'facts' produced in an environmental mediation are likely to be incomplete and inaccurate."

---

16. For an overview of major environmental disputes in which ADR methods were used, see Allan R. Talbot, Settling Things (1983), and Lawrence Susskind, Lawrence Bacow & Michael Wheeler, Resolving Environmental Regulatory Disputes (1983).

17. This mode has been called "front-loading" or anticipatory consensus-building.

18. Mays, Alternative Dispute Resolution and Environmental Enforcement: A Noble Experiment or a Lost Cause?, 18 Envtl. L. Rep. 10,087, 10,088 (1988).

19. Brunet, The Costs of Environmental Alternative Dispute Resolution, 18 Envtl. L. Rep. 10,515, 10,516 (1988). See also Fiss, Against Settlement, 93 Yale L.J. 1073 (1984), and Fiss, Out of Eden, 94 Yale L.J. 1669 (1985), arguing that, among other major shortcomings, ADR undermines the important law-building, law-applying functions of judicial litigation.

On the other hand, ADR sometimes promotes effective joint fact-finding techniques, producing facts faster and with greater accuracy than traditional discovery. If parties can develop a mutually acceptable fact-finding agenda and methodology, then the traditional "battle of the experts" can be averted and questions shifted from a position-based to a broader interest-based resolution process on the merits.[20]

2. Environmental ADR

An array of alternative methods is available in the environmental setting to parties seeking to resolve their differences through ADR.

National Institute for Dispute Resolution, Paths to Justice: Major Public Policy Issues of Dispute Resolution

Administrative Conference of the United States, Sourcebook:
Federal Agency Use of Alternative Means of Dispute
Resolution 5-47 (1983, 1987)

Some conflict contributes to and, indeed, is essential to a healthy, functioning society. Social change occurs through dispute and controversy. Some observers attribute the long-term stability of the country to its ability to hear and reconcile the disagreements of its diverse population. Thus one should focus not only on avoiding disputes, but also on finding suitable ways of hearing and resolving those that inevitably arise. . . .

Dispute resolution techniques can be arrayed along on a continuum ranging from the most rulebound and coercive to the most informal. Specific techniques differ in many significant ways, including:

- whether participation is voluntary;
- whether parties represent themselves or are represented by counsel;
- whether decisions are made by the disputants or by a third party;
- whether the procedure employed is formal or informal;
- whether the basis for the decisions is law or some other criteria; and
- whether the settlement is legally enforceable.

At one end of the continuum is adjudication (including both judicial and administrative hearings): parties can be compelled to participate; they are usually represented by counsel; the matter follows specified procedure; the case is decided by a judge in accordance with previously established rules; and the decisions are enforceable by law. . . .

At the other end of the continuum are negotiations in which disputants represent and arrange settlements for themselves: participation is voluntary, and the

> **Alternative Methods of Environmental ADR:**
>
> 1. Arbitration
> 2. Conciliation
> 3. Facilitation
> 4. Fact-finding
> 5. Med-arb
> 6. Mediation
> 7. Mini-trial
> 8. Multi-door center
> 9. Neighborhood justice centers
> 10. Ombudsman
> 11. Public policy dialogue and negotiation
> 12. Rent-a-judge

---

20. See Lawrence Susskind & Jeffrey Cruikshank, Breaking the Impasse: Consensual Approaches to Resolving Public Disputes (1987); see also Roger Fisher & William Ury, Getting to Yes (1981).

disputants determine the process to be employed and criteria for making the decision. Somewhere in the middle of the continuum is mediation, in which an impartial party facilitates an exchange among disputants, suggests possible solutions, and otherwise assists the parties in reaching a voluntary agreement . . .
[Here follows a definitional survey of forms of ADR:]

Arbitration, involves the submission of the dispute to a third party who renders a decision after hearing arguments and reviewing evidence. It is less formal and less complex and often can be concluded more quickly than court proceedings. In its most common form, binding arbitration, the parties select the arbitrator and are bound by the decision, either by prior agreement or by statute.[21] In last-offer arbitration, the arbitrator is required to choose between the final positions of the two parties. . . .

Court-annexed arbitration, a newer development, judges refer civil suits to arbitrators who render prompt, non-binding decisions. If a party does not accept an arbitrated award, some systems require they better their position at trial by some fixed percentage, or court costs are assessed against them. Even when these decisions are not accepted, they sometimes lead to further negotiations and pretrial settlement.

Conciliation, an informal process in which the third party tries to bring the parties to agreement by lowering tensions, improving communications, interpreting issues, providing technical assistance, exploring potential solutions and bringing about a negotiated settlement, either informally or, in a subsequent step, through formal mediation. Conciliation is frequently used in volatile conflicts and in disputes where the parties are unable, unwilling or unprepared to come to the table to negotiate their differences.

Facilitation, a collaborative process used to help a group of individuals or parties with divergent views reach a goal or complete a task to the mutual satisfaction of the participants. The facilitator functions as a neutral process expert and avoids making substantive contributions, [helping] bring the parties to consensus. . . .

Fact-finding, a process used from time to time primarily in public sector collective bargaining. The fact finder, drawing on information provided by the parties and additional research, recommends a resolution of each outstanding issue. It is typically non-binding and paves the way for further negotiations and mediation.

Med-arb, an innovation in dispute resolution under which the med-arbiter is authorized by the parties to serve first as a mediator and, secondly, as an arbitrator empowered to decide any issues not resolved through mediation.

Mediation, a structured process in which the mediator assists the disputants to reach a negotiated settlement of their differences. Mediation is usually a voluntary process that results in a signed agreement which defines the future behavior of the parties. The mediator uses a variety of skills and techniques to help the parties reach a settlement but is not empowered to render a decision.[22]

The Mini-trial, a privately developed method of helping to bring about a negotiated settlement in lieu of corporate litigation. A typical mini-trial might entail a period of limited discovery after which attorneys present their best case before managers with authority to settle and, most often, a neutral advisor who may be a retired judge or other lawyer. The managers then

---

21. In a somewhat surprising 1990 case, representatives of a Phillips 66 petrochemical plant and citizens of a Texas Gulf Coast community agreed to arbitration to resolve a dispute over the company's discharge of polluted waste water into Linnville Bayou. Under the terms of the agreement assenting to arbitration, a panel of three scientists was given binding authority to determine the extent of pollution in the bayou and to set out the best clean-up method. The decision of the arbitration panel could be appealed only to a retired judge, and appeal was limited to the narrow issue of whether the decision was arbitrary.

22. Mediation has been a particularly successful method for reaching settlement and allocating responsibility among potentially responsible parties in dozens of EPA Superfund toxic waste clean-up cases.

D. Alternative Dispute Resolution Process

enter settlement negotiations. They may call on the neutral advisor if they wish to obtain an opinion on how a court might decide the matter.[23]

The Multi-door center (or Multi-door courthouse), a proposal [by Professor Sander] to offer a variety of dispute resolution services in one place with a single intake desk which would screen clients. Under one model, a screening clerk would refer cases for mediation, arbitration, fact-finding, ombudsman or adjudication. . . .

[Negotiation, is the generic process that recurs in many of these ADR forms. In its simplest incarnation, however, negotiation constitutes discussions between the parties, with no formalized format, ground rules, or third party participation.]

Neighborhood justice centers (NJCs), the title given to . . . about 180 local centers now operating through the country under the sponsorship of local or state governments, bar associations and foundations. . . . They are also known as Community Mediation Centers, Citizen Dispute Centers, etc.

Ombudsman, a third party [on the Scandinavian model] who receives and investigates complaints or grievances aimed at an institution by its constituents, clients or employees. The Ombudsman may take actions such as bringing an apparent injustice to the attention of high-level officials, advising the complainant of available options and recourses, proposing a settlement of the dispute or proposing systemic changes in the institution. . . .

Public policy dialogue and negotiation, aimed at bringing together affected representatives of business, public interest groups and government to explore regulatory matters. The dialogue is intended to identify areas of agreement, narrow the areas of disagreement, and identify general areas and specific topics for negotiation. A facilitator guides the process.

[Reg-neg, is the term given to a process of intensive multiparty negotiations leading to governmental issuance of regulatory rules, noted in the next excerpt.]

Rent-a-judge, the popular name given to a procedure, presently authorized by legislation in six states, in which the court, on stipulation of the parties, can refer a pending lawsuit to a private neutral party for trial with the same effect as though the case were tried in the courtroom before a judge. The verdict can be appealed through the regular court appellate system.

3. Negotiated Rulemaking

Lawrence Susskind and Gerard McMahon, The Theory and Practice of Negotiated Rulemaking

3 Yale J. on Reg. 133, 140-141, 142-146 (1985)[24]

Since the late 1970s, advocates of negotiated approaches to rulemaking have argued that the legitimacy of proposed rules could be restored—and time-consuming court challenges avoided—if informal, face-to-face negotiations were used to supplement the traditional review and comment process. Critics, however, have responded quite negatively to what they perceive as the dangers of "deal-making behind closed doors." Nevertheless, proponents of the innovation have persisted, and during the last few years several federal agencies have experimented with negotiated approaches to rulemaking. . . .

---

23. Since the mid-1980s, the Army Corps of Engineers has used the mini-trial technique in resolving a number of regulatory environmental disputes.

24. Copyright 1985 by Yale Journal on Regulation, Box 401A Yale Station, New Haven, CT 06520; reprinted from Volume 3:133 by permission. Other useful works on reg-neg include Philip Matter's Negotiated Regulations: A Cure for Malaise, 71 Georgetown L. Rev. 1 (1982) and Perritt, Negotiated Rulemaking Before Federal Agencies, 74 Georgetown L. Rev. 1625 (1986). The Administrative Conference has published a useful collection: Negotiated Rulemaking Sourcebook (1990).

Negotiated rulemaking will only be utilized more broadly if it achieves better results than the traditional rulemaking process. . . . Each party must feel that the negotiated rule serves its interest at least as well as the version of the rule most likely to be developed through conventional process. . . . A negotiation should yield realistic commitments from all of those involved. A rule that satisfies everyone in principle but cannot be implemented is of little use. Not only is the support of the participants important, but so too is the support of any interested party. . . . The interests of the parties should be so well-reconciled that no possible joint gains are left unrealized. Changes which would help a party without harming another party should not be missed. If a more elegant method of reconciling conflicting interests of the parties is possible, it will probably emerge once the draft of the agreement is publicized. . . . The agency should be able to demonstrate that it has upheld its statutory mandate, and the public-at-large should feel satisfied that both the process and outcome were fair. . . . Relationships among the participants in the negotiations should improve, not deteriorate, as a result of their interactions. The parties should be in a better position to deal with their differences in the future. . . . The negotiated rule should take account of the best scientific and technological information available at the time of the negotiation.

EPA's Regulatory Negotiation Demonstrations. The notion of using a negotiated approach to rulemaking at EPA first emerged during the Carter Administration. . . . While the change of Administration slowed the momentum, appointment of Joseph Cannon as Acting Associate Administrator of EPA's Office of Planning and Resource Management in 1981 brought renewed interest. . . . In February 1983, EPA published a notice in the Federal Register indicating that it intended to pursue the idea of negotiated rulemaking and used solicitation letters to invite interested parties to suggest candidate rules. . . .

In December 1983, David Doniger of the Natural Resources Defense Council (NRDC) formally proposed [rulemaking on CAA motor vehicle emissions] nonconformance penalties [NCPs] as a candidate rule for negotiated rulemaking. Between December 1983 and March 1984, [EPA] found widespread support for negotiating the NCP rule among potential stakeholders. Charles Freed, Director of EPA's Manufacturers Operations Division, the program office responsible for the rule, enthusiastically supported using a negotiated approach, as did the EPA Office of General Counsel and Office of Program Planning and Evaluation. Environmentalists were generally supportive, viewing NCPs as a means to accommodate temporary industry needs while holding industry to technology-forcing standards. Smaller manufacturers were somewhat wary of the costs of participating in a negotiated rulemaking and felt that any NCP rule had to preserve their competitiveness. Larger manufacturers generally supported the proposed process and felt that they had adequate staff to participate in the process. In general, all stakeholders felt that the rule was important enough to merit their involvement and that it did not involve the type of "life and death" value questions that would have made negotiation—an unfamiliar process at any rate—appear less workable.

In an April 1984 Federal Register notice, EPA announced its intention to develop an NCP rule using a regulatory negotiation. At an organizational meeting . . . some twenty participants met to learn more about the proposed process and to discuss how the negotiations would proceed. At that time, EPA announced the creation of a $50,000 resource pool—a fund that any or all of the participants would be able to draw upon to cover the costs of technical studies or other costs related to their participation.

Negotiations began June 14, 1984, and ended October 12, 1984. In order to develop some structure for the process, a negotiation facilitator opened the June session by asking participants to produce a statement of issues reflecting their interests. A final list often

D. Alternative Dispute Resolution Process

issues was synthesized to help organize the work of the negotiating committee. Three work groups were formed. . . .

Five one-day negotiating sessions dealing with substantive aspects of the NCP rule and numerous work group sessions dealing with specific technical and administrative issues were held during a four month period. The NCP negotiating committee used over $10,000 to fund an independent study of a proposed engine testing plan. Other collaborative technical work was done by committee members who designed a micro-computer-based spreadsheet model to test the impacts of parameter changes in the penalty formula.

The negotiations were conducted under a Federal Advisory Committee Act (FACA) charter. Notice of the NCP negotiating committee sessions was given in the Federal Register, and meetings were open to the public. The committee eventually reached consensus on all of the issues it originally identified in the first meeting.

In reaching this consensus, EPA's choice of a facilitator was crucial. The ERM-McGlennon team, which had extensive mediation experience, took the lead in generating agreement on a detailed agenda and work schedule, organizing work group meetings at which components of the final version of the regulation were drafted, and convening the full group to review these work group drafts. . . . [T]he facilitation team initiated caucuses during and outside of meetings, maintained frequent contact with all participants, and intervened quite actively during several of the sessions.

After the last negotiation session on October 12, 1984, in which all the issues were resolved, a four-member subcommittee—consisting of EPA, state, environmental, and industry representatives—was given the responsibility of translating the tentative agreement into a consensus document. A first draft was circulated in mid-October, and comments were solicited. The subcommittee then used several conference calls to prepare the final draft that was signed by the entire committee in December 1984. With the consensus statement signed by all participants, EPA published its notice of proposed rulemaking on March 6, 1985. Only thirteen comments were received during the comment period, all in support of the committee's proposal. The final rule was promulgated without opposition on August 30, 1985. . . .

COMMENTARY & QUESTIONS

1. Statutory ADR and reg-neg. In 1990, Congress formally recognized the utility of ADR and negotiated rulemaking, and made them federal policy. The 101st Congress passed the Administrative Dispute Resolution Act, Pub. L. No. 101-552, and the Negotiated Rulemaking Act, Pub. L. No. 101-648, as amendments to the adjudication section of the APA. Under the ADRA, agencies are required to appoint resolution specialists and to develop policy addressing the potential uses of ADR in that agency. The Act does not force agencies to use ADR mechanisms, but each agency must review its litigation and administrative disputes to determine where ADR techniques may be useful. The second statute explicitly establishes the authority of federal regulatory agencies to use negotiated rulemaking and permits the use of federal funds to cover the expenses of private party participants. These policies may give ADR methods new legitimacy and force, although temperaments and practical constraints do not change automatically. FRCP Rules 16 and 68 also promote nonlitigation resolutions in cases filed in federal court.

2. Technical details. The ERA reg-neg illustrates several technical issues. It is always a question, for instance, who pays—especially where citizen groups are involved. How many participants are too many? Federal rules may well directly affect thousands. What about the records of an ADR process (this issue applies equally to nonreg-neg cases)? ADR specialists typically try to keep as few records as possible and get the parties to contract to confidentiality, to avoid the disruptive possibility that information may be subpoenaed and used in other more litigious forums. (In some jurisdictions, a nascent "mediation privilege" is being recognized, analogous to an attorney-client privilege.)

And what about the administrative law consequences? Does reg-neg violate the delegation doctrine because nonofficials effectively make the decision?[25] Do split caucuses in reg-neg violate the ban on ex parte contacts with agency decisionmakers?[26] Will courts still feel obliged to scrutinize closely to assure that agencies gave a "hard look" to the facts and law?[27]

3. Evaluating ADR. Ultimately, evaluation of ADR depends not only on whether cases reach settlement, but also upon what it is intended to achieve. And different observers have very different views. Justice Burger wanted to unclog the courts. Professor Fiss discerns a questionable political goal "to insulate the status quo from the judiciary."[28] Professors McThenia and Shaffer likewise focus on more holistic goals, quoting Socrates: "Justice is what we discover—you and I—when we walk together, listen together, and even love one another, in our curiosity about what justice is and where justice comes from."[29] (Fiss replied that he's as much for love as anybody, but dispute resolution has broader goals and constraints.) Are a governing system's needs adequately fulfilled when the interests of all parties involved in a particular conflict are satisfied, or are there further systemic goals such as establishing precedent?

E. THE IMPETUS TO SELF-GENERATED CORPORATE COMPLIANCE

In recent years, with the exponential growth in the scope and complexity of the environmental laws, the debate over the effectiveness of environmental enforcement has entered a new phase. As even those responsible for environmental enforcement have come to recognize, a major change has taken place in the attitudes and business priorities of American business:

> Even the most curmudgeonly old enforcer must recognize . . . that the general attitudes of the regulated sector have altered over time. Deliberate efforts to evade environmental controls have become rarer (although by no means unknown), the importance attached to compliance has increased, and the resources and management attention devoted to the environmental protection has greatly expanded. Environmental management was once commonly considered a nuisance activity to be conducted and supervised as a corporate backwater function. It has now taken a much more central role, becoming a core part of many companies' management

---

25. Susskind argues that it doesn't because agency officials have the last word. 3 Yale J. Reg. at 158.
26. Perritt argues that it doesn't. Negotiated Rulemaking before Federal Agencies: Evaluation of Recommendations by the Administrative Conference of the United States, 74 Geo. L. Rev. 1625, 1697 (1986).
27. Susskind argues that the hard look will be satisfied if the reg-neg incorporates notice; equal footing, including funding of citizens; reasonable record; round-robin review of the final draft; full discussion of comments; procedural equality; clear statement of agency negotiation positions; and an opportunity for all parties to sign off on the final rule. 3 Yale J. Reg. at 164. Cf. Wald, Negotiation of Environmental Disputes: A New Role for the Courts?, 10 Colum. J. Envtl. L. 1 (1985).
28. Fiss, Out of Eden, 94 Yale L.J. 1669, 1670 (1985).
29. McThenia & Shaffer, For Reconciliation, 94 Yale L.J. 1660, 1665 (1985).

E. Self-Generated Corporate Compliance

structures. Diamond, Confessions of an Environmental Enforcer, 26 Envtl. L. Rep. 10252, 10254 (1996).

Because environmental compliance has now made the transition from a corporate backwater function to a top business priority, what implications does this have for the future of environmental enforcement? Because many corporations are now reducing emissions and achieving compliance on their own initiative, will this self-generated compliance continue, or is the credible threat of continued governmental and citizen enforcement still required in order to "induce" compliance?

> **Triggers for Self-Generated Corporate Environmental Compliance:**
> 1. permitting and reporting,
> 2. SEC disclosure requirements for public companies,
> 3. satisfying corporate management information needs,
> 4. borrowing for ongoing business needs, and
> 5. purchasing or selling a business or property.

1. The Five Primary Triggers for Environmental Compliance

Today, buyers, sellers, borrowers, and lenders almost invariably confront environmental issues when engaging in their regular business activities. While the magnitude of potential liability, and the likelihood of its occurrence, may be greater in certain business sectors (e.g., chemical manufacturers) than in others, the scope of environmental regulation now covers almost every type of property or business. Environmental risks, costs, and benefits have become a factor in virtually every transaction.

Environmental issues typically arise in connection with five key types of business events that trigger attention to the need for environmental compliance in order to avoid environmental liabilities and risks. These five triggers are summarized and detailed below:

a. Permitting and Reporting

Hundreds of thousands of dischargers and waste management facilities are subject to the permit programs established under federal and state environmental laws.[30] Permits define and facilitate compliance and enforcement by transforming generally applicable limitations promulgated by governmental enforcers (e.g., "discharges shall be treated in accordance with BAT") into specific obligations, including a timetable for compliance for the individual discharger. Permits thus provide an effective means of assuring that the permittee is on notice of its obligations as spelled out in the permit, that regulators are notified of releases and discharges by permitters as required by the terms of the permit, and that the specific requirements applicable to a particular discharge or activity are identified and clarified.

By applying federal and state requirements to individual pollution sources and hazardous waste management activities, permits play a crucial role, and the inability or failure to obtain a necessary permit can be fatal to business operations. Thus, obtaining permits in the first instance, and then complying with their reporting and other standards, are key events triggering attention to environmental concerns. For these reasons, the need to obtain and comply with permits is taken as a given by business executives today.

---

30. Federal statutes creating one or more permit systems include CAA §110(a)(2), 42 U.S.C. §7410(a)(2); CWA §412(b), 33 U.S.C. §1342(b); SDWA §1422(b), 33 U.S.C. §300h-1(b); and RCRA §3006(b), 42 U.S.C. §6929(b). State agencies will issue the permits either when EPA has delegated its authority to implement a program to the state, or when the state has adopted an independent regulatory program.

b. SEC Disclosure Requirements for Public Companies

There are two events that may trigger a company's duty to disclose certain of its environmental liabilities under the federal securities laws. First, disclosure may be required as part of a publicly held company's mandated securities filings. See Regulation S-K, 17 C.F.R. pt. 229. Second, disclosure may be required when a company is subject to SEC Rule 10b-5, an anti-fraud rule that usually comes into play as a result of a company selling its securities, such as in a stock purchase agreement in which the company makes representations and warranties concerning its operations, its compliance with laws, and other material facts in the agreement. The importance of compliance with these disclosure obligations is detailed below.

Frank Friedman and David Giannotti, Environmental Self Assessment, in Environmental Law Institute, Law of Environmental Protection

7-28 to 7-33 (1998)

Publicly held companies must also identify environmental problems to ensure timely and accurate reports under the securities and exchange laws and SEC regulations. An SEC finding that a company failed to disclose environmentally related matters, thereby deceiving investors, could jeopardize the company's ability to raise capital through new stock offerings or debt instruments. It can also result in SEC initiation of costly and time-consuming administrative proceedings. Any such action by the SEC can give rise to shareholders' class actions and derivative suits. Thus, SEC enforcement of environmental laws and regulations, although indirect, is potentially more powerful than that of direct agency enforcement of environmental laws and regulations. Included within the scope of required SEC reporting are environmentally related matters, such as: (1) two-year estimates of capital expenditures for environmental compliance, or for a longer period if such estimates have been developed and a failure to disclose would be misleading; (2) particular types of environmental proceedings; and (3) circumstances under which companies must disclose their policies or approaches concerning environmental compliance.

With respect to proceedings, any governmental administrative or judicial proceedings arising or known to be contemplated under any federal, state, or local provisions regulating the discharge of materials into the environment or otherwise relating to the protection of the environment must be disclosed if any one of three conditions exist. Any private or governmental proceeding that is material to the business or financial condition of the corporation must be reported. Any private or governmental proceeding for damages, potential monetary sanctions, capital expenditures, deferred charges or charges to income is reportable if the amount involved (exclusive of interest and costs) exceeds 10 percent of the current assets of the corporation. And any governmental proceeding must be reported if monetary sanctions (exclusive of interest and costs) will or reasonably are expected to exceed $100,000. . . .

The SEC's May 1989 interpretative release concerning the disclosure required in Management's Discussion and Analysis of Financial Condition and Results of Operations (MD&A) in SEC filings further details the scope of disclosure. The MD&A release states

E. Self-Generated Corporate Compliance 831

that "once management knows of a potentially material environmental problem, it must disclose it unless it can determine that the problem is not reasonably likely to cause a material effect, either because the event is not likely to happen or if it does happen, the effect is not likely to be material."[31] Thus, in preparing SEC filings, data developed during routine assessments and assessments made for acquisition and sale of properties becomes important. . . .

The basis for measuring environmental liability is very important and is worth quoting in detail.

In measuring its environmental liability, a registrant should consider available evidence including the registrant's prior experience in remediation of contaminated sites, other companies' cleanup experience, and data released by the Environmental Protection Agency or other organizations. Information necessary to support a reasonable estimate or range of loss maybe available prior to the performance of any detailed remediation study. Even in situations in which the registrant has not determined the specific strategy for remediation, estimates of the costs associated with the various alternative remediation strategies considered for a site maybe available or reasonably estimable. While the range of costs associated with the alternatives may be broad, the minimum clean-up cost is unlikely to be zero. SEC Staff Accounting Bulletin No. 92. . . .

[The] tightening interpretation of what financial information must be disclosed greatly increases the potential liability exposure for failure to disclose or properly accrue. Legal involvement is critical as these issues are examined. . . .

c. Satisfying Corporate Management Information Needs

Environmental considerations are also triggered by a company's corporate management information needs, which can include financial planning, risk management, the setting of appropriate accounting reserves, consideration of new product lines, and the acquisition of appropriate amounts and type of insurance coverage for environmental risk.

Assume, for example, that, in developing a new product line, a company will be developing a product utilizing a new chemical substance. Under ToSCA (see Chapter 15), a company would need to consider whether there maybe limitations on the product's use or safety associated with the product's manufacture or processing. Such concerns obviously affect the cost of the product and the ability to market it. Alternatively, assume that a company seeks to establish, under RCRA (see Chapter 17), that it can provide the financial assurance necessary to operate a TSD facility. Evaluation of environmental risks may be essential to establishing that the company qualifies as financially responsible, including covering (through bonds, insurance, and the like) both closure and post-closure costs. As another example, assume that a company is seeking to open another facility. Under the CAA, the company must identify whether the new facility will be in an attainment or nonattainment area, a factor that can affect preconstruction review. Similarly, the company must evaluate whether, under CERCLA (see Chapter 16), the new facility maybe near a waste disposal site requiring potential cost and expense of remediation.

As the Frankel article below concludes, sound corporate management especially requires gathering information to address the needs of company auditors. The reporting of environmental contingencies is now a permanent part of the financial landscape within which a business must operate.

---

31. SEC Act Release No. 6835, 54 Fed. Reg. 22,427 (May 24, 1989)

Stuart B. Frankel, Full Disclosure: Financial Statement Disclosures under CERCLA

3 Duke Environmental Law & Policy Forum 57, 65-67 (1993)

Companies typically prepare their financial statements in accordance with Generally Accepted Accounting Principles (GAAP). GAAP is a hierarchy of accounting standards promulgated by various professional accounting bodies, most notably the Financial Accounting Standards Board (FASB) and the American Institute of Certified Public Accountants (AICPA). SFAS-5 is the primary source of guidance available to companies for estimating and disclosing environmental liabilities in their financial statements.

SFAS-5 uses probabilities to determine the likelihood that a loss contingency will eventually be realized. There are three levels of probability at which a contingency may be classified by a business entity:

1. Probable. The future event or events are likely to occur.
2. Reasonably possible. The chance of future event or events occurring is more than remote but less than likely.
3. Remote. The chance of the future event or events occurring is slight.

SFAS-5 delineates appropriate treatment of financial statements based upon each contingency classification. If a loss contingency appears probable and the amount of the loss can be reasonably estimated, the contingency "shall be accrued by a charge to income." This means the estimated amount will be recognized as a loss as well as disclosed in the financial statement. If the loss cannot be estimated but the likelihood of it occurring is probable, the contingency should be disclosed with an explanation of why no estimate can be made. If the loss is reasonably possible, accrual of the expense is not required, but disclosure of the nature of the contingency and an estimate of the potential loss is necessary. Finally, if the contingency is classified as remote, there is generally no impact reflected in financial statements.

In Appendix A to SFAS-5, FASB gives several examples of the application of SFAS-5 to specific situations. With respect to Superfund disclosures, the most appropriate example is set out under the heading "Litigation, Claims, and Assessments." In the discussion, SFAS-5 indicates that the decision to accrue and/or disclose a loss that may result from pending and potential litigation should be based in large part on the "degree of probability of an unfavorable outcome." Several factors are listed that should be considered in assessing the probability of litigation outcome:

> The nature of the litigation, claim, or assessment, the progress of the case . . . , the opinions or views of legal counsel and other advisers, the experience of the enterprise in similar cases, the experience of other enterprises, and any decision of the enterprise's management as to how the enterprise intends to respond to the lawsuit, claim or assessment. . . .

Once it is determined that an unfavorable litigation outcome is either probable or reasonably possible, the company must derive an estimate for disclosure. In the context of Superfund, that task is even more challenging. Factors such as the number of PRPs, their respective financial resources, joint and several liability, allocation of liability to each PRP, existence of insurance coverage, time frame of the investigation, and related litigation all make the estimation process very difficult and imprecise. Added to the obstacles posed by the estimation process is the fact that companies are generally loath to report information that may attract negative publicity, especially if it is not clear that the loss or other liability will materialize. Consequently, disclosure policies among companies regarding environmental contingencies vary greatly. . . .

E. Self-Generated Corporate Compliance

d. Borrowing for Ongoing Business Needs

In order to continue existing operations, to expand to new operations, or to meet capital obligations, companies must consider borrowing to satisfy their ongoing business needs. As a practical matter, without such financing, many private undertakings cannot be pursued.

Lenders typically seek information about environmental issues affecting the property or business that is the subject of the contemplated loan; it is extremely important for both creditworthiness considerations and assessment of potential collateral. Conducting a due diligence investigation, or requiring the borrower to conduct one as a condition precedent to the loan, is often a necessity for assessing, to the extent possible, the value of the property. Likewise, a borrower's ability to repay the loan may be impaired if the borrower must spend significant sums to comply with environmental laws or to clean up historic contamination.

Representations and warranties can be used by a lender to create a mechanism in the event of default should the representation turn out to be false; representations and warranties also can be used to cut off a borrower's ability to make further draws under a revolving credit facility, when something has happened during the term of the loan and the borrower is no longer able to reaffirm the validity of the representations as would be required at the time of the draw request. Also, representations can be used to elicit due diligence information on the target company. Lenders typically require the borrower to provide notice of certain events during the life of the loan (such as receipt of a notice of violation or an information request pertaining to off-site disposal of hazardous substances) to enable the lender to reevaluate its position in light of new events.

In lending for ongoing business needs, lenders are also concerned about their own potential liabilities under the environmental laws. In 1996, after several years of lobbying by the financial services and real estate industries, Congress adopted significant amendments to CERCLA's security interest exemption in an effort to limit the risks to lenders arising from the environmental liabilities of their borrowers.[32] Nonetheless, concerns about lender liability persist, adding additional motivation to lenders' desire to require their borrowers to engage in environmental compliance.

e. The Purchase and Sale of a Business or Real Estate

Under CERCLA, and some analogous state laws, present owners of real property may be strictly liable for remediation of contamination that exists on or beneath, or that flows from, acquired property, despite their lack of participation in or knowledge of activities that caused the contamination. Common law damage actions by neighboring landowners based on common law trespass, nuisance, or negligence grounds may also be brought against the present owners on the theory that they are continuing the tortious interference. In addition, compliance deficiencies and enforcement actions that are directed at ongoing conduct may become the burden of new owners either of the property or of the operations that are maintained on the property. Thus, one who acquires a corporation that owns real

---

32. These amendments were codified in the Asset Conservation, Lender Liability, and Deposit Insurance Protection Act of 1996 (Act), which essentially codified into law EPA's Lender Liability Rule pertaining to the scope of the secured creditor exemption under CERCLA, See Final Rule on Lender Liability under CERCLA, 57 Fed. Reg. 18,344 (Apr. 29, 1992). That rule had not enjoyed smooth going in the courts. In February 1994, the D.C. Circuit struck down that rule, concluding that Congress made the federal courts, not EPA, the ultimate arbiter of CERCLA's liability provisions. See *Kelley v. EPA*, 15 F.3d 1100 (D.C. Cir. 1994), reh'g denied, 25 F.3d 1088 (D.C. Or. 1994). Thereafter, Congress passed the Act, which defines what is (and what is not) "participation in management" sufficient to subject a lender to CERCLA liability. See 42 U.S.C. §9601(20)(E)-(G).

property or an entity that merges or consolidates with a corporate property owner may, in appropriate circumstances, succeed to the liabilities of the predecessor.

Identifying, analyzing, and allocating the risks of these potential liabilities among the parties to the purchase or sale of a business or real estate brings environmental considerations into virtually every transaction. The assessment and allocation of the risks of a transaction requires an understanding of both the nature of the environmental liabilities and the types of contract provisions available for incorporation into an agreement as a mechanism for risk allocation among the parties to the transaction. Examples of the types of contract provisions available for allocation of financial responsibility and risk include (1) purchase price adjustments, (2) cost-sharing arrangements, (3) escrowed monies, (4) representations and warranties, (5) indemnification provisions, and (6) conditions precedent and subsequent to the transaction.

Increasingly, buyers are requiring, as a condition precedent to transactions, that environmental risks be identified and either eliminated or minimized before a transaction will close. This type of contractual provision implements the buyer's requirement that, before closing, a property or business come into compliance with the environmental laws, so that the buyer may avoid or limit environmental liability and risk. A simple example of such a condition precedent to closing, in a real estate transaction in Illinois, is set forth below.

> Environmental Remediation. . . . Seller has advised Purchaser that environmental remediation has commenced on the Property. Such remediation shall be subject to the following conditions:
> (a) Seller has advised Purchaser that Seller is undertaking remediation of certain hazardous contamination on a portion of the Property, with the goal that, upon completion of such remediation, the Property will not pose a threat to Purchaser's intended use of the Property or to the environment. Seller shall seek to obtain a letter from the Illinois Environmental Protection Agency (IEPA) confirming that no further remediation of said contamination will be necessary with respect to the Property (the IEPA Letter).
> (b) Seller shall pay all costs associated with the remediation of the Property. In the event that Seller cannot accomplish the site remediation (including the delivery to Purchaser of the IEPA Letter) by (date), Purchaser may elect any of the following options: (i) to terminate the Contract, in which event the escrowee shall release the earnest money and all interest earned thereon to Purchaser immediately and neither party shall have any further obligations or liabilities to each other hereunder; (ii) to waive receipt of the IEPA Letter, provided all site remediation has otherwise been completed and Purchaser has given at least ten (10) business days advance written notice of such waiver; or (iii) to extend in writing the date by which the site remediation may be completed and the IEPA Letter obtained to (date).

This contractual provision is a form of self-generated compliance. Buyers are increasingly insisting that businesses and properties that are the target of a transaction come into compliance with federal and state environmental laws before the transaction can proceed. From the buyer's perspective, achieving compliance beforehand is obviously preferable to participating in a transaction that exposes the buyer to potential governmental or citizen enforcement.

COMMENTARY & QUESTIONS

1. SEC Guidance regarding climate change disclosures. On January 27, 2010, pursuant to its authority under Regulation S-K of the Securities Act of 1933, the SEC voted to issue an interpretive release to provide guidance on existing climate change disclosure obligations. The SEC's January 27, 2010 decision (by a vote of 3-2) reflected the view that

E. Self-Generated Corporate Compliance

public companies need assistance in determining their disclosure obligations in light of the changing legislative and regulatory landscape concerning climate change. Following that vote, the SEC then published, on February 2, 2010, a new interpretive release, which informed companies of their obligations to disclose both the positive and negative impacts of climate change on their businesses.[33]

In its interpretive release, the SEC addressed four particular categories of information that reporting companies should take into account when deciding whether to include information in Management's Discussion and Analysis of Financial Condition and Results of Operations. First, the SEC concluded that, when assessing potential disclosure obligations, a public company should consider whether the impact of existing laws and regulations regarding climate change is material. Second, the SEC concluded that a public company should consider, and disclose when material, the risks or effects on its business of international accords and treaties relating to climate change. Third, the SEC concluded that companies should consider legal, technological, political, and scientific developments regarding climate change that may cause new opportunities or risks for companies (such as new legislation and regulation that could cause a shift in consumer demand for products that create or reduce greenhouse gas emissions). Finally, the SEC concluded that management must also disclose material information about the physical consequences of climate change on a company's business (for example, varying sea levels, changing weather patterns, and the availability and quality of water, which may disrupt a company's supply lines, affect costs, affect access to certain resources, or damage property and equipment).

In issuing this interpretive release, did the SEC, in fact, make substantive changes in existing disclosure law? Although the majority of the Commissioners emphasized that there was no intent to change or modify existing law (including materiality standards), the two dissenting Commissioners asserted that the SEC has now "taken sides" in the policy debate about climate change, and that reporting companies and investors will pay the price in terms of additional compliance costs and in inundation of information of questionable value. In issuing the interpretive release, did the SEC engage in impermissible speculation as to the possibility of potential legislation and international treaties? Again, the dissenters claimed that this was the case, contending that the SEC is now seeking disclosure of information that only "might" be relevant. Finally, and more broadly, was this interpretive release necessary? The dissenters expressed the view that the interpretive release was not necessary, on the grounds that there is no evidence of systemic deficiencies with respect to environmental disclosures. But the majority of Commissioners determined otherwise, concluding that the changing legislative and regulatory landscape relating to climate change warranted the interpretive release.

How will the foregoing disagreements among the SEC Commissioners affect the debate about the need for environmental enforcement with respect to climate change issues? Have any changes in business practices developed as a result of the SEC's decision to issue the interpretive release requiring these disclosures pertaining to climate change?

2. The disparity between EPA reporting and SFAS-5 disclosures. SEC reporting requirements have historically been more stringent than GAAP. For an SEC registered

---

33. The SEC took this action, aware that an increasing number of companies already incorporate climate change issues in their existing SEC disclosures. The SEC has also repeatedly been asked to clarify when climate-related risks should be disclosed. In 2009, for example, a group of investors with over $1.4 billion under management petitioned the SEC to expand disclosures pertaining to climate change. Two years earlier, a group of investors and state government officials filed a similar petition also seeking an expansion of disclosure concerning climate change.

company, there can be a significant disparity between information disclosed in its SEC filings and information disclosed under GAAP in the Notes to the Consolidated Financial Statements. For a company not subject to the SEC reporting requirements, this often means that environmental contingencies either are not disclosed or are underdisclosed in the financial statements. See Frankel, Full Disclosure: Financial Statement Disclosures Under CERCLA, 93 Duke Envtl. L. & Pol'y F. 57, 70-71 (1993).

3. Private arrangements for loss allocation. What is the relationship of private agreements that shift or allocate losses and the law's allocation of liability? For example, can a generator PRP escape liability through an indemnity agreement with a transporter or TSD operator, or could a seller, by agreement, agree to assume the CERCLA liability of the facility purchaser? CERCLA §107(e)(l), despite seeming ambiguity, gives a perfectly clear answer, "yes and no." It states:

> No indemnification, hold harmless, or similar agreement or conveyance shall be effective to transfer from [a PRP] to any other person the liability imposed under this section. Nothing in this subsection shall bar any agreement to insure, hold harmless, or indemnify a party to such agreement for liability under this section.

As the courts eventually realized, the statute does not allow private arrangements to limit the legal liability of the parties, which would plainly contravene the statute's policy, but the statute expressly allows the enforcement inter sese of the parties to those private agreements. In short, private arrangements for post-liability loss shifting are allowed and can be enforced. See, e.g., *AM Int'l v. International Forging Equip. Corp.*, 982 F.2d 989 (6th Cir. 1993); *Jones-Hamilton v. Beazer Materials & Servs., Inc.*, 973 F.2d 688 (9th Cir. 1992).

2. Due Diligence, Audits, and Other Avenues Toward Voluntary Compliance

As business events trigger the need for environmental compliance, companies have increasingly relied on two key tools to evaluate such compliance: environmental due diligence and environmental audits.

Environmental Due Diligence. Due diligence has long been standard practice for companies considering the purchase of the stock, assets, or real estate of a target company. In the environmental context, due diligence essentially involves the examination of a company's compliance with environmental requirements and the assessment

> **Evaluating Voluntary Environmental Compliance:**
>
> - Environmental due diligence
> - Environmental audits

of the target's potential or contingent environmental liabilities. The information obtained from the due diligence investigation maybe used for different purposes by the various parties to the transaction. For example, due diligence may reveal potential problems that will make a target unattractive to the buyer and suggest abandoning the transaction. Alternatively, it may allow the purchaser to negotiate adjustments to the price, to change the structure of the deal, or to redraft other important contractual provisions,[34] seeking to

---

34. In May 1993, the American Society for Testing and Materials (ASTM) promulgated standards for environmental site assessments, or environmental due diligence investigations. The first standard sets out a "Transaction Screen" process for commercial property transactions where environmental problems are unlikely to be of major concern. See ASTM, Standard Practice for Environmental Site Assessment, Transaction Screen Process, E-528-93. The second standard is designed for use in transactions where a more thorough inquiry into environmental issues

E. Self-Generated Corporate Compliance

satisfy the "appropriate inquiry" requirement of CERCLA's innocent purchaser defense. See CERCLA §101(35)(A), 42 U.S.C. §9601(35)(A). ASTM has also produced a guide to due diligence inquiry, providing checklists for document reviews and questionnaires for use in environmental due diligence reviews.

Environmental due diligence also helps a potential lender determine whether to proceed with a loan. It permits a lender to assess whether contingent environmental liabilities may impair a borrower's ability to repay the loan or damage the borrower's credit rating, making it difficult or impossible for the lender to sell the loan. It also enables the lender to identify any environmental contamination that could affect the desirability of foreclosing on property or affect securing the loan. Furthermore, an environmental due diligence investigation can serve to alert the purchaser or lender to present or future environmental problems that may require management or remedial action.

Recently, environmental due diligence has included not just a focus on potential environmental pitfalls, but also a focus on previously latent environmental benefits. New tools are being developed to measure both positive and negative environmental factors impacting a company's valuation. Methodologies have been employed, for example, in certain recent acquisitions, that measure greenhouse gas emissions, water use, waste management, forest products consumption, and primary chemicals use. By this means, a target company's business activities are assessed, including the potential not only for risk mitigation, but also for cost savings and revenue expansion. This approach allows for an evaluation of not just how a company has been doing, but also how well it will do in the future, including its ability to cope with the potential regulation of carbon dioxide emissions and other climate change factors. For more on this development, see Miller, The Cost of Clean, The Deal Magazine, April 21, 2010, at pp. 1-4.

Environmental Audits. Environmental audits are somewhat more formal and extended than due diligence inquiries. EPA defines an environmental audit as a "systematic, documented, periodic and objective review by regulated entities of facility operations and practices related to meeting environmental requirements."[35] An audit represents a "snapshot" of a company's environmental compliance at a moment in time, enabling a company to assess its state of environmental compliance and to identify what, if anything, is necessary to achieve full compliance. Audits generally involve a review of past and present operations; the history of compliance with federal, state, and local environmental laws; permits; waste practices; disclosure and reporting practices; operations and processes; budgets for environmental expenditures; and developing environmental strategies.

EPA generally considers the need for penalties in the context of a company's good faith efforts to comply with environmental laws and regulations. Although the existence of an audit program is not a mitigating factor, EPA may consider honest and genuine efforts of regulated entities to avoid and promptly correct violations discovered through audits when fashioning penalties for regulatory violations.

While the existence of an auditing program may have a mitigating effect in enforcement proceedings, there is also a risk that an audit report may be used against a company in administrative, civil or criminal enforcement actions. Consequently, both EPA and DOJ have been reluctant to provide explicit assurances that the results of any audits will not be used as the basis for criminal prosecution. Historically, EPA's position has been that it is free to seek disclosure of internal environmental audit reports on a case-by-case basis.

---

is necessary. See ASTM, Standard Practice for Environmental Assessments; Phase I Environmental Site Assessment Process, E-527-93.

35. EPA Environmental Audit Policy Statement, 51 Fed. Reg. 25,004, 25,005 (July 9, 1986).

In July 1991, DOJ issued a long-awaited guidance document entitled "Factors in Decisions on Criminal Prosecutions for Environmental Violations in the Context of Significant Voluntary Disclosure of Compliance Efforts by the Violator." To promote self-auditing, self-policing, and voluntary disclosure of environmental regulation by the regulated community, the DOJ delineated several factors that it will review in considering whether, and to what extent, to prosecute criminally under the environmental laws.

In recent years, EPA and DOJ policies have come under close scrutiny. There is significant concern in the business community that the risk that environmental audit reports may be used against a company in enforcement proceedings is a disincentive to candid, self-evaluative environmental auditing. As a result, numerous states have enacted statutes establishing a privilege for environmental audit reports and granting immunity from prosecution for violations discovered by an environmental audit and then promptly fixed and reported to appropriate authorities. In general, three conditions must be met under most state audit-privilege laws in order to invoke the privilege or qualify for reduced penalties or immunity: (1) the regulated entity must conduct an audit that uncovers environmental violations, (2) the entity must voluntarily report the violations to authorities within a certain period of time, and (3) the entity must expeditiously correct the violation.

In December 1995, EPA responded to the concerns raised in the business community that environmental audit laws will be used on the federal level to assist in enforcement proceedings. EPA replaced its 1986 Environmental Audit Policy Statement with a new guidance document (effective January 22, 1996) entitled "Incentives for Self-Policing: Discovery, Disclosure, Correction and Prevention of Violations" (Incentives Policy).[36] The Incentives Policy does not provide absolute protection from discovery or an evidentiary privilege. Instead, the policy provides that EPA will not request or use an environmental report to initiate a civil or criminal investigation, but if EPA has an independent reason to believe that a violation has occurred, EPA may seek any information relevant to identifying violations or determining liability or extent of harm. The Incentives Policy provides only that EPA will seek reduced civil fines if certain outcomes are met (e.g., the company discovers the violation through a self-audit, voluntarily discloses the violation within 10 days, corrects the violation promptly, and cooperates with EPA) and will not refer the matter for criminal enforcement if certain other criteria are met (e.g., EPA determines that the violation does not involve a corporate philosophy or practice, or does not involve higher level corporate involvement in, or willful blindness to, the violation).

Rather than aligning with the trend in the states toward developing audit privileges, however, EPA remains staunchly opposed to such privileges. In the Incentives Policy, EPA has stated its opposition to any state legislation that jeopardizes the fundamental interest in assuring that violations of federal law do not threaten the public health or the environment, or make it profitable not to comply. EPA has further stated that it reserves its right to bring independent action against regulated entities for violations of federal law that threaten human health or the environment, reflect criminal conduct, represent repeated noncompliance, or allow one company to make a substantial profit at the expense of its law-abiding competitors. EPA has also requested that some states revise existing audit-privilege laws and has informed certain states that failure to amend privilege and immunity laws may jeopardize their federally delegated authority.

---

36. Incentives for Self-Policing: Discovery, Disclosure, Correction, and Prevention of Violations—Final Policy Statement, 60 Fed. Reg. 66,706 (Dec. 22, 1995); see also ELR Admin. Mat. 135639. In addition, on June 3, 1996, EPA issued a policy designed to provide small businesses with an incentive to conduct environmental audits and engage in compliance activities. See 61 Fed. Reg. 27, 984 (June 3, 1996).

E. Self-Generated Corporate Compliance

COMMENTARY & QUESTIONS

1. EPA and audit privileges. Critics view EPA's actions limiting the scope of protection it will allow to information discovered through environmental audits as an attempt to coerce states into rescinding, altering, or declining to enact audit-privilege legislation. One pair of commentators has in the past referred to this type of opposition by EPA as "delegation blackmail" because EPA has in the past threatened to rescind delegation of enforcement authority in states where audit privileges immunize many of the violations uncovered in the audit. See Wilkins & Stroman, Delegation Blackmail: EPA's Use of Program Delegation to Combat State Audit Privilege Statutes 11, 16th Annual RCRA/CERCLA and Private Litigation Update, A.B.A. Sec. Nat. Res., Energy & Envtl. L, 25th Annual Conference on Environmental Law (Dec. 12-13, 1996).

2. Citizen groups and environmental audits. The citizen's right of access to information is often forgotten in the debate over environmental audits. Local citizen groups have fought extensively for greater access to information about corporate environmental compliance, and these groups are reluctant to concede to business any additional control over information on corporate compliance with environmental regulations. Citizen groups view business' desire for self-regulation as a means to avoid environmental disclosure, on the ground that providing business with more secrecy for environmental audits is like the "fox guarding the hen house." Can the views of citizen groups be reconciled with the desire of business to monitor its own compliance with the environmental laws? Could an auditing privilege be fashioned that excludes audits as admissible evidence in civil suits or government enforcement actions but still allows the results to be available to the public?

3. Corporate infighting over environmental principle? Environmental law creates some unusual twists in corporate law as well as every other part of the field it touches. Imagine a publicly held lumber company run for generations on principles of sustain-able silviculture, conserving its mountain acreage, cutting selectively, and enjoying a mutually rewarding partnership with the local communities that supply its workforce. Then comes a Wall Street raider who launches a hostile takeover planning to strip the company of its capital assets and clearcut the forests with no thought of sustainability, to maximize short-term profits, close down the company, and move on. Are there principles of corporate law taking account of such severe environmental consequences that could be mobilized to fend off the raider? See the Pacific Lumber corporate law materials on the coursebook Web site.

4. Striking the right enforcement balance. Simply doing business in the United States today involves engaging in activities that trigger material attention to environmental concerns. The development and increasing use of environmental due diligence and auditing, as tools to measure and enhance compliance efforts, reflect these realities. Marketplace priorities have changed. Industry is internalizing new environmental priorities because the business risks and costs of environmental noncompliance are a fundamental factor in business planning; and there is a growing awareness within the federal government and the states that certain types of cooperative approaches with the regulated community have their place in furthering environmental enforcement and compliance. But even if more cooperative approaches are desirable, does that cooperation still need to be tempered by the threat of credible environmental enforcement? In answering this question, consider the remarks of former EPA Administrator William D. Ruckelshaus, who has observed that "environmentalism is here to stay" and "paying attention to the environmental impact of technology or processes benefits the bottom line." See Ruckelshaus, Stopping the Pendulum, Envtl. F, Nov./Dec. 1995, at 25-26.

19

Environmental Criminal Law

A. Tactical Rediscovery of Criminal Provisions: The 1899 Refuse Act
B. An Increasing Tendency to Prosecute Environmental Crimes
C. Criminal Liability: Problems of Knowledge and Intent
D. Problems Raised in Corporate and Executive Prosecutions

Criminal punishment is an ancient societal instinct and includes the levying of fines, imprisonment, and corporal punishments, including death. In legal process terms, the criminal law is often a crude blunt instrument, in comparison to civil remedies. Yet, even in highly developed modern regulatory systems, the force of the criminal law remains an important functional component. In environmental law, despite its highly developed civil and administrative complexity and the growing culture of compliance within the industrial community, the importance of criminal law continues to grow.

Prior to the 1960s, virtually no criminal law was applied in environmental cases. In the late 1960s and early 1970s, although statutes such as the federal Refuse Act raised the prospect of criminal fines, and some violators of the newly amended federal Clean Water Act were in fact sanctioned with substantial criminal fines, no one went to jail. By the late 1970s and early 1980s, the federal government, and prosecutors in some states, were becoming increasingly sophisticated in using evidence from a variety of sources, including civil litigation, in seeking meaningful criminal sanctions.[1] Typical prosecutions at this time involved false statement cases based upon the failure to report toxic discharges. Still, short of life-threatening acts, prosecutors rarely sought jail time for criminal violations of the environmental laws. By the 1990s, however, criminal prosecution of the environmental laws was much more vigorous. Even when environmental crimes did not directly endanger health or safety, prosecutors were much more likely to seek jail time for those convicted of felonies.[2] Today, it is not unusual for convicted environmental defendants to face actual personal

---

1. Largely in response to Love Canal and other notorious waste sites, Congress amended RCRA in 1980 by strengthening its criminal provisions, resulting in the first federal felony penalties for an environmental crime. See 42 U.S.C. §6928. In the 1980s, CERCLA was enacted and also included substantial criminal penalties. See 42 U.S.C. §9603.
2. In the years following environmental catastrophes (like the massive oil spill by the *Exxon-Valdez* in 1989, or the recent *Deepwater Horizon* oil spill that began in 2010 off the coast of Louisiana), public opinion tends increasingly to favor criminal prosecutions and harsh penalties. For example, right after the *Exxon-Valdez* spill, criminal

time in jail as well as large punitive fines that cannot be charged to insurance or deducted from income taxes as business expenses. Moreover, U.S. EPA's criminal enforcement activities have increasingly become both more sophisticated and more international in focus, now even including responses to environmental terrorism.[3]

The Public Policy Objectives of Criminal Law

Criminal law seeks to punish bad actors in order to accomplish several different public policy objectives not so directly involved in civil law:

- incapacitation (the prevention of repeat offenses by holding perpetrators in prison or controlled probation);
- specific deterrence, by making the defendant apprehensive about future conduct;
- general deterrence, by showing other potential culprits that crime does not pay;
- revenge and retribution, through physical and fiscal punishment, for defendants' bad actions; and
- rehabilitation (although, in some settings, this is merely theoretical).

Regulatory enforcement attorneys consider the utility of potential criminal charges in designing their enforcement agendas, despite the increased difficulties of proof. All the listed rationales for criminal punishment can apply in environmental prosecutions, and to the list should be added the "club-in-the-closet" function: For environmental regulatory agencies, the background threat of criminal sanctions against violators strongly reinforces negotiations on administrative civil penalties, and compliance.

Criminal prosecutions, more than civil, reflect the governing moral climate of the moment. Criminal law was enlisted in legal efforts to protect the environment when a broadened environmental consciousness infiltrated the general public. Although for some Americans, "Throw the bums in jail" was always at least as natural as "Sue the bastards" as a gut reaction to many pollution controversies, only since the 1980s have environmental prosecutions ceased being rare occurrences. However, the broad availability of criminal punishment remains important practically as well as conceptually. Often criminal proceedings proceed parallel to civil proceedings brought by citizen plaintiffs or the government, with obvious tactical consequences.

Although there originally was a lack of federal criminal prosecution, states have always had general crimes such as battery and homicide that could have been applied. Today, however, most of the major federal environmental statutes contain criminal penalty provisions along with civil penalties. Many other state and federal penal laws with potential application to environmental cases, particularly those in the area of public health, still remain underutilized. Nevertheless, as detailed below, criminal law prosecutions of environmental offenses play an increasing and special role in the legal system's response to problems of pollution and environmental quality.

---

enforcement became the fastest growing enforcement component at EPA, as EPA made it a top priority to prosecute the worst polluters and target the most significant threats to public health and the environment.

3. For example, in 2001, EPA provided assistance to the FBI in response to the September 11 2001 attacks at the World Trade Center and the Pentagon, as well as helping to address the anthrax contamination of Capitol Hill buildings, U.S. Postal Service facilities, and other sites.

A. Rediscovery of Criminal Sanctions

Federal Environmental Crimes, By Statute

The list of federal statutes having environmental criminal provisions continues to grow. As detailed below, these statutes basically fall into two primary categories—those providing for the prosecution of acts involving pollution ("Pollution Crimes"), and those providing for the prosecution of acts involving wildlife ("Wildlife Crimes")—

Pollution Crimes:

- Act to Prevent Pollution from Ships (APPS), 33 U.S.C. §§1901-1912
- Atomic Energy Act, 42 U.S.C. §§2011-2296
- Clean Air Act (CAA), 42 U.S.C. §§7401-7671
- Comprehensive Environmental Response, Compensation & Liability Act (CERCLA), 42 U.S.C. §§9601-9675
- Deepwater Port Act, 33 U.S.C. §§1501-1524
- Emergency Planning and Community Right to Know Act (EPCRA) (also known as SARA Title III), 42 U.S.C. §§11001-11050
- Energy Supply and Environmental Coordination Act, 15 U.S.C. §§791-798
- Federal Hazardous Material Transportation Law, 49 U.S.C. §§5101-5127
- Federal Insecticide, Fungicide and Rodenticide Act (FIFRA), 7 U.S.C. §136-136y
- Federal Water Pollution Control Act (FWPCA) (also known as the Clean Water Act (CWA)), 33 U.S.C. §§1251-1387
- Noise Control Act, 42 U.S.C. §§4901-4918, 42 U.S.C. §4910 (criminal provision)
- Ocean Dumping Act (ODA), 33 U.S.C. §§1401-1445
- Outer Continental Shelf Lands Act (OCSLA), 43 U.S.C. §§1331-1356
- Ports and Waterways Safety Act, 33 U.S.C. §§1221-1236
- Rivers and Harbors Appropriations Act, 33 U.S.C. §§401-467
- Resource Conservation and Recovery Act (RCRA), 42 U.S.C. §§6901-6992k
- Safe Drinking Water Act (SDWA), 42 U.S.C. §§300f-300j-26
- Surface Mining Control and Reclamation Act (SMCRA), 30 U.S.C. §§1201-1328
- Toxic Substances Control Act (ToSCA), 15 U.S.C. §§2601-2692

Wildlife Crimes:

- Endangered Species Act, 16 U.S.C. §§1531-1544
- Bald and Golden Eagle Protection Act (BGEPA), 16 U.S.C. §668
- Migratory Bird Treaty Act (MBTA), 16 U.S.C. §703-712
- The Lacey Act, 16 U.S.C. §§3371-3378

A. TACTICAL REDISCOVERY OF CRIMINAL PROVISIONS: THE 1899 REFUSE ACT

Here is an illuminating example of how criminal laws lingering on the statute books can have dramatic application in the environmental setting.

The first federal environmental statute (known as The Rivers and Harbors Act of 1899, commonly known as the "Refuse Act") prescribed, in pertinent part, misdemeanor penalties for depositing, without a permit, any refuse matter of any kind or description whatever into the navigable waters of the United States or their tributaries. Nonetheless, the Refuse Act remained virtually unused for decades.

In the 1960s, however, with the reawakening in the United States of significant interest in environmental protection, environmental activists rediscovered the Refuse Act, and they read its terms with pleased anticipation:

33 U.S.C. §407. Deposit of Refuse in Navigable Waters Generally. It shall not be lawful to throw, discharge, or deposit or cause, suffer, or procure to be thrown, discharged, or deposited either from or out of any ship, barge, or other floating craft of any kind, or from the shore, wharf, manufacturing establishment, or mill of any kind, any refuse matter of any kind or description whatever other than that flowing from streets and sewers and passing therefrom in a liquid state, into any navigable water of the United States, or into any tributary of any navigable water from which the same shall float or be washed into such navigable water . . . or on the bank of any tributary of any navigable water, where the same shall be liable to be washed into such navigable water . . . whereby navigation shall or may be impeded or obstructed: Provided, That . . . the Secretary of the Army, whenever in the judgment of the Chief of Engineers anchorage and navigation will not be injured thereby, may permit the deposit of any material above mentioned in navigable waters, within limits to be defined and under conditions to be prescribed by him. . . .

33 U.S.C. §411. Penalty for Wrongful Deposit of Refuse: Use of or Injury to Harbor Improvements, and Obstruction of Navigable Waters Generally. Every person and every corporation that shall violate or that shall knowingly aid, abet, authorize, or instigate a violation of the provisions of . . . this title shall be guilty of a misdemeanor, and on conviction thereof shall be punished by a fine of up to $25,000 per day, or by imprisonment (in the case of a natural person) for not less than thirty days nor more than one year, or by both such fine and imprisonment . . . one-half of said fine to be paid to the person or persons giving information which shall lead to conviction.

COMMENTARY & QUESTIONS

1. The Refuse Act. With the explosion in the late 1960s of environmental consciousness in the media and the electorate, a number of prosecutions were begun across the country as U.S. Attorneys responded by invoking the provisions of the Refuse Act. In part, the Refuse Act's strategic novelty was due to the fact that it even existed as an actionable pollution statute, not that it was criminal. Most activists in the 1960s had presumed that there were no existing environmental laws with teeth in them, and that legal action would therefore have to await further legislative action. But by invoking the Refuse Act, prosecutors were able to go immediately against a wide range of defendants, from small dumpers to major corporations, obtaining convictions quickly and decisively, and levying substantial fines. Consequently, in the years right before and following the creation in 1970 of the EPA, the Refuse Act enjoyed a renaissance. At the same time, however, the American Chamber of Commerce and the National Association of Manufacturers began to urge repeal of the Refuse Act. Ultimately, with the passage of the Federal Water Pollution Control Act of 1972 and later the passage of RCRA in 1976 (and RCRA's amendments in 1980), these other federal statutes took over most of the Refuse Act's pollution coverage, and the enforcement of the Refuse Act again became relatively infrequent. For a time, however, the Refuse Act was undoubtedly the nation's most direct and effective environmental statute.

2. Ease of prosecution. If you were an environmentally minded U.S. Attorney in the 1960s, and the Refuse Act was brought to your attention along with bottles and samples of muck from a particular water pollution outfall pipe, why would you find your case against

A. Rediscovery of Criminal Sanctions

the suspect dumper so easy to prove? Note first of all the geographical scope of the statute. To what geographical areas does it not apply? To what polluting materials does it apply? Is it clear that it applies to liquid pollutants? And what are the elements of the criminal offense? Virtually no dischargers had obtained a permit from the U.S. Army Corps of Engineers. Not much more had to be proved. The Supreme Court helped by holding, in *United States v. Republic Steel Corp.*, 362 U.S. 482, 491 (1960), that the Act meant what it said in plain words: Pollution was "refuse," and where there were doubts, the Act should be read "charitably in light of the purpose to be served." (What was the 1899 Act's purpose?) What about the question of criminal *mens rea* or intent? Section 411 contains the requirement that defendants who aid and abet must be acting "knowingly," but that seems to apply only to aiding and abetting, not to direct violations of §407. To what extent can we punish persons who did not know what they were doing was wrong? What does *knowing* mean? Does it mean that a person was not acting unconsciously? Does it mean that a defendant must know that she does not have a permit and that federal law requires one? These questions are considered later in this chapter.

3. Citizen prosecution—qui tam? If federal (and potentially state) prosecutors decline to prosecute a particular action, for whatever prosecutorial discretion reason, the violation is unlikely to be criminally prosecuted. In some circumstances, citizens attempted to obtain prosecution of particularly egregious polluters by seeking to file qui tam actions themselves against polluters. The qui tam action is a traditional remedy by which a citizen can bring a lawsuit "in the name of the King," particularly where the citizen has a direct personal stake in the prosecution. The potential reward offered in §411 of the Refuse Act appears to be sufficient to establish a standing basis for citizen prosecutors. As it happened, the courts were generally inhospitable to citizen qui tam actions under the Refuse Act, so that initiation of prosecution depended upon political, social, and media pressures applied to prosecutorial authorities.

4. Statutory interpretation issues. What is "refuse"? If it includes pollution (which is indeed a leap of sorts), what about the argument that it does not include oil spills because oil is a valuable commodity that is not being disposed of as waste, but rather was lost by accident? See *United States v. Standard Oil Co.*, 384 U.S. 224 (1966). As the courts developed the doctrines of the Refuse Act, ultimately even temperature changes came to be regarded as "refuse" and thereby as violations of the statute.

What does the Refuse Act teach about the life history of statutory enactments? Industrial corporations were the primary targets of Refuse Act prosecutions in the 1960s. Is there any question in your mind what would have happened if someone had told the Congress in 1899 that the statute would be applied against manufacturers producing liquid pollution wastes?

A criminal statute is a potent piece of legislatively created law. As applied, however, it can be both a crude blunt instrument and a relatively unguided missile. The words that it embodies continue to be law while surrounding circumstances may change. The legislators who write a statute do not thereafter act as judges determining how it should be applied; the separation of powers sees to that. If the words of the statute are perfectly clear, its application follows, even 70 years after the statute was written. If the citizen activists who pushed prosecutions of the Refuse Act knew that the legislature that had passed the law intended that it have no application to circumstances like pollution, were they being unethical in seeking prosecutions under the Act?

5. Permits. Even if prosecutions under the Refuse Act were not certain to follow, many polluters in the 1960s understandably wanted to avoid the possibility of being prosecuted and consequently started seeking permits from the Corps of Engineers to cover their effluent outfall pipes. Under the terms of the statute, can or must the Corps of Engineers' Chief of Engineers issue permits? Must a permit's issuance or denial be based solely on questions of anchorage and navigation, or can the Corps include other public concerns such as pollution, especially after 1970, when NEPA became law? NEPA declared, in broad terms, the responsibility of all federal government agencies to improve environmental quality. See *Zabel v. Tabb*, 430 F.2d 199 (5th Cir. 1970). Must the Corps of Engineers base its permit issuance on considerations of public health and environmental quality?

6. Implied civil remedies? Injunctions? Why did the 1898 Congress make violation of the Refuse Act a criminal offense rather than providing for civil penalties, damages, and injunctions? Can a court that finds a polluter in violation of the criminal offense tack on civil remedies such as injunctions and damages as well, by "implying civil remedies" from the penal statute? Some 1960s Refuse Act cases did so. *United States v. Jellico Indus.*, 3 BNA Env't Rep. Cas. 1519 (M.D. Tenn. 1971).

7. Juries. In virtually all environmental prosecutions, the defendants will have the right to a jury. How is that likely to affect the course and outcome of criminal proceedings? Is it any surprise that most of the reported criminal appellate cases are cases initially tried to a judge without a jury? In all probability, why were juries not requested in those cases?

Prophesying jury reactions and jury verdicts has become a major feature of the defense attorney's art. Besides the individual proclivities of each juror, there are situational differences that can have great bearing. How dramatic is the environmental consequence of the indicted offense? How readily can the jury see itself in the role of the defendant rather than the victims? What deference attaches to corporate white collar defendants? Is jury nullification—always a possibility in the Anglo-American jury system—a reasonable tactic, or is the jury's hyper-vindictiveness rather to be feared?

8. The effectiveness of the Refuse Act. The initial impact of the Refuse Act was extraordinary in getting the attention of American polluters. Why does criminal law have this effect? In reality, not many executives can expect to go to jail, and their corporations certainly can be expected to pay any individual fines that corporate officers are assessed in criminal prosecutions. Conviction of a criminal offense, even a misdemeanor, seems to attach some special stigma to corporate officials, unlike civil penalties that are often merely perceived as a cost of doing business. Even though the chance of being convicted may be relatively small, the uncertain possibility is something that no executive lives with easily.

Some of the provisions of the Refuse Act were amended by the CWA, which established a more direct, comprehensive federal water pollution control system, albeit with less decisive teeth than the Refuse Act. Some of the provisions of the Refuse Act set out here are still in force. Ten to fifteen major Refuse Act prosecutions are initiated each year by the Department of Justice, mostly under §407. According to one federal prosecutor, the old statute has major advantages over comparable provisions of the modern CWA. Under the latter statute, for example, defendants can gain immunity from prosecution by self-reporting; the Refuse Act includes no such immunity. The Act continues to serve as an indication of the perils and potential of environmental criminal statutes.

9. Questioning the effectiveness of criminal prosecutions. What particular effectiveness does a criminal statute add to the system of pollution laws? Often environmental crimes are "accidental." In such cases, is it clear that criminal penalties are appropriate? When criminal prosecutions are filed, they certainly pack a punch. But when do they constitute overkill? Criminal fines bear no necessary relationship to the amount of harm caused by pollution, and they are not paid into a pollution control fund. Jail sentences can vary widely from judge to judge, although now the federal sentencing guidelines (discussed later in this chapter) provide an advisory scheme that arguably reduces the variations between sentences for similar offenses.

Even in the most dramatic cases, criminal prosecutions pose logistical and political problems. For example, the *Exxon-Valdez* oil spill of March 24, 1989 was at that time the worst oil spill in the history of the United States, with environmental consequences that to some extent remain irreparable even today. Social and economic dislocations have likewise been drastic. It now appears probable that the Alaska spill was not caused only or even primarily by the known alcoholism of the tanker's captain. At least in part, there also appears to have been a consistent course of corporate conduct shortcutting safety procedures, cutting back on necessary shipboard personnel to save on payrolls, and perhaps even using financial incentives to encourage ships to run at higher speeds regardless of weather and water conditions. If these and other assertions were proved true and causative, the corporation and its officers would face criminal charges under the Refuse Act §407 and other federal statutes, as well as state laws. But the wreck was not an intentional act; it was "accidental." What further purpose was served by criminal prosecution, especially in light of the civil costs and loss of goodwill that the corporation had already sustained? What does it say about environmental criminal prosecutions that both the federal and Alaska state governments strenuously avoided criminal trials against Exxon, Alyeska, and their executives?[4] By contrast (as discussed later in this chapter), the 2010 *Deepwater Horizon* oil spill is now the worst oil spill in our history, and criminal, as well as civil, prosecutions have been a major focus of both federal and state governments. In light of the readings below, consider why that shift in focus has resulted in an increasing willingness to prosecute serious, pervasive, and well-publicized environmental crimes.

B. AN INCREASING TENDENCY TO PROSECUTE ENVIRONMENTAL CRIMES

People v. Film Recovery Systems, Inc., Metallic Marketing Inc., Charles Kirschbaum, Daniel Rodriguez, Steven O'Neil

Circuit Court, Cook County, Illinois, Fourth Division No. 83-11091
(involuntary manslaughter); No. 84-5064 (murder), June 14, 1985
Oral Verdict from the Bench

BANKS, J. This court is being reconvened this afternoon in order for me to render a decision in the case against Film Recovery Systems, Inc., Metallic Marketing Systems, Inc., Steven O'Neil, Charles Kirschbaum, and Daniel Rodriguez.

The record should be clear the defendants are charged with the following offenses: Steven O'Neil, Charles Kirschbaum, and Daniel Rodriguez are charged by way of indictment No. 84 C-5064 with murder as defined in Chapter 38 Section 9-1-a-2, that being "A person who kills an individual without lawful justification commits murder if, in performing the acts which cause the death, such person knows that such acts create a strong

---

4. The federal government ultimately negotiated a criminal settlement out of court with Exxon, by which a fine of $100 million was remitted down to $25 million in light of the civil responsibility the defendant had taken on. Captain Hazelwood was not prosecuted under the federal water pollution act because the CWA provides immunity for self-reported acts, and Hazelwood had self-reported the spill when he had radioed the Coast Guard, "Uh . . . we seem to have got stuck on Bligh Reef, and are losing a little oil. . . ."

probability of death or great bodily harm to the individual or another." Also, the defendants Film Recovery Systems, and Metallic Marketing Systems, Inc. are charged by way of indictment No. 83 C-11091 with involuntary manslaughter and fourteen counts of reckless conduct. Also, Steven O'Neil, Daniel Rodriguez, and Charles Kirschbaum are charged in the same indictment with fourteen counts of reckless conduct.

Before I render a decision in this case, I would like to set forth some of the reasons for my decision. I would like to make it known and make it perfectly clear that the reasons I state are not the total basis for my decision in this case. My decision in this case is based on total review of all evidence presented in this case by both the State and Defense. . . .

During my deliberations and evaluations of all the evidence, let it be known that I never forgot the most important concept in criminal law, that being the defendants are presumed innocent and that it is the burden of the State that they must prove guilt beyond a reasonable doubt.

I hereby make the following findings: No. 1: Stefan Golab died of acute cyanide toxicity. I arrived at that conclusion in the following way: many witnesses testified to the conditions of the air in the plant; not only workers, but independent witnesses as well, such as insurance inspectors, OSHA inspectors, Environmental Protection Agency inspectors, police officers and other service representatives. The testimony of the police investigators is the most important because although we do not know the actual amount of hydrogen cyanide gas in the air on February 10, 1983, the date of the death of Stefan Golab. . . . The symptoms were classical symptoms, which, according to the Material Safety Data Sheet, would occur if exposed to hydrogen cyanide gas at high levels — nausea, burning throat, burning eyes, difficulty breathing, plus others.

No. 2: I believe also the Medical Examiner, because in the Medical Examiner and toxicologist reports, the victim had a blood cyanide level of 3.45 micrograms per milliliter, which is a lethal dose and can be fatal. The manufacturer states that sodium cyanide . . . when mixed with a weak alkali, with water in this case, having a pH of approximately seven, will create hydrogen cyanide gas.

I find that the conditions under which the workers in the plant performed their duties was totally unsafe. There was an insufficient amount of safety equipment present on the premises. There were no safety instructions given to the workers. The workers were not properly warned of the hazards and dangers of working with cyanide. The warning signs were totally inadequate. The warning signs were written in Spanish and English. The warning signs stated the words "poison," or "veneno" meaning poison in Spanish. The problem with that is that . . . aside from the Spanish and American workers, there was Stefan Golab, plus other Polish workers. The evidence has shown that Stefan Golab did not speak English, could not read or write English, so a sign in Spanish had no benefit to that man at all.

The Cyanogran label . . . states that there are three ways in which cyanide can be fatal; one being inhalation of the gas hydrogen cyanide, one being ingestion of sodium cyanide, and third, the absorption into the skin of the sodium cyanide. . . . This was not told to the workers. . . .

I also find the defendants were totally knowledgeable in the dangers which are associated with the use of cyanide. . . . The defendants knew that the workers were becoming nauseated and vomiting. The workers complained to all three of the defendants. Steven O'Neil knew hydrogen cyanide gas was present. He knew hydrogen cyanide gas, if inhaled, could be fatal. Charles Kirschbaum saw workers vomiting. He was given a Material Safety Data Sheet. He read the label, and he knew what it said. He said that he did not wear the same equipment the workers did because he did not do the same work as the workers, even though he testified to the contrary. . . . I also find that Steven O'Neil, who was the President of Film Recovery Systems and Metallic Marketing Systems, was in control and exercised control over both Film Recovery Systems and Metallic Marketing Systems before and after the death of Stefan Golab, which was on February 10, 1983.

Using all the facts stated above and all other evidence pertinent to this case, I find that the conditions present in the work place which caused sickness and injury to workers was reckless conduct. I also find that the death of Stefan Golab was not accidental but in fact murder. I also find that the defendants created the conditions present in the plant by their acts of omission and commission. . . .

Therefore, it is the decision of this Court that the defendants Steven O'Neil, Charles Kirschbaum and Daniel Rodriguez are guilty of murder both as individuals and also as officers and high managerial personnel of Film Recovery Systems and Metallic Marketing Systems, Inc. I also find that they are guilty of murder and reckless conduct. . . .

I also find that because of the negligence and reckless behavior of both Film Recovery Systems, Inc. and Metallic Marketing Systems . . . the corporations are guilty of involuntary manslaughter and fourteen counts of reckless conduct. . . .

Finally, and this is the most important part and most difficult part for a Judge, I believe because the cloak of innocence has been removed from the accused and because the charge of murder, which the defendants have been found guilty of, does not carry probation and carries a minimum of twenty years in the penitentiary, it is my duty to revoke all bail and the defendants shall be remanded to the custody of the Sheriff's Office, awaiting sentencing, and it is the order of this Court that the bonds be revoked.

At this time, gentlemen, I am going to set a date for sentencing. . . .

Steven Ferrey, Hard Time: Criminal Prosecution for Polluters
10.4 Amicus Journal 11 (Fall 1988)

On the surface, it was a model company. It recycled valuable minerals from waste materials, and had a stellar record on hiring minorities. But beyond the facade lurked a darker, more ominous, and deadly story.

Film Recovery Systems . . . extracted trace amounts of silver from hospitals' discarded X-ray film by using sodium cyanide. In its heyday, the company employed eighty workers and earned about $18 million annually. But in its unventilated workroom, employees hunched over 140 bubbling, foaming cauldrons of sodium cyanide. They were issued no protective gear and were not instructed in safety measures. While manually stirring these vats, sodium cyanide slopped over the sides, soaking the workers' clothing and skin. The air was choked with the fumes of hydrogen cyanide gas.

Film Recovery employed illegal Mexican and Polish immigrant laborers almost exclusively in its silver-recovery process. . . . Few workers spoke English; even fewer could read. The common antidote for cyanide poisoning, amyl nitrite, was not available at the facility. Even the skull-and-crossbones warning labels on the drums of the cyanide were covered over or obscured by management. One day in February 1983, Stefan Golab, a Polish immigrant, stumbled into the lunchroom, fell to the floor with nausea, and died from acute cyanide poisoning. He was fifty-nine years old. . . .

Jay Magnuson, of the Cook County State's Attorney's Office [who obtained the original indictments] prosecuted Film Recovery President Steven O'Neil, the plant manager, and the foreman, for murder. "Callously, they knowingly maintained an unsafe plant environment that was likely to cause death to workers," Magnuson remarks. "I never had a second thought that they should be convicted for murder." . . .

Investigators later discovered almost 15 million pounds of cyanide waste from Film Recovery that had been dumped illegally in rented truck trailers parked in other parts of Illinois. The EPA used $4.5 million of taxpayer's funds to clean up this toxic debris. Decontamination of the facility cost the building's landlord $250,000.

[Before Film Recovery,] jail sentences for polluters were unheard of. At worst, the penalty for violating environmental or workplace safety laws was a modest fine. On the remote chance of getting caught, the fines could be rationalized as just another cost of doing business.

But times are changing. Federal and state laws covering hazardous waste, clean air, clean water, and workplace safety impose stiff civil and criminal penalties of up to $25,000 per violation. Like expanding reflections in a carnival mirror, one transgression magnifies into multiple dimensions. A single polluting action can violate several laws simultaneously, and each day of violation is counted by the courts as if it were a new violation. A single act of pollution becomes a serious and compounded felony. "Corporate America will readily take notice of environmental statutes when they start going to jail for their violations," says Glenn Sechen, assistant prosecutor for Cook County. "It simply ceases to be a cost of doing business when it becomes their own necks."

The impact of environmental prosecution has been refocused on individuals. The protective wall between corporate actions and corporate executives is eroding. . . . The U.S. Department of Justice has brought criminal indictments against 328 individuals and 117 corporations for environmental pollution. The courts have imposed 203 years of jail time and collected $12 million in fines. Sixty-four years of those sentences already have been served. Of those sentenced, about one-third were corporate presidents, 12 percent were vice-presidents, an additional 5 percent were corporate officers, and 20 percent were managers or foremen. Less than 25 percent of those sentenced to jail were the workers who actually released the pollution.

How high in the corporate hierarchy prosecutions reach is a function of employee cooperation in providing evidence against co-workers. An emerging lesson is that the middle of a large corporate ladder can be a perilous place to perch in a company that ignores environmental requirements. At the lower end of the corporation, the "Nuremberg defense" can be an effective escape. Prosecutors are reticent to indict lower-level personnel who claim that they unknowingly were "just following orders" when breaking an environmental law.

Correspondingly, in large corporations, the top-level management may not have direct knowledge of polluting activities. The buck often stops on the desk of middle-level managers, identified by employees as the ones giving the orders to engage in polluting activities. Ironically, a large corporation, with a diffuse management structure and unclear lines of responsibility, may shield executives from potential criminal liability.

In a survey of environmental prosecutions on the East Coast . . . the typical company cited was small, employing less than fifty persons. . . . About a quarter are dismissed before a verdict, about half result in guilty pleas by defendants, and of the remaining cases that proceed through a trial, three quarters result in convictions while about a quarter result in acquittals.

Despite successful prosecutorial records in several states, most local prosecutors do not actively pursue criminal environmental polluters. The barriers can be daunting. "Judges understand a smoking gun and a bag of heroin as criminal. They do not understand environmental pollution," laments Lieutenant Gary Long of the Illinois State Police environmental unit—some prosecutors argue privately that criminal court judges, experienced in dealing with common criminals, are uncomfortable with prosecution of executives in

B. Prosecuting Environmental Crimes

Gucci loafers [and with] the very large penalties in environmental statutes ($25,000 per violation per day)....

Problems of proof can be substantial. Documenting the facts and dates of actual polluting activities can prove elusive without help from informants. Allegations against criminal defendants must be proved beyond reasonable doubt. Not all convictions result in jail sentences, and not all jail sentences actually are served. Liberal use of suspended sentences, immediate probation, sentences served on weekends only, and other "innovative" programs mitigate the service of "hard" time. A typical jail sentence is about sixty to ninety days.

Environmental criminals often qualify for treatment that Lynch describes as "commit a crime, go to your room." With jails overcrowded, convicted executives typically fit the profile for release programs: they have ties to the community, references from prominent persons, and are not violent or likely to flee. Consequently, some serve time by wearing an identification bracelet and confining their activities to their homes.

Despite practical problems, criminal prosecution has assumed center stage in environmental enforcement. For an executive, the prospect of incarceration with violent felons focuses the attention like few other sanctions. In return for no jail time, defendants often are willing to plead guilty to violations carrying very large fines.... Until the corporation also can serve time, criminal prosecution of individual corporate executives will remain the most potent weapon in the expanding arsenal of environmental enforcement.

COMMENTARY & QUESTIONS

1. The aftermath of the *Film Recovery* convictions. *Film Recovery* was a strategic environmental prosecution because of the dramatic way its precedent-setting homicide charge was covered by the press (the first time that a corporate executive had been prosecuted for murder in connection with environmental pollution). Less press attention was paid to the aftermath: Judge Banks sentenced Steven O'Neil to 25 years in jail for murder and reckless conduct, but after several unsuccessful appeals urging that the state homicide statute was preempted by the federal OSHA statute, an Illinois appellate court overturned the convictions in 1991. The court held:

> Because the offenses of murder and reckless conduct require mutually exclusive mental states, and because we conclude [that the trial court used] the same evidence of the individual defendants' conduct ... to support both offenses and does not establish, separately, each of the requisite mental states, we conclude that the convictions are legally inconsistent. *People v. O'Neil*, 550 N.E.2d 1090, 1098 (Ill. App. 1990).

Do you see the problem? In most states, murder in the first or second degree requires proof of an intent to kill, while negligent homicide (involuntary manslaughter) and the lesser charge of reckless conduct are based on unintentional harms. The trial judge may have based his verdicts on the wording of part of the Illinois murder statute, which seems to allow a murder conviction without intent to kill if a person "knows that such acts create a strong probability of death or great bodily harm to that individual or another," Chap. 720 ILCS 5/9-1, but the appeals court rejected that logic.

To avoid a retrial, the Film Recovery executives cut a deal. On the factual record found in Judge Banks's opinion, in 1993 O'Neil, Kirschbaum, and Rodriguez pleaded guilty to involuntary manslaughter. O'Neil served three years in prison, Kirschbaum got two years in prison, and Rodriguez received two years probation. Another executive, David McKay, pleaded down to one misdemeanor charge of reckless conduct, and received six months probation, 100 hours of community service, and a $1,000 fine. The new Cook County state's attorney apparently made the deals because he did not believe murder charges were warranted on these environmental facts. Given the murder count, it is not clear why the executives had not also initially been charged with involuntary manslaughter, instead of the lesser reckless conduct. (In this regard, note the remarkably different options available to state prosecutors in environmental cases, ranging here from reckless conduct, with simple misdemeanor fines, up to first degree murder for which O'Neil could theoretically have been executed.) With regard to criminal intent, how would you have chosen among the relevant variables of (1) whether to charge murder, (2) what range of penalties was appropriate, and (3) whether the fact that harm was caused by an indirect environmental exposure lessens the criminality of the act?

The media coverage of *Film Recovery*'s original murder convictions encouraged both federal and state prosecutions throughout the country for environmental crimes. In a more recent echo of *Film Recovery*, a district court in Idaho held industrialist Alan Elias, owner of Evergreen Resources, Inc., liable for knowingly exposing a worker to hazardous waste. *United States v. Elias*, No. CR 98-00070-E-BLW, 2000 WL 489732 (D. Idaho Mar. 16, 2000). The exposure, which resulted in brain damage to the employee, followed the defendant's order to wash down a 25,000-gallon tank of waste containing phosphoric acid and cyanide. This combination of chemicals produces a gas like that used in the World War II Nazi death camps. Elias was ordered to pay a criminal fine of $5.9 million.

By contrast, in May 2009, following an 11-week trial, a federal jury acquitted W.R. Grace and three of its former executives of charges that they violated the CAA by knowingly endangering and contaminating a small Montana town with asbestos from mining operations and by their conspiracy to cover it up. There was no doubt that the mine, operated by W.R. Grace from 1963 to 1990, was the source of the asbestos and that over 200 people had died, and hundreds of others were made ill, by asbestos related diseases, but the jury decided that the contamination was not criminal. The company faced millions of dollars of fines if convicted, and the executives faced prison time of up to 15 years on the most serious charges.

2. *Film Recovery* and preemption. What is your assessment of the reliability of law enforcement efforts by the federal OSHA in the *Film Recovery* case? Should the existence of OSHA preclude other remedies like the state's criminal charges? As Professor Ferrey has noted, "The tragedy of Stefan Golab's death is compounded by the fact that OSHA had given the firm a clean bill of health only months before. In the fall of 1982, OSHA inspectors visited the plant, but they never got past the front office, where they saw nothing out of the ordinary in the company's paperwork. They did not walk the additional 25 feet beyond the office doors to observe Golab and others hunched over gurgling vats of cyanide. After Golab's death, OSHA inspectors descended on the plant, fining management the seemingly arbitrary and insignificant amount of $4855. Film Recovery refused to pay, so OSHA reduced it by half, though to this day it has not collected."

Despite an agency's general fecklessness, however, defendants are sometimes successful in persuading courts that the existence of federal statutory remedies precludes and preempts application of general state criminal statutes. See *People v. Chicago Magnet Wire Corp.*, 510 N.E.2d 1173 (Ill. App. Ct. 1st Dist. 1987) (reversed in 1989 by the Illinois Supreme Court).

3. Trends in environmental criminal prosecutions. Environmental prosecutions have been heating up for many years on both the federal and state level, and that trend has continued. During the 1970s, under avowed conservationist Jimmy Carter, only 25 federal environmental prosecutions were commenced. Between 1982 and 1989 under Ronald Reagan's

B. Prosecuting Environmental Crimes

law-and-order policies, there were more than 450 indictments, more than 325 pleas or convictions, almost 100 of them against corporations, with assessed fines of over $13 million (although 20% or more of these appear to have been suspended) and jail terms of more than 200 years (mostly against noncorporate individual offenders), with nearly 65 years of jail time actually being served. Through the Clinton Administration years, the rate of criminal prosecutions continued to rise. The majority of environmental prosecutions, however, unlike *Film Recovery*'s murder indictment, were straightforward regulatory enforcement actions brought by state and federal agencies based on alleged violations of permits and statutory requirements under federal law, and their state equivalents.

In the Bush II and Obama Administrations, criminal prosecutions have become a standard, if not increasing, part of the enforcement arsenal, considered as a necessary backup to regulatory compliance programs.

The Increasing Tendency to Prosecute Environmental Crimes

As data collected by the U.S. EPA shows, environmental criminal prosecution has now become a standard part of environmental enforcement. In fiscal year 2011, for example, EPA's criminal enforcement program exceeded 2010 outcomes for new environmental crime investigations opened and the total level of incarceration, as shown by the chart below.

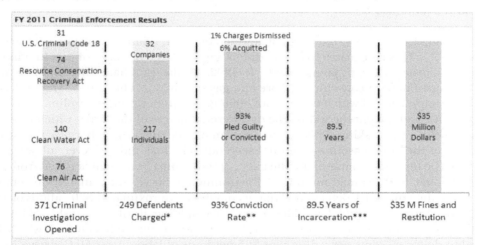

* 249 Criminal Defendants Charged: Eighty-seven percent of the charged cases included at least one individual defendant, as opposed to a company. The charging of individuals, where warranted by the evidence, is important, because the possibility of being incarcerated for an environmental crime provides significant deterrent effect.
** 93% Conviction Rate: The conviction rate was in line with EPA's historical average of approximately 90 percent. Defendants can be acquitted for a variety of reasons, e.g., found not guilty at trial or have convictions overturned on appeal, or charges can be dropped after exculpatory evidence in their favor was entered into the record.
*** The total level of incarceration in FY 2011 was reduced by 43 years as a consequence of prior Supreme Court decisions which made the U.S. federal sentencing guidelines discretionary rather than mandatory for use by federal district court judges.

As the chart indicates, 371 environmental crime cases were opened in 2011—a 7% increase from 2010. But there was also a decrease in the number of defendants charged (217 individuals and 32 companies)—a 14% decrease from the prior year. This resulted in a total of 89.5 years of incarceration and $35 million in fines and restitution.

Although criminal enforcement statistics from the EPA provide a quantitative picture of criminal enforcement results, they provide little insight into perhaps the more substantive question—whether the quality of justice resulting from environmental criminal enforcement has improved. Though useful, the bean counting of cases opened and criminal sanctions imposed does not necessarily measure true environmental progress.

C. Criminal Liability: Problems of Knowledge and Intent

Underlying the criminal enforcement of the environmental laws is an implicit question: How much "criminal intent," a.k.a. "*mens rea* knowledge" or "scienter," must be proved in order to convict a defendant of an environmental crime? Where a statute requires proof of a "knowing" or "willful" violation, how much knowledge does that mean? And what type of knowledge is required? (And where a statute contains no expressed requirement of knowledge or willfulness, like §411 of the Refuse Act, when can a defendant constitutionally be convicted without any proof of criminal intent?)

United States v. Ahmad
101 F.3d 386 (5th Cir. 1996)

Attique Ahmad appeals his conviction of, and sentence for, criminal violations of the Clean Water Act. . . . This case arises from the discharge of a large quantity of gasoline into the sewers of Conroe, Texas, in January 1994. In 1992, Ahmad purchased the "Spin-N-Market No. 12," a combination convenience store and gas station. . . . The Spin-N-Market has two gasoline pumps, each of which is fed by an 8000-gallon underground gasoline tank. Some time after Ahmad bought the station, he discovered that one of the tanks, which held high-octane gasoline, was leaking. This did not pose an immediate hazard, because the leak was at the top of the tank; gasoline could not seep out. The leak did, however, allow water to enter into the tank and contaminate the gas . . . [and] Ahmad was unable to sell from it. . . .

In October 1993, Ahmad hired CTT Environmental Services, a tank testing company, to examine the tank. CTT determined that it contained approximately 800 gallons of water, and the rest mostly gasoline. Jewel McCoy, a CTT employee, testified that she told Ahmad that the leak could not be repaired until the tank was completely emptied, which CTT offered to do for 65 cents per gallon plus $65 per hour of labor. After McCoy gave Ahmad this estimate, he inquired whether he could empty the tank himself. She replied that it would be dangerous and illegal to do so. On her testimony, he responded, "Well, if I don't get caught, what then?"

On January 25, 1994, Ahmad rented a hand-held motorized water pump from a local hardware store, telling a hardware store employee that he was planning to use it to remove water from his backyard. Victor Fonseca, however, identified Ahmad and the pump, and testified that he had seen Ahmad pumping gasoline into the street. Oscar Alvarez stated that he had seen Ahmad and another person discharging gasoline into a manhole. Tereso Uribe testified that he had confronted Ahmad and asked him what was going on, to which Ahmad responded that he was simply removing the water from the tank. . . . In all, 5,220 gallons of fluid were pumped from the leaky tank, of which approximately 4,690 gallons were gasoline. . . .

C. Problems of Knowledge and Intent

The gasoline discharged onto Lewis Street . . . entered a storm drain and . . . flowed through a pipe . . . into Possum Creek [which] feeds into the San Jacinto River, which eventually flows into Lake Houston. The gasoline that Ahmad discharged into the manhole . . . entered the city sewage treatment plant. . . . The plant supervisor ordered that non-essential personnel be evacuated from the plant and called firefighters and a hazardous materials crew to the scene. The Conroe fire department determined the gasoline was creating a risk of explosion and ordered that two nearby schools be evacuated. Although no one was injured as a result of the discharge, fire officials testified at trial that Ahmad had created a "tremendous explosion hazard" that could have led to "hundreds, if not thousands, of deaths and injuries" and millions of dollars of property damage. By 9:00 a.m. on January 26, investigators had traced the source of the gasoline back to the manhole directly in front of the Spin-N-Market. . . . The investigators questioned Ahmad, who at first denied having operated a pump. . . . Soon, however, his story changed: He admitted to having used a pump but denied having pumped anything from his tanks.

Ahmad was indicted for three violations of the CWA: knowingly discharging a pollutant from a point source into a navigable water of the United States without a permit, knowingly [discharging into a public sewage works] in violation of a pretreatment standard, and knowingly placing another person in imminent danger of death or serious bodily injury by discharging a pollutant. . . . [33 U.S.C.A. §1319 says that "any person . . . commits a felony . . . who knowingly violates" any of a number of other sections of the CWA [including §§1311(a), 1317(d), and 1319(c)(3) which comprise the three charges].

At trial, Ahmad did not dispute that he had discharged gasoline from the tank or that eventually it had found its way to Possum Creek and the sewage treatment plant. Instead, he contended that his discharge of the gasoline was not "knowing," because he had believed he was discharging water. . . .

The [jury] instruction on count one stated in relevant part: For you to find Mr. Ahmad guilty of this crime, you must be convinced that the government has proved each of the following beyond a reasonable doubt:

> (1) That on or about the date set forth in the indictment, (2) the defendant knowingly discharged, (3) a pollutant, (4) from a point source, (5) into the navigable waters of the United States, (6) without a permit to do so.

Ahmad contends that the jury should have been instructed that the statutory *mens rea*—knowledge—was required as to each element of the offenses, rather than only with regard to discharge . . . The principal issue is to which elements of the offense the modifier "knowingly" applies. . . . Ahmad argues that within this context, "knowingly violates" should be read to require him knowingly to have acted with regard to each element of the offenses. The government . . . contends that "knowingly violates" requires it to prove only that Ahmad knew the nature of his acts and that he performed them intentionally. Particularly at issue is whether "knowingly" applies to the . . . discharge's being a pollutant, for Ahmad's main theory at trial was that he thought he was discharging water, not gasoline. . . .

In *Staples v. United States*, 511 U.S. 600 (1994), the Court found that statutes criminalizing knowing possession of a machinegun require that defendants know not only that they possess a firearm but that it actually is a machinegun. . . . Statutory crimes carrying severe penalties are presumed to require that a defendant know the facts that make his conduct illegal. . . . In *United States v. Baytank (Houston), Inc.*, 934 F.2d 599 (5th Cir. 1991), we concluded that a conviction for knowing and improper storage of hazardous wastes . . . requires "that the defendant know . . . factually what he is doing: storing, what is being stored, and that what is being stored factually has the potential for harm to others or the environment, and that he has no permit. . . ." This is directly analogous to the interpretation of the CWA that Ahmad urges upon us. Indeed, we find it eminently sensible that the phrase "knowingly violates" in §1319, when referring to . . . offenses . . . should uniformly require knowledge as to each of those elements rather than only one or two. To hold otherwise would require an explanation as to why some elements should be treated differently from others, which neither the parties nor the caselaw seems able to provide. . . .

[Are] CWA violations . . . "public welfare offenses," under which some regulatory crimes have been held not to require a showing of *mens rea*[?] . . . The exception is narrow. . . . The possession of machineguns fell outside the exception. . . . [As] Staples held, the key to the public welfare offense analysis is whether . . . the defendant [is being punished for acts that are] traditionally lawful conduct . . . We hold that the offenses charged . . . are not public welfare offenses.

At best, the jury charge made it uncertain to which elements "knowingly" applied. At worst, and considerably more likely, it indicated that only the element of discharge need be knowing. The instructions listed each element on a separate line, with the word "knowingly" present only in the line corresponding to the element that something was discharged. . . . Knowledge was required only as to the fact that something was discharged, and not as to any other fact. In effect, with regard to the other elements of the crimes, the instructions implied that the requisite *mens rea* was strict liability rather than knowledge. . . .

We conclude that the instructions . . . withdrew from the jury's consideration facts that it should have been permitted to find or not find. . . . The district court's instructions . . . indicate that it thought "knowingly" modified only the element that something was discharged. . . . Ahmad's defense . . . was built around the idea that he thought water, rather than gasoline, was being discharged. A rational jury could so have found. . . .

We reverse Ahmad's convictions.

United States v. Weitzenhoff

35 F.3d 1275 (9th Cir, 1994), cert. denied, 115 S. Ct. 939 (1995)

Michael H. Weitzenhoff and Thomas W. Mariani . . . appeal their convictions for violations of the Clean Water Act . . . contending that the district court misconstrued the word "knowingly" under §1319. . . .

In 1988 and 1989 Weitzenhoff was the manager and Mariani the assistant manager of the East Honolulu Community Services Sewage Treatment Plant located not far from Sandy Beach, a popular swimming and surfing beach on Oahu. The plant is designed to treat some 4 million gallons of residential wastewater each day. . . .

Weitzenhoff and Mariani instructed two employees at the [East Honolulu sewage treatment] plant to dispose of [waste activated sludge] on a regular basis by pumping it from the storage tanks directly into the outfall, that is, directly into the ocean. The [sludge] thereby bypassed the plant's effluent sampler so that the samples taken and reported to Hawaii's Department of Health and the EPA did not reflect . . . some 436,000 pounds of pollutant solids being discharged into the ocean. . . . Most of the [] discharges occurred during the night. . . . Inspectors contacted the plant on several occasions in 1988 in response to complaints by lifeguards at Sandy Beach that sewage was being emitted from the outfall, but Weitzenhoff and Mariani repeatedly denied that there was any problem at the plant. . . . One of the plant employees who participated in the dumping operation testified that Weitzenhoff instructed him not to say anything about the discharges, because if they all stuck together and did not reveal anything, "they [couldn't] do anything to us." . . .

C. Problems of Knowledge and Intent

The district court construed "knowingly" in §1319(c)(2) as requiring only that Weitzenhoff and Mariani were aware that they were discharging the pollutants in question, not that they knew they were violating the terms of the statute or permit. According to appellants, the district court erred in its interpretation of the CWA and in instructing the jury that "the government is not required to prove that the defendant knew that his act or omissions were unlawful...."

As with certain other criminal statutes that employ the term "knowingly," it is not apparent from the face of the statute whether "knowingly" means a knowing violation of the law or simply knowing conduct that is violative of the law.... Our conclusion that "knowingly" does not refer to the legal violation is fortified by decisions interpreting analogous public welfare statutes. The leading case in this area is *United States v. International Minerals & Chem. Corp.*, 402 U.S. 558 (1971). In *International Minerals*, the Supreme Court construed a statute which made it a crime to "knowingly violate any . . . regulation" promulgated by the ICC . . . for the safe transport of corrosive liquids. The Court held that the term "knowingly" referred to the acts made criminal rather than a violation of the regulation, and that "regulation" was a shorthand designation for the specific acts or omissions contemplated by the Act. "Where . . . dangerous or deleterious devices or products or obnoxious waste materials are involved, the probability of regulation is so great that anyone who is aware that he is in possession of them or dealing with them must be presumed to be aware of the regulation."...

Parties such as Weitzenhoff are closely regulated and are discharging waste materials that affect public health. The International Minerals rationale requires that we impute to these parties knowledge of their operating permit.[5] This was recognized by the Court in *Staples v. United States*, 511 U.S. 600 (1994) . . . holding . . . that the government is required to prove that a defendant charged with possession of a machine gun knew that the weapon he possessed had the characteristics that brought it within the statutory definition of a machine gun. But the Court . . . explicitly contrasted the mere possession of guns to public welfare offenses, which include statutes that regulate "dangerous or deleterious devices or products or obnoxious waste materials," and confirmed the continued vitality of statutes covering public welfare offenses, which "regulate potentially harmful or injurious items" and place a defendant on notice that he is dealing with a device or a substance "that places him in responsible relation to a public danger. In such cases Congress intended to place the burden on the defendant to ascertain at his peril whether [his conduct] comes within the inhibition of the statute...."

The dumping of sewage and other pollutants into our nation's waters is precisely the type of activity that puts the discharger on notice that his acts may pose a public danger. Like other public welfare offenses that regulate the discharge of pollutants into the air, the disposal of hazardous wastes, the undocumented shipping of acids, and the use of pesticides on our food, the improper and excessive discharge of sewage causes cholera, hepatitis, and other serious illnesses, and can have serious repercussions for public health and welfare.

---

5. [In] *United States v. Speach*, 968 F.2d 795, 796-97 [(9th Cir. 1992)] . . . we held that 42 U.S.C. §6928(d)(1), which imposes criminal liability on parties who "knowingly transport . . . hazardous waste . . . to a facility which does not have a permit," requires that the transporter know that he acted in violation of the statute.... *Speach* recognizes the general rule that public welfare offenses are not to be construed to require proof that the defendant knew he was violating the law in the absence of clear evidence of contrary congressional intent, and finds only a narrow exception to this general rule . . . that the defendant was not the permittee but simply the individual who transported waste to the permittee, and . . . was not . . . in the best position to know the facility's permit status.

The criminal provisions of the CWA are clearly designed to protect the public at large from the potentially dire consequences of water pollution, and as such fall within the category of public welfare legislation. . . . The government did not need to prove that Weitzenhoff and Mariani knew that their acts violated the permit or the CWA. We affirm both the convictions. . . .

COMMENTARY & QUESTIONS

1. *Ahmad* and *Weitzenhoff*. Are these two cases inconsistent? The *Ahmad* court did not think so, concluding that *Weitzenhoff* "was concerned almost exclusively with whether the language of the CWA creates a mistake-of-law defense, [and did not address the] mistake of fact or the statutory construction issues raised by *Ahmad*." 101 F.3d at 390. If a jury decided that Ahmad truly did not realize that he was discharging gasoline, does the *Ahmad* decision make sense on mistake of fact grounds? (You may suspect that Ahmad actually did know he was discharging gasoline, but the court reminds us that this issue was contested and had not yet been decided by a jury.) Or would it be enough that he knew he was discharging something dangerous or illegal (which McCoy's evidence indicated), which would bring him closer to *Weitzenhoff*? The two cases also reach contrary conclusions about whether CWA violations are "public welfare offenses."

2. Differing criminal statutory liability standards. Federal environmental criminal statutes utilize different standards to establish criminal liability. Depending upon the federal statute at issue, the differing standards include:

The Spectrum of Federal Criminal Environmental Liability Standards

- Negligence,
- Knowledge,
- Willfulness, or
- Knowing endangerment

— negligence (the least stringent standard, found in the CWA), which imposes criminal penalties for "negligent" violations—see, e.g., CWA §309(c)(1);
— knowledge (found in the CWA as well as in the federal hazardous waste statutes, including RCRA, CERCLA and ToSCA), which make proof of knowledge a minimum prerequisite to criminal liability—see, e.g., CWA §309(c)(2); RCRA §3008(d); CERCLA §103(b); ToSCA §16(b);
— willfulness (found in ToSCA), for the purpose of assessing criminal penalties—see, e.g., ToSCA § 16(b); and
— knowing endangerment (found in RCRA and in the CWA), which augment criminal penalties for any offender who both knowingly violates certain provisions and, as a result, knowingly places another in imminent danger of death or injury—see, e.g., RCRA §3008(e)-(f); and CWA §309(c).

3. Degrees of knowledge. There is also a spectrum of interpretation of the different degrees of knowledge that may be applied, in those cases where a statute requires proof that defendants "knowingly" violated its provisions. The range analytically extends from defendants' mere consciousness of the fact of their physical action, to highly specific and willed violation of particular known laws. Here is a rough progression of possible interpretations of what amount of "knowledge" or "scienter" of defendants is required to be proved in order to convict:

C. Problems of Knowledge and Intent

(a) "Knowledge" only that they are doing a specific physical action,[6] while not realizing at all that the action happens to fit the description of a crime. (This is the lowest level of "knowledge," only requiring proof that they did the physical act consciously and amounts to liability with no proof of intent. Proof of at least this level of knowledge is probably necessary in every crime.)

(b) Knowledge of the identity of an instrument to some degree of specificity—e.g., knowing that a liquid being discharged is gasoline, or a toxic chemical, or a sludge—without knowing that dumping of such liquids is illegal or possibly harmful.

(c) Knowledge of a specific necessary element of a particular violation, as for discharges under an invalid permit, where defendants say they did not know the permit lacked validity.

(d) Knowledge, actual or constructive, that such an act might harm individuals or the public (with different degrees of probability ranging from trivial to high likelihood; this often constitutes a negligence-based rather than intent-based culpability).

(e) Knowledge that an act would harm individuals or the public, and specifically intending so to hurt them.

(f) Knowledge that an action is probably illegal because it may harm individuals or the public.

(g) Knowledge that an action is illegal and harmful, but not knowing what specific law is violated (this may also include different degrees of knowledge about degrees of seriousness of the offense, as in acting in the belief that a serious felony is just a trivial misdemeanor).

(h) Knowledge that what they are doing specifically violates a particular provision, e.g., "Hah, what I'm doing here will violate 40 C.F.R. §129.102(b)(3)(i) under 33 U.S.C.A. §1317(a)(2)!"

It is highly likely that virtually no defendants will have the highest degree of specialized knowledge. But the question is where a court will draw the line—based on statutory interpretation, the common law of a statute, and constitutional due process—defining the minimum necessary degree of proof of knowledge.

Defendants have regularly challenged courts to define knowledge requirements strictly. By contrast, the prosecution regularly argues for a more relaxed interpretation of such requirements, often contending that public welfare statutes must be interpreted liberally in order to fulfill their statutory purpose. Courts tend to accept decreased degrees of knowledge when the offense is recognized as a "public welfare offense" and tend to require greater degrees of knowledge when penalties are severe and include incarceration. When a court concludes the prosecution must prove "specific intent," however, it is not necessarily clear which kind of "knowledge" or specific intent is being required. Would the *Ahmad* court, after holding that Ahmad had to know his discharge was gasoline (on the mistake-of-fact defense), also require proof that he specifically knew Lake Houston was navigable and that Possum Creek flowed into it? Or that his pump was legally a "point source" (on a mistake-of-law defense)? If not, the court implicitly concedes that not all the elements of a crime must be known by the defendant in order to convict.

4. Is specific intent a proxy for "knowingly" violating the CWA? In *United States v. Metalite Corp.*, No. 99-008-CR-BIN, 2000 U.S. Dist. LEXIS 11507 (S.D. Ind. July 28, 2000), a federal district court discussed *Ahmad* and *Wilson* in the context of a mistake-of-fact defense in CWA criminal cases. The indictment charged the defendant Metalite Corp.

---

6. Acts of omission add another level of subtlety: Where defendants can violate a law by failing to act, how much in each case do they have to know of the duty to act and how it may be breached?

with "knowingly discharging and causing the discharge of a pollutant, chemical wastes . . . into waters of the United States" in violation of CWA §309(c)(2)(A), also known as 33 U.S.C. §1319(c)(2)(A). In rejecting the defendant's argument that the relevant sections of the CWA outline a specific intent crime, the court relied on decisions by five other circuit courts to analyze what constituted a "knowing violation" under the CWA:

> **BARKER, J.** . . . Although the words "knowingly violate" seem clear in the context of §1319(c)(2)(A) itself, their meaning is less clear when the statute is read as a whole. . . . When the CWA enforcement provisions are read as a whole, it seems likely that Congress intended "knowingly violates [certain sections]" to be "construed as a shorthand designation for specific acts or omissions which violate the Act." . . . The change by the amendment of the CWA's criminal intent language from "willful" to "knowing" suggests Congress did not intend a "knowing violation" to require specific intent of illegality. . . .
>
> None of the five Circuit Court opinions to address the issue of the CWA's *mens rea* requirement has held that a defendant must know he is violating the law or a permit to be convicted of a knowing violation of the CWA under §1319(c)(2)(A). Most share the view that "requiring the government to prove that a defendant knew he was violating the law or the conditions of a permit would allow defendants to assert a 'mistake of law' defense." . . . Drawing on the prevailing law in other circuits as described above, we are persuaded that §1319(c)(2)(A) does not create a specific intent crime and we therefore reject defendants' contentions. . . .
>
> For the reasons stated above, we find that the defendants are not entitled to dismissal of the indictment. We reject defendants' argument that the relevant sections of the CWA outline a specific intent crime and find that the indictment sufficiently communicates the offense being charged, as well as implies the correct scienter requirement, "knowingly," to the offense. . . .

5. Syntax as part of deciding which elements must be "knowingly" violated. In *United States v. Hoflin*, 880 F.2d 1033 (9th Cir. 1989), a city's Director of Public Works was convicted under RCRA §6928(d)(2)(A) of ordering his workers to take 14 barrels filled with waste highway paint to the grounds of the sewage treatment plant, dig a hole, and dump the drums in. Some of the drums were rusted and leaking, and at least one burst open in the process. The hole was not deep enough, so the employees crushed the drums with a front-end loader to make them fit, and they were then covered with sand. Hoflin appealed on the grounds that the jury should have been required to find that he knew the city did not have a permit to dispose of the barrels. RCRA §6928(d)(2)(A) provides:

> (d) **Criminal Penalties.** . . . Any person who . . . (2) knowingly treats, stores or disposes of any hazardous waste identified or listed under this subtitle 42 USCS §§6921 et seq. — (A) without a permit . . . ; or (B) in knowing violation of any material condition or requirement of such permit; . . . shall, upon conviction, be subject to [fines, imprisonment, or both].

The Ninth Circuit interpreted this provision only to require proof that Hoflin knew the paint wastes were hazardous, not to require proof that he knew there was no permit. The Third Circuit, in *United States v. Johnson & Towers, Inc.*, 741 F.2d 662 (3d Cir. 1984), decided the other way—at least as regards prosecution of subordinate employees, the "knowingly" requirement pours over from the first clause of subsection (d)(2) into (d)(2)(A). Which court has the better of the statutory interpretation, in terms of the provision's syntax? (The word *knowing* is left out of the middle clause.)

Do you see also that, in cases like *Hoflin*, ignorance of the law is no defense? The court did not require proof that Hoflin knew the hazardous dumping was illegal. It used the argument that, for regulatory "public welfare" statutes involving grave issues of public health, there is no need to prove *mens rea* unless statutory terms require it. Does the "public welfare offense argument" presume that when something is so noxious, everyone must know it is

C. Problems of Knowledge and Intent

likely to be illegal? [7] Many other environmental statutes besides RCRA would seem to fit this category.

6. Constitutional dimensions: "void for vagueness." As in many criminal cases, Weitzenhoff argued that the statute as applied was void for vagueness because it did not provide adequate notice of what permit requirements would ground violations. In rejecting the vagueness defense, along with an entrapment claim, the court concluded, "A defendant is deemed to have fair notice of an offense if a reasonable person of ordinary intelligence would understand that his or her conduct is prohibited by the law in question," and the standard is even easier if the defendants have specialized training:

> Weitzenhoff and Mariani were knowledgeable in the wastewater field and can be expected to have understood what the permit meant. In particular, they should have known that it did not give them license to dump thousands of gallons of partially treated sewage into the ocean on a regular basis. We are further persuaded that appellants had adequate notice of the illegality of their dumping by the considerable pains they took to conceal their activities.

The "void for vagueness" challenge is a serious due process argument, but generally "in the field of regulatory statutes governing business activities, where the acts limited are in a narrow category, greater leeway [in required specificity of notice] is allowed than in statutes applicable to the general public." *People v. Martin*, 211 Cal. App. 3d 699, 706 (Cal. App. 2d Dist. 1989) (a dumper of toxics disputed the specificity of "hazardous wastes"); *United States v. Protex Indus., Inc.*, 874 F.2d 740 (10th Cir. 1989) (a chemical company was convicted of "knowing endangerment" of workers who suffered solvent poisoning, under 42 U.S.C.A. §6928(e), of RCRA).

7. Constitutional dimensions: due process. Does due process nevertheless require proof of criminal knowledge, intent, or negligent fault, in no-fault crimes where the legislature expressly excludes it?

Contrast two oil spill cases: The Exxon Corporation paid $200 million in criminal fines for the unintended *Exxon-Valdez* oil spill, but that penalty did not seem to shock fundamental fairness, perhaps because defendants' behavior showed elements of fault: Exxon should have known its operating practices were unsafe. On the other hand, in *United States v. White Fuel Corp.*, 498 F.2d 619 (1st Cir. 1974), a company had to pay a $1000 fine for violating §407 of the Refuse Act, for oil seepage from a half a million gallon underground

---

7. In cases under 42 U.S.C. §6928(d) involving charges that a defendant "knowingly" treated, stored, or disposed of hazardous waste without a permit, liability often turns on the determination by the court of which elements of the offense are modified by the term "knowingly." Most courts have concluded that "knowingly" modifies "treats, stores, or disposes" in §6928(d)(2), on the theory that it is not likely that a party would treat, store, or dispose of waste without knowledge of that action. See *United States v. Johnson & Towers, Inc.*, 741 F.2d 662, 668 (3d Cir. 1984). Courts have also consistently recognized that "knowingly" modifies the term "hazardous waste." See, e.g., *United States v. Laughlin*, 10 F.3d 961, 966 (2d Cir. 1993), cert. denied 511 U.S. 1071 (1994). But, as noted in the text above, some courts have also held that the government need not prove that the defendant knew that the waste was a "hazardous waste" under RCRA, but instead only that the defendant knew that the waste had the potential to be harmful to others or the environment. See *Hoflin* at 1039. Courts have also disagreed over whether "knowingly" applies to the requirement in §6928(d)(2)(A) that treating, storing, or disposing of hazardous waste must be done "without a permit." In the Third Circuit, for example, the term "knowingly" in this context applies to "without a permit" so that, in order to convict, a jury must find that each defendant knew that the corporation involved was required to have a permit, and also knew that the corporation did not have a permit. See *Johnson & Towers*, 741 F.2d at 669. But in the Second, Fourth, Sixth, Seventh, Ninth and Eleventh Circuits, the view is that §6928(d) does not require the government to prove that the defendant knew that a permit was required or that the corporation did not have a permit. See, e.g., *Laughlin*, 10 F.3d at 966; *United States v. Wolfgang Wagner*, 29 F.3d 264, 265-266 (7th Cir. 1994).

leakage under their tank farm abutting Boston Harbor. White Fuel had no warning of the leakage, worked diligently to drain the accumulation, and paid for the cleanup. The court upheld criminal liability because public welfare offenses "are in the nature of neglect where the law requires care, or inaction where it imposes a duty.... The accused, if he does not will the violation, usually is in a position to prevent it with no more care than society might reasonably expect and no more exertion than society might reasonably exact from one who assumed his responsibilities. *Morissette v. U.S.*, 342 U.S. 246, 255-256 (1952)." 498 F.2d at 622. Skepticism of this standard arises in cases like *White Fuel*, where no such neglect and no prior duty were ever proved. When there is truly "no fault" in such cases, is there a sense of violated due process? This sense of constitutional unfairness may seem assuaged if (1) the criminal penalty is small, like White Fuel's $1000 fine, and (b) it is a corporation, not a person, that faces criminal penalties.

Contrast two endangered wildlife cases raising the tougher problem—where individual persons faced no-fault jail time: In *United States v. Wulff*, 758 F.2d 1121 (6th Cir. 1985), the defendant sold a necklace made of red-tailed hawk and great-horned owl talons to a special agent of the U.S. Fish and Wildlife Service. In *United States v. Engler*, 806 F.2d 425 (3d Cir. 1986), cert. denied, 481 U.S. 1019 (1987), the defendant was convicted under the same Act for the innocent sale of a protected falcon in interstate commerce. The Migratory Bird Treaty Act (MBTA, 16 U.S.C.A. §701) provides strict liability for sale of raptors. Without proof of knowledge or intent, defendants "shall be guilty of a felony and fined not more than $2,000 or imprisoned not more than two years, or both...." 758 F.2d at 1122.

Both courts considered the crimes "public welfare offenses," so that proof of criminal intent was not necessarily required by the Constitution. The *Wulff* court, however, found that no-fault convictions violated due process unless "the penalty is relatively small, and conviction does not gravely besmirch" an individual's reputation, quoting a test from Judge Blackmun in *Holdridge v. United States*, 282 F.2d 302 (8th Cir. 1960). But, it held, the MBTA's fines and two-year jail sentences "were not 'relatively small penalties.' A convicted felon loses his right to vote, his right to sit on a jury and his right to possess a gun, among other civil rights, for the rest of his life."

The *Engler* court, on the other hand, upheld the MBTA conviction, quoting the Supreme Court that "public policy may require in prohibition or punishment of particular acts ... that he who shall do them shall do them at his peril and will not be heard to plead good faith or ignorance in defense.... This court cannot set aside legislation because it is harsh. *Shevlin-Carpenter v. State of Minn.*, 218 U.S. 57, 70 (1910)." 806 F.2d at 434. *Engler* held that "Due process is not violated by the imposition of strict liability as part of a regulatory measure in the interest of public safety, which may well be premised on the theory that one would hardly be surprised to learn that the prohibited conduct is not an innocent act." Does this imply constructive knowledge? Is the sale of endangered wildlife an act that is obviously not innocent, and an offense against public welfare? Does the prohibition of such sales, as the court said, serve "a national interest of very nearly the first magnitude"? 806 F.2d at 436.

The *Engler* court ridiculed Wulff's "besmirchment" line drawing between felonies and misdemeanors, and went on to add a practical element to the due process balance: "Where the offenses prohibited and made punishable are capable of inflicting widespread injury, and where the requirement of proof of the offender's guilty knowledge and wrongful intent would render enforcement of the prohibition difficult if not impossible, the legislative intent to dispense with *mens rea* as an element of the offense has justifiable basis." 806 F.2d at 434. (A practical argument in the other direction is that, insofar as a statute is designed to deter proscribed acts, proof of knowing, or at least careless, acts is necessary.)

C. Problems of Knowledge and Intent

The issues involved in no-fault crimes, as addressed in *Wulff* and *Engler* remain a focus of environmental litigation. Recently, for example, the Fifth Circuit reversed the convictions of Citgo Petroleum Corp. for alleged violations of the Clean Air Act (CAA) and the Migratory Bird Treaty Act (MBTA), arising from Citgo's wastewater treatment program at its Corpus Christi Oil Refinery, where Citgo allegedly used uncovered equalization tanks as oil-water separators. The government charged Citgo with violation of the CAA (which requires that oil-water separators have emission control devices, like roofs, to limit VOC emissions) and with "taking" migratory birds in violation of the MBTA (because the government suspected that birds had died in the uncovered tanks). Specifically, the MBTA imposes strict liability on violators by making it "unlawful at any time, by any means or in any manner to pursue, hunt, take, capture, or kill . . . any migratory bird" in violation of applicable regulations and permits. See 16 U.S.C. §703(a); §704(a). After the district court sentenced Citgo to a $2 million fine for the CAA counts and $15,000 for each MBTA violation, the Fifth Circuit reversed the convictions. *United States v. Citgo Petroleum Corp.*, No. 14-40128 (5th Cir., Sep. 4, 2015).

The Fifth Circuit reversed the CAA convictions based on faulty jury instructions. As to the MBTA counts, the Fifth Circuit agreed with Citgo's argument that illegally "taking" migratory birds involves only conduct intentionally directed at birds, such as hunting and trapping, not commercial activity that unintentionally and indirectly causes migratory bird deaths. In reaching this result, the Fifth Circuit recognized that there is a circuit split on whether and to what degree proof of intentional conduct is essential to a conviction under the MBTA. Compare *Newton Cnty. Wildlife Ass'n v. U.S. Forest Serv.*, 113 F.3d 110, 115 (8th Cir. 1997), and *Seattle Audobon Soc'y v. Evans*, 952 F.2d 297, 302 (9th Cir. 1991), with *United States v. Apollo Energies, Inc.*, 611 F.3d 679, 686 (10th Cir. 2010); and *United States v. FMC Corp.*, 572 F.2d 902, 905 (2d Cir. 1978). Emphasizing its view that proof of intent is essential under the MBTA, the Fifth Circuit held that the MBTA's ban on "takings" only prohibits intentional acts (not omissions) that directly (not indirectly or accidentally) kill migratory birds.

8. A scienter requirement balance? Are some public welfare offenses more dramatic than others, so "less" scienter is required, or in such cases does more "besmirchment" of individual reputation occur, thus requiring proof of "more" scienter? Should distinctions be drawn between protections of endangered birds and protections of human health against toxic pollution? In *Weitzenhoff*, the court noted that in the *Staples* machine gun case, the Supreme Court had acknowledged a changing balance: "The penalty attached to a violation of a criminal statute in the past has been a relevant factor in determining whether the statute defines a public welfare offense. . . . Public welfare offenses originally involved statutes that provided only light penalties such as fines or short jail sentences, but modern statutes now punish public welfare offenses with much more significant terms of imprisonment." 35 F.3d at 1281. See also *United States v. X-Citement Video, Inc.*, 513 U.S. 64 (1994) (required "knowingly to apply to each element of the offense," despite the "most natural grammatical reading" indicating otherwise); dissent of J. Thomas, joined by J. O'Connor, to denial of certiorari in *Hanousek v. United States*, 528 U.S. 1102 (2000) (the "narrow" public welfare offense doctrine should not be used in CAA conviction for negligence with respect to "ordinary industrial and commercial activities" such as railroad track construction work near petroleum pipeline that was accidentally ruptured during the course of such work; dissent also noted that the severity of the penalty (a felony) distinguishes crimes where knowledge must be proved from public welfare offenses, and that the circuit courts invoke the doctrine too readily).

9. Strict liability and sentencing options. In strict liability crime cases, would you feel differently about convictions that lead only to fines and convictions that could lead to incarceration? Note also that, although fines and imprisonment are the standard criminal sanctions available to environmental prosecutors, injunctions are also available as remedies for many crimes. The field of criminal injunctions is little studied but has particular utility in the field of environmental crimes. Where due process concerns are implicated in no-fault crimes, moreover, the prospective nature of a criminal injunction intrudes far less upon defendant's rights.

D. PROBLEMS RAISED IN CORPORATE AND EXECUTIVE PROSECUTIONS

Much of the pollution dumped into the air and waters of the United States historically comes from corporate polluters, especially the most toxic of such waste streams. In *Film Recovery*, the corporation had folded, but in many cases prosecutors target established ongoing corporate enterprises in their tactical gunsights. Successful prosecution of criminal environmental violations always faces an array of difficulties not encountered in civil lawsuits, notably in Fifth Amendment and other limitations on discovery, and also with respect to the special burden of proof required to prove defendants guilty "beyond a reasonable doubt." These difficulties are particularly pronounced in the case of prosecutions of corporations and corporate executives.

Prosecution of environmental crimes against corporations and their executives typically raises three common sets of issues: (1) the proof required to establish criminal intent, a topic addressed earlier in this chapter; (2) the extent to which the actions and intentions of the corporate agent may properly be attributable to the corporation; and (3) the criminal liability of individuals, particularly corporate officers, for environmental violations by the corporation carried out on their individual watch.

> **Key Issues in the Prosecution of Environmental Crimes Against Corporations and their Executives:**
>
> - The Fifth Amendment
> - Difficulties in Proving Collective Activity Crimes
> - Executive Liability for Acts or Omissions of Subordinates

1. THE FIFTH AMENDMENT AND THE CORPORATION

A corporation can claim Fifth Amendment protections against regulatory takings and violations of procedural due process. Can a corporation take the Fifth, refusing to produce documents that may tend to incriminate it, as a natural person can? The Supreme Court's answer is "no." See *Bellis v. United States*, 417 U.S. 85 (1974). See also *Hale v. Henkel*, 201 U.S. 43, 74-75 (1906); *Wilson v. United States*, 221 U.S. 361, 383-384 (1911); *United States v. White*, 322 U.S. 694, 698-704 (1944).

In some cases, the corporation may not be able to claim attorney-client privilege. See, e.g., *People v. Superior Court (Keuffel & Esser Co.)*, 181 Cal. App. 3d 785 (Cal. App. 2d Dist. 1986) (upholding the prosecution's request for discovery of corporate records and information, despite claims of privilege). In the absence of applicable privileges, the corporation (if subpoenaed, if subject to discovery requests, or if otherwise willing to cooperate) must typically deliver up documents, including witness statements, in its possession, even if the documents or statements directly incriminate the individuals who serve as executives of the

D. Corporate and Executive Prosecutions

corporation. In such circumstances, by virtue of their corporate positions, corporate officers can effectively lose the protections of the Fifth Amendment. See, e.g., *United States v. Ruehle*, 583 F.3d 600 (9th Cir. 2009) (holding that a corporate officer's statements to attorneys hired by the corporation to conduct an internal investigation and defend the officer were not privileged, because the officer knew they would be shared with the corporation's outside auditor).

In an effort to motivate corporations to cooperate and to avoid harsh sentences, the DOJ traditionally has applied a set of key factors in determining whether to prosecute criminal violations of the environmental laws, including: (1) whether the corporation voluntarily discloses its violation, (2) whether the corporation has a pervasive level of noncompliance, (3) whether the corporation establishes preventative measures and compliance programs, and (4) whether the corporation promulgates its own internal disciplinary actions and produces subsequent compliance. EPA has adopted similar criteria in determining whether to pursue investigations for self-disclosed violations identified during voluntary environmental audits.[8]

The purpose of such criteria is essentially the same—to provide significant incentives inducing corporate self-disclosure. But they also drive a wedge between the corporations (which are incentivized to disclose) and their executives (who may be targeted based upon corporate disclosures). Accordingly, although voluntary self-disclosures by corporations may prove very helpful to the corporation in mitigating corporate criminal and civil liabilities, such disclosures may also well provide the evidence needed to prosecute individual corporate officials, whose personal Fifth Amendment rights do not prohibit disclosures by the corporations for which they work.

2. Difficulties in Proving Collective Activity Crimes

The following excerpt notes some of the key issues raised by criminal indictments of corporate and individual defendants charged with environmental crimes based upon their collective activities.

William Goldfarb, Kepone: A Case Study
8 Environmental Law 645 (1978)

On May 7, 1976, the Federal grand jury in Richmond, Virginia, handed down two indictments charging Allied, LSP, the City of Hopewell, and six individuals with a total of 1,097 counts (separate offenses) relating to the Kepone incident at Hopewell. Then on July 28th, the grand jury was reconvened to hear further evidence; and the result was a third indictment issued on August 2, 1976.

Indictment #1 charged Allied with 941 counts: 940 alleged violations of the Refuse Act and FWPCA for discharging Kepone, TAIC, and THEIC from Allied's Semi-Works without permits; and one count for an alleged conspiracy to violate control laws among Allied and

---

8. The factors which the DOJ considers in determining whether to bring criminal charges are similar to the factors typically addressed under applicable environmental laws for mitigating civil penalties: the seriousness of the violation; the efforts made to comply with the regulations; the harm caused by the violations; the economic benefit derived from noncompliance; the violator's ability to pay; the government's conduct, including delay in enforcement; and the clarity of the obligation involved. See *United States v. WCI Steel, Inc.*, 72 F. Supp. 2d 810, 828 (N.D. Ohio 1999) (citing *United States v. Ekco Housewares, Inc.*, 62 F.3d 806, 815 (6th Cir. 1995)).

five of its employees. Each of the individual defendants was also charged with conspiracy to defraud the United States by providing false information regarding the Semi-Works effluent.

Indictment #2 charged Allied, LSP, Hundtofte, Moore, and the City of Hopewell with 153 counts apiece relating to the unlawful discharge of Kepone by LSP into the Hopewell sewer system. In addition, Hopewell was charged with three counts of failure to report the presence of Kepone in its municipal treatment works.

[I]ndictment #3 contained only one count, charging Allied, LSP, Hundtofte, and Moore with conspiracy relating to the discharge of Kepone of LSP.

None of the indictments related to conditions within the LSP plant, because the Federal Occupational Safety and Health Act does not provide for criminal sanctions for such occupational hazards.

The corporate and individual defendants were confronted by the prospect of heavy fines and jail terms if found guilty and accorded maximum sentences. Allied faced a maximum fine of more than $17 million; LSP and its co-owners $3.8 million each; the City of Hopewell $3.9 million; and the alleged co-conspirators $10,000 on each conspiracy count. The more serious potential penalty, however, was imprisonment. The counts for discharging without a permit—940 counts in Indictment #1 and 153 in Indictment #2—carried a maximum jail term of one year on each count. The possible penalty on the conspiracy counts was up to five years on each count. . . .

The FWPCA goes beyond the Refuse Act by explicitly extending liability to a "responsible corporate officer" for the illegal acts of his corporation. LSP as discharger and Hundtofte and Moore as its only officers obviously contravened the FWPCA by discharging pollutants which interfered with the Hopewell treatment plant, [] and continuously violating pretreatment standards—all with the knowledge of Hundtofte and Moore. The City of Hopewell was clearly in violation of its own NPDES permit by discharging an unpermitted and unreported substance (Kepone) with knowledge of its presence in the system.

Given the clearcut direct criminal liability in this case, it is not surprising that the defendants, after having made some unsuccessful preliminary motions, chose to change their pleas from "not guilty" to *nolo contendere* on the direct liability counts.[9]. . .

[Virgil Hundtofte] was permitted to plead *nolo* on 79 of the 153 counts of Indictment #2 (the remaining 74 counts were dismissed), and to plead "guilty" to a reduced charge of conspiring to furnish false information to the Federal government. Hundtofte also pleaded *nolo* to the single conspiracy count of Indictment #3. Hundtofte also consented to appear as a witness for the United States against Allied.

Allied unexpectedly requested permission to plead *nolo* on 940 counts of Indictment #1. The prosecutor objected vehemently to Allied's request, but Judge Merhige accepted the *nolo* plea "in the interest of justice. . . . " Judge Merhige, in accepting Allied's *nolo* plea, afforded Allied a profound tactical advantage in subsequent civil suits.

As a result of plea bargaining, all relevant defendants had pleaded *nolo* to all outstanding counts charging direct violations of pollution control laws. . . . However, the ease with which the United States obtained convictions on the counts involving direct violations of

---

9. There are two main reasons for entering a *nolo* plea. First, carrying less of a stigma than "guilty," it may be part of a plea bargaining process in which a prosecutor agrees that in return for avoiding the delay and expense of a trial he will accept a *nolo* plea and request the judge to impose a sentence which is lighter than the maximum. Second, the conviction of a defendant after a *nolo* plea cannot be used as evidence in another legal proceeding arising out of the same set of facts—e.g, in a civil action for damages. Had the defendant pleaded or been found guilty, on the other hand, such a conviction would make a prima facie case for the plaintiffs in a related case.

D. Corporate and Executive Prosecutions

law, stands in stark contrast to its inability to establish any vicarious liability or conspiracy regarding Allied.

[As to vicarious liability, by pretrial motion,] Allied sought a ruling dismissing the "conspiracy to provide false information" count on the ground that, as a matter of law, a corporation cannot be in conspiracy with its own employees who are acting within the scope of their authority. . . . Allied was arguing that it could not be in conspiracy with itself. The court agreed, and dismissed the count as to Allied. . . .

Although the 153 counts of Indictment #2 and the single conspiracy count of Indictment #3 represented less than ten percent of the total number of counts in the three indictments, they were undoubtedly the most controversial and significant from the standpoint of law and public policy since they held Allied responsible for the criminal acts of LSP. . . .

In attempting to hold Allied criminally liable for LSP's discharges, the United States relied upon four legal theories: (1) that LSP was an instrumentality of Allied; (2) that LSP was an agent of Allied; (3) that Allied was an accomplice of LSP; and (4) that Allied and LSP were engaged in a conspiracy to violate pollution control laws.

Under the instrumentality theory, the United States was called upon to prove "actual domination" of LSP by Allied. Somewhat less was necessary to establish an agency relationship: a continuous right of control by Allied (rather than actual domination), along with a consent by LSP to produce Kepone primarily for the benefit of Allied, and at least a tacit acceptance by Allied, if not an explicit condonation, of LSP's unlawful acts. Imposing accomplice liability depended upon proving that Allied "aided and abetted" LSP's illegal discharges. Accomplice liability moves from the realm of control to that of association and assistance, preserving the autonomy of accomplice and perpetrator. It is a kind of vicarious liability that does not require the corporate veil to be pierced. Finally, a conspiracy is a formal or informal agreement to commit another crime. Under a conspiracy theory, Allied and LSP would also be treated as distinct entities.

At the trial, witnesses for the United States, including Hundtofte and Moore, emphasized Allied's close knowledge of Kepone production and toxicity; the relationship of Allied to Hundtofte and Moore; the onesideness of the tolling agreement; Allied's provision of services to LSP—including sampling its effluent on a regular basis, and tours of the LSP plant by Allied's employees and consultants; and Allied's constant urging of LSP to greater Kepone production. . . .

The defense relied on letters from LSP to Allied, allegedly written over a period of years, reassuring Allied that LSP was not discharging in violation of the law. Allied's reasonable reliance on these letters, it was urged, refuted the "instrumentality" and "agency" theories and also precluded the requisite criminal intent to aid and abet LSP's illegal discharges and to agree upon an illegal course of conduct (conspire). Counsel for Allied also highlighted Allied's willingness to pay for LSP's pollution control equipment, claiming that Allied could not have intended to break the law when it was spending money to ensure LSP's compliance.

Without a formal opinion in the case, the court exonerated Allied on all counts involving vicarious liability for LSP. While Judge Merhige's remarks during and after the trial were cryptic, he did indicate that he was not convinced beyond a reasonable doubt of Allied's having possessed the necessary intent upon which to base a conviction, [a holding which might encourage corporations to enter into tolling agreements in order to evade the costs of pollution control].

Much greater publicity was accorded to the imposition of the maximum fine on Allied for its own discharges. For its conviction on the 940 counts of Indictment #1 (to which it pleaded "*nolo*"), Allied was fined $13.2 million. However . . . Allied sought a reduction in sentence based on its having set aside $8 million to fund the Virginia Environmental Endowment, a nonprofit corporation which would perform research and implement programs to mitigate the environmental effects of Kepone. Judge Merhige then adjusted the fine down to $5 million. . . .

Hundtofte and Moore were fined $25,000 each. LSP received a fine of close to $4 million, a meaningless gesture in light of LSP's lack of assets. Finally, the city of Hopewell was fined $10,000. . . .

Did the *Kepone* sentences actually do justice? Did they achieve the retribution and deterrence (both for the defendants and prospective violators) for which the criminal law strives? . . . Was Allied's "corporate image" tarnished, as its attorneys claimed prior to sentencing? This argument would deserve greater credence if Allied's operations were more closely related to the general public; but in fact Allied sells almost all of its chemicals to other corporations. . . . Would it have better served the purposes of the criminal law to have imposed jail terms on some of Allied's executives, and perhaps Hundtofte and Moore? The American public does not look favorably upon the imprisonment of corporate officers for corporate crimes. This explains why jail terms were never a viable alternative in the Kepone case. (Judge Merhige commented early on that "nobody is going to jail in this case.") Moreover, the imprisonment of corporate officers frequently does more harm than good, fostering a "demonology myth" that a few greedy industrialists are responsible for the pollution problem, whereas pollution is a pervasive result of our economic system's "externalization" of certain costs of production. The light fines imposed upon Hundtofte and Moore typify the generous treatment which cooperating corporate officials can expect to receive at the hands of the law.

But is not the function of the criminal law in pollution cases really a symbolic one? To stigmatize an offender so as to achieve deterrence? And to effectuate a catharsis of public outrage?

COMMENTARY & QUESTIONS

1. The judge, and the absence of a jury. Where was the jury in this criminal prosecution? Obviously Allied and its indicted executives chose to waive their constitutional right to a jury. Was this a good move? Note the effect of Judge Merhige's rulings on pleadings, on required elements of collective action crimes, and on sentencing, as well as his comments at the early stages of trial ("Nobody is going to jail . . . "). What effect did these have on the parties? If there had been a jury, would there have been a different judicial posture?

2. The perils of plea bargaining. The negotiations between the U.S. Attorney's office and Hundtofte, Moore, and the City of Hopewell illustrate the potential benefits of plea bargaining to both prosecutor and defendants. Note, however, that bargains struck between the parties do not per se bind the judge. A tough judge could have refused to dismiss the original counts or to allow the lesser pleas, or could have ignored the prosecutors' recommendations for lighter sentences. Judges can go softer on defendants than the terms of a bargain as well. Judge Merhige felt free to ignore the U.S. Attorney's opposition to Allied's *nolo* plea, even though it undermined the prosecutors' basis for the prior plea bargains. Can defendants or prosecutors whose plea bargains have not been followed by the trial judge get relief from an appellate court? Not likely because trial judges, within applicable guidelines, have substantial discretion as to whether to accept a plea bargain. In environmental cases, where criminal liability remains a relatively novel phenomenon for many judges, the reliability of plea bargaining for both sides may be relatively unpredictable.

D. Corporate and Executive Prosecutions

3. Allied's vicarious liability. It is not clear why Judge Merhige dismissed all the vicarious liability counts against Allied. Does it appear that Allied was a stranger to the sloppy operations at Life Science's plant? Did Allied not have the requisite knowledge of what was going on? Should "tolling" and "*maquiladora*" agreements legally insulate corporate principals from the pollution of their "independent" subcontractors? If the United States had appealed dismissal of the counts holding Allied vicariously liable for LSP's pollution, which argument on the Kepone facts—instrumentality, agency, accomplice, or conspiracy—would have appeared strongest?

4. The *Kepone* fines and taxes. Defendant industries that negotiate SEPs (supplemental environmental projects) as setoff alternatives to larger penalties often do so in order to write the sums off on their income tax returns as business expenditures under 26 U.S.C. §162 of the Internal Revenue Code, or as charitable deductions under 26 U.S.C. §170. As noted, Allied agreed with the judge to set up an $8 million Virginia Environmental Endowment, and the fines were then reduced from $13.2 million to $5 million. When Allied deducted the $8 million as a business expense, the IRS balked. When the tax case came to trial almost 20 years later, the court had to decide:

> Whether petitioner's payment of $8,000,000 in 1977 to the Virginia Environmental Endowment Fund is deductible under §162(a) as an "ordinary and necessary business expense" or whether such payment is a "fine or similar penalty" [like the $5 million] the deductibility of which is proscribed by 26 U.S.C. §162(f). . . .
>
> We accept petitioner's characterization of a "fine or similar penalty" as an involuntary payment [but] in the present case, petitioner made the $8 million payment to the Endowment with the virtual guarantee that the sentencing judge would reduce the criminal fine by at least that amount. Petitioner's characterization of this payment as "voluntary" is simply not borne out by the record as a whole. . . . We hold that the payment by petitioner to the Endowment was in substance a "fine or similar penalty" within the meaning of 26 U.S.C. §162(f). *Allied-Signal, Inc. v. Comm'r*, 63 T.C.M. (CCH) 2672 (1992), aff'd, 54 F.3d 767 (3d Cir. 1995) (unpublished table decision).

If prosecutors negotiating penalties wish to have penalty funds used for onsite remedies rather than merely pouring into the federal treasury, tax deductibility is a settlement incentive. Can such SEPs be made deductible? Does it make a difference if the remediation fund is set up before a judge issues a penalty ruling? Is tax deductibility sound public policy?

5. Further Developments Concerning the Deductibility of Environmental Fines and Penalties. As the discussion above demonstrates, the deductibility of environmental fines and penalties is an issue that has long engaged the courts, as well as the parties seeking to fashion a plea agreement.

Generally, a criminal fine, including one paid pursuant to a plea of *nolo contendere*, is not deductible from gross income as an ordinary and necessary business expense under Section 162(a) of the Internal Revenue Code. *See also* 26 U.S.C. §162(f); Treas. Reg. 1.162-21(b)(1)(i). Nonetheless, applicable federal tax regulations provide that, when amounts are paid to the government as "compensatory damages," they do not constitute fines or penalties and, consequently, may be deducted from gross income.

Given the potential ambiguity over what constitutes "compensatory damages," the case law has been less than definitive concerning what factors in a criminal case allow a restitution payment, like a SEP, to be tax deductible. The case law generally turns on whether a restitution payment is characterized as "punitive" (and therefore non-deductible) or "compensatory" (and therefore deductible). However, it is not the label attached to a payment either as "punitive" or "compensatory" which is determinative under Section 165(2)(c) of the Internal Revenue Code. *See Kraft v. United States*, 991 F.2d 292 (6th Cir. 1993), *cert.*

denied, 510 U.S. 976 (1973); *see also Bailey v. Commissioner*, 756 F.2d 44 (6th Cir. 1985) (restitution payment under a sentence was disallowed as deductible, even when the fine was labeled and applied as restitution in settlement).

The leading case of *Waldman v. Commissioner*, 88 T.C. 1384 (1987), *aff'd* 850 F.2d 611 (9th Cir. 1988), is instructive. There, the court concluded that when a payment serves both a law enforcement function and a compensatory function, the key is to determine what purpose the payment is to serve. In *Waldman*, the court looked to state law and concluded that, because the payment was in satisfaction of a criminal liability, it was not tax deductible.

Likewise, in *Allied Signal, Inc. v. Commissioner*, 63 T.C.M. (CCH) 2672 (1992), *aff'd* 54 F.3d 767 (3d. Cir. 1995), the tax court deemed non-deductible a payment involuntarily made as a *quid pro quo* for a lower fine, concluding that the primary purpose of the payment was to resolve a punishment. The defendant had entered a *nolo contendere* plea and then contended that its multi-million-dollar payment was a contribution to an environmental trust that benefitted the state rather than a payment made to satisfy a criminal fine. But the court rejected this argument, concluding that the payment was, in fact, made to resolve a criminal fine. *See also Colt Industries, Inc. v. United States*, 880 F.2d 1311 (Fed. Cir. 1989) (rejecting the argument that an environmental payment was tax deductible, where (i) the defendant had not convincingly articulated how its $1.6 million payment to the Pennsylvania Clean Air and Clean Water Fund would benefit the government, and (ii) the court also found that, under the CWA and CAA, the EPA was not authorized to seek compensatory damages).

The claim that SEPs should be deductible has fallen into greater disfavor since the *Kepone* case. In 2008, the IRS noted that "because [Section] 162(f) [of the Internal Revenue Code] represents a codification of ... public policy doctrine, the analyses used by the courts and the Service in determining whether certain expenses meet the definition of a fine or similar penalty for purposes of [Section] 162(f) are relevant for determining whether any [SEP] expenditure, or a portion thereof, constitutes a fine or penalty whose allowance as a tax benefit would frustrate public policy." IRS Issue Paper LMSB-04-0608-036 (July 9, 2008).

As a consequence, it is important for parties involved in the negotiation of SEPS that they identify which part of the SEP is intended to be compensatory and, therefore, beyond the amount that would otherwise be paid in a civil or criminal penalty. The parties could then contend that the compensatory portion of the SEP should be deemed remedial and deductible. For example, in the *Exxon Valdez* plea agreement, the parties sought to design an agreement which would take advantage of the tax deductibility of compensatory payments. To that end, the parties' agreement characterized the restitution to be paid as "exclusively remedial, compensatory, and non-punitive and ... separate and distinct from the fines ..." Does this language succeed in structuring a restitution payment that is deductible? If so, would a court be bound by this agreement? In persuading a court to endorse this agreement, how would a defendant obtain the cooperation and support of the prosecutor? How important would it be to obtain the prosecutor's support?

3. Executive Liability for Acts or Omissions by Subordinates

United States v. Park

421 U.S. 658 (1975)

BURGER, C.J. Acme Markets, Inc., is a national retail food chain with approximately 36,000 employees, 874 retail outlets, 12 general warehouses, and four special warehouses. Its headquarters, including the office of the president, respondent Park, who is chief executive officer of the corporation, are located in Philadelphia, Pa. In a five-count information filed

D. Corporate and Executive Prosecutions

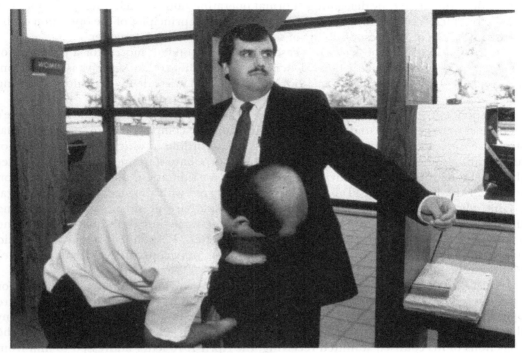

FIGURE 19-1. *Former president of Film Recovery Systems, Inc., Steven O'Neil, being frisked before being sentenced to 25 years in prison for the job-related death of an employee at his Elk Grove Village plant. Prosecutors said O'Neil and two other executives were "motivated by greed and greed alone." Convicted of murder, he theoretically could have faced execution in Illinois. Photo: Scott Sanders/Daily Herald, Arlington Heights, Illinois.*

in the United States District Court for the District of Maryland, the Government charged Acme and respondent with violations of the Federal Food, Drug and Cosmetic Act. Each count of the information alleged that the defendants had received food that had been shipped in interstate commerce and that, while the food was being held for sale in Acme's Baltimore warehouse following shipment in interstate commerce, they caused it to be held in a building accessible to rodents and to be exposed to contamination by rodents. These acts were alleged to have resulted in the food's being adulterated within the meaning of 21 U.S.C. §§342(a)(3) and (4), in violation of 21 U.S.C. §331(k).

Acme pleaded guilty to each count of the information. Respondent pleaded not guilty. The evidence at trial demonstrated that in April 1970 the Food and Drug Administration (FDA) advised respondent by letter of insanitary conditions in Acme's Philadelphia warehouse. In 1971 the FDA found that similar conditions existed in the firm's Baltimore warehouse. An FDA consumer safety officer testified concerning evidence of rodent infestation and other insanitary conditions discovered during a 12-day inspection of the Baltimore warehouse in November and December 1971. He also related that a second inspection of the warehouse had been conducted in March 1972. On that occasion the inspectors found that there had been improvement in the sanitary conditions, but that "there was still evidence of rodent activity in the building and in the warehouse and we found some rodent-contaminated lots of food items." . . .

The Government's final witness, Acme's vice president for legal affairs and assistant secretary, identified respondent as the president and chief executive officer of the company and read a bylaw prescribing the duties of the chief executive officer. He testified that respondent functioned by delegating "normal operating duties," including sanitation, but that he retained "certain things, which are the big, broad, principles of the operation of the company," and had "the responsibility of seeing that they all work together."

At the close of the Government's case in chief, respondent moved for a judgment of acquittal on the ground that "the evidence in chief has shown that Mr. Park is not personally concerned in this Food and Drug violation." The trial judge denied the motion, stating that *United States v. Dotterweich*, 320 U.S. 277 (1943), was controlling.

Respondent was the only defense witness. He testified that, although all of Acme's employees were in a sense under his general direction, the company had an "organizational structure for responsibilities for certain functions" according to which different phases of its operation were "assigned to individuals who, in turn, have staff and departments under them." He identified those individuals responsible for sanitation, and related that upon receipt of the January 1972 FDA letter, he had conferred with the vice president for legal affairs, who informed him that the Baltimore division vice president "was investigating the situation immediately and would be taking corrective action and would be preparing a summary of the corrective action to reply to the letter." Respondent stated that he did not "believe there was anything [he] could have done more constructively than what [he] found was being done."

On cross-examination, respondent conceded that providing sanitary conditions for food offered for sale to the public was something that he was "responsible for in the entire operation of the company," and he stated that it was one of many phases of the company that he assigned to "dependable subordinates." Respondent was asked about and, over the objections of his counsel, admitted receiving, the April 1970 letter addressed to him from the FDA regarding insanitary conditions at Acme's Philadelphia warehouse.... Finally, in response to questions concerning the Philadelphia and Baltimore incidents, respondent admitted that the Baltimore problem indicated the system for handling sanitation "wasn't working perfectly" and that as Acme's chief executive officer he was responsible for "any result which occurs in our company." ...

The jury found respondent guilty on all counts of the information, and he was subsequently sentenced to pay a fine of $50 on each count.

The Court of Appeals reversed [saying] as "a general proposition, some act of commission or omission is an essential element of every crime." ... It reasoned that, although our decision in *United States v. Dotterweich*, 320 U.S. at 281, had construed the statutory provisions under which respondent was tried to dispense with the traditional element of "awareness of some wrongdoing," the Court had not construed them as dispensing with the element of "wrongful action." The Court of Appeals concluded that ... proof of this element was required by due process.... We reverse.

In *Dotterweich* [on similar facts to *Park* concerning contaminated drugs] a jury ... convicted Dotterweich, the corporation's president and general manager.... This Court ... observed that the Act ... "dispenses with the conventional requirement for criminal conduct—awareness of some wrongdoing. In the interest of the larger good it puts the burden of acting at hazard upon a person otherwise innocent but standing in responsible relation to a public danger." ... The interpretation given the Act in *Dotterweich*, as holding criminally accountable the persons whose failure to exercise the authority and supervisory responsibility reposed in them by the business organization resulted in the violation complained of, has been confirmed in our subsequent cases.... "The public interest in the purity of its food is so great as to warrant the imposition of the highest standard of care on distributors." ... The Act punishes "neglect where the law requires care, or inaction where it imposes a duty." *Morissette v. United States*, at 255. "The accused, if he does not will the

D. Corporate and Executive Prosecutions

violation, usually is in a position to prevent it with no more care than society might reasonably expect and no more exertion than it might reasonably exact from one who assumed his responsibilities." . . .

Congress has seen fit to enforce the accountability of responsible corporate agents dealing with products which may affect the health of consumers by penal sanctions cast in rigorous terms, and the obligation of the courts is to give them effect so long as they do not violate the Constitution.

The concept of a "responsible relationship" to, or a "responsible share" in, a violation of the Act indeed imports some measure of blameworthiness; but it is equally clear that the Government establishes a prima facie case when it introduces evidence sufficient to warrant a finding by the trier of the facts that the defendant had, by reason of his position in the corporation, responsibility and authority either to prevent in the first instance, or promptly to correct, the violation complained of, and that he failed to do so.

COMMENTARY & QUESTIONS

1. Fighting over principles? Note that this case went up to the Supreme Court of the United States on appeal of a sentence of $50 for each of five counts. Why did Park bother? The corporation itself was also prosecuted but did not attempt to fight the conviction.

2. Who gets targeted? The "responsible corporate officer" doctrine. The government, if it had wished, could have prosecuted the actual workers whose acts or omissions had caused the contamination. Many statutes can be so applied, but governmental prosecutors often understandably choose to prosecute higher up the corporate chain of command if they can. The DOJ's environmental crimes division has long had a policy of prosecuting in each case the highest-ranking corporate officer it can reach. See Starr, Countering Environmental Crimes, 13 B.C. Envtl. Aff. L. Rev. 379 (1986).

The last line in the *Park* excerpt seems to set out an extremely inclusive definition for "responsible corporate officer" liability. Is it really that broad? The presidents of auto companies, for example, arguably have authority to prevent or correct violations of a far-off subsidiary if they are brought to their attention; the question is the interpretation to be given to the word *responsibility*. Two later cases imposed much stricter requirements for the prosecution of corporate executives: In *United States v. MacDonald & Watson Waste Oil Co.*, 933 F.2d 35 (1st Cir. 1991), and *United States v. White*, 766 F. Supp. 873 (E.D. Wash. 1991), the courts held that, at least for crimes for which knowledge is an element, a mere showing of official responsibility is not an adequate substitute for direct or circumstantial proof of actual knowledge. A recent analysis concluded this:

> No cases under the CWA have held a responsible corporate officer liable merely because of his or her position and it is unlikely that such a holding would occur for violations that require proof of some culpable knowledge. Such a decision may be possible, however, where the violation is based on strict liability or negligence, since there would be no scienter requirement and the conduct of the responsible corporate officer could be portrayed as deficient or negligent in some respect. . . . Courts have been extremely reticent to punish criminally those with only an attenuated relationship to wrongdoing. Executives must remain wary, however because decisions offering broad definitions of the rule are still being developed, particularly where hazardous substances are involved. Donald A. Carr et al., Environmental Criminal Liability: Avoiding and Defending Enforcement Actions 329 (1995).

The DOJ prosecutorial guidelines have long advised federal prosecutors to make a particularized scienter showing (direct or circumstantial) even where a statute does not by its plain terms specifically require knowledge.

3. Defensive organizational responses. Aware of new liabilities as well as the growing public concern for the environment, and as detailed in Chapter 18, many corporations have modified their internal structures to ensure environmental compliance. One common change is creation of a centralized office charged with companywide oversight, to try to ensure that pollution standards are not compromised for the sake of production, particularly given the pressures to cut corners common in times of recession. After *Park*, would you accept appointment as a major corporation's vice president responsible for pollution control?

4. Executive liability, civil as well as criminal. *Park* demonstrates judicial willingness to extend individual criminal liability far up the corporate executive ladder. Under the "responsible corporate officer doctrine," corporate officers may be held criminally liable not only for their direct actions or instructions to others, but also indirectly, by virtue of their responsibility for corporate compliance with applicable laws pertaining to hazardous waste. Although this chapter focuses on criminal liability, it is appropriate to note the similarities to executive civil liability issues.

As with civil liability, corporate officers can be held criminally liable for their individual acts where they themselves dumped toxics or directly ordered employees to do so (this is obvious but is rarely easy to prove). They also can be held liable, both civilly and criminally, for actions that take place within areas of their corporate responsibility and authority.[10] In some cases, where a corporate officer is in active daily managerial control of the area of corporate activity that caused a statutory violation, liability may reflect an inference that the executive in fact personally ordered, encouraged, or winked at the acts—where these facts cannot be directly proved.[11] See, e.g. *United States v. Hansen*, 262 F.3d 1217 (11th Cir. 2001), where the court upheld the sufficiency of the evidence in affirming the criminal convictions of corporate officers.

In other cases, liability appears to be based on a more indirect nexus—the officer's status and general authority over corporate matters. In *Dotterweich*, Justice Frankfurter held that, at least with regard to public health crimes, it is permissible to place the burden on corporate individuals who are in a position to prevent the harm from occurring "rather than to throw the hazard on the innocent public who are wholly helpless." 320 U.S. at 285. In a Vermont case, the court based liability on a finding that "each individual defendant here was either personally involved in corporate acts of Staco, *or was in a position as a corporate officer or majority stockholder to have ultimate control.*" *Vermont v. Staco Inc.*, 684 F. Supp. 822 (D. Vt. 1988) (emphasis added). In a Ninth Circuit decision, the court sent a clear message that corporate executives, directors, supervisors, and managers of construction projects are personally vulnerable to the risk of criminal prosecutions for CWA violations by those under their supervision. In *United States v. Hanousek*, 176 F.3d 1116 (9th Cir. 1999), the court affirmed the conviction of a rock-quarrying project supervisor, holding him personally liable for negligent supervision despite the fact that the supervisor was not directly regulated under the Act and did not physically cause the violation. The oil was illegally discharged when a backhoe operator accidentally struck an oil pipeline while working at the site alone at night. Hanousek received a sentence of six months in prison, six months in a halfway house, and six months of supervised release. See also Seymour, Civil and Criminal Liability of Corporate Officers Under Federal

---

10. The concept of piercing the corporate veil is rarely relevant to the question of officer liability in the criminal setting, where proof of individual responsibility rather than availability of assets is the issue.

11. This may explain the liability found against certain officers in the cases of *United States v. Carolawn Co. Inc.*, 21 ERC (BNA) 2124 (D.S.C. 1984); *United States v. Pollution Abatement Servs. of Oswego Inc.*, 763 F.2d 133 (2d Cir. 1985); and *In re BED*, EPA No. TSCA-IV-860001 (Dec. 8, 1988).

D. Corporate and Executive Prosecutions

Environmental Laws, 20 Env't Rep. (BNA) 337 (1989). John F. Seymour notes that "even though . . . actual operating functions had been delegated to subordinate employees who exercised responsibility over the everyday operations of the company, the court . . . in *Park* . . . indicated that with the power to delegate comes a corresponding obligation on the part of high-level corporate officers to control the behavior of subordinates. . . ."

Failure to discover and correct violations, as well as failure to provide adequate supervision, can be the basis of criminal as well as civil liability. How far up the ladder does such responsibility go? The indirect theory of executive responsibility, which comes closest to executive strict liability, raises special problems in the criminal setting. What if the defendant has no specific knowledge of the illegal acts? Some statutes are written without a requirement of specific proof of knowledge, but constitutional questions arise as to whether knowledge is nevertheless required. Civil liability is freer of such constraints. Into which liability theory does *Park* fall, or defendant Michaels's circumstances in *NEPACCO* (see Chapter 16)?

The same defenses that may be available to executives in criminal actions—inability to prevent the violation or ignorance of the violation—are sometimes available in the civil context as well. In any case, criminal sanctions, because of their stigma and potential severity, are generally more credible as deterrents than civil penalties.

5. Corporate ignorance as a defense. In *Park* the defendant admitted knowing fairly specifically that there was a violation of federal law that was not being corrected. What if, as in most cases, executives say they did not know that the criminal violation was occurring? How far does the criminal responsibility set out in *Park* and *Dotterweich* extend beyond the facts of those two cases? Could prosecutors—who are continually amazed by how little, according to litigation affidavits, corporate executives know about what really goes on in their factories—base executive criminal liability on a theory of "willful ignorance"? Some executives surely instruct their employees that they "don't want to know" how certain things get done, "just get it done."

In 1991, the California Corporate Criminal Liability Act went into effect, making it a crime whenever a corporation or manager has "actual knowledge" of a serious concealed danger associated with a product or business practice and knowingly fails within 15 days (or immediately, if there is imminent risk of great bodily harm or death) to notify the state occupational safety and health agency and affected employees. Cal. Pen. Code § 387. The statute provides that knowledge need not be actual awareness but may simply be possession of facts that would lead a reasonable person to believe that a danger exists.

6. Nonprosecution agreements. The U.S. Department of Justice is increasingly offering deferred prosecution and nonprosecution agreements to resolve corporate criminal investigations, rather than the all-or-nothing choice between indictment and no charge at all. These agreements have their place in prosecutions involving environmental crimes.

Nonprosecution agreements can be useful weapons against corporate misconduct. They avoid what may be an unwarranted corporate "death sentence", while providing deterrent impact and punishment that can be proportional to the conduct at issue. Indeed, many criticized DOJ's decision to charge the accounting firm Arthur Andersen, after it turned down a deferred prosecution agreement, precisely because the indictment alone was viewed as causing the company to go out of business and as exacting a toll on so many who had nothing to do with the charged conduct.

Prosecutors face a complex determination in considering whether an entire business should be prosecuted for committing a crime. For individuals, prosecutors typically consider whether the person committed a "bad act" and whether that person had the intent to perform the act. By contrast, many prosecutors would argue that an entire business can be liable for the actions of any single, low-level employee, even if the employee acted in contravention of a clear company policy. A company may try to deter such conduct through a robust compliance program, but no company can usually control completely the actions of the employees for whom it could always be held criminally liable.

As a result, having alternatives to indicting a whole company is extremely important. Deferred prosecution and nonprosecution agreements are alternatives that, if properly utilized, can meet law-enforcement goals. The former results in a public charge against the organization, but commits the government to dismiss the charge if the defendant complies with the agreed-upon requirements during a set period of time, e.g., from 18 to 36 months. A nonprosecution agreement works in much the same way, except that charges are not filed, but can be brought if the company does not comply with the terms of the agreement.

These agreements avoid the risks of trial and the expenditure of considerable prosecutorial resources. They usually result in payment of fines and restitution that can be orders of magnitude higher than those awarded after conviction. Deferred prosecution agreements can be used to achieve results that are rarely imposed following a trial and conviction, including the appointment of corporate monitors who oversee a company's reforms and report to the government.

The use of deferred prosecution and nonprosecution agreements has grown in recent years. That use is widely viewed as the result of DOJ's increased focus on corporate crime, in the wake of corporate scandals since Enron's demise in December 2001.

7. The invalidation of the mandatory provisions of the federal sentencing guidelines. The Sentencing Reform Act of 1984, 18 U.S.C. §3551, et seq., eliminated the system of indeterminate sentencing and parole formerly applied in the federal criminal justice system, by replacing it with mandatory sentencing guidelines, supplemented by nonbinding policy statements. These guidelines were designed with the goal of treating all classes of offenses committed by all categories of offenders consistently. The Sentencing Reform Act also created the U.S. Sentencing Commission, to which it delegated the task of devising the guidelines and policies to be used in sentencing, and abolished the Parole Commission. On November 1, 1987, the guidelines promulgated by the Sentencing Commission concerning the sentencing of individuals took effect. Four years later, on November 1, 1991, the guidelines for corporations became effective.

Although the sentencing guidelines for individuals applied across the board to all federal convictions, they were criticized when they were issued as having a disproportionately harsh impact on environmental offenders, particularly white collar defendants. At the same time, the guidelines were praised for making it possible for federal prosecutors to address three key problems that had previously hampered sentencing: (1) sentencing disparity; (2) misleading sentences which were shorter than they appeared (as a result of parole and unduly generous good time allowances); and (3) inadequate sentences involving crimes of violence, white collar crimes, drug trafficking crimes, and environmental offenses.[12]

Eighteen years later, however, the U.S. Supreme Court struck down the mandatory provisions of the Federal Sentencing Guidelines, while also preserving the remaining guidelines law as an essentially advisory scheme to be considered by federal district judges in sentencing defendants. *United States v. Booker*, 543 U.S. 220 (2005). As now modified by *Booker*, federal judges must nevertheless still consider the guidelines--particularly the factors outlined under 18 U.S.C. §553(a)—in tailoring appropriate sentences, subject to a "reasonableness" standard of review by appellate courts. Thus, a sentence must still reflect the seriousness of the offense, promote respect for the law, provide just punishment, provide

---

12. See Enforcement: Sentencing Guidelines Will Mean More Trials, Stiffer Penalties, EPA, DOJ Officials Predict, 12 Chem. Reg. Rep. (BNA) 1633 (Feb. 10, 1989).

D. Corporate and Executive Prosecutions

adequate deterrence, and protect the public. The *Booker* Court stated that the basic goal which Congress intended in promulgating the guidelines was to move the federal sentencing scheme in the direction of increased uniformity. The Court further concluded that the excision of the mandatory aspects of the guidelines still leaves the federal sentencing system consistent with original legislative intent.

8. Criminal enforcement after the BP *Deepwater Horizon* oil spill. In addition to facing private lawsuits and civil governmental actions, those allegedly responsible for the *Deepwater Horizon* oil spill have also faced criminal liability.

The Justice Department filed the first criminal charge against a BP engineer in April 2012, for obstructing justice by allegedly deleting messages purporting to show that BP knew that: (1) the flow rate from the ruptured well was three times higher than initially claimed by the company, and (2) "Top Kill" was unlikely to succeed, but claimed otherwise. Three more BP employees were charged in November 2012: two site managers aboard the *Deepwater Horizon* were charged with manslaughter for acting negligently in their supervision of key safety tests performed on the rig prior to the explosion and for failure to alert onshore engineers of problems in the drilling operation; and BP's former vice-president for exploration in the Gulf of Mexico was charged with obstruction of Congress. Two other employees were also charged with obstruction of justice and for lying to federal investigators.

In November 2012, BP agreed to plead guilty in federal district court in New Orleans to 11 felony counts related to the deaths of 11 workers and paid $4 billion in penalties (to be paid over a period of 5 years) for the oil well blowout and spill. BP also agreed to serve a term of 5 years probation. The plea deal included payment of about $2.4 billion to the National Fish and Wildlife Foundation, $350 million to the National Academy of Sciences, and roughly $500 million to the Securities and Exchange Commission.

Pursuant to the terms of the plea agreement, the federal district court in New Orleans also ordered certain equitable relief against BP, including ordering additional actions related to BP's risk management processes, as well as requiring several initiatives with academia and regulators to develop new technologies related to deepwater drilling safety. In addition, as outlined in BP's plea agreement with the DOJ, BP was required to appoint a process safety monitor and an ethics monitor, both with a term of four years, and an independent auditor is reporting annually on BP's compliance with the remedial terms of probation.

The charges to which BP pled guilty also included one misdemeanor count under the CAA, which triggers a debarment. Mandatory debarment prevents a company from entering into new contracts or new leases with the U.S. government that would be performed at the facility where the CWA violation occurred. A mandatory debarment does not affect any existing contracts or leases a company has with the U.S. government.

A second corporate defendant, Transocean, also agreed to settle its criminal liability with the federal government. Transocean pled guilty to an information, previously filed in federal court in New Orleans, charging the company with violating the CWA. During the guilty plea proceeding, Transocean admitted that members of its crew on board the *Deepwater Horizon*, acting at the direction of BP's well site leaders, known as "company men," were negligent in failing to investigate fully indications that the Macondo well was not secure and that oil and gas were flowing into the well. This criminal resolution is also structured to benefit directly the Gulf region. Under the order entered by the federal district court pursuant to the plea agreement, $150 million of the $400 million criminal recovery is dedicated to acquiring, restoring, preserving, and conserving—in consultation with appropriate state and other resource managers—the marine and coastal environments, ecosystems, and bird and wildlife habitat in the Gulf of Mexico and bordering states harmed by the *Deepwater Horizon* oil spill. This portion of the criminal recovery is also being directed to significant barrier island restoration and/or river diversion off the coast of Louisiana to benefit further and improve coastal wetlands affected by the spill. An additional $150 million is being used to fund improved oil spill prevention and response efforts in the Gulf through research, development, education, and training. Transocean was also sentenced, according to the plea agreement, to five years of probation.

In connection with criminal environmental enforcement, one of the key issues is whether these criminal sanctions meaningfully affect the corporate behavior of BP, Transocean, and others involved in deepwater oil drilling. In this regard, it is worth evaluating BP's position on whether the sanctions have already made a difference and caused reform in its business processes.

In making the case that it has reformed, BP has cited significant changes to enhance safety throughout its global operations. BP launched an internal investigation immediately after the spill began and has claimed that it is implementing the investigation's recommendations. BP has also made leadership changes, reorganized its upstream business, created a centralized Safety and Operational Risk organization, and adopted voluntary deepwater drilling standards in the Gulf of Mexico that, BP contends, exceed current regulatory requirements.

9. Individual accountability for corporate crimes. The U.S. Department of Justice UNITED STATES ATTORNEYS' MANUAL states: "Prosecution of a corporation is not a substitute for the prosecution of criminally culpable individuals within or without the corporation." See *United States Attorneys' Manual* 9-28.200 (2008). Nonetheless, as a recent book by a noted University of Maryland School of Law professor suggests, only a relatively low number of individual prosecutions have recently been undertaken in connection with the investigation and prosecution of large corporate entities. See Rena Steinzor, WHY NOT JAIL? INDUSTRIAL CATASTROPHES, CORPORATE MANAGEMENT AND GOVERNMENT INACTION (Cambridge University Press, 2014).

James Stewart makes the case that "[h]ardly any top executives at the financial firms paying multi-million and billion-dollar-plus firms for engaging in criminal behavior have been charged or convicted." See Stewart, In Corporate Crimes, Individual Accountability Is Elusive, New York Times (February 19, 2015),

To back up his thesis, Stewart references the work of Professor Brandon Garrett of University of Virginia Law School, who found that only 34% of cases of corporate non-prosecution or deferred prosecution agreements resulted in individual criminal charges. Furthermore, Professor Garrett found that, of that 34%, only 42% received any jail time. Professor Garrett's book, TOO BIG TO JAIL, HOW PROSECUTORS COMPROMISE WITH CORPORATIONS (2014), discusses a pattern of negotiation and settlement in which prosecutors demand admissions of wrongdoing, impose penalties, and require structural reforms, but many companies ultimately pay no criminal fines, and high-level employees tend to avoid prosecution.

Significantly, Professor Garrett has concluded that:

> Prosecutors have made some changes already in response to the "too big to jail" concerns that people have raised, but much more needs to be done. It is crucial that we get corporate prosecutions right, given the size, seriousness, and complexity of the crimes that can occur in the corporate setting. Corporate prosecutions are themselves too big to fail. Id. at 288.

This issue has obvious environmental law reverberations.

Those wishing to exploit the land for their own private benefit never cease their political efforts. Those who would protect the natural world cannot afford to do less.

—R.F. Dasmann

20

Public Environmental Rights and Duties: The Public Trust Doctrine

A. Beyond Direct Threats to Human Health & Property: Modern Rediscovery of the Public Trust Doctrine
B. Applying the Modern Public Trust Doctrine

By the law of nature, these things are common to mankind: the air, running water, the sea, and consequently the shores of the sea. . . .

—Institutes of Emperor Justinian, 2.1.1 (A.D. 529)

So neither can the king intrude upon the common property, thus understood, and appropriate it to himself or to the fiscal purposes of the nation. . . . The enjoyment of it is a natural right which cannot be infringed or taken away, unless by arbitrary power, and that, in theory at least, [can]not exist in a free government. . . .

—*Arnold v. Mundy*, 6 N.J.L. 1, 87-88 (1821)

We do not inherit the earth from our fathers. We borrow it from our children.

—David Brower

A. BEYOND DIRECT THREATS TO HUMAN HEALTH & PROPERTY: MODERN REDISCOVERY OF THE PUBLIC TRUST DOCTRINE

The resurrection of the public trust doctrine (PTD) from relative obscurity is environmental law's unique contribution to the modern legal system, and the trust's continuing background presence is felt throughout the field.

At its heart, environmental law has come to incorporate a set of principles representing and accounting for present and future natural and civic values that lie beyond the daily marketplace and current events. It is perhaps only in environmental law that the legal system directly incorporates measures of long-term societal needs into today's operative norms and doctrinal provisions.

The "sustainable development" principle of domestic and global natural resources management is a prime example. The PTD embodies this perspective and goes further, incorporating societal protections that range beyond strict human utility.

Most environmental cases, of course, are built upon the ultimate social utility of environmental protection. By keeping Allied's Kepone wastes out of the river and bay, human and economic health are protected along with natural resources.[1] We protect birds from pesticides in part to protect human genetics. We protect stratospheric ozone and the CO_2 functions of global forests on behalf of long-term human and planetary health. But the PTD, drawing upon ancient roots of heritage legacy principles reflecting themes of continuing intergenerational equity, touches virtually every area of environmental protection law.

> Professor Joseph Sax has said that the Public Trust Doctrine, descending from codified customary law in the ancient Byzantine Empire, is perhaps the only truly innovative legal doctrine that environmental law has brought into the modern legal system; the rest is more familiar old wine in new bottles. For his part, Justice Scalia has regarded the PTD as a dangerous legal affliction from across the seas that threatens established rights and norms of corporate and private property.

As noted in Chapter 1, public trust concepts are found in the protection of endangered species, PSD in air quality far cleaner than necessary for health, restoration of mined lands despite low locational values, safeguards for groundwater purity even where no one uses the groundwater resource, and so on.

Here's a quartet of evocative public trust examples:

The Methusaleh Tree. What is lost when an ancient forest is gone, or an ancient tree? A number of years ago a geography professor set off on a summer grant project to find the oldest living thing on the face of the earth. What would that be? Not a great whale, not a giant redwood. It seems the oldest living things on earth are bristlecone pine trees. Bristlecone pines are not majestic monoliths but rather small scraggly survivors, some more than 4000 years old, twisted and gnarled with the winds of time, surviving ice storms, droughts, and wildfires, clinging to a ridge in a federal forest reserve in a remote region of eastern Nevada.

The professor, however, did not have a modern microscopic coring tool for dating trees. The only method he had available to determine a tree's age was to cut it down and count the cross-section rings. So with the approval of the government official in charge of the forest, he found the oldest living thing on the face of the earth and dated it in that way. It was 4990 years old. To be certain he had found the real Methuselah tree, moreover, he also dated — killed — the next two oldest living things on earth.

What did we lose by the death of those bristlecone pine trees? Since the next-oldest was automatically made the oldest living thing by the professor's actions, what difference did it make? But if you feel something move in the pit of your stomach from the death of the Methusaleh tree, it may be the PTD. If you could have brought this issue to a court in time, seeking to stop the cutting, you would need to find some cause of action to ground

---

1. Hit by Allied's pesticide contamination in the 1970s, noted in Chapter 2, Chesapeake Bay has since then been cursed by nutrient runoffs from chicken-processing plants in the Chesapeake Bay watershed, triggering outbreaks of the toxic *Pfiesteria piscicida* organism that not only has caused the death of hundreds of thousands of fish but also human skin lesions and illness. Hog wastes in North Carolina rivers have done the same.

A. Rediscovery of the Public Trust Doctrine

an injunction. Analytically the cause of action would probably be, expressly or implicitly, the legal theory of public trust.

Selling Lake Michigan. The classic public trust case in U.S. law arose from a scandalous case of political corruption in the 1890s, when the Illinois state legislature was induced by railroad lawyers to pass a statute selling two square miles of submerged lands along the Chicago waterfront, at a very cheap price, to the Illinois Central Railroad Company, which planned to fill and develop the submerged lands for multimillion-dollar profits. When a subsequent (presumably less corrupt) legislature tried to rescind the statute, the state faced the prospect of paying huge compensation awards to get the waterfront back. In *Illinois Central Railroad v. Illinois*,[2] the Supreme Court had to figure out how to avoid the takings claim without spreading out on the public record the unseemly story of how the state had made the deal in the first place. The Court seized upon the unwritten ancient PTD: The state never had unbridled authority to give away such trust lands in the first place, the Court explained, so the statutory transfer was simply void. Lake Michigan remained a public trust resource owned by all.

FIGURE 20-1. *Surviving the death of Methusaleh: A bristlecone pine on "The Table" formation, Snake Mountain Range, Nevada. PHOTO CREDIT: G. Thomas.*

The Idaho Shoshone County River Oil-Sheen Case. Can a state require a million-dollar restoration effort to remove a slight oil sheen from a river, if there is no likelihood of any harm to humans or the ecosystem? In the mid-1990s, it was discovered that a small amount of petroleum was leaching underground from an old railroad switching area into Idaho's St. Joe River, causing a rainbow effect on the downstream water surface. The Rock Island Railroad Company argued that the sheen was totally insignificant and didn't come from a regulatable "point source." What did it matter that viewed from one angle the water looked a little different, if no other invidious effects could be shown?[3] The State of Idaho, however, prepared a lawsuit "as the trustee of the natural resources within the state . . . entrusted with the management and protection of said natural resources . . . and as *parens patriae* [likewise a trusteeship sounding in public trust] on behalf of all residents of the state," alleging injury to, among other things, "ecological" and "aesthetic qualities." Faced with the public trust claim for broad affirmative injunctive relief as well as natural resource damages, the defendants ultimately settled, agreeing to fund and carry out a long-term treatment protocol under state oversight.

---

2. 146 U.S. 387 (1892). A virtually identical but more recent case is *Lake Mich. Fed'n v. U.S. Army Corps of Eng'rs*, 742 F. Supp. 441 (N.D. Ill. 1990).

3. In fact it seems to the authors, who are trout fishers, that entomologists could have been found to demonstrate a lethal effect on subimago stages of certain aquatic insect species, which would impact the river's food chain.

Natural Resources Damages: *Steuart Transportation.* The PTD has frequently surfaced, expressly or implicitly, in the blossoming area of natural resources damages. In one typical case, a badly maintained oil barge foundered while being towed, dumping thousands of gallons of crude oil into coastal marshes of the Chesapeake Bay, killing or injuring wildlife and habitat:

> Approximately 30,000 migratory birds allegedly were destroyed as a result of the oil spill. . . . Steuart contends that . . . to recover money damages for the loss of property one must establish an ownership interest, and . . . neither the state nor the federal Government has an ownership interest in migratory waterfowl. . . . The Commonwealth and the U.S., on the other hand, maintain . . . their right to recover for the loss of migratory waterfowl . . . upon the sovereign right to protect the public interest in preserving wildlife resources. This sovereign right derives from . . . the public trust doctrine and the doctrine of parens patriae. . . .
>
> This Court is of the opinion that both of these doctrines are viable and support the State and the Federal claims for the waterfowl. . . . Under the public trust doctrine, the State of Virginia and the U.S. have the right and the duty to protect and preserve the public's interest in natural wildlife resources. Such right does not derive from ownership of the resources but from a duty owing to the people. . . . *In re Steuart Transp. Co., Owner of the Tank Barge STC-101,* 495 F. Supp. 38, 40 (E.D. Va. 1980).

Similar natural resources damages were claimed on common law public trust principles after the *Exxon-Valdez* oil spill in Alaska and in a host of cases under resource damage provisions of several federal pollution statutes. The legal aftermath of the 2010 BP Deepwater Gulf oil spill is likely to reawaken public trust precedents, as well as push statutory boundaries under OPA-90.

Three Legal Public Trust Settings. Public trust law, coming from constitutional and statutory sources as well as nonstatutory judicial holdings,[4] is discernable in a wide range of legal settings but can be roughly categorized into three basic legal formats.

- *"Alienation"* cases, limiting government attempts to sell public trust assets to a private party, which was the basis of the *Illinois Central* Chicago waterfront case.[5]
- *"Diversion"* cases, limiting agency attempts to divert ownership and use of public trust assets from one public use like parkland to other more exploitive uses like government buildings, dumps, or parking lots.[6]
- *"Resource-defense"* or *"prevention-of-derogation"* issues, often seen in the water pollution setting but including land-based cases like the bristlecone pines, where human actors threaten to pollute or destroy trust resources.[7]

What the PTD contributes to each setting is an abstract societal interest framed in present and future legacy terms. Its extent is particularly significant, however, in its

---

4. See Cal. Const. art. XV, §§2, 3; Mass. Const. art. IX, §1; Pa. Const. art. I, §27; Mass. Gen. Laws ch. 214, §7A; Mich. Comp. Laws §§691-1201; Tenn. Code Ann. §70.324.

5. The classic example of restricted alienability of public trust assets, *Illinois Central Ry. v. Illinois,* 146 U.S. 387 (1892) is noted later in this chapter.

6. An example of the diversion issue is the *Paepke* case, discussed in Section B of this chapter, where the court reviewed a diversion in Chicago's Washington Park. Lying in a gray area between the alienation and diversion categories are cases such as *Vermont v. Cent. Vt. Ry.,* 571 A.2d 1128 (Vt. 1989), where the state supreme court held that a public utility railroad company's grant of lands on the shores of Lake Champlain would be restricted to public trust uses, where the company, which held title, wanted to undertake resort and commercial development of the lands.

7. See, e.g., Tenn. Code Ann. §§70.324 et seq.; beyond water resources, see the redwood cases, invoking the trust to protect redwoods against erosion and destruction. *Sierra Club v. Dep't of Interior,* 376 F. Supp. 90 (N.D. Cal. 1974); *Sierra Club v. Dep't of Interior,* 398 F. Supp. 284 (N.D. Cal. 1975).

A. Rediscovery of the Public Trust Doctrine

representation of the social and cultural values of natural conditions, going beyond traditional definitions of harm.

The trust's primary remedies are equitable—prohibitory or affirmative restoration injunctions and other orders—but can include monetary damages for remediation or natural resources losses as well.

> The PTD, as a revolutionary new legal concept, was pulled into the modern legal system from ancient fifth-century roots by the 1970 writings of Professor Sax that follow here. It has extraordinary resonance within modern environmental consciousness, from endangered butterflies to anthropogenic global climate change, and as such it can have major reverberations in the political arena as well as in law and philosophy.

Joseph L. Sax, Defending the Environment: A Strategy for Citizen Action
163-165 (1970)

Long ago there developed in the law of the Roman Empire a legal theory known as the "doctrine of the public trust." It was founded upon the very sensible idea that certain common properties, such as rivers, the seashore, and the air, were held by government in trusteeship for the free and unimpeded use of the general public. Our contemporary concerns about "the environment" bear a very close conceptual relationship to this venerable legal doctrine.

Under the Roman law, perpetual use of common properties "was dedicated to the public." As one scholar, R.W. Lee, noted: "In general the shore was not owned by individuals. One text suggests that it was the property of the Roman people. More often it is regarded as owned by no one, the public having undefined rights of use and enjoyment."[8] Similarly in England . . . the law developed that "the ownership of the shore, as between the public and the King, has been settled in favor of the King: but . . . this ownership is, and had been immemorially, liable to certain general rights of egress and regress, for fishing, trading, and other uses claimed and used by his subjects."

American law adopted the general idea of trusteeship but rarely applied it to any but a few sorts of public properties such as shorelands and parks. The content and purpose of the doctrine never received a careful explication, though occasionally a comment can be found in the cases to the effect that it is "inconceivable" that any person would claim a private-property interest in the navigable waters of the U.S., assertable against the free and general use of the public at large. And from time to time provisions can be found, as in the Northwest Ordinance of 1787, which stated that "the navigable waters leading into the

---

8. The Latin concepts are *res communes* and *res nullius*. The former referred to such things that, while not susceptible to exclusive ownership, can be enjoyed and used by everyone (such as water, air, and light); the latter referred to things that belonged to no one, "either because they were unappropriated by anyone, such as unoccupied lands or wild animals, or things similar to *res sacrae* or *res religiosae* 'to which a religious character prevents any human right of property attaching.'" Coquillette, Mosses from an Old Manse: Another Look at Some Historic Property Cases about the Environment, 64 Cornell L. Rev. 761, 803 n. 196 (1979); Black's Law Dictionary 1304-1305, 1306 (6th ed. 1990). For more from Justinian's Institutes, see H.F. Jolowicz, Historical Introduction to the Study of Roman Law 502-503 (2d ed. 1954). [EDS.]

Mississippi . . . shall be common highways and forever free . . . to the citizens of the United States. . . ."

The scattered evidence, taken together, suggests that the idea of a public trusteeship rests upon three related principles. First, that certain interests—like the air and the sea—have such importance to the citizenry as a whole that is would be unwise to make them the subject of private ownership. Second, that they partake so much of the bounty of nature, rather than of individual enterprise, that they should be made freely available to the entire citizenry without regard to economic status. And, finally, that it is a principal purpose of government to promote the interests of the general public rather than to redistribute public goods from broad public uses to restricted private benefit. . . .

Joseph L. Sax, The Public Trust Doctrine in Natural Resource Law: Effective Judicial Intervention
68 Mich. L. Rev. 471, 489-502 (1970)

The most celebrated public trust case in American law is the decision of the U.S. Supreme Court in *Illinois Central Railroad Company v. Illinois*, 146 U.S. 387 (1892). . . . The Court did not actually prohibit the disposition of trust lands to private parties. Its holding was much more limited. What a state may not do, the Court said, is to divest itself of authority to govern the whole of an area in which it has responsibility to exercise its police power. To grant almost the entire waterfront of a major city to a private company is, in effect, to abdicate legislative authority over navigation. . . . The Court determined that the states have special regulatory obligations over shorelands, obligations which are inconsistent with large-scale private ownership. The Court stated that the title under which Illinois held the navigable waters of Lake Michigan—

> is different in character from that which the state holds in lands intended for sale. . . . It is a title held in trust for the people of the state that they may enjoy the navigation of the waters, carry on commerce over them, and have liberty of fishing therein freed from the obstruction or interference of private parties.

With this language, the Court articulated a principle that has become the central substantive thought in public trust litigation: When a state holds a resource which is available for the free use of the general public, a court will look with considerable skepticism upon *any* governmental conduct which is calculated *either* to reallocate the resource to more restricted uses *or* to subject public uses to the self-interest of private parties.

The Court in *Illinois Central* did not specify reasons for adopting its position, but the attitude implicit in the decision is fairly obvious. . . . While there may be good reason to use governmental resources to benefit some group smaller than the whole citizenry, there is usually some relatively obvious reason for the subsidy, such as a need to assist the farmer or the urban poor. In addition, there is ordinarily some plainly rational basis for the reallocative structure of any such programs—whether it be taxing the more affluent to support the poor or using the tax base of a large community to sustain programs in a smaller unit of government. Although courts are disinclined to examine these issues through a rigorous economic analysis, it seems fair to say that the foregoing observations are consistent with a general view of the function of government. Accordingly, the court's suspicions are naturally aroused when they are faced with a program which seems quite at odds with such a view of government.

A. Rediscovery of the Public Trust Doctrine

In *Illinois Central* . . . everything seems to have been backwards. There appears to have been no good reason for taxing the general public in order to support a substantial private enterprise in obtaining control of the waterfront. There was no reason to believe that private ownership would have provided incentives for needed developments, as might have been the case with land grants in remote areas of the country; and if the resource was to be maintained for traditional uses, it was unlikely that private management would have produced more efficient or attractive services to the public. Indeed, the public benefits that could have been achieved by private ownership are not easy to identify.

Although the facts of *Illinois Central* were highly unusual — and the grant in that case was particularly egregious — the case remains an important precedent. The model for judicial skepticism it built poses a set of relevant standards for current, less dramatic instances of dubious governmental conduct. . . .

A court should look skeptically at programs which infringe broad public uses in favor of narrower ones. Similarly there should be a special burden of justification on government when such results are brought into question. But *Illinois Central* also raises more far-reaching issues. For example, what are the implications for the workings of the democratic process when such programs, although ultimately found to be unjustifiable, are nonetheless promulgated through democratic institutions? Furthermore, what does the existence of those seeming imperfections in the democratic process imply about the role of the courts, which, *Illinois Central* notwithstanding, are generally reluctant to hold invalid the acts of co-equal branches of government?

THE CONTEMPORARY DOCTRINE OF THE PUBLIC TRUST: AN INSTRUMENT FOR DEMOCRATIZATION . . . The [Massachusetts] Supreme Judicial Court has shown a clear recognition of the potential for abuse which exists whenever power over lands is given to a body which is not directly responsive to the electorate. To counteract the influence which private interest groups may have with administrative agencies and to encourage policy decisions to be made openly at the legislative level, the Massachusetts court has developed a rule that a change in the use of public lands is impermissible without a clear showing of legislative approval.

In *Gould v. Greylock Reservation Commission*,[9] the Supreme Judicial Court of Massachusetts took the major step in developing the doctrine applicable to changes in the use of lands dedicated to the public interest. . . . Mount Greylock, about which the controversy centered, is the highest summit of an isolated range which is surrounded by lands of considerably lower elevation. In 1888, a group of citizens, interested in preserving the mountain as an unspoiled natural forest, promoted the creation of an association for the purpose of laying out a public park on it. The state ultimately acquired about 9,000 acres, and the legislature enacted a statute creating the Greylock Reservation Commission and giving it certain of the powers of a park commission. By 1953, the reservation contained a campground, a few ski trails, a small lodge, a memorial tower, some TV and radio facilities, and a parking area and garage. In that year, the legislature enacted a statute creating an Authority to construct and operate on Mount Greylock an aerial tramway and certain other facilities, and it authorized the original commission to lease to the Authority "any portion of the Mount Greylock Reservation." . . .

A joint venture corporation called American Resort Services [was] to lease 4,000 acres of the reservation from the Commission . . . to build and manage an elaborate ski

---

9. 215 N.E.2d 114 (Mass. 1966).

development, for which it was to receive forty percent of the net operations revenue of the enterprise. . . .

Five citizens of the county in which the reservation is located brought an action against both the Greylock Reservation Commission and the Tramway Authority . . . as beneficiaries of the public trust under which the reservation was said to be held, and they asked that the court declare invalid both the lease of the 4,000 acres of reservation land and the agreement between the Authority and the management corporation. They asked the court to examine the statutes authorizing the project, and to interpret them narrowly to prevent both the extensive development contemplated and the transfer of supervisory powers into the hands of a profit-making corporation. The case seemed an exceedingly difficult one for the plaintiffs, both because the statutes creating the Authority were phrased in extremely general terms, and because legislative grants of power to administrative agencies are usually read quite broadly. . . . Nonetheless, the court held both the lease and the management agreement invalid. . . . The critical passage in the decision is that in which the court stated:

> The profit sharing feature and some aspects of the project itself strongly suggest a commercial enterprise. In addition to the absence of any clear or express statutory authorization of as broad a delegation of responsibility by the Authority as is given by the management agreement, we find no express grant to the Authority of power to permit use of public lands and of the Authority's borrowed funds for what seems, in part at least, a commercial venture for private profit.

In coming to this recognition, the court took note of the unusual developments which led to the project. What had begun as authorization to a public agency to construct a tramway had developed into a proposal for an elaborate ski area. Since ski resorts are popular and profitable private enterprises, it seems slightly odd in itself that a state would undertake such a development. Furthermore, the public authority had gradually turned over most of its supervisory powers to a private consortium and had been compelled by economic circumstances to agree to a bargain which heavily favored the private investment house.

It hardly seems surprising, then, that the court questioned why a state should subordinate a public park, serving a useful purpose as relatively undeveloped land, to the demands of private investors for building such a commercial facility. . . . Yet the court was unwilling to invalidate an act of the legislature on the sole ground that it involved a modification of the use of public trust land. Instead, the court devised a legal rule which imposed a presumption that the state does not ordinarily intend to divert trust properties in such a manner as to lessen public uses. . . . Under the Massachusetts courts' rule, that assumption . . . is to be altered only if the legislature clearly indicates that it has a different view of the public interest. . . .

Although such a rule may seem to be an elaborate example of judicial indirection, it is in fact directly responsive to the central problem of public trust controversies. There must be some means by which a court can keep a check on legislative grants of public lands while ensuring that historical uses may be modified to accommodate contemporary public needs and that the power to make such modifications resides in a branch of government which is responsive to public demands. . . .

While it will seldom be true that a particular governmental act can be termed corrupt, it will often be the case that the whole of the public interest has not been adequately considered by the legislative or administrative officials whose conduct has been brought into question. In those cases, which are at the center of concern with the public trust, there is a strong, if not demonstrable, implication that the acts in question represent a response to limited and self-interested proponents of public action. It is not difficult to perceive

A. Rediscovery of the Public Trust Doctrine

the reason for the legislative and administrative actions which give rise to such cases, for public officials are frequently subjected to intensive representations on behalf of interests seeking official concessions to support proposed enterprises. The concessions desired by those interests are often of limited visibility to the general public so that public sentiment is not aroused; but the importance of the grants to those who seek them may lead to extraordinarily vigorous and persistent efforts. It is in these situations that public trust lands are likely to be put in jeopardy and that legislative watchfulness is likely to be at the lowest levels. To send such a case back for express legislative authority is to create through the courts an openness and visibility which is the public's principal protection against overreaching, but which is often absent in the routine political process.[10]

COMMENTARY & QUESTIONS

1. The history of the PTD in the U.S. Professor Sax's article can claim most of the credit for the active presence of the PTD in U.S. environmental law. (It has been so often cited as the seminal work in the field that Professor Sax was recently introduced at a conference on western public interest law as "Seminal Sax" and received a standing ovation on the point.) But the PTD did exist earlier in the case law of the U.S., waiting to be rediscovered (somewhat like the Refuse Act of 1899). In 1810, in *Carson v. Glazer*, 2 Binn. 475, the Pennsylvania court asserted the PTD to affirm that no one could own the rights to fish in a river as against the public. That case is notable, moreover, not only for the fact that it used the term *trust* in the very modern sense that Sax uses it, but also that the court quite matter of factly extended the traditional trust from navigable waters and ocean waters to inland waterways with no suggestion of navigability. The New Jersey Supreme Court followed in *Arnold v. Mundy*, 6 N.J.L. 1 (1821), asserting that no one could own shellfishing beds as against the public. Other cases prior to *Illinois Central* had established the same principle. *Martin v. Waddell*, 41 U.S. 367 (1842). Accordingly, the questions that have arisen about the PTD are not debating its existence but rather the terms upon which the trust exists and applies.

2. The public trust as trust law. The PTD is an equitable doctrine that shares its elements with the far more commonly litigated doctrine of private trusts. There must be a "thing" about which the trust is concerned: the "corpus" or "res," the defined bundle of assets to be

---

10. [Sax notes the common problem of agency insulation and the low visibility of official decisions:] After the massive oil leakage off the Santa Barbara coast . . . , the governmental agency charged with protecting the public interest decided against holding public hearings prior to granting approval for a project because the agency "preferred not to stir the natives up any more than possible [sic]," Interoffice Memo from Eugene W. Standley, Staff Engineer, U.S. Dept. of the Interior, Feb. 15, 1968. When questions were raised, the agency publicly responded by saying, "we feel maximum provision has been made for the local environment and that further delay in the lease sale would not be consistent with the national interest." N.Y. Times, March 25, 1969, at 30, col. 6 (quoting from a letter from the Undersecretary of the Interior to the chairman of the board of supervisors of Santa Barbara County). But the agency privately indicated that "The 'heat' has not died down but we can keep trying to alleviate the fears of the people," id. at col. 3, and noted that pressures were being applied by the oil company whose equipment worth "millions of dollars" was being held "in anticipation."

There are a variety of other ways in which agencies minimize public participation in their deliberations. For example, the duty to hold a public hearing may technically be satisfied by holding a hearing which is "announced" to the public by posting a notice on an obscure bulletin board in a post office. *Nashville I-40 Steering Comm. v. Ellington*, 387 F.2d 179, 183 (6th Cir. 1967), cert. denied, 390 U.S. 921 (1968). Alternatively, a statutory hearing requirement may simply be ignored, and the argument later made that despite the omission no citizen has legal standing to challenge the agency's action. See *D.C. Fed'n of Civic Ass'ns v. Airis*, 391 F.2d 478 (D.C. Cir. 1968).

owned and managed under the trust framework. Then there must be a *trustee*, a person or entity legally charged with responsibilities and rights. Trustees in Anglo-American law actually own the resources in terms of legal title. They accordingly have the right to manage, sell, lease, and develop the trust assets, but only insofar as a careful fiduciary would so as to protect the existence of the assets and achieve the purposes of the trust, and always answerable to the equity court. The *terms* of a trust are critically important and differ from trust to trust. The trustees must follow the precise dictates and terms of the trust stipulations set up by the trustor or settlor. If a trust is mandated to maximize the financial security of family members, then the management of the assets will be judged by the careful economic standards necessary to achieve that end. If the trust is set up to care for a park or an educational institution, then the primary trust standard is to maintain the character and use of the trust property. While the legal title of a trust rests with the trustee, the real equitable or beneficial title to the property, enforceable in court, is held by the beneficiaries. In most trusts, the court's enforcement and oversight comes at the request of beneficiaries, any one of whom has standing to call for an accounting from the trustees, in court.

These, then, are the generic elements of a trust. Can you roughly identify how each of them is to be defined in the case of the PTD? In a public trust, who is the trustee, who are the beneficiaries, what is the corpus, and, perhaps most important, what are the terms? (The theorized identity of the settlor may depend upon your theological inclinations.)

> The public trust's ancient lineage and essential societal role do not mean that it is uncontroversial. For instance, just as environmental conditions do not stop at international borders, note that sometimes, as in the following milestone case, the PTD does not shy away from private property boundaries.

Marks v. Whitney
491 P.2d 374 (Cal. Sup. Ct. 1971)

McComb, J. This is a quiet title action. . . . A part of Marks' property on the westerly side of Tomales Bay in Marin County is tidelands acquired under an 1874 patent issued pursuant to the Act of March 28, 1868. . . . A small [strip] of these tidelands adjoins almost the entire shoreline of Whitney's upland property. Marks asserted complete ownership of the tidelands and the right to fill and develop them. Whitney opposed on the ground that this would cut off his rights as a littoral owner and as a member of the public. . . . He requested a declaration in the decree that Marks' title was burdened with a public trust easement. . . . This matter is of great public importance, particularly in view of population pressures, demands for recreational property, and the increasing development of seashore and waterfront property. . . .

The title of Marks in these tidelands is burdened with a public easement. . . . The state holds tidelands in trust for public purposes. . . . Public trust easements are traditionally defined in terms of navigation, commerce and fisheries. They have been held to include the right to fish, hunt, bathe, swim, to use for boating and general recreation purposes the navigable waters of the state, and to use the bottom of the navigable waters for anchoring, standing, or other purposes. . . .

The public uses to which tidelands are subject are sufficiently flexible to encompass changing public needs. In administering the trust the state is not burdened with an outmoded classification favoring one mode of utilization over another. There is a growing

B. Applying the Modern Public Trust Doctrine

public recognition that one of the most important public uses of the tidelands—a use encompassed within the tidelands trust—is the preservation of those lands in their natural state, so that they may serve as ecological units for scientific study, as open space, and as environments which provide food and habitat for birds and marine life, and which favorably affect the scenery and climate of the area....

The power of the state to control, regulate and utilize its navigable waterways and the lands lying beneath them, when acting within the terms of the trust, is absolute, except as limited by the paramount supervisory power of the federal government over navigable waters.... There has been no official act of either sovereignty to modify or extinguish the public trust servitude upon Marks' tidelands [and accordingly] the court may not bar members of the public from lawfully asserting or exercising public trust rights on this privately owned tidelands....

COMMENTARY & QUESTIONS

1. The evolving public trust. Note how the court matter-of-factly states that "the public uses to which tidelands are subject are sufficiently flexible to encompass changing public needs." As constitutional jurisprudence constantly demonstrates, the definition of any significant basic doctrine capable of evolving in ongoing societal contexts is bound to be fascinating and controversial, especially if public rights are held to be evolving on private titled property.

2. How is the public trust a trust? The PTD echoes the elements of private trusts, construing governments as the trustees of the public commons, rights, and resources, with a duty to protect the trust assets in a balanced fiduciary fashion, with only a qualified right to sell, develop, or permit exploitation. The terms of the public trust thus generally reflect a presumption in favor of preservation of the natural and cultural legacy received from past generations, to be passed to the future. The beneficiaries, it then might be said, are all the citizens of the jurisdiction—of the present, the future, and even the past.

B. APPLYING THE MODERN PUBLIC TRUST DOCTRINE

1. Public Trust Balancing: Diversion

The following decision, denying the environmental plaintiffs' claims, involved a diversion of public parkland to a more intensive narrowed public use. It echoes Sax's analysis of the trust's procedural requirements but also experiments, perhaps inexactly, with the process of defining *substantive* public trust standards.

Paepke v. Building Commission
263 N.E.2d 11 (Ill. Sup. Ct. 1970)

BURT, J. . . . A site has been designated in Washington Park for the erection of a school-park facility. The Chicago Park District proposes to convey to the Public Building Commission of Chicago for such purposes a total of 3.839 acres located in the northwest portion of the park about 250 feet from the northern boundary. On 2.586 acres of this site the building commission proposes to construct a middle school for approximately 1500 students to be leased to the Board of Education of the City of Chicago. The remaining 1.253 acres would be utilized in the construction of a gymnasium and recreational facilities which will be leased to the Chicago Park District. . . .

It is plaintiffs' theory that the parks in question are so dedicated that they are held in public trust for use only as park or recreational grounds and that those of them who are property owners adjacent to or in the vicinity of a park dedicated by the acts of 1869 have a private property right to the continuation of the park use of which even the legislature cannot deprive them. They further contend that all plaintiffs who are citizens and residents of any area of the city have a public property right to enforce the public trust existing by reason of the dedication of the parks as aforesaid and to require that no change of park use be permitted because the legislature has not explicitly and openly so provided by statute. . . .

Such dedication having been made by the sovereign, the agencies created by it hold the properties in trust for the uses and purposes specified and for the benefit of the public. See *Illinois Central*; Sax, The Public Trust Doctrine in Natural Resource Law: Effective Judicial Intervention, 68 Mich. L. Rev. 471-566.[11] [The plaintiffs have standing to enforce the trust.[12]]

As to . . . whether there has been a sufficient manifestation of legislative intent to permit the diversion and reallocation contemplated by the plan proposed by defendants, it . . . is our conclusion [that the] legislation is sufficiently broad, comprehensive and definite to allow the diversion in use involved here.

In passing we think it appropriate to refer to the [substantive balancing] approach developed by the courts of our sister state, Wisconsin, in dealing with diversion problems. . . . The Supreme Court of Wisconsin [has] approved proposed diversions in the use of public trust lands under conditions which demonstrate (1) that public bodies would control use of the area in question, (2) that the area would be devoted to public purposes and open to the public, (3) the diminution of the area of original use would be small compared with the entire area, (4) that none of the public uses of the original area would be destroyed or greatly impaired and (5) that the disappointment of those wanting to use the area of new use for former purposes is negligible when compared to the greater convenience to be afforded those members of the public using the new facility. We believe that the present plans for Washington Park meet all of these tests. . . .

The issues presented in this case illustrate the classic struggle between those members of the public who would preserve our parks and open lands in their pristine purity and those charged with administrative responsibilities who, under the pressures of the changing needs of an increasingly complex society, find it necessary, in good faith and for the public good, to encroach to some extent upon lands heretofore considered inviolate to change. The resolution of this conflict in any given case is for the legislature and not the courts. . . .

COMMENTARY & QUESTIONS

1. The scope of the trust. Note in the *Paepke* case how matter-of-factly the court accepts the assumption that the PTD, developed in the oceans of the Roman Empire, applies to a

---

11. Extensive quotations from Professor Sax's article are omitted. [EDS.]
12. "If the public trust doctrine is to have any meaning or vitality at all, . . . the members of the public . . . must have the right and standing to enforce it."

B. Applying the Modern Public Trust Doctrine

public parkland, and that citizens have standing to sue. The PTD has three strategic advantages over common law remedies: (1) automatic standing (unlike public nuisance, which the lower court in *Paepke* relied on to deny standing); (2) a presumption in favor of public uses, transferring the burden of proof to the public trustee to justify a diversion or alienation; and (3) an ability to avoid sovereign immunity (in this sense at least the public trust clearly acts like a constitutional provision). In fact, there has been little serious argument in the public trust cases over the past decades about whether the PTD can appropriately be applied to dedicated parklands. The fundamental idea of a park, it appears, is a long-term special management relationship between land, people, and government. (This may help to explain why Professor Sax's public trust scholarship moved quite naturally into an extensive study of the meaning of parks and wilderness in the twentieth century. See J. Sax, MOUNTAINS WITHOUT HANDRAILS (1981).) What is a "park"? The U.S. invented the idea of national parks, but there is a continuing debate about what they mean. If the PTD applies to "parks," does it apply to all state or federal forests? Is a concept of express or implied terms of special "dedication" the distinguishing factor?

2. The *Paepke* court's balancing process: a substantive, not merely a procedural, standard? Is the *Paepke* court's holding based on the Wisconsin (substantive) or the Massachusetts (procedural) trust analysis? If, based on Professor Sax's description of the Massachusetts cases, the public trust balance is merely procedural, all a development-minded legislature has to do to override the trust would be to pass exceedingly specific authorization for a favored project. (In *Paepke*, in contrast to Sax's prescription, the court did not even require specific authorization: "The legislation is sufficiently broad, comprehensive and definite to allow the diversion.") The *Paepke* case implies, however, that governments also have substantive trusteeship duties as well as procedural requirements—if the court had found that the Wisconsin trust tests were violated, the school development would have been enjoined despite its statutory authorization.

Under the Wisconsin tests, proposed alterations of trust resources will apparently be tested by scrutiny of the actual balance struck between trust obligations and values on one hand and economic or other legislative development motives on the other. The public trust's long-term legacy value is presumed to be primary. Departures from the trust bear the substantive burden of persuasion. When the government is acting as a trustee, it comes before the equity court as a fiduciary subject to special scrutiny.[13] Although courts review the acts of other branches of government deferentially, equity precedents for trust accountings from public officials as in charitable trusts argue for less deference.

The standards applied by the *Paepke* court, and the process by which it applied them, have the ring of good common sense. The court recognizes that parklands are important public trust resources and takes seriously its role of determining whether the diversion ordered by the governmental process will be permitted to chop a piece out of Washington Park. What do you think of the Wisconsin standards, and of the way the *Paepke* court applied them to the case? Take the five tests one by one and ask yourself whether they sufficiently capture the protective ideas of the public trust. Is there anything missing that could be added as a litigable standard in *Paepke*?

---

13. See *People ex rel. Scott v. Chicago Park Dist.*, 360 N.E.2d 773 (Ill. 1977). The Illinois legislature wanted to convey 194.6 acres of submerged lands under Lake Michigan to U.S. Steel—remarkably like the circumstances of *Illinois Central*. Despite a legislative assertion in the bill that the conveyance would result in "the conversion of otherwise useless and unproductive submerged land into an important commercial development to the benefit of the people of the State of Illinois," the court wasn't biting. "The self-serving recitation of a public purpose within a legislative enactment is not conclusive of the existence of such purpose." Id. at 781.

Why was the city of Chicago diverting this section of parkland to its school department's use? Is this the only place in this area of Chicago where the school board could build a new school and facilities? Or is it rather an economic tradeoff? Presumably, since they have the power of eminent domain, the school board and city authorities could take 3.8 acres anywhere in this part of the city. The only problem is cost, because it would surely cost a great deal more to take private property than to grab public property for free. But that motive—saving cash—will in *every* case result in diversion or destruction of public trust resources. In the *Overton Park* case, analyzed in Chapter 6, the Supreme Court strictly interpreted the Parklands §4(f) statutory provision in which Congress, faced with the same dilemma of automatic tradeoffs, declared that no parkland shall be taken for a federal-aid highway unless there is "no feasible and prudent alternative." Professor Sax clearly would not object to that standard.

For another formulation of the balance, see *Payne v. Kassab*, 312 A.2d 86, 94 (Pa. Commw. Ct. 1973). The *Payne* court, citing no precedent, asserted that a change in use of public trust parkland must meet three standards: (1) compliance with applicable statutes and regulations, (2) a reasonable effort to minimize environmental "incursions" resulting from the change in use, and (3) benefits must outweigh any resulting harms. The third test is clearly the key to determining whether there will be a meaningful trust balance or a mere conclusory bureaucratic write-off: Will harms be weighed in terms of long-term intangible trust values, or market dollars? Will project benefits be accounted realistically, or in the promoters' hyperbolic terms? Will alternatives be scrupulously weighed against the proposal? Only with a balance weighing the full range of societal legacy values will the sensitive principles of the trust be honored. Note too that the terms of the trust balance, weighing how much, if any, modification is permissible, may be quite different in the three different trust settings of resource derogation, alienation, and diversion.

3. A diversity of values: environmental justice tradeoffs? If the City of Chicago was merely trying to save a few dollars and could just as well have condemned private land near the park for its school, that surely should be weighed against the city's proposal. But shouldn't the court also consider the environmental justice question whether particular proposed alternative locations would disrupt stable, low-income, minority neighborhoods?

2. Public Trust Protections Against Derogation

Or what if protection of the public trust resource imposes heavy burdens and expenses on millions of citizens, rich and poor, in a major U.S. city?

National Audubon Society v. Superior Court of Alpine County *The Mono Lake Case*
658 P.2d 709 (Cal. Sup. Ct. 1983)

[The County of Los Angeles, located in its dry coastal enclave on the southern California coast, has 13 million inhabitants, and continues to grow each year. To assure that water supplies critical to its survival and growth would remain available, city officials thought that they had locked up sufficient appropriated/contract water rights in the Sierra Nevada Mountains[14] to last well into the twenty-first century. Using the PTD, environmentalists filed

---

14. The bitter battles over those water rights formed part of the political backdrop for Roman Polanski's movie *Chinatown*.

B. Applying the Modern Public Trust Doctrine

a lawsuit against Los Angeles's water diversions. The case eventually came to the California Supreme Court on a federal trial judge's request for clarification of the state's PTD.]

Broussard, J. . . . Mono Lake, the second largest lake in California, sits at the base of the Sierra Nevada escarpment near the eastern entrance to Yosemite National Park. The lake is saline; it contains no fish but supports a large population of brine shrimp which

FIGURE 20-2. *Views of Mono Lake: top photograph shows the setting and tufa spires rising from the lake bed; bottom photograph shows land bridge to Negit Island created by falling water levels in 1979—because of feeder stream diversions to Los Angeles—allowing invading predators to cross over and destroy the island's nesting population of 38,000 California gulls, three-fourths of the gull's total population in the state. Photo: ©Jim Stroup/Mono Lake Committee.*

feed vast numbers of nesting and migratory birds. Islands in the lake protect a large breeding colony of California gulls, and the lake itself serves as a haven on the migration route for thousands of Northern Phalarope, Wilson's Phalarope, and Eared Grebe. Towers and spires of tufa on the north and south shores are matters of geological interest and a tourist attraction.

Although Mono Lake receives some water from rain and snow on the lake surface, historically most of its supply came from snowmelt in the Sierra Nevada. Five freshwater streams — Mill, Lee Vining, Walker, Parker and Rush Creeks — arise near the crest of the range and carry the annual runoff to the west shore of the lake. In 1940, however, the state Division of Water Resources granted the Department of Water and Power of the City of Los Angeles (DWP) a permit to appropriate virtually the entire flow of four of the five streams flowing into the lake. DWP promptly constructed facilities to divert about half the flow of these streams into DWP's Owens Valley aqueduct. In 1970 DWP completed a second diversion tunnel, and since that time has taken virtually the entire flow of these streams.... The ultimate effect of continued diversions is a matter of intense dispute, but there seems little doubt that both the scenic beauty and the ecological values of Mono Lake are imperiled....

The case brings together for the first time two systems of legal thought: the appropriative water rights system which since the days of the gold rush has dominated California water law, and the public trust doctrine which, after evolving as a shield for the protection of tidelands, now extends its protective scope to navigable lakes. Ever since we first recognized that the public trust protects environmental and recreational values [citing *Marks v. Whitney*] ... the two systems of legal thought have been on a collision course. Johnson, Public Trust Protection for Stream Flows and Lake Levels, 14 U.C. Davis L. Rev. 233 (1980). They meet in a unique and dramatic setting which highlights the clash of values. Mono Lake is a scenic and ecological treasure of national significance, imperiled by continued diversions of water; yet, the need of Los Angeles for water is apparent, its reliance on rights granted by the board evident, the cost of curtailing diversions substantial....

The core of the public trust doctrine is the state's authority as sovereign to exercise a continuous supervision and control over the navigable waters of the state and the lands underlying those waters. This authority applies to the waters tributary to Mono Lake and bars DWP or any other party from claiming a vested right to divert waters once it becomes clear that such diversions harm the interests protected by the public trust.... The prosperity and habitability of much of this state [however] requires the diversion of great quantities of water from its streams for purposes unconnected to any navigation, commerce, fishing, recreation, or ecological use relating to the source stream. The state must have the power to grant nonvested usufructuary rights to appropriate water even if diversions harm public trust uses.... We believe that before state courts and agencies approve water diversions they should consider the effect of such diversions upon interests protected by the public trust, and attempt, so far as feasible, to avoid or minimize any harm to those interests....

DWP expects that its future diversions of about 100,000 acre-feet per year will lower the lake's surface level another 43 feet and reduce its surface area by about 22 square miles over the next 80 to 100 years.... By DWP's own estimates, unabated diversions will ultimately produce a lake that is about 56 percent smaller on the surface and 42 percent shallower than its natural size. Plaintiffs consider these projections unrealistically optimistic. They allege that, 50 years hence, the lake will be at least 50 feet shallower than it now is, and hold less than 20 percent of its natural volume. Further, plaintiffs fear that "the lake will not stabilize at this level [but] may continue to reduce in size until it is dried up."...

As noted above, Mono Lake has no outlets. The lake loses water only by evaporation and seepage. Natural salts do not evaporate with water, but are left behind. Prior to

B. Applying the Modern Public Trust Doctrine

commencement of the DWP diversions, this naturally rising salinity was balanced by a constant and substantial supply of fresh water from the tributaries. Now, however, DWP diverts most of the fresh water inflow. The resultant imbalance between inflow and outflow not only diminishes the lake's size, but also drastically increases its salinity....

Plaintiffs predict that the lake's steadily increasing salinity, if unchecked, will wreck havoc throughout the local food chain. They contend that the lake's algae, and the brine shrimp and brine flies that feed on it, cannot survive the projected salinity increase.... DWP's diversions also present several threats to the millions of local and migratory birds using the lake.... Any reduction in shrimp population allegedly caused by rising salinity endangers a major avian food source.... The California gull is especially endangered, both by the increase in salinity and by loss of nesting sites. Ninety-five percent of this state's gull population and 25 percent of the total species population nests at the lake. Most of the gulls nest on islands in the lake. As the lake recedes, land between the shore and some of the islands has been exposed, offering such predators as the coyote easy access to the gull nests and chicks. In 1979, coyotes reached Negit Island, once the most popular nesting site, and the number of gull nests at the lake declined sharply. In 1981, 95 percent of the hatched chicks did not survive to maturity....

Plaintiffs allege that DWP's diversions adversely affect the human species and its activities as well. First, as the lake recedes, it has exposed more than 18,000 acres of lake bed composed of very fine silt which, once dry, easily becomes airborne in winds. This silt contains a high concentration of alkali and other minerals that irritate the mucous membranes and respiratory systems of humans and other animals. While the precise extent of this threat to public health has yet to be determined, such threat as exists can be expected to increase with the exposure of additional lake bed.... Furthermore, the lake's recession obviously diminishes its value as an economic, recreational, and scenic resource, ... there will be less lake to use and enjoy. The declining shrimp hatch depresses a local shrimping industry.... Mono Lake has long been treasured as a unique scenic, recreational and scientific resource, but continued diversions threaten to turn it into a desert wasteland like the dry bed of Owens Lake....

THE PUBLIC TRUST DOCTRINE IN CALIFORNIA... "By the law of nature these things are common to mankind—the air, running water, the sea and consequently the shores of the sea." (Institutes of Justinian 2.1.1.) From this origin in Roman law, the English common law evolved the concept of the public trust, under which the sovereign owns "all of its navigable waterways and the lands lying beneath them 'as trustee of a public trust for the benefit of the people.'" The State of California acquired title as trustee to such lands and waterways upon its admission to the union (see *City of Berkeley v. Superior Court* (1980) 26 Cal. 3d at 521 and cases there cited). From the earliest days (see *Eldridge v. Cowell* (1854) 4 Cal. at 87) its judicial decisions have recognized and enforced the trust obligation....

THE PURPOSE OF THE PUBLIC TRUST... The objective of the public trust has evolved in tandem with the changing public perception of the values and uses of waterways. As we observed in *Marks v. Whitney*, ... the traditional triad of uses—navigation, commerce and fishing—did not limit the public interest in the trust res.[15] ... Mono Lake is a navigable waterway. It supports a small local industry which harvests brine shrimp for sale as fish food,

---

15. The public trust doctrine, like all common law principles, should not be considered fixed or static, but should be molded and extended to meet changing conditions and needs of the public it was created to benefit." *Neptune City v. Avon-by-the-Sea*, 294 A.2d 47, 54 (N.J. 1972).

which endeavor probably qualifies the lake as a "fishery" under the traditional public trust cases. The principal values plaintiffs seek to protect, however, are recreational and ecological—the scenic views of the lake and its shore, the purity of the air, and the use of the lake for nesting and feeding by birds. Under *Marks v. Whitney* it is clear that protection of these values is among the purposes of the public trust.

THE SCOPE OF THE PUBLIC TRUST ... The beds, shores and waters of the lake are without question protected by the public trust. The streams diverted by DWP, however, are not themselves navigable. Accordingly, we must address in this case a question not discussed in any recent public trust case—whether the public trust limits conduct affecting nonnavigable tributaries to navigable waterways. ...

The principles recognized by [our early public trust dambuilding and stream bed gold mining] decisions apply fully to a case in which diversions from a nonnavigable tributary impair the public trust in a downstream river or lake. "If the public trust doctrine applies to constrain fills which destroy navigation and other public trust uses in navigable waters, it should equally apply to constrain the extraction of water that destroys navigation and other public interests. Both actions result in the same damage to the public interest." Johnson, 14 U.C. Davis L. Rev. at 257-258. ... We conclude that the public trust doctrine, as recognized and developed in California decisions, protects navigable waters from harm caused by diversion of nonnavigable tributaries.

DUTIES AND POWERS OF THE STATE AS TRUSTEE ... The dominant theme is the state's sovereign power and duty to exercise continued supervision over the trust. One consequence ... is that parties acquiring rights in trust property generally hold those rights subject to the trust, and can assert no vested right to use those rights in a manner harmful to the trust. ... The continuing power of the state as administrator of the public trust ... extends to the revocation of previously granted right or to the enforcement of the trust against lands long thought free of the trust. ...

The Attorney General of California, seeking to maximize state power under the trust, argues [that] "trust uses" encompass all public uses, so that in practical effect the doctrine would impose no restrictions on the state's ability to allocate trust property. We know of no authority which supports this view of the public trust. ... The public trust is more than an affirmation of state power to use public property for public purposes. It is an affirmation of the duty of the state to protect the people's common heritage of streams, lakes, marshlands and tidelands, surrendering that right of protection only in rare cases when the abandonment of that right is consistent with the purposes of the trust. ...

THE RELATIONSHIP BETWEEN THE PUBLIC TRUST DOCTRINE AND THE CALIFORNIA WATER RIGHTS SYSTEM ... Plaintiffs ... argue that the public trust is antecedent to and thus limits all appropriative water rights, an argument which implies that most appropriative water rights in California were acquired and are presently being used unlawfully. Defendant DWP, on the other hand, argues that the public trust doctrine as to stream waters has been "subsumed" into the appropriative water rights system and, absorbed by that body of law, quietly disappeared: according to DWP, the recipient of a board license enjoys a vested right in perpetuity to take water without concern for the consequences to the trust.

We are unable to accept either position. In our opinion, both the public trust doctrine and the water rights system embody important precepts which make the law more responsive to the diverse needs and interests involved in the planning and allocation of water resources. ... Seeking an accommodation which will make use of the pertinent principles of both the public trust doctrine and the appropriative water rights system, and drawing

B. Applying the Modern Public Trust Doctrine

upon the history of the public trust and the water rights system, the body of judicial precedent, and the views of expert commentators, we reach the following conclusions:

- The state as sovereign retains continuing supervisory control over its navigable waters and the lands beneath those waters. This principle, fundamental to the concept of the public trust, applies to rights in flowing waters as well as to rights in tidelands and lakeshores; it prevents any party from acquiring a vested right to appropriate water in a manner harmful to the interests protected by the public trust.
- As a matter of current and historical necessity, the legislature, acting directly or through an authorized agency . . . has the power to . . . permit an appropriator to take water from flowing streams and use that water in a distant part of the state, even though this taking does not promote, and may unavoidably harm, the trust uses at the source stream. . . . Now that the economy and population centers of this state have developed in reliance upon appropriated water, it would be disingenuous to hold that such appropriations are and have always been improper. . . .
- The state has an affirmative duty to take the public trust into account in the planning and allocation of water resources, and to protect public trust uses whenever feasible. Just as the history of this state shows that appropriation may be necessary for efficient use of water despite unavoidable harm to public trust values, it demonstrates that an appropriative water rights system administered without consideration of the public trust may cause unnecessary and unjustified harm to trust interests. As a matter of practical necessity the state may have to approve appropriations despite foreseeable harm to public trust uses. In so doing, however, the state must bear in mind its duty as trustee to consider the effect of the taking on the public trust and to preserve, so far as consistent with the public interest, the uses protected by the trust.

Once the state has approved an appropriation, the public trust imposes a duty of continuing supervision over the taking and use of the appropriated water. In exercising its sovereign power to allocate water resources in the public interest, the state is not confined by past allocation decisions which may be incorrect in light of current knowledge or inconsistent with current needs.

The state accordingly has the power to reconsider allocation decisions even though those decisions were made after due consideration of their effect on the public trust. . . . No responsible body has ever determined the impact of diverting the entire flow of the Mono Lake tributaries into the Los Angeles Aqueduct. This is not a case in which the Legislature, the Water Board, or any judicial body has determined that the needs of Los Angeles outweigh the needs of the Mono Basin, that the benefit gained is worth the price. . . . DWP acquired rights to the entire flow in 1940 from a water board which believed it lacked both the power and the duty to protect the Mono Lake environment, and continues to exercise those rights in apparent disregard for the resulting damage to the scenery, ecology, and human uses of Mono Lake. . . .

We recognize the substantial concerns voiced by Los Angeles. . . . We hold only that they do not preclude a reconsideration and reallocation which also takes into account the impact of water diversion on the Mono Lake environment. . . . The federal court inquired . . . whether the "public trust doctrine in this context [is] subsumed in the California water rights system, or . . . function[s] independently of that system?" Our answer is "neither." The public trust doctrine and the appropriative water rights system are parts of an integrated system of water law. . . . We hope by integrating these two doctrines to clear away the legal barriers which have so far prevented either the Water Board or the courts from taking a new and objective look at the water resources of the Mono Basin. The human and environmental uses of Mono Lake—uses protected by the public trust doctrine—deserve to be taken into account. Such uses should not be destroyed because the state mistakenly thought itself powerless to protect them.

COMMENTARY & QUESTIONS

1. The terms of the trust balance. Note that in this case, the state's Attorney General argued against the applicability of public trust restrictions on the state's ability to allocate water. Why? Ultimately the court defined a public trust role for the state government that held it to a new and higher standard of decisionmaking. The state could no longer merely be a mechanism of majoritarian politics; it apparently now had enforceable long-term fiduciary obligations to an indefinite constituency including generations unborn.

After the decision in *Mono Lake*, what are the standards by which the public trust balance will be struck to determine how much of Los Angeles's private water rights and how much of Mono Lake's public trust assets will be legally protected? A serious apples and oranges problem presents itself. How can two such disparate public interests be balanced? It is notable that the courts have declared that the PTD cannot be abrogated, which apparently asserts that the trust obligations, whatever they are, must be substantively fulfilled. After *Mono Lake*, if you were an attorney for the Los Angeles Water Board or, on the other hand, for the environmental coalition, how would you go about preparing for subsequent proceedings in state court to determine what actually would happen to Mono Lake? To what extent in that balance does the lack of prior notice of the trust's existence to owners of the water rights matter to you? Are public trust rights necessarily superior to private property rights, if indeed they conflict? If the trust balance results in a restriction of private water rights, do the losers have a right to compensation for an unconstitutional "taking"? See the next chapter on this.

2. Scope of the PTD. Just what is the public trust resource that is being protected in *Mono Lake*? It clearly has not much to do with navigability. Is it the lake itself that is the public trust asset? If so, is it the lake in its original form, as it is today, or at some intermediate point? Is it the economic use of the water, based on harvesting brine shrimp? Is it the brine shrimp themselves? The California gulls?

Mono Lake may stand for the proposition that the PTD is capable of reaching out and encompassing the ecological values of an entire functioning ecosystem. Does this mean all ecosystems, or just those ecosystems fortunate enough to inhabit a photogenic environment?

Note something else striking about *Mono Lake*. The decision apparently applies to *private* rights. True, the water rights to the various streams flowing into Mono Lake are owned by the government of Los Angeles, but it owns them by purchasing water rights in the same way that those rights would be obtained and held by a private citizen. Does the public trust lie latent within private property rights? *Marks v. Whitney*, excerpted above and cited in the main opinion, held precisely that there was an inherent public right in privately owned submerged lands, so that the private property owner was completely restricted unless the government gave permission to fill in the submerged lands and make them economically useful. What if you owned the oldest burr oak tree in Illinois, or the house in which Benjamin Franklin was born, or the land on which the state's oldest church was located, and in each case you wanted to bulldoze the property to make a profitable parking lot? Might the PTD apply with full force and litigibility to your case as well? What standards would apply?

B. Applying the Modern Public Trust Doctrine

3. A reprise on *Mono Lake*. What further developments in California public trust law followed the decision in *Mono Lake*? The years initially following the California Supreme Court decision were unusually wet and the level of Mono Lake actually rose. Then there was an extended drought. The court had sent the case back to the Water Board to determine whether and to what extent Los Angeles should cut back its diversions from the Mono Lake tributaries in order to protect public trust values. Even if that task had been undertaken with maximum dispatch, it would have taken years before any final order actually changing the flows into Mono Lake would have been forthcoming. In 1989, officials for the City of Los Angeles and the Mono Lake Committee reached an agreement whereby Los Angeles would abide by a court-set lake level and would give up some of its water rights, in exchange for assistance from the state in finding alternate sources of water. But controversy continued. An entirely new suit to protect the lake was successfully brought under two obscure provisions of the Fish and Game Code requiring releases from dams sufficient to reestablish and maintain fish populations below the dams.

In the late 1980s, rain levels were again high and the lake level gained. While awaiting the Water Board studies on Mono Lake, the trial court issued a preliminary injunction in 1989 requiring that the lake be maintained at 6377 feet above sea level, some 2 feet above its existing level but still more than 40 feet below the historic average level prior to L.A.'s diversion project. That case was then expanded to encompass issues other than the balance between public trust and municipal supply needs (the plaintiffs had been concerned that their doctrinal public trust victory might be "balanced away"). One such issue is violation of air quality requirements resulting from blowing dust created by exposure of shoreland flats as the lake level declined. Another is a claim to lake level maintenance on behalf of the U.S. government. The interest of the federal government has come to the fore because in 1984 Congress established a Mono Basin National Forest Scenic Area in order to protect the geological, ecological, and cultural resources of Mono Basin. The Scenic Area statute provides, however, that "nothing in [this law] shall be construed to . . . affect the present (or prospective) water rights of any person . . . including the City of Los Angeles." 16 U.S.C. §543c(h).

On September 28, 1994, the Water Board issued D-1631, its landmark decision amending the City of Los Angeles's water diversion licenses in the Mono Basin. The Water Board's decision addressed both the issues with water release below the dams and the public trust values originally raised by the California Supreme Court over ten years earlier. D-1631 calls for a lake level of 6392 feet above sea level, 15 feet higher than the level required in the 1989 preliminary injunction. The City of Los Angeles could still divert some water while the lake regenerated, and then could divert, on average, 31,000 acre-feet of water, or about one-third of the City's historical diversion from the Mono Basin. The Water Board committed to aiding the City in finding alternative water sources to make up for the loss. After the Water Board decision, the trial court continued to exercise jurisdiction over the Mono Lake matter until 1998, when the City reached a settlement agreement regarding lake restoration and the Water Board issued an order for stream and waterfowl habitat restoration.

The case that reinvigorated the PTD in California has actually led to a relative success story for the lake and city that started it all. By early 2010, Mono Lake was still 9 feet short of the D-1631 required lake level, but had added 11 feet from the historic low level. The Water Board and the City continue to use adaptive management principles to work toward full regeneration of the lake. The City of Los Angeles currently diverts 16,000 acre-feet of water per year from the Mono Lake tributaries, which represents less than a fourth of the amount it historically diverted from the lake. In response, the City has found some replacement water since the *Mono Lake* decision, in part with the help of $60 million in funds the State of California dedicated to finding alternatives to Mono Lake tributaries. More significant, though, the City has instituted a number of successful water conservation efforts in the past several decades that have decreased per capita water demand. While the population of Los Angeles continued to grow, total water use each year was roughly the same in the late 2000s as it was in the 1970s when the Mono Lake litigation began.

3. How Far Does the Public Trust Doctrine Go?

The PTD asserts that certain special public rights and duties lie latent within various natural resources, whether publicly or privately owned, with consequences that can be dramatic. The following case unfolded in 1969, a short distance west of Colorado Springs where an accident of geology 10 million years ago created a remarkably rich 6000-acre area of fossil beds. The Florissant Fossil Beds, layer upon layer of paper-thin shales filled with biological artifacts, was a unique and nationally famous archaeological site, featured in many junior high school textbooks. Congress, in desultory fashion, had been discussing whether to purchase the beds in order to create a national monument. Meanwhile, a group of private developers contracted to purchase the 6000-acre tract, figuring that in marketplace terms the area's best commercial use lay in subdivision construction. The bulldozers were poised and ready to roll, to carve roads, driveways, and split-level foundations into the fragile fossil beds. The Florissant story is dramatically told in E. Leopold, et al., SAVED IN TIME: THE FIGHT TO SAVE FLORISSANT FOSSIL BEDS (2011).

Defenders of Florissant v. Park Land Development Co.

from Victor J. Yannacone, Jr., Bernard Cohen & Steven Davison, Environmental Rights and Remedies 47-60 (1972) (unreported case)

IN THE UNITED STATES DISTRICT COURT
FOR THE DISTRICT OF COLORADO

DEFENDERS of Florissant, Inc., individually and on behalf of all those entitled to the full benefit use and enjoyment of the national natural resource that is the proposed FLORISSANT FOSSIL BEDS NATIONAL MONUMENT, and all those similarly situated,
 	
                                          Plaintiffs,
vs.
Park Land Company, CENTRAL ENTERPRISES, INC., CLAUDE R. BLUE, KENNETH C. WOFFARD; J.R. FONTAN, M.L. BARNES; W. NATE SNARE, A.W. GREGG, R. MITSCHELE, MARILDA NELSON; DELBERT and EMMA WELLS; E.D. KELLY, JOHN BAKER, and their successors in interest, if any, as their interest may appear,
                                         Defendants.
	))))))))))))))))

NOTICE OF MOTION

PLEASE TAKE NOTICE that the Plaintiffs will move this Court at the United States District Court House, Denver, Colorado, on the 8th day of July, 1969, at half past nine o'clock in the forenoon of that day, or as soon thereafter as counsel can be heard, for an order:

B. Applying the Modern Public Trust Doctrine

RESTRAINING the Defendants from any actions which may cause serious permanent or irreparable damage to the national natural resource that is the area included within the proposed Florissant Fossil Beds National Monument; or in the alternative,

DIRECTING the immediate hearing on the merits of the Plaintiff's application for a temporary injunction,

TOGETHER with such other and further relief as to the Court shall seem just and proper under the circumstances.

Respectfully submitted,
Victor J. Yannacone, Jr., Attorney for Plaintiff

VERIFIED COMPLAINT

The Plaintiffs, complaining of the Defendants by their attorney, Victor J. Yannacone, Jr., set forth and allege:

1. JURISDICTION: Jurisdiction of this Court is invoked under Title 28 U.S.C. §1331(a), "The district courts shall have original jurisdiction of all civil actions wherein the matter in controversy exceeds the sum or value of $10,000, exclusive of interest and costs, and arises under the Constitution, laws, or treaties of the United States." . . .

2. JURISDICTION: Jurisdiction of this Court is invoked under Title 28 U.S.C. §343(3): "To redress the deprivation, under color of any State law, statute, ordinance, regulation, custom or usage, of any right, privilege or immunity secured by the Constitution of the United States or by any Act of Congress providing for equal rights of citizens or of all persons within jurisdiction of the United States." . . .

3. JURISDICTION: This is also a proceeding for Declaratory Judgment under Title 28 U.S.C. §§2201, and 2202, declaring the rights and legal relations of the parties to the matter in controversy, specifically:

   (a) That the proposed Florissant Fossil Beds National Monument is a national natural resource.
   (b) The right of all the people of the United States in and to the full benefit, use and enjoyment of the unique values of the proposed Florissant Fossil Beds National Monument, without diminution or degradation resulting from any of the activities of the Defendants or their Successors in interest, sought to be restrained herein.
   (c) That the degradation of the unique National Natural Resources of the proposed Florissant Fossil Beds National Monument by the Defendants or their Successors in interest violates the rights of the Plaintiffs, guaranteed under the Ninth Amendment of the Constitution of the United States and protected by the due process and equal protection clauses of the Fifth and Fourteenth Amendments of the Constitution of the United States. . . .

5. THE PROPOSED FLORISSANT FOSSIL BEDS NATIONAL MONUMENT: The proposed national monument comprises an area of 6,000 acres on the east slope of the Rocky Mountains. Located in a region of high recreation use and relatively close to a fast growing metropolitan complex, heavy visitation is expected.

The primary resources are the unique Oligocene lake beds with their plant and insect fossil-bearing layers and related geological features. These resources, combined with a scenic setting and secondary recreational and biological resources, constitute a relatively compact natural unit.

The ancient lake beds of Florissant preserve more species of terrestrial fossils than any other known site in the world. . . . The beds have been a famous collecting ground by numerous scientists for nearly a century and continue to be of great value for paleontological research.

The present-day vegetation is one of pine-covered hills and grassy meadows. In good years the wildflower display in June and July may be spectacular and is an acknowledged tourist attraction. . . .

Geological History: Subsequent to the birth of the Rocky Mountains, 60 million years, ago, a period of erosion ensued. By Oligocene time, 40 million years ago, the mountains in the Florissant region had been reduced generally to a broad, gently rolling hill land—a piedmont of low relief and moderate elevation.

Volcanic eruptions covered the region with pyroclastics to a depth of 40 to 60 feet or more, and the drainage of the area was blocked, thus forming the Florissant Lake. The rolling slopes and the lakeshore were mantled by many types of deciduous trees and immense Sequoia groves.

Explosive eruptions and mud flows eventually filled the lake. The mud flows engulfed and buried the lakeshore trees which were gradually petrified. Insects, leaves, and other forms of life were carried to the lake bottom and preserved between alternating layers of volcanic ash. . . . A number of tree stumps, including large Sequoias, are exposed at the two commercially operated petrified forest areas. . . .

Significance of Geological Resources: These deposits represent a small chapter of the geological history of the earth, but one very closely related to the present. What happened here in Oligocene times—the environment conditions that existed, the life forms that prevailed, the whole story—is written into the Florissant deposits. Scientists have revealed parts of this story; more remains to be told.

The rare quality of the Florissant site lies in the delicacy with which thousands of fragile insects, tree foliage, and other forms of life—completely absent, or extremely rare in most paleontological sites—have been preserved. There is no known locality in the world where so many terrestrial species of one time have been preserved. . . . Approximately 60,000 specimens of insect fossils have been collected here. . . . Probably no formation of such limited extent has ever been the subject of as large a body of literature as the Florissant lake beds (226 papers). . . .

6. THE DEFENDANT: That upon information and belief, the defendants, individually and collectively, as their interests may appear, are the owners in fee of lands included within the proposed Florissant Fossil Beds National Monument.

Upon information and belief the defendants individually and collectively as their interests may appear are subject to the exercise of eminent domain by the United States of America upon final action by the Congress of the United States which, upon information and belief, should occur during the current session of the Congress.

7. DEFENDANTS' ACTIONS: That upon information and belief, unless restrained by order of this Court, the Defendants, individually, or their Successors in Interest, will develop the area to be included within the proposed Florissant Fossil Beds National Monument, in such a way as to cause serious, permanent and irreparable damage to the unique national natural resource that is the Florissant Fossil Beds.

That the development of the region of the Florissant Fossil Beds in any way which involves road building, excavation, or covering the fossil beds with permanent dwelling

B. Applying the Modern Public Trust Doctrine

units or building structures, will cause serious permanent and irreparable damage to the unique paleontological resource that is the Florissant Fossil Beds. . . .

That upon information and belief the operation of conventional building construction methods will cause serious permanent and irreparable damage to the unique national paleontological resource represented by the Florissant Fossil Beds. . . .

Upon information and belief, the defendant Park Land Company, Claude R. Blue, Kenneth C. Woffard, J.R. Fontan, and M.L. Barnes, jointly or severally intend to commence construction operations immediately which will cause serious permanent and irreparable damage to the National Natural Resource which is the Florissant Fossil Beds. . . .

8. EQUITABLE JURISDICTION: That this action is properly brought in equity before this court on the following grounds:

(a) This action is brought for the purpose of restraining the Defendants individually, and their Successors in Interest, from damaging or degrading the unique national natural resource that is, the Florissant Fossil Beds, within the area proposed for inclusion in the Florissant Fossil Beds National Monument. The injury which may be inflicted by the Defendants individually or their successors in Interest, if they are permitted to develop the area without regard for the unique national natural resources represented thereby, will be irreparable, in that it cannot be adequately compensated in damages. The declaratory judgment demanded by the Plaintiffs, together with the equitable relief related thereto are equitable remedies in the substance of character of the rights sought to be enforced or historically in the province of the Court of Chancery. . . .

9. TRUST: That the Defendants individually and their Successors in Interest, hold the unique national natural resource of the Florissant Fossil Beds, with respect to its

COURTESY FLORISSANT FOSSIL BEDS NATIONAL MONUMENT

FIGURE 22-2
A view of today's Florissant Fossil Beds National Monument showing an area in which ditch excavations have revealed rich layering of fossils going back 50 million years.

paleontological, paleobotanical and palynological values in trust for the full benefit, use and enjoyment of all the people of this generation, and those generations yet unborn.

That the maintenance of this trust is compatible with the proper efficient development of the resource represented by the area encompassed within the proposed Florissant Fossil Beds National Monument area.

That the administrative agencies of the Federal and State governments are incapable of preventing the irreparable damage which will result from the improper development of the region by the Defendants. . . .

That the maintenance of the trust is consistent with private ownership of the property and does not constitute any taking of the Defendant's property.

WHEREFORE, the plaintiffs individually and on behalf of all those entitled to the full benefit, use and enjoyment of the national resource that are the proposed Florissant Fossil Beds National Moment, respectfully pray:

That this Court take jurisdiction of the matter, and that a three judge court be convened to hear and determine this cause as provided by Title 28 U.S. Code, §2281, et seq. and upon such hearing:

(a) Grant judgment declaring the right of the Plaintiff and all others to the full benefit, use and enjoyment of the national natural resources that are the proposed Florissant Fossil Beds National Monument, without any degradation resulting from the improper development thereof by the Defendants and/or their Successors in Interest.

(b) That the Court issue such orders as will protect the unique paleontological, paleobotanical and palynological values encompassed within the Florissant Fossil Beds, pending the final hearing of determination of this action.

(c) That the Court issue such orders as will protect the unique paleontological and palynological values encompassed within the Florissant Fossil Beds.

(d) Together with all such other and further relief as to the Court may seem just, proper, and necessary under the circumstances to protect the unique national natural resources that are in the Florissant Fossil Beds.

(Signed) Victor Yannacone, *Attorney for Plaintiff*

[AFFIDAVIT]
STATE OF COLORADO, CITY AND COUNTY OF DENVER

Estella B. Leopold, being duly sworn deposes and says:

1. That she is a Paleontologist presently employed by the U.S. Geological Survey, and is personally familiar as a research scientist with the area to be included within the proposed Florissant Fossil Beds National Monument, and in particular the land and area presently being threatened by the activities of the Defendants with respect to excavation and road building. . . .

[Dr. Leopold's affidavit provided detailed description and analysis, and was the source of most of the material set out in the Complaint. The District Court, however, dismissed the action for failure to state a claim upon which relief could be granted. The plaintiffs quickly appealed to the Tenth Circuit for temporary injunctive relief.]

• • •

B. Applying the Modern Public Trust Doctrine

UNITED STATES COURT OF APPEALS FOR THE TENTH CIRCUIT

DEFENDERS of FLORISSANT, Inc., individually)
and on behalf of all those entitled to the full)
benefit, use and enjoyment of the national)
natural resource that is the proposed)
FLORISSANT FOSSIL BEDS NATIONAL) <u>No.00341-69</u>
MONUMENT, and all those similarly situated,)
                  Plaintiffs,)
        vs.)
PARK LAND COMPANY, et al.)
                  Defendants.)

ORDER

Upon reading and filing the application of the plaintiffs herein for a temporary restraining order, together with the transcript of the hearing on the application of plaintiffs for similar relief before the U.S. District Court, District of Colorado on July 9, 1969, together with the oral application of counsel for the plaintiffs before this Court on this date, including a complete recital of all the efforts by counsel for the plaintiffs to secure the appearance of the defendants, Claude R. Blue and J.R. Thornton, individually and as partners of the Park Land Company, the principal defendant herein, including recital of the substance of the conference held among the parties in the U.S. District Courthouse . . . on July 10, 1969 . . . and representations by counsel for the defendants, Robert Johnson of Colorado Springs, that he would not enter a formal appearance under any circumstances in this action at this time, together with telegraphic notice . . . to which no reply had been received.

AND IT APPEARING TO THE COURT from the representations of counsel and the information contained in the verified complaint and exhibits annexed thereto, the affidavits submitted therewith of Dr. Estella Leopold, Paleontologist for the U.S. Geological Survey, that the Florissant Fossil Beds represent a unique national natural resource, and that the excavation with road building or other construction equipment of these fossil beds will result in serious, permanent, irreparable damage and render the action for preliminary injunction pending for trial in the U.S. District Court on July 29, 1969, moot, and it appearing from the uncontradicted statements contained in the transcript of the hearing of July 9, 1969, conducted in the presence of defendants and their counsel and the similar representations of plaintiff's counsel before this Court, and that there will be no damage to the defendants by order of this Court restraining construction activities at the area of the Florissant Fossil Beds,

IT IS ORDERED that the defendants, jointly or severally, individually or collectively, or by their agents, servants or employees, their contract vendees or their successors in interest, be and are hereby restrained from disturbing the soil, or sub-soil or geologic formations at the Florissant Fossil Beds by any physical or mechanical means including, but not limited to excavation, grading, roadbuilding activity or other construction practice until a hearing on the merits of the plaintiff's application for preliminary injunction to be heard in the U.S. District Court, District of Colorado, on July 29, 1969, at 9:30 A.M.

IT IS FURTHER ORDERED that service of this order shall be made by the U.S. Marshal on any workman engaged in construction activities at the Florissant Fossil Beds forthwith and that personal service shall also be made on each of the defendants subject to the jurisdiction of the Court. . . .

> ALFRED P. MURRAH, Chief Judge;
> JEAN S. BREITENSTEIN,
> JOHN J. HICKEY

[On remand, at the hearing for a preliminary injunction, the district court again dismissed the case. On appeal to the Tenth Circuit again, the appellate judges ordered that the above injunction be continued indefinitely, until further order of the Court of Appeals. The federal government authorized eminent domain purchase by a bill signed on August 14, 1969, Pub. L. No. 91-60, and the injunction remained in effect during the time that the federal government was acquiring the lands in question. The fossil beds are now a National Monument.]

COMMENTARY & QUESTIONS

1. The basis of the injunction? The injunction issued in the *Florissant Fossil Beds* case (which, it should be noted, is hardly a typical run-of-the-mill environmental case) froze the use of the private land pending possible governmental purchase. What was the basis of the injunction? The court never issued an opinion, so the precise rationale is not clear. An injunction, in modern legal practice, is not itself a cause of action. It requires a foundation tort or other cause of action in order to be issued. In the course of oral argument in the trial court, the attorney for the fossil beds was asked by the judge what his cause of action was, and he replied that he did not have a clear cause of action. He was dismissed. The Tenth Circuit Court of Appeals panel later asked the same question, and attorney Yannacone replied in essence, "Your Honors, if I told you that the original U.S. Constitution somehow lay buried there in the fossil beds, would you let the bulldozers roll?" When the court said, "Of course not, we'd issue an injunction," the attorney said, "Whatever you'd use there, I'm using here." Was it, in fact, the public trust?

The complaint uses the word *trust* in substantially the same manner as the PTD might be applied. Is that the basis of the case? Note that the trustee, according to the plaintiffs' allegation, was not the government but the private owner, certainly a most disgruntled potential trustee.

2. The balancing process in *Florissant*. In *Florissant*, the environmentalists were attempting to hold up bulldozing of the fossil bed area until such time as the federal Congress would pony up the money to pay for purchasing it from the owners. Bills were proceeding in both the House and the Senate to that end, but the private developer, with an instinct, perhaps, for playing the role of environmental defendant to the hilt, reportedly announced that it was going to bulldoze some of the fragile areas immediately. The defendant corporation's only concession to the existence of the fossil beds was to offer to sell them to the environmental coalition for a price double what it had itself paid for the property the week before. If the environmentalists would not pay the 100% markup, the defendants clearly wished to proceed quickly because eminent domain proceedings for governmental purchase, as we will see in the next chapter, would pay them fair market value only, which was presumptively the amount that they themselves had just paid for the land. In *Florissant*, the trust balance might have been very different if plaintiffs had sought to freeze the fossil beds permanently from development, without the imminent likelihood of governmental purchase that in fact settled the case. The trust balance in that case may have been a process

B. Applying the Modern Public Trust Doctrine

of weighing the strategic time values of maintaining the status quo, as well as public and private rights.

Does it shock you that these *privately-owned* fossil beds were protected by the court with an injunctive order, freezing them from development, for aesthetic public reasons with no compensation required by the injunction? The following chapter considers such constitutional takings issues at length.

3. Governmental use of the trust. Governments have often used the trust doctrine, most often to affirm the existence of their governmental powers to regulate, as in wildlife cases, where the state acts as trustee. In the *Steuart Transportation* oil spill case, for example, countering defendant's argument that neither the federal nor the state government plaintiffs "owned" the birds and ducks destroyed by oil, both governments successfully argued the public trust doctrine to win standing for recovery of damages. The trust can aid in defending against regulatory takings challenges as well. When governments cite the trust in affirming their authority over a matter, however, they may concurrently expand their active liabilities, opening themselves to trust suits by disgruntled environmentalist "beneficiaries." This scenario may help explain the California Attorney General's hesitation in *Mono Lake*, and why public trust law has generally been developed, like so many other areas of environmental law, through citizen rather than governmental efforts.

4. Familiarizing the trust. An initial obstacle to courts' active adoption of public trust theories, understandably, was the fact that many judges had never heard of the trust. Attorneys often faced the task of establishing the existence of the doctrine in their state's common law heritage. Consider the following on researching public trust case law:

> In 1970 the public trust was an unfamiliar principle in Tennessee practice. The drafters of the 1972 water pollution act inserted the public trust concept into that statute (as to water quality only) but the effect of the trust language was not clear. When environmental law classes focused upon the public trust doctrine, however, they came up with a wealth of public trust law starting in the earliest days of statehood. More than 50 cases were found dealing with the trust (often in direct and express terms) in state parklands, lakes and watercourses, wildlife, roads and streets, railroad rights of way, subterranean water, and school lands. When the state's regional prison program subsequently proposed a diversion of state forest lands, cutting approximately 50 acres out of the center of a wild public preserve, the student researchers and local attorneys were able to marshal sufficient federal and state case law to convince the trial court that the trust existed, that citizens had standing as beneficiaries to enforce it, and that trust standards had to be complied with prior to any diversion of the resource.[16] Plater, The Nonstatutory Public Trust: Affirmative New Environmental Powers for Attorneys-General, Nat'l Ass'n of Attorneys-General Envtl. Control J., Apr. 1976, at 13-14.

5. The public trust doctrine: Is it amphibious?[17] As the excerpt from *Marks v. Whitney* in *Mono Lake* demonstrates, the public trust in water resources has grown far beyond the traditional trust terms of Roman law. To what extent does it apply beyond water-based resources? Parklands are obviously included today, though unknown to Justinian. During the Pigeon River Forest litigation on the State of Michigan's duty to keep oil wells out of a state forest preserve, the Assistant Attorney General, arguing for the oil companies, asked, "Is all publicly-owned land now invested with the public trust, even dumps and highway

---

16. *Marion County v. Luttrell*, No. A-3586 (Chancery Ct., Davidson County, Tenn., June 28, 1974). The case was finally resolved extrajudicially, without a statement by higher courts, through dynamite threats against the contractors. Citizen standing was also upheld on trust beneficiary principles in *State ex rel. SOCM v. Fowinkle*, No. A-2914-A (Chancery Ct., Davidson County, Tenn., Nov. 2, 1973).

17. See Scott Reed's article of the same name, 1 J. Envtl. L. & Litig. 107 (1986).

yards?" *West Mich. Envtl. Action Council v. NRC*, 275 N.W.2d 538 (Mich. 1978). It's a good question. If they aren't, where is the line to be drawn?

Above the water line, the trust doctrine has been applied, at various times, to parks (*Paepke*, etc.); wildlife and archaeological artifacts (*In re Steuart Transp. Co.*, 495 F. Supp. 38 (E.D. Va. 1980), and *Wade v. Kramer*, 459 N.E.2d 1025 (Ill. 1984)); beach access over uplands (*Matthews v. Bay Head Improvement Ass'n*, 471 A.2d 355 (N.J. 1984));[18] stream access, including the right to portage around barriers by traversing adjacent private land (*Montana Coalition for Stream Access v. Hildreth*, 684 P.2d 1088 (Mont. 1984)); critical upland areas surrounding a redwood forest (*Sierra Club v. Dep't of Interior*, 376 F. Supp. 90 (N.D. Cal. 1974); *Sierra Club v. Dep't of Interior*, 398 F. Supp. 284 (N.D. Cal. 1975)); trees threatened by resort developments (*Irish v. Green*, 4 Env't Rep. Cas. (BNA) 1402 (Mich. Cir. Ct. 1972)); trees damaged by oil spills (*P.R. v. S.S. Zoe Colocotroni*, 628 F.2d 652 (1st Cir. 1980) (mangrove trees); fossil beds, as we have seen; and more.

Take this not-so-hypothetical: What if, after purchasing a painting by the renowned post-Impressionist Paul Cézanne for $800,000, two entrepreneurial MBAs announce that they have decided to cut it up into one-inch squares because their marketing analysis indicates they can sell off the tiny "authentic Cézannes" for more than $1.5 million? See Held, Alteration and Mutilation of Works of Art, 62 S. Atl. Q. 1, 19 (1963) (noting commercial "butchery" chop-jobs on works of Van Eyck, VanderWeyden, and Pollock); The Case of the Dismembered Masterpieces, ARTnews, Sept. 1980, at 68; Cal. Civ. Code §987, Protection of Fine Art against Alteration or Destruction (1997); J.L. Sax, PLAYING DARTS WITH A REMBRANDT: PUBLIC AND PRIVATE RIGHTS IN CULTURAL TREASURES 85 (1999). Could a public trust be argued here, or public nuisance? Who has standing to sue? What remedy — an injunction pending imminent public purchase, as in *Florissant*? Would the same kind of theory be applicable to the protection of ancient petroglyphs — prehistoric human rock paintings — from willful destruction? Once started on this road, the trust's complications abound, but the doctrine's recognition of intangible public values undeniably captures a piece of reality, the legal significance of a society's common cultural heritage.

6. The public trust doctrine: Is it stratospheric? Professor Mary Wood has explored the possibilities for deploying Justinian's PTD to address climate change in "atmospheric trust" litigation.[19] Wood's theory is premised on the "obligation of all governments to protect a shared atmosphere that is vital to human welfare and survival." Just as sovereign governments hold other natural resources (e.g., shorelines) in trust for the public, they should also be acknowledged as trustees of the atmosphere. The logic of atmospheric trust litigation would impose a form of legal "carbon responsibility" upon every nation and enable citizens to sue governments for failing to protect the atmospheric trust. Application of an atmospheric trust doctrine is both innovative and speculative, but the history and potential power of the PTD make this initiative worth exploring.

---

18. An active case law has developed around the question of public access to beaches, generally asserting the public's rights to use all beaches, sometimes including even the right to go over private land to reach the public beach area. See *Matthews v. Bay Head Improvement Ass'n*, 471 A.2d 355 (N.J. 1984); Note, Public Trust Doctrine — Beach Access . . . , 15 Seton Hall L. Rev. 344 (1985); D. Brower, Access to the Nation's Beaches: Legal and Planning Perspectives (1978). Massachusetts and Maine are anomalies, due to the courts' interpretation of a 1647 colonial ordinance issued under authority granted by the King purporting to convey private property grants down to the low-water mark, subject only to a public easement for "fyshynge, fowleing, and navigation," but not for beach use. Opinion of the Justices, 313 N.E.2d 561 (Mass. 1974). There is some question whether the King himself possessed such authority.

19. See Mary Christina Wood, NATURE'S TRUST ENVIRONMENTAL LAW FOR A NEW ECOLOGICAL AGE (2013).

B. Applying the Modern Public Trust Doctrine

On Mother's Day 2011, in an initiative organized by Our Children's Trust, an Oregon climate action group drawing upon Professor Wood's work, lawsuits or petitions for rulemaking were filed in 49 of 50 states[20] plus a federal action in an Oregon district court. In each case, the legal actions were filed by minors who sought to force the official structures of the older generation to meaningfully address the impending climate-induced calamities that their younger generation would suffer and have to handle. The initiative thrust the public trust concept into public debate in many locations, and gained some traction in several courts. Is this long shot initiative a David & Goliath story, launching a little known ancient legal concept into the biggest, most politicized, most existential threat being faced by modern societies? (Remember, it was David's superior understanding of technology and strategy that ultimately downed the Philistine.) For background and updates on the PTD climate initiative, see ourchildrenstrust.org.

7. The third category of public trust situations. Whenever the trust is used to support antipollution efforts (see Water Pollution Control Act, Tenn. Code Ann. §§70.324 et seq., and *State v. Amerada Hess*, 350 F. Supp. 1060 (Md. 1972)), to prevent destruction of trust resources by public or private actors (see the redwood cases in note 5), or to recover damages for the destruction of trust assets as in *Steuart Transp.*, or the state of Alaska's oil spill litigation noted in Chapter 3, it is analytically focused on defense of the quality of the resource against derogation rather than protecting the character of ownership. Emperor Justinian, remember, began his list of public trust resources with air, for which issues of ownership are irrelevant but issues of quality essential. In practice, however, the application of the trust analysis in this third resource-defense, or derogation, category parallels the alienation and diversion cases and is the implicit basis for state pollution laws. The issue in each setting is to determine to what extent the qualities of the trust resources are to be preserved and stewarded against short-term exploitation.

8. The public trust: so how far does it go? The trust doctrine is not absolute. Private property rights obviously must be weighed in the trust balance, and the balance struck in the *Florissant Fossil Beds* case appears to be an appropriate balance. But in some cases the conflict between public rights and private property will produce bitter political confrontations: how far can the system go in regulating private business decisions in favor of protecting cultural and natural values where nobody is going to be hurt except for fossils, or antelope, or a historic battlefield, or. . . . Where does it stop?

9. Cultural values beyond market values. The ultimate measure of a society would seem to be based upon more than just the essential physical needs for survival — to this should be added the full quality of its people's life, and the legacy of ideas, accomplishments, and potentials it seeks to pass on to successor generations. The public trust, whether incorporated in statutes or existing within our nonstatutory jurisprudence, represents and gives legal force to many of the unmarketized present and future social values that often get overlooked in the immediacy of daily life but are part of the ultimate measure.

In emphasizing stewardship, intergenerational equity, and sustainability, the public trust embodies fundamentally conservative principles. If a society is to survive and advance over time, like species competing in the Darwinian process of replicating and prolonging their genetic identity over succeeding generations, it must incorporate present realities and the needs of future generations into its present legal norms. Ethical concepts of environmental stewardship described by ecophilosophers evoke concepts of legacy — nations, like most nondysfunctional families, honoring what they have received from the past, and

---

20. Surprisingly, a petition was not successfully filed in Massachusetts until a year later.

trying to pass it on, enhanced, to their posterity. The ancient public trust doctrine thus fits well with principles and technologies of sustainability.

10. What kind of law is the public trust and does it apply to the federal government? There is little controversy about the existence of the public trust historically in the U.S. But what, exactly, is it? Is the public trust a common law doctrine? If so, how is it that it can overturn a *statutory* enactment, as in *Illinois Central*? Is it a federal or state doctrine? Note that in *Illinois Central*, the doctrine was used by a federal court to overcome the action of a sovereign state. Does the doctrine apply to the federal government as well? In several cases, courts have asserted that the federal government is equally accountable and restricted under the terms of the PTD. See *Steuart Transportation*, above, and *U.S. v. 1.8 Acres*, 523 F. Supp. 120, 124 (D. Mass. 1981). The federal government is a creature of the states by delegation through the Act of Union and the federal Constitution. If the federal government is therefore exercising delegated powers, it would appear straightforward that it cannot have greater rights and fewer limitations than the entities that created it. On the other hand, in the federal PTD climate suit noted above, a strong position against its federal applicability was taken by the Obama Administration.[21] A number of courts and commentators have indicated that neither the federal government nor the state governments can act to abolish it, so it seems the PTD isn't just federal common law. See *Marks v. Whitney*, 491 P.2d at 380-381. As trustees, if the state sovereignties and federal government are bound by the terms of the trust, is it then a principle of federal constitutional law? If so, where does it lie?

And on a grander scale, is the PTD a Rawlsian, Lockian, "pre-political" natural right? Is it an implicit constitutional right? Is it intergenerational democracy, a charge to protect the "common heritage of humankind," mediating resource legacies over the years? Is it enforceable? Is it merely an administrative law "hard look" doctrine applied to natural resources? Is it like Burke's tree: We honor it for its years of growth, but also because we don't understand exactly whence it comes?

11. Where is the public trust going? If it is clear that governments—state and perhaps federal—are the trustees, then what is the scope of the assets held in trust? The doctrine has already spread far beyond tidal waters and now applies on dry land as well, but the ultimate scope of the doctrine is not yet clearly delineated.[22]

Does the public trust require absolute protection of all trust resources? Like standard trust law, variations of the public trust are permissible through a careful fiduciary balancing process. This is more than merely a procedural requirement of specific statutory authorization described by Professor Sax. Simple legislative or referendum majorities are probably not enough to alter trust protections. A substantive trust balance seems necessary under traditional equity standards. After the *Illinois Central* case, the U.S. Supreme Court and state supreme courts have sometimes found that a conscientious substantive balancing of public trust interests permitted alteration of trust assets. In *State v. Public Service Comm'n*, 81 N.W.2d 71 (Wis. 1957), the issue was the proposed filling of a small percentage of Lake Wingra in the town of Madison, Wisconsin, for the purposes of making a park area more enjoyable and accessible. The court held, after a careful balancing of public trust considerations, that this action would not violate the trust. See also *Milwaukee v. State*, 214 N.W. 820 (Wis. 1927).

---

21. *Alec L. et al. v. Administrator of US EPA*, No. 13-5192, DC Circuit (June 5, 2014), cert. denied Dec. 7, 2014.
22. See Rieser, Ecological Preservation as a Public Property Right: An Emerging Doctrine in Search of a Theory, 15 Harv. Envtl. L. Rev. 393 (1991); Coastal States Org., Putting the Public Trust to Work (symposium proceedings, 1990) (including a 29-state survey); Symposium, 19 Envtl. L. 425 (1990).

B. Applying the Modern Public Trust Doctrine

An interesting reprise to *Illinois Central* played out on the Lake Michigan shoreline only a few miles north of the site of the famous case. In *Lake Michigan Fed'n v. Army Corps of Eng'rs*, 742 F. Supp. 441 (N.D. Ill. 1990), Loyola University proposed an 18.5-acre lakefill project that would be owned by the University, with a 35-foot public promenade on the outer rim, and athletic fields on the interior likewise available to the public. The district court held that because the main purpose of the project was for a private interest, the trust land could not be alienated. The court looked solely to the original motivation of the project, rather than balancing the benefits of the public use of the project against the loss of trust land. The University abandoned the project without appealing the decision. Could a trust balancing process have been argued that would have validated the project? See *People ex rel. Moloney v. Kirk*, 45 N.E. 830 (Ill. 1896).

As environmental consciousness grows, public conceptions of public rights inevitably expand, and public and private property expectations follow suit. The U.S. has been learning to accept the end of the myths of the frontier, of unlimited resources, of the ability to walk away from mistakes to fresh terrain. The PTD reflects societal realities long accepted in other modern nation states, which have had to deal with problems of limited resources and high population densities. If, as some leaders of the ABA said after the original Earth Day, "Environmental law is what will give the legal profession a soul," it will probably be the PTD that supplies the conceptual and spiritual compass.

PTD into the stratosphere? In April 2016 a federal magistrate judge in Oregon issued findings substantially advancing the "atmospheric public trust" theories noted in C&Q Note 6 on pages 908-909 above. In the case of *Juliana et al. v. U.S.*, (6:15-cv-1517-TC, D. Ore. April 8, 2016) the magistrate judge asserted that the federal government was subject to the public trust doctrine. He upheld the youth plaintiffs' Fifth and Ninth Amendment claims and their assertion of violations under the public trust doctrine, ruling that there is a federal public trust and that plaintiffs' claims can proceed. For ongoing details on this litigation and each of the other youth initiatives, google Our Children's Trust.

12. Environmental rights from constitutions and statutes: Pennsylvania's *Robinson Township* public trust doctrine decision. In a number of states, constitutional or statutory provisions establish environmental rights and duties, often expressly incorporating the PTD. For a time, a number of environmental attorneys held the hope that federal courts could be persuaded to recognize an implicit right to environmental quality lying latent somewhere within the U.S. Constitution. Cases such as *Tanner v. Armco Steel*[23] put a quick end to this wistful premise. In *Robinson Township v. Commonwealth of Pennsylvania*,[24] the Pennsylvania Supreme Court held unconstitutional several portions of the state's "Act 13," a statute intended by the oil and gas industry to severely limit municipal attempts to regulate oil and gas extraction.[25] The court's plurality based their decision on Article I §27 of the Pennsylvania Constitution, the public trust provision: "The people have a right to clean air, pure water, and to the preservation of the natural, scenic, historic and esthetic values of the environment. Pennsylvania's public natural resources are the common property

---

23. For a dramatic example of Pennsylvania's constitutional public trust provision and an analysis of whether constitutional provisions are "self-executing" or require further legislative action, see the unit on State Constitutional Rights on the coursebook website in the supplementary materials for this chapter.

24. 340 F. Supp. 532 (S.D. Tex. 1972).

25. Federal jurisprudence has not been a promising seedbed for environmental rights. Although the idea of federal rights periodically resurfaces (see Krier, The Environment, the Constitution, and the Coupling Fallacy, 32 Mich. L. Quad. Notes 35 (1988), and Soifer, Protecting Posterity, 7 Nova L. Rev. 39, 45 (1982)), the field of evolving environmental rights has centered on the states.

of all the people, including generations yet to come. As trustee of these resources, the Commonwealth shall conserve and maintain them for the benefit of all the people. . . ." The *Robinson Township* decision implicitly gave §27 the same constitutional status as the other provisions of the state constitution's Declaration of Rights. The holding may well propel the PTD in other states as well. (An extended text on public trust rights under state constitutional provisions is available on the coursebook website in the supplementary materials for this chapter. See also John Dernbach, The Potential Meanings of a Constitutional Public Trust, 45 Envtl. Law 463 (2015).)

13. Justice Scalia and the PTD. Especially where it can impact upon corporate and other private property rights, the PTD raises the specter of lessening those rights through the imposition of public values and environmental science concerns that previously had no traction within the established economic framework. In the *Nollan* case (in Chapter 21) Justice Scalia reportedly threatened to write a majority opinion cutting the PTD back to its narrowest water rights elements, and was only dissuaded by Justice Brennan's agreement to remove the PTD from his dissent.[26] In the *Stop-the-Beach* case (also in Chapter 21) it appeared to observers that it was the PTD again as his target when he suggested that judges who apply new interpretations of public rights may be themselves subject to liability for unconstitutional "judicial takings."

14. The ongoing evolution and institutionalization of the public trust doctrine. For an authoritative and illuminating survey of the PTD in all 50 states see Professor Robin Craig's two-part analysis of public trust jurisprudence, East and West: A Comparative Guide to the Eastern Public Trust Doctrines: Classification of States, Property Rights, and State Summaries, 16 Penn State Envtl L. Rev. 1 (2007), and A Comparative Guide to the Western States' Public Trust Doctrines: Public Values, Private Rights, and the Evolution Toward an Ecological Public Trust, 37 Ecol. L.Q. 53 (2010). Each article includes a substantial Appendix setting out each state's configuration of the trust.

The law locks up both man and woman Who steal the goose from off the common, But lets the greater felon loose Who steals the common from the goose.

— Old English quatrain

As the man said, "Money can always wait."

— Joseph Sax, Defending the Environment, 51 (1970)

We abuse land because we regard it as a commodity belonging to us. When we see land as a community to which we belong, we may begin to use it with love and respect.

— Aldo Leopold

---

26. This may explain the first line of Justice Blackmun's cryptic dissent: "I do not understand the Court's opinion in this case to implicate in any way the public trust doctrine."

21

Private Property and Public Rights: Constitutional Limits on Physical and Regulatory Takings

A. Eminent Domain Condemnations
B. Inverse Condemnation: A Constitutional Tort?
C. Challenges to Regulations as "Invalid Takings"

> Physical appropriations by government—eminent domain condemnations where a government agency takes a right of possession and pays just compensation—can be environmentally harmful and difficult to resist. Government regulatory actions at all levels, uncompensated, are part of the fabric of all modern societies; regulations play a huge part in environmental protection and continually are subject to critical analysis and resistance. Property rights-based cases arise in three main settings. In the eminent domain setting, environmental law presents substantive challenges to questionable physical condemnations (Section A). "Inverse condemnation" imposes property rights liability on governments for nuisance-like physical invasions (Section B). Arguments that environmental rules are "invalid regulatory takings" of private property (Section C), are a pervasive theme in environmental regulation and politics, reflecting fundamental clashing concepts of democratic governance. Although the inverse condemnation label is now sometimes used in claims against regulations as well as against physical acts by government, its application in the regulatory setting follows the tests for regulatory takings.

How far can government go in imposing public values and requirements upon the private property rights of corporations and individuals? That intensely political question, a central issue of democratic governance, lies latent or explosively obvious within a vast number of environmental issues. Whether by physical appropriations or regulatory restrictions on individual and corporate behavior, the imposition of public values and needs upon private property and private actions sets up political confrontations of constitutional proportions.

Local, state, and federal governments each functionally possess the coercive "police power" as a basic and necessary attribute of sovereignty,[1] the power in appropriate cases to force anyone within their jurisdiction to do or not to do things that the government believes would affect the health, safety, or general welfare of its citizens. The police power includes both physical condemnation and regulatory powers. Government can prohibit you from dumping pollutants or filling a wetland, force you to sell your land for a public park or airport, or regulate your use of wilderness areas and wildlife.

The constitutional tensions between public rights and private property rights are based on the language of the Fifth Amendment to the U.S. Constitution (as incorporated in the Fourteenth Amendment for state actions and substantially replicated in corresponding provisions in most state constitutions):

> No person shall be . . . deprived of life, liberty, or property, without due process of law; nor shall private property be taken for public use, without just compensation.

The Five Basic Police Power Inquiries.[2] Virtually all challenges to governmental mandates, whether federal, state, or local, can be subjected to the same five inquiries of constitutional scrutiny, the first four sounding in *substantive* due process (with "takings," the fourth, often separated out as a special inquiry), and the fifth in *procedural* due process. These five inquiries are discernible throughout the case law, and encompass virtually all substantial nonstatutory questions typically raised in judicial review of governmental actions.

1. **Authority.** A challenger to a zoning decision can assert the government's lack of general or specific authority to act. Such a challenge presents the *ultra vires* ("beyond the authorized powers") question, a constitutional issue. *Ultra vires* challenges involve substantive constitutional inquiry because they dispositively review the foundation of the right by which the government constrains private interests in the possession, use, and enjoyment of an individual parcel of property.

2. **Proper Public Purpose.** The second category of challenges addresses proper public purpose in regulatory actions as well as condemnations. Until *Euclid v. Ambler*, 272 U.S. 365 (1926), for example, zoning laws were attacked as not fitting within the "general welfare" component of the police power's classic triad of basic regulatory purposes: health, safety, and welfare. Narrower "poison purpose" allegations have included,

> **FIVE BASIC TESTS OF THE VALIDITY OF GOVERNMENT ACTIONS:**
>
> 1. Authority?
> 2. Proper Public Purpose? (and no "poison purpose"?)
> 3. Means Reasonably Related to Ends?
> 4. Excessive Burden Imposed on Individual?
> 5. Procedural Due Process?

---

1. The police power resides in all state governments by definition, from which it is broadly delegated to local governments for various health, safety, and welfare purposes. The federal government does not possess a general police power, but exercises a similar range of powers through its commerce, national defense, property, and other delegated authorities, and its exercises of these powers are also at times referred to as "police power" actions.

2. Plater & Norine, Through the Looking Glass of Eminent Domain: Exploring the "Arbitrary and Capricious" Test and Substantive Rationality Review of Governmental Decisions,"16 B.C. Envtl. Aff. L. Rev. 661, 707-712 (1989) (cited hereafter as Looking Glass).

with varying degrees of success, claims that regulations were "purely aesthetic," were for "purely private purposes," were motivated by a desire to drive down land prices for future condemnation, were racially exclusionary or otherwise invidiously intended to discriminate, or, like some motorcycle helmet prohibitions, impermissibly protected individuals against their own rugged wills. The proper public purpose inquiry is a threshold question, testing the propriety of the governmental objective rather than the nature of the actual decision itself.

3. **Merits Review: Means Rationally Related to Ends.** The third category of challenges involves attacking a governmental action on its merits for lack of rational relationship of the chosen means to accomplishment of the proper purposes. Even if the purposes of challenged governmental actions are perfectly proper, the design of an ordinance or the factual reasoning supporting a decision may nevertheless be insufficiently, illogically, or erroneously related to achieving those purposes. Analytically, moreover, this third means-end inquiry may also incorporate "least drastic means" and equal protection review, and can be widely discerned in judicial declarations that governmental determinations and classifications must "have reasonable relation to a proper legislative purpose, and [be] neither arbitrary nor discriminatory [to satisfy] the requirements of due process," and must "rationally advance . . . a reasonable and identifiable governmental objective."[3]

4. **Excessive Private Burden.** Because compensation is automatically owed in condemnation cases, in eminent domain the fourth inquiry is less a balancing than an evaluation of the appropriate amount of governmental payment to compensate burdened individuals for property rights taken.

But especially when applied to government regulations—challenged as "invalid regulatory takings"—the fourth inquiry, the degree of burden imposed on the individual, is often the emotional heart of substantive review and a particular tactical focus. Its most common manifestation is the allegation of "confiscatory" takings burdens in regulatory cases, asking a question basic to justice and democracy: How far can the collective power of the majority erode the property of the individual for the sake of public well-being? A common approach in regulatory takings cases is some form of "residuum" or "diminution" takings test: Property owners lose value from regulatory restrictions but must be left with a "reasonable" remaining benefit of their regulated property. The various versions of a diminution test usually do not explicitly weigh public harms avoided, but if implicit or explicit balancing of potential public harms against private property losses is included, the hybrid offers a workable and philosophically defensible test, for application far beyond the field of environmental and land use regulations.

5. **Procedural Due Process.** Courts also apply procedural due process requirements. One form considers a contextual balance whether government has given enough process—questions of notice, opportunity to contest issues at a hearing, the quantity of hearing procedures available, the clarity of legal standards to be applied, and the opportunity to obtain review of the application of a law to a particular case. The constitutional procedural balance is nicely set out in *Mathews v. Eldridge*.[4] A second form of procedural requirements is owed to the courts themselves. As in *Overton Park*, in

---

3. *Schweiker v. Wilson*, 450 U.S. 221, 235 (1981). The latter part of the quotation is clearly directed at establishing a proper public purpose.

4. *Mathews v. Eldridge*, 424 U.S. 319 (1976) —a court reviewing how much procedure an agency must constitutionally give a claimant should weigh (1) the hardship to the claimant in not receiving additional process, (2) the

order for courts to fulfill their judicial review functions government processes must produce a meaningful reviewable record, showing the basis of official actions and that officials have considered all relevant factors in reaching determinations.

These five diagnostic categories are not carved in stone but offer a useful analytical organization that can be applied to the often complex and confusing controversies surrounding the imposition of public power upon private property, as noted in the following materials of this chapter. Governmental actions that violate Inquiries Number 1, 2, and 3 often are declared "void on their face," while violations of 4 and 5 usually are voided "as applied" to that particular land.

A. EMINENT DOMAIN CONDEMNATIONS

1. The Domain of Deference

The power of the public to appropriate private property via condemnation is clearly necessary to the functioning of all governments—taking land from unwilling individuals for highways, airports, public hospitals, flood control constructions, and many more public enterprises.[5] As a result, governmental eminent domain decisions in the U.S. have generally received a most respectful reception in courts, both state and federal. Given that the government concedes that it will pay just compensation for a taking, many courts in effect declare that they have no further questions.[6] As the Supreme Court held in *Berman v. Parker*, the government's assertions of condemning authority, proper public purpose, and rational choice of means are, in practice, "well-nigh unassailable." *Berman v. Parker*, 348 U.S. 26, 35 (1954), is the Supreme Court's classic eminent domain case, upholding a condemnation for private corporate urban renewal economic development.

The usual eminent domain case is cut and dried. The condemning entity files a complaint in court against a parcel of land; the "remedy" requested is a court order transferring title. For the condemnation to succeed, the court need only be convinced that—

1. the condemning entity, which is normally either a unit of government or a public utility, has the power of eminent domain under the applicable statutes and follows the necessary procedures for its exercise;
2. the condemnation is for a stated proper public purpose;
3. the condemnation decision is not "arbitrary and capricious" (or, in some states, whether the condemnation is "necessary," usually an inquiry at the level of "are

---

hardship to the government in having to provide additional process, and (3) the risk of error in not having particular additional procedures apply. The last of these is the key argument.

5. See *Kohl v. U.S.*, 91 U.S. 367, 371-372 (1875), where the Court assumed for the first time that the federal government had inherent eminent domain authority.

6. The general invulnerability of eminent domain appears to exist irrespective of which level of condemning authority is involved—federal, state, or local government, or public utility corporation. Analytically, as well, there are no meaningful differences between these condemners. Each must have a proper grant of authority and must satisfy the other three categories of police power tests. Judicial review of the rationality of the condemner's site-selection choice is typically very deferential. In most cases, condemnees cannot require a specific showing why a particular site was not chosen. The Colorado Supreme Court, however, has suggested that public utility condemnations may deserve more scrutiny than governmental takings. *Ariz.-Colo. Land & Cattle Co. v. Dist. Ct.*, 511 P.2d 23, 24-25 (Colo. 1975).

highways necessary?" rather than "is this particular land essential if a highway is to be built?");
4. appropriate just compensation will be paid; and
5. all required procedures were followed.

The location, amount of land to be taken, and ecological effects of condemnations normally are not open to question. Thus in the vast majority of cases the opponents of condemnation can only stand and fight on the amount of compensation, a jury award, trying to make the taking more expensive. This tack is practically useless for environmentalists when they oppose a condemnation but don't own the subject property. And it is not very satisfying anyway, since money is small comfort for the unnecessary loss of a beautiful marsh or forest.

2. Challenging an Eminent Domain Condemnation

Over the decades since *Berman v. Parker*, most significant challenges to eminent domain takings have been political rather than legal. As in the highly publicized case noted below, *Kelo v. New London*, the political rhetoric reflects a gut reaction standoff. Private property groups and talk radio argue that government should keep its hands off private property, sometimes asserting the illegitimacy of all eminent domain. Government agencies argue that whatever they propose is strict public necessity. Politicians and legislatures may react in their spheres, but the constitutional validity of most takings is matter-of-factly upheld in court.

Environmentalists involved in eminent domain controversies in some cases support condemnations: There wouldn't be a Central Park in New York City or most national parks if eminent domain wasn't used. More frequently, however, they are found in opposition to projects that may not take sufficient account of environmental values—cutting highways through wilderness, building publicly owned office towers in low-income neighborhoods, siting regional trash dumps or power plants, creating development parks in bucolic areas to attract industry, or (through delegation of power to private companies), condemning rights of way for power lines, pipelines, ditches, and drains, or taking private lands so that mining companies can operate strip mines. In many such cases, environmentalists raise legal as well as political issues. The wonder is that eminent domain condemnation has been subjected to so little active judicial scrutiny on substantive rationality grounds, beyond the usual reviews of how much compensation is owed.[7]

The primary target of substantive environmental challenges to eminent domain is the question of rationality or arbitrariness. If a court allows property owners a serious hearing on their claim of irrationality, and weighs that defense according to the standard tests of arbitrariness applied in other administrative law settings, substantive challenges can be credible.[8]

---

7. The reason that relatively few condemnations are challenged, though they would appear to present attractive targets for "conservative" opposition, may be that condemnations typically are levied for "establishment" initiatives such as airports and industrial development projects, and the design plans for what property will be taken often avoid land parcels where owners are likely to be able to mount substantial legal defenses.

8. Some state courts matter-of-factly allow defenses alleging that a particular taking is "unnecessary." See Plater & Norine, Looking Glass, 16 B.C. Envtl. Aff. L. Rev. at 689-693. Another approach is available where property owners can claim that their land serves quasi-public environmental purposes. When one government tries to condemn another governmental entity's property, courts determine the winner under the "paramount public use" balance. Several courts have extended this defense to private lands. See *Texas E. Transmission Co. v. Wildlife Preserves*, 225 A.2d 130 (N.J. 1966); *Merrill v. Manchester*, 499 A.2d 216 (N.H. 1985) (the court weighed the "recreational, scenic and ecological importance" of the private land dedicated to open space preservation, against a proposed town industrial park taking); *Oxford County Agric. Soc'y v. Sch. Dist.*, 211 A.2d 893 (Me. 1965); *Middlebury Coll. v. Cent. Power Corp.*, 143 A. 384 (Vt. 1928).

Two hypothetical cases[9] help to set out the legal basis for serious substantive review of condemnation decisions.

A Means-Ends Factual Implausibility Case. Assume that a federal agency with an express statutory mandate to "promote regional economic development" decides to condemn 38,000 acres of farmland to build a regional industrial park for future corporate tenants.[10] The 300+ farm families who own the land typically would respond by making a barrage of complaints—that this is a "land-grab," a taking of private land to be turned over to other private interests, a taking of "excess" land, a "socialistic" governmental land speculation, and so on. Defense attorneys in eminent domain cases turn these verbal complaints into defensive legal arguments—most focusing on the alleged improper "private use," not "public use" as in the Fifth Amendment — and as in *Kelo*, all such regularly lose where there is a valid public *purpose*.[11]

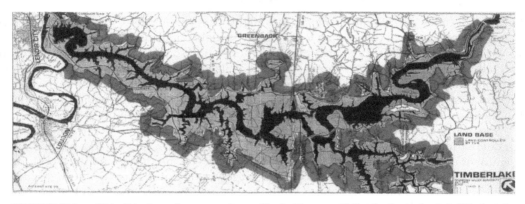

FIGURE 21-1. *This slide shows the area condemned by the Tennessee Valley Authority for their "Timberlake New Town" development project, a key element in the agency's justification for its Tellico Dam (see Chapter 10). The black area is the flooded lake; the rest of the area taken by or under threat of eminent domain—300 farms, almost 40 square miles—was taken for the model-city and associated development. After the Boeing Corp. pulled out of the project, the city was never built.*

Assume, however, that the agency previously had used exactly the same rationale to condemn a total of more than 200 square miles of farmland for other industrial development projects, *and virtually no development occurred.* The condemnation defendants realistically cannot argue that industrial development is not a proper public policy or public purpose, but they have a further argument: that they should be allowed to try to prove that condemnation of their lands is not rationally related to the accomplishment of the agency's expressed public purpose. Whereas a court initially could well have deferred to the agency

---

9. These are set out at greater length in Plater & Norine, Looking Glass, 16 B.C. Envtl. Aff. L. Rev. at 671-677.
10. This hypothetical is, in fact, the case of TVA's Columbia and Tellico Dam projects. See Chapter 10. By acquiring more than 60 square miles for the Tellico project, only 16,000 acres of which would be flooded, TVA projected that it could resell up to 35 square miles of condemned farmlands to a hypothetical industrial city to be called Timberlake, theoretically to be built by the Boeing Corporation with congressional subsidies. The speculative resale income and the future economic activity value were key economic underpinnings of the project, without which it would have failed to have a benefit-cost ratio in excess of 1:1.
11. *Berman v. Parker*, 348 U.S. 26, 35 (1954), declared that government can condemn private property to give to private redevelopers even where the land was not derelict, so long as the redevelopment served public *purposes.* This effectively killed the strict "public use" interpretation as a matter of constitutional law, though condemnees and politicians continue to argue it, and some state legislatures have statutorily modified it.

A. Eminent Domain Condemnations

on its first industrial development projects, now that the factual record clearly shows their implausibility, private property owners must be allowed at least a practical chance to allege the arbitrariness of such condemnations in court. Based on this factual record, no governmental official could reasonably believe that the governmental choice of means—condemnation of these lands—would achieve the avowed governmental ends of industrial development. Under the deferential standard of review applied in condemnation takings, however, most courts today would not undertake even this first step. Normally agencies' discretion and the rationality of their decisions to condemn, short of lunacy, are supported in court by the strongest presumption of constitutionality.[12]

A Rational Alternatives Case. The second paradigm requires the reviewing court to apply the rationality rule in a contextual setting, reviewing how an agency has chosen between several competing alternatives that admittedly would each achieve a public purpose but are irrational when viewed in context. *Poletown Neighborhood Council v. City of Detroit* illustrates this paradigm:[13]

Assume that a federal redevelopment agency, working through the auspices of a city government, decides to encourage the construction of a new job-creating, manufacturing plant within city limits. It decides to condemn and raze an urban neighborhood of 50 square blocks that contains 1100 homes, 144 businesses, 16 churches (including 2 cathedrals), 2 schools, and a hospital. The project would cause a substantial amount of personal and commercial distress, all in order to turn over the 500-acre parcel to a major automobile manufacturer for construction of a Cadillac assembly plant.

The property owners might, as usual, attack the taking as based on an improper public purpose—a "private use," for example—and, as usual, would lose. They might argue further that condemnation payments will never provide sufficient funds for replacement of their homes and businesses at relocated sites, but, in the absence of special statutory provisions, this argument also fails because just compensation is assessed according to the market value of what is taken with no guarantee of relocation or replacement costs.

Assume further, however, that at the time the officials decided to condemn and raze the neighborhood at least four other empty industrial sites of 500 acres each are available within city limits with equivalent access to rail, highways, and utilities. The landowners may now make a further argument: Given the drastic burden imposed upon them, and the available alternative sites that cannot be rationally distinguished from their neighborhood's site (except that they are less expensive to develop given the cost of condemnation to the city), no official could rationally have chosen to condemn their homes and businesses rather than go to one of the other four open sites.[14]

---

12. Some state courts allow review of the rationality of condemnation decisions, though most have followed the federal courts' extremely deferential example. Use of the federal APA §706 and its state corollaries could help open up such judicial review in the future.

13. See 304 N.W.2d 455 (Mich. 1981) (per curiam); see also *Crosby v. Young*, 512 F. Supp. 1363, 1374 (E.D. Mich. 1981). For a factual chronicle of Poletown, see *Poletown*, 304 N.W.2d at 464-471 (Ryan, J., dissenting). See Wylie, Poletown: Community Betrayed (1989); Bukowczyk, The Decline and Fall of a Detroit Neighborhood: Poletown vs. GM and the City of Detroit, 41 Wash. & Lee L. Rev. 49 (1984); Poletown Lives (documentary film), Information Factory, 3512 Courville St., Detroit MI 48224. General Motors, despite the desperate efforts of property owners and Ralph Nader, successfully induced a federally funded redevelopment condemnation project to give the corporation land in Poletown, a stable, mixed-race, low-income neighborhood of Detroit, to build a Cadillac plant.

14. The Poletown environmental impact statement identified nine potential sites for the Cadillac factory, but, from the beginning, General Motors' site criteria were so particular to the Poletown site that only it would fit. The company demanded "an area of between 450 and 500 acres; a rectangular shape (¾ mile by 1 mile); access to a long-haul railroad line; and access to the freeway system." 304 N.W.2d at 460 (Fitzgerald, J., dissenting). Never clarified in the legal

FIGURE 21-2. *Detroit's Poletown area, before and after. General Motors and the city used eminent domain powers to eliminate everything standing on the 465 acres of this integrated low-income residential-commercial neighborhood — the homes of 4,200 people, 144 local businesses, 16 churches, 2 schools, and a hospital — in order to build a Cadillac assembly plant, despite the existence of alternative undeveloped industrial park sites in the area. Photo credit: David Turnley/Corbis Historical/Getty Images.*

Such an argument is not a means-end argument that the condemnation of Parcel A will not in fact or logic serve the avowed public purpose of industrial development, but rather that, viewed in the factual context of drastic social costs and available alternative sites at

---

battle was the fact that others of the nine potential sites were basically "greenfield" sites empty of houses, churches, and small businesses and thus available without the massive disruption of Poletown; but they all were rejected at GM's insistence. Was shape a critical or a superficial requirement? When Detroit's planning office staffers inquired informally of GM, they were told that the corporation was insisting on a rectangle so that it could use the same blueprint layout of parking lots and assembly units as at an existing GM plant in Oklahoma. GM adamantly refused to consider a parking structure or shifting the parking lot layout at Poletown. One of the GM attorneys said they couldn't figure out why their CEO was insisting on the Poletown location, except that he wanted to see the new Cadillac plant, and that was the only site visible from his office. See Plater & Norine, Looking Glass, 16 B.C. Envtl. Aff. L. Rev. at 675 n. 37.

A. Eminent Domain Condemnations

B, C, D, and E, no rational official could have picked A. This version of rationality review is analytically more complex and difficult, dealing not with basic factual implausibility but with a judicial cost-benefit-alternatives review. In effect, it involves judicial acknowledgment of a "less-drastic-means" inquiry in review of some governmental condemnation actions. Deference to governmental decisions is an even greater consideration here, but the fundamental question remains: If to serve the legitimate, expressed public purpose of industrial development a site must be chosen, but in light of the disproportionate private and public burdens no rational official could have thought that Parcel A was preferable for that legitimate purpose, doesn't a defendant have the right to ask a court to scrutinize the substance of the condemnation decision and rescind it if it fails the test?

These two paradigms present instances in which private property owners would want at least the opportunity to go forward with the burden of proving that a governmental decision is not rational, in terms showing that a rational official could not so have decided. In both these cases, however, the "arbitrary and capricious" standard would be honored in the breach. Federal courts currently do not take on a particularized rational basis scrutiny of governmental condemnation decisions, but instead defer in general terms to the exercise of official discretion, leaving condemnation defendants with no practical substantive review of takings decisions.

The paradigms are admittedly rather extreme examples of eminent domain condemnation, but such cases permit clearer insights into condemnation review. Lest they be thought hyperbolic, moreover, remember that both have actually occurred and may well occur again.

COMMENTARY & QUESTIONS

1. Legal bases for more active substantive review: *Midkiff.* In the two paradigms above, the theoretical basis for substantive review can be seen in the Supreme Court decision upholding Hawaii's land reform act. The decision provided a substantive due process test for eminent domain decisions: In order to meet constitutional requirements it must be shown that "the Legislature *rationally could have believed* that the [Act] would promote its objective." *Hawaii v. Midkiff,* 467 U.S. 229, 242 (1984) (O'Connor, J., emphasis in original). It is a high burden for challengers to shoulder, but it at least allows challenges drawing on precedents of administrative law. Under administrative procedure acts courts review and occasionally rescind government agency actions found to be "arbitrary and capricious." 5 U.S.C. §706(a)(2). Administrative law interprets that test more rigorously than eminent domain case law's general deference to agencies, so the door is open for administrative law challenges of ill-considered agency and public utility condemnations.

2. Legal bases for more active substantive review: *Kelo* **and** *Hathcock.* In the *Poletown* case, the unsuccessful constitutional arguments made in court for the neighborhood were based on challenges to the public *purpose*—that giving land to a private corporation was not a "public use." In *Kelo v. New London,* 545 U.S. 469 (2005), the U.S. Supreme Court likewise upheld a challenge to an economically depressed city's attempt to revive itself with a waterfront-oriented economic renewal project based on transfer of condemned land to a private development corporation.

3. *Kelo* aroused renewed arguments that transfers of condemned private property to private corporations violated the Public Use Clause of the Fifth Amendment. But even the strenuous dissenting opinion by Justice O'Connor did not resurrect the "public use" test. She reaffirmed the prior holdings in *Berman* and *Midkiff*: "Because each taking directly

FIGURE 21-3. *The New London, Connecticut area focused upon for economic development. The porkchop-shaped parcel below the arrow is the Pfizer ex-World Headquarters intended to provide customers for the planned harborside park, restaurants, stores and other development reinvestments. The aerial photo arrow marks Susette Kelo's house. One of the flags on the home says "Don't Tread on Me" and a sign on the front of the house says "Not For Sale." The house, pink in color, was in good condition before condemnation.*

achieved a *public benefit*, it did not matter that the property was turned over to private use. . . . A public purpose was realized when the harmful use was eliminated." 545 U.S. at 500 (emphasis added). She said the taking was unjustified because Susette Kelo's house was not a harmful blighted property. (Mr. Berman had proved exactly the same thing in 1948, but lost to an expressed need for area-wide renewal.) The significance of *Kelo*, however, was that the swing vote, Justice Kennedy, shared the conviction that condemnations transferring title to a private corporation deserved greater scrutiny of their fairness. Justice Kennedy gave heightened scrutiny to the city's taking, but concluded that it was not irrational:

> A court applying rational-basis review, . . . confronted with a plausible accusation of impermissible favoritism to private parties should treat the objection as a serious one and review the record to see if it has merit, though with the presumption that the government's actions were reasonable. . . . Here, the trial court . . . considered testimony from government officials and corporate officers; . . . awareness of New London's depressed economic condition and evidence corroborating the validity of this concern; the substantial commitment of public funds by the State to the development project before most of the private beneficiaries were known; evidence that respondents reviewed a variety of development plans and chose a private developer from a group of applicants rather than picking out a particular transferee beforehand. . . . This case, then, survives the meaningful rational basis review that in my view is required under the Public Use Clause. 545 U.S. at 491-492.[15]

---

15. Ironically, the hopes for New London's public development initiative were cast into doubt by the decision of Pfizer, the city's prime "anchor enterprise" on the waterfront, to close its headquarters offices there in the wake of economic downturn. Susette Kelo angrily accepted compensation for her house and moved away.

Justice Kennedy's concurrence echoed the heightened-scrutiny logic of the Michigan Supreme Court in *Wayne County v. Hathcock*, 684 N.W.2d 765 (Mich. 2004), reversing their prior holding in *Poletown*. In *Hathcock*, an airport buffer zone was not allowed to transfer private lands to private commercial uses. *Hathcock* stated three somewhat jumbled tests to be satisfied in such takings. The Michigan court said for such takings to be valid:

> First [they must involve] public necessity of the extreme sort [for] . . . enterprises generating public benefits . . . [needing] land that can be assembled only by the coordination . . . government alone is capable of achieving. . . .
>
> Second . . . the private entity remains accountable to the public in its use of that property. . . .
>
> Finally . . . the property must be selected on the basis of "facts of independent public significance." . . . 684 N.W.2d at 781-784.

In Justice Kennedy's take, did the facts in *Kelo* pass the Michigan *Hathcock* test?

4. The politics of eminent domain. On one hand, eminent domain is a longstanding rhetorical bugbear of "conservatives." On the other, as in the *Poletown* case, private corporate interests often stand foursquare with government in favor of condemnation, opposing private property owners. Indeed, as in *Poletown*, the company appears to have initiated and controlled the government's exercise of eminent domain from the start.

Although it was a relatively straightforward application of prior law, *Kelo* was seized upon by a national coalition of antiregulatory interests, backed by nascent Tea Party organizations, as a focused issue for stirring anti-governmental popular wrath. In the political turmoil that followed, a number of state legislatures were prompted to pass statutes forbidding condemnations for economic development, for unblighted parcels, for transfer to private parties, and the like. Several bills also tacked on provisions requiring property owners to be compensated for *regulations* that lowered market values. Though *Kelo* did not alter the constitutional law of eminent domain, the *Kelo* backlash has clearly served anti-governmental agendas.

B. INVERSE CONDEMNATION: A CONSTITUTIONAL TORT?

At first glance, inverse condemnation scarcely resembles eminent domain. The facts in physical inverse condemnation cases—governmental actions resulting in noise, vibrations, smells, and general disruptions to the neighboring environs—resemble tort cases, not constitutional law.

Why then make these into constitutional cases? The simple answer is: to get around sovereign immunity. If the federal, state, or local government performing a governmental function hasn't consented to be sued, the immunity doctrine is a defense to tort actions.[16] The right to challenge government action on *constitutional* grounds, however, remains available.

Why call it "inverse" condemnation? In an ordinary condemnation case, the government decides it wants someone's property and sues to get it, as a plaintiff willing to pay just compensation. But what if, instead of suing to get the property, the government in effect simply goes ahead and takes it physically? In that case, the victim of the taking usually cannot sue in tort because of sovereign immunity. It can file a *constitutional* suit for compensation, however, effectively saying, "The government has in reality condemned my property by physically taking it, without admitting it, so I want to sue them in court to make them

---

16. The availability and extent of governmental liability, short of constitutional claims, depends on the vagaries of statutory and common law exceptions to immunity.

exercise eminent domain against me and pay compensation." Hence inverse condemnation, or "reverse condemnation," is defined by the reversal of roles.

As in the following case, the government is doing something, such as running an airport, without acknowledging its significant physical appropriation of private property uses. In the usual eminent domain case, the amount of compensation is usually the dominant issue. In inverse condemnation cases, however, there is a prior threshold issue: Was there a taking at all?

Thornburg v. Port of Portland
376 P.2d 100 (Or. Sup. Ct. 1962)

GOODWIN, J. The issues in their broadest sense concern rights of landowners adjacent to airports and the rights of the public in the airspace near the ground. Specifically, we must decide whether a noise-nuisance can amount to a taking.

The Port of Portland owns and operates the Portland International Airport. It has the power of eminent domain. It has used this power to surround itself with a substantial curtilage, but its formal acquisition stopped short of the land of the plaintiffs. For the purposes of this case, the parties have assumed that the Port is immune from ordinary tort liability....

The plaintiffs own and reside in a dwelling house located about 6,000 feet beyond the end of one runway and directly under the glide path of aircraft using it. Their land lies about 1,500 feet beyond the end of a second runway, but about 1,000 feet to one side of the glide path of aircraft using that runway. The plaintiffs contend that flights from both runways have resulted in a taking of their property. Their principal complaint is that the noise from jet aircraft makes their land unusable. The jets use a runway the center line of which, if extended, would pass about 1,000 feet to one side of the plaintiffs' land. Some planes pass directly over the plaintiffs' land, but these are not, for the most part, the civilian and military jets which cause the most noise.

FIGURE 21-4. *The Port of Portland airport. The white line indicates schematically the area overtly taken by eminent domain for the airport, with adjacent privately-owned areas not purchased by the Port Authority, but impacted by overflights; the white square is a schematic representation of the Thornburg property's location.*

B. Inverse Condemnation: A Constitutional Tort?

The plaintiffs own and reside in a dwelling house located about 6,000 feet beyond the end of one runway and directly under the glide path of aircraft using it. Their land lies about 1,500 feet beyond the end of a second runway, but about 1,000 feet to one side of the glide path of aircraft using that runway. The plaintiffs contend that flights from both runways have resulted in a taking of their property. Their principal complaint is that the noise from jet aircraft makes their land unusable. The jets use a runway the center line of which, if extended, would pass about 1,000 feet to one side of the plaintiffs' land. Some planes pass directly over the plaintiffs' land, but these are not, for the most part, the civilian and military jets which cause the most noise.

The plaintiffs' case proceeded on two theories: (1) Systematic flights directly over their land cause a substantial interference with their use and enjoyment of that land. This interference constitutes a nuisance. Such a nuisance, if persisted in by a private party, could ripen into a prescription. Such a continuing nuisance, when maintained by government, amounts to the taking of an easement, or, more precisely, presents a jury question whether there is a taking. (2) Systematic flights which pass close to their land, even though not directly overhead, likewise constitute the taking of an easement, for the same reasons, and upon the same authority.

The Port of Portland contends that its activities do not constitute the taking of easements in the plaintiffs' land. The Port argues: (1) The plaintiffs have no right to exclude or protest flights directly over their land, if such flights are so high as to be in the public domain, i.e., within navigable airspace as defined by federal law.[17] (2) The plaintiffs have no right to protest flights which do not cross the airspace above their land, since these could commit no trespass. . . . Accordingly, the Port contends, there is no interference with any legally protected interest of the plaintiffs and thus no taking of any property for which the plaintiffs are entitled to compensation. . . .

The trial court proceeded as if the rights of the plaintiffs were limited by the imaginary lines that would describe a cube of airspace exactly 500 feet high and bounded on four sides by perpendicular extensions of the surface boundaries of their land. The trial court thus in effect adapted the law of trespass to the issues presented in this case, and held that unless there was a continuing trespass within the described cube of space there could be no recovery. The trial court [held] that . . . a nuisance could not give rise to a taking. . . .

Since *U.S. v. Causby*, 328 U.S. 256 (1946), and particularly since *Griggs v. Allegheny County*, 369 U.S. 84 (1962), we know that easements can be taken by repeated low-level flights over private land . . . [and] compensation must be paid to the owners of the lands thus burdened. . . .

It is not so well settled, however, that the easements discussed in the *Causby* and *Griggs* cases are easements to impose upon lands *near* an airport a servitude of noise. . . . It must be remembered that in both the *Causby* and *Griggs* cases the flights were virtually at tree-top level. Accordingly, both decisions could perhaps be supported on trespass theories exclusively. . . . The Tenth Circuit . . . held . . . that there must be a trespass before there can be a taking. *Batten v. U.S.*, 306 F.2d 580 (10th Cir. 1962). As pointed out in a dissent by Chief Judge Murrah, the interference proven was substantial enough to impose a servitude upon the lands of the plaintiffs, and under the *Causby* and *Griggs* cases equally could

---

17. See Civil Aeronautics Act, 49 U.S.C. §551(a)(7) (1952). One FAA rule fixed 500 feet as the minimum safe altitude over persons, vehicles, and structures. 14 C.F.R. §60.107. Congress has, during all material times, denominated the airspace 500 feet above any person, vessel, vehicle or structure in other than congested areas as navigable airspace which is subject to a public right of transit.

have constituted a taking.... We believe the dissenting view in the *Batten* case presents the better-reasoned analysis of the legal principles involved....

In cases of governmental nuisance as a matter of law, there is a question, in each case, as a matter of fact, whether or not the governmental activity complained of has resulted in so substantial an interference with use and enjoyment of one's land as to amount to a taking of private property for public use. This factual question ... is equally relevant whether the taking is trespassory or by a nuisance....

The plaintiffs concede that single-instance torts ... are not compensable. Inverse condemnation, however, provides the remedy where ... the continued interference amounts to a taking for which the constitution demands a remedy....

If we accept ... that a noise can be a nuisance; that a nuisance can give rise to an easement; and that a noise coming straight down from above one's land can ripen into a taking if it is persistent enough and aggravated enough, then logically the same kind and degree of interference with the use and enjoyment of one's land can also be a taking even though the noise vector may come from some direction other than the perpendicular.

If a landowner has a right to be free from unreasonable interference caused by noise, as we hold that he has, then when does the noise burden become so unreasonable that the government must pay for the privilege of being permitted to continue to make the noise? Logically, the answer has to be given by the trier of fact....

Logically, it makes no difference to a plaintiff disturbed in the use of his property whether the disturbing flights pass 501 feet or 499 feet above his land.... Whether a plaintiff is entitled to recover should depend upon the fact of a taking, and not upon an arbitrary rule. The ultimate question is whether there was a sufficient interference with the landowner's use and enjoyment to be a taking.... Congress may very properly declare certain airspace to be in the public domain for navigational purposes, but it does not necessarily follow that rights of navigation may be exercised unreasonably.... There is a point beyond which such power may not be exercised without compensation....

PERRY, J., DISSENTING. ... I am unable to find any evidence that would support a judgment of a taking, based on interference with the plaintiffs' use and enjoyment of the land by airplane flights above the 500-foot level.... The majority rely upon the law of nuisance.... Trespass of property which, as has been pointed out, effects a taking in a constitutional sense, comprehends a physical invasion of the property either by the person or by causing a physical object to enter upon or over the property of another.... Therefore, it is the taking of an owner's possessory interest in land as compared with interfering with an owner's use and enjoyment of his land that distinguishes a trespass which is a "taking" from a nuisance, which is not.... A nuisance takes none of the title in the property....

COMMENTARY & QUESTIONS

1. Physical easements taken: beyond trespasses? Should substantial physical burdens on neighbors, beyond physical trespasses, be compensated by the government as a cost of doing business? The majority and dissent agree that a plane's *physical trespass* constitutes the compensable taking of a servitude (more properly labeled an "easement"). They were split over the rather technical point of whether nuisance-like impacts can likewise give rise to prescriptive easements.[18] Today a well-established line of cases holds that nuisances can

---

18. The dissent's argument echoed a principle of eminent domain compensation where, as in highway corridor condemnations, if government physically takes any piece of your real property, however tiny, payment for all

B. Inverse Condemnation: A Constitutional Tort?

create prescriptive easements to pollute, so airport inverse condemnation cases can apparently be based on noise and vibration nuisance effects creating easement-like burdens upon private property, even where planes don't physically penetrate plaintiffs' airspace.

2. Extending physical inverse condemnation theories. The inverse condemnation cause of action can potentially be applied far beyond airports in cases where tort claims are barred by sovereign tort immunity (because federal and state laws waiving sovereign tort immunity are quite narrow).

Highway and railroad noise? The agency in *Thornburg* argued that "plaintiffs must endure the noise of the nearby airport with the same forbearance that is required of those who live near highways and railroads." Could the inverse condemnation remedy extend to highways and railroads? Compensation has been ordered for loss of access (where a public road was converted to a limited-access highway) and loss of light and air (where a bridge or overpass was built alongside a house), even though no part of the plaintiffs' land or airspace was physically invaded. The court notes "the forbearance that is required of those who live near highways and railroads," likewise facing dust, noise, vibrations, flashing lights, and severe losses in property value. Should these be compensable now? If so, the costs could bankrupt public transit programs.

Intentional or negligent flooding? In the *Arkansas Game & Fish Commission* case, 133 S. Ct. 511 (2012), the Court held that flood control actions that cause temporary downstream flooding are compensable in the event that they meet the usual tests applied in cases alleging physical takings. After the Katrina hurricane, New Orleans plaintiffs argued that the U.S. Army Corps' negligent maintenance of the MR-GO ship channel caused an inverse condemnation taking by pouring flood waters into the city, and in 2015 a federal judge agreed. *St. Bernard Parish v. United States*, U.S Court of Federal Claims, No. 05-1119 L (May 1, 2015).

Wildlife? Inverse condemnation claims can also arise in the wild. Can't it be argued that the government takes an easement in my property without compensation when it forbids me from fencing out the antelope that want to eat my grass (giving the antelope an easement of access over my land), or when I am forbidden to shoot the endangered gray wolf that still thinks my property is her territory and eats one of my calves, or when the USFS adopts a "let-burn" policy for national forests so that my private trees and vacation cabin are destroyed by fire?[19]

Challenging non-physical government actions? Inverse condemnation is now also often used in challenges to non-physical "*regulatory* takings" (as in the next section). Do you see the legal and political advantages produced for those attacking government regulations if the constitutional test is considered the same for physical and non-physical government actions? Should *all regulatory reductions* of property use require compensation as takings of an "easement"? That would practically end all government regulation. So even when inverse condemnation claims are used to challenge regulations, the tests of validity for physical and non-physical government actions are necessarily substantially different.

---

resulting "consequential" damages must be made, but if no bit of land is taken, no compensation will be paid for the sometimes huge loss of adjacent property values caused by the new highway.

19. See *U.S. v. Lawrence*, 848 F.2d 1502 (10th Cir. 1988) (antelope); *Christy v. Hodel*, 857 F.2d 1324 (9th Cir. 1988) (grizzlies); Wiener, Uncle Sam and Forest Fires, 15 Envtl. L. 623 (1985); Keiter & Holscher, Wolf Recovery Under the Endangered Species Act: A Study in Contemporary Federalism, 11 Pub. Land L. Rev. 19 (1990). For a remarkable video chronicling the effects of wolf reintroduction see https://www.youtube.com/embed/ysa5OBhXz-Q?feature=player_embedded.

C. Challenges to Regulations as "Invalid Takings"

1. Regulatory Takings

The "crazy-quilt pattern" of Supreme Court doctrine has effectively been acknowledged by the Court itself, which has developed the habit of introducing its uniformly unsatisfactory opinions in this area with the understatement that "no rigid rules" or "set formula" are available to determine where [valid] regulation ends and [invalid] taking begins.[20]

> Sweeping attacks against government regulation have become a major characteristic of modern politics, arising in virtually all areas of governance. Private property rights-based attacks on environmental protection rules have frequently played a major role. It's a fundamental question of democracy: Where do you draw the line? How far can the collective power of the majority intrude upon an individual's property rights, especially where compensation is not paid? Takings challenges, claiming that a governmental *regulatory* action has taken private property for public use without compensation in contravention of the Fifth Amendment, can be significant in all areas of government, but nowhere more pressingly and vividly than in the field of environmental protection. The Supreme Court's decisions continue to be vague and erratic, but recent environmental cases present a slow movement toward clarity.

The politics and rhetoric of regulatory takings debates are intense. When a state prohibits development in wetlands, when the federal government prohibits billboards on interstate highways, when a local town council prohibits junkyards, when the EPA imposes a new tough pollution standard or restricts sale of a commodity, when post-strip mining reclamation standards are imposed, or when government entities propose to regulate any of a host of other concerns whereby property values and profits are restricted, in each case the "invalid takings" argument is likely to be heard loudly in the legislative, administrative, and ultimately in the judicial process. These complaints about government high-handedness are sometimes coupled with a dire warning from lobbyists that if the restriction is passed, those who vote for it as well as the agency regulators may find themselves personally liable for damages for violating the regulatees' civil rights. Because the legal lines for judging the validity of regulations have been so poorly defined, often the mere threat of a lawsuit raising a takings challenge is enough to dissuade legislators and city councils from passing environmental measures, even where the proposed regulation clearly would comply with judicial takings tests.

When a restriction is actually challenged in court, the argument typically begins with allegation of economic loss, the fourth area of constitutional inquiry. (The first three areas of police power tests are relevant but usually in effect conceded.) The attack alleges that even though the restriction does not take physical possession of all or part of the private property (which in virtually all cases would clearly require eminent domain compensation), it so excessively restricts property rights that it amounts to a taking under the due process clause and eminent domain clause of the Fifth Amendment and their state corollaries. The test classically turned in some manner on the amount of property loss, viewed in a vacuum.

---

20. Sax, Takings and the Police Power, 74 Yale L.J. 36, 37 (1964).

C. Challenges to Regulations as "Invalid Takings"

If a court finds a restriction excessive or confiscatory, the regulating agency can accept an equitable remedy nullifying the law as applied to the subject property, or agree to pay damages for the invalid taking (these cases are often confusingly filed as "inverse condemnation" or "eminent domain" actions, focusing on monetary relief).[21]

Paradoxically, although courts go to extraordinary lengths to defer to and uphold eminent domain actions, as seen earlier in this chapter, the judicial approach to regulatory acts has been discernibly more critical, especially in the past three decades of the political Right's marked ascendancy. In recent years, courts—when presented with losses of property value, a frequent occurrence in most police power settings—often have shifted the burden to government, ignoring the usual presumption of constitutionality for governmental acts.

> *Pennsylvania Coal,* the classic takings decision that follows, is cited in almost all regulatory takings cases since 1922. It is the very first case in the history of the Republic in which the 1789 constitutional prohibition on uncompensated *physical* takings was extended by the Supreme Court to *non*-physical regulatory actions.[22] As the commentary and questions that follow *Pennsylvania Coal* will note, the decision raises but doesn't resolve many of the issues already encountered in environmental cases. Like its author Oliver Wendell Holmes, the decision is both eminent and enigmatic. It purports to set out a "general rule," but does it?

Pennsylvania Coal Co. v. Mahon
260 U.S. 393 (1922)

HOLMES, J. This is a bill in equity brought by the defendants in error to prevent the Pennsylvania Coal Company from mining under their property in such way as to remove the supports and cause a subsidence of the surface and of their house. The [homeowner's] deed conveys the surface but in express terms reserves the right to remove all the coal under the same and the grantee takes the premises with the risk and waives all claim for damages that may arise from mining out the coal. But the plaintiffs say that whatever may have been the Coal Company's rights, they were taken away by an Act of Pennsylvania, approved May 27, 1921 (P. L. 1198), commonly known there as the Kohler Act. . . . The statute forbids the mining of anthracite coal in such a way as to cause the subsidence of, among other things, any structure used as a human habitation [preventing coal companies nearing the end of mining in underground coal seams from quarrying away parts of the supportive "pillars" of coal that are kept in place to hold up the ceilings of working mines if there were homes, public buildings, roads, lakes, or streams above]. . . . As applied to this case the statute is admitted to destroy previously existing rights of property and contract. The question is whether the police power can be stretched so far.

---

21. The *remedies* sought in regulatory challenges can be the same as in inverse condemnation and eminent domain cases: damages for the taking or injunctions to block the government action. But the substantive elements of the claims are very different in the regulatory and the physical taking settings.

22. The Founding Fathers quite clearly did not think that regulations could ever be compensable takings. See F. Bosselman, D. Callies & J. Banta, The Taking Issue (1973). This fact of constitutional history is often ignored by individuals on the Right who are otherwise strict "original intent" constructionists.

FIGURE 21-5. *Photograph from Scranton, Pennsylvania, showing coal mine subsidence cave-ins caused by removal of coal pillars beneath the city. The photo above, taken shortly before 1920, was presented to the state legislature as part of the city's case for passage of the 1921 Kohler Act, which was declared unconstitutional in* Pennsylvania Coal. *The bottom photograph was taken in the first decade of the twentieth century. The residents of the home, Mr. & Mrs. Buckley, escaped safely by ladder up to the surface from their attic window.*

Government hardly could go on if to some extent values incident to property could not be diminished without paying for every such change in the general law. As long recognized some values are enjoyed under an implied limitation and must yield to the police power. But obviously the implied limitation must have its limits or the contract and due process clauses are gone. One fact for consideration in determining such limits is the extent of the

C. Challenges to Regulations as "Invalid Takings"

diminution. When it reaches a certain magnitude, in most if not in all cases there must be an exercise of eminent domain and compensation to sustain the act. So the question depends upon the particular facts. The greatest weight is given to the judgment of the legislature but it always is open to interested parties to contend that the legislature has gone beyond its constitutional power. . . .

This is a case of a single private house. . . . The extent of the public interest [in the statute] is not justified as a protection of personal safety. That could be provided for by notice. Indeed the very foundation of this bill is that the defendant gave timely notice of its intent to mine under the house. On the other hand the extent of the taking is great. It purports to abolish what is recognized in Pennsylvania as an estate in land—a very valuable estate—and what is declared by the Court below to be a contract hitherto binding the plaintiffs. If we were called upon to deal with the plaintiffs' position alone we should think it clear that the statute does not disclose a public interest sufficient to warrant so extensive a destruction of the defendant's constitutionally protected rights.

But the case has been treated as one in which the general validity of the act should be discussed. . . . It is our opinion that the Act cannot be sustained as an exercise of the police power, so far as it affects the mining of coal under streets or cities in places where the right to mine such coal has been reserved. As said in a Pennsylvania case, "For practical purposes, the right to coal consists in the right to mine it." What makes the right to mine coal valuable is that it can be exercised with profit. To make it commercially impracticable to mine certain coal has very nearly the same effect for constitutional purposes as appropriating or destroying it. This we think that we are warranted in assuming that the statute does.

The protection of private property in the Fifth Amendment . . . provides that it shall not be taken for [public] use without compensation. A similar assumption is made in the decisions upon the Fourteenth Amendment. When this seemingly absolute protection is found to be qualified by the police power, the natural tendency of human nature is to extend the qualification more and more until at last private property disappears. But that cannot be accomplished in this way under the Constitution of the United States.

The general rule at least is that while property may be regulated to a certain extent, if regulation goes too far it will be recognized as a taking. It may be doubted how far exceptional cases, like the blowing up of a house to stop a conflagration, go—and if they go beyond the general rule, whether they do not stand as much upon tradition as upon principle. In general it is not plain that a man's misfortunes or necessities will justify his shifting the damages to his neighbor's shoulders. We are in danger of forgetting that a strong public desire to improve the public condition is not enough to warrant achieving the desire by a shorter cut than the constitutional way of paying for the change. As we already have said this is a question of degree—and therefore cannot be disposed of by general propositions. But we regard this as going beyond any of the cases decided by this Court. We assume, of course, that the statute was passed upon the conviction that an exigency existed that would warrant it, and we assume that an exigency exists that would warrant the exercise of eminent domain. But the question at bottom is upon whom the loss of the changes desired should fall. So far as private persons or communities have seen fit to take the risk of acquiring only surface rights, we cannot see that the fact that their risk has become a danger warrants the giving to them greater rights than they bought. Decree reversed.

BRANDEIS, J., dissenting. . . . The right of the owner to use his land is not absolute. He may not so use it as to create a public nuisance, and uses once harmless may, owing to changed conditions, seriously threaten the public welfare. Whenever they do, the Legislature has power to prohibit such uses without paying compensation. . . . If by mining anthracite coal the owner would necessarily unloose poisonous gases, I suppose no one would doubt the power of the state to prevent the mining without buying his coal fields. And why may not the state, likewise, without paying compensation, prohibit one from digging so deep or excavating so near the surface, as to expose the community to like dangers? In the latter case, as in the former, carrying on the business would be a public nuisance.

It is said that one fact for consideration in determining whether the limits of the police power have been exceeded is the extent of the resulting diminution in value, and that here the restriction destroys existing rights of property and contract. But values are relative. If we are to consider the value of the coal kept in place by the restriction, we should compare it with the value of all other parts of the land. That is, with the value not of the coal alone, but with the value of the whole property. The rights of an owner as against the public are not increased by dividing the interests in his property into surface and subsoil. The sum of the rights in the parts cannot be greater than the rights in the whole.... For aught that appears the value of the coal kept in place by the restriction may be negligible as compared with the value of the whole property, or even as compared with that part of it which is represented by the coal remaining in place and which may be extracted despite the statute.

COMMENTARY & QUESTIONS

1. The various contested elements of regulatory takings cases. How to define the limit beyond which government regulations on private property must be compensated? When government authority *physically* appropriates private property, the line normally is passed, a distinction reaffirmed in the 1978 *Loretto* case where a regulation forcing apartment buildings to allot physical space to TV cable boxes required compensation.[23] And it has been well established that property uses that are nuisances or noxious uses can be abated without compensation.[24] But where the regulatory impact on private property is not physical, clarity disappears and a welter of complex issues arises.

There are at least eight major questions that regularly arise or lie latent within regulatory takings challenges:

- **Does the property rights diminution go "too far"?** What is the ultimate legal standard of takings validity? In most takings cases, courts cite Justice Holmes's dictum that "the extent of the diminution" of private property rights is highly significant, and if it goes "too far" the regulation will be an invalid taking. But this standard, though it comports with common sense, is impossible to apply objectively. Asking whether the property owner retains a "reasonable remaining use or value," also a common phrasing of the standard of takings validity, likewise invites subjective judgments. Only recently have the standards been somewhat clarified.
- **Setting the physical baseline for the judicial inquiry into property value diminution: the parcel as a whole?** Since virtually all agree with Holmes that diminution

---

23. *Loretto v. Teleprompter Manhattan CATV Corp.*, 458 U.S. 419 (1982). Even this line on physical taking is not consistent. Justice Holmes acknowledged "exceptional cases, like the blowing up of a house to stop a conflagration," 216 U.S. at 416, and upheld regulations requiring nuisance properties such as diseased cattle or trees to be physically appropriated or destroyed without compensation. See *Miller v. Schoene*, 276 U.S. 272 (1928).

24. Since no individual has a right to use his property so as to create a nuisance or otherwise harm others, the State has not 'taken' anything when it asserts its power to enjoin ... nuisance-like activity." Stevens, J., in *Keystone Bituminous Coal Ass'n v. DeBenedictis*, 480 U.S. 470, 491 (1987). See also *Penn Central Transp. Co. v. N.Y.*, 438 U.S. 104, 144-146 (1978) (dissent by Rehnquist, J.), citing *Mugler v. Kansas*, 123 U.S. 623, 668-669 (1887), and *Hadacheck v. Sebastian*, 239 U.S. 394 (1915).

C. Challenges to Regulations as "Invalid Takings"

(the degree of private loss caused by a regulation) is relevant to determining regulatory validity, on what physical property baseline is the degree of loss to be calculated—on the property as a whole as Brandeis argued (presumably the entire coal field, not just the restricted pillars) or just on the regulated pillar portion as Holmes' majority held? The latter perspective, a divide-and-conquer definition, dramatically increases the prospects for invalidity. After *Keystone Bituminous*, noted below, the law now generally adopts Brandeis' dissenting view of the conceptual baseline rather than that of Holmes.

- **The time baselines:** There are two timing issues: retrospective economic accounting and time-of-purchase notice-based estoppel. In *Pennsylvania Coal*, the mining company had made huge profits prior to the date that the regulation prohibiting removal of support pillars was passed. Can the reviewing court take the *past economic returns* from the company's investment into account when weighing the regulation's validity (see the next paragraph on IBEs)? Second, if property owners buy regulated land knowing that it is restricted (therefore often paying less for it) (ditto), are they thereafter estopped from turning around and seeking to overturn the regulation because it lessens their full potential property value?

- **Investment-backed expectations (IBEs).** To what extent does constitutional fairness require consideration of the property owner's IBEs?[25] When the Pennsylvania Coal Company originally bought the mine, it based its investment on overall profits from the entire mine, not on the last marginal coal left in the support pillars. Today, weighing the property-owners' original IBEs can on one hand reinforce property owners' challenges by emphasizing when reasonable expectations are unfairly frustrated, and on the other hand support challenged regulations by defining the physical and time baselines broadly, according to the property owners' original overall investment planning, and weighing whether the property-owner had bought with notice of the restrictive regulation, therefore creating a "self-imposed hardship."

- **Measuring land *value* or active *use*?** In virtually all takings reviews, the courts must consider how much economic diminution the private interest has suffered. Generally this measure looks not to how much has been lost but to how much was gained or remains. There is an issue, however, whether this residuum private interest is to be measured in terms of land *value* (if an undevelopable wetland, for instance, nevertheless has market value of $2000 an acre as a buffer, or for aesthetics), or whether there must remain an ability to make *active commercial use* of the land, as Justice Scalia has sometimes insisted.[26] The distinction, only recently clarified—it's *value*—obviously can make a great difference in takings outcomes.

- **To balance or not to balance?** In the twentieth century, some takings decisions validated regulations by considering only whether government restrictions had been passed with proper authority. Others instead looked only at the impact on private property, making gestalt judgments of whether the restrictions went "too far." Over the years, with occasional departures like the *Lucas* case's exceptional "categorical" rule noted below, the common-sense conviction has grown that constitutional

---

25. The IBE phrase comes from Michelman, Property, Utility, and Fairness: Comments on the Ethical Foundations of Just Compensation Law, 80 Harv. L. Rev. 1165, 1192 (1967), and was not originally intended as a constitutional test, although as noted in this chapter IBEs have potential utility for both attackers and defenders of regulations.

26. See *Suitum v. Tahoe Reg'l Planning Agency*, 520 U.S. 725, 747-750 (1997) (Scalia, J. concurring), and Scro, Navigating the Takings Maze, 19 Ocean & Coastal L.J. 219 at n. 27 (2014).

determinations of takings validity require a balancing of *both* the public rights and the private rights implicated in a case.[27]

- **How to weigh public rights?** Even if we achieve consensus that takings tests require balancing, how to do so can never be a completely objective technical process. It is far easier to quantify private market value impacts than public interests. As considered below, in weighing this balance do all public benefits of a regulation weigh in its favor, or only those that represent the prevention of harms to the public, and how are these to be measured? Ultimately it will make a great difference which party bears the burden of proof. If properly promulgated government regulations are presumed valid unless the presumption is successfully overridden, they will tend to survive. If private rights are presumed dominant, or the presumption of governmental validity is rebuttable merely by showing economic loss, then regulations often will fail, unless compensation can be paid. The takings issue tends to force us all to define what we consider to be the proper character and role of government.
- **If a regulation is found to be invalid, what remedy?** If a decision is reached that a regulation impacts too greatly upon private property, further decisions must be made about what form of relief to issue for the excessive taking. One remedy is declaratory or injunctive nullification of the regulation on its face, or as applied to the property. Another is the payment of compensation by government, as an inverse condemnation, while keeping the regulation in force. The government defendant usually has the choice. (A further possibility, noted in *First English*[28] below, is that even if the regulation is voided, government may have to pay "interim damages" for the economic losses suffered during the time that the invalid regulation was on the books.) Compensation remedies also raise complex issues of valuation.

2. "Diminution"—what does it mean? A continuing quandary begun by Justice Holmes is how diminution of private property interests by regulations is to be measured, before a court asks whether it has gone "too far." Most courts take evidence of market values—with and without the regulation—as well as of "reasonable remaining use." Market value is the highest price a willing buyer would pay a willing seller for title to a piece of property today. It is usually determined by asking several real estate appraiser witnesses to estimate that price by analyzing "comps"—recent sales of comparable pieces of property in the same vicinity. (Some attorneys and courts mistakenly ask for valuation of the "highest and best use," a planning and development concept that is not the same as market value.) The *Pennsylvania Coal* diminution principle does not require compensation for every regulatory deflation of a parcel's market value, but only when that reduction goes too far. In practice, that has required proof of quite dramatic private losses, as noted below.

3. The baseline game: setting a baseline in takings cases—"the parcel as a whole." Note the games that can be played in determining the "baseline" against which to weigh property value diminution in order to measure whether there is a reasonable remaining use. Justice Brandeis in *Pennsylvania Coal*, suggested that judicial review should weigh the regulations' effect on the plaintiffs' contiguous property as a whole, not merely the regulated portion. Not coincidentally, a focus on the regulated portion alone in wetland cases (and many other environmental settings) typically reveals that the regulation has eliminated virtually all economic value, while a focus on the property owner's parcel as a whole

---

27. See, e.g., the third prong of the test announced by *Penn Central Transp. Co. v. City of N.Y.*, 438 U.S. 104 (1978) which is described in the following materials.

28. *First English Evangelical Lutheran Church v. Los Angeles*, 482 U.S. 304 (1987) (decided on other grounds).

C. Challenges to Regulations as "Invalid Takings"

often reveals a substantial profit that has been made in the past or may be made in the future on the property as a whole, rendering the regulation valid. The question of what to consider as the property baseline for judicial review of takings (or the "denominator" of the diminution fraction) can be critical.

4. Balancing? In wetlands cases, as for example in the *Palazzolo* coastal wetlands case that follows, judges typically are not oblivious to ecological values. (Recent coastal flooding, where protective barrier island wetlands had been destroyed, may expand recognition of eco-system services—how economics and wetland ecology go together.) In many cases, however, the courts note the value of protecting wetlands only as a basis for establishing that the act served a proper public purpose.[29] Having done so, they then focus exclusively on the private loss, without any process of constitutional balancing that would take some account of the public rights in the environmental context. Courts have found it easy to recognize the costs "externalized" onto private property by regulation, but less obvious that there should be a weighing of harms externalized onto the public by private action. For example, the "loss" to the landowner of flood plain zoning limitations that prevent property development can be measured with comparative ease, but the potential cost to the public of development in the flood plain is far more difficult to evaluate. Taking it a step further and introducing what the late Professor Joseph Sax described as the nibbling phenomenon, the cost externalized by a single parcel may be slight, and thus not figure weightily in a balance. That calculation, however, is true for all parcels, but taken together cumulatively their development would lead to massive additional damage during flood events. Not knowing how to account properly for the harm to the public, many courts focus primarily on private diminution of value, the market loss figure, and miss the full constitutional context.[30] In *Palazzolo*, below, Justice O'Connor lays the groundwork for a more overt weighing of public as well as private rights.

5. Regulations that "physically take" or take title—*Loretto* and the *Horne* raisin case. The *Loretto* case[31] makes it clear that regulations imposing direct physical impact on private property require compensation. (The New York regulation had required owners of apartment buildings to provide physical space for TV cable companies to install their cable boxes in order to encourage public Internet access.) In *Horne v. U.S. Dep't of Agriculture*,[32] a rather antiquated Depression-era law artificially raised prices of raisins by restricting the amount of raisins on the market. Producers were required to transfer to a government agency the *title* for their excess raisins above their allotted (restricted) amounts. The Hornes, raisin farmers, argued that this reserve was the equivalent of a physical taking of their excess raisins, necessitating compensation for those excess raisins at fair market value. Citing *Loretto*, the Court unanimously agreed.

2. The U.S. Supreme Court's Classic Takings Cases: An Emerging Consensus on Takings Balancing?

Here follow brief summaries of some of the most important environmental regulatory takings cases in the Supreme Court:

---

29. See *Maine v. Johnson*, 265 A.2d 711 (Me. 1970).
30. Plater, The Takings Issue in a Natural Setting: Floodlines and the Police Power, 52 Tex. L. Rev. 201, 244-252 (1974).
31. *Loretto* v. *Teleprompter Manhattan CATV Corp.*, 458 U.S. 419 (1982)
32. 133 S.Ct. 2053 (2015) (reviewing the Agricultural Marketing Agreement Act of 1937).

- *Pennsylvania Coal*,[33] noted above, in 1922 was the first Court case to hold a regulation invalid as a taking, basing its holding on property value diminution, focusing on the virtual elimination of the market value of each individual coal pillar.
- The *Penn Central* Triad: *Penn Central*,[34] 1978, likewise weighed the amount of private diminution loss, but viewed "the parcel as a whole," defining the baseline denominator as plaintiffs' entire property (Grand Central Station, which the Landmark Commission had designated a historic landmark, prohibiting construction in the air space above the terminal) as in Justice Brandeis's dissent in *Pennsylvania Coal*, not just the regulated portion (the air space). The Court's three balancing considerations upholding the restrictions have become totemic in modern takings cases: judicially weighing (1) the economic impact on the property owner (i.e. diminution), (2) the property owner's IBEs, and (3) the character of the governmental action—The *Penn Central* triad.

> **JUDICIAL POLITICS IN TAKINGS**
>
> For 50+ years after *Pennsylvania Coal*, Supreme Court Justices avoided virtually all takings cases. Since the 1970s, takings attacks on regulation, often spearheaded by Justices Rehnquist and Scalia, have been frequent.

- *Keystone Bituminous*,[35] 1987—on almost exactly the same facts as *Pennsylvania Coal*, the Court without saying so effectively overruled the way *Pennsylvania Coal* had framed the baseline diminution denominator. Justice Stevens's majority opinion viewed the private loss within the context of the *entire* coalfield, not just the regulated pillars, "the parcel as a whole," as in Justice Brandeis's dissent in *Pennsylvania Coal*, and upheld the law. *Keystone Bituminous* also explicitly assumed that takings reviews must go beyond a focus on individual loss, in addition incorporating a balancing of public interests through consideration of public harms, "noxiousness," a "nuisance exception," and the like.
- In *Lucas v. South Carolina Coastal Council*,[36] 1992, Justice Scalia struck down a South Carolina coastal protection act's prohibition of building on barrier beach lots, based on the trial court's finding that the restriction rendered the land completely "valueless." He asserted a "categorical rule" requiring compensation for regulatory wipeout where no economic value remains.

> [As to] regulations that prohibit all economically beneficial use of land: Any limitation so severe cannot be newly legislated or decreed (without compensation), but must inhere in the title itself, in the restrictions that background principles of the State's law of property and nuisance already place upon land ownership, . . . in other words do no more than duplicate the result that could have been achieved in the [state's] courts. 505 U.S. at 1018, 1027-1029.

Lucas may have been narrow on its facts, but its forceful rhetoric and attractive clarity invited a subsequent series of antiregulatory decisions in the lower courts, and a number of unsophisticated courts took *Lucas* as authority to strike down regulations, requiring compensation not only for "wipeouts" but also for regulations that eliminated profitability. (We note later how this "categorical" rule allowed exceptions for

---

33. *Pennsylvania Coal Co. v. Mahon*, 260 U.S. 393 (1922).
34. *Penn Central Transp. Co. v. City of N.Y.*, 438 U.S. 104 (1978).
35. *Keystone Bituminous Coal Ass'n v. DeBenedictis*, 480 U.S. 470 (1987).
36. *Lucas v. S.C. Coastal Council*, 505 U.S. 1003 (1992).

C. Challenges to Regulations as "Invalid Takings"

regulations of nuisance-like public harms, and for situations where private property rights are limited, for instance by the public trust doctrine (PTD).)

- In *Palazzolo*,[37] 2001, the notable case studied below, a property owner proposed to build between 70-90 small homes, or alternatively a beach club, on a coastal marsh. Both requests were turned down under a state wetlands regulation. The Court held that Mr. Palazzolo had standing to attack the regulation even if he had taken title to the land knowing it was restricted, but refused to apply *Lucas*'s "categorical" rule because the land still retained more than "token" value and remanded for a judicial balancing of public and private interests—establishing the *Penn Central* balance as the presumptive legal test to be applied in all takings cases other than total wipe-outs. Justice O'Connor's concurrence significantly clarified the constitutional balance by noting that *Penn Central's* "character of the governmental action" required courts to weigh private diminution in light of the public *purpose* for which the law was passed. On remand, the Rhode Island court found that the public harms of putting houses in a coastal marsh outweighed the private property loss.
- *Tahoe-Sierra Preservation Council*,[38] 2002, arose from longstanding governmental attempts to protect the purity of Lake Tahoe from the effects of prolific development in the crater area around the lake. In *Tahoe-Sierra*, landowners brought suit against the Tahoe Regional Planning Agency, claiming that temporary moratoria on development (a total of 32 months) constituted an uncompensated regulatory taking on its face. Extensively quoting Justice O'Connor's concurrence in *Palazzolo*, noted below, Justice Stevens's majority opinion refused to apply the harsh *Lucas* test. The 32 months were not a 100% taking of a 32-month "lease," but rather the basis for an overall *Penn Central* balance of a sort of *parcel-[of time]-as-a-whole*. The Court dismissed the takings suit, holding that the time baseline, like the physical baseline, should be viewed overall, not focusing merely upon the regulated time portion. The Court also limited the categorical *Lucas* compensation rule to cases where land value was *totally* wiped out—which virtually never occurs—and that the measure of post-regulation private rights is to be made in terms of land's remaining market *value*, not a requirement that it retain active market *uses*.
- *Stop the Beach Renourishment, Inc. v. Florida*,[39] the Court unanimously rejected coastal property-owners' taking challenge to a Florida law that allowed the public to use sand beach areas created by governmental beach reconstruction efforts after hurricanes. The Court deferred to the Florida Supreme Court's application of "core principles" of Florida property law including the PTD. Justice Scalia's plurality opinion, however, asserted a novel theory that when judges define new limitations on private property, the changing of prior law might require compensation as an unconstitutional "judicial taking."[40]

---

37. *Palazzolo v. R.I.*, 533 U.S. 606 (2001).
38. *Tahoe-Sierra Pres. Council v. Tahoe Reg'l Planning Agency*, 535 U.S. 302 (2002).
39. *Stop the Beach Renourishment v. Florida*, 560 U.S. 702 (2010).
40. For more on the "judicial takings" theory, see below.

> The following classic regulatory takings case arose on the interior wetlands of an Atlantic coast barrier beach; it not only presents a modern array of takings issues, but also potentially marks a significant turning point in our understanding of constitutional balancing in these situations, and beyond.[41]

Anthony Palazzolo v. State of Rhode Island
533 U.S. 606 (2011)

KENNEDY, J. Petitioner Anthony Palazzolo owns a waterfront parcel of land in the town of Westerly, Rhode Island. Almost all of the property is designated as coastal wetlands under Rhode Island law. After petitioner's development proposals were rejected by respondent Rhode Island Coastal Resources Management Council (Council), he sued in state court, asserting the Council's application of its wetlands regulations took the property without compensation in violation of the Takings Clause of the Fifth Amendment, binding upon the State through the Due Process Clause of the Fourteenth Amendment... In 1959 petitioner ... and associates ... purchased the property, [18-plus acres, as Shore Gardens, Inc., (SGI); and in 1960] petitioner bought out his associates and became the sole shareholder. ...

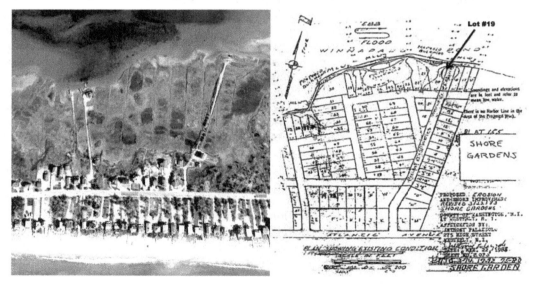

FIGURE 21-6. *The Palazzolo property in aerial view, and a very rough subdivision plan submitted by Mr. Palazzolo, with roughly 90 lots. To the north, the property borders upon Winnapaug Pond, a salty embayment lying behind the barrier beach. To the south, the property faces Atlantic Avenue and beachfront homes abutting it on the other side, and beyond that, are the dunes and the ocean beach. Lot #19, indicated by an arrow, is the small "upland portion" that might be developed. The beach community was completely destroyed by a 1938 hurricane. Since then, many seasonal homes have been reconstructed along the beach road.*

---

41. For a detailed chronology of the *Palazzolo* setting, see Cole, An Analytical Chronology of *Palazzolo v. Rhode Island*, 30 B.C. Envtl. Aff. L. Rev. 171 (2002), and the *Palazzolo* Symposium issue incorporating it.

C. Challenges to Regulations as "Invalid Takings"

Most of the property was then, as it is now, salt marsh subject to tidal flooding. The wet ground and permeable soil would require considerable fill—as much as six feet in some places—before significant structures could be built. . . .

SGI's proposal, submitted in 1962 to the Rhode Island Division of Harbors and Rivers, sought to dredge from Winnapaug Pond and fill the entire property. The application was denied. . . . In 1971, Rhode Island enacted legislation creating the Council, an agency charged with the duty of protecting the State's coastal properties, [which] designated salt marshes like those on SGI's property as protected "coastal wetlands." . . . In 1978 SGI's corporate charter was revoked for failure to pay corporate income taxes; and title to the property passed, by operation of state law, to petitioner as the corporation's sole shareholder. In 1983 petitioner, now the owner, . . . requested permission . . . to fill the entire marsh land area. The Council rejected the application, [finding] that "the proposed activities will have significant impacts upon the waters and wetlands of Winnapaug Pond." [A 1985 permit request was likewise denied.]

Petitioner filed an inverse condemnation action in Rhode Island Superior Court, asserting that the State's wetlands regulations, as applied by the Council to his parcel, had taken the property without compensation in violation of the Fifth and Fourteenth Amendments. The suit alleged the Council's action deprived him of "all economically beneficial use" of his property, resulting in a total taking requiring compensation under *Lucas* [and] sought damages in the amount of $3,150,000, a figure derived from an appraiser's estimate as to the value of a 74-lot residential subdivision. The . . . Superior Court ruled against petitioner; the Rhode Island Supreme Court affirmed . . . , recit[ing] multiple grounds for rejecting petitioner's suit. The court held, first, that petitioner's takings claim was not ripe; second, that petitioner had no right to challenge regulations predating 1978, when he succeeded to legal ownership of the property from SGI; and third, that the claim of deprivation of all economically beneficial use was contradicted by undisputed evidence that he had $200,000 in development value remaining on an upland parcel of the property, [Lot #19; and] could not recover under the more general test of *Penn Central*. . . .

We disagree with the Supreme Court of Rhode Island as to the first two of these conclusions; and, we hold, the court was correct to conclude that the owner is not deprived of all economic use of his property because the value of upland portions is substantial. [The Court then holds that the issue was ripe for review.]

We turn to the second asserted basis for declining to address petitioner's takings claim on the merits. When the Council promulgated its wetlands regulations, the disputed parcel was owned not by petitioner but by the corporation of which he was sole shareholder. When title was transferred to petitioner by operation of law, the wetlands regulations were in force. The state court held the postregulation acquisition of title was fatal to the claim for deprivation [as a standing estoppel, because he took title with notice and thus is] barred from claiming that it effects a taking. . . . The State may not put so potent a Hobbesian stick into the Lockean bundle. . . . Were we to accept the State's rule, the postenactment transfer of title would absolve the State of its obligation to defend any action restricting land use, no matter how extreme or unreasonable. . . .

The state court must address, however, the merits of petitioner's claim under *Penn Central*. That claim is not barred by the mere fact that title was acquired after the effective date of the state-imposed restriction. In Justice Holmes' well-known, if less than self-defining, formulation, "while property may be regulated to a certain extent, if a regulation goes too far it will be recognized as a taking." . . . We hold that the court was correct to conclude that the owner is not deprived of all economic use of his property because the value of upland portions is substantial. We remand for further consideration of the claim under the principles set forth in *Penn Central.*

O'CONNOR, J., concurring. . . . As the Court holds, . . . petitioner's claim under *Penn Central* "is not barred by the mere fact that title was acquired after the effective date of the state-imposed restriction." . . . [However,] today's holding does not mean that the timing of the regulation's enactment relative to the acquisition of title is immaterial to the *Penn Central* analysis. Indeed, it would be just as much error to expunge this consideration from the takings inquiry as it would be to accord it exclusive significance. . . .

The concepts of "fairness and justice" that underlie the Takings Clause, of course, are less than fully determinate. Accordingly, we have eschewed "any 'set formula' for determining when 'justice and fairness' require that economic injuries caused by public action be compensated by the government. . . . The outcome instead "depends largely 'upon the particular circumstances [in that] case.'" *Penn Central.* We have "identified several factors that have particular significance" in these "essentially ad hoc, factual inquiries." *Penn Central.* Two such factors are "the economic impact of the regulation on the claimant and, particularly, the extent to which the regulation has interfered with distinct investment-backed expectations." Another is "the character of the governmental action." The purposes served, as well as the effects produced, by a particular regulation inform the takings analysis. . . . Regulatory takings cases "necessarily entail complex factual assessments of the purposes and economic effects of government actions."

The Rhode Island Supreme Court concluded that, because the wetlands regulations predated petitioner's acquisition of the property at issue, petitioner lacked reasonable investment-backed expectations and hence lacked a viable takings claim. The court erred in elevating what it believed to be "[petitioner's] lack of reasonable investment-backed expectations" to "dispositive" status. . . . Evaluation of the degree of interference with investment-backed expectations instead is *one* factor that points toward the answer to the question whether the application of a particular regulation to particular property "goes too far." . . . Our decision today does not remove the regulatory backdrop against which an owner takes title to property from the purview of the *Penn Central* inquiry. It simply restores balance to that inquiry. Courts properly consider the effect of existing regulations under the rubric of investment-backed expectations in determining whether a compensable taking has occurred.

SCALIA, J., concurring. I write separately to make clear that my understanding of how the issues discussed in [the prior notice portion] of the Court's opinion must be considered on remand is not Justice O'Connor's. The principle that underlies her separate concurrence [i.e. as to buyers' knowledge of prior-existing regulatory restrictions] is that it may in some (unspecified) circumstances be "unfair" and produce unacceptable "windfalls" to allow a subsequent purchaser to nullify an unconstitutional partial taking. . . . The polar horrible, presumably, is the situation in which a sharp real estate developer, realizing (or indeed, simply gambling on) the unconstitutional excessiveness of a development restriction that a naive landowner assumes to be valid, purchases property at what it would be worth subject to the restriction, and then develops it to its full value (or resells it at its full value) after getting the unconstitutional restriction invalidated. This can, I suppose, be called a windfall. . . . There is something to be said (though in my view not much) for pursuing abstract "fairness" by requiring part or all of that windfall to be returned to the naive original owner, who presumably is the "rightful" owner of it. But there is nothing to be said for giving it instead to the *government*—which not only did not lose something it owned, but is both the *cause* of the miscarriage of "fairness" and the only one of the three parties involved in the miscarriage (government, naive original owner, and sharp real estate developer)

C. Challenges to Regulations as "Invalid Takings"

which *acted unlawfully*—indeed *unconstitutionally*. Justice O'Connor would eliminate the windfall by giving the malefactor the benefit of its malefaction. It is rather like eliminating the windfall that accrued to a purchaser who bought property at a bargain rate from a thief clothed with the indicia of title, by making him turn over the "unjust" profit *to the thief*.

> The *Palazzolo* case was remanded to the Rhode Island courts, presumably only on the *Penn Central* diminution question of whether there was sufficient remaining value after the regulation (particularly the Lot #19 "upland portion") to avoid a finding of an excessive regulatory taking requiring compensation. In the remand decision below, however, note how far the court goes, perhaps at Justice O'Connor's invitation, beyond simple diminution.

Anthony Palazzolo v. State of Rhode Island
C.A. NO. WM 88-0297, 2005 R.I. Super LEXIS 108
Superior Court of Rhode Island, filed July 5, 2005

GALE, J. This case is back before the Superior Court on remand. . . . The United States Supreme Court found the case ripe for decision, . . . and remanded the case for the purpose of a *Penn Central* analysis. The Rhode Island Supreme Court entered an Order remanding the case to the Superior Court with express guidelines . . . for the purpose of determining "the claim of Anthony Palazzolo for monetary damages against the State of Rhode Island for an alleged regulatory taking of his property by analyzing his reasonable investment-backed expectations in accordance with the principle enunciated in [the *Penn Central* case]." . . .

The 446-acre Winnapaug Pond is a shallow, tidal pond used for fishing, boating and shell fishing. Its size and shallow depth make it a particularly fragile ecosystem. The adjacent salt marsh provides, inter alia, a valuable filtering system regarding water runoff containing pollutants and nitrogen from adjacent land. The ISDS[42] systems from the proposed subdivision would add significant nitrogen to the pond. Filling of the Palazzolo site would result in 12% less salt marsh and a reduction of pollutant and nitrogen filtering by the pond's salt marsh ecosystem. The effect of the denigration of the natural purifying salt marsh is viewed by experts as significant. Loss of the marsh filtering effect, together with the loss of wildlife habitat which would occur if Plaintiff's planned subdivision was constructed, was previously found by this Superior Court to constitute a nuisance. Moreover, there can be no doubt that the pond and its surroundings, particularly the undeveloped salt marsh, have an amenity value to both the land owners in the area as well as the entire vacation/recreation community in Westerly. This Court likewise finds that the evidence is to the effect that not only has there never been a subdivision near Winnapaug Pond which rivals the scope of that proposed by Palazzolo, but none exists anywhere on the Rhode Island shore.

Prior to discussing Plaintiff's takings claim in the context of a *Penn Central* analysis, it is necessary to consider certain background legal principles which bear on the extent of plaintiff's property interest. *Lucas v. South Carolina*, makes clear that, for purposes of takings analysis, . . . the government need not compensate the property owner if the regulated or prohibited use was "not part of his title to begin with."

---

42. ISDS is an acronym for "individual sewerage disposal systems," i.e. septic tanks. [EDS.]

The State contends that this Court's [prior] conclusion . . . that Plaintiff's proposed development would constitute a public nuisance, precludes a Plaintiff's verdict on his takings claim. . . . The State also contends that a strong Public Trust Doctrine in Rhode Island must result in a finding that the subject parcel is not capable of being developed economically. This is because, the State maintains, approximately one-half of Plaintiff's property lies below the mean high water mark and is, therefore, not Plaintiff's to develop, at least in contravention to the wishes of the state.

In the case at bar, Palazzolo's proposed development has been shown to have significant and predictable negative effects on Winnapaug Pond and the adjacent salt water marsh. The State has presented evidence as to various effects that the development will have including increasing nitrogen levels in the pond, both by reason of the nitrogen produced by the attendant residential septic systems, and the reduced marsh area which actually filters and cleans runoff. This Court finds that the effects of increased nitrogen levels constitute a predictable (anticipatory) nuisance which would almost certainly result in an ecological disaster to the pond. Both water quality and wildlife habitat would be substantially harmed. Nor is the proposed high density subdivision suitable for the salt marsh environs presented here. This Court agrees with the first trial justice. Because clear and convincing evidence demonstrates that Palazzolo's development would constitute a public nuisance, he had no right to develop the site as he has proposed. Accordingly, the State's denial to permit such development cannot constitute a taking. . . .

A second significant issue is to what extent the Public Trust Doctrine would have limited the title originally acquired by Plaintiff. . . . After receiving voluminous evidence on the issue, this Court finds that Winnapaug Pond is a tidal body of water [and] almost exactly 50% of Plaintiff's property is below mean high water. Thus, the pond and Plaintiff's adjacent property are subject to the Public Trust Doctrine. . . . The Public Trust Doctrine dictates that, "the state holds title to all land below the high-water mark in a proprietary capacity for the benefit of the public." . . . Although the Public Trust Doctrine cannot be a total bar to recovery as to this takings claim, it substantially impacts Plaintiff's title to the parcel in question and has a direct relationship to Plaintiff's reasonable investment-backed expectations. . . .

***PENN CENTRAL* ANALYSIS** This Court now turns to the focus of the Rhode Island Supreme Court's remand and the United States Supreme Court's mandate, to consider whether or not Plaintiff has proved a compensable taking under the three part analysis set forth in *Penn Central*. The factors which provide the framework for analysis under *Penn Central* are (1) the economic impact of the action on the claimant, (2) the extent to which the action interfered with the claimant's reasonable investment-backed expectations, and (3) the character of governmental action.

This Court is mindful that the analysis requires an ad hoc consideration of a number of other relevant factors often unique to the case at hand, including the temporal relationship between Plaintiff's acquisition of title and the regulations giving rise to the takings claim. *Palazzolo*, (O'Connor, J., concurring).

In conducting the takings analysis, this Court must focus on the "parcel as a whole." The denominator or "parcel as a whole" is that property in which Palazzolo invested that is subject to the regulations. . . .

Plaintiff asserts that he has lost a profit of over three million dollars as a result of the State's denial of his planned development. . . . Palazzolo's monetary claim is based upon the premise that he is entitled to be compensated based upon the highest and best use of his property. . . . The testimony of the State's engineering expert cast grave doubt on the

C. Challenges to Regulations as "Invalid Takings" 943

viability of Plaintiff's [development] proposals. . . . The expert concluded that for a 50-lot subdivision, development costs would be $3,893,750. . . . The ultimate conclusion is that Plaintiff will be better off financially by selling the site in its current undeveloped state, knowing that a single residence will be allowed to be built on the upland area near the pond shoreline. . . . Site development costs unique to the parcel in question would result in an economic loss to Plaintiff if he were to build either of the high density residential developments he has proposed. Thus, as to Palazzolo's claim, the regulations complained of do not have an adverse economic impact. . . .

Moreover, although Plaintiff is entitled to compensation based upon the highest and best use of the subject property if there is a taking, diminution of property value, standing alone can not establish a taking. . . . Determination of the takings issue depends in large part on Plaintiff's reasonable investment-backed expectations, and whether or not the property owner has been unfairly economically impacted. "Pecuniary loss or diminution in value is not controlling on the issue of confiscation because a property owner does not have a vested property right in maximizing the value of his property."

This Court now turns to . . . consideration of Plaintiff's reasonable, investment-backed expectations. . . . In the words of Plaintiff, he acquired an interest in "the worst of them [lots], what's left." Thus, even from the time of his initial investment, Palazzolo had doubts about the value of the remaining property. While Palazzolo hoped that some variation of the 74-lot subdivision would eventually be approved, the [investment-backed expectations] prong of the *Penn Central* analysis clearly requires a determination of *realistically achievable* economic goals. . . . Massive filling of the site was required and permission of the state would be needed for such filling. These problems were known, or reasonably should have been known, by Palazzolo as early as his initial investment and must be factored into any determination of "reasonable investment-backed expectations." . . . This Court finds that Plaintiff's investment-backed expectations were not realistically achievable; accordingly he fails to satisfy [that] prong of the *Penn Central* test. . . . Despite wishful thinking on Palazzolo's part, he paid a modest sum to invest in a proposed subdivision that he must have known from the outset was problematic at best. . . . Constitutional law does not require the state to guarantee a bad investment.

Regarding the character of the governmental action, this is clearly neither a categorical physical takings case nor a regulatory takings case in which a statutory scheme has taken all "economically beneficial use" of the subject property. . . . It is all too obvious that government need not compensate a property owner each and every time it enacts regulations which are designed to promote the health, safety, and welfare of the people. In fact, the legitimacy of the regulatory scheme at issue here militates against a finding that a taking has occurred. . . .

In sum, Plaintiff has failed to prove by a preponderance of the evidence that there has been a regulatory taking of his property.

COMMENTARY & QUESTIONS

1. An expansive remand! Note that the *Palazzolo* Supreme Court majority clearly thought that the remand to Rhode Island would simply apply the diminution inquiry from *Penn Central*, only looking to see if the Lot #19 "upland portion" would provide sufficient economic value. The remand barely noted that, and instead weighed an array of other factors as noted in the following paragraphs, including a heavy emphasis on investment-backed expectations, explicitly citing the O'Connor concurrence as authoritative. Could the remand court's expansive view be partly explained by the fact that the "upland" Lot #19 was probably unbuildable due to sewerage difficulties? Did Justice O'Connor's pointed concurrence help set up a more expansive balancing on remand?

2. Some clarifications from *Palazzolo*: notice estoppel and investment-backed expectations. The majority opinion forcefully rejected the state's argument that Anthony Palazzolo lacked standing to challenge the regulation because he'd taken title with notice of the land's restrictions. As Justice Scalia fumed, a citizen always has the right to challenge the constitutionality of a rule; there's no notice estoppel against constitutional rights. But note how Justice O'Connor's concurrence blunted the force of the majority's words: she agreed that a property-owner's knowledge of land restrictions before purchasing doesn't absolutely block a challenge, but she insisted it was nevertheless a substantial consideration in determining fairness—and she used the familiar logic of investment-backed expectations to say that prior knowledge of restrictions should weigh in the takings balance. Despite Justice Scalia's argument that this favored the government as "thief," note how the state court on remand defined O'Connor's investment-backed expectation phrasing as its primary *Penn Central* focus. Is Scalia's "thief" characterization accurate? After the coastal devastation to the over-built New York and New Jersey coasts that accompanied Super Storm Sandy, it should be clear that wetland regulation is a bulwark that prevents imprudent (albeit highly profitable) building by private parties, construction that externalizes the costs of such storms in the form of increased damage to others. Is government stealing when it proscribes actions that harm others?

3. Some loopholes in *Lucas*. Justice Scalia's "categorical" rule in *Lucas*, the *Palazzolo* Court held, applied only where restrictions left the property owner with merely "a token interest"—an extremely rare situation with any regulation—so the default test, *Penn Central*, applied instead. His *Lucas* opinion also served here as a basic *validation* of the *Palazzolo* regulation, as Judge Gray on remand examined whether the wetland development would be a tort, and a violation of the public trust, thus using the Justice's own words to undercut any "categorical rule" requiring compensation. And Justice Scalia's *Lucas* initiative was cast further into marginality by the clear adoption of the "parcel as a whole" baseline. "Conceptual severance," as Professor Margaret Radin labeled it—viewing only the restricted part of the property in order to increase the chances of finding excessive diminution[43] –was firmly rejected.

4. Balancing the expanded third prong of *Penn Central*. The most intriguing aspect of the *Palazzolo* case can also be traced to a few more words in Justice O'Connor's concurrence. The Court majority had declared the three-pronged *Penn Central* balancing test to be the canonic methodology for reviewing regulatory takings challenges. It had never been clear, however, how public and private interests in wetlands are to be weighed against one another in a *Penn Central* balancing. *Penn Central's* first two prongs are quite tangible—diminution, and its corollary IBE, both focused on the private party. But what is the third prong, "the character of the government action"? *Penn Central* merely noted whether the government action was a physical taking or not.

But the third prong of *Penn Central* could be an invitation to weigh public values against the private regulatory loss, and Justice O'Connor provided the small but significant clarifying key. Quoting *Penn Central* extensively in addressing "the character of the governmental

---

43. On remand, Palazzolo's attorneys had tried to narrow the baseline to the regulated portion of the property alone, instead of the whole investment parcel. "Conceptual severance" the divide-and-conquer antiregulatory strategy of defining narrowed baselines, was coined in Radin, The Liberal Conception of Property: Cross Currents in the Jurisprudence of Takings, 88 Colum. L. Rev. 1667, 1676 (1988).

C. Challenges to Regulations as "Invalid Takings"

action," she wrote, "The *purposes served* . . . by a particular regulation, . . . as well as the effects produced, . . . inform the takings analysis. Regulatory takings cases "necessarily entai[l] *complex factual assessments of the purposes* and economic effects of government actions." 533 U.S. at 633-634, commenting on *Penn Central*, 438 U.S. at 124 (*emphasis added*).

This latter statement, overlooked in Justice Scalia's fiery *Palazzolo* opinion, provides the first explicit acknowledgment in a Court opinion that the constitutional balances in regulatory takings cases must conscientiously weigh not only the private market value loss from restrictions, but also the public purposes (typically various impending harms) that had prompted the legislature to authorize those regulations in the first place. It makes no sense to ignore the public harms that a regulation is intended to prevent when weighing whether regulated private property is unconstitutionally burdened.[44]

This express invitation to balance public concerns against private diminution goes far beyond the "nuisance exception" noted in some takings cases and incorporated in *Lucas*'s "categorical rule." Consider: Could most regulatory protection settings in the environmental field be practically litigated as nuisance torts? The most challenging problem facing would-be-plaintiffs victimized by increased harm is likely to be proving causation: linking each landowner's action in developing their parcel to the harm the victim has suffered. Does the relaxed causation standard used in joint tortfeasor cases such as *Velsicol* (Chapter 3) make that proof any more feasible? If the goal is to avoid the potentially devastating harm rather than suffer it and seek compensation, would a court, as in *Wilsonville* (Chapter 3), be likely to grant an injunction seeing the building activity as an anticipatory nuisance? If not, isn't it valid government regulation, or nothing?

The *Palazzolo* remand incorporates an explicit balance of public harms against the petitioner's private rights. The court emphasizes the many public harms for which wetlands were restricted, including the wetland's ecosystem services that would be lost — the loss of marsh filtration, shellfish mortality, drainage effects on public health, and other public concerns that would occur absent the restrictions — a number of which could never practically be litigated as torts.[45]

3. A Takings Role for the Public Trust Doctrine?

In *Lucas*, Justice Scalia held that where property values were fully wiped out, "any limitation so severe . . . must inhere in the title itself, in the restrictions that background principles of the State's law of property and nuisance already place upon land ownership."[46] But to Justice Scalia's undoubted dismay, as in *Palazzolo* on remand, that phrasing has operated

---

44. Some courts, however, have been surprisingly avoidant in acknowledging public harms in the balance. See *Dooley v. Fairfield*, 226 A.2d 509 (Conn. 1967) (striking down floodplain restrictions where a developer planned to put 300 homes in coastal lowlands repeatedly hit by hurricane flooding). In *First English*, Justice Rehnquist even posited that a flood hazard ordinance would be an unconstitutional confiscation where it eliminated the economic value of a canyon parcel used as a riverside camp for handicapped children. This amounted to saying that because the land's market valuation ignored the dangers, the property owner had a constitutional right to house 200 children in the path of recurring floods where ten people had recently been drowned, or be compensated fully for the banning of that use. On remand, the California Supreme Court seemed astonished by that premise, noting that the lives of children surely weighed more heavily constitutionally than the loss of property value. 210 Cal. App. 3d 1353 (1989). See also Plater, The Takings Issue in a Natural Setting: Floodlines and the Police Power, 52 Tex. L. Rev. 201, 244-252 (1974).

45. The remand opinion closely tracked but didn't cite Prof. Parenteau's anticipatory article, Unreasonable Expectations: Why *Palazzolo* Has No Right to Turn a Silk Purse into a Sow's Ear, 30 B.C. Envtl. Aff. L. Rev. 101 (2002).

46. *Lucas v. S.C.*, 505 U.S. at 1029.

to validate rather than restrict governmental regulations. Did Justice Scalia inadvertently open the door to additional consideration of public rights (and perhaps even of the "natural economy") against private marketplace rights by allowing the PTD into the takings balance?

Shortly after *Lucas*, Professor Babcock prophesized that the PTD, as a property law principle, like nuisance law, was likely to circumvent Justice Scalia's "categorical" compensation rule. "Public trust principles may well be employed by government regulators in their attempts to justify their actions under the *Lucas* takings rule.... The PTD helps to harmonize the laws of nature and the law of property, bringing the expectations of landowners into harmony with the needs of nature,... infusing an ecological perspective into property law.... The doctrines of custom and public trust [underscore] the public's superior right to access and use certain resources, but this is not as destabilizing as it sounds because both common law doctrines are a reflection of public expectations."[47]

Professor Sax likewise has emphasized that the public trust fits into takings balances as part of a society's fairness expectations:[48]

> The essence of property law is respect for reasonable expectations. The idea of justice at the root of private property protection calls for identification of those expectations which the legal system ought to recognize. We all appreciate the importance of expectations as an idea of justice, but our concern for expectations has traditionally been confined to private owners.... The central idea of the public trust is preventing the destabilizing disappointment of expectations held in common but without formal recognition such as title. The function of the public trust as a legal doctrine is to protect... public expectations against destabilizing changes, just as we protect conventional private property from such changes.[49]

Sax also argued that a society's expectations about what are unfair impositions on private property change over time.[50] In *Sanderson v. Penn Coal*,[51] a coal company was mining and dumping its wastes in a river, and a downstream landowner objected, claiming traditional riparian rights and protections under nuisance law. The court agreed with the company that "the law should be adjusted to the exigencies of the great industrial interests of the Commonwealth and that the production of an indispensable mineral... should not be crippled and endangered by adopting a rule that would make colliers answerable in damages for corrupting a stream."[52] In 1886, this assertion of marketplace needs did not arouse a horrified reaction in defenders of private property rights, but it surely would today. Indeed, the same court that decided *Sanderson* repudiated it early in the age of heightened

---

47. Babcock, Has the U.S. Supreme Court Finally Drained the Swamp of Takings Jurisprudence? The Impact of *Lucas v. South Carolina* Coastal Council on Wetlands and Coastal Barrier Beaches, 19 Harv. Envtl. L. Rev. 1 (1994).

48. Sax, Property Rights and the Economy of Nature: Understanding *Lucas v. South Carolina Coastal Council*, 45 Stan. L. Rev. 1433 (1993).

49. Sax, Liberating the Public Trust Doctrine from Its Historical Shackles, 14 U.C. Davis L. Rev. 185, 186-194 (1980). A 1988 Supreme Court public trust case turned upon whether a state's assertion that it owned certain tidal wetlands upset "settled private expectations." *Philips Petroleum Co. v. Miss.*, 484 U.S. 469 (1988), decided that it did not, in an opinion emphasizing the traditional role of the states in defining their public trust; see also, e.g., *Shively v. Bowlby*, 152 U.S. 1, 26 (1894).

50. Sax, The Limits of Private Rights in Public Waters, 19 Envtl. L. 473 (1989).

51. 6 A. 453 (1886). See also Horwitz, The Transformation in the Conception of Property in American Law 1780-1860, 40 U. Chi. L. Rev. 248 (1973).

52. The court held:

> We are of opinion that mere private personal inconvenience... must yield to the necessities of a great public industry, which... subserves a great public interest. To encourage the development of the great natural resources of a country, trifling inconveniences to particular persons must sometimes give way to the necessities of a great community. 6 A. at 459.

C. Challenges to Regulations as "Invalid Takings"

environmental awareness: "[W]e find that even with regard to the facts of *Sanderson*, the legal doctrine enunciated in that case is no longer viable."[53]

Since *Palazzolo*, as in the remand in that case, a number of courts have used the public trust doctrine to validate regulations even where they substantially eliminate market value.[54]

COMMENTARY & QUESTIONS

1. Can governmental negligence be an unconstitutional taking? In the aftermath of Hurricane Katrina's devastation of New Orleans and much of the adjacent Gulf coast, it has appeared that a substantial portion of the causation of flooding in the city was attributable to the U.S. Army Corps of Engineers, negligent design and maintenance of MRGO, the Mississippi River Gulf Outlet, a channel that accelerated the storm surge's race up into the city.[55] When the Fifth Circuit rejected tort claims against the Corps on the basis of sovereign immunity, plaintiffs filed an inverse condemnation takings claim against the Corps in the U.S. Federal Court of Claims, which awarded compensation. As Professor Peter Byrne wrote:

> The ... decision of the U.S. Court of Federal Claims in the *St. Bernard Parish* case[56] may provide "just" compensation to the residents harmed by the Army Corps' negligent design and maintenance of the MRGO, but it also marks a troubling expansion of takings liability for the government.... Government liability for takings through flooding have been based on deliberate government action that had the foreseeable effect of flooding the plaintiff's land. *Pumpelly v. Green Bay Co.*, 13 Wall. 166 (1872). In *St. Bernard*, the Corps did not construct MRGO in the 1950s and '60s with the intent or even expectation that it would flood the plaintiffs' property. What the Court found was that by 2004-05, before Katrina, the Corps had recognized that MRGO, now tripled in width due to erosion, created a serious risk of flooding that should be addressed. At that point the risk of harm from a major storm was foreseeable. Nothing was done. That inaction in the face of risks exacerbated by the defendants conduct sounds on tort, but how can it amount to a taking? Takings generally involve authorized and permissible government action that so invades the defendant's property that the government can proceed only by paying compensation.... It is hard to see how the negligent design and lack of a response to erosion 40 years later could be the kind of government action that could be held a taking under prior doctrine. We seem to have entered [Prof. Christopher] Serkin's imaginative world of "Passive Takings," where government inaction can create takings liability. 113 Mich. L. Rev. 345 (2014).... It may be that the MRGO is one of a kind, given its notoriety and the appalling

---

53. *Commonwealth. v. Barnes & Tucker Co.*, 455 Pa. 392, 410-411, 319 A.2d 871, 881 (1974).

54. The Supreme Court of South Carolina found that a prohibition on filling tideland below the MHW issued by the state Coastal Council was *not* a taking, despite the uncontested fact that the land retained no value as a result of the prohibition. The *Lucas* background principles of South Carolina's public trust property law preserving marine life, water quality, and public access absolved the state from having to compensate the plaintiff. *McQueen v. S.C. Coastal Council*, 580 S.E.2d 116 (S.C. 2003).

55. The facts are laid out in *In re Katrina Breaches Consol. Litig.*, 647 F. Supp. 2d 644 (E.D. La. 2009), rendered irrelevant by the eventual decision of the Fifth Circuit applying the Corps' statutory immunity from tort claims. *In re Katrina Breaches Litig.*, 674 F. 3d 436 (5th Cir. 2012).

56. St. Bernard Parish Government and other Owners of Real Property in St. Bernard Parish, the Lower Ninth Ward of the City of New Orleans v. U.S., (No. 05-1119L, Federal Ct. of Claims, May 1, 2015).

losses from Katrina. . . . I suppose the government will push back hard to preserve the distinction between tort and takings. And the Takings Clause continues to be fashioned into a general tool for judicial control of government.[57]

This expansion of governmental takings liability could become a tangible constraint on a number of environmental protection efforts.

2. Justice Scalia's endeavor to assert "judicial takings." The most controversial aspect of the *Stop the Beach* case noted above[58] arises in the plurality opinion of Justice Scalia (joined by Roberts, Thomas, and Alito) novelly hypothesizing the availability of "judicial taking" claims — that *the state judges themselves* can violate the Fifth and Fourteenth Amendments by defining new applications of legal doctrines like the public trust doctrine. The littoral owners had argued that the state supreme court had redefined, or made a sudden, unpredictable, major change in, common law rights. They cited language in Justice Scalia's *Lucas* opinion constraining state courts' ability to recast evolving common law property rules, and parts of a concurring opinion by Justice Stewart in a different beach accretion setting.[59] Justice Scalia said there was no judicial taking, in the *Stop the Beach* setting, but used the plurality opinion to plant his notion that "judicial takings" could be found in the future if challengers showed that a court-modified right had been "well established" under state law; his new test of invalidity would not require showing "sudden or unpredictable" change. Justices Kennedy and Sotomajor said this case did not require a discussion of principles for evaluating "judicial taking" claims; Justices Breyer and Ginsburg concurred, noting the problems posed if federal judges oversee state court pronouncements of state law. Not noted was how judges would be forced to pay, and how chilling that prospect might be to their judicial judgments.

4. Other Property Regulation Issues: Remedies, Exactions & Innocent Landowner Liability

a. Remedies: If Regulations Are Held to Be Invalid Takings

In the *First English* case,[60] the U.S. Supreme Court announced important dicta on the question of what remedies were theoretically available if a takings challenge succeeds, although on remand to the California Supreme Court the challenged land use regulations were ultimately held valid without compensation. The majority opinion stated that if a regulation is ultimately determined to be an invalid taking, two remedy options are generally available: (1) an equitable injunction or declaration that the regulation is void on its face or as applied to that particular parcel, or (2) payment by the government for the taking under the rubric of "inverse condemnation" applied to regulatory takings. Governments have the choice: to pay compensation while continuing to apply a regulation that has been found to go too far, or to accept its nullification as to the challenger's property, thereby avoiding the need to pay (although temporary interim damages might be assessed).

---

57. Post by Prof. Peter Byrne, Univ. of Oregon Environmental Professors Listserv, May 7, 2015; used with permission.

58. *Stop the Beach Renourishment v. Florida,* 560 U.S. 702 (2010).

59. In *Hughes v. Washington,* 389 U.S. 290, 295-297 (1967), the Stewart concurrence had said, "To the extent that the decision of the [state] Supreme Court on [the property issue in dispute] arguably conforms to reasonable expectations, we must of course accept it as conclusive. But to the extent that it constitutes a *sudden change in state law, unpredictable* in terms of the relevant precedents, no such deference would be appropriate." (Emphasis added.) The Framers would have been astonished by the judicial takings theory, as they would by regulatory takings arguments generally. See F. Bosselman, et al., The Taking Issue (1973).

60. *First English Evangelical Lutheran Church v. County of Los Angeles,* 482 U.S. 304 (1987).

C. Challenges to Regulations as "Invalid Takings"   949

Governments only rarely will choose to buy off a regulated property owner if regulation has been found to be a taking. If it does so, it is not clear how compensation should be measured. Take a zoning example, with regard to a parcel that would have a full fee simple market value of $100,000 if unregulated. Assume that a court is willing to make especially precise findings of fact, and determines that market value after zoning is $20,000 and that is too little, and hence unconstitutional, but that a remaining value of $60,000 would have been constitutional. How much would government have to pay, if it is not taking possession but only maintaining the regulation? $80,000? $40,000?

Even tougher is the question of valuing temporary takings, where the state decides to give up and suspend the regulation's application to the parcel, but the landowner, using the further element of *First English*'s majority decision, demands compensation for the "temporary" taking between the time the regulation was applied and the time that it is suspended. What should the measure of such temporary damages be? If it is the difference in market value, that often will have increased between the time of the initial regulation and the time the regulation is released. Some courts have argued that "rent," or even "lost profits," must be paid by the government. These latter figures could become huge, thereby chilling the exercise of the police power from the start, which may be the deregulatory result desired in some quarters in the first place. What local government wants to undertake an environmental regulation when affected property owners can argue that it confiscates their property and can then force payment of millions in lost profits if a court agrees with them?[61] Does the result in *Sierra Tahoe*, focusing on the temporary moratorium in relation to the longer run value of a parcel and finding no taking, diminish the likelihood that temporary taking damages are less likely to be awarded and, if awarded, be for a more limited amount?

b. Amortization, and Offset Alternatives?

One way governments can attempt to secure regulations against takings challenges is by providing a period of delay before enforcement, to allow the property owner to "amortize" and recoup her investment before it is shut down. If state or local governments wish to ban billboards, for example, they may provide a four-year amortization period. The billboard industry, one of the strongest lobbies in the nation, is sure to challenge the ban as a regulatory taking. How is amortization, which has been upheld in a wide variety of other property land use regulations, likely to fare against billboards? See *New Castle v. Rollins Outdoor Adver.*, 459 A.2d 541 (Del. 1983) (three years, insufficient); *Village of Skokie v. Walton*, 456 N.E.2d 293 (Ill. App. 1983) (seven years, OK). Is it relevant that a billboard company has long since written off the billboard in depreciation credits on its tax books for the IRS? *National Adver. Co. v. County of Monterey*, 464 P.2d 33 (Cal. 1970) (tax depreciation can be considered); *Art Neon v. Denver*, 488 F.2d 118 (10th Cir. 1973) (amortization need not await depreciation); *Modjeska Sign Studios v. Berle*, 373 N.E.2d 255 (N.Y. 1977) (same).

Another possibility is a takings compensation offset. If, for example, the state and federal governments created thousands of acres of private agricultural land out of Florida swamps by channelizing the Kissimmee River at public expense, must they now, many years later, pay full dryland market value when they decide that groundwater levels must be raised, returning some of the lands to wetlands (because the loss of marshes turned out to cause

---

61. In *Almota Farmer's Elevator & Warehouse Co. v. U.S.*, 409 U.S. 470 (1973), rental value was used as the measure of damages in a physical appropriation case.

massive pollution effects in downstream water supplies and Lake Okeechobee)? Can a state condemning a billboard agree to pay its fair market value minus an offset amount attributable to public expenditures, i.e., excluding all value attributable to the highway? See *U.S. v. Cors*, 337 U.S. 325 (1949) (government expropriating a vessel need not pay higher values attributable to demand caused by government program); *U.S. v. Miller*, 317 U.S. 369 (1943).

In the *Horne* raisin case noted above,[62] the Supreme Court majority declined to use the logic of offsetting in setting compensation for the federal government's quasi-physical taking of title. The Agricultural Marketing Agreement Act of 1937 artificially raised prices of raisins by restricting the amount of raisins sold on the market, taking title to the excess raisins in a reserve that would dispose of them off-market. When the Court unanimously held that taking title to the excess raisins was the equivalent of an invalid physical taking of their excess raisins that required compensation for those excess raisins, it gave the Hornes the *full market value* of their raisins, refusing to discount the Hornes' compensation by the amount which the government itself had created by stabilizing the artificially high market value of those raisins. Was it logical, in economic terms, to fail to subtract the rule-enhanced value as an offset against the compensation price, given that all the Hornes' raisins clearly would have had a lower market value but for the regulation that they attacked?

c. Exactions: *Nollan, Dolan,* and *Koontz*

Physical appropriations by the public, as opposed to mere regulatory prohibitions, are virtually always a taking. See *Loretto*. In many so-called "exaction" cases, however, government regulations have been upheld when they have required regulated landowners to provide free property for public parks, public schools, roadways, and the like for public ownership and use — in return for the privilege of getting development permits, as in subdivision regulation and urban "linkage" programs.

In *Nollan v. California Coastal Comm'n*, 483 U.S. 825 (1987), the California Coastal Commission had denied the owners of a one-tenth acre lot permission to expand their seashore cabin into a three-bedroom home unless they allowed members of the public using the beach to walk alongside the Nollans' seawall. The Commission said it needed this right-of-way easement exaction for pedestrian passage along the rocky coastline, because without it beachgoers would not have a "visual access" visibly linking public sandy beaches north and south of the Nollans' property.[63]

Exaction cases are not regulatory takings cases. Instead they turn on the question of exactions' substantive due process validity when a regulation is otherwise clearly valid as a takings matter. The Supreme Court struck down the *Nollan* exaction. But it held that exactions in general are valid if they (a) occur in a case where an outright denial of the entire permit application would not be an invalid taking,[64] and (b) if there is a sufficient nexus relationship between the exaction and the regulation — in effect, to assure that the exaction is not arbitrary extortion. The definition of this latter "sufficient relationship" was and is the difficult part. Writing for the Court, Justice Scalia did not question the first step; the

---

62. *Horne v. U.S. Dep't of Agriculture*, 133 S. Ct. 2053 (2015).

63. This is as hard to visualize as it was to litigate. Apparently the state commission argued that, lacking a declared easement, beachgoers looking along the shore to the next beach would see only private cabins, seawalls, and rocks coming down to the edge of the sea, and would not realize that there was actually an existing narrow path through the rocks on public property (below the MHW) along the shore linking the two beaches. By opening up a declared easement, the implied visual barrier would be eliminated.

64. "The Commission argues that a permit condition that serves the same legitimate police-power purpose as a refusal to issue the permit should not be found to be a taking if the refusal to issue the permit would not constitute a taking. We agree." 483 U.S. at 836.

C. Challenges to Regulations as "Invalid Takings" 951

Commission apparently could validly have prohibited the application outright because the Nollans had a reasonable remaining use of the cabin as it was. But he rejected the second step:

> The evident constitutional propriety disappears . . . if the condition substituted for the prohibition utterly fails to further the end advanced as the justification for the prohibition. When that essential nexus is eliminated, [the exaction is void]. . . . Unless the permit condition serves the same governmental purpose as the development ban, the building restriction is not a valid regulation of land use but "an out-and-out plan of extortion. . . ." It is quite impossible to understand how a requirement that people already on public beaches be able to walk across the Nollans' property reduces any obstacles to viewing the beach created by the new house. . . . 483 U.S. at 837-838.

Justice Scalia indicated that if the exaction had been to require an easement of visual access across Nollan's property to the beach from the shore road, that might well have been sufficiently related and acceptable. But the exaction apparently must have a nexus to the *burdens* that would be directly created and imposed upon the public by the proposed development.

In *Dolan v. City of Tigard*, 512 U.S. 374 (1994), Justice Rehnquist tightened the terms of how much nexus had to be shown in exactions. The city, acting through its Land Use Board of Appeals, gave petitioners a special permit to double the size of their electric and plumbing supply store and to create a small shopping mall, but required exaction conditions: (a) dedication of a narrow strip of land within the 100-year floodplain for a low-density "greenway" to protect against flooding that might be caused by the new structure's closeness to a creek, and (b) dedication of an additional 15-foot strip of land adjacent to the floodplain as a pedestrian/bicycle pathway as an alternative route to alleviate some of the car traffic that the new shopping area would cause. Writing for the majority, Justice Rehnquist said the city had to show more than a causal nexus:

> We think a term such as "rough proportionality" best encapsulates what we hold to be the requirement of the Fifth Amendment, . . . some sort of individualized determination that the required dedication is related both in nature and extent to the impact of the proposed development. . . . We conclude that the findings upon which the city relies do not show the required reasonable relationship between the floodplain easement and the petitioner's proposed new building . . . [and] the city has not met its burden of demonstrating that the additional number of vehicle and bicycle trips generated by the petitioner's development reasonably relate to the city's requirement for a dedication of the pedestrian/bicycle pathway easement. . . . 512 U.S. 389-396.

The 2013 case of *Koontz v. St. Johns River Water Management District*[65] was a Florida land use case scrutinizing the quite common management agency practice of attaching required mitigating "offsets," "exactions," or other specific or general conditions as part of the permitting process in which government agencies approve or deny private development requests. Mr. Koontz wanted to develop a small mall on 3½ acres of a 14-acre mostly wetland parcel.[66] The water district agency probably could have denied the permit outright—and it wouldn't have been an invalid taking—because, as in *Palazzolo*, there was a buildable upland portion

---

65. 133 S. Ct. 2586 (2013).
66. The property is sited at 28°33'46.69" N x 81°11'16.46" W.

of the property. But the agency instead gave the owner four exaction options that would allow him to fill and develop part of the wetlands:

The agency said Mr. Koontz (1) could develop one acre if he restricted the remainder for water management, (2) could fill 3.7 acres of wetland if he restricted the remainder and paid for fixing a water-blocking culvert off-site, four miles away, (3) could fill 3.7 acres of wetland if he restricted the remainder and paid for fixing a water-blocking ditch off-site, seven miles away, or (4) could fill 3.7 acres if he could propose any other exaction that the agency believed would mitigate the loss of water-retaining wetlands. Koontz objected and went to court.[67]

On this record, the Florida Supreme Court held there was no constitutional violation, and said that *Nollan-Dolan* did not apply. On appeal the U.S. Supreme Court majority reversed on the *Nollan-Dolan* point, holding that *Nollan-Dolan* did apply, and remanded the case back to the Florida courts. Justice Alito was noticeably dubious about the *Koontz* situation, in part because either of the off-site 3.7 acre exaction proposals clearing water-blocking obstructions would improve the wetland conditions of roughly 50 acres—an amount that for him strained the idea of "proportionality." As to the "nexus" requirement of *Nollan-Dolan*, the Koontz property is sited at 28°33'46.69" North x 81°11'16.46" West—and viewing a satellite image of that area on Google Earth reveals the water-vegetation corridors that make the Koontz parcel a wetland property, and the locations of the two off-site exaction options, are all parts of a larger contiguous portion of the St. Johns River watershed drainage area.

At publication time *Koontz* has not been resolved, but the case is nevertheless instructive. The Alito majority allowed the challenge to proceed despite the fact that the agency had never made a final demand for an exaction—an unusual ripeness holding.[68] The Court held that it was appropriate to apply the *Nollan-Dolan* unconstitutional conditions inquiry to monetary exactions, a conclusion bitterly contested by Justice Kagan and the dissenters but quite consistent with the *Eastern Enterprises* case noted below. Both the majority and the dissenters agreed that a straight-out denial of Mr. Koontz's request to fill his 3.7 acres would not involve *Nollan-Dolan*. It would be handled as a straight takings question under the *Penn Central* takings test. And each agreed that *Nollan-Dolan* is an "unconstitutional conditions" case, not a case of excessive regulatory diminution of private property value.

Both the Alito and the Kagan opinions, however—and this is a critical semantic and analytical flaw in both—also framed the concept of "unconstitutional conditions" into the rubric of "takings" tests, thereby bollixing their reasoning, as noted in the following commentary and questions.

COMMENTARY & QUESTIONS

1. *Nollan-Dolan* is the test—but what exactly is it? After these three cases it's clear that the *Nollan-Dolan* nexus/proportionality inquiry is the authoritative test for detemining the validity of exactions, offsets, and "unconstitutional conditions." The nexus part of the test from *Nollan* is relatively straightforward. More complicated is the *Dolan* issue, *how much*

---

67. The two proposed off-site mitigation exactions are located at the Hal Scott Preserve, four miles from the Koontz property and the Little Big Econlockhatchee State Forest seven miles away, in the same watershed.

68. The Court didn't make clear whether or when proposed potential offsetting exaction conditions constitute a sufficient governmental "demand" to be tested if a negotiated agreement was never achieved.

C. Challenges to Regulations as "Invalid Takings"

nexus is required? "Rough proportionality" is a concept that will require a good deal of further judicial elaboration. Does validity of an exaction require proof that public harms caused by a permitted action are roughly proportional to the property owner's costs attributable to the exaction—or rather that the benefits of the exaction are roughly proportional to the harms attributable the permitted action? A further question is who has the burden of proving their case? The presumption of constitutionality typically casts the burden on private parties attacking government, but the Rehnquist opinion in *Dolan* attempts to shift the burden, holding that at least in that case it was up to the government to show rough proportionality. He justified the shift by saying the city's negotiated exaction decision was "adjudicative," for which more evidence was necessary.[69] The vast majority of governmental regulatory actions (e.g., permits) are informal "adjudications." If indeed *Dolan* marked a shift toward putting the burden of proof of constitutionality upon regulatory government, its consequences could substantially change the administrative process.

After *Koontz* applied the *Nollan-Dolan* test to exactions, some commentators considered it an unprecedentedly tragic imposition on land use managers; others considered it an appropriate process already quite familiar in the analogous judicial review of land development fees.[70] Faced with the difficulties of defending negotiated conditions against *Nollan-Dolan* challenges, however, will some agencies just deny permits outright, forswearing the negotiation flexibility and adjustments previously available under exactions law?

2. Severability. An interesting *severability* question deserves further study: Should land use permits be considered null-and-void if the exactions that induced them are struck down as unconstitutional conditions? When a component provision of a legal document like a permit is stricken as illegal or unconstitutional, reviewing courts are supposed to analyze the document's authors' intent: would the drafters have considered the stricken provision essential to the survival of the permit, or would they intend the remaining provisions to remain valid even if the faulty provision was severed?[71] In *Nollan* and *Dolan*, without analyzing the question, Justices Rehnquist and Scalia held the exactions severable, so that the permits were automatically treated as valid authorizations to build in spite of the loss of the exactions.

3. The takings/substantive due process jumble. The Due Process Clause offers a general protection of property, and includes the Takings Clause as a particularized incorporated inquiry. But courts repeatedly conflate the takings test—which focuses on the diminution of property-owner's value, balanced against the regulatory purpose—with quite different considerations of substantive due process.

There is a fundamental distinction between cases making a "takings test" review of the validity of government actions—based on property value diminution under *Pennsylvania Coal* and *Penn Central*—and cases addressing other due process considerations like the causative nexus inquiries in *Nollan, Dolan,* and *Koontz*. Those latter cases, and *Eastern Enterprises* which follows below, are not regulatory takings cases, instead they turn on substantive due process considerations.

In a 1980 takings decision, *Agins v. City of Tiburon*,[72] the Court had added a new element—whether a regulation actually "substantially advanced a legitimate state

---

69. Justice Rehnquist appeared to be applying a distinction made by the Oregon Supreme Court in *Fasano v. Bd. of County Comm'rs of Wash. County*, 507 P.2d 23 (Or. 1973), which was later overruled by the same court. *Neuberger v. Portland*, 607 P.2d 722 (Or. 1980).

70. Prof. John Echeverria, an eminent takings scholar, expressed the conclusion that *Koontz* is the very worst land use decision ever. See Echeverria, The Costs of *Koontz*, 39 Vt. L. Rev. 573 (2015). Prof. J.B. Ruhl, another eminent scholar, demurs. See Ruhl, Who's Afraid of the Big Bad *Koontz?* 22 Vt. J. Envtl. Law (2014).

71. Permit-issuing agencies, when including exactions, might well consider phrasing the permit as "No, unless . . ." rather than "Yes, if . . . ," to make clear whether exactions are to be considered severable from the permit in general.

72. 447 U.S. 255 (1980).

interest"—to its takings test diminution analysis holding an ordinance constitutionally valid. "Substantially advanced . . . " was quite clearly a nexus-like substantive due process inquiry. In 2005, *Lingle v. Chevron*[73] clarified that whether a statute actually "substantially advanced a legitimate state interest" was not a valid judicial inquiry for identifying invalid regulatory takings. For a unanimous Court Justice O'Connor declared the statutory restriction was not a regulatory taking because there had not been a showing of an excessive diminution of Chevron's property value.

> On occasion, a would-be doctrinal rule or test finds its way into our case law through simple repetition of a phrase, however fortuitously coined. A quarter century ago, in *Agins*, the Court declared that government regulation of private property "effects a taking if it does not substantially advance legitimate state interests.". . . Through reiteration in a half dozen or so decisions since *Agins*, this language has been ensconced in our Fifth Amendment takings jurisprudence. . . . This case requires us to decide whether the "substantially-advances" formula announced in *Agins* is an appropriate test for determining whether a regulation effects a Fifth Amendment taking. We conclude that it is not. . . . This formula prescribes an inquiry in the nature of a due process, not a takings, test, and that it has no proper place in our takings jurisprudence. . . . The Due Process Clause is intended, in part, to protect the individual against the exercise of power without any reasonable justification in the service of a legitimate governmental objective. But such a test is not a valid method of discerning whether private property has been 'taken' for purposes of the Fifth Amendment." 544 U.S. at 542.

And as to substantive due process inquiries, Justice O'Connor added, "*Nollan* and *Dolan* cannot be characterized as applying the 'substantially advances' test . . . , and our decision should not be read to disturb these precedents." The *Nollan* and *Dolan* exactions decisions both called themselves "takings" cases because they were decided after *Agins* and before *Lingle*.

The semantic conflation has continued after *Lingle*, as many court decisions like *Koontz* apply the "takings" label to cases challenging regulatory actions on grounds other than property value diminution. In *Koontz*, the Alito opinion acknowledged that the case's facts did not present a taking. "Where the permit is denied and the [putatively unconstitutional] condition is never imposed, nothing has been taken," but then goes on to say that "the unconstitutional conditions doctrine recognizes that this burdens a constitutional right" posing a test of what he labeled "per se *takings*." The *Lingle* case should have broadly clarified the semantic "takings" conflation reflected in the *Nollan* and *Dolan* exaction decisions, but it didn't.

The remedy issue illustrates problems in conflating takings with the other due process tests. If a court strikes down a regulation as an invalid taking, the remedy is either monetary just compensation or injunction against applying the restriction. If a court strikes down a permit's exaction as an unconstitutional condition, presumably there has been no loss of property rights and no just compensation owed, and a severability question of whether the basic permit is rendered void or is still valid. Even farther from takings jurisprudence, what remedy makes sense if a merely-discussed condition later adjudged to violate *Nollan-Dolan* was discussed *prior to a permit denial* as in *Koontz*?

4. Substantive Due Process and the Innocent Landowner— n.b. *Eastern Enterprises.* In a variety of environmental situations, regulations apply heavy burdens on defendants who can say that they themselves did not cause the problem. This often occurs in the case of toxic contamination of land. Should courts acknowledge the legitimacy of substantive due process tests of fairness in such situations? For years conventional wisdom had been that the courts should not apply substantive due process to strike down legislation,[73]

---

73. 544 U.S. 528 (2005).

C. Challenges to Regulations as "Invalid Takings"

though the courts nevertheless continually have utilized substantive due process in latent fashion (e.g. "rational basis," "arbitrary & capricious," "ultra vires").[74] Does the imposition of severe toxic cleanup burdens on innocent land owners, especially on those who lack an industry nexus to the original dumping, trigger substantive due process concerns?[75] The appropriate test would seem to require some consideration of *causation* or the lack thereof, evoking the "rational relationship" police power test, rather than testing whether the takings burden is excessive, viewed in the context of public harms. To make non-causative innocent landowners liable for massive cleanup costs presents an obvious fairness problem that, given the heritage of the American bench and bar, should probably on its own terms be litigatable.[76]

Eastern Enterprises,[77] a case on coal miners' illness compensation established a substantive due process analysis: Eastern Enterprises, a utility company with a subsidiary that was involved in coal mining prior to passage of the Coal Industry Retiree Health Benefit Act of 1992, challenged the Act's imposition of retroactive liability for payments to former employee coal miners and their families suffering the effects of black lung disease (pneumoconiosis) and associated work-related illnesses. Liability could total between $50 and $100 million. Eastern objected—on the ground that the miners had been employed in the distant past, when there was no expectation that companies would have to cover lifetime health effects—and claimed that the law was (a) an invalid regulatory taking, and (b) a violation of substantive due process. The company won but, as so often, Justice Kennedy tilted the vote: Justices Rehnquist, Scalia, Thomas, and O'Connor said it was an invalid taking, but Justice Kennedy, joined by the four dissenters, said it wasn't an issue of a regulatory takings diminution of value, but rather whether there was a sufficient rational nexus between the company and the long latent illnesses. He said there wasn't; the four dissenters

---

74. Aversion to express recognition of substantive due process arises from the reversal of a regressive run of cases where anti–New Deal judges used economic due process to void federal economic recovery legislation. See *Ferguson v. Skrupa*, 372 U.S. 726, 731, (1963) (noting "our abandonment of the use of the 'vague contours' of the Due Process Clause to nullify laws which a majority of the Court believed to be economically unwise"); see also *Williamson v. Lee Optical of Okla.*, 348 U.S. 483, 488 (1955) ("The day is gone when this Court uses the Due Process Clause . . . to strike down . . . laws, regulatory of business and industrial conditions, because they may be unwise, improvident, or out of harmony with a particular school of thought").

75. There is an implicit "recognition that substantive due process inquiry is not anathema; it is an established component of the courts' constitutional jurisdiction. Substantive due process occurs in present-day reviews of public purposes, authority, and bad faith, as well as in [reviews of] arbitrariness." Plater & Norine, Exploring the "Arbitrary and Capricious" Test and Substantive Rationality Review of Governmental Decisions, 16 B.C. Envtl. Aff. L. Rev. 661, 697 (1986).

76. See Jordan, Substantive Due Process after *Eastern Enterprises*, with New Defenses Based on Lack of Causative Nexus—the Superfund Example, 32 B.C. Envtl. Aff. L. Rev. 395 (2005).

77. There are a number of situations where burdens are imposed on non-causative parties without recourse. In an acid mine pollution case, *Commonwealth v. Barnes & Tucker Co.*, 371 A.2d 461 (Pa. 1977), the mining company proved that virtually all of the acid mine water draining from its mine came from the past wrongful activities of neighboring coal mines now abandoned. The court nevertheless held the defendant liable to pay for the entire cleanup, perhaps under some sort of theory of "enterprise liability," an approach that has been followed by other courts. A similar situation occurs with the forfeiture of private property used in crimes, even where the property owners are totally innocent, as in *Bennis v. Mich.*, 516 U.S. 442 (1996), although many consider such cases grossly unfair. Professor Laitos has pioneered this inquiry into the constitutional invalidity of liability without fault. See Laitos, Causation and the Unconstitutional Conditions Doctrine: Why the City of Tigard's Exaction Was a Taking, 72 U. Denver L. Rev. 893 (1995).

said there was. Accordingly, given the five-vote alignment, *Eastern Enterprises* has stood for the proposition that the nexus inquiry is not a takings issue, but rather is a substantive due process inquest, a clarification and application of doctrine that should be applicable in cases brought by innocent owners of contaminated land, those subjected to exactions, and beyond.

5. Groundwater: Regulating aquifer depletion is unconstitutional in Texas? One of the most pressing national hydrogeological concerns is the fact that groundwater aquifers (subterranean reservoirs of "fossil water," deposited in the age of glaciers and very slowly enhanced by rainfall over the centuries), are now being massively depleted at extraordinarily unsustainable rates by urban water supply and agricultural irrigation pumping—*see* Robert Glennon's WATER FOLLIES: GROUNDWATER PUMPING AND THE FATE OF AMERICA'S FRESH WATERS (2012)—and, more recently, by the hydrofracking boom, which in addition extensively pollutes groundwater by reinjecting chemical-laden post-production fracking fluids into the earth.

Is groundwater management operationally and politically infeasible? To date, surface waters are the major focus of governmental concern. The SDWA does virtually nothing to protect the majority of the nation's groundwater against pollution and depletion. Can government agencies meaningfully monitor and attempt to sustain the availability and purity of the nation's groundwaters?

In 2012, the Texas Supreme Court decided that surface landowners possessed unlimited ownership of the "groundwater in place" beneath their land, and authorized awards of constitutional compensation against regulations "condemning" the unlimited right to withdraw. *Edwards Aquifer Authority v. Day*, 274 SW.3d 742 (Tex. 2012, reversing 100 years of state water law which had adhered to the "rule of capture"). The Edwards aquifer underlies 300+ square miles in southwest Texas including San Antonio and is the sole source of water for more than two million people. In 2015 the Texas Supreme Court (No. 13-1023, (Tex. 2015)) let stand a decision of the San Antonio Court of Appeals that interpreted *Penn Central* to require the Aquifer Authority to pay commodity-based compensation for denying permits for substantial withdrawals by owners of a pecan orchard. *Edwards Aquifer Auth. v. Bragg*, 421 S.W.3d 118 (Tex. App.-San Antonio 2013). A jury gave the Braggs $2.5 million in March of 2016 No. 06-11-18170-CV (38th Dist. Ct., Medina Cnty., Tex. Decision March 2016.)

These cases appear to apply an outmoded understanding of the *Penn Central* triad, and seemingly ignore several physical realities: Aquifer groundwater is *not* a perpetual, limitless resource continually replenished by a divine hand for unlimited human use (as in another setting for many years we assumed the unlimited existence of fish and whales in the seas). And groundwater does not exist statically beneath a surface owner's property—unlike coal or other minerals it can move underground like oil and gas, "fugacious" like ferae naturae, so the Braggs, pumping water for their pecans, were pumping water out from under a wide swathe of other landowners.

On groundwater regulatory takings challenges, see Dave Owen, Taking Groundwater, 91 Wash. U. L. Rev. 253 (2013), arguing that groundwater users' rights don't deserve such heightened constitutional protection against regulatory takings. Requiring compensation for aquifer protection restrictions is not supported by past groundwater/takings caselaw, and no property theory justifies adopting such an approach. Groundwater rights can be treated as property, but substantial government regulation of groundwater use is both traditionally and constitutionally justifiable. On *Bragg*, see Owen, Groundwater Regulation and the Takings Clause: A Case Study, goo.gl/cWMTqx. On groundwater valuation issues, see Wade, *Bragg*: Wrong Question, Wrong Result In Texas, to the Detriment of Sustainable Water Supply, at goo.gl/ph3F17.

C. Challenges to Regulations as "Invalid Takings"

> In the following article analyzing the takings validity of TDRs—transfers of development rights noted earlier at page 357—Jennifer Scro discovered several tactical semantic moves that Justice Scalia made to undercut this and other regulatory designs. Note the "use" versus "value" argument, as well as the narrowed geographic scope of where TDRs could be counted in the constitutional balance.

Jennifer Scro, Navigating the Takings Maze: The Use of Transfers of Development Rights in Defending Regulations Against Takings Challenges
19 Ocean & Coastal L.J. 219 (2014)

... **Justice Scalia versus Penn Central**. ... TDR programs ... allow regulated landowners to sell blocks of their development rights, unusable on the regulated sites under the terms of the challenged regulations, to purchasers who can use them to expand allowable development rights on designated off-site receiving parcels. The sale of TDRs can thus generate significant revenues for regulated property owners because purchasers are often willing to pay large sums for the right to use the TDR credits to build at much greater intensity than otherwise allowed under existing land use regulations.

If TDRs are weighed as part of a court's constitutional takings balance under the Penn Central formulation, then many such challenged land use regulations will be upheld, and the utility and market value of TDR programs will remain secure. If, instead, the market value of TDRs is excluded from the regulatory validity balance, then many regulations would in all likelihood be struck down as excessively diminishing the regulated landowners' property values. Most courts follow the holding in *Penn Central*, written by Justice Brennan, and include TDRs as part of the landowner's retained post-regulation property value in constitutional takings balances. Conversely, Justice Scalia argued in a strongly-worded concurring opinion [in *Suitum v. Tahoe Reg'l Planning Agency*, 520 U.S. 725, 747-48 (1997)], that TDRs should not be considered in determining the amount of property values lost by regulated landowners; rather, they should only be considered as part of a landowner's compensation package *after the courts, have found the challenged regulations unconstitutional by disregarding the value of TDRs.*

... For Justice Brennan, the value of TDRs was a factor in the initial judicial determination of whether a regulation has "gone too far" leaving the landowner with no reasonable economic return. ... [In *Suitum*,] Justice Scalia attacked the *Penn Central* majority's formulation of the role of TDRs ..., arguing that ...

TDRs [were] nothing more than a "peculiar type of chit" or "coupon" from the government, not representing relevant value to the regulated landowner. ... Justice Scalia attempted to align his view with *Penn Central's* holding by teasing out a distinction on the *Penn Central* facts [where] the affected corporate property owner [*himself*] happened to have been able to use the TDR air rights from the regulated historic train station to substantially expand development on other properties it owned ... thereby separating TDRs from their status as "market value" rights and asserting that TDRs "have nothing to do with the use or development of the land to which they are (by regulatory decree) 'attached.'" ...

As a corollary semantic distinction, he sought to define ... takings challenges in terms of the regulated landowners' diminished property *use* rather than diminished *value*. Unless the landowners themselves could "use" the TDRs, ... their market value to the landowner would not be acknowledged under the Scalian takings formulation. ...

TDRs . . . allow regulated landowners to recapture lost value by selling them in the marketplace. . . . If, as Justice Scalia argues, TDRs cannot be weighed toward the validity of regulatory programs, there is little practical governmental motivation [for TDRs, and] the usefulness and functionality of TDR programs would be lost. TDR programs are only viable if the TDRs themselves are rightfully considered by courts to be both an essential property right and a fungible market asset. . . .

Viewed in context, Justice Scalia's semantic formulations fundamentally multiply a regulation's negative effect on a regulated landowner, excluding the very real retained private values attributable to transferable credits in well-designed TDR programs.

COMMENTARY & QUESTIONS

1. Justice Scalia's Strategic focus on remaining "use" rather than remaining "value" to regulated propertyowners. Defining the nature and quantum of property rights left to propertyowners after the application of police power regulations is the essence of the first two elements in *Penn Central* takings tests, typically focused on whether private property owners have been left with a reasonable remaining *value* from the regulated property. Justice Scalia's use-focused standard, on the other hand, (scarcely noticed by scholars, but also discernable in *Lucas* and *Palazzolo*), implies a requirement for some remaining active development use, perhaps even a structural use, and would often tend to be defined by the propertyowner's intentions for the land. The Scro article implies that Justice Scalia advocated his requirement for active remaining *uses*, realizing that it would certainly make it much easier to strike down regulations. (*See also* Brian Crossman, The Use-Value Distinction in Regulatory Takings Law: Which Property Interest is Protected by the Constitution? in the coursebook's supplementary materials.)

2. Why does Scalia ignore market value? To support TDRs' continuing utility, Scro argues that courts appropriately should consider TDRs based on their actual ascertained market value. Although TDRs alone might not fully constitute "just" compensation, they properly would be included in the final compensation package. For example, if "just compensation" is $100,000 and a regulated landowner has $30,000 in TDR credits, then the TDRs could be included as compensation, with the government obliged to pay the difference—$70,000. The amount that TDRs contribute toward the regulated landowner's compensation, as in the constitutionality balance, would depend on their actual market value. In light of Justice Scalia's usual adherence to market-based reasoning in other takings cases, his argument for selective non-acknowledgment of market values in TDRs would seem to reflect a selective departure from principles, in order to undercut regulations.

"Property" is that which is peculiarly yours, whether it is your money, your wife, your children, your house, your car, or your real estate.

—Don Gerdts, founder, Property Rights Council of America [a proto-Tea Party organization], Albany Times-Union, April 11, 1992

22

International and Comparative Environmental Law

A. Customary International Law
B. International Conferences & Soft Law
C. Comparative Environmental Law
D. Multilateral Environmental Agreements & Global Climate Change
E. International Institutions

> Public international law is the law governing the relations between states. In international law, states make the law, states apply the law, and the law applies to interactions among states.

This coursebook began with the metaphor of Spaceship Earth, emphasizing the interconnectedness of the planet's geophysical, ecological, and human components, and the law. Slowly circling the globe, an observing eye could catalog a depressingly long list of planetary environmental threats, more daunting than the problems encountered in any single nation. International environmental governance, however, is not just public international law on the level of relations between nation-states and within international organizations. Just as global environmental problems are built by an aggregation of dozens or billions of individual actions, the legal responses to global problems must inevitably draw upon multiple levels of law and governance—national, subnational, and supra-national forces intersecting with the marketplace, governments and "transgovernmental" linkages, and citizen groups.

Like domestic environmental law, the global setting presents the same tensions and interconnections between the dominant marketplace economy, the economy of Nature, and civic-societal imperatives for sustainability, but on an almost incomprehensibly immense scale. Sustainable development, one of the most important "principles" of international environmental law, is becoming a dominant focusing concept for law and policymaking at national, regional, and local levels as well. As the First Law of Ecology says, everything is connected to everything else.

Over the past two decades, environmental organizations (known in international jargon as NGOs (nongovernmental organizations)) have played an increasingly prominent role in an area previously reserved almost exclusively to states[1] and governments. Environmental activists from every corner of the world have become increasingly energized in publicizing international environmental issues,[2] in lobbying for international rules to protect the global environment, and in utilizing newly created mechanisms for enforcing those rules at the international and domestic levels.

At the same time, international environmental law has increasingly penetrated into national legal systems, as we saw in Chapter 7, which over time promotes coherence and consistency in environmental law and policy from one state to another. International environmental law is no longer confined strictly to rights and obligations exercised by states, but increasingly is a vehicle for crafting international standards and enforceable national policies simultaneously. International environmental law has established new directions and precedents that have profoundly affected how states deal with each other in every aspect of international relations.

While pessimism about the fate of the world in general, and the environment in particular, may be the order of the day in the U.S. and abroad, lawyers and others with legal training are uniquely well positioned to alter the trajectory of the future. Notwithstanding the serious challenges facing us as a planet, there is reason for optimism about the potential for meaningful solutions. This chapter presents international environmental law and policy not as an abstract, amorphous, and enormous problem—although it is all of those. Instead, we proceed from the perspective that complex interrelated international linkages can be demystified and mastered by identifying the forces that drive them and the junctures at which they can be effectively influenced. Just as previous generations of lawyers, activists, advocates, and environmental professionals molded the domestic law of the environment from next to nothing, the international environmental lawyers of the present and future face the exhilarating opportunity and profound responsibility of shaping the world to come.

A. CUSTOMARY INTERNATIONAL LAW

> Customary international law is created by a pattern and practice of states motivated by a sense of legal obligation or right (*opinion juris*). Because it derives from state behavior, customary law is not necessarily written, nor reciprocal. One can think of customary law as a collection of legally binding norms that are created by states, and apply to states, as a result of their cumulative interactions over time.

Transboundary pollution is the simplest form of international environmental problem. Toxic by-products from a manufacturing process in one state may cause harm in another state because a factory may be located at or near the border between the two countries. Typically such situations involve the transmission of a physical pollutant into a passive, and perhaps unknowing, "victim" state. The international setting, however, raises complexities that are not encountered in a purely domestic context like the U.S. What standards apply to

---

1. The word *state* is the standard term in international jurisprudence for a country or nation-state.
2. See, e.g., Wirth, Legitimacy, Accountability, and Partnership: A Model for Advocacy on Third World Environmental Issues, 100 Yale L.J. 2645 (1991).

the activity, if any? Does the victim state have the authority to enforce that standard, or any rights at all? What about impacts on private parties, including landowners and citizens, in the victim state? Just such a situation arose in the early twentieth century along the western border between the U.S. and Canada.

Trail Smelter Arbitration (U.S. v. Canada)
3 U.N.R.I.A.A. 1965 (1941)

[A privately owned metal smelter operating in Trail, British Columbia, had been belching sulfur dioxide fumes into Washington State, causing considerable damage to orchards and other property on the U.S. side of the border. No private remedy was available to the injured U.S. citizens: The courts of British Columbia did not have jurisdiction to hear the case because the injury was physically located across the border, and the courts of Washington lacked jurisdiction because the polluters had no business presence in their state. The U.S. intervened—somewhat unusually because the case did not directly concern the interests or conduct of either national government—filing what amounted to a novel international nuisance claim. At first, the issue was referred for study to the International Joint Commission, a standing international organization established under a 1909 treaty on boundary waters between the U.S. and Canada. In 1931, the Commission identified a figure of $350,000 (U.S. dollars) in accrued damages, together with a finding expressing the Tribunal's expectation that further harm would not occur. Canada accepted the report, but the U.S. did not. The two countries negotiated an agreement to settle the dispute, a type of international legal instrument often known by the French term *compromis*. The *compromis* referred the disagreement to a three-member arbitral tribunal established specifically to deal with this case, consisting of one Canadian, one American, and a Belgian national. Article III of the *compromis* instructed the arbitral tribunal to decide the following four questions:

1. Whether damage caused by the Trail Smelter in the State of Washington has occurred since the first day of January 1932, and, if so, what indemnity should be paid therefor?
2. In the event of the answer to the first part of the preceding question being in the affirmative, whether the Trail Smelter should be required to refrain from causing damage in the State of Washington in the future and, if so, to what extent?
3. In the light of the answer to the preceding question, what measures or regime, if any, should be adopted or maintained by the Trail Smelter?
4. What indemnity or compensation, if any, should be paid on account of any decision or decisions rendered by the Tribunal pursuant to the preceding two questions?

Article IV of the *compromis* stated: "The Tribunal shall apply the law and practice followed in dealing with cognate question in the U.S. of America as well as international law and practice, and shall give consideration to the desire of the high contracting parties to reach a solution just to all parties concerned." In 1938, the tribunal rendered a preliminary decision establishing interim restrictions for the smelter's operation and issued the following final decision in 1941.[3]]

---

3. See Read, The Trail Smelter Dispute, 1 Can. Y.B. Int'l L. 213 (1963); Rubin, Pollution by Analogy: The Trail Smelter Arbitration, 50 Or. L. Rev. 259 (1971). The citation for the 1938 order is 3 U.N.R.I.A.A. 1905 (1938).

DECISION OF THE TRIBUNAL. The first problem which arises is whether the question should be answered on the basis of the law followed in the U.S. or on the basis of international law. The Tribunal, however, finds that this problem need not be solved here as the law followed in the U.S. in dealing with the quasi-sovereign rights of the States of the Union, in the matter of air pollution, whilst more definite, is in conformity with the general rules of international law. . . .

No case of air pollution dealt with by an international tribunal has been brought to the attention of the Tribunal nor does the Tribunal know of any such case. The nearest analogy is that of water pollution. But, here also, no decision of an international tribunal has been cited or has been found.

There are, however, as regards both air pollution and water pollution, certain decisions of the Supreme Court of the U.S. which may legitimately be taken as a guide in this field of international law, for it is reasonable to follow by analogy, in international cases, precedents established by that court in dealing with controversies between States of the Union or with other controversies concerning the quasi-sovereign rights of such States, where no contrary rule prevails in international law and no reason for rejecting such precedents can be adduced from the limitations of sovereignty inherent in the Constitution of the U.S..

In the suit of the *Missouri v. Illinois* (200 U.S. 496, 521) concerning the pollution, within the boundaries of Illinois, of the Illinois River, an affluent of the Mississippi flowing into the latter where it forms the boundary between that State and Missouri, an injunction was refused. "Before this court ought to intervene," said the court, "the case should be of serious magnitude, clearly and fully proved, and the principle to be applied should be one which the court is prepared deliberately to maintain against all considerations on the other side." The court found that the practice complained of was general along the shores of the Mississippi River at that time, that it was followed by Missouri itself and that thus a standard was set up by the defendant which the claimant was entitled to invoke.

As the claims of public health became more exacting and methods for removing impurities from the water were perfected, complaints ceased. It is significant that Missouri sided with Illinois when the other riparians of the Great Lakes' system sought to enjoin it to desist from diverting the waters of that system into that of the Illinois and Mississippi for the very purpose of disposing of the Chicago sewage. . . .

What the Supreme Court says there of its power under the Constitution equally applies to the extraordinary power granted this Tribunal under the Convention. What is true between States of the Union is, at least, equally true concerning the relations between the U.S. and the Dominion of Canada.

In another recent case concerning water pollution (283 U.S. 473), the complainant was successful. The City of New York was enjoined, at the request of the State of New Jersey, to desist, within a reasonable time limit, from the practice of disposing of sewage by dumping it into the sea, a practice which was injurious to the coastal waters of New Jersey in the vicinity of her bathing resorts.

In the matter of air pollution itself, the leading decisions are those of the Supreme Court in the *Georgia v. Tennessee Copper Company and Ducktown Sulphur, Copper and Iron Company, Limited*. Although dealing with a suit against private companies, the decisions were on questions cognate to those here at issue. Georgia stated that it had in vain sought relief from the State of Tennessee, on whose territory the smelters were located, and the court defined the nature of the suit by saying: "This is a suit by a State for an injury to it in its capacity of quasi-sovereign. In that capacity, the State has an interest independent of and behind the titles of its citizens, in all the earth and air within its domain."

A. Customary International Law

On the question whether an injunction should be granted or not, the court said (206 U.S. 230):

> It [the State] has the last word as to whether its mountains shall be stripped of their forests and its inhabitants shall breathe pure air.... It is not lightly to be presumed to give up quasi-sovereign rights for pay and ... if that be its choice, it may insist that an infraction of them shall be stopped. This court has not quite the same freedom to balance the harm that will be done by an injunction against that of which the plaintiff complains, that it would have in deciding between two subjects of a single political power. Without excluding the considerations that equity always takes into account ... it is a fair and reasonable demand on the part of a sovereign that the air over its territory should not be polluted on a great scale by sulphurous acid gas, that the forests on its mountains, be they better or worse, and whatever domestic destruction they may have suffered, should not be further destroyed or threatened by the act of persons beyond its control, that the crops and orchards on its hills should not be endangered from the same source.... Whether Georgia, by insisting upon this claim, is doing more harm than good to her own citizens, is for her to determine. The possible disaster to those outside the State must be accepted as a consequence of her standing upon her extreme rights.

Later on, however, when the court actually framed an injunction, in the case of the Ducktown Company (237 U.S. 474, 477) (an agreement on the basis of an annual compensation was reached with the most important of the two smelters, the Tennessee Copper Company), they did not go beyond a decree "adequate to diminish materially the present probability of damage to its (Georgia's) citizens."

Great progress in the control of fumes has been made by science in the last few years and this progress should be taken into account.

The Tribunal, therefore, finds that the above decisions, taken as a whole, constitute an adequate basis for its conclusions, namely, that, under the principles of international law, as well as of the law of the U.S., no State has the right to use or permit the use of its territory in such a manner as to cause injury by fumes in or to the territory of another or the properties or persons therein, when the case is of serious consequence and the injury is established by clear and convincing evidence....

Considering the circumstances of the case, the Tribunal holds that the Dominion of Canada is responsible in international law for the conduct of the Trail Smelter. Apart from the undertakings in the Convention, it is, therefore, the duty of the Government of the Dominion of Canada to see to it that this conduct should be in conformity with the obligation of the Dominion under international law as herein determined.

COMMENTARY & QUESTIONS

1. Customary international law. In Chapter 7 we encountered treaties as the international equivalent of contracts between states that create law for the parties to them. The *Trail Smelter* arbitration relies on the other principal kind or "source" of international law, known as "custom." Unlike the law in the U.S. and many other countries, customary international law is not based on a text in the form of a constitution or a statute. Rather, customary international law accumulates over time through a pattern of practice of states based on a sense of legal right or obligation (*opinio juris*). At least in principle, states adopt patterns of behaviors in dealing with other states that are in those states' mutual interests. As those patterns are reinforced over time and states come to rely on them as predicting future state behavior, those habits crystallize into legally enforceable norms or rules. The legal status of the high seas as a global commons, beyond the jurisdictional reach of any state, is originally of customary origin, arising because all states have an interest in freedom of the seas to facilitate global commerce. At a more micro level, for obvious practical reasons it became a uniform customary legal rule that ships passing on the right had priority. Proving the existence of a customary rule involves two steps. The first is identifying the pattern of state behavior. While the pattern need not be universal without departures, it must be discernibly consistent. Second, the pattern must be motivated by a sense of legal obligation. The evidence of both factors can be drawn from various actions and inactions by states that are not ordinarily considered lawmaking, including statements of government officials in press releases and news conferences, actions of regulatory authorities in an enforcement setting, and news stories reporting factual events. If you were representing the U.S., how would you confirm the existence of a customary rule governing a situation like that encountered in the *Trail Smelter* arbitration? If you were representing Canada, how would you attempt to demonstrate the absence of a rule? What are the relative advantages and disadvantages of custom as opposed to treaties as legal vehicles for making international environmental law? Although customary law would appear to develop slowly, that is not necessarily so. So long as acceptance of a new principle is widespread, the law may change quite quickly, a phenomenon sometimes called "instant custom."[4]

2. State responsibility for internationally wrongful acts. International claims typically are framed in terms of "state responsibility." The regime of state responsibility is the approximate international analogue of a tort system, with the important distinction that the law applies to, and can be invoked by, states and not private actors such as individuals or corporations. As with many international environmental issues, the real parties in interest in the *Trail Smelter* dispute are not states, but individuals. On their behalf, how could you overcome the doctrine that international law does not regulate the behavior of the Canadian smelter because the owner of the smelter is not a "subject" of international law? Similarly, how would you establish standing (*locus standi*), given that your client is an individual and not a state? The international system deals with these structural problems through a legal construct known as "espousal." In principle, the Tribunal in the *Trail Smelter* arbitration is not adjudicating a dispute between two private parties, but between two states—the U.S. and Canada. The claimant state, in this case the U.S., has espoused the claim of the Washington landowners, in effect adopting the injuries of its nationals as its own. If you represent the Washington landowners, what difficulties might you have in persuading the U.S. government to "espouse" your clients' claims or to resolve them satisfactorily once espoused? If you represent the government of Canada, what arguments might you make that Canada ought not be responsible for the behavior of private parties under its jurisdiction, such as the smelter at Trail?

3. International adjudication. Like the law of treaties, customary international law governs relations between states even if there is no obvious forum in which to apply it. The U.S. could have asserted an international "claim" against Canada through bilateral diplomatic channels even if Canada had refused to agree to establish an arbitral tribunal. In a domestic setting, we think of taking disputes to court as the norm. In the international system, in which there are no courts of general jurisdiction, that is not necessarily the case. In the *Trail Smelter* arbitration, the two governments took the step of contractually agreeing to arbitrate

---

4. As discussed below in regard to the Rio UNCED and similar conclaves, international conference statements endorsed by most or all states on the planet may rapidly change the law. As a nonenvironmental example, widespread acceptance of, or at least acquiescence in, the need for the military operations in Afghanistan after the terrorist attacks of September 11, 2001, arguably tended to solidify the proposition that states have an obligation to refrain from harboring terrorists—a principle not widely understood as international law before then.

A. Customary International Law

the dispute before a neutral, impartial tribunal and to accept the result as binding. In international jurisprudence, opinions of international courts and tribunals like the one in this dispute are evidence of the state of the law. But international tribunals, in contrast to common law courts, cannot make international law, which is created strictly by states and a few other subjects of international law, including international organizations. The International Court of Justice (ICJ), sitting in The Hague, Netherlands, has a strictly delimited scope of law that it can apply.[5] Taken together with the requirement for espousal, the hurdles to binding international dispute settlement of transboundary pollution issues such as sulfur fumes from a smelter in British Columbia are high indeed. Based on your insights from domestic environmental law, what recommendations could you make to modify international law to facilitate binding resolution of international pollution controversies, consistent with the basic principle that only states may make international law?

4. The rule of the *Trail Smelter*. Before the *Trail Smelter* decision, as noted by the Tribunal, international law appeared to provide no rule of decision dealing with harm to a private party in one jurisdiction by a private party in another. The *Trail Smelter* arbitration is consequently most famous for articulating the rule that "under the principles of international law, as well as of the law of the U.S., no State has the right to use or permit the use of its territory in such a manner as to cause injury by fumes in or to the territory of another or the properties or persons therein, when the case is of serious consequence and the injury is established by clear and convincing evidence." This teaching is similar to the common law maxim *sic utere tuo ut alienum non laedas*—one should use one's own property so as not to injure that of another. According to the Tribunal, what is the source of this customary rule? Why does the Tribunal rely on cases from the U.S.? How convincing do you consider its reasoning? Comparing the Tribunal's articulation of this principle to the tasks that the U.S. and Canadian governments assigned the Tribunal in the *compromis*, how would you characterize the famous language as an analytical matter? To what extent is this "principle" necessary to the tasks the Tribunal was instructed to perform? If you are representing the polluting state, Ruritania, in a different dispute initiated by the "victim" state of Fredonia, how might you argue that the rule of the *Trail Smelter* is not good law? If it does apply to Ruritania and Fredonia, how might you envisage distinguishing that situation from that in the *Trail Smelter* dispute? What do you think of the wisdom of the *Trail Smelter* rule from an international environmental policy point of view? What are the benefits of the rule? What might be its drawbacks? How would you evaluate it from an economic perspective? Is it effective as a rule of environmental protection?

5. Extraterritorial reach of U.S. law. Decades after the famous international arbitration, the smelter at Trail made a reappearance on the international environmental law scene. Lake Roosevelt is the reservoir created by the Grand Coulee Dam, one of the largest dams in the world, on the Columbia River in Washington State. This immense reservoir reaches all the way into Canada and is used for recreational purposes, such as fishing and boating. In 2002, EPA conducted a sediment study of Lake Roosevelt and found slag contaminated with heavy metals, including lead, arsenic, and mercury. Potentially responsible parties identified the largest likely contributor as a Canadian smelting company, Teck

---

5. According to Article 36 of the Statute of the International Court of Justice, a multilateral agreement appended to the Charter of the United Nations, the ICJ may obtain jurisdiction over a "contentious" case by (1) special agreement or *compromis*; (2) a clause in a treaty specifying that disputes arising under the agreement may be referred to the Court; or (3) the prior general consent of a state to the Court's exercise of jurisdiction in all cases or particular classes of cases, the misleadingly named "compulsory" jurisdiction of the Court. Article 65 also authorizes the ICJ, unlike federal courts in the U.S., to issue advisory opinions.

Cominco Metals Ltd., the world's largest zinc producer—and operating a smelter at the same location in British Columbia that gave rise to the *Trail Smelter* arbitration! After being sued by Native American tribes from Washington State, the company—now known as Teck Resources, Ltd.—admitted to discharging toxic slag into the Columbia River between 1896 and 1995, causing environmental harm in the United States.

B. International Conferences & Soft Law

Customary international law of the *Trail Smelter* variety may be too slow in evolving to meet the urgent environmental threats of the twenty-first century. Based on a pattern of often unilateral actions, and frequently reflecting existing power relationships among the international community, customary principles often leave little room for bargaining and deal-making of the sort necessary to engage many or all states in a collective solution to a common problem. As demonstrated by the *Trail Smelter* rule, the content of customary norms may be vague or uncertain, or formulated as adjective tests—attributes that are not necessarily helpful when the practical, real-world need may be, for example, emissions reductions of a specified amount. Because the existence of a customary rule depends on a pattern of state behavior that may be difficult to discern, the very existence of a customary norm may be subject to dispute. International agreements, as discussed in Chapter 7, overcome many of these impediments but are themselves subject to other weaknesses due to the twin downward drags of consent and consensus that characterize most international processes.

Jump-starting progress on international environmental policy at high-profile, global meetings is a recent response to these problems. The first of these events, the United Nations Conference on the Human Environment held in Stockholm, Sweden, in 1972, is generally considered the catalytic event signaling the internationalization of environmental policy and law. Delegations representing 114 of the then-131 UN member states participated in the 1972 event. The Stockholm Conference advocated the creation of a new UN effort that became the United Nations Environment Program (UNEP), virtually the sole international institution whose mission is strictly environmental. More generally, the Stockholm Conference left a lasting legacy as a clarion call for cooperative action on environmental problems of international and even global concern.

The Stockholm meeting adopted a conference declaration containing 26 principles and an action plan including 109 recommendations for future implementation at the international level. Unlike a formal international agreement like those discussed in Chapter 7, the Stockholm Declaration does not have identifiable parties, did not have a date certain for entry into force, and was not subject to ratification. The Stockholm Declaration is an advisory statement of purpose—so-called soft law, in contrast to binding or "hard" legal obligations contained in bilateral or multilateral treaties or whose origin is custom. Although frequently encountered, the term *soft law* is itself an oxymoron because international law governs only binding obligations, whose origin is typically treaty or custom. In the international system, nonbinding standards or expectations are not law at all.

The Stockholm Declaration is an example of a very large number of these nonbinding international instruments, whose form may vary significantly but that nonetheless set out normative expectations for behavior by states. Conference declarations like the Stockholm Declaration, recommendations, guidelines and principles adopted by international organizations, and multi- and bilateral summit statements are but a few of the vehicles for

B. International Conferences & Soft Law

governments to undertake commitments or to create expectations that are politically significant but not legally binding.

Nonbinding documents may serve a number of purposes. Perhaps the most important function of soft law is consciously to establish normative expectations — to be contrasted with binding obligations, which in principle are the realm of "hard" law. Nonbinding instruments often function as "good practice standards," phrased in terms of advisory "shoulds" rather than obligatory "shalls." While not creating formal international legal obligations, these advisory instruments can nonetheless establish widely accepted standards for desirable or sound state practice. Adjectives typically applied to this category of instruments include *hortatory, precatory,* and *aspirational.*

On the twentieth anniversary of the Stockholm Conference (nearly to the day), the United Nations Conference on Environment and Development (UNCED), the so-called Earth Summit, was held in Rio de Janeiro, Brazil, in 1992. The Earth Summit was expressly planned as a successor to the Stockholm Conference. Continuity was assured by the selection of Maurice Strong, Secretary General of the Stockholm Conference, to serve in the same capacity for UNCED. More than 180 countries sent delegations to the Rio meeting, which, due to the presence of over 100 heads of state or government, was the largest summit-level conference to that date. Like the earlier Stockholm meeting, the Rio conference was preceded by extensive preparatory meetings. The principal theme of UNCED was reconciling environmental protection and economic development, an approach encapsulated in the term *sustainable development.*

While there is no agreed definition for *sustainable development,* a widely accepted description was provided by a precursor body, the World Commission on Environment and Development:

> Sustainable development is development that meets the needs of the present without compromising the ability of future generations to meet their own needs. It contains within it two key concepts:
>
> - the concept of "needs," in particular the essential needs of the world's poor, to which overriding priority should be given; and
> - the idea of limitations imposed by the state of technology and social organization on the environment's ability to meet present and future needs.

UNCED produced four major pieces of "deliverables" (work product). Two major multilateral conventions were opened for signature at the Earth Summit: the United Nations Framework Convention on Climate Change, discussed in Section D below, and a Convention on Biological Diversity. The nonbinding Rio Declaration on Environment and Development, consisting of 27 principles, originally planned as an "Earth Charter," was purposefully crafted as a successor to the Stockholm Declaration. The nonbinding Agenda 21, the action plan for the future adopted at UNCED, is the analogue of the Stockholm action plan.[6]

---

6. See generally Wirth, The Rio Declaration on Environment and Development: Two Steps Forward and One Back, or Vice Versa?, 29 Ga. L. Rev. 599 (1994); Kovar, A Short Guide to the Rio Declaration, 4 Colum. J. Int'l Envtl. L. & Pol'y 119 (1993). The text of the Rio Declaration was drafted in private toward the end of the preparatory meetings leading up to UNCED by a small group of seven industrialized and seven developing countries, with the direct input of Preparatory Committee chairman Tommy Koh from Singapore. That text was adopted by the Rio conference without alteration.

Rio Declaration on Environment and Development
31 I.L.M. 876 (1992)

The United Nations Conference on Environment and Development. . . .
Reaffirming the Declaration of the United Nations Conference on the Human Environment, adopted at Stockholm on 16 June 1972, and seeking to build upon it. . . .
Proclaims that:

Principle 1. Human beings are at the centre of concerns for sustainable development. They are entitled to a healthy and productive life in harmony with nature.

Principle 2. States have, in accordance with the Charter of the United Nations and the principles of international law, the sovereign right to exploit their own resources pursuant to their own environmental and developmental policies, and the responsibility to ensure that activities within their jurisdiction or control do not cause damage to the environment of other States or of areas beyond the limits of national jurisdiction.

Principle 3. The right to development must be fulfilled so as to equitably meet developmental and environmental needs of present and future generations.

Principle 4. In order to achieve sustainable development, environmental protection shall constitute an integral part of the development process and cannot be considered in isolation from it. . . .

Principle 6. The special situation and needs of developing countries, particularly the least developed and those most environmentally vulnerable, shall be given special priority. International actions in the field of environment and development should also address the interests and needs of all countries.

Principle 7. States shall cooperate in a spirit of global partnership to conserve, protect and restore the health and integrity of the Earth's ecosystem. In view of the different contributions to global environmental degradation, States have common but differentiated responsibilities. The developed countries acknowledge the responsibility that they bear in the international pursuit of sustainable development in view of the pressures their societies place on the global environment and of the technologies and financial resources they command. . . .

Principle 10. Environmental issues are best handled with the participation of all concerned citizens, at the relevant level. At the national level, each individual shall have appropriate access to information concerning the environment that is held by public authorities, including information on hazardous materials and activities in their communities, and the opportunity to participate in decision-making processes. States shall facilitate and encourage public awareness and participation by making information widely available. Effective access to judicial and administrative proceedings, including redress and remedy, shall be provided. . . .

Principle 12. States should cooperate to promote a supportive and open international economic system that would lead to economic growth and sustainable development in all countries, to better address the problems of environmental degradation. Trade policy measures for environmental purposes should not constitute a means of arbitrary or unjustifiable discrimination or a disguised restriction on international trade. Unilateral actions to deal with environmental challenges outside the jurisdiction of the importing country should be avoided. Environmental measures addressing transboundary or global environmental problems should, as far as possible, be based on an international consensus. . . .

B. International Conferences & Soft Law

Principle 14. States should effectively cooperate to discourage or prevent the relocation and transfer to other States of any activities and substances that cause severe environmental degradation or are found to be harmful to human health.

Principle 15. In order to protect the environment, the precautionary approach shall be widely applied by States according to their capabilities. Where there are threats of serious or irreversible damage, lack of full scientific certainty shall not be used as a reason for postponing cost-effective measures to prevent environmental degradation.

Principle 16. National authorities should endeavour to promote the internalization of environmental costs and the use of economic instruments, taking into account the approach that the polluter should, in principle, bear the cost of pollution, with due regard to the public interest and without distorting international trade and investment.

Principle 17. Environmental impact assessment, as a national instrument, shall be undertaken for proposed activities that are likely to have a significant adverse impact on the environment and are subject to a decision of a competent national authority. . . .

COMMENTARY & QUESTIONS

1. What's soft law good for? Nonbinding principles and declarations such as the Stockholm and Rio Declarations are not necessarily second-best alternatives to hard or binding law. Soft law is different in kind from treaties and custom and sometimes facilitates better compliance. Because the obligations are perceived as requiring a lower level of commitment on the part of states, a soft instrument may be appropriate in controversial situations in which a high degree of consensus is impossible to obtain. What other situations can you identify in which a soft law approach might be particularly desirable? What might be the benefits of employing a soft approach as opposed to hard law? The benefits? What criteria would you apply in determining whether a particular subject matter ought to be addressed through a hard or soft instrument? On occasion, the position of the U.S. with respect to soft law instruments has been to treat them as de facto hard. That is, the U.S. will not agree to a multilateral soft law document like the Stockholm Declaration unless the U.S. is able, and prepared, to implement that instrument fully. Does this policy tend to further the purposes of soft law by giving greater weight to such instruments? Or does it tend to undermine the advantages of the soft approach?

2. *Trail Smelter* revisited: Stockholm Principle 21, first among equals. The *Trail Smelter*'s rule governing transboundary pollution reappeared in 1972 as Principle 21 of the Stockholm Declaration, which specifies that:

> States have, in accordance with the Charter of the United Nations and the principles of international law, the sovereign right to exploit their own resources pursuant to their own environmental policies, and the responsibility to ensure that activities within their jurisdiction or control do not cause damage to the environment of other States or of areas beyond the limits of national jurisdiction.

How does this formulation of the basic rule governing transboundary pollution differ from the *Trail Smelter*'s language? What does the first clause in Principle 21—"the sovereign right to exploit their resources pursuant to their own environmental policies"—mean when juxtaposed with the second—"the responsibility to ensure that activities within their jurisdiction or control do not cause damage to the environment of other States or of areas beyond the limits of national jurisdiction?" Does the Principle give with one hand and take away with the other? How viable do you think this rule is as an aspirational principle in international relations?

Stockholm's Principle 21, although originally framed as a nonbinding exhortation, over time has been accepted as a substantive rule of customary international law, the only one of the Stockholm Declaration's 26 principles to have achieved that status. Can you explain as an analytical matter how a nonbinding principle can metamorphose into binding customary international law? From a policy point of view, what do you think of Principle 21 as a binding directive of international law creating rights for aggrieved states? Would you regard Principle 21 as sufficient to serve as the central organizing doctrine of international environmental law and policy, as has sometimes been asserted? Is it adequate for that purpose, or is it perhaps underinclusive in the sense of failing to address some important international issues? If not Principle 21, what should be the overarching goal or goals of international environmental law?

3. Stockholm Principle 21 goes Latin. Stockholm Principle 21 reappears in substantially similar—but not identical—form as Principle 2 of the Rio Declaration. The change in language relates to the expansion in the later text of states' "sovereign right to exploit their own resources pursuant to their own environmental *and developmental* policies. . . ." Since 1972, innumerable international authorities, including binding treaties and nonbinding principles and guidelines, allude to and incorporate Principle 21 by reference. The addition of the phrase "and developmental" in Rio might be taken to disrupt and skew the already delicate balance between the two clauses somewhat uncomfortably juxtaposed in Stockholm Principle 21, inconsistent with at least some post-Stockholm codifications and reaffirmations of the earlier Principle. Alternatively, maybe the drafters of Rio Principle 2 simply updated the Stockholm formulation. If Stockholm Principle 21 was customary law before the Rio Conference, as many scholars have asserted, of what legal significance is the modification to that Principle in the Rio Declaration? What arguments can you make to support the position that Rio Principle 2 is now binding law? Or that, alternatively, Rio Principle 2 fails to displace Stockholm Principle 21, which continues to be the statement of governing international law? (Welcome to the ambiguities of international law.)

4. Precaution, principle or approach? Concepts of "precaution," with roots in domestic approaches such as the German *Vorsorgeprinzip*,[7] have rapidly become the subject of a wide variety of international instruments. Rio Principle 15 codified a perspective that has gained considerable currency in recent years. This exhortation to "precautious" decision-making is characteristic of a recent upsurge in the importance of "principles" such as sustainable development in international environmental law and policy. Even the terminology employed—for instance, references to "the precautionary principle" as opposed to "a precautionary approach"— can be an occasion for vigorous international disagreements. The U.S., for example, has asserted that "the precautionary principle" is an invitation to disregard science, while at the same time supporting "a precautionary approach." The EU, for its part, has forcefully argued for the acceptance of "principle" over "approach," asserting that a principle enjoys a higher status than an approach. What is the status of the precautionary principle in international law? Of other principles such as sustainable development? How would you approach these questions from an analytical point of view?

5. Precaution at home in the U.S. Consider the following classic statement of precaution in domestic environmental law:

---

7. *Vorsorgeprinzip* is the straightforward German phrase for "precautionary principle."

B. International Conferences & Soft Law

Where a statute is precautionary in nature, the evidence difficult to come by, uncertain, or conflicting because it is on the frontiers of scientific knowledge, the regulations designed to protect the public health, and the decision that of an expert administrator, we will not demand rigorous step-by-step proof of cause and effect. Such proof may be impossible to obtain if the precautionary purpose of the statute is to be served. *Ethyl Corp. v. EPA*, 541 F.2d 1, 28 (D.C. Cir. 1976) (en banc).

What domestic regulatory approaches would you describe as precautionary? What regulatory approaches to the environment employed in U.S. law would not qualify as precautionary?

6. The Rio Declaration and U.S. law. One of the purposes of the Rio Declaration is to catalyze the development of national legislation. Based on your study of the domestic environmental law of the U.S. in the previous portions of this coursebook, to what extent would you say that our domestic environmental law conforms to the requirements of the Rio Declaration? Specifically, by reference to Rio Principle 3, does U.S. law assure the goal of "equitably meet[ing] developmental and environmental needs of present and future generations?" Principle 4's standard that "environmental protection shall constitute an integral part of the development process and cannot be considered in isolation from it"? Principle 14's exhortation to "discourage or prevent the relocation and transfer to other States of any activities and substances that cause severe environmental degradation or are found to be harmful to human health"? Principle 10 addresses public participation in the processes of environmental law. Principle 16 is an international formulation of the basic principle of environmental economics asserting the need to internalize environmental externalities, in a precept known as the Polluter Pays Principle. Similarly, Principle 17 generalizes the National Environmental Policy Act to the international level, where the analogous methodology is known as "environmental impact assessment." To what extent would you say that the expectations of these principles have been met by the U.S.? As an environmental advocate at the domestic level, how might you use the Rio Declaration to argue for changes to domestic law? See Stumbling Toward Sustainability (J.C. Dernbach ed., 2002).

7. What is "sustainability" anyway? International environmental law has been criticized for lack of any readily identifiable, coherent central principles. "Sustainable development," the central theme of the 1992 UNCED, probably comes closest to a broad-gauge theme. Despite numerous attempts, however, there has yet to be a consensus statement of the meaning of this amorphous term, with many diverse interests projecting their own agendas onto it. As used in the 1987 report of the World Commission on Environment and Development, the term suggests confining development options to those that preserve environmental integrity. As articulated in the Rio Declaration from the Earth Summit, however, the term seems to suggest an entirely different sort of approach that balances economic and environmental interests, trading one off against the other. What should be the overarching goal or goals of international environmental law and policy? If not sustainable development, prohibitions on transboundary pollution, or the precautionary principle, then what?

8. Subsequent sustainability summits. Another of these global events, the World Summit on Sustainable Development (WSSD), the so-called Rio+10 meeting, a ten-year follow-up to UNCED, was held in Johannesburg, South Africa, in 2002. The WSSD was intended to be different in kind from its predecessors, the 1972 Stockholm Conference and the 1992 Earth Summit. Instead of serving as an agenda-setting vehicle, the emphasis at the WSSD was on effectiveness in implementation. Delegates from 193 countries attended the Summit, which was addressed by some 100 world leaders. The June 2012 United Nations Conference on Sustainable Development in Rio de Janeiro, also known as Rio+20, produced an outcome document "The Future We Want," which set out further goals designed to motivate further momentum in achieving sustainable development. Rio+20, attended by nearly 10,000 representatives of civil society, mobilized more than $500 billion in voluntary commitments in the sectors of energy, transport, green economy, disaster reduction, desertification, water, forests and agriculture.

C. Comparative Environmental Law

Triggering positive developments in national law and policy by setting aspirational good practice standards is a central goal of the Rio Declaration and many other nonbinding instruments. To date, this approach has had little impact in the U.S., where national legislative priorities established by Congress and domestic agencies such as EPA tend to be interpreted as establishing not only minimum standards but also maximum expectations for private parties such as industry. While the U.S. can lay claim to taking an early lead as a pace setter in shaping and molding environmental policy early in the development of the modern environmental era, other countries more recently have been crucibles for domestic implementation of more up-to-date innovations in environmental policy like sustainability and precaution. For example, the constitutions of a number of states—including Brazil, Chile, Ecuador, Honduras, Nicaragua, Peru, Portugal, South Korea, and Spain—explicitly pronounce an individual right to a clean and healthy environment. Comparative approaches, examining foreign law and policy, have much to teach us here in the U.S. as we move into the dizzyingly globalized world of the twenty-first century.

International law and comparative law are two very different enterprises, although many internationally focused jurists concern themselves with both. International law governs relationships at the level of nation-states and international organizations such as the UN. Comparative law instead considers what goes on *within* states. Comparisons between foreign legal traditions and our own in some cases can shed light on deeper structural dynamics common to both; in others, comparisons explain divergences in terms of differing legal traditions or cultures. The methods and skills of comparative analysis are also useful to attorneys practicing between different states in a federal system like ours. Different legal systems naturally find themselves addressing domestic implementation of common principles or international agreements quite differently. The following case, an example of "social action litigation," deals with urban air pollution in India, a country where environmental law is a constitutional issue.

Mehta v. Union of India
2 Law Reports of India 1 (2002)

[The Constitution of India directs that:

> The State shall endeavour to protect and improve the environment and to safeguard the forests and wild life of the country.... It further shall be the duty of every citizen of India ... to protect and improve the natural environment including forests, lakes, rivers and wild life, and to have compassion for living creatures. Article 51A, Fundamental Duties.

M.C. Mehta, a public interest lawyer practicing by himself, filed suit against the government of India in 1986 challenging unhealthy levels of air pollution in Delhi. As the case dragged on over the years, orders issued by the Supreme Court of India between 1986 and 1996 resulted in the introduction of unleaded gasoline, catalytic converters, low-sulfur diesel fuel, and government vehicles fired by compressed natural gas (CNG). A special committee

C. Comparative Environmental Law

established during the course of the litigation under India's Environment (Protection) Act of 1986 recommended a conversion of all buses to CNG, and the Environment Pollution (Prevention and Control) Authority, India's version of the U.S. EPA, adopted a binding direction implementing the recommendation. As part of the relief in the case, the Court in 1998 ordered the conversion of all buses in Delhi to CNG by a deadline of January 31, 2002, a target that had been delayed by the court twice before. The government requested yet another extension of the deadline, claiming shortage of CNG and disruption of bus service to the public. In response, the Court issued the following extraordinary order, imposing a fine of 500 rupees per day per bus on diesel bus operators from the original deadline and literally overnight removing as many as 6000 diesel-fueled buses from the streets of Delhi.]

DECISION OF THE COURT. Articles 39(e), 47 and 48A [of the Indian Constitution] by themselves and collectively cast a duty on the State to secure the health of the people, improve public health and protect and improve the environment. It was by reason of the lack of effort on the part of the enforcement agencies, notwithstanding adequate laws being in place, that this Court has been concerned with the state of air pollution in the capital of this country. Lack of concern or effort on the part of various governmental agencies had resulted in spiralling pollution levels. The quality of air was steadily decreasing and no effective steps were being taken by the administration in this behalf. It was by reason of the failure to discharge its constitutional obligations, and with a view to protect the health of the present and future generations, that this Court, for the first time, on 23rd September, 1986, directed the Delhi Administration to file an affidavit specifying steps taken by it for controlling pollution emission of smoke, noise, etc. from vehicles plying in Delhi.

The concern of this Court in passing various orders since 1986 has only been one, namely, to protect the health of the people of Delhi . . . , [although to avoid] disruption in bus services . . . and unnecessary hardship . . . this Court has been extending the time with regard to the conversion of commercial vehicles. . . . Action has been taken by the [Government] of India which leaves us with no doubt that its intention, clearly, is to frustrate the orders passed by this Court with regard to conversion of commercial vehicles to CNG. The manner in which it has sought to achieve this object is to try and dis-credit CNG as the proper fuel and, secondly, to represent to this Court that CNG is in short supply and, thirdly, delay the setting of adequate dispensing stations.

One of the principles underlying environmental law is that of sustainable development. This principle requires such development to take place which is ecologically sustainable. The two essential features of sustainable development are the precautionary principle and the polluter pays principle.

The "precautionary principle" was elucidated thus by this Court in *Vellore Citizens' Welfare Forum vs. Union of India and Others*, (1996) 5 SCC 647, inter alia, as follows: The State Government and the statutory authorities must anticipate, prevent and attack the causes of environmental degradation. Where there are threats of serious and irreversible damage, lack of scientific certainty should not be used as a reason for postponing measures to prevent environmental degradation. The "onus of proof" is on the actor or the developer to show that his action is environmentally benign. It cannot be gainsaid that permission to use automobiles has environmental implications, and thus any "auto policy" framed by the Government must, therefore, of necessity conform to the Constitutional principles as well as over-riding statutory duties can upon the Government under the EPA. The "auto policy" must, therefore, focus upon measures to

(a) "Anticipate, prevent and attack" the cause of environmental degradation in this field. (b) In the absence of adequate information, lean in favour of environmental protection by refusing rather than permitting activities likely to be detrimental. (c) Adopt the "precautionary principle" and thereby ensure that unless an activity is proved to be environmentally benign in real and practical terms, it is to be presumed to be environmentally harmful. (d) Make informed recommendations which balance the needs of transportation with the need to protect the environment and reverse the large scale degradation that has resulted over the years, priority being given to the environment over economic issues.

The plea of the Government that CNG is in short supply, and that it is unable to supply adequate quantity is incorrect, and this is clearly a deliberate attempt to frustrate the orders passed by this Court. . . .

During the course of arguments, literature was filed in Court giving data from cities all over the world which co-relates increased air pollution with increase in cardiovascular and respiratory diseases and also shows the carcinogenic nature of Respirable Particulate Matter (RSPM). The scientific studies indicate that air pollution leads to considerable levels of mortality and morbidity. Fine particulate matter, or RSPM-PM10 (i.e. matter less than 10 microns in size), is particularly dangerous.

The Journal of American Medical Association (JAMA) has published in its recent issue the findings of a study involving over 500,000 people, conducted over 16 years, in different cities of the US. The researchers find that fine particle related pollution leads to lung cancer and cardiopulmonary mortality. Their research indicates that with an increase of every 10 micro-gramme per cum (mg/cum) of fine particles, the risk of lung cancer increases by 8 per cent.

The USEPA has mandated that annual average levels of PM 2.5 particles in the air should not exceed 15 mg/cum. The Indian annual national average standard for PM10 is 60 mg/cum, but most cities, including Delhi register PM10 levels above 150-200 mg/cum on an annual basis. . . .

The increase in respiratory diseases specially amongst the children should normally be a cause of concern for any responsible government. The precautionary principle enshrined in the concept of sustainable development would have expected the government and the health authorities to take appropriate action and arrest the air pollution. However, children do not agitate or hold rallies and, therefore, their sound is not heard and the only concern of the Government now appears to be is to protect the financial health of the polluters, including the oil companies who by present international desirable standards produce low quality petrol and diesel at the cost of public health. The statistics show that the continuing air pollution is having a more devastating effect on the people than what was caused by the Bhopal gas tragedy. . . . Under these circumstances, it becomes the duty of this Court to direct such steps being taken as are necessary for cleaning the air so that the future generations do not suffer from ill-health.

It was repeatedly contended on behalf of the Union of India that no other city in the world had introduced CNG buses at the scale directed by this Court. Both the State Government and the Union of India had urged that the CNG technology was still evolving and experimental. It is no doubt true that most of the cities of the industrialised world do not have large numbers of CNG buses, but the share of natural gas buses, needed to meet the stringent norms in the future, are growing. The data filed indicates that in the U.S., CNG buses account for 18 per cent of the current bus orders and 28 per cent of the potential orders. Under pressure to clean up the air because of the approaching Olympic Games in 2004, Beijing has resorted to an alternative fuel strategy. Latest figures from Beijing indicates that there will be 18,000 buses fuelled by CNG, LPG and electricity in that city. By 1999, Beijing had 1300 CNG buses and the numbers are growing rapidly to meet the Olympic deadline. Similarly, the Ministry of Environment in South Korea, partly to meet

C. Comparative Environmental Law

the targets in time for World Cup Soccer, aims to induct 20,000 natural gas buses in its fleet and already 3000 such buses are plying. From the aforesaid, it is clear that the alternative fuel of CNG, LPG and electricity is a preferred technology which critically polluted cities like Delhi need as a leapfrogging technological option. . . .

[The request] of the Union of India for extension of time to run diesel buses is dismissed. . . . It is made clear, and it is obvious in our constitutional setup, that orders and directions of this Court cannot be nullified or modified or in any way altered by any administrative decision of the Central or the State Governments. The administrative decision to continue to ply diesel buses is, therefore, clearly in violation of this Court's orders.

COMMENTARY & QUESTIONS

1. Judicial activism in other jurisdictions. The Supreme Court of India has been described as "India's main catalyst of environmental reform." From a U.S. viewpoint, the Court's approach in this case is highly unusual. The Court appears to decide many scientific questions for itself, or at least feels comfortable evaluating the public policy significance of scientific data. The Court unashamedly scolds the government of India, overruling governmental determinations, substituting its conclusions for those of the government, and accusing governmental authorities of outright deception. The Court's order, in addition to removing diesel buses from the streets of Delhi, instructed the government to give preference to CNG vehicles throughout India, directed the government to make a minimum amount of CNG available to Delhi, required the city of Delhi to phase out 800 diesel buses per month, and ordered that permits of bus owners cancelled for nonconversion to CNG be reallocated to "weaker sections of society." These are all attributes that we associate with judicial activism. Is this an appropriate role for courts to play? If you think so, what limits would you identify for the judicial function?

2. Constitutionalization of environmental law. Over the years, there have been proposals for an environmental amendment to the U.S. Constitution, but they have never gained much momentum. Would you consider a constitutional amendment along the lines of the constitution of India to be a useful addition to U.S. environmental jurisprudence? What might be some of the drawbacks to such an approach? The constitutions of some U.S. states contain environmental guarantees. For example, the Virginia Constitution establishes a conservation policy of the Commonwealth "[t]o the end that the people have clean air, pure water, and the use and enjoyment for recreation of adequate public lands, waters, and other natural resources. . . ." Many state constitutional provisions, however, have been held to be nonjusticiable, meaning that they cannot be enforced in court. See, e.g., *Robb v. Shockoe Slip Found.*, 324 S.E.2d 674, 676 n. 2, 677 (Va. 1985). The provisions cited by the Supreme Court in the first sentence of its order, which fall under the heading "Directive Principles of State Policy," according to the Indian Constitution "shall not be enforced by any court, but the principles therein laid down are nevertheless fundamental in the governance of the country and it shall be the duty of the State to apply these principles in making laws." The Court does not seem to consider this an impediment to relying on these constitutional provisions in its order. Can you craft an argument on behalf of the citizen plaintiff in this case that overcomes the apparent prohibition on judicial application of these constitutional principles? See H. Steiner, R. Goodman, & P. Alston, International Human Rights in Context: Law, Politics, Morals 321-322 (3d ed. 2008).

3. International environmental law in national courts. The Supreme Court of India refers to principles of precaution and sustainability familiar from the Rio Declaration, a nonbinding soft law instrument. What role do those principles play in the Court's reasoning, and how do they affect the outcome in the case? As an analytical matter, how did they metamorphose from nonbinding international exhortations to enforceable domestic rules of decision against which the Court measures the performance of the Indian government?

4. Regional impacts outside India. Actions in one jurisdiction can lead by example, spurring other states to apply laws and policies that have worked elsewhere. The *Mehta* decision has already had this effect in other countries of South Asia. The Supreme Court of Bangladesh is requiring classes of vehicles there to use CNG. In July 2003, the Lahore High Court established the Lahore Clean Air Commission (LCAC) for the State of Punjab, Pakistan, which advised the court about measures to improve urban air quality. The LCAC will recommended, among other measures, that public transportation vehicles using diesel fuel convert to the use of CNG. What does this case have to teach us here in the U.S. about air pollution policy and law, or environmental law more generally?

5. Who is M.C. Mehta? In early 1984, M.C. Mehta, a public interest attorney, visited the Taj Mahal for the first time. He saw that the famed monument's marble had turned yellow and was pitted as a result of pollutants from nearby industries. This spurred Mehta to file his first environmental case in the Supreme Court of India. The following year, Mehta learned that the Ganges River, considered to be the holiest river in India and used by millions of people every day for bathing and drinking water, caught fire due to industrial effluents in the river. Once again Mehta filed a petition in the Supreme Court against the polluting factories, and the scope of the case was broadened to include all the industries and municipalities in the river basin.

For years, every Friday, a courtroom has been set aside just for Mehta's cases. In 1993, after a decade of court battles and threats from factory owners, the Supreme Court ordered 212 small factories surrounding the Taj Mahal to close because they had not installed pollution control devices. Another 300 factories were put on notice to do the same. While the Ganges cases continued to be heard every week, 5000 factories along the river were directed to install pollution control devices and 300 factories were closed. Approximately 250 towns and cities in the Ganges Basin have been ordered to set up sewage treatment plants.

Mehta has won additional precedent-setting suits against industries that generate hazardous waste and has succeeded in obtaining a court order to make lead-free gasoline available. He has also been working to ban intensive shrimp farming and other damaging activities along India's 7000-kilometer coast. Mehta has succeeded in getting new environmental policies initiated and has brought environmental protection into India's constitutional framework. He has almost singlehandedly obtained about 40 landmark judgments and numerous orders from the Supreme Court against polluters, a record that may be unequaled by any other environmental lawyer in the world.[8]

D. Multilateral Environmental Agreements & Global Climate Change

> International agreements, much like domestic contracts, are a source of binding international law for the states parties to them.

---

8. Information from the website of the Goldman Environmental Prize, awarded annually to six "environmental heroes," and received by Mr. Mehta in 1996. See www.goldmanprize.org.

D. Multilateral Environmental Agreements & Global Climate Change

Some problems of the international environment are immensely challenging to address with only the simple model of bilateral transboundary pollution set out above in *Trail Smelter*. Harm may be long-term and diffuse, instead of palpable and substantial as in the smelter dispute. It may be difficult to prove relationships between emissions in one state and impacts in another, or there may be multiple sources from a multiplicity of states, as is the case with acid precipitation in Europe. Some environmental risks even threaten the entire globe. Scientific evidence may be equivocal, or scientific opinion divided or in a state of evolution, which should suggest the application of precautionary methodology. Such challenges are truly multilateral and require the cooperation of all states in implementing solutions.

Although complex challenges often call for creative use of some or all of the legal and policy options in the international toolbox, many of them are unsuited to serious global environmental challenges requiring concrete policy responses. Customary law is of limited utility in response to urgent, controversial threats. Global summits, while useful for elevating the profile of international environmental hazards, have largely become "talking shops" for articulating aspirational goals and general principles. The adoption of national laws and policies, while helpful, must be coordinated multilaterally to address threats of global proportions.

Multilateral agreements consequently have become the principal workhorse of international law and policy. Chapter 7 notes the effect of environmental treaties as domestic law in the U.S. This section analyzes the equally complex operation of multilateral environmental agreements to prevent disruption of the earth's climate from the phenomenon of global warming to illustrate the innumerable opportunities and frustrating challenges encountered in protecting our fragile planet.

1. Stratospheric Ozone Depletion

The protection of the stratospheric ozone layer is routinely cited as the biggest success story of international environmental law. Ozone is an unstable, triatomic form of oxygen, which at ground level is a criteria pollutant under the Clean Air Act (CAA), where it is a component of photochemical smog. In the stratosphere, 40 km above the earth's surface, however, ozone performs the essential function of absorbing harmful levels of high-energy ultraviolet (UV) radiation emanating from the sun, preventing excess levels of those destructive rays from endangering our fragile planet. Terrestrial and oceanic life forms evolved in an environment of an intact ozone layer. Unnaturally high levels of UV radiation can disrupt biological processes, leading to elevated levels of skin cancer—including life-threatening melanoma—cataracts, and immune system suppression. In addition to these threats to human health, an increase in UV radiation has also been shown to damage crops and marine resources.

In 1974, scientists hypothesized that the stratospheric ozone layer was being destroyed by CFCs used in refrigeration systems, air conditioners, and other pressurized products.[9] While these economically useful chemicals, which are strictly man-made, are stable and essentially nontoxic at ground level, they eventually drift higher into the stratosphere. Chlorine atoms are split off in this high-energy environment, where they go on to destroy

---

9. Molina & Rowland, Stratospheric Sink for Chlorofluoromethanes: Chlorine Atom-Catalysed Destruction of Ozone, 249 Nature 810 (1974). Drs. Molina and Rowland received the 1995 Nobel Prize in chemistry for this research.

ozone in a chain reaction, each molecule of CFC potentially annihilating tens of thousands of molecules of stratospheric ozone.

Due to their chemical stability, CFCs remain in the atmosphere for many years after being emitted, some for well over a century. As a result, the atmospheric concentrations of these gases are essentially the same everywhere. Emissions anywhere on the planet have the same impact on stratospheric ozone, regardless of their geographic origin, so that ozone depletion is truly a global issue. The distribution of CFC emissions, moreover, presents issues of global equity, with most coming from wealthy industrialized countries and relatively little from poor, developing countries that might use these substances for essential purposes such as refrigeration. Stratospheric ozone depletion threatens long-term, potentially catastrophic harm, whose precise delineation—like many environmental issues—is complicated by a range of uncertainty.

States negotiating under UN auspices to reduce threats to the stratospheric ozone layer in the early 1980s made an explicit decision to undertake a two-component process. One product of this process was to be a so-called *framework* multilateral convention. Ancillary agreements, known as *protocols*, containing substantive regulatory measures would be appended to this convention. Although not required by any legal constraints, this framework convention-plus-protocols model has since become standard in international environmental policy.

The ozone "umbrella" treaty evolved into the Vienna Convention, which was concluded in March 1985. The Vienna Convention itself contains no substantive requirements for specific measures to protect stratospheric ozone. Instead, it embodies only a vague, unenforceable exhortation to protect the stratospheric ozone layer through the implementation of "appropriate measures."

When negotiations on the CFC Protocol broke down, the Convention alone was adopted. In 1985 a huge "hole"—a dramatic seasonal thinning in the ozone layer not predicted by computer models—was discovered over Antarctica. Renegotiation of the Protocol after a scheduled one-year "cooling off" period coincided with an upsurge in public concern about the Antarctic ozone hole, which broke the deadlock and facilitated adoption of the Montreal Protocol in September 1987.

The ozone Vienna Convention/Montreal Protocol system is intended to be a dynamic, evolving regime responsive to new scientific discovery and novel policy challenges. Consequently, both the Convention and the Protocol provide for regular reassessment and revision, most recently in 2007. Despite numerous impediments and setbacks, the legal history of stratospheric ozone has largely been a success story. As dramatically demonstrated by Figure 1, the ozone layer is now expected to recover by the middle of this century.

COMMENTARY & QUESTIONS

1. Lessons from ozone. The legal history of stratospheric ozone holds many crucial lessons for the future of Earth. The underlying problem originally seemed intractable and immensely costly to tackle. Alternatives to cheap and useful CFCs were not readily at hand, necessitating a leap of faith in industry's innovative capacity to identify substitutes. Crafting a solution required a global bargain, delicately balancing the needs of industrialized and developing countries. Fraught with scientific uncertainty, saving the ozone layer required governmental negotiators and scientists to communicate with each other in new and unfamiliar ways. Connections to apparently unrelated issues such as trade created additional complications. Since no state had domestic mechanisms in place adequate to the task, all

D. Multilateral Environmental Agreements & Global Climate Change

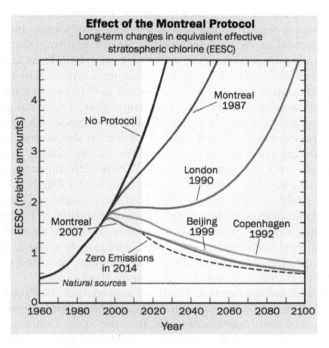

FIGURE 22-1 *Impact of international agreements on chlorine levels in the stratosphere. This figure shows that, because of the long atmospheric lifetimes of CFCs, the 50% reductions called for in the unrevised 1987 Protocol would have been useful but insufficient to protect the ozone layer. The assessment and review procedure in the Protocol provided a basis for the parties to the agreement to take the further, more aggressive action incorporated in subsequent revisions. See World Meteorological Organization Report, http://goo.gle/g4FLHG (2014).*

the participating governments were simultaneously creating new domestic environmental law as well. The interplay among all these factors without doubt will characterize the next generations of environmental treaties.

The stratospheric ozone negotiations also invigorated a public culture of global lawmaking. Extensive press coverage of threats to the ozone layer created an unprecedented sense of public apprehension and urgency. As one of the first major environmental agreements with serious consequences for industry, the ozone negotiations became a policy battleground to an extent never before experienced on the international level. The ozone negotiations were also a watershed for vastly expanded participation in international negotiations by environmental organizations—in international parlance, NGOs. Governmental negotiators accustomed to working largely behind closed doors faced new demands for accountability and transparency. Although all of this might go without saying in the U.S., active public involvement in international environmental policymaking had been infrequent and sporadic before the ozone negotiations. Now that the debate is largely concluded, and resolved in favor of strict environmental controls, it is all too easy to forget how contentious this issue was during the 1980s—a cautionary lesson about currently controversial threats such as climate warming.

2. Science in international diplomacy. Scientific understanding of the stratospheric ozone problem was and is central to the task of crafting a responsive international policy, but diplomatic negotiators rarely have technical scientific training. Consequently, UNEP organized a Coordinating Committee on the Ozone Layer (CCOL) as an institutional link to provide scientific and technical advice to the ozone negotiations. The members of CCOL were scientific experts appointed in their individual and personal capacities. Although some of the individual members might have been employees of national governments, they were expected to operate in a purely collegial, scientific mode. The goal was to create a body that could provide objective and neutral advice on the underlying science to the negotiators who would interpret its policy significance in negotiating instruments such as the Vienna Convention and the Montreal Protocol. Scientific input into the multilateral process continues to this day. If you were the chairperson of CCOL, how would you resolve the disputes that inevitably arise between scientists? How would you deal with a scientist who disputed the Rowland-Molina theory and hence the existence of the problem? With a scientist who asserted that the problem was much more severe than the majority view? Despite the potential tensions in such a role, the model largely worked, with the scientific explanation for such phenomena as the ozone hole, whether provided through CCOL or otherwise, a principal driver in the ozone negotiations, then as now.

3. International technology-forcing. The basic approach of the Protocol as adopted in 1987 was to reduce and, in light of the subsequent amendments and adjustments, eventually eliminate production and consumption of CFCs. Because at the time there were no known substitutes for these cheap, useful, and nontoxic (at least at ground level) chemicals, the Protocol is often cited as an example of a ban designed to create incentives for technological innovation. The 1987 Protocol, however, did not eliminate these chemicals entirely but instead required a 50% reduction in consumption by 1999. Soon after the adoption of the Protocol, the ozone "hole" over Antarctica was connected to CFCs, adding momentum to demands for further reductions and ultimately elimination of these compounds. Beyond the policy challenges to any public policy involving technology-forcing, as discussed in Chapter 11, what additional impediments can you imagine on the international level? How would you propose to overcome them?

4. Laggards, holdouts, and free riders. A persistent structural impediment in international law, heavily tilted toward consent and consensus, is how to deal with states that are not parties to a particular agreement. Any state may avoid the obligations of the Montreal Protocol, or any other agreement, merely by refraining from signing and ratifying. In the case of the Montreal Protocol, the problem of nonparties was particularly acute because the parties to the agreement were undertaking expensive obligations in purely economic terms. Nonparties would not incur those costs, putting parties to the agreement at a competitive disadvantage. Article 4 of the Montreal Protocol, entitled "Control of Trade with Non-parties," addresses this issue. The agreement's trade provisions require parties to the Protocol to prohibit imports from and exports to nonparties of bulk CFCs; products containing CFCs, such as refrigerators and air conditioners; and products manufactured with CFCs that do not contain them, such as computer chips. At the same time, trade in those products was freely permitted among parties during the phaseout period. Can you explain why negotiators believed this provision was essential? What would you expect the effect of these requirements to be on relations among parties and nonparties? What beneficial results would you expect for the environment?

5. COPs and MOPs. Like its predecessor, the Vienna Convention, the Montreal Protocol is an organic instrument that sets out a framework for future cooperative action by the parties to the instrument. Article 6, entitled "Assessment and Review of Control Measures," specifies periodic reviews of the science with an eye to revising the Protocol. Article 11 calls for regular meetings of the parties to the Protocol (MOPs), which in practice are held simultaneously with the conferences of the parties to the Vienna Convention (COPs). The first revisions to the Protocol were adopted in 1990. Even before that, at the first MOP held in 1989, the parties to the then-new Protocol, which had just entered into force, adopted a decision entitled the "Helsinki Declaration on the Protection of the Ozone Layer." This document states that the Protocol parties "agree to phase out the production and the consumption of CFC's controlled by the Montreal Protocol as soon as possible but not later than the year 2000." In other words, the Helsinki Declaration states the same goal as the London amendments and adjustments of a year later. What do you think is the purpose of the Helsinki Declaration? What is the Declaration's legal status? If the Helsinki Declaration accomplished this goal in 1989, what need was there for the London amendments and adjustments? Can you identify a legal relationship among the Protocol, the Declaration, and the London adjustments and amendments?

6. Revising the Protocol and a novel twist. Customary international law specifies that an amendment to a multilateral treaty is binding only on those states that indicate their affirmative intent to accept those new obligations, ordinarily through ratification or acceptance of the amendment. In effect, an amendment is a new agreement under international law. The drafters of the Protocol, however, saw that the customary rule is an unattractive option for issues such as stratospheric ozone depletion, in which the scientific knowledge underlying treaty provisions is in a constant state of evolution and reassessing international obligations is often desirable, if not necessary. Under the customary rule, there is a serious risk that repeated amendment of an agreement in light of new scientific developments will result in classes of parties, each with its own configuration of obligations depending upon the amendments to which it has acceded. This danger is particularly grave in the case of complex, delicately balanced regulatory regimes such as the Montreal Protocol, where the costs to states parties are high.

In a "sleeper" provision little noticed at the time of its drafting, Article 2, Paragraph 9 of the Montreal Protocol modifies the customary rule by providing for "adjustments"—a term otherwise unknown to international law—that are binding on all parties to be adopted by a two-thirds majority vote. There is no opt-out provision, as with the Whaling Convention discussed in Chapter 7. True majority voting of this sort is virtually unknown to the international legal system, which almost always operates by consensus or unanimity. Can you see why there is a preference in international relations for acquiescence by every state, in effect giving every country a veto? What drawbacks can you see to the adjustment process? In an approach worthy of Solomon, but understandable in light of the international bias in favor of consensus, the parties to the Protocol split the difference, adopting adjustments on the streamlined, nonconsensus model for those substances already covered by the agreement, but requiring full-blown amendments to add new substances.

7. Developing countries. Article 5 of the Protocol responds to the demands of developing countries by giving them a ten-year grace period for implementing the obligations in the Protocol. Why do you think the negotiators might have chosen this particular formula? From the point of view of environmental efficacy, is this a helpful provision or a harmful one? Does it reflect an appropriate balance of competing factors?

8. The rule of law: confronting scofflaws. Article 8 of the Protocol directs the MOP to adopt noncompliance procedures "for treatment of Parties found to be in non-compliance." In recognition of the fact that there is little to be done if a state party chooses flagrantly to violate its international obligations, the Protocol prefers the term *compliance* to the stronger concept of *enforcement*. Can you imagine why that might be so? In 1992, the

MOP adopted a compliance mechanism, administered by an Implementation Committee, that can be triggered either by a third party or by the noncomplying state itself. Why might a state choose to, in effect, accuse itself of noncompliance? If you were the diplomatic representative of a party admittedly not in compliance, how would you frame your presentation to the Implementation Committee? The first two cases considered by the Implementation Committee concerned Russia and Bulgaria, both of which identified serious impediments to compliance. Nonetheless, the Committee declined to recommend cutting off multilateral aid or trade sanctions, probably the two most serious punishments available to the Committee. Can you imagine why the Implementation Committee might have taken such a lenient approach? If you were representing Russia or Bulgaria, can you make an argument that it would be environmentally counterproductive to sanction your client in that manner?

2. Global Warming

Earth averaged 57.9 degrees, or 1.6 degrees hotter, in the 1990s than in 1860. Atmospheric carbon dioxide now measures 360 ppm [and in 2015: over 400 ppm — EDS.]; . . . that's 30 percent higher than at the start of the industrial era, higher, in fact, than in the past 160,000 years. In half a century, that could double. . . . Atmospheric layers of gases (water vapor, methane, nitrous oxide and carbon dioxide) let in sunlight, then trap heat. . . . Trouble comes when humans artificially pump up the volume to unnatural levels. Concentrating carbon dioxide . . . trap[s] more heat. Can we "think global, act local" regarding climate change? No. But we can invert the slogan to think about what we may lose locally, then act at a global forum. Bruce Babbitt, Park's Retreating Glaciers Signal a Climate Warning, Denver Post, Nov. 16, 1997, at H-08. Cf. T.M. Moore, Climate of Fear: Why We Shouldn't Worry about Global Warming (1997).

> "From the standpoint of meteorologists and oceanographers we are carrying out a tremendous geophysical experiment of a kind that could not have happened in the past or be reproduced in the future." Testimony of Roger Revelle, Second Supplemental Appropriation Bill, 1956: Hearing Before Subcommittees of the Committee on Appropriations, House of Representatives, Eighty-fourth Congress, Second Session 467 (Testimony of Roger Revelle).

Climate change is perhaps the most daunting of the global threats currently facing humankind. Human activities since the Industrial Revolution have dramatically altered the composition of the global atmosphere, increasing average global temperatures by at least 0.8° C (1.4° F). A number of gases, emitted in small but significant amounts, absorb infrared radiation reflected from the surface of the earth, causing average temperature to rise. The impact of these changes is highly unpredictable, but almost certainly detrimental to both the health of ecosystems and quality of life for human beings. Fourteen of the fifteen warmest years on record have occurred during the present century, and 2015 has been confirmed as the hottest on record. Ocean uptake of CO_2 from anthropogenic sources since 1750 has acidified the oceans, with an average decrease in pH of 0.1 unit—an increase in acidity of 26%, reducing the capacity of marine life such as corals to access carbonate necessary to producing and maintain their shells.

Emissions of CO_2 are the single largest cause of elevated temperatures from the greenhouse effect, accounting for approximately half of the problem. For millions of years concentrations of CO_2 in the range of 280 parts per million (ppm), together with water vapor in the atmosphere, established the pre-industrial equilibrium temperature of the planet.

D. Multilateral Environmental Agreements & Global Climate Change

FIGURE 22-2. *Climate change today is probably the single most urgent environmental issue subject to international law. Addressing climate change effectively will be far more difficult than the remarkably successful international legal initiative to protect stratospheric ozone in the Montreal Protocol. The effects of climate change are increasingly visible. The Grinnell Glacier in Glacier National Park, photographed from the same vantage point in 1910, 1931, and 1997 (top to bottom at left), as average temperatures around the globe continue to rise by small increments over the decades. A considerable portion of what formerly was glacier is now a lake with ice in the middle. Scientists predict that all the glaciers in Glacier National Park will have vanished within a decade.*

Beginning with the start of the Industrial Revolution, however, atmospheric CO_2 levels have increased by over 40% to approximately 400 ppm as of 2015.[10] Elevated CO_2 concentrations result primarily from the intensified burning of fossil fuels—coal, oil, and natural gas—which liberates the chemical in varying amounts. Coal burning releases the most CO_2, while the combustion of quantities of natural gas and oil needed to produce the same amount of energy results in only about 57% and 83% as much CO_2, respectively.

---

10. Methane, the principal component of natural gas, is another significant climate-modifying chemical. Atmospheric methane reached a new high of about 1819 parts per billion (ppb) in 2012, or 260% of the pre-industrial level. Animal husbandry and rice cultivation have been identified as major sources of increased methane emissions. Coal mining, landfills and pipeline leaks are also significant sources, with large potential for rapid growth in the future. On a weight basis, methane is more than 25 times more potent a greenhouse gas (GHG) than carbon dioxide.

The world's forests are vast storehouses or "sinks" for carbon. Worldwide loss of forest cover releases this vast stockpile of carbon into the atmosphere as CO_2, aggravating the greenhouse problem. Deforestation in Third World countries is particularly severe, from activities such as burning, logging, and conversion to agricultural and pastureland. As of 2014, the total annual global loss of forest cover amounted to more than 32 million acres.

The accumulation in the atmosphere of CO_2, methane, and other GHGs could have sweeping and far-reaching effects on the earth's climate. By as early as the year 2030, the heat-retaining capacity of the atmosphere may have doubled in relation to pre-industrial concentrations of CO_2. By 2100, the annual global mean surface temperatures may have risen by as much as 1.8-6.4° C, 3.2°-11.5° F. The absolute magnitude of these temperatures, as well as the rapidity of temperature change, will exceed any ever experienced previously in human history.

The effects of a greenhouse-driven climate disruption will be characterized with complete certainty only after significant damage has already occurred. However, among the most dramatic effects likely to ensue from greenhouse warming is an unprecedented rise in sea level resulting from thermal expansion of the oceans and melting of glaciers and polar ice. Over the twentieth century, the average global sea level increased less than 2 mm. By contrast, by 2100 the sea level rise will accelerate considerably, producing a total increase up to 4 feet, depending on the degree of global warming that occurs.

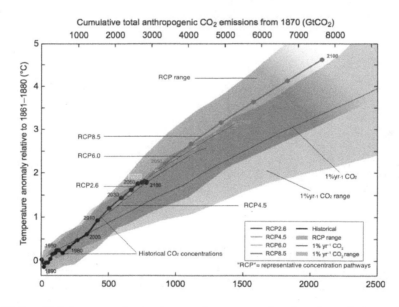

FIGURE 22-3. *Global mean surface temperature increase as a function of cumulative total global CO_2 emissions based on a variety of emissions scenarios.* Source: Working Group I, Intergovernmental Panel on Climate Change, Climate Change 2013: The Physical Science Basis (5th Assessment Report), http://www.climatechange2013.org/images/report/WG1AR5_ALL_FINAL.pdf.

The dramatic anticipated increases in global temperature are virtually certain to cause a wide variety of modifications in regional climates, affecting agriculture in particular. Forests, many of them economically productive, could begin to die off if they prove unable to adjust to rapidly shifting climatic zones. Regions of agricultural productivity could shift. Computer models predict continental drying in middle latitudes, which means that parched soils, scorching droughts, and massive heat waves could become commonplace.

D. Multilateral Environmental Agreements & Global Climate Change

Extreme temperatures have been shown to elevate human mortality. Some models also project disruptions in atmospheric and ocean circulation patterns. The impact of these changes is highly unpredictable.

Because of their long atmospheric lifetimes, GHGs—like CFCs, which contribute to stratospheric ozone depletion—are "well-mixed," meaning that their concentrations are essentially the same around the world. A molecule of carbon dioxide released in the United States has global impacts, as does a molecule in China or anywhere else. Climate change is consequently literally a global problem requiring a universal solution.

The long atmospheric lifetimes of the principal GHGs—CO_2 can remain in the atmosphere for decades after its release and methane for about 12 years—necessitate major reductions in emissions of these pollutants in order to have a meaningful impact in slowing the growth in their concentration. Merely to stabilize global concentrations of CO_2 gas, it will be necessary to cut global emissions of CO_2 by 50-85%.[11] Burning fossil fuels releases most of the excess CO_2 into the atmosphere, and because currently there is no known economical technology for removing CO_2 from waste-gas streams, cutting back releases of CO_2 will require a lower total energy consumption and a shift in energy sources toward low- or non-CO_2-emitting technologies.

Reversing deforestation and creating new forested areas will help to offset current levels of CO_2 emissions. New forests, in absorbing CO_2 from the air during photosynthesis, will contribute to climate stabilization by serving as supplementary reservoirs for carbon. Aggressive policies to conserve existing forests and create new forested areas will yield other significant environmental benefits, including erosion control and the preservation of a rich diversity of species whose genetic potential is only now becoming accessible to humankind. Nevertheless, the key element in ensuring the integrity of the global climate is a massive reduction in emissions of GHGs.

3. The Global Warming Framework Convention

The global warming problem is a model case study in the formation of international consensus through international conferences, nonbinding statements and declarations, and involvement of nongovernmental stakeholders and experts, including scientists, representatives of industry, and environmental activists. Expectations about the prospects for a convention to limit emissions of carbon dioxide and other GHGs arose in large measure from progress in negotiating and implementing the Montreal Protocol. It is consequently natural that discussions concerning multilateral instruments on climate have explicitly relied on the structures established in the ozone negotiations.

The connection between the stratospheric ozone and "greenhouse" issues is of more than mere precedential significance. CFCs are themselves potent contributors to global warming. Despite their relatively low concentrations, CFCs and a related class of chemicals called halons, also controlled by the Montreal Protocol, are responsible for upwards of 15% of current contributions to the greenhouse effect. Per molecule in the atmosphere, these

---

11. To understand why major *cuts* in *emissions* are required merely to *stabilize* ambient *concentrations*, it helps to analogize the earth's atmosphere to a home or apartment into which a stove is leaking gas. Opening the window—the equivalent of natural removal processes for carbon dioxide and methane—will alleviate the problem somewhat. However, if gas continues to gush from the stove—corresponding to emissions of polluting chemicals—faster than it leaves through the window, there will still be a net accumulation of gas, resulting in an increase in concentration, which is the indicator to which the climate system responds. In the case of GHGs, natural decomposition occurs very slowly, particularly by comparison with the rate at which pollutants have been released into the environment, a figure that has increased dramatically since the Industrial Revolution.

chemicals are up to 20,000 times more potent in absorbing infrared radiation than carbon dioxide (CO_2), the most important anthropogenic GHG. Indeed, Montreal Protocol parties have agreed to eliminate hydrochlorofluorocarbons (HCFCs), alternatives to chlorofluorocarbons that are themselves potent GHGs, by 2030, and are currently considering similar measures with respect to hydrofluorocarbons (HFCs).

In response to mounting concerns about the integrity of the global climate, the United Nations Environment Program (UNEP) and the World Meteorological Organization (WMO) created the Intergovernmental Panel on Climate Change (IPCC) with a mandate to study the climate change issue primarily from a scientific perspective. The principal activities of the IPCC, which met for the first time in November 1988, were and are divided among three working groups: a scientific one that addresses the causes of climate change (Working Group I, the physical science basis); one that studies the social and environmental impact of climate change (Working Group II, impacts, adaptation, and vulnerability); and one that addresses response options for limiting GHG emissions and reducing the effects of climate change (Working Group III, mitigation of climate change).

The IPCC's First Assessment Report, released in 1990, established much of the scientific basis for subsequent international work on the global warming problem that took place during the run-up to the United Nations Conference on Environment and Development (UNCED), the so-called Earth Summit. Now literally thousands of scientists from all over the world participate in IPCC activities, and the institution's broadly international character and consensus decisionmaking processes account for much of its well-earned perception of legitimacy and impartiality. More than 830 coordinating lead authors and review editors from over 80 countries, along with over 1000 contributing authors, were responsible for producing the Fifth Assessment Report, the IPCC's latest, in 2013 to 2014. See www.ipcc.ch. The IPCC received the Nobel Peace Prize in 2007, sharing it with former U.S. Vice President Al Gore.

The UN Framework Convention on Climate Change (FCCC) was one of the two global treaties to emerge from the 1992 Earth Summit. Following the framework convention-plus-protocols model that appeared to be successful in addressing stratospheric ozone, the Convention is primarily a procedural vehicle for further cooperation on scientific matters and identification of policy options. Reflecting the need perceived by at least some states for "targets and timetables," the Convention also includes a goal for industrialized countries of limiting GHG emissions to 1990 levels.[12] Another important feature of the framework-convention-with protocols model found in the FCCC is a requirement for periodic review of the science and policy related to protection of the global climate at an annual conference of the parties (COP).

The yearly COPs have since served as the institutional juncture at which major new pieces of the climate regime have been put in place, for instance the Kyoto Protocol adopted at COP-3. Virtually every state on the planet sends a reasonable level of representation to what continues to be an occasion for vigorous policy debate. The annual COPs have also acquired a larger cultural significance, attracting thousands of individuals representing hundreds of nongovernmental organizations from all over the world. On an even higher level of generality, the annual COPs are an occasion for the entire world to debate an important component of the future well-being of the planet, with extensive press coverage. While the negotiations leading to the Rio Convention attracted some attention, the interest in what might very well be perceived as a routine international meeting has now become staggering.

Apart from the U.S., which has historically been the single largest national emitter of GHGs, developing countries are probably the biggest "hot spot" in the climate regime.

---

12. As noted above, even if this goal were achieved, it would have only a modestly beneficial effect on the climate system.

D. Multilateral Environmental Agreements & Global Climate Change

While developing countries have caused little of the existing problem, as economic development accelerates, Third World countries may account for the preponderance of GHG emissions by the middle of this century. An international solution that provides incentives for the participation of developing countries while fairly distributing the responsibility for implementing solutions is essential to a successful global strategy for combating greenhouse warming. Both the Convention and the subsequent Kyoto Protocol exempt developing countries from substantive control and reduction obligations, but it is clear that that situation will not be suitable for the long term. At the same time, the Convention recognizes the special needs of developing countries for external assistance to fund adaptation, mitigation, and emission reduction efforts.

As of this writing, 195 states—virtually every one on the planet, including the U.S. and the EU—are parties to the Convention. For a negotiating history of the Convention, see Bodansky, The United Nations Framework Convention on Climate Change: A Commentary, 18 Yale J. Int'l L. 451 (1993).

United Nations Framework Convention on Climate Change
31 I.L.M. 851 (1992)

The Parties to this Convention . . . have agreed as follows . . .

ARTICLE 2. Objective. The ultimate objective of this Convention and any related legal instruments that the Conference of the Parties may adopt is to achieve, in accordance with the relevant provisions of the Convention, stabilization of greenhouse gas concentrations in the atmosphere at a level that would prevent dangerous anthropogenic interference with the climate system. Such a level should be achieved within a time-frame sufficient to allow ecosystems to adapt naturally to climate change, to ensure that food production is not threatened and to enable economic development to proceed in a sustainable manner.

ARTICLE 3. Principles. In their actions to achieve the objective of the Convention and to implement its provisions, the Parties shall be guided, inter alia, by the following:

1. The Parties should protect the climate system for the benefit of present and future generations of humankind, on the basis of equity and in accordance with their common but differentiated responsibilities and respective capabilities. Accordingly, the developed country Parties should take the lead in combating climate change and the adverse effects thereof.
2. The specific needs and special circumstances of developing country Parties, especially those that are particularly vulnerable to the adverse effects of climate change, and of those Parties, especially developing country Parties, that would have to bear a disproportionate or abnormal burden under the Convention, should be given full consideration.
3. The Parties should take precautionary measures to anticipate, prevent or minimize the causes of climate change and mitigate its adverse effects. Where there are threats of serious or irreversible damage, lack of full scientific certainty should not be used as a reason for postponing such measures, taking into account that policies and measures to deal with climate change should be cost-effective so as to ensure global benefits at the lowest possible cost. To achieve this, such policies and measures should take into account different socio-economic contexts, be comprehensive, cover all

relevant sources, sinks and reservoirs of greenhouse gases and adaptation, and comprise all economic sectors. Efforts to address climate change may be carried out cooperatively by interested Parties.

4. The Parties have a right to, and should, promote sustainable development. Policies and measures to protect the climate system against human-induced change should be appropriate for the specific conditions of each Party and should be integrated with national development programmes, taking into account that economic development is essential for adopting measures to address climate change.

5. The Parties should cooperate to promote a supportive and open international economic system that would lead to sustainable economic growth and development in all Parties, particularly developing country Parties, thus enabling them better to address the problems of climate change. Measures taken to combat climate change, including unilateral ones, should not constitute a means of arbitrary or unjustifiable discrimination or a disguised restriction on international trade.

ARTICLE 4. COMMITMENTS . . . 2. The developed country Parties and other Parties included in Annex I commit themselves specifically as provided for in the following:

(a) Each of these Parties shall adopt national policies and take corresponding measures on the mitigation of climate change, by limiting its anthropogenic emissions of greenhouse gases and protecting and enhancing its greenhouse gas sinks and reservoirs. These policies and measures will demonstrate that developed countries are taking the lead in modifying longer-term trends in anthropogenic emissions consistent with the objective of the Convention, recognizing that the return by the end of the present decade to earlier levels of anthropogenic emissions of carbon dioxide and other greenhouse gases not controlled by the Montreal Protocol would contribute to such modification, and taking into account the differences in these Parties' starting points and approaches, economic structures and resource bases, the need to maintain strong and sustainable economic growth, available technologies and other individual circumstances, as well as the need for equitable and appropriate contributions by each of these Parties to the global effort regarding that objective. These Parties may implement such policies and measures jointly with other Parties and may assist other Parties in contributing to the achievement of the objective of the Convention and, in particular, that of this subparagraph.

(b) In order to promote progress to this end, each of these Parties shall communicate, within six months of the entry into force of the Convention for it and periodically thereafter, and in accordance with Article 12, detailed information on its policies and measures referred to in subparagraph (a) above, as well as on its resulting projected anthropogenic emissions by sources and removals by sinks of greenhouse gases not controlled by the Montreal Protocol for the period referred to in subparagraph (a), with the aim of returning individually or jointly to their 1990 levels these anthropogenic emissions of carbon dioxide and other greenhouse gases not controlled by the Montreal Protocol. This information will be reviewed by the Conference of the Parties, at its first session and periodically thereafter, in accordance with Article 7. . . .

7. The extent to which developing country Parties will effectively implement their commitments under the Convention will depend on the effective implementation by developed country Parties of their commitments under the Convention related to financial resources and transfer of technology and will take fully into account that economic and social development and poverty eradication are the first and overriding priorities of the developing country Parties.

D. Multilateral Environmental Agreements & Global Climate Change

COMMENTARY & QUESTIONS

1. Soft or hard law—which is more environmentally friendly? A major international meeting hosted by the Government of Canada in 1988 and attended by more than 300 individuals from 46 countries, including government officials, scientists, and representatives of industry and environmental organizations, adopted a nonbinding recommendation for a "reduc[tion in] CO_2 emissions by approximately 20 percent of 1988 levels by the year 2005" as an initial goal. The Convention, by contrast, requires at most stabilization of emissions of GHGs from industrialized countries at 1990 levels, a less ambitious target. After the adoption of the Convention, what is left of the earlier commitment? Was it just a waste of time or—considering the carbon emissions associated with the air travel that many delegates used to get there—worse than nothing? What insight does the relationship between the two instruments provide into the relationship between hard (binding) and soft (nonbinding) law?

2. The Convention and the Rio Declaration. Article 3 of the Convention, entitled "Principles," was considered very important by many delegations and was extensively scrutinized and reworked during the negotiations. What is the relationship between the "principles" of Article 3 and the "obligations" of Article 4? Of what practical utility, if any, are Articles 2 and 3? Many provisions in the Convention, and Article 3 in particular, have exact analogues in the Rio Declaration, which was adopted more or less simultaneously. Compare, for instance, Rio Principle 15 with Convention Article 3, paragraph 3, both of which deal with precaution. Negotiations on the Convention, however, were complete by the time serious discussions on the Rio Declaration had begun. What is the legal relationship between the two instruments? Of what significance are the divergences in language between the Rio Principles and the Convention in treatment of the same subject matter, such as precaution? Can you imagine a scenario in which each influenced the development of the other?

3. The Convention as substantive law. At the time it was negotiated, the principal policy debate over the FCCC concerned the question of "targets and timetables"—that is, to what extent the Convention would contain substantive policy measures or be confined to the framework or "umbrella" role for which the Vienna Convention on ozone depletion was the model. The result was the language in Article 4.2(a) and (b). Predictably, states have interpreted this hard-fought language as either mandatory or hortatory, depending on their domestic policies. Based strictly on the language of these two provisions, can you argue that the Convention articulates a binding target of stabilizing emissions of GHGs by the year 2000? Alternatively, how would you argue that this is a nonbinding "soft" target, identified as helpful guidance for states to aim for, but not enforceable under international law?

4. The Convention as U.S. law. As discussed below, after the adoption of the Kyoto Protocol, the debate over the binding character of the Convention's stabilization goal was largely irrelevant for all parties to the Convention save one—the U.S., which stated its intent not to become a party to the Protocol. Recall that under Article VI of the Constitution, ratified treaties such as the FCCC are "the supreme Law of the Land." A U.S. EPA routine report submitted in 2002 to the Convention Secretariat, the professional staff serving the parties to the agreement, identified numerous consequences of global warming that were "likely, very likely, or projected" to occur, including temperature increases of up to 9° F; rises in sea level of up to 35 inches; loss of sensitive ecosystems such as barrier islands, alpine meadows, coral reefs, and coastal wetlands; and dramatic increases in heat indices during the summer that could trigger heat-related illnesses and deaths. Several months later, Massachusetts, Connecticut, and Maine filed suit against EPA, alleging that the Agency had violated the CAA by failing to list CO_2 as a pollutant under §108. Assuming you are a lawyer for the plaintiff states, how would you weave together the Convention and the CAA as legal authorities to obtain the desired relief? If you represent EPA, what defenses would you raise to the states' suit? Even if the states are successful in securing the listing of CO_2 as a pollutant, to what extent would you expect the CAA to serve as a successful vehicle for reducing carbon emissions from the U.S.? What other goals do you think the states might have? What legal theories other than a violation of the CAA might they have employed?

5. Role of the press. Because there is no court of general jurisdiction to engage in judicial review of the actions of government, in international environmental law and policy the "court of public opinion" assumes relatively greater importance than in the domestic setting. The media are major factors in shaping public opinion on the environment. In Europe, the press routinely connects extreme weather events such as the extreme heat wave during the summer of 2003, which was documented to have claimed 70,000 lives, with greenhouse warming. In the U.S., by contrast, the admitted uncertainties linking the causes of the phenomenon with local effects have tended to discourage reporting from this perspective. Which do you consider the more responsible approach, and why? The press, as a matter of journalistic ethics, routinely quotes global warming skeptics, despite the overwhelming weight of scientific evidence. Some journalists have criticized this approach as misleading the public, on the theory that "it is not reasonable to be in the middle of the road on a one-sided question." Do you agree with this perspective? If so, how would you propose to assure more "balanced" reporting?

4. The Kyoto Protocol and the Road to Paris

The first protocol to the Convention is the Kyoto Protocol, adopted in 1997, which specifies quantitative emissions reductions in gases that contribute to climate change, notably carbon dioxide, by 38 enumerated industrialized countries and economies in transition identified in Annex I to the Convention, transposed into Annex B of the Protocol. Early in the negotiations, it was agreed that there would be no new emissions reduction commitments for non-Annex I parties to the Convention. The Protocol controls emissions of six GHGs — most notably carbon dioxide, methane, and nitrous oxide—weighted according to their relative contributions to climate disruption as measured by "carbon equivalents" based on global warming potentials established by the IPCC.

The overall goal of the Protocol is to lower global releases of these gases by those states with quantified emissions limitation or reduction (mitigation) commitments by about 5% by reference to 1990 levels. The multilaterally agreed regulatory vehicle for accomplishing this initial reduction goal was a first commitment period commencing in 2008 and ending in 2012. The Protocol anticipates additional reductions in subsequent commitment periods. The reduction goals accepted by Annex I parties to the Convention are set out on a state-by-state basis in an annex to the Protocol.

Among the novel features of the Kyoto Protocol is its "cap and trade" architecture. The principal vehicles for implementing this regulatory design are the Protocol's "flexible mechanisms," designed to reduce the cost of implementation by expanding the range of options available to states in fulfilling their obligations under the agreement. The Protocol specifies that rights to emit may be traded among parties to the Protocol with quantified emissions reductions obligations. Second, the Protocol permits Annex I parties to undertake cooperative projects that reduce emissions of GHGs in other Annex I parties and to obtain credit for those reductions, an option known as "joint implementation." The resulting "emissions reduction units" are also tradable. Third, the Protocol establishes a "clean

D. Multilateral Environmental Agreements & Global Climate Change

development mechanism" (CDM), which provides a basis for those countries with emission reduction obligations to implement those commitments by undertaking projects in developing countries. "Certified emissions reductions units" generated by such projects may also be traded.

In 2001, the infrastructure for implementation of the Protocol was completed with the adoption of the Marrakesh Accords, a set of rules governing important aspects of the operation of the agreement such as accounting for GHG emissions and reductions. The Accords, a group of decisions of the meeting of the parties to the Protocol, also adopted a compliance mechanism.

The Kyoto Protocol was negotiated for the United States by the Clinton Administration, and the agreement owes much of its content, including the concept behind the flexible mechanisms, to U.S. governmental input. But even before the Protocol's adoption, the Senate had expressed its objection to the agreement in a resolution sponsored by Senators Byrd and Hagel and adopted by a vote of 95-0. The Clinton Administration consequently had relatively little expectation of obtaining Senate advice and consent to ratification of the Protocol by the two-thirds majority required by Article II, §2 of the Constitution. Vice President Albert Gore nonetheless signed the Kyoto Protocol in November 1998, toward the end of the Clinton presidency, presumably on the expectation that the composition of the Senate in the future would shift in a direction more receptive to the agreement.

After the Protocol's First Commitment Period. In late March 2001, the prospects for the Kyoto Protocol darkened considerably when President George W. Bush announced that the United States would not ratify the Kyoto Protocol. That action affected not only the international legal obligations of the United States, but also endangered the prospects of the Protocol's taking effect for any state. One of the conditions precedent for the Protocol's entry into force was ratification by states representing 55% of 1990 global emissions of carbon dioxide. Of that amount, the United States represented about 35%, meaning that a shortfall in ratifications from states representing only 10% of total Annex I emissions would preclude the Protocol's entry into force. After much uncertainty, the Protocol entered into force in February 2005, following the Russian Federation's ratification.

Unsurprisingly, subsequent negotiations on mitigation (emission reductions) commitments focused on next steps after the expiration of the Kyoto Protocol's first commitment period in 2012. The endpoint of that process was anticipated to be COP 15 held in Copenhagen. In the event, that meeting turned out to be at best inconclusive, and in retrospect is probably best understood as an intermediate juncture on the way to the Paris meeting at the end of 2015.

The negotiations were divided into two tracks. The first, under the Kyoto Protocol, focused on the adoption of new binding mitigation (emissions reductions) commitments by developed (Annex I) countries that are party to that instrument, known as the Ad Hoc Working Group on Further Commitments for Annex I Parties under the Kyoto Protocol. A parallel process under the Framework Convention, which involved all parties to the Convention, including the United States, was known as the Ad Hoc Working Group on Long-Term Cooperative Action Under the Convention.

After the election of President Obama, the United States vowed to reengage with the UN-sponsored multilateral process. Obama appointed Todd Stern special envoy on climate change, reporting to then-Secretary of State Hillary Rodham Clinton. Despite the high expectations and general atmosphere of goodwill, the United States went into the Copenhagen meeting in an arguably weak position. The legal authority in the U.S. Clean

Air Act, if any, for a comprehensive, nationwide cap-and-trade scheme of the sort anticipated by the Kyoto Protocol is less than clear.

The new Obama EPA nonetheless signaled its intention of utilizing existing statutory authority by also initiating the process of moving forward on motor vehicle emission standards called for by *Massachusetts v. EPA*. See Chapter 11. A bill cosponsored by Congressmen Waxman and Markey, H.R. 2454, establishing a Kyoto-style nationwide cap-and-trade scheme, had been adopted in the U.S. House of Representatives. But at the time of the Copenhagen meeting in December 2009 (and as of this writing), no analogous bill had passed the Senate. The Waxman-Markey bill established a goal of a 17% reduction in GHG emissions by 2020 and 83% by 2050, but with a reference year of 2005 arguably incommensurate with the Convention/Protocol scheme, which employs a 1990 baseline. See Chapter 14. Additionally, a proliferation of state and local initiatives had already been undertaken.

Despite all this, the U.S. proposal going into Copenhagen failed to identify quantified mitigation (emission reduction) goals. The U.S. submission uses the curious (from the perspective of the Convention and the Protocol) term "implementing agreement," impliedly suggesting that the outcome might be adopted as an executive agreement not requiring Senate advice and consent to ratification. See text on Executive Agreements in Chapter 7.

The principal issues in the multilateral negotiations culminating in the Copenhagen summit included mitigation actions (emissions reductions) for Annex I (developed) countries. Reductions on the order of 50% in CO_2 equivalents from 1990 levels by 2050 received serious discussion. Interim targets, as for 2020, were more problematic because of the near-term impacts, both political and economic.

Mitigation actions for non-Annex I (developing) countries were important because of the increasing contributions of those countries to the problem. China has now surpassed the United States as the single largest national emitter of GHGs, and there is widespread recognition that without the participation of developing countries, multilateral efforts to protect the climate will likely not be effective. Unlike the discussions of quantifiable emissions reductions for Annex I countries, the discussion for developing countries focused on "nationally appropriate mitigation actions" (NAMAs), together with funding for achieving those goals.

Despite initial gridlock at the meeting, something of a breakthrough was achieved when 20 to 25 heads of state, who very rarely engage personally in face-to-face wordsmithing at a multilateral meeting, privately negotiated what is now known as the Copenhagen Accord does not identify any global numerical targets, nor does it allude to either a second commitment period, a new agreement, or any successor instrument, either binding or nonbinding. According to news reports, the deal was clinched by a meeting between U.S. President Obama and the heads of state of the four BASIC countries: Brazil, South Africa, India, and China. The resulting Copenhagen Accord, strictly speaking, is not part of the formal UN process. Some states objected to the "undemocratic" process that had produced it. The FCCC's rules of procedure require the adoption of decisions, nonbinding though they are, by consensus, meaning the absence of objection, but in effect unanimity. Continued objections by a few states such as Venezuela, Sudan, Bolivia, and Nicaragua meant that the COP was able merely to "take[] note" of the Copenhagen Accord.

Despite defects in its legal status, its unruly drafting history and opaque language, the Copenhagen Accord collects all the strands in the negotiation in a single instrument, in effect a snapshot reflecting the status of most of the issues to that point. Although there is much rhetoric about the importance of addressing climate change, in operative terms the salient points are few and vague.

Specifically with respect to mitigation, the Accord articulates a goal of limiting the increase in global average temperature to 2° Celsius, with the possibility of more aggressive action to limit warming to no more than 1.5° Celsius after a review of the Accord's efficacy. The Copenhagen Accord is vague as to targets for both the level of emissions cuts and the date for achieving them. In contrast to the Kyoto Protocol, which specifies numerical economy-wide emissions reductions, the Copenhagen Accord does not identify any global numerical targets, nor does it allude to either a second commitment period, a new agreement, or any successor instrument, either binding or nonbinding.

The Copenhagen Accord invites non–Annex I Parties to the Convention to implement NAMAs, even though these parties do not have quantified emissions reductions obligations under the Protocol. Unlike subsequent submissions expected of Annex I states, NAMAs were not anticipated to be, and have not been, framed in terms of quantified reduction targets. Rather, NAMAs have tended to be phrased in sector-specific terms—as in reduction in deforestation or implementation of best practices in manufacturing (Brazil), as a reduction in energy intensity per unit GDP (China, India), or as curtailing emissions that otherwise would have taken place in a business-as-usual scenario without promising actual reductions (South Africa, Mexico).

COP 15 and its principal output, the Copenhagen Accord, snatched out of a chaotic soup, may have muddied the legal and policy situation more than clarified it. The uncertain and indeterminate legal form of the Accord and its nearly incoherent text mirror the turbulent setting that gave rise to it. The Accord addresses both mitigation and adaptation by developing countries, which in the FCCC context are understood to be distinct from one another. Similarly, the two-track process, one expressly confined to the Protocol and the other under the Convention, appears to have been conflated into a single product, without clear distinctions between the two undertakings. The Accord's legal status does not even rise to that of a decision, itself understood to be formally nonbinding. Instead, the Accord exists in a legal limbo, at least formally disconnected from the FCCC process. Perhaps most importantly, the Accord is critically lacking in the sort of precision with respect to mitigation obligations required to retard, reduce, and reverse the worst effects of anthropogenically induced climate warming.

Consequently, the text of the Copenhagen Accord was largely a disappointment, in failing to articulate meaningful consensus-based global goals going forward. By comparison with the structure of the Kyoto Protocol, the Accord, indeed, amounts to backtracking in terms of precision and ambition. But if nothing else, the Copenhagen Accord served as a vehicle for both Annex I and non–Annex I states voluntarily to identify their intentions with respect to mitigation in a pledge-and-review mode.

In its submission to Annex I of the Copenhagen Accord, in which states with economy-wide mitigation (emissions reduction) obligations in the Kyoto Protocol identified subsequent goals in a nonbinding mode, the United States pledged, using a base year of 2005, emissions reductions for the year 2020 "[i]n the range of 17%, in conformity with anticipated U.S. energy and climate legislation, recognizing that the final target will be reported to the Secretariat in light of enacted legislation." In a footnote, the United States clarified that "[t]he pathway set forth in pending legislation would entail a 30% reduction in 2025 and a 42% reduction in 2030, in line with the goal to reduce emissions by 83% by 2050."

From Durban to Paris. The 2009 Copenhagen meeting was at best inconclusive. Although it fell well short of producing the hoped-for major breakthrough in the form of a new, comprehensive agreement, it did serve as an occasion for 46 non–Annex I states to offer mitigation commitments for the first time in the form of nonbinding NAMAs and for

Annex I states to identify their future mitigation goals, also—and in contrast to the Kyoto Protocol—in a nonbinding format.

After that, multilateral efforts regrouped around a new goal of Paris in 2015, this time in a more structured manner with clearer goals agreed in incremental fashion along the way. After the disappointing Copenhagen outputs, the FCCC negotiations were somewhat reinvigorated at COP 17 held in Durban, South Africa at the end of 2011. There, the parties to both the Convention and the Protocol embarked on a stopgap effort to address the then-looming end of the first commitment period under Kyoto, as well as further collective action thereafter.

The Durban meeting took a nonbinding decision proposing an amendment to extend the Kyoto Protocol for a second commitment period, beginning on January 1, 2013, the day after the expiration of the first commitment period, through the end of 2017 or 2020. Consistent with the requirements of the Convention and Protocol, the Amendment was formally adopted the next year in Doha, Qatar, clarifying that the second commitment period extends until 2020. A total of 144 instruments of acceptance are required for the entry into force of the Amendment.

In less auspicious developments, Canada formally withdrew from the Kyoto Protocol on the day after the end of COP 17, after widespread acknowledgment that it would not achieve its Kyoto target of a 6% reduction in GHG emissions by reference to the base year of 1990. Among other things, this action might reduce the likelihood of sanctions against Canada by the Compliance Committee established by the Marrakesh Rules. Informal reports suggested that Canadian emissions have increased during that period by 35% or more. Moreover, Japan and the Russian Federation stated that they did not intend to accept new obligations in a second commitment period, positions indicated by black boxes in the proposed new reduction schedule for all three countries. The United States, still not a party to the Kyoto Protocol, was formally not part of this process, despite having made nonbinding representations in 2009 in Copenhagen.

COP 17 created an Ad Hoc Working Group on the Durban Platform for Enhanced Action (ADP). The ADP was mandated "to develop a protocol, another legal instrument or an agreed outcome with legal force under the Convention applicable to all Parties," to be adopted at COP 21 in Paris at the end of 2015 and to take effect in 2020—that is, at the end of the Kyoto Protocol's second commitment period as set out in the Doha Amendment to that instrument. In the same decision, the COP launched a related undertaking at closing the "ambition gap with a view to ensuring the highest possible mitigation efforts by all Parties"—that is, encouraging more aggressive emission reduction commitments.

COP 19, held in Warsaw in 2013, instructed the ADP to identify "elements for a draft negotiating text . . . including . . . mitigation, adaptation, finance, technology development and transfer, capacity-building and transparency of action and support." The same decision anticipates that "intended nationally determined contributions" (INDCs) will be identified by the first quarter of 2015 "by those Parties ready to do so" with a view to ensuring the highest possible mitigation efforts by all Parties. National submissions are "without prejudice to the legal nature of the contributions."

The United States released its INDC on March 31, 2015. After years of the President's reiterating the 17% goal to be achieved by 2020, originally identified in the Waxman-Markey bill, the United States set out "an economy-wide target of reducing its greenhouse gas emissions by 26-28% below its 2005 level in 2025 and to make best efforts to reduce its emissions by 28%." This was not unexpected, as those numerical targets track those in the understanding with China reached in November 2014. Under the heading, "Domestic laws, regulations, and measures relevant to implementation," the U.S. INDC identifies

D. Multilateral Environmental Agreements & Global Climate Change

"completed" regulatory actions, including mandated increases in vehicle fuel efficiency. Proposed actions underway include EPA's proposed regulations, to be "finalize[d] by summer 2015 . . . to cut carbon pollution from new and existing power plants," which was formally released at the beginning of August 2015 as the Clean Power Plan. Unlike the European Union and Norwegian INDCs, both of which identify their contributions as "binding," the U.S. INDC does not identify the legal force of its proposed targets.[13]

The United States position as to the legal form of what came to be known as the Paris Outcome was set out by Mr. Stern shortly before the Paris meeting:

> We have strongly backed the notion of non-legally binding targets as the best way to ensure broad participation in the agreement. We concluded early on that many countries would be unwilling to put forward legally binding targets and, as noted, we are not willing to accept the Kyoto approach of binding targets for developed countries only. Also—contrary to much conventional wisdom—we think that non-binding targets will produce greater ambition because many countries would low-ball legally binding commitments out of fear for the consequences of missing their targets.[14]

The resulting Paris Agreement—even the potential title of "protocol" proved to be controversial, thanks to Kyoto—marks the reengagement of the United States with the multilateral climate regime. Requiring submissions in the form of "nationally determined contributions" from all parties to the on a five-year cycle, the Paris Agreement among other things is intended to overcome the "original sin" of the Kyoto Protocol, the cleavage of the world into those states that have emissions reductions obligations (mitigation) undertakings, and those that do not.

Paris Agreement

Dec. 12, 2015, http://unfccc.int/resource/docs/2015/cop21/eng/l09r01.pdf

Article 2

1. This Agreement, in enhancing the implementation of the Convention, including its objective, aims to strengthen the global response to the threat of climate change, in the context of sustainable development and efforts to eradicate poverty, including by:

(a) Holding the increase in the global average temperature to well below 2°C above pre-industrial levels and to pursue efforts to limit the temperature increase to 1.5°C above pre-industrial levels, recognizing that this would significantly reduce the risks and impacts of climate change;

(b) Increasing the ability to adapt to the adverse impacts of climate change and foster climate resilience and low greenhouse gas emissions development, in a manner that does not threaten food production;

---

13. Much of this material is taken from Wirth, The International and Domestic Law of Climate Change: A Binding International Agreement Without the Senate or Congress?, 39 Harv. Envtl. L. Rev. 515 (2015).

14. Testimony of Special Envoy for Climate Change Todd D. Stern, Senate Foreign Relation Committee Subcommittee on Multilateral International Development, Multilateral Institutions, and International Economic, Energy, and Environmental Policy, Oct. 20, 2015.

(c) Making finance flows consistent with a pathway towards low greenhouse gas emissions and climate resilient development.

2. This Agreement will be implemented to reflect equity and the principle of common but differentiated responsibilities and respective capabilities, in the light of different national circumstances . . .

Article 4

1. . . . Parties aim to reach global peaking of greenhouse gas emissions as soon as possible, recognizing that peaking will take longer for developing country Parties, and to undertake rapid reductions thereafter in accordance with best available science, so as to achieve a balance between anthropogenic emissions by sources and removals by sinks of greenhouse gases in the second half of this century, on the basis of equity, and in the context of sustainable development and efforts to eradicate poverty.

2. Each Party shall prepare, communicate and maintain successive nationally determined contributions that it intends to achieve. Parties shall pursue domestic mitigation measures with the aim of achieving the objectives of such contributions.

3. Each Party's successive nationally determined contribution will represent a progression beyond the Party's then current nationally determined contribution and reflect its highest possible ambition, reflecting its common but differentiated responsibilities and respective capabilities, in the light of different national circumstances.

4. Developed country Parties should continue taking the lead by undertaking economy-wide absolute emission reduction targets. Developing country Parties should continue enhancing their mitigation efforts, and are encouraged to move over time towards economy-wide emission reduction or limitation targets in the light of different national circumstances . . .

Article 9

1. Developed country Parties shall provide financial resources to assist developing country Parties with respect to both mitigation and adaptation in continuation of their existing obligations under the Convention.

2. Other Parties are encouraged to provide or continue to provide such support voluntarily . . .

Article 13

1. In order to build mutual trust and confidence and to promote effective implementation, an enhanced transparency framework for action and support, with built-in flexibility which takes into account Parties' different capacities and builds upon collective experience is hereby established . . .

4. The transparency arrangements under the Convention, including national communications, biennial reports and biennial update reports, international assessment and review and international consultation and analysis, shall form part of the experience drawn upon for the development of the modalities, procedures and guidelines under . . . this Article.

5. The purpose of the framework for transparency of action is to provide a clear understanding of climate change action in the light of the objective of the Convention as set out in its Article 2, including clarity and tracking of progress towards achieving Parties' individual nationally determined contributions under Article 4 . . .

Article 15

1. A mechanism to facilitate implementation of and promote compliance with the provisions of this Agreement is hereby established.

2. The mechanism referred to in paragraph 1 of this Article shall consist of a committee that shall be expert-based and facilitative in nature and function in a manner that is

D. Multilateral Environmental Agreements & Global Climate Change

transparent, non-adversarial and non-punitive. The committee shall pay particular attention to the respective national capabilities and circumstances of Parties....

3. The committee shall operate under the modalities and procedures adopted by the Conference of the Parties serving as the meeting of the Parties to the Paris Agreement at its first session and report annually to the Conference of the Parties serving as the meeting of the Parties to the Paris Agreement.

COMMENTARY & QUESTIONS

1. Leaving a 2°C world to future generations? The 2° goal in article 2, paragraph 1(a) was articulated, as in Copenhagen, as an important goal from the beginning of the negotiations. The inclusion of the 1.5° option was a coup for countries such as small island states likely to be most severely affected by climate-induced sea level rise. Yet the IPCC's Fifth Assessment Report identifies limiting warming to 1.5° as virtually impossible, and a COP decision accompanying the Paris Agreement acknowledges "with concern that the estimated aggregate greenhouse gas emission levels in 2025 and 2030 resulting from the intended nationally determined contributions [submitted by 188 states by the end of the Paris meeting] do not fall within least-cost 2° scenarios." What mechanisms, if any, are contained in the Paris Agreement to close the gap between the ambition represented by these anticipated efforts and the 2° goal?

2. Few words, much meaning. Take a close look at article 4, paragraph 1. IPCC scenarios identify the concept of emissions "peaking"—starting on a downward trajectory—as a critical component of achieving the 2° goal, let alone achieving a carbon-neutral world. For instance, China's pre-Paris INDC identifies a goal of peaking that country's emissions by 2030, an aim identified a year earlier in a bilateral undertaking with the U.S. How does the Paris Agreement address this issue? The Copenhagen Accord dealt with the question similarly. The language "so as to achieve a balance between anthropogenic emissions by sources and removals by sinks of greenhouse gases in the second half of this century" was understood as articulating a goal of net carbon neutrality, although not necessary zero emissions, in the second half of the twenty-first century. What does the qualifying language "on the basis of equity, and in the context of sustainable development and efforts to eradicate poverty" mean in operational terms? To what extent does the operative structure of the Paris Agreement assure that the world will achieve these goals?

3. The Paris Agreement in U.S. law. The Obama Administration, presumably based on the learning of Kyoto and consistent with other recent multilateral initiatives such as the nuclear deal with Iran, has made every effort to steer clear of concluding an agreement that could be considered a "treaty" under article II, §2 of the Constitution. It simultaneously had to "thread the needle" to comply with the Doha mandate of achieving an "an agreed outcome with legal force." This issue blew up in the press before the Paris meeting, and then receded into the background after the Paris terror attacks of November 13, 2015. As documented by multiple news accounts, the U.S. delegation held up final adoption of the Paris Agreement, insisting on the hortatory "should" as opposed to the obligatory "shall" in the forward-looking undertaking of article 4, paragraph 4, requiring Parties progressively to ratchet the level of ambition in identifying subsequent nationally-determined contributions.

As identified in Chapter 7's notes on executive agreements, the reporting and other "procedural" obligations in the Paris Agreement are presumably authorized by the Senate's prior advice and consent to the Framework Convention and therefore can be undertaken by the U.S. as an executive agreement without Congressional participation. With respect to the pre-Paris INDC, the U.S. arguably could have made a binding commitment as to the substantive numerical mitigation commitment, which as a domestic matter are supported by legal authority already delegated to the President by Congress, in the form of an executive agreement. See Wirth, The International and Domestic Law of Climate Change: A Binding International Agreement Without the Senate or Congress?, 39 Harv. Envtl. L. Rev. 515 (2015). What difference does the domestic legal form of the Paris Agreement make internationally? At the national level?

4. Common but differentiated responsibilities redux. One of the major accomplishments of the Paris Agreement is to overcome what one commentator has described as the "rigid, debilitating divide between industrial and developing countries," in major part by including *all* parties to the Agreement in the successive identification of mitigation undertaking in the form of nonbinding nationally determined contributions. Presumably this approach is something closer to the structure of article 5 of the Montreal Protocol, which gives low-CFC-consuming countries a grace period while including them in the agreement's broader reduction obligations. But consistent with Principle 7 of the Rio Declaration, the Paris Agreement continues to recognize the principle of common but differentiated responsibilities. Based on your reading of the excerpt above where and, in an operational sense, exactly how would you see the Principle at work?

5. Putting U.S. money where our mouth is. At the 2009 Copenhagen meeting, then-Secretary of State Hilary Rodham Clinton promised a $100 billion contribution to the Green Climate Fund and other financial mechanisms designed to help developing countries to undertake mitigation efforts, to conserve and enhance forest cover, and to deal with the consequences of climate change (adaptation). Before the Paris meeting, President Obama reiterated that commitment, with a goal of 2020. In the nonbinding decision accompanying the Paris Agreement, developed countries agreed to "set a new collective quantified goal from a floor of USD 100 billion *per year*" (emphasis added). The $100 billion annual figure has taken on immense significance in the negotiations, but it is uncertain which countries will contribute how much, and when. Why might that be a particularly difficult part of the deal for the United States to implement domestically?

6. A celestial perspective on the climate negotiations. Several months in advance of the Paris meeting, Pope Francis released a new encyclical focusing on climate, "Laudato si'," http://w2.vatican.va/content/francesco/en/encyclicals/documents/papa-francesco_20150524_enciclica-laudato-si.html. In addition to stressing the moral and ethical dimension of climate change, the encyclical drew attention to climate change's impact on the poor and the potential inequity of relying on market mechanisms for implementation of climate-related mitigation goals. How would you evaluate the Pope's unprecedented role in the negotiations, plainly designed to influence their outcome? To what extent might the encyclical catalyze the development of an international customary law of climate? Intensely-negotiated multilateral environmental instruments like the Paris Agreement, reliant on precise, often numerical commitments, are generally taken to be the antithesis of custom because of their expressly negotiated character. But from the time of the seventeenth century international legal scholar Hugo Grotius[15] or earlier, international law—the "law of nations"—was understood to reflect a higher moral, ethical, and even divinely-inspired legal order than might be captured by the collective self-interest of sovereign states.

---

15. A voice from the beginning of public international law as a legal regime, as noted in Chapter 7.

E. International Institutions

International environmental agreements such as the UNFCCC and the Paris Agreement exist in a larger international legal universe in which they are embedded within other international institutions and commitments. As an emerging environmental problem like global warming begins to penetrate the consciousness of the public, environmental activists, and governmental decisionmakers, tensions or even outright clashes between public policy goals as pursued by other mission-oriented international institutions may appear—a problem antiseptically dubbed "multilateral coherence" in international bureaucratese. Friction with two international institutions created to promote economic development, the World Bank and the World Trade Organization, has provoked fierce criticism of those institutions from environmental NGOs and equally vigorous defenses by the institutions themselves and constituencies whose interests they promote. The First Law of Ecology—everything is connected to everything else—applies not only to ecosystems but also to international institutions such as the Bank and the WTO.

1. The World Bank

One of the World Bank's principal functions, according to its constitutive multilateral treaty, is "to promote economic development, increase productivity and thus raise standards of living in the less-developed areas of the world . . . in particular by providing financing to meet their important developmental requirements." Similar international institutions, designed on the model of the World Bank—including the Inter-American Development Bank, the African Development Bank, the Asian Development Bank, and the European Bank for Reconstruction and Development—perform similar functions on a regional basis.

The World Bank consists of a number of "windows," each of which technically is a separate international organization established by a distinct treaty entitled the "Articles of Agreement." The two most important of these windows are the International Bank for Reconstruction and Development (IBRD), established in 1945, which lends roughly at prevailing market rates of interest; and the International Development Association (IDA), established in 1965, which lends to the very poorest countries in the form of concessional "credits" that carry very low interest rates or no interest whatsoever. As of this writing, the IBRD has 188 member states and IDA 173. In fiscal year 2015, the IBRD and IDA together approved over 300 "operations" in the form of loans and credits totaling more than U.S. $42 billion, many of which financed major development projects. The IBRD and IDA together are often known simply as the "World Bank."

The IBRD and IDA share common institutions within the Bank. One Governor, ordinarily that country's finance minister, represents each member state at the Bank. The U.S. Governor is the Secretary of the Treasury. The Board of Governors meets as a body only once a year and in practice gives only very general guidance to the Bank's professional staff. Twenty-five Executive Directors, appointed or elected by member country governments, have offices physically located in the World Bank headquarters complex in Washington and exercise day-to-day authority on behalf of the Governors by approving staff proposals for individual loans. The U.S., Japan, Germany, the United Kingdom, France, and China each have a single Executive Director. Other Executive Directors represent groups of states, some of them quite odd, for example, the Netherlands, Armenia, Bosnia & Herzegovina, Bulgaria, Croatia, Cyprus, Georgia, Israel, Macedonia, Moldova, Montenegro, Romania, and Ukraine. The individual commonly identified as the Executive Director for Canada also represents most of the Caribbean countries.

The Board of Executive Directors takes decisions by weighted majority voting. Votes are allocated according to a formula that depends on the number of a member state's shares and its capital contribution to the institution. So, among the current IBRD members, the U.S. now exercises somewhat more than 16% of the total voting power in the IBRD, more than twice as much as the next largest shareholder, Japan. No single shareholder holds enough votes unilaterally to direct the Bank as an institution to take a particular action, including the approval or rejection of a particular lending proposal. Both the IBRD and IDA Articles of Agreement prohibit political activity by specifying that "[t]he [Bank] and its officers shall not interfere in the political affairs of any member; nor shall they be influenced in their decisions by the political character of the member or members concerned. Only economic considerations shall be relevant to their decisions, and these considerations shall be weighed impartially in order to achieve the purposes stated [in the Articles of Agreement]."

Only the governments of member states may borrow from the IBRD and IDA, which do not lend to private parties. Loan agreements between borrowing country governments on the one hand and the IBRD or IDA on the other have the status of binding treaties under international law. Loan agreements may contain certain promises or "conditions" that the borrowing country government agrees to perform in return for the loan — including, of course, repayment of the loan proceeds — but perhaps other requirements as well. In recent years, the Bank's increasing tendency to include environmental or "green" conditionality in its lending program has created some friction with borrowing country governments.

The World Bank's professional staff, headed by the President of the Bank, is somewhat analogous to the secretariat of other international organizations. Bank staff work for the international institution of the World Bank and do not represent the interests of their own national governments. Bank staff are specifically charged with the operational task of preparing or "appraising" specific loan proposals for approval by the Bank's Board of Executive Directors. Lending proposals must be agreed between the professional staff and the borrowing country government before presentation to the Board of Executive Directors for subsequent approval. Bank staff may choose not to pursue negotiations on a loan proposal, or negotiations between the borrowing country government and the Bank may break down. For either of these reasons, a particular loan proposal may not reach the Board.

In the fall of 1993, in response to continued criticism about the Bank's environmental performance, the World Bank's Board of Executive Directors adopted a resolution creating a new Inspection Panel. The Panel is intended to serve as a vehicle for ensuring full implementation by Bank staff of Bank Operational Directives (ODs) and other internal Bank policies. The Panel provides new opportunities for private parties — principally NGOs — to initiate proceedings to encourage performance of international standards. NGOs may seek review of both failures by the Bank's professional staff to observe that institution's own internal standards and inadequate supervision by Bank staff on the implementation of loan covenants by borrowing country governments. The Panel consists of three independent experts appointed in their personal capacities. Although created as an investigatory body, many of its pronouncements have an adjudicatory character. By creating rights of access for NGOs, the Panel is a major innovation in public international law. The Inspection Panel is also the first time an international institution has created a mechanism for independent oversight of its own operations.

Nonetheless, the resolution creating the Panel establishes some potentially significant limitations to its authority. Only organizations, and not individuals, may file a "request for inspection." The Panel is confined to considering "failure of the Bank to follow its operational policies and procedures with respect to the design, appraisal and/or implementation of a project financed by the Bank." These internal Bank standards, which govern such issues as the prior evaluation of environmental impacts, involuntary resettlement, and indigenous peoples, do not necessarily reflect customary norms in areas such as human rights. The Panel, after receiving a request for inspection, may proceed only with the subsequent approval of the Bank's Board of Executive Directors. Despite these weaknesses, the Inspection Panel creates entirely new formal opportunities for nonstate actors to assure compliance with international standards, both by the Bank's professional staff and, indirectly, by borrowing country governments.

In June 1999, the International Campaign for Tibet, a U.S. NGO, filed a request for inspection of the Bank's proposed Western Poverty Reduction Project in China. The request challenged one component of the $311 million project located in Qinghai Province, which included resettling nearly 58,000 subsistence farmers earning about $60 a year from the hillsides of eastern Qinghai (the "move-out" area) to a new irrigation project involving construction of a new 400-foot high dam (the "move-in" area). The requesters complained that the project would involve the relocation of other ethnic groups into a traditionally Tibetan area and that the project would have adverse environmental effects. The Panel reported its findings less than a year after receiving the request.

Inspection Panel's Report and Findings on the Qinghai Project: Executive Summary

World Bank RQ99/3 (2000)

If there is no alternative there can be no choice.... One of the most noticeable and significant weaknesses of the [environmental] assessments [EAs] is that investment and project alternatives are neither identified nor systematically compared. For all practical purposes, the Environmental Assessment avoids consideration of alternatives, both for poverty reduction in the Move-out areas and for sites in the Move-in area. From the documentation, it is not possible to deduce whether the Qinghai Project as proposed is the best way for the Bank to meet the Project's objectives or to ensure that the Bank's safeguard policies are being respected.

Management failed to ensure that those responsible for the EA understood their brief to include an examination of alternatives to resettlement in both the Move-out and Move-in areas. Instead, the Panel found that they understood the main purpose of their studies to be to assist the optimal resettlement of around 60,000 people from the Move-out area into the Balong-Xiangride irrigation area. The same is true of the Social Assessment. There is no systematic study of *in situ* alternatives to resettlement, or of alternative resettlement sites, or of alternative development plans for the national minorities affected within the Move-in area.

Why the Bank accepted Assessments conducted in such circumscribed and limiting manner is unclear. Whatever the reasons, the Panel finds that the Assessments do not make any meaningful analysis of realistic project alternatives as required by Bank policy.

One of the most important decisions (perhaps the most crucial) that Management must make concerning the environmental assessment of any project is the category of the assessment that will be undertaken. Under OD 4.01 [on environmental assessment], this critical judgment is made in the first instance by the Task Manager (now Task Team Leader), with the concurrence of the regional environment unit. The project is assigned to Category "A," in which case a full Environment Assessment (EA) is required, or a Category "B," in which case a full EA is not required, but an environmental analysis is, or a Category "C," in which case no environmental analysis is required. . . . The OD further provides that a full EA is required if a project is likely to have significant adverse impacts that may be sensitive, irreversible, and diverse. . . . This critical decision of the category of the EA is made at a very early stage in the project cycle, but the OD permits a later revision of the category as new information becomes available. . . .

The initial decision to assign "B," taken on January 8, 1998, was made before the Task Team leader, or any other Bank official associated with the decision, had an opportunity to visit the Move-in area. . . . The first Bank official involved in the decision to visit the Project site was the consultant who was engaged to be responsible for the environmental impact assessment aspects of the Project. Following his visit, on March 13, 1998, he raised a number of issues with senior staff and recommended the re-classification of the Qinghai component as an "A." Senior staff responded at length, citing reasons why it should remain a "B." Management was aware of the A/B debate, but did not intervene. The Project concept Document meeting of April 14, 1998, in effect confirmed a "B. . . ."

After reviewing the screening process, the Panel finds that management's decision to classify the project as a "B" was not in compliance with OD 4.01. Several components of the Project fall within the illustrative list of "A" projects in Annex E, i.e., dams and reservoirs, irrigation, and resettlement. And the impacts qualify as "sensitive" since vulnerable ethnic minorities are affected and involuntary resettlement is involved. . . .

The proposed in-migration to Dulan county will more than double its population. The proposed new towns will each have populations five times as large as Xiangride, the nearest established town to the main irrigation site. This will lead to further induced development, on which OD 4.01 lays great stress. The dam, irrigation and resettlement parts of the Qinghai Project are treated as though they were to take place in a regional vacuum. The potential impact of this development on the network of social, commercial and political interactions that exists in Dulan county and Xiangride Township has not been considered. There is no indication of how these communities and their populations will be affected, for better or worse, by the Project. Without this assessment, the Bank's policy goal of enhancing Project benefits has no substance or meaning.

The EA and other Project documents fail to consider the appropriateness of implanting large-scale irrigated agriculture in this Region. It does not examine its suitability or viability in comparison with the traditional forms of land use, including agropastoralism, sedentary pastoralism, semi-sedentary pastoralism (semi-nomadism), and migratory pastoralism involving the herding of sheep and other animals. There appears simply to be an assumption that irrigated agriculture is "a good thing" without consideration of alternatives and relative costs. . . .

The information on the biodiversity of the area is very sketchy and inadequate. It does not incorporate an assessment of the diversity encountered with regard to distribution, frequency/rarity and conservation status. . . . Extensive exploitation of oil, natural gas and minerals is carried out in parts of the Qaidam basin and test drillings have been undertaken near the Project area. No mention is made in the EA of the general economic importance of oil and minerals in the Province, or its possible effects on the Project areas, or of any drilling activities in the Region.

Given the scale of absolute habitat conversion in the Project area, involving 19,000 hectares of land that will be irrigated, and construction developments such as the dam, canals, townships, villages and roads—all adding up to an estimated 21,444 hectares—it cannot be asserted with confidence that possible critical natural habitats will not be lost. The necessary baseline information is not available in the Assessment. The Panel is therefore of

E. International Institutions

the view that the Project is in contravention of the Bank's policy OP 4.04, in regard to the significant conversion of critical natural habitats.

The Panel finds that the Environmental Assessment of the Qinghai Project is not in compliance with Bank policies as set out in OD 4.01.

COMMENTARY & QUESTIONS

1. Environmental impact assessment and foreign aid. The Bank's loan preparation process is governed by a series of instruments known as Operational Policies (OPs), Bank Procedures (BPs), and Good Practices (GPs). In principle, the first two categories are binding and the third advisory, but the force of the instruments may vary depending on their terms. Two of those instruments, OP 4.01 and BP 4.01, require environmental assessments to be conducted as part of the loan appraisal process. This process is the equivalent of NEPA in the U.S. or environmental impact assessment as specified in Principle 17 of the Rio Declaration. Indeed, the Inspection Panel's report reads very much like a U.S. court opinion in NEPA cases involving judicial review of federal agency action, as in Chapter 8. The U.S. bilateral assistance agency, the Agency for International Development, has similar requirements. As described by the Inspection Panel, the World Bank—like the regional development banks for Latin America, Asia, and Eastern Europe and the former Soviet Union—categorizes projects according to the magnitude of their impacts and pegs the detail of the analysis to that determination. A setting involving external financing presents somewhat different issues from a purely domestic project. For example, the Bank's policies specify that the borrowing country government is responsible for carrying out the EA, including hiring consultants, while Bank staff exercise an oversight role. What might be the weak links in the multilateral aid process from the point of view of the environment? From the point of view of an individual in a borrowing country whose livelihood might be affected by a Bank-financed project?

2. Unilateralism at the World Bank. In 1987 the U.S., in response to concerns about the World Bank's environmental performance, adopted new legislation addressing the role of environment in the U.S.'s future participation in the World Bank. The legislation is specifically targeted at the U.S. Executive Director to the World Bank and the Department of the Treasury, to which the U.S. Executive Director reports. For example, 22 U.S.C. §262m-7, the so-called Pelosi Amendment, establishes standards of performance in the area of environmental impact assessment by the multilateral development banks as a condition of favorable votes by the U.S. Executive Director to those institutions. Partially as a result of the legislation, but also on his own initiative, in 1988 then-Secretary of the Treasury James Baker issued instructions to the U.S. Executive Director to the World Bank concerning the manner in which the U.S. would exercise its vote within that institution on projects that could affect tropical forests. The World Bank's staff and other countries have on occasion vehemently protested the congressional legislation and Baker instructions as unilateral attempts to leverage change at the Bank. In particular, these actions of both the Congress and the executive branch have been labeled by the Bank's professional staff as "inconsistent with multilateralism." What arguments can you make in support of that assertion? As a representative of U.S. Department of the Treasury, how would you respond?

3. Foreign aid for the global environment. Article 11 of the UNFCCC, entitled "Financial Mechanism," responds to the demands of developing countries during the negotiation of the Climate Convention for additional resources to facilitate their contributions to reducing global warming. Paragraph 1 of that provision specifies that the operation of the financial mechanism "shall be entrusted to one or more existing international entities," a reference at that time to the Global Environment Facility (GEF). The GEF is a multilateral entity whose projects are developed and implemented by the World Bank, the United Nations Development Program, and the United Nations Environment Program. It provides developing countries with grant and concessional (low or zero interest) funding on climate change, stratospheric ozone depletion, biological diversity, international waters, land degradation, and persistent organic pollutants. The GEF has allocated $14.5 billion in grants and mobilized $75.4 billion in additional financing from other sources, including bilateral donors such as the U.S. Agency for International Development, to support almost 4000 projects. In April 2014, 30 donor-states pledged $4.43 billion more to fund the work of the GEF for the following 4 years. Notwithstanding its environmentally beneficial mission, the GEF has come under criticism from developing countries as reflecting the priorities of wealthy, industrialized donor countries and from environmentalists and human rights advocates as nothing more than a fig leaf that masks the much larger problem of environmentally and socially harmful projects like that in China. What factors would you identify as key to effective deployment of environmentally beneficial aid, and how would you structure a multilateral institution to reflect them? Or is it impossible, as some have asserted, for foreign aid to reduce global environmental threats?

4. The Inspection Panel fights for independence. The interim juncture of the inspection process at which the Bank's Board of Executive Directors must approve a request for inspection before the inspection may go forward created a great deal of tension between the Board and the Panel. Members of the Panel were publicly and vocally critical of the Bank Management's attempts to circumvent or hobble the Panel. In at least two cases, Bank Management cited remedial action plans identified by the borrower as reasons for disapproving a request for inspection. In a third, it authorized only a limited "desk study" investigation confined to information already available at the Bank's headquarters in Washington. Not coincidentally, these cases involved large and influential borrowers, Brazil and India. See The World Bank Inspection Panel: The First Four Years (1994-1998) (A. Umaña ed., 1998); Bissell, Recent Practice of the Inspection Panel of the World Bank, 91 Am. J. Int'l L. 741 (1997). In the end, the Board accepted a "tacit approval" or "nonobjection" procedure in which the Board is deemed to have consented to the Panel's recommendation to proceed with an investigation unless that recommendation is expressly disapproved by the Board. The Panel, however, is still confined to considering only compliance with internal Bank policies, a factor some critics have identified as creating an incentive to weaken those requirements. On behalf of an NGO submitting a request for inspection, what arguments could you make that the Panel nonetheless must consider customary international legal norms, multilateral treaties of general application, and widely accepted nonbinding instruments such as the Rio Declaration?

5. Are alternatives to the Bank worse? In response to the Inspection Panel's report, China announced that it intended to go forward with the Qinghai component of the Western Poverty Reduction Project without Bank funding. The Chinese Executive Director stated that "[i]t is unacceptable to my authorities that other Bank shareholders would insist on imposing additional conditions on Management's recommendations. . . . China will therefore turn to its own resources to implement the Qinghai Component of the project, and in its own way. . . . [C]ompliance policies have been interpreted by some to an extreme and used for political purposes. . . . From the very start, the whole process has been under enormous political pressure." Bank staff have often asserted that the environmental and human rights goals are better served by having the Bank involved in major projects such

E. International Institutions

as the Western Poverty Reduction Project, even if some concessions to borrowing country governments are necessary. If the Bank pulls out, they say, there will be no external checks to assure that even minimal standards are met. Do you agree with this argument? If not, how would you respond to it?

WORLD BANK PROBLEM EXERCISE

Since 2001, Bank staff have been discussing a new projected entitled "Forest Exploitation III" with the Government of Ruritania, a developing country that is a member of both the IBRD and IDA. Exploitation III would be financed by a $60 million IBRD loan to the Government of Ruritania. As suggested by the name, this project, if approved, would be the third in a series of World Bank-funded projects designed to build penetration roads into tropical forests and to facilitate commercial timbering operations in Ruritania's dwindling primary tropical rainforests, which are a significant repository for biological diversity. Exploitation III, according to Bank staff, is expected to produce considerable economic growth in Ruritania primarily through increased exportation of raw and semiprocessed timber to markets in industrialized countries. Bank staff estimate that the Government of Ruritania should be able to repay the loan at prevailing market rates of interest within 10 years, primarily as a result of fees to be charged by the Government for leases issued to foreign corporations granting those corporations permission to log identified tracts of government lands containing primary forest.

About a month ago, Bank staff announced that Exploitation III was ready for presentation to the Bank's Board of Executive Directors for that body's approval. The Government of Ruritania has prepared an environmental assessment, and Bank staff and the Government of Ruritania have asserted that all requirements of the Bank's operational policy on environmental assessment and all other Bank environmental criteria have been satisfied. In particular, the Government of Ruritania has stated that it is prepared to agree, as a condition of the World Bank's approval of Exploitation III, to measures that the Government and the Bank's professional staff believe would reduce, but not eliminate, adverse environmental impacts from the project.

After being lobbied heavily by a coalition of British and Ruritanian NGOs calling itself End Unsustainable Funding (ENUF), the Government of the United Kingdom and the UK Executive Director concluded that the UK could not support Exploitation III. Indeed, the British Government was so convinced of the environmental defects in the loan that it engaged in some last-minute but highly effective diplomacy to muster opposition to the loan among other important donor countries, including the U.S.

Accordingly, at its meeting held last Thursday, the Bank's Board of Executive Directors—over the vociferous objections of the Executive Director for Ruritania—narrowly disapproved the staff's proposal to finance Forest Exploitation III, the first time the Board had ever formally disapproved a loan proposal by recorded vote for environmental reasons. Every Executive Director who voted against the loan publicly stated that he or she was doing so strictly because of concerns about environmental defects in the project. Many of the Executive Directors, moreover, referenced the loan's failure to meet the standards set out in the Nonlegally Binding Authoritative Statement of Principles for a Global Consensus on the Management, Conservation, and Sustainable Development of All Types of Forests, a soft law instrument similar in form to the Rio Declaration that was adopted at the UNCED in 1992.

Outraged, the Executive Director for Ruritania immediately sent a memorandum to the Chairman of the Board of Executive Directors and the President of the World Bank, which reads in its entirety as follows:

> I respectfully request you to declare today's vote on Forest Exploitation III to be illegal and to present this loan for reconsideration to the Board of Executive Directors as soon as possible. In particular, the disapproval of Forest Exploitation III based on false allegations by the United Kingdom and other donor states:
>
> (1) violates the sovereignty of Ruritania and illegally intrudes into the Government of Ruritania's exclusive prerogative to govern within its territory;
> (2) violates Article 2, ¶7, of the Charter of the United Nations, which provides that "[n]othing . . . shall authorize the United Nations [or any specialized agency thereof such as the World Bank] to intervene in matters that are essentially within the domestic jurisdiction of any state";
> (3) violates the prohibition in the IBRD and IDA Articles of Agreement specifying that "[t]he [Bank] and its officers shall not interfere in the political affairs of any member";
> (4) violates the provision in the IBRD and IDA Articles of Agreement specifying that "[o]nly economic considerations shall be relevant to [the Bank's] decisions"; and
> (5) violates fundamental principles of international law in attempting to apply the UNCED forest principles—a nonbinding instrument not accepted by the Government of Ruritania—as a condition of a World Bank loan.

As a staff lawyer at the World Bank, how would you respond on behalf of the Chairman of the Board and the President to the Executive Director for Ruritania defending the validity of the Board of Executive Directors' vote on Forest Exploitation III? You should be prepared to argue on behalf of your client that each of the five points raised in the Executive Director for Ruritania's letter is incorrect.

2. The World Trade Organization

> *Free trade is not a principle, it is an expedient.*
> —Benjamin Disraeli, Speech on import duties, April 25, 1843

Until the mid-1990s, the principal multilateral instrument governing trade relationships among states was the General Agreement on Tariffs and Trade (GATT). The GATT was adopted soon after World War II to encourage liberalized trade relations among states. Originally a formal International Trade Organization (ITO) was envisioned to be established by what came to be known as the Havana Charter. In the event, there was no agreement on the establishment of a new international organization, and the agreement now known as the GATT was provisionally adopted. Over time, it acquired the status of a de facto international organization, with a secretariat located in Geneva.

The basic obligations or "disciplines" found in the GATT that relate to environment, also noted in Chapter 7, are:

- the most-favored nation (MFN) obligation in Article I, which prohibits discrimination among imported products on the basis of their national origin;
- the national treatment requirement in Article III, which prohibits discrimination between foreign products and "like" domestic products; and
- a prohibition on quantitative restrictions in Article XI, which precludes numerical restrictions on imports and exports.

E. International Institutions

Article XX of the GATT contains a number of exemptions from the General Agreement for specific categories of national measures that otherwise would violate these three basic disciplines. Of particular importance in the fields of environment and public health are two express exceptions: one in paragraph (b) for measures "necessary to protect human, animal or plant life or health"; and another in paragraph (g) for measures "relating to the conservation of exhaustible natural resources if such measures are made effective in conjunction with restrictions on domestic production or consumption."

The potential for these international obligations substantially to constrain domestic environmental policies hit home in 1991 when a GATT dispute settlement panel issued its report reviewing a challenge initiated by Mexico. The challenge objected to a U.S. ban on importation of tuna that had been caught through the use of fishing practices that injure and kill dolphins. In the Eastern Tropical Pacific Ocean (ETP), schools of tuna often travel below pods of air-breathing dolphin, which are visible at or just below the surface of the water as they break the surface to breathe and leap into the air. Taking advantage of this relationship, tuna fishing fleets from several nations, including the U.S. and numerous South and Central American states such as Ecuador, Mexico, Panama, and Venezuela, typically targeted the visible dolphin herds to locate schools of yellowfin tuna below. In a practice known as "setting on dolphin," fishing boats encircle pods of air-breathing dolphin with a "purse-seine" net to capture the tuna below. Setting on dolphin entangles many dolphin in the nets above the tuna, holding them below the surface so they cannot breathe, resulting in widespread injury and death to dolphin. Although dolphin-safe netting devices and methods exist, they cost more and require more attention, so that unregulated fishing fleets have tended to continue slaughtering dolphin to catch tuna.

In response to this problem, the MMPA, enacted in 1972, establishes industrywide practices for tuna harvesting designed to prevent the incidental "taking" of marine mammals, specifically various species of dolphins. The law prohibits the incidental taking of marine mammals by U.S. fishermen unless a permit has been issued by the National Marine Fisheries Service (NMFS) of the NOAA, located within the Department of Commerce. Under the permitting program, no more than 20,500 dolphins may be incidentally killed or injured each year by the U.S. fleet fishing in the ETP. These provisions apply as well to all entities and vessels subject to U.S. jurisdiction, on the high seas and in U.S. territory, including the territorial sea of the U.S. and the U.S. exclusive economic zone.

The U.S. fleet is generally in compliance with these requirements. Foreign fleets not subject to U.S. jurisdiction, however, have had considerably higher dolphin mortality rates. To address this problem, the MMPA contains provisions that apply specifically to imports of tuna and that require the U.S. Customs Service to "ban the importation of commercial fish or products from fish which have been caught with commercial fishing technology which results in the incidental kill or incidental serious injury of ocean mammals in excess of U.S. standards." Dissatisfied with executive branch inaction with respect to foreign tuna, Congress amended the statute in 1984 and 1988 with increasingly specific requirements that require that the harvesting country's tuna fleet does not exceed 1.25 times the average taking rate for U.S. vessels.

By 1990, the Secretary of Commerce had neither issued findings of comparability nor banned tuna imports from the offending nations. Frustrated with this delay, the Earth Island Institute, a private environmental organization, brought suit in the U.S. District Court for the Northern District of California to compel the executive branch to comply with the MMPA. The court enjoined executive branch officials from permitting further tuna imports into the U.S. because no findings of comparability had been made. *Earth Island Inst. v. Mosbacher*, 746 F. Supp. 964 (N.D. Cal. 1990). The court's order affected tuna imports from Ecuador, Mexico, Panama, Vanuatu, and Venezuela. Panama and Ecuador later prohibited their fleets from setting on dolphin and were consequently exempted from the embargo. Mexico did not, and a ban on imports of Mexican tuna took effect in 1991. Mexico then challenged the ban in the GATT.

The GATT's dispute resolution mechanisms first encourage contracting parties to the General Agreement to settle differences through consultation and negotiation. If negotiations and consultations are unsuccessful, as they were in this case, an aggrieved party may submit a complaint requesting appointment of a panel of experts to hear the dispute. The panel constituted to consider Mexico's complaint issued the following report, the most controversial in its history, prompting a representative of the Humane Society of the U.S. to utter the plaintive rhetorical question, "How many more of these gentle creatures will have to die in the name of free trade?"

U.S.—Restrictions on Imports of Tuna

30 I.L.M. 1594 (1991)

The Panel . . . concluded that . . . the U.S. import prohibition would not meet the requirements of Article III [requiring national treatment of "like" products, in this case tuna]. Article III:4 calls for a comparison of the treatment of imported tuna as a product with that of domestic tuna as a product. Regulations governing the taking of dolphins incidental to the taking of tuna could not possibly affect tuna as a product. Article III:4 therefore obliges the U.S. to accord treatment to Mexican tuna no less favourable than that accorded to U.S. tuna, whether or not the incidental taking of dolphins by Mexican vessels corresponds to that of U.S. vessels. . . .

The Panel noted that the U.S. had argued that its direct embargo under the MMPA could be justified under Article XX(b) or Article XX(g). . . . The Panel recalled that previous panels had established that Article XX is a limited and conditional exception from obligations under other provisions of the General Agreement, and not a positive rule establishing obligations in itself. Therefore, the practice of panels has been to interpret Article XX narrowly, to place the burden on the party invoking Article XX to justify its invocation, and not to examine Article XX exceptions unless invoked. . . .

The Panel proceeded to examine whether Article XX(b) or Article XX(g) could justify the MMPA provisions on imports of certain yellowfin tuna and yellowfin tuna products, and the import ban imposed under these provisions. The Panel noted that Article XX provides that:

> Subject to the requirement that such measures are not applied in a manner which would constitute a means of arbitrary or unjustifiable discrimination between countries where the same conditions prevail, or a disguised restriction on international trade, nothing in this Agreement shall be construed to prevent the adoption or enforcement by any contracting party of measures . . .
> (b) necessary to protect human, animal or plant life or health; . . .
> (g) relating to the conservation of exhaustible natural resources if such measures are made effective in conjunction with restrictions on domestic production or consumption. . . .

The Panel noted that the U.S. considered the prohibition of imports of certain yellowfin tuna and certain yellowfin tuna products from Mexico, and the provisions of the MMPA on which this prohibition is based, to be justified by Article XX(b) because they served solely the purpose of protecting dolphin life and health and were "necessary" within the

E. International Institutions

meaning of that provision because, in respect of the protection of dolphin life and health outside its jurisdiction, there was no alternative measure reasonably available to the U.S. to achieve this objective. Mexico considered that Article XX(b) was not applicable to a measure imposed to protect the life or health of animals outside the jurisdiction of the contracting party taking it and that the import prohibition imposed by the U.S. was not necessary because alternative means consistent with the General Agreement were available to it to protect dolphin lives or health, namely international co-operation between the countries concerned.

The Panel noted that the basic question raised by these arguments, namely whether Article XX(b) covers measures necessary to protect human, animal or plant life or health outside the jurisdiction of the contracting party taking the measure, is not clearly answered by the text of that provision. It refers to life and health protection generally without expressly limiting that protection to the jurisdiction of the contracting party concerned. The Panel therefore decided to analyze this issue in the light of the drafting history of Article XX(b), the purpose of this provision, and the consequences that the interpretations proposed by the parties would have for the operation of the General Agreement as a whole....

The Panel ... noted that Article XX(b) allows each contracting party to set its human, animal or plant life or health standards. The conditions set out in Article XX(b) which limit resort to this exception, namely that the measure taken must be "necessary" and not "constitute a means of arbitrary or unjustifiable discrimination or a disguised restriction on international trade," refer to the trade measure requiring justification under Article XX(b), not however to the life or health standard chosen by the contracting party.... The Panel considered that if the broad interpretation of Article XX(b) suggested by the U.S. were accepted, each contracting party could unilaterally determine the life or health protection policies from which other contracting parties could not deviate without jeopardizing their rights under the General Agreement. The General Agreement would then no longer constitute a multilateral framework for trade among all contracting parties but would provide legal security only in respect of trade between a limited number of contracting parties with identical internal regulations.

The Panel considered that the U.S.' measures, even if Article XX(b) were interpreted to permit extrajurisdictional protection of life and health, would not meet the requirement of necessity set out in that provision. The U.S. had not demonstrated to the Panel—as required of the party invoking an Article XX exception—that it had exhausted all options reasonably available to it to pursue its dolphin protection objectives through measures consistent with the General Agreement, in particular through the negotiation of international cooperative arrangements, which would seem to be desirable in view of the fact that dolphins roam the waters of many states and the high seas. Moreover, even assuming that an import prohibition were the only resort reasonably available to the U.S., the particular measure chosen by the U.S. could in the Panel's view not be considered to be necessary within the meaning of Article XX(b). The U.S. linked the maximum incidental dolphin taking rate which Mexico had to meet during a particular period in order to be able to export tuna to the U.S. to the taking rate actually recorded for U.S. fishermen during the same period. Consequently, the Mexican authorities could not know whether, at a given point of time, their policies conformed to the U.S.' dolphin protection standards. The Panel considered that a limitation on trade based on such unpredictable conditions could not be regarded as necessary to protect the health or life of dolphins.

On the basis of the above considerations, the Panel found that the U.S.' direct import prohibition imposed on certain yellowfin tuna and certain yellowfin tuna products of

Mexico and the provisions of the MMPA under which it is imposed could not be justified under the exception in Article XX(b).

[For similar reasons, the Panel found that the exception in Article XX(g) for the conservation of exhaustible natural resources was inapplicable.]

The Panel wished to underline that its task was limited to the examination of this matter "in the light of the relevant GATT provisions," and therefore did not call for a finding on the appropriateness of the U.S.' and Mexico's conservation policies as such.

The Panel wished to note the fact, made evident during its consideration of this case, that the provisions of the General Agreement impose few constraints on a contracting party's implementation of domestic environmental policies. . . . [However,] a contracting party may not restrict imports of a product merely because it originates in a country with environmental policies different from its own. The Panel further recalled its finding that the import restrictions examined in this dispute, imposed to respond to differences in environmental regulation of producers, could not be justified under the exceptions in Articles XX(b) or XX(g). These exceptions did not specify criteria limiting the range of life or health protection policies, or resource conservation policies, for the sake of which they could be invoked. It seemed evident to the Panel that, if the [GATT] were to permit import restrictions in response to differences in environmental policies under the General Agreement, they would need to impose limits on the range of policy differences justifying such responses and to develop criteria so as to prevent abuse. . . .

These considerations led the Panel to the view that the adoption of its report would affect neither the rights of individual contracting parties to pursue their internal environmental policies and to co-operate with one another in harmonizing such policies, nor the right of the [GATT parties] acting jointly to address international environmental problems which can only be resolved through measures in conflict with the present rules of the General Agreement.

COMMENTARY & QUESTIONS

1. Process and production methods (PPMs). In the first paragraph of its report quoted above, the GATT Panel makes a distinction between the content of an imported product and the method by which it is produced—so-called process and production methods (PPMs)—even when a manufacturing process creates environmental externalities. If tuna from Mexico had been tainted with mercury, for example, it would not be a "like" product by comparison with uncontaminated tuna. According to the Panel, however, tuna caught by methods that harm dolphin is comparable to dolphin-safe tuna. The Panel's conclusion necessarily means that states of import may not discriminate among products based on manufacturing methodologies that do not cause environmental harm within the state of import's jurisdiction. How did the Panel justify this conclusion? According the Panel, what harm would result to the international trading system if the U.S. had been permitted to discriminate against dolphin-unsafe tuna? Do you agree or disagree with the Panel's conclusion? If you disagree, how would you respond to the Panel's concern about the adverse effects on international trade?

2. An escape valve for the environment. The bulk of the excerpt above is devoted to the Panel's analysis of Article XX of the GATT, which permits the U.S. to attempt to justify the tuna embargo despite the fact that it violates the basic GATT disciplines. At the time the GATT was adopted, protection of the environment was not widely understood as a basis for national policies. Consequently, environmentally related measures are most likely to fall

E. International Institutions

under the exceptions in Article XX(b) addressing "human, animal or plant life or health" or in Article XX(g) dealing with "conservation of exhaustible natural resources." As with the U.S. arguments concerning the "likeness" of dolphin-safe and dolphin-unsafe tuna, the U.S. lost on this point, meaning that it lost the overall dispute. According to the Panel, why do neither of these two exceptions justify the tuna embargo? Accepting this conclusion at least for the sake of argument, what alternatives would be available to the U.S. to protect dolphin outside its jurisdiction? How do those alternatives compare with the trade ban in their effectiveness in protecting dolphin?

3. Baptists, bootleggers, and Flipper. One of the GATT Panel's concerns seems to be the willingness of the U.S. to utilize a trade ban to achieve its conservation purposes when less coercive approaches might have accomplished a similar result without disadvantaging Mexico or foreign fishing interests. If you were a representative of the U.S. tuna fishing industry, which had already been subjected to regulatory requirements that limited dolphin "bycatch" (unwanted species caught incidentally and dumped at sea), why might you find a ban on imports of tuna from countries that did not have comparable requirements a particularly attractive alternative? Trade policy analysts sometimes speak of "Baptist-bootlegger" coalitions, referring to political dynamics during the era of prohibition when both teetotalers and smugglers supported a ban on alcohol, one group out of principle and the other motivated by self-interest. The U.S. in defending the tuna ban argued that its purpose was benign (i.e., aimed at protecting dolphins) and not protectionist (i.e., designed to protect the domestic tuna industry from foreign competition). Should this have made a difference to the Panel? If so, what should be the role of intent in analyzing the validity of a trade barrier such as the tuna ban? How would you go about determining the intent of Congress in passing the MMPA? As a matter of principle, why might a GATT panel conclude, as it did, that intent is immaterial and that the relevant question is the effect of the measure?

4. PPMs in the WTO. In the GATT system, panel reports such as that on the U.S. tuna embargo did not have legal effect unless they were adopted by consensus by the GATT Council, which represented all the GATT "contracting parties." Mexico declined to present the tuna report to the GATT Council, presumably because of concerns that the intense public outcry over the most publicized panel report ever could threaten then-ongoing negotiations with the U.S. and Canada over NAFTA. The EU and the Netherlands then challenged a secondary embargo designed to prevent "tuna laundering," with a result similar to Mexico's challenge. U.S.—Restrictions on Imports of Tuna, 33 I.L.M. 839 (1994). Because both reports remained unadopted at the end of 1994, when the GATT as a legal matter ceased to exist, neither is a definitive statement of GATT law. One of the principal innovations in the WTO, which came into existence as the successor to the GATT on January 1, 1995, was the dispute settlement process through the creation of a standing Appellate Body that could consider appeals of panel decisions on questions of law. It was no longer possible, as in the GATT, for a losing party with political clout such as the U.S. unilaterally to block the adoption of an adverse panel report. The WTO Appellate Body confronted the issue of PPMs in a dispute very similar to the tuna/dolphin case, which was initiated by India, Malaysia, Pakistan, and Thailand concerning a U.S. ban on importation of shrimp harvested by methods that harm endangered sea turtles. The new Appellate Body concluded that the shrimp ban, like the tuna embargo, violated the trading rights of the complainants and the obligations of the U.S. In contrast to both tuna panels, however, the Appellate Body strongly suggested that the deficiencies in the U.S. scheme were not inherent in the "extraterritorial" reach of the import ban but instead could be corrected through a more careful design and implementation of the program. After the U.S. State Department amended its guidelines for implementation of the program, the Appellate Body held the ban consistent with GATT/WTO rules. U.S.—Import Prohibition of Certain Shrimp and Shrimp Products, available at www.wto.org/english/tratop_e/dispu_e/cases_e/ds58_e.htm.

5. **Unilateralism versus multilateralism.** The MMPA, like the Pelly and Packwood Amendments described in Chapter 7, is an example of a unilateral measure taken to fill gaps in, and to reinforce, international cooperative regimes such as the Inter-American Tropical Tuna Commission, which has the authority to regulate tuna on a multilateral basis. The executive branch embargoed tuna imports from Mexico only after two amendments to the MMPA and a court order obtained by a domestic environmental organization. With the ban in place, the U.S. government continued to negotiate with Mexico and other governments in an attempt to identify an alternative to the ban. Soon after the imposition of the tuna embargo, ten states, negotiating under the auspices of the Inter-American Tropical Tuna Commission, entered into an agreement to reduce dolphin mortality, the so-called La Jolla Agreement. This instrument was intended to phase down the maximum permissible take of dolphins in the Eastern Pacific Ocean to 5000 in 1999 while continuing to allow the practice of dolphin sets. In October 1995, a configuration of states similar to those party to the La Jolla Agreement adopted the Declaration of Panama, which anticipated further binding international commitments with the goal of eliminating dolphin mortality and further tightened standards beyond those identified in the earlier La Jolla Agreement. After Congress amended the MMPA, the embargoes were lifted after the State Department's finding that an agreement meeting the requirements of the legislation is in effect for countries that are in compliance with the agreement—virtually all countries with vessels setting on dolphins in the region. Is this what the tuna panel had in mind when it referred to "the negotiation of international cooperative arrangements"? What practical difference is there between approaching Mexico in the first instance about the possibility of an international agreement and proposing negotiations against the backdrop of a ban already in place? Which is better for dolphins, a unilateral embargo or a multilateral agreement such as the La Jolla Agreement or the Panama Declaration? As a representative of the Earth Island Institute, how would you decide whether such a multilateral agreement made sufficient progress such that your organization could support lifting the embargo? As a government official, what incentive would you have to consult with the Earth Island Institute during negotiations with Mexico and other countries? In the event, the Panama Declaration seriously divided the U.S. conservation community.

6. **WTO dispute settlement and democratic participation.** In contrast to the opportunities for public input into the legislative, administrative, and judicial fora in which this dispute was treated on the domestic level, but consistent with standard GATT procedures, the documents and oral proceedings in the case were not accessible to the public. Dispute settlement in GATT did not allow for participation by private parties such as the Earth Island Institute. According to anecdotal reports, the Earth Island Institute's lawyer was shut out and forced to wait in the corridor while the Panel heard arguments from Mexico and the U.S. Ten other GATT parties and the European Union nonetheless were permitted to make written submissions to the Panel, all of which were critical of the ban, arguing that it violated the GATT. The Uruguay Round made some changes toward a more transparent process in the WTO, principally by permitting—although not requiring—publication of nonconfidential summaries of parties' written submissions to panels and the Appellate Body. The Appellate Body's jurisprudence has moved toward a more open process, principally by creating entry points for submissions by NGOs in a role analogous to amici curiae in domestic courts. The WTO Council, however, has expressed virtually unanimous dissatisfaction with this practice. In contrast with many other international organizations such as

E. International Institutions

UNEP, NGO "observers" are still excluded from formal negotiating sessions of new WTO agreements. As a representative of the Earth Island Institute, what are the costs if members of the public—including NGOs, industry, and the public—are excluded from WTO panels, the Appellate Body, and the negotiation of new agreements? What principled arguments can you make in support of the proposition that trade agreement negotiation and dispute settlement processes, unlike multilateral environmental agreements, should not be conducted "in a fishbowl"? How might the potential adverse effects from greater transparency be minimized or eliminated?

7. Trade and climate. From time to time there have been proposals to impose at-the-border measures designed to reinforce the climate regime. Fuels, for instance, differ in their relative contribution to the problem. Coal burning releases the most CO_2, while the combustion of quantities of natural gas and oil needed to produce the same amount of energy results in only about 57% and 83% as much CO_2 respectively. Suppose Ruritania were to impose differential tariffs on these three fuels, based on their "carbon intensity." How would you expect the GATT/WTO regime to treat such a measure? Some fuels, while identical in composition to other fuels, may nonetheless be extracted in a manner that exacerbates climate change. For example, Canada's current CO_2 emissions are 35% above their 1990 level, primarily due to increases of emissions from the production of oil from the Alberta tar sands, which according to Greenpeace releases five times as much CO_2 per barrel than conventional extraction methods. How would you expect the GATT/WTO regime to treat a measure that differentiates among fuels based on such factors? Every piece of climate legislation introduced into the U.S. Congress has contained at the border offsets designed to protect U.S. industry from unfair competition from energy-intensive goods imported from countries that do not have similar measures in place. By contrast, the Paris Agreement and its accompanying COP decision do not mention trade even once.

8. Greening the WTO. The trade and environment debate highlights competing visions of the interrelationship between these two aspirational goals, both of which are intended to promote human welfare. One perspective is that excessively zealous attempts to address environmental and public health measures as potential nontariff trade barriers may excessively constrain legitimate national regulatory measures through a process of "deregulation from abroad." From this perspective, trade-based restrictions on environmental measures may justify or promote a downward spiral—a race-to-the-bottom—toward weak, least common denominator domestic regulatory standards or chill the adoption of new regulatory measures out of fear of a trade-based challenge. An alternative view is that trade promotes wealth, which in turn becomes available for "investment" in environmental protection. According to this view, "protectionist practices might well be viewed as generally promoting environmental degradation because they provide no incentive to use resources efficiently. Free trade might justifiably be viewed as promoting environmental protection, because countries will generate more wealth with which to protect the environment." Weiss, Environment and Trade as Partners in Sustainable Development: A Commentary, 86 Am. J. Int'l L. 728, 729-730 (1992). Principle 12 of the Rio Declaration, reproduced in Section B above, is a response to the GATT tuna-dolphin decision of the previous year. What proposals could you make for reconciling environmental and trade policy? One solution that has been proposed is to treat environmental laxity—the failure of certain countries to require compliance with minimum international environmental standards—as an impermissible de facto "subsidy" that can be offset through at-the-border measures such as tariffs. This would appear to be consistent with Rio Principle 16, which encourages states to "promote the internalization of environmental costs and the use of economic instruments, taking into account the approach that the polluter should, in principle, bear the cost of pollution, with due regard to the public interest and without distorting international trade and investment." What do you think of such a proposal? How might it be written into GATT/WTO rules? What difficulties could you imagine in implementing it, and how might they be resolved?

TRADE AND ENVIRONMENT PROBLEM EXERCISE

The GATT tuna-dolphin report appeared to call into question the validity of major existing multilateral environmental agreements (MEAs) that rely on trade measures as regulatory tools. These include the trade provisions in the Montreal Protocol (discussed in Chapter 7), the Convention on International Trade in Endangered Species (CITES, the linchpin of international efforts to protect endangered species), and the Basel Convention on the Control of Transboundary Movements of Hazardous Wastes and Their Disposal (the principal multilateral instrument governing international shipments of toxic waste). These agreements discriminate between trade with parties and with nonparties, sometimes to the point of prohibiting trade in CFCs, endangered species, or waste with nonparties, in an effort to enhance the environmental efficacy of the agreement and to create incentives for nonparty states to accept the obligations of the agreement. Why and exactly how could restrictions on trade between nonparties and parties, all of them WTO members, violate the basic GATT/WTO disciplines?

Two solutions that have been suggested to the "MEA problem" are provided by GATT 1947 and NAFTA. The first is a "waiver" for specific multilateral environmental agreements employing trade measures, as provided in Article XXV of GATT 1947:

Article XXV. Joint Action by the Contracting Parties

5. In exceptional circumstances not elsewhere provided for in this agreement, the CONTRACTING PARTIES may waive an obligation imposed upon a contracting party by this Agreement; Provided that any such decision shall be approved by a two-thirds majority of the votes cast and that such majority shall comprise more than half of the contracting parties. The CONTRACTING PARTIES may also by such a vote
   (i) define certain categories of exceptional circumstances to which other voting requirements shall apply for the waiver of obligations, and
   (ii) prescribe such criteria as may be necessary for the application of this paragraph.

The following is the text of Article 104 of NAFTA:

Article 104. Relation to Environmental and Conservation Agreements

1. In the event of any inconsistency between this Agreement and the specific trade obligations set out in:
   (a) the Convention on International Trade in Endangered Species of Wild Fauna and Flora, done at Washington, March 3, 1973, as amended June 22, 1979,
   (b) the Montreal Protocol on Substances that Deplete the Ozone Layer, done at Montreal, September 16, 1987, as amended June 29, 1990,
   (c) the Basel Convention on the Control of Transboundary Movements of Hazardous Wastes and Their Disposal, done at Basel, March 22, 1989, on its entry into force for Canada, Mexico and the U.S.,[16] or

---

16. Canada and Mexico are currently parties to the Basel Convention. The U.S. has signed but not ratified, and is consequently not yet a party to the Convention as of this writing.

E. International Institutions

(d) the agreements set out in Annex 104.1 [which you may assume currently contains no entries],

such obligations shall prevail to the extent of the inconsistency, provided that where a Party has a choice among equally effective and reasonably available means of complying with such obligations, the Party chooses the alternative that is the least inconsistent with the other provisions of this Agreement.

2. The Parties may agree in writing to modify Annex 104.1 to include any amendment to an agreement referred to in paragraph 1, and any other environmental or conservation agreement.

COMMENTARY & QUESTIONS

Dealing with multilateral environmental agreements: GATT versus NAFTA. Identify the differences, from a legal and policy perspective, in the operation and effect of these two approaches. By identifying and analyzing different situations to which the two approaches might apply, discuss the relative merits and disadvantages of the two approaches in resolving the "MEA problem."

The Uruguay Round created a new WTO Committee on Trade and Environment that, despite repeated attempts, has been unable to reach agreement on a "legislative" solution to the "MEA problem." Assuming neither GATT Article XXV nor NAFTA Article 104 applies to a hypothetical dispute between a nonparty and a party to the Montreal Protocol over the application of the trade provisions in that agreement, what role, if any, would the multilateral nature of the measures at issue play in applying Article XX? To date, there have been no trade-based challenges to national measures relying on an MEA. Why do you think that is?

To secure our common future, we need a new international vision based on cooperation and a new environmental ethic based on the realization that the issues with which we wrestle are globally interconnected. This is not only a moral ethic but also a practical one—the only way we can pursue our own self interests on a small and closely knit planet.

—Gro Harlem Brundtland

Of all possible worlds, we only got one We gotta ride it, whatever we've done, We'll never get far from what we leave behind Baby, we can run, run, run, but we can't hide. . . .

—The Grateful Dead, We Can Run (IceNine Publishing Co., Inc. 1989)

TABLE OF ACRONYMS, REFERENTS, PAGES WITH DEFINITIONS

AAU, Assigned Amount Unit (Kyoto), 630

ABEL, Ability to Pay for Environmental Liability, 802

ADRs, Alternative Dispute Resolution Mechanisms, 821

AEA, Atomic Energy Act of 1954, 260

AEC, Atomic Energy Commission, 224

AICPA, American Institute of Certified Public Accountants, 832

ALJ, Administrative Law Judge, 797

AMA, Alaska Miners Association, 539

AMSA, Association of Metropolitan Sewerage Agencies, 566

ANSI, American National Standards Institute, 643

APA, Administrative Procedures Act, 200

AQCR, Air Quality Control Regions, 468

AR, Attributable Risk, 167

ARARs, Applicable, Relevant and Appropriate requirements drawn from other environmental laws, 738

ASC, Area Source Credits, 623

ASTM, American Society for Testing and Materials, 836

ATTAINS, Assessment TMDL Tracking and Implementation System, 524

AWG-KP, Ad Hoc Working Group on Further Commitments for Annex I Parties Under the Kyoto Protocol, 991

AWG-LCA, Ad Hoc Working Group on Long-Term Cooperative Action Under the Convention, 991

BACT, Best Available Control Technology, 253

BADT, Best Available Demonstrated Control Technology, 519

BANANA, Build Absolutely Nothing Anywhere Near Anybody, 122

BASIC (Carbon) Major Negotiating Countries (Brazil, South Africa, India, and China), 992

BAT, Best Available Technology (economically achievable), 56

BCT, Best Conventional Pollutant Control Technology, 519

BEN, Economic Benefit of Noncompliance, 802

BLM, Bureau of Land Management, 219

BMPs, Best Management Practices, 529

BOD, Biochemical Oxygen Demand, 522

BPJ, Best Professional Judgment, 543

BPs, Bank Procedures, 1003

CAA, Clean Air Act, 174

CAFE, Corporate Average Fuel Economy Standards, 346

CAFO, Concentrated Animal Feeding Operation (CWA), 530

CAIR, Clean Air Interstate Rule, 479

CAMR, Clean Air Mercury Rule, 490

CBO, Congressional Budget Office, 202

CCAAs, Candidate Conservation Agreements with Assurances, 450

CCAs, Candidate Conservation Agreements, 450

CCC, California Coastal Commission, 266

CCOL, Coordinating Committee on the Ozone Layer, 980

CDC, Center for Disease Control, 48

CDM, Clean Development Mechanism, 630

CEC, Commission for Environmental Cooperation, 303

CEMS, Continuous Emissions Monitoring Systems, 617

CEQ, Council on Environmental Quality, 317

CERCLA, Comprehensive Environmental Response, Compensation, and Liability Act (Superfund), 58

CERCLIS, CERCLA Information System, 738

CFATS, Chemical Facility Anti-terrorism Standards, 340

CFB, Circulating Fluidized Bed, 497

CFR, Code of Federal Regulations, 205

CIPS, Central Illinois Public Service Company, 158

CITES, Convention on International Trade in Endangered Species, 457

CMA, Calcium Magnesium Acetate, 37

CMA, Chemical Manufacturers Association, 665

CMA, Cooperative Management Agreement (BLM), 385

CNG, Compressed Natural Gas, 972

COD, Chemical Oxygen Demand, 522

COPs, Conferences of the Parties to the Vienna Convention, 981

CSOs, Combined Sewer Overflows, 547

CVM, Contingent Valuation Methods, 140

CWA, Clean Water Act, 51

CZMA, Coastal Zone Management Act, 59

DEC, Department of Environmental Conservation, 90

DEIS, Draft Environmental Impact Statement, 321

DMRs, Discharge Monitoring Reports, 819

DOJ, U.S. Department of Justice, 792

DOT, Department of Transportation, 220

DWP, Department of Water and Power of the City of Los Angeles, 896

EAB, Environmental Appeals Board, 797

EBEs, Environmentally Beneficial Expenditures, 800

ECHA, European Chemicals Agency, 680

ECJ, European Court of Justice, 681

EDF, Environmental Defense Fund, 654

EGU, Electric Utility Steam Generating Unit, 491

EIS, Environmental Impact Statement, 59

EMF, Electromagnetic Field, 156

EMS, Environmental Management Systems, 644

ENUF, End Unsustainable Funding, 1005

EPA, U.S. Environmental Protection Agency, 21

EPCA, Energy Policy and Conservation Act of 1975, 325

EPCRA, Emergency Planning and Community Right-To-Know Act, 58

ERDA, Energy Research and Development Agency, 224

ESA, Endangered Species Act, 59

ET, Emissions Trading, 179

ETP, Eastern Tropical Pacific Ocean, 1007

EU ETS, European Union's Emissions Trading Scheme, 630

FACA, Federal Advisory Committee Act, 827

FASB, Financial Accounting Standards Board, 832

Table of Acronyms, Referents, Pages With Definitions

FCCC, UN Framework Convention on Climate Change, 986

FDA, Food and Drug Administration, 872

FDCA, Food, Drug, and Cosmetics Act, 58

FDF, Fundamentally Different Factor, 542

FEIS, Final Environmental Impact Statement, 321

FELA, Federal Employers' Liability Act, 153

FEPCA, Fed. Env. Pesticide Control Act, 653

FERC, Federal Energy Regulatory Commission, 265

FHWA, Federal Highways Administration, 213

FIFRA, Federal Insecticide, Fungicide, and Rodenticide Act, 60

FIP, Federal Implementation Plan, 461

FOIA, Freedom of Information Act, 247

FONSI, Finding of NO Significant Impact (NEPA), 324

FPC, Federal Power Commission, 227

FQPA, Food Quality Protection Act of 1996, 420

FRCP, Federal Rules of Civil Procedure, 818

FWPCA, Federal Water Pollution Control Act (CWA), 45

GAAP, Generally Accepted Accounting Principles, 832

GAO, General Accounting Office, 202

GATT, General Agreement on Tariffs and Trade, 297

GEF, Global Environment Facility, 1004

GHGs, Greenhouse Gases, 82

gpm, Grams per Mile, 511

GPs, Good Practices, 1003

GRAS List, Generally Regarded As Safe

HAPs, Hazardous Air Pollutants, 489

HAZMEC, Hazardous Materials Export Controls Statute, 60

HCs, Hydrocarbons, 489

HFCs, Hydrofluorocarbons, 516

HMTA, Hazardous Materials Transportation Act, 60

HRRCA, Health Risk Reduction and Cost Analysis, 590

HRS, Hazard Ranking System, 735

HSWA, Hazardous & Solid Waste Amendments of 1984, 757

HWIR, Hazardous Waste Identification Rule, 771

IBRD, International Bank for Reconstruction and Development, 999

ICC, Interstate Commerce Commission, 200

ICJ, International Court of Justice, 290

ICS, Industrial Chemical Survey, 551

IDA, International Development Association, 999

IEPA, Illinois Environmental Protection Agency, 117

IET, International Emissions Trading, 629

IPCC, Intergovernmental Panel on Climate Change, 986

IPM, Integrated Pest Management, 661

ISGS, Illinois State Geological Survey, 119

ISO, International Organization for Standardization, 643

ITC, Interagency Testing Committee (toxics), 669

ITO, International Trade Organization, 1006

JAMA, Journal of American Medical Association, 974

JI, Joint Implementation, 630

LAER, Lowest Achievable Emissions Rate, 463

LAPP, Limited Access Privilege Programs, 621

LCA, Life Cycle Assessment, 773

LCAC, Lahore Clean Air Commission, 976

LIA, Lead Industry Association, 474

LSP, Life Science Products Company, 46

LULU, Locally Unwanted Land Use, 122

LUST, Large (or Leaking) Underground Storage Tank Program, 773

MACT, Maximum Available Control Technology, 460

MBTU, Million British Thermal Units of Heat Input, 477

MCL, Maximum Contaminant Level, 549

MCLGs, Maximum Contaminant Level Goals, 549

MCLs, Maximum Contaminant Loads

MDEQ, Michigan Department of Environmental Quality,

MEAs, Multilateral Environmental Agreements, 497

MFN, Most-Favored Nation, 297

MMPA, Marine Mammal Protection Act, 1005

MOAs, Memorandums of Agreement, 807

MOPs, Meetings of the Parties to the Protocol, 979

MSERC, Mobile Source Emission Reduction Credits, 623

MSW, Municipal Solid Waste, 771

MTBE, Methyl Tertiary Butyl Ether, 264

MUSY, Multiple Use Sustained Yield, 379

NAAEC, North American Agreement on Environmental Cooperation, 303

NAAQS, National Ambient Air Quality Standards, 160

NACEPT, National Advisory Council for Environmental Policy and Technology, 812

NAFTA, North American Free Trade Agreement, 297

NAHB, National Association of Home Builders, 453

NAMAs, Nationally Appropriate Mitigation Actions, 992

NAS, National Academy of Sciences, 326

NCP, National Contingency Plan, 704

NCPs, Nonconformance Penalties, 826

NEPA, National Environmental Policy Act, 59

NESHAPs, National Emissions Standards for Hazardous Air Pollutants, 489

NFMA, National Forest Management Act, 194

NFR, Notice of Final Rulemaking, 22

NGO, Nongovernmental Organization, 64

NHTSA, National Highway Traffic Safety Administration, 325

NIMBY, "Not In My Back Yard!", 122

NJCs, Neighborhood Justice Centers, 825

NMFS, National Marine Fisheries Service, 1005

NMPs, Nutrient Management Plans, 545

NMU, Northern Michigan University, 497

NOAA, National Oceanic and Atmospheric Administration, 59

NOIS, Notice of Intent to Sue, 820

NOV, Notice of Violation, 797

NPDES, National Pollutant Discharge Elimination System, 45

Table of Acronyms, Referents, Pages With Definitions

NPL, National Priorities List, 735

NPR, Notice of Proposed Rulemaking, 207

NRC, National Research Council, 577

NRC, Nuclear Regulatory Commission, 224

NRDC, Natural Resource Defense Council, 242

NRDs, Natural Resource Damages, 137

NSPSs, New Source Performance Standards, 461

NSR, New Source Review, 464

NTAs, Negotiated Testing Agreements, 669

OCR, EPA's Office of Civil Rights, 482

ODs, Operational Directives, 998

OECD, Organisation for Economic Cooperation and Development, 63

OIRA, OMB's Office of Information and Regulatory Affairs, 465

OMB, Office of Management and Budget, 319

OPA-90, Oil Pollution Act of 1990, 345

Ops, Operational Policies, 1001

ORV, Off-Road Vehicle, 220

OSHA, Occupational Safety and Health Administration, 47

OTA, Office of Technology Assessment, 202

OTAG, Ozone Transport Advisory Group, 479

OTC, Ozone Transport Commission, NO HITS

PA, Removal Preliminary Assessment, 738

PAH, Polynuclear Organic (Aromatic) Hydrocarbons, 159

PBT, Persistent, Bioaccumulative, and Toxic Chemicals, 336

PCBs, Polychlorinated biphenyls, 524

PFCs, Perfluorocarbons, 516

PIC, Prior Informed Consent, 63

PM, Particulate Matter, 467

PNSCP, Pre-Notice Site Cleanup Program (CERCLA), 810

POCLAD, Program on Corporations, Law & Democracy, 51

POP, Persistent Organic Pollutants, 64

POTW, Publicly-Owned Treatment Works, 47

PPA, Pollution Prevention Act, 59

ppm, Parts per Million, 469

PPMs, Process and Production Methods, 1008

PRIA, Public Rangelands Improvement Act, 384

PRP, Potentially Responsible Party (CERCLA), 157

PRTRs, Pollutant Release and Transfer Registers, 340

PSD, Prevention of Significant Deterioration, 463

PTD, Public Trust Doctrine, 879

PWSA, Ports and Waterways Safety Act of 1972, 263

RACT, Reasonably Available Control Technology, 463

RCACs, Regional Citizens Advisory Councils (OPA-90), 416

RCC, Resource Conservation Challenge, 774

RCRA, Resource Conservation and Recovery Act, 58

RD, Remedial Design, 737

REACH (Europe) Registration, Evaluation, Authorisation, and Restriction of Chemicals, 651

RECLAIM, Regional Clean Air Incentives Market, 621

RI/FS, Remedial Investigation/Feasibility Study, 737

RIA, Regulatory Impact Analysis, 597

RIPs, REACH Implementation Projects, 681

ROD, Record of Decision, 737

RPAR, Rebuttable Presumption Against Registration, 658

RR, Relative Risk, 167

SCAQMD, South Coast Air Quality Management District, 621

SDWA, Safe Drinking Water Act, 59

SEER, National Cancer Institute Surveillance Epidemiology and End Results Program Rates, 163

SEIS, Supplemental EIS, 368

SEP, Supplemental Environmental Project, 800

SI, Removal Site Inspection, 738

SIP, State Implementation Plan (CAA), 58

SIU, Significant Industrial Users, 548

SLAPP, Strategic Lawsuit Against Public Participation, 99

SMPs, Stormwater Management Plans, 546

SPDES, State Pollutant Discharge Elimination System, 550

SSOs, Sanitary Sewer Overflows, 547

SWRCB, California State Water Resource Control Board, 265

TBELs, Technology-Based Effluent Limitations, 520

TBT, Technical Barriers to Trade, 647

TC, Technical Committee (ISO), 644

TCE, Trichloroethylene, 90

TCLP, Toxicity Characteristic Leaching Procedure, 762

ToSCA, Toxic Substances Control Act, 51

TPP, Trans Pacific Partnership, 297

TRI, Toxic Release Inventory (EPCRA), 58

TSDFs, Treatment, Storage, and Disposal Facilities, 180

TSS, Total Suspended Solids, 541

TVA, Tennessee Valley Authority, 208

UIC, Underground Injection Control, 781

UNCED, United Nations Conference on Environment and Development, 965

UNEP, United Nations Environment Program, 63

US EPA, U.S. Environmental Protection Agency, 809

USDA, U.S. Department of Agriculture, 652

USTs, Underground Storage Tanks, 773

UV, Ultraviolet, 975

VATIP, Voluntary Advanced Technology Incentives Program, 537

VOC, Volatile Organic Compounds, 159

WLA, Waste-Load Allocation, 558

WMO, World Meteorological Organization, 984

WQBELs, Water Quality-Based Effluent Limitations, 520

WQSs, Water Quality Standards, 535

WTO, World Trade Organization, 297

TABLE OF CASES

Abbott Laboratories. v. Gardner, 149, 214, 219

Abilene v. EPA, see City of Abilene v. EPA

Abreu v. U.S., 786

Acton v. Blundell, 87

Acuna v. Brown & Root, 83

Adkins v. Thomas Solvent, 156

AFL-CIO v. OSHA, 814

Agere Sys., Inc. v. Advanced Envtl. Tech. Corp , 729

Air Courier Conference v. American Postal Workers Union, 232

Air Pollution Control Dist. v. EPA, 477

Air Transport Association of America et al. v. Secretary of State for Energy and Climate Change, 631-634

Akzo Coatings v. Aigner Corp., 728

Alaska Dep't of Envtl. Conservation (ADEC) v. EPA, 253, 507

Alaska v. Exxon Corp., 139

Albany Bank & Trust Co. v. Exxon Mobil Corp., 786

Albuquerque v. EPA, 567

Alec L. et al. v. Administrator of U.S. EPA, 910

Alexander v. Sandoval, 369, 485

Allen v. U.S., 168

Allen v. Wright, 232

Allied Chemical Kepone case, see Kepone,

Allied-Signal v. Commissioner, 42, 54

Allstate Ins. Co. v. Klock Oil Co., 716

Almota Farmer's Elevator & Warehouse Co. v. U.S., 947

Alsea Valley Alliance v. Lautenbacher, 446

AM International v. International Forging Equip. Corp., 836

Amcast Indus. Corp. v. Detrex Corp., 711

American Chem. Council v. EPA, 771

American Dental Ass'n v. Martin, 575

American Electric Power et al., States of Ct., N.Y., Cal., Iowa, N.J., R.I., Vt., Wis., and City of N.Y., see Connecticut et al. v. American Electric Power, and Connecticut, N.Y., Cal., Iowa, N.J., R.I., Vt., Wis., and City of N.Y. v. American Electric Power, 94, 96

American Lung Ass'n v. EPA, 475

American Mining Congress v. EPA, 757, 771

American Petroleum Inst. (API) v. EPA, 300

American Textile Mfg. Inst. v. Donovan (Cotton Dust), 203, 254, 586

American Trucking Associations v. Browner, Brief Amici Curiae, 597-599

American Trucking Assoc. v. City of Los Angeles, 268

American Trucking v. Whitman, 203, 470-472, 493, 593, 596-597, 599

Aminoil, Inc. v. EPA, 733

Anderson v. W.R. Grace and Anderson v. Beatrice Foods Co., 149

Anspec Co. v. Johnson Controls, Inc., 715

Antarctic Whaling case, see Australia v. Japan, 288-291

Appalachian Power Co. v. EPA (Title V permits), 803

Appleton Papers v. George A. Whiting Paper Co., No. 08-C-16, 2009 WL, 709

ARCO Industries, 708

Ariz.-Colo. Land & Cattle Co. v. Dist. Ct., 914

Arkansas v. Oklahoma, 567

Arkansas Game & Fish Commission v. U.S., 927

Arlington Heights v. Metro. Hous. Dev. Corp., 369

Arnold v. Mundy, 879, 885

Art Neon v. Denver, 947

Ashcroft v. Iqbal, 83

Ass'n of Data Processing Servs. v. Camp, 229

Ass'n of Pacific Fisheries v. EPA, 540

Ass'n to Protect Hammersley, Eld & Totten Inlets v. Taylor Res., 532

Atchison, Topeka & Santa Fe Ry. v. Brown & Bryant Inc., 723

Atlantic Cement Co. v. Fidelity Cas. Co. of N.Y., 114

Atlantic Research Corp. v. U.S., 725

Atlantic States Legal Found. v. Tyson Foods, 817, 819

Atlantic States Legal Foundation v. Eastman Kodak Company, 550-553

Atlas Chemical Indus. v. Anderson, 87

Audritz Sprout-Bauer v. Beazer East, Inc., 786

Auer v. Robbins, 253

Ausimont U.S.A., Inc. v. EPA, 667

Australia v. Japan, New Zealand intervening, 288-291

Avenal v. State, 394

Aviall. see Cooper Industries

Avondale Fed. Sav. Bank v. Amoco Oil Co., 786

Ayers v. Township of Jackson, 155

Babbitt v. Sweet Home Communities for a Great Oregon, 432-435

Baldwin v. see lig, 270

Baltimore Gas & Elec. v. NRDC, 246

Bates v. Dow Agrosciences, 659

Baughman v. Bradford Coal Co., 818

Baur v. Veneman, 206, 678

Bays' Legal Fund v. Browner, 444

Bell Atlantic v. Twombly, 83

Bellis v. United States, 864

Bennett v. Spear, 234, 239

Bennis v. Michigan, 955

Berkeley v. Superior Court, see City of Berkeley v. Superior Court

Berman v. Parker, 914-916

Berry v. Armstrong Rubber Co., 123

Bersani v. U.S. Environmental Protection Agency, 360-361, 362, 363

BestFoods, U.S. v., see U.S. v. BestFoods Corp.

Bixby Ranch Co. v. Spectrol Elec. Corp., 156

Boomer et al. v. Atlantic Cement Company, 78, 91, 108-112, 114

Borland v. Sanders Lead Company, 76-78, 114, 115, 132, 136, 145

Bowman v. Chicago & Northwestern R. Co., 272

Boyes v. Shell Oil Prods. Co., 264

BP Deepwater Horizon blowout spill, see Gulf of Mexico BP Deepwater blowout spill

Branch v. Oconto County, 411

Branch v. Western Petroleum, Inc., 85-87, 131-132

Briggs & Stanton Corp. v. Concrete Sales & Servs., 786

Table of Cases

British Petroleum Deepwater Horizon blowout spill, see Gulf of Mexico BP Deepwater Horizon blowout spill

Burke v. Dow Chem. Co., 662

Burlington Northern & Santa Fe Railway Company v. U.S., 697-700, 709, 710

Burlington Truck Lines v. U.S., 217

Buttrey v. U.S., 364

C&A Carbone v. Town of Clarkstown, 274-275

California Coastal Comm'n v. Granite Rock Co., 265, 412

California v. Federal Energy Regulatory Comm'n (FERC), 265

Calvert Cliffs Coordinating Comm. v. AEC, 232

Camfield v. U.S., 408, 409, 410

Carson v. Glazer, 885

Carson-Truckee Water Conservancy Dist. v. Clark, 430

Catellus Dev. Corp. v. U.S., 711

Catskills Mt. Chapter of Trout Unlimited v. City of N.Y., 532

Center for Biological Diversity v. National Highway Traffic Safety Administration, 325-332

Chem-Dyne, see U.S. v. Chem-Dyne Corp

Chemical Mfrs. Ass'n v. EPA, 586, 665-669, 671

Chemical Waste Mgmt. Inc. v. Hunt, 273

Chesapeake & Potomac Tel. Co. of Va. v. Peck Iron & Metal Co., 711

Chevron Chemical Co. v. Ferebee, 166

Chevron U.S.A., Inc. v. NRDC, 249-254, 294, 295, 553, 560

Chevron v. Costle, 676

Chicago v. Commonwealth Edison, see City of Chicago v. Commonwealth Edison

Chicago v. EDF, see City of Chicago v. EDF

Chisholm v. Georgia, 257

Christy v. Hodel, 410, 925

Cimino v. Milford Keg, Inc., 151

Citizens Against the Refinery's Effects (CARE) v. EPA, 489, 619, 635

Citizens to Preserve Overton Park, Inc. v. Volpe, 7, 38, 211, 212-222, 224, 238, 242, 250, 252, 419, 429, 439

City Envtl. Inc. v. U.S. Chem. Co., 723

City of Abilene v. EPA, 547

City of Chicago v. Commonwealth Edison, 164

City of Chicago v. EDF, 772

City of Philadelphia v. New Jersey, 270-273

Clapper v. Amnesty, 236

Clarke v. Securities Indus. Ass'n, 230

Clean Air Markets Group v. Pataki, 620

Coalition for Health Concern v. LWD, Inc., 368

Coburn v. Sun Chem. Co., 818

Coeur Alaska, Inc. v. S.E. Alaska Conservation Council, 363

Columbia Falls Aluminum Co. v. EPA, 762

Combustion Eng'g v. Johansen, 134, 137,

Comer v. Murphy Oil Company, 95

Comm. to Save the Mokelumne River v. E. Bay Mun. Util. Dist., 531

Commonwealth of Pennsylvania v. National Gettysburg Tower, Inc., 410

Commonwealth v. Allied Chemical, et al., (criminal), 54

Commonwealth v. Barnes & Tucker Co., 945, 954

Concerned Area Residents for the Environment (CARE) v. Southview Farms, 530, 531, 545

Connecticut Coastal Fishermen's Ass'n v. Remington Arms Co., 819

Connecticut v. American Electric Power Co., 96

Conservancy, Inc., Audubon Soc'y of N.H. v. Am. Elec. Power Co., Am. Elec. Power Serv. Corp., Southern Co., Tenn. Valley Auth., Xcel Energy, Inc., and Cinergy Corp., 94, 96

Conservation Law Found. v. Watt, 401

Consol. Coal Co. v. Georgia Power Co. cases, 720

Consolidated Edison Co. of N.Y. v. UGI Util., Inc., 698, 725, 726,

Consolidated Rail Corp. v. Gottshall, 154

Cook Inlet Keeper v. Alaska, 401

Cooper Indus. v. Aviall Servs., 724, 725, 726, 729, 730

Copart Indus. v. Cons. Edison Co., 91

Corrosion Proof Fittings v. U.S. Environmental Protection Agency, 584-586, 593, 672-673

County Line Inv. Co. v. Tinney, 137

Courtaulds Fibers v. Long, 98

Criscuola v. Power Auth. of the State of N.Y., 156

Crosby v. Young, 917

Cross Oil Co. v. Phillips Petroleum Co., 786

CSX Transp. v. Pub. Util. Comm'n of Ohio, 264

Ctr. for Biological Diversity v. Norton, 446

CTS Corp. v. Waldburger, 730

D.C. Fed'n of Civic Ass'ns v. Airis, 885

Daubert v. Merrell Dow Pharmaceuticals, Inc., 123-124, 685

Davenport v. Neely, 786

Decker v. Northwest Envtl. Defense Ctr., 253

Dedham Water Co. v. Cumberland Farms Dairy Inc., 698, 728

Defenders of Florissant v. Park Land Development Co., 898-906

Defenders of Wildlife v. EPA, 547

Delta Smelt Consolidated Cases, 456

Dental Ass'n v. Martin, 575

Dep't of Transp. v. Public Citizen, 454

Dolan v. City of Tigard, 949-951

Dole v. Dow Chem., 105

Donaldson v. Central Illinois Public Service Company, 158-165, 166, 168

Donsco, Inc. v. Casper Corp., 706-707

Dooley v. Fairfield, 944

Dow Chem. Co. v. Blum, 657

Dubois v. Thomas (Administrator of EPA), 817

Ducktown Copper cases, 113, 126, 127-128, 958-959

Duke Power v. Carolina Envtl. Study Group, 219, 231

E. I. du Pont de Nemours & Co. v. Train, 543

E.I. DuPont de Nemours & Co. v. U.S., 725, 726

Earth Island Inst. v. Mosbacher, 1003-1004, 1008

Eastern Enterprises v. Apfel, 950, 951, 953

EDF v. EPA, 654-657, 658, 674

EDF v. Hardin, 49, 238

EDF v. Ruckelshaus, 49

EDF v. TVA (Tellico Dam), 424

Edwards Aquifer Authority v. Day, 956

Edwards Aquifer Auth. v. Bragg, 956

Eldridge v. Cowell, 893

EME Homer City Generation v. EPA, 468, 479-480

Endangered Species Committee Decision (snail darter/TVA Tellico Dam), 430

English v. General Elec. Co., 262, 263

ENSCO Inc. v. Dumas, 730

Entergy Corp. v. Riverkeeper, Inc., 493, 495, 599

Environmental Def. Ctr., Inc. v. EPA, 547

EPA v. California, 532-534

EPA v. Nat'l Crushed Stone Ass'n, 538

Escamilla v. Asarco, Inc., 129

Ethyl Corp. v. EPA, 658, 967

Euclid v. Ambler, see Village of Euclid v. Ambler Realty Co.

Evans v. Johnstown, 137,

Express Car Wash Corp. v. Irinaga Bros., 786

Exxon Corp. v. Hunt, 730

Exxon Corp. v. Yarema, 156

Exxon Mobil, 135

Exxon Shipping Co. v. Baker, 134

Exxon v. Train, 529

Exxon Valdez v. Exxon Mobil, 136

Exxon-Valdez oil spill, 68, 138, 814, 847, 861, 880

Fasano v. Bd. of County Comm'rs of Wash. County, 951

FCC v. Schreiber, 244

Federal Lands Legal Consortium v. Agriculture Dep't, 410

Fédération des entreprises du commerce et de la distribution (FCD) & Fédération des magasins de bricolage et de l'aménagement de la maison (FMB) v. Ministry of Ecology, Sustainable Development, and Energy, 682-684

Fednav. Ltd. v. Chester, 268

FERC v. Miss., 277

Ferebee, see Chevron Chemical Co. v. Ferebee.

Ferguson v. Skrupa, 955

Film Recovery, see People v. Film Recovery

Final Creek Group v. Newmont Mining Corp., 728

First Iowa Hydro-Elec. Coop. v. FPC, 265

Fischer v. Johns Manville Corp., 133

Fishermen Against the Destruction of the Environment v. Closter Farms, 531

Fisser v. International Bank, 720

Florida Key Deer v. Paulson, 454

Florida Lime & Avocado Growers, Inc. v. Paul, 260

Florissant Fossil Beds, see Defenders of Florissant v. Park Land Development Company.

Forester v. CPSC, 585

Fort Gratiot Sanitary Landfill Inc. v. Michigan Dep't of Natural Res., 273

Foster-Fountain Packing Co. v. Haydel, 272

Freeman v. Glaxo Wellcome, Inc., 711

Frew v. Hawkins, 811

Fri v. Sierra Club, see Sierra Club v. Ruckelshaus

Friends of the Earth v. Laidlaw Envtl. Servs., 234-238, 820

Friends of the Earth v. Consolidated Rail Corp., 818

Friends of the Earth v. EPA, 559

Friends of the Everglades v. S. Fla. Water Mgmt. Dist., 532

Frontier Communications Corp. v. Barrett Paving Matls., 709

Fund for Animals et al. v. Norton, 395

Fund for Animals v. Army Dep't, 362

Garcia v. San Antonio Metro. Transit Auth., 277

Geer v. Connecticut, 269, 284

Geier v. Am. Honda Motor Co., 264

General Elec. Co. v. Dep't of Commerce, 744

General Elec. Co. v. EPA, 253

General Elec. Co. v. Jackson, 733

General Electric Co. v. Joiner, 124

General Elec. Co. v. Litton Indus. Automation Sys., Inc., 727

Georgia v. Tennessee Copper Company and Ducktown Sulphur, Copper and Iron Company Limited, 94, 960

Geraghty & Miller, Inc. v. Conoco Inc., 711

Gibbons v. Ogden, 258, 260

Gilbert v. Allied Chem. (personal injury), 42

Goldstein v. Potomac Elec. Power Co., 98

Good v. U.S., 357

Gordon v. Marrone, 100

Gould v. Greylock Reservation Commission, 885

Granite Rock, see California Coastal Comm'n v. Granite Rock Co.

Greyrocks Dam case, 439

Griggs v. Allegheny County, 927

Gulf of Mexico BP Deepwater blowout spill, 75, 142-143, 804-805, 877-878, 882

Gwaltney of Smithfield v. Chesapeake Bay Found., 231, 232, 818-819

H.P. Hood & Sons, Inc. v. Du Mond, 270

Hadacheck v. Sebastian, 932

Hagy v. Allied Chem., 84

Hale v. Henkel, 864

Hallstrom v. Tillamook County, 231, 818

Hanousek v. U.S., 863, 875

Harmon Indus. v. Browner, 797

Haslip (Pac. Mut. Life Ins. Co. v. Haslip), 133-134, 137

Hawaii v. Midkiff, 921

Hazardous Waste Treatment Council v. U.S. Environmental Protection Agency, 776-780

Hearst v. NLRB, 250

Heckler v. Chaney, 239, 514, 817

Hells Canyon Alliance v. USFS, 395

Hercules v. EPA, 253

Hill et al. v. TVA (the Snail Darter case), see Tennessee Valley Authority v. Hill et al.

Hines v. Davidowitz, 258, 261

Hirsch v. CSX, 88-89

Hodel v. Va. Surface Mining & Reclamation Ass'n, 259, 277

Holdridge v. U.S., 862

Holly Farms v. NLRB, 251

Homer City, see EME Homer City

Honda Motors v. Oberg, 134

Horne v. U.S. Dep't of Agriculture, 935, 950

Horsehead Res. Dev. Co. v. Browner, 771

Hughes v. Alexandria Scrap, 608

Hughes v. Okla., 269

Hughes v. Washington, 948

Hulbert v. California Portland Cement Co., 111

Hurley v. Lederle Lab. Div. of American Cyanamid, 662

Huron Portland Cement Co. v. Detroit, 262

Idaho Watersheds Project v. Hahn, 386

Table of Cases

IIT Indus., Inc. v. BorgWarner, Inc., 729

Illinois Central Railroad Company v. Illinois, 883-884

In re Bell Petroleum Servs., 695

In re Bergsoe Metal Corp., 713

In re Dant & Russell, 728

In re Deseret Power Elec. Coop., 504

In re GEMS Landfill Super. Ct. Litig., 156

In re Katrina Breaches Consolidated Litigation, 947

In re Northern Michigan University Ripley Heating Plant, 497-503

In re Oil Spill by the Oil Rig Deepwater Horizon, 805

In re Select Steel, 482, 485

In re Steuart Transp. Co., Owner of the Tank Barge STC-101, 884-885, 907-910

Indiana-Michigan Power Co. v. DOE, 369

Industrial Union Dep't, AFL-CIO v. Am. Petroleum Inst. ("Benzene"), 472, 495, 576

INS v. Cardoza-Fonseca, 252

International Harvester v. Ruckelshaus, 508-510, 685

International Paper Co. v. Ouellette, 94, 567

Irish v. Green, 908

Ironbound Health Rights Advisory Comm'n v. Diamond Shamrock Chems. Co., 153

Japan Whaling Association v. American Cetacean Society, 293-296, 301

Johansen v. Combustion Eng'g, 134, 137

Jones-Hamilton Co. v. Beazer Materials & Servs., 711, 836

Juliana et al. v. U.S. (atmospheric PTD), 911, 913

Kaiser Aluminum & Chem. Corp. v. Catellus Dev. Corp., 735

Karlen v. Harris, 318

Kelley ex rel. Mich. Natural Res. Comm'n v. ARCO Indus. Corp., 708

Kelley v. EPA, 713-714, 833

Kelo v. City of New London, 115, 917-923

Kennecott Utah Copper Corp. v. U.S. Dep't of the Interior, 744

Kepone, 42-69, 105-106, 865-869

Key Tronic Corp v. U.S., 724

Keystone Bituminous Coal Ass'n v. DeBenedictis, 932-933, 936

KFC Western, Inc. v. Meghrig, 698, 783-786

Kinley v. Atlantic Cement, 114

Klamath Basin case, 443

Kleppe v. New Mexico, 407-412

Kohl v. U.S., 916

Koos v. Roth, 89

Koontz v. St. Johns River Water Management District, 951-954

Kumho Tire Co. v. Carmichael, 124

Ky.-Ohio Gas Co. v. Bowling, 111

La Raza Unida v. Volpe, 231

Lake Mich. Fed'n v. U.S. Army Corps of Eng'rs, 881

Landers v. East Texas Salt Water Disposal Co., 102-103

Landrigan v. Celotex Corp., 166-169

Langan v. Valicopters, 89

Lead Industries Association v. EPA, 469, 474-475

Leo Sheep Co. v. U.S., 411

Les v. Reilly, 420

Lingle v. Chevron, 956

Lochner v. New York, 273-275

Loe v. Lenhard, 89

Lone Pine, 82-83

Lopez v. U.S., 285

Loretto v. Teleprompter, 932, 935, 950

Louisiana v. Lujan, 401

Louisiana-Pacific Corp. v. Asarco, Inc., 723

Lucas v. South Carolina Coastal Council, 936-941, 944-948, 958

Lujan I (Lujan v. National Wildlife Fed'n), 232

Lujan II (Lujan v. Defenders of Wildlife), 233-238

Lusk v. Foxmeyer Health Corp., 719

Lykins v. Westinghouse Electric Corp., 818

Madison v. Ducktown Sulphur, Copper & Iron Co., 113, 126-129, 958-959

Maine v. Johnson. see State of Maine v. Johnson

Maine v. Taylor, 275

Mangan v. Landmark 4, LLC, 87-88, 123

Marbury v. Madison, 241, 253

Mardan Corp. v. C.G.C. Music, Ltd., 723

Marion County v. Luttrell, 907

Marks v. Whitney, 888-896, 907, 910

Martin v. Reynolds Metals Co., 77

Martin v. Waddell, 887

Maryland Waste Coalition v. SCM Corp., 818

Massachusetts v. EPA, 513-518, 990

Mathews v. Eldridge, 205, 917

Matthews v. Bay Head Improvement Ass'n, 908

Mayo Found. v. STB, 324

McElwain v. Georgia Pacific Corp., 132-133, 136

McQueen v. S.C. Coastal Council, 947

Meghrig v. KFC Western, 698, 783, 786

Mehta v. Union of India, 970-973

Menard v. Collins, 151

Merrill v. Manchester, 917

Merryweather v. Nixon, 103

Metro-North Commuter R.R. v. Buckley, 154, 155

Metro. Water Reclamation Dist. of Greater Chicago v. N. Am. Galvanizing & Coatings., 725

Michie v. Great Lakes Steel, 102-103

Michigan v. US EPA, 473, 491-495, 597, 599

Mid-States Coalition for Progress v. Surface Transportation Board, 320-323, 325

Middlebury Coll. v. Cent. Power Corp., 917

Millennium Pipeline Co. v. Gutierrez, 405

Miller v. Schoene, 932

Milwaukee v. State, 910

Mineral King Mountain, see Sierra Club v. Morton

Minnesota v. Clover Leaf Creamery Co., 274

Mississippi v. EPA, 476

Missouri v. Holland, 283-286

Missouri v. Illinois, 960

Modjeska Sign Studios v. Berle, 951

Mono Lake, 384, 892-898, 907

Monsanto v. Geertson Seed Farms, 236

Montana Coalition for Stream Access v. Hildreth, 908

Monterey v. Del Monte Dunes Corp., 908

Moore v. Allied, 52

Moore, Hundtofte & LSP v. Occupational Safety & Health Rev. Comm'n, 42, 50

Table of Cases

Morissette v. U.S., 862, 873

Morrison Enters., LLC v. Dravo Corp., 729

Mortellite v. Novartis, 660

Morton Int'l v. A.E. Staley Mfg., 710

Motor Vehicle Mfrs. Ass'n v. State Farm Mutual Life Ins. Co., 221-222, 251

Mount Laurel, see Township of Mount Laurel v. NAACP

Mountain States Legal Found. v. Hodel, 410

Mugler v. Kansas, 932

NAHB v. EPA, 453-455

Nashville I-40 Steering Comm. v. Ellington, 887

National Adver. Co. v. County of Monterey, 949

National Association of Home Builders (NAHB) v. Defenders of Wildlife, 453-455

National Audubon Society v. Superior Court of Alpine County (Mono Lake), 384, 892-900, 907

National Cotton Council v. EPA, 531

National Envtl. Dev. Ass'ns Clean Air Project v. EPA, 475

National League of Cities v. Usery, 277

National Parks & Conservation Ass'n v. Babbitt, 327

National Parks & Conservation Ass'n v. Morton, 247

National Solid Waste Mgmt. Ass'n v. Meyer, 275

National Wildlife Fed'n v. Exxon Corp., Alyeska Pipeline Serv. Co., 139-142, 847

National Wildlife Fed'n v. Gorsuch, 531, 807

Natural Resources Defense Council. See NRDC

Nebraska v. EPA, 593

NEPACCO. See U.S. v. Northeastern Pharm.

Neptune City v. Avon-by-the-Sea, 895

Neuberger v. Portland, 954

Nevada State Bd. of Agric. v. U.S., 411

New Castle v. Rollins Outdoor Adver., 949

New Jersey v. U.S. EPA, 490

New York v. Lashins Arcade, 716

New York v. Schenectady Chemical Company, 89, 90-94, 96-99, 113, 367

New York v. Shore Realty Corp., 705, 707

Newton Cnty. Wildlife Ass'n v. U.S. Forest Serv., 863

Niagara Mohawk Power Corp. v. Chevron U.S.A., Inc., 729

NLRB v. United Food & Comm'l Wkrs. Union, 242

Nollan v. California Coastal Comm'n, 911, 950-954

Norfolk & Western Railway v. Ayers, 153

North Carolina v. Brown, 405

North Carolina v. EPA, 479

North Carolina v. Federal Energy Reg. Comm'n, 531

North Shore Gas Co. v. EPA, 733

North. Cal. River Watch v. City of Healdsburg, 528

Northern States Power Co. v. Minnesota, 261

Northwest Airlines, Inc. v. Transport Workers Union of America, 714

Northwest Envtl. Advocates v. Portland, 253, 547, 555

Northwest Forest Resource Council, 240

Norton v. Southern Utah Wilderness Alliance (SUWA), 220, 390-392, 395

NRDC v. Costle, 348, 699

NRDC v. EPA (HAPs), 231

NRDC v. EPA (NAAQS), 476

NRDC v. EPA (NGO's attorneys fees),

NRDC v. EPA, 771

NRDC v. Hodel, 385

NRDC v. Morton, 376

NRDC v. Texaco Ref. & Mktg., 555

NRDC v. Train (listing air pollutants), 206, 462, 517, 544

NRDC v. U.S. Dep't of the Interior, 444

Nuclear Energy Institute, Inc. v. EPA, 370

Nugget Hydroelectric Co. v. SWRCB, 265

Nurad Inc. v. William E. Hooper & Sons. Co., 716

O'Neil v. Picillo, 695, 746, 747-750

Office of Communication of United Church of Christ v. FCC, 247

Ohio Forestry v. Sierra Club, 238

Ohio v. U.S. Dep't of Interior, 140, 744

Open Space Inst., Inc., Open Space Conservancy, Inc., Audubon Soc'y of N.H. v. Am. Elec. Power Co., et al., see American Electric Power

Opinion of the Justices (Mass. beach rights), 908

Oregon Nat. Res. Council v. Jack Ward Thomas, 240

Oregon Nat'l Desert Ass'n v. Dombeck, 568

Oregon Waste Sys. Inc. v. Oregon Dep't of Envtl. Quality, 273

Overton Park. See Citizens to Preserve Overton Park v. Volpe

Oxford County Agric. Soc'y v. Sch. Dist., 917

Oxygenated Fuels Ass'n v. Davis, 264

Pac. Gas & Elec. v. Cal. Energy Res. Conservation & Dev. Comm'n, 260, 261

Pacific Mut. Life Ins. Co. v. Haslip, 133-134, 137

Paepke v. Building Commission, 880, 887-889, 906

Palazzolo v. Rhode Island, 394, 935, 937-945, 949-958

Palila v. Hawaii Dep't of Land & Natural Res., 430

Palsgraf v. Long Island R.R. Co., 106

Paoli R.R. Yard PCB Litig., 155

Payne v. Kassab, 892

Payton v. Abbott Labs., 149-150

Pebble Limited Partnership v. EPA, 239

Penn Central Transp. Co. v. New York, 357, 932-945, 952-953, 956-958

Pennsylvania Coal v. Mahon, 929-932, 936

Pennsylvania v. Union Gas, 260

People ex rel. Moloney v. Kirk, 909

People ex rel. Scott v. Chicago Park Dist, 891

People v. Chicago Magnet Wire, 852

People v. Film Recovery Systems, Inc., 847-853, 864

People v. Keuffel & Esser Co., 864

People v. Martin, 861

People v. O'Neill et al., 847-53, 864

Petition of Kinsman Transit Co., 106

Philadelphia v. New Jersey. See City of Philadelphia v. New Jersey

Phillip Morris USA v. Williams, 134

Philips Petroleum Co. v. Mississippi, 946

Phillip Morris USA v. Williams, 134

Pike v. Bruce Church, Inc., 271, 274, 275

Table of Cases

Pneumo Abex Corp. v. High Point, Thomasville & Denton R.R., 711

Poletown Neighborhood Council v. City of Detroit, 919-924

Polumbo v. Waste Techs., 368

Portland Audubon Soc'y v. Endangered Species Comm., 439

Potter v. Firestone Tire & Rubber Co., 153

Prairie State Generating Co., 505

Price v. U.S. Navy, 785

Pronsolino v. Nastri, 556-565

Pruitt v. Allied Chem. Corp., 42, 54, 105-107, 137, 141, 152

Public Citizen v. Office of the U.S. Trade Representative, 454

Public Util. Dist. No. 1 of Jefferson County & City of Tacoma v. Wash. Dep't of Ecology, 568

Puerto Rico v. S.S. Zoe Colocotroni, 908

Pullen v. Boston Elevated Ry. Co., 151

Rapanos v. United States, 360, 526-529, 539

Ray v. Atlantic Richfield Co., 263, 268

Reeves Inc. v. Stake, 276

Regina v. Prospec Chems., 647

Republican Nat'l Comm. v. FEC, 300

Rice v. Santa Fe Elevator Corp., 260

Richardson et al. v. BLM (Otero Mesa), 210, 388

Rio Grande Silvery Minnow v. Keys, 440

Robb v. Shockoe Slip Found., 975

Roberson v. DuPont, 662

Robins Drydock & Repair Co. v. Flint, 107

Robinson Township v. Comm. of Pennsylvania, 911

Rosemere Neighborhood Ass'n v. EPA, 485-486

Roth v. Cabot Oil & Gas Corp, 79-82

Ruckelshaus v. Monsanto, 676

Rumpke of Ind. v. Cummins Engine Co., Inc., 728

Rybachek v. U.S. Environmental Protection Agency, 206, 208-209, 532, 536-550

Rylands v. Fletcher, 86, 88

S.D. Warren Co. v. Me. Bd. of Envtl. Protection, 568-569

Sackett v. EPA, 239, 734

St. Bernard Parish Government and other Owners of Real Property in St. Bernard Parish, the Lower Ninth Ward of the City of New Orleans v. U.S., 927, 947

Sanderson v. Penn Coal, 946-949

Santa Rosa v. EPA, 462

Save Our Community v. EPA, 364

Scenic Hudson Preservation Conference v. FPC, 227-229, 235, 246-250

Schenectady Chemical, see New York v. Schenectady Chemical Company

Schwarzenbach v. Oneonta Light & Power Co., 112

Schweiker v. Wilson, 915

Seattle Audubon v. Evans, 863

Seattle Audubon v. Robertson, 240

Secretary of Interior v. Cal., 402

Select Steel, (U.S. EPA Office of Civil Rights decision), 482-483, 485

Shell Oil Co. v. EPA, 771

Shevlin-Carpenter v. Minn., 862

Sierra Club v. Block (public trust doctrine), 384

Sierra Club v. Chevron U.S.A., Inc. (notice in citizen suits), 817-818

Sierra Club v. Clark, 396

Sierra Club v. Dep't of Interior (public trust doctrine), 384, 882, 908

Sierra Club v. FWS (ESA critical habitats), 444

Sierra Club v. Morton (Mineral King), 219, 228

Sierra Club v. Ruckelshaus, 223, 463

Sierra Club v. Thomas, 382

Sierra Club v. Union Oil, 819

Sierra Club v. Yeutter (public trust doctrine), 384

Silkwood v. Kerr-McGee, 261, 263

Simon v. Eastern Ky. Welfare Rights Org., 233

Sindell v. Abbot Labs., 104, 169

Skidmore v. Swift & Co., 254

Smith Land & Improvement Corp. v. Celotex Corp., 723

Solid Waste Agency of N. Cook County (SWANNC) v. U.S. Army Corps of Eng'rs, 360

Solutia, Inc. Pharmacia Corp. v. McWane, Inc., 729

Soucie v. David, 247

South African Airways v. Dole, 301

South Camden Citizens in Action v. Shinn, 369

South Carolina Dep't of Health & Envtl. Control v. Commerce & Indus. Ins. Co., 786

South Carolina State Highway Dept. v. Barnwell Bros., 270

South Fla. Water Mgmt. Dist. v. Montalvo, 711

South-Central Timber Dev. Co. v. Wunnicke, 274

Southern Utah Wilderness Alliance case, see Norton v. Southern Utah Wilderness Alliance (SUWA)

Southview Farms, see Concerned Area Residents v. Southview Farms

Spur Industries v. Del Webb Development Co., 89, 98

Staples v. U.S., 855-857

State ex rel. SOCM v. Fowinkle, 907

State Farm Mut. Auto. Ins. Co. v. Campbell, 134

State of Maine v. Johnson, 935

State v. Amerada Hess, 909

State v. Public Service Comm'n, 910

Steel Co. v. Citizens for a Better Env't (CBE), 232, 234, 338, 819

Sterling v. Velsicol, 153

Steuart Transportation, see U.S. v. Steuart Transp. Co.

Stop the Beach Renourishment, Inc. v. Florida, 911, 937, 949

Storm King case, see Scenic Hudson Preservation Conference v. FPC

Strahan v. Coxe, 210

Strahan v. Linnon, 210

Strawn v. Incollingo, 156

Strycker's Bay Neighborhood Council v. Karlen, 317

Stupak-Thrall v. U.S., 410

Suitum v. Tahoe Regional Planning Agency, 357-358, 933, 957-958

Summers v. Earth Island Institute, 236

Summers v. Tice, 104

Superior Air Prods. v. NL Indus., 753

Swin Res. Sys. v. Lycoming County Pa., 276

Tahoe Pub. Util. Dist. v. Atlantic Richfield Co., 93

Tahoe-Sierra Preservation Council v. Tahoe Reg'l Planning Agency, 937

Tanner v. Armco Steel, 911

Table of Cases

Tennessee Valley Authority v. Hill et al., see also Hill et al. v. Tennessee Valley Authority, 208-209, 125, 250, 423-432, 433, 438, 444, 448, 454

Terry v. Zions Coop., 132

Texas E. Transmission Co. v. Wildlife Preserves, 917

The Schooner Charming Betsy, 301

Thomasville & Denton R.R., 711

Thornburg v. Port of Portland, 924-927

Thorpe v. Housing Auth., 216

Tillamook County. see Hallstrom v. Tillamook County, 231, 818

Township of Mount Laurel v. NAACP, 354

Trail Smelter Arbitration (U.S. v. Canada), 959-962

Train v. Colo. Pub. Interest Research Group, 544

TVA v. Hill, see Tennessee Valley Authority v. Hill et al.

Tyson Foods, see Atl. States Legal Found. v. Tyson Foods.

U.S. EPA v. California, 532

U.S. Steel v. Train (groundwater), 529

U.S. v. 1.8 Acres, 910

U.S. v. A&F Matls. Co., 732

U.S. v. Aceto Agric. Chems. Corp., 710

U.S. v. Ahmad, 854-856, 858, 859

U.S. v. Alcan Aluminum Corp., 695

U.S. v. Allegheny-Ludlum Steel Corp., 242

U.S. v. Allied Chem. (criminal case), 42-56, 865-868, 880

U.S. v. Apex Oil, 787

U.S. v. Apollo Energies, 863

U.S. v. Atlantic Research Corporation, 725-727, 728, 729-730

U.S. v. Baytank (Houston), Inc., 855

U.S. v. BestFoods Corporation, 698, 717-723

U.S. v. BP Exploration & Prod. Inc., 805

U.S. v. Booker, 877

U.S. v. Cannons Eng'g Corp., 753

U.S. v. Carolawn Co., 874

U.S. v. Carroll Towing Co., 85

U.S. v. Causby, 925

U.S. v. CDMG Realty Co., 716

U.S. v. Cello-Foil Prods., 711

U.S. v. Chem-Dyne Corp., 695, 697, 698, 748

U.S. v. v. Citgo Petroleum Corp., 863

U.S. v. Darby, 276

U.S. v. Domestic Indus., 786

U.S. v. Dotterweich (burden of proof), 872-873, 875

U.S. v. Ekco Housewares, 865

U.S. v. Elias, 852

U.S. v. Engler, 862-863

U.S. v. Fleet Factors Corp., 713

U.S. v. Florida E. Coast Ry. Co., 242

U.S. v. FMC Corp, 863

U.S. v. Gardner, 411

U.S. v. Gen. Elec. Co., 709

U.S. v. Hanousek, 875

U.S. v. Hansen, 874

U.S. v. Hoflin, 860-861

U.S. v. Int'l Minerals & Chem. Corp., 857

U.S. v. Jellico Indus., 846

U.S. v. Johnson & Towers, Inc., 860-861

U.S. v. Kramer, 696, 713

U.S. v. Laughlin, 861

U.S. v. Lawrence, 410, 927

U.S. v. Locke, 263, 268

U.S. v. MacDonald & Watson Waste Oil Co., 873

U.S. v. McCullagh, 284

U.S. v. Mead Corp., 252, 254

U.S. v. Metalite Corp., 859

U.S. v. Mexico Feed & Seed Co., 723

U.S. v. Midwest Oil Co., 384

U.S. v. Miller, 950

U.S. v. Monsanto Co., 695

U.S. v. Morgan, 217

U.S. v. Northeastern Pharm. & Chem. Co. (NEPACCO), 692, 703-710, 735, 783, 875

U.S. v. Nye County, Nev., 411

U.S. v. Park., 869-873

U.S. v. Parsons, 734

U.S. v. Plaza Health Labs., 530

U.S. v. Pollution Abatement Servs., Inc. of Oswego, 874

U.S. v. Power Eng'g Co., 797

U.S. v. Protex, 861

U.S. v. Republic Steel, 845

U.S. v. Robinson, 528

U.S. v. Ruehle, 865

U.S. v. San Francisco, 408

U.S. v. SCRAP, 219

U.S. v. Shauver, 284

U.S. v. Shimer, 250

U.S. v. Smithfield Foods, 58

U.S. v. Standard Oil Co., 845

In Re Steuart Transportation Co., 882, 907-910

U.S. v. Stringfellow, 712

U.S. v. TIC Inv. Corp., 709

U.S. v. Wade (Wade II), 701-703, 708

U.S. v. Ward, 705

U.S. v. Wash. State Dep't of Transp., 709

U.S. v. WCI Steel, 865

U.S. v. Weitzenhoff, 856-858, 861, 863

U.S. v. White, 864

U.S. v. White Fuel Corp., 861-862

U.S. v. Winstar Corp., 449

U.S. v. Wulff, 862

U.S. v. X-Citement Video, 863

U.S. Army Corps of Engineers v. Hawkes Co., 239

Union Elec. Co. v. EPA, 471-472, 474

Union Oil Co. v. Oppen, 106

United Techs. Corp. v. Browning-Ferris Indus., 728

Utah Power & Light Co. v. U.S., 408

Utilex, In Re (Michigan DNR file), 185-188, 189, 198

Utility Air Regulatory Group (UARG) v. EPA, 516-517

Vellore Citizens' Welfare Forum v. Union of India and Others, 971

Velsicol Chemical Corporation v. Rowe, 101-103, 945

Vermont v. Cent. Vt. Ry, 882

Vermont v. Staco Inc., 875

Vermont Yankee Nuclear Power Corporation v. NRDC, 201, 242-246, 248

Village of Euclid v. Ambler Realty Co., 121, 171, 351, 914

Village of Skokie v. Walton, 949

Village of Wilsonville v. SCA Services, Inc., 116-125, 366, 945

Vimar Seguros y Reaseguros, S.A. v. M/V Sky Reefer, 301

Wade v. Kramer, 908

Table of Cases

Walls v. Waste Res. Corp., 708

Walton County v. Stop the Beach Renourishment, Inc., 911, 937, 949

Warth v. Seldin, 232

Waterkeeper Alliance v. EPA, 546

Wayne County v. Hathcock, 923

West Mich. Envtl. Action Council v. NRC (Pigeon River case), 212, 907-908

Westling v. County of Mille Lacs, 156

Weyerhaeuser v. Costle, 543

Whalen v. Union Bag & Paper Co., 109, 112-113, 129

Whitman v. American Trucking Ass'ns. See American Trucking, 203, 470-474, 476, 493, 593, 596-597, 599

Wickard v. Filburn, 258

Williams v. Phillip Morris Inc, 134

Williamson v. Lee Optical of Okla., 955

Wilson v. United States, 864

Wilsonville v. SCA Services, see Village of Wilsonville v. SCA Services

Winter v. Natural Resources Defense Council, 236

Wisc. Pub. Intervenor v. Mortier, 660

Wisconsin v. EPA, 567

Wong Yang Sung v. McGrath, 242, 245

Wood v. Picillo, 87

WTO, U.S., Import Prohibition of Certain Shrimp and Shrimp Products, 999-1010

WTO, U.S., Restrictions on Imports of Tuna, 1006-1009

Wuebker v. Wilber Ellis Co., 660

Wyoming v. U.S., 412

Yannacone v. Dennison, 49

Zabel v. Tabb, 846

TABLE OF AUTHORITIES: BOOKS, ARTICLES, SPEECHES

ABA, Brownfields Redevelopment: Cleaning Up the Urban Environment, 807

Abrams, Binding Agreements with Governmental Entities, 811

Abrams, Robert H., & Hall, Noah D., Framing Water Policy in a Carbon Affected and Carbon Constrained Environment, 394

Ackerman, Bruce & Stewart, Richard, Reforming Environmental Law, 197

Ackerman, Frank, & Heinzerling, Lisa, Priceless, On Knowing the Price of Everything and the Value of Nothing, 581

Ackerman, Frank, & Heinzerling, Lisa, Pricing the Priceless: Cost-Benefit Analysis of Environmental Protection, 572-574, 600-605

Adelson, Glenn, et al., ENVIRONMENT: AN INTERDISCIPLINARY ANTHOLOGY, xxvii

Adler, Robert, et al., The Clean Water Act 20 Years Later, 548

Administrative Conference of the U.S., Negotiated Rulemaking Sourcebook, 825

Ahern, L.R. & Marsh, D.T., Environmental Obligations in Bankruptcy, 717

Akers, New Tools for Environmental Justice: Articulating a Net Health Effects Challenge to Emissions Trading Markets, 628

Alaska Oil Spill Comm'n, Spill: The Wreck of the Exxon-Valdez: Lessons for the Safe Transportation of Oil, 138

Allaby, M., BASICS OF ENVIRONMENTAL SCIENCE, 9

American Planning Ass'n, A GUIDE TO WELLHEAD PROTECTION, 349

American WaterWorks Ass'n, SOURCE WATER PROTECTION: EFFECTIVE TOOLS AND TECHNIQUES YOU CAN USE, 349

Anderson, Below-Cost Timber Sales & Community Economic Subsidies: A Conflict of Values, 385

Anderson, J. & Hirsch, D., ENVIRONMENTAL LAW PRACTICE, xxviii, 205

Andreen, The Evolution of Water Pollution Control in the United States: State, Local, and Federal Efforts, 535

Andrews, R.N.L., MANAGING THE ENVIRONMENT, MANAGING OURSELVES, A HISTORY OF AMERICAN ENVIRONMENTAL POLICY, 465

Appellate Body Report, European Communities, Trade Description of Sardines, 647

Applegate, The Perils of Unreasonable Risk: Information, Regulatory Policy, and Toxic Substances Control, 660-661, 669, 670, 671-672

Araiza, Text, Purpose, and Facts: The Relationship Between CERCLA Sections, 728

ARTNews, The Case of the Dismembered Masterpieces, 908

Ashford, Nicholas, & Charles Caldart, ENVIRONMENTAL LAW, POLICY, AND ECONOMICS: RECLAIMING THE ENVIRONMENTAL AGENDA, xxvii

ASTM, STANDARD PRACTICE FOR ENVIRONMENTAL ASSESSMENTS; Phase I Environmental Site Assessment Process, 836-837

Avi-Yonah & Uhlmann, Why a Carbon Tax Is a Better Response to Global Warming than Cap-and-Trade, 639

Babbitt, Park's Retreating Glaciers Signal a Climate Warning, Denver Post, 982

Babcock, Dual Regulation, Collaborative Management, or Layered Federalism: Can Cooperative Federalism Models from Other Laws Save Our Public Lands?, 278

Barnett, Gov. Ross, 1965 Speech at Princeton University, 191

Barrett, Mirage, 351

Been, Locally Undesirable Land Uses in Minority Neighborhoods: Disproportionate Siting or Market Dynamics?, 368

Benson, Adaptive Management Approaches by Resource Management Agencies in the U.S., 416

Bissell, Recent Practice of the Inspection Panel of the World Bank, 104

Black & Lilienfeld, Epidemiologic Proof in Toxic Tort Litigation, 166

BLACK'S LAW DICTIONARY, 726, 885

Blasser & Kentopp, Impact Fees: The Second Generation, 358

Bleich, Chrome on the Range: Off-Road Vehicles on Public Lands, 395

Blumm & Bosse, Norton v. SUWA and the Unraveling of Federal Public Land Planning, 392

Blumm, Public Choice Theory and the Public Lands: Why "Multiple Use" Failed, 382

BNA, New Records for Actions, Fines Set by EPA Despite Restructuring Program, 792

Bodansky, The United Nations Framework Convention on Climate Change: A Commentary, 987

Bolt, A Man for All Seasons, 427

Bosselman, F., D. Callies & J. Banta, THE TAKING ISSUE, 929, 948

Bosselman, The Statutory and Constitutional Mandate for a No Surprises Policy, 449

Breyer, Judicial Review of Questions of Law and Policy, 435

Broome, Trying to Value a Life, 601

Brower, Access to the Nation's Beaches: Legal and Planning Perspectives, 908

Brown, Greenhouse Economics: Think Before You Count, 587

Brunet, The Costs of Environmental Alternative Dispute Resolution, 822

Budnick, L., Toothpick-Related Injuries in the U.S., 1979 Through 1982, 586

Bukowczyk, The Decline and Fall of a Detroit Neighborhood, 921

Bullard, Robert, Dumping in Dixie: Race, Class & Environmental Quality, 55, 368

Butzel, Intervention and Class Actions Before the Agencies and the Courts, 246

Buzbee, Expanding the Zone, Tilting the Field: Zone of Interests and Article III Standing Analysis After Bennett v. Spear, 235

Byrne, Peter, post on Reg. Takings, 947

Calvin Center for Christian Scholarship, EARTHKEEPING: CHRISTIAN STEWARDSHIP OF NATURAL RESOURCES, 26

Camacho, Can Regulation Evolve? Lessons from a Study in Maladaptive Management, 415, 443

Camerer, Colin and George LOEWENSTEIN, BEHAVIORAL ECONOMICS: PAST, PRESENT, AND FUTURE, 611

Campbell-Mohn, Objectives and Tools of Environmental Law, in ENVIRONMENTAL LAW: FROM RESOURCES TO RECOVERY, 21

Canan & Pring, Studying Strategic Lawsuits Against Public Participation, 99

Carbon Tax Center, Where Carbon is Taxed, 640

Carlson, Standing for the Environment, 235

Carr et al., ENVIRONMENTAL CRIMINAL LIABILITY: AVOIDING AND DEFENDING ENFORCEMENT ACTIONS, 874

Carson, Rachel, SILENT SPRING, 8-10, 11, 14, 49, 67, 189, 459, 651

Center for Biological Diversity, Petition to Establish National Pollution Limits for Greenhouse Gases, 517

Centner, Terence, Anti-Nuisance Legislation, 99

Chekouras, Balancing National Security with a Community's Right to Know: Maintaining Public Access to Environmental Information Through EPCRA's Non-preemption Clause, 340

Chertow & Esty, Environmental Policy: The Next Generation, 442

Cicchetti & Peck, Assessing Natural Resource Damages: The Case Against Contingent Value Survey Methods, 140

Clapham, Japan's Whaling Following the International Court of Justice Ruling: Brave New World—Or Business as Usual?, 290

Clay, The EPA's Proposed Phase III Expansion of the Toxic Release Inventory (TRI) Reporting Requirements, 339

Clean Air Trust, Debunking the Myth of Emission Trading, 627

CMP Adaptive Management Process, Conservation Measures Partnership, 414

Coase, The Problem of Social Cost, 33

Coastal States Org., Putting the Public Trust to Work, 20

Coggins & Lindeberg-Johnson, The Law of Public Rangeland Management II: The Commons and the Taylor Act, 375

Coggins, Commentary: Overcoming the Unfortunate Legacies of Western Public Land Law, 381

Coggins, Conserving Wildlife Resources: An Overview of the Endangered Species Act of 1973, 426

Coggins, The Law of Public Rangeland Management IV: FLPMA, PRIA, and the Multiple Use Mandate, 14 Environmental Law 1, 5-6 (1983), 377-381

Colborn, T., D. Dumanoski & J. P. Myers, OUR STOLEN FUTURE, 11, 63, 156

Cole, Civil Rights, Environmental Justice and the EPA, 369

Cole, Empowerment as a Key to Environmental Protection, The Need for Environmental Poverty Law, 55, 368

Comment, Counterclaim and Countersuit Harassment of Private Environmental Plaintiffs, 99

Comment, Primary Jurisdiction in Environmental Cases, 97

Comment, Superfund at Square One: Promising Statutory Framework Requires Forceful EPA Implementation, 689

Congressional Budget Office, Issues in the Design of a Cap-and-Trade Program for Carbon Emissions, 643

Congressional Research Service, Library of Congress, A Legislative History of the Federal Water Pollution Control Act Amendments of 1972, 535

Copeland & Simpson, Considering Risk in Environmental Protection, 17

Coplan, Refracting the Spectrum of Clean Water Act Standing in Light of Lujan v. Defenders, 235

Coquillette, Mosses from an Old Manse: Another Look at Some Historic Property Cases about the Environment, 883

Costanza & Daly, Natural Capital and Sustainable Development, 19, 142

Costanza et al., The Value of the World's Ecosystem Services and Natural Capital, 19, 142, 394

Costonis, Development Rights Transfers: An Exploratory Essay, 357

Council on Environmental Quality, ENVIRONMENTAL QUALITY: 25th Annual Report, 465

Cowart & Fairfax, Public Lands Federalism: Judicial Theory and Administrative Reality, 267

Cox, No Tragedy of the Commons, 32-33,

Cox, Reforming the Law Applicable to the Award of Restoration Damages as a Remedy for Environmental Torts, 129, 130

Craig & Miller, Ocean Discharge Criteria and Marine Protection Areas, 526

Craig, Robin, A Comparative Guide to the Eastern Public Trust Doctrines: Classification of States, Property Rights, and State Summaries, 912

Craig, Robin, A Comparative Guide to the Western States' Public Trust Doctrines: Public Values, Private Rights, and the Evolution Toward an Ecological Public Trust, 912

Craig, Robin, Notice Letters and Notice Pleading, 818

Cross, Natural Resource Damage Valuation, 140

Cross, The Public Role in Risk Control, 17

Culhane et al., Forecasts and Environmental Decisionmaking, 335

Currie, Air Pollution: Federal Law and Analysis, 470

Daily, ed., Nature's Services: Societal Dependence on Natural Ecosystems, 19, 141

Dalai Lama & G. Rowell, MY TIBET, 26

Daly, A Glimpse of the Past, A Vision for the Future: Senator Henry M. Jackson and National Land-Use Legislation, 396

Daly, Herman, Beyond Growth: The Economics of Sustainable Development, 23

Darwin, Charles, The Formation of Vegetable Mould, through the Action of Worms, with Observations on Their Habits, 9

Davis, Groundwater Pollution, 87

Davis, K.C., & R. Pierce, ADMINISTRATIVE LAW Treatise, 235

Defenders of Wildlife White Paper, The Dunes Sagebrush Lizard: The Cautionary Tale of a Candidate Species Denied, 447

Denison, Evaluating Environmental Impacts, 774

Dernbach, J., Citizen Suits and Sustainability, 21

Dernbach, J., The Potential Meanings of a Constitutional Public Trust, 911

Dernbach, J., "Reflexive" law and governance, 417

Dernbach, J., and May, J., Shale Gas & the Future of Energy, 83

Dernbach, J., ed., STUMBLING TOWARD SUSTAINABILITY, 968

Dernbach, J. The Unfocused Regulation of Toxic and Hazardous Pollutants, 670

Derzko, Using Intellectual Property Law and Regulatory Processes to Foster the Innovation and Diffusion of Environmental Technologies, 536

Developments, Toxic Waste Litigation, 750

Diamond, Confessions of an Environmental Enforcer, 792, 801, 828-829

Dintzer & Mosher, Epidemiological Evidence in Toxic Tort Cases, 167

Diver, Statutory Interpretation in the Administrative State, 252

Donald, Defending Against Daily Fines and Punitive Damages Under CERCLA, 733

Doremus, Adaptive Management, the Endangered Species Act, and the Institutional Challenges of "New Age" Environmental Protection, 450

Doremus, Patching the Ark: Improving Legal Protection of Biological Diversity, 412

Dorsey, A Brief History of the New England Fisheries Crisis, 387

Driesen, Does Emissions Trading Encourage Innovation?, 197

Driesen, Free Lunch or Cheap Fix? The Emissions Trading Idea and the Climate Change Convention, 627

Driesen, Is Emissions Trading an Economic Incentive Program?, 197

Druley, Ray M., & Girard L. Ordway, The Toxic Substances Control Act, 663-665

Drury, Richard Toshiyuki and Michael E. Belliveau, J. Scott Kuhn & Shipra Bansal, Pollution Trading & Environmental Injustice, 622-626, 628

Duany, Plater-Zyberk, et al., SUBURBAN NATION: THE RISE OF SPRAWL AND THE DECLINE OF THE AMERICAN DREAM, 355

Dubuc & Evans, Recent Developments Under CERCLA: Toward a More Equitable Distribution of Liability, 751

Duff, The Coastal Zone Management Act, 401, 402

Echeverria & Kaplan, Poisonous Procedural "Reform", 248

Echeverria & Zeidler, Barely Standing: The Erosion of Citizen "Standing" to Sue and Enforce Environmental Law, 235

Echeverria, The Costs of *Koontz*, 953

Economist, The, Stopping Climate Change, 639

Economist, The, What Price Posterity?, 584

Egan, Wingtip "Cowboys" in Last Stand to Hold on to Low Grazing Fees, 385

Ellerman, Denny, et al., Emissions Trading in the United States, 609, 612-618

Elliott, Donald, Ackerman, Bruce & Millian, John, The Federalization of Environmental Law, 188-189, 193

Emanuel, James, Letter to the Editor, The Economist, 640

Engel, State Environmental Standard-Setting: Is There a "Race" and Is It "to the Bottom?", 192

Environmental Defense (ED), online database, "Scorecard", 336

Estes, The Public Cost of Private Corporations, 51

Esty, Revitalizing Environmental Federalism, 192

European Community, Measures Concerning Meat and Meat Products, 580

Evans, The Phantom PRP in CERCLA Contribution Litigation, 728

Fairlie, The Establishment at Work, 226

Farber, Ecopragmatism, 421

Farber, Taking Slippage Seriously, 421, 436

Farnsworth, Do Parties to Nuisance Cases Bargain After Judgment?, 33

Feldman, D.L., Water Resources Management: In Search of an Environmental Ethic, 10

Feller, 'Til the Cows Come Home: The Fatal Flaw in the Clinton Administration's Public Lands Grazing Policy, 385-386

Ferrer, The Application of Statutes of Repose to Environmentally-Related Injuries, 98

Ferrey, Hard Time: Criminal Prosecution for Polluters, 849-851, 852

Fink, Structuring a Program for the Lake Tahoe Basin, 357

Fischman, Biological Diversity and Environmental Protection: Authorities to Reduce Risk, 365

Fisher, R. & W. Ury, Getting to Yes, 823

Fiss, Against Settlement, 822

Fiss, Out of Eden, 822, 828

Flint Water Advisory Task Force Final Report, 72

Flippen, THE NIXON ADMINISTRATION, POLITICS, AND THE ENVIRONMENT, 399

Florio, Congress as Reluctant Regulator: Hazardous Waste Policy, 758, 775

Frank & Sunstein, Cost-Benefit Analysis and Relative Position, 598

Frank, Robert H., Of Individual Liberty and Cap-and-Trade, 642

Frankel, Stuart, Full Disclosure: Financial Statement Disclosures Under CERCLA, 831-832, 836

Freeman, Collaborative Governance in the Administrative State, 814-815

Freyfogle, Granite Rock: Institutional Competence and the State Role in Federal Land Planning, 267

Friedan, Betty, THE FEMININE MYSTIQUE, 11

Friedman, Frank & David Giannotti, Environmental Self-Assessment, 830-831

Friedman, T., Hot, Flat, and Crowded: Why We Need a Green Revolution, and How It Can Renew America, 347-348

Fuhrman, Almost Always ABEL: EPA Treatment of Ability-to-Pay Issues in Civil Penalty Cases, 802

Gale & Goyer, Recovery for Cancerphobia and Increased Rick of Cancer, 153

GAO, Better Data and Evaluation of Urban Runoff Programs Needed to Assess Effectiveness, 547

GAO, EPA Should Strengthen Its Efforts to Measure and Encourage Pollution Prevention, 338

GAO, Poor Quality Assurance and Limited Pollutant Coverage Undermine EPA's Control of Toxic Substances, 550

GAO, Rulemaking: OMB's Role in Reviews of Agencies' Draft Rules and the Transparency of Those Reviews, 595

Garber, Federal Common Law of Contribution Under the 1986 CERCLA Amendments, 751

Garcia, Remittitur in Environmental Cases, 136

Garcia, M.J., Cong. Research Serv., International Law and Agreements: The Effect Upon U.S. Law 5 (2014), 292

Gardner, Banking on Entrepreneurs: Wetlands, Mitigation Banking, and Takings, 363, 364

Garrett, Brandon, Too Big to Jail, How Prosecutors Compromise With Corporations, 879

Garrett, Theodore, Reinventing EPA Enforcement, 792

Geltman, Recycling Land: Encouraging the Redevelopment of Contaminated Property, 808

Gibbons, Too Much of a Good Thing? Federal Supremacy & Devolution of Regulatory Power: The Case of the Coastal Zone Management Act, 401

Gibeaut, SECRET JUSTICE, 52

Glass, Superfund and SARA: Are There Any Defenses Left?, 713

Glennon, WATER FOLLIES: GROUNDWATER PUMPING AND THE FATE OF AMERICA'S FRESH WATERS, 956

Global Change Research Program, 70

Goldfarb, Changes in the Clean Water Act Since Kepone, 42, 52

Goldfarb, et al., Unsafe Sewage Sludge or Beneficial Biosolids?, 549

Goldfarb, William, Kepone: A Case Study, 42, 865-868

Goodstein & Hodges, Polluted Data, 575

Greenwald, Noah, Center for Biological Diversity, message to authors, 446, 449

Greve, The Private Enforcement of Environmental Law, 815

Gros, The ICJ's Handling of Science in the Whaling in the Antarctic Case: A Whale of a Case?, 290

Grotius, THE FREEDOM OF THE SEAS, 286

Hahn, Getting More Environmental Protection for Less Money, 536,

Hahn, The Impact of Economics on Environmental Policy, 618

Hall, N.D., Political Externalities, Federalism, and a Proposal for an Interstate Environmental Impact Assessment Policy, 333-335

Hardin, G., Sweet-Singing Economists, Exploring New Ethics for Survival: The Voyage of the Spaceship Beagle, 22

Hardin, The Tragedy of the Commons, 28-31, 286

Harper & James, LAW OF TORTS, 102

Harr, Jonathan, A CIVIL ACTION, 149

Harvard Business School, Allied Chemical Corporation Case, 49

Hasselman, Alaska's Nuisance Statute Revisited: Federal Substantive Due Process Limits to Common Law Abrogation, 97

Hasselman, Holes in the Endangered Species Act Safety Net: The Role of Agency "Discretion" in §7 Consultation, 455

Hasselman, National Association of Home Builders v. Defenders of Wildlife: The Supreme Court's Endangered Species Act Decision Should Have Limited Impacts, 455

Hawken, P., et al., Natural Capitalism: Creating the Next Industrial Revolution, 142

Hawken, P., et al., Natural Capitalism: The Coming Efficiency Revolution, 19

Heinzerling, Discounting Life, 602

Heinzerling, Discounting Our Future, 602

Heinzerling, Pragmatists and Environmentalists, 421

Heinzerling, Regulatory Costs of Mythic Proportions, 587, 673

Heinzerling, The Commercial Constitution, 273

Heinzerling, Inside EPA: A Former Insider's Reflections on the Relationship Between the Obama EPA and the Obama White House, 595

Heinzerling, The Rights of Statistical People, 593, 602

Held, Alteration and Mutilation of Works of Art, 908

Hensler et al., Compensation for Accidental Injuries in the U.S., 85

Hiley, Involuntary Sale Damages in Permanent Nuisance Cases: A Bigger Bang from Boomer, 115

Hood, Frayed Safety Nets: Conservation Planning under the ESA, 441

Horner & Brenner, Environmental Evaluation of Calcium Magnesium Acetate for Highway Deicing Applications, 39

Hornstein, Lessons from Federal Pesticide Regulation on the Paradigms and Politics of Environmental Law Reform, 661, 662, 663

Houck & Rolland, Federalism in Wetlands Regulation, 363, 405

Houck, Hard Choices: The Analysis of Alternatives Under §404 of the Clean Water Act and Similar Environmental Laws, 362

Houck, Is That All? A Review of the National Environmental Policy Act, an Agenda for the Future, by Lynton Keith Caldwell, 317

Houck, Regulation of Toxic Pollutants Under the Clean Water Act, 549-550

Houck, The "Institutionalization of Caution" under §7 of the Endangered Species Act: What Do You Do When You Don't Know?, 444

Houck, The Clean Water Act TMDL Program, 564

Houck, TMDLs III: A New Framework for the Clean Water Act's Ambient Standards Program, 565

Houck, TMDLs IV: The Final Frontier, 566

Houck, TMDLs, Are We There Yet? The Long Road Toward Water Quality-Based Regulation Under the Clean Water Act, 565

Houck, TMDLs: The Resurrection of Water Quality Standards-Based Regulation Under the Clean Water Act, 556

Houck, Why Do We Protect Endangered Species, and What Does That Say About Whether Restrictions on Private Property to Protect Them Constitute "Takings"?, 445

Hsu, The Case for a Carbon Tax: Getting Past Our Hang-ups to Effective Climate Policy, 641-642

Huber, Safety and the Second Best: The Hazards of Public Risk Management in the Courts, 148

Huffman, Public Lands: The Case for Privatization, 382

Inspection Panel's Report and Findings on the Qinghai Project: Executive Summary, 999

Interagency Group, Economic Analysis of Federal Regulations Under Executive Order 12,866, 602

IPCC, Fifth Assessment Report, 984, 995

IRS, Issue Paper LMSB-04-0608-036, 870

Irvin, When Survival Is at Stake: A Proposal for Expanding the Emergency Exception to the ESA Sixty-Day Notice Requirement, 231

Jackson, Joint Torts & Several Liability, 102

Jacobs, Jane, THE DEATH AND LIFE OF GREAT AMERICAN CITIES, 11, 355

James, Limitations of Liability for Economic Loss Caused by Negligence: A Pragmatic Appraisal, 105

Jehl, On Environmental Rules, Bush Sees a Balance, Critics a Threat, 793

Jesup, Endless War or End This War? The History of Deadline Litigation Under Section 4 of the Endangered Species Act and The Multi-District Litigation Settlements, 447

Johnson, Ralph, Public Trust Protection for Stream Flows and Lake Levels, 894

Jolowicz, Historical Introduction to the Study of Roman Law, 883

Jordan, Substantive Due Process after Eastern Enterprises, with New Defenses Based on Lack of Causative Nexus—the Superfund Example, 955

Justinian, THE INSTITUTES OF EMPEROR JUSTINIAN, 27, 881, 885, 895

Kagan, Presidential Administration, 477

Kappler, Off-Roading Without a Map: The Supreme Court Drives over NEPA in Southern Utah Wilderness Alliance, 392

Karkkainen, Information as Environmental Regulation: TRI and Performance Benchmarking, Precursor to a New Paradigm?, 335, 339

Katu, Michio, whatis.techtarget.com, 571

Keep, D., & D. Parker, Tests Clear Snow, Path for Use of Liquid Anti-icing in Northwest, Roads & Bridges, 39

Keeton, W.P., & W.L. Prosser, PROSSER AND KEETON ON TORTS, 76

Keiter & Holscher, Wolf Recovery Under the Endangered Species Act: A Study in Contemporary Federalism, 394, 927

Keiter, Breaking Faith with Nature: The Bush Administration and Public Land Policy, 392

Kelly, D., & G. Braasch, SECRETS OF THE OLD GROWTH FOREST, 429

Kendig, Lane, et al., Performance Zoning, 357

Kirchblum, NLUPA: Senator Henry Jackson's Ill-Fated National Land Use Planning Act, and Its Continuing Echoes in the Coastal Zone Management Act, 396

Konrad, The Shrinking Scope of Judicial Review in SUWA, 392

Kopf, Steamrolling §7(d) of the ESA: How Sunk Costs Undermine Environmental Regulations, 444

Kostyack, Surprise, 450

Kovar, A Short Guide to the Rio Declaration, 965

Krier, James, The Environment, the Constitution, and the Coupling Fallacy, 911

Krier, James, and Clayton Gillette, Risks, Courts, and Agencies, 78

Krugman, Paul, Building a Green Economy, 23, 607, 642-643

Kuhse, The Federal Consistency Requirement of the Coastal Zone Management Act of 1972, 401

Kuiper, The Courts, Daubert, and Willingness to Pay: The Doubtful Future of Hedonic Damages Testimony, 130-131

Kysar and Salzman, Environmental Tribalism, 71

Laitos, Jan & Carr, Transformation on Public Lands, 382

Laitos, Jan, Causation and the Unconstitutional Conditions Doctrine: Why the City of Tigard's Exaction Was a Taking, 955

Laitos, Jan, Legal Institutions & Pollution: Some Intersections Between Law & History, 181

LaLonde, Note, Allocating the CZMA Burden of Proof, 401

Langston, Toxic Bodies: Hormone Disruptors and the Legacy of DES, 156

Latin, Howard, Ideal versus Real Regulatory Efficiency Implementation of Uniform Standards and "Fine-Tuning" Regulatory Reforms, 197

Lazarus, Litigating Suitum . . . , 357-358

Lee, Charles, Toxic Wastes and Race in the United States, 55-56, 368

Leonard, Annie, web-video cartoon lambasting cap-and-trade, 641

Leonard, Sovereignty, Self-Determination, and Environmental Justice in the Mescalero Apache's Decision to Store Nuclear Waste, 369

Leopold, Aldo, A SAND COUNTY ALMANAC, 7-8, 10, 24-25

Leopold, E., et al., SAVED IN TIME: THE FIGHT TO SAVE FLORISSANT FOSSIL BEDS, 900

Leventhal, Environmental Decisionmaking and the Role of the Courts, 657

Lichatowich, James, It's the Economies, Mr. President, 22

Limbaugh, Rush, The Rush Limbaugh Show, 422

Loomis & White, Economic Benefits of Rare and Endangered Species: Summary and Meta-analysis, 573

Lopez, Barry, ARCTIC DREAMS: TORNARSSUK, 451

Lopez, Cost Recovery for Petroleum Contamination: Will RCRA Citizen Plaintiffs Be Cookin' with KFC or Relegated to a State Law Jungle?, 786

Lovelock, THE AGES OF GAIA, 26

Low, Bobbi, and Matt Ridley, Can Selfishness Save the Environment?, 21

Luban, A Flawed Case Against Punitive Damages, 135

Lyndon, Information Economics and Chemical Toxicity, 670

Malcolm and Ya-Wei Li, Data Contradict Common Perceptions About a Controversial Provision of the US Endangered Species Act, 448-449

Malloy, Timothy, Regulating by Incentive: Myths, Models, and Micromarkets, 610-611

Mandelker, NEPA Law and Litigation, 333

Manko & Cozine, The Battle over Municipal Liability under CERCLA Heats Up: An Analysis of Proposed Congressional Amendments to Superfund, 696

Mann, Polluter-Financed Environmentally Beneficial Expenditures: Effective Use or Improper Abuse of Citizen Suits Under the Clean Water Act?, 816, 819

Maples, Reforming Judicial Interpretation of the Diligent Prosecution Bar: Ensuring an Effective Citizen Role in Achieving the Goals of the Clean Water Act, 816

Marketing Failure: The Experience with Air Pollution Trading in the U.S., 627

Martens & Getto, Medical Monitoring and Class Actions, 155

Marzulla, Superfund 1991: How Insurance Firms Can Help Clean Up the Nation's Hazardous Waste, 713

Matter, Negotiated Regulations: A Cure for Malaise, 825

May, Alternative Dispute Resolution and Environmental Enforcement: A Noble Experiment or a Lost Cause?, 822

McEleney, Using Transferable Development Rights to Preserve Vanishing Landscapes and Landmarks, 357

McGarity & Ruttenberg, Counting the Cost of Health, Safety, and Environmental Regulation, 575

McGarity & Shapiro, The Trade Secret Status of Health and Safety Testing Information: Reforming Agency Disclosure Policies, 676

McGarity, Politics by Other Means: Law, Science, and Policy in EPA's Implementation of the Food Quality Protection Act, 650

McGarity, Professor Sunstein's Fuzzy Math, 594

McGinnis, Collective Bads: The Case of Low-Level Radioactive Waste Compacts, 370

McPhee, ENCOUNTERS WITH THE ARCHDRUID, 3

MDEQ, Operational Memorandum No. 20, 500

Meadows, et al., Beyond the Limits, 23

Melville, Herman, MOBY DICK, 295

Michelman, Property, Utility, and Fairness: Comments on the Ethical Foundations of Just Compensation Law, 933

Miller, G. Tyler, Living in the Environment: Principles, Connections, & Solutions, 17-19

Miller, Marshall, Federal Regulation of Pesticides, Environmental Law Handbook, 651-654

Miller, OCCUPATIONAL SAFETY AND HEALTH ACT, ENVIRONMENTAL LAW HANDBOOK, 49

Miller, Private Enforcement of Federal Pollution Control Laws, 816

Miller, The Cost of Clean, 837

Mintz & Klaidman, Creative Settlement or Improper Deal?, 42

Mintz, Joel A., State and Local Government Environmental Liability, 487-488

Mintz, Joel, Agencies, Congress, and Regulatory Enforcement: A Review of EPA Hazardous Waste Enforcement Effort, 737

Mintz, Joel, Enforcement at the EPA, 795-796

Mitchell, When Mountains Move, 364

Mohai et al., Racial and Socioeconomic Disparities in Residential Proximity to Polluting Industrial Facilities, 341

Molina & Rowland, Stratospheric Sink for Chlorofluoromethanes: Chlorine Atom-Catalysed Destruction of Ozone, 975

Moore, T.M., Climate of Fear: Why We Shouldn't Worry about Global Warming, 982

Morrall, John F., III, Cotton Dust: An Economist's View, 587

Mugdan, The Use of CERCLA Section 106 Administrative Orders to Secure Remedial Action, 734

Muir, John, MY FIRST SUMMER IN THE SIERRA, xxv

Mulhern, Marine Pollution: A Tort Recovery Standard for Pure Economic Losses, 107

Murphy, Old Maxims Never Die: The Plain Meaning Rule and Statutory Interpretation in Modern Federal Courts, 253

Muskie, Edumund, Statement of Sen. Muskie, principal author of the CWA and the Chair of the Senate's Public Works Committee, 562

Nafta CEC, Final Factual Record for Submission (Migratory Birds), 304-307

Naselsky, Charles, Note, Public Trust Doctrine, Beach Access, 908

Nash, Jonathan Remy & Richard L. Revesz, Markets and Geography: Designing Marketable Permit Schemes to Control Local and Regional Pollutants, 627

Nash, R., RIGHTS OF NATURE: A HISTORY OF ENVIRONMENTAL ETHICS, 25

National Academy of Sciences RED BOOK, 576-577

National Governors' Association, Statement Concerning Development, 370

National Institute for Dispute Resolution: Paths to Justice, 823-825

National Public Radio, Declining Fisheries, 388

National Research Council, Compensating for Wetland Losses under the Clean Water Act, 364

National Research Council, Risk Assessment in the Federal Government, 576-579

National Research Council "Silver Book," 577

National Research Council, Science and Judgment in Risk Assessment, 578

Nesson, Agent Orange Meets the Blue Bus: Factfinding at the Frontier of Knowledge, 104, 169

New Jersey Dep't of Envtl. Protection, Creating Indicators of Wetland Status (Quantity and Quality), 364

New York Times Editorial, 281

Nichol, Justice Scalia, Standing, and Public Law Litigation, 234

Nixon, Richard M., State of the Union Message to the Congress on Natural Resources & Environment, 399

NOAA, A Brief History of the Groundfishing Industry of New England, 387

NOAA, Catchshare Draft Policy, 621

Nolon, Comparative Land Use Law: Patterns of Sustainability, 398

Nolon, Fusing Economic and Environmental Policy: The Need for Framework Laws in the United States and Argentina, 396

Nolon, New Ground: The Advent of Local Environmental Law, 60

Nordhaus, The Climate Casino: Risk, Uncertainty, and Economics for a Warming World, 638-639

Nozick, Anarchy, State and Utopia, 25

OECD, Evaluating Economic Instruments for Environmental Policy, 607

OIRA-OMB, 2008, 2013 Reports to Congress on the Costs and Benefits of Federal Regulations and Unfunded Mandates on State, Local, and Tribal Entities, 465

Olney, Letter from Attorney General Richard Olney to Charles Perkins, in Jaffe, The Effective Limits of the Administrative Process, 200

OMB, Economic Analysis of Federal Regulations Under Executive Order 12,866, 602

OMB, OIRA, 2008, 2013 Reports to Congress on the Costs and Benefits of Federal Regulations, 465

Ophuls, Ecology and the Politics of Scarcity, 32

OregonWild, Commercial Agriculture on Klamath Refuges, 383

Osnos, Green Giant, 347

Owen, Groundwater Regulation and the Takings Clause: A Case Study, 956

Owen, Probabilities, Planning Failures, and Environmental Law, 344

Owen, Punitive Damages in Products Liability Litigation, 133

Owen, Taking Groundwater, 956

Page, Talbot, A Generic View of Toxic Chemicals & Similar Risks, 12-14

Pang, J., and N. Greenwald, THE POLITICS OF EXTINCTION, 445

Pardy, Changing Nature: The Myth of the Inevitability of Ecosystem Management, 11

Parenteau, Cities on Stilts: The Myth of Large-Scale Climate Adaptation and the Limits of Sustainability, in J. Owley & K. Hirokawa, RETHINKING SUSTAINABILITY TO MEET THE CLIMATE CHANGE CHALLENGE, 76, 417

Parenteau, Letter to New England Senators, 442

Parenteau, Rearranging the Deck Chairs: Endangered Species Act Reforms in an Era of Mass Extinction, 443-444

Parenteau, Whatever Industry Wants . . . The Bush Environmental Record, 450, 456

Passell, Experts Question Staggering Costs of Toxic Cleanups, 743

Passmore, Man's Responsibility for Nature, 26

Payne, C., UN Commission Awards Compensation for Environmental and Public Health Damage from 1990-91 Gulf War, 141-142

Pedersen, Regulation and Information Disclosure, 338

PEER, EPA Ignored Employees' Objections on Louisiana Program, 629

Pelham, Innovative Growth Control Measures: The Potential Impacts of Recent Federal Legislation and the Lucas Decision, 406

Perlman, D., & G. Adelson, BIODIVERSITY: EXPLORING VALUES & PRIORITIES IN CONSERVATION, 442

Perritt, Negotiated Rulemaking Before Federal Agencies, 825, 828

Pew Oceans Comm'n, AMERICA'S LIVING OCEANS: CHARTING A COURSE FOR SEA CHANGE, 526

Phillips, Contribution and Indemnity in Products Liability, 105

Pianin, Study Assesses Risk of Attack on Chemical Plant, 340

Picou, J.S., et al., The Exxon Valdez Disaster: Readings on a Modern Social Problem, 140

Pierce, *Lujan v. Defenders*, 234

Plater & Norine, Through the Looking Glass of Eminent Domain: Exploring the "Arbitrary and Capricious" Test and Substantive Rationality Review of Governmental Decisions," 221, 917-918, 920, 955

Plater, A Modern Political Tribalism in Natural Resources, 71

Plater, Coal Law from the Old World, 347

Plater, Environmental Law and Three Economies, 22

Plater, Environmental Law as a Mirror of the Future, 20, 344

Plater, Facing a Time of Counter-Revolution, The Kepone Incident and a Review of First Principles, 387

Plater, Statutory Violations and Equitable Discretion, 122, 125-128

Plater, The Embattled Social Utilities of the Endangered Species Act, A Noah Presumption, and a Caution Against Putting Gas Masks on the Canaries in the Coal Mine, 430

Plater, The Non-statutory Public Trust: Affirmative New Environmental Powers for Attorneys-General, 907

Plater, Z., THE SNAIL DARTER & THE DAM, 423

Plater, The Takings Issue in a Natural Setting: Floodlines and the Police Power, 935, 937

POCLAD, Ending Corporate Dominance, 51

Polesetsky, A Study of the South Coast Air Quality Management District's Regional Clean Air Incentives Market, 621

Poletown Lives (documentary film), 919

Pollard, Oliver A., Smart Growth, 370-373

Posner, R., Economic Analysis of Law, 155

Potoski & Prakash, Cross-National Adoptions of ISO 14001 Certifications, 647

Powell, Lewis, The Powell Memorandum, 69, 399

Powledge, WATER: THE NATURE, USES, AND FUTURE OF OUR MOST PRECIOUS AND ABUSED RESOURCE, 424

Presidential-Congressional Comm'n on Risk Assessment & Risk Management, 16-17

Pring, Intimidation Suits Against Citizens: A Risk for Public Policy Advocates, 99

Quarles & Steinberg, The Superfund Program at Its 25th Anniversary, 745

Radin, The Liberal Conception of Property: Cross Currents in the Jurisprudence of Takings, 944

Raffensperger & Tarlock, The Wild and Scenic Rivers Act at 25: The Need for a New Focus, 365

Rand Corporation Institute for Civil Justice, Understanding Superfund, 737

Read, The Trail Smelter Dispute, 959

Reed, Scott, The Public Trust Doctrine: Is It Amphibious?, 907

Reitze & Schell, Self-Monitoring and Self-Reporting of Routine Air Pollution Releases, 505

Reitze, Environmental Policy, It Is Time for a New Beginning, 20

RESTATEMENT 2D OF TORTS, 77, 82, 85-86, 88, 93, 120-121, 129, 151-152, 154, 695-698, 727, 748, 751

RESTATEMENT 3D OF TORTS, 154

RESTATEMENT OF THE FOREIGN RELATIONS LAW OF THE U.S., 293

Revesz, Richard, Rehabilitating Interstate Competition: Rethinking the "Race-to-the-Bottom" Rationale for Federal Environmental Regulation, 192

Revesz, The Race-to-the-Bottom and Federal Environmental Regulation: A Response to Critics, 192

Rich, David, Personal Liability for Hazardous Waste Cleanup: An Examination of CERCLA, 691-694

Riesenberg, The Inalienability of Sovereignty in Medieval Political Thought, 26

Rieser, Ecological Preservation as a Public Property Right: An Emerging Doctrine in Search of a Theory, 910

Robertson, Restitution Under RCRA §6972(a)(1)(B): The Courts Finally Grant What Congress Authorized, 786

Rodgers, Benefits, Costs and Risks: Oversight of Health and Environmental Decisionmaking, 657

Rodgers, W., M. Robinson-Dorn, A. Moritz, and J. Barcelos, eds., Climate Change: A Reader, 70

Rodgers, William, HANDBOOK ON ENVIRONMENTAL LAW, xxviii

Rolston, Environmental Ethics: Duties to and Values in the Natural World, 25

Rosbe & Gulley, The Hazardous and Solid Waste Amendments of 1984: A Dramatic Overhaul of the Way America Manages Its Hazardous Wastes, 775

Rose, The Comedy of the Commons, 33

Rubin, Pollution by Analogy: The Trail Smelter Arbitration, 959

Ruckelshaus, Stopping the Pendulum, 839

Ruhl, J.B., The "Background Principles" of Natural Capital and Ecosystem Services, 394

Ruhl, J.B., Biodiversity Conservation and the Ever-Expanding Web of Federal Laws Regulating Nonfederal Lands: Time for Something Completely Different?, 402-404

Ruhl, Climate Change Adaptation & the Structural Transformation of Environmental Law, 70, 452

Ruhl, Keeping the Endangered Species Act Relevant, 452

Ruhl, J.B., S.E. Kraft & C.L. Lant, The Law and Policy of Ecosystem Services, 141, 394

Ruhl & Salzman, The Law and Policy Beginnings of Ecosystem Services, 19

Ruhl, A Manifesto for the Radical Middle, 421

Ruhl, Toward a Common Law of Ecosystem Services, 19

Ruhl, Who's Afraid of the Big Bad Koontz?, 953

Ruhl, Working Both (Positivist) Ends Toward a New (Pragmatist) Middle in Environmental Law, 421

Russell, Cries and Whispers: Environmental Hazards, Model Rule 1.6, and the Attorney's Conflicting Duties to Clients and Others, 55

Russo, Contribution Under CERCLA: Judicial Treatment After SARA, 751

Sagoff, Mark, THE ECONOMY OF THE EARTH, 22, 603

Sakashita, . . . A Failure to Protect Wilderness in Redrock Country, 392

Salkin, P.E., Authority to Enact Land Use Regulations: Delegation of Power; The Enabling Acts, 351

Salzman & Ruhl, Currencies and the Commodification of Environmental Law, 609-610

Salzman, A Field of Green? The Past and Future of Ecosystem Services, 141

Salzman, Thompson & Daily, Protecting Ecosystem Services: Science, Economics, and Law, 19

Sanders, The Lockean Proviso, 32

Sandman, Peter, Risk Communication: Facing Public Outrage, 15-16, 155-156

Sarnoff, The Continuing Imperative (But Only from a National Perspective) for Environmental Protection, 192

Sax, Joseph L., B. Thompson, J. Leshy & R. Abrams, LEGAL CONTROL OF WATER RESOURCES, 374, 384

Sax, Joseph L., DEFENDING THE ENVIRONMENT: A STRATEGY FOR CITIZEN ACTION, xxviii, 365, 883-884, 912

Sax, Joseph L., Helpless Giants: The National Parks and the Regulation of Private Lands, 393, 410

Sax, Joseph L., MOUNTAINS WITHOUT HANDRAILS: REFLECTIONS ON THE NATIONAL PARKS, 393, 893

Sax, Joseph L., PLAYING DARTS WITH A REMBRANDT: PUBLIC AND PRIVATE RIGHTS IN CULTURAL TREASURES, 908

Sax, Joseph L., Property Rights and the Economy of Nature, 22, 946

Sax, Joseph L., Takings and the Police Power, 928

Sax, Joseph L., The (Unhappy) Truth about NEPA, 317

Sax, Joseph L., The Public Trust Doctrine in Natural Resource Law: Effective Judicial Intervention, 884-887, 890

Scalia, Antonin, The Doctrine of Standing as an Essential Element of the Separation of Powers, 201, 232

Schapiro, Mark, CARBON SHOCK: A TALE OF RISK AND CALCULUS ON THE FRONT LINES OF THE DISRUPTED GLOBAL ECONOMY, 635

Schapiro, Mark, EXPOSED: THE TOXIC CHEMISTRY OF EVERYDAY PRODUCTS AND WHAT'S AT STAKE FOR AMERICAN POWER, 684

Schmalensee, et al., An Interim Evaluation of Sulfur Dioxide Emissions Trading, 618

Schoenbrod, The Delegation Doctrine: Could the Court Give It Substance?, 254

Scro, Navigating the Takings Maze, 933

Seymour, Civil and Criminal Liability of Corporate Officers under Federal Environmental Laws, 875

Sher & Hunting, Eroding the Landscape, Eroding the Laws: Congressional Exemptions from Judicial Review of Environmental Laws, 241

Sheridan, Off-Road Vehicles on Public Lands, 388-389

Shrader-Frechette, K.S. & E.D. McCoy, Method in Ecology, 10

Smith, Shields for the King's Men: Official Immunity and Other Obstacles to Effective Prosecution of Federal Officials for Environmental Crimes, 211

Soifer, Aviam, Protecting Posterity, 911

Solley et al., Estimated Use of Water in the United States, 394

Starfield, Lawrence, The 1990 National Contingency Plan, 738-742

Starr, Countering Environmental Crimes, 873

Stavins, What Can We Learn from the Grand Policy Experiment: Positive and Normative Lessons from the SO2 Allowance Trading, 618

Steiner, H., R. Goodman, & P. Alston, International Human Rights in Context: Law, Politics, 973

Steinzor, EPA and Its Sisters at 30: Devolution, Revolution, or Reform?, 198

Steinzor, Toward Better Bubbles and Future Lives: A Progressive Response to the Conservative Agenda for Reforming Environmental Law, 197

Steinzor, Why Not Jail? Industrial Catastrophes, Corporate Management and Government Inaction, 878

Stern, Todd D, Testimony of Special Envoy for Climate Change, Senate Foreign Relation Committee Subcommittee on Multilateral International Development, Multilateral Institutions, and International Economic, Energy, and Environmental Policy, 993

Stever, The Law of Chemical Regulation and Hazardous Waste, 669

Stewart, James, In Corporate Crimes, Individual Accountability is Elusive, 879

Stewart, Richard, The Reformation of American Administrative Law, 199, 225-226

Stone, A Slap on the Wrist for the Kepone Mob, 42

Stone, SHOULD TREES HAVE STANDING?, 25, 229

Strahan, Max, A New Paradigm for Conservation of Great Whales, 211

Sunstein, The Arithmetic of Arsenic, 593

Sunstein, Simpler: The Future of Government, 596

Sunstein, What's Standing after Lujan?, 234, 238

Susskind, L. & J. Cruikshank, Breaking the Impasse: Consensual Approaches to Resolving Public Disputes, 823

Susskind, L. and Gerard McMahon, The Theory & Practice of Negotiated Rulemaking, 825-827

Susskind, L., L. Bacow & M. Wheeler, Resolving Environmental Regulatory Disputes, 822

Swire, The Race of Laxity and the Race to Undesirability, 192

Talbot, A., Settling Things, 822

Talbot, Power Along the Hudson: The Storm King Case & the Birth of Environmentalism, 228

Tarlock, The Nonequilibrium Paradigm in Ecology and the Partial Unraveling of Environmental Law, 10

Tear, et al., Status and Prospects for Success of the Endangered Species Act: A Look at Recovery Plans, 441

Tengs & Graham, The Opportunity Costs of Haphazard Social Investments in Life-Saving, 597, 600

Thode, Tort Analysis: Duty-Risk v. Proximate Cause and the Rational Allocation of Functions Between Judge and Jury, 168

Thomas, Environmental Progress and Challenges, 21

Thompson, Tragically Difficult: The Obstacles to Governing the Commons, 374

Thorson, On Thin Ice: The Failure of the United States and the World Heritage Committee to Take Climate Change Mitigation Pursuant to the World Heritage Convention Seriously, 413

Thurmon, Reconsidering the Precedential Value of Supreme Court Plurality Decisions, 527

Toscano, Note, Forbearance Agreements: Invalid Contracts for the Surrender of Sovereignty, 811

Title VI of the Civil Rights Act, see U.S. EPA, Title VI of the Civil Rights Act

Toxics L. Reptr., High Court Dismisses Suit by Superior Air, 753

Toxics Law Reporter, Need Protection from Rolls-Royce Cleanup, 727

Transportation Research Board/National Research Council, Highway De-icing: Comparing Salt and Calcium Magnesium Acetate, 39

Tribe, Trial by Mathematics: Precision and Ritual in the Legal Process, 169

Tucker, Environmentalism and the Leisure Class, 228

Turner, Delaney Lives! Reports of Delaney's Death Are Greatly Exaggerated, 650

Twomey, Breaking the Silence: Examining the Enforceability of Private Settlements Which Conceal Environmental Hazards, 52

United Nations Conference on Sustainable Development in Rio de Janeiro, Rio+20, THE FUTURE WE WANT, 969

U.S. Dept. of Justice, UNITED STATES ATTORNEYS' MANUAL, 878

U.S. Dep't of Interior, Adaptive Management Tech Guide, 414

U.S. Department of Interior, Fact Sheet: BLM, USFS Greater Sage-Grouse Conservation Effort, 447

U.S. EPA Region 5, Office of Pub. Affairs, Basic Brownfields Fact Sheet, 629

U.S. EPA, 2004 Report to Congress: Impacts and Controls of CSOs and SSOs, 547

U.S. EPA, 2008 TRI National Analysis webpage, 336

U.S. EPA, Agreements with Prospective Purchasers of Contaminated Property and Model Prospective Purchaser Agreement, 807

U.S. EPA, Arsenic in Drinking Water Rule: Economic Analysis, 574

U.S. EPA, Brownfields Action Agenda, 806-807

U.S. EPA, Comprehensive TRI Database, 336

U.S. EPA, Environmental Audit Policy Statement, 837-838

U.S. EPA, Fact Sheet: Coal Combustion Residues (CCR), Surface Impoundments with High Hazard Potential Rating, 339

U.S. EPA, Land Use in the CERCLA Remedy Selection Process, 807

U.S. EPA, Memorandum from Deputy Assistant Administrator for Water Enforcement Jeffrey G. Miller to Regional Enforcement Director, 552

U.S. EPA, National Water Quality Inventory: 1994 Report to Congress, 522-524

U.S. EPA, New Source Review Workshop Manual, 499

U.S. EPA, Policy Toward Owners of Property Containing Contaminated Aquifers, 807

U.S. EPA, Project XL, 812-814

U.S. EPA, Study of Clean Air Act, 174

U.S. EPA, Surface Impoundment Assessment, 769

U.S. EPA, Sustainable Materials Management: The Road Ahead, 774-775

U.S. EPA, The Benefits and Costs of the Clean Air Act, 465, 574

U.S. EPA, Title VI of the Civil Rights Act of 1964: Adversity and Compliance with Environmental Health-Based Thresholds, 481-485

U.S. EPA, Toxics Release Inventory, Summary of Key Findings, 337

U.S. EPA, Wetlands, Status and Trends, 359

U.S. GAO, Differences Among the States in Issuing Permits Limiting the Discharge of Pollutants, 191

U.S. GAO, Ecosystem Management: Additional Actions Needed to Adequately Test a Promising Approach, 412

U.S. GAO, EPA's Chemical Testing Program Has Made Little Progress, 669

U.S. GAO, Key EPA and State Decisions Limited by Inconsistent and Incomplete Data, 566

U.S. GAO, Radioactive Waste: Status of Commercial Low-Level Facilities, 370

U.S. GAO, Report—Hazardous Waste: The Cost and Availability of Pollution Insurance, 769

U.S. GAO, Wetlands Protection Assessments Needed to Determine Effectiveness of In-Lieu Fee Mitigation, 364

U.S. GAO, Wetlands Protection: The Scope of the §404 Program Remains Uncertain, 359, 363-364

University of Maryland Environmental Law Center, Environmental Science for Lawyers, 10

USFS Adaptive Management Services Unit, 414

Van Houtven & Cropper, When Is a Life Too Costly to Save? The Evidence From Environmental Regulations, 673

Vanik, Rep., Failure to Establish National Air Quality Standards, 191

Verdiccio, Environmental Restoration Orders, 129

Viscusi, The Social Costs of Punitive Damages Against Corporations in Environmental and Safety Torts, 135

Wade, *Bragg*: Wrong Question, Wrong Result In Texas, to the Detriment of Sustainable Water Supply, 956

Wald, C., Negotiation of Environmental Disputes: A New Role for the Courts?, 828

Warrick, Study Finds More Hazards at Paducah, Discord Greets Draft Report on Uranium Workers' Radiation Exposure, 57

Webster's THIRD NEW INTERNATIONAL DICTIONARY, 470, 526, 785

Weiss, Environment and Trade as Partners in Sustainable Development: A Commentary, 1011

Westbrook, Liberal Environmental Jurisprudence, 11

Wheeler, Negotiating NIMBYs: Learning from the Failure of the Massachusetts Siting Law, 367

Wiener, Uncle Sam and Forest Fires, 927

Wilkins & Stroman, Delegation Blackmail: EPA's Use of Program Delegation to Combat State Audit Privilege Statutes, 839

Wilkinson, Crossing the Next Meridian, 383-385

Williams, M. and J.E. Cannon, Rethinking the Resource Conservation and Recovery Act for the 1990s, 772, 776

Wirth & Silbergeld, Risky Reform, 578

Wirth, The International and Domestic Law of Climate Change: A Binding International Agreement Without the Senate or Congress?, 292

Wirth, David, Legitimacy, Accountability, and Partnership: A Model for Advocacy on Third World Environmental Issues, 958

Wirth, David, The EU's New Impact on American Environmental Regulation, 680

Wirth, David, The International Organization for Standardization: Private Voluntary Standards as Swords and Shields, 646

Wirth, David, The Rio Declaration on Environment and Development: Two Steps Forward and One Back or Vice Versa?, 965

Wirth, David, The Sixth Session, Part Two, and Seventh Session of the Conference of the Parties to the Framework Convention on Climate Change, 630

Wise, Steven, Science and the Case for Animal Rights, 25

Witten & Curtin, Windfalls, Wipeouts, Givings, and Takings in Dramatic Redevelopment Projects: Bargaining for Better Zoning on Density, Views, and Public Access, 352

Witten, Jon, Carrying Capacity and the Comprehensive Plan: Establishing and Defending Limits to Growth, 18, 349

Wolf, Taxation Can Give the Earth a Chance, 640

Wood, Mary, NATURE'S TRUST: ENVIRONMENTAL LAW FOR A NEW ECOLOGICAL AGE, 908

Wooley, D., & E. Morss, CLEAN AIR HANDBOOK, 505

World Bank Inspection Panel Report and Findings on the Qinghai Project: Executive Summary, 999-1001

World Bank Inspection Panel: The First Four Years (1994-1998), 1002

World Commission on Environment and Development, Report, 21, 969

Wright, The Cost-Internalization Case for Class Actions, 116

Wright, Introduction to the Law of Torts, 76

Wurster, Charles, Of Salt . . . , 35-36

Wylie, Poletown: Community Betrayed, 919

Yaffee, The Wisdom of the Spotted Owl, 384

Yang, The Form and Substance of Environmental Justice, 485

Yannacone, Victor J., Jr., Bernard Cohen & Steven Davison, ENVIRONMENTAL RIGHTS AND REMEDIES, 900-906

Young, Determining the Economic Value of Water, 394

Yudkowsky, An Intuitive Explanation of Bayesian Reasoning, 415

Zakaria, Swing for the Fences, 609

Zim, Allied Chemical's $20-Million Ordeal with Kepone, Fortune, 42

Znaniecki, Cancerphobia, Damages in Medical Malpractice Claims, 153

TABLE OF AUTHORITIES: STATUTES, REGULATIONS, CONSTITUTIONS, TREATIES

ABA Model Rule Prof. Conduct, 55

Administrative Dispute Resolution Act (ADRA), 813, 827-828

Administrative Procedures Act, see Chapter 6

Air Quality Act of 1967, 188, 460, 470, 535

Alaska Statute §24.20.160 et seq. (1990), 814

American Recovery & Reinvestment Act of 2009, 455

APA, see Administrative Procedure Act, Chapter 6

Arhaus Convention, 340

Asset Conservation, Lender Liability, and Deposit Insurance Protection Act of 1996, 714, 833

Atomic Energy Act of 1954 (AEA), 245, 260, 761, 843

Bankruptcy Code, 787

Basel Convention on the Control of Transboundary Movements of Hazardous Wastes and Their Disposal, 64, 282, 1012

British Town & Country Planning Act of 1948, 347

CAA, Clean Air Act, Chapter 11, and 58, 83, 94, 95, 128, 174, 188, 189, 190, 230, 264, 300, 321, 323, 330, 373, 405, 566, 574, 599, 615, 616, 620, 677, 791, 843, 975, 992

CAFO rules (CWA), 196, 530, 531, 545, 546,

California Civ. Code §987, Protection of Fine Art against Alteration or Destruction, 908

California Const. art. XV, §§2, 3, 882

California Corporate Criminal Liability Act, 875

Canada, Environmental Assessment Act, 335

CERCLA, Comprehensive Environmental Response, Compensation, and Liability Act, Chapter 16, and 58, 104, 137, 157, 180, 504, 608, 658, 755, 757, 780, 782, 783, 784, 785, 786, 787, 799, 804, 806, 807, 808, 810, 811, 815, 821, 831, 832, 833, 836, 837, 839, 841, 843, 858

Chemical Facility Anti-Terrorism Standards (CFATS), 340

Civil Aeronautics Act, 925

Civil Rights Act of 1964, 369, 481, 485

Clean Air Act, CAA, Chapter 11, and 58, 83, 94, 128, 174, 175, 178, 188, 189, 190, 193, 197, 223, 230, 231, 249, 253, 254, 264, 278, 299, 300, 301, 321, 323, 330, 340, 344, 376, 373, 404, 405, 406, 419, 450, 453, 454, 519, 535, 536, 544, 566, 574, 575, 583, 593, 596, 599, 609, 615, 616, 620, 621, 627, 641, 677, 756, 757, 791, 794, 801, 815, 821, 826, 829, 831, 843, 852, 863, 878, 975, 988, 990

Clean Power Plan Final Rule (2015), 345, 620, 993

Clean Water Act, CWA, Chapter 12, and 45, 47, 51, 52, 56, 57, 58, 59, 137, 140, 142, 174, 177, 178, 182, 183, 186, 195, 207, 230, 231, 232, 234, 235, 236, 237, 239, 250, 264, 276, 278, 314, 344, 348, 349, 350, 351, 359, 360, 362, 363, 364, 402, 405, 453, 454, 455, 505, 511, 595, 596, 599, 600, 636, 644, 690, 729, 734,

756, 757, 791, 801, 802, 803, 804, 805, 806, 812, 814, 815, 816, 817, 818, 819, 821, 841, 843, 846, 847, 854, 855, 856, 857, 858, 859, 860, 874, 875, 878.

Coastal Zone Management Act, 59, 177, 344, 350, 396, 398, 400, 401, 402, 403, 404, 405, 406

Commerce Clause, 258, 259, 260, 261, 268, 269, 270, 272, 273, 274, 275, 276, 277, 285, 297, 593, 620, 684

Comprehensive Environmental Response, Compensation, and Liability Act, see CERCLA

Convention for the Protection of Migratory Birds, 281

Convention on Biological Diversity, 292, 457, 963

Convention on Environmental Impact in a Transboundary Context, 334

Convention on International Trade in Endangered Species, CITES, 292, 422, 457, 965, 1012

Copenhagen Accord, 990-991, 995

CWA, see Clean Water Act

CZMA, see Coastal Zone Management Act

Deep Seabed Hard Mineral Resources Act, 230

Deepwater Port Act of 1974, 137, 230, 843

Department of Interior and Related Agencies Appropriations Act, 240

Department of Justice "Petite Policy," 304

Department of Transportation Act, §4(f), 419

Detroit's Smoke Abatement Code, 262

Disposal of Polychlorinated Biphenyls (PCBs) Rule, 674

Dormant Commerce Clause, 258, 259, 260, 261, 268, 269, 274, 276, 297, 620, 684

Electric Consumers Protection Act, 265

Electronic Waste Recycling Act (California), 683-684

Emergency Planning & Community Right to Know Act, EPCRA, 345, 368, 554-555, 756, 819, 820, 843

Endangered Species Act, Chapter 10, 12, 59, 176, 208-210, 230, 313, 394, 402, 843, 927

Endangered Species Act, God Committee Amendments, Chapter 10, and see 423, 430, 437-440, 444, 456

Endangered Species Act, Habitat Conservation Plans, HCP Handbook, 415, 437, 440, 443, 452

Energy and Water Development Appropriations Act of 2004, 440

Energy Independence and Security Act of 2007, 332

Energy Policy Act, 346, 347, 370

Energy Policy and Conservation Act of 1975, 230, 325, 346

Energy Sources Development Act, 230

ESA, Safe Harbor Policy (Dept. of Interior, ESA), 450

ESA, see Endangered Species Act

European Climate Change Programme (ECCP), 630

European Union, Restriction of Hazardous Substances (RoHS), 684

European Union Directive 2008/101, 631-634

Executive Order 12898, Federal Actions To Address Environmental Justice in Minority Populations and Low-Income Populations, 481, 485

Executive Order No. 12866, "Regulatory Planning and Review," 594, 595, 596, 597

FDCA, see Federal Food, Drug and Cosmetic Act

Table of Authorities: Statutes, Regulations, Constitutions, Treaties

Federal Advisory Committee Act (FACA), 812, 827

Federal Aid to Highways Act of 1968, 213

Federal Aviation Administration Authorization Act, FAAAA, 268

Federal Environmental Pesticide Control Act (FEPCA), 653

Federal Insecticide, Fungicide, and Rodenticide Act (FIFRA), 43, 60, 531, 583, 650, 652, 653, 654, 655, 656, 657, 658, 659, 660, 661, 662, 663, 670, 671, 676, 815, 843

Federal Land Policy & Management Act (FLPMA), 344, 375, 376, 377, 378, 379, 380, 381, 384, 385, 388, 389, 390, 391, 392, 393, 395, 411

Federal Power Act, 227, 265, 568

Federal Rules of Civil Procedure, 818

Federal Rules of Evidence, 124, 131

Federal Water Pollution Control Act Amendments of 1972 (FWPCA), 45, 54, 56, 190, 230, 519, 535, 843, 865, 866

Federal Water Pollution Control Act, 45, 190, 230, 405, 519, 533, 535, 692, 761, 843, 844

FIFRA, see Federal Insecticide, Fungicide, and Rodenticide Act

Fifth Amendment, 351, 864-65, 901, 914, 918, 921, 928-29, 938, 951, 954

FOIA, see Freedom of Information Act

Food Quality Protection Act of 1996 (FQPA), 420, 650

Food, Drug, and Cosmetics Act, 58

Food, Drug, Cosmetic Act, Delaney Clause, 420, 436, 650, 673

Freedom of Information Act, 247, 305, 333, 626

General Agreement on Tariffs and Trade (GATT), 297, 1002

General Mining Law of 1872, 383

Halliburton Amendments, Cheney-Bush pro-fossil energy, 82, 517

Hazardous and Solid Waste Amendments of 1984 (HSWA), 757, 775

Hazardous Materials Export Controls Statute, 60

Hazardous Materials Transportation Act, 60, 766

Health Risk Reduction and Cost Analysis (HRRCA), 590, 591

Healthy Forests Restoration Act of 2003, 456

Helsinki Declaration on the Protection of the Ozone Layer, 977

House Rule 23, 240

Illinois Environmental Protection Act, 165

Insecticide Act of 1910, 652

Institutes of Emperor Justinian, 27, 879, 883, 895

Intermodal Surface Transportation Efficiency Act (ISTEA), 39, 345, 373, 406

Internal Revenue Code, 869-870

International Convention for the Regulation of Whaling, 287-296, 979

Justinian, Emperor, *see* Institutes of Emperor Justinian

Kohler Act (Penn.), 929, 930

Kyoto Protocol, 292, 347, 629, 630, 633, 634, 635, 639, 643, 984-985, 987, 990-995

Laudato sí Encyclical, Pope Francis, 629, 996

Lender Liability Rule Under CERCLA, 713-714, 833

Low Level Radioactive Waste Policy Act, 370

Magnuson-Stevens Fishery Conservation and Management Act, 621

Marine Mammal Protection Act (MMPA), 236, 1005-1006, 1010

Marine Protection, Research, and Sanctuaries Act, 138

Marrakesh Accords, 630, 634, 635, 991

Maryland's Priority Funding Areas Act, 371

Massachusetts Siting Statute, 366-367

Michigan Water Resources Commission Act, 182, 183

Migratory Bird Treaty Act, 282, 283, 843, 862

Migratory Birds Convention Act, 281, 282, 283, 284, 285

Military Readiness Act, 456

Mineral Leasing Act of 1920, 383

Minnesota Siting Statute, 366-367

Minnesota Stat. §116D.04, 334

Montreal Protocol on Substances that Deplete the Ozone Layer, 299, 302, 978-988, 998, 1014

Motor Vehicle Pollution Control Act of 1965, 188

Multiple-Use, Sustained Yield Act, 379

NAFTA, 297, 302, 303, 307, 339, 1009, 1012, 1013

National Environmental Policy Act, NEPA, see Chapter 8, 59, 176, 376, 386, 388, 398, 422, 455, 846, 969

National Forest Management Act (NFMA), 194, 345, 377, 388, 412,

National Forest Management [Planning] Act, NFMA, 194, 345, 377, 384, 388-389, 412, 439

National Land Use Policy Act (NLUPA), 344, 358, 396, 397, 398, 398-399, 404

National Primary Drinking Water Regulations; Arsenic, 589

National Technology Transfer and Advancement Act of 1995, 646

National Wildlife Refuge Administration Act, 383

National Wildlife System Improvement Act of 1997, 412

Negotiated Rulemaking Act, 813, 827

NEPA, see National Environmental Policy Act

New Jersey Environmental Cleanup Responsibility Act, 753

New Jersey Siting Stat., 366-367

New Jersey Stat. Ann. §58:10A-3 (water), 529

New York Envtl. Conserv. Law §8-0105, 335

Noise Control Act of 1972, 230

North American Agreement on Environmental Cooperation (NAAEC), 303, 307, 308

North Carolina Gen. Stat. Ann. § 1-52(16), 98, 154, 730-731

Northwest Forests Initiative, 439

Northwest Ordinance of 1787, 883

Nuclear Waste Policy Act (NWPA), 369

Occupational Safety and Health Administration Act (OSHA), 59, 254, 576, 813, 814, 852

Ocean Thermal Energy Conservation Act, 230

Off-Road Vehicles Exec. Order No. 11989, 395

Oil Pollution Act of 1990 (OPA-90), 143, 263, 345, 416, 814

OMB Circular No. A-119, 646

OMB/OIRA, 465, 594, 595, 596

OPA-90, see Oil Pollution Act of 1990

Outer Continental Shelf Lands Act, 843

Paris Agreement of 2015, 345, 417, 633-635, 643, 986, 993-999, 1011

Parklands Act, §4(f) of the Department of Transportation Act of 1966, 213, 223, 224

Payment in Lieu of Taxes Act, 379

PCB Mega Rule, 673-674

PCB Spill Cleanup Policy, 674

Pelly and Packwood Amendments, 291-292, 294-296, 1010

Pennsylvania Constitution, 911-912

Pennsylvania Consol. Stats., §3218(c)(1), 81

Policy on CERCLA Settlements Involving Municipalities and Municipal Wastes, 756, 770

Pollution Prevention Act of 1990, 59, 180, 675, 757

Ports and Waterways Safety Act of 1972 (PWSA), 263, 268, 843

Prevention of Significant Deterioration and Title V Greenhouse Gas Tailoring Rule, 28, 463

Price-Anderson Act, 261

Proposed National Emission Standards for Hazardous Air Pollutants, 462-464, 489-495

Proposed Standards of Performance for New and Existing Stationary Sources: Electric Utility Steam Generating Units, 491

Protocol on Pollutant Release and Transfer Registers (PRTRs), 340

Public Rangelands Improvement Act of 1978, 384-385

RCRA, see Resource Conservation and Recovery Act

REACH, see Registration, Evaluation, Authorisation, and Restriction of Chemicals

RECLAIM, 621-623, 626-629

Refuse Act of 1899, 45, 50, 55-56, 419, 533, 841-847, 854, 861, 865-866, 885

Registration, Evaluation, Authorisation, and Restriction of Chemicals, 651, 679-85,

Regulation S-K of the Securities Act of 1933, 834

Regulatory Reform Act, 812

Reinventing Government, Executive Order on Regulatory Planning and Review, 812

Reorganization Order No. 3 creating the Environmental Protection Agency, 653

Resource Conservation and Recovery Act, RCRA, Chapter 17, 51, 58, 124, 180, 196, 203, 217, 278, 366-368, 549-550, 658, 672, 700-709, 730, 735, 743, 746, 797, 806, 810, 816, 818, 821, 831, 841, 858, 860-861

Rio Conference on the Environment of 1992, See Rio Declaration

Rio Declaration on Environment and Development, 65, 334, 636, 965-970, 984, 987, 1003-1004

Rio Declaration on Environment and Development, Principle 15, 579, 967, 968, 987

Rivers and Harbors Act of 1899, See Refuse Act

Rotterdam Convention on the Prior Informed Consent Procedure, 64

Safe Drinking Water Act (SDWA), 59, 71-72, 348-349, 549, 572, 588-593, 781, 843

Sarbanes-Oxley Act, 683

Senate Rule 16, 240

Sentencing Reform Act of 1984, 876

Siting statutes (state hazardous waste siting), 366-367

Small Business Liability Relief and Brownfields Revitalization Act, 715, 811

Solid Waste Disposal Act (SWDA), 58, 230, 757

Spotted Owl Record of Decision, Amendments to Forest Service and Bureau of Land Management Planning Documents, 432, 439-440

Standard State Zoning Enabling Act (SSZEA), 351

Standards for Reformulated and Conventional Gasoline, 299

Stockholm Convention on Persistent Organic Pollutants, 64

Stockholm Declaration, 964-68

Superfund Amendments and Reauthorization Act of 1986 (SARA), see CERCLA, 711, 746

Superfund Recycling Equity Act (SREA), 711

Surface Mining Control and Reclamation Act of 1977, 277, 843

Taylor Grazing Act of 1934, 375-376

Technical Barriers to Trade Agreement (TBT), 647

Tennessee Code Ann. §70.324, 28, 882, 909

Tennessee Water Pollution Control Act, 28

Toxic Substances Control Act (ToSCA), Chapters 13, 15, and see 51, 59-60, 230, 555, 572, 581-594, 650-651, 662-679, 681, 685, 756, 815, 831, 843, 858

Toxic Substances Control Act Chemical Substance Inventory, 552

Transportation Equity Act of the 21st Century (TEA-21), 406

U.S. Army Corps of Engineers 2015 Clean Water Rule, 528-529

U.S. Bureau of Land Management, 194, 210, 219-220, 240, 324, 375-386, 388-392, 395, 407-412, 439-440

U.S. Constitution, Article II §2, 291

U.S. Constitution, Compact Clause, 193

U.S. Constitution, Fifth Amendment, Chapter 21, and 351, 864-865, 901, 914, 918, 921, 928-929, 938, 951, 954

U.S. Constitution, Ninth Amendment, 901

U.S. Constitution, Eleventh Amendment, 257, 260, 276, 696, 811

U.S. Constitution, Fourteenth Amendment, 351, 901, 914, 931, 938-939, 949

U.S. Constitution, Property Clause, 267, 407-410

U.S. Constitution, Supremacy Clause, 259-262, 276, 278, 283, 405, 409

U.S. Constitution, Tenth Amendment, 258, 262, 276-277, 283-285, 412, 547, 593,

U.S. EPA, Clarifications to Compliance & New Source Contaminants Monitoring, 589-594

U.S. EPA, Definition of Solid Waste under RCRA, 761

U.S. EPA, Pesticide General Permit for Discharges from the Application of Pesticides, 531

U.S. EPA Guidance, Incentives for Self-Policing: Discovery, Disclosure, Correction, and Prevention of Violations, 838

U.S. EPA Guidance, Investigating Title VI Administrative Complaints Challenging Permits, 482, 485

U.S. EPA Lead & Copper Rule (LCR), 71-72

U.S. EPA, NSR Manual, 499-500, 503, 505

Table of Authorities: Statutes, Regulations, Constitutions, Treaties 1065

U.S. EPA, Pesticide General Permit for Discharges from the Application of Pesticides, 531

U.S. EPA, Proposed Regulation of Land Application of Sludge from Pulp and Paper Mills Using Chlorine, 536, 672

U.S. EPA Public Involvement Policy, 248

U.S. EPA, Settleable Solids Rule, 207-208

U.S. EPA, Water Quality Trading Policy, 566, 620-21

U.S. Forest Service, 194, 240, 345, 377, 381-382, 385, 388, 395, 412, 414, 439-440, 927

U.S. GAO, Key EPA and State Decisions Limited by Inconsistent and Incomplete Data, 566

Unfunded Mandates Reform Act, 812

Uniform Comparative Fault Act, 99, 105

Uniform Contribution Among Tortfeasors Act, 99, 103, 105

United Nations Conference on Environment and Development (UNCED), see Rio Declaration

United Nations Convention on Biological Diversity, 292, 965

United Nations Framework Convention on Climate Change (FCCC), 984-987, 991-993, 997, 1001

Unlawful Enclosures Act, 410

Vienna Convention, 976, 978-979, 987

Virginia Code Annotated, 154

Washington Administrative Code, 334

Waxman-Markey cap-and-trade bill, 990

Wetlands Regulations (EPA/CWA), 58, 359-365, 526-528, 610, 935, 938-945

Whaling Convention of 1949, 291, 295-296

Wild and Scenic Rivers Act of 1968 (WSRA), 365

Wild Free-Roaming Horses and Burros Act, 16 U.S.C. §§133, 407-412

Wilderness Act of 1964, 220, 383, 389-396, 419

Wisconsin Siting Statute, 366

WTO, U.S. Import Prohibition of Certain Shrimp and Shrimp Products, 1009-1011

WTO, U.S., Restrictions on Imports of Tuna (1991), 1005-1010

INDEX

See separate Tables of Cases, Statutes & Regulations, Books & Articles, and Acronyms

9/11 attacks, 143, 340, 964

Abnormally dangerous activities, *see* strict liability

Acid precipitation, 279, 331, 464, 490, 575, 608-609, 613, 616-617, 620, 629, 977

Ackerman, Bruce, 188, 197

Adaptation (climate change), 986-988, 993-998

Adelson, Glenn, 443

Administrative law, *see* Chapters 5, 6, 21

Administrative Orders, 700, 732-737, 746-747, 797, 799-800

Admiralty law, 401, 105, 134-136, 267

Advocate General (European Court of Justice), 681, 685

Affirmative defenses, 84, 705, 712

Afghanistan, 964

Aflatoxin, 16

African Development Bank, 999

Agency for International Development (AID), 1003-1004

Agenda 21, 967

Air pollution, *see* Chapters 5, 11, 14

Air, hazardous, see NESHAPs

Airports, 399, 918-920, 926-929

Alaska oil spill, 137-142, 144

Aldrin, 43, 653-658

Allied Chemical, *see* Kepone episode

Alternative dispute resolution, *see* Chapter 18(D)

Ambient standards, *see* Chapter 11

Animal bioassays, 17, 576-581

Annex I countries (Framework Convention on Climate Change), 983-996

Antarctica, 33, 978, 980

Anti-degradation, *see* Prevention of Significant Deterioration

Antitrust, 684

Anyway credits, 619

Appellate Body (of World Trade Organization)

Aquifers, 28, 35, 86-89, 90, 122-123, 157, 169, 359, 388, 394, 662, 807

Arbitrary and capricious, 147, 220-222, 300, 314, 328, 331-332, 393, 489, 583, 593, 742, 762, 918, 923, 957

Arhaus Convention, 340

Armenia, 999

Arranger liability, 709-711

Arsenic, 90, 117, 339, 363, 460, 520, 538, 574, 589-594, 603, 755, 965

"Article," definition, 679-685

Artificial pollution markets, *see* Market-enlisting

Asbestos, 6, 57, 96, 117, 147, 153-161, 166, 575, 578, 581-588, 672-673, 852

Asian Development Bank, 999

Asphalt, 489, 619

Atmospheric public trust, 910-911, 913

Attorneys' fees, 136, 231-232, 237-238, 248, 506, 555, 724, 727, 820-821

Audits and audit privilege, 337, 644-645, 802, 831, 836-839, 865, 872

Authority, *see* Chapters 5 and 6

1067

Automobile emissions, 190-193, 460, 508-517

Babbitt, Bruce, 327, 444, 982

Babcock, Hope, 278, 948

Backlash, 421, 925

Baitfish, 275

Balancing the equities, *see also* Remedies

Bangladesh, 976

Banking of pollution credits, 197, 363, 609-618, 628

Bankruptcy, 711-712, 716-717, 787

Baptist-bootlegger coalitions, 1014

Basel Convention on Transboundary Movements of Hazardous Wastes and Their Disposal, 64, 1014

BASIC countries (Brazil, South Africa, India, China), 992

BDAT, 768, 776-782

Benefit-cost analysis, Chapter 13, *see also* Cost-benefit analysis, 13, 179, 325, 330, 469, 494-495, 511, 539-540, 611

Benzene, 90, 203, 254, 460, 576-577, 624-625, 813

Bhopal incident, 16, 58, 68, 336, 770, 974

Bioassays, 17, 576-581, 661

Biodiversity, 15, 18, 20, 67, 365, 402-405, 412, 436, 442, 601, 1002

Bioreserves, 436

Biosolids, 548-549, 570

Blue bus hypo, 104, 169

Bonds, 86, 768

BP Deepwater blowout spill, *see* Gulf of Mexico BP Deepwater blowout spill

Breach of warranty, 659-660

British Petroleum Deepwater blowout spill, *see* Gulf of Mexico BP Deepwater blowout spill

Brower, David, 3-4, 19, 881

Brownfields, 372, 482, 689-690, 715

Brundtland, 1015

Bubbles, 197, 249-251, 609, 615-616, 630

Bureau of Land Management, 194, 219, 240, 324, 375, 390-394, 440

Burros, *see* Wild horses and burros

Byrd-Hagel resolution, 991

CAA, Clean Air Act, *see* Chapters 11 and 14, 58, 83, 174-175, 178, 190-193, 197, 223, 231, 249- 250, 253-254, 278, 299, 340, 376, 404-406, 453, 519, 535, 566-567, 593, 596, 599, 608, 641, 794, 801, 815, 826, 831, 863, 878, 975, 992

Cadillac cleanup, 727, 743

Cadillac plant (Poletown), 919-920

"California effect," 683

California public trust (Mono Lake), 384, 894-902, 909

Camacho, Alejandro, 415, 443

Cancer risk assessment, 420, 580, 586, 590-592

Cancerphobia, 153

Candidate conservation agreements (ESA), 450

Cap-and-trade, Chapter 14, and 990-1000

Capture phenomenon, 225-226

Carcinogens, 5, 14, 16, 49, 88, 117, 149-166, 420, 575-581, 625, 652-655, 672-674, 679-685, 779, 974

Carrying capacity, 17-19, 28, 33-34, 349, 355, 374-376, 386-388

Carson, Rachel, 8-10, 11, 14, 49, 67, 189, 459, 651

Causation, 65-66, 81, 93, 96-97, 100-107, *see also* Proximate cause

CERCLA (Superfund), Chapter 16, *see also* , 58, 104, 137, 157, 180, 504, 608,

Index

658, 755, 757, 780-787, 799, 804, 806-812, 816, 821, 831-841

CERCLIS, 738, 807, 810

Checkerboard land grants, 410-411

Chesapeake Bay, 42-54, 58, 105-107, 129, 137, 522, 620-621, 880-882

Chevron deference, 252-253, 294, 300-301, 435-436, 480, 531-532, 599

China, 347-348, 630, 684, 990-995, 997, 999, 1002

Clean Power Plan, 345, 620, 995

Clinton, Hillary Rodham, 991, 998

Chlorofluorocarbons, 6, 178, 977-986, 1014-1015

CITES, *see* Convention on Biological Diversity

Citizen intervention in agency actions, 62, 212, 247

Citizen litigation, 68, 223, 226-248, 313, 319, *see also* Standing, and Citizen statutory enforcement suits

Citizen oversight councils, 814

Citizen statutory enforcement suits, 62, 230-231

Civil Action, A, by Jn. Harr, *see* Woburn toxics episode

Civil penalties, 50, 75, 140, 236, 734, 797-799, 802, 819-820, 842, 846, 865, 875

Class action, 50, 52, 83, 93, 116, 136, 155, 246

Clean Air Act, *see* CAA

Clean Development Mechanism (CDM, Kyoto Protocol), 988-1000

Clean Power Plan (2015), 345, 620, 995

Clean Water Act, *see* CWA

Clean Water Rule, 2015, 528-529

Cleanup of hazardous materials, *see* Chapter 16

Climate Central interactive mapping, 416

Climate disruption, Climate change, Climate change mitigation, Climate change adaptation, 11, 20, 29, 70-71, 96, 156, 173, 327-332, 345, 398-417, 429, 451-453, 513-518, 633-635, 643, 986-998

CMA, Calcium magnesium acetate, 37-39

Coal ash, 339

Coase theorem, 31-33, 66, 620, 642

Coliform, 543

Collective activity crimes, 864-869

Combined sewer overflows (CSOs), 547

Coming to the nuisance defense, 98-99, 126

Comity, 190

Command-and-control, *see* Chapters 11, 12 & 15, 197, 636

Common but differentiated responsibilities, 968, 981, 987, 996-998

Common heritage of humankind, 28, 896, 910

Common law actions, *see* Chapters 3 & 4

Common law remedies, 105-123

Common Sense Initiative (CSI), 812-813

Commoner, Barry, 757

Commons, 28-34, 54, 66, 68, 286-288, 374-376, 388, 467, 608-609, 621, 636, 889-891, 963

Compacts, 193, 279, 292, 357, 370

Comparative risk assessment, 579

Compensatory damages, 105-123, 148

Comprehensive Environmental Response, Cleanup, and Liability Act, *see* CERCLA

Concurrent regulation, 260, 264

Condemnation, *see* Eminent domain, and Chapter 21A

Congressional-Executive Agreement, 298

Conseil d'Etat (France), 681

Consistency (with plan requirements), 177, 278, 352, 392, 397-406, 724-728

Constitutional issues, *see* Chapters 6, 7, 21

Consultation (ESA), 233, 423, 436-437, 443-449, 455

Contract law, 281

Contribution among tortfeasors, PRPs, 99-105, 154, 695-697, 724-730, 746, 748-753, 784

Convention for the Protection of Migratory Birds, 281-286, 304-307, 863

Convention on Biological Diversity, 292, 457, 967

Convention on International Trade in Endangered Species, CITES, 1014-1015

Cooperative federalism, 45, 56, 174, 196, 277-279, 358, 467, 809, 812

Cooperative management, 384-385

COP-21, *see* Paris Agreement

Copenhagen Accord, 991-998

Corporate Average Fuel Economy (CAFE) Standards, 325-333, 346-347

Corporate law, *see* Parent corporation; Subsidiary corporation; Successor corporation

Corporate officers and employees, liability, 694, 703-708, 846, 864-865, 868, 872-873

Corrosivity, 762-764

Cost-benefit analysis, *see* Chapter 13, *see also* 13, 179, 325, 330, 469, 494-495, 511, 539-540, 611

Cost-internalization, 84, 116, 180, 248, 608, 688

Cotton dust case, 203, 254, 586-587

Council on Environmental Quality (CEQ), 317-320, 322-324, 455

Council of European Union, 679-680

Court of Justice of the European Union, 679-680, 682-685

Cows and cattle, 33, 89, 206, 374-376, 678

Criminal intent, *see* Intent, criminal

Criminal law, Chapter 19

Criminal liability, vicarious, 707, 867-869 *see also* Chapter 19

Criteria pollutants, 461-467, 487, 504, 512

Critical areas management, 177, 359-365

Crop-dusting, 89

Cumulative impacts, 329-330, 364, 368

Customary international law, 960-977, 981-1004

Customary practice, 716

Cuyahoga River, 189, 520-521, 535

CWA, Clean Water Act, *see* Chapter 12, and 45-47, 51-52, 57-59, 137, 231, 250, 344, 348-351, 359-365, 453-455, 511, 596, 636, 801-805, 812, 814, 817, 819, 846-847, 854-861, 872, 878

Damages, *see* Compensatory damages; Hedonic damages; Indirect damages; Permanent damages; Punitive damages

DDT, 11, 43, 49, 64, 238, 430, 524, 653, 659

Declaration of Panama (on tuna conservation), 1012

Deductibility of environmental fines and penalties, 54, 99, 204, 842, 869-870

Deepwater blowout spill, *see* Gulf of Mexico BP Deepwater blowout spill

Defamation, 99

Defenses, 84, 90-93, 96-100, 126, 219-220, 308, 320, 691-692, 712-713, 730, 751, 811, 875, 955-957

Index

Deforestation, 7, 20, 506, 984-985

Delaney clause, 419-420

Delegation of power, 65, 176, 181-194, 196, 201-203, 238, 254, 351, 363, 469-473, 758, 828, 839, 910-912, 917-919

Démarche (diplomatic representation), 685

Descartes, 26

Desert, and Desertification, 5, 113, 126, 279, 386-389, 394, 456

Di-polar system, traditional corporate/agency societal governance, 62, 69, 416

Directive (in European Union), 679-680

Directive on Strategic Environmental Assessment, EU, 347

Discount rate, 574, 584-587, 604-605

Doha Amendment (to Kyoto Protocol), 629, 994

Dolphins, 1007-1015

Dominant use, 177, 377-386, 412

Dormant Commerce Clause, 258-259, 268-274, 276, 297, 620, 684

Dose-response assessment, 162, 577-579, 589, 594

Drinking water standards, 59, 230, 348-349, 517, 523, 549-550, 555, 572-574, 588-594, 676, 740, 779, 781

Due diligence, 689, 811, 833, 836-839

Due Process Clause, 859, 861-864, 916-923, 930-957, *see also* Fifth Amendment, Takings issues

Durban Platform (climate change), 993-994

E-coli, 523

Earth Island Institute, 1007, 1012-1013

Earth Summit, 21, 964, 967-972, 986, *see also* UNCED

Earthworms, 9

Easements, 114-116, 372, 411, 890, 910, 927-929, 952-953

Ecology, First Law of, xxv, 12, 18, 959, 999

Economic analysis, *see* Chapter 13, and Benefit-Cost analysis

Economic incentive systems, *see* Chapter 14

Ecosystem management, 11, 412

Ecosystem services, 17-19, 135, 141-142, 394, 453, 947

Ecosystems, 10-12, 17-21, 25, 63, 67, 139, 187, 322, 365, 394, 405, 412-417, 433-436, 524, 601, 629, 878, 900, 982, 987-990

Effluent taxes, 608-609

EISs, *see* Environmental impact statements

Electronic Waste Recycling (California), 683-684

Elements of a tort, 79, 81, 83, 115, 131

Elephants, 233, 457

Eleventh Amendment, 257, 259, 276, 696, 811

Emergency Planning and Community Right-to-Know Act, 58, 176, 234, 336-41, 345, 368, 554-555, 756, 819-820

Eminent domain, Chapters 21A & 21B, *see also* 115, 221, 894, 908

Emissions reduction units, 630, 966, 990-995

Emissions Trading Schemes (CAA, EU, Kyoto), 464, 605, 630-631, 990-998

Emotional distress; 52, 138, 148-154, 263, *see also* Cancerphobia, Intangible costs

Endangered Species Act, Chapter 10, *and see* 415, 423, 430, 437-444, 452, 456

Endangered Species Act, Habitat Conservation Plans, HCP Handbook, 415, 437, 440, 443, 452

Endangered species de-listing, 445-448

Endangered species, reintroduction, 393, 929

Endocrine-disrupting chemicals, 679-685

Energy planning, 345-348, 351

Energy, 8, 34-35, 77, 80, 83-84, 224, 227, 260, 325-332, 345-346-348, 394, 413, 499-500, 506, 638, 767, 793, 983-985, 91-993

Enforcement, *see* Chapter 18

Enhanced risk, 154

Environmental accounting, 324

Environmental assessments, 332, 644, 837, 1001-1003

Environmental audits, 836-839, 865

Environmental ethics, 24-28

Environmental impact statements & assessments, Chapter 8, and 59, 222, 233, 376, 386, 388-397, 424, 455, 969, 971, 1001-1006

Environmental justice, 5-6, 14, 55, 67-68, 129, 196, 337, 341, 368-369, 481-486, 581, 622, 793, 802, 812, 892

EPCRA, *see* Emergency Planning and Community Right-to-Know Act

ESA, *see* Endangered Species Act

European Bank for Reconstruction and Development, 999

European Chemicals Agency, 680-685

European Commission, 679-680

European Parliament, 679-680, 685

European Union , 679-685, 995, 1011-1012

Executive agreements, 280, 286, 291-296, 992, 997-998

Export, 6, 51, 55, 60, 63, 269, 274, 457, 528, 659, 680, 681-684, 772-773, 1006, 1009

Exposure assessment, 577

Externalities, 15, 23, 34, 42, 51, 131, 326, 333-335, 353, 636-638, 971, 1010

Extinction, *see* Chapter 10, and 5, 15, 25, 281, 286-294, 573, 601, 621

Extraterritorial laws, 275, 278, 405, 683, 965, 1011

Exxon-Valdez oil spill, 68, 75, 107, 134-143, 263, 416, 814, 847, 861

False negatives, 12-15, 511, 649

False positives, 12-15, 511, 649

Fast track, 143, 298-299, 812

Fear of increased risk of cancer, *see* Cancerphobia

Fee shifting, *see* Attorneys' fees

Feedlots, 89, 98

FIFRA, 43, 60, 583, 649-663, 670-671, 676

First Law of Ecology, xxv, 12, 18, 959, 999

Fishable-swimmable, 520-521, 570

Flexible mechanisms, 629-630, 635, 990-991

Flint, Michigan toxic lead water contamination, 71-72

Florissant fossil beds, 6, 900-911

FONSI, 324-332

Forbearance credits, 619

Foresee ability, 76, 79-82, 106, 161

Forests, 5-6, 8, 142, 240-241, 280, 319, 374, 381-385, 393, 412, 429, 439, 456, 839, 882, 891, 907, 927, 982-983, 1001

Fossils, 28, 900-911

Four Horsemen of the Eco-palypse, The, 20

Fracking, 79-89, 101, 345, 517, 674-676

Fracking proposed rule, 675-676

Framework convention, 978

Framework Convention on Climate, Chapter 12, 28, 37, 45, 48, 50-52, 56, 61, 87, 94, 103, 174, 182, 189, 190, 194, 195, 207, 231, 232, 331, 348, 371, 401,

Index

406, 453, 467, 511, 608, 612, 620, 770, 846, 858, 884, 909, 962, 967

Free trade agreements, 296-302, 1006-1013

Frontiers of scientific knowledge doctrine, 971

Game theory, 192-193

General Agreement on Tariffs and Trade, GATT, 297-302, 1006-1015

Genetics, 413, 880

Gettysburg tower, 410

GHGs, *see* Greenhouse Gases

Glaciers, 416, 982-984

Global commons, 286-291, 963

Global Environment Facility (GEF), 1004

Global Monitoring for Environment and Security programs, GMES, (EU), 347

Global warming, *see* Climate disruption

Goldman Environmental Prize, 976

God Committee, "God Squad" (ESA), 430, 437-440, 444, 456

Good Practices (World Bank), 1003

Gore, Albert, 986, 991

Gore factors (CERCLA), 751-752

Gravity component, 799-803

Grazing, 11, 23, 29, 34, 194, 374-386, 392-393, 407-411, 568, 815

Greenhouse gases (GHGs), 6, 20, 82, 95, 323, 326-331, 451, 464, 467, 504, 512-518, 608-609, 612-614, 628-630, 636, 639-640, 982-992, 994-997

Greenhouse gases Petition to Establish National Pollution Limits for GHGs, Center for Biological Diversity & 350.org, 517

Greenpeace, 1013

Greylock, Mt., 885-886

Greyrocks Dam, 439

Grizzly bears, 410

Gross National Product, GNP, 19, 142, 382, 587, 792

Grotius, Hugo, 286, 998

Groundwater, 85-88, 116-125, 958

Gulf of Mexico BP Deepwater blowout spill, 5, 75, 137, 142-143, 347, 416, 804-806, 841, 847, 877-878, 882

Habitat conservation plans, HCPs, 440-443, 449-450

Halliburton Amendments, Cheney-Bush pro-fossil energy, 82, 517

Halons, 985

Hammer clauses, 180, 278, 370, 510-511, 757, 768, 775-782

Hardin, Garrett, 286, 636

Harm-based standards, 58, 175-178, 198, 459-477, 489-490, 519-520, 535, 544, 566-567, 599, 620, 768, 781

Harmonization, 683-684

Hazard identification, 577

Hazardous air pollutants, *see* NESHAPS

Hazardous Waste Identification Rule (HWIR), 771

Hazardous waste siting, 117-122, 125, 177, 341, 351, 366-370, 767, 776, 917

Hazardous waste, Chapters 3, 9, 16, and 17, and *see also* Hazardous waste siting

Hazardous waste, export of, 43, 51, 60, 63, 659, 680-684, 772-773, 980

Hedonic damages, 130-131, 140

Helsinki Declaration on the Protection of the Ozone Layer, 981

High seas, 286, 294, 631-632, 963, 1007

Hormone-disrupting chemicals, 679-685

Hot air credits, 618, 626-629, 635

Hot spots, 190, 264, 481-484, 620-628

Houck, Ollie, 317, 362-634, 405-406, 444-445, 549-550, 556, 564-566

Hydraulic fracturing, *see* Fracking

Hydrofluorocarbons (HFCs), 986

Ignorance, 14, 860-862, 875-876

Impact fees, 358

Incidental take permits, 423, 437, 440-444, 449, 452

Indemnity, 104-105, 659, 723, 751, 836

Independent contractors, 90, 93-94

Indirect damages, 107

Injunctions, 89, 112, 116, 122, 124-130, 138, 211, 240-241, 787, 799-800, 846, 864, 883, 899-901, 905-908, 948, 962-963

Innocent purchasers of contaminated property, 712, 837

Insecticide, 9, 43, 60, 531, 583, 649-663

Insolvency, 49, 103-104, 697, 716, 754, 767

Inspections, 59, 144, 201, 262, 337, 463, 664, 678, 738, 773, 792-797, 1000-1005

Insurance, 155, 158, 713-716, 768-769, 773, 831-833, 842

Integrated environmental management, 21

Intended Nationally Determined Contributions (INDCs, to Paris Agreement), 994-998

Intent, criminal, 800, 845, 852-867

Intentional torts, 78-85, 89, 114, 132, 165, 263

Inter-American Development Bank, 999

Inter-American Tropical Tuna Commission, 1012

Intergenerational equity, 21, 28, 65, 70, 380, 880, 909-911, 968, 987

Intergovernmental Panel on Climate Change (IPCC), 513, 986, 990, 997

Internal Revenue Service: deductibility of pollution fines, 869-870

Internalities, *see* Cost-internalization

International agreements, 974-998

International Bank for Reconstruction and Development (IBRD), 997-1006

International Convention for the Regulation of Whaling, 287-296, 981

International Court of Justice, ICJ, 288-291, 965

International Development Association (IDA), 999-1005

International environmental law, Chapter 22, *and see also* 14, 21, 28, 63-65, 69, 174, 224, 267, 279-309, 333-335, 339-341, 358, 374, 404, 422, 428, 457, 629-635, 639-643

International law, Chapter 22

International Organization for Standardization, 643-648

International trade agreements, 296-309

International Trade Organization, 1006

International Whaling Commission, IWC, 287-296

Interstate compacts, 193, 357, 370

Interstate pollution, 94, 190-193, 333-335, 464, 477-481, 567-568

Intervention, 184, 195, 212, 223, 246-247, 884-888

"Instant" custom, 964, 990

Inverse condemnation, Chapter 21B, *and see also* 111, 410, 915, 925-931, 936, 941, 949-950

Iron triangles, 224, 374, 415, 454

Irrigation, 96, 265, 383, 394, 443, 524, 530-531, 570, 760, 956, 1001-1002

IRS, *see* Internal Revenue Service

Isocyanate, 68, 336, 770

Index

Ivory, 457

Jacobs, Jane, 18

Japan, 281, 288-296, 629, 678, 774, 994, 997

JARPA, Japanese purported "scientific whaling" program, 288-291

Joinder, 103-104

Joint and several liability, 100-104, 153-154, 169, 180, 692-702, 725-729, 747, 751-753, 832

Joint Implementation, 629-630, 990

Judicial review of agency action, 203, 206-223, 227, 780

Jury trial, 158

Justinian, Emperor, The Institutes of Emperor Justinian, 27, 879, 881, 885, 895, 907-909

Katrina, hurricane, 95, 240, 927, 947-948

Kepone episode, 41-64, 67-69, 105-106, 137, 141, 189, 387, 519-520, 549, 553-554, 856-858, 865-869, 880

Kissimmee, 949

Knowledge, criminal, *see* Criminal intent

Korea, 5, 683, 685, 972, 974-975

Krugman, Paul, 23, 607, 640, 642-643

Kyoto Protocol, 292, 347, 609, 629-630, 633-635, 639-643, 986-997

Laches, 98, 126

Laissez-faire, 67, 344-345, 375

La Jolla Agreement (on tuna conservation), 1012

Land ban, 180, 550, 768, 775-781

Land use, Chapters 9 & 21, *and see also* 24-25, 60, 71, 122, 177, 194, 233, 266-267, 334, 443, 486, 506, 529-530, 769, 807, 809

Landfills, 5, 117-122, 124, 179, 196, 270-274, 371, 549, 608, 762, 775-776, 983

Latency, latent effects, 14, 16, 98, 147, 152, 155, 593, 602, 731, 955

Laudato si´ Encyclical, Pope Francis, 629, 998

Leaching, 11, 37, 65, 85-87, 124-125, 169, 268, 661-662, 716, 762, 768, 775, 883

Legionnaires' disease, legionellosis, 71-72

Lender liability, 712-714, 808, 833

Lichatowich, James, 22

Life Cycle Assessment (LCA), 773

Limbaugh, Rush, 422

Limited access privilege programs (LAPPs), 621

Local land use controls, 351, 396, 405

Local permits, 60

Lodestar fee awards, 136

Logging, 241, 304-307, 319, 382-385, 393, 433-434, 523, 555, 565, 984

Lone Pine orders, 82-83

Low-dose extrapolation, 578-579

Mad cow, 678-679

Malaysia, 685

Maquiladoras, 46, 51, 869

Marine Mammal Protection Act, 230, 815, 1007-1015

Maritime law, *see* Admiralty

Markey, Ed, 992, 994

Market access regulation, Chapter 15, *and see also* 59-60, 314, 581, 583, 768

Market participant doctrine, 193, 276, 287, 626

Market-based pollution controls, *see* Market-enlisting regulatory strategies

Market-enlisting regulatory strategies, Chapters 11 & 14

Marrakesh Accords, 630, 634, 991-994

Maximum sustainable yield, 387

Means-ends relationship, 920, *see also* Eminent domain, Regulatory takings issues

Media, role of, 40, 42, 48, 64, 67-70, 189, 195, 205, 248, 313, 336, 366, 384, 399, 411, 424, 428, 430-431, 437, 459, 463, 506, 812, 844-845, 852, 990

Medical monitoring, surveillance fund, 155

Mehta, M.C., 972-976

Memorandum of Agreement, 807-810

Mens rea, *see* Intent, criminal

Mercury, 117, 207, 234-236, 321, 323-324, 336, 339, 370, 464, 490-496, 523, 525-526, 551, 609-610, 710-711, 755, 965, 1010

Mesothelioma, 157, 584

Methane, 982-984

Methuselah (ancient bristlecone pine), 880-883

Methyl-isocyanate, 16, 58, 68, 336, 770, 974

Mexico, 46, 51, 281, 303, 339-340, 773, 993, 1007-1014

Migratory birds, and Migratory Bird Treaty Act, MBTA, 280-287, 303-309, 374, 506, 843, 862-863, 882, 894-895

Mining, 28, 34, 127, 207-208, 232, 259, 264, 266, 277, 319, 338, 348, 364, 376, 382-383, 388, 432, 507, 524, 537-544, 584, 596, 760, 762, 815, 843, 852, 896, 917, 928-933, 946, 955, 981

Mitigation, 16, 70, 142, 321-324, 334-335, 360-364, 406, 413, 416, 439-442, 452-453, 559, 610, 633-635, 643, 952-953, 986-998, 1014-1015

Molina, Mario, 977, 980

Mono Lake, 384, 892-900, 907

Montreal Protocol on Substances That Deplete the Ozone Layer, 299, 302, 978-985, 988, 998, 1014-1015

Most-favored nation obligation, 297, 1006-1007

Motor vehicle emissions, 461, 507-518, 826

MTBE additive, 264, 773

Multilateral environmental agreements, 965-969, 976-998, 1012-1015

Muir, John, xxv

Multi-centric pluralism, *see* Pluralism

Multilateral treaties, 64, 280, 286-297, 301-303, 629, 633, 643, 965-969, 976-982, 985, 990-998, 999, 1004, 1006, 1012-1015

Multimedia permitting, 537, 812-813

Multiparty litigation, 746, 825

Multiple use sustained yield, 10, 177, 233, 266, 377-385, 390-395, 411-412

Municipal wastewater, 344, 349, 548, 566, 856-858, 861

Muskie, Edmund, 473, 510, 562

Mutagenicity, 679-685

NAAQSs (CAA), *see* Chapter 11, *see also* 160-162, 566-567, 595-596, 598-599, 620

Nader, Ralph, 919

NAFTA, 296-298, 302-303, 339, 1011, 1014-1015

National Academy of Sciences, 326, 448, 509, 576, 590,

National ambient air quality standards, *see* NAAQSs

National contingency plan (NCP), 704, 724, 727-728, 735-743

National Environmental Policy Act, *see* NEPA

National forests, 19, 194, 228-229, 240-241, 264-266, 374, 381-382, 384-385, 412

National Highway Traffic Safety Administration [NHTSA], 325-332

Index

National Land Use Policy Act, bill, *see* NLUPA

National Marine Fisheries Service, 1007

National Oceanic and Atmospheric Administration, 1007

National Research Council, 576-577, 579, 590

National treatment obligation, 297-302, 1006-1015

Nationally appropriate mitigation actions, 992-993

Native Americans, 966

Natural capital, 19, 141-142, 394, 452-453

Natural resources damages, 54, 63, 107, 137-144, 884

Natural resources, ethical values, 34, 141-142, 556, 909-912, 998

Natural resources, remedies, 108, 128, 137-144

Navigable waters, *see* Chapter 12, *see also* 45-47, 359-361, 692, 844, 883-884, 887-889, 895-897

Necessary and proper clause, 259, 276, 284

Negligence, 76-85, 947-949

Negotiated rulemaking (reg-neg), 812-813, 825-828

NEPA, Chapter 8, *see also* 59, 176, 455, 845-846, 1003, *and see* the classic early-NEPA *Chicod Creek* case materials on the website

NESHAPS, 58, 468, 46-464, 489-495, 600

New source, 460-464, *and see* NSR, NSPS

NIMBY, 122, 365-369, 776, 782

NLUPA, National Land Use Policy Act (bill), 344, 358, 396-400, 404

No migration variance, 781

Nonattainment areas, 463, 486-489

Nondeterioration, 223, *and see* PSD

Nondiscriminatory state laws, 270-273, 297

Nongovernmental organizations, 194-196, 345, 417, 814, 959-960, 979, 985, 999-1000, 1013

Nonlegally Binding Authoritative Statement of All Types of Forests, 1005-1006

Nonpoint source pollution, 56, 348-349, 520-521, 525-526, 529-531, 546-547, 555-568, 620-621

Nordhaus, William, 638-640

North American Commission for Environmental Cooperation, 339-340

North American Free Trade Agreement (NAFTA, and NAFTA side agreement), 297, 302-309, 1014-1015

NSPS, 461, 538-539, 543, 567

NSR, 464, 499-500

Nuclear power, 242-244, 261-262, 369-370, 544

Nuisance, private, 78-83

Nuisance, public, 89-96, 137, 164-165, 910, 933-937, 941-942, 945-946, 961ff.

Occupational safety, 873-874

Ocean acidification, 416

Office of Management and Budget, 646

Off-road vehicles, 219-220, 383-395, 623

Offsets, 363, 448, 463, 488-489, 615-616, 619, 949-950

Oil Pollution Act of 1990, *see* OPA-90

One-shot technology, 11

"Only representative" (REACH), 680, 684

OPA-90, 137, 142-144, 263-264, 345, 416, 814

Opinio juris, 963

ORVs, *see* Off-road vehicles

Our Children's Trust, 910-911, 913

Outfalls, 45, 47, 58-59, 519-520, 550-554, 856-858

Outrage, 15-17, 68-69, 122-123, 367

Overton Park case, 211-223, 242, 252, 892

Ozone-depletion (stratospheric ozone), 977-984, 989

Ozone, 460, 462-464, 466-469, 476-477, 479, 488, 497-498, 512-513, 595-597

Packwood Amendment (to Magnuson-Stevens Fishery Conservation and Management Act), 291-296, 1012

Paramount public use, 917

Parent corporation, liability, 713, 717-723

Parenteau, Patrick, 442-444, 450, 456

Paris Agreement/Accord, COP-21 (on climate change), 345, 417, 633-635, 643, 990-999, 1013

Parks, 7, 213-223, 374, 395, 883, 887-891

Particulate matter, 77, 111, 122, 159-162, 321, 464-469, 492, 497, 597, 600, 622, 627, 974

Pathogens, 523, 525, 547

PCBs, 64, 523-525, 551, 673-674, 679

Pebble Mine, Alaska, 239

Pelly Amendment (to Magnuson-Stevens Fishery Conservation and Management Act), 291-296, 302-303, 1012

Peppercorn, 4

Performance standards, 196-198, 325-332, 385, 460-461, 507, 519-520, 535-536, 537-543

Performance Track, 647-648

Permanent damages, 109-116, 130

Permit defense, 97

Permit processes, 187-188, 812-813

Personal liability, 694, 703-706

Perverse incentives, 535-536

Pesticides, 9, 11, 14, 42-52, 60, 63-64, 88-89, 531, 583, 649-663

Pesticides, export of, 42-43, 63-64

Pfisteria piscicida, 522

Philippines, 685

Pigou, Arthur, 636

Pike test, 274

Pinchot, Gifford, 34, 381

Placer mining, 207-208, 537-542

Planning, Chapter 9

Plater, Marika, 396

Plea bargaining, 868

Pluralism, citizen empowerment, as opposed to di-polar corporate-agency establishment, 62, 69, 267

Point source, 519-521, 526, 529-531, 532, 539-540, 545-547, 566

Polar bears, 451-453

Police power tests, 916-919, 956-957

Political questions, 95-96

Polluter Pays Principle, 31, 64, 688-689, 731, 969, 971, 973

Pollution exclusion, 716

Pollution prevention, *see* Chapter 15, *see also* 59, 337-338, 525

Pope Francis, 629, 998

Population, 20-21, 315, 394-395, 989-900

Potentially responsible party (PRP), 157

Powder River Basin coal mining, 320-323, 416

Powell Memorandum (1972), 69, 399

Practicable alternative, 360-362

Precautionary Principle, 14, 65, 579, 604, 649, 658, 691, 696-971, 969-974, 977, 987, 989

Index

Precursors, 464, 624, 627

Predecessor landowners' liability, 712, 716, 833-834

Preemption, 259-268, 659-660, 852

Pre-market approval, Chapter 15, and 679-685

Prescriptive easements, 926-927

Prevention of significant deterioration, 463, 486-487, 503-504

Primary jurisdiction, 97

Private attorneys general, 62, 68, 238, 442

Private litigation for response costs, 708, 724-731

Private voluntary standards, 643-648

Privatizing, 382

Process and production methods (PPMs), 1010-1015

Project Relief, 192

Project XL, EPA, 812-813

Project XL, *see* Multimedia permitting

Proof disparity—civil/criminal, 145

Proper public purpose, 915-916, 919

Property Clause, 267, 407-410

Property law, Chapter 21, *see also* 32

Proportionality, 683

Prosecutorial discretion, 239-240

Prospective nuisance, *see* Anticipatory nuisance

Prospective purchaser agreements, 807

Protectionism, 268-273

Protocol on Pollutant Release and Transfer Registers, 339-340

Proximate cause, 105-107

Public Land Law Review Commission, 377-381

Public goods, 636-638

Public lands, 267, 374-396, 406-412

Public parks, 214-218, 887-893

Public trust doctrine, Chapter 20, *see also* 27-28, 70, 384

Punitive damages, 131-137

Purse-seine nets, 1007-1015

Qinghai Project (China), 1001-1005

Quantitative risk assessment, 575-581

Quarantine, 274-275

Qui tam actions, 845

Race of laxity, 190-193, 468

Race-to-the-bottom, 68, 190-193, 1013-1014

Radioactivity, 370

Rangeland, 374-386

Rationality tests, 147, 916-925, 955

REACH, (Registration, Evaluation, Authorisation and Restriction of Chemicals (REACH), Chapter 15(B), 651, 679-685

REACH Implementation Projects (RIPs), 681

RCACs, 416, 814

RCRA, *see* Chapter 17, *see also* 58, 180, 703-709, 735

Recycling, 275, 711

Red Book, 576, 579

Red-cockaded woodpecker, 433-434

Redressability, 238

Refineries, 787

Reformulated gasoline, 299-302

Refuse Act, 843-847

Reg-neg, *see* Negotiated rulemaking

Registration, Evaluation, Authorisation, and Restriction of Chemicals (REACH), 679-685

Regulatory takings issues, *see* Chapter 21, *and* 122, 125-128

Reitze, Arnold, 20-21

Releases of liability, 99

Remedies, 108-144, 147-156, 694-695, 929, 948-950

Remittitur, 137, 847

Remote damages, *See* Proximate cause

Rent-a-judge, 825

Reproductive effects, 679-685

Resource Conservation and Recovery Act, *see* RCRA

Restitution, 128, 783-787

Restoration, 129-130, 142, 883

Retroactive liability, 956-957

Restriction of Hazardous Substances (RoHS) Directive (EU), 683-684

Review-and-permit, 182-184, 198

Right-to-farm laws, 99

Right-to-know, 58, 176, 336-341

Rio Conference on the Environment/Declaration, 65, 964, 967-972, 976, 989, 998, 1003-1005, 1013-1014

Risk assessment, 12-17, 575-581, 662, 740

Risk characterization, 577

Risk management, 12-17, 124, 576-581

Road salt, 34-40

Roadblock statutes, *see* Chapter 10, *see also* 177

Rowland, Sherwood, 977, 980

Ruckelshaus, William, 508-512

Rulemaking, 201-212, 242-246, 455, 825-828

Safe Drinking Water Act, SDWA, 71-72

Sage grouse, 386, 447

Sagebrush Rebellion, 411-412

Salt marsh, 940-949

Sandman, Peter, 15-17

SARA, 713

Sarbanes-Oxley Act, 683

Savings clauses, 263-264

Sax, Joseph L., *passim; and, more specifically*, 22, 317, 365, 374, 384, 393, 410, 880-892, 908, 910, 912, 928, 935, 946

Scalia, Antonin, 231-237, 390-392, 470-472, 491-495, 880, 912, 933, 936-937, 950, 957-958

Schapiro, Mark, 635, 684-685

Schroth, Peter, xxix

Scienter, 854-864

Sea turtles, 1011-1012

Sedimentation, 523

Segmentation, 217-219

Sentencing guidelines, 876-877

Septic systems, 569-570, 941-943

Servitude on land, 108-112

Settlements, 52, 746-747, 752-753, 799-806, 823-825

Seveso toxic incident, 68

Sewerage, 355-356, 547-548

Shared Natural Resources, 280-286

Shellfish, 139, 522, 943-945

Shrimp, 894-900, 1011-1012

Sic utere maxim, 965

Side Agreement (NAFTA), 302-309

Significant deterioration, 462-463

Siltation, 523

Siting statutes (state hazardous waste siting), 366-367

SLAPP suits, 99-100

Slippage, regulatory, 198, *and see* Chapter 10

Index

Sludge, 548-549, 760-761, 856-858

Sluicing, 206-208, 537-544

Smart growth, 370-373

Smog, 508-511, 622-627

Smoking, 167

Snail darter endangered fish, 208-212, 423-432

Snowmobiles, *see* Off-road vehicles

Soft law, 966-972, 989, *and see* Chapter 22

Solid waste, 760-764

Sources of international law, Chapter 22

Sovereign immunity, 219, 923-927, 947

Spotted owls, 240-241

Standard-setting, 61-62, 187-188, 191, 474-475, 519-520

Standing, Chapter 6, *and see* 68, 89-93, 890-891, 907-908, 937, 944-946

State implementation plans, 58, 460-461

State of the art, 96

State responsibility, 964

Stationary sources, 460-464, 487-488

Statistical proof, 180

Statutes of limitations, 97-98, 154

Statutes of repose, 98, 154, 730-731

Statutory construction, 249-255

Statutory enforcement suits, *see* citizen statutory enforcement suits

Stevenson, Adlai, xxv

Stewart, Richard, 197-198, 225-226

Stockholm Conference/Declaration (United Nations Conference on the Human Environment), 966-971

Storm King Mountain, 227-228

Storm water, 546-547

Strahan, Richard "Max," 210-211

Stratospheric ozone, *see* Ozone depletion

Streambeds, 537-539

Strict liability, 85-89

Strip-mining, 364

Subdivision regulation, 355-356

Subsidiarity Principle, 358

Subsidiary corporation, liability, 717-723

Subsidies, 179-180, 607-608

Substantial factor test, 158-169

Substances of very high concern (REACH), 681, 684

Substantive due process, 914-918, 919, 953-957

Successor corporation, 723

Sunk costs, 217-219, 444

Sunset provisions, 445

Sunstein, Cass, 593, 596

Superfund Amendment and Reauthorization Act, *see* SARA

Superfund, *see* CERCLA

Supertanker, 134, 267-268

Supplemental environmental projects (SEPs), 800-802, 869

Supply and demand, law of, 637

Supremacy Clause, 258-264, 278, 283, 401, 409, 989

Supremacy of international law 285, 296

Surface Transportation Board, 320-324

Susskind, Lawrence, 825-827

Sustainability, xxv, 17-18, 21, 33, 63, 70, 345, 376, 398, 417, 909-910, 959, 967-975, 988

Sustained yield, Chapter 9(B)

Taj Mahal, 976

Taking, endangered species, 282, 294, 306, 422, 432-436, 440-444, 609

Takings Clause, 351, Chapter 21

Takings issues, *see* Regulatory takings issues

TBELs, *see* Chapter 12

TDRs, 357-358, 957-958

Technology-based standards, Chapters 11, 12, *and see* 178, 777, 781

Technology-forcing, 178-179, 768, 826, 980, *and see* Chapter 11

Technology transfer, 988

Teck Resources, Ltd., 965-966

Tellico Dam, 208-209, 423-439, 918

Tenth Amendment, 258-259, 262, 276-277, 283-285, 370, 411, 412, 547

Teratogenicity, 679-685

Tetrachloroethylene, 149

Thailand, 685

Third party defense, 103

Three economies, 19, 21-24

Thrillcraft, *see* Off-road vehicles

Tidelands, 888-891, 894, 897, 947

Timber cutting, 240

THMs, trihalomethanes, 71-72

Tort actions, Chapters 3 & 4, *and see* 659-660, 925

ToSCA, Chapters 13 & 15, *and see* Toxic Substances Control Act, 59-60, 230, 555, 581-594, 663-679, 685, 756, 815, 831, 843, 858

Total Maximum Daily Loads (TMDLs), 349, 556-567

Toxic Release Inventory, 58, 336, 339

Toxic substances regulation, Chapters 13 & 15, and 59-60, 550, 552-555, 581-594, 663-679, 685, 756, 815, 831, 843, 858

Toxic torts, Chapter 4, 685, 703, 731

Toxiprox, 155

Tradable credits, Chapter 14 *and* 197

Trade promotion authority 298

Trading emissions rights, *see* Market-enlisting regulatory approaches

Tragedy of the Commons, 28-34, 55-55, 66, 68, 223, 286, 287-291, 374, 388, 467, 609, 621

Trans-Alaska pipeline, 137

Trans-Pacific Partnership (TPP), 297

Transboundary pollution, 190, 334, 477-481, 960-966, 969, 971, 977

Transfers of development rights, *see* TDRs

Treaties, 280-287, *and see* Chapter 22

Trespass, 76-78, 102, 926-927

Triad, takings, *Penn Central,* 936, 944-945, 956

Trichloroethylene, 90, 551

TSDs (TSDFs), 180, 711-713, 756, 764-771, 781-782, 831, 836

TTP, trial-type procedure, 204

Tuna-dolphin, 1007-1015

UIC, Underground Injection Control, 781-782

Ultra hazardous activity, *see* strict liability

Umaña, Alvaro, 1004

UNCED, 964, 967, 1005

Uncertainty, *see* Risk

Underground storage tank regulation, 58, 524, 672, 756, 773

Unfunded Mandates, 812

Uniform hazardous waste manifest, 765-766

Unilateralism, 1003, 1012

United Nations Charter, 1006

United Nations Conference on Environment and Development (Earth Summit), 964, 967-972, 986, 1005

Index

United Nations Conference on the Human Environment (Stockholm Conference), 966-971

United Nations Conference on Sustainable Development (Rio + 20), 971-972

United Nations Development Program, 1004

United Nations Environment Program, 966, 980, 986, 1004, 1013

United Nations Framework Convention on Climate Change, 986-990, 999, 1003-1004

U.S. Department of Commerce, 681

Utilex plating company, 185-187, 198

Variability, 146

Vicarious liability, 93-94, 707, 867, 869

Vienna Convention on the Protection of the Ozone Layer, 978, 989

Vorsorgeprinzip (precautionary principle), 970

Wastewater, Chapter 12, 80, 84, 88, 207, 344, 349, 856-58, 861, 863

Water rights, 374, 384, 440, 894, 896, 898-901

Water use and supply, and irrigation, 96, 265, 383, 394, 443, 524, 530-531, 570, 760, 1001-1002

Watersheds, 281, 348-349, 386, 800

Waxman, Henry, 643, 992-994

Weiss, Edith Brown, 1013

Western Poverty Reduction Project (China), 999-1003

Wetlands, 24,58, 139, 140, 174, 177, 223, 271, 276, 353, 359-365, 371, 383, 405, 406, 437, 526-528, 546, 610, 734, 793, 878, 928, 935-946, 949, 952, 987

Whales and Whaling, 286-296

Whistleblower protection, 263

Wild horses and burros, 391, 407-409, 412

Wilderness, 28, 189, 220, 383, 388, 389, 390, 392,393, 419, 442, 486, 603, 891, 913

Wise Users, 34

Woburn toxics episode, 149-153, 157, 173, *and see more* on book's website

Wolves, 24-25, 393-394, 446-448, 573, 927

Wood, Mary, 908-909, 911

Workplace hazards, *see also Kepone* and the *Film Recovery* case

World Bank, 997-1004

World Commission on Environment and Development (Brundtland Commission), 21, 965, 969

World Meterological Organization (WMO), 984

World Summit on Sustainable Development, *see also* Johannesburg summit,), 967, 969

World Trade Organization, *see* WTO

WQBELs, 520, 555-556, 565-567

WTO, 290, 297-302, 580, 647, 684, 863, 997, 1007-1013

Zero emission vehicles, 623

Zero-discharge, 525, 536, 537, 542, 543, 550

Zero-infinity problem, 14, 66

Zone-of-interests test, 230-232, 235

Zoning, Chapter 9, *and see* 61, 177, 261, 914, 935, 949

Zooplankton, 138